Neiman Marcus	www.neimanmarcus.com
Nordstrom	www.nordstrom.com
Office Depot	www.officedepot.com
OfficeMax	www.officemax.com
Pantry, Inc.	www.thepantry.com
Pathmark	www.pathmark.com
Payless ShoeSource	www.payless.com
J.C. Penney	www.jcpenney.com
Pep Boys	www.pepboys.com
PetsMart	www.petsmart.com
Publix	www.publix.com
QVC	www.qvc.com
Radio Shack	www.radioshack.com
Raleys	www.raleys.com
Rite Aid	www.riteaid.com
Ross Stores	www.rossstores.com
Safeway	www.safeway.com
Saks, Inc.	www.saksincorporated.com
Schnucks	www.schnucks.com
Sears	www.sears.com
Sherwin-Williams	www.sherwin-williams.com
Shopko	www.shopko.com
Smart & Final	www.smartandfinal.com
Sonic Automotive	www.sonicautomotive.com
Spiegel	www.spiegel.com
Staples	www.staples.com
Stater Bros.	www.staterbros.com
Super Valu	www.supervalu.com
Target	www.target.com
Tiffany	www.tiffany.com
TJX Cos.	www.tjx.com
Toys "R" Us	www.tru.com
United Auto Group	www.uag.com
Value City	www.valuecity.com
Walgreen	www.walgreens.com
Wal-Mart	www.walmart.com
Wegman's	www.wegmans.com
Williams-Sonoma	www.williams-sonoma.com
Winn-Dixie	www.winndixie.com
Yum Restaurants	www.yum.com
Zale	www.zale.com

JAPAN (J MEANS SITE IS IN JAPANESE)

Aeon (Jusco)	www.aeon.info/aeoncorp/english
Best Denki	www.bestdenki.ne.jp (J)
Co-op Kobe	www.kobe.coop.or.jp (J)
Daiei	www.daiei.co.jp (J)
Daimaru	www.daimaru.co.jp (J)
Hankyu Department Stores	www.hankyu-dept.co.jp (J)
Heiwado	www.heiwado.co.jp (J)
Isetan	www.isetan.co.jp (J)
Ito-Yokado	www.itoyokado.iyg.co.jp/iy/index1_e.htm
Izumi	www.izumi.co.jp (J)
Izumiya	www.izumiya.co.jp (J)
Kojima	www.kojima.net (J)
Kotobukiya	www.kotobukiya.co.jp (J)
Maruetsu	www.maruetsu.co.jp (J)
Marui	www.marui-imai.co.jp/sapporo (J)
Matsuzakaya	www.matsuzakaya.co.jp (J)
Mitsukoshi	www.mitsukoshi.co.jp (J)
Mycal	www.mycal.co.jp (J)
Odakyu Electric Railway	www.odakyu-group.co.jp/english/index.htm
Seibu	www.seibu.co.jp (J)
Seiyu	www.seiyu.co.jp (J)
Skylark	www.skylark.co.jp (J)
Spar	www.spar.co.jp (J)
Takashimaya	www.takashimaya.co.jp (J)
Tokyu Department Store	www.tokyu-depart.co.jp (J)
Tokyu Store Chain	www.tokyu-store.co.jp (J)
Uny	www.uny.co.jp (J)

Retail Management

A Strategic Approach

NINTH EDITION

Barry Berman
Hofstra University

Joel R. Evans
Hofstra University

PEARSON
Prentice Hall

Prentice Hall
Upper Saddle River, NJ 07458

Library of Congress Cataloging-in-Publication Data

Berman, Barry.
    Retail management: a strategic approach/Barry Berman, Joel R. Evans.—9th ed.
        p. cm
    Includes indexes.
    ISBN 0-13-100944-3
        1. Retail trade—Management. I. Evans, Joel R. II. Title.

HF5429.B45 2004
658.8′7—dc21

                                                    2003040595

Editor-in-Chief: Jeff Shelstad
Acquisitions Editor: Katie Stevens
Assistant Editor: Melissa Pellerano
Editorial Assistant: Danielle Serra
Media Project Manager: Anthony Palmiotto
Marketing Manager: Michelle O'Brien
Senior Managing Editor (Production): Judy Leale
Production Editor: Marcela Maslanczuk
Production Assistant: Joseph DeProspero
Permissions Supervisor: Suzanne Grappi
Associate Director, Manufacturing: Vincent Scelta
Manufacturing Buyer: Diane Peirano
Design Manager: Maria Lange
Interior Design: Blair Brown
Cover Design: Blair Brown
Cover Photo: Jonelle Weaver, Getty Images
Illustrator (Interior): Electragraphics
Manager, Print Production: Christy Mahon
Project Management: Heidi Allgair, UG / GGS Information Services, Inc.
Printer/Binder: R.R. Donnelley—Willard

Credits and acknowledgments borrowed from other sources and reproduced, with permission, in this textbook appear on appropriate page within text or on pages 554–555.

Pearson Education LTD.
Pearson Education Singapore, Pte. Ltd
Pearson Education, Canada, Ltd
Pearson Education–Japan

Pearson Education Australia PTY, Limited
Pearson Education North Asia Ltd
Pearson Educación de Mexico, S.A. de C.V.
Pearson Education Malaysia, Pte. Ltd

10 9 8 7 6 5 4 3 2 1
ISBN 0-13-100944-3

Brief Contents

Preface   *xv*
About the Authors   *xxi*
Acknowledgments   *xxiii*

 PART ONE

AN OVERVIEW OF STRATEGIC RETAIL MANAGEMENT   1

1. An Introduction to Retailing   2
2. Building and Sustaining Relationships in Retailing   19
3. Strategic Planning in Retailing   48

PART TWO

SITUATION ANALYSIS   83

4. Retail Institutions by Ownership   84
5. Retail Institutions by Store-Based Strategy Mix   104
6. Web, Nonstore-Based, and Other Forms of Nontraditional Retailing   127

 PART THREE

TARGETING CUSTOMERS AND GATHERING INFORMATION   159

7. Identifying and Understanding Consumers   160
8. Information Gathering and Processing in Retailing   184

PART FOUR

CHOOSING A STORE LOCATION   213

9. Trading-Area Analysis   214
10. Site Selection   240

 PART FIVE

MANAGING A RETAIL BUSINESS   267

11. Retail Organization and Human Resource Management   268

12. Operations Management: Financial Dimensions   294
13. Operations Management: Operational Dimensions   313

 PART SIX

MERCHANDISE MANAGEMENT AND PRICING   337

14. Developing Merchandise Plans   338
15. Implementing Merchandise Plans   365
16. Financial Merchandise Management   389
17. Pricing in Retailing   414

PART SEVEN

COMMUNICATING WITH THE CUSTOMER   449

18. Establishing and Maintaining a Retail Image   450
19. Promotional Strategy   473

 PART EIGHT

PUTTING IT ALL TOGETHER   505

20. Integrating and Controlling the Retail Strategy   506

APPENDIXES

A   Careers in Retailing   531
B   About the Web Site That Accompanies *Retail Management* (**http://www.prenhall.com/bermanevans**)   538
C   Glossary   540

PHOTO CREDITS   554

NAME INDEX   556

SUBJECT INDEX   563

v

Contents

Preface xv
About the Authors xxi
Acknowledgments xxiii

1 PART ONE

AN OVERVIEW OF STRATEGIC RETAIL MANAGEMENT 1

1. AN INTRODUCTION TO RETAILING 2

Chapter Objectives 2
Overview 3
The Framework of Retailing 3
 Reasons for Studying Retailing 4
 The Special Characteristics of Retailing 9
The Importance of Developing and Applying a Retail
 Strategy 10
 Target Stores: A Retail Strategy That Aims
  and Scores! 11
 The Retailing Concept 12
The Focus and Format of the Text 16
Summary 17
Key Terms 17
Questions for Discussion 17
Web-Based Exercise: About Retail Industry
 (http://retailindustry.about.com) 18

2. BUILDING AND SUSTAINING RELATIONSHIPS IN RETAILING 19

Chapter Objectives 19
Overview 20
Value and the Value Chain 20
Retailer Relationships 22
 Customer Relationships 23
 Channel Relationships 30
The Difference in Relationship Building Between
 Goods and Service Retailers 32
Technology and Relationships in Retailing 34
 Electronic Banking 34
 Customer and Supplier Interactions 35
Ethical Performance and Relationships
 in Retailing 36
 Ethics 37
 Social Responsibility 38
 Consumerism 39

Summary 41
Key Terms 42
Questions for Discussion 43
Web-Based Exercise: Nordstrom
 (www.nordstrom.com) 43
• Appendix on Planning for the Unique Aspects
 of Service Retailing 44
Abilities Required to Be a Successful Service
 Retailer 44
Improving the Performance of Service Retailers 45
The Strategy of Pal's Sudden Service:
 A Recent Baldrige Award Winner 47

3. STRATEGIC PLANNING IN RETAILING 48

Chapter Objectives 48
Overview 49
Situation Analysis 50
 Organizational Mission 50
 Ownership and Management Alternatives 52
 Goods/Service Category 54
 Personal Abilities 54
 Financial Resources 55
 Time Demands 57
Objectives 57
 Sales 57
 Profit 58
 Satisfaction of Publics 58
 Image (Positioning) 59
 Selection of Objectives 61
Identification of Consumer Characteristics
 and Needs 61
Overall Strategy 63
 Controllable Variables 63
 Uncontrollable Variables 65
 Integrating Overall Strategy 67
Specific Activities 68
Control 68
Feedback 68
Summary 68
Key Terms 69
Questions for Discussion 69
Web-Based Exercise: Carrefour
 (www.carrefour.com) 70
• Appendix on the Special Dimensions of Strategic
 Planning in a Global Retailing Environment 70
The Strategic Planning Process and Global
 Retailing 71

Opportunities and Threats in Global Retailing 72
Opportunities 72
Threats 72
Standardization: An Opportunity
and a Threat 72
**Factors Affecting the Success of a Global Retailing
Strategy** 73
U.S. Retailers in Foreign Markets 73
Foreign Retailers in the U.S. Market 75

Part One Short Cases 77
1: Schlotzsky's Deli Raises the Bar with Its Total
Retail Experience 77
2: Drugstores Work on Their Customer Loyalty
Programs 77
3: The Positioning Approach of High-End Jewelry
Stores 78
4: Is the Sears-Lands' End Merger a Match Made in
Heaven? 79

PART ONE • COMPREHENSIVE CASE
Zane's Cycles: Creating Lifetime Customers 80

2 PART TWO

SITUATION ANALYSIS 83

4. RETAIL INSTITUTIONS
BY OWNERSHIP 84

Chapter Objectives 84
Overview 85
Retail Institutions Categorized by Ownership 85
Independent 86
Chain 89
Franchising 91
Leased Department 94
Vertical Marketing System 95
Consumer Cooperative 96
Summary 97
Key Terms 98
Questions for Discussion 98
**Web-Based Exercise: Subway
(www.subway.com)** 98
• **Appendix on the Dynamics of Franchising** 99
Managerial Issues in Franchising 100
Franchisor–Franchisee Relationships 101

5. RETAIL INSTITUTIONS BY STORE-BASED
STRATEGY MIX 104

Chapter Objectives 104
Overview 105
**Considerations in Planning a Retail Strategy
Mix** 105
The Wheel of Retailing 105

Scrambled Merchandising 106
The Retail Life Cycle 108
How Retail Institutions Are Evolving 110
Mergers, Diversification, and Downsizing 110
Cost Containment and Value-Driven Retailing 111
**Retail Institutions Categorized by Store-Based
Strategy Mix** 112
Food-Oriented Retailers 112
General Merchandise Retailers 118
Summary 124
Key Terms 125
Questions for Discussion 125
**Web-Based Exercise: Amazon.com
(www.amazon.com)** 126

6. WEB, NONSTORE-BASED, AND OTHER
FORMS OF NONTRADITIONAL
RETAILING 127

Chapter Objectives 127
Overview 128
Direct Marketing 129
The Domain of Direct Marketing 131
The Customer Data Base: Key to Successful Direct
Marketing 132
Emerging Trends 132
The Steps in a Direct Marketing Strategy 135
Key Issues Facing Direct Marketers 137
Direct Selling 138
Vending Machines 139
**Electronic Retailing: The Emergence of the
World Wide Web** 140
The Role of the Web 140
The Scope of Web Retailing 141
Characteristics of Web Users 142
Factors to Consider in Planning Whether to Have
a Web Site 143
Examples of Web Retailing in Action 145
Other Nontraditional Forms of Retailing 147
Video Kiosks 147
Airport Retailing 149
Summary 150
Key Terms 151
Questions for Discussion 151
**Web-Based Exercise: CyberAtlas
(www.cyberatlas.internet.com)** 151

Part Two Short Cases 153
1: Piggly Wiggly: A Supermarket Franchising
Giant 153
2: Can Traditional Department Stores Revive
Themselves? 153
3: J. Jill Moves into Multi-Channel Retailing 154
4: Can eBay Keep Booming? 155

PART TWO • COMPREHENSIVE CASE
Addressing E-Retail Operational Issues 156

3 PART THREE

TARGETING CUSTOMERS AND GATHERING INFORMATION 159

7. IDENTIFYING AND UNDERSTANDING CONSUMERS 160

Chapter Objectives 160
Overview 161
Consumer Demographics and Life-Styles 161
    Consumer Demographics 162
    Consumer Life-Styles 164
    Retailing Implications of Consumer Demographics and Life-Styles 166
    Consumer Profiles 168
Consumer Needs and Desires 168
Shopping Attitudes and Behavior 170
    Attitudes Toward Shopping 170
    Where People Shop 171
    The Consumer Decision Process 172
    Types of Consumer Decision Making 176
    Impulse Purchases and Customer Loyalty 177
Retailer Actions 178
    Retailers with Mass Marketing Strategies 179
    Retailers with Concentrated Marketing Strategies 179
    Retailers with Differentiated Marketing Strategies 180
Environmental Factors Affecting Consumers 180
Summary 181
Key Terms 182
Questions for Discussion 182
Web-Based Exercise: J.C. Penney (www.jcpenney.com) 182

8. INFORMATION GATHERING AND PROCESSING IN RETAILING 184

Chapter Objectives 184
Overview 185
Information Flows in a Retail Distribution Channel 185
Avoiding Retail Strategies Based on Inadequate Information 186
The Retail Information System 188
    Building and Using a Retail Information System 188
    Data-Base Management 191
    Gathering Information Through the UPC and EDI 194
The Marketing Research Process 196
    Secondary Data 198
    Primary Data 201
Summary 205
Key Terms 205

Questions for Discussion 206
Web-Based Exercise: A.C. Nielsen (www.acnielsen.com) 206

Part Three Short Cases 207
    1: Should Retailers Ask Customers What They Want—and Give It to Them? 207
    2: Lowe's: Drawing Women to Home Improvement Stores 207
    3: Justifying an Investment in Retail Information Systems 208
    4: 3-D Computer-Assisted Design Comes to Retailing 209
PART THREE • COMPREHENSIVE CASE
    A Retailer's Guide to Meeting Consumer Expectations 210

4 PART FOUR

CHOOSING A STORE LOCATION 213

9. TRADING-AREA ANALYSIS 214

Chapter Objectives 214
Overview 215
The Importance of Location to a Retailer 215
Trading-Area Analysis 217
    The Use of Geographic Information Systems in Trading-Area Delineation and Analysis 218
    The Size and Shape of Trading Areas 220
    Delineating the Trading Area of an Existing Store 224
    Delineating the Trading Area of a New Store 225
Characteristics of Trading Areas 228
    Characteristics of the Population 231
    The Nature of Competition and the Level of Saturation 235
Summary 236
Key Terms 237
Questions for Discussion 237
Web-Based Exercise: Site Selection Magazine (www.siteselection.com) 238

10. SITE SELECTION 240

Chapter Objectives 240
Overview 241
Types of Locations 241
    The Isolated Store 241
    The Unplanned Business District 242
    The Planned Shopping Center 246
The Choice of a General Location 250
Location and Site Evaluation 251
    Pedestrian Traffic 252
    Vehicular Traffic 253

Parking Facilities 253
Transportation 253
Store Composition 254
Specific Site 254
Terms of Occupancy 255
Overall Rating 257
Summary 257
Key Terms 258
Questions for Discussion 258
**Web-Based Exercise: Underground Atlanta
(www.underatl.com) 259**

Part Four Short Cases 260
1: Jones Lang Lasalle's Property Watch: A New Tool
for Retail Site Selection 260
2: Wal-Mart's Search for Growth Outside the
United States 260
3: The Waterfront: Pittsburgh's New Mixed-Use
Center 261
4: Quizno's: A Strip-Center Strategy
for Restaurants 261

PART FOUR • COMPREHENSIVE CASE
Mall Retailers: The Search for Growth 263

5 PART FIVE

MANAGING A RETAIL BUSINESS 267

**11. RETAIL ORGANIZATION AND HUMAN
RESOURCE MANAGEMENT 268**

Chapter Objectives 268
Overview 269
Setting Up a Retail Organization 269
Specifying Tasks to Be Performed 270
Dividing Tasks Among Channel Members and
Customers 270
Grouping Tasks into Jobs 271
Classifying Jobs 273
Developing an Organization Chart 273
Organizational Patterns in Retailing 274
Organizational Arrangements Used by Small
Independent Retailers 275
Organizational Arrangements Used by Department
Stores 275
Organizational Arrangements Used by Chain
Retailers 277
Organizational Arrangements Used by Diversified
Retailers 278
**Human Resource Management
in Retailing 279**
The Special Human Resource Environment of
Retailing 280

The Human Resource Management Process in
Retailing 283
Summary 291
Key Terms 292
Questions for Discussion 292
**Web-Based Exercise: Federated Department Stores
(www.retailology.com/college/home.asp) 293**

**12. OPERATIONS MANAGEMENT:
FINANCIAL DIMENSIONS 294**

Chapter Objectives 294
Overview 295
Profit Planning 295
Asset Management 297
The Strategic Profit Model 298
Other Key Business Ratios 300
Financial Trends in Retailing 300
Budgeting 305
Preliminary Budgeting Decisions 306
Ongoing Budgeting Process 306
Resource Allocation 308
The Magnitude of Various Costs 308
Productivity 309
Summary 310
Key Terms 311
Questions for Discussion 311
**Web-Based Exercise: QuickBooks
(www.quickbooks.com/products/pro) 311**

**13. OPERATIONS MANAGEMENT:
OPERATIONAL DIMENSIONS 313**

Chapter Objectives 313
Overview 314
Operating a Retail Business 314
Operations Blueprint 314
Store Format, Size, and Space Allocation 316
Personnel Utilization 317
Store Maintenance, Energy Management, and
Renovations 318
Inventory Management 320
Store Security 321
Insurance 321
Credit Management 322
Computerization 323
Outsourcing 326
Crisis Management 327
Summary 327
Key Terms 328
Questions for Discussion 328
**Web-Based Exercise: Category Management Systems
(www.cmsinc.on.ca) 328**

Part Five Short Cases 330
1: The New Hiring System
of Sherwin-Williams 330

2: Dollar General Seeks to Bounce Back from Financial Woes   330
3: Toys "R" Us Tightens Its Belt   331
4: Beall's: Using Software to Track Employee Theft   331

PART FIVE • COMPREHENSIVE CASE
Developing Employees with Good Communication Skills   333

PART SIX

MERCHANDISE MANAGEMENT AND PRICING   337

14. DEVELOPING MERCHANDISE PLANS   338

Chapter Objectives   338
Overview   339
Merchandising Philosophy   339
Buying Organization Formats and Processes   341
  Level of Formality   341
  Degree of Centralization   342
  Organizational Breadth   342
  Personnel Resources   343
  Functions Performed   344
  Staffing   344
Devising Merchandise Plans   346
  Forecasts   346
  Innovativeness   347
  Assortment   350
  Brands   353
  Timing   356
  Allocation   357
Category Management   357
Merchandising Software   360
  General Merchandise Planning Software   360
  Forecasting Software   360
  Innovativeness Software   360
  Assortment Software   361
  Allocation Software   361
  Category Management Software   361
Summary   362
Key Terms   363
Questions for Discussion   363
Web-Based Exercise: Sports Authority (www.sportsauthority.com)   363

15. IMPLEMENTING MERCHANDISE PLANS   365

Chapter Objectives   365
Overview   366
Implementing Merchandise Plans   366
  Gathering Information   366
  Selecting and Interacting with Merchandise Sources   368
  Evaluating Merchandise   371
  Negotiating the Purchase   371
  Concluding Purchases   372
  Receiving and Stocking Merchandise   372
  Reordering Merchandise   375
  Re-Evaluating on a Regular Basis   375
Logistics   375
  Performance Goals   376
  Supply Chain Management   377
  Order Processing and Fulfillment   378
  Transportation and Warehousing   379
  Customer Transactions and Customer Service   381
Inventory Management   381
  Retailer Tasks   382
  Inventory Levels   382
  Merchandise Security   383
  Reverse Logistics   384
  Inventory Analysis   385
Summary   386
Key Terms   387
Questions for Discussion   387
Web-Based Exercise: UPS e-Logistics (www.e-logistics.ups.com)   387

16. FINANCIAL MERCHANDISE MANAGEMENT   389

Chapter Objectives   389
Overview   390
Inventory Valuation: The Cost and Retail Methods of Accounting   390
  The Cost Method   391
  The Retail Method   394
Merchandise Forecasting and Budgeting: Dollar Control   397
  Designating Control Units   397
  Sales Forecasting   398
  Inventory-Level Planning   400
  Reduction Planning   401
  Planning Purchases   402
  Planning Profit Margins   404
Unit Control Systems   405
  Physical Inventory Systems   405
  Perpetual Inventory Systems   406
  Unit Control Systems in Practice   407
Financial Inventory Control: Integrating Dollar and Unit Concepts   407
  Stock Turnover and Gross Margin Return on Investment   407
  When to Reorder   409
  How Much to Reorder   411
Summary   412
Key Terms   412
Questions for Discussion   413
Web-Based Exercise: e-Data Technologies (www.geodata.com)   413

17. PRICING IN RETAILING   414

Chapter Objectives   414
Overview   415
External Factors Affecting a Retail Price
   Strategy   416
   The Consumer and Retail Pricing   416
   The Government and Retail Pricing   418
   Manufacturers, Wholesalers, and Other Suppliers—
     and Retail Pricing   421
   Competition and Retail Pricing   422
Developing a Retail Price Strategy   422
   Retail Objectives and Pricing   422
   Broad Price Policy   425
   Price Strategy   426
   Implementation of Price Strategy   431
   Price Adjustments   435
Summary   438
Key Terms   438
Questions for Discussion   439
Web-Based Exercise: Costco (www.costco.com)   439

Part Six Short Cases   441
  1: Product Innovations and Burger King   441
  2: Wet Seal Stays Ahead of the Fashion Curve   441
  3: The Bottom Line on Reverse Logistics   442
  4: Can Retailers Successfully Exploit the Power of
     Optimal Pricing?   442

PART SIX • COMPREHENSIVE CASE
   Kohl's: Keeping the Momentum Going   444

PART SEVEN

COMMUNICATING WITH THE CUSTOMER   449

**18. ESTABLISHING AND MAINTAINING
    A RETAIL IMAGE   450**

Chapter Objectives   450
Overview   451
The Significance of Retail Image   452
   Components of a Retail Image   452
   The Dynamics of Creating and Maintaining a Retail
     Image   452
Atmosphere   454
   A Store-Based Retailing Perspective   454
   A Nonstore-Based Retailing Perspective   464
Encouraging Customers to Spend More Time
   Shopping   466
Community Relations   469
Summary   470
Key Terms   471
Questions for Discussion   471
Web-Based Exercise: Godiva Chocolatier
   (www.godiva.com)   471

19. PROMOTIONAL STRATEGY   473

Chapter Objectives   473
Overview   474
Elements of the Retail Promotional Mix   474
   Advertising   475
   Public Relations   480
   Personal Selling   482
   Sales Promotion   484
Planning a Retail Promotional Strategy   488
   Determining Promotional Objectives   488
   Establishing an Overall Promotional Budget   490
   Selecting the Promotional Mix   491
   Implementing the Promotional Mix   493
   Reviewing and Revising the Promotional Plan   495
Summary   496
Key Terms   496
Questions for Discussion   497
Web-Based Exercise: Point-of-Purchase Advertising
   International (www.popai.com)   497

Part Seven Short Cases   499
  1: Paco Underhill, Consulting Guru, on Retail
     Atmospherics   499
  2: Sports Authority: Upgrading the In-Store
     Experience   499
  3: Can Gap Regain Its Advertising Luster?   500
  4: Best Buy Uses Promotions to Pump Up
     the Sales   500

PART SEVEN • COMPREHENSIVE CASE
   Build-A-Bear Workshop: Putting the Heart Back
     in Retailing   502

PART EIGHT

PUTTING IT ALL TOGETHER   505

**20. INTEGRATING AND CONTROLLING
    THE RETAIL STRATEGY   506**

Chapter Objectives   506
Overview   507
Integrating the Retail Strategy   507
   Planning Procedures and Opportunity
     Analysis   507
   Defining Productivity in a Manner Consistent
     with the Strategy   509
   Performance Measures   511
   Scenario Analysis   515
Control: Using the Retail Audit   518
   Undertaking an Audit   518
   Responding to an Audit   521
   Possible Difficulties in Conducting a Retail
     Audit   521
   Illustrations of Retail Audit Forms   523

Summary 524
Key Terms 524
Questions for Discussion 524
**Web-Based Exercise: American Customer
  Satisfaction Index (www.theacsi.org/
  industry_scores.htm)** 525

Part Eight Short Cases 526
  1: Looking Ahead with 7-Eleven 526
  2: Can Jiffy Lube Continue Getting the Job
     Done? 526

PART EIGHT • COMPREHENSIVE CASE
  Who's Minding the Future? 528

APPENDIXES

A: Careers in Retailing 531

Overview 531
The Bright Future of a Career in Retailing 531
Owning a Business 532
Opportunities as a Retail Employee 533
  Types of Positions in Retailing 533
  Career Paths and Compensation in
    Retailing 535
Getting Your First Position as a Retail Professional 535

Searching for Career Opportunities
  in Retailing 535
Preparing for the Interview 537
Evaluating Retail Career Opportunities 537

B: About the Web Site That Accompanies
   Retail Management (www.prenhall.com/
   bermanevans) 538

Overview 538
Web Site Components 538
  Interactive Study Guide 539
  Chapter Objectives/Chapter Overviews 539
  Key Terms and Glossary 539
  Text-Related Web Site Links 539
  Careers in Retailing 539
  Retail Resources on the Web 539
  Web Exercises 539
  Computer Exercises 539
  Trade Associations 539

C: Glossary 540

PHOTO CREDITS 554

NAME INDEX 556

SUBJECT INDEX 563

Preface

As we move further into the new millennium, we are delighted by the continuing positive response to our book as evidenced by adoptions at hundreds of colleges and universities around the world. In this edition, we have raised the bar higher for ourselves—in a way that we hope you find rewarding. Our goal is to seamlessly meld the traditional framework of retailing with the realities of the competitive environment and the emergence of high-tech as a backbone for retailing.

We have worked hard to produce a cutting-edge text, while retaining the coverage and features most desired by professors and students, and reducing the length of prior editions. We have spent many hours eliminating the "middle age spread" that occurs in books, without eliminating any important content or examples.

The concepts of a strategic approach and a retail strategy remain our cornerstones. With a strategic approach, the fundamental principle is that the retailer has to plan for and adapt to a complex, changing environment. Both opportunities and constraints must be considered. A retail strategy is the overall plan or framework of action that guides a retailer. Ideally, it will be at least one year in duration and outline the mission, goals, consumer market, overall and specific activities, and control mechanisms of the retailer. Without a pre-defined and well-integrated strategy, the firm may flounder and be unable to cope with the environment that surrounds it. Through our text, we want the reader to become a good retail planner and decision maker, and to be able to adapt to change.

Retail Management is designed as a one-semester text for students of retailing or retail management. In many cases, such students will have already been exposed to marketing principles. We believe retailing should be viewed as one form of marketing and not distinct from it.

BUILDING ON THE E-VOLUTION OF *RETAIL MANAGEMENT: A STRATEGIC APPROACH*

As Bob Dylan once said, "The times, they are a changing." What does this all mean? The "E" word—electronic—now permeates our lives. From a consumer perspective, gone are the old Smith-Corona typewriters, replaced by word processing software on PCs. Snail mail is giving way to E-mail. Looking for a new music CD? Well, we can go to the store—or we can order it from CDNow (**www.cdnow.com**) or Amazon.com (**www.amazon.com**) or maybe even download some tracks as we create our own CDs. Are you doing research? Then hop on the Internet express and have access to millions of facts at your fingertips. The Web is a 24/7/365 medium that is transforming and will continue to transform our behavior.

From a retailer perspective, we see four formats—all covered in *Retail Management*—competing in the new millennium (cited in descending order of importance):

- **Combined "bricks-and-mortar" and "clicks-and-mortar" retailers.** These are store-based retailers that also offer Web shopping, thus providing customers the ultimate in choice and convenience. Over 90 percent of the world's largest retailers, as well as many medium and small firms, fall into this category or will shortly. This is clearly the fast-growing format in retailing, exemplified by such different firms as Barnes & Noble (**www.barnesandnoble.com**), Costco (**www.costco.com**), and Target (**www.target.com**).
- **Clicks-and-mortar retailers.** These are the new breed of Web-only retailers that have emerged in recent years, led by Amazon.com. Rather than utilize their own physical store facilities, these companies

promote a "virtual" shopping experience: wide selections, low prices, and convenience. Among the firms in this category are Priceline (**www.priceline.com**)—the discount airfare, hotel, and more retailer, and toy retailer, eToys (**www.etoys.com**).

- **Direct marketers with clicks-and-mortar retailing operations.** These are firms that have relied on traditional nonstore media such as print catalogs, direct selling in homes, and TV infomercials to generate business. Almost all of them have added Web sites, or will be shortly, to enhance their businesses. Leaders include Lands' End (**www.landsend.com**) and Spiegel (**www.spiegel.com**). These direct marketers will see a dramatic increase in the proportion of sales coming from the Web.
- **Bricks-and-mortar retailers.** These are companies that rely on their physical facilities to draw customers. They do not sell online, but use the Web for customer service and image building. Bloomingdale's (**www.bloomingdales.com**) mostly offers customer service and a gift registry. Firms in this category represent the smallest grouping of retailers. Many will need to rethink their approach as online competition intensifies.

We have access to more information sources than ever before, from global trade associations to government agencies. The information in *Retail Management*, Ninth Edition, is more current than ever because we are using the original sources themselves and not waiting for data to be published months or a year after being compiled. We are also able to include a greater range of real-world examples because of the information at company Web sites.

Will this help you, the reader? You bet. Our philosophy has always been to make *Retail Management* as reader-friendly, up-to-date, and useful as possible. In addition, we want you to benefit from our experiences, in this case, our E-xperiences.

E-XCITING E-FEATURES

To reflect these E-xciting times, *Retail Management: A Strategic Approach*, Ninth Edition, incorporates a host of E-features throughout the book—and at our wide-ranging, interactive Web site (**www.prenhall.com/bermanevans**).

This edition has a very strong integration of the book with its Web site:

- A special section of the Web site is devoted to each chapter.
- In each chapter, there are multiple references to Web links regarding particular topics (such as free online sources of secondary data).
- Every chapter has a number of margin notes that refer to company and company Web sites.
- Every chapter concludes with a short Web exercise.
- At our Web site, for each chapter, there are chapter objectives, a chapter overview, a listing of key terms, interactive study guide questions, hot links to relevant Web sites, and more.
- Our Web site contains extra math exercises for Chapters 9, 12, 16, and 17.
- Our Web site includes in-depth exercises that apply key course concepts through free company downloads and demonstrations. There are several for each part of the book.
- We have moved some material to our Web site for better currency and visualization, including hints for solving cases, a listing of key online secondary data sources, and descriptions of retail job opportunities and career ladders.

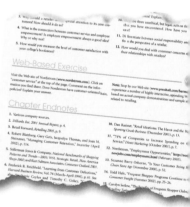

But, that's not all! *Retail Management*, Ninth Edition, is packed with other E-features:

- Our Web site has an interactive study guide (with feedback on the correct answers and text page references).
- Our Web site has more than 1,000 "hot links," a glossary, and much more.
- The end papers of *Retail Management* show the Web addresses for 200 retailers around the globe.
- There is a "Technology in Retailing" box in each chapter that cover various E-applications.
- Many cases have E-components.

NEW TO THE NINTH EDITION

Since the first edition of *Retail Management: A Strategic Approach*, we have sought to be as contemporary and forward-looking as possible. We are proactive rather than reactive in our preparation of each edition. That is why we still take this adage of Wal-Mart's founder, the late Sam Walton, so seriously: "Commit to your business. Believe in it more than anybody else."

For the ninth edition, there are many changes in *Retail Management*:

1. There is a livelier writing style, and the length of the book has been reduced.
2. The all-new opening vignettes highlighting the titans of retailing:

Chapter 1—**Wal-Mart**	Chapter 11—**Nordstrom**
Chapter 2—**Stew Leonard's**	Chapter 12—**Federated Department Stores**
Chapter 3—**Limited Brands**	Chapter 13—**Starbucks**
Chapter 4—**McDonald's**	Chapter 14—**Gap Inc.**
Chapter 5—**Ikea**	Chapter 15—**Pearle Vision**
Chapter 6—**Amazon.com**	Chapter 16—**eBay**
Chapter 7—**Staples**	Chapter 17—**Costco**
Chapter 8—**Mrs. Fields**	Chapter 18—**Target**
Chapter 9—**Blockbuster**	Chapter 19—**Mary Kay**
Chapter 10—**Dunkin' Donuts**	Chapter 20—**Home Depot**

3. All of the applied boxes in each chapter are new: "Technology in Retailing," "Retailing Around the World," "Ethics in Retailing," and "Careers in Retailing."
4. There is greater use of line art and fewer table "lists."
5. All of the cases are new and based on real companies and situations; and the cases have been repositioned to the end of each part (rather than each chapter).
6. These substantive chapter changes have been made:

- **Chapter 1, An Introduction to Retailing**—We introduce multi-channel retailing much earlier in the book and look, in-depth, at Target Corporation's successful retail strategy.
- **Chapter 2, Building and Sustaining Relationships in Retailing**—There is enhanced coverage of "value" and relationships in retailing, as well as new material on the American with Disabilities Act. The appendix includes a discussion of a small retailer as a Baldrige award winner for Quality.
- **Chapter 3, Strategic Planning in Retailing**—There is a streamlined, more applications-oriented emphasis on the strategic planning process in retailing. The appendix on global retailing is closely linked to strategic planning concepts.
- **Chapter 4, Retail Institutions by Ownership**—All of the data on retail ownership formats have been updated. The appendix on franchising opportunities is presented in a planning format.
- **Chapter 5, Retail Institutions by Store-Based Strategy Mix**—All of the data on store-based retail strategies have been updated, and the chapter is keyed to today's economic conditions and trends.
- **Chapter 6, Web, Nonstore-Based, and Other Forms of Nontraditional Retailing**—There is new material on single-channel retailing versus multi-channel retailing, and their interrelation with nonstore retailing. The Internet discussion reflects the present state of Web retailing.
- **Chapter 7, Identifying and Understanding Consumers**—There is greater emphasis on the retailing ramifications of consumer characteristics, attitudes, and behavior; and we include current data on where America shops.
- **Chapter 8, Information Gathering and Processing in Retailing**—We have a new section on "Information Flows in a Retail Distribution Channel."

- **Chapter 9, Trading-Area Analysis**—There is new material on geographic information systems, as well as many new retail applications.
- **Chapter 10, Site Selection**—We include many new retail applications.
- **Chapter 11, Retail Organization and Human Resource Management**—There is a streamlined, more strategic emphasis on the human resource environment in retailing.
- **Chapter 12, Operations Management: Financial Dimensions**—We have new material on events relating to asset management: the state of the U.S. economy; funding sources; mergers, consolidations, and spinoffs; bankruptcies and liquidations; and questionable accounting and financial reporting practices.
- **Chapter 13, Operations Management: Operational Dimensions**—There is a streamlined, more strategic emphasis on operations issues in retailing.
- **Chapter 14, Developing Merchandise Plans**—We make a sharper distinction between the roles of buyers and sales managers, with illustrative (and real) career ladders. There is enhanced coverage of private brands.
- **Chapter 15, Implementing Merchandise Plans**—There is a streamlined, more strategic emphasis on implementing merchandise plans, including logistics and inventory management.
- **Chapter 16, Financial Merchandise Management**—There is a streamlined, more strategic emphasis on financial merchandise management.
- **Chapter 17, Pricing in Retailing**—We emphasize the retailer's need to provide value to customers, regardless of price orientation.
- **Chapter 18, Establishing and Maintaining a Retail Image**—We place more focus on the total retail experience and retail positioning. There is enhanced material on atmospherics and Web-based retailers.
- **Chapter 19, Promotional Strategy**—There is a streamlined, more strategic emphasis on the retail promotional strategy.
- **Chapter 20, Integrating and Controlling the Retail Strategy**—There is a better, tighter discussion on integrating the retail strategy and how to assess it. The retail audit forms are more focused.

BUILDING ON A STRONG TRADITION

Besides introducing the new features previously mentioned, *Retail Management*, Ninth Edition carefully builds on its heritage as the market leader. At the request of our reviewers, these features have been retained from earlier editions:

- A strategic decision-making orientation, with many illustrative flowcharts, figures, tables, and photos. The chapter coverage is geared to the six steps used in developing and applying a retail strategy, which are first described in Chapter 1.
- Full coverage of all major retailing topics—including merchandising, consumer behavior, information systems, store location, operations, logistics, service retailing, the retail audit, retail institutions, franchising, human resource management, computerization, and retailing in a changing environment.
- A real-world approach focusing on both small and large retailers. Among the well-known firms discussed are Amazon.com, Bloomingdale's, Costco, Gap, Home Depot, Kohl's, Limited Brands, McDonald's, Neiman Marcus, Spiegel, Starbucks, Target Stores, and Wal-Mart.
- Real-world boxes on current retailing issues in each chapter. These boxes further illustrate the concepts presented in the text by focusing on real firms and situations.
- A numbered summary keyed to chapter objectives, a key terms listing, and discussion questions at the end of each chapter.
- Thirty-two short cases involving a wide range of retailers and retail practices.
- Eight comprehensive cases (one per part).

- Up-to-date information from such sources as *Advertising Age, Business Week, Chain Store Age, Direct Marketing, DSN Retailing Today, Entrepreneur, Fortune, Inc., Journal of Retailing, Progressive Grocer, Stores,* and *Wall Street Journal.*
- "How to Solve a Case Study" (now online at **www.prenhall.com/bermanevans**).
- End-of-chapter appendixes on service retailing (following Chapter 2), global retailing (following Chapter 3), and franchising (following Chapter 4).
- Three end-of-text appendixes: "Careers in Retailing," "About the Web Site," and "Glossary."

WWW.PRENHALL.COM/BERMANEVANS: A WEB SITE FOR THE 21ST CENTURY

We are E-xtremely E-nergized about the Web site that accompanies *Retail Management: A Strategic Approach,* Ninth Edition. The site is a lively learning, studying, interactive tool. It is easy to use (see Appendix B for more details), provides hands-on applications, and has easy downloads and hot links. We believe the supplement will be of great value to you. It is completely revamped and has separate student and instructor sections.

The student section of the Web site has several elements, including:

- **Important "Hot Links":** Applications broken down by chapter.
- **Career and Company Information:** Advice on resumé writing, how to take an interview, jobs in retailing, retail career ladders, and a comprehensive listing of retailers. There are "hot links" that go directly to the career sections of the Web sites of numerous retailers.
- **Study Materials:** Chapter objectives and summaries and chapter-by-chapter listings of key terms with their definitions.
- **Interactive Study Guide:** 20 multiple choice, 20 true-false, and 15 fill-in questions per chapter. You can get page references for wrong answers, check your score, and send the results to yourself or your professor.
- **Glossary:** All of the key terms from *Retail Management* with their definitions. Terms may be accessed alphabetically through an easy-to-use search feature.
- **Web Site Directory:** Hundreds of retailing-related Web sites, divided by topic. The sites range from search engines to government agencies to retail firms to trade associations.
- **Computer-Based Exercises in Retail Management:** Sixteen exercises keyed to parts in the text. These exercises reinforce your knowledge of basic retail concepts and enable you to gain "hands-on" experience with computerized software and spreadsheets. An icon ▬ in the text shows the best use for each exercise.
- **Strategic Planning Template for Retail Management:** Places the retail planning process into a series of steps that are integrated with Figure 3-1 on page 49 of this text. This in-depth exercise is built around 8 scenarios involving different types of retailers. Each retailer has unique strengths and weaknesses and faces a different set of opportunities and threats.
- **Web Exercises:** Dozens of user-friendly exercises. These are keyed to parts in the text and involve real company Web materials.
- **Free Downloads and Demos:** We encourage you to visit specific Web sites to gather useful information and try out innovative software.
- **Extra Math Problems:** For Chapters 9, 12, 16, and 17. These exercises help you to better understand complex retail mathematical concepts.

The instructor's section of the Web site includes teaching notes, hundreds of colorful PowerPoint slides, electronic versions of instructor support materials, and a whole lot more at the password-protected section of our Web site.

HOW THE TEXT IS ORGANIZED

Retail Management: A Strategic Approach has eight parts. Part One introduces the field of retailing, the basics of strategic planning, the importance of building and maintaining relations, and the decisions to be made in owning or managing a retail business. In Part Two, retail institutions are examined in terms of ownership types, as well as store-based, nonstore-based, electronic, and nontraditional strategy mixes. The wheel of retailing, scrambled merchandising, the retail life cycle, and the Web are covered. Part Three focuses on target marketing and information gathering methods, including discussions of why and how consumers shop, and the retailing information system and data warehouse. Part Four presents a four-step approach to location planning: trading-area analysis, choosing the most desirable type of location, selecting a general locale, and deciding on a specific site.

Part Five discusses the elements involved in managing a retail business: the retail organization structure, human resource management, and operations management (both financial and operational). Part Six deals with merchandise management—developing and implementing merchandise plans, the financial aspects of merchandising, and pricing. In Part Seven, the ways to communicate with customers are analyzed, with special attention paid to retail image, atmosphere, and promotion. Part Eight deals with integrating and controlling a retail strategy.

At the end of the text, Appendix A highlights career opportunities in retailing, Appendix B explains the components of the Web site and how to use it, and Appendix C is a comprehensive glossary.

ABOUT THE VIDEOS THAT ACCOMPANY *RETAIL MANAGEMENT: A STRATEGIC APPROACH*

Retail Management is accompanied by a video package, which consists of 25 videos that comprise over 5 hours of viewing. Of the 25 videos, seven are teaching videos on such topics as mass merchandising, franchising, retailing in Europe, retail site selection, planned purchases and open-to-buy, managing merchandise assortments, and visual merchandising. These are designed to supplement class lectures on these important topics. The other 18 videos involve a variety of retailers or retailers' suppliers, such as Starbucks, Lands' End, Lillian Vernon, Fresh Brands, Ritz Carlton, Maaco, Shopping 4 Sure, Atlas GIS, Mall of America, Supervalu, APL Logistics, NCR, Sensormatic, Bojangles, and Patagonia. Several of the videos are completely new to this edition, a number of others have been revised and updated.

FOR THE CLASSROOM

A complete teaching package is available. It includes:

- A detailed, password-protected section of our Web site devoted to instructor materials. After securing a password from Prentice Hall, please visit **www.prenhall.com/bermanevans** for more details. The site contains student material, as well.
- A comprehensive, several-hundred-page instructor's manual, complete with sample syllabi, lecture notes, and a lot more.
- Hundreds of colorful PowerPoint slides.
- A large test bank in computerized and print versions.
- A number of videos on a wide variety of retailing topics and companies, complete with teaching notes.
- A companion book, *Great Ideas in Retailing*, with additional cases, exercises, and more.

As always, the authors have remained extremely "hands on" in the development of these instructor materials.

Please feel free to send us comments regarding any aspect of *Retail Management* or its package: Barry Berman (E-mail at **mktbxb@hofstra.edu**) or Joel R. Evans (E-mail at **mktjre@hofstra.edu**), Department of Marketing and International Business, Hofstra University, Hempstead, N.Y., 11549. We promise to reply to any correspondence.

B.B.
J.R.E.

About the Authors

Barry Berman

Joel R. Evans

Barry Berman (Ph.D. in Business with majors in Marketing and Behavioral Science) is the Walter H. "Bud" Miller Distinguished Professor of Business and Professor of Marketing and International Business at Hofstra University. He is also the director of Hofstra's Executive M.B.A. program. **Joel R. Evans** (Ph.D. in Business with majors in Marketing and Public Policy) is the RMI Distinguished Professor of Business and Professor of Marketing and International Business at Hofstra University. He is also the coordinator for Hofstra's Master of Science programs in Marketing and Marketing Research.

While at Hofstra, each has been honored as a faculty inductee in Beta Gamma Sigma honor society, received multiple Dean's Awards for service, and been selected as the Teacher of the Year by the Hofstra M.B.A. Association. For several years, Drs. Berman and Evans were co-directors of Hofstra's Retail Management Institute and Business Research Institute. Both regularly teach undergraduate and graduate courses to a wide range of students.

Barry Berman and Joel R. Evans have worked together for 25 years in co-authoring several best-selling texts, including *Retail Management: A Strategic Approach*, Ninth Edition. They have also consulted for a variety of clients, from "mom-and-pop" retailers to *Fortune 500* companies. They are co-founders of the American Marketing Association's Special Interest Group in Retailing and Retail Management, and currently serve on its board. They have co-chaired the Academy of Marketing Science/American Collegiate Retailing Association's triennial conference. They have been featured speakers at the annual meeting of the National Retail Federation, the world's largest retailing trade association. Each has a chapter on retailing in the most recent edition of Dartnell's *Marketing Manager's Handbook*.

Barry and Joel are both active Web practitioners (and surfers), and they have written and developed all of the content for the comprehensive, interactive Web site that accompanies *Retail Management* (**www.prenhall.com/bermanevans**). They may be reached through the Web site or by writing to **mktbxb@Hofstra.edu** (Barry Berman) and **mktjre@Hofstra.edu** (Joel R. Evans).

Acknowledgments

Many people have assisted us in the preparation of this book, and to them we extend our warmest appreciation.

We thank the following reviewers, who have reacted to this or earlier editions of the text. Each has provided us with perceptive comments that have helped us to crystallize our thoughts and to make *Retail Management* the best book possible:

M. Wayne Alexander, Morehead State University

Larry Audler, University of New Orleans

Ramon Avila, Ball State University

Betty V. Balevic, Skidmore College

Stephen Batory, Bloomsburg University

Joseph J. Belonax, Western Michigan University

Ronald Bernard, Diablo Valley College

Charlane Bomrad, Onondaga Community College

John J. Buckley, Orange County Community College

David J. Burns, Youngstown State University

Joseph A. Davidson, Cuyahoga Community College

Peter T. Doukas, Westchester Community College

Jack D. Eure, Jr., Southwest Texas State University

Phyllis Fein, Westchester Community College

Letty Fisher, Westchester Community College

Myron Gable, Shippensburg University

Linda L. Golden, University of Texas at Austin

James Gray, Florida Atlantic University

J. Duncan Herrington, Radford University

Mary Higby, University of Detroit, Mercy

Charles A. Ingene, University of Mississippi

Marvin A. Jolson, University of Maryland

David C. Jones, Otterbein College

Carol Kaufman-Scarborough, Rutgers University

Ruth Keyes, SUNY College of Technology

Maryon King, Southern Illinois University

John Lanasa, Duquesne University

J. Ford Laumer, Jr., Auburn University

Richard C. Leventhal, Metropolitan State College

Michael Little, Virginia Commonwealth University

John Lloyd, Monroe Community College

James O. McCann, Henry Ford Community College

Frank McDaniels, Delaware County Community College

Ronald Michman, Shippensburg University

Howard C. Paul, Mercyhurst College

Roy B. Payne, Purdue University

Dawn I. Pysarchik, Michigan State University

Curtis Reierson, Baylor University

Barry Rudin, Loras College

Julie Toner Schrader, North Dakota State University

Steven J. Shaw, University of South Carolina

Ruth K. Shelton, James Madison University

Gladys S. Sherdell, Bellarmine College

Jill F. Slomski, Gannon University

John E. Swan, University of Alabama, Birmingham

Anthony Urbanisk, Northern State University

Lillian Werner, University of Minnesota

Kaylene C. Williams, California State University, Stanislaus

Terrell G. Williams, Western Washington State University

Ugur Yucelt, Penn State University, Harrisburg

Special thanks and acknowledgment are due to our Prentice Hall colleagues who have worked on this edition, especially editors Katie Stevens and Bruce Kaplan, production editor Marcela Maslanczuk, media project manager Anthony Palmiotto, assistant editor Melissa Pellerano, and editorial assistant Danielle Serra. We also appreciate the efforts of Diane Schoenberg, Juan Gomez, and Jeff Roth for their editorial assistance; and Linda Berman for compiling the indexes.

We would also like to recognize the contributions of Kenneth McLeod, who recently passed away. Ken was our first editor and was a great friend.

Barry Berman
Joel R. Evans
HOFSTRA UNIVERSITY

part one

An Overview of Strategic Retail Management

Welcome to *Retail Management: A Strategic Approach, 9e.* We hope you find this book to be as informative and reader-friendly as possible. Please visit our Web site (**www.prenhall.com/bermanevans**) for interactive, useful, up-to-date features that complement the text—including chapter-by-chapter hot links, a study guide, and a whole lot more!

In Part One, we explore the field of retailing, establishing and maintaining relationships, and the basic principles of strategic planning and the decisions made in owning or managing a retail business.

■ **Chapter 1** describes retailing, shows why it should be studied, and examines its special characteristics. We note the value of strategic planning, including a detailed review of Target Stores. The retailing concept is presented, along with the total retail experience, customer service, and relationship retailing. The focus and format of the text are detailed.

■ **Chapter 2** looks at the complexities of retailers' relationships—with both customers and other channel members. We examine value and the value chain, customer relationships and channel relationships, the differences in relationship-building between goods and service retailers, the impact of technology on retailing relationships, and the interplay between ethical performance and relationships in retailing. The chapter ends with an appendix on planning for the unique aspects of service retailing.

■ **Chapter 3** shows the usefulness of strategic planning for all kinds of retailers. We focus on the planning process: situation analysis, objectives, identifying consumers, overall strategy, specific activities, control, and feedback. We also look at the controllable and uncontrollable parts of a retail strategy. Strategic planning is shown as a series of interrelated steps that are continuously reviewed. At the end of the chapter, there is an appendix on the strategic implications of international retailing.

AN INTRODUCTION TO RETAILING

Reprinted by permission.

A perfect example of a dream come true is the story of Sam Walton, the founder of Wal-Mart (**www.walmart.com**). From a single store, Wal-Mart has grown to become the largest company in the United States (in terms of revenues). And today it dwarfs every other retailer.

In 1992, President George Bush presented Sam Walton with the Medal of Freedom and said he was "an American original who embodied the entrepreneurial spirit and epitomized the American dream." As a store owner in Bentonville, Arkansas, Sam Walton had a simple strategy: to take his retail stores to rural areas of the United States and then sell goods at the lowest prices around. Sam was convinced that a large discount format would work in rural communities.

Walton's first discount store opened in 1962 and used such slogans as "We sell for less" and "Satisfaction guaranteed," two of the current hallmarks of the company. By the end of 1969, Wal-Mart had expanded to 31 locations. Within a year, Wal-Mart became a public corporation and rapidly grew on the basis of additional discount stores, its supercenter format, and global expansion. Wal-Mart has become a true textbook example of how a retailer can maintain growth without losing sight of its original core values of low overhead, the use of innovative distribution systems, and customer orientation—whereby employees swear to serve the customer. "So help me, Sam."[1]

chapter objectives

1. To define retailing, consider it from various perspectives, demonstrate its impact, and note its special characteristics

2. To introduce the concept of strategic planning and apply it

3. To show why the retailing concept is the foundation of a successful business, with an emphasis on the total retail experience, customer service, and relationship retailing

4. To indicate the focus and format of the text

OVERVIEW

Retailing encompasses the business activities involved in selling goods and services to consumers for their personal, family, or household use. It includes every sale to the *final* consumer—ranging from cars to apparel to meals at restaurants to theater tickets. Retailing is the last stage in the distribution process.

Retailing today is at an interesting crossroads. On the one hand, retail sales are at their highest point in history. Wal-Mart is now the leading company in the world in terms of sales—ahead of ExxonMobil, General Motors, and other manufacturing giants. New technologies are improving retail productivity. There are lots of opportunities to start a new retail business—or work for an existing one—and to become a franchisee. Global retailing possibilities abound. On the other hand, retailers face numerous challenges. Many consumers are bored with shopping or do not have much time for it. Some locales have too many stores, and retailers often spur one another into frequent price cutting (and low profit margins). Customer service expectations are high at a time when more retailers offer self-service and automated systems. At the same time, many retailers remain unsure what to do with the Web; they are still grappling with the emphasis to place on image enhancement, customer information and feedback, and sales transactions.

These are the issues that retailers must resolve: "How can we best serve our customers while earning a fair profit?" "How can we stand out in a highly competitive environment where consumers have so many choices?" "How can we grow our business while retaining a core of loyal customers?" Our point of view: Retail decision makers can best address these questions by fully understanding and applying the basic principles of retailing in a well-structured, systematic, and focused retail strategy. That is the philosophy behind *Retail Management: A Strategic Approach.*

Visit Krispy Kreme (www.krispykreme.com) and see what drives one of the world's "hot" retailers.

Can retailers flourish in today's tough marketplace? You bet! Just look at your favorite restaurant, gift shop, and food store. Look at the growth of Costco, Kohl's, and Krispy Kreme Doughnuts. What do they have in common? A desire to please the customer and a strong market niche. To prosper in the long term, they all need a strategic plan and a willingness to adapt, both central thrusts of this book. See Figure 1-1.

In Chapter 1, we will look at the framework of retailing, the importance of developing and applying a sound retail stategy, and the focus and format of the text.

THE FRAMEWORK OF RETAILING

To better appreciate retailing's role and the range of retailing activities, let us view it from three different perspectives:

- Suppose we manage a manufacturing firm that makes vacuum cleaners. How should we sell these items? We could distribute via big chains such as Circuit City or small neighborhood

FIGURE 1-1

Boom Times for Costco

By consistently fulfilling its simple mission statement— "to continually provide our members with quality goods and services at the lowest possible prices"— Costco has grown into a retailing dynamo. It now operates hundreds of membership stores in the United States, Canada, Great Britain, Taiwan, Korea, Japan, and Mexico.

Photo reprinted by permission of Retail Forward, Inc.

appliance stores, have our own sales force visit people in their homes (as Aerus—formerly Electrolux—does), or set up our own stores (if we have the ability and resources to do so). We could sponsor TV infomercials or magazine ads, complete with a toll-free phone number.

● Suppose we have an idea for a new way to teach first graders how to use computer software for spelling and vocabulary. How should we implement this idea? We could lease a store in a strip shopping center and run ads in a local paper, rent space in a Y and rely on teacher referrals, or do mailings to parents and visit children in their homes. In each case, the service is offered "live." But there is another option: We could use an animated Web site to teach children online.

● Suppose that we, as consumers, want to buy apparel. What choices do we have? We could go to a department store or an apparel store. We could shop with a full-service retailer or a discounter. We could go to a shopping center or order from a catalog. We could look to retailers that carry a wide range of clothing (from outerwear to jeans to suits) or look to firms that specialize in one clothing category (such as leather coats). We could zip around the Web and visit retailers around the globe.

Service businesses such as Lawn Doctor (www. lawndoctor.com) often engage in retailing.

There is a tendency to think of retailing as primarily involving the sale of tangible (physical) goods. However, retailing also includes the sale of services. And this is a big part of retailing! A service may be the shopper's primary purchase (such as a haircut) or it may be part of the shopper's purchase of a good (such as delivery). Retailing does not have to involve a store. Mail and phone orders, direct selling to consumers in their homes and offices, Web transactions, and vending machine sales all fall within the scope of retailing. Retailing does not even have to include a "retailer." Manufacturers, importers, nonprofit firms, and wholesalers act as retailers when they sell to final consumers.

Let us now examine various reasons for studying retailing and its special characteristics.

REASONS FOR STUDYING RETAILING

Learn more about the exciting array of retailing career opportunities (www. careersinretailing.com).

Retailing is an important field to study because of its impact on the economy, its functions in distribution, and its relationship with firms selling goods and services to retailers for their resale or use. These factors are discussed next. A fourth factor for students of retailing is the broad range of career opportunities, as highlighted with a "Careers in Retailing" box in each chapter, Appendix A at the end of this book, and our Web site (**www.prenhall.com/bermanevans**). See Figure 1-2.

The Impact of Retailing on the Economy

Retailing is a major part of U.S. and world commerce. Retail sales and employment are vital economic contributors, and retail trends often mirror trends in a nation's overall economy.

Careers in RETAILING
Many Career Opportunities Are Available in Retailing

Although the typical entry-level positions in retailing for a college graduate include retail management trainee, department/sales manager, and assistant buyer, it is generally difficult to classify retail career opportunites—because there are so many of them. Most large retail organizations can be described as "small cities." As such, these retailers offer career paths in almost every aspect of business, such as buying, store operations, accounting, financial management, human resources, advertising, public relations, marketing research, and so on.

The ideal candidate pursing a retail career should possess the following qualities:

● Be a "people person" to understand customer needs and be an effective team member.
● Be flexible to be able to perform a variety of tasks throughout the workday.

● Be decisive to make quick decisions that are well thought out.
● Have analytical skills to analyze data and predict trends.
● Have stamina to be able to work under pressure for long time periods.

What makes retailing so fascinating is the constant change that a retail executive must understand and manage. Among the areas of retailing that are now undergoing rapid change are the increased importance on nonstore retailing, the focus on customer satisfaction, and the application of technology to all areas of retailing. These changes represent both opportunities and challenges.

Source: "Careers in Retailing," **www.nrf.com** (January 27, 2003).

FIGURE 1-2
Career Pathways
to Success

Photo reprinted by permission
of *DSN Retailing Today*.

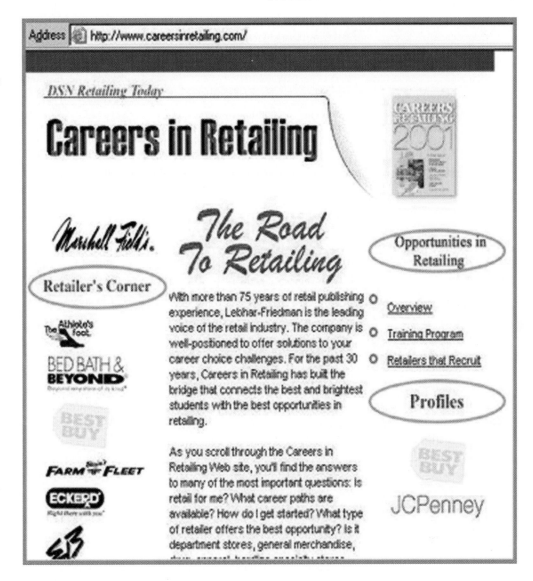

According to the Department of Commerce, annual U.S. retail store sales exceed $3.5 trillion—representing 31 percent of the total economy. Telephone and mail-order sales by non-store retailers, vending machines, direct selling, and the Web generate hundreds of billions of dollars in additional yearly revenues. And personal consumption expenditures on financial, medical, legal, educational, and other services account for another several hundred billion dollars in annual retail revenues. Outside the United States, retail sales are trillions of dollars per year.

Durable goods stores—including the auto group; furniture and appliance group; and lumber, building materials, and hardware group—make up 42 percent of U.S. retail store sales. Nondurable goods and services stores—including the general merchandise group, apparel group, gasoline service stations, eating and drinking places, food group, drug and proprietary stores, and liquor stores—together account for 58 percent of U.S. retail store sales.

The world's 100 largest retailers generate $2 trillion in annual revenues. They represent 16 nations. Forty-three of the 100 are based in the United States, 11 in Great Britain, 10 in Japan, 9 in France, and 8 in Germany.[2] Table 1-1 shows the 2001 performance of the 10 largest U.S. retailers. They produced $580 billion in sales, operated 24,000-plus stores, and employed 3.5 million people. Visit our Web site for links to a lot of current information on retailing (**www.prenhall. com/bermanevans**).

The Occupational Outlook Handbook (www.bls.gov/oco) is a great source of information on employment trends.

Retailing is a major source of jobs. In the United States alone, 23 million people—about one-sixth of the total labor force—work for traditional retailers. Yet this figure understates the true

TABLE 1-1		The 10 Largest Retailers in the United States, 2001					
Rank	Company	Web Address	Major Retail Emphasis	Sales (million)	After-Tax Earnings (millions)	Number of Stores	Number of Employees
1	Wal-Mart	www.walmart.com	Full-line discount stores, membership clubs	$219,812	$6,671	4,414	1,383,000
2	Home Depot	www.homedepot.com	Home centers, design centers	53,553	3,044	1,348	256,300
3	Kroger	www.kroger.com	Supermarkets, convenience stores, jewelry stores	50,098	1,043	3,534	288,000
4	Sears Roebuck	www.sears.com	Department stores, specialty stores	41,078	735	2,960	310,000
5	Target	www.target.com	Full-line discount stores, department stores	39,362	1,368	1,381	223,500
6	Albertson's	www.albertsons.com	Supermarkets, drugstores	37,931	501	2,400	220,000
7	Kmart	www.kmart.com	Full-line discount stores	37,028	(244)	2,150	240,525
8	Costco	www.costco.com	Membership clubs	34,797	602	369	64,500
9	Safeway	www.safeway.com	Supermarkets	34,301	1,284	1,773	193,000
10	J.C. Penney	www.jcpenney.com	Department stores, drugstores, catalog	32,004	98	3,770	270,000

Sources: "Triversity Top 100 Retailers," *Stores* (July 2002); and company annual reports.

number of people who work in retailing because it does not include the several million persons employed by service firms, seasonal employees, proprietors, and unreported workers in family businesses or partnerships.

From a cost perspective, retailing is a significant field of study. In the United States, on average, 31 cents of every dollar spent in department stores, 44 cents spent in furniture and home furnishings stores, and 27 cents spent in grocery stores go to the retailers to cover operating costs, activities performed, and profits. Costs include rent, displays, wages, ads, and maintenance. Only a small part of each dollar is profit. In 2001, the 10 largest U.S. retailers' after-tax profits averaged 2.6 percent of sales.[3] Figure 1-3 shows costs and profits for Kroger, a food-based retailer that also operates some jewelry businesses.

FIGURE 1-3
The High Costs and Low Profits of Retailing—Where the Typical $100 Spent with Kroger Went in 2001

Source: Computed by the authors from *Kroger 2001 Annual Report.*

Manufacturer's costs and profits

Retailer's operating, personnel, advertising, and other costs

Retailer's income taxes

Retailer's after-tax profits

$72.65 $23.94 $1.33 $2.08

FIGURE 1-4
A Typical Channel of
Distribution

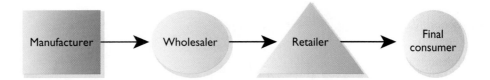

FIGURE 1-4
A Typical Channel of
Distribution

Retail Functions in Distribution

Retailing is the last stage in a **channel of distribution**—all of the businesses and people involved in the physical movement and transfer of ownership of goods and services from producer to consumer. A typical distribution channel is shown in Figure 1-4. Retailers often act as the contact between manufacturers, wholesalers, and the consumer. Many manufacturers would like to make one basic type of item and sell their entire inventory to as few buyers as possible, but consumers usually want to choose from a variety of goods and services and purchase a limited quantity. Retailers collect an assortment from various sources, buy in large quantity, and sell in small amounts. This is the **sorting process**. See Figure 1-5.

Another job for retailers is communicating both with customers and with manufacturers and wholesalers. Shoppers learn about the availability and characteristics of goods and services, store hours, sales, and so on from retailer ads, salespeople, and displays. Manufacturers and wholesalers are informed by their retailers with regard to sales forecasts, delivery delays, customer complaints, defective items, inventory turnover, and more. Many goods and services have been modified due to retailer feedback.

For small suppliers, retailers can provide assistance by transporting, storing, marking, advertising, and pre-paying for products. Small retailers may need the same type of help from their suppliers. The functions performed by retailers affect the percentage of each sales dollar they need to cover costs and profits.

Retailers also complete transactions with customers. This means having convenient locations, filling orders promptly and accurately, and processing credit purchases. Some retailers also provide customer services such as gift wrapping, delivery and installation. To make themselves even more appealing, many firms now engage in **multi-channel retailing** whereby a retailer sells to consumers through multiple retail formats (points of contact). Most large retailers operate both physical stores and Web sites to make shopping easier and to accommodate consumer desires. Firms such as J.C. Penney sell to customers through retail stores, mail-order catalogs, a Web site, and a toll-free phone number. See Figure 1-6.

FIGURE 1-5
The Retailer's Role in the
Sorting Process

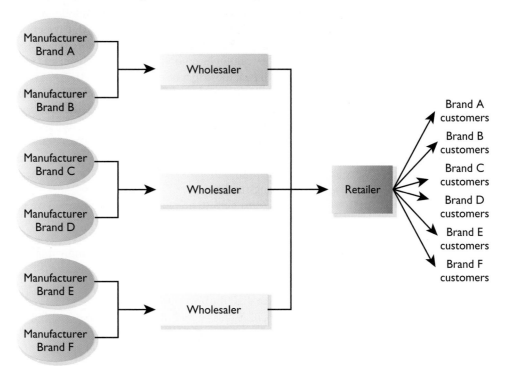

Polo Ralph Lauren
(www.polo.com) is not
only a designer but
also a retailer.

For these reasons, products are usually sold through retailers not owned by manufacturers (wholesalers). This lets manufacturers reach more customers, reduce costs, improve cash flow, increase sales more rapidly, and focus on their area of expertise. Select manufacturers such as Sherwin-Williams and Polo Ralph Lauren do operate retail facilities (besides selling at traditional retailers). In running their stores, these firms complete the full range of retailing functions and compete with conventional retailers.

The Relationships Among Retailers and Their Suppliers

Relationships among retailers and suppliers can be complex. Because retailers are part of a distribution channel, manufacturers and wholesalers must be concerned about the caliber of displays, customer service, store hours, and retailers' reliability as business partners. Retailers are also major customers of goods and services for resale, store fixtures, computers, management consulting, and insurance.

These are some issues over which retailers and suppliers have different priorities: control over the distribution channel, profit allocation, the number of competing retailers handling suppliers' products, product displays, promotion support, payment terms, and operating flexibility. Due to the growth of retail chains, retailers have more power than ever. Unless suppliers know retailers' needs, they cannot have good rapport with them; and as long as retailers have a choice of suppliers, they will pick those that offer them more.

Channel relations tend to be smoothest with **exclusive distribution**, whereby suppliers make agreements with one or a few retailers that designate the latter as the only ones in specified geographic areas to carry certain brands or products. This stimulates both parties to work together to maintain an image, assign shelf space, allot profits and costs, and advertise. It also usually requires that retailers limit their brand selection in the specified product lines; they might have to decline to handle other suppliers' brands. From the manufacturers' perspective, exclusive distribution may limit their long-run total sales.

Channel relations tend to be most volatile with **intensive distribution**, whereby suppliers sell through as many retailers as possible. This often maximizes suppliers' sales and lets retailers offer many brands and product versions. Competition among retailers selling the same items is high; and retailers may use tactics not beneficial to individual suppliers, as they are more concerned about their own results. Retailers may assign little shelf space to specific brands, set very high prices on them, and not advertise them.

With **selective distribution**, suppliers sell through a moderate number of retailers. This combines aspects of exclusive and intensive distribution. Suppliers have higher sales than in exclusive distribution, and retailers carry some competing brands. It encourages suppliers to provide some marketing support and retailers to give adequate shelf space. See Figure 1-7.

FIGURE 1-7
Comparing Exclusive,
Intensive, and Selective
Distribution

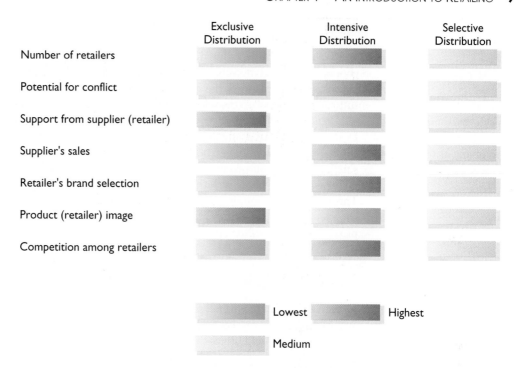

THE SPECIAL CHARACTERISTICS OF RETAILING

Three factors that distinguish retailing from other types of business are noted in Figure 1-8 and discussed here. Each factor imposes unique requirements on retail firms.

The average amount of a sales transaction for retailers is much less than for manufacturers: The average sales transaction per shopping trip is well under $100 for department stores, specialty stores, and supermarkets. This low amount creates a need to tightly control the costs associated with each transaction (such as credit verification, sales personnel, and bagging); to maximize the number of customers drawn to the retailer, which may place more emphasis on ads and special promotions; and to increase impulse sales by more aggressive selling. However, cost control can be tough. For instance, inventory management is often expensive due to the many small transactions to a large number of customers. A typical supermarket has several thousand customer transactions *per week*, which makes it harder to find the proper in-stock level and product selection. Thus, retailers are expanding their use of computerized inventory systems.

Final consumers make many unplanned or impulse purchases: Surveys show that a large percentage of consumers do not look at ads before shopping, do not prepare shopping lists (or

FIGURE 1-8
Special Characteristics
Affecting Retailers

deviate from the lists once in stores), and make fully unplanned purchases. This behavior indicates the value of in-store displays, attractive store layouts, and well-organized stores, catalogs, and Web sites. Candy, cosmetics, snack foods, magazines, and other items are sold as impulse goods when placed in visible, high-traffic areas in a store, catalog, or Web site. Because so many purchases are unplanned, the retailer's ability to forecast, budget, order merchandise, and have sufficient personnel on the selling floor is more difficult.

Macy's (www.macys.com) has a Web site to accompany its traditional stores and catalogs.

Retail customers usually visit a store, even though mail, phone, and Web sales have increased: Despite the inroads made by nonstore retailers, most retail transactions are still conducted in stores—and will continue to be in the future. Many people like to shop in person; want to touch, smell, and/or try on products; like to browse for unplanned purchases; feel more comfortable taking a purchase home with them than waiting for a delivery; and desire privacy while at home. This store-based shopping orientation has implications for retailers; they must work to attract shoppers to their stores and consider such factors as store location, transportation, store hours, proximity of competitors, product selection, parking, and ads.

THE IMPORTANCE OF DEVELOPING AND APPLYING A RETAIL STRATEGY

A **retail strategy** is the overall plan guiding a retail firm. It influences the firm's business activities and its response to market forces, such as competition and the economy. Any retailer, regardless of size or type, should utilize these six steps in strategic planning:

1. Define the type of business in terms of the goods or service category and the company's specific orientation (such as full service or "no frills").
2. Set long-run and short-run objectives for sales and profit, market share, image, and so on.
3. Determine the customer market to target on the basis of its characteristics (such as gender and income level) and needs (such as product and brand preferences).
4. Devise an overall, long-run plan that gives general direction to the firm and its employees.
5. Implement an integrated strategy that combines such factors as store location, product assortment, pricing, and advertising and displays to achieve objectives.
6. Regularly evaluate performance and correct weaknesses or problems when observed.

To illustrate these points, the background and strategy of Target Stores—one of the world's foremost retailers—are presented. Then the retailing concept is explained and applied.

Ethics in RETAILING
Lands' End: A High Standard of Business Conduct

Lands' End (**www.landsend.com**) is so serious about its business conduct that it will stop all future orders with a partner if the partner does not correct a practice Land's End deems unacceptable. Of particular concern are its partners' labor practices.

Lands' End does not tolerate partners that employ child workers under 16 years of age, pay less than minimum wages, practice discrimination, or have unsafe working conditions. To enforce its standards, Lands' End requires that business partners provide it with full access to both their facilities and to their employment records. Lands' End then makes unannounced visits.

Lands' End's ethical standards also extend to customers. The firm proudly promotes its "principles of doing business" as one of its core values. Among its principles are:

● "We price our products fairly and honestly. We do not, have not, and will not participate in the common retailing practice of inflating markups to set up a phony 'sale'."
● "We believe that what is best for our customer is best for all of us. Everyone here understands that concept. Our sales and service staff are urged to take all the time necessary to take care of you. We even pay for your call, for whatever reason you call."

Sources: "Lands' End's Standards of Business Conduct," **www.landsend.com** (September 27, 2002); and "Lands' End Principles of Doing Business," **www.landsend.com** (September 27, 2002).

TARGET STORES: A RETAIL STRATEGY THAT AIMS AND SCORES![4]

Company Background

See the mass/class approach of Target Stores (www.target.com).

Target Stores is the leading division of Target Corporation (which also operates Marshall Field's and Mervyn's). A brief history of the chain appears at its Web site (**www.target.com**):

> In 1961, Dayton's department store identified a demand for a store that sold less expensive goods in a quick, convenient format. In 1962, the first Target store opened in Roseville, Minnesota. We were the first retail store to offer well-known national brands at discounted prices. During the 1970s, we paved new ground by using electronic cash registers to monitor inventory and speed up service. And we began an annual shopping event for seniors and those with disabilities, and a toy safety campaign. In the 1980s, opening new stores all the time, we rolled out electronic scanning nationwide. The 1990s saw our first Target Greatland store. Our Club Wedd bridal gift registry went nationwide in 1995, followed by Lullaby Club. We opened our first SuperTarget, combining groceries and special services with a Target Greatland store. We introduced our own credit card. And that's just the beginning!

Today, Target Stores has about 1,000 stores in 47 states with 214,000 employees. It also operates a popular Web shopping site of its own and is a partner of Amazon.com. In 2001, Target Stores had sales of $32.6 billion, which would have placed it 10th among the largest U.S. retailers.

The Target Stores' Strategy: Keys to Success

Throughout its existence, Target has followed a consistent, far-sighted, customer-oriented strategy—one that has paved the way for its long-term achievements:

- *Growth-oriented objectives.* The chain seeks annual long-run growth of 8 percent to 12 percent. To reach that goal, it has invested billions of dollars to increase total store square footage by more than 50 percent over the past five years. In 2002 alone, it opened about 110 new stores.

- *Appeal to a prime market.* The firm is strong with middle-income, well-educated adults, who have an average income that is about 20 percent higher than the typical Wal-Mart shopper. It is quite popular among female shoppers, parents with children under 18, and 25- to 44-year-olds.

- *Distinctive company image.* Target Stores has done a superb job of positioning itself: "Pay Less + Expect More." See Figure 1-9. It is a true discount department store chain with every-day low prices. Along with Wal-Mart and Kmart, Target Stores makes up the "big three" of discounting. It has linoleum floors, shopping carts, and a simple store layout. But Target is also perceived as an "upscale discounter." It carries products from such designers as Michael

FIGURE 1-9

"Pay Less + Expect More" at Target

This well-admired chain projects a strong image for both low prices and plentiful, quality merchandise.

Photo reprinted by permission of Retail Forward, Inc.

Graves (home products), Todd Oldham (apparel), Mikasa (dinnerware), and Michael Sprouse (apparel, accessories, and home products).

- *Focus.* The chain never loses sight of its discount store niche: "Value always wins." Target "has succeeded in impressing on consumers that spending $8 on a basic white T-shirt in its stores, rather than $18 at Gap stores, is not only smart, it's cool."

- *Strong customer service for its retail category.* The firm prides itself on offering excellent customer service for a discount store: "At the end of most aisles is a red service phone that customers can use to get help in finding the Gulden's mustard or the Philippe Starck chocolate spread." And "If an item is out of stock, Target will offer a substitute item of equal or greater value at the same discount, or give a rain check for the original item."

- *Multiple points of contact.* Target reaches its customers through extensive advertising, stores in 47 states, and a toll-free telephone service center (open 7 days a week, 17 hours per day).

- *Employee relations.* "Target believes in celebrating success, applauding risk, and bringing out the best in teams and individuals." It "encourages personal and career development through individual growth plans designed by team members, an array of training programs, performance feedback, and more."

- *Innovation.* The chain "has long embraced the concepts of innovation and newness, recognizing the importance of creating unique ways to delight our guests every time they visit our stores."

- *Commitment to technology.* Target Stores is devoted to new technologies. Consider the new Target Visa card: It "has a built-in computer chip, called a smart chip. Today, you can use your Target Visa with an in-home smart card reader to access exclusive offers. And soon, you'll see exciting new smart chip features popping up! The chip makes the Target Visa smart."

- *Community involvement.* Target believes in giving back. One of its popular programs is School Fundraising: "You can support your school just by shopping with your Target Visa or Target Guest Card. Target will donate an amount equal to 1 percent of your qualifying purchases at Target Stores or target.com to the eligible K–12 school of your choice."

- *Constant performance monitoring.* "In recent years, we have become increasingly flexible in our site selection and store design—without compromising our Target brand or our financial discipline."

THE RETAILING CONCEPT

As we just described, Target Stores has a sincere long-term desire to please customers. In doing so, it uses a customer-centered, chainwide approach to strategy development and implementation; it is value-driven and it has clear goals. Together, these four principles form the **retailing concept** (depicted in Figure 1-10), which should be understood and applied by all retailers:

1. *Customer orientation.* The retailer determines the attributes and needs of its customers and endeavors to satisfy these needs to the fullest.

FIGURE 1-10
Applying the Retailing Concept

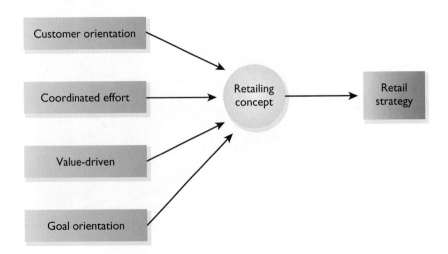

2. *Coordinated effort.* The retailer integrates all plans and activities to maximize efficiency.
3. *Value-driven.* The retailer offers good value to customers, whether it be upscale or discount. This means having prices appropriate for the level of products and customer service.
4. *Goal orientation.* The retailer sets goals and then uses its strategy to attain them.

Unfortunately, this concept is not grasped by every retailer. Some are indifferent to customer needs, plan haphazardly, have prices that do not reflect the value offered, and have unclear goals. Some are not receptive to change, or they blindly follow strategies enacted by competitors. Some do not get feedback from customers; they rely on supplier reports or their own past sales trends.

The retailing concept is fairly easy to adopt. It means communicating with shoppers and viewing their desires as critical to the firm's success, having a consistent strategy (such as offering designer brands, plentiful sales personnel, attractive displays, and above-average prices in an upscale store), offering prices perceived as "fair" (a good value for the money) by customers, and working to achieve meaningful, specific, and reachable goals. However, the retailing concept is only a strategic guide. It does not deal with a firm's internal capabilities or competitive advantages but offers a broad planning framework.

Let's look at three issues that relate to a retailer's performance in terms of the retailing concept: the total retail experience, customer service, and relationship retailing.

The Total Retail Experience

While one consumer may shop at a discount retailer, another at a neighborhood store, and a third at a full-service firm, these diverse customers all have something crucial in common: They each encounter a total retail experience (including everything from parking to checkout counter) in making a purchase. According to WSL Strategic Retail's *How America Shops 2002*, "When asked about the characteristics of 'their most favorite' outlet, shoppers rated appearance and cleanliness highest, followed by convenience, 'a good place to spend time browsing,' and 'attracts customers I feel comfortable with.'"[5]

The **total retail experience** includes all the elements in a retail offering that encourage or inhibit consumers during their contact with a retailer. Many elements, such as the number of salespeople, displays, prices, the brands carried, and inventory on hand, are controllable by a retailer; others, such as the adequacy of on-street parking, the speed of a consumer's modem, and sales taxes, are not. If some part of the total retail experience is unsatisfactory, consumers may not make a purchase—they may even decide not to patronize a retailer again: "Everyone has stories to tell about disrespectful retailing. You're in an electronics store, looking for assistance to buy a DVD player or a laptop computer. You spot a couple of employees by their uniforms and badges, but they're deep in conversation. They glance in your direction but continue to ignore you. After a while, you walk out, never to return."[6]

Technology in RETAILING

Paw Paw Shopping Center: High Touch and High Tech

Marv Imus, vice-president of the family-owned Paw Paw Shopping Center (**www.pawpawshop.com**) in Paw Paw, Michigan, has developed a customer-friendly frequent shopping card. The center's Super1card, which is involved with 88 percent of total sales, enables Imus to better understand the shopping behavior of his firm's 12,000 weekly supermarket customers.

Imus spends three hours daily studying his frequent shopper data base so he can develop innovative store promotions. He typically creates three different target promotions per month, which are then distributed by mail to 2,500 specific customers. Other promotions are focused on a smaller target audience of 500 cardholders. Although the redemption rate on the larger mailings averages 20 percent, Imus has achieved redemption rates as high as 80 percent on his smaller, more targeted offerings.

Even though Imus extensively uses technology, he sees himself more as a technology implementer than a technology expert. In addition to his frequent shopper card, his supermarket has a Web site that receives over 1,000 hits per week and an electronic customer newsletter. Imus agrees with his father, who started the supermarket 50 years ago, that his relationships with customers and employees are more valuable than his company's data base: "The secret today is to combine both—people and technology—to become a better retailer."

Source: Jane Olszeski Tortola, "Coming Full Circle: Michigan Operator Marv Imus Takes a High-Tech Approach to Maintaining a 50-Year Tradition of Connecting with Customers," *Progressive Grocer* (February 1, 2002), pp. 48–50.

In planning its strategy, a retailer must be sure that all strategic elements are in place. *For the shopper segment to which it appeals*, the total retail experience must be aimed at fulfilling that segment's expectations. A discounter should have ample stock on hand when it runs sales but not plush carpeting, and a full-service store should have superior personnel but not have them perceived as haughty by customers. Some retailers have not learned this lesson, which is why some theme restaurants are in trouble. Their novelty has worn off, and many people believe that the food is only fair while prices are high.

A big challenge for today's retailers is generating customer "excitement" because many people are bored with shopping or have little time for it. Here is what one retailer, highlighted in Figure 1-11, is doing:

> Build-A-Bear Workshop utilizes its physical space as a forum to interact with the customer. Heavily experience-oriented, customers come into the store and are involved in every step of the process of creating their own bear, from designing to dressing. The appeal of this type of environment is that customers can experience the product—they can see, touch, and interact with their creation, thereby interacting with the brand. In this way, Build-A-Bear uses its stores to personalize the experience and forge an emotional bond with its customers.[7]

Customer Service

Customer service refers to the identifiable, but sometimes intangible, activities undertaken by a retailer in conjunction with the basic goods and services it sells. It has a strong impact on the total retail experience. Among the factors comprising a customer service strategy are store hours, parking, shopper friendliness of the store layout, credit acceptance, salespeople, amenities such as gift wrapping, rest rooms, employee politeness, delivery policies, the time shoppers spend on checkout lines, and customer follow-up. This list is not all inclusive, and it differs in terms of the retail strategy undertaken. Customer service is discussed further in Chapter 2, "Building and Sustaining Relationships in Retailing."

Satisfaction with customer service is affected by expectations (based on the type of retailer) and past experience, and people's assessment of customer service depends on their perceptions—not necessarily reality. Different people may evaluate the same service quite differently. The same person may even rate a firm's customer service differently over time due to its intangibility, though the service stays constant:

> Costco shoppers don't expect anyone to help them to their car with bundles of commodities. Teens at Abercrombie & Fitch would be pretty turned off if a tuxedo-clad piano player serenaded them while they shopped. And Wal-Mart customers would protest loudly if the company traded its shopping carts for oversized nylon tote bags. On the other hand, helping shoppers to their cars when they have an oversized purchase is

part of the service package at P.C. Richard & Sons, piano music sets the mood at Nordstrom, and nylon totes jammed full of value-priced apparel are in sync with the Old Navy image. Service varies widely from one retailer to the next, and from one shopping channel to the next. The challenge for retailers is to ask shoppers what they expect in the way of service, listen to what they say, and then make every attempt to satisfy them.[8]

Interestingly, despite a desire to provide excellent customer service, a number of outstanding retailers now wonder if "the customer is always right." Are there limits? Ponder this scenario: Companies such as Home Depot, Saks Fifth Avenue, and Old Navy are among those that have tightened their return policies. Furthermore, "Gap, which used to exchange pretty much anything at anytime, now requires clothes kept longer than two weeks to come back unworn, unwashed, and with the tags on." Gap also no longer accepts returns at its U.S. stores of merchandise bought overseas. Some leading retailers are using software programs to determine "habitual returners." Why the policy change? "With growth slowing in the retail business, companies are scrambling to plug the leaks. About 6 percent of all retail purchases are returned every year."[9]

Relationship Retailing

Today's best retailers realize it is in their interest to engage in **relationship retailing**, whereby they seek to establish and maintain long-term bonds with customers, rather than act as if each sales transaction is a completely new encounter. This means concentrating on the total retail experience, monitoring satisfaction with customer service, and staying in touch with customers. Figure 1-12 shows a customer respect checklist that retailers could use to assess their relationship efforts.

To be effective in relationship retailing, a firm should keep two points in mind: (1) Because it is harder to lure new customers than to make existing ones happy, a "win-win" approach is critical. For a retailer to "win" in the long run (attract shoppers, make sales, earn profits), the customer must also "win" in the long run (receive good value, be treated with respect, feel welcome by the firm). Otherwise, that retailer loses (shoppers patronize competitors) and customers lose

As with the retailers profiled in this book, we want to engage in relationship retailing. So please visit our Web site (www.prenhall.com/bermanevans). ☺

FIGURE 1-12

A Customer Respect Checklist

Source: Adapted by the authors from Leonard L. Berry, "Retailers with a Future," *Marketing Management* (Spring 1996), p. 43. Reprinted by permission of the American Marketing Association.

√ Do we trust our customers?

√ Do we stand behind what we sell? Are we easy to deal with if a customer has a problem? Are frontline workers empowered to respond properly to a problem? Do we guarantee what we sell?

√ Is keeping commitments to customers—from being in stock on advertised goods to being on time for appointments—important in our company?

√ Do we value customer time? Are our facilities and service systems convenient and efficient for customers to use? Do we teach employees that serving customers supersedes all other priorities, such as paperwork or stocking shelves?

√ Do we communicate with customers respectfully? Are signs informative and helpful? Is advertising above reproach in truthfulness and taste? Are contact personnel professional? Do we answer and return calls promptly—with a smile in our voice? Is our voice mail caller-friendly?

√ Do we treat all customers with respect, regardless of their appearance, age, race, gender, status, or size of purchase or account? Have we taken any special precautions to minimize discriminatory treatment of certain customers?

√ Do we thank customers for their business? Do we say "thank you" at times other than after a purchase?

√ Do we respect employees? Do employees, who are expected to respect customers, get respectful treatment themselves?

RETAILING
Around the World   ASDA Profits from the Wal-Mart Business Model

Even though ASDA's combination food and clothing stores (**www.asda.com**) in Great Britain were successful before Wal-Mart (**www.walmart.com**) acquired the chain in 1999, ASDA's sales and profits rose as it began to incorporate Wal-Mart's merchandising strategies. For example, during one 12-week period, same-store sales for apparel and general merchandise increased by 30 percent. According to an ASDA spokesperson, "The process we are going through is making our space work harder."

In following the Wal-Mart business model, ASDA created a specialty division to oversee its pharmacy, optical, jewelry, photography, and shoe departments. ASDA began 2001 with no jewelry departments, six vision centers, and 36 pharmacies and ended the year with 12 jewelry departments, 50 vision centers,

and 84 pharmacies. It now has more than 150 jewelry departments, 150 vision centers, and 130 pharmacies.

ASDA's sales also improved with the introduction of 5,000 new nonfood items aimed at home and leisure use. The chain introduced various specialty departments so that consumers now view ASDA as a one-stop shopping destination. Much of the space for the larger assortment of general merchandise and the new specialty departments has been generated by offering smaller package sizes and fewer shelf facings for each item.

Source: "ASDA Reaps Rewards for International Division," *DSN Retailing Today* (February 25, 2002), pp. 1, 28.

(by spending time and money to learn about other retailers). (2) Due to the advances in computer technology, it is now much easier to develop a customer data base with information on people's attributes and past shopping behavior. Ongoing customer contact can be better, more frequent, and more focused. This topic is covered further in Chapter 2, "Building and Sustaining Relationships in Retailing."

THE FOCUS AND FORMAT OF THE TEXT

There are various approaches to the study of retailing: an institutional approach, which describes the types of retailers and their development; a functional approach, which concentrates on the activities that retailers perform (such as buying, pricing, and personnel practices); and a strategic approach, which centers on defining the retail business, setting objectives, appealing to an appropriate customer market, developing an overall plan, implementing an integrated strategy, and regularly reviewing operations.

We will study retailing from each perspective but center on a *strategic approach*. Our basic premise is that the retailer has to plan for and adapt to a complex, changing environment. Both opportunities and threats must be considered. By engaging in strategic retail management, the retailer is encouraged to study competitors, suppliers, economic factors, consumer changes, marketplace trends, legal restrictions, and other elements. A firm prospers if its competitive strengths match the opportunities in the environment, weaknesses are eliminated or minimized, and plans look to the future (as well as the past).

Retail Management: A Strategic Approach is divided into eight parts. The balance of Part One looks at building relationships and strategic planning in retailing. Part Two characterizes retailing institutions on the basis of their ownership; store-based strategy mix; and Web, nonstore-based, and other nontraditional retailing format. Part Three deals with consumer behavior and information gathering in retailing. Parts Four to Seven discuss the specific elements of a retailing strategy: planning the store location; managing a retail business; planning, handling, and pricing merchandise; and communicating with the customer. Part Eight shows how a retailing strategy may be integrated, analyzed, and improved. These topics have special end-of-chapter appendixes: service retailing (Chapter 2), international retailing (Chapter 3), and franchising (Chapter 4). There are three end-of-text appendixes: retailing careers, about the Web site accompanying *Retail Management*, and a glossary. And our Web site includes "How to Solve a Case Study" (**www.prenhall.com/bermanevans**), which will aid you in your case analyses.

To underscore retailing's exciting nature, four real-world boxes appear in each chapter: "Careers in Retailing," "Ethics in Retailing," "Retailing Around the World," and "Technology in Retailing."

Summary

In this and every chapter, the summary is related to the objectives stated at the beginning of the chapter.

1. *To define retailing, consider it from various perspectives, demonstrate its impact, and note its special characteristics.* Retailing comprises the business activities involved in selling goods and services to consumers for personal, family, or household use. It is the last stage in the distribution process. Today, retailing is at an interesting crossroads, with many challenges ahead.

   Retailing may be viewed from multiple perspectives. It includes tangible and intangible items, does not have to involve a store, and can be done by manufacturers and others—as well as by retailers.

   Annual U.S. store sales exceed $3.5 trillion, with other forms of retailing accounting for hundreds of billions of dollars more. The world's 100 largest retailers generate $2 trillion in yearly revenues. About 23 million people in the United States work for retailers, which understates the number of those actually employed in a retailing capacity. Retail firms receive up to 40 cents or more of every sales dollar as compensation for operating costs, the functions performed, and the profits earned.

   Retailing encompasses all of the business and people involved in physically moving and transferring ownership of goods and services from producer to consumer. In a distribution channel, retailers perform valuable functions as the contact for manufacturers, wholesalers, and final consumers. They collect assortments from various suppliers and offer them to customers. They communicate with both customers and other channel members. They may ship, store, mark, advertise, and pre-pay for items. They complete transactions with customers and often provide customer services. They may offer multiple formats (multi-channel retailing) to facilitate shopping.

   Retailers and their suppliers have complex relationships because retailers serve in two capacities. They are part of a distribution channel aimed at the final consumer, and they are major customers for suppliers. Channel relations are smoothest with exclusive distribution; they are most volatile with intensive distribution. Selective distribution is a way to balance sales goals and channel cooperation.

   Retailing has several special characteristics. The average sales transaction is small. Final consumers make many unplanned purchases. Most customers visit a store location.

2. *To introduce the concept of strategic planning and apply it.* A retail strategy is the overall plan guiding the firm. It has six basic steps: defining the business, setting objectives, defining the customer market, developing an overall plan, enacting an integrated strategy, and evaluating performance and making modifications. Target Stores' strategy has been particularly well designed and enacted.

3. *To show why the retailing concept is the foundation of a successful business, with an emphasis on the total retail experience, customer service, and relationship retailing.* The retailing concept should be understood and used by all retailers. It requires a firm to have a customer orientation, use a coordinated effort, and be value driven and goal oriented. Despite its ease of use, many firms do not adhere to one or more elements of the retailing concept.

   The total retail experience consists of all the elements in a retail offering that encourage or inhibit consumers during their contact with a retailer. Some elements are controllable by the retailer; others are not. Customer service includes identifiable, but sometimes intangible, activities undertaken by a retailer in association with the basic goods and services sold. It has an effect on the total retail experience. In relationship retailing, a firm seeks long-term bonds with customers rather than acting as if each sales transaction is a totally new encounter with them.

4. *To indicate the focus and format of the text.* Retailing may be studied by using an institutional approach, a functional approach, and a strategic approach. Although all three approaches are covered in this book, our focus is on the strategic approach. The underlying principle is that a retail firm needs to plan for and adapt to a complex, changing environment.

Key Terms

retailing (p. 3)
channel of distribution (p. 7)
sorting process (p. 7)
multi-channel retailing (p. 7)

exclusive distribution (p. 8)
intensive distribution (p. 8)
selective distribution (p. 8)
retail strategy (p. 10)

retailing concept (p. 12)
total retail experience (p. 13)
customer service (p. 14)
relationship retailing (p. 15)

Questions for Discussion

1. What is your favorite retailer? Discuss the criteria you have used in making your selection. What can a competing firm do to lure you away from your favorite firm? Apply your answer to retailing in general.

2. What kinds of information do retailers communicate to customers? To suppliers?

3. What are the pros and cons of a firm such as Polo Ralph Lauren having its own retail facilities, as well as selling through traditional retailers?

4. Why would one retailer seek to be part of an exclusive distribution channel while another seeks to be part of an intensive distribution channel?

5. Describe how the special characteristics of retailing offer unique opportunities and problems for drugstores.

6. What is the purpose of developing a formal retail strategy? How could a strategic plan be used by your college bookstore?

7. On the basis of the chapter description of Target Stores, present five suggestions that a new retailer should consider.

8. Explain the retailing concept. Apply it to a local Ford or Chevrolet dealer.

9. Define the term *total retail experience*. Then describe a recent retail situation in which you were dissatisfied and state why.

10. Do you believe that customer service in retailing is improving or declining? Why?

11. How could a small Web-based retailer engage in relationship retailing?

12. What checklist item(s) in Figure 1-12 do you think would be most difficult for Wal-Mart, as the world's largest retailer, to address? Why?

Web-Based Exercise

Visit the Web site of About Retail Industry (**http://retailindustry. about.com**). Describe the site and give several examples of what a prospective retailer could learn from this site.

Note: Stop by our Web site (**www.prenhall.com/bermanevans**) to experience a number of highly interactive, appealing Web exercises

based on actual company demonstrations and sample materials related to retailing.

Chapter Endnotes

1. Various company sources.

2. Estimated by the authors from data in "2002 Global Powers of Retailing," *Stores* (January 2002), Section 2.

3. *Annual Retail Trade Survey 2001* (Washington, DC: U.S. Census Bureau, 2002); and retailer annual reports.

4. The material in this section is drawn from **www.target.com**; *Target Corporation Annual Report 2001*; "Target at 40," *DSN Retailing Today* (April 8, 2002), special section; Constance L. Hays, "Can Target Survive in Wal-Mart's Cross Hairs?" *New York Times* (June 9, 2002), Section 3, pp. 1, 12; Teri Agins, "Todd Does Target," *Wall Street Journal* (April 11, 2002), pp. B1, B6; and Mathew Grimm, "Target Hits Its Mark," *American Demographics* (November 2002), pp. 42–43.

5. Marianne Wilson, "Satiated, Not Satisfied," *Chain Store Age* (April 2002), p. 86.

6. Leonard L. Berry, "The Old Pillars of New Retailing," *Harvard Business Review*, Vol. 79 (April 2001), p. 7.

7. "Creating an Interactive Experience," *Chain Store Age* (August 2001), p. 19A.

8. Susan Reda, "Saving Customer Service: Are Retailers Up to the Challenge?" *Stores* (January 2001), p. 50.

9. Jane Spencer, "The Point of No Return—Stores from Gap to Target Tighten Refund Rules," *Wall Street Journal* (May 14, 2002), p. D1.

Chapter 2

BUILDING AND SUSTAINING RELATIONSHIPS IN RETAILING

Reprinted by permission.

Stew Leonard's (**www. stewleonards.com**) is a four-store supermarket chain (as of 2004) with units in Connecticut and New York. It has been featured in Tom Peters' best-selling book, *A Passion for Excellence.* Each square foot of selling space yields over $2,500 in sales; that's probably the highest figure of any retail store in the country and about seven times higher than the average supermarket.

Stew Leonard's bases its store strategy on "retailtainment" and on building and maintaining customer relationships. Supermarket executives have flown in from as far away as Japan to see what makes Stew Leonard's a "mecca of merchandising." One of Stew Leonard's tactics is to make each of its stores as exciting as possible for shoppers of all ages—by having everything from an animal petting zoo and tours of an in-house dairy for children to selling adult cashmere sweaters valued at $149 for $49.

The retailer's shopper relationships are built on the concept that the "Customer Is Always Right." Carved into 6-foot-high, 6,000-pound boulders at the entrance to the firm's Norwalk and Danbury, Connecticut, stores are two rules: "Rule 1: The customer is always right. Rule 2: If the customer is wrong, reread Rule 1." Stew Leonard's really prides itself on its customer service. In one instance, a store manager dropped off a free package of chicken breasts at a customer's home after getting a note in the firm's suggestion box complaining that the outlet was sold out.[1]

chapter objectives

1. To explain what "value" really means and highlight its pivotal role in retailers' building and sustaining relationships

2. To describe how both customer relationships and channel relationships may be nurtured in today's highly competitive marketplace

3. To examine the differences in relationship building between goods and service retailers

4. To discuss the impact of technology on relationships in retailing

5. To consider the interplay between retailers' ethical performance and relationships in retailing

OVERVIEW

To prosper, a retailer must properly apply the concepts of "value" and "relationship" so (a) customers strongly believe the firm offers a good value for the money and (b) both customers and channel members want to do business with that retailer. Some firms grasp this well. Others still have some work to do. Consider the view of Dillard's, a discount department store chain:

Dillard's (www.dillards.com) is—first and foremost—a value-driven retailer.

> The word "value" has become a staple in retailing. But what exactly IS value? At Dillard's, we believe value is defined not only in consistently offering customers the finest quality merchandise at fair prices, but also in creating a totally satisfying one-stop shopping experience with all the conveniences and services they've come to expect from Dillard's. We start by asking ourselves, "What does our customer want?" through the execution of our Product First Buying Philosophy. This quest for value has prompted us to build our private-brand program and to seek exclusive relationships with talented designers and product specialists. And it keeps us focused on enhancing the total shopping experience with exceptional customer attention and convenient services.[2]

As retailers look to the future, this is the looming bottom line on value:

> Consumers will demand more for less from the shopping experience. Time and budget constrained consumers will spend less time shopping, make fewer trips, visit fewer stores, and shop more purposefully. Different strokes will satisfy different folks. Consumers will shop different formats for different needs. Specifically, they will split the commodity shopping trip from the value-added shopping trip. Consumers are becoming more skeptical about price. Under the barrage of sales, price has lost its meaning; gimmicks have lost their appeal. To regain consumer confidence, pricing by retailers and manufacturers alike will become clearer, more sensible, and more sophisticated.[3] (See Figure 2-1.)

This chapter looks at value and the value chain, relationship retailing with regard to customers and channel partners, the differences in relationship building between goods and service retailers, technology and relationships, and ethics and relationships. There is also a chapter appendix on service retailing.

VALUE AND THE VALUE CHAIN

In many channels of distribution, there are several parties: manufacturer, wholesaler, retailer, and customer. These parties are most apt to be satisfied with their interactions when they have similar beliefs about the value provided and received and agree on the payment for that level of value.

FIGURE 2-1
Kroger: Providing Extra Value for Customers

Kroger supermarkets offer a lot of services for customers to accommodate their desire for one-stop, time-conserving shopping.

Photo reprinted by permission of Retail Forward, Inc.

From the perspective of the manufacturer, wholesaler, and retailer, **value** is embodied by a series of activities and processes—a value chain—that *provides* a certain value for the consumer. It is the totality of the tangible and intangible product and customer service attributes offered to shoppers. The level of value relates to each firm's desire for a fair profit and its niche (such as discount vs. upscale). Where firms may differ is in rewarding the value each provides and in allocating the activities undertaken.

From the customer's perspective, **value** is the *perception* the shopper has of a value chain. It is the customer's view of all the benefits from a purchase (formed by the total retail experience). Value is based on the perceived benefits received versus the price paid. It varies by type of shopper. Price-oriented shoppers want low prices, service-oriented shoppers will pay more for superior customer service, and status-oriented shoppers will pay a lot to patronize prestigious stores.

Why is "value" such a meaningful concept for every retailer in any kind of setting?

- Customers must always believe they got their money's worth, whether the retailer sells $20,000 Rolex watches or $40 Casio watches.

- A strong retail effort is required so that customers perceive the level of value provided in the manner the firm intends.

- Value is desired by all customers; however, it means different things to different customers.

- Consumer comparison shopping for prices is easy through ads and the World Wide Web. Thus, prices have moved closer together for different types of retailers.

- Retail differentiation is essential so a firm is not perceived as a "me-too" retailer.

- A specific value/price level must be set. A retailer can offer $100 worth of benefits for a $100 item or $125 worth of benefits (through better ambience and customer service) for the same item and a $125 price. Either approach can work if properly enacted and marketed.

Peapod (www.peapod.com) offers a unique value chain with its home delivery service.

A retail **value chain** represents the total bundle of benefits offered to consumers through a channel of distribution. It comprises store location and parking, retailer ambience, the level of customer service, the products/brands carried, product quality, the retailer's in-stock position, shipping, prices, the retailer's image, and other elements. As a rule, consumers are concerned with the results of a value chain, not the process. Food shoppers who buy online via Peapod care only that they receive the brands ordered when desired, not about the stops needed for home delivery at the neighborhood level.

Some elements of a retail value chain are visible to shoppers, such as display windows, store hours, sales personnel, and point-of-sale equipment. Other elements are not visible, such as store location planning, credit processing, company warehouses, and many merchandising decisions. In the latter case, various cues are surrogates for value: upscale store ambience and plentiful sales personnel for high-end stores; shopping carts and self-service for discounters.

RETAILING Around the World — Costco Grows in Japan

Costco (**www.costco.com**), the membership club chain, never assumed that the Japanese market would be easy. One of the firm's major tasks has been to adapt its U.S. concept of selling large package sizes to the Japanese marketplace where consumers typically live in small houses and apartments with very limited storage space. A strategy that appears to be working well is to sell products in multi-packs instead of in a single large box. This also enables Japanese shoppers to visit a Costco store together and to then divide their purchases.

Costco has also had to learn the shopping habits of Japanese shoppers and then fine-tune its merchandise selection to address them. Some of Costco's most popular products in Japan are U.S. items such as basketball hoops and housewares; yet, others are quite different—such as seaweed and dried fish. Surprisingly, donuts have become one of the most popular items in Costco's Japanese stores.

Despite its use of two-story buildings in Japan, due to high real-estate costs and the low availability of retail sites, Costco still finds it tough to find appropriate new locations. As one Japanese retailing analyst explains, "That's why you don't see many foreign retailers in Japan."

Source: Doug Desjardins, "Costco Forges Ahead with Clubs No. 3 and 4," *Retailing Today* (May 6, 2002), pp. 4–5.

There are three aspects of a value-oriented retail strategy: expected, augmented, and potential. An *expected retail strategy* represents the minimum value chain elements a given customer segment (e.g., young women) expects from a type of retailer (e.g., a midpriced apparel retailer). In most cases, these are expected value chain elements: store cleanliness, convenient hours, well-informed employees, timely service, popular products in stock, parking, and return privileges. If applied poorly, expected elements cause customer dissatisfaction and relate to why shoppers avoid certain retailers.

An *augmented retail strategy* includes the extra elements in a value chain that differentiate one retailer from another. As an example, how is Sears different from Nordstrom? These are often augmented elements: exclusive brands, superior salespeople, loyalty programs, delivery, personal shoppers and other special services, and valet parking. Augmented features complement expected value chain elements, and they are the key to continued customer patronage.

A *potential retail strategy* comprises value chain elements not yet perfected by a competing firm in the retailer's category. For example, what customer services could a new upscale apparel chain offer that no other chain offers? In many situations, these are potential value chain elements: 24/7 store hours (an augmented strategy for supermarkets), unlimited customer return privileges, full-scale product customization, instant fulfillment of rain checks through in-store orders accompanied by free delivery, and in-mall trams to make it easier for shoppers to move through enormous regional shopping centers. The first firms to capitalize on potential features gain a head start over their adversaries. Barnes & Noble and Borders accomplished this by opening the first book superstores, and Amazon.com has become a major player by opening the first online bookstore. Yet, even as pioneers, firms must excel at meeting customers' basic expectations and offering differentiated features from competitors if they are to grow.

There are five potential pitfalls to avoid in planning a value-oriented retail strategy:

- *Planning value with just a price perspective:* Value is tied to two factors: benefits and prices. Most discounters accept credit cards because shoppers want to purchase with them.
- *Providing value-enhancing services that customers do not want or will not pay extra for:* Ikea knows most of its customers want to save money by assembling furniture themselves.
- *Competing in the wrong value/price segment:* Neighborhood retailers generally have a tough time competing in the low-price part of the market. They are better off providing augmented benefits and charging somewhat more than large chains.
- *Believing augmented elements alone create value:* Many retailers think that if they offer a benefit not available from competitors that they will automatically prosper. Yet, they must never lose sight of the importance of expected benefits. A movie theater with limited parking will have problems even if it features first-run movies.
- *Paying lip service to customer service:* Most firms say, and even believe, that customers are always right. Yet, they act contrary to this philosophy—by having a high turnover of salespeople, charging for returned goods that have been opened, and not giving rain checks if items are out of stock.

To sidestep these pitfalls, a retailer could use the checklist in Figure 2-2, which poses a number of questions that must be addressed. The checklist can be answered by an owner/corporate president, a team of executives, or an independent consultant. It should be reviewed at least once a year or more often if a major development, such as the emergence of a strong competitor, occurs.

Compare Sears (www.sears.com) and Nordstrom (www.nordstrom.com).

Today Barnes & Noble (www.bn.com) relies on both its stores and its Web site for revenues.

RETAILER RELATIONSHIPS

In Chapter 1, we introduced the concept of *relationship retailing,* whereby retailers seek to form and maintain long-term bonds with customers, rather than act as if each sales transaction is a new encounter with them. For relationship retailing to work, enduring value-driven relationships are needed with other channel members, as well as with customers. Both jobs are challenging. See Figure 2-3. Visit our Web site for links related to relationship retailing issues (**www.prenhall.com/bermanevans**).

FIGURE 2-2
A Value-Oriented
Retailing Checklist

Answer yes or no to each
question.

✓ Is value defined from a consumer perspective?

✓ Does the retailer have a clear value/price point?

✓ Is the retailer's value position competitively defensible?

✓ Are channel partners capable of delivering value-enhancing services?

✓ Does the retailer distinguish between expected and augmented value chain elements?

✓ Has the retailer identified meaningful potential value chain elements?

✓ Is the retailer's value-oriented approach aimed at a distinct market segment?

✓ Is the retailer's value-oriented approach consistent?

✓ Is the retailer's value-oriented approach effectively communicated to the target market?

✓ Can the target market clearly identify the retailer's positioning strategy?

✓ Does the retailer's positioning strategy consider trade-offs in sales versus profits?

✓ Does the retailer set customer satisfaction goals?

✓ Does the retailer periodically measure customer satisfaction levels?

✓ Is the retailer careful to avoid the pitfalls in value-oriented retailing?

✓ Is the retailer always looking out for new opportunities that will create customer value?

CUSTOMER RELATIONSHIPS

Loyal customers are the backbone of a business:

> The top management of a major Midwest grocery retailer met to evaluate the information
> gathered through the firm's frequent shopper program. The discussion included some
> astounding data: 30 percent of the company's customers represented over 75 percent of
> its profits. The president told the group, "We're in a new era of retailing. We must under-
> stand and manage our key customers much better than we have before. Our future rests
> on the ability to retain our customers. Competitors like Wal-Mart are making major
> inroads into our customer base. It is no longer enough to bring customers in with our
> weekly ads; we must learn how to provide a unique environment for our top customers."[4]

FIGURE 2-3

4,200 Places to Bring the Care Back to Health Care

In conjunction with its channel partners, CVS uses the latest technology to service its customers and foster relationships with
them. Since its introduction in 1994, CVS has invested over
$200 million in its proprietary Rx2000 pharmacy system. One
of the most successful innovations has been CVS' launch of the
Rapid Refill system, which enables customers to order prescription refills using a touch-tone phone. Rapid Refill now accounts
for more than 50 percent of refills. In addition to providing an
added convenience for customers, one of the most important
benefits of Rapid Refill is that it significantly reduces the time
pharmacists spend on the phone, so they can spend more time
counseling patients on medications and addressing their total
health care needs.

Reprinted by permission.

In relationship retailing, there are four factors to keep in mind: the customer base, customer service, customer satisfaction, and loyalty programs and defection rates. Let's explore these next.

The Customer Base

Retailers must regularly analyze their customer base in terms of population and life-style trends, attitudes toward and reasons for shopping, the level of loyalty, and the mix of new versus loyal customers.

The U.S. population is aging. One-fourth of all households have only one person, one-sixth of the population moves annually, most people live in urban and suburban areas, the number of working women is high, middle-class income has been rising slowly, and African-American, Hispanic-American, and Asian-American segments are expanding. Thus, gender roles are changing, shoppers demand more, market segments are more diverse, there is less interest in shopping, and time-saving goods and services are desirable.

There are various factors that influence shopping behavior:

- More women than men enjoy shopping, and men shop more quickly than women. However, the shopping behavior of younger men (ages 18 to 34) is more similar to their female counterparts.
- Due to their time constraints, consumers now spend an average of only 75 minutes when visiting a shopping mall. Working women account for 42 percent of all mall purchases.
- Consumers' most important reasons to shop at a given *apparel retailer* are product availability, ease in finding products, confidence in products, ease of shopping, and convenience of the location.
- Consumers' most important reasons to shop at a given *discount department store* are convenience, price, and assortment and quality of merchandise.
- Consumers' most important reasons to shop at a given *supermarket* are cleanliness, prices, accuracy in price scanning at the register, and how clearly prices are labeled.[5]

It is more worth nurturing relationships with some shoppers than with others; they are the retailer's **core customers**—its best customers. And they should be singled out:

The most practical way to get started is by answering three questions. First, which of your customers are the most profitable and the most loyal? Look for those who spend more money, pay their bills promptly, are reasonable in their customer service requests, and seem to prefer stable, long-term relationships. Second, which customers place the greatest value on what you have to offer? Some customers will have found that your products, customers services, and special strengths are simply the best fit for them. Third, which customers are worth more to you than to your competitors? Some warrant extra effort and investment. Yet, no firm can be all things to all people: Customers who are worth more to a competitor will eventually defect.[6]

A retailer's desired mix of new versus loyal customers depends on that firm's stage in its life cycle, goals, and resources, and its competitors' actions. A mature firm is more apt to rely on core customers and supplement its revenues with new shoppers. A new firm faces the dual tasks of attracting shoppers and building a loyal following; it cannot do the latter without the former. If goals are growth-oriented, the customer base must be expanded by adding stores, increasing advertising, and so on; the challenge is to do this in a way that does not deflect attention from core customers. Although it is more costly to attract new customers than to serve existing ones, core customers are not cost-free. If competitors try to take away a firm's existing customers with price cuts and special promotions, a retailer may feel it must pursue competitors' customers in the same way. Again, it must be careful not to alienate core customers.

Customer Service

As described in Chapter 1, *customer service* refers to the identifiable, but sometimes intangible, activities undertaken by a retailer in conjunction with the goods and services it sells. It impacts on the total retail experience. Consistent with a value chain philosophy, retailers must apply two elements of customer service: **Expected customer service** is the service level that customers want to receive from any retailer, such as basic employee courtesy. **Augmented customer service** includes the activities that enhance the shopping experience and give retailers a competitive advantage. AutoZone does a good job with both expected and augmented customer services:

AutoZone (www.autozone.com) has a unique style of customer service.

> Tools have also always been an essential part of car repair, but some jobs require more than just a socket set and a wrench. For instance, a customer might need a tie-rod end puller. Already strapped for cash, he or she may not have the option of shelling out additional dollars for a tool that may be used only once in the life of the car. So we offer our Loan-a-Tool service, which makes available approximately 75 obscure tools—some costing as much as $100—to people who need a temporary loaner to get the job done right. It helps them do the work, and it helps us make the sale.[7]

The attributes of personnel who interact with customers (such as politeness and knowledge), as well as the number and variety of customer services offered, have a strong effect on the relationship created.[8] Here are two opposite consumer perceptions related to their customer service experiences:

> My wife likes to shop at the local Safeway. Is it because of the prices? Yes, that's part of it. Is it because of the location? Yes, that's part of it too. She also likes the produce department. But the biggest reason she likes to shop at the local Safeway is "Marshall," who is a very good checkout person. He's fast, efficient, and seldom makes a mistake. But his competency is not why my wife keeps going back. She goes back because Marshall always has a warm and friendly smile. And because when Marshall asks, "How are you today?" you know he's sincere about it.[9]

> Enticed by an ad to visit the store, I spent 10 minutes inside without being greeted. Two employees were tossing a sponge football around while talking about their previous night's adventure. Another employee was busy shopping for himself and soliciting fashion advice from the previous two. As I interrupted them to help direct me to the item that was in the ad, they were clueless about the ad but pointed me in the direction where I might be able to help myself. The scene at the checkout didn't improve. There was no greeting and the young lady never looked at me.[10]

Planning the best customer service strategy can be complex: "Although the current state of retailing is causing firms to cut costs in many areas of their businesses, customers still expect the same level of service," said one expert. Customer service satisfaction "has always been a key for positive financial results. Businesses must not make customer service investments only to keep pace with growth—they should view their spending as a strategic benefit to bring greater customer satisfaction and retention."[11]

Home Depot (www.homedepot.com) really believes in empowering its employees to better serve customers.

Some retailers realize that customer service is better when they utilize **employee empowerment**, whereby workers have the discretion to do what they believe is necessary—within reason—to satisfy the customer, even if this means bending some rules. At Nordstrom, "Our company is our people. That's why we are dedicated to hiring outstanding individuals and empowering them to unlock their talent and creativity with a career they feel passionate about."[12] At Home Depot, each worker on the selling floor gets several weeks training prior to meeting customers. Employees have wide latitude in making on-the-spot decisions. They can act as consultants and problem solvers. Consider these industrywide statistics: "73 percent of consumers attribute their best customer-service experience to retail employees. Conversely, 81 percent attribute their worst customer-service experience to retail employees."[13]

To apply customer service effectively, a firm must first develop an overall service strategy and then plan individual services. Figure 2-4 shows one way a retailer may view the customer services it offers.

DEVELOPING A CUSTOMER SERVICE STRATEGY A retailer must make the following fundamental decisions.

What customer services are expected and what customer services are augmented for a particular retailer? Examples of expected customer services are credit for a furniture retailer, new-car preparation for an auto dealer, and a liberal return policy for a gift shop. Those retailers could not stay in business without them. Because augmented customer services are extra elements, a firm could serve its target market without such services; however, using them enhances its com-

FIGURE 2-4

Classifying Customer Services

Source: Adapted by the authors from Albert D. Bates, "Rethinking the Service Offer," *Retailing Issues Letter* (December 1986), p. 3. Reprinted by permission.

Cost of Offering the Customer Service

	High	**Low**
High (Value of the Customer Service to the Shopper)	**Patronage Builders** High-cost activities that are the primary factors behind customer loyalties. Examples: transaction speed, credit, gift registry	**Patronage Solidifiers** The "low-cost little things" that increase loyalty. Examples: courtesy (referring to the customer by name and saying thank you), suggestion selling
Low	**Disappointers** Expensive activities that do no real good. Examples: weekday deliveries for two-earner families, home economists	**Basics** Low-cost activities that are "naturally expected." They don't build patronage, but their absence could reduce patronage. Examples: free parking, in-store directories

petitive standing. Examples are delivery for a supermarket, an extra warranty for an auto dealer, and gift wrapping for a toy store. Each firm needs to determine which customer services are expected and which are augmented for its situation. Expected customer services for one retailer, such as delivery, may be augmented for another. See Figure 2-5.

What level of customer service is proper to complement a firm's image? An upscale retailer would offer more customer services than a discounter because people expect the upscale firm to have a wider range of customer services as part of its basic strategy. In addition, performance would be different. Customers of an upscale retailer may expect elaborate gift wrapping, valet parking, a restaurant, and a ladies' room attendant, whereas discount shoppers may expect cardboard gift boxes, self-service parking, a lunch counter, and an unattended ladies' room. Customer service categories are the same; performance is not.

Should there be a choice of customer services? Some firms let customers select from various levels of customer service; others provide only one level. A retailer may honor several credit cards or only its own. Trade-ins may be allowed on some items or all. Warranties may have optional extensions or fixed lengths. A firm may offer one-, three-, and six-month payment plans or insist on immediate payment.

FIGURE 2-5

Augmented Services: Going Above and Beyond

To better serve its supermarket customers, Giant Food has partnered with Peapod to provide online ordering and home delivery.

Reprinted by permission of Giant Food, Inc.

Staples (www.staples.com) offers free delivery on orders of $50 or more.

Should customer services be free? Two factors cause retailers to charge for some customer services: (1) Delivery, gift wrapping, and some other customer services are labor intensive. (2) People are more apt to be home for a delivery or service call if a fee is imposed. Without a fee, a retailer may have to attempt a delivery twice. In settling on a free or fee-based strategy, a firm must determine which customer services are expected (these are often free) and which are augmented (these may be offered for a fee), monitor competitors and profit margins, and study the target market. In setting fees, a retailer must also decide if its goal is to break even or to make a profit on certain customer services.

How can a retailer measure the benefits of providing customer services against their costs? The purpose of customer services is to enhance the shopping experience in a manner that attracts and retains shoppers while maximizing sales and profits. Thus, augmented customer services should not be offered unless they raise total sales and profits. A retailer should plan augmented customer services based on experience, competitors' actions, and customer comments; and when the costs of providing these customer services increase, higher prices should be passed on to the consumer.

How can customer services be terminated? Once a customer service strategy is set, shoppers are likely to react negatively to any customer service reduction. Nonetheless, some costly augmented customer services may have to be dropped. In that case, the best approach is to be forthright by explaining why the customer services are being terminated and how customers will benefit via lower prices. Sometimes a firm may use a middle ground, charging for previously free customer services (such as clothing alterations) to allow those who want the services to still receive them.

PLANNING INDIVIDUAL CUSTOMER SERVICES Once a broad customer service plan is outlined, individual customer services are planned. A department store may offer credit, layaway, gift wrapping, a bridal registry, free parking, a restaurant, a beauty salon, carpet installation, dressing rooms, clothing alterations, pay phones, rest rooms and sitting areas, the use of baby strollers, delivery, and fur storage. The range of typical customer services is shown in Table 2-1 and described next.

Most retailers let customers make credit purchases, and many firms accept personal checks with proper identification. Consumers' use of credit rises as the purchase amount goes up. Retailer-sponsored credit cards have three key advantages: (1) The retailer saves the fee it would pay for outside card sales, (2) people are encouraged to shop with a given retailer because its card is usually not accepted elsewhere, and (3) contact can be maintained with customers and information learned about them. There are also disadvantages to retailer cards: Startup costs are high, the firm must worry about unpaid bills and slow cash flow, credit checks and follow-up tasks must be performed, and customers without the firm's card may be discouraged from shopping.

TABLE 2-1	Typical Customer Services	
Credit	Miscellaneous	
Delivery	• Bridal registry	• Rest rooms
Alterations and installations	• Interior designers	• Restaurant
Packaging (gift wrapping)	• Personal shoppers	• Baby-sitting
Complaints and returns handling	• Ticket outlets	• Fitting rooms
Gift certificates	• Parking	• Beauty salon
Trade-ins	• Water fountains	• Fur storage
Trial purchases	• Pay phones	• Shopping bags
Special sales for regular customers	• Baby strollers	• Information
Extended store hours		
Mail and phone orders		

Bank and other commercial credit cards enable small and medium retailers to offer credit, generate added business for all types of retailers, appeal to mobile shoppers, provide advertising support from the sponsor, reduce bad debts, eliminate startup costs for the retailer, and provide data. Yet, these cards charge a transaction fee and do not yield loyalty to the retailer.

All bank cards and most retailer cards involve a **revolving credit account**, whereby a customer charges items and is billed monthly on the basis of the outstanding cumulative balance. An **option credit account** is a form of revolving account; no interest is assessed if a person pays a bill in full when it is due. Should a person make a partial payment, he or she is assessed interest monthly on the unpaid balance. Some credit card firms (such as American Express) and some retailers offer an **open credit account**, whereby a consumer must pay the bill in full when it is due. Partial, revolving payments are not permitted. A person with an open account also has a credit limit.

For a retailer that offers delivery, there are three decisions: the transportation method, equipment ownership versus rental, and timing. The shipping method can be car, van, truck, rail, mail, and so forth. The costs and appropriateness of the methods depend on the products. Large retailers often find it economical to own their delivery vehicles. This also lets them advertise the company name, have control over schedules, and use their employees for deliveries. Small retailers serving limited trading areas may use personal vehicles. Many small, medium, and even large retailers use firms such as United Parcel Service if consumers live away from a delivery area and shipments are not otherwise efficient. Finally, the retailer must decide how quickly to process orders and how often to deliver to different locales.

For some retailers, alterations and installations are expected customer services, although more retailers now charge fees. However, many discounters have stopped offering alterations of clothing and installations of heavy appliances on both a free and a fee basis. They feel the services are too ancillary to their business and not worth the effort. Other retailers offer only basic alterations: shortening pants, taking in the waist, and lengthening jacket sleeves. They do not adjust jacket shoulders or width. Some appliance retailers may hook up washing machines but not do plumbing work.

Within a store, packaging (gift wrapping)—as well as complaints and returns handling—can be centrally located or decentralized. Centralized packaging counters and complaints and returns areas have key advantages: They may be situated in otherwise dead spaces; the main selling areas are not cluttered; specialized personnel can be used; and a common policy is enacted. The advantages of decentralized facilities are that shoppers are not inconvenienced; people are kept in the selling area, where a salesperson may resolve a problem or offer different merchandise; and extra personnel are not required. In either case, clear guidelines as to the handling of complaints and returns are needed.

Gift certificates encourage shopping with a given retailer. Many firms require gift certificates to be spent and not redeemed for cash. Trade-ins also induce new and regular shoppers to shop.

Careers in RETAILING — What Can We Learn from Stanley Marcus and Dave Thomas?

Stanley Marcus, the former chairperson of Neiman Marcus Group (**www.neimanmarcus.com**), an upscale department store chain, and Dave Thomas, the founder of Wendy's (**www.wendys.com**), both left a rich retailing legacy when they passed away in 2002.

On the surface, Marcus and Thomas had few similarities. Stanley Marcus, with his newly minted Harvard M.B.A., joined the family department store business as a director at the age of 21. His family's business specialized in the sale of designer apparel and precious jewelry to affluent consumers who wanted "the best, regardless of price." In contrast, Dave Thomas, who was adopted at six weeks old, founded a family-oriented restaurant chain that specialized in offering value meals to middle-class families. It is quite possible that the two men never visited or shopped in each other's stores.

Yet, these premier retailers shared a number of fundamentals in managing their businesses:

- *Leadership:* Both men spent much of their time in their stores and sought to "lead by example."
- *Differentiation:* Marcus introduced unusual gifts in his Christmas catalog (such as his and hers aircraft), whereas Thomas was the first fast-food operator to introduce salad bars.
- *Customer Service:* Both were obsessed with creating a pleasurable shopping environment.

Source: Tony Lisanti, "A Tribute to Two Retail Leaders," *DSN Retailing Today* (February 25, 2002), p. 13.

People get the feeling of a bargain. Trial purchases let shoppers test products before purchases are final to reduce risks.

Retailers increasingly offer special customer services to regular customers. Sales events (not open to the general public) and extended hours are provided. Mail and phone orders are handled for convenience.

Other useful customer services include a bridal registry, interior designers, personal shoppers, ticket outlets, free (or low-cost) and plentiful parking, water fountains, pay phones, baby strollers, rest rooms, a restaurant, baby-sitting, fitting rooms, a beauty salon, fur storage, shopping bags, and information counters. A retailer's willingness to offer some or all of these services indicates to customers a concern for them. Therefore, firms need to consider the impact of excessive self-service.

Customer Satisfaction

Customer satisfaction occurs when the value and customer service provided through a retailing experience meet or exceed consumer expectations. If the expectations of value and customer service are not met, the consumer will be dissatisfied. Only "very satisfied" customers are likely to remain loyal in the long run. How well are retailers doing in customer satisfaction? Many have much work to do. The American Customer Satisfaction Index annually questions thousands of people to link customer expectations, perceived quality, and perceived value to satisfaction. Over all, retailers consistently score only about 75 on a scale of 100. Fast-food firms usually rate lowest in the retailing category (with scores around 70). To improve matters, retailers should engage in the process shown in Figure 2-6.

Most consumers do not complain when dissatisfied. They just shop elsewhere. Why don't shoppers complain more? (1) Because most people feel complaining produces little or no positive results, they do not bother to complain. (2) Complaining is not easy. Consumers have to find the party to whom they should complain, access to that party may be restricted, and written forms may have to be completed.

Try out some of CustomerSat.com's (www.customersat.com) tools for measuring customer satisfaction.

To obtain more feedback, retailers must make it easier for shoppers to complain, make sure shoppers believe their concerns are being addressed, and sponsor ongoing customer satisfaction surveys. As suggested by consulting firm CustomerSat.com, retailers should ask such questions as these and then take corrective actions reflecting their shoppers' feelings:

1. "Please rate our customer service."
2. "How often does our customer service exceed expectations?"
3. "What do you like most about our customer service?" "What do you like least?"

Loyalty Programs

Consumer loyalty (frequent shopper) programs reward a retailer's best customers, those with whom it wants long-lasting relationships. According to A.C. Nielsen surveys, 78 percent of all U.S. households participate in at least one loyalty program.[14] And here's what consumers want:

> When structuring a frequent shoppers club, retailers should keep in mind what consumers see as the chief benefit: getting a deal. For almost two-thirds of the public, receiving

FIGURE 2-6
Turning Around Weak Customer Service

Source: Figure and its discussion developed by the authors from information in Jeff Mowatt, "Keeping Customers When Things Go Wrong," *Canadian Manager* (Summer 2001), pp. s23, 28.

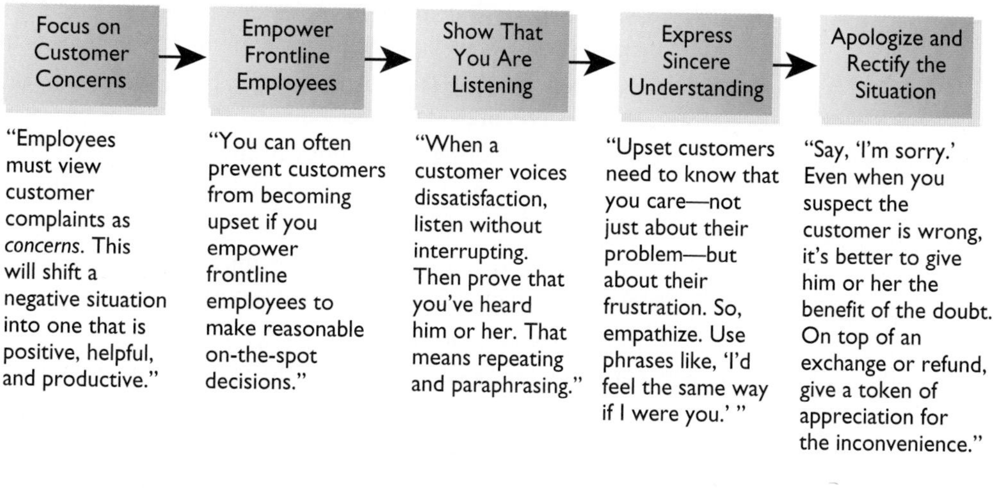

Focus on Customer Concerns	Empower Frontline Employees	Show That You Are Listening	Express Sincere Understanding	Apologize and Rectify the Situation
"Employees must view customer complaints as *concerns*. This will shift a negative situation into one that is positive, helpful, and productive."	"You can often prevent customers from becoming upset if you empower frontline employees to make reasonable on-the-spot decisions."	"When a customer voices dissatisfaction, listen without interrupting. Then prove that you've heard him or her. That means repeating and paraphrasing."	"Upset customers need to know that you care—not just about their problem—but about their frustration. So, empathize. Use phrases like, 'I'd feel the same way if I were you.'"	"Say, 'I'm sorry.' Even when you suspect the customer is wrong, it's better to give him or her the benefit of the doubt. On top of an exchange or refund, give a token of appreciation for the inconvenience."

"a percentage discount on all purchases" is the feature that would "most likely" encourage them to participate. One-third would be attracted by "advance notice of upcoming sales"; 31 percent would look for either "special coupons for new products" or "coupons or discounts on goods and services from other vendors"; 29 percent are attracted by "cash-back offers"; and almost a quarter want a "free gift with purchase." Relatively few over all are attracted by invitations to special events or parties (10 percent), preferred parking (10 percent), or personal shopping assistance (9 percent). Just as important as the attractions are the turnoffs. In a time when headlines often are devoted to privacy issues, it should come as no surprise that the top consumer negative has to do with this topic.[15]

Safeway (www.safeway.com) has a substantial loyalty program (Safeway Club) for its supermarket customers.

What do good customer loyalty programs have in common? Their rewards are useful and appealing, and they are attainable in a reasonable time. The programs honor shopping behavior (the greater the purchases, the greater the benefits). A data base tracks behavior. There are features that are unique to particular retailers and not redeemable elsewhere. Rewards stimulate both short- and long-run purchases. Customer communications are personalized. Frequent shoppers feel "special." Participation rules are publicized and rarely change.

When a retailer studies customer defections (by tracking data bases or surveying consumers), it can learn how many customers it is losing and why they no longer patronize the firm. Customer defections may be viewed in absolute terms (people who no longer buy from the firm at all) and in relative terms (people who shop less often). Each retailer must define its acceptable defection rate. Furthermore, not all shoppers are "good" customers. A retailer may feel it is okay if shoppers who always look for sales, return items without receipts, and expect fee-based services to be free decide to defect. Unfortunately, too few retailers review defection data or survey defecting customers because of the complexity of doing so and an unwillingness to hear "bad news."

CHANNEL RELATIONSHIPS

Within a value chain, the members of a distribution channel (manufacturers, wholesalers, and retailers) jointly represent a **value delivery system**, which comprises all the parties that develop, produce, deliver, and sell and service particular goods and services. The ramifications for retailers follow:

- Each channel member is dependent on the others. When consumers shop with a certain retailer, they often do so because of both the retailer and the products it carries.
- All value delivery system activities must be enumerated and responsibility assigned for them.
- Small retailers may have to use suppliers outside the normal distribution channel to get the products they want and gain adequate supplier support. Although large retailers may be able to buy directly from manufacturers, smaller retailers may have to buy through wholesalers that handle small accounts.
- A value delivery system is as good as its weakest link. No matter how well a retailer performs its activities, it will still have unhappy shoppers if suppliers deliver late or do not honor warranties.
- The nature of a given value delivery system must be related to target market expectations.
- Channel member costs and functions are influenced by each party's role. Long-term cooperation and two-way information flows foster efficiency.
- Value delivery systems are complex due to the vast product assortment of superstores, the many forms of retailing, and the use of multiple distribution channels by some manufacturers.
- Nonstore retailing (such as mail-order, phone, and Web transactions) requires a different delivery system than store retailing.
- Due to conflicting goals about profit margins, shelf space, and so on, some channel members are adversarial—to the detriment of the value delivery system and channel relationships.

When they forge strong positive channel relationships, members of a value delivery system better serve each other and the final consumer. Here's how:

Traditionally, the relationship between retailers and suppliers was, at best, arm's length. The manufacturers' goal was to move the greatest volume of goods at the highest price. The retailers' goal was to negotiate the lowest price for the goods. Competitive pressures led to a new paradigm. It focused on a simple idea: make sure the right product at the right price is on the shelf when the customer enters the store, while maintaining the lowest possible inventory at all points in the pipeline from suppliers to retailer. This requires cooperation between retailers and upstream suppliers.[16]

Blockbuster (www.blockbuster.com) guarantees that popular movies will be in stock, due to its novel approach with vendors.

The new strategy for Blockbuster is simple: stock more of the new releases that customers want. Before, the average customer had to visit a store five consecutive weekends to get the movie wanted. To change that, Blockbuster overhauled its business model. In the past, it bought tapes from studios for about $65 apiece. Inventory got expensive, limiting its willingness to invest in too many copies of one film. Now Blockbuster has revenue sharing with most major studios. The deals dramatically lower Blockbuster's up-front costs. In exchange, Blockbuster hands over about one-half of revenue.[17]

For Ace Hardware, the benefits of cooperation are real. By allowing both retailer and partner to see the same data, sales increases are a result. "Our vendors that have been on the program for more than a year had a 10.3 percent annual sales increase versus our corporate sales rates, which were basically flat," said Scott Smith, Ace collaborative project leader. Ace has also seen expense reduction on the traffic side, with one manufacturer reducing freight cost as a percentage of the production cost from 7 to 2.5 percent. "I firmly believe when you have more than one person looking at a business decision and you take a team approach, you really come up with a better decision," Smith added.[18]

One relationship-oriented practice that some manufacturers and retailers use, especially supermarket chains, is *category management*, whereby channel members collaborate to manage products by category rather than by individual item. Category management is based on these principles: (1) Retailers listen more to customers and stock what they want. (2) Profitability is improved because inventory matches demand more closely. (3) By being better focused, each department is more desirable for shoppers. (4) Retail buyers are given more responsibilities and accountability for category results. (5) Retailers and suppliers must share data and be more computerized. (6) Retailers and suppliers must plan together. Category management is discussed further in Chapter 14.

Figure 2-7 shows various factors that contribute to effective channel relationships.

FIGURE 2-7
Elements Contributing to
Effective Channel
Relationships

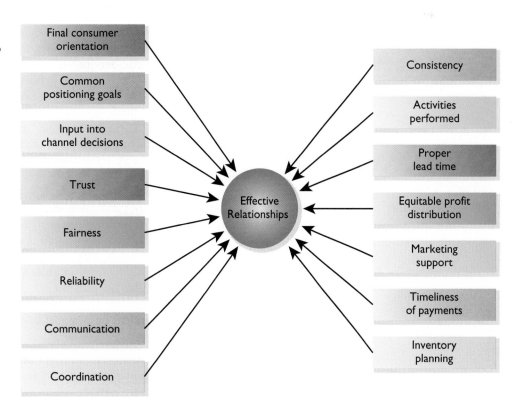

THE DIFFERENCES IN RELATIONSHIP BUILDING BETWEEN GOODS AND SERVICE RETAILERS

The consumer interest in services makes it crucial to understand the differences in relationship building between retailers that market services and those that market goods. This applies to store-based and nonstore-based firms, those offering only goods *or* services, and those offering goods *and* services.

Goods retailing focuses on the sale of tangible (physical) products. **Service retailing** involves transactions in which consumers do not purchase or acquire ownership of tangible products. Some retailers engage in either goods retailing (such as hardware stores) or service retailing (such as travel agencies); others offer a combination of the two (such as video stores that rent, as well as sell movies). The latter format is the fastest-growing. Consider how many pharmacies offer film developing, how many department stores have beauty salons, how many hotels have gift shops, and so on.

Service retailing encompasses such diverse businesses as personal services, hotels and motels, auto repair and rental, and recreational services. In addition, although several services have not been commonly considered a part of retailing (such as medical, dental, legal, and educational services), they should be when they entail final consumer sales. There are three kinds of service retailing:

- **Rented-goods services**, whereby consumers lease and use goods for specified periods of time. Tangible goods are leased for a fixed time, but ownership is not obtained and the good must be returned when the rental period is up. Examples are Hertz car rentals, carpet cleaner rentals at a supermarket, and video rentals at a 7-Eleven.

- **Owned-goods services**, whereby goods owned by consumers are repaired, improved, or maintained. In this grouping, the retailer providing the service never owns the good involved. Illustrations include watch repair, lawn care, and an annual air-conditioner tune-up.

- **Nongoods services**, whereby intangible personal services are offered to consumers, who then experience the services rather than possess them. The seller offers personal expertise for a specified time in return for a fee; tangible goods are not involved. Some examples are stockbrokers, travel agents, real-estate brokers, and personal trainers.

Please note: The terms *customer service* and *service retailing* are not interchangeable. Customer service refers to the activities undertaken *in conjunction with* the retailer's main business; they are part of the total retail experience. Service retailing refers to situations in which services *are sold to* consumers.

There are four unique aspects of service retailing that influence relationship building and customer retention: (1) The intangibility of many services makes a consumer's choice of competitive offerings tougher than with goods. (2) The service provider and his or her services are sometimes inseparable (thereby localizing marketing efforts). (3) The perishability of many services prevents storage and increases risks. (4) The aspect of human nature involved in many services makes them more variable.

Cheap Tickets (www.cheaptickets.com) makes itself more tangible through its descriptive name.

The intangible (and possibly abstract) nature of services makes it harder for a firm to develop a clear consumer-oriented strategy, particularly because many retailers (such as opticians, repairpeople, and landscapers) start service businesses on the basis of their product expertise. The inseparability of the service provider and his or her services means the owner-operator is often indispensable and good customer relations are pivotal. Perishability presents a risk that in many cases cannot be overcome. Thus, revenues from an unrented hotel room are forever lost. Variability means service quality may differ for each shopping experience, store, or service provider. See Figure 2-8.

Service retailing is much more dependent on personal interactions and word-of-mouth communication than goods retailing:

Relationship marketing benefits the customer, as well as the firm. For services that are personally important, variable in quality, and/or complex, many customers will

FIGURE 2-8

Characteristics of Service Retailing That Differentiate It from Goods Retailing and Their Strategic Implications

Source: Adapted by the authors from Valarie A. Zeithaml, A. Parasuraman, and Leonard L. Berry, "Problems and Strategies in Service Marketing," *Journal of Marketing,* Vol. 49 (Spring 1985), p. 35. Reprinted by permission of the American Marketing Association.

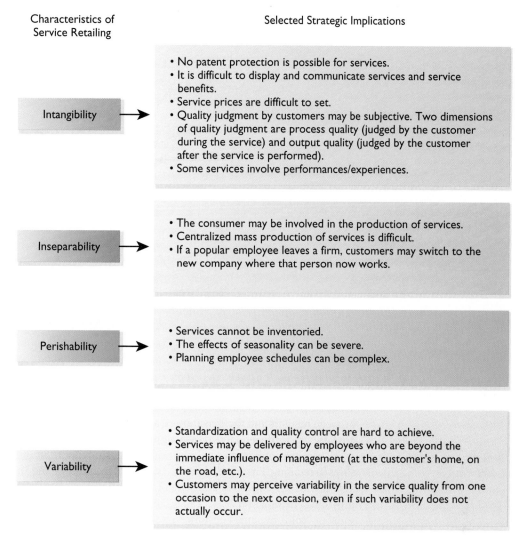

Characteristics of Service Retailing

Selected Strategic Implications

Intangibility
- No patent protection is possible for services.
- It is difficult to display and communicate services and service benefits.
- Service prices are difficult to set.
- Quality judgment by customers may be subjective. Two dimensions of quality judgment are process quality (judged by the customer during the service) and output quality (judged by the customer after the service is performed).
- Some services involve performances/experiences.

Inseparability
- The consumer may be involved in the production of services.
- Centralized mass production of services is difficult.
- If a popular employee leaves a firm, customers may switch to the new company where that person now works.

Perishability
- Services cannot be inventoried.
- The effects of seasonality can be severe.
- Planning employee schedules can be complex.

Variability
- Standardization and quality control are hard to achieve.
- Services may be delivered by employees who are beyond the immediate influence of management (at the customer's home, on the road, etc.).
- Customers may perceive variability in the service quality from one occasion to the next occasion, even if such variability does not actually occur.

desire to be "relationship customers." Medical, banking, insurance, and hairstyling services illustrate some or all of the significant factors—importance, variability, and complexity— that would cause many customers to desire continuity with the same provider, a proactive service attitude, and customized service delivery. The intangible nature of services makes them difficult for customers to evaluate prior to purchase. The heterogeneity of labor-intensive services encourages customer loyalty when excellent service is experienced. Not only does the auto repair firm want to find customers who will be loyal, but customers want to find an auto repair firm that evokes their loyalty. Knowledge of the customer combined with social rapport built over a series of service encounters facilitate the tailoring of service to customer specifications. Relationship marketing does not apply to every service situation. However, for those services distinguished by the characteristics discussed here, it is potent.[19]

Figure 2-9 highlights several factors that consumers may consider in forming their perceptions about the caliber of the service retailing experience offered by a particular firm. The appendix at the end of this chapter presents an additional discussion on the unique aspects of operating a service retailing business.

FIGURE 2-9

Selected Factors
Affecting Consumer
Perceptions of Service
Retailing

Source: Adapted by the
authors from Leonard L. Berry,
Kathleen Seiders, and Dhruv
Grewal, "Understanding
Service Convenience," *Journal
of Marketing,* Vol. 66 (July
2002), pp. 1–17; and Hung-
Chang Chiu, "A Study on
the Cognitive and Affective
Components of Service
Quality," *Total Quality
Management,* Vol. 13 (March
2002), pp. 265–274.

TECHNOLOGY AND RELATIONSHIPS IN RETAILING

Technology is beneficial to retailing relationships if it facilitates a better communication flow between retailers and their customers, as well as between retailers and their suppliers, and if there are faster, more dependable transactions.

These two points should be considered in studying technology and its impact on relationships in retailing. First, in each firm, the roles of technology and "humans" must be clear and consistent with the objectives and style of that business. Although technology can be a great aid in providing customer service, it can become overloaded and break down. It is also viewed as impersonal or "cold" by some consumers. New technology must be set up as efficiently as possible with minimal disruptions to suppliers, employees, and customers. Second, customers expect certain operations to be in place, so they can rapidly complete credit transactions, get feedback on product availability, and so on. Firms have to deploy some advances (such as a computerized checkout system) simply to be competitive. By enacting other advances, they can carve out differential advantages. For instance, consider the paint store with computerized paint-matching equipment for customers who want to buy paint to touch up old jobs.[20]

Throughout this book, we devote a lot of attention to technological advances through "Technology in Retailing" boxes and in-chapter discussions. Here, we look at technology's effects in terms of electronic banking and customer/supplier interactions.

ELECTRONIC BANKING

Electronic banking involves both the use of automatic teller machines (ATMs) and the instant processing of retail purchases. It allows centralized recordkeeping and lets customers complete transactions 24 hours a day, 7 days a week at bank and nonbank locations—including home or office. Besides its use in typical financial transactions (such as check cashing, deposits, withdrawals, and transfers), electronic banking is now used in retailing. Many retailers accept some form of electronic debit payment plan (discussed further in Chapter 13) whereby the purchase price is immediately deducted from a consumer's bank account by computer and transferred to the retailer's account.

Worldwide, there are 1 billion ATMs—350,000 in the United States alone—and people make billions of ATM transactions yearly.[21] ATMs are located in banks, shopping centers, department stores, supermarkets, convenience stores, hotels, and airports; on college campuses; and at other sites. With sharing systems, such as the Cirrus and Plus networks, consumers can make transactions at ATMs outside their local banking areas and around the world.

A highly touted, but thus far limited in use, new version of electronic payment is called the *smart card* by industry observers. The smart card contains an electronic strip that stores and modifies customer information as transactions take place. It is similar to pre-paid phone cards, whereby consumers buy computer-coded cards in denominations of $10, $20, $50, $100, and more. As they shop, card readers deduct the purchase amount from the cards. After they are used up, the cards are thrown away or are recoded. However, unlike with cash payments, retailers pay a fee for smart card transactions. In the future, "smarter" smart cards are expected to be more permanent and store more information (such as frequent shopper points). MasterCard has been experimenting with a smart card that can reward loyal shoppers with coupons, gifts, and other incentives.[22]

CUSTOMER AND SUPPLIER INTERACTIONS

Technology is changing the nature of retailer–customer and retailer–supplier interactions. If applied well, benefits accrue to all parties. If not, there are negative ramifications. Here are several illustrations.

Retailers widely use point-of-sale scanning equipment. Why? By electronically scanning products (rather than having cashiers "ring up" each product), retailers can quickly complete transactions, amass sales data, give feedback to suppliers, place and receive orders faster, reduce costs, and adjust inventory. There is a downside to scanning: the error rate. This can upset consumers, especially if they perceive scanning to be inaccurate. Yet, according to a Federal Trade Commission (FTC) study, scanner errors in reading prices occurred only 3.4 percent of the time; and although consumers believe that most errors result in overcharges, the FTC found that overcharges and undercharges were equally likely.[23] One way to assure consumers is to display more information at the point of purchase.

A popular new point-of-sale system involves self-scanning (which is discussed further in Chapter 13). Here's how a basic system works:

> A supermarket customer scans the groceries and sacks them. The sacking area is built atop a scale linked to the scanner that alerts the customers if an item was scanned twice or not at all. After all items are scanned, the customer scans in any coupons and selects a payment method. The machine accepts cash, credit, and debit cards, and electronic benefits transfers. Customers can use checks and food stamps but will need assistance from a cashier. Additionally, a cashier monitoring the checkout stations will be required to enter the birth date of customers purchasing alcohol or cigarettes.[24]

Figure 2-10 shows a self-scanning station.

FIGURE 2-10
A Self-Checkout Station

This self-checkout, from Stores Automated Systems, Inc., is stationary. Shoppers scan goods across a scanner and place them into a bag on a scale. The weight of the bagged items is compared to the weight of the scanned items, ensuring the shopper has scanned all items. A signature-capture device lets shoppers pay for purchases by credit or debit card without needing a cashier.

Reprinted by permission.

Technology in RETAILING — Self-Checkouts: Scanning for Fun

A focus group survey by Opinion Research Corp. International (**www.opinionresearch.com**) found that 33 percent of the consumers who were interviewed prefer a self-checkout over a cashier for simple checkout transactions. The consumers cite three major advantages of the self-checkout over traditional cashiers: shorter lines, increased speed, and privacy.

According to a spokesperson for Shaw's Supermarkets (**www.shaws.com**), "It's all a matter of perception on the part of the consumer. If there were a race between self-checkout and one of our store associates, I contend the store cashier would win the race. However, 56 percent of consumers polled in the Opinion Research survey were confident that they could scan supermarket purchases as quickly as the cashier could." Shoppers who are moving through the self-checkout lane, even if they are going at a slower pace than a cashier in the next lane, may perceive that they are being served more quickly than if they were standing in line waiting their turn.

An NCR (**www.ncr.com**) spokesperson says that certain categories of merchandise also lend themselves better to self-checkout due to a customer's concern for privacy. For example, many consumers may feel more comfortable purchasing incontinence products through self-checkout stations than cashiers.

Source: "Time Flies When You're Scanning for Fun: Is Self-Checkout the Next Retail Standard?" *Chain Store Age Executive* (February 2002), pp. 2C2–2C4.

Other technological innovations are also influencing retail interactions. Here are three examples:

Neiman Marcus pioneered the electronic gift card (www.neimanmarcus.com).

- Many retailers think they have the answer to the problem of finding the perfect gift—the electronic gift card. They have become so popular that 50 million Americans buy them each year: "They're easy to use, cutting-edge enough to appeal to kids, and with a big advantage to retailers. If the recipient buys less than the full value of the gift, the balance stays on the card." Neiman Marcus was the first retailer to issue gift cards in 1994. But today "they're as ubiquitous as credit cards and, for some retailers, as important a sales tool as incentive coupons."[25]

- Interactive electronic kiosks (discussed further in Chapter 6) are gaining in use: "You arrive at an airport and use electronic check-ins to board the plane. You reach your destination, electronically access your rental car, and are on the road. Now, some hotels are betting they can speed up one of traveling's great ordeals with check-in kiosks."[26]

- More retailers are using Web portals to exchange information with suppliers: "ChainDrugStore.net gives member retailers and suppliers quick access to each other. Created as a subsidiary of the National Association of Chain Drug Stores, the Web site boasts more than 110 retailers on its network, including supermarket chains like Safeway, Albertson's, Wegmans, and Price Chopper. The retailers are connected to major pharmaceutical suppliers including Bristol-Meyers Squibb, Pfizer, and Procter & Gamble. While it comes in handy when the speed and accuracy of information are crucial, ChainDrugStore.net also offers a way for merchandising and marketing data and retailer requests to flow through the Internet to the desks of the people who need the information."[27]

ETHICAL PERFORMANCE AND RELATIONSHIPS IN RETAILING

Ethical challenges fall into three interconnected categories: *Ethics* relates to the retailer's moral principles and values. *Social responsibility* involves acts benefiting society. *Consumerism* entails protecting consumer rights. "Good" behavior depends not only on the retailer but also on the expectations of the community in which it does business.

Throughout this book, in "Ethics in Retailing" boxes and chapter discussions, we look at many ethical issues. Here we study the broader effects of ethics, social responsibility, and consumerism. Visit our Web site for links on retailers' ethical challenges (**www.prenhall.com/bermanevans**).

ETHICS

In dealing with their constituencies (customers, the general public, employees, suppliers, competitors, and others), retailers have a moral obligation to act ethically. Furthermore, due to the attention paid to firms' behavior and the high expectations people have today, a failure to be ethical may lead to adverse publicity, lawsuits, the loss of customers, and a lack of self-respect among employees.

When a retailer has a sense of **ethics**, it acts in a trustworthy, fair, honest, and respectful manner with each of its constituencies. Executives must articulate to employees and channel partners which kinds of behavior are acceptable and which are not. The best way to avoid unethical acts is for firms to have written ethics codes, to distribute them to employees and channel partners, to monitor behavior, and to punish poor behavior—and for top managers to be highly ethical in their own conduct. See Figure 2-11.

Often society may deem certain behavior to be unethical even if laws do not forbid it. Most observers would agree that practices such as these are unethical (and sometimes illegal, too):

- Raising prices on scarce products after a natural disaster such as a hurricane.
- Not having adequate stock when a sale is advertised.
- Charging high prices in low-income areas because consumers there do not have the transportation mobility to shop out of their neighborhoods.

FIGURE 2-11
Eddie Bauer: Strong
Ethical Sensibilities

Reprinted by permission of
Eddie Bauer, Inc.

- Selling alcohol and tobacco products to children.
- Having a salesperson pose as a market researcher when engaged in telemarketing.
- Defaming competitors.
- Selling refurbished merchandise as new.
- Pressuring employees to push high-profit items to shoppers, even if these items are not the best products for them.
- Selling information from a customer data base.

The Direct Marketing Association makes its complete ethics code available at its Web site (www.the-dma.org/library/guidelines/index.shtml).

Many trade associations promote ethics codes to member firms. For example, the Direct Marketing Association has a code that it encourages members to use. Here are some of its provisions: *Article 1:* All offers should be clear, honest, and complete. *Article 5:* Disparagement of anyone on grounds of race, color, religion, national origin, gender, marital status, or age is unacceptable. *Article 8:* All contacts should disclose the sponsor and the purpose of the contact; no one should make offers or solicitations in the guise of one purpose when the intent is another purpose. *Article 24:* Sweepstakes prizes should be advertised in a clear, honest, and complete way so the consumer may know the exact offer. *Article 27:* Merchandise should not be shipped without receiving customer permission. *Article 39:* A telemarketer should not knowingly call a consumer with an unlisted or unpublished phone number.[28]

SOCIAL RESPONSIBILITY

A retailer exhibiting **social responsibility** acts in the best interests of society—as well as itself. The challenge is to balance corporate citizenship with a fair level of profits for stockholders, management, and employees. Some forms of social responsibility are virtually cost-free, such as having employees participate in community events or disposing of waste products in a more careful way. Some are more costly, such as making donations to charitable groups or giving away goods and services to a school. Still others mean going above and beyond the letter of the law, such as having free loaner wheelchairs for persons with disabilities besides legally mandated wheelchair accessibility to retail premises.

The Ronald McDonald House program (www.ronald-mcdonald-house.com) is one of the most respected community outreach efforts in retailing.

Most retailers know socially responsible acts do not go unnoticed. Though the acts may not stimulate greater patronage for firms with weak strategies, they can be a customer inducement for those otherwise viewed as "me-too" entities. It may also be possible to profit from good deeds. If a retailer donates excess inventory to a charity that cares for the ill, it can take a tax deduction equal to the cost of the goods plus one-half the difference between the cost and the retail price. To do this, a retailer must be a corporation and the charity must use the goods and not sell or trade them.

This is what some retailers are doing. McDonald's founded Ronald McDonald House so families can stay at a low-cost facility instead of a costly hotel when their seriously ill children get medical treatment outside their community. Target Stores no longer sells cigarettes. At Wal-Mart,

Ethics in RETAILING
Better Business Bureau Seals: Helping to Reduce Online Problems

The Better Business Bureau (**www.bbb.org**) has developed both reliability and privacy seals for Web-based retailers. Currently, more than 11,000 Web sites display one or more of these seals. Although member firms agree to comply with a number of rules, the programs do not constitute legal enforcement. Thus, the Better Business Bureau's seals are a form of self-regulation.

A retailer can earn the reliability seal by joining the local Better Business Bureau office, agreeing to adhere to the Bureau's online business practices, and committing to participate in its dispute resolution program. To be eligible to join this program, a retailer must be in business for at least one year; however, the retailer does not have to have its Web operations for that long.

The privacy seal signifies that a retailer will honor the customer's privacy concerns.

According to a spokesperson for the Council of Better Business Bureaus, the most common Web complaints involve return policies. For example, consumers sometimes incorrectly assume that they can return goods purchased on the Web to a nearby retailer store or that the retailer would reimburse the consumer for return shipping and insurance costs. Another common complaint involves either late or nondelivery of merchandise.

Source: "Better Business Bureau Seal Helps Resolve Online Trouble," *Knight Ridder/Tribune Business News* (May 2, 2002).

"We recognize the importance of preserving our natural resources whenever and wherever possible. That's why we pursue environmentally sound business practices and get involved in local recycling and other environmental efforts."[29] J.C. Penney requires all suppliers to sign a code of conduct that underage labor is not used. Hannaford Bros.' pledge sums up the role of a socially involved retailer:

> To be successful, we must satisfy our customers, our associates, our communities, and our shareholders. To achieve this, we must practice the highest level of ethical, social, legal, and professional behavior. We must constantly anticipate the changing needs and desires of our customers and respond quickly and effectively to those needs and desires. We are committed to distributing the goods and services consumers want with prices and quality that represent superior value. We are committed to the growth of all associates. To accomplish this, we need a growing business, a sharing of common goals and an atmosphere of mutual trust, openness, and encouragement. We will support and participate in the efforts of local, state, and national organizations which best contribute to the quality of life. In the long run, we will best serve the interests of our shareholders by serving well our customers, associates and communities.[30]

CONSUMERISM

Consumerism involves the activities of government, business, and other organizations to protect people from practices infringing upon their rights as consumers. These actions recognize that consumers have basic rights that should be safeguarded. As President Kennedy said more than 40 years ago, consumers have the *right to safety* (protection against unsafe conditions and hazardous goods and services), the *right to be informed* (protection against fraudulent, deceptive, and incomplete information, advertising, and labeling), the *right to choose* (access to a variety of goods, services, and retailers), and the *right to be heard* (consumer feedback, both positive and negative, to the firm and to government agencies).

Retailers and their channel partners need to avoid business practices violating these rights and to do all they can to understand and protect them. These are some reasons why:

Learn more about ADA (www.usdoj.gov/crt/ada/adahom1.htm).

- Some retail practices are covered by legislation. One major law is the **Americans with Disabilities Act (ADA)**, which mandates that persons with disabilities be given appropriate access to retailing facilities. As Title III of the Act states: "Public accommodations [retail stores] must comply with basic nondiscrimination requirements that prohibit exclusion, segregation, and unequal treatment. They also must comply with specific requirements related to architectural standards for new and altered buildings; reasonable modifications to policies, practices, and procedures; effective communication with people with hearing, vision, or speech disabilities; and other access requirements. Additionally, public accommodations must remove barriers in existing buildings where it is easy to do so without much difficulty or expense, given the public accommodations' resources." ADA affects entrances, vertical transportation, width of aisles, and stores displays.[31] See Figure 2-12.
- People are more apt to patronize firms perceived as customer-oriented and not to shop with ones seen as greedy.
- Consumers are more knowledgeable, price-conscious, and selective than in the past.
- Large retailers may be viewed as indifferent to consumers. They may not provide enough personal attention for shoppers or may have inadequate control over employees.
- The use of self-service is increasing, and it can cause frustration for some shoppers.
- Innovative technology is unsettling to many consumers, who must learn new shopping behavior (such as how to use electronic video kiosks).
- Retailers are in direct customer contact, so they are often blamed for and asked to resolve problems caused by manufacturers (such as defective products).

One of the most worrisome issues for consumers involves how retailers handle *customer privacy*. A consumer-oriented approach, comprising these elements, can alleviate negative shopper feelings: (1) Notice—"A company should provide consumers with a clear and con-

FIGURE 2-12
Understanding the
Americans with
Disabilities Act

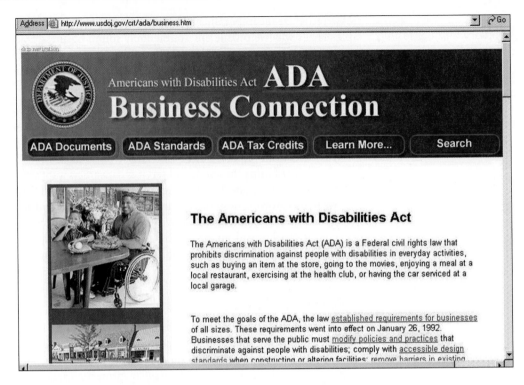

spicuous notice regarding its information practices." (2) Consumer choice—"A company should provide consumers with an opportunity to decide whether it may disclose personal information about them to unaffiliated third parties." (3) Access and correction—"Companies should provide consumers with an opportunity to access and correct personal information that they have collected about the consumers." (4) Security—"Companies should adopt reasonable security measures to protect the privacy of personal information." (5) Enforcement—"The firm should have in place a system by which it can enforce its privacy policy."[32]

To avoid customer relations problems, many retailers have devised programs to protect consumer rights without waiting for government or consumer pressure to do so. Here are examples.

For more than 90 years J.C. Penney has adhered to the "Penney Idea":

> To serve the public, as nearly as we can, to its complete satisfaction; to expect for the service we render a fair remuneration and not all the profit the traffic will bear; to do all in our power to pack the customer dollar with value, quality, and satisfaction; to continue training ourselves and our associates so the service we give will be more intelligently performed; to improve constantly the human factor in our business; to reward men and women in our firm by participation in what the business produces; and to test our every policy, method, and act—"Does it square with what is right and just?[33]

Thirty-five years ago, the Giant Food supermarket chain devised a consumer bill of rights (based on President Kennedy's), which it still follows today: (1) Right to safety—Giant's product safety standards, such as age-labeling toys, go beyond those required by the government. (2) Right to be informed—Giant has a detailed labeling system. (3) Right to choose—Consumers who want to purchase possibly harmful or hazardous products (such as foods with additives) can do so. (4) Right to be heard—A continuing dialogue with reputable consumer groups is in place. (5) Right to redress—There is a money-back guarantee policy on products. (6) Right to service—Customers should receive good in-store service.[34]

A number of retailers have enacted their own programs to test merchandise for such attributes as value, quality, misrepresentation of contents, safety, and durability. Sears, Wal-Mart, A&P, Macy's, and Target Stores are just a few of those doing testing. See Figure 2-13. Among the other consumerism activities undertaken by many retailers are setting clear procedures for handling

FIGURE 2-13
Voluntary Product Testing
at Target Stores

Reprinted by permission of
Target Stores.

Target's Responsibility
At Target, toys are an important part of our business. We want the toys you buy to meet Target's and the U.S. Government's high standards of quality, value, and safety. Therefore, we abide by all U.S. Consumer Product Safety Regulations. Target also utilizes an independent testing agency. They test samples of all toys we sell to help ensure your child's safe play.

All toys sold at Target are tested to be certain they are free from these dangers:

 Sharp edges

Toys of brittle plastic or glass can be broken to expose cutting edges. Poorly made metal or wood toys may have sharp edges.

 Small parts

Tiny toys and toys with removable parts can be swallowed or lodged in child's windpipe, ears, or nose.

 Loud noises

Noise-making guns and other toys can produce sounds at noise levels that can damage hearing.

 Sharp points

Broken toys can expose dangerous points. Stuffed toys can have barbed eyes or wired limbs that can cut.

 Propelled objects

Projectiles and similar flying toys can injure eyes in particular. Arrows or darts should have protective soft tips.

 Electrical shock

Electrically operated toys that are improperly constructed can shock or cause burns. Electric toys must meet mandatory safety requirements.

 Wrong toys for the wrong age

Toys that may be safe for older children can be dangerous when played with by little ones.

customer complaints, sponsoring consumer education programs, and training personnel to interact properly with customers.

Consumer-oriented activities are not limited to large chains; small firms can also be involved. A local toy store can separate toys by age group. A grocery store can set up displays featuring environmentally safe detergents. A neighborhood restaurant can cook foods in low-fat vegetable oil. A sporting goods store can give a money-back guarantee on exercise equipment, so people can try it at home.

Summary

1. *To explain what "value" really means and highlight its pivotal role in retailers' building and sustaining relationships.* Sellers undertake a series of activities and processes to provide a given level of value for the consumer. Consumers then perceive the value offered by sellers, based on the perceived benefits received versus the prices paid. Perceived value varies by type of shopper.

A retail value chain represents the total bundle of benefits offered by a channel of distribution. It comprises store location, ambience, customer service, the products/brands carried, product quality, the in-stock position, shipping, prices, the retailer's image, and so forth. Some elements of a retail value chain are visible to shoppers. Others are not. An expected retail strategy represents the minimum value chain elements a given customer segment expects from a given retailer type. An augmented retail strategy includes the extra elements that differentiate retailers. A potential retail strategy includes value chain elements not yet perfected in the retailer's industry category.

2. *To describe how both customer relationships and channel relationships may be nurtured in today's highly competitive marketplace.* For relationship retailing to work, enduring relationships are needed with other channel members, as well as with customers. More retailers now realize loyal customers are the backbone of their business.

In applying relationship retailing with consumers, these factors should be considered: the customer base, customer service, customer satisfaction, and loyalty programs and defection rates. In terms of the customer base, all customers are not equal. Some shoppers are more worth nurturing than others; they are a retailer's core customers.

Customer service has two components: expected services and augmented services. The attributes of personnel who interact with customers, as well as the number and variety of customer services offered, have a big impact on the relationship created. Some firms have improved customer service by empowering personnel, giving them the authority to bend some rules. In devising a strategy, a retailer must make broad decisions and then enact specific tactics as to credit, delivery, and so forth.

Customer satisfaction occurs when the value and customer service provided in a retail experience meet or exceed expectations. Otherwise, the consumer will be dissatisfied.

Loyalty programs reward the best customers, those with whom a retailer wants to develop long-lasting relationships. To succeed, they must complement a sound value-driven retail strategy. By studying defections, a firm can learn how many customers it is losing and why they no longer patronize it.

Members of a distribution channel jointly represent a value delivery system. Each one depends on the others, and every activity must be enumerated and responsibility assigned. Small retailers may have to use suppliers outside the normal channel to get the items they want and gain supplier support. A delivery system is as good as its weakest link. A relationship-oriented technique that some manufacturers and retailers are trying, especially supermarket chains, is category management.

3. *To examine the differences in relationship building between goods and service retailers.* Goods retailing focuses on selling tangible products. Service retailing involves transactions in which consumers do not purchase or acquire ownership of tangible products.

There are three kinds of service retailing: rented-goods services—consumers lease goods for a given time; owned-goods services—goods owned by consumers are repaired, improved, or maintained; and nongoods services—consumers experience personal services rather than possess them. Customer service refers to activities that are part of the total retail experience. With service retailing, services are sold to the consumer.

The unique features of service retailing that influence relationship building and retention are the intangible nature of many services, the inseparability of some service providers and their services, the perishability of many services, and the variability of many services.

4. *To discuss the impact of technology on relationships in retailing.* Technology is advantageous when it leads to an improved information flow between retailers and suppliers, and between retailers and customers, and to faster, smoother transactions.

Electronic banking involves both the use of automatic teller machines and the instant processing of retail purchases. It allows centralized records and lets customers complete transactions 24 hours a day, 7 days a week at various sites. Technology is also changing the nature of supplier/retailer/customer interactions via point-of-sale equipment, self-scanning, electronic gift cards, interactive kiosks, and other innovations.

5. *To consider the interplay between retailers' ethical performance and relationships in retailing.* Retailer challenges fall into three related categories: Ethics relates to a firm's moral principles and values. Social responsibility has to do with benefiting society. Consumerism entails the protection of consumer rights. "Good" behavior is based not only on the firm's practices but also on the expectations of the community in which it does business.

Ethical retailers act in a trustworthy, fair, honest, and respectful way. Firms are more apt to avoid unethical behavior if they have written ethics codes, communicate them to employees, monitor and punish poor behavior, and have ethical executives. Retailers perform in a socially responsible manner when they act in the best interests of society through recycling and conservation programs and other efforts. Consumerism activities involve government, business, and independent organizations. Four consumer rights are basic: to safety, to be informed, to choose, and to be heard.

Key Terms

value (p. 21)
value chain (p. 21)
core customers (p. 24)
expected customer service (p. 25)
augmented customer service (p. 25)
employee empowerment (p. 25)
revolving credit account (p. 28)
option credit account (p. 28)

open credit account (p. 28)
customer satisfaction (p. 29)
consumer loyalty (frequent shopper) programs (p. 29)
value delivery system (p. 30)
goods retailing (p. 32)
service retailing (p. 32)
rented-goods services (p. 32)

owned-goods services (p. 32)
nongoods services (p. 32)
electronic banking (p. 34)
ethics (p. 37)
social responsibility (p. 38)
consumerism (p. 39)
Americans with Disabilities Act (ADA) (p. 39)

Questions for Discussion

1. When a consumer shops at an upscale apparel store, what factors determine whether the consumer feels that he or she got a fair value? How does the perception of value differ when that same consumer shops at a discount apparel store?

2. What are the expected and augmented value chain elements for each of these retailers?
   a. Fast-food restaurant.
   b. Motel.
   c. Local pharmacy.

3. Why should a retailer devote special attention to its core customers? How should it do so?

4. What is the connection between customer service and employee empowerment? Is employee empowerment always a good idea? Why or why not?

5. How would you measure the level of customer satisfaction with your college's bookstore?

6. Devise a consumer loyalty program for a national consumer electronics chain.

7. What are the unique aspects of service retailing? Give an example of each.

8. What are the pros and cons of ATMs? As a retailer, would you want an ATM in your store? Why or why not?

9. Will the time come when most consumer purchases are made with self-scanners? Explain your answer.

10. Describe three unethical, but legal, acts on the part of retailers that you have encountered. How have you reacted in each case?

11. Differentiate between social responsibility and consumerism from the perspective of a retailer.

12. How would you deal with consumer concerns about privacy in their relationships with retailers?

Web-Based Exercise

Visit the Web site of Nordstrom (**www.nordstrom.com**). Click on "customer service" at the top of the page. Comment on the information you find there. Does Nordstrom have customer-oriented policies? Explain your answer.

Note: Stop by our Web site (**www.prenhall.com/bermanevans**) to experience a number of highly interactive, appealing Web exercises based on actual company demonstrations and sample materials related to retailing.

Chapter Endnotes

1. Various company sources.

2. *Dillards, Inc. 2001 Annual Report*, p. 4.

3. Retail Forward, *Retailing 2005*, p. 9.

4. Robert Blattberg, Gary Getz, Jacquelyn Thomas, and Joan M. Steinauer, "Managing Customer Retention," *Incentive* (April 2002), p. 114.

5. Stillerman Jones & Company, *National Benchmarks of Shopping Patterns and Trends—2001*; WSL Strategic Retail, *How America Shops 2002*; and Kurt Salmon Associates, *Consumer Outlook 2001*.

6. Frederick R. Reichheld, "Learning from Customer Defections," *Harvard Business Review*, Vol. 74 (March–April 1996), p. 61. See also Stephanie Coyles and Timothy C. Gokey, "Customer Retention Is Not Enough," *McKinsey Quarterly* (Number 2, 2002), pp. 80–89.

7. *AutoZone 2000 Annual Report*, p. 5.

8. Susan Reda, "Saving Customer Service: Are Retailers Up to the Task?" *Stores* (January 2001), pp. 46–52.

9. Ernest W. Nicastro, "The 'Marshall' Plan—Or Customer After-Care: How to Spend Less and Sell More," *Direct Marketing* (April 1999), p. 62.

10. Dan Bazinet, "Retail Ideations: The Haves and the Have-Nots," *Sporting Goods Business* (December 2001), p. 13.

11. "74% of Companies to Increase Spending on Customer Service," *Direct Marketing* (October 2001), p. 7.

12. Nordstrom, "Employment Opportunities," **http://nordstrom. newjobs.com/employment.html** (February 2003).

13. Suzanne Barry Osborne, "Is Your Customer Being Served?" *Chain Store Age* (November 2000), p. 52.

14. Todd Hale, "Frequent Shopper Programs Continue to Grow," *Consumer Insight* (Summer 2002), pp. 25–26.

15. Carolyn Setlow, "The Benefits of Frequent Shopper Clubs," *DSN Retailing Today* (March 25, 2002), p. 11.

16. Robert D. Buzzell, "Channel Partnerships Streamline Distribution," *Sloan Management Review*, Vol. 36 (Spring 1995), p. 86.

17. Daniel Kadlec, "How Blockbuster Changed the Rules," *Time* (August 3, 1998), p. 48; and Gérard P. Cachon and Martin A. Lariviere, "Turning the Supply Chain into a Revenue Chain," *Harvard Business Review*, Vol. 79 (March 2001), pp. 20–21.

18. Ken Clark, "Collaborators, and Proud of It," *Chain Store Age* (March 2002), p. 76.

19. Leonard L. Berry, "Relationship Marketing of Services—Growing Interest, Emerging Prospects," *Journal of the Academy of Marketing Science*, Vol. 23 (Fall 1995), pp. 237–38. See also Charlene Pleger Bebko, "Service Intangibility and Its Impact on Consumer Expectations of Service Quality," *Journal of Services Marketing*, Vol. 14 (Number 1, 2000), pp. 9–26.

20. See Len Lewis, "Technology at Retail: Enhancing Customer Service?" *Consumer Insight* (Summer 2002), pp. 27–35.

21. Bill Koch, "1,200 ATMs for Every Million Americans," *ATMmarketplace.com* (April 22, 2002).

22. "In Brief: MasterCard in Chip Loyalty System Pact," *American Banker* (May 7, 2002), p. 12; and Ken Clark, "Chips and Nationalism," *Chain Store Age* (July 2002), p. 66.

23. Federal Trade Commission, "Price Check II Shows Scanner Accuracy Has Improved Since 1996" (December 16, 1998), press release.

24. "Omaha, Neb., Grocery Joins Growing Number to Add Self-Checkout Stands," *Omaha World-Herald* (February 18, 2002).

25. "Flush with Gift Cards, Retailers Found a Cash Bonanza in Reloadable Plastic Presents," *News Tribune* (May 5, 2002); Lisa Cornell, Associated Press, "Retailers Have High Hopes for Electronic Gift Cards," *Marketing News* (January 4, 1999), p. 33; and "Gift Cards: The Next Generation," *Chain Store Age* (February 2002), Supplement.

26. Neal Templin, "Electronic Kiosk Checks in Guests at More Hotels," *Wall Street Journal* (February 16, 1999), p. B1. See also "FYI: Gee-Whiz Technology Backs Up Trans World's New Banner, FYE," *Chain Store Age* (January 2002), p. 81.

27. Bob Vavra, "Pharmacy Link," *Progressive Grocer* (January 2002), p. 80.

28. *Direct Marketing Association Guidelines for Ethical Business Practices* (New York: Direct Marketing Association, revised April 2002).

29. "Wal-Mart: Welcome to Good Works: Our Environment," **www.walmartfoundation.org** (January 10, 2003).

30. "Hannaford Values & Mission," **www.hannaford.com/about/values.htm** (January 17, 2003).

31. See Marianne Wilson, "ADA: Open to Interpretation," *Chain Store Age* (July 2002), p. 110.

32. Susan Haller, "Privacy: What Every Manager Should Know," *Information Management Journal*, Vol. 36 (May–June 2002), pp. 38–39.

33. J.C. Penney, public relations.

34. Giant Food, public relations.

Appendix on Planning for the Unique Aspects of Service Retailing

We present this appendix because service retailing in the United States and around the world is growing steadily and represents a large portion of overall retailing. In the United States, consumers spend 60 percent of their after-tax income on such services as travel, recreation, personal care, education, medical care, and housing. Three-quarters of the labor force works in services. Consumers spend billions of dollars each year to rent such products as power tools and party goods (coffee urns, silverware, wine glasses, etc.). People annually spend $150 billion to maintain their cars. There are 90,000 beauty and barber shops, 45,000 laundry and cleaning outlets, 60,000 hotels and motels, 21,000 video-rental stores, and 17,000 sports and recreation clubs. During the past 30 years, the prices of services have risen more than the prices of many goods. Due to technological advances, automation has substantially reduced manufacturing labor costs, but many services remain labor-intensive due to their personal nature.[1]

Here we will look at the abilities required to be a successful service retailer, how to improve the performance of service retailers, and the strategy of a recent Baldrige Award winner.

ABILITIES REQUIRED TO BE A SUCCESSFUL SERVICE RETAILER

The personal abilities required in service retailing are usually quite distinct from those in goods retailing:

• With service retailing, the major value provided to the customer is some type of retailer service, not the ownership of a physical product produced by a manufacturer.

- Specific skills are often required, and these skills may not be transferable from one type of service to another. TV repairpeople, beauticians, and accountants cannot easily change businesses or transfer skills. The owners of appliance stores, cosmetics stores, and toy stores (all goods retailers) would have an easier time than others in changing and transferring their skills to another area.

- More service operators must possess licenses or certification to run their businesses. Barbers, real-estate brokers, dentists, attorneys, plumbers, and others must pass exams in their fields.

- Owners of service businesses must enjoy their jobs and have the aptitude for them. Because of the close personal contact with customers, these elements are essential and difficult to feign.

Many service retailers can operate on lower overall investments and succeed on less yearly revenues than goods retailers. A firm with four outdoor tennis courts can operate with one worker who functions as clerk/cashier and maintenance person. A tax-preparation firm can succeed with one accountant. A watch repair business needs one repairperson. In each case, the owner may be the only skilled worker. Costs can be held down accordingly. On the other hand, a goods retailer needs a good product assortment and inventory on hand, which may be costly and require storage facilities.

The time commitment of a service retailer differs by type of business opportunity. Some businesses, such as a self-service laundromat or a movie theater, require a low time commitment. Other businesses, such as house painting or a travel agency, require a large time commitment because personal service is the key to profitability. More service retailers fall into the high rather than the low time-investment category.

IMPROVING THE PERFORMANCE OF SERVICE RETAILERS[2]

Service tangibility can be increased by stressing service provider reliability, promoting a continuous slogan (the Hertz #1 Club), describing specific results (a car tune-up's improving gas consumption by one mile per gallon), and offering warranties (hotels giving automatic refunds to unhappy guests). Most airlines have Web sties where customers can select flights and make their reservations interactively. These sites are a tangible representation of the airlines and their logos.

Demand and supply can be better matched by offering similar services to market segments with different demand patterns (Manhattan tourists versus residents), new services with demand patterns that are countercyclical from existing services (cross-country skiing during the winter at Denver golf resorts), new services that complement existing ones (beauty salons adding tanning booths), special deals during nonpeak times (midweek movie theater prices), and new services not subject to existing capacity constraints (a 10-table restaurant starting a home catering service).

Standardizing services reduces their variability, makes it easier to set prices, and improves efficiency. Services can be standardized by clearly defining each of the tasks involved, determining the minimum and maximum times needed to complete each task, selecting the best order for tasks to be done, and noting the optimum time and quality of the entire service. Standardization has been successfully applied to such firms as quick-auto-service providers (oil change and tune-up firms), legal services (for house closings and similar proceedings), and emergency medical care centers. If services are standardized, there is often a trade-off (e.g., more consistent quality and convenience in exchange for less of a personal touch).

Besides standardizing services, retailers may be able to make services more efficient by automating them and substituting machinery for labor. Thus, attorneys often use computerized word-processing templates for common paragraphs in wills and house closings. This means more consistency in the way documents look, time savings, and neater documents with fewer errors. Among the service firms that automate at least part of their operations are banks, car washes, bowling alleys, airlines, phone services, real-estate brokers, and hotels.

The location of a service retailer must be carefully considered. Sometimes, as with TV repairs, house painting, and lawn care, the service is "delivered" to the customer. The firm's location becomes a client's home, and the actual retail office is rather insignificant. Many clients might never even see a service firm's office; they make contact by phone or personal visits, and customer convenience is optimized. The firm incurs travel expenses, but it also has low (or no) rent and does not have to maintain store facilities, set up displays, and so on. Other service retailers are visited on "specific-intent" shopping trips. Although a customer may be concerned about the convenience of a service location, he or she usually does not select a skilled practitioner such as a doctor or a lawyer based on the location. It is common for doctors and attorneys to have offices in their homes or near hospitals or court buildings. A small store can often be used because little or no room is needed for displaying merchandise. A travel agency may have 6 salespeople and book millions of dollars in trips, but fit into a 500-square-foot store.

To improve their pricing decisions, service retailers can apply these principles to "capture and communicate value through their pricing":[3] Satisfaction-based pricing recognizes and reduces customer perceptions of uncertainty that service intangibility magnifies. It involves service guarantees, benefit-driven pricing, and flat-rate pricing. Relationship pricing encourages long-term relationships with valuable customers. It entails long-term contracts and price bundling. Efficiency pricing shares cost savings with customers that arise from the firm's efficiently executing service tasks. It is related to the concept of cost leadership.

Negotiated pricing occurs when a retailer works out pricing arrangements with individual customers because a unique or complex service is involved and a one-time price must be agreed on. Unlike traditional pricing (whereby each consumer pays the same price for a standard service), each consumer may pay a different price under negotiated pricing (depending on the nature of the unique service). A moving company charges different fees, depending on the distance of the move, who packs the breakable furniture, the use of stairs versus an elevator, access to highways, and the weight of the furniture.

Contingency pricing is an arrangement whereby the retailer does not get paid until after the service is performed and payment is contingent on the service's being satisfactory. A real-estate broker earns a fee only when a house purchaser (who is ready, willing, and able to buy) is presented to the house seller. Several brokers may show a house to prospective buyers, but only the broker who actually sells the house earns a commission. This technique presents risks to a retailer because considerable time and effort may be spent without payment. A broker may show a house 25 times, not sell it, and, therefore, not be paid.

One customer type is often beyond the reach of some service firms: the do-it-yourselfer. And the number of do-it-yourselfers in the United States is growing, as service costs increase. The do-it-yourselfer does a car tune-up, paints the house, mows the lawn, makes all vacation plans, and/or sets up a darkroom for developing film. Goods-oriented discount retailers do well by selling supplies to these people, but service retailers suffer because the labor is done by the customer.

Figure A2-1 highlights 10 lessons that service retailers can learn from the best in the business, such as Walt Disney Company, Marriott International, Ritz-Carlton, and Southwest Airlines.

FIGURE A2-1

Lessons in Service Retailing from the Best Firms

Source: Figure developed by the authors based on information in Robert C. Ford, Cherrill P. Heaton, and Stephen W. Brown, "Delivering Excellent Service: Lessons from the Best Firms," *California Management Review,* Vol. 44 (Fall 2001), pp. 39–56.

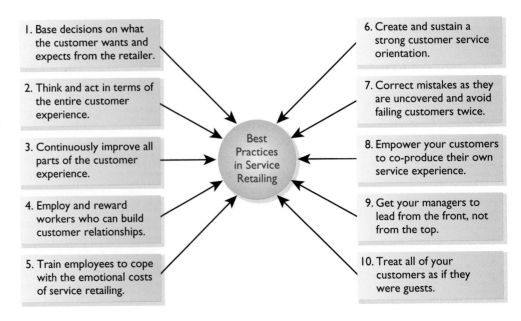

1. Base decisions on what the customer wants and expects from the retailer.
2. Think and act in terms of the entire customer experience.
3. Continuously improve all parts of the customer experience.
4. Employ and reward workers who can build customer relationships.
5. Train employees to cope with the emotional costs of service retailing.

Best Practices in Service Retailing

6. Create and sustain a strong customer service orientation.
7. Correct mistakes as they are uncovered and avoid failing customers twice.
8. Empower your customers to co-produce their own service experience.
9. Get your managers to lead from the front, not from the top.
10. Treat all of your customers as if they were guests.

THE STRATEGY OF PAL'S SUDDEN SERVICE: A RECENT BALDRIGE AWARD WINNER[4]

The Baldrige Award is given by the president of the United States to businesses—manufacturing and service, small and large—and to education and health care organizations that apply and are judged to be outstanding in seven areas: leadership, strategic planning, customer and market focus, information and analysis, human resource focus, process management, and business results. One of the few retailers to win this award is Pal's Sudden Service, a privately owned, quick-service restaurant chain with 17 locations, all within 60 miles of Kingsport, Tennessee. The firm distinguishes itself by offering competitively priced food of consistently high quality, delivered rapidly, cheerfully, and without error.

Hop over to Pal's Sudden Service (www.palsweb.com). See why it's a big winner!

For everything organizational and operational, Pal's has a process. Its Business Excellence Process is the key integrating element, an approach to ensuring that customer requirements are met in each transaction. Carried out under the leadership of Pal's two top executives and its 17 store owner-operators, the Business Excellence Process spans all facets of operations from strategic planning (done annually) to online quality control.

Pal's goal is to provide the "quickest, friendliest, most accurate service available." Achieving this is a challenge in an industry with annual employee turnover rates of more than 200 percent. The company's success in reducing turnover among frontline production and service personnel, most of whom are between the ages of 16 and 32, has become a key advantage. Owner-operators and assistant managers have primary responsibility for training based on a four-step model: show, do it, evaluate, and perform again. Employees must demonstrate 100 percent competence before they can work at a specific job task.

Pal's order handout speed has improved more than 30 percent since 1995, decreasing from 31 seconds to 20 seconds, almost four times faster than its top competitor. Errors in orders are rare, averaging less than one for every 2,000 transactions. The company aims to reduce its error rate to one in every 5,000 transactions. In addition, Pal's has consistently received the highest health inspection scores in its market and in the entire state of Tennessee.

Appendix Endnotes

1. *Statistical Abstract of the United States 2002* (Washington, D.C.: U.S. Department of Commerce, 2002), various pages.

2. See J. Joseph Cronin, Jr., Michael K. Brady, and G. Tomas M. Hult, "Assessing the Effects of Quality, Value, and Customer Satisfaction on Consumer Behavioral Intentions in Service Environments," *Journal of Retailing*, Vol. 76 (Summer 2000), pp. 193–218; and Valarie A. Zeithaml, Roland T. Rust, and Katherine N. Lemon, "The Customer Pyramid: Creating and Serving Profitable Customers," *California Management Review*, Vol. 43 (Summer 2001), pp. 118–142.

3. Leonard L. Berry and Manjit S. Yadav, "Capture and Communicate Value in the Pricing of Services," *Sloan Management Review*, Vol. 37 (Summer 1996), pp. 41–51.

4. The material in this section is excerpted from "Baldrige Award Recipient Profile: Pal's Sudden Service," **www.nist.gov/ public_affairs/pals.htm** (January 21, 2003.)

Chapter 3

STRATEGIC PLANNING IN RETAILING

Reprinted by permission.

While working at his father's clothing store, Leslie Wexner urged his father to concentrate on sportswear due to its higher sales rates. His father insisted that a clothing store needed a wide variety of merchandise, including formal and business clothing. He angrily told Leslie, "You'll never be a merchant." So, at the age of 26, Leslie Wexner founded The Limited—now Limited Brands (**www.limitedbrands.com**). He started in 1963 with a small store after getting a $5,000 loan from an aunt.

Clearly, Wexner's focused strategy has worked. Today, Limited Brands operates thousands of stores in the United States (including Express, Lerner New York, The Limited, Structure, and Victoria's Secret). Wexner has definitely turned out to be an ace merchant.

As a merchandiser, Leslie Wexner was one of the first retailing executives to understand the importance of developing a network of foreign suppliers that could manufacture goods at low cost and at blazing speed. This enabled his stores to rapidly respond to hot fashion trends without the risks associated with large inventories. Wexner also is known for creatively positioning retail stores by using timely fashions, distinctive store design, and powerful advertising. For example, after one acquisition, he immediately placed more emphasis on fashion. As a result, sales per store grew about 20 percent per year. He also had the insight to reposition Victoria's Secret, which was a rather sleazy six-store chain based in San Francisco at the time Wexner bought it. Today, it is the leader in intimate apparel.[1]

chapter objectives

1. To show the value of strategic planning for all types of retailers
2. To explain the steps in strategic planning for retailers
3. To examine the individual controllable and uncontrollable elements of a retail strategy
4. To present strategic planning as a series of integrated steps

OVERVIEW

In this chapter, we cover strategic retail planning—the underpinning of our book—in detail. As we noted in Chapter 1, a **retail strategy** is the overall plan or framework of action that guides a retailer. Ideally, it will be at least one year in duration and outline the mission, goals, consumer market, overall and specific activities, and control mechanisms of the retailer. Without a defined and well-integrated strategy, a firm can flounder and be unable to cope with the marketplace: "Ask people who advise small business owners about the biggest mistakes their clients make and they come up with a variety of answers—but they all have a common thread: a lack of planning or thinking in advance."[2]

The U.S. Small Business Administration (www.sba.gov) has a lot of useful planning tools for retailers at its Web site.

The process of strategic retail planning has several attractive features:

- It provides a thorough analysis of the requirements for doing business for different types of retailers.
- It outlines retailer goals.
- A firm determines how to differentiate itself from competitors and develop an offering that appeals to a group of customers.
- The legal, economic, and competitive environment is studied.
- A firm's total efforts are coordinated.
- Crises are anticipated and often avoided.

Strategic planning can be done by the owner of a firm, professional management, or a combination of the two. Even among family businesses, the majority of high-growth companies have strategic plans.

The steps in planning and enacting a retail strategy are interdependent; a firm often starts with a general plan that gets more specific as options and payoffs become clearer. In this chapter,

FIGURE 3-1

Elements of a Retail Strategy

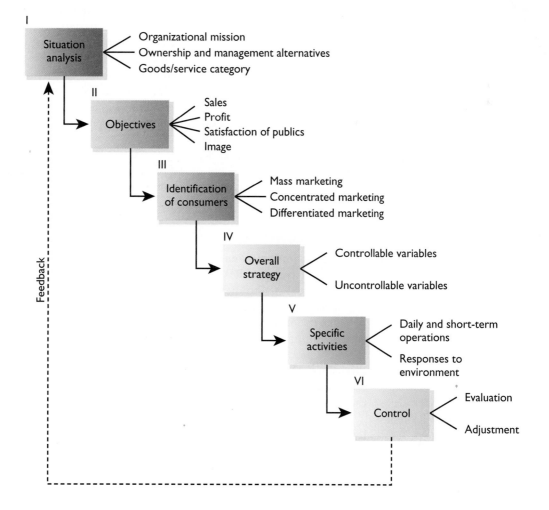

we cover each step in developing a retail strategy, as shown in Figure 3-1. Given the importance of global retailing, a chapter appendix explores the special dimensions of strategic planning in a global retailing environment. Visit our Web site (**www.prenhall.com/bermanevans**) for several links on strategic planning.

Please Note: An in-depth user-friendly strategic planning template, *Computer-Assisted Strategic Retail Management Planning*, appears on our Web site (**www.prenhall.com/bermanevans**). This template uses a series of drop-down menus, based on Figure 3-1. A sample plan is provided. As a planning exercise, you may be asked to apply the template to one of the 7 retail business scenarios that are provided—or to another scenario. You have the option of printing each facet of the planning process individually, or printing the entire plan as an integrated whole.

SITUATION ANALYSIS

Situation analysis is a candid evaluation of the opportunities and threats facing a prospective or existing retailer. It seeks to answer two general questions: What is the firm's current status? In which direction should it be heading? Situation analysis means being guided by an organizational mission, evaluating ownership and management options, and outlining the goods/service category to be sold.

A good strategy anticipates and adapts to both the opportunities and threats in the changing business environment. **Opportunities** are marketplace openings that exist because other retailers have not yet not capitalized on them. Ikea does well because it is the pioneer firm in offering a huge selection of furniture at discount prices. **Threats** are environmental and marketplace factors that can adversely affect retailers if they do not react to them (and, sometimes, even if they do). Single-screen movie theaters have virtually disappeared in most areas because they have been unable to fend off the inroads made by multiscreen theaters.

A firm needs to spot trends early enough to satisfy customers and stay ahead of competitors, yet not so early that shoppers are not ready for changes or that false trends are perceived. Merchandising shifts—like stocking popular fad items—are more quickly enacted than adjustments in a firm's overall location, price, or promotion strategy. A new retailer can adapt to trends more easily than existing firms with established images, ongoing leases, and space limitations. Small firms that prepare well can compete in a market with large retailers.

During situation analysis, especially for a new retailer or one thinking about making a major strategic change, an honest, in-depth self-assessment is vital. It is all right for a person or company to be ambitious and aggressive, but overestimating one's abilities and prospects may be harmful—if the results are entry into the wrong retail business, inadequate resources, or misjudgment of competitors.

ORGANIZATIONAL MISSION

An **organizational mission** is a retailer's commitment to a type of business and to a distinctive role in the marketplace. It is reflected in the firm's attitude toward consumers, employees, suppliers, competitors, government, and others. A clear mission lets a firm gain a customer following and distinguish itself from competitors. See Figure 3-2.

One major decision is whether to base a business around the goods and services sold or around consumer needs. A person opening a hardware business must decide if, in addition to hardware products, a line of bathroom vanities should be stocked. A traditionalist might not carry vanities because they seem unconnected to the proposed business. But if the store is to be a do-it-yourself home improvement center, vanities are a logical part of the mix. That store would carry any relevant items the consumer wants.

By focusing on quick-serve Mexican food, available at convenient locations, Taco Bell (www.tacobell.com) has become the leading retailer in its category.

A second major decision is whether a retailer wants a place in the market as a leader or a follower. It could seek to offer a unique strategy, such as Taco Bell becoming the first national quick-serve Mexican food chain. Or it could emulate the practices of competitors but do a better job in executing them, such as a local fast-food Mexican restaurant offering five-minute guaranteed service and a cleanliness pledge.

FIGURE 3-2

The Focused Organizational Mission of Frisch's Restaurants

The company operates and licenses family restaurants under the trade name Frisch's Big Boy. These facilities are located in Ohio, Indiana, and Kentucky. Additionally, the firm operates two hotels with restaurants in metropolitan Cincinnati, where it is headquartered. Trademarks that the company has the right to use include "Frisch's," "Big Boy," "Quality Hotel," and "Golden Corral."

Reprinted by permission.

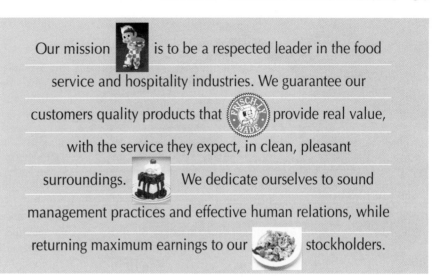

Our mission is to be a respected leader in the food service and hospitality industries. We guarantee our customers quality products that provide real value, with the service they expect, in clean, pleasant surroundings. We dedicate ourselves to sound management practices and effective human relations, while returning maximum earnings to our stockholders.

A third basic decision involves market scope. Large chains often seek a broad customer base (due to their resources and recognition). It is usually best for small retailers and startups to focus on a narrower customer base, so they can compete with bigger firms that tend not to adapt strategies as well to local markets.

Although the development of an organizational mission is the first step in the planning process, the mission should be continually reviewed and adjusted to reflect changing company goals and a dynamic retail environment. Here are examples of well-conceived retail organizational missions:[3]

Burlington Coat Factory department stores feature a broad range of the latest, first-quality, brand name and designer clothing for the entire family at everyday low prices that are significantly below those found at other department stores and specialty stores.

PetsMart operates retail stores, the Internet's most popular pet E-commerce sites, and several major branded catalogs and Web sites that market supplies for pets and horses. PetsMart offers a broad line of products for all the life stages of pets and is the nation's

Careers in RETAILING
What Does It Take for a Successful Retail Career?

An executive recruiter with 28 years of experience working with retail executives says that today's successful retail executives need an expanded skill set that understands the modern global business environment. Why? Twenty years ago, a retail buyer was primarily responsible for the selection of merchandise, in-store marketing, and the handling of reorders. Now the buyer has become a "category manager" with the added responsibilities of obtaining deliveries on time and reacting to the changing value of the dollar in international markets. In addition, merchandise lines are often more complex than in the past.

To be successful, a retailing executive needs to be knowledgeable in such areas as merchandising, logistics, operations, and finance. According to the executive recruiter, "Success is

achieved by recognizing that mastering one area of the business is not enough. Today's successful retail executive is not one-dimensional."

A retail executive with a diverse background better understands the overall environment facing his or her firm, as well as what it takes to be successful in the current competitive and economic market. This broad-based background can be obtained through education (both degree and continuing education programs) and experience (with different retailers and in different functional areas of the firm).

Source: Eric Segal, "Successful Retail Career Requires Multitude of Skills," *Retail Merchandiser* (June 2001), p. 34.

largest provider of high-quality grooming and pet training services. Veterinary care is offered at about half of PetsMart's stores.

Sam Goody is a mall-based specialty music retailer offering a broad product selection in a youthful, consumer-friendly shopping environment. Stores carry DVDs, videos, audiocassettes, music and movie videos, sheet music, music-inspired apparel, posters, and other music-related accessories.

OWNERSHIP AND MANAGEMENT ALTERNATIVES

An essential aspect of situation analysis is assessing ownership and management alternatives, including whether to form a sole proprietorship, partnership, or corporation—and whether to start a new business, buy an existing business, or become a franchisee.[4] Management options include owner-manager versus professional manager and centralized versus decentralized structures. As two experts noted, "Customers may not notice if a firm is a sole proprietorship, a partnership, or a corporation. The form chosen, though, can make a difference when it's time to pay taxes, respond to a lawsuit, or split up the business."[5]

A **sole proprietorship** is an unincorporated retail firm owned by one person. All benefits, profits, risks, and costs accrue to that individual. It is simple to form, fully controlled by the owner, operationally flexible, easy to dissolve, and subject to single taxation by the government. It makes the owner personally liable for legal claims from suppliers, creditors, and others; and it can lead to limited capital and expertise.

A **partnership** is an unincorporated retail firm owned by two or more persons, each with a financial interest. Partners share benefits, profits, risks, and costs. Responsibility and expertise are divided among multiple principals, there is a greater capability for raising funds than with a proprietorship, the format is simpler to form than a corporation, and it is subject to single taxation by the government. Depending on the type of partnership, it, too, can make owners personally liable for legal claims, can be dissolved due to a partner's death or a disagreement, binds all partners to actions made by any individual partner acting on behalf of the firm, and usually has less ability to raise capital than a corporation.

A **corporation** is a retail firm that is formally incorporated under state law. It is a legal entity apart from individual officers (or stockholders). Funds can be raised through the sale of stock, legal claims against individuals are not usually allowed, ownership transfer is relatively easy, the firm is assured of long-term existence (if a founder leaves, retires, or dies), the use of professional managers is encouraged, and unambiguous operating authority is outlined. Depending on the type of corporation, it is subject to double taxation (company earnings and stockholder dividends), faces more government rules, can require a complex process when established, may be viewed as impersonal, and may separate ownership from management. A closed corporation is run by a limited number of persons who control ownership; stock is not available to the public. In an open corporation, stock is widely traded and available to the public.

Sole proprietorships account for 77 percent of all U.S. retail firms that file tax returns, partnerships for 3 percent, and corporations for 20 percent. In terms of sales volume, sole proprietorships account for just 7 percent of total U.S. retail store sales, partnerships for 6 percent, and corporations for 87 percent.[6]

Starting a new business—being entrepreneurial—offers a retailer flexibility in location, operating style, product lines, customer markets, and other factors; and a strategy is fully tailored to the owner's desires and strengths. There may be high construction costs, a time lag until the business is opened and then until profits are earned, beginning with an unknown name, and having to form supplier relationships and amass an inventory of goods. Figure 3-3 presents a checklist to consider when starting a business.

Buying an existing business allows a retailer to acquire an established company name, a customer following, a good location, trained personnel, and facilities; to operate immediately; to generate ongoing sales and profits; and to possibly get good lease terms or financing (at favorable interest rates) from the seller. Fixtures may be older, there is less flexibility in enacting a strategy tailored to the new owner's desires and strengths, and the growth potential of the

FIGURE 3-3

A Checklist to Consider When Starting a New Retail Business

Source: Adapted by the authors from *Small Business Management Training Instructor's Guide,* No. 109 (Washington, D.C.: U.S. Small Business Administration, n.d.).

Name of Business _____

A. Self-Assessment and Business Choice

✓ Evaluate your strengths and weaknesses.
✓ Commitment paragraph: Why should you be in business for yourself? Why open a new business rather than acquire an existing one or become a member of a franchise chain?
✓ Describe the type of retail business that fits your strengths and desires. What will make it unique? What will the business offer customers? How will you capitalize on the weaknesses of competitors?

B. Overall Retail Plan

✓ State your philosophy of business.
✓ Choose an ownership form (sole proprietorship, partnership, or corporation).
✓ State your long- and short-run goals.
✓ Analyze your customers from their point of view.
✓ Research your market size and store location.
✓ Quantify the total retail sales of your goods/service category in your trading area.
✓ Analyze your competition.
✓ Quantify your potential market share.
✓ Develop your retail strategy: store location and operations, merchandising, pricing, and store image and promotion.

C. Financial Plan

✓ What level of funds will you need to get started and to get through the first year? Where will they come from?
✓ Determine the first-year profit, return on investment, and salary that you need/want.
✓ Project monthly cash flow and profit-and-loss statements for the first two years.
✓ What sales will be needed to break even during the first year? What will you do if these sales are not reached?

D. Organizational Details Plan

✓ Describe your personnel plan (hats to wear), organizational plan, and policies.
✓ List the jobs you like and want to do and those you dislike, cannot do, or do not want to do.
✓ Outline your accounting and inventory systems.
✓ Note your insurance plans.
✓ Specify how day-to-day operations would be conducted for each aspect of your strategy.
✓ Review the risks you face and how you plan to cope with them.

business may be limited. Figure 3-4 shows a checklist to consider when purchasing an existing retail business.

By being a franchisee, a retailer can combine independent ownership with franchisor support: strategic planning assistance; a known company name and loyal customer following; cooperative advertising and buying; and a regional, national, or global (rather than local) image. However, a franchisee contract may specify rigid operating standards, limit the product lines sold, and restrict supplier choice; the franchisor company is usually paid continuously (royalties); advertising fees may be required; and there is a possibility of termination by the franchisor if the agreement is not followed satisfactorily.

Strategically, the management format also has a dramatic impact. With an owner-manager, planning tends to be less formal and more intuitive, and many tasks are reserved for that person (such as employee supervision and cash management). With professional management, planning tends to be more formal and systematic. Yet, professional managers are more constrained in their authority than an owner-manager. In a centralized structure, planning clout lies with top management or ownership; managers in individual departments have major input into decisions with a decentralized structure.

A comprehensive discussion of independent retailers, chains, franchises, leased departments, vertical marketing systems, and consumer cooperatives is included in Chapter 4.

FIGURE 3-4
A Checklist for
Purchasing an Existing
Retail Business

NAME OF BUSINESS _____

✓ Why is the seller placing the business up for sale?

✓ How much are you paying for goodwill (the cost of the business above its tangible asset value)?

✓ Have sales, inventory levels, and profit figures been confirmed by your accountant?

✓ Will the seller introduce you to his or her customers and stay on during the transition period?

✓ Will the seller sign a statement that he or she will not open a directly competing business in the same trading area for a reasonable time period?

✓ If sales are seasonal, are you purchasing the business at the right time of the year?

✓ In the purchase of the business, are you assuming existing debts of the seller?

✓ Who receives proceeds from transactions made prior to the sale of the business but not yet paid by customers?

✓ What is the length of the lease if property is rented?

✓ If property is to be purchased along with the business, has it been inspected by a professional engineer?

✓ How modern are the storefront and store fixtures?

✓ Is inventory fresh? Does it contain a full merchandise assortment?

✓ Are the advertising policy, customer service policy, and pricing policy of the past owner similar to yours? Can you continue old policies?

✓ If the business is to be part of a chain, is the new unit compatible with existing units?

✓ How much trading-area overlap is there with existing stores?

✓ Has a lawyer examined the proposed contract?

✓ What effect will owning this business have on your life-style and on your family relationships?

GOODS/SERVICE CATEGORY

Entrepreneur Magazine (www.entrepreneurmag. com) addresses many of the issues facing new and growing firms as they plan their strategies.

Before a prospective retail firm can fully design a strategic plan, it selects a **goods/service category**—the line of business—in which to operate. Figure 3-5 shows the diversity of goods/service categories. Chapter 5 examines the attributes of food-based and general merchandise store retailers. Chapter 6 focuses on Web, nonstore, and other forms of nontraditional retailing.

It is advisable to specify both a general goods/service category and a niche within that category. Jaguar dealers are luxury auto retailers catering to upscale customers. Wendy's is an eating and drinking chain known for its quality fast food with a menu that emphasizes hamburgers. Motel 6 is a chain whose forte is inexpensive rooms with few frills.

A potential retail business owner should select a type of business that will allow him or her to match personal abilities, financial resources, and time availability with the requirements of that kind of business. Visit our Web site (**www.prenhall.com/bermanevans**) for links to many retail trade associations, which represent various goods/service categories.

PERSONAL ABILITIES

Personal abilities depend on an individual's aptitude—the preference for a type of business and the potential to do well; education—formal learning about retail practices and policies; and experience—practical learning about retail practices and policies.

An individual who wants to run a business, likes to use initiative, and has the ability to react quickly to competitive developments will be suited to a different type of situation than a person who depends on others for advice and does not like to make decisions. The first individual could be an independent operator, in a dynamic business such as apparel; the second might seek partners or a franchise and a stable business, such as a stationery store. Some people enjoy customer

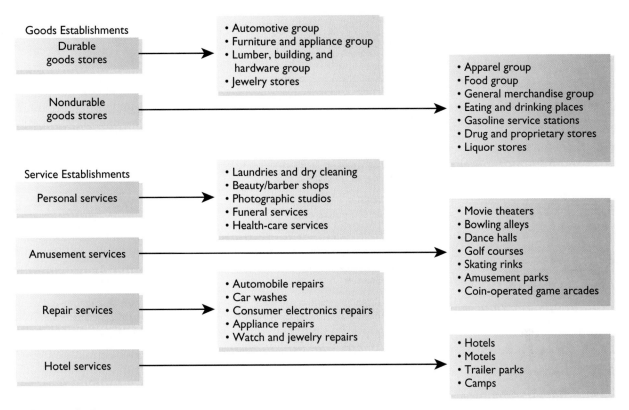

FIGURE 3-5
Selected Kinds of Retail Goods and Service Establishments

interaction; they would dislike the impersonality of a self-service operation. Others enjoy the impersonality of mail-order or Web retailing.

In certain fields, education and experience requirements are specified by law. Stockbrokers, real-estate brokers, beauticians, pharmacists, and opticians must all satisfy educational or experience standards to show competency. For example, real-estate brokers are licensed after a review of their knowledge of real-estate practices and their ethical character. The designation "broker" does not depend on the ability to sell or have a customer-oriented demeanor.

Some skills can be learned; others are inborn. Accordingly, potential retail owners have to assess their skills and match them with the demands of a given business. This involves careful reflection about oneself. Partnerships may be best when two or more parties possess complementary skills. A person with selling experience may join with someone who has the operating skills to start a retail business. Each partner has valued skills, but each may be unable to operate a retail entity without the expertise of the other.

FINANCIAL RESOURCES

Many retail enterprises, especially new, independent ones, fail because the owners do not adequately project the financial resources needed to open and operate the firm. Table 3-1 outlines some of the typical investments for a new retail venture.

Novice retailers tend to underestimate the value of a personal drawing account, which is used for the living expenses of the owner and his or her family in the early, unprofitable stage of a business. Because few new ventures are immediately profitable, the budget must include such expenditures. In addition, the costs of renovating an existing facility often are miscalculated. Underfunded firms usually invest in only essential renovations. This practice reduces the initial investment, but it may give the retailer a poor image. Merchandise assortment, as well as the types of goods and services sold, also affects the financial outlay. Finally, the use of a partnership, corporation, or franchise agreement will affect the investment.

TABLE 3-1	Some Typical Financial Investments for a New Retail Venture
Use of Funds	**Source of Funds**
Land and building (lease or purchase)	Personal savings, bank loan, commercial finance company
Inventory	Personal savings, manufacturer credit, commercial finance company, sales revenues
Fixtures (display cases, storage facilities, signs, lighting, carpeting, etc.)	Personal savings, manufacturer credit, bank loan, commercial finance company
Equipment (cash register, marking machine, office equipment, computers, etc.)	Personal savings, manufacturer credit, bank loan, commercial finance company
Personnel (salespeople, cashiers, stockpeople, etc.)	Personal savings, bank loan, sales revenues
Promotion	Personal savings, sales revenues
Personal drawing account	Personal savings, life insurance loan
Miscellaneous (equipment repair, credit sales [bad debts], professional services, repayment of loans)	Personal savings, manufacturer and wholesaler credit, bank credit plan, bank loan, commercial finance company

Note: Collateral for a bank loan may be a building, fixtures, land, inventory, or a personal residence.

Table 3-2 illustrates the financial requirements for a hypothetical used-car dealer. The initial personal savings investment of $300,000 would force many potential owners to rethink the choice of product category and the format of the firm. First, the plans for a 32-car inventory reflect this owner's desire for a balanced product line. If the firm concentrates on subcompact, compact, and intermediate cars, it can reduce inventory size and lower the investment. Second, the initial investment can be reduced by seeking a location whose facilities do not have to be

TABLE 3-2	Financial Requirements for a Used-Car Dealer	
Total investments (first year)		
Lease (10 years, $60,000 per year)		$ 60,000
Beginning inventory (32 cars, average cost of $12,500)		400,000
Replacement inventory (32 cars, average cost of $12,500)[a]		400,000
Fixtures and equipment (painting, paneling, carpeting, lighting, signs, heating and air-conditioning system, electronic cash register, service bay)		60,000
Replacement parts		75,000
Personnel (one mechanic)		45,000
Promotion (brochures and newspaper advertising)		35,000
Drawing account (to cover owner's personal expenses for one year; all selling and operating functions except mechanical ones performed by the owner)		40,000
Accountant		15,000
Miscellaneous (loan payments, etc.)		100,000
Profit (projected)		40,000
		$1,270,000
Source of funds		
Personal savings		$ 300,000
Bank loan		426,000
Sales revenues (based on expected sales of 32 cars, average price of $17,000)		544,000
		$1,270,000

[a]Assumes that 32 cars are sold during the year. As each type of car is sold, a replacement is bought by the dealer and placed in inventory. At the end of the year, inventory on hand remains at 32 units.

modified. Third, fewer financial resources are needed if a partnership or corporation is set up with other individuals, so that costs—and profits—are shared.

The U.S. Small Business Administration (**www.sba.gov/financing**) assists businesses by guaranteeing tens of thousands of loans each year. Such private companies as Wells Fargo and American Express also have financing programs specifically aimed at small businesses.

American Express
(www.americanexpress.com/
homepage/smallbusiness.
shtml) offers financial
support and advice for
small firms.

TIME DEMANDS

Time demands on retail owners (or managers) differ significantly by goods or service category. They are influenced both by consumer shopping patterns and by the ability of the owner or manager to automate operations or delegate activities to others.

Many retailers must have regular weekend and evening hours to serve time-pressed shoppers. Gift shops, toy stores, and others have extreme seasonal shifts in their hours. Mail-order firms and those selling through the Web, which can process orders during any part of the day, have more flexible hours.

Some businesses require less owner involvement, including gas stations with no repair services, coin-operated laundries, and movie theaters. The emphasis on automation, self-service, standardization, and financial controls lets the owner reduce the time investment. Other businesses, such as hair salons, restaurants, and jewelry stores, require more active owner involvement.

Intensive owner participation can be the result of several factors:

- The owner may be the key service provider, with patrons attracted by his or her skills (the major competitive advantage). Delegating work to others will lessen consumer loyalty.

- Personal services are not easy to automate.

- Due to limited funds, the owner and his or her family must often undertake all operating functions for a small retail firm. Spouses and children work in 40 percent of family-owned businesses.

- In a business that operates on a cash basis, the owner must be around to avoid being cheated.

Off-hours activities are often essential. At a restaurant, some foods must be prepared in advance of the posted dining hours. An antique dealer spends nonstore hours hunting for goods. An owner of a small computer store cleans, stocks shelves, and does the books during the hours the firm is closed. A prospective retail owner also has to examine his or her time preferences regarding stability versus seasonality, ideal working hours, and personal involvement.

OBJECTIVES

After situation analysis, a retailer sets **objectives**, the long-run and short-run performance targets it hopes to attain. This helps mold a strategy and translates the organizational mission into action. A firm can pursue goals related to one or more of these areas: sales, profit, satisfaction of publics, and image. Some retailers strive to achieve all the goals fully; others attend to a few and want to achieve them really well. Think about this array of goals for the Kroger Company:

Kroger (www.kroger.com)
is the leading food-based
retailer in the United
States.

Kroger has a new strategic growth plan through which the company will: (1) Increase its identical food store sales growth target. (2) Reduce operating and administrative costs by more than $500 million. (3) Further leverage its size to achieve even greater economies of scale. (4) Reinvest in its core business to increase sales and market share. As part of the plan, Kroger has set a long-term, sustainable earnings per share growth target of 13 to 15 percent per year beginning in fiscal 2004. For fiscal 2002 and 2003, the firm expected annual earnings per share growth of 10 to 12 percent.[7]

SALES

Sales objectives are related to the volume of goods and services a retailer sells. Growth, stability, and market share are the sales goals more often sought.

Some retailers set sales growth as a top priority. They want to expand their business. There may be less emphasis on short-run profits. The assumption is that investments in the present will yield future profits. A firm that does well often becomes interested in opening new units and enlarging revenues. However, management skills and the personal touch are sometimes lost with overly fast expansion.

Stability is the goal of retailers that emphasize maintaining their sales volume, market share, price lines, and so on. Small retailers often seek stable sales that enable the owners to make a satisfactory living every year without downswings or upsurges. And certain firms develop a loyal customer following and are intent not on expanding but on continuing the approach that attracted the original consumers.

For some firms, market share—the percentage of total retail-category sales contributed by a given company—is another goal. It is often an objective only for large retailers or retail chains. The small retailer is more concerned with competition across the street than with total sales in a metropolitan area.

Sales objectives may be expressed in dollars and units. To reach dollar goals, a retailer can engage in a discount strategy (low prices and high unit sales), a moderate strategy (medium prices and medium unit sales), or a prestige strategy (high prices and low unit sales). In the long run, having unit sales as a performance target is vital. Dollar sales by year may be difficult to compare due to changing retail prices and inflation; unit sales are easier to compare. A firm with sales of $350,000 three years ago and $500,000 today might assume it is doing well, until unit sales are computed: 10,000 then and 8,000 now.

PROFIT

With profitability objectives, retailers seek at least a minimum profit level during a designated period, usually a year. Profit may be expressed in dollars or as a percentage of sales. For a firm with yearly sales of $5 million and total costs of $4.2 million, pre-tax dollar profit is $800,000 and profits as a percentage of sales are 16 percent. If the profit goal is equal to or less than $800,000, or 16 percent, the retailer is satisfied. If the goal is higher, the firm has not attained the minimum desired profit and is dissatisfied.

Firms with large capital expenditures in land, buildings, and equipment often set return on investment (ROI) as a goal. ROI is the relationship between profits and the investment in capital items. A satisfactory rate of return is pre-defined and compared with the actual return at the end of the year or other period. For a retailer with annual sales of $5 million and expenditures (including payments for capital items) of $4 million, the yearly profit is $1 million. If the total capital investment is $10 million, ROI is $1 million/$10 million, or 10 percent per year. The goal must be 10 percent or less for the firm to be satisfied.

Operating efficiency may be expressed as $1 -$ (operating expenses/company sales). The higher the result, the more efficient the firm. A retailer with sales of $2 million and operating costs of $1 million has a 50 percent efficiency rating ($[1 -$ ($1 million/$2 million)$]$). Of every sales dollar, 50 cents goes for nonoperating costs and profits, and 50 cents for operating expenses. The retailer might set a goal to increase efficiency to 60 percent. On sales of $2 million, operating costs would have to drop to $800,000 ($[1 -$ ($800,000/$2 million)$]$). Sixty cents of every sales dollar would then go for nonoperating costs and profits, and 40 cents for operations, which would lead to better profits. If a firm cuts expenses too much, customer service may decline; this may lead to a decline in sales and profit.

SATISFACTION OF PUBLICS

Retailers typically strive to satisfy their publics: stockholders, customers, suppliers, employees, and government. Stockholder satisfaction is a goal for any publicly owned retailer. Some firms set policies leading to small annual increases in sales and profits (because these goals can be sustained over the long run and indicate good management) rather than ones based on innovative ideas that may lead to peaks and valleys in sales and profits (indicating poor management). Stable earnings lead to stable dividends.

Customer satisfaction with the total retail experience is a well-entrenched goal at most firms now. A policy of *caveat emptor* ("Let the buyer beware") will not work in today's competitive marketplace. Retailers must listen to criticism and adapt. If shoppers are pleased, other goals are more easily reached. Yet, for many retailers, other objectives rate higher in their list of priorities.

Good supplier relations is also a key goal. Retailers must understand and work with their suppliers to secure favorable purchase terms, new products, good return policies, prompt shipments, and cooperation. Relationships are very important for small retailers due to the many services that suppliers offer them.

Cordial labor relations is another goal that is often critical to retailer's performance. Good employee morale means less absenteeism, better treatment of customers, and lower staffing turnover. Relations can be improved by effective selection, training, and motivation.

Because all levels of government impose rules affecting retailing practices, another goal should be to understand and adapt to these rules. In some cases, firms can influence rules by acting as members of large groups, such as trade associations or chambers of commerce.

IMAGE (POSITIONING)

An **image** represents how a given retailer is perceived by consumers and others. A firm may be seen as innovative or conservative, specialized or broad-based, discount-oriented or upscale. The key to a successful image is that consumers view the retailer in the manner the firm intends.

Through **positioning**, a retailer devises its strategy in a way that projects an image relative to its retail category and its competitors and that elicits a positive consumer response. A firm selling women's apparel could generally position itself as an upscale or midpriced specialty retailer, a department store, a discount department store, or a discount specialty retailer, and it could specifically position itself with regard to other retailers carrying women's apparel.

Two opposite positioning philosophies have gained popularity in recent years: mass merchandising and niche retailing. **Mass merchandising** is a positioning approach whereby retailers offer a discount or value-oriented image, a wide and/or deep merchandise selection, and large store facilities. Wal-Mart has a wide, deep merchandise mix whereas Sports Authority has a narrower, deeper assortment. These firms appeal to a broad customer market, attract a lot of customer traffic, and generate high stock turnover. Because mass merchants have relatively low operating costs, achieve economies in operations, and appeal to value-conscious shoppers, their continuing popularity is forecast.

In **niche retailing**, retailers identify specific customer segments and deploy unique strategies to address the desires of those segments rather than the mass market. Niching creates a high level of loyalty and shields retailers from more conventional competitors. Babies "R" Us appeals to parents with very young children whereas Catherine's Stores has fashions for plus-size women. This approach will have a strong future because it lets retailers stress factors other than price and have a better focus. See Figure 3-6.

Babies "R" Us (www.babiesrus.com) has a very focused strategy and an online partnership with Amazon.com.

FIGURE 3-6

Niche Retailing by American Outpost

As its Web site (**www.americanoutpost.com**) notes, American Outpost operates stores in outlet shopping centers. The firms "sells first-quality merchandise at value prices, aimed to compete with other leading retailers, offering quality merchandise at prices below the competitors. For example, the company's basic denim jeans sell for $16.99 while the same quality jeans at our competitors may sell for $25 or more."

Photo reprinted by permission of Retail Forward, Inc.

Because both mass merchandising and niche retailing are popular, some observers call this the era of **bifurcated retailing**. They believe this may mean the decline of middle-of-the-market retailing. Firms that are neither competitively priced nor particularly individualistic may have difficulty competing.

Let us further examine the concept of positioning through these examples:

- "J.C. Penney dedicates itself to satisfying the needs and expectations of targeted customer segments. We offer fashion and basic apparel, accessories, and home furnishings in a customer-friendly environment in our stores, in our catalog, and on the Internet. We provide our customers with timely and competitive selections of fashionable, quality merchandise with day-in, day-out value. Within this positioning framework, we begin with our target customers' point of view in developing merchandise offerings, quality standards, branding and pricing strategies, visual merchandising, and service levels. We want to be positioned uniquely in a niche of our own by exceeding the fashion, quality, selection, and service components of the discounter; equaling the merchandise intensity of the specialty store; and providing the selection and under-one-roof shopping of the department store."[8]

Big Lots (www.biglots. com) is a shopping haven for consumers looking for bargains in closeouts and end-of-season goods.

- "A focus on becoming the best in the business at selling brand name closeouts is starting to pay off for Big Lots as part of a singular, unified strategy. Formerly known as Consolidated Stores, the firm changed its name during 2002 in line with plans to convert all of its stores to its strongest banner, Big Lots. Stores previously called Pic 'N Save and Mac Frugal's were changed to Big Lots. Once an operator of different retail formats, Big Lots sold its K-B Toys division in late 2000 as part of its new strategy. The firm also updated fixtures and lighting, and worked on other cosmetic refurbishments in stores to make them brighter and more inviting. It also completed the final phase of a new supply-chain management system, which made it more efficient at tracking inventory and being in stock."[9]

- Figure 3-7 shows a retail positioning map based on two shopping criteria: (1) price and service and (2) product lines offered. Our assumption: There is a link between price and service (high price equals excellent service). Upscale department stores (Neiman Marcus) offer outstanding customer service and carry several product lines. Traditional department stores

FIGURE 3-7
Selected Retail
Positioning Strategies

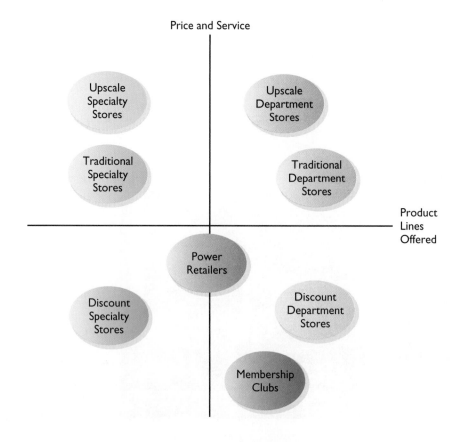

Technology in RETAILING — Smart Cards: Are They Dumb to Consumers and Retailers?

Although smart cards look like traditional credit or debit cards, unlike regular credit or debit cards, smart cards can be refilled. A metallic chip integrated into the smart card enables the card to store its remaining value. While the smart card's widespread use has been predicted for years, expectations have not been realized.

Despite high levels of advertising by banks aimed at getting European consumers to use their smart cards, these cards have not taken off in the Benelux counties where they were first introduced. For example, smart card usage has remained at less than 1 percent of retail sales in the Netherlands since being launched in 1995. According to a spokesperson for a major department store chain in the Netherlands, "Consumers just don't see much of an advantage to using smart cards rather than cash. Consumers know how much cash they have in their pockets, but they often don't know how much value is on their smart cards. And refilling them is a chore."

Another problem with smart cards is the high fees to retailers. These fees are significant because smart cards are often targeted at small purchases that do not warrant a credit or debit card. To further complicate matters, there are two smart card standards in countries such as the Netherlands that are incompatible (which causes difficulties for retailers).

Source: Matt Nannery, "Smart Cards Are No Dutch Treat," *Chain Store Age* (May 2001), p. 258.

(Sears) carry more electronics and other product lines than upscale stores. They have a trained sales staff to help customers. Discount department stores (Wal-Mart) carry a lot of product lines and rely on self-service. Membership clubs (Costco) have a limited selection in a number of product categories. They have very low prices and plain surroundings. Upscale specialty stores (Tiffany) offer outstanding customer service and focus on one general product category. Traditional specialty stores (Gap) have a trained sales staff to help customers and focus on one general product category. Discount specialty stores (Old Navy) rely more on self-service and focus on one general product category. Power retailers (Home Depot) offer moderate service and prices and a huge assortment within one general product category.

SELECTION OF OBJECTIVES

A firm that clearly sets its goals and devises a strategy to achieve them improves its chances of success.

An example of a retailer with clear goals and a proper strategy to attain them is Papa John's, the nearly 3,000-outlet pizza chain. As reported at its Web site (**www.papajohns.com**):

Customers: Papa John's will create superior brand loyalty—"raving fans"—through (a) authentic, superior-quality products, (b) legendary customer service, and (c) exceptional community service. *Team Members:* People are our most important asset. Papa John's will provide clear, consistent, strategic leadership and career opportunities for team members who (a) exhibit passion toward their work, (b) uphold our core values, (c) take pride of ownership in building the long-term value of the Papa John's brand, and (d) have ethical business practices. *Franchisees:* We will partner with our franchisees to create continued opportunity for outstanding financial returns to those franchisees who (a) adhere to Papa John's proven core values and systems, (b) exhibit passion in running their businesses, and (c) take pride of ownership in building the long-term value of the Papa John's brand. *Shareholders:* We will produce superior long-term value for our shareholders.

IDENTIFICATION OF CONSUMER CHARACTERISTICS AND NEEDS

The customer group sought by a retailer is called the **target market**. In selecting its target market, a firm may use one of three techniques: **mass marketing**, selling goods and services to a broad spectrum of consumers; **concentrated marketing**, zeroing in on one specific group; or

TABLE 3-3	Target Marketing Techniques and Their Strategic Implications		
	TARGET MARKET TECHNIQUES		
Strategic Implications	Mass Marketing	Concentrated Marketing	Differentiated Marketing
Retailer's location	Near a large population base	Near a small or medium population base	Near a large population base
Goods and service mix	Wide selection of medium-quality items	Selection geared to market segment—high- or low-quality items	Distinct goods/services aimed at each market segment
Promotion efforts	Mass advertising	Direct mail, E-mail, subscription	Different media and messages for each segment
Price orientation	Popular prices	High or low	High, medium, and low—depending on market segment
Strategy	One general strategy for a large homogeneous (similar) group of consumers	One specific strategy directed at a specific, limited group of customers	Multiple specific strategies, each directed at different (heterogeneous) groups of consumers

differentiated marketing, aiming at two or more distinct consumer groups, with different retailing approaches for each group.

Supermarkets and drugstores define their target markets broadly. They sell a wide assortment of medium-quality items at popular prices. In contrast, a small upscale men's shoe store appeals to a specific consumer group by offering a narrow, deep product assortment at above-average prices (or in other cases, below-average prices). A retailer aiming at one segment does not try to appeal to everyone.

Department stores are among the retailers seeking multiple market segments. They cater to several customer groups, with unique goods and services for each. Apparel may be sold in a number of distinctive boutiques in the store. Also, large retail chains frequently have divisions that appeal to different market segments. Target Corporation operates Marshall Field's (traditional department stores) for customers interested in full service and Target Stores (discount department stores) for those interested in low prices.

After choosing the target market, a firm can determine its best competitive advantages and devise a strategy mix. See Table 3-3. The significance of **competitive advantages**—the distinct competencies of a retailer relative to competitors—must not be overlooked. Some examples will demonstrate this.

Is the T.J. Maxx Web site (www.tjmaxx.com) consistent with the image it wants to project?

Tiffany seeks affluent, status-conscious consumers. It places stores in prestigious shopping areas, offers high-quality products, uses elegant ads, has extensive customer services, and sets rather high prices. Kohl's targets middle-class, value-conscious shoppers. It locates mostly in suburban shopping areas, offers national brands and Kohl's brands of medium quality, features good values in ads, has some customer services, and charges below-average to average prices. T.J. Maxx, a chain of off-price stores, aims at extremely price-conscious consumers. It locates in low-rent strip shopping centers or districts, offers national brands (sometimes overruns and seconds) of average to below-average quality, emphasizes low prices, offers few customer services, and sets very low prices. The key to the success of each of these retailers is its ability to define customers and cater to their needs in a distinctive manner. See Figure 3-8.

A retailer is better able to select a target market and satisfy customer needs if it has a good understanding of consumer behavior. This topic is discussed in Chapter 7.

FIGURE 3-8

Albertson's: Keeping a Competitive Edge

Albertson's (**www1.albertsons.com/corporate**) is quite proud of its heritage: "In 1939, our founder, Joe Albertson, opened a small grocery store in Boise, Idaho. Joe changed the rules in the grocery business by introducing unheard of services like a scratch bakery, magazine racks, home-made ice cream, popcorn, nuts, and an automatic donut machine. He based his store on high quality, good value, and excellent service. Joe's original philosophy of giving the customers the merchandise they want, at a price they can afford, in clean stores with great service from friendly personnel still applies today."

Photo reprinted by permission of Retail Forward, Inc.

OVERALL STRATEGY

Next, the retailer develops an in-depth overall strategy. This involves two components: the aspects of business the firm can directly affect and those to which the retailer must adapt. The former are called **controllable variables**, and the latter are called **uncontrollable variables**. See Figure 3-9.

A strategy must be devised with both variables in mind. The ability of retailers to grasp and predict the effects of controllable and uncontrollable variables is greatly aided by the use of suitable data. In Chapter 8, information gathering and processing in retailing are described.

CONTROLLABLE VARIABLES

The controllable parts of a retail strategy consist of the basic categories shown in Figure 3-9: store location, managing a business, merchandise management and pricing, and communicating with the customer. A good strategy integrates these areas. These elements are covered in Chapters 9 to 19.

FIGURE 3-9
Developing an Overall
Retail Strategy

Controllable variables
• Store location
• Managing a business
• Merchandise management and pricing
• Communicating with the customer

→ Retail strategy ←

Uncontrollable variables
• Consumers
• Competition
• Technology
• Economic conditions
• Seasonality
• Legal restrictions

FIGURE 3-10

The Sheraton Safari Hotel: Capitalizing on Its Location

This very successful hotel is situated just outside the entrance to Walt Disney World in Florida. It has 489 rooms, a lush décor inside and out, and meeting facilities for conventions. The location is appealing because of its proximity to Walt Disney World, despite the large number of competing hotels and motels.

Reprinted by permission of MeriStar Hospitality Corporation.

Store Location

A retailer has several store location decisions to make. The initial one is whether to use a store or nonstore format. Then, for store-based retailers, a general location and a specific site are determined. Competitors, transportation access, population density, the type of neighborhood, nearness to suppliers, pedestrian traffic, and store composition are considered in picking a location. See Figure 3-10.

The terms of tenancy (such as rent and operating flexibility) are reviewed and a build, buy, or rent decision is made. The locations of multiple outlets are considered if expansion is a goal.

Managing a Business

Two major elements are involved in managing a business: the retail organization and human resource management, and operations management. Tasks, policies, resources, authority, responsibility, and rewards are outlined via a retail organization structure. Practices regarding employee hiring, training, compensation, and supervision are instituted through human resource management. Job descriptions and functions are communicated, along with the responsibility of all personnel and the chain of command.

Operations management oversees the tasks that satisfy customer, employee, and management goals. The financial aspects of operations involve asset management, budgeting, and resource allocation. Other elements include store format and size, personnel use, store maintenance, energy management, store security, insurance, credit management, computerization, and crisis management.

Merchandise Management and Pricing

In merchandise management, the general quality of the goods and services offering is set. Decisions are made as to the width of assortment (the number of product categories carried) and the depth of assortment (the variety of products carried in any category). Policies are set with respect to introducing new items. Criteria for buying decisions (how often, what terms, and which suppliers) are established. Forecasting, budgeting, and accounting procedures are outlined, as is the level of inventory for each type of merchandise. Finally, the retailer devises procedures to assess the success or failure of each item sold.

With regard to pricing, a retailer chooses from among several techniques, and it decides what range of prices to set, consistent with the firm's image and the quality of goods and services offered. The number of prices within each product category is determined, such as how many prices of luggage to carry. And the use of markdowns is planned in advance.

San Francisco-based Esprit de Corp. (**www.esprit.com**) recently sold its trademark rights to its Hong Kong-based partner. Under founders Doug and Susie Tomkins, Esprit grew rapidly from the late 1970s to the late 1980s. During this time, Esprit's international partners also made the firm into a global brand.

Although Esprit's Asian and European businesses came together in 1997 with a design headquarters in Germany and retail headquarters located in Hong Kong, the American unit continued to have its own sourcing and distribution facilities. However, during the late 1990s and early 2000s, the European and Asian retail businesses thrived while the American unit continued its decline.

Esprit's new owners want to apply the European model to the U.S. operation. They want to position Esprit as a contemporary and affordable life-style brand with an international flavor. Esprit now plans to sell its products to discounters, general merchandise stores, and full-service department stores. To avoid oversaturating the market, one store may receive Esprit's junior line while a neighboring store may get its children's line. Esprit will also continue to have company-owned and franchised stores that feature the brand's full range of offerings, including licensed goods such as watches and jewelry.

Source: Marianne Wilson, "Shopping Esprit," *Chain Store Age* (May 2002), pp. 51–52.

Communicating with the Customer

An image can be created and sustained by applying various techniques.

The physical attributes, or atmosphere, of a store and its surrounding area greatly influence consumer perceptions. The impact of the storefront (the building's exterior or the home page for a Web retailer) should not be undervalued, as it is the first physical element seen by customers. Once inside, layouts and displays, floor colors, lighting, scents, music, and the kind of sales personnel also contribute to a retailer's image. Customer services and community relations generate a favorable image for the retailer.

The right use of promotional tools enhances sales performance. These tools range from inexpensive flyers for a take-out restaurant to an expensive national ad campaign for a franchise chain. Three forms of paid promotion are available: advertising, personal selling, and sales promotion. In addition, a retailer can obtain free publicity when stories about it are written, televised, or broadcast.

While the preceding discussion outlined the controllable parts of a retail strategy, uncontrollable variables (discussed next) must also be kept in mind.

UNCONTROLLABLE VARIABLES

The uncontrollable parts of a strategy are composed of the factors shown in Figure 3-9: consumers, competition, technology, economic conditions, seasonality, and legal restrictions. Farsighted retailers monitor the external environment and adapt the controllable parts of their strategies to take into account elements beyond their immediate control.

Consumers

A skillful retailer knows it cannot alter demographic trends or life-style patterns, impose tastes, or "force" goods and services on people. The firm learns about its target market and forms a strategy consistent with consumer trends and desires. It cannot sell goods or services that are beyond the price range of customers, that are not wanted, or that are not displayed or advertised in the proper manner.

Competition

There is often little that retailers can do to limit the entry of competitors. In fact, a retailer's success may encourage the entry of new firms or cause established competitors to modify their strategies to capitalize on the popularity of a successful retailer. A major increase in competition should lead a company to re-examine its strategy, including its target market and merchandising focus, to ensure that it sustains a competitive edge. A continued willingness to satisfy the target market better than any competitor is fundamental.

Technology

Computer systems are available for inventory control and checkout operations. There are more high-tech ways to warehouse and transport merchandise. Toll-free 800 numbers are popular for consumer ordering. And, of course, there is the Web. Nonetheless, some advancements are expensive and may be beyond the reach of small retailers. For example, although small firms might have computerized checkouts, they will probably be unable to use fully automated inventory systems. As a result, their efficiency may be less than that of larger competitors. They must adapt by providing more personalized service.

Economic Conditions

Economic conditions are beyond any retailer's control, no matter how large it is. Unemployment, interest rates, inflation, tax levels, and the annual gross domestic product (GDP) are just some economic factors with which a retailer copes. In outlining the controllable parts of its strategy, a retailer needs to consider forecasts about international, national, state, and local economies.

Seasonality

A constraint on certain retailers is their seasonality and the possibility that unpredictable weather will play havoc with sales forecasts. Retailers selling sports equipment, fresh food, travel services, and car rentals cannot control the seasonality of demand or bad weather. They can diversify offerings to carry a goods/service mix with items that are popular in different seasons. Thus, a sporting goods retailer can emphasize ski equipment and snowmobiles in the winter, baseball and golf equipment in the spring, scuba equipment and fishing gear in the summer, and basketball and football supplies in the fall.

Legal Restrictions

The Federal Trade Commission has a section of its Web site (www.ftc.gov/ftc/business. htm) devoted to do's and don'ts for business.

Table 3-4 shows how each controllable aspect of a retail strategy is affected by the legal environment.

Retailers that operate in more than one state are subject to federal laws and agencies. For example, the Sherman Act and the Clayton Act deal with monopolies and restraints of trade. The Federal Trade Commission deals with unfair trade practices and consumer complaints. The Robinson-Patman Act prohibits suppliers from giving unjust merchandise discounts to large retailers that could adversely affect small ones. The Telemarketing Sales Rule protects consumers.

At the state and local levels, retailers have to deal with many restrictions. Zoning laws prohibit firms from operating at certain sites and demand that building specifications be met. Blue

---

Ethics in RETAILING
What Does the Telemarketing Rule Mean for Consumers?

With some exceptions, all firms that sell goods or services through interstate telephone must comply with the Telemarketing Sales Rule (**www.ftc.gov/bcp/telemark/ rule.htm**). This rule requires telemarketers to provide important information to avoid misleading consumers before they pay for goods or services.

Telemarketers must promptly tell consumers that they are making a sales call, the nature of the products being offered, and in the case of prize promotions, that no purchase is necessary to be eligible to win. Telemarketers must also disclose the total costs to purchase, receive, or use the good or service offered. Telemarketers that fail to comply with this rule are subject to a $10,000 fine for each violation.

Two common areas of abuse that this rule seeks to prevent are vacation certificates and prize promotions. Sellers of vacation certificates have to disclose the limits on using the certificates during peak seasons or the requirements that buyers have to purchase meals at the resort. Prize promotions have to disclose the odds of winning. Furthermore, sellers or telemarketers also have to tell consumers that they can participate in the prize promotion without buying any products and to explain how a consumer can enter the contest without buying.

Source: "Telemarketing Sales Rule," **www.ftc.gov/bcp/rulemaking/tsr** (January 4, 2003).

TABLE 3-4	The Impact of the Legal Environment on Retailing[a]

Controllable Factor Affected	Selected Legal Constraints on Retailers
Store Location	*Zoning laws* restrict the potential choices for a location and the type of facilities constructed. *Blue laws* restrict the days and hours during which retailers may operate. *Environmental laws* limit the retail uses of certain sites. *Door-to-door (direct) selling laws* protect consumer privacy. *Local ordinances* involve fire, smoking, outside lighting, capacity, and other rules. *Leases and mortgages* require parties to abide by stipulations in tenancy documents.
Managing the Business	*Licensing provisions* mandate minimum education and/or experience for certain personnel. *Personnel laws* involve nondiscriminatory hiring, promoting, and firing of employees. *Antitrust laws* limit large firm mergers and expansion. *Franchise agreements* require parties to abide by various legal provisions. *Business taxes* include real-estate and income taxes. *Recycling laws* mandate that retailers participate in the recycling process for various materials.
Merchandise Management and Pricing	*Trademarks* provide retailers with exclusive rights to the brand names they develop. *Merchandise restrictions* forbid some retailers from selling specified goods or services. *Product liability laws* allow retailers to be sued if they sell defective products. *Lemon laws* specify consumer rights if products, such as autos, require continuing repairs. *Sales taxes* are required in most states, although *tax-free days* have been introduced in some locales to encourage consumer shopping. *Unit-pricing laws* require price per unit to be displayed (most often applied to supermarkets). *Collusion laws* prohibit retailers from discussing selling prices with competitors. *Sales prices* must be a reduction from the retailer's normal selling prices. *Price discrimination laws* prohibit suppliers from offering unjustified discounts to large retailers that are unavailable to smaller ones.
Communicating with the Customer	*Truth-in-advertising and -selling laws* require retailers to be honest and not omit key facts. *Truth-in-credit laws* require that shoppers be informed of all terms when buying on credit. *Telemarketing laws* protect the privacy and rights of consumers regarding telephone sales. *Bait-and-switch laws* make it illegal to lure shoppers into a store to buy low-priced items and then to aggressively try to switch them to higher-priced ones. *Inventory laws* mandate that retailers must have sufficient stock when running sales. *Labeling laws* require merchandise to be correctly labeled and displayed. *Cooling-off laws* let customers cancel completed orders, often made by in-home sales, within three days of a contract date.

[a]This table is broad in nature and omits a law-by-law description. Many laws are state or locally oriented and apply only to certain locations; the laws in each place differ widely. The intent here is to give the reader some understanding of the current legal environment as it affects retail management.

laws limit the times during which retailers can conduct business. Construction, smoking, and other codes are imposed by the state and city. The licenses to operate some businesses are under state or city jurisdiction.

For more information, contact the Federal Trade Commission (**www.ftc.gov**), state and local bodies, the Better Business Bureau (**www.bbb.org**), the National Retail Federation (**www.nrf.com**), or a specialized group such as the Direct Marketing Association (**www.the-dma.org**).

INTEGRATING OVERALL STRATEGY

What do you think about the overall strategy of Hertz (www.hertz.com)?

At this point, the retailer has devised on overall strategy. It has chosen a mission, an ownership and management style, and a goods/service category. Long- and short-run goals have been set. A consumer market has been designated and studied. General decisions have been made about store location, managing the business, merchandise management and pricing, and communications. These elements must be coordinated to have a consistent, integrated strategy and to systematically account for uncontrollable variables (consumers, competition, technology, economic conditions, seasonality, and legal restrictions).

The company is then ready to perform the specific tasks to carry out its strategy productively.

SPECIFIC ACTIVITIES

Chain Store Age (www. chainstoreage.com) tracks all kinds of tactical moves made by retailers.

Short-run decisions are now made and enacted for each controllable part of the strategy in Figure 3-9. These actions are known as **tactics** and encompass a retailer's daily and short-term operations. They must be responsive to the uncontrollable environment. Here are some tactical moves a retailer may make:

- *Store location:* Trading-area analysis gauges the area from which a firm draws its customers. The level of saturation in a trading area is studied regularly. Relationships with nearby retailers are optimized. A chain carefully decides on the sites of new outlets. Facilities are actually built or modified.

- *Managing the business:* There is a clear chain of command from managers to workers. An organization structure is set into place. Personnel are hired, trained, and supervised. Asset management tracks assets and liabilities. The budget is spent properly. Operations are systemized and adjusted as required.

- *Merchandise management and pricing:* The assortments within departments and the space allotted to each department require constant decision making. Innovative firms look for new merchandise and clear out slow-moving items. Purchase terms are negotiated and suppliers sought. Selling prices reflect the firm's image and target market. Prices offer consumers some choice. Adaptive actions are needed to respond to higher supplier prices and react to competitors' prices.

- *Communicating with the customer:* The storefront and display windows, store layout, and merchandise displays need regular attention. These elements help gain consumer enthusiasm, present a fresh look, introduce new products, and reflect changing seasons. Ads are placed during the proper time and in the proper media. The deployment of sales personnel varies by merchandise category and season.

The essence of excellent retailing is building a sound strategy and fine-tuning it. A firm that stands still is often moving backward. Tactical decision making is discussed in detail in Chapters 9 through 19.

CONTROL

In the **control** phase, a review takes place (Step VI in Figure 3-1), as the strategy and tactics (Steps IV and V) are assessed against the business mission, objectives, and target market (Steps, I, II, and III). This procedure is called a retail audit, which is a systematic process for analyzing the performance of a retailer. The retail audit is covered in Chapter 20.

The strengths and weaknesses of a retailer are revealed as performance is reviewed. The aspects of a strategy that have gone well are continued; those that have gone poorly are revised, consistent with the mission, goals, and target market. The adjustments are reviewed in the firm's next retail audit.

FEEDBACK

During each stage in a strategy, an observant management receives signals or cues, known as **feedback**, as to the success or failure of that part of the strategy. Refer to Figure 3-1. Positive feedback includes high sales, no problems with the government, and low employee turnover. Negative feedback includes falling sales, government sanctions (such as fines), and high turnover.

Retail executives look for positive and negative feedback so they can determine the causes and then capitalize on opportunities or rectify problems.

Summary

1. *To show the value of strategic planning for all types of retailers.* A retail strategy is the overall plan that guides a firm. It consists of situation analysis, objectives, identification of a customer market, broad strategy, specific activities, control, and feedback. Without a well-conceived strategy, a retailer may stumble or be unable to cope with environmental factors.

2. *To explain the steps in strategic planning for retailers.* Situation analysis is the candid evaluation of opportunities and threats. It looks at the firm's current position and where it should be heading. This analysis includes defining an organizational mission, evaluating ownership and management options, and outlining the goods/service category. An organizational mission is a commitment to a type of business and a place in the market. Ownership/management options include sole proprietorship, partnership, or corporation; starting a business, buying an existing one, or being a franchisee; owner management or professional management; and being centralized or decentralized. The goods/service category depends on personal abilities, finances, and time resources.

Objectives are the retailer's long- and short-run goals. A firm may pursue one or more of these goals: sales (growth, stability, and market share), profit (level, return on investment, and efficiency), satisfaction of publics (stockholders, consumers, and others), and image/positioning (customer and industry perceptions).

Next, consumer characteristics and needs are determined, and a retailer selects a target market. A firm can sell to a broad spectrum of consumers (mass marketing); zero in on one customer group (concentrated marketing); or aim at two or more distinct groups of consumers (differentiated marketing), with separate retailing approaches for each.

A broad strategy is then formed. It involves controllable variables (aspects of business a firm can directly affect) and uncontrollable variables (factors a firm cannot control and to which it must adapt).

After a general strategy is set, a firm makes and implements short-run decisions (tactics) for each controllable part of that strategy. Tactics must be forward-looking and respond to the environment.

Through a control process, strategy and tactics are evaluated and revised continuously. A retail audit systematically reviews a strategy and its execution on a regular basis. Strengths are emphasized and weaknesses minimized or eliminated.

An alert firm seeks out signals or cues, known as feedback, that indicate the level of performance at each step in the strategy.

3. *To examine the individual controllable and uncontrollable elements of a retail strategy.* There are four major controllable factors in retail planning: store location, managing the business, merchandise management and pricing, and communicating with the customer. The principal uncontrollable factors affecting retail planning are consumers, competition, technology, economic conditions, seasonality, and legal restrictions.

4. *To present strategic planning as a series of integrated steps.* Each stage in the strategic planning process needs to be performed, undertaken sequentially, and coordinated in order to have a consistent, integrated, unified strategy.

Key Terms

retail strategy (p. 49)
situation analysis (p. 50)
opportunities (p. 50)
threats (p. 50)
organizational mission (p. 50)
sole proprietorship (p. 52)
partnership (p. 52)
corporation (p. 52)
goods/service category (p. 54)

objectives (p. 57)
image (p. 59)
positioning (p. 59)
mass merchandising (p. 59)
niche retailing (p. 59)
bifurcated retailing (p. 60)
target market (p. 61)
mass marketing (p. 61)
concentrated marketing (p. 61)

differentiated marketing (p. 62)
competitive advantages (p. 62)
controllable variables (p. 63)
uncontrollable variables (p. 63)
tactics (p. 68)
control (p. 68)
feedback (p. 68)

Questions for Discussion

1. Why is it necessary to develop a thorough, well-integrated retail strategy? What could happen if a firm does not develop such a strategy?

2. How would situation analysis differ for a consumer electronics store chain and an online consumer electronics retailer?

3. What are the pros and cons of starting a new restaurant versus buying an existing one?

4. Develop a checklist to help a prospective service retailer choose the proper service category in which to operate. Include personal abilities, financial resources, and time demands.

5. Why do retailers frequently underestimate the financial and time requirements of a business?

6. Draw and explain a positioning map showing the kinds of retailers selling food products.

7. Discuss local examples of retailers applying mass marketing, concentrated marketing, and differentiated marketing.

8. Marsha Hill is the store manager at a popular gift store. She has saved $100,000 and wants to open her own store. Devise an overall strategy for Marsha, including each of the controllable factors listed in Figure 3-9 in your answer.

9. A competing toy store has a better location than yours. It is in a modern shopping center with a lot of customer traffic. Your store is in an older neighborhood and requires customers to travel further to reach you. How could you use a merchandising, pricing, and communications strategy to overcome your disadvantageous location?

10. Describe how a retailer can use fine-tuning in strategic planning.

11. How are the control and feedback phases of retail strategy planning interrelated? Give an example.

12. Should a store-based camping equipment retailer use the strategic planning process differently from a catalog retailer? Why or why not?

Web-Based Exercise

Visit the Web site of Carrefour (**www.carrefour.com**), the largest retailer outside the United States. Describe and evaluate the company based on the information you find there. What U.S. firm does it most resemble? Why?

Note: Stop by our Web site (**www.prenhall.com/bermanevans**) to experience a number of highly interactive, appealing Web exercises based on actual company demonstrations and sample materials related to retailing.

Chapter Endnotes

1. Various company sources.

2. Associated Press, "Planning Essential in Small Business" (April 25, 2002).

3. *Burlington Coat Factory 2001 Annual Report*, p. 1; *PetsMart 2000 Annual Report*, inside cover; and *Best Buy Inc. 2001 10K Report*, p. 4.

4. For additional information about the pros and cons of ownership formats, beyond that provided in this chapter, go to *Inc.'s* "General Business Law" site (**www.inc.com/articles/legal/gen_biz_law**).

5. Steven C. Bahls and Jane Easter Bahls, "In Good Form," *Entrepreneur* (September 1996), pp. 75–79.

6. Computed by the authors from data in *Statistical Abstract of the United States 2002* (Washington, DC: U.S. Department of Commerce, 2002).

7. "Kroger Company Financial Information," **www.kroger.com/financialinfo.htm** (December 11, 2001 announcement).

8. "Positioning Statement," **www.jcpenney.net/company/position/index.htm** (January 18, 2003).

9. Debbie Howell, "Big Lots Starts to See Dividends of Single-Banner, Closeout-Only Strategy," *DSN Retailing Today* (April 8, 2002), p. 8.

Appendix on the Special Dimensions of Strategic Planning in a Global Retailing Environment

There are about 270 countries—with 6.5 billion people and a $35 trillion economy—in the world. The United States accounts for less than 5 percent of the world's population and about 30 percent of the worldwide economy. Although the United States is an attractive marketplace, there are also many other appealing markets. Annual worldwide retailing sales have already reached $8 trillion—and they are growing.[1] When we talk about the global environment of retailing, we mean both U.S. firms operating in foreign markets and foreign retailers operating in U.S. markets.

Michigan State University's CIBER (http://ciber.bus.msu.edu) is an excellent source of information on global business practices.

The strategic planning challenge is clear: "Every global retail strategy must be built on three pillars: (1) The retailer must offer a competitively superior product as defined by local consumers. (2) The retailer must develop superior economics across the value chain that delivers the product to the local consumer. (3) The retailer must execute in the local environment. These pillars are much more difficult to create in retailing than in manufacturing."[2] In embarking on an international retailing strategy, firms should consider the factors shown in Figure A3-1.

FIGURE A3-1
Factors to Consider
When Engaging in
Global Retailing

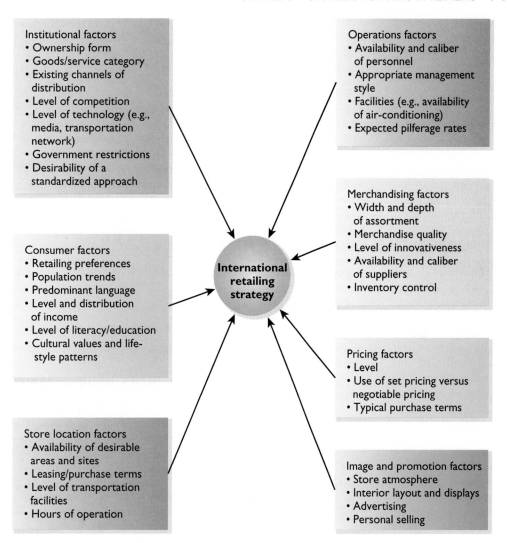

THE STRATEGIC PLANNING PROCESS AND GLOBAL RETAILING

Retailers looking to operate globally should follow these four steps in *in conjunction with* the strategic planning process described in Chapter 3:

1. *Assess Your International Potential:* "You must first focus on assessing your international potential to get a picture of the trends in your industry, your domestic position in that industry, the effects that international activity may have on current operations, the status of your resources, and an estimate of your sales potential. Find out about candidate countries by using research. It's easy to ruin a good plan by making fundamental cultural, partnering, or resource allocation mistakes."

2. *Get Expert Advice and Counseling:* "Many groups in the private sector and government provide guidance to those planning to go international. Trade associations are also useful, as are consulting firms and the business departments of universities. If you are entirely new to international retailing, contact the U.S. Trade Information Center (**www.ita.doc.gov/tic**) at (800) USA-TRADE (800-872-8723). If you are further along, contact a district office of the Commerce Department's International Trade Administration (**www.ita.doc.gov**). State governments are another source of assistance."

The United Nations (www.un.org) has a wealth of useful data about the international environment.

3. *Select Your Countries:* "You need to prioritize information about each country's economic strength, political stability, regulatory environment, tax policy, infrastructure development, population size, and cultural factors. For example, the economy of a country is generally

considered critical to most businesses. Equally critical are political factors, particularly government regulations. Others are more dependent on which product you market. The technological stage of a country has a more influential role for computers than for cosmetics."

4. *Develop, Implement, and Review an International Retailing Strategy:* "In general, a successful strategy identifies and manages your objectives, both immediate and long range; specifies tactics you will use; schedules activities and deadlines; and allocates resources among those activities. The plan should cover a two- to five-year period, depending on what you are selling, competitors' strength, conditions in target countries, and other factors. Keep your strategy flexible because often it is only after entering a country that you realize that your way of doing business needs modification. The best strategies can be changed to exploit unique local conditions and circumstances. Don't underestimate the local competition, but don't overestimate it either."[3]

OPPORTUNITIES AND THREATS IN GLOBAL RETAILING

For participating firms, there are wide-ranging opportunities and threats in global retailing.

OPPORTUNITIES

- Foreign markets may be used to supplement domestic sales.
- Foreign markets may represent good growth opportunities when domestic markets are saturated or stagnant.
- A retailer may be able to offer goods, services, or technology not yet available in foreign markets.
- Competition may be less in foreign markets.
- There may be tax or investment advantages in foreign markets.
- Due to government and economic shifts, many countries are more open to the entry of foreign firms.
- Communications are easier than before. The World Wide Web enables retailers to reach customers and suppliers well outside their domestic markets.

THREATS

- There may be cultural differences between domestic and foreign markets.
- Management styles may not be easily adaptable.
- Foreign governments may place restrictions on some operations.
- Personal income may be poorly distributed among consumers in foreign markets.
- Distribution systems and technology may be inadequate (for example, poor roads and lack of refrigeration). This may minimize the effectiveness of the Web as a selling tool.
- Institutional formats vary greatly among countries.
- Currencies are different. The countries in the European Union have sought to alleviate this problem by introducing the euro, a common currency, in most of their member nations.

STANDARDIZATION: AN OPPORTUNITY AND A THREAT

When devising a global strategy, a retailer must pay attention to the concept of *standardization*. Can the strategy in the home market be standardized and directly applied to foreign markets, or do personnel, physical facilities, operations, advertising messages, product lines, and other factors have to be adapted to local conditions and needs? Table A3-1 shows how the economies differ in 15 countries. And consider this: If you intend to enter a foreign market, you must be very sensitive to local cultural issues, and then be humble enough to accept that no matter how well you have prepared, some aspect of local culture will probably surprise you. Your entry plans must consist of some measure of humility and flexibility. You will inevitably be facing execution challenges that you had not adequately considered in the planning stage of your market entry.[4]

TABLE A3-1	The Global Economy, Selected Countries					
Country	2001 Population (millions)	2001 Population Density (per sq. kilometer)	2000 Per Capita GDP (U.S. $)	Annual GDP Growth Rate (%)	2000 Per Capita Retail Sales (U.S. $)	2002 World Competitiveness Ranking Among the 15 Countries Listed
Brazil	174	20	6,500	4.2	555	8
Canada	32	3	22,800	4.3	4,278	2
China	1,273	134	3,600	8.0	307	10
France	60	108	24,400	3.1	4,833	5
Germany	83	234	23,400	3.0	5,448	3
Great Britain	60	244	22,800	3.0	5,268	4
India	1,030	337	2,200	6.0	220	12
Indonesia	228	118	2,900	4.8	119	15
Italy	58	195	22,100	2.7	4,484	9
Japan	127	336	24,900	1.3	8,578	6
Mexico	102	52	9,100	7.1	962	11
Russia	145	9	7,700	6.3	456	14
South Africa	44	36	8,500	3.0	580	13
South Korea	48	475	16,100	9.0	1,908	7
United States	278	30	36,200	5.0	8,135	1

GDP is a country's gross domestic product. Per capita GDP is expressed in terms of purchasing power parity.
World Competitiveness Ranking is based on a country's economic performance, government efficiency, business efficiency, and infrastructure.

Sources: Compiled by the authors from *CIA World Factbook 2002*; IMD, *2002 World Competitiveness Yearbook*; and *Euromonitor*.

FACTORS AFFECTING THE SUCCESS OF A GLOBAL RETAILING STRATEGY

Several factors can affect the level of success of an international retailing strategy:

- *Timing:* "Being first in a market doesn't ensure success, but being there before the serious competition does increase one's chances."
- *A balanced international program:* "Market selection is critical."
- *A growing middle class:* "A rapidly growing middle class means expandable income, which translates into sales."
- *Matching concept to market:* "In *developed* markets, where quality and fashion are more appreciated, specialty operations are entering with success. In *developing* markets, discount/combination (food and general merchandise) retailers have been successful. Consumers there are more interested in price, assortment, value, and convenience." See Table A3-2.
- *Solo or partnering:* "When establishing a presence, retailers have often chosen the route of joint ventures with local partners. This makes it easier to establish government contacts and learn the ways of getting things done."
- *Store location and facilities:* "Foreign retailers often have to adapt their concepts to different real estate configurations in other markets." Shopping malls may be rare in some places.
- *Product selection:* "Consumers in most parts of the world would be overwhelmed by the product assortment in North American stores."
- *Service levels:* "Consumers in some areas do not expect anything close to the level of service American shoppers demand." This can be a real point of distinction.[5]

U.S. RETAILERS IN FOREIGN MARKETS

Here are examples of U.S. retailers with high involvement in foreign markets.

Until 1991, when it opened a store in Mexico, Wal-Mart only operated U.S. stores. By 2002, it had 1,200 stores in Argentina, Brazil, Canada, China, Germany, Korea, Mexico, and Great Britain (and in

TABLE A3-2	Preparing for Different Global Markets

Developed, Mature Markets

Issues

- Increasing competition, deteriorating margins, and saturation
- Consolidation and rationalization (cost cutting), forcing poor performers out of the market
- New enabling technologies
- Demanding customers
- Limited growth

Implications

- Retailers must focus on maximizing operational efficiencies, vendor relationships, infrastructure, and technology
- For growth, large retailers are expanding regionally and then globally into developed or developing markets

Developing, Immature Markets

Issues

- Minimal purchasing power per capita, yet strong economic growth and pent-up demand
- Huge customer base, representing up to 70 percent of the world's population
- Infrastructure issues—transportation, communication, etc.—may pose problems
- Disorganized, fragmented retail structures that are vulnerable to new entrants
- The number of indigenous large retailers is small to none
- Strong protectionist measures may exist

Implications

- Tremendous opportunity for large retailers, limited competition, huge growth potential
- Initial entry may need to be through intermediary; joint venture, etc.

Source: Deloitte & Touche, "Global Powers of Retailing," *Stores* (January 1998), Section 3, p. S15. Reprinted by permission.

2002, it also acquired a stake in Japan's Seiyu supermarket chain)—reaching annual sales of more than $35 billion outside the United States. According to its Web site (**www.walmart.com**): "Wal-Mart International has achieved global expansion through a combination of new-store construction and acquisitions. This strategy has given the company excellent market penetration and positioned it for future development. The company sees its development throughout North America, Latin America, Asia, and Europe as a good beginning with many promising areas for further expansion."

Toys "R" Us has been active internationally for years and now has more than 500 stores abroad. Among the nearly 30 nations in which it has well-established stores are Australia, Canada, France, Germany, Great Britain, Japan, Singapore, Spain, and Sweden. In some of its markets, such as Indonesia, Italy, South Africa, Turkey, and United Arab Emirates, the firm emphasizes franchising rather than direct corporate ownership. Why? As its Web site (**www.tru.com**) said, "Their local knowledge of the retail market combined with the Toys "R" Us expertise in the management of megastores provides a powerful combination to fully cover the potential of the market and increase the availability of toys."

Many of the world's leading mail-order retailers are U.S.-based, including American Express, Avon, Franklin Mint, and Reader's Digest. They are efficient and have a clear handle on customers and distribution methods. Because total worldwide mail-order sales (for both U.S. and foreign firms) outside the United States are less than those in the United States, there is great potential in foreign markets.

For nearly two decades, the majority of McDonald's new restaurants have opened outside the United States. Sales at the 17,000 outlets in 120 foreign nations account for more than one-half of total revenues. Besides Western Europe, McDonald's has outlets in Argentina, Australia, Brazil, Brunei, Canada, China, Czech Republic, Hungary, India, Japan, Malaysia, Mexico, New Zealand, Philippines, Russia, Turkey, Venezuela, and Yugoslavia. The restaurants in India are distinctive: "McDonald's worked with its local Indian partners to adapt the menu to local tastes and needs. As the old advertising jingle goes, the 'Maharaja Mac' is made of 'two all lamb patties, special sauce, lettuce, cheese, pickles, onions on a sesame seed bun.' The famous sandwich's main ingredient, beef, was replaced out of respect for the local Hindu population of India."[6]

FOREIGN RETAILERS IN THE U.S. MARKET

A large number of foreign retailers have entered the United States to appeal to the world's most affluent mass market. Here are three examples.

Ikea (**www.ikea.com**) is a Swedish-based home-furnishings retailer with stores in 35 countries. In 1985, Ikea opened its first U.S. store in Pennsylvania. Since then, it has added stores in such cities as Baltimore, Chicago, Elizabeth (New Jersey), Hicksville (Long Island, New York), Houston, Los Angeles, San Francisco, Seattle, and Washington, D.C. The firm offers durable, stylish, ready-to-assemble furniture at low prices. Stores are huge, have enormous selections, and include a playroom for children and other amenities. Today, Ikea generates 93 percent of its sales from international operations, and 13 percent of total company sales (more than $1 billion per year) are from its U.S. stores.

The Netherlands' Royal Ahold (**www.ahold.com**) ranks among the world's top retailers with more than $50 billion in annual retail sales. It has food stores in 28 countries and serves 40 million shoppers weekly. In the United States, Royal Ahold has acquired several chains, making it the leading supermarket firm on the East Coast. Its more than 1,600 U.S. stores include Stop & Shop, Giant Food, Tops Markets, Bruno's, and Bi-Lo.

Body Shop International (**www.the-body-shop.com**) is a British-based chain that sells natural cosmetics and lotions that "cleanse, beautify, and soothe the human form." There are 1,900 Body Shop stores in 50 countries, including the United States. The firm has more than 300 U.S. stores (60 percent company-owned and 40 percent franchised), which generate one-fifth of total company revenues.

Although the revenues of U.S.-based retailers owned by foreign firms are hard to measure, they exceed $150 billion annually. Foreign ownership in U.S. retailers is highest for general merchandise stores, food stores, and apparel and accessory stores. Examples of U.S.-based retailers owned by foreign firms are shown in Table A3-3.

TABLE A3-3	Selected Ownership of U.S. Retailers by Foreign Firms		
U.S. Retailer	Principal Business	Foreign Owner	Country of Owner
Eddie Bauer	Mail order and specialty stores	Otto Versand Gmbh	Germany
Crate & Barrel	Housewares stores	Otto Versand Gmbh	Germany
Food Lion	Supermarkets	Delhaize Le Lion	Belgium
Giant Food	Supermarkets	Royal Ahold	Netherlands
Great Atlantic & Pacific (A&P)	Supermarkets	Tengelmann	Germany
LensCrafters	Optical stores	Luxottica	Italy
Motel 6	Economy motels	Accor	France
7-Eleven	Convenience stores	Ito-Yokado	Japan
Spiegel	Mail order	Otto Versand Gmbh	Germany
Stop & Shop	Supermarkets	Royal Ahold	Netherlands
Talbots	Apparel	Aeon	Japan

Appendix Endnotes

1. Deloitte Touche Tohmatsu, "2002 Global Powers of Retailing," *Stores* (January 2002), Section 2.

2. John C. Koopman, "Successful Global Retailers a Rare Breed," *Canadian Manager* (Spring 2000), p. 22.

3. William J. McDonald, "Five Steps to International Success," *Direct Marketing* (November 1998), pp. 32–36.

4. Koopman, "Successful Global Retailers a Rare Breed," p. 25.

5. "Global Powers of Retailing," *Chain Store Age* (December 1996), Section 3, pp. 10B–13B.

6. "Maharaja Mac," **www.media.mcdonalds.com/secured/products/international/maharajamac.html** (August 18, 2002); and *McDonald's 2002 Annual Report.*

part one
Short Cases

1: SCHLOTZSKY'S DELI RAISES THE BAR WITH ITS TOTAL RETAIL EXPERIENCE

Schlotzsky's (www.schlotzsky.com) is a 700-unit fast-food chain that uses technology as a major competitive advantage. According to some retailing analysts, when a customer orders a deli sandwich at Schlotzsky's, "It comes with a side order of technology."

To integrate technology into the total retail experience offered by the chain, Schlotzsky's hired Robin Hanna, a former IBM and Dell Computer executive, as its chief information officer. By working with vendors, Hanna is striving to turn Schlotzsky's into a "leading-edge" retailer and to introduce wireless and hand-held technology applications. Let's see how Schlotzsky's has been experimenting with dramatic innovations to enhance the retail experience for its customers both before and during their meals.

At select restaurants, Schlotzsky's customers could use their personal digital assistants (PDAs) or Internet-enabled cell phones to view menus and specials. And they could place an order, pick up a meal (without having to wait on a line), and pay for an order with their PDAs or Internet-enabled cell phones. For those without PDAs or Internet-enabled cell phones, Schlotzsky's tested interactive kiosks that were located in the outlets. Customers could use the kiosks to place orders by making selections on touchscreen windows and going immediately to the counter to pick up a meal (without having to wait on a line).

As the firm's chief executive said, "It's not just [speed] for the customer, speed of service is where your volume comes from. Every time you increase speed, sales goes up." Schlotzsky's also plans to use its Web site and the kiosks to conduct surveys of customers directly after they have placed an order. Through these surveys, the company will gain valuable information about the individual tastes of its customers and their long-term behavior by tracking PDA, cell phone, and kiosk transactions over time.

In addition, Schlotzsky's is in the early stages of devising a system whereby consumers can use their credit cards to pay for their sandwiches by merely touching the keypad of their PDA or cell phone or using an RFID (radio frequency identification device) located near a cash register in the restaurant. With this system, IBM technology links an identification code to the customer's credit card account.

Last but not least, Schlotzsky's is testing technology to redefine the eating experience. At various company-owned and franchisee-owned outlets in Texas and elsewhere, customers can surf the Web at these "cyber-delis." Schlotzsky's chief executive views the cyber-deli as "the playground of the future. It can be both entertaining and time-saving." The cyber-deli experience lets customers check their E-mail, view the latest stock prices, or send a note to a friend through either iMac or IBM NetVista. As the chain's chief information officer says, "It's hard to put an ROI [return on investment] figure on the cyber-deli. It's about the customer experience. That said, we do feel it's helping to spark repeat business."

Although many industry analysts applaud Schlotzsky's efforts in applying technology to enrich the total retail experience, others remain skeptical. They wonder how customers in suburban areas will respond, and they doubt whether Schlotzsky's franchised outlets will either understand the technology or decide to adopt it.

Questions

1. What are the major differences between customer service and the total retail experience? Why does this matter?
2. Compare the total retail experience at Schlotzsky's for customers who have PDAs or Internet-enabled cell phones with those who do not.
3. In communicating its enhanced total retail experience, what can Schlotzsky's do to raise the comfort level among customers who are not technologically savvy?
4. What are the potential disadvantages of Schlotzsky's current total retail experience strategy for the retailer and for its customers?

The material in this case is drawn from Shirley Leung, "E-Commerce (A Special Report): Selling Strategies—Fast Food," *Wall Street Journal* (January 14, 2002), p. R14; and Susan Reda, "Schlotzsky's Gets Serious About Customer Technology," *Stores* (February 2002), pp. 44–48.

2: DRUGSTORES WORK ON THEIR CUSTOMER LOYALTY PROGRAMS

Supermarkets have had formal customer loyalty programs in place for years. But drugstore chains, such as CVS (www.cvs.com), Duane Reade (www.duanereade.com), and Rite Aid (www.riteaid.com), have only recently introduced these programs. Nonetheless, drugstore retailers have always had one of the most effective informal loyalty programs—their pharmacy counter. Because customers have typically returned to the same pharmacy to fill their prescriptions, these customers often purchased their health-and-beauty products at that drugstore.

Now, with the growth of health maintenance organizations (HMOs), the buying habits of drugstore customers are changing. Shoppers are more apt to choose a pharmacy on the basis of its convenience or cost. New competitors have also emerged, such as pharmacy departments in supermarkets, mail-order pharmacies, and online pharmacies. According to one study, only 53 percent of shoppers purchased prescription drugs at a drugstore in 2001, down from 61 percent in 1995. Similarly, drugstores have lost market share in the over-the-counter drug, cosmetics, and fragrances and colognes categories to supermarkets, discounters, and others. Drugstores do remain as the leading sellers of prescription drugs, film, and film processing. Let's see how drugstore customer loyalty programs work at three large chains.

After more than four years of market testing, CVS introduced its ExtraCare loyalty card at the beginning of 2001. By April 2002, over 27 million consumers had signed up for the program, which includes discounts at the point of sale, rewards based on spending, and targeted informational newsletters. The data base of ExtraCare provides vital marketing research information on customer buying habits over time. Unlike other loyalty programs, the CVS approach is to charge the same price to noncardholders as cardholders, because it does not want to alienate those who have not signed up.

Duane Reade, a regional chain based in New York, has 2 million customers in its Dollars Rewards program. Members receive special discounts on a number of items that are offered weekly. Like CVS, Duane Reade plans to use loyalty card data for research purposes and to target consumers. According to a Duane Reade senior vice-president, "We've found that 65 to 85 percent of the sales in the non-pharmacy area are driven by 30 percent of the shoppers. With that information, we can do direct marketing to those individuals who are most valuable to us. Over time, we'll continue to treat these customers differently in terms of pricing and attention, with the intent of keeping them loyal to Duane Reade."

Rite Aid's Rite Rewards loyalty card has 6 million members in the nine markets where it is available. This program entitles members to 10 percent off on all Rite Aid brand products, unadvertised specials that are available only to members, and in some markets a photography benefit. Rite Aid has found that in every market in which Rite Rewards is available, there is a positive effect that results in average transaction size, shopping frequency, and/or sales revenues.

Some retail analysts do not expect that drugstore customer loyalty programs will become as widespread as supermarket ones. Many drugstore chains do not have the information systems technology to analyze customer data. Few drugstores have their own credit card programs. In the pharmacy area, data cannot be used for analysis on an individual customer basis due to privacy laws. Finally, most drugstore chains have limited experience with customer data bases.

Questions

1. Evaluate the pros and cons of CVS' policy of charging the same price to noncardholders and cardholders.
2. Explain how a drugstore chain could switch customers to private-label products on the basis of targeted mailings and offers.
3. What are the best uses of the information gathered in a customer loyalty program?
4. How can a small pharmacy develop an effective customer loyalty program?

The material in this case is drawn from Susan Reda, "Customer Loyalty: Cure for the Drug Store Flu?" *Stores* (April 2002), pp. 44–48.

3: THE POSITIONING APPROACH OF HIGH-END JEWELRY STORES

Some industry experts strongly believe that retailers have contributed to an increasing confusion in the positioning of jewelry: "The mass merchants have gone class by making diamonds more affordable to all levels of the income stream, and the upscale merchants have reached down to the masses a bit."

The blurred positioning of diamond jewelry can be seen by reviewing the sales approaches by retail firms as disparate as Wal-Mart (**www.walmart.com**), department stores, and Tiffany (**www.tiffany.com**). Wal-Mart, a chain more associated in buyers' minds with the sale of inexpensive housewares and clothing, is now the leading seller of diamonds costing about $100 or so. Department stores also tend to sell a wide range of popularly priced jewelry to a

broad-based market. Tiffany has recently broadened its appeal (and moved somewhat downscale) by opening more stores at mall locations, introducing a Web site, and promoting items ranging in price from $200 to $100,000. Why? A Tiffany spokesperson says, "We believe advertising a wide range of price points helps build long-term relationships with people, including those who merely aspire to be Tiffany customers." In response, a critic of Tiffany's mass market shift asserts that "by making itself accessible to the lower end, Tiffany has watered down what was once a truly exclusive brand—and there's no going back."

Unlike other luxury goods retailers that have responded to increased competition and a fragile economy with price reductions, high-end jewelry stores have not used a deep discounting strategy. They recognize that they cannot win price wars against discounters or department stores. These jewelers also fear that price reductions might "tarnish their high-luster image." They agree with retail analysts who suggest that discounting "becomes a downward spiral. As soon as stores start discounting, people wait for the sales. With luxury jewelry, some of what you're paying for is exclusivity, and part of the exclusivity is bolstered by the price point. Discounting is completely inconsistent with maintaining that image."

Instead of following the Tiffany strategy, some high-end jewelers have modified their advertising plans to better target their promotions through media with an affluent readership. For some, this has meant using direct mail, mail-order catalogs, and data-base marketing more intensively. The House of Harry Winston, a two-store chain, draws attention to its merchandise by getting celebrities to wear its jewelry at major televised awards shows. It then faxes and E-mails its best prospects to tell them which items are worn by specific celebrities.

As one senior retail advertising executive states, "I think that quality is more important than ever right now. I think cachet is just as important, but cachet because people believe there's value there, not because there's just a name." There is some statistical evidence of this position. In a recent online survey of 25- to 54-year-olds with household incomes of more than $100,000 a year, the two leading purchase motivators were to (1) buy "things I know will last" and (2) to buy things "for my well-being."

There are still limits in price setting to the wealthy. The House of Harry Winston's global marketing director recently reported that it must be concerned with the "anxiety threshold" that customers encounter when shopping for jewelry priced between $6,500 and $10 million. Despite the firm's appeal to people with a net worth exceeding $2 million, some of these shoppers "quiver with fear" as they enter a store.

Questions

1. Develop a positioning chart for jewelry. Include Wal-Mart, Tiffany, and department stores with jewelry departments on the chart. Explain your choice of axes, as well as each store's positioning.
2. Do you agree that the events described in this case are contributing to the blurred positioning of jewelry retailing? Explain your answer and its ramifications.
3. What are the pros and cons of Tiffany selling items priced as low as $200?

4. As a jewelry shopper, how would you expect the total retail experience to differ in Wal-Mart, department stores, and high-end retailers?

The material in this case is drawn from Kate Fitzgerald, "Jewelers Out to Protect Cachet," *Advertising Age* (March 11, 2002), p. S-2.

4: IS THE SEARS–LANDS' END MERGER A MATCH MADE IN HEAVEN?

In May 2002, Sears, Roebuck and Company (**www.sears.com**) announced that it would buy Lands' End (**www.landsend.com**), the mail-order clothing retailer, for $1.9 billion in cash. Although Lands' End is to be a wholly owned subsidiary of Sears, Lands' End remains at its Dodgeville, Wisconsin, headquarters. The companies are to operate as separate businesses, with no Sears merchandise available for sale in Lands' End catalogs or on its Web site. However, Land's End merchandise is to be sold at Sears stores and each of the companies' Web sites is to have links to the other retailer.

One of the main goals of the merger is for the two firms to have a fully integrated, multi-channel strategy. Lands' End merchandise ordered on the Web could be delivered to a local Sears store for customer pickup, and Sears stores will accept Lands' End returns. Retail analysts view the purchase as advantageous to both firms: "This is a great brand name for Sears to associate with. One of their [Sears'] challenges is to have names that the consumer recognizes and associates with Sears."

The acquisition gives Sears access to Lands' End's products, as well as access to Lands' End's 30-million household data base. Sears will position the Land's End line as its top pricing point. Sears' chairperson plans for 15 to 20 percent of all apparel at Sears to carry the Land's End label. Sears is banking on Lands' End to build up Sears' apparel business. Before the acquisition, about 70 percent of consumers who shopped for appliances at Sears shopped at other stores for apparel. Sears hopes that the Lands' End acquisition will result in shoppers buying appliances and apparel on the same trip. In addition, Sears will benefit from Lands' End's expertise in managing a Web and catalog-based business. Lands' End executives will now manage these business units for Sears.

The acquisition also provides key benefits for Lands' End. Before the acquisition, Lands' End had only 16 discount outlets and one test store. After the acquisition, Lands' End goods are to be in Sears' 870 retail stores, as well as on Sears' Web site. (Sears.com had three times the traffic as the Landsend.com Web site before the merger.) This should boost Lands' End's Web business. Sears also sends out 25 million credit card statements monthly; this is an efficient way to promote a special Land's End offer.

Some analysts who question the merger are concerned about how Land's End's customers will react to seeing Lands' End merchandise in Sears stores. They believe that Lands' End's image could easily be tarnished if Sears does not manage the brand effectively. For example, Sears must be careful not to reduce Lands' End's quality as a means of becoming more price competitive. Lands' End's smaller suppliers may also be incapable of expanding their current production quantities. Finally, Lands' End's higher price levels may alienate Sears' current shoppers, and its younger, more clothes-conscious shoppers may decide not to shop at Sears. As one analyst remarked, "I don't think Lands' End unto itself is the final answer to Sears' problems in apparel."

Questions

1. What do you think are pros and cons of the acquisition from Sears' perspective? Why?
2. What do you think are pros and cons of the acquisition from Lands' End's perspective? Why?
3. What impact do you think the acquisition will have on the positioning of Sears and Lands' End? Why?
4. How would you integrate the management and employees of the two firms to best attain the goals noted in the case?

The material in this case is drawn from Maryanne Murray Buechner, "Recharging Sears," *Time* (May 27, 2002), pp. 46–47; Lorrie Grant and Jon Swartz, "'A Really Good Fit'; Sears Buys Lands' End to Gussy Up Image," *USA Today* (May 14, 2002), p. B1; and Constance L. Hays, "Sears to Buy Lands' End in a $1.9 Billion Deal," *New York Times* (May 14, 2002), p. A1.

part one
Comprehensive Case

Zane's Cycles: Creating Lifetime Customers*

INTRODUCTION

Zane's Cycles is a bicycle retailer similar to the one just down the street from you. So why would you be interested in Zane's and my style of doing business? Because I promise that if you use any of our "points of difference" programs, your firm and employees will grow and benefit in a way you never imagined.

The Zane's Philosophy in a Nutshell

I would love to show you the service we offer, but since I can't and everyone knows service costs money, I will tell you why I give away money during my live presentations. As I walk in the audience with a bowl of quarters, I invite attendees to help themselves. Most people take a few quarters; some take a handful. When allowed unlimited access to the quarters and offered more than seems reasonable, participants always self-regulate their desire and need. How does this analogy translate into the customer service I offer in my store? The quarters in the bowl represent how much money I am willing to spend on any one customer. Since I don't explain that and I know that most customers are reasonable people, I am able to serve many people for the same amount that I am willing to spend on just one.

After demonstrating that most customers are reasonable and fair, I then proceed back to those attendees who took coins and I hand each a few more. Giving customers more service than they perceive as reasonable has made Zane's Cycles an internationally recognized customer service leader.

I founded Zane's Cycles in 1981 as a junior in high school at the age of 16. I was working at a bike store, and the owner decided to liquidate the inventory because of high operating costs. This gave me the opportunity to buy an operating business for the cost of the inventory. I first had to convince my parents that it was time for me to operate a storefront business. I figured I could persuade them because I also had been running Foxon Bike Shop, a repair business, from our garage since I was 12. Let me tell you, this took a lot of convincing. After my agreeing to pay back a $20,000 loan with interest to my grandfather, regardless of the success or failure of the business, my parents endorsed my desire to become a small business retailer. First year's sales were $56,000. This year's sales were a respectable $4.5 million.

The Best Offer in Town

Lifetime free service, lifetime parts warranty, and 90-day price protection differentiate Zane's Cycles. While we use several strategies, these three are the most recognized. The usual new bicycle purchase includes the store's offer of a short-term service warranty so it can build in profit from the maintenance and servicing of the products sold. But what happens if you offer lifetime free service and maintenance to guarantee future sales? Only 20 percent of the bicycles sold need service the first year. The need for service diminishes exponentially over the next 10 years, the life of a typical bicycle. Manufacturers offer a one-year parts warranty on bicycles, parts, and accessories.

How about extending the offer to a lifetime warranty on everything you sell? Defects usually appear in the first month of use, which is within the warranty period. With some persuading of the manufacturer, "If you credit me for a $20 out-of-warranty part, I will give you a $5,000 order for the parts I can buy from one of 10 suppliers," you can satisfy customers with the cost absorbed by the manufacturer.

Many customers at first assumed that this service must mean that products cost more than if buying from someone not offering these warranties. However, our 90-day price protection plan allows customers to purchase without worrying about the price. They have 90 days to find the product for less, and we will refund the difference plus 10 percent of the difference. If we're willing to give customers 90 days to find the product for less, then we must be competitive. We promote Zane's as willing to serve customers at all costs. We price products to ensure that we are profitable. Sometimes, we're less and other times, we're not. We are not concerned with what competitors charge since the number of people who take advantage of this policy is low compared to what we are prepared to spend. Don't forget the quarters—people are reasonable. When is the last time you really shopped for something after you made that purchase?

If we offer lifetime free warranties, why would customers ever go into another bike shop? The irony is that when we do give a rebate, the customer often buys additional merchandise from Zane's. This lets us use the profits from that new transaction to fund half the real cost of the program. We also have found that people use this program only once. They are so impressed that they stay out of our competitor's store. Since we were more expensive at first and it was so easy to get the rebate, you would think that they would price compare every future purchase, but they don't. We have never given a rebate to the same person twice; 90 percent of those who get one make at least two more purchases within a year of a rebate.

Coming Back for More

Every time my customers walk into my store for their free service, they find hundreds of new items not in the store during their previous visit. I would love to see a computer company offer a lifetime warranty. Imagine it—a customer who buys a Zany PC actually talks to a Zany employee every time rather than to a third-party service center. Each "service" call would open up new lines of communication with consumers and give Zany the opportunity to sell its latest upgrades, software, and peripherals—immediately. In the real world, however, by allowing the third party to provide service, the opportunity for added sales is lost.

Give Away the First Dollar

I decided a long time ago to develop programs that are good for the customers first and then figure out how to make the long-term relationships profitable. At Zane's Cycles, we don't charge for anything under $1. Usually a customer comes in for a small part needed to solve a frustrating problem. The master link on a child's bike has broken, and the child is upset because he or she can't use a bike. Or, while changing a flat tire, a customer loses an axle nut. We give customers the small parts they need for free.

Why? By giving the customer the part for free (and an extra, just in case it happens again), that customer is so overwhelmed by the gesture that he or she will never go to anyone else's bike shop again. The parent tells the child, who is in turn able to fix and ride the bike, and we have just captured two lifetime customers for 25 cents in parts. Fast-food restaurants capture customers early on with toy surprises and banks with lollypops and dog treats. I do it with master links, axle nuts, and ball bearings. This program costs less than $100 a year, equivalent to one bad print advertisement that no one ever mentioned seeing.

The chance to give customers something extra may come unexpectedly. When the "new" VW Beetle first arrived, it generated considerable excitement. My first experience with this car happened during our annual "Big Wheel Sale," our largest promotion. We spend half of our annual ad budget to promote the event and attendance exceeds 3,000 people. With a store full of customers collectively participating in a feeding frenzy, a hush came over the store. Suddenly, I was alone, watching my customers and staff standing 10 deep, trying to get a look at the new Beetle outside the store. My first thought, "I have to get one!" Soon after the Beetle departed, the frenzy regenerated and the event was a huge success.

I frantically called in every favor I had in my arsenal, and a week later, we had a logoed yellow Beetle in front of the store. People drove from all over to see it. Marketing is fun when you're the first one on the block with something that everyone wants to see.

Okay, you have eliminated your competition by introducing policies that no one can beat. What next? Get all those customers who are loyal to your competitor to come to you. Contact the Yellow Pages in your area and ask them about Directory Connect, available in most areas—even though your local Yellow Pages salesperson may not know about it. This service allows you to forward the phone number of your "out of business" competitor to your business. The cost is negotiable but usually runs about 50 percent of the cost of the ad until that current book expires. Each time we acquired a new number, the cost was paid for the first day of the month. At one point, we had three former competitors' numbers forwarded to us. This is the simplest way to capture new customers guaranteed to be seeking your goods and services.

A Mahogany Coffee Bar in a Bike Shop?

On my travels, I explore unique stores. So, I'm in Lucerne, Switzerland, before the Barnes & Noble–Starbucks affiliation, and the local bicycle/ski store has a coffee/espresso/cappuccino bar. Pretty cool. So, after careful consideration, Zane's now has a mahogany coffee bar. Everyone loves coffee, and why would we charge for coffee if we don't charge for bicycle service? The customers will spend more time in our store. Employees don't leave the store for coffee breaks, making them accessible to customers. It's a place for people to wait without becoming frustrated if we are a little too busy to offer immediate help.

The coffee bar is just one interesting feature of our environment. A children's play area provides fun, clean toys to entertain children. Clean dressing rooms? That's one you don't see very often. How many times do you go into a beautiful store, load your arms with merchandise, and walk into a messy dressing room? At Zane's, an outdoor neighborhood setting helps to create the attitude of enjoying the bike in the outdoors. These amenities show our way of

creating a unique environment and establishing the Zane's Cycles "brand" in the mind of our customers—extremely difficult for competitors to penetrate.

Form Thriving Partnership with Your Community

Zane's Cycles has a very strong partnership with our community. We receive many requests for donations from nonprofit organizations. We have implemented a successful strategy: sell to nonprofits at our cost. Most requests are for fund-raisers and auctions. By selling merchandise at our cost, we can offer our support without any out-of-pocket expense besides labor. We receive incredible feedback from the public about our generosity. This year, we will sell at cost more than 200 bicycles, which is a lot of labor, but we will be recognized as a supporter of more than 200 nonprofit events. As a result, we receive many "thanks for supporting our favorite charity" comments, even from new customers.

Since out-of-pocket costs are low and we can capture a huge audience, we award scholarships to graduating students at our local high school awards night. It began with one $1,000 scholarship and has grown to five such awards. The Zane Foundation awards scholarships to the top five graduating seniors who display character and goodwill in the community. Zane's both supports the graduating class and displays its commitment to the community before 300 students, their families, and their friends. Furthermore, new bicycles are one of the 10 items most desired by a student going away to college.

Scholarship funds are generated by selling M&M candies through 50 gumball-style candy machines we have placed throughout the market. The community goodwill generated by a "Zane Foundation" candy machine was the benefit we sought. Soon after awarding the first scholarship, we recognized a huge increase in our back-to-school business. Today, August is the second largest sales month of the year.

Know Customers Better Than They Know Themselves

Whether huge or small, a retailer can use information technology, training, and a customer-oriented culture to provide great service. At Zane's Cycles, you never need a receipt to return merchandise. We capture every transaction of every customer. For example, a customer came into my store looking for a "Trail-a-bike," an accessory that would allow him to connect his daughter's bike to his. During our conversation, he explained that he had purchased a $350 trailer a couple of years earlier but had never used it because his daughter didn't like riding in it. I credited him the full amount of the purchase and asked him to return the trailer when it was convenient. I knew I could easily resell the merchandise. Although I would need to discount the trailer, the difference would be covered by the profit on the $180 "Trail-a-bike." Because he received a full credit for the trailer, he could purchase the "Trail-a-bike," a new helmet for his growing daughter, and a few other accessories.

Because I know my customers, I was aware that he had three daughters all under the age of seven. Since the initial trailer transaction, he has made four purchases, and in three years as a customer, he has never asked for a discount, even during a multiple-bike transaction. To complete the story, we actually sold the trailer at a discount to a valuable customer within a week of having it returned.

Because we capture all customer transactions, we can offer attractive savings. When we are able to buy discounted inventory from manufacturers, we can create a promotion with that inventory by focusing on only those customers who potentially need that product. For example, I can often get clothing in one particular size at a discount. We then run a transaction search of everyone who has previously purchased that size. We send a postcard or E-mail, informing targeted customers about the discounted merchandise.

Employees Make It Happen

Employees need to understand and want to spend time in this customer-friendly environment. Once they see the results, they help make the place better and more distinctive. How do you inspire people? Zane's Cycles offers tools, systems, and programs that will excite employees, and they are motivated to create a one-of-a-kind environment. I pay them well, thank them a lot, and let them have fun.

Pay: easy. Thanks: easy. Fun: not so easy. It takes a great management team to ensure fun. About five years ago, Tom Girard, my awesome general manager, explained that the staff was getting burned out. He told me that on July 14th we would close a couple of hours early to go to an amusement park. I thought, "July is one of our busiest months and you want to close early. Are you nuts?"

We put a note on the door explaining that in observance of Bastille Day (no significance except that it was printed on the calendar of the day he picked when everyone could attend), we were closing early. The note also explained that in consideration for customers' inconvenience, we would give them 10 percent off their next purchase if they mentioned the note. The result: no loss of employees and the greatest increase in morale and profit we have seen to date. Customers, happy for the discount, never mentioned any inconvenience. Today, the staff eagerly anticipates our annual trip.

Questions

1. What can *any* retailer learn from Zane's Cycles?
2. Relate the retailing concept to Zane's.
3. Discuss which elements of Zane's customer service are expected and which are augmented.
4. Is Zane's socially responsible? Explain your answer.
5. Present several specific goals for Zane's as it looks to the future.
6. How would you compete with Zane's if you owned a nearby bicycle store? Explain your reasoning.
7. Are there any of Zane's policies with which you disagree? Why or why not?

*The material in this case is adapted by the authors from Christopher J. Zane, President, Zane's Cycles, "Creating Lifetime Customers," *Retailing Issues Letter* (September 2000), pp. 1–5. Reprinted by permission.

part two

Situation Analysis

In Part Two, we present the organizational missions, ownership and management alternatives, goods/service categories, and objectives of a broad range of retail institutions. By understanding the unique attributes of these institutions, better retail strategies can be developed and implemented.

- ■ **Chapter 4** examines the characteristics of retail institutions on the basis of ownership type: independent, chain, franchise, leased department, vertical marketing system, and consumer cooperative. We also discuss the methods used by manufacturers, wholesalers, and retailers to obtain control in a distribution channel. A chapter appendix has added information on franchising.

- ■ **Chapter 5** describes retail institutions in terms of their strategy mix. We introduce three key concepts: the wheel of retailing, scrambled merchandising, and the retail life cycle. Strategic responses to the evolving marketplace are noted. Several strategy mixes are then studied, with food and general merchandise retailers reviewed separately.

- ■ **Chapter 6** focuses on nonstore retailing, electronic retailing, and nontraditional retailing approaches. We cover direct marketing, direct selling, vending machines, the World Wide Web, video kiosks, and airport retailing. The dynamics of Web-based retailing are featured.

Reprinted by permission.

In 1954, Ray Kroc, then a salesman of milkshake mixers, visited two of his best customers—Maurice and Richard McDonald—in San Bernadino, California. The McDonald brothers had just purchased eight Multimixers, one of Kroc's largest orders, and he wanted to see their operations in action. What Kroc saw astounded him. Although many burger places of that era were dirty and had poor reputations, the McDonald brothers' operation was clean and modern and even had a burger production line.

The following day, Kroc approached the brothers and came to an agreement with them whereby he would sell franchises for $950 each and 1.4 percent of the sales while the brothers received 0.5 percent. Shortly thereafter, Kroc became so obsessed with the business that he was often quoted as saying, "I believe in God, family, and McDonald's." He soon bought out the McDonald brothers.

As the chain expanded, Kroc was careful to ensure that the eating experience was identical at each restaurant. McDonald's (**www.mcdonalds.com**) controlled franchisees' menu items and décor, automated many of the operations, instituted training programs at Hamburger University, and developed precise operating standards. Kroc passed on his obsession with quality and cleanliness to franchisees. An often quoted motto was "if you have time to lean, you have time to clean."

Today, McDonald's has thousands of fast-food restaurants around the world. It is by far the leader in the hamburger-based segment of the business. And yes, it costs a lot more to become a franchisee—both in the initial costs and the ongoing royalties.[1]

chapter objectives

1. To show the ways in which retail institutions can be classified
2. To study retailers on the basis of ownership type and examine the characteristics of each
3. To explore the methods used by manufacturers, wholesalers, and retailers to exert influence in the distribution channel

OVERVIEW

The term **retail institution** refers to the basic format or structure of a business. In the United States, there are 2.2 million retail firms (including those with no payroll, whereby only the owner and/or family members work for the firm), and they operate 2.8 million establishments. An institutional discussion shows the relative sizes and diversity of different kinds of retailing, and indicates how various types of retailers are affected by the external environment. Institutional analysis is important in strategic planning when selecting an organizational mission, choosing an ownership alternative, defining the goods/service category, and setting objectives.

We examine retail institutions from these perspectives: ownership (Chapter 4); store-based strategy mix (Chapter 5); and nonstore-based, electronic, and nontraditional retailing (Chapter 6). Figure 4-1 shows a breakdown. An institution may be correctly placed in more than one category: A department store may be part of a chain, have a store-based strategy, accept mail-order sales, and operate a Web site.

Please interpret the data in Chapters 4 to 6 carefully. Because some institutional categories are not mutually exclusive, care should be taken in combining statistics so double counting does not occur. Although data are as current as possible, not all information corresponds to a common date. *Census of Retail Trade* data are only collected twice a decade. Furthermore, our numbers are based on the broad interpretation of retailing used in this book, which includes auto repair shops, hotels and motels, movie theaters, real-estate brokers, and others who sell to the final consumer.

RETAIL INSTITUTIONS CHARACTERIZED BY OWNERSHIP

Retail firms may be independently owned, chain-owned, franchisee-operated, leased departments, owned by manufacturers or wholesalers, or consumer-owned.

Although retailers are primarily small (three-quarters of all stores are operated by firms with one outlet and over one-half of all firms have two or fewer paid employees), there are also very

FIGURE 4-1
A Classification Method for Retail Institutions

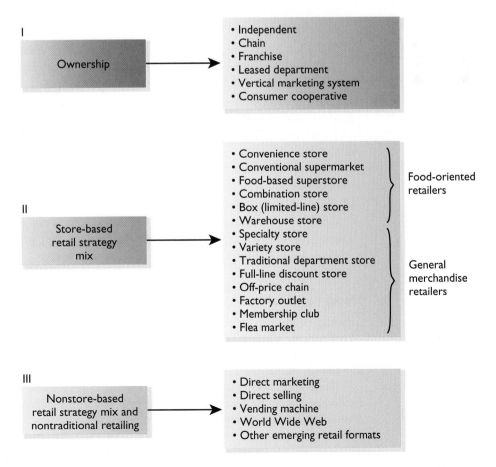

Ethics in RETAILING
For Small Bookstores, There Is More Bad News

The American Booksellers Association (**www.bookweb.org/aba**), the trade association for about 3,000 independent bookstores, recently lost a major antitrust court battle against Barnes & Noble (**www.barnesandnoble.com**) and Borders (**www.bordersstores.com**). Why has litigation been so important to the independent bookseller? During the last decade alone, the independents' share of the consumer book market has dropped to 15 percent from 33 percent.

Lawyers for the booksellers' association alleged during the trial that both of these chains sometimes bought books at prices that were a few percentage points lower than the independent stores or lower than the publishers' publicly stated prices. Lawyers for the chains argued that their preferential purchase prices were due to their size and in-house distribution functions. This marks the end of 20 years of legal challenges by the independent booksellers.

Under the settlement, both Barnes & Noble and Borders paid $2.35 million to the independents—less than the cost to the chains of finishing their trial. According to Leonard Riggio, chairperson of Barnes & Noble, "Every day for 15 years, you are accused, accused—it is not a nice environment for us to work in. We have been indirectly maligned for so many years, and this was our first chance to face our accusers."

Source: David D. Kirkpatrick, "Small Bookshops End Fight, Dropping Suit Against Chains," *New York Times on the Web* (April 20, 2001).

large retailers. In 2001, the five leading U.S. retailers totaled $404 billion in sales and employed 2.5 million people. Ownership opportunities abound. For example, according to the U.S. Census Bureau (**www.census.gov**), women own about 1 million retail firms, African-Americans (men and women) own about 100,00 retail firms, and Asian-Americans (men and women) own about 200,000 retail firms.

Each ownership format serves a marketplace niche, if the strategy is executed well:

- Independent retailers capitalize on a very targeted customer base and please shoppers in a friendly, folksy way. Word-of-mouth communication is important. These retailers should not try to serve too many customers or enter into price wars.
- Chain retailers benefit from their widely known image and from economies of scales and mass promotion possibilities. They should maintain their image chainwide and not be inflexible in adapting to changes in the marketplace.
- Franchisors have strong geographic coverage—due to franchisee investments—and the motivation of franchisees as owner-operators. They should not get bogged down in policy disputes with franchisees or charge excessive royalty fees.
- Leased departments enable store operators and outside parties to join forces and enhance the shopping experience, while sharing expertise and expenses. They should not hurt the image of the store or place too much pressure on the lessee to bring in store traffic.
- A vertically integrated channel gives a firm greater control over sources of supply, but it should not provide consumers with too little choice of products or too few outlets.
- Cooperatives provide members with price savings. They should not expect too much involvement by members or add facilities that raise costs too much.

INDEPENDENT

The CCH Business Owner's Toolkit (http://toolkit.cch.com) is an excellent resource for the independent retailer.

An **independent** retailer owns one retail unit. There are 2.1 million independent U.S. retailers—accounting for nearly 40 percent of total store sales. One-half of independents are run by the owners and their families; these firms generate just 3 percent of U.S. store sales (averaging under $100,000 in annual revenues) and have no paid workers (there is no payroll).

The high number of independents is associated with the **ease of entry** into the marketplace, due to low capital requirements and no, or relatively simple, licensing provisions for many small retail firms. The investment per worker in retailing is usually much lower than for manufacturers, and licensing is pretty routine. Each year, tens of thousands of new retailers, mostly independents, open in the United States.

The ease of entry, which leads to intense competition, is a big factor in the high rate of failures among newer firms. One-third of new U.S. retailers do not survive the first year and two-thirds do not continue beyond the third year. Most failures involve independents. Annually, thousands of U.S. retailers (of all sizes) file for bankruptcy protection besides the thousands of small firms that simply close.[2]

The U.S. Small Business Administration (SBA) has a Small Business Development Center (SBDC) Program to provide assistance for current and prospective small business owners (**www.sba.gov/sbdc**). There are 58 regional SBDCs and 1,000 local SBDCs, satellites, and specialty centers. The purpose "is to provide basic business counseling and management assistance to current and prospective small business owners." Centers offer individual counseling, seminars and training sessions, conferences, information through the Internet, as well as in person and by phone, and generally "assist anyone seeking advice about operating a small business." The SBA also has many free downloadable publications at its Web site. See Figure 4-2.

Competitive Advantages and Disadvantages of Independents

Read the Mrs. Fields story (www.mrsfields.com/about)—from one cookie store to a worldwide chain.

Independent retailers have a variety of advantages and disadvantages. These are among their advantages:

- There is flexibility in choosing retail formats and locations, and in devising strategy. Because only one location is involved, detailed specifications can be set for the best site and a thorough search undertaken. Uniform location standards are not needed, as they are for chains, and independents do not have to worry about company stores being too close. Independents have great latitude in selecting target markets. Because they often have modest goals, small segments may be selected rather than the mass market. Assortments, prices, hours, and other factors are then set consistent with the segment.

FIGURE 4-2
Useful Online Publications for Small Retailers

Go to **www.sba.gov/library/pubs.html** and download any of the U.S. Small Business Administration's publications at this Web site. They're free!

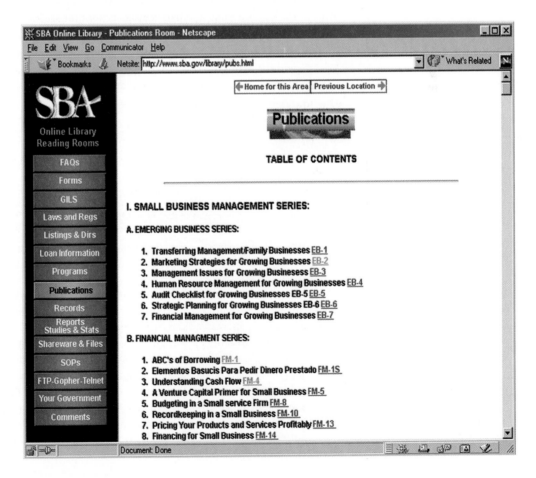

- Investment costs for leases, fixtures, workers, and merchandise can be held down; and there is no duplication of stock or personnel functions. Responsibilities are clearly delineated within a store.

- Independents frequently act as specialists in a niche of a particular goods/service category. They are then more efficient and can lure shoppers interested in specialized retailers.

- Independents exert strong control over their strategies, and the owner-operator is typically on the premises. Decision making is centralized and layers of management personnel are minimized.

- There is a certain image attached to independents, particularly small ones, that chains cannot readily capture. This is the image of a personable retailer with a comfortable atmosphere in which to shop.

- Independents can easily sustain consistency in their efforts because only one store is operated.

- Independents have "independence." They do not have to fret about stockholders, board of directors meetings, and labor unrest. They are often free from unions and seniority rules.

- Owner-operators typically have a strong entrepreneurial drive. They have made a personal investment and there is a lot of ego involvement. According to a recent National Small Business Poll, 81 percent of small business owners rate their firms a success.[3]

These are some of the disadvantages of independent retailing:

- In bargaining with suppliers, independents may not have much power because they often buy in small quantities. Suppliers may even bypass them. Reordering may be hard if minimum order requirements are high. Some independents, such as hardware stores, belong to buying groups to increase their clout.

- Independents generally cannot gain economies of scale in buying and maintaining inventory. Due to financial constraints, small assortments are bought several times per year. Transportation, ordering, and handling costs per unit are high.

- Operations are labor intensive, sometimes with little computerization. Ordering, taking inventory, marking items, ringing up sales, and bookkeeping may be done manually. This is less efficient than computerization. In many cases, owner-operators are unwilling or unable to spend time learning how to set up and apply computerized procedures.

- Due to the relatively high costs of TV ads and the large geographic coverage of magazines and some newspapers (too large for firms with one outlet), independents are limited in their access to certain media. Yet, there are various promotion tools available for creative independents (see Chapter 19).

Technology in RETAILING — Independent Retailers: Using Software to Stay Strong

In order to remain competitive against Home Depot (**www.homedepot.com**) and other chain competitors, member stores at retail cooperatives such as Ace Hardware (**www. acehardware.com**) are honing their logistics-related skills. Since Ace began a Web-based vendor-managed inventory (VMI) replenishment program, it has been able to increase inventory turnover rates and have more consistent deliveries. In the first 60 days of this system, Ace reduced its freight costs by 18 percent and lowered its distribution costs by 28 percent—while being able to fill 99 percent of its member stores' orders.

As an Ace spokesperson points out, each vendor needs an Internet connection to dial into its network and review sales rates for its goods. "Essentially, they are cutting themselves an electronic purchase order." Currently, about 40 manufacturers, representing about 25 percent of Ace's retail sales, use its VMI system.

Ace plans to extend the VMI system to the store level, so that inventory carried over from previous seasons at the retail level can be incorporated into the inventory replenishment model. Ace estimates that its inventory at the wholesale level is valued at $300 million, with another $300 million at the retail store level. Reducing inventory by 5 to 10 percent will have a major impact on inventory holding costs.

Source: "Nailing the Big Boxes," *Chain Store Age* (March 2001), p. 126.

- A crucial problem for family-run independents is overdependence on the owner. Often all decisions are made by that person, and there is no management continuity when the owner-boss is ill, on vacation, or retires. Long-run success and employee morale can be affected by this. As one small business owner said, "A succession plan must be implemented for legal and tax purposes or we risk losing everything."[4]
- A limited amount of time is allotted to long-run planning, since the owner is intimately involved in daily operations of the firm.

CHAIN

A **chain** retailer operates multiple outlets (store units) under common ownership; it usually engages in some level of centralized (or coordinated) purchasing and decision making. In the United States, there are roughly 100,000 retail chains that operate about 750,000 establishments.

There are more than 7,200 Radio Shack (www.radioshack.com) stores in the United States. See if there is one near you.

The relative strength of chain retailing is great, even though the number of firms is small (less than 5 percent of all U.S. retail firms). Chains today operate about one-quarter of retail establishments, and because stores in chains tend to be considerably larger than those run by independents, chains account for more than 60 percent of total U.S. store sales and employment. Although the majority of chains have 5 or fewer outlets, the several hundred firms with 100 or more outlets account for well over one-third of U.S. retail sales. Some big U.S. chains have at least 1,000 outlets each. There are also many large foreign chains. See Figure 4-3.

The dominance of chains varies by type of retailer. Chains generate at least 75 percent of total U.S. category sales for department stores, discount department stores, and grocery stores. On the other hand, stationery, beauty salon, furniture, and liquor store chains produce far less than 50 percent of U.S. retail sales in their categories.

Competitive Advantages and Disadvantages of Chains

There are abundant competitive advantages for chain retailers:

Sears' Craftsman brand (www.craftsman.com) is so powerful that different tools are sold under the Craftsman name.

- Many chains have bargaining power due to their purchase volume. They receive new items when introduced, have orders promptly filled, get sales support, and obtain volume discounts. Large chains may also gain exclusive rights to certain items and have goods produced under the chains' brands.
- Chains achieve cost efficiencies when they buy directly from manufacturers and in large volume, ship and store goods, and attend trade shows sponsored by suppliers to learn about new offerings. They can sometimes bypass wholesalers, with the result being lower supplier prices.
- Efficiency is gained by sharing warehouse facilities; purchasing standardized store fixtures; centralized buying and decision making; and other practices. Chains typically give headquarters executives broad authority for personnel policies and for buying, pricing, and advertising decisions.

FIGURE 4-3

Carrefour: The Largest Foreign-Based Retailer in the World

Carrefour is the leading retailer in Europe and the second-largest worldwide. It operates more than 9,200 stores in 30 countries. It relies on three major formats: hypermarket (combination of a discount store and a supermarket), supermarket, and discount store.

Photo reprinted by permission of Retail Forward, Inc.

FIGURE 4-4

MasterCuts: A Well-Defined Management Philosophy

MasterCuts Family Haircutters is a provider of value-priced hair-cuts within the shopping mall environment. Professionally trained stylists are available on a walk-in basis to serve price-sensitive families looking for fast and convenient quality haircutting services. There is a strong emphasis on staff training, field management, and the presentation of retail products. Artistic training is very important to the success of MasterCuts. Stylists are encouraged to keep abreast of new trends, techniques, and professional hair care products through regularly scheduled workshops. "We are working to deliver great value and consistently good customer service."

Reprinted by permission of Regis Corporation.

- Chains use computers in ordering merchandise, taking inventory, forecasting, ringing up sales, and bookkeeping. This increases efficiency and reduces overall costs.

- Chains, particularly national or regional ones, can take advantage of a variety of media, from TV to magazines to newspapers.

- Most chains have defined management philosophies, with detailed strategies and clear employee responsibilities. There is continuity when managerial personnel are absent or retire because there are qualified people to fill in and succession plans in place. See Figure 4-4.

- Many chains expend considerable time in long-run planning and assign specific staff to planning on a permanent basis. Opportunities and threats are carefully monitored.

Chain retailers do have a number of disadvantages:

- Once chains are established, flexibility may be limited. New nonoverlapping store locations may be hard to find. Consistent strategies must be maintained throughout all units, including prices, promotions, and product assortments. It may be difficult to adapt to local diverse markets.

- Investments are higher due to multiple leases and fixtures. The purchase of merchandise is more costly because a number of store branches must be stocked.

- Managerial control is complex, especially for chains with geographically dispersed branches. Top management cannot maintain the control over each branch that independents have over

Careers in RETAILING
The Container Store Empowers Employees Throughout the Chain

As manager of a 19,000-square-foot Container Store (**www.containerstore.com**) in Houston, Danielle Raska is responsible for a staff of between 90 and 120 employees. Her unit is the chain's highest-volume store. Unlike most retail chains, Container Store believes in empowering all of its employees. As Raska explains, "I don't have any assistant store managers, and I don't have to appoint somebody to be in charge when I'm away."

The firm's corporate culture is well communicated to its employees. For example, when Houston suffered from flooding, many of the chain's customers did not have flood insurance. If shoppers purchased plastic containers to stow their belongings, the cashier decided not to charge them. Unlike at other stores,

where the cashier would probably be fired, Container Store assumed that the shoppers would become lifetime customers because of its generosity.

Also unlike other retailers that have high personnel turnover, Container Store has high employee retention. Raska says, "That's because we have very high standards about who we hire. We want people who love customer service." Part-time employees working as little as 18 hours a week are entitled to paid vacation time.

Source: Matt Nannery, "Minding the Stores," *Chain Store Age* (September 2001), pp. 45–54.

their single outlet. Lack of communication and delays in making and enacting decisions are particular problems.

- Personnel in large chains often have limited independence because there are several management layers and unionized employees. Some chains empower personnel to give them more authority.

FRANCHISING[5]

The International Franchise Association (www.franchise.org) is the leading source of information about franchising.

Franchising involves a contractual arrangement between a *franchisor* (a manufacturer, wholesaler, or service sponsor) and a retail *franchisee*, which allows the franchisee to conduct business under an established name and according to a given pattern of business. The franchisee typically pays an initial fee and a monthly percentage of gross sales in exchange for the exclusive rights to sell goods and services in an area. Small businesses benefit by being part of a large, chain-type retail institution.

In **product/trademark franchising**, a franchisee acquires the identity of a franchisor by agreeing to sell the latter's products and/or operate under the latter's name. The franchisee operates rather autonomously. There are certain operating rules, but the franchisee sets store hours, chooses a location, and determines facilities and displays. Product/trademark franchising represents two-thirds of retail franchising sales. Examples are auto dealers and many gasoline service stations.

With **business format franchising**, there is a more interactive relationship between a franchisor and a franchisee. The franchisee receives assistance on site location, quality control, accounting systems, startup practices, management training, and responding to problems besides the right to sell goods and services. Prototype stores, standardized product lines, and cooperative advertising foster a level of coordination previously found only in chains. Business format franchising arrangements are common for restaurants and other food outlets, real estate, and service retailing. Due to the small size of many franchisees, business format franchising accounts for about 70 percent of franchised outlets, although only 30 percent of total sales.

McDonald's (**www.mcdonalds.com/corporate/franchise**) is a good example of a business format franchise arrangement. The firm provides franchisee training at "Hamburger U," a detailed operating manual, regular visits by service managers, and brush-up training. In return for a 20-year franchising agreement with McDonald's, a traditional franchisee has an initial cash investment of $175,000 and pays ongoing royalty fees totaling at least 12.5 percent of gross sales to McDonald's. See Figure 4-5.

FIGURE 4-5
Business Qualifications Sought by McDonald's for Potential Franchisees

Source: Figure developed by the authors based on information in McDonald's "Franchising Frequently Asked Questions," **www.mcdonalds.com/ corporate/franchise/faq/ index.html** (January 27, 2003).

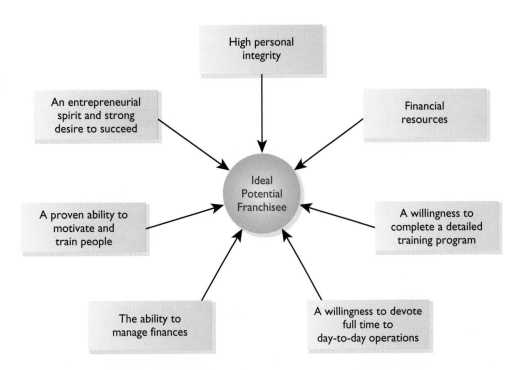

Size and Structural Arrangements

Although auto and truck dealers provide more than one-half of all U.S. retail franchise sales, few sectors of retailing have not been affected by franchising's growth. In the United States, there are 3,000 retail franchisors doing business with 320,000 franchisees. They operate 750,000 franchisee- and franchisor-owned outlets, employ several million people, and generate over one-third of total store sales. In addition, hundreds of U.S.-based franchisors have foreign operations, with tens of thousands of outlets.

About 85 percent of U.S. franchising sales and franchised outlets involve franchisee-owned units; the rest involve franchisor-owned outlets. If franchisees operate one outlet, they are independents; if they operate two or more outlets, they are chains. Today, a large number of franchisees operate as chains.

Three structural arrangements dominate retail franchising. See Figure 4-6:

1. *Manufacturer-retailer*. A manufacturer gives independent franchisees the right to sell goods and related services through a licensing agreement.
2. *Wholesaler-retailer*.
   a. *Voluntary*. A wholesaler sets up a franchise system and grants franchises to individual retailers.
   b. *Cooperative*. A group of retailers sets up a franchise system and shares the ownership and operations of a wholesaling organization.
3. *Service sponsor-retailer*. A service firm licenses individual retailers so they can offer specific service packages to consumers.

Competitive Advantages and Disadvantages of Franchising

Franchisees receive several benefits by investing in successful franchise operations:

- They own a retail enterprise with a relatively small capital investment.
- They acquire well-known names and goods/service lines.
- Standard operating procedures and management skills may be taught to them.
- Cooperative marketing efforts (such as national advertising) are facilitated.
- They obtain exclusive selling rights for specified geographical territories.
- Their purchases may be less costly per unit due to the volume of the overall franchise.

Want to learn more about what it takes to be a franchisee? Check out the Jazzercise Web site (www.jazzercise.com/franchise.html).

FIGURE 4-6
Structural Arrangements in Retail Franchising

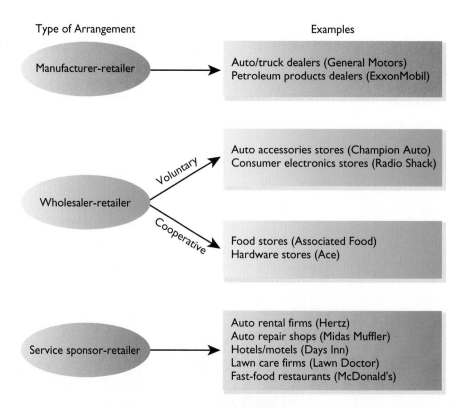

Some potential problems do exist for franchisees:

- Oversaturation could occur if too many franchisees are in one geographic area.
- Due to overzealous selling by some franchisors, franchisees' income potential, required managerial ability, and investment may be incorrectly stated.
- They may be locked into contracts requiring purchases from franchisors or certain vendors.
- Cancellation clauses may give franchisors the right to void agreements if provisions are not satisfied.
- In some industries, franchise agreements are of short duration.
- Royalties are often a percentage of gross sales, regardless of franchisee profits.

The preceding factors contribute to **constrained decision making**, whereby franchisors limit franchisee involvement in the strategic planning process.

The Federal Trade Commission (FTC) has a rule regarding disclosure requirements and business opportunities that applies to all U.S. franchisors. It is intended to provide adequate information to potential franchisees prior to their making an investment. Though the FTC does not regularly review disclosure statements, several states do check them and may require corrections. Also, 14 states (including Arizona, California, Indiana, New Jersey, Virginia, Washington, and Wisconsin) have fair practice laws that do not permit franchisors to terminate, cancel, or fail to renew franchisees without just cause. The FTC has an excellent franchising Web site (**www.ftc.gov/bcp/franchise/netfran.htm**), as highlighted in Figure 4-7.

Franchisors accrue lots of benefits by having franchise arrangements:

- A national or global presence is developed more quickly and with less franchisor investment.
- Franchisee qualifications for ownership are set and enforced.
- Agreements require franchisees to abide by stringent operating rules set by franchisors.
- Money is obtained when goods are delivered rather than when they are sold.

FIGURE 4-7

Franchises and Business Opportunities

At the FTC's franchising site, **www.ftc.gov/bcp/franchise/netfran.htm**, there are many free downloads about opportunities—and warnings, as well.

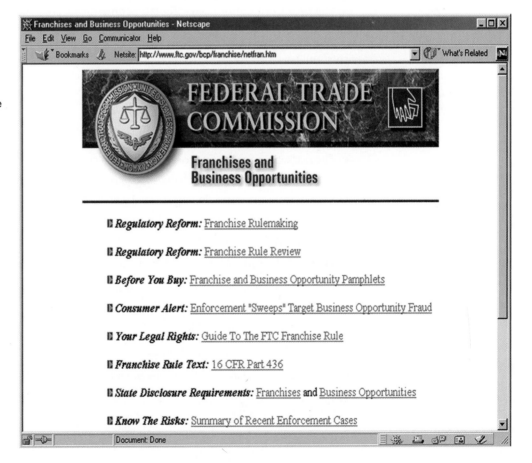

- Because franchisees are owners and not employees, they have a greater incentive to work hard.
- Even after franchisees have paid for their outlets, franchisors receive royalties and may sell products to the individual proprietors.

Franchisors also face potential problems:

- Franchisees harm the overall reputation if they do not adhere to company standards.
- A lack of uniformity among outlets adversely affects customer loyalty.
- Intrafranchise competition is not desirable.
- The resale value of individual units is injured if franchisees perform poorly.
- Ineffective franchised units directly injure franchisors' profitability that results from selling services, materials, or products to the franchisees and from royalty fees.
- Franchisees, in greater numbers, are seeking to limit franchisors' rules and regulations.

Additional information on franchising is contained in the appendix at the end of this chapter. Also, visit our Web site for a lot of links on this topic (**www.prenhall.com/bermanevans**).

LEASED DEPARTMENT

A **leased department** is a department in a retail store—usually a department, discount, or specialty store—that is rented to an outside party. The leased department proprietor is responsible for all aspects of its business (including fixtures) and normally pays a percentage of sales as rent. The store sets operating restrictions for the leased department to ensure overall consistency and coordination.[6]

Leased departments are used by store-based retailers to broaden their offerings into product categories that often are on the fringe of the store's major product lines. They are most common for in-store beauty salons, banks, photographic studios, and shoe, jewelry, cosmetics, watch repair, and shoe repair departments. Leased departments are also popular in shopping center food courts. They account for $15 billion in annual department store sales. Data on overall leased department sales are not available.

Meldisco Corporation (**www.footstar.com**) runs leased shoe departments in more than 6,500 stores (especially Kmart, Federated Department Stores, and Rite Aid) and has annual sales of $1.5 billion. It owns the inventory and display fixtures, staffs and merchandises the departments, and pays a fee for the space occupied. The stores where Meldisco operates typically cover the costs of utilities, maintenance, advertising, and checkout services.

Competitive Advantages and Disadvantages of Leased Departments

From the *stores' perspective*, leased departments offer a number of benefits:

- The market is enlarged by providing one-stop customer shopping.
- Personnel management, merchandise displays, and reordering items are undertaken by lessees.
- Regular store personnel do not have to be involved.
- Leased department operators pay for some expenses, thus reducing store costs.
- A percentage of revenues is received regularly.

There are also some potential pitfalls, from the stores' perspective:

- Leased department operating procedures may conflict with store procedures.
- Lessees may adversely affect stores' images.
- Customers may blame problems on the stores rather than on the lessees.

For *leased department operators*, there are these advantages:

- Stores are known, have steady customers, and generate immediate sales for leased departments.
- Some costs are reduced through shared facilities, such as security equipment and display windows.
- Their image is enhanced by their relationships with popular stores.

Lessees face these possible problems:

- There may be inflexibility as to the hours they must be open and the operating style.
- The goods/service lines are usually restricted.
- If they are successful, stores may raise rent or not renew leases when they expire.
- In-store locations may not generate the sales expected.

An example of a thriving long-term lease arrangement is one between CPI Corporation and Sears. For 45 years, CPI has had photo studios in Sears stores. In exchange for space in the nearly 1,000 U.S. and Canadian Sears stores, CPI pays 15 percent of its sales. Its annual sales per square foot are much higher than Sears' overall average. CPI's agreement with Sears has been renewed several times. Annual revenues through Sears exceed $320 million.

CPI (www.cpicorp.com) has flourished with its leased department relationship at Sears.

VERTICAL MARKETING SYSTEM

A **vertical marketing system** consists of all the levels of independently owned businesses along a channel of distribution. Goods and services are normally distributed through one of these systems: independent, partially integrated, and fully integrated. See Figure 4-8.

In an *independent vertical marketing system*, there are three levels of independently owned firms: manufacturers, wholesalers, and retailers. Such a system is most often used if manufacturers or retailers are small, intensive distribution is sought, customers are widely dispersed, unit sales are high, company resources are low, channel members seek to share costs and risks, and task specialization is desirable. Independent vertical marketing systems are used by many stationery stores, gift shops, hardware stores, food stores, drugstores, and many other firms. They are the leading form of vertical marketing system.

With a *partially integrated system*, two independently owned businesses along a channel perform all production and distribution functions. It is most common when a manufacturer and a retailer complete transactions and shipping, storing, and other distribution functions in the absence of a

FIGURE 4-8
Vertical Marketing Systems: Functions and Ownership

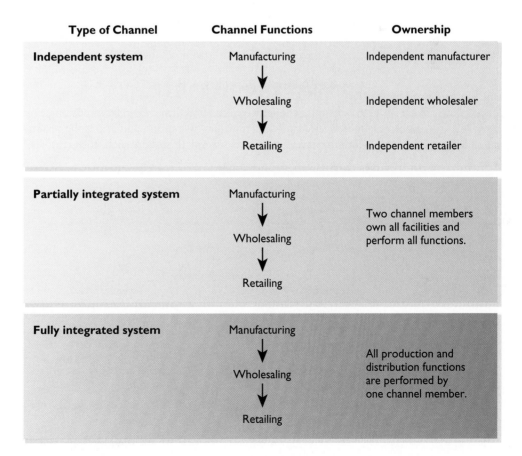

wholesaler. This system is most apt if manufacturers and retailers are large, selective or exclusive distribution is sought, unit sales are moderate, company resources are high, greater channel control is desired, and existing wholesalers are too expensive or unavailable. Partially integrated systems are often used by furniture stores, appliance stores, restaurants, computer retailers, and mail-order firms.

Through a *fully integrated system*, one firm performs all production and distribution functions. The firm has total control over its strategy, direct customer contact, and exclusivity over its offering; and it keeps all profits. This system can be costly and requires a lot of expertise. In the past, vertical marketing was employed mostly by manufacturers, such as Avon and Sherwin-Williams. At Sherwin-Williams, its own 2,600 paint stores account for 63 percent of total company sales.[7] Today, more retailers (such as Kroger) use fully integrated systems for at least some products.

Kroger, the food *retailer*, manufacturers 3,500 food and nonfood products in over 40 plants (www.kroger. com/operations.htm).

Some firms use **dual marketing** (a form of *multi-channel retailing*) and engage in more than one type of distribution arrangement. In this way, firms appeal to different consumers, increase sales, share some costs, and retain a good degree of strategic control. Here are two examples: (1) Sherwin-Williams sells Sherwin-Williams paints at company stores. It sells Dutch Boy paints in home improvement stores, full-line discount stores, hardware stores, and others. See Figure 4-9. (2) Sears recently acquired Lands' End, the mail-order and Web firm, mostly so that it could also sell Lands' End apparel in Sears stores.[8]

Besides partially or fully integrating a vertical marketing system, a firm can exert power in a distribution channel because of its economic, legal, or political strength; superior knowledge and abilities; customer loyalty; or other factors. With **channel control**, one member of a distribution channel dominates the decisions made in that channel due to the power it possesses. Manufacturers, wholesalers, and retailers each have a combination of tools to improve their positions relative to one another.

Manufacturers exert control by franchising, developing strong brand loyalty, pre-ticketing items (to designate suggested prices), and using exclusive distribution with retailers that agree to certain standards in exchange for sole distribution rights in an area. *Wholesalers* exert influence when they are large, introduce their own brands, sponsor franchises, and are the most efficient members in the channel for tasks such as processing reorders. *Retailers* exert clout when they represent a large percentage of a supplier's sales volume and when they foster their own brands. Private brands let retailers switch vendors with no impact on customer loyalty, as long as the same product features are included.

Strong long-term channel relationships often benefit all parties. They lead to scheduling efficiencies and cost savings. Advertising, financing, billing, and other tasks are dramatically simplified.

CONSUMER COOPERATIVE

As an REI member (www.rei.com/rei/help/ membership.html), look at what $15 will get you!

A **consumer cooperative** is a retail firm owned by its customer members. A group of consumers invests, elects officers, manages operations, and shares the profits or savings that accrue.[9] In the United States, there are several thousand such cooperatives, from small buying clubs to

FIGURE 4-9
Sherwin-Williams' Dual
Vertical Marketing
System

Recreational Equipment Inc. (**www.rei.com**), a U.S. retail cooperative chain, had a head start before it opened its first retail store in Tokyo. Due to its Web site (**www.rea.co.jp**), the chain already had a customer base of 80,000 Japanese shoppers.

Unlike many other retailers, REI understands the potential synergies of maintaining a presence at retail stores, as well as through catalogs and the Web. For example, REI knows that 45 percent of its Web customers also make store, phone, or catalog purchases. According to an REI spokesperson, "Channel synchronization does not necessarily mean channel cannibalization."

Unlike its stores—which have a limited amount of space—REI is able to place new products on an experimental basis on its Web site without having to prune existing products. Products that do well on the Web can then be placed into its stores. The Web also enables REI to quickly respond to market needs. It recently added an online fitness boutique to its Web site in 10 weeks and a virtual fly-fishing shop in five weeks. In contrast, building these departments into its stores would have taken least six months. REI's stores provide credibility for the cooperative's Web operations.

Source: Eric Chabrow, "Biz Model: Recreational Equipment Inc.—Outdoor Retailer REI Gets a Head Start in the Clicks-and-Mortar Race," *Informationweek* (May 1, 2002), pp. RB24–RB26.

Recreational Equipment Inc. (REI), with $750 million in annual sales. Consumer cooperatives have been most popular in food retailing. Yet, the 500 or so U.S. food cooperatives account for less than 1 percent of total grocery sales.

Consumer cooperatives exist for these basic reasons: Some consumers feel they can operate stores as well as or better than traditional retailers. They think existing retailers inadequately fulfill customer needs for healthful, environmentally safe products. They also assume existing retailers make excessive profits and that they can sell merchandise for lower prices.

REI sells outdoor recreational equipment to 2 million active members. It has 60 stores, a mail-order business, and a Web site (**www.rei.com**). Unlike other cooperatives, REI is operated by a professional staff that adheres to policies set by the member-elected board. There is a $15 one-time membership fee, which entitles customers to shop at REI, vote for the board of directors, and share in profits (based on the amount spent by each member). REI's goal is to distribute a 10 percent dividend to members.

Cooperatives are only a small part of retailing because they involve consumer initiative and drive, consumers are usually not expert in retailing functions, cost savings and low selling prices are often not as expected, and consumer boredom in running a cooperative frequently occurs.

Summary

1. *To show the ways in which retail institutions can be classified.* There are 2.2 million retail firms in the United States operating 2.8 million establishments. They can be classified on the basis of ownership, store-based strategy mix, and nonstore-based and nontraditional retailing. Many retailers can be placed in more than one category. This chapter deals with retail ownership. Chapters 5 and 6 report on the other classifications.

2. *To study retailers on the basis of ownership type and examine the characteristics of each.* Three-quarters of U.S. retail establishments are independents, each operating one store. This is mostly due to the ease of entry. Independents' competitive advantages include their flexibility, low investments, specialized offerings, direct strategy control, image, consistency, independence, and entrepreneurial spirit. Disadvantages include limited bargaining power, few economies of scale, labor intensity, reduced media access, overdependence on owner, and limited planning.

Chains are multiple stores under common ownership, with some centralized buying and decision making. They account for a quarter of U.S. retail outlets but over 60 percent of retail sales. Chains' advantages are bargaining power, functional efficiencies, multiple-store operations, computerization, media access, well-defined management, and planning. They face these potential problems: inflexibility, high investments, reduced control, and limited independence of personnel.

Franchising embodies arrangements between franchisors and franchisees that let the latter do business under established names and according to detailed rules. It accounts for over one-third of U.S. store sales. Franchisees benefit from small investments, popular company names, standardized operations and training, cooperative marketing, exclusive selling rights, and volume purchases. They may face constrained decision making, resulting in oversaturation, lower than promised profits, strict contract terms, cancellation clauses, short-term contracts, and royalty fees. Franchisors benefit by expanding their businesses, setting franchisee qualifications, improving cash flow, outlining procedures, gaining motivated franchisees, and receiving ongoing royalties. They may suffer if franchisees hurt the company image, do not operate uniformly, compete with one another, lower resale values and franchisor profits, or seek greater independence.

Leased departments are in-store locations rented to outside parties. They usually exist in categories on the fringe of their stores' major product lines. Stores gain from the expertise of lessees, greater traffic, reduced costs, merchandising support, and revenues. Potential store disadvantages are conflicts with lessees and adverse effects on store image. Lessee benefits are well-known store names, steady customers, immediate sales, reduced expenses, economies of scale, and an image associated with the store. Potential lessee problems are operating inflexibility, restrictions on items sold, lease nonrenewal, and poorer results than expected.

Vertical marketing systems consist of all the levels of independently owned firms along a channel of distribution. Independent systems have separately owned manufacturers, wholesalers, and retailers. In partially integrated systems, two separately owned firms, usually manufacturers and retailers,

perform all production and distribution functions. With fully integrated systems, single firms do all production and distribution functions. Some firms use dual marketing, whereby they are involved in more than one type of system.

Consumer cooperatives are owned by their customers, who invest, elect officers, manage operations, and share savings or profits. They account for a tiny piece of retail sales. Cooperatives are formed because consumers think they can do retailing functions, traditional retailers are inadequate, and prices are high. They have not grown because consumer initiative is required, expertise may be lacking, expectations have frequently not been met, and boredom occurs.

3. *To explore the methods used by manufacturers, wholesalers, and retailers to exert influence in the distribution channel.* Even without an integrated vertical marketing system, channel control can be exerted by the most powerful firm(s) in a channel. Manufacturers, wholesalers, and retailers each have ways to increase their impact. Retailers' influence is greatest when they are a large part of their vendors' sales and private brands are used.

Key Terms

retail institution (p. 85)

independent (p. 86)

ease of entry (p. 86)

chain (p. 89)

franchising (p. 91)

product/trademark franchising (p. 91)

business format franchising (p. 91)

constrained decision making (p. 93)

leased department (p. 94)

vertical marketing system (p. 95)

dual marketing (p. 96)

channel control (p. 96)

consumer cooperative (p. 96)

Questions for Discussion

1. What are the characteristics of each of the ownership forms discussed in this chapter?

2. Do you believe that independent retailers will soon disappear with the retail landscape? Explain your answer.

3. Why does the concept of ease of entry usually have a greater impact on independent retailers than on chain retailers?

4. How can an independent retailer overcome the problem of overdependence on the owner?

5. What difficulties might an independent encounter if it tries to expand into a chain?

6. What competitive advantages and disadvantages do regional chains have in comparison with national chains?

7. What are the similarities and differences between chains and franchising?

8. From the franchisee's perspective, under what circumstances would product/trademark franchising be advantageous? When would business format franchising be better?

9. Why would a department store want to lease space to an outside operator rather than run a business, such as shoes, itself? What would be its risks in this approach?

10. What are the pros and cons of Sherwin-Williams using dual marketing?

11. How could a small independent restaurant increase its channel power?

12. Why have consumer cooperatives not expanded much? What would you recommend to change this?

Web-Based Exercise

Visit the Web site of Subway (**www.subway.com**), one of the largest retail franchisors in the world. Click on "Franchise Opportunities." Based on the information you find there, would you be interested in becoming a Subway franchisee? Why or why not?

Note: Stop by our Web site (**www.prenhall.com/bermanevans**) to experience a number of highly interactive, appealing Web exercises based on actual company demonstrations and sample materials related to retailing.

Chapter Endnotes

1. Various company sources.

2. *Statistical Abstract of the United States 2002* (Washington, DC: U.S. Department of Commerce, 2002).

3. "Small Business Owners Mostly Satisfied, NFIB Survey Finds," *Business Credit* (February 2002).

4. Jane Olszeski Tortola, "Your Stores Without You," *Progressive Grocer* (January 2002), p. 83.

5. For a good overview of franchising and franchising opportunities, see *Entrepreneur's* "Annual Franchise 500" issue, which appears each January.

6. For more information on leased departments, see Connie Robbins Gentry, "Retailers as Landlords," *Chain Store Age* (May 2002), pp. 55–58; and Ken Clark, "Store-in-Store Concept Gains Ground," *Chain Store Age* (June 2001), pp. 43–45.

7. *Sherwin-Williams 2002 Annual Report.*

8. Amy Merrick, "Sears to Buy Lands' End in Deal That Unites Bricks and Clicks," *Wall Street Journal* (May 14, 2002), pp. A1, A8.

9. For more information on cooperatives, see Nicole L. Torres, "Examine Your Co-Op(tions)," *Entrepreneur* (July 2002), pp. 120, 128.

Appendix on the Dynamics of Franchising

This appendix is presented because of franchising's strong growth and exciting opportunities. Over the past two decades, annual U.S. franchising sales have more than tripled! We go beyond the discussion of franchising in Chapter 4 and provide information on managerial issues in franchising and on franchisor–franchisee relationships.

Consider: In 1986, the Serruya brothers (Aaron, Michael, and Simon, who then ranged in age from 14 to 20) opened their first Yogen Früz frozen yogurt stand in Toronto. Now, due to franchising, CoolBrands International (**www.coolbrandsinternational.com**) has 5,200 outlets, of which less than 50 are company-owned, including Yogen Früz, I Can't Believe It's Yogurt, Bresler's Ice Cream and Premium Frozen Yogurt, Swensen's Ice Cream, Steve's Ice Cream, and Java Coast Fine Coffees. Its outlets have revenues in the hundreds of millions of dollars (U.S.), and there are stores throughout the United States and Canada and in 80 other nations.

Visit Blockbuster's "Franchise Opportunities" (www.blockbuster.com/bb/about/franchisingops) section of its Web site.

How about Blockbuster? Although it has a base of company-owned outlets, it also has nearly 1,500 franchised stores. Consider this:

> If you become a Blockbuster franchisee, you will be in very good company. We have more than 8,000 corporate and franchise stores in 27 countries. The Blockbuster franchising initiative is one of the fastest and most exciting ways to grow in attractive new markets and in underserved existing markets. Our franchisees get to associate with a world leader in home entertainment. In return, we're assured high-quality, on-site management to service Blockbuster customers. We anticipate that all new franchisees will have retail backgrounds as owner-operators. Financial requirements are a minimum net worth of $400,000 and a minimum liquidity of $100,000.

U.S. franchisors are situated in well over 150 countries, a number that keeps on rising due to these factors: U.S. firms see the potential in foreign markets. Franchising is accepted as a retailing format in more nations. Trade barriers are fewer due to such pacts as the North American Free Trade Agreement, which makes it easier for firms based in the United States, Canada, and Mexico to operate in each other's marketplaces.

Here are three Web sites for you to get more information on franchising. And, remember, we have a special listing of franchising links at our Web site (**www.prenhall.com/bermanevans**):

- International Franchise Association's Resource (**www.franchise.org/resourcectr/resourcectr.asp**)
- Franchising.org (**www.franchising.org**)
- Small Business Administration Franchise Workshop (**www.sbaonline.sba.gov/workshops/franchises**)

MANAGERIAL ISSUES IN FRANCHISING

Franchising appeals to franchisees for several reasons. Most franchisors have easy-to-learn, standardized operating methods that they have perfected. New franchisees do not have to learn from their own trial-and-error methods. Franchisors often have facilities where franchisees are trained to operate equipment, manage employees, maintain records, and improve customer relations; there are usually follow-up field visits.

A new outlet of a nationally advertised franchise (such as Subway fast food) can attract a large customer following rather quickly and easily because of the reputation of the firm. And not only does franchising result in good initial sales and profits, it also reduces franchisees' risk of failure *if the franchisees affiliate with strong, supportive franchisors.*

What kind of individual is best suited to being a franchisee? This is what one expert says:

One of the myths that has been perpetuated is that franchise ownership is easy. This is just simply not true! While the franchisor will give the startup training and offer ongoing support, you, the franchisee, must be prepared to manage the business. While some franchises may lend themselves to absentee ownership, most are best run by hands-on management. You must be willing to work harder than you have perhaps ever worked before. Forty-hour weeks are also a myth, particularly in the startup phase of the business. It is more like 60- to 70-hour weeks. You must also be willing to mop floors, empty garbage, fire employees, and handle upset customers.[1]

What makes McDonald's such an admired franchise operator? Read on:

McDonald's succeeds by applying both system standards and individual opportunities. As a franchisee, you agree to work within the system. You must devote your full time and best efforts to daily operations. The franchise agreement allows you to operate a specific McDonald's restaurant, according to McDonald's standards, for a period of years (usually 20). McDonald's locates, develops, and constructs the restaurant based on a nationwide development plan that seeks to be responsive to changing demographics, customer convenience, and competition. McDonald's retains control of the restaurant facilities. You equip the restaurant at your expense with kitchen equipment, lighting, signs, seating, and decor. While none of this equipment is bought from McDonald's, it must meet the firm's specifications. To maintain uniformity, franchisees must use McDonald's formulas and specifications for menu items; methods of operation, inventory control, bookkeeping, accounting, and marketing; trademarks and service marks; and concepts for restaurant design, signs, and equipment layout.[2]

Investment and startup costs for a franchised outlet can be as low as a few thousand dollars for a personal service business to as high as several million dollars for a hotel. In return for its expenditures, a franchisee gets exclusive selling rights for an area; a business format franchisee also gets training, equipment and fixtures, and support in site selection, supplier negotiations, advertising, and so on. Half of U.S. business format franchisors require franchisees to be owner-operators and work full-time. Besides receiving fees and royalties from franchisees, franchisors may sell goods and services to them. This may be required; more often, for legal reasons, such purchases are at the franchisees' discretion (subject to franchisor specifications). Each year, franchisors sell billions of dollars worth of items to franchisees.

Table A4-1 shows the franchise fees, startup costs, and royalty fees for new franchisees at 10 leading franchisors in a variety of business categories. Financing support—either through in-house financing or third-party financing—is offered by almost all the firms cited in Table A4-1. In addition, through its guaranteed loan program, the U.S. Small Business Administration is a good financing option for prospective franchisees, and some banks offer special interest rates for franchisees affiliated with established franchisors.

Franchised outlets can be bought (leased) from franchisors, master franchisees, or existing franchisees. Franchisors sell either new locations or company-owned outlets (some of which may have been taken back from unsuccessful franchisees). At times, they sell the rights in entire regions or counties to master franchisees, which then deal with individual franchisees. Existing franchisees usually have the right to sell their units if they first offer them to their franchisor, if

TABLE A4-1	The Costs of Becoming a New Franchisee with Selected Franchisors (as of 2002)				
Franchising Company	Franchise Fee	Other Startup Costs	Royalty Fee as a % of Sales	Franchisee-Owned Outlets as a % of All Outlets	Offers Financing Support
Aamco Transmissions	$30,000	$181,000–$190,600	7	99 +	Third party
CoolBrands International[a]	$25,000	$0–$225,000	6	99 +	Third party
Dunkin' Donuts	$50,000	$242,800–$1,300,000	5.9	100	Third party
Fantastic Sams	$25,000	$75,000–$164,000	$215/week fee	99 +	Third party
Jazzercise	$325–$650	$1,800–20,600	up to 20	99 +	None
Mail Boxes Etc.	$29,995	$125,900–$195,900	5	99 +	Third party
Medicine Shoppe	$10,000–$18,000	$76,800–$152,500	2–5.5	99 +	Third party
Moto Photo	$35,000	$225,000–$310,000	6	89	None
Petland	$25,000	$403,500–$892,700	4.5	99 +	Third party
Super 8 Motels	$24,000 and up	$288,100–$2,300,000	5	100	In-house and third party

[a]Formerly Yogen Früz Worldwide.

Source: Computed by the authors from "23rd Annual Franchise 500," *Entrepreneur* (January 2002), various pages.

potential buyers meet all financial and other criteria, and/or if buyers undergo training. Of interest to prospective franchisees is the emphasis a firm places on franchisee-owned outlets versus franchisor-owned ones. This indicates the commitment to franchising. As indicated in Table A4-1, leading franchisors typically own a small percentage of outlets.

One last point regarding managerial issues in franchising concerns the failure rate of new franchisees. For many years, it was believed that success as a franchisee was a "sure thing"—and much safer than starting a business—due to the franchisor's well-known name, its experience, and its training programs. However, some recent research has shown franchising to be as risky as opening a new business. Why? Some franchisors have oversaturated the market and not provided promised support, and unscrupulous franchisors have preyed on unsuspecting investors.

With the preceding in mind, Figure A4-1 has a checklist by which potential franchisees can assess opportunities. In using the checklist, franchisees should also obtain full prospectuses and financial reports from all franchisors under consideration, and talk to existing franchise operators and customers.

FRANCHISOR–FRANCHISEE RELATIONSHIPS

Taco John's (www.tacojohns.com) prides itself on its collegial relationships with franchisees.

Many franchisors and franchisees have good relationships because they share goals for company image, operations, the goods and services offered, cooperative ads, and sales and profit growth. This two-way relationship is illustrated by the actions of Taco John's International, a firm with 450 franchised pizza restaurants in about 25 states. As the franchisor says at its Web site:

Our customers are our franchisees, their employees, and their customers. Everything we do is aimed at helping franchisees better serve customers:

- *Franchise Development.* Our restaurant design is the result of careful research and development with company prototypes. We provide conceptual floor plans and site sketches. We also provide construction consultation.

FIGURE A4-1

A Checklist of Questions
for Prospective
Franchisees Considering
Franchise Opportunities

✓ What are the required franchise fees: initial fee, advertising appropriations, and royalties?
✓ What degree of technical knowledge is required of the franchisee?
✓ What is the required investment of time by the franchisee? Does the franchisee have to be actively involved in the day-to-day operations of the franchise?
✓ How much control does the franchisor exert in terms of materials purchased, sales quotas, space requirements, pricing, the range of goods sold, required inventory levels, and so on?
✓ Can the franchisee tolerate the regimentation and rules of the franchisor?
✓ Are the costs of required supplies and materials purchased from the franchisor at market value, above market value, or below market value?
✓ What degree of name recognition do consumers have of the franchise? Does the franchisor have a meaningful advertising program?
✓ What image does the franchise have among consumers and among current franchisees?
✓ What are the level and quality of services provided by the franchisor: site selection, training, bookkeeping, human relations, equipment maintenance, and trouble-shooting?
✓ What is the franchisor policy in terminating franchisees? What are the conditions of franchise termination? What is the rate of franchise termination and nonrenewal?
✓ What is the franchisor's legal history?
✓ What is the length of the franchise agreement?
✓ What is the failure rate of existing franchises?
✓ What is the franchisor's policy with regard to company-owned and franchisee-owned outlets?
✓ What policy does the franchisor have in allowing franchisees to sell their business?
✓ What is the franchisor's policy with regard to territorial protection for existing franchisees? With regard to new franchisees and new company-owned establishments?
✓ What is the earning potential of the franchise during the first year? The first five years?

- *Marketing and Advertising.* The Marketing Department is responsible for planning, producing, and distributing effective and impactful programs and materials to help you grow your business and build Taco John's brand image. The Marketing Department plans and distributes materials to help you grow and to build the Taco John's brand image. Our national campaign is funded by Taco John's, suppliers, and franchisees. Each restaurant also belongs to a regional marketing co-op to participate in advertising that would otherwise not be cost-effective.

- *Franchise Business Consultants.* Each restaurant is assigned a Franchise Business Consultant.

- *Human Resources.* Our Human Resources Department will provide you with materials to help attract, motivate, and retain people. The Training Department teaches franchisees and their team members our operating system and how to best deliver the Taco John's promise to each customer.

- *Your New Restaurant Opening.* A Grand Opening Team will work with you in your restaurant, just before and during your opening.

- *Research and Development.* The Research and Development Department's focus is consumer research, operations testing, and customer feedback.

- *Purchasing and Distribution.* Company personnel negotiate to make sure our system receives good quality, service, and prices. A nationwide system of approved distributors warehouse all the products needed to operate a restaurant. Weekly orders are delivered to each restaurant's door.

Nonetheless, for several reasons, tensions do exist between various franchisors and their franchisees:

- The franchisor–franchisee relationship is not one of employer to employee. Franchisor controls are often viewed as rigid.

- Many agreements are considered too short by franchisees. Nearly half of U.S. agreements are 10 years or less (one-sixth are 5 years or less), usually at the franchisor's request.

- The loss of a franchise generally means eviction, and the franchisee gets nothing for "goodwill."

- Some franchisors believe their franchisees do not reinvest enough in their outlets or care enough about the consistency of operations from one outlet to another.
- Franchisors may not give adequate territorial protection and may open new outlets near existing ones.
- Franchisees may refuse to participate in cooperative advertising programs.
- Franchised outlets up for sale must usually be offered first to franchisors, which also have approval of sales to third parties.
- Some franchisees believe franchisor marketing support is low.
- Franchisees may be prohibited from operating competing businesses.
- Restrictions on suppliers may cause franchisees to pay higher prices and have limited choices.
- Franchisees may band together to force changes in policies and exert pressure on franchisors.
- Sales and profit expectations may not be realized.

Tensions can lead to conflicts—even litigation. Potential negative franchisor actions include terminating agreements; reducing marketing support; and adding red tape for orders, information requests, and warranty work. Potential negative franchisee actions include terminating agreements, adding competitors' products, refusing to promote goods and services, and not complying with data requests. Each year, business format franchisors terminate the contracts of 10 percent of the franchisee-owned stores that opened within the preceding five years.

Although franchising has been characterized by franchisors having more power than franchisees, this inequality is being reduced. First, franchisees affiliated with specific franchisors have joined together. For example, the Association of Kentucky Fried Chicken Franchisees, Supercuts Franchisee Association, and Vision Care Franchisee Association represent thousands of franchisees. Second, large umbrella groups, such as the American Franchisee Association (**www.franchisee.org**) and the American Association of Franchisees and Dealers (**www.aafd.org**), have been formed. Third, many franchisees now operate more than one outlet, so they have greater clout. Fourth, there has been a substantial rise in litigation.

Better communication and better cooperation are necessary to resolve problems. Here are two progressive approaches: First, the International Franchise Association has an ethics code for its franchisor and franchisee members, founded on these principles (**www.franchise.org/welcome_about/code.asp**):

> Every franchise relationship is founded on the mutual commitment of both parties to fulfill their obligations under the franchise agreement. Each party will fulfill its obligations, will act consistently with the interests of the brand, and will not act so as to harm the brand and system. This willing interdependence between franchisors and franchisees, and the trust and honesty upon which it is founded, has made franchising a worldwide success as a strategy for business growth. Honesty embodies openness, candor, and truthfulness. Franchisees and franchisors commit to sharing ideas and information and to face challenges in clear and direct terms. Our members will be sincere in word, act, and character—reputable and without deception.

Second, the National Franchise Mediation Program (**www.franchisemediation.org**) was established "by an ad hoc group of franchisors who sought a way to resolve disputes between franchisors and franchisees without the rancor and cost of litigation, wherever possible. Its goal is to resolve such conflicts fairly, amicably and cost-effectively." The program is overseen by an equal number of franchisee and franchisor representatives. "Thus far, a success rate of 90 percent has been achieved in cases in which the franchisee agreed to participate, and in which a mediator was needed. Many more disputes have been resolved prior to a mediator's intervention."

Appendix Endnotes

1. Robert McIntosh, "Self-Evaluation: Is Franchising for You?" **www.franchise.org/resourcectr/faq/abc/selfeval.asp** (January 28, 2003).

2. *McDonald's Franchising Brochure*, p. 3.

Chapter 5
RETAIL INSTITUTIONS BY STORE-BASED STRATEGY MIX

Reprinted by permission.

Although Ikea (**www.ikea.com**) has had stores in the United States for only 20 years, Ingvar Kamprad began selling furniture in Almhult, Sweden, under the Ikea name about 60 years ago. Kamprad got the idea for producing ready-to-assemble furniture to reduce his delivery costs when the milk wagon that was used to ship his small orders changed its route. In 1953, he purchased an empty factory and opened a showroom. Five years later, when he opened a large store, Kamprad cleverly added roof racks to the inventory mix so that customers could take their purchases home.

Today, Ikea strives to facilitate the shopping process. Most stores have a spacious, open layout, a cafeteria, and even a playroom that offers baby-sitting assistance for customers. The layout encourages browsing and increases impulse purchases. The inexpensive cafeteria, which serves Swedish-style delicacies at cost, encourages customers to spend more time on the premises. The playroom enables shoppers to go through the store without their children tagging behind them.

Ikea constantly fine-tunes its merchandise assortment to keep its "furniture as fashion" image. For example, it recently designed a colorful $10 plastic drawer unit on wheels that snaps together like Legos, as well as a ready-to-assemble upholstered sofa. The retailer Ikea currently has nearly 170 stores in more than 30 countries, including roughly two dozen in the United States and Canada.[1]

chapter objectives

1. To describe the wheel of retailing, scrambled merchandising, and the retail life cycle and show how they can help explain the performance of retail strategy mixes

2. To discuss some ways in which retail strategy mixes are evolving

3. To examine a wide variety of food-oriented retailers involved with store-based strategy mixes

4. To study a wide range of general merchandise retailers involved with store-based strategy mixes

OVERVIEW

In Chapter 4, retail institutions were described by type of ownership. In this chapter, we discuss three key concepts in planning retail strategy mixes: the wheel of retailing, scrambled merchandising, and the retail life cycle. We then look at how retail strategies are evolving and study the basic strategies of several store-based institutions. Chapter 6 deals with nonstore-based, electronic, and nontraditional strategies.

CONSIDERATIONS IN PLANNING A RETAIL STRATEGY MIX

A retailer may be categorized by its **strategy mix**, the firm's particular combination of store location, operating procedures, goods/services offered, pricing tactics, store atmosphere and customer services, and promotional methods.

Store location refers to the use of a store or nonstore format, placement in a geographic area, and the kind of site (such as a shopping center). Operating procedures include the kinds of personnel employed, management style, store hours, and other factors. The goods/services offered may encompass several product categories or just one, and quality may be low, medium, or high. Pricing refers to a retailer's use of prestige pricing (creating a quality image), competitive pricing (setting prices at the level of rivals), or penetration pricing (underpricing other retailers). Store atmosphere and customer services are reflected by the physical facilities and personal attention provided, return policies, delivery, and other factors. Promotion involves activities in such areas as advertising, displays, personal selling, and sales promotion. By combining these elements, a retailer can develop a unique strategy.

To flourish today, a retailer should strive to be dominant in some way. The firm may then reach **destination retailer** status—whereby consumers view the company as distinctive enough to become loyal to it and go out of their way to shop there. We tend to link "dominant" with "large." Yet, both small and large retailers can dominate in their own way. As follows, there are many ways to be a destination retailer, and combining two or more approaches can yield even greater appeal for a given retailer:

- Be price-oriented and cost-efficient to attract price-sensitive shoppers.
- Be upscale to attract full-service, status-conscious consumers.
- Be convenient to attract those wanting shopping ease, nearby locations, or long hours.
- Offer a dominant assortment in the product lines carried to appeal to consumers interested in variety and in-store shopping comparisons.
- Offer superior customer service to attract those frustrated by the decline in retail service.
- Be innovative or exclusive and provide a unique way of operating (such as kiosks at airports) or carry products/brands not stocked by others to reach people who are innovators or bored.

Before looking at specific strategy mixes, let us look at three concepts that help explain the use of these mixes: the wheel of retailing, scrambled merchandising, and the retail life cycle—as well as the ways in which retail strategies are evolving.

THE WHEEL OF RETAILING

According to the **wheel of retailing** theory, retail innovators often first appear as low-price operators with low costs and low profit margin requirements. Over time, the innovators upgrade the products they carry and improve their facilities and customer service (by adding better-quality items, locating in higher-rent sites, providing credit and delivery, and so on), and prices rise. As innovators mature, they become vulnerable to new discounters with lower costs, hence, the wheel of retailing.[2] See Figure 5-1.

The wheel of retailing is grounded on four principles: (1) There are many price-sensitive shoppers who will trade customer services, wide selections, and convenient locations for lower prices. (2) Price-sensitive shoppers are often not loyal and will switch to retailers with lower prices. However, prestige-sensitive customers like shopping at retailers with high-end strategies.

FIGURE 5-1

The Wheel of Retailing

As a low-end retailer upgrades its strategy to increase sales and profit margins, a new form of discounter takes its place.

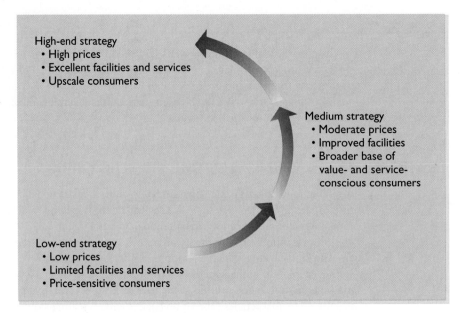

Where would you place Jo-Ann's fabrics and crafts stores (www.joann.com) along the wheel of retailing?

(3) New institutions are frequently able to have lower operating costs than existing institutions. (4) As retailers move up the wheel, they typically do so to increase sales, broaden the target market, and improve their image.

For example, when traditional department store prices became too high for many consumers, the growth of the full-line discount store (led by Wal-Mart) was the result.[3] The full-line discount store stressed low prices because of such cost-cutting techniques as having a small sales force, situating in lower-rent store locations, using inexpensive fixtures, emphasizing high stock turnover, and accepting only cash or check payments for goods. Then, as full-line discount stores prospered, they typically sought to move up a little along the wheel. This meant enlarging the sales force, improving locations, upgrading fixtures, carrying a greater selection of merchandise, and accepting credit. These improvements led to higher costs, which led to somewhat higher prices. The wheel of retailing again came into play as newer discounters, such as off-price chains, factory outlets, and permanent flea markets, expanded to satisfy the needs of the most price-conscious consumer. More recently, we have witnessed the birth of discount Web retailers, some of which have very low costs because they do not have "bricks-and-mortar" facilities.

As indicated in Figure 5-1, the wheel of retailing reveals three basic strategic positions: low end, medium, and high end. The medium strategy may have some difficulties if retailers in this position are not perceived as distinctive: "With specialty stores siphoning customers from above and discounters siphoning from below, J.C. Penney and Sears are stuck in the very skinny middle."[4] Figure 5-2 shows the opposing alternatives in considering a strategy mix.

The wheel of retailing suggests that established firms should be wary in adding services or converting a strategy from low end to high end. Because price-conscious shoppers are not usually loyal, they are apt to switch to lower-priced firms. Furthermore, retailers may then eliminate the competitive advantages that have led to profitability. This occurred with the retail catalog showroom, which is now a defunct format.

SCRAMBLED MERCHANDISING

Whereas the wheel of retailing focuses on product quality, prices, and customer service, scrambled merchandising involves a retailer increasing its width of assortment (the number of different product lines carried). **Scrambled merchandising** occurs when a retailer adds goods and services that may be unrelated to each other and to the firm's original business. See Figure 5-3.

Scrambled merchandising is popular for many reasons: Retailers want to increase overall revenues; fast-selling, highly profitable goods and services are usually the ones added; consumers make more impulse purchases; people like one-stop shopping; different target markets may be reached; and the impact of seasonality and competition is reduced. In addition, the popularity of

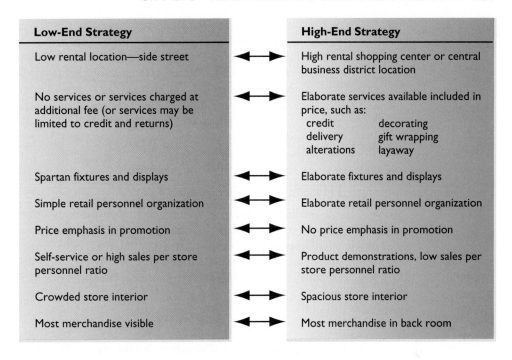

FIGURE 5-2
Retail Strategy
Alternatives

a retailer's original product line(s) may fall, causing it to scramble to maintain and grow the customer base. Blockbuster, due to the advent of pay-per-view and premium movie channels on cable and satellite TV, now carries CDs, magazines, movie merchandise, candy, video games, game players, DVD players, and more.

How much of a practitioner of scrambled merchandising is Sharper Image (www. sharperimage.com)?

Scambled merchandising is contagious. Drugstores, bookstores, florists, video stores, and photo-developing firms are all affected by supermarkets' scrambled merchandising. About one-eighth of U.S. supermarket sales are from general merchandise, health and beauty aids, and other nongrocery items, such as pharmacy products, magazines, flowers, and video rentals.

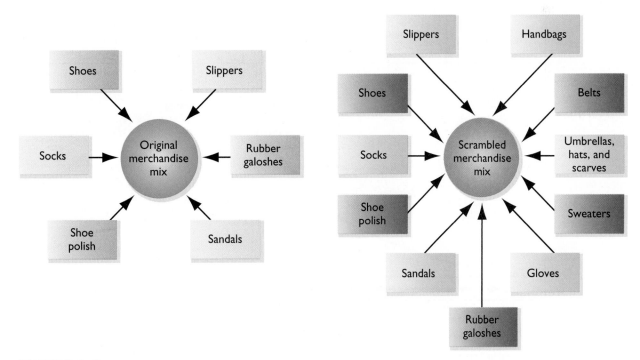

FIGURE 5-3
Scrambled Merchandising by a Shoe Store

In response, retailers such as drugstores are pushed into scrambled merchandising to fill the sales void caused by supermarkets. They have added toys and gift items, greeting cards, batteries, and cameras. This then creates a void for other retailers, which are also forced to scramble.

The prevalence of scrambled merchandising means greater competition among different types of retailers and that distribution costs are affected as sales are dispersed over more retailers. There are other limitations to scrambled merchandising, including the potential lack of retailer expertise in buying, selling, and servicing unfamiliar items; the costs associated with a broader assortment (including lower inventory turnover); and the possible harm to a retailer's image if scrambled merchandising is ineffective.

THE RETAIL LIFE CYCLE

The **retail life cycle** concept states that retail institutions—like the goods and services they sell— pass through identifiable life stages: introduction (early growth), growth (accelerated development), maturity, and decline. The direction and speed of institutional changes can be interpreted from this concept. Take a look at Figure 5-4. Figure 5-4(a) shows the business characteristics of the four stages, and Figure 5-4(b) indicates the stages in which several mall-based retail formats are now operating.

(a) Key Business Characteristics During the Stages of the Retail Life Cycle

	Life Cycle Stage			
	Introduction	Growth	Maturity	Decline
Sales	Low/growing	Rapid acceleration	High, leveling off	Dropping
Profitability	Negative to break even	High yield	High/declining	Low to break even
Positioning	Concept innovation	Special need	Broad market	Niche
Competition	None	Limited	Extensive/ saturation	Intensive/ consolidated

(b) Applying the Retail Life Cycle to Mall Retailers

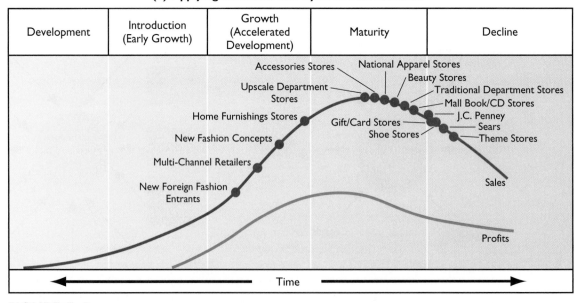

FIGURE 5-4

The Retail Life Cycle

Source: Retail Forward, "Mall Retailers—The Search for Growth," *Industry Outlook* (October 2001), p. 3. Reprinted by permission of Retail Forward, Inc. (**www.retailforward.com**).

Let us examine the stages of the retail life cycle as they apply to individual institutional formats and show specific examples. During the first stage of the cycle (introduction), there is a strong departure from the strategy mixes of existing retail institutions. A firm in this stage significantly alters at least one element of the strategy mix from that of traditional competitors. Sales and then profits often rise sharply for the first firms in a category. There are risks that new institutions will not be accepted by shoppers, and there may be large initial losses due to heavy investments. At this stage, long-run success is not assured.

One institution in the innovation stage is the online grocery store. How will the format do?

Thanks to her ZIP code and Peapod (**www.peapod.com**) by Stop & Shop, Jill Simpson does the majority of her weekly marketing online. It's an alternative that is, she said, "perfect for me." It is, however, an alternative fraught with obstacles, and one that has been defeated in various incarnations over the last few years. Webvan, a California firm begun in 1999, closed in 2001. Other efforts that met similar fates were Kozmo, which serviced nine cities, including New York, and Streamline.com, from which Peapod bought operations in Chicago and Washington. The biggest problem for the other dot.com grocers was the huge expense of warehousing. They had a great concept, but they hadn't accounted for how much the warehouse, shipping, and delivery costs would cut into their margins. Peapod surmounts this by forming partnerships with supermarkets that stock its warehouses, which are within or next to these stores.[5]

In the second stage (growth), both sales and profits exhibit rapid growth. Existing firms expand geographically, and new companies of the same type enter. Toward the end of accelerated development, cost pressure (to cover a larger staff, a more complex inventory system, and extensive controls) may begin to affect profits.

See TouchVision's (www.touchvision.com) view of the future for video kiosks.

The interactive electronic video kiosk is an institution in the growth stage. Today, kiosks sell everything from clothing to magazines to insurance to PCs. According to *Kiosk* and Jupiter Media Metrix, U.S. retail sales revenues generated by kiosks are expected to rise from $370 million in 1996 and $1.1 billion in 2001 to $6.5 billion in 2006. Worldwide, the number of installed kiosks is projected to go from 246,000 in 2001 to 598,000 in 2006.[6] This institution is examined further in Chapter 6.

The third stage (maturity) is characterized by slow sales growth for the institutional type. Though overall sales may continue to go up, that rise is at a much lower rate than during prior stages. Profit margins may have to be reduced to stimulate purchases. Maturity is brought on by market saturation caused by the high number of firms in an institutional format, competition from newer institutions, changing societal interests, and inadequate management skills to lead mature or larger firms. Once maturity is reached, the goal is to sustain it as long as possible and not to fall into decline.

The liquor store, a form of specialty store, is an institution in the maturity stage; sales are rising, but very slowly as compared to earlier years. From 1993 to 2002, U.S. liquor store sales went up an average of just under 4 percent annually, which was far less than the rate for all U.S. retailers. This is due to competition from membership clubs, mail-order wine retailers, and supermarkets (in states allowing wine or liquor sales); changing life-styles and attitudes regarding liquor; the national 21-year-old drinking age requirement; and limits on the nonalcoholic items that liquor stores are permitted to sell in some locales.

The final stage in the retail life cycle is decline, whereby industrywide sales and profits for a format fall off, many firms abandon the format, and newer formats attract consumers previously committed to that retailer type. In some cases, a decline may be hard or almost impossible to reverse. In others, it may be avoided or postponed by repositioning the institution.

With the retail catalog showroom, consumers chose items from a catalog, shopped in a warehouse setting, and wrote up orders. After peaking in the 1980s and seeing a steady sales decline thereafter, the format finally vanished in 1998. Best Products and Consumers Distributing went out of business and Service Merchandise switched to a traditional store format (in 2002, it too closed down). Why? Many other retailers aggressively cut costs and prices, so showrooms were no longer low-price leaders. Catalogs had to be printed far in advance. Too many items were slow-sellers or had low profit margins. Some consumers found showrooms crowded and disliked writing orders, the lack of displays reduced browsing time, and the paucity of apparel goods also held down revenues.[7]

On the other hand, conventional supermarkets have slowed their decline by placing new units in suburban shopping centers, redesigning interiors, lengthening store hours, having low prices, expanding the use of scrambled merchandising, closing unprofitable smaller units, and converting to larger outlets.

The life cycle concept highlights the proper retailer response as institutions evolve. Expansion should be the focus initially, administrative skills and operations become critical in maturity, and adaptation is essential at the end of the cycle.

HOW RETAIL INSTITUTIONS ARE EVOLVING

Forward-looking firms know their individual strategies must be modified as retail institutions evolve over time. Complacency is not desirable. Many retailers have witnessed shrinking profit margins due to intense competition and consumer interest in lower prices. This puts pressure on them to tighten internal cost controls and to promote higher-margin goods and services while eliminating unprofitable items. Let us see how firms are reacting to this formidable environment through mergers, diversification, and downsizing, as well as cost containment and value-driven retailing.

MERGERS, DIVERSIFICATION, AND DOWNSIZING

Some firms use mergers and diversification to sustain sales growth in a highly competitive environment (or when the institutional category in which they operate matures). For stronger firms, this trend is expected to carry over into the future.

Mergers involve the combination of separately owned retail firms. Some mergers take place between retailers of different types, such as the ones between Sears (the department store chain) and Lands' End (the catalog and online apparel retailer). Other mergers occur between similar types of retailers, such as two local banks or two auto parts chains (as took place when Advance Auto Parts acquired Discount Auto Parts). By merging, retailers hope to jointly maximize resources, enlarge their customer base, improve productivity and bargaining power, limit weaknesses, and gain competitive advantages. This is a way for resourceful retailers to grow more rapidly and for weaker ones to enhance their long-term prospects for survival (or gain some return on investment by selling assets). See Figure 5-5.

With **diversification**, retailers become active in businesses outside their normal operations and add stores in different goods/services categories. To expand beyond its core business,

Technology in RETAILING | Grocery Stores: Top Drawer or Bottom Rung in Technology?

A common question among retailing analysts is whether supermarkets are innovators or laggards with regard to technology. Evidence of the innovator perspective is the early use of barcode scanners, as well as the high degree of current usage of self-checkout systems and electronic shelf labels. Many supermarkets also extensively manage large customer data bases and frequent customer programs.

On the other hand, many supermarkets are leery of sharing their data bases with buyers, category managers, and suppliers. A spokesperson for a major retail consulting firm says that, although many supermarkets have a large amount of information and understand its value, they often do not have either the staff or expertise to "pull it all together just yet." The large num-

ber of supermarket mergers (such as Kroger/Fred Meyer) also complicates the use of technology by U.S. retailers.

Hannaford Bros. (**www.hannaford.com**), a Maine-based supermarket chain recently acquired by Delhaize America (**www. delhaize.com/en/co_us.asp**), is an example of a supermarket retailer that effectively uses technology. Its new data warehouse architecture enables it to monitor inventory and buying trends. This system captures data on a weekly basis, and the chain soon hopes to review sales and inventory data several times per day.

Source: Susan Reda, "Grocery Stores: Leaders or Laggards on Technology?" *Stores* (February 2001), pp. 18–22.

FIGURE 5-5

J.C. Penney's Eckerd: A Growing Drugstore Power Through Mergers

J.C. Penney has been in the drugstore business since 1969 when it acquired Thrift Drug. In 1996, the company acquired Eckerd, Fay, Kerr, and a number of Rite Aid drugstores. In 1997, it purchased Revco drugstores; and in 1999, it acquired Genovese drugstores. As of now, J.C. Penney operates nearly 3,000 drugstores—most converted to the powerful Eckerd name.

Reprinted by permission of Eckerd Corporation.

Through its various divisions, Limited Brands (www.limitedbrands.com) is an apparel retailing dynamo.

Limited Brands (parent of The Limited) developed Express (targeting young women), Structure and Express for Men (targeting men), and Bath & Body Works (toiletries). It also acquired Victoria's Secret (a mail-order, store, and Web lingerie business) and Henri Bendel (upscale women's clothing).

The size of many retail chains has grown dramatically because of mergers and diversification. All have not done well with that approach. Thus, even though stronger firms are expanding, we are also witnessing **downsizing**—whereby unprofitable stores are closed or divisions are sold off—by retailers unhappy with performance. Because Kmart's diversification had poor results, it closed or sold its ventures outside the discount department store field (including Borders' bookstores, Builders Square, OfficeMax, Pay Less drugstores, and Sports Authority). It has also closed a number of Kmart stores as part of its bankruptcy reorganization. This is discussed further in Chapter 12.

The interest in downsizing should continue. Various retailers have overextended themselves and do not have the resources or management talent to succeed without retrenching. In their quest to open new stores, certain firms have chosen poor sites (having already saturated the best locations). Retailers such as Barnes & Noble are more interested in operating fewer, but much larger, stores and using the Web. Retailers such as supermarkets are finding they can do better if they are regional rather than national.

COST CONTAINMENT AND VALUE-DRIVEN RETAILING

With a cost-containment approach, retailers strive to hold down both initial investments and operating costs. Many firms use this strategy because of intense competition from discounters, the need to control complicated chain or franchise operations, high land and construction costs, the volatility of the economy, and a desire to maximize productivity: "In today's business environment, more firms are looking for ways to expand the value they deliver to customers without adding costs that detract from the bottom line."[8]

BJ's membership club chain has a cost-containment approach that even extends to its austere Web site (www.bjswholesale.com).

Cost containment can be accomplished through one or more of these strategic decisions:

- Standardizing operating procedures, store layouts, store size, and product offerings.
- Using secondary locations, freestanding units, and locations in older strip centers and by occupying sites abandoned by others (second-use locations).
- Placing stores in smaller communities where building regulations are less strict, labor costs are lower, and construction and operating costs are reduced.
- Using inexpensive construction materials, such as bare cinder-block walls and concrete floors.
- Using plainer fixtures and lower-cost displays.

- Buying refurbished equipment.
- Joining cooperative buying and advertising groups.
- Encouraging manufacturers to finance inventories.

A driving force behind cost containment is the quest to provide good value to customers:

The retailing buzzword of the day is value. The word's meaning, however, is subjective—it can mean price, quality, service, convenience, or a combination thereof. Price clearly plays a big role in what consumers buy and where they buy it. Retailers' pricing policies—particularly for discounters—have encouraged consumers to shop for bargains and to distrust traditional sales and sale prices. Today's pragmatic consumers know they can get reasonable quality at everyday low prices. Many consumers no longer trust high prices as being an accurate reflection of value.[9]

RETAIL INSTITUTIONS CATEGORIZED BY STORE-BASED STRATEGY MIX

Selected aspects of the strategy mixes of 14 store-based retail institutions, divided into food-oriented and general merchandise groups, are highlighted in this section and Table 5-1. Although not all-inclusive, the strategy mixes do provide a good overview of store-based strategies. Please note that *width of assortment* is the number of different product lines carried by a retailer; *depth of assortment* is the selection within the product lines stocked. Visit our Web site (**www.prenhall.com/bermanevans**) for many links related to retail institutions' strategies.

FOOD-ORIENTED RETAILERS

The following food-oriented strategic retail formats are described next: convenience store, conventional supermarket, food-based superstore, combination store, box (limited-line) store, and warehouse store. Visit our Web site (**www.prenhall.com/bermanevans**) for many links related to retail institutions' food-based strategies.

Convenience Store

7-Eleven (www.7-eleven.com) dominates the convenience store category.

A **convenience store** is typically a well-located, food-oriented retailer that is open long hours and carries a moderate number of items. The store facility is small (only a fraction of the size of a conventional supermarket), has average to above-average prices, and average atmosphere and customer services. The ease of shopping at convenience stores and the impersonal nature of many large supermarkets make convenience stores particularly appealing to their customers, many of whom are male.

There are 100,000 U.S. convenience stores (excluding the stores where food is a small fraction of revenues), and their total annual sales are $90 billion (excluding gasoline).[10] 7-Eleven, Circle K, and Casey's General Store are major food-based U.S. convenience store chains. Speedway SuperAmerica is a leading gasoline service station–based convenience store chain with more than 2,000 outlets.

Items such as milk, eggs, and bread once represented the major portion of sales; now sandwiches, tobacco products, snack foods, soft drinks, newspapers and magazines, beer and wine, video rentals, ATMs, and lottery tickets are also key items. And gasoline generates 30 percent or more of total sales at most of the convenience stores that carry it. See Figure 5-6.

The convenience store's advantages are its usefulness when a consumer does not want to travel to or shop at a supermarket, the availability of both fill-in items and gas, long hours, and drive-through windows. Many customers shop there multiple times a week, and the average transaction is small. Due to limited shelf space, stores receive frequent deliveries and there are high handling costs. Customers are less price-sensitive than those at other food-oriented retailers.

The industry does have problems: Some areas are saturated with stores; supermarkets have longer hours and more nonfood items; some stores are too big, making shopping less convenient; the traditional market (blue-collar workers) has shrunk; and some chains have had financial woes.

TABLE 5-1	Selected Aspects of Store-Based Retail Strategy Mixes				
Type of Retailer	Location	Merchandise	Prices	Atmosphere and Services	Promotion
Food-Oriented					
Convenience store	Neighborhood	Medium width and low depth of assortment; average quality	Average to above average	Average	Moderate
Conventional supermarket	Neighborhood	Extensive width and depth of assortment; average quality; manufacturer, private, and generic brands	Competitive	Average	Heavy use of newspapers, flyers, and coupons; self-service
Food-based superstore	Community shopping center or isolated site	Full assortment of supermarket items, plus health and beauty aids and general merchandise	Competitive	Average	Heavy use of newspapers and flyers; self-service
Combination store	Community shopping center or isolated site	Full selection of supermarket and drugstore items or supermarket and general merchandise; average quality	Competitive	Average	Heavy use of newspapers and flyers; self-service
Box (limited-line) store	Neighborhood	Low width and depth of assortment; few perishables; few national brands	Very low	Low	Little or none
Warehouse store	Secondary site, often in industrial area	Moderate width and low depth; emphasis on manufacturer brands bought at discounts	Very low	Low	Little or none
General Merchandise					
Specialty store	Business district or shopping center	Very narrow width and extensive depth of assortment; average to good quality	Competitive to above average	Average to excellent	Heavy use of displays; extensive sales force
Traditional department store	Business district, shopping center, or isolated store	Extensive width and depth of assortment; average to good quality	Average to above average	Good to excellent	Heavy ad and catalog use, direct mail; personal selling
Full-line discount store	Business district, shopping center, or isolated store	Extensive width and depth of assortment; average to good quality	Competitive	Slightly below average to average	Heavy use of newspapers; price-oriented; moderate sales force
Variety store	Business district, shopping center, or isolated store	Good width and some depth of assortment; below-average to average quality	Average	Below average	Heavy use of newspapers; self-service

(continued)

| TABLE 5-1 | (Continued) | | | | |

Type of Retailer	Location	Merchandise	Prices	Atmosphere and Services	Promotion
Off-price chain	Business district, suburban shopping strip, or isolated store	Moderate width but poor depth of assortment; average to good quality; lower continuity	Low	Below average	Use of newspapers; brands not advertised; limited sales force
Factory outlet	Out-of-the-way site or discount mall	Moderate width but poor depth of assortment; some irregular merchandise; lower continuity	Very low	Very low	Little; self-service
Membership club	Isolated store or secondary site (industrial park)	Moderate width but poor depth of assortment; lower continuity	Very low	Very low	Little; some direct mail; limited sales force
Flea market	Isolated site, racetrack, or arena	Extensive width but poor depth of assortment; variable quality; lower continuity	Very low	Very low	Limited; self-service

Conventional Supermarket

The Food Marketing Institute (www.fmi.org) is the leading industry association for food retailers.

A **supermarket** is a self-service food store with grocery, meat, and produce departments and minimum annual sales of $2 million. Included are conventional supermarkets, food-based superstores, combination stores, box (limited-line) stores, and warehouse stores. See Figure 5-7.

A **conventional supermarket** is a departmentalized food store with a wide range of food and related products; sales of general merchandise are rather limited. This institution started 70 years ago when it was recognized that large-scale operations would let a retailer combine volume sales, self-service, and low prices. Self-service enabled supermarkets to both cut costs and increase volume. Personnel costs were reduced, and impulse buying increased. The car and the refrigerator contributed to the supermarket's success by lowering travel costs and adding to the life span of perishables.

FIGURE 5-6
Wendy's and Pilot: A New Combination for Convenience Stores

Wendy's and Pilot have combined their facilities in some locales to offer expanded products for convenience store customers.

Reprinted by permission of Wendy's International.

FIGURE 5-7

Supermarkets Have
Come a Long Way

"Today, Albertson's offers a
design with several 'stores
within a store.' Shoppers
will find the finest fresh
foods like homemade
breads, abundant produce,
a well-stocked international
deli, and delicious cut-to-
order meats. Our Better
Care center offers over-the-
counter and prescription
medications along with
friendly, knowledgeable
pharmacists and certified
technicians to assist customers with health-care
needs. Baby care products
and pet care items each
have their own special
areas to make shopping
trips more efficient. Stores
also offer such varied services as meals-to-go, full-
service in-store banks,
video rentals, film developing, fresh flowers, and
wine stewards." [**www1.
albertsons.com/corporate**]

Photo reprinted by permission
of Retail Forward, Inc.

For several decades, overall supermarket sales have been about three-quarters of U.S. grocery sales, with conventional supermarkets now yielding 36 percent of total supermarket sales. There are 17,000 conventional units, with annual sales of $145 billion.[11] Chains account for the majority of sales. Among the leaders are Kroger, Safeway, Albertson's, and Winn-Dixie. Many independent supermarkets are affiliated with cooperative or voluntary organizations, such as IGA and Supervalu.

Conventional supermarkets generally rely on high inventory turnover (volume sales). Their profit margins are low. In general, average gross margins (selling price less merchandise cost) are 20 to 22 percent of sales and net profits are 1 to 3 percent of sales.

These stores face intense competition from other food stores: Convenience stores offer greater customer convenience; food-based superstores and combination stores have more product lines and greater variety within them, as well as better margins; and box and warehouse stores have lower operating costs and prices. Membership clubs (discussed later), with their low prices, also provide competition—especially now that they have much expanded food lines. Variations of the supermarket are covered next.

Food-Based Superstore

A **food-based superstore** is larger and more diversified than a conventional supermarket but usually smaller and less diversified than a combination store. This format originated in the 1970s as supermarkets sought to stem sales declines by expanding store size and the number of nonfood items carried. Some supermarkets merged with drugstores or general merchandise stores but more grew into food-based superstores. There are 8,400 food-based U.S. superstores, with sales of $160 billion.[12]

The typical food-based superstore occupies at least 30,000 to 50,000 square feet of space and 20 to 25 percent of sales are from general merchandise, including garden supplies, flowers, small appliances, and film developing. It caters to consumers' complete grocery needs, along with fill-in general merchandise.

Like combination stores, food-based superstores are efficient, offer a degree of one-stop shopping, stimulate impulse purchases, and feature high-profit general merchandise. But they also offer other advantages: It is easier and less costly to redesign and convert supermarkets into food-based superstores than into combination stores. Many consumers feel more comfortable shopping in true food stores than in huge combination stores. Management expertise is better focused.

Over the past two decades, U.S. supermarket chains have turned more to food-based superstores. They have expanded and remodeled existing supermarkets and built numerous new stores. Many independents have also converted to food-based superstores.

Combination Store

A **combination store** unites supermarket and general merchandise in one facility, with general merchandise accounting for 25 to 40 percent of sales. The format began in the late 1960s and early 1970s, as common checkout areas were set up for separately owned supermarkets and drugstores or supermarkets and general merchandise stores. The natural offshoot was integrating operations under one management. There are 3,300 U.S. combination stores (including supercenters), and annual sales are $70 billion.[13] Among those with combination stores are Meijer, Fred Meyer, and Albertson's.

Meijer's (www.meijer.com) combination stores are quite popular with shoppers. They carry 120,000 items.

Combination stores are large, from 30,000 up to 100,000 or more square feet. This leads to operating efficiencies and cost savings. Consumers like one-stop shopping and will travel to get there. Impulse sales are high. Many general merchandise items have better margins than food items. Supermarkets and drugstores have commonalities in the customers served and the low-price, high-turnover items sold. Drugstore and general merchandise customers are drawn to the store more often.

A **supercenter** is a combination store blending an economy supermarket with a discount department store. It is the U.S. version of the even larger **hypermarket** (the European institution pioneered by firms such as Carrefour that did not succeed in the United States). As a rule, the majority of supercenter sales are from nonfood items. Stores usually range from 75,000 to 150,000 square feet in size and they stock up to 50,000 and more items, much more than the 30,000 or so items carried by other combination stores. Wal-Mart, Kmart, and Target all operate some supercenters.

Box (Limited-Line) Store

The **box (limited-line) store** is a food-based discounter that focuses on a small selection of items, moderate hours of operation (compared to other supermarkets), few services, and limited manufacturer brands. It carries less than 2,000 items, few refrigerated perishables, and few sizes and brands per item. Prices are on shelves or overhead signs. Items are displayed in cut cases. Customers bag their purchases. Box stores rely on low-priced private-label brands. Their prices are 20 to 30 percent below supermarkets.

The box store originated in Europe and was exported to the United States in the mid-1970s. The growth of these stores has not been as anticipated, as sales rose modestly over the last decade. Some other food stores have matched box-store prices. Many people are loyal to manufacturer brands, and box stores cannot fulfill one-stop shopping needs. There are 2,500 box stores in the United States, with sales of $10 billion.[14] The leading box store operators are Save-A-Lot and Aldi.

Warehouse Store

A **warehouse store** is a food-based discounter offering a moderate number of food items in a no-frills setting. It appeals to one-stop food shoppers, concentrates on special purchases of popular brands, uses cut-case displays, offers little service, posts prices on shelves, and locates in secondary sites. Warehouse stores began in the late 1970s. There are now 900 U.S. stores with $16 billion in annual sales.[15]

The largest warehouse store is known as a super warehouse. There are 500 of them in the United States. They have annual sales exceeding $20 million each and they contain a variety of departments,

Ethics in RETAILING
Good Neighbor Award Honors a Local Supermarket Manger

The Good Neighbor Award was first established by former President George H. W. Bush as a way to honor volunteers in industry. One recent national winner was Jay Dickey, a store manager of the Publix Super Market (**www.publix.com**) in Cartsville, Georgia. Dickey is a board member, as well as vice-chairperson, of the Noble Wheeler Foundation (**http://notatlanta.org/noblehill.html**). This foundation has raised monies to finish refurbishing the first African-American school in Bartow County, Georgia.

According to Jay Dickey, "Publix is big-time into United Way, so I joined the allocations board, and the light was so bright it blinded me. I couldn't believe the need that was in our community." After serving on the allocations board for four years and being named "Volunteer of the Year," he stepped down to join the Hickory Log Foundation "because they needed help more than any other organization." This organization offers a nonprofit program that provides housing and care for men with mental disabilities.

Another project that helped Jay Dickey earn the Good Neighbor Award was the Publix Learning Lab that he established at an elementary school. The lab is a little grocery store, about the size of a classroom, in which children can learn math and science in a mini-store environment.

Source: "12th Annual Good Neighbor Awards," *Supermarket Business* (April 15, 2000), pp. 38–44.

including produce. High ceilings accommodate pallet loads of groceries. Shipments are made directly to the store. Customers pack their own groceries. Super warehouses are profitable at gross margins far lower than those for conventional supermarkets. The leading super warehouse chain is Cub Foods.

Many consumers do not like shopping in warehouse settings. Furthermore, because products are usually acquired when special deals are available, brands may be temporarily or permanently out of stock.

Table 5-2 shows selected operating data for the food-oriented retailers just described.

TABLE 5-2	Selected Typical Operating Data for Food-Oriented Retailers, as of 2002					
Factor	Convenience Stores	Conventional Supermarkets	Food-Based Superstores	Combination Stores	Box (Limited-Line) Stores	Warehouse Stores
Number of stores	100,000	17,000	8,400	3,300	2,500	900
Total annual sales	$90 billion[a]	$145 billion	$160 billion	$70 billion[b]	$10 billion	$16 billion
Average store selling area (sq. ft.)	5,000 or less	15,000–20,000	30,000–50,000+	30,000–100,000+	5,000–9,000	15,000+
Number of checkouts per store	1–3	6–10	10+	10+	3–5	5+
Gross margin	25–30%	20–22%	20–25%	25%	10–12%	12–15%
Number of items stocked per store	3,000–4,000	12,000–17,000	20,000+	30,000+	Under 2,000	2,500+
Major emphasis	Daily fill-in needs; dairy, sandwiches, tobacco, gas, beverages, magazines	Food; only 5–10% of sales from general merchandise	Positioned between supermarket and combo store; 20–25% of sales from general merchandise	One-stop shopping; general merchandise is 25–40% of sales	Low prices; few or no perishables	Low prices; variable assortments; may or may not stock perishables

[a]Excluding gasoline.
[b]Including supermarket sales at the supercenters of Wal-Mart, Kmart, and Target (which are more heavily oriented to general merchandise than other combination stores).

Sources: Various issues of *Progressive Grocer*; Food Marketing Institute, "Facts & Figures," **www.fmi.org/facts_figs/superfact.htm**; *Convenience Store News Online*, **www.csnews.com**; and author's estimates.

GENERAL MERCHANDISE RETAILERS

We now examine these general merchandise strategic retail formats highlighted in Table 5-1: specialty store, traditional department store, full-line discount store, variety store, off-price chain, factory outlet, membership club, and flea market. Visit our Web site (**www.prenhall.com/bermanevans**) for many links related to retail institutions' general merchandise strategies.

Specialty Store

A **specialty store** concentrates on selling one goods or service line, such as young women's apparel. It usually carries a narrow but deep assortment in the chosen category and tailors the strategy to a given market segment. This enables the store to maintain a better selection and sales expertise than competitors, which are often department stores. Investments are controlled, and there is a certain amount of flexibility. Among the most popular categories of specialty stores are apparel, personal care, auto supply, home furnishings, electronics, books, toys, home improvement, pet supplies, jewelry, and sporting goods.

Consumers often shop at specialty stores because of the knowledgeable sales personnel, the variety of choices within the given category, customer service policies, intimate store size and atmosphere (although this is not true of the category killer store), the lack of crowds (also not true of category killer stores), and the absence of aisles of unrelated merchandise that they must pass through. Some specialty stores have elaborate fixtures and upscale merchandise for affluent shoppers, whereas others are discount-oriented and aim at price-conscious consumers.

Total specialty store sales are difficult to determine because these stores sell virtually all kinds of goods and services, and aggregate specialty store data are not compiled by the government. We do estimate that annual nonfood specialty store sales in the United States exceed $1 trillion (including auto dealers). The top 100 specialty store chains (excluding auto dealers) have sales of more than $250 billion and operate about 100,000 outlets. Among those chains, about one-third are involved with apparel. Specialty store leaders include Toys "R" Us and K-B (toys), The Limited and Gap (apparel), Best Buy and Circuit City (consumer electronics), and Barnes & Noble and Borders (books).[16]

As noted earlier in the chapter, one type of specialty store—the category killer—has gained particular strength. A **category killer** (also known as a **power retailer**) is an especially large specialty store. It features an enormous selection in its category and relatively low prices. Consumers are drawn from wide geographic areas. Toys "R" Us, The Limited, Gap, Sam Goody, and Barnes & Noble are just some of the specialty store chains that have category killer stores to complement existing stores. Blockbuster, Sephora, Home Depot, Sports Authority, and Staples are among the chains almost fully based on the concept. See Figure 5-8. Sports Authority's 200 stores usually have more than 40,000 square feet of selling space: "This format enables the

FIGURE 5-8

Home Depot: A Power in Home Improvement

At its enormous stores, Home Depot offers thousands of goods and services—including truck rentals.

Reprinted by permission.

company to provide under one roof an extensive selection of merchandise for sports and leisure activities, including golf, tennis, snow skiing, cycling, hunting, fishing, bowling, archery, boating and water sports, team sports, physical fitness, and men's, women's, and children's athletic and active apparel and footwear. The average store offers over 40,000 active items (excluding discontinued items). Its assortment includes over 700 brand names, including Nike, New Balance, Titleist, Taylor Made, Reebok, Wilson, Russell, Diamondback, Salomon, and others."[17]

Sometimes the focus of specialty stores is as narrow as the Joy of Socks (www.joyofsocks.com).

Nonetheless, smaller specialty stores (even ones with under 1,000 square feet of space) can prosper if they are focused, offer strong customer service, and avoid imitating larger firms. Many consumers do not like shopping in category killer stores: "Consumers who are looking for just one or a few basic items and a quick checkout may not want to spend time scouring through a cavernous warehouse with a seemingly endless volume of merchandise to find what they need." That is why we are seeing the emergence of another specialty store format: "Nicknamed 'gnategory killers' by industry analysts, these micro-specialty stores specialize in one item within an already narrow category. Their extremely narrow focus allows them to stock deep assortments of a particular item while operating small-size stores. A pioneer of this concept is Sunglass Hut. Until recently, the retailer sold over 1,000 models of just one item—sunglasses. Other participants in this trend today include Tie Rack and Joy of Socks."[18]

Any size specialty store can be adversely affected by seasonality or a decline in the popularity of its product category. This type of store may also fail to attract consumers who are interested in one-stop shopping for multiple product categories.

Traditional Department Store

A **department store** is a large retail unit with an extensive assortment (width and depth) of goods and services that is organized into separate departments for purposes of buying, promotion, customer service, and control. It has the most selection of any general merchandise retailer, often serves as the anchor store in a shopping center or district, has strong credit card penetration, and is usually part of a chain. To be classified as a department store, a retailer must sell a wide range of products—such as apparel, furniture, appliances and home furnishing; and selected other items, such as paint, hardware, toiletries, cosmetics, photo equipment, jewelry, toys, and sporting goods—with no one merchandise line predominating.

Two basic types of retailers meet the preceding criteria: the traditional department store and the full-line discount store. They account for more than $325 billion in annual sales (including supercenters where general merchandise sales exceed food sales and leased departments), about 9 percent of all U.S. retail sales.[19] The traditional department store is discussed here; the full-line discount store is examined next.

Saks Incorporated (www.saksincorporated.com) operates several department store chains around the country, including Carson Pirie Scott, Parisian, Profitt's, and Saks Fifth Avenue.

At a **traditional department store**, merchandise quality ranges from average to quite good. Pricing is moderate to above average. Customer service ranges from medium levels of sales help, credit, delivery, and so forth to high levels of each. For example, Macy's targets middle-class shoppers interested in assortment and moderate prices, whereas Bloomingdale's aims at upscale consumers through more trendy merchandise and higher prices. Few traditional department stores sell all of the product lines that the category used to carry. Many place great emphasis on apparel and may not carry such lines as furniture, electronics, and major appliances.

Over its history, the traditional department store has been responsible for many innovations, including advertising prices, enacting a one-price policy (whereby all shoppers pay the same price for the same item), developing computerized checkouts, offering money-back guarantees, adding branch stores, decentralizing management, and moving into suburban shopping centers. However, in recent years, the performance of traditional department stores has lagged behind that of full-line discount stores. Today, traditional department store sales ($95 billion annually) represent less than 30 percent of total department store sales. These are some reasons for traditional department stores' difficulties:

- They no longer have brand exclusivity for a lot of the popular items they sell.
- Instead of creating more of their own brands, they have signed exclusive licensing agreements with fashion designers to use the designers' names. This generates loyalty to the designer, not the retailer.

- Price-conscious consumers are more attracted to discounters than to traditional department stores.
- The popularity of shopping centers has aided specialty stores because consumers can engage in one-stop shopping at several specialty stores in the same shopping center. Department stores do not dominate the smaller stores around them as they once did.
- Specialty stores often have better assortments in the lines they carry.
- Customer service has deteriorated. Store personnel are not as loyal, helpful, or knowledgeable.
- Some stores are too big and have too much unproductive selling space and low-turnover merchandise.
- Unlike specialty stores, many department stores have had a weak focus on customer market segments and a fuzzy image.
- Such chains as Sears have repeatedly changed strategic orientation, confusing consumers as to their image. (Is Sears a traditional department store chain or a full-line discount store chain?)
- Some companies are not as innovative in their merchandise decisions as they once were.

Traditional department stores need to clarify their niche in the marketplace (retail positioning); place greater emphasis on customer service and sales personnel; present more exciting, better-organized store interiors; use space better by downsizing stores and eliminating slow-selling items (such as J.C. Penney dropping consumer electronics); and open outlets in smaller, less-developed towns and cities (as Sears has done). They can also centralize more buying and promotion functions, do better research, and reach customers more efficiently (by such tools as targeted mailing pieces).

Full-Line Discount Store

A **full-line discount store** is a type of department store with these features:

- It conveys the image of a high-volume, low-cost outlet selling a broad product assortment for less than conventional prices.
- It is more apt to carry the range of product lines once expected at department stores, including electronics, furniture, and appliances—as well as auto accessories, gardening tools, and housewares.
- Shopping carts and centralized checkout service are provided.
- Customer service is not usually provided within store departments but at a centralized area. Products are normally sold via self-service with minimal assistance in any single department.
- Nondurable (soft) goods feature private brands, whereas durable (hard) goods emphasize well-known manufacturer brands.
- Less fashion-sensitive merchandise is carried.
- Buildings, equipment, and fixtures are less expensive, and operating costs are lower than for traditional department stores and specialty stores.

Annual U.S. full-line discount store revenues are $230 billion (including general merchandise-based supercenters and leased departments), more than 70 percent of all U.S. department store sales. Together, Wal-Mart, Kmart, and Target Stores operate 6,000 full-line discount stores (including supercenters) with $200 billion in full-line discount store sales.[20]

The success of full-line discount stores is due to many factors. They have a clear customer focus: middle-class and lower-middle-class shoppers looking for good value. The stores feature popular brands of average- to good-quality merchandise at competitive prices. They have expanded their goods and service categories and often have their own private brands. Firms have worked hard to improve their image and provide more customer services. The average outlet (not the supercenter) tends to be smaller than a traditional department store and sales per square foot are usually higher, which improves productivity. Many full-line discount stores are located in small towns where competition is less intense. Facilities may be newer than those of many traditional department stores.

The year 2001 marked the first time that the chief executive officers (CEOs) of Wal-Mart (**www.walmart.com**), Target (**www.target.com**), and Kmart (**www.kmart.com**) each earned salaries of more than $1 million. That's only part of the story, as these numbers do not include bonus payments or earnings from exercising stock options:

- Target's chairperson and CEO had the highest overall compensation package. Although his salary was $1.4 million and his bonus amounted to $3.7 million, the real money was from his 625,000 stock options (worth $16 million at the time they were issued).
- Wal-Mart's president and CEO had total compensation that may appear to be somewhat modest, given the retailer's size. However, in addition to his salary of $1.123 million and $1.784 million bonus, the CEO received 521,634 stock options worth an estimated $13.6 million at the time the options were granted.
- Kmart's chairperson and CEO had his compensation package approved by the court, since Kmart was in bankruptcy. His annual salary of $1.5 million was greater than that of either of the CEOs at Target or Wal-Mart. He also was to get a bonus of $2.5 million just for coming to work, and he was eligible to receive an additional bonus of $1.875 million.

Source: Mike Troy, "Big Three CEOs Cross $1 Million Threshold: Big Money Lies in Options and 'Other,' " *DSN Retailing Today* (May 6, 2002), p. 3.

The greatest challenges facing full-line discount stores are the competition from other retailers (especially lower-priced discounters and category killers), too rapid expansion of some firms, saturation of prime locations, and the dominance of Wal-Mart, Kmart, and Target Stores. The industry has undergone a number of consolidations, bankruptcies, and liquidations.

Variety Store

A **variety store** handles an assortment of inexpensive and popularly priced goods and services, such as apparel and accessories, costume jewelry, notions and small wares, candy, toys, and other items in the price range. There are open displays and few salespeople. The stores do not carry full product lines, may not be departmentalized, and do not deliver products. Although the conventional variety store format has faded away, there are two successful spin-offs from it: dollar discount stores and closeout chains.

Dollar discount stores sell similar items to those in conventional variety stores but in plainer surroundings and at much lower prices. Thus, they are much more competitive and generate $12 to $15 billion in yearly sales. Dollar General and Family Dollar are the two leading dollar discount store chains. *Closeout chains* sell items to those in conventional variety stores but feature closeouts and overruns. They account for $5 billion annually. Big Lots is the leader in that category.[21]

The conventional variety store format (led by Woolworth and McCrory) disappeared from the U.S. marketplace in the mid-1990s after a long, successful run. What happened? There was heavy competition from specialty stores and discounters, most of the stores were older facilities, and some items had low profit margins. At one time, Woolworth had 1,200 variety stores with annual sales of $2 billion.

Off-Price Chain

An **off-price chain** features brand-name (sometimes designer) apparel and accessories, footwear (primarily women's and family), linens, fabrics, cosmetics, and/or housewares and sells them at everyday low prices in an efficient, limited-service environment. It frequently has community dressing rooms, centralized checkout counters, no gift wrapping, and extra charges for alterations. The chains buy merchandise opportunistically, as special deals occur. Other retailers' canceled orders, manufacturers' irregulars and overruns, and end-of-season items are often purchased for a fraction of their original wholesale prices. The total sales of U.S. off-price apparel stores are $33 billion. The four biggest chains are T.J. Maxx and Marshalls (both owned by TJX), Ross Stores, and Burlington Coat Factory.

TJX (www.tjx.com) operates two of the biggest off-price apparel chains: T.J. Maxx and Marshall's.

Off-price chains usually aim at the same shoppers as traditional department stores but with prices reduced by 40 to 50 percent. Shoppers are also lured by the promise of new merchandise on a regular basis: "They get new shipments every week. Go every week. If you see something you like, pick it up and don't put it down. Because if you don't buy it, someone else will."[22] In addition, off-price shopping centers now appeal to people's interest in one-stop shopping.

The most crucial strategic element for off-price chains involves buying merchandise and establishing long-term relationships with suppliers. To succeed, the chains must secure large quantities of merchandise at reduced wholesale prices and have a regular flow of goods into the stores. Sometimes manufacturers use off-price chains to sell samples, products that are not doing well when they are introduced, and merchandise remaining near the end of a season. At other times, off-price chains employ a more active buying strategy. Instead of waiting for closeouts and canceled orders, they convince manufacturers to make merchandise during off-seasons and pay cash for items early. Off-price chains are less demanding in terms of the support requested from suppliers, they do not return products, and they pay promptly.

Off-price chains face some market pressure because of competition from other institutional formats that run frequent sales throughout the year, the discontinuity of merchandise, poor management at some firms, insufficient customer service for some shoppers, and the shakeout of underfinanced companies.

Factory Outlet

A **factory outlet** is a manufacturer-owned store selling closeouts, discontinued merchandise, irregulars, canceled orders, and, sometimes, in-season, first-quality merchandise. Manufacturers' interest in outlet stores has risen for four basic reasons: (1) Manufacturers can control where their discounted merchandise is sold. By placing outlets in out-of-the-way spots with low sales penetration of the firm's brands, outlet revenues do not affect sales at key specialty and department store accounts. (2) Outlets are profitable despite prices up to 60 percent less than customary retail prices due to low operating costs—few services, low rent, limited displays, and plain store fixtures. (3) The manufacturer decides on store visibility, sets promotion policies, removes labels, and ensures that discontinued items and irregulars are disposed of properly. (4) Because many specialty and department stores are increasing private-label sales, manufacturers need revenue from outlet stores to sustain their own growth.

More factory stores now operate in clusters or in outlet malls to expand customer traffic, and they use cooperative ads. Large outlet malls are in Connecticut, Florida, Georgia, New York, Pennsylvania, Tennessee, and other states. There are 14,000 U.S. factory outlet stores representing 450 manufacturers, many in the 260 outlet malls nationwide, and these stores account for $14 billion in yearly sales with three-quarters from apparel and accessories.[23] Manufacturers with a major outlet presence include Bass (footwear), Brooks Brothers (apparel), Harry and David (fruits and gift items), Levi's (apparel), Liz Claiborne (apparel), Pepperidge Farm (food), Samsonite (luggage), and Totes (rain gear). See Figure 5-9.

FIGURE 5-9

Brooks Brothers: Realizing the Value of Factory Outlet Stores

The upscale Brooks Brothers has a number of outlet stores to attract value-driven shoppers.

Photo reprinted by permission of Retail Forward, Inc.

RETAILING Around the World — Factory Outlet Centers Are Booming Abroad

Factory outlet centers have been popular in the United States for years. However, this institutional format is only now starting to catch on in Europe. Today, there are nearly 100 factory outlets in Europe, compared with about 300 such centers in the United States.

One possible explanation is that in Europe the factory outlet center is run by developers, whereas in the United States, these centers are operated by individual retailers. Many experts believe that, unlike retailers, developers do not understand that "value hunter" outlet shoppers want to shop in comfort and expect a high level of customer support in their search for bargains. In addition, the lack of European outlet centers is due to restrictive zoning in several European countries and the power-

ful opposition of local retailers and manufacturers to the construction of outlet centers.

Recently, the number of European outlet centers has begun to rapidly increase. Although most U.S. factory outlet malls are located between two retail areas, over one-half of the European factory outlet malls are located at edge-of-town locations. About one-quarter of European shopping centers are located "in the middle of nowhere."

Source: Norma Cohen, "Creating a Warm, Fuzzy Feeling: Factory Outlet Centres Are Set to Do Well in Europe Only If They Are Able to Master the Art of U.S. Style Customer Service," *Financial Times* (August 31, 2001), p. 20.

When deciding whether to utilize factory outlets, manufacturers must be cautious. They must evaluate their retailing expertise, the investment costs, the impact on existing retailers that buy from them, and the response of consumers. Manufacturers do not want to jeopardize their products' sales at full retail prices.

Membership Club

A **membership (warehouse) club** appeals to price-conscious consumers, who must be members to shop there. It straddles the line between wholesaling and retailing. Some members are small business owners and employees who pay a membership fee to buy merchandise at wholesale prices. They make purchases for use in operating their firms or for personal use and yield 60 percent of club sales. Most members are final consumers who buy for their own use; they represent 40 percent of club sales. They also pay a fee and must belong to a union, be municipal employees, work for educational institutions, or belong to other specific groups to be members (in reality, eligibility is so broad as to exclude few people). Prices may be slightly more than for business customers. There are 1,200 U.S. membership clubs, with annual sales to final consumers of $30 billion. Costco and Sam's generate 90 percent of industry sales.[24]

Sam's (www.samsclub.com) is Wal-Mart's membership club division. It has lower prices and plainer settings than Wal-Mart's full-line discount stores.

The operating strategy of the modern membership club centers on large stores (up to 100,000 or more square feet), inexpensive isolated or industrial locations, opportunistic buying (with some merchandise discontinuity), a fraction of the items stocked by full-line discount stores, little advertising, plain fixtures, wide aisles to give forklift trucks access to shelves, concrete floors, limited delivery, fewer credit options, and very low prices. A typical club carries general merchandise, such as consumer electronics, appliances, computers, housewares, tires, and apparel (35 to 60 percent of sales); food (20 to 35 percent of sales); and sundries, such as health and beauty aids, tobacco, liquor, and candy (15 to 30 percent of sales). It may also have a pharmacy, photo developing, a car-buying service, a gasoline service station, and other items once viewed as frills for this format. Inventory turnover is several times that of a department store.

The major retailing challenges relate to the allocation of company efforts between business and final consumer accounts (without antagonizing one group or the other and without presenting a blurred store image), the lack of interest by many consumers in shopping at warehouse-type stores, the power of the two industry leaders, and the potential for saturation caused by overexpansion.

Flea Market

At a **flea market**, many retail vendors sell a range of products at discount prices in plain surroundings. It is rooted in the centuries-old tradition of street selling—shoppers touch and sample items, and haggle over prices. Vendors used to sell only antiques, bric-a-brac, and assorted used merchandise. Today, they also frequently sell new goods, such as clothing, cosmetics, watches, consumer electronics, housewares, and gift items. Many flea markets are located in non-traditional sites such as racetracks, stadiums, and arenas. Some are at sites abandoned by other retailers. Typically, vendors rent space. A flea market might rent individual spaces for $30 to $100 or more per day, depending on location. Some flea markets impose a parking fee or admission charge for shoppers.

There are a few hundred major U.S. flea markets, but overall sales data are not available. The credibility of permanent flea markets, consumer interest in bargaining, the broader product mix, the availability of brand-name goods, and the low prices all contribute to the format's appeal. The Rose Bowl Flea Market (**www.rgcshows.com/rosebowl.asp**) has 2,000 vendors and attracts 20,000 shoppers a day:

> The flea market is held the second Sunday of every month. The only restricted items are food, animals, guns, ammunition, and pornography. The price of available selling space is as follows: Our best available high-traffic spaces are $100.00 reserved pink spaces located around the main perimeter. Also, for new merchandise sellers, we have $60.00 yellow spaces located in a section by the front of the main entrance. We also have $80.00 reserved white spaces located across a bridge from our other flea market areas, in the front half and prime areas of the white section. Any type of merchandise can be sold, including antiques, used clothing, and new merchandise. The $50.00 unreserved white spaces are assigned the morning of the event. They are located in the rear portion of the white section. Regular admission for the general public is $7.00 per person; children under 12 are free with an adult.

At a flea market, price haggling is encouraged, cash is the predominant currency, and many vendors gain their first real experience as retail entrepreneurs. The newest trend involves nonstore, Web-based flea markets such as eBay (**www.ebay.com**) and Amazon.com with its zShops.

Many traditional retailers believe flea markets represent an unfair method of competition because the quality of merchandise may be misrepresented, consumers may buy items at flea markets and return them to other retailers for higher refunds, suppliers are often unaware their products are sold there, sales taxes can be easily avoided, and operating costs are quite low. Flea markets may also cause traffic congestion.

The high sales volume from off-price chains, factory outlets, membership clubs, and flea markets is explained by the wheel of retailing. These institutions are low-cost operators appealing the price-conscious consumers who are not totally satisfied with other retail formats that have upgraded their merchandise and customer service, raised prices, and moved along the wheel.

Summary

1. *To describe the wheel of retailing, scrambled merchandising, and the retail life cycle and show how they can help explain the performance of retail strategy mixes.* In Chapter 4, retail institutions were examined by ownership. This chapter uses a store-based strategic retailing perspective. A retail strategy mix involves a combination of factors: location, operations, goods/services offered, pricing, atmosphere and customer services, and promotion. To flourish, a firm should strive to be dominant in some way and, thus, reach destination retailer status.

Three important concepts help explain the performance of diverse retail strategies. According to the wheel of retailing, retail innovators often first appear as low-price operators with low costs and low profit margins. Over time, they upgrade their offerings and customer services and raise prices. They are then vulnerable to new discounters with lower costs that take their place along the wheel. With scrambled merchandising, a retailer adds goods and services that are unrelated to each other and its original business to increase overall sales and profits. Scrambled merchandising is contagious and often used in self-defense. The retail life cycle states that institutions pass through identifiable stages of introduction, growth, maturity, and decline. Strategies change as institutions mature.

2. *To discuss some ways in which retail strategy mixes are evolving.* Many institutions are adapting to marketplace dynamics. These approaches have been popular for various firms, depending on their strengths, weaknesses, and goals: mergers—by which separately owned retailers join together; diversification—by which a retailer becomes active in business outside its normal operations; and downsizing—whereby unprofitable stores are closed

or divisions sold. Sometimes, single companies use all three approaches. More firms also utilize cost containment and value-driven retailing. They strive to hold down both investment and operating costs. There are many ways to do this.

3. *To examine a wide variety of food-oriented retailers involved with store-based strategy mixes.* Retail institutions may be classified by store-based strategy mix and divided into food-oriented and general merchandise groups. Fourteen store-based strategy mixes are covered in this chapter.

These are the food-oriented store-based retailers: A convenience store is well located, is open long hours, and offers a moderate number of fill-in items at average to above-average prices. A conventional supermarket is departmentalized and carries a wide range of food and related items, there is little general merchandise, and prices are competitive. A food-based superstore is larger and more diversified than a conventional supermarket but smaller and less diversified than a combination store. A combination store unites supermarket and general merchandise in a large facility and sets competitive prices; the food-based supercenter (hypermarket) is a type of combination store. The box (limited-line)

store is a discounter focusing on a small selection, moderate hours, few services, and few manufacturer brands. A warehouse store is a discounter offering a moderate number of food items in a no-frills setting that can be quite large.

4. *To study a wide range of general merchandise retailers involved with store-based strategy mixes.* These are the general merchandise store-based retailers: A specialty store concentrates on one goods or service line and has a tailored strategy; the category killer is a special kind of specialty store. A department store is a large retailer with an extensive assortment of goods and services. The traditional one has a range of customer services and average to above-average prices. A full-line discount store is a department store with a low-cost, low-price strategy. A variety store has inexpensive and popularly priced items in a plain setting. An off-price chain features brand-name items and sells them at low prices in an austere environment. A factory outlet is manufacturer-owned and sells closeouts, discontinued merchandise, and irregulars at very low prices. A membership club appeals to price-conscious shoppers who must be members to shop. A flea market has many vendors offering items at discount prices in nontraditional venues.

Key Terms

strategy mix (p. 105)
destination retailer (p. 105)
wheel of retailing (p. 105)
scrambled merchandising (p. 106)
retail life cycle (p. 108)
mergers (p. 110)
diversification (p. 110)
downsizing (p. 111)
convenience store (p. 112)

supermarket (p. 114)
conventional supermarket (p. 114)
food-based superstore (p. 115)
combination store (p. 116)
supercenter (p. 116)
hypermarket (p. 116)
box (limited-line) store (p. 116)
warehouse store (p. 116)
specialty store (p. 118)

category killer (power retailer) (p. 118)
department store (p. 119)
traditional department store (p. 119)
full-line discount store (p. 120)
variety store (p. 121)
off-price chain (p. 121)
factory outlet (p. 122)
membership (warehouse) club (p. 123)
flea market (p. 123)

Questions for Discussion

1. Describe how a small TV repair store could be a destination retailer.

2. Explain the wheel of retailing. Is this theory applicable today? Why or why not?

3. Develop a high-end retail strategy mix for a shoe store. Include location, operating procedures, goods/services offered, pricing tactics, and promotion methods.

4. How could these retailers best apply scrambled merchandising? Explain your answers.
   a. Diner.
   b. Dry cleaner.
   c. Car wash.
   d. Music store.

5. What strategic emphasis should be used by institutions in the growth stage of the retail life cycle compared with the emphasis by institutions in the decline stage?

6. Contrast the strategy mixes of convenience stores, conventional supermarkets, food-based superstores, and warehouse stores. Is there room for each? Explain your answer.

7. Do you think U.S. combination stores (supercenters) will dominate grocery retailing? Why or why not?

8. What are the pros and cons of Sports Authority operating 40,000+-square-foot stores?

9. Contrast the strategy mixes of specialty stores, traditional department stores, and full-line discount stores.

10. What must the off-price chain do to succeed in the future?

11. Do you expect factory outlet stores to keep growing? Explain your answer.

12. Comment on the decision of many membership clubs to begin selling gasoline.

Web-Based Exercise

Visit the Web site of Amazon.com (**www.amazon.com**). In your view, (a) where is Amazon.com positioned along the wheel of retailing and (b) how would you describe its use of scrambled merchandising? Explain whether you think that Amazon.com is doing the right thing in terms of these two concepts.

Note: Stop by our Web site (**www.prenhall.com/bermanevans/ webexercises**) to experience a number of highly interactive, appealing Web exercises based on actual company demonstrations and sample materials related to retailing.

Chapter Endnotes

1. Various company sources.

2. The pioneering works on the wheel of retailing are Malcolm P. McNair, "Significant Trends and Developments in the Postwar Period," in A. B. Smith (Editor), *Competitive Distribution in a Free High Level Economy and Its Implications for the University* (Pittsburgh: University of Pittsburgh Press, 1958), pp. 17–18; and Stanley Hollander, "The Wheel of Retailing," *Journal of Marketing*, Vol. 25 (July 1960), pp. 37–42. For further analysis of the concept, see Stephen Brown, "The Wheel of Retailing: Past and Future," *Journal of Retailing*, Vol. 66 (Summer 1990), pp. 143–149; and Stephen Brown, "Postmodernism, the Wheel of Retailing, and Will to Power," *International Review of Retail, Distribution, and Consumer Research*, Vol. 5 (July 1995), pp. 387–414.

3. For an interesting review of Wal-Mart's founding and evolution, see "The Class of '62," *Chain Store Age* (August 2002), pp. 41–79.

4. Dina Elboghdady, "Sears, J.C. Penney Taking Different Paths to Survival," *Houston Chronicle* (April 21, 2002), p. 6.

5. Susan Hodara, "Bananas. Click. Paper Towels. Click." *New York Times* (June 9, 2002), Section 14WC, p. 3.

6. "Projected Retail Revenues Earned Via Kiosks, 2000–2006," **www.kiomag.com/sf9** (February 17, 2003).

7. "Last Catalog Showroom Retailer Now in Liquidation," *Knight Ridder/Tribune Business News* (February 3, 2002).

8. Elaine Pollack, "Asset Intensification: Doing More with What You Have in the Next Economy," 2002 Strategic Outlook Conference (Columbus, OH: Retail Forward, Inc., 2002), p. 14.

9. "Retailing: General," *Standard & Poor's Industry Surveys* (May 9, 2002), p. 12.

10. *2002 State of the Industry* (Alexandria, VA: National Association of Convenience Stores, 2002).

11. Various issues of *Progressive Grocer*; and Food Marketing Institute, "Facts & Figures," **www.fmi.org/facts_figs/superfact.htm**.

12. Ibid.

13. Ibid.

14. Ibid.

15. Ibid.

16. Computed by the authors from David P. Schulz, "Triversity Top 100 Specialty Stores," *Stores* (August 2002), various pages.

17. "Sports Authority," *Standard & Poor's Corporate Descriptions Plus News* (August 3, 2002).

18. "Retailing: Specialty," *Standard & Poor's Industry Surveys* (January 31, 2002), p. 16.

19. *Annual Benchmark Report for Retail Trade and Food Services: January 1992 to March 2002* (Washington, DC: Department of Commerce, 2002).

20. "The DSN Retailing Today Annual Industry Report," *DSN Retailing Today* (July 8, 2002), various pages.

21. Ibid.

22. Chris Reidy, "T.J. Maxx Aims for More Returns," *Boston Globe* (May 25, 2001), p. C3.

23. "Outlet Industry Data," **www.valueretailnews.com/research/ research_index.htm** (January 18, 2003).

24. "The DSN Retailing Today Annual Industry Report," various pages.

Chapter 6

WEB, NONSTORE-BASED, AND OTHER FORMS OF NONTRADITIONAL RETAILING

Reprinted by permission.

A decade ago, after learning that Web usage was growing at 2,300 percent per year, Jeff Bezos analyzed a list of the 20 best products to sell online. Books topped the list, in large part due to the vast number of titles available. After deciding to sell books, Bezos moved to Seattle, due to the large number of computer professionals located there. He created an online strategy based on the concept of creating a place where people could not only find and buy any book they wanted but also get great customer service. To Bezos, the three most important components of this strategy were and still are service, selection, and price.

Sales for Amazon.com (**www.amazon.com**) took off immediately, as the firm concentrated on books and sought to have the largest selection of books that could be found anywhere.

Almost from the start, industry analysts believed that Amazon.com's Web site had several distinctive advantages: an emphasis on information over graphics; a separate page for each book, including a brief description; customer reviews; and, sometimes, author interviews.

Although Amazon.com started off selling books, it has since branched out into many other product lines, such as electronics, small appliances, a bridal registry, and toys from Toys "R" Us. It also partners with Target Stores. In essence, it is now an online department store.

Because of its heavy investment in technology, infrastructure, and expansion, Amazon.com did not earn an operating profit until the first quarter of 2002—after losing $545 million in 2001. Through productivity enhancements, Amazon.com reduced operating expenses by 30 percent, while still maintaining double-digit revenue growth.[1]

chapter objectives

1. To contrast single-channel and multi-channel retailing
2. To look at the characteristics of the three major retail institutions involved with nonstore-based strategy mixes: direct marketing, direct selling, and vending machines—with an emphasis on direct marketing
3. To explore the emergence of electronic retailing through the World Wide Web
4. To discuss two other nontraditional forms of retailing: video kiosks and airport retailing

OVERVIEW

In this chapter, we contrast single-channel and multi-channel retailing and then examine non-store-based retailing, electronic retailing, and two other types of nontraditional retailing: video kiosks and airport retailing. These formats influence the strategies of current store retailers and newly formed retailers. Visit our Web site (**www.prenhall.com/bermanevans**) for links on a variety of nonstore and nontraditional topics.

When it begins, a retailer often relies on **single-channel retailing**, whereby it sells to consumers through one retail format. That one format may be store-based (a corner shoe store) or nonstore-based (catalog retailing, direct selling, or Web retailing). As the firm grows, it may turn to **multi-channel retailing**, whereby a retailer sells to consumers through multiple retail formats. Retail leader Wal-Mart sells through stores (including Wal-Mart stores, Sam's Club, and Neighborhood Market) and a Web site (**www.walmart.com**). Multi-channel retailing enables a firm to reach different customer groups, share costs among various formats, and diversify its supplier base. Figure 6-1 shows examples of single-channel and multi-channel retailing.

From its roots as a full-line discount store chain, Wal-Mart (www.walmart.com) has become a master of multi-channel retailing.

Why have we introduced this concept here? Because even though some nonstore-based firms are "pure players" (single-channel retailers), a rapidly growing number of firms are combining store and nonstore retailing to actively pursue multi-channel retailing:

With the advent of the World Wide Web and E-Commerce, consumers have more ways to shop, select, and buy products than before. From department stores to specialty retailers to independent shops, firms are using two to three channels in bringing merchandise to customers, as well as attracting new and existing customers to their real and virtual stores. Besides their physical stores, many retailers use direct communications including mailers, catalogs, Web sites, and E-mail to drive sales. Operating with multiple channels creates numerous challenges and the decision making also becomes more complex, since the channels often interact at the discretion of the customer.[2]

The technologies that offer this kind of integrated experience also facilitate more efficient uses of personnel, warehousing, and fulfillment resources by providing "anytime, anywhere, any way" access to data. Instead of inefficiently calling store after store to find an item that a customer has requested, store personnel can find it online at another store or the warehouse and have it shipped to the customer or another physical store. Retailers are also able to better leverage their distributed inventories, reducing out-of-stocks and markdowns while improving margins and inventory turns.[3]

FIGURE 6-1

Approaches to Retailing Channels

Examples of Single-Channel Retailing

Store-based retailer, such as a local apparel store, operating only one store format	Mail-order sporting goods retailer selling only through catalogs	Online CD/DVD retailer that only does business through the Web

Examples of Multi-Channel Retailing

Store-based retailer, such as a local gift store, also selling through catalogs	Store-based retailer, such as a jewelry store, also selling through the Web	Store-based retailer, such as Toys "R" Us, affiliating with a Web-based firm, such as Amazon.com
Store-based retailer, such as a local gift store, also selling through catalogs and the Web	Store-based retailer, such as a jewelry store, also selling through the Web and leased departments in select department stores	Store-based retailer, such as Toys "R" Us, affiliating with a Web-based firm, such as Amazon.com, and operating multiple store formats (Kids "R" Us)

FIGURE 6-2

Home Depot: Combining Bricks-and-Mortar with Clicks-and-Mortar

Home Depot uses a full-feature Web site (**www.homedepot.com**) to complement its category killer chain of stores. The site serves several purposes, besides selling products. It offers gift cards, provides detailed hints on how to undertake various do-it-yourself home improvement projects (with suggestions about the best tools and supplies to complete these projects), and gives store locations and directions.

Reprinted by permission.

The ever-popular eBay (www.ebay.com) is a pure Web retailer.

Retailers—single-channel or multi-channel—engage in **nonstore retailing** when they use strategy mixes that are not store-based to reach consumers and complete transactions. Nonstore retailing sales exceed $300 billion annually, with 78 percent of that from direct marketing (hence, the direct marketing emphasis in this chapter). The fastest-growing form of direct marketing involves electronic (Web-based) retailing. From sales of $500 million in 1996 and $50 billion in 2001, Web retailing is expected to reach revenues of $150 billion in 2006. As one expert says: "There is still a perception that online retailing is faltering, but it is actually the reverse. Consumers love buying online and are shifting purchases from offline to online—even though their overall spending might not be growing."[4] See Figure 6-2.

Nontraditional retailing also comprises video kiosks and airport retailing, two key formats not fitting neatly into "store-based" or "nonstore-based" retailing. Sometimes they are store-based; other times they are not. What they have in common is their departure from traditional retailing strategies.

DIRECT MARKETING

Direct (www.directmag.com) and *Catalog Age* (www.catalogagemag.com) are two vital sources of direct marketing information.

In **direct marketing**, a customer is first exposed to a good or service through a nonpersonal medium (direct mail, TV, radio, magazine, newspaper, or computer) and then orders by mail, phone or fax—and increasingly by computer. Annual U.S. sales are $235 billion (including the Web), and more than half of adults make at least one such purchase a year. Japan, Germany, Great Britain, France, and Italy are among the direct marketing leaders outside the United States.[5] Popular products are gift items, apparel, magazines, books and music, sports equipment, home accessories, food, and insurance.

In the United States, direct marketing customers are more apt to be married, upper middle class, and 36 to 50 years of age. Mail shoppers are more likely to live in areas far from malls. Phone shoppers are more likely to live in upscale metropolitan areas, and they want to avoid traffic and save time. Although the share of direct marketing purchases made by men has been small, it is growing: Nearly 40 percent of catalog shoppers are now men. The average consumer who buys direct spends several hundred dollars per year, and he or she most desires convenience, unique merchandise, and good prices.[6]

FIGURE 6-3

Micro Warehouse: Specializing in Personal Computers and Accessories

Micro Warehouse is a specialty direct marketer. But specialty does not mean small. The company offers more than 30,000 different microcomputer hardware, software, and peripheral products and supplies. As one satisfied customer says, "It doesn't matter what I need or when I need it, Micro Warehouse has the products, and it's always able to deliver them immediately."

Reprinted by permission.

Direct marketers can be divided into two broad categories: general and specialty. General direct marketing firms offer a full line of products and sell everything from clothing to housewares. J.C. Penney (with its mail-order and Web businesses) and QVC (with its cable TV and Web businesses) are general direct marketers. Specialty direct marketers focus on more narrow product lines. L.L. Bean, Publishers Clearinghouse, and Franklin Mint are among the thousands of U.S. specialty firms. See Figure 6-3.

Direct marketing has a number of strategic business advantages:

- Many costs are reduced—low startup costs are possible; inventories are reduced; no displays are needed; a prime location is unnecessary; regularly staffed store hours are not important; a sales force may not be needed; and business may be run out of a garage or basement.

- It is possible for direct marketers to have lower prices (due to reduced costs) than store-based retailers with the same items. A huge area can be covered inexpensively and efficiently.

- Customers shop conveniently—without crowds, parking congestion, or checkout lines. And they do not have safety concerns about shopping early in the morning or late at night.

- Specific consumer segments are pinpointed through targeted mailings.

- Consumers may sometimes legally avoid sales tax by buying from direct marketers not having retail facilities in their state (however, some states want to eliminate this loophole).

- A store-based firm can supplement its regular business and expand its trading area (even becoming national or global) without adding outlets.

Careers in RETAILING — Founding an Online MVP

Mary Naylor operates an Internet concierge service, VIPdesk (**www.vipdesk.com**), that secures theater and sporting event tickets, sends flowers, and does other chores for its corporate client customers. In its first two years of business, VIPdesk's revenues nearly tripled. Today, it has nearly 100 employees. About 10.5 million people now have access to VIPdesk. This performance is remarkable given that it has occurred during a time when many Web firms have gone out of business or drastically curtailed their operations.

Among VIPdesk's corporate clients are MasterCard International and Citibank. Customers of those corporate clients who have access to VIPdesk as a benefit can place a request for one of its concierge services via phone, a wireless handheld device, or the Web. The request goes directly to a VIPdesk employee located in the field or to VIPdesk's call center, and it is ultimately processed by one of VIPdesk's local business partners in an average of 30 minutes.

VIPdesk started out by raising $7.5 million, about one-third of Naylor's initial goal. Because the firm was prepared, it had several different marketing plans based on funding levels, so Naylor reduced her spending on technology and marketing. She also had to reduce her expansion plans. Naylor hopes to soon work with more strategic partners.

Source: Toddi Gutner, "A Dot-Com's Survival Store," *Business Week* (May 13, 2002), p. 122.

Direct marketing also has its limits, but they are not as critical as those for direct selling:

- Products cannot be examined before purchase. Thus, the range of items purchased is more limited than in stores, and firms need liberal return policies to attract and keep customers.
- Prospective firms may underestimate costs. Catalogs can be expensive. A computer system is required to track shipments, monitor purchases and returns, and keep mailing lists current. A 24-hour phone staff may be needed.
- Even successful catalogs draw purchases from less than 10 percent of recipients.
- Clutter exists. Each year, billions of catalogs are mailed in the United States alone.
- Printed catalogs are prepared well in advance, causing difficulties in price and style planning.
- Some firms have given the industry a bad name due to delivery delays and shoddy goods.

The full 30-day rule is available online (www. ftc.gov/bcp/conline/pubs/ buspubs/mailorder.htm).

The Federal Trade Commission's "30-day rule" is a U.S. regulation that affects direct marketers. It requires firms to ship orders within 30 days of their receipt or notify customers of delays. If an order cannot be shipped in 60 days, the customer must be given a specific delivery date and offered the option of canceling an order or waiting for it to be filled. The rule covers mail, phone, fax, and computer orders.

Despite its limitations, good long-run growth for direct marketing is projected. Consumer interest in convenience and the difficulty in setting aside shopping time will continue. More direct marketers will offer 24-hour ordering and improve their efficiency. Greater product standardization and the prominence of well-known brands will reduce consumer perceptions of risk when buying from a catalog or the Web. Technological breakthroughs, such as purchases on the Web, will attract more consumer shopping.

Due to its vast presence and immense potential, our detailed discussion is intended to give you an in-depth look into direct marketing. Let us study the domain of direct marketing, emerging trends, steps in a direct marketing strategy, and key issues facing direct marketers.

THE DOMAIN OF DIRECT MARKETING

As defined earlier, *direct marketing* is a form of retailing in which a consumer is exposed to a good or service through a nonpersonal medium and then orders by mail, phone, fax, or computer. It may also be viewed as "an interactive system that uses one or more advertising media to effect a measurable response and/or transaction at any location, with this activity stored on a data base."[7]

Accordingly, we *do* include these as forms of direct marketing: any catalog; any mail, TV, radio, magazine, newspaper, phone directory, fax, or other ad; any computer-based transaction; or any other nonpersonal contact that stimulates customers to place orders by mail, phone, fax, or computer.

We *do not* include these as forms of direct marketing: direct selling, whereby consumers are solicited by in-person sales efforts or seller-originated phone calls, and the firm uses personal

---

Technology in RETAILING | Petco: Making Online Searching Easier for Customers

Petco (**www.petco.com**) is a leading retailer of premium pet food, supplies, and services. Petco, a publicly-held company, currently operates hundreds of stores in more than 40 states and in Washington, D.C. The chain recently selected the IntuiFind software package from Mercado (**www.mercado.com**) for its Web site's search engine. As a Petco spokesperson said, "We have installed Mercado Software's IntuiFind search engine software to help us provide superior customer service. With IntuiFind, our online customers get relevant results as they search through one of the most complete selections of pet-related products online."

IntuiFind enables consumers to easily find desired items or information on a content-rich Web site. For example, a Petco customer can type such words as "birds" and "food" in the search field. The search engine then produces the most relevant articles on bird foods, as well as articles on bird feeding and care.

The search engine is equipped to handle spelling errors and alternative terms through its use of both a powerful thesaurus and alternative spelling data bases. IntuiFind can be utilized for structured and unstructured Web content. A demonstration of IntuiFind software can be found at the Mercado Web site (**www.mercado.com/customers/demos**).

Source: "Petco.com Selected Mercado Software's IntuiFind; Software Helps Petco's Online Customers Find Relevant Search Results Faster," *Business Wire* (January 14, 2002).

communication to initiate contact; and conventional vending machines, whereby consumers are exposed to nonpersonal media but do not complete transactions via mail, phone, fax, or computer, and do not interact with the firm in a manner that allows a data base to be generated and kept.

Direct marketing *is* involved in many computerized kiosk transactions; when items are mailed to consumers, there is a company–customer interaction and a data base can be formed. Direct marketing is also in play when consumers originate phone calls, based on catalogs or ads they have seen.

THE CUSTOMER DATA BASE: KEY TO SUCCESSFUL DIRECT MARKETING

Because direct marketers initiate contact with customers (in contrast to store shopping trips that are initiated by the consumer), it is imperative that they develop and maintain a comprehensive customer data base. They can then pinpoint their best customers, make offers aimed at specific customer needs, avoid costly mailings to nonresponsive shoppers, and track sales by customer. A good data base is the major asset of most direct marketers; and *every* thriving direct marketer has a strong data base.

Data-base retailing is a way to collect, store, and use relevant information about customers. Such information typically includes a person's name, address, background data, shopping interests, and purchase behavior. Though data bases are often compiled through large computerized information systems, they may also be used by small firms that are not overly computerized.

Here's how data-base retailing can be beneficial:

> In many situations, 80 percent of sales are made to 20 percent of customers. With data-base retailing, a firm could identify those 20 percent and better satisfy them by superior product selection, special sales, and more personalized correspondence. The firm could also identify and pay greater attention to the next 40 percent of its customers, an often-ignored group. In addition, the company could learn which people no longer patronize it and which shop less often. Those people may be called or sent cordial letters to see why they are no longer shopping or shopping less; and the retailer could then undertake special promotions. What's the key to successful data-base retailing? It must be viewed as a beneficial tool—not as a burdensome chore. Knowledge is power and power leads to profits.[8]

Data-base retailing is discussed further in Chapter 8.

EMERGING TRENDS

Several trends are relevant for direct marketing: the evolving activities of direct marketers, changing consumer life-styles, increased competition, the greater use of dual distribution channels, the newer roles for catalogs and TV, technological advances, and the interest in global direct marketing.

Evolving Activities of Direct Marketers

Over the past 25 years, these direct marketing activities have evolved:

- Technology has moved to the forefront in all aspects of direct marketing—from lead generation to order processing.
- Multi-channel retailing is utilized by many more firms today.
- There is an increased focus on data-base retailing.
- Many more firms now have well-articulated and widely communicated privacy policies.[9]

Changing Consumer Life-Styles

American consumers' life-styles have shifted dramatically over the past 35 years, mostly due to the large number of women who are now in the labor force and the longer commuting time to and from work for suburban residents. Many consumers no longer have the time or inclination to shop at stores. They are attracted by the ease of purchasing through direct marketing. A recent survey of catalog shoppers found that 33 percent feel catalog shopping is more satisfying than store shopping, 56 percent think the two formats are equally satisfying, and only 11 percent believe store shopping is more satisfying.[10]

These are some of the factors consumers consider in selecting a direct marketer:

- Company reputation (image).
- Ability to shop whenever the consumer wants.
- Types of goods and services, as well as the assortment and brand names carried.
- Availability of a toll-free phone number or Web site for ordering.
- Credit card acceptance.
- Speed of promised delivery time.
- Competitive prices.
- Satisfaction with past purchases and good return policies.

Increased Competition Among Firms

As direct marketing sales have risen, so has competition; and although there are a number of big firms, such as J.C. Penney and Spiegel, there are also thousands of small ones. The Direct Marketing Association estimates that there are over 10,000 U.S. mail-order companies.

Spiegel (www.spiegel.com) has largely been a direct marketer since the early 1900s. It faces more competition now than ever before.

Intense competition exists because entry into direct marketing is easier and less costly than entry into store retailing. A firm does not need a store; can operate with a small staff; and can use low-cost one-inch magazine ads, send brochures to targeted shoppers, and have an inexpensive Web site. It can keep a low inventory and place orders with suppliers after people buy items (as long as it meets the 30-day rule).

About one out of every two new direct marketers fails. Direct marketing lures many small firms that may poorly define their market niche, offer nondistinctive goods and services, have limited experience, misjudge the needed effort, have trouble with supplier continuity, and attract many consumer complaints.

Greater Use of Multi-Channel Retailing

Today, many stores add to their revenues by using ads, brochures, catalogs, and Web sites to obtain mail-order, phone, and computer-generated sales. They see that direct marketing is efficient, targets specific segments, appeals to people who might not otherwise shop with those firms, and needs a lower investment to reach other geographic areas than opening branch outlets.

Bloomingdale's and Nordstrom are two store-based retailers that have successfully entered direct marketing. Bloomingdale's by Mail has a loyal target market and a customer data base of 3 million people. Nordstrom's The Catalog capitalizes on the firm's customer service reputation: toll-free 24-hour shopping, delivery by Federal Express, and complimentary gift boxes. Yet, while Nordstrom's Web site (**www.nordstrom.com**) has had good sales results, in 2002, Bloomingdale's Web site (**www.bloomingdales.com**) was dramatically scaled back. Today, it is used mostly for customer relations and image purchases—and does very little selling.

Newer Roles for Catalogs and TV

Direct marketers are recasting the ways in which they use their catalogs and their approach to TV retailing. Here's how.

We are witnessing three key changes in long-standing catalog tactics: (1) Many firms now print "specialogs" in addition to or instead of the annual catalogs showing all of their products. With a **specialog**, a retailer caters to a particular customer segment, emphasizes a limited number of items, and reduces production and postage costs (as a specialog is much shorter than a general catalog). Each year, such firms as Spiegel, L.L. Bean, and Travelsmith send out separate specialogs by market segment or occasion. (2) To help defray costs, some companies accept ads from non-competing firms that are compatible with their image. For instance, Bloomingdale's by Mail has had ads for fine liquors and luxury cars. (3) To stimulate sales and defray costs, some catalogs are sold in bookstores, supermarkets, and airports, and at company Web sites. The percentage of consumers buying a catalog who actually make a product purchase is many times higher than that for those who get catalogs in the mail.

TV retailing has two components: shopping networks and infomercials. On a *shopping network*, the programming focuses on merchandise presentations and their sales (usually by phone). The two biggest players are cable giants QVC and Home Shopping Network (HSN), with combined annual worldwide revenues of $6 billion. Each firm has access to a global TV audience of 125 million households. About 10 percent of U.S. consumers buy goods through TV shopping programs each year. Once regarded as a medium primarily for shut-ins and the lower middle class, the typical TV-based shopper is now younger, more fashion-conscious, and as apt to be from a high-income household as the overall U.S. population. QVC and HSN feature jewelry, women's clothing, and personal-care products, and do not stress nationally recognized brands. Most items must be bought as they are advertised to encourage consumers to act immediately. The firms also have active Web sites (**www.qvc.com** and **www.hsn.com**).[11]

An **infomercial** is a program-length TV commercial (typically, 30 minutes) for a specific good or service that airs on cable or broadcast television, often at a fringe time. As they watch an infomercial, shoppers call in orders, which are delivered to them. Infomercials work well for products that benefit from demonstrations. The best infomercials present detailed information, include customer testimonials, are entertaining, and are divided into timed segments (since the average viewer watches only a few minutes of the "show" at a time) with ordering information displayed in every segment. Infomercials account for over $1 billion in annual U.S. revenues. Extremely successful infomercials include those for the Ronco Rotisserie, the George Foreman Grill, Time-Life books, and a variety of exercise equipment. The Electronic Retailing Association (**www.retailing.org**) is the trade association for infomercial firms.

Ron Popeil has become a very rich man through his Ronco (http://shop. ronco.com) infomercials.

Technological Advances

A technological revolution is improving operating efficiency and offering enhanced sales opportunities:

- Market segments can be better targeted. Through selective binding, longer catalogs are sent to the best customers and shorter catalogs to new prospects.
- Firms inexpensively use computers to enter mail and phone orders, arrange for shipments, and monitor inventory on hand.
- It is simple to set up and maintain computerized data bases using inexpensive software.
- Huge, automated distribution centers efficiently accumulate and ship orders.
- Customers dial toll-free phone numbers or visit Web sites to place orders and get information. The cost per call for the direct marketer is quite low.
- Consumers can conclude transactions from more sites, including kiosks at airports and train stations.
- Cable TV programming and the Web offer 24-hour shopping and ordering.
- Both in-home and at-work Web-based shopping transactions can be conducted.

Mounting Interest in Global Direct Marketing

Lands' End has many different Web sites to service customers around the world, such as its German site (www.landsend.de). Because of Lands' End's customer commitment, this site is in German.

More retailers are involved with global direct marketing because of the growing consumer acceptance of nonstore retailing in other countries. Among the U.S.-based direct marketers with a significant international presence are Eddie Bauer, Lands' End, Sharper Image, and Williams-Sonoma.

Outside the United States, annual retail mail-order sales (by both domestic and foreign firms) exceed $150 billion. Although German and Japanese consumers account for nearly half of that spending, there are a number of emerging areas, including China, Brazil, South Africa, France, and Spain. Consider this:

With proper research, and country-specific execution, global direct marketing can pay big dividends. For U.S. retailers seeking to connect with overseas customers, response rates can

According to a study by Gartner (**www.gartner.com**), a marketing research firm that specializes in online sales, the online retail market in Europe is forecast to grow from 2.3 percent of total retail sales in 2002 to 5.6 percent in 2005. Nonetheless, the firm warns European retailers to carefully focus their efforts at a specific target market rather than use a broader approach.

A Gartner executive says, "The true opportunity comes from using real-time interactivity with shoppers to drive customers to the most convenient sales channel for them, on or offline, and to drive loyalty, branding, and customer satisfaction." Gartner predicts that, as of 2005, 73 percent of online shopping will be conducted via the PC, 17 percent via digital television, and 10 percent through mobile devices.

Gartner believes that the European retailer needs to better understand the benefits of a multi-channel approach to online sales. For example, although digital television may not be the ideal medium for selling and the mobile phone does not have display capability, they each have a role in improving and maintaining customer relationships. Their contribution to the firm should be measured in objectives other than sales. Retailers also need to create the proper balance between online and offline channels.

Source: "European Online Shopping Market Prediction," *Gartner Press Release* (March 19, 2002).

double the numbers typically received in the United States. Why? There is much less mailbox clutter worldwide. The stability of a market and its currency are important when determining where to implement your international direct mail strategy. Other market considerations include the regulatory environment, political situation, fiscal and tax policies, population spread, and infrastructure development.[12]

THE STEPS IN A DIRECT MARKETING STRATEGY

A direct marketing strategy has eight steps: business definition, generating customers, media selection, presenting the message, customer contact, customer response, order fulfillment, and measuring results and maintaining the data base. See Figure 6-4.

Business Definition

First, a company makes two decisions regarding its business definition: (1) Is the firm going to be a pure direct marketer or is it going to engage in multi-channel retailing? If the firm chooses the latter, it must clarify the role of direct marketing in its overall retail strategy. (2) Is the firm going to be a general direct marketer and carry a broad product assortment, or will it specialize in one goods/service category?

FIGURE 6-4
Executing a Direct
Marketing Strategy

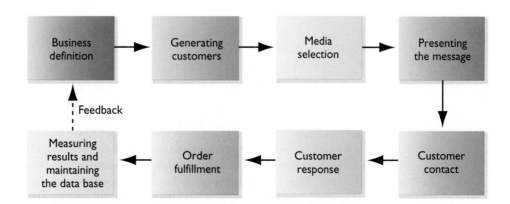

Generating Customers

A mechanism for generating business is devised next. A firm can

- Buy a printed mailing list from a broker. For one mailing, a list usually costs $50 to $100 or more per 1,000 names and addresses; it is supplied in mailing-label format. Lists may be broad or broken down by gender, location, and so on. In purchasing a list, the direct marketer should check its currency.

- Download a mailing list from the Web that is sold by a firm such as infoUSA (**www.infoUSA.com**), which has data on 120 million U.S. households. With a download, a firm can use the list multiple times, but it is responsible for selecting names and printing labels.

- Send out a blind mailing to all the residents in a particular area. This method can be expensive (unless done through E-mail) and may receive a very low response rate.

- Advertise in a newspaper, magazine, Web site, or other medium and ask customers to order by mail, phone, fax, or computer.

- Contact consumers who have bought from the firm or requested information. This is efficient, but it takes a while to develop a data base. To grow, a firm cannot rely solely on past customers.

Media Selection

Several media are available to the direct marketer:

- Printed catalogs.
- Direct mail ads and brochures.
- Inserts with monthly credit card and other bills ("statement stuffers").
- Freestanding displays with coupons, brochures, or catalogs (such as magazine subscription cards at the supermarket checkout counter).
- Ads or programs in the mass media—newspapers, magazines, radio, TV.
- Banner ads or "hot links" on the World Wide Web.
- Video kiosks.

In choosing among media, costs, distribution, lead time, and other factors should be considered.

Presenting the Message

Now, the firm prepares and presents its message in a way that engenders interest, creates (or sustains) the proper image, points out compelling reasons to purchase, and provides data about goods or services (such as prices and sizes). The message must also contain ordering instructions, including the payment method, how to designate the chosen items, shipping fees, and a firm's address, phone number, and Web address.

The message, and the medium in which it is presented, should be planned in the same way that a traditional retailer plans a store. The latter uses a storefront, lighting, carpeting, the store layout, and displays to foster an image. In direct marketing, the headlines, message content, use of color, paper quality, personalization of mail, space devoted to each item, and other elements affect a firm's image.

Customer Contact

For each campaign, a direct marketer decides whether to contact all customers in its data base or to seek specific market segments (with different messages and/or media for each). It can classify prospective customers as *regulars* (those who buy continuously); *nonregulars* (those who buy infrequently); *new contacts* (those who have never been sought before by the firm); and *nonrespondents* (those who have been contacted but never made a purchase).

Regulars and nonregulars are the most apt to respond to a firm's future offerings, and they can be better targeted since the firm has their purchase histories. Customers who have bought clothing before are prime prospects for specialogs. New contacts probably know little about the firm. Messages to them must build interest, accurately portray the firm, and present meaningful reasons for consumers to buy. This group is important if growth is sought.

Nonrespondents who have been contacted repeatedly without purchasing are unlikely to ever buy. Unless a firm can present a very different message, it is inefficient to pursue this group. Firms such as Publishers Clearinghouse send mailings to millions of people who have never bought from them; this is okay since they sell inexpensive impulse items and need only a small response rate to succeed.

Customer Response

Customers respond to direct marketers in one of three ways: (1) They buy through the mail, phone, fax, or computer. (2) They request further information, such as a catalog. (3) They ignore the message. Purchases are generally made by no more than 2 to 3 percent of those contacted. The rate is higher for specialogs, mail-order clubs (e.g., for music), and firms focusing on repeat customers.

Order Fulfillment

A system is needed for order fulfillment. If orders are received by mail or fax, the firm must sort them, determine if payment is enclosed, see whether the item is in stock, mail announcements if items cannot be sent on time, coordinate shipments, and replenish inventory. If phone orders are placed, a trained sales staff must be available when people may call. Salespeople answer questions, make suggestions, enter orders, note the payment method, see whether items are in stock, coordinate shipments, and replenish inventory. If orders are placed by computer, there must be a process to promptly and efficiently handle credit transactions, issue receipts, and forward orders to a warehouse. In all cases, names, addresses, and purchase data are added to the data base for future reference.

In peak seasons, additional warehouse, shipping, order processing, and sales workers supplement regular employees. Direct marketers that are highly regarded by consumers fill orders promptly, have knowledgeable and courteous personnel, do not misrepresent quality, and provide liberal return policies.

Measuring Results and Maintaining the Data Base

The last step is analyzing results and maintaining the data base. Direct marketing often yields clear outcomes:

- Overall response rate—The number and percentage of people who make a purchase after viewing a particular brochure, catalog, or Web site.
- Average purchase amount—By customer location, gender, and so forth.
- Sales volume by product category—Revenues correlated with the space allotted to each product in brochures, catalogs, and so forth.
- Value of list brokers—The revenues generated by various mailing lists.

After measuring results, the firm reviews its data base and makes sure that new shoppers are added, address changes are noted for existing customers, purchase and consumer information is current and available in segmentation categories, and nonrespondents are purged (when desirable).

This stage provides feedback for the direct marketer as it plans each new campaign.

KEY ISSUES FACING DIRECT MARKETERS

In planning and applying their strategies, direct marketers must keep the following in mind.

Many people dislike one or more aspects of direct marketing. They are the most dissatisfied with late delivery or nondelivery, deceptive claims, broken or damaged items, the wrong items being sent, and the lack of information. Nonetheless, in most cases, leading direct marketers are highly rated by consumers.

Most U.S. households report that they open all direct mail, but many would like to receive less of it. Since the average American household is sent 200 catalogs a year, besides hundreds of other mailings, firms must be concerned about marketplace clutter. It is hard to be distinctive in this environment.

A lot of consumers are concerned that their names and other information are being sold by list brokers, as well as by some retailers. They feel this is an invasion of privacy and that their decision to purchase does not constitute permission to pass on personal data. To counteract this, members of the Direct Marketing Association remove people's names from list circulation if they make a request.

Multiple-channel retailers need a consistent image for both store-based and direct marketing efforts. They must also perceive the similarities and differences in each approach's strategy. The steady increase in postal rates makes mailing catalogs, brochures, and other promotional materials costly for some firms. Numerous direct marketers are turning more to newspapers, magazines, and cable TV—and the Web.

Direct marketers must monitor the legal environment. They must be aware that, in the future, more states will probably require residents to pay sales tax on out-of-state direct marketing purchases; the firms would have to remit the tax payments to the affected states.

DIRECT SELLING

Direct selling includes both personal contact with consumers in their homes (and other non-store locations such as offices) and phone solicitations initiated by a retailer. Cosmetics, jewelry, vitamins, household goods and services (such as carpet cleaning), vacuum cleaners, and magazines and newspapers are among the items sometimes sold in this way. The industry has $27 billion in annual U.S. sales and employs 11 million people (more than 80 percent part-time).[13] Table 6-1 shows an industry overview.

The Direct Selling Association (www.dsa.org) is working hard to promote the image and professionalism of this retail format.

The direct selling strategy mix emphasizes convenient shopping and a personal touch, and detailed demonstrations can be made. Consumers often relax more in their homes than in stores. They are also likely to be attentive and are not exposed to competing brands (as they are in stores). For some shoppers, such as older consumers and those with young children, in-store shopping is hard due to limited mobility. For the retailer, direct selling has lower overhead costs because stores and fixtures are not necessary.

TABLE 6-1	A Snapshot of the U.S. Direct Selling Industry

Major Product Groups (as a percent of sales dollars)

Home/family care products (cleaning products, cookware, cutlery, etc.)	33.7
Personal care products (cosmetics, jewelry, skin care, etc.)	26.4
Services/miscellaneous/other	16.9
Wellness products (weight loss products, vitamins, etc.)	16.5
Leisure/educational products (books, encyclopedias, toys/games, etc.)	6.5

Place of Sales (as a percent of sales dollars)

In the home	64.4
Over the phone	14.7
In a workplace	8.7
Over the Internet	5.5
At a temporary location (such as a fair, exhibition, shopping mall, etc.)	4.1
Other locations	2.6

Sales Approach (method used to generate sales, as a percent of sales dollars)

Individual/one-to-one selling	70.3
Party plan/group sales	27.7
Customer placing order directly with firm	1.7
Other	0.3

Demographics of Salespeople (as a percent of all salespeople)

Independent contractors/employees	99.8/0.2
Female/male	72.5/27.5
Part-time/full-time (30 hours and up per week)	81.6/18.4

Source: Direct Selling Association, "Selling by the Numbers," **www.dsa.org/research/numbers.htm** (January 27, 2003).

FIGURE 6-5

Direct Selling and Mary Kay

Throughout the world (in nearly 35 countries), Mary Kay Cosmetics employs more than 900,000 direct sales "consultants," who mostly visit customers in their homes and account for $1.5 billion in revenues. Through its Web site, **www.marykay.com**, the company even provides links to the home pages of its U.S. consultants.

Reprinted by permission of Mary Kay Cosmetics.

Despite its advantages, direct selling in the United States is growing slowly:

- More women work, and they may not be interested in or available for in-home selling.
- Improved job opportunities in other fields and the interest in full-time careers have reduced the pool of people interested in direct selling jobs.
- A firm's market coverage is limited by the size of its sales force.
- Sales productivity is low since the average transaction is small and most consumers are unreceptive—many will not open their doors to salespeople or talk to telemarketers.
- Sales force turnover is high because employees are often poorly supervised part-timers.
- To stimulate sales personnel, compensation is usually 25 to 50 percent of the revenues they generate. This means average to above-average prices.
- There are various legal restrictions due to deceptive and high-pressure sales tactics. One such restriction is the FTC's Telemarketing Sales Rule (**www.ftc.gov/bcp/telemark/rule.htm**), which mandates that firms must disclose their identity and that the purpose of the call is selling.
- Because *door-to-door* has a poor image, the industry prefers the term *direct selling*.

Firms are reacting to these issues. Avon places greater emphasis on workplace sales, offers free training to sales personnel, rewards the best workers with better territories, pursues more global sales, and places cosmetics kiosks in shopping centers. Mary Kay hires community residents as salespeople and has a party atmosphere rather than a strict door-to-door approach; this requires networks of family, friends, and neighbors. Tupperware has an arrangement with Target Stores to host Tupperware parties at SuperTarget stores. And every major direct selling firm has a Web site to supplement its revenues.

Among the leading direct sellers are Avon and Mary Kay (cosmetics), Amway (household supplies), Tupperware (plastic containers), Shaklee (health products), Fuller Brush (small household products), Kirby (vacuum cleaners), and Welcome Wagon (greetings for new residents sponsored by groups of local retailers). Some stores, such as J.C. Penney, also use direct selling. Penney's decorator consultants sell a complete line of furnishings, not available in its stores, to consumers in their homes. See Figure 6-5.

VENDING MACHINES

A **vending machine** is a cash- or card-operated retailing format that dispenses goods (such as beverages) and services (such as electronic arcade games). It eliminates the use of sales personnel and allows 24-hour sales. Machines can be placed wherever convenient for consumers—inside or outside stores, in motel corridors, at train stations, or on street corners.

Aramark (www.
refreshment.aramark.com)
vending machines sell
hundreds of millions of
servings of soda and
snacks every year.

Although there have been many attempts to "vend" clothing, magazines, and other general merchandise, 85 percent of the $40 billion in annual U.S. vending machine sales involve hot and cold beverages and food items. Because of health issues, over the past 25 years, cigarettes' share of sales has gone from 25 to just 2 percent. The greatest sales are achieved in factory, office, and school lunchrooms and refreshment areas; public places such as service stations are also popular sites. Newspapers on street corners and sidewalks, various machines in hotels and motels, and candy machines in restaurants and at train stations are visible aspects of vending but account for a small percentage of U.S. vending machine sales.[14] Leading vending machine operators are Canteen Corporation and Aramark Refreshment Services.

Items priced above $1.50 have not sold well; too many coins are required and most vending machines do not have dollar bill changers. Consumers are reluctant to buy more expensive items that they cannot see displayed or have explained. However, their expanded access to and use of debit cards are expected to have a major impact on resolving the payment issue, and the video-kiosk type of vending machine lets people see product displays and get detailed information (and then place a credit or debit card order). Popular brands and standardized nonfood items are best suited to increasing sales via vending machines.

To improve productivity and customer relations, vending operators are applying several innovations. Popular products such as French fries are being made fresh in vending machines. Machine malfunctions are reduced by applying electronic mechanisms to cash-handling controls. Microprocessors track consumer preferences, trace malfunctions, and record receipts. Some machines have voice synthesizers that are programmed to say "Thank you, come again" or "Your change is 25 cents."

Operators must still deal with theft, vandalism, stockouts, above-average prices, and the perception that vending machines should be patronized only when a fill-in convenience item is needed.

ELECTRONIC RETAILING: THE EMERGENCE OF THE WORLD WIDE WEB

We are living through enormous changes from the days when retailing simply meant visiting a store, shopping from a printed catalog, greeting the Avon lady in one's home, or buying candy from a vending machine. Who would have thought that a person could "surf the Web" to research a stock, learn about a new product, search for bargains, save a trip to the store, and complain about customer service? Well, these activities are real and they're here to stay. Let's take a look at the World Wide Web from a retailing perspective, remembering that selling on the Web is a form of direct marketing.

Let us define two terms that may be confusing: The **Internet** is a global electronic superhighway of computer networks that use a common protocol and that are linked by telecommunications lines and satellite. It acts as a single, cooperative virtual network and is maintained by universities, governments, and businesses. The **World Wide Web (Web)** is one way to access information on the Internet, whereby people work with easy-to-use Web addresses (sites) and pages. Web users see words, charts, pictures, and video, and hear audio—which turn their computers into interactive multimedia centers. People can easily move from site to site by pointing at the proper spot on the monitor and clicking a mouse button. Web browsing software, such as Microsoft Internet Explorer and Netscape, facilitate surfing the Web.

Both *Internet* and *World Wide Web* convey the same central theme: online interactive retailing. Since almost all online retailing is done by the World Wide Web, we use *Web* in our discussion, which is comprised of these topics: the role of the Web, the scope of Web retailing, characteristics of Web users, factors to consider in planning whether to have a Web site, and examples of Web retailers. Visit our Web site (**www.prenhall.com/bermanevans**) for several valuable links on E-retailing.

THE ROLE OF THE WEB

From the vantage point of the retailer, the World Wide Web can serve one or more roles:

- Project a retail presence and enhance the retailer's image.
- Generate sales as the major source of revenue for an online retailer or as a complementary source of revenue for a store-based retailer.
- Reach geographically dispersed consumers, including foreign ones.

- Provide information to consumers about products carried, store locations, usage information, answers to common questions, customer loyalty programs, and so on.
- Promote new products and fully explain and demonstrate their features.
- Furnish customer service in the form of E-mail, "hot links," and other communications.
- Be more "personal" with consumers by letting them point and click on topics they choose.
- Conduct a retail business in a cost-efficient manner.
- Obtain customer feedback.
- Promote special offers and send coupons to Web customers.
- Describe employment opportunities.
- Present information to potential investors, potential franchisees, and the media.

The role a retailer assigns to the Web depends on (1) whether its major goal is to communicate interactively with consumers or to sell goods and services, (2) whether it is predominantly a traditional retailer that wants to have a Web presence or a newer firm that wants to derive most or all of its sales from the Web, and (3) the level of resources the retailer wants to commit to site development and maintenance. There are millions of Web sites worldwide and hundreds of thousands in retailing.

THE SCOPE OF WEB RETAILING

Forrester Research (www.forrester.com/NRF) tracks online retailing through a monthly index.

The potential of the Web is enormous: By 2004, there will be about 185 million Web users in North America, 220 million in Europe, 230 million in Asia-Pacific, 61 million in Latin America, and 11 million in the Middle East/Africa. One-fifth of all U.S. households purchase online at least once a year. Five years ago, U.S. shoppers generated 75 percent of worldwide online retail sales; the amount is now less than 50 percent and falling. European shoppers currently generate 30 percent of global Web revenues. As we noted earlier, U.S. retail Web sales should rise from $50 billion in 2001 to $150 billion in 2006. At least 5 percent or more of the U.S. sales of these goods and services are made online: apparel, banking, books, computer hardware and software, consumer electronics, gifts, greeting cards, insurance, music, newspapers/magazines, sporting goods, toys, travel, and videos. And a real milestone was recently achieved in Web retailing as—for the first time—the majority of U.S. E-retailers reported a profit.[15] Figure 6-6 indicates the percentage of online sales by product category.

FIGURE 6-6
Web-Based U.S. Retail Sales by Product Category

Source: Computed by the authors based on data in U.S. Department of Commerce, *E-Stats,* www.census.gov/estats (October 11, 2002).

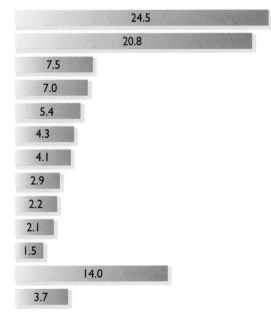

Product Category	% of Total Web-Based Retail Sales
Computer hardware and software	24.5
Travel arrangement and reservation services	20.8
Apparel (including shoes)	7.5
Books and magazines	7.0
Electronics and appliances	5.4
Music and videos	4.3
Toys, hobby goods, sporting goods, and games	4.1
Furniture and home furnishings	2.9
Drugs and health and beauty aids	2.2
Food and beverages	2.1
Building materials and garden supplies	1.5
Other merchandise	14.0
Other nonmerchandise	3.7

Despite the foregoing figures, the Web accounts for less than 3 percent of U.S. retail sales! It will not be the death knell of store-based retailing but another choice for shoppers, like other forms of direct marketing:

> Yes, there is a lot of growth, excitement, and substance to the Web economy. There is also a lot of hype and many failures. That is part of the process of entrepreneurial endeavor. Hype encourages investment, which accelerates the innovation cycle of trial and error. For all the attention given to Web firms, they are mainly an innovative ferment on the surface of the U.S. economy. As Kevin Kelly (author of *New Rules for the New Economy*) notes, the new economy doesn't replace the old economy; it builds on top of the old, and its technologies eventually permeate underlying layers.[16]

There is much higher sales growth for "clicks-and-mortar" Web retailing (multi-channel retailing) than "bricks-and-mortar" stores (single-channel retailing) and "clicks-only" Web firms (single-channel retailing). Store-based retailers account for three-quarters of U.S. online sales:

> Incumbents are major offline players that can effectively leverage existing assets—a recognized name, an established infrastructure, strong operating capabilities—in the online space. These retailers can use name recognition to generate traffic and online relationships with current customers. They can use their established retail and distribution networks to serve their online customers efficiently and profitably. And once they have established a multi-channel relationship, they can continually improve and refine online offerings by using what they know about their offline customers to better understand and anticipate online customers' needs and preferences. The result can be a multi-channel customer relationship that blurs the distinctions between channels and alters the way people shop.[17]

CHARACTERISTICS OF WEB USERS

U.S. Web users have these characteristics, some of which are highlighted in Figure 6-7:

- Gender and age—There are about as many males as females surfing the Web; however, males are somewhat more apt to purchase (a gap that is rapidly disappearing). Three-quarters of adults age 39 and younger are Web users; two-thirds of adults ages 40 to 59 are Web users; and one-quarter of adults age 60 and older are Web users.

- Income and education—Households with an annual income of at least $50,000 account for two-thirds of all Web users (although they represent only 45 percent of total households). Three-quarters of Web users have attended college. About 95 percent of college students say they use the Web.

FIGURE 6-7
A Snapshot of U.S. Web Customers

Sources: Chart developed by the authors based on data in Taylor Nelson Sofres Interactive, *Global E-Commerce Report 2002;* "MRI Cyberstats," **www.mriplus. com/resources.cyberstats.html** (August 19, 2002); and Ernst & Young, *Global Online Retailing* (New York: 2001).

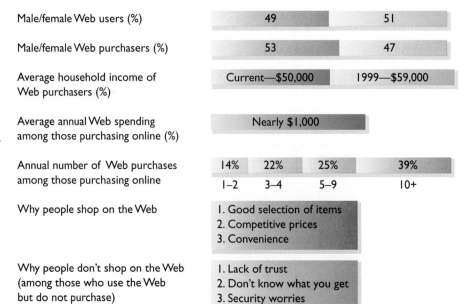

Male/female Web users (%)	49	51
Male/female Web purchasers (%)	53	47
Average household income of Web purchasers (%)	Current—$50,000	1999—$59,000
Average annual Web spending among those purchasing online (%)	Nearly $1,000	

Annual number of Web purchases among those purchasing online

14%	22%	25%	39%
1–2	3–4	5–9	10+

Why people shop on the Web
1. Good selection of items
2. Competitive prices
3. Convenience

Why people don't shop on the Web (among those who use the Web but do not purchase)
1. Lack of trust
2. Don't know what you get
3. Security worries

- Purchase behavior—Among those making Web purchases, almost one-half spend $250 or more on the Web each year and two-thirds shop at least 5 times.
- Reasons for *using* the Web—People seek information, entertainment, and interactive communications.
- Reasons for *shopping* on the Web—Shoppers are attracted by the selection, prices, convenience, and "fun" of Web retailing.
- Reasons for *not shopping* on the Web—Nonshoppers do not trust online retailers, worry about transmitting credit data, like to see products, do not feel secure shopping online, like talking to salespeople, and do not want to be surprised by the lack of shipping cost information.[18]

Shoppers say the most important aspects for their continued patronage are value and customer service: "If an online retailer is true to its value proposition, shopper loyalty will follow. But today's shoppers are fickle, eclectic, value-driven, and searching for new experiences. That puts pressure on retailers to be consistent in their value propositions and vigilant of the fulfillment activities that weigh heavily on the likelihood to buy again. Loyalty on the Web remains suspect. If online firms want to turn the tide, they must offer loyalty programs based on rewards, personalization, quality customer support for the online shopping experience, and privacy policies that protect customers and establish trust."[19]

Web users can be enticed to shop more often if they are assured of privacy, retailers are perceived as trustworthy, sites are easy to maneuver, prices are lower than at stores, there are strong money-back guarantees, they can return a product to a store, shipping costs are not hidden until the end of a purchase, transactions are secure, they can speak with sales representatives, and download time is faster.

FACTORS TO CONSIDER IN PLANNING WHETHER TO HAVE A WEB SITE

The Web generally offers many *advantages* for retailers. It is usually less costly to have a Web site than a store. The potential marketplace is huge and dispersed, yet relatively easy to reach. Web sites can be quite exciting, due to their multimedia capabilities. People can visit Web sites at any time, and their visits can be as short or long as they desire. Information can be targeted, so that, for example, a person visiting a toy store Web site could click on the icon labeled "Educational Toys—ages three to six." A customer data base can be established and customer feedback obtained.

The Web also has *disadvantages* for retailers. If consumers do not know a firm's Web address, it may be hard to find. For various reasons, many people are not yet willing to buy online. There is tremendous clutter with regard to the number of Web sites. Because Web surfers are easily bored, a Web site must be regularly updated to ensure repeat visits. The more multimedia features a Web site has, the slower it may be for people to access. Some firms have been overwhelmed with

Ethics in RETAILING

Retailers Spin a Complex Web for Consumer Trust

Consumer WebWatch (**www.consumerwebwatch.org**), a non-profit research project funded by Consumers Union, recently undertook a research project on U.S. consumer impressions of news and information on Web sites. The study involved 1,500 interviews with Internet users aged 18 and older.

These are among the major findings of the study.

- 80 percent of respondents say it is important to trust the information provided on a Web site.
- 95 percent of respondents say it is very important that sites disclose their fees.
- 93 percent of respondents say it is very important that sites disclose how they protect credit card information.
- 80 percent of respondents want search engines to reveal that they are paid to list some sites more prominently than others.

Despite their desires, only 20 percent of respondents trust Web sites that sell goods and services. And 60 percent of respondents do not know about payments to search engines for preferential placement. According to the director of Consumer WebWatch, "Using the Web should not be a game of 20 questions. Consumer WebWatch will encourage sites to be more transparent about the financial interests behind the content they publish, and provide tools to help consumers feel more confident about using the Web."

Source: "Consumer Trust Alarmingly Low," **http:retailindustry.about. com** (August 29, 2002).

customer service requests and questions from E-mail. It may be hard to coordinate store and Web transactions. There are few standards or rules as to what may be portrayed at Web sites. Consumers expect online services to be free and are reluctant to pay for them.

There is a large gulf between full-scale, integrated Web selling and a basic "telling"—rather than "selling"—Web site. To better understand this gulf, the model highlighted in Figure 6-8 was introduced at a National Retail Federation Information Technology Power Summit so that retailers can envision Web site development as a five-step process: "Many large, successful retailers are happy to be at Stage 2, and find that it brings them new customers and increased visibility. Stage 3, where the Web becomes simply another channel, was, for a time, the ideal that retailers sought. Stages 4 and 5 represent the next steps on the road to retail nirvana—the total integration of the virtual with the physical. Yet, as history tells us, Stages 6, 7, 8, and beyond are out there, waiting for technology to mature and new applications."[20]

Keep current on E-retailing news with Retail Forward's information-rich Web site (http://eretail.retailforward.com).

Web retailers should carefully consider these recommendations from several industry experts:

- Develop (or exploit) a well-known, trustworthy retailer name.
- Tailor the product assortment for Web shoppers.
- With download speed in mind, provide pictures and ample product information.
- Enable the shopper to make as few clicks as possible to get product information and place orders.
- Provide the best possible on-site search engine.
- Capitalize on customer information and relationships.
- Integrate online and offline businesses, and look for partnering opportunities.
- Save customer data to make future shopping trips easier.
- Indicate shipping fees early and be clear about delivery options.

FIGURE 6-8
The Five Stages of Developing a Retail Web Presence

Source: Chart developed by the authors from the discussion in Tracy Mullin, "Determining Web Presence," *Chain Store Age* (October 1999), p. 42.

Stage 1: Brochure Web Site

A site is built rapidly on a small budget. It may sell a few items but really exists to see if Web sales will work for the retailer. Customers are directed to the nearest store. These sites may move to Stage 2.

Stage 2: Commerce Web Site

This site involves full-scale selling. It has customer service support and describes the retailer's history and community efforts. It is not integrated with information systems. As a result, customers may order and later find an item is not in stock.

Stage 3: Web Site Integrated with Existing Processes

The site is integrated with the firm's buying, inventory, and accounting systems. That lessens the need to have separate reports and ensures that out-of-stock items are automatically deleted from the site.

Stage 4: The "Webified" Store

Network systems bring Web connectivity to browser-based point-of-sale, kiosk, or in-store terminals. This lets the retailer sell items that are not being carried in a given store, directs customers to the items at other stores where they are available, enables Web-assisted sales, and provides information from manufacturer Web sites.

Stage 5: Site Integrated with Manufacturer Systems

The site now combines all the information sources needed for collaborative sales. Manufacturers automatically replenish fast-selling items and ship directly to consumers, if so desired by the retailer.

- Do not promote items that are out of stock.
- Offer online order tracking.
- Use a secure order entry system for shoppers.
- Prominently state the firm's return and privacy policies.[21]

See Figures 6-9 and Figures 6-10.

Consistent with the preceding discussion, a firm has many decisions to make if it wants to utilize the Web. These are enumerated in Figure 6-9. A firm cannot just put up a site and wait for consumers to visit it in droves and then expect them to happily return. In many cases: (1) It is still difficult for people to find exactly what they are looking for. (2) Once the person finds what he or she wants, it may be hard to envision the product. "Subtleties of color and texture often don't come across well on the Web. Until someone figures out how to send a cashmere scarf digitally, you won't be able to touch it." (3) Customer service is sometimes lacking. (4) Web sites and their store siblings may not be in sync. "Send someone a gift from CompanyA.com and the recipient may be surprised to find it can't be returned or exchanged at a CompanyA store." (5) Privacy policies may not be consumer-oriented. "Order from a site, fill out a survey, or merely browse, and you find your E-mail box swamped with unsolicited ads and other junk."[22]

EXAMPLES OF WEB RETAILING IN ACTION

These examples show the breadth of retailing on the World Wide Web.

Amazon.com (**www.amazon.com**) is probably the most famous pure Web retailer in the world, with revenues exceeding $4 billion and 30 million customers purchasing from the firm each year. See Figure 6-10. This is how *Hoover's Online* sums up the Amazon.com phenomenon:

> What started as Earth's biggest bookstore is rapidly becoming Earth's biggest anything store. Amazon.com's main site offers millions of books, CDs, DVDs, and videos (which still

FIGURE 6-9
A Checklist of Retailer Decisions in Utilizing the Web

✓ What are the company's Web goals? At what point is it expected that the site will be profitable?
✓ What budget will be allocated to developing and maintaining a Web site?
✓ Who will develop and maintain the Web site, the retailer itself or an outside specialist?
✓ Should the firm set up an independent Web site for itself or should it be part of a "cybermall?"
✓ What features will the Web site have? What level of customer service will be offered?
✓ What information will the Web site provide?
✓ How will the goods and services assortment differ at the Web site from the firm's store?
✓ Will the Web site offer benefits not available elsewhere?
✓ Will prices reflect a good value for the consumer?
✓ How fast will the user be able to download the text and images from the Web site, and point and click from screen to screen?
✓ How often will Web site content be changed?
✓ What staff will handle Web inquiries and transactions?
✓ How fast will turnaround time be for Web inquiries and transactions?
✓ How will the firm coordinate store and Web transactions and customer interactions?
✓ What will be done to avoid crashes and slow site features during peak shopping hours and seasons?
✓ How will online orders be processed?
✓ How easy will it be for shoppers to enter and complete orders?
✓ What online payment methods will be accepted?
✓ What search engines (such as Yahoo!) will list the retailer's Web site?
✓ How will the site be promoted: (a) on the Web and (b) by the company?
✓ How will Web data be stored and arranged? How will all of the firm's information systems be integrated?
✓ How will Web success be measured?
✓ How will the firm determine which Web shoppers are new customers and which are customers who would otherwise visit a company store?
✓ How will the firm ensure secure (encrypted) transactions?
✓ How will consumer privacy concerns be handled?
✓ How will returns and customer complaints be handled?

FIGURE 6-10

Amazon.com: A Pure
Web Retailer

"Amazon.com opened its
virtual doors in July 1995
with a mission to use the
Internet to transform book
buying into the fastest, easi-
est, and most enjoyable
shopping experience possible. While our customer
base and product offerings
have grown considerably
since our early days, we
still maintain our founding
commitment to customer
satisfaction and the delivery of an educational and
inspiring shopping experience." [www.amazon.com]

Reprinted by permission.

account for most of its sales), not to mention toys, tools, electronics, health and beauty products, prescription drugs, and services such as film processing. Expansion is propelling the
company in many directions; it owns stakes in online sellers of prescription drugs, hand-
crafted items, and more. Long a model for Internet companies that put market share ahead of
profits and make acquisitions funded by meteoric market capitalization, Amazon.com is now
focusing on profits. Founder Jeff Bezos and his family own about one-third of the firm.[23]

At the opposite end of the spectrum from Amazon.com is the tiny business of Rosa
Simon. In 1998, she opened a Web site (**www.blindsdepot.com**) for her window-treatments
business, which she had operated by herself through direct selling: "A technology neophyte,
Simon looked first at Yahoo! Store. As with other firms, Yahoo enables users to build a Web site
in minutes by filling out a series of forms online. What Ms. Simon could not get from Yahoo
was placement high on the results pages of search engines. Seeking more shoppers, she opted
for an all-in-one package from iMall, which guaranteed placement on its shopping site. When
that failed to generate sales, she built an online store using software from Concentric Network,
an Internet service provider that hosted the site. Concentric software was limited, so she spent
$500 more for ShopSite software. With the aid of a consultant, she also learned how to increase
site visibility on search engines. Then came the payoff: 'I'm making more than before. And I'm
working less.'" The Blinds Depot Web site is now maintained and hosted by BuildHost.com.[24]

Netflix (**www.netflix.com**) is an online service retailer. It rents DVDs in a customer-
friendly way:

With no due dates and no late fees, Netflix lets you choose movies over the Internet from our
extensive selection of DVDs—over 11,500 titles. Every week we add new titles, enough to
keep even the biggest movie buff busy. Movies are delivered to your address by U.S. mail in
postage-paid return envelopes and you can keep them as long as you like for a flat fee of
$19.95 per month. When you're done watching one movie, drop it back in the mail and
Netflix will send your next choice. You can have three movies out at a time—so you always
have a good movie ready to watch. Want to see one of your movies again? Just keep it and
return the other two, Netflix will send you two more. No more late evening trips to stand in
line at the video store and no more frantic runs to get movies back in time to avoid late fees.[25]

Finally, here are two other exciting Web retailing illustrations: First, eBay (**www.ebay.com**), Priceline.com (**www.priceline.com**), and uBid.com (**www.ubid.com**) are just three of the retailers with online auctions, featuring everything from consumer electronics and textbooks to hotel rates and air fares. See Figure 6-11. Even nonprofit Goodwill has an auction Web site (**www.shopgoodwill.com**) to sell donated items. Second, Starbucks is offering high-speed wireless Internet service at more than 1,000 of its outlets: "Travel at blazing speeds on the Internet—all from the comfort of your favorite cozy chair. With high-speed wireless Internet service from T-Mobile HotSpot, your search for phone jacks is over and the opportunity to stay connected has just begun. The T-Mobile HotSpot service at Starbucks gives you the speed you need to quickly and easily check your E-mail, download that file you need for your next meeting, surf the Web, and get work done in coffeehouse comfort."[26]

OTHER NONTRADITIONAL FORMS OF RETAILING

Two other nontraditional institutions merit discussion: video kiosks and airport retailing. Although both formats have existed for years, they are now much more noteworthy. They appeal to retailers' desires to use new technology (video kiosks) and to locate in sites with high pedestrian traffic (airports).

VIDEO KIOSKS

The **video kiosk** is a freestanding, interactive, electronic computer terminal that displays products and related information on a video screen; it often has a touchscreen for consumers to make selections. Some kiosks are located in stores to enhance customer service; others let consumers place orders, complete transactions (typically with a credit card), and arrange for shipping. Kiosks can be linked to retailers' computer networks or to the Web. There are 1.5 million video kiosks in use throughout the United States, 250,000 of which are Internet connected; and they account for $3 billion in annual sales. Worldwide, it is estimated that kiosks *influence* $40 to $50 billion in retail sales—by providing product and warranty information, showing product assort-

FIGURE 6-11

Priceline.com: Online Auctions for Travel

"If you like to save money, you've come to the right place! Since we opened for business in April 1998, we've sold over 12 million airline tickets, 6 million hotel room nights, and 6 million rental car days. In the process, we've saved our customers millions and millions of dollars!" [www.priceline.com]

Reprinted by permission.

ments, displaying out-of-stock products, listing products by price, and so forth—and *generate* $5 billion in retail sales annually. North America accounts for the bulk of kiosk sales, followed by the Pacific Rim, Europe, and the rest of the world.[27]

Kiosks.org (www.kiosks. org) is tracking the phenomenal growth of video kiosks.

What exactly is an electronic kiosk? It "is distinguished by several minimum characteristics: a powerful CPU, often linked to a proprietary telecommunications system or the Internet, with full-motion video and audio, usually with MPEG hardware, a receipt printer, and magstripe card reader. Kiosks appear in bewildering variety now, with high-resolution laser printers, video tele-conferencing, fingerprint and barcode readers, smart cards, and more."[28] Yet, as *Kiosk* says:

> An interactive kiosk is more than just a computer; it is an extension of a great communications process that assists companies, marketers, customers, and the public to come together. Francis Mendelsohn, a veteran consultant to the kiosk industry, has stated, "The most exciting factor that will lead many retailers into new kiosk projects are compelling and easy-to-use applications that use touchscreens to conduct transactions while viewing product demonstrations and other attention-grabbers on the upper screen." If getting and holding the interest of customers is important, then the kiosk of tomorrow will have to provide the ultimate dynamic experience.[29]

Video kiosks can be placed almost anywhere (from a store aisle to the lobby of a college dormitory to a hotel lobby), require few employees, and are an entertaining and easy way to shop. See Figure 6-12. Many shopping centers and individual stores are putting their space to better, more profitable use by setting up video kiosks in previously underutilized areas. These kiosks carry everything from gift certificates to concert tickets to airline tickets. Take the case of Staples: "Employees can now say, 'Yeah, we've got that,' and mean it. Shoppers who don't find what they're looking for amongst the 9,000 SKUs in a typical Staples can order from an inventory of 100,000 items offered via in-store kiosks. And Staples has a key incentive for store managers to direct

FIGURE 6-12

Border's Title Sleuth Video Kiosk

At each of Borders' nearly 400 book superstores, there are 5 to 10 Title Sleuth kiosks. Each week, nearly 1 million searches are conducted at these kiosks as customers track down the books they are most interested in buying. Shoppers can locate nearby stores that have their selections in stock or place an order for delivery.

Reprinted by permission.

shoppers to the kiosks: Online sales are credited to the stores from which they're placed. 'Our motto is *Don't lose the sale*,' Staples' George Lamson said."[30]

The average hardware cost to a retailer for a video kiosk is $5,000. This does not include content development and kiosk maintenance. Hardware prices range from under $500 per kiosk to $10,000 to $15,000 per kiosk, depending on its functions—the more "razzle dazzle," the higher the price.[31]

AIRPORT RETAILING

In the past, the leading airport retailers were fast-food outlets, tiny gift stores, and newspaper/magazine stands. Today, airports are a major mecca of retailing. At virtually every large airport, as well as at many medium ones, there are full-blown shopping areas. And most small airports have at least a fast-food retailer and vending machines for newspapers, candy, and so forth. See Figure 6-13.

New York's Kennedy Airport (www.panynj. gov/aviation/jfkshopsframe. htm) typifies the retailing environment at the world's major airports.

The potential retail market is huge. U.S. airports alone fly 3 million passengers a day and employ more than 1 million people (who often buy something for their personal use at the airport). There are over 400 primary commercial U.S. airports, 30 of which are large hubs, 40 of which are medium hubs, 70 of which are small hubs, and 270 of which are nonhubs. Over all, U.S. airport retailing generates $6 billion in sales annually.[32] Consider this:

> After Pittsburgh pioneered the airport-as-shopping-mall concept in the United States, a flurry of retail projects is transforming the airport-going experience throughout the country. As important, in their store designs, retailers are figuring out how to meld their familiar names with what travelers are seeking. Thus, while it's great for travelers to encounter global brands like McDonald's and Gap, the retail environment needs to be customized to the locale so the comfort of seeing familiar names is balanced by a sense of local charm, color and flavor, and the excitement and discovery of the new, even the exotic. It all should give passengers a sense of place, conveyed through the spatial personality of the environment.[33]

FIGURE 6-13

Airport Retailing and Waldenbooks

As airport retailing has grown, more nationally recognized retailers have located stores there. This Waldenbooks store is situated at Newark Liberty International Airport in New Jersey.

Reprinted by permission.

These are some of the distinctive features of airport retailing:

- There is a large group of prospective shoppers. In a typical year, a big airport may have 20 million people passing through its concourses. A regional mall attracts 5 million to 6 million annual visits.

- Air travelers are a temporarily captive audience at the airport, looking to fill their waiting time, which could be up to several hours. They tend to have above-average incomes.

- Sales per square foot of retail space are usually three to four times higher than at regional malls. Rent is about 20 to 30 percent higher per square foot for airport retailers.

- Airport stores are smaller, carry fewer items, and have higher prices than traditional stores.

- Replenishing merchandise and stocking shelves may be difficult at airport stores because they are physically removed from delivery areas and space is limited.

- The sales of gift items and forgotten travel items, from travelers not having the time to shop elsewhere, are excellent. Brookstone, which sells garment bags and travel clocks at airport shops, calls these products "I forgot" merchandise.

- Passengers are at airports at all times of the day. Thus, longer store hours are possible.

- International travelers are often interested in duty-free shopping.

- There is much tighter security at airports than before, which has had a dampening effect on some shopping.

Summary

1. *To contrast single-channel and multi-channel retailing.* A new retailer often relies on single-channel retailing, whereby it sells to consumers through one retail format. As the firm grows, it may turn to multi-channel retailing and sell to consumers through multiple retail formats. This allows the firm to reach different customers, share costs among various formats, and diversify its supplier base.

2. *To look at the characteristics of the three major retail institutions involved with nonstore-based strategy mixes: direct marketing, direct selling, and vending machines—with an emphasis on direct marketing.* Firms employ nonstore retailing to reach customers and complete transactions. Nonstore retailing encompasses direct marketing, direct selling, and vending machines.

In direct marketing, a consumer is exposed to a good or service through a nonpersonal medium and orders by mail, phone, fax, or computer. Annual U.S. retail sales from direct marketing are $235 billion. Direct marketers fall into two categories: general and specialty. Among the strengths of direct marketing are its reduced operating costs, large geographic coverage, customer convenience, and targeted segments. Among the weaknesses are the shopper's inability to examine items before purchase, the costs of printing and mailing, the low response rate, and marketplace clutter. Under the "30-day rule," there are legal requirements that a firm must follow as to shipping speed. The long-run prospects for direct marketing are strong due to consumer interest in reduced shopping time, 24-hour ordering, the sales of well-known brands, improvements in operating efficiency, and technology.

The key to successful direct marketing is the customer data base, with data-base retailing being a way to collect, store, and use relevant information. Several trends are vital to direct mar-keters: their attitudes and activities, changing consumer lifestyles, increased competition, the use of dual distribution, the roles for catalogs and TV, technological advances, and the growth in global direct marketing. Specialogs and infomercials are two tools being used more by direct marketers.

A direct marketing plan has eight stages: business definition, generating customers, media selection, presenting the message, customer contact, customer response, order fulfillment, and measuring results and maintaining the data base. Firms must consider that many people dislike shopping this way, feel overwhelmed by the amount of direct mail, and are concerned about privacy.

Direct selling includes personal contact with consumers in their homes (and other nonstore sites) and phone calls by the seller. It yields $27 billion in annual U.S. retail sales, covering many goods and services. The strategy mix stresses convenience, a personal touch, demonstrations, and relaxed consumers. U.S. sales are not going up much due to the rise in working women, the labor intensity of the business, sales force turnover, government rules, and the poor image of some firms.

A vending machine uses coin- and card-operated dispensing of goods and services. It eliminates salespeople, allows 24-hour sales, and may be put almost anywhere. Beverages and food represent 85 percent of the $40 billion in annual U.S. vending revenues. Efforts in other product categories have met with customer resistance, and items priced above $1.50 have not done well.

3. *To explore the emergence of electronic retailing through the World Wide Web.* The Internet is a global electronic superhighway that acts as a single, cooperative virtual network. The World Wide Web (Web) is a way to access information on the Internet, whereby people turn their computers into interactive multimedia centers. The Web can serve one or more retailer purposes, from projecting an image to presenting information to investors. The purpose chosen depends on the goals and focus. There is a great contrast between store retailing and Web retailing.

The growth of Web-based retailing has been enormous. U.S. revenues from retailing on the Web will reach $150 billion in 2006. Nevertheless, the Web currently still garners less than 3 percent of total U.S. retail sales.

Somewhat more males than females shop on the Web, and purchasers are above-average in income and education. Shoppers are attracted by selection, prices, and convenience. Nonshoppers worry about the trustworthiness of online firms, transmitting credit information, and not seeing products first.

The Web offers these positive features for retailers: It can be inexpensive to have a Web site. The potential marketplace is huge and dispersed, yet easy to reach. Sites can be quite exciting. People can visit a site at any time. Information can be targeted. A customer data base can be established and customer feedback obtained. Yet, if consumers do not know a firm's Web address, it may be hard to find. Many people will not buy online. There is clutter with regard to the number of retail sties. Because Web surfers are easily bored, a firm must regularly update its site to ensure repeat visits. The more multimedia features a site has, the slower it may be to access. Some firms have been deluged with customer service requests. Improvements are needed to coordinate store and Web transactions. There are few standards or rules as to what may be portrayed at Web sites. Consumers expect online services to be free and are reluctant to pay for them.

A Web strategy can move through five stages: brochure site, commerce site, site integrated with existing processes, "Webified" store, and site integrated with manufacturer systems.

4. *To discuss two other nontraditional forms of retailing: video kiosks and airport retailing.* The video kiosk is a freestanding, interactive computer terminal that displays products and other information on a video screen; it often has a touchscreen for people to make selections. Although some kiosks are in stores to upgrade customer service, others let consumers place orders, complete transactions, and arrange shipping. Kiosks can be put almost anywhere, require few personnel, and are an entertaining and easy way for people to shop. They yield $3 billion in annual U.S. revenues.

Due to the huge size of the air travel marketplace, airports are popular as retail shopping areas. Travelers (and workers) are temporarily captive at the airport, often with a lot of time to fill. Sales per square foot, as well as rent, are high. Gift items and "I forgot" merchandise sell especially well. Annual retail revenues are $6 billion at U.S. airports.

Key Terms

single-channel retailing (p. 128)
multi-channel retailing (p. 128)
nonstore retailing (p. 129)
direct marketing (p. 129)

data-base retailing (p. 132)
specialog (p. 133)
infomercial (p. 134)
direct selling (p. 138)

vending machine (p. 139)
Internet (p. 140)
World Wide Web (Web) (p. 140)
video kiosk (p. 147)

Questions for Discussion

1. Contrast single-channel and multi-channel retailing. What do you think are the advantages of each?

2. Do you think nonstore retailing will continue to grow faster than store-based retailing? Explain your answer.

3. How would you increase a direct marketer's response rate from less than 1 percent of those receiving E-mail sales offers by the firm to 3 percent?

4. Explain the "30-day rule" for direct marketers.

5. What are the two main decisions to be made in the business definition stage of planning a direct marketing strategy?

6. How should a university that uses direct marketing handle consumer concerns about their privacy?

7. Differentiate between direct selling and direct marketing. What are the strengths and weaknesses of each?

8. Select a product not heavily sold through vending machines and present a brief plan for doing so.

9. From a consumer's perspective, what are the advantages and disadvantages of the World Wide Web?

10. From a retailer's perspective, what are the advantages and disadvantages of having a Web site?

11. What must retailers do to improve customer service on the Web?

12. What future role do you see for airport retailing? Why?

Web-Based Exercise

Visit the Web site of CyberAtlas (**www.cyberatlas.internet.com**). Scroll down the toolbar on the left and click on "Stats Toolbox." Describe three key facts that a retailer could learn from this site.

Note: Stop by our Web site (**www.prenhall.com/bermanevans**) to experience a number of highly interactive, appealing Web exercises based on actual company demonstrations and sample materials related to retailing.

Chapter Endnotes

1. Various company sources.

2. Behram J. Hansotia and Bradley Rukstales, "Direct Marketing for Multi-Channel Retailers: Issues, Challenges, and Solutions," *Journal of Database Marketing*, Vol. 9 (March 2002), pp. 259–260.

3. Richard Lawson, "Integrating Multiple Channels," *Chain Store Age* (April 2001), p. 58.

4. "E-Commerce's Growth Is Accelerating," *Business Wire* (April 11, 2002).

5. Direct Marketing Association, *Economic Impact: Direct Marketing in 30 Countries Worldwide* (New York: Direct Marketing Association, 2002).

6. Sherry Chiger, "Consumer Catalog Shopping Survey: Parts I to III," *Catalog Age* (August, October, and November 2001).

7. "Direct Marketing: An Aspect of Total Marketing," *Direct Marketing* (November 2001), p. 2.

8. Joel R. Evans and Barry Berman, "Using Data-Base Marketing to Target Repeat (Loyal) Customers," *Tips for Better Retailing*, Vol. 1 (Number 3, 1995).

9. See Alicia Orr Suman, "Celebrating 25 Years of Change in Direct Marketing," *Target Marketing* (May 2002), pp. 36–46, 99.

10. Chiger, "Consumer Catalog Shopping Survey: Part II," *Catalog Age* (October 2001).

11. "QVC Corporate Facts," **www.qvc.com/mainhqfact.html** (February 11, 2003); and "HSN Company Info," **www.hsn.com/cnt/article/default.aspx?aid=14** (February 11, 2003).

12. Jennifer Derryberry, "Europe Hails Snail Mail," *Sales & Marketing Management* (September 2000), p. 118. See also Laus Pike, "The 10 Most-Common Mistakes Americans Make When Direct Marketing in Europe," *Target Marketing* (March 2002), pp. 61–65.

13. *2002 Direct Selling Industrywide Growth & Outlook Survey* (Washington, D.C.: Direct Selling Association, 2002).

14. National Automatic Merchandising Association, "About Vending," **www.vending.org/about_vending** (January 29, 2003); and *Vending Times Census of the Industry 2002*.

15. eMarketer, "North America Online," **www.emarketer.com/products/report.php?online_no_am** (January 27, 2003); Taylor Nelson Sofres Interactive, "Global eCommerce Report 2002," **www.tnsofres.com/ger2002/home.cfm** (January 30, 2003); Boston Consulting Group, *The State of Retailing Online 5.0* (June 12, 2002); Michael Pastore, "New Records Predicted for Holiday E-Commerce," **www.cyberatlas.internet.com/markets/retailing** (October 12, 2001); Hyokjin Kwak, Richard J. Fox, and George M. Zinkhan, "What Products Can Be Successfully Promoted and Sold Via the Internet?" *Journal of Advertising Research*, Vol. 42 (January–February 2002), pp. 23–38; and "E-Retail Profitability, Revenues Grew in 2001," *Chain Store Age* (July 2002), p. 62.

16. Steve Lohr, "The Web Hasn't Replaced the Storefront Quite Yet," *New York Times on the Web* (October 3, 1999).

17. Boston Consulting Group, *The Next Chapter in Business-to-Consumer E-Commerce: Advantage Incumbent* (May 2001), p. 16.

18. eMarketer, "North America Online"; Taylor Nelson Sofres Interactive, "Global eCommerce Report 2002"; Boston Consulting Group, *The State of Retailing Online 5.0*; "MRI Cyberstats," **www.mriplus.com/resources.cyberstats.html** (February 19, 2003); and Ernst & Young, *Global Online Retailing* (New York: 2001).

19. Susan Reda, "Research Probes Links Between Online Satisfaction and Customer Loyalty," *Stores* (August 1999), p. 65.

20. Tracy Mullin, "Determining Web Presence," *Chain Store Age* (October 1999), p. 42.

21. Boston Consulting Group, *The State of Retailing Online 5.0*; "Top 10 Rules for Holiday (or Any Day) E-Commerce Success," *Sales & Marketing Management* (December 2001), p. 26; Bill Baird, "Web Site Best Practices," *Target Marketing* (March 2001), p. 16; and Retail Forward, "Lessons Worth Learning," *E-Retail Intelligence Update* (March 2002).

22. Jodi Mardesich, "The Web Is No Shopper's Paradise," *Fortune* (November 8, 1999), pp. 188–198.

23. "Amazon.com, Inc," **www.hoovers.com/co/capsule/3/0,2163,51493,00.html** (February 21, 2003).

24. Bob Tedeschi, "Turning Small Businesses, Web Dreams into Reality," *New York Times on the Web* (October 11, 1999); BuildHost.com, **www.buildhost.com** (January 27, 2003).

25. "About Netflix," **www.netflix.com/PressRoom?id=1005** (January 22, 2003).

26. "High-Speed Internet Access at Starbucks," **www.starbucks.com/retail/wireless.asp** (February 14, 2003).

27. "Stats N' Facts Research Area," **www.kiomag.com/statfactoptions** (January 18, 2003); and Retail Forward, *The Ongoing Evolution of E-Retailing* (June 2002).

28. North Communications, **www.kioskstore.com** (1998).

29. "Future Kiosk Interface: The Dynamic Experience," *Kiosk* (November 2001), p. 19. See also "The Top 12 Areas Your Retail Business Can Use a Kiosk," *Kiosk* (Issue 1, 2002).

30. "Staples Touts Kiosk, POS Link," *Chain Store Age* (July 2001), p. 66.

31. "Thinking Inside the Box," **www.kiomag.com/kioskcpu** (August 20, 2002); and "Future Kiosk Interface: The Dynamic Experience."

32. Nicole Harris, "A Time of Turbulence for Concourse Shops," *Wall Street Journal* (March 27, 2002), pp. B1, B6; and *Economic Impact of U.S. Airports* (Washington, D.C.: Airports Council International—North America, 1998).

33. Jacqueline T. DeLise, "Elaborate Retail Environments Taking Off at U.S. Airports," *Brandweek* (April 10, 2000).

part two
Short Cases

1: PIGGLY WIGGLY: A SUPERMARKET FRANCHISING GIANT

Piggly Wiggly (**www.pigglywiggly.com**) is a franchisor with over 600 supermarket units that span the southern states from Louisiana to North Carolina. In addition, Piggly Wiggly franchises about 20 stores in Wisconsin that are owned and operated by Fresh Brands (**www.fresh-brands.com**), a wholesaler that uses the Fresh Brands name. Any independent supermarket can become a Piggly Wiggly franchisee by signing a franchise agreement and paying a percentage of sales as a royalty.

In 2002, *Progressive Grocer* honored Piggly Wiggly with an Award of Excellence, based on the firm's successful marketing efforts for its franchisees. The company pays strict attention to such elements as developing specifications for store signs to assure a uniform image, managing a private-label program, arranging for special purchases for its franchisees, planning special promotions, and so on.

Piggly Wiggly provides extensive purchasing assistance for its franchises by arranging for both private-label and national-brand programs. Piggly Wiggly's private-label program includes about 1,000 products in more than 200 categories. The franchisor handles all of the management responsibilities for its private-label line, including setting product specifications, choosing suppliers, monitoring quality, and package design. Although Piggly Wiggly is owned by Fleming Companies (**www.fleming.com**), a major grocery wholesaler, its franchised stores do not have to purchase from Fleming. Some of the private-label products are bought from Fleming; others are acquired from various sources.

Through a centralized purchasing program for national brands, Piggly Wiggly franchisees have access to deals that would be otherwise unavailable to them. According to Piggly Wiggly's president, "We do top-to-top meetings with manufacturers in which we present ourselves as a conventional chain. If you counted all our stores as a single chain, we'd be at $4 billion in sales. That gets the attention of the Coca-Colas and the Frito-Lays."

Through the franchisor's efforts, its independently owned franchised units can better compete against national chains. As Piggly Wiggly's president says, "Nothing will replace running a store efficiently. A store has to be clean, well-stocked, safe, have an easily accessible parking lot—that's the cost of doing business. But, when you're on your own, you need a few things that you can't provide yourself in order to compete with the big chains. You need buying power, a recognizable name, and marketing power that goes beyond one store in one market. That's where we come in. We're the icing on the cake."

Piggly Wiggly's mascot, Mr. Pig, has high awareness throughout the South. Franchisees can even borrow a Mr. Pig costume to use at local parades and events. Piggly Wiggly employs field representatives to periodically visit each franchise location and apprise franchisee operators and their staffs of its current marketing programs. Store operators can also review the programs at a dedicated Web site, Pignet.com. One recent program featured a Mr. Pig Pack of three Kellogg cereal varieties—and Coca-Cola vending machines at Piggly Wiggly locations showing Mr. Pig drinking an ice-cold bottle of Coke Classic.

In contrast with its southern stores, the units in Wisconsin use the Fresh Brands name and do not participate in some promotions with a distinct southern emphasis. However, these units use the same logos and trademarks as the southern stores. Many of their promotions involve the Green Bay Packers, the Milwaukee Bucks, and the Milwaukee Brewers sports teams.

Questions

1. As an independent supermarket operator, would you want to become a Piggly Wiggly franchisee? Why or why not?
2. What are the advantages to Piggly Wiggly of having franchised outlets instead of its own stores? The disadvantages?
3. What criteria should Piggly Wiggly use in evaluating potential franchisees?
4. Should Fleming require Fresh Brands to use the Piggly Wiggly name and all of its promotions? Explain your answer.

The material in this case is drawn from Al Urbanski, "Piggly Wiggly: Branding the Virtual Chain," *Progressive Grocer* (January 1, 2002), pp. 55–57.

2: CAN TRADITIONAL DEPARTMENT STORES REVIVE THEMSELVES?

When the first department stores appeared 150 years ago, they were hailed as one-stop shopping outlets where people could purchase a wide range of goods for their homes and apparel for the entire family in a full-service environment. Today, a question that is often raised among retailing experts is whether department stores, or at least some of them, are bordering on extinction.

Analysts who challenge the long-term viability of department stores typically point out these stores are now subject to competition on multiple fronts. According to a spokesperson for the International Council of Shopping Centers (**www.icsc.org**), "Department stores find themselves stuck between specialty retailers and discounters." The specialty store is able to effectively compete against department stores on the basis of selection, exclusive merchandise, well-trained salespeople, and customer service and support. The discount store chain, through its purchasing power, low-rent locations, centralized purchasing, and self-service merchandising, can generally outprice the department store. In addition, Web retailers offer 24/7 conveniences, a high level of product information, and freedom from local sales taxes.

Due to the extensive competition from these formats, many department stores have stopped selling such merchandise lines as cameras, consumer electronics, and large appliances. In addition, a number of department stores have closed their doors forever. These include such notables as Abraham & Straus, John Wanamaker's, Stern's, and Montgomery Ward. Many of the remaining department stores have also been experiencing declining same-store sales.

Department stores have a number of operational issues that need to be addressed. These include their being too jammed with clothes to easily allow browsing, the use of centralized buying that results in inappropriate merchandise at some stores (such as winter clothing stocked in Florida department stores), and a lack of a distinctive image (it may sometimes be difficult to figure out if you are in Macy's or Bloomingdale's based on merchandise, displays, and store interiors).

Many department stores are "not sitting still" in light of these criticisms and declining sales. Sears' (**www.sears.com**) merger with Lands' End (**www.landsend.com**) is an attempt to increase its apparel business and appeal to a more affluent target market. In addition, Sears is trying to reposition itself somewhere between a department store and a discount store. It is remodeling its largest stores, installing central banks of cash registers, and displaying easy-to-read signs to facilitate browsing and self-service.

The chief executive officer of Bloomingdale's (**www. bloomingdales.com**) acknowledges that too many department stores sell nondistinctive merchandise: "I believe the biggest challenge that we have is how we continue to give uniqueness of product." Bloomingdale's goal is to better attract the young male segment, while continuing to keep its traditional middle-aged female shopper. To appeal to the younger high-fashion shopper, Bloomingdale's has proposed opening a new store in New York City's trendy Soho neighborhood. The chain is also planning on increasing the number of salespeople on the floor.

Department stores are also experimenting with ways to make their stores a better shopping environment for families with young children. A Canadian chain now has a lounge for children and parents that includes a play area for children and a sitting area that includes current newspapers. Federated Department Stores (**www.federated-fds.com**) recently opened a laboratory store that offers free child care, a salon and spa, a coffee bar, and even a demonstration kitchen.

Questions

1. Evaluate department stores in terms of the wheel of retailing. How can they better apply this concept?
2. Given the age of this institution and the competitive environment it faces, are department stores doomed to continue their downward spiral? Explain your answer.
3. As a retail executive, how would you better differentiate your department store from specialty stores?
4. As a retail executive, how would you better differentiate your department store from the full-line discount store?

The material in this case is drawn from "Department Stores to Reinvent Themselves," *Record-Bergen County* (March 17, 2002).

3: J. JILL MOVES INTO MULTI-CHANNEL RETAILING

In addition to its successful catalog operations, J. Jill operates more than 70 stores in 25 states (as of 2002) and has a successful Web site (**www.jjill.com**). While the merchandise collections for its catalog, stores, and Web site are identical, the catalog offers the largest selection. The firm strongly believes that its multi-channel retail strategy is the key to its future growth.

There is a high degree of integration among its catalog, store, and Web businesses. Each store has a concierge desk with a Web portal wherein customers can place orders for out-of-stock merchandise or special sizes. Items ordered at these sites are the first items shipped the following morning. About 8 percent of each store's total sales occur at the concierge desk. J. Jill's Web site enables viewers to view the retailer's latest catalogs. In addition, a customer can order an item from its Web site by using the catalog order number for that product.

J. Jill's Web site has a real-time connection to its warehouse. To ensure that ordered goods are available to Web shoppers, items are deleted from the firm's Web site after inventory levels fall below a certain level. The Web site has been enhanced to handle E-mails from customers, as well as a "live chat room." J. Jill also uses its Web site as a clearinghouse for markdowns on odd lots, discontinued items, and end-of-season specials. The firm maintains a customer data base to notify shoppers of these specials.

Gordon R. Cooke, J. Jill's current president and chief executive, joined J. Jill in 1996. Previously, he was executive vice-president of sales promotion and marketing at Bloomingdale's and founded Bloomingdale's By Mail. In 1997, Cooke decided that J. Jill would increase the circulation of its catalog, appeal to a younger audience, and hire a new creative director. These efforts were so successful that in 1997 sales at J. Jill increased to $73.8 million from $22.6 million in the previous year. In 1998, sales rose again to $165 million and the company changed its name to J. Jill Group.

J. Jill—with 2002 sales exceeding $300 million—now appeals to 35- to 55-year-old women with household incomes over $75,000. While its customer profile is similar to Talbots (**www. talbots.com**), J. Jill focuses more on casual, relaxed, and unstructured clothing. J. Jill's clothing can be best described as taking the middle ground between being fashion-forward and conservative. Most of its garments have a signature style consisting of a unique set of buttons, special embroidery, or select fabrics. Almost all of its clothing is private label and is developed and designed by an in-house staff.

Even though J. Jill is committed to a multi-channel strategy, it believes that most of its future growth will come primarily from stores, which accounted for 31 percent of total sales in 2002. (Catalogs and the Web site accounted for 50 and 19 percent, respectively.) According to Gordon Cooke, a major advantage of the store relative to the catalog or Web site is that a fabric's texture and detail can be better visualized. J. Jill hopes to grow to 300 stores in the next five years. Petite-sized merchandise does especially well at J. Jill's stores and has a separate department in most of the stores.

Questions

1. What are the pros and cons of J. Jill's multi-channel strategy?
2. How can J. Jill better integrate its catalog, store, and Web operations in the future?
3. Evaluate J. Jill's Web site (**www.jjill.com**).
4. What criteria can J. Jill use to assess its Web site? Explain your answer.

The material in this case is drawn from Marianne Wilson, "J. Jill Gets Physical," *Chain Store Age* (January 2002), pp. 42–46; and Jennifer Weitzman, "J. Jill Net Balloons as Margins Grow, Petites to Expand," *Women's Wear Daily* (July 26, 2002), p. 2.

4: CAN EBAY KEEP BOOMING?

According to Meg Whitman, eBay's chief executive, the online firm (**www.ebay.com**) has come a long way in its quest "to build the world's largest online trading platform where practically anyone can trade practically anything." Sales on eBay generate more than $10 billion annually. Over $1 billion in sales come from auto sales alone, a category that did not even exist on eBay a few years ago.

eBay is the largest online seller of autos, collectibles, computers, photo equipment and supplies, and sporting goods. In addition to traditional goods, eBay has literally created a market for products that did not previously exist (such as unused wedding presents and cases for discontinued cameras). eBay takes advantage of the low communication and transaction costs of the Web to bring buyers and sellers together. The more buyers who visit eBay, the more sellers that are attracted to use the service. eBay earns its own revenues from listing fees, as well as the 1 to 5 percent commission from every trade.

The company is often credited with coming closer than any other firm to establishing a virtual corporation that can flourish without inventories, warehouses, stores, fixtures, or a sales force. As eBay's chief financial officer says, "We have no real cost of goods, and customer acquisition is largely driven by word of mouth." Even an efficient firm like Wal-Mart has close to $16 billion in long-term debt; in contrast, eBay is virtually debt free. Since eBay is free of most retailing expenses, it generates a profit margin percentage that is three to four times higher than Wal-Mart's.

eBay organizes its operations by having a separate manager responsible for each of its major categories (such as books, music, and real-estate) and for each of its major global markets. These managers are responsible for growing their units, for making sure that nothing impedes sales in their units, and for determining when a category needs to be split into new categories to maximize sales potential. A recent innovation is eBay's "Buy It Now" feature. This enables a buyer to avoid the traditional bidding process by paying a pre-selected price on a product.

Another major avenue of growth is the use of eBay by Disney, IBM, Home Depot, and Dell as a channel to sell discontinued, shopworn, and refurbished goods. A number of state governments also now use eBay to sell off assets seized in foreclosure judgments.

Despite its continued success, a number of retail analysts have begun to question whether eBay can continue to grow at its hyper pace. Clearly, eBay needs to expand into new product categories and new geographic markets. This will be increasingly difficult. Furthermore, although eBay has usually taken a neutral stance when there is a dispute between a buyer and seller, some sellers argue that eBay needs to take their side when dealing with such issues as deadbeat buyers who bid and then refuse to purchase the goods. And some sellers are concerned that eBay has been so effective that their prices have actually dropped. The Internet Antique Shop reported that the average selling prices for collectibles and antiques declined by 30 percent between 2001 and 2002. Says one appraiser, "They [eBay] leveled the playing field, but unfortunately they leveled it underwater."

Questions

1. Visit eBay (**www.ebay.com**). Evaluate the site from the perspective of both (a) prospective sellers and (b) prospective buyers.
2. What are the pros and cons of Dell's selling discontinued equipment through an eBay store versus its own Web site?
3. What type of infrastructure must a local camera store develop to effectively sell collectible cameras on the Web through eBay?
4. What can eBay do to better manage buyer–seller relationships and to make sure that both parties are protected and satisfied in the exchange process?

The material in this case is drawn from Erick Schonfeld, "eBay's Secret Ingredient," *Business 2.0* (March 2002), pp. 52–58.

part two
Comprehensive Case
Addressing E-Retail Operational Issues*

INTRODUCTION

Historians will portray the early 21st century as the period when E-retailers focused on improving the shopping experience. Operational enhancements principally encompass expediting purchases, improving the efficiency of shopping trips, trying to overcome online purchase barriers for certain products by using better product imaging (such as 3-D images and virtual models), and enhancing customer service.

More Difficult Online

Difficult problems on the part of E-retailers are taken for granted by store shoppers and operators. If a store shopper has a customer service question, he or she goes to a nearby employee and poses the inquiry. Online shoppers can call a 1-800 number, write and E-mail (and wait for a response), or engage in online chat (if available). From the shopper's perspective, it takes more time to locate the appropriate link/person and get an answer online, while there are complications and costs surrounding solutions for E-retailers.

Decisions on which products to display as key items and product adjacencies affect store shopability. These decisions are more complicated within the E-retailing space. E-retailers have a limited amount of "virtual shelf space" to feature products on the home page or category-level pages. In a store, items not displayed prominently are just steps away, which may impact sales; but the situation is unlike the online predicament in which products displayed on secondary Web pages see a huge reduction in "foot traffic."

It's also fairly easy in stores to move a product to a different fixture or update a display. Online, any product movement needs coordination across the merchandising, technology, and marketing departments. Furthermore, an employee can't just go and "pick up" and "move" a product, as the process requires a highly skilled (and well-compensated) programmer.

Shoppers Noticing Recent Enhancements

E-retailers are trying to address their shortcomings, and their actions are generating improvements in online shopping satisfaction. According to Retail Forward's Internet Users Consumer Panels, 73 percent of online holiday shoppers were satisfied with all of their online holiday gift shopping experiences in 2001, up 18 points from 2000. Still, much work remains, as more than one in four holiday shoppers was dissatisfied with at least one online shopping experience in 2001. The majority of online holiday shoppers either strongly agreed or agreed that, compared to prior years, most online shopping sites had simplified the checkout process (61 percent), it was easier to find what they were looking for (61 percent), and the "search" function on most online shopping sites had improved (52 percent).

Leading Operational Issues

Online shoppers say the most significant feature at Web shopping sites is product availability information (in-stock status), from both a usefulness and online shopping satisfaction perspective. Following product availability are product imaging and search functionality. Certain product imaging features, such as close-up images and product images themselves, are perceived as being useful and satisfaction drivers by a large proportion of the online shopping community, while the opposite is true for 3-D images of products.

Features such as online chat and site personalization capabilities are considered very useful by less than one in four online shoppers and selected by less than 10 percent as a satisfaction driver. These features are relatively recent additions to online shopping and less well known than features like product availability, product images, and search functionality. In addition, there are many shopping sites where it rarely makes sense to have online chat or site personalization due to the needs of people shopping there.

Product Imaging: Bigger Is Better—Generally

Large, accurate product images are an expectation of online shoppers. However, some E-retailers have taken this to the next level by providing views that entail product images from multiple angles, the ability to view a product in all available colors and styles, and 3-D rotations. E-retailers have reported marked improvements to key performance metrics from the technology:

- Utilizing RichFX's ZoomFX, Coach.com provides online shoppers with access to key product features, including leather texture, logo, stitching, and hardware.
- EddieBauer.com introduced Viewpoint technology to create a 3-D interactive environment for a daypack backpack collection, so shoppers could see, "touch," and "try" every flap, pocket, and pouch. It has since applied the technology to a new line of home and outdoor gadgets, armoires, and men's and women's shoes. Eddie Bauer was the first firm to use Viewpoint's ZoomView technology, featuring pan and zoom capabilities, for over 30 apparel, luggage, and home furnishing products.
- Spiegel.com also features RichFX's ZoomFX to highlight a selection of apparel. The firm expects the technology to facilitate cross-selling since multiple products can be viewed simultaneously.

Despite the success stories, product imaging has experienced a few black eyes. Saks launched its online shopping site in fall 2000 with 360-degree technology that allowed users to view product details at different angles. However, the functionality was ultimately removed because no one used it.

Other complications include slow load times due to large product files. This is particularly so for 3-D imaging, especially for shoppers accessing the Internet via dial-up modems. Some 3-D technologies can minimize load times. For example, a 3-D image from Kaon Interactive takes 10 to 15 seconds to access with a dial-up connection. Yet, there is a trade-off between load times and image quality, as Kaon images are grainy. For many 3-D imaging technologies, users must download a plug-in to view the images. Some technologies have compatibility problems and only work with certain Web browsers. These complications increase the likelihood of a user experiencing technical difficulties and deciding to leave the site.

From a consumer perspective, many products don't require sophisticated imaging to improve the online experience. The technology is best for specialized products that generally feature high price points, where shoppers need to learn everything about the products before making purchases. The technology is not appropriate for E-retailers that sell products featuring a low price and/or well-understood feature(s).

Virtual Models and Fit Predictors: Taking Off

In some respects, online shopping is inferior to the store experience; and clothing is often more "behind the eight ball." Online shoppers can't touch and feel clothes or try them on. The typical online apparel retailer has a return rate in excess of 20 percent, compared to 10 percent at a typical apparel store.

To address the problem, online retailers have debuted technology that lets shoppers create a virtual representation of themselves: Shoppers answer basic questions (like height and weight) and more difficult inquiries (like body shape and waist definition), and choose a face, eyes, and skin color to create a model that looks like them. They can "try on clothes" and rotate the virtual model before making a decision. The first online retailer to adopt the capability was Lands' End in 1998. More recently, it has been debuted by several firms, including American Eagle, FUBU, Lane Bryant, Maxim, and PlusSize.com.

The primary provider of the technology is My Virtual Model. At the end of 2001, over 3 million My Virtual Models had been created, about two-thirds of them at Lands' End. In June 2001, My Virtual Model acquired EZsize, a provider of fit and size technology. EZsize's technology was integrated with My Virtual Model to create the My Virtual Model Fit service, which advises shoppers how well a specific product fits on a five-star rating and recommends the best size. At sites with this capability, shoppers enter detailed body measurements. The impact of the technology on key performance metrics has been impressive. According to My Virtual Model, the technology helps E-retailers reduce over 50 percent of returns due to fit problems, as well as increase conversion rates.

The technology is not perfect. First, it is a complex online application, creating slow load times for shoppers, especially those lacking broadband connections. Second, the virtual model itself isn't a fit predictor, but a virtual dressing room. The core technology provides shoppers with an idea of how products look together and which ones might be flattering for different body shapes but requires another application (My Virtual Model Fit) to determine whether a specific product will fit well. As a result, a small number of firms have removed the technology, including Limited Too and J.C. Penney.

Search: The Next Generation

The terms *search* and *shop* are frequently interchangeable when it comes to shopping online. According to Forrester Research, more than half of online purchasers use a search function to find products, and the search results page is typically the second most highly visited page at online shopping sites, trailing the home page. Given the importance of the search function, it's understandable why firms have focused on improving its efficiency and the quality of results. According to Jupiter Media Metrix, 80 percent of online users will abandon a site if the search function doesn't work well.

Online search functionality is seeing a metamorphosis. Technology now helps guide the shopping process by aggregating results into logical groups by product category or product attribute. "Intelligent" search software is becoming more mainstream, which can significantly improve the function's efficiency and E-retailers' ability to convert searchers into buyers.

EasyAsk search technology responds to "natural language" search requests (e.g., red sweaters under $100, men's red polo shirts from Tommy Hilfiger) that are posed as full sentences, phrases, or keywords. The technology lets shoppers pose a second question to refine the original search results (e.g., show me dresses under $100, followed by ones in orange). It understands six languages (English, Spanish, German, French, Italian, and Dutch) and can interpret different terminology, consider synonyms, and correct spelling errors. It can also associate relationships between different products, leading to cross-selling possibilities.

IntuiFind is an integrated search-and-browse technology that accommodates both shoppers who know exactly what they want and those who need additional assistance in finding the appropriate product. It features an intuitive free text search, which indexes the contents of an E-retailer's product data base and applies linguistic modules to ensure relevant results regardless of spelling, terminology, or wording. The search can be further narrowed by providing the ability to drill down at the category or attribute level.

These are examples of firms reporting performance improvements due to better search capabilities:

- Coach.com did a four-week test in which half of all search queries were handled by EasyAsk and the remainder by the site's existing search engine. Reportedly, for every $1 of sales generated by the existing search engine, EasyAsk produced $4.
- After redesigning its site, which included deploying IntuiFind and installing other enhancements, Macys.com reportedly increased its conversion rate and number of orders by 150 percent and 200 percent, respectively, compared to the prior year.

Going forward, more firms will continue to devote resources to sites' search capability. However, they would be wise to be cautious. Implementing intelligent search technology can cost into the millions of dollars, depending on Web site size and search parameters, along with a maintenance fee. More importantly, intelligent search is not for all E-retailers. Many of the first-movers sell clothing and related items, in which there are many product categories and each product has multiple attributes. For E-retailers with less complicated products, the return from optimizing the search function will be less attractive.

Customer Service: There When Needed

At multiple points during the online shopping process, consumers may need access to information, such as product information, shipping and handling charges, privacy and return policies, and so on. This is a challenge. Traditional solutions, such as a Web page of customer service policies or FAQs (frequently asked questions), can take a lot of time to locate the specific piece of information, potentially frustrating shoppers and causing them to leave the site. The ability to contact a customer service representative via E-mail or a 1-800 number is also a standard feature. Yet, these solutions are frequently not timely or not possible at all, as is the case for dial-up shoppers who want to call a customer service representative but are using the household's sole phone line to get online. New online customer service capabilities are debuting that try to be more convenient, more timely, and more efficient.

Online chat is becoming more popular. According to LivePerson, one of the largest providers of online chat, an estimated 4 percent of online shopping sites utilized the service as of early 2002, including Alloy.com, L.L. Bean, Lands' End, Neiman Marcus, MSN eShop, iQVC, RedEnvelope, and Staples.

LivePerson's Live Engage is a technology that makes it possible for firms to automatically send a proactive chat invitation to site visitors. Invitations can feature a sale, promotion, or gift. When users click on an icon, online chat is commenced. eStara's Push to Talk makes it possible for users to initiate voice conversation with a customer service representative. Users can enter a phone number to initiate a phone-to-phone call or they can talk to a representative via their PC, as long as it has a microphone and speakers. The technology can be deployed on a Web page or within E-mails.

Some E-retailers use automated or self-service customer service solutions. Buy.com utilizes Finali's netSage software that takes shoppers through an exchange resembling a conversation with "Ian Stone," a techno-savvy 20-something. The virtual agent uses still images of an actor doing tasks. OfficeDepot.com uses Ask Jeeves, a natural language self-service question answering software that provides shoppers with a list of the best possible answers to inquiries. Self-service solutions are becoming more popular because they cost less than other customer service options.

Personalization: Making It Sticky

Several firms have unveiled initiatives to create a personal shopping experience and/or personal E-mail communications based on demographics, past purchasing behavior, and other data. The ultimate goals of these initiatives are to create site stickiness and customer loyalty—to build "switching costs" into users' site selection. When a specific site has a good understanding of shopping preferences and the capability to incorporate that information into future shopping trips to increase the efficiency of those trips, why would customers go elsewhere? Financial goals for personalization include increasing the productivity of high-traffic Web pages and E-mail campaigns, average order size, and conversion rates.

Amazon.com has been at the forefront of personalization for years. It has a personalized store for every customer, with each person's name in a tab next to the Welcome tab on the main menu. The personalization requires no action by customers, featuring relevant products and content based on past purchases, products customers have rated, and areas of the site customers have marked as favorites. Store sections include Your Recommendations (based on previous purchases, ratings, etc.), Your Bargains (items on sale), New for You (product recommendations), Your Favorite Stores (recommendations by product category), The Page You Made (a tracking system for previously viewed products that presents related items), Friends & Favorites (reviews, recommendations, and opinions from others), and Just Like You (purchases and ratings from other customers who have made a number of the same purchases).

E-retailers are trying to increase E-mail effectiveness by personalizing communications. Examples include Amazon.com distributing E-mails to prior Disney video/DVD purchasers when a new animated feature is released, and British grocery retailer Tesco and personal care manufacturer Unilever distributing targeted E-mails to increase sales for Unilever products at Tesco.com.

Firms can also use personalization technology to assist with product recalls, repair, and warranty information; and online personalization technology can have a positive impact on other distribution channels. For example, Guitar Center utilizes its online personalization software at MusiciansFriend.com to assist in determining what products should be featured in upcoming catalogs.

The potential stumbling block for personalization is privacy concerns. It's impossible to provide a personal shopping experience without acquiring customer data. The onus falls on E-retailers to properly use the data. Long-term relationships must be built on trust and understanding.

Questions

1. What could a small independent retailer learn from this case?
2. What could a store-based chain retailer learn from this case as it prepares to upgrade its Web site?
3. Comment on the value of the emerging technologies described here for retailers using the Web.
4. Do you expect these technologies to be popular with consumers within the next few years? Why or why not?
5. Discuss the implications of the trends noted in the case in terms of the retail life cycle concept.
6. Will the new customer service technologies improve the quality of online customer service to a high level?
7. What are the implications of the emerging technologies for multi-channel retailers?

*The material in this case is adapted by the authors from Retail Forward, "Addressing E-Retail Operational Issues," *Hot Topics* (March 2002), pp. 1–15. Reprinted by permission of Retail Forward, Inc. (**www.retailforward.com**).

part three

Targeting Customers and Gathering Information

In Part Three, we first present various concepts related to identifying and understanding consumers, and developing an appropriate target market plan. Information-gathering methods—which can be used in identifying and understanding consumers, as well as in developing and implementing a retail strategy—are then described.

- **Chapter 7** discusses many influences on retail shoppers: demographics, life-styles, needs and desires, shopping attitudes and behavior, retailer actions that influence shopping, and environmental factors. We place these elements within a target marketing framework, because it is critical for retailers to recognize what makes their customers and potential customers tick—and for them to act accordingly.

- **Chapter 8** deals with information gathering and processing in retailing. We first consider the information flows in a retail distribution channel and review the difficulties that may arise from basing a retail strategy on inadequate information. Then we examine in depth the retail information system, its components, and recent advances in information systems—with particular emphasis on data warehousing and data mining. The last part of the chapter describes the marketing research process.

Chapter 7

IDENTIFYING AND UNDERSTANDING CONSUMERS

Reprinted by permission.

Thomas Stemberg, a Harvard M.B.A. (he went to business school after being turned down for the law school), was working on a business plan in his home during summer 1985. While printing spreadsheets, he realized that his printer ribbon was broken. Attempts to purchase a new ribbon over the Fourth of July weekend were unsuccessful. His local stationery store and a nearby computer store were both closed, and the nearest BJ's did not carry the correct ribbon. All of a sudden, a thought occurred to Stemberg: What the world needed was a superstore selling nothing but office supplies at great prices.

On May 1, 1986, Staples (**www.staples.com**) opened its first superstore in Brighton, Massachusetts. The store was so successful that about 20 competitors launched similar store formats within the next two years. Today, there are only three major players in this business— Staples, Office Depot (**www.officedepot.com**), and OfficeMax (**www.officemax.com**)—with about 2,500 superstores worldwide.

Staples appeals to three distinct market segments: small and large businesses, home offices, and final consumers. Its stores have changed the way each of these consumers purchases supplies. Let's look at the back-to-school shopper. To increase its sales of back-to-school supplies, Staples has placed these goods in the front of stores. It has also introduced a freestanding kiosk that displays special promotions, as well as school lists. The lists state suggested purchases for each nearby school; in addition, there are generic school lists for each grade.[1]

chapter objectives

1. To discuss why it is important for a retailer to properly identify, understand, and appeal to its customers

2. To enumerate and describe a number of consumer demographics, life-style factors, and needs and desires—and to explain how these concepts can be applied to retailing

3. To examine consumer attitudes toward shopping and consumer shopping behavior, including the consumer decision process and its stages

4. To look at retailer actions based on target market planning

5. To note some of the environmental factors that affect consumer shopping

OVERVIEW

The quality of a retail strategy depends on how well a firm identifies and understands its customers and forms its strategy mix to appeal to them. This entails identifying consumer characteristics, needs, and attitudes; recognizing how people make decisions; and then devising the proper target market plan. It also means studying the environmental factors that affect purchase decisions. Consider the following:

Each consumer segment has its own value equation and shops accordingly. Understanding what drives different groups is critical to creating an experience and product offering that satisfies their individual value equations. The biggest problem is that some retailers want to be "all things to all people," striving to offer the best price, service, and product. While commendable, this often causes them to compromise their core value propositions and miss their goal.

Retailers must examine consumers on different levels to identify and understand their target market and generate relevant, actionable business strategies. Firms aiming to understand the whole consumer picture must first obtain demographic information and then delve into questions designed to uncover purchase behavior drivers. Once a company knows who it has the most potential to reach, it can determine which segments are the bull's-eye within the broader spectrum. By focusing the majority of its efforts on the bull's-eye—rather than gambling on a handful of loosely understood consumer groups—the retailer can transform target consumers' needs into true competitive advantages; and it can begin to create deep and profitable long-term relationships.[2]

In this chapter, we explore—in a retailing context—the impact on shoppers of each of the elements shown in Figure 7-1: demographics, life-styles, needs and desires, shopping attitudes and behavior, retailer actions that influence shopping, and environmental factors. By studying these elements, a retailer can devise the best possible target market plan and do so in the context of its overall strategy.

Please note: We use the terms *consumer*, *customer*, and *shopper* interchangeably in this chapter.

CONSUMER DEMOGRAPHICS AND LIFE-STYLES

Demographics are objective, quantifiable, easily identifiable, and measurable population data. **Life-styles** are the ways in which individual consumers and families (households) live and spend time and money. Visit our Web site (**www.prenhall.com/bermanevans**) for several useful links on these topics.

FIGURE 7-1
What Makes Retail
Shoppers Tick

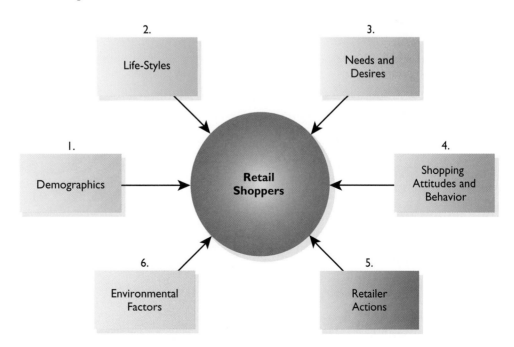

CONSUMER DEMOGRAPHICS

At *The Rite Site* (http://easidemographics.com/reports/easi_free_reports.phtml), retailers can access lots of demographic data. Just click "Go!" Then enter your ZIP code.

Both groups of consumers and individual consumers can be identified by such demographics as gender, age, population growth rate, life expectancy, literacy, language spoken, household size, marital and family status, income, retail sales, mobility, place of residence, occupation, education, and ethnic/racial background. These factors affect people's retail shopping and retailer actions.

A retailer should have some knowledge of overall trends, as well as the demographics of its own target market. Table 7-1 indicates broad demographics for 10 nations around the world and Table 7-2 shows U.S. demographics by region. Regional data are useful since most retailers are local and regional.

In understanding U.S. demographics, it is helpful to know these facts:

- The typical household has an annual income of $45,000. The top one-quarter of households earn $75,000 or more; the lowest one-sixth earn under $15,000. If income is high, people are apt to have **discretionary income**—money left after paying taxes and buying necessities.

- One-sixth of people move each year, yet 60 percent of all moves are in the same county.

- There are 5 million more females than males, and three-fifths of females aged 16 and older are in the labor force (many full-time).

- Most U.S. employment is in services. In addition, there are now more professionals and white-collar workers than before and fewer blue-collar and agricultural workers.

- More adults have attended some level of college, with one-quarter of all U.S. adults aged 25 and older at least graduating from a four-year college.

- The population comprises many ethnic and racial groups. African-Americans, Hispanic-Americans, and Asian-Americans account for 30 percent of U.S. residents—a steadily rising figure. Each of these groups represents a large potential target market; their total annual buying power is $1.2 trillion.[3]

| TABLE 7-1 | Population Demographics: A Global Perspective—Selected Countries (2001 Data) |

Country	Male/Female (%)	AGE DISTRIBUTION (%)			Annual Population Growth (%)	Life Expectancy in Years	Literacy Rate (%)	Principal Languages Spoken
		0–14 Years	15–64 Years	65 Years and Over				
Canada	49.5/50.5	19	68	13	0.99	79.6	97	English, French
China	51.5/48.5	25	68	7	0.88	71.6	82	More than a dozen versions of Chinese
Great Britain	49.2/50.8	19	65	16	0.23	77.8	99	English, Welsh
India	51.7/48.3	33	62	5	1.55	62.8	52	Hindi, English, 22 other languages spoken by at least 1 million people
Italy	48.5/51.5	14	68	18	−0.07	79.1	98	Italian, German, French, Slovene
Japan	49.0/51.0	15	68	17	0.17	80.8	99	Japanese
Mexico	49.2/50.8	33	62	5	1.50	71.8	90	Spanish
Poland	48.5/51.5	18	69	13	−0.03	73.4	99	Polish
South Africa	48.5/51.5	32	63	5	0.26	48.1	82	Afrikaans, English, 9 other languages
United States	49.0/51.0	21	66	13	0.90	77.3	97	English, Spanish

Note: The literacy rate is the percentage of people ages 15 and older who can read and write.

Sources: Compiled by the authors from *CIA World Factbook 2001*.

TABLE 7-2	Selected U.S. Demographics by Region (2001 Data)					
Region	Percent of Population	Percent of Household Income	Percent of Retail Sales	Percent Ages 18–34	Percent Ages 50 and Older	Population Per Square Mile
NE	4.9	5.7	5.7	23.6	29.3	222.5
MA	13.9	14.9	12.9	22.4	30.7	400.4
ENC	15.9	15.9	15.9	22.4	28.5	186.4
WNC	6.8	6.5	7.4	21.8	29.3	38.1
SA	18.6	18.5	18.2	22.8	29.4	196.8
ESC	6.0	5.2	5.4	22.1	28.9	90.5
WSC	11.2	10.4	11.1	23.2	25.7	74.6
M	6.6	6.4	6.8	22.5	25.9	21.6
P	16.1	16.5	16.6	24.2	25.3	50.6

NE (New England) = Connecticut, Maine, Massachusetts, New Hampshire, Rhode Island, Vermont
MA (Middle Atlantic) = New Jersey, New York, Pennsylvania
ENC (East North Central) = Illinois, Indiana, Michigan, Ohio, Wisconsin
WNC (West North Central) = Iowa, Kansas, Minnesota, Missouri, Nebraska, North Dakota, South Dakota
SA (South Atlantic) = Delaware, District of Columbia, Florida, Georgia, Maryland, North Carolina, South Carolina, Virginia, West Virginia
ESC (East South Central) = Alabama, Kentucky, Mississippi, Tennessee
WSC (West South Central) = Arkansas, Louisiana, Oklahoma, Texas
M (Mountain) = Arizona, Colorado, Idaho, Montana, Nevada, New Mexico, Utah, Wyoming
P (Pacific) = Alaska, California, Hawaii, Oregon, Washington

Sources: Computed by the authors from U.S. Bureau of the Census data, except for household income and retail sales data, which are from "2002 Survey of Buying Power," *Sales & Marketing Management* (September 2002).

Although the preceding gives an overview of the United States, demographics vary by area. Within a state or city, some locales have larger populations and more affluent, older, and better-educated residents. Because most retailers are local or operate in only part of a region, they must compile data about the people living in their trading areas and those most apt to shop there. *For a given business and location,* the characteristics of the target market (the customer group to be sought by the retailer) can be studied on the basis of some combination of these demographic factors—and a retail strategy planned accordingly:

- Market size—How many people are in the potential target market?
- Gender—Is the potential target market more male or female, or are they equal in proportion?
- Age—What are the prime age groups to which the firm wants to appeal?
- Household size—What is the average household size of potential consumers?
- Marital and family status—Are potential consumers single or married? Do families have children?
- Income—Is the potential target market lower income, middle income, or upper income? Is discretionary income available for luxury purchases?
- Retail sales—What is the area's sales forecast for the retailer's goods/services category?
- Birth rate—How important is the birth rate for the retailer's goods/services category?
- Mobility—What percent of the potential target market moves into and out of the trading area yearly?
- Where people live—How large is the trading area from which potential customers can be drawn?
- Employment status—Does the potential target market include working women?

- Occupation—In what industries and occupations are people in the area working? Are they professionals, office workers, or of some other designation?
- Education—Are potential customers college-educated?
- Ethnic/racial background—Does the potential target market cover a distinctive racial or ethnic group?

CONSUMER LIFE-STYLES

Consumer Insight Magazine (www.acnielsen.com/pubs/ci) provides a good perspective on emerging consumer trends.

Consumer life-styles are based on social and psychological factors, and influenced by demographics. As with demographics, a retailer should first have some knowledge of consumer life-style concepts and then determine the life-style attributes of its own target market.

These *social factors* are useful in identifying and understanding consumer life-styles.

- A **culture** is a distinctive heritage shared by a group of people that passes on a series of beliefs, norms, and customs. The U.S. culture stresses individuality, success, education, and material comfort; there are also various subcultures (such as African-, Hispanic-, and Asian-Americans) due to the many countries from which residents have come.
- **Social class** involves an informal ranking of people based on income, occupation, education, and other factors. People often have similar values in each social class.
- **Reference groups** influence people's thoughts and behavior: aspirational groups—a person does not belong but wishes to join; membership groups—a person does belong; and dissociative groups—a person does not want to belong. Face-to-face groups, such as families, have the most impact. Within reference groups, there are opinion leaders whose views are well respected and sought.
- The **family life cycle** describes how a traditional family moves from bachelorhood to children to solitary retirement. At each stage, attitudes, needs, purchases, and income change. Retailers must also be alert to the many adults who never marry, divorced adults, single-parent families, and childless couples. The **household life cycle** incorporates life stages for both family and nonfamily households.
- *Time utilization* refer to the activities in which a person is involved and the amount of time allocated to them. The broad categories are work, transportation, eating, recreation, entertainment, parenting, sleeping, and (retailers hope) shopping. Today, many consumers allocate less time to shopping.

R E T A I L I N G
Around the World | The Life-Styles and Shopping Behavior of Global Consumers Are Changing

The Cap Gemini Ernst & Young marketing research firm (**www.capgemini.com**) recently conducted a study of 6,000 consumers in nine European countries. The findings of the European study were similar to those conducted with 10,000 consumers in the United States and 1,000 consumers in Asia Pacific.

These are the major conclusions:

- Consumers do not feel that retailers are sufficiently differentiated. Four of 10 consumers in Spain and one-third of Norwegian shoppers could not provide the name of their favorite supermarket.
- The most important values that consumers look for in a company are honesty, respect, and reliability. European shoppers identified the same five factors as U.S. consumers:

courteous employees, consistency in merchandise quality, a clean store environment, easy return of merchandise, and a visible process.

- An "honest price" is far more important to shoppers than the "lowest price"; and "consistent good-quality merchandise" is more important than "top-quality merchandise."
- There are some important national differences that retailers need to understand. For example, German shoppers are almost twice as likely to visit a discounter at least once a week than the average European shopper.

Source: "What Consumers Value Most," *Cap Gemini Ernst & Young press release* (April 23, 2002).

Consumer psychology can be studied with tools such as the Keirsey Temperament Sorter. Take the online test (www. keirsey.com/cgi-bin/ keirsey/newkts.cgi) to learn about yourself.

These *psychological factors* help in identifying and understanding consumer life-styles:

- A **personality** is the sum total of an individual's traits, which make that individual unique. They include a person's level of self-confidence, innovativeness, autonomy, sociability, emotional stability, and assertiveness.

- **Class consciousness** is the extent to which a person desires and pursues social status. It helps determine the use of reference groups and the importance of prestige purchases. A class-conscious person values the status of goods, services, and retailers.

- **Attitudes (opinions)** are the positive, neutral, or negative feelings a person has about different topics. They are also feelings consumers have about a given retailer and its activities. Does the consumer feel a retailer is desirable, unique, and fairly priced?

- **Perceived risk** is the level of risk a consumer believes exists regarding the purchase of a specific good or service from a given retailer, whether or not the belief is correct. There are six types: *functional* (Will a good or service perform well?), *physical* (Can a good or service hurt me?), *financial* (Can I afford to buy?), *social* (What will peers think of my shopping here?), *psychological* (Am I doing the right thing?), and *time* (How much effort must I exert in shopping?). Perceived risk is high if the retailer or its brands are new, a person is on a budget, a person has little experience, there are many choices, and a purchase is socially visible or complex. See Figure 7-2. Retailers can reduce perceived risk through information.

- *The importance of a purchase* to the consumer affects the amount of time he or she will spend to make a decision and the range of alternatives considered. If a purchase is important, perceived risk tends to be higher, and the retailer must adapt to this.

A retailer can develop a life-style profile of its target market by answering these questions and then use the answers in developing its strategy:

- Culture—What values, norms, and customs are most important to the potential target market?

- Social class—Are potential consumers lower, middle, or upper class? Are they socially mobile?

FIGURE 7-2
The Impact of Perceived Risk on Consumers

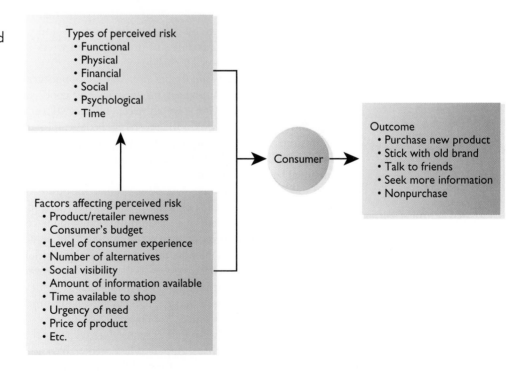

- Reference groups—To whom do people look for purchasing advice? Does this differ by good or service category? How can a firm target opinion leaders?
- Family (or household) life cycle—In what stage(s) of the cycle are the bulk of potential customers?
- Time utilization—How do people spend time? How do they view their shopping time?
- Personality—Do potential customers have identifiable personality traits?
- Class consciousness—Are potential consumers status-conscious? How does this affect purchases?
- Attitudes—How does the potential target market feel about the retailer and its offerings in terms of specific strategy components?
- Perceived risk—Do potential customers feel risk in connection with the retailer? Which goods and services have the greatest perceived risk?
- Importance of the purchase—How important are the goods/services offered to potential customers?

RETAILING IMPLICATIONS OF CONSUMER DEMOGRAPHICS AND LIFE-STYLES

Demographic and life-style factors need to be considered from several perspectives. Here are some illustrations. By no means do the examples cover the full domain of retailing.

Gender Roles: The huge number of working women, who put in 60 to 70 hours or more each week between their job and home responsibilities, is altering life-styles significantly. Compared to women who have not worked outside the home, they tend to be more self-confident and individualistic, more concerned with convenience, more interested in sharing household and family tasks with spouses or significant others, more knowledgeable and demanding as consumers, more interested in leisure activities and travel, more involved with self-improvement and education, more appearance-conscious, and more indifferent to small price differences among retailers. They are less interested in unhurried shopping trips.

Due to the trend toward working women, the life-styles of males are also changing. More men now take care of their children, shop for food, do laundry, wash dishes, cook for the family, vacuum the house, and clean the bathroom. Today, 31 percent of U.S. males are either the primary grocery shopper in the family (20 percent) or share that responsibility (11 percent).[4] See Figure 7-3. The future will see still more changes in men's and women's roles—and in the conflicts over them. The clout and duties of husbands and wives will be shared with greater frequency. Retailers need to appreciate this trend.

Consumer Sophistication and Confidence: Many shoppers are now more knowledgeable and cosmopolitan; more aware of trends in tastes, styles, and goods and services; and more sophisticated. Nonconforming behavior is widely accepted since consumers are self-assured and better appreciate the available choices. Confident shoppers depend less on brands and they will experiment: "Consumers view shopping as part necessity and part adventure, part pragmatism and part emotion. For retail companies to succeed they must satisfy the consumers' requirements for both. The functional basics are a given."[5]

Poverty of Time: The increase in working women, the desire for personal fulfillment, the daily job commute, and the tendency of some people to have second jobs contribute to many consumers feeling time-pressured: "No matter how rich or poor consumers are, time is the great social equalizer. A new priority of making the most of the limited time we have is taking over. Consumers are looking at all the ways they spend their time, including shopping, and demanding a more time-efficient, time-conscious way to shop."[6] There are ways for retailers to respond to the poverty-of-time concept. Firms can add branch stores to limit customer travel time; be open longer hours; add on-floor sales personnel; reduce checkout time; and use mail order, Web sites, and other direct marketing practices. See Figure 7-4.

Component Life-Styles: In the past, shoppers were typecast, based on demographics and life-styles. Now, it is recognized that shopping is less predictable and more individualistic. It is more situation-based, hence, the term *component life-style*: "Have you wondered what's going on with

consumers? Why the contradictions when it comes to spending money? Why they will buy a $500 leather jacket at full price but wait for a $50 sweater to go on sale? Will buy a top-line sports utility vehicle then go to Costco for tires? Will pay $3.50 for a cup of coffee but think $1.29 is too much for a hamburger? Will spend $2.00 for a strawberry-smelling bath soap but wait for a coupon to buy a $0.99 twin pack of toilet soap?"[7]

CONSUMER PROFILES

VALS (www.sric-bi.com/ VALS) classifies life-styles into several profiles. Visit the site to learn about the profiles and take the "VALS Survey" to see where you fit.

Considerable research has been aimed at describing consumer profiles in a way that is useful for retailers. Here are three examples:

Demographically, the typical outlet shopper is a married, career woman who's 43 years old, with a family income of $53,000. Four times a year she travels about 45 minutes to outlet shop, and spends more than $100 each visit.[8]

Today's men 18 to 34 shop more like women their age than like older men. Younger men make 3.6 shopping trips a week, compared to 4.1 by younger women. Younger men visit an average of 1.6 stores, nearly as many as visited by younger women (1.9). These young men were the first to grow up in households with working, liberated moms who did not have time to do all the shopping for them. Mom sent them to the mall to get their own jeans and sneakers. Mom delegated grocery shopping and errands. They received shopping gift cards from Old Navy and Gap.[9]

One-third of shoppers drive the majority of sales, and it is these "heavy shoppers" that retailers should take into consideration. Who are they? Convenience stores and drugstores tend to attract smaller households (one or two members), while heavy grocery store shopper households tend to be larger (three or four members). Drugstores have heavy shoppers who are older—more than one-quarter are aged 65 and older, while other channels see their heavy shoppers primarily coming from households headed by under 55-year-olds. Upscale shoppers are more likely to shop heavily at membership clubs, while the poor are more apt to be heavy convenience store shoppers than any other segment.[10]

CONSUMER NEEDS AND DESIRES

Catherines (www. catherines.com), a retailer of plus-size women's apparel, works hard to satisfy both consumer needs and desires, especially the latter.

When developing a target market profile, a retailer should identify key consumer needs and desires. From a retailing perspective, *needs* are a person's basic shopping requirements consistent with his or her present demographics and life-style. *Desires* are discretionary shopping goals that have an impact on attitudes and behavior. A person may need a new car to get to and from work and seek a dealer with Saturday service hours. The person may desire a Porsche and a free loaner car when the vehicle is serviced but be satisfied with a Saturn that can be serviced on the weekend and fits within the budget.

Consider this: "Consumers today spend proportionately less on basic necessities, such as food, clothing, and shelter, than they did 25, 35, or 50 years ago. But they spend more on discre-

Careers in
RETAILING
Taking on McDonald's in the Philippines

When McDonald's (www.mcdonalds.com) first entered the Philippines in 1981, many retailing analysts assumed that it would soon dominate the Philippine market. Little did anyone imagine that Tony Tan, the local owner of a few ice cream parlors that had converted into burger kitchens, would soon become the Philippines' fast-food burger market leader.

Tan's chain, Jollibee (www.jollibee.com.ph), became so dominant in the Philippines that McDonald's only choice seemed to be either to retreat or imitate it. And although McDonald's would probably deny it, it clearly has sought an imitation-based strategy.

To appeal to Philippine palates, Jollibee offers such foods as burgers that are sweet and juicy, spaghetti that is topped with

hot dogs, and beef with honey and rice. And unlike McDonald's icon, Ronald McDonald, Jollibee's icon is the bee. The bee was chosen because it epitomizes the Philippine spirit of light-hearted, everyday happiness. Lastly, Jollibee's staff has been known to outsmile McDonald's employees. Jollibee's employees greet customers with a sign language-based gesture made up of a vertical stroke for "bee" and hands going toward the heart for "happy." They also refer to each other and to customers by "sir" or "mom," terms that are viewed as casual, yet, respectful.

Source: "A Busy Bee in the Hamburger Hive," *Economist* (March 2, 2002), p. 62.

tionary purchases that are motivated by emotion and desire."[11] And this: "Because of their life stage needs and inherent attitudes, first-wave baby boomers are in their peak spending years. Those aged 45 to 54 spend at a level far exceeding their share of the population. They are particularly strong spenders on 'desires' (wants) as opposed to 'needs'—categories such as gifts, entertainment, and personal care products. Retailers that want to benefit from this group's fat wallets will work to make the shopping experience easier through new location strategies, new approaches to merchandising, and upgraded service."[12]

When a retail strategy aims to satisfy consumer needs and desires, it appeals to consumer **motives**, the reasons for their behavior. These are just a few of the questions to resolve:

- How far will customers travel to get to the retailer?
- How important is convenience?
- What hours are desired? Are evening and weekend hours required?
- What level of customer services is preferred?
- How extensive a goods/service assortment is desired?
- What level of goods/service quality is preferred?
- How important is price?
- What retailer actions are necessary to reduce perceived risk?
- Do different market segments have special needs? If so, what are they?

Let us address the last question by looking at three particular market segments that attract retailer attention: in-home shoppers, online shoppers, and outshoppers.

In-Home Shopping: The in-home shopper is not always a captive audience. Shopping is often discretionary, not necessary. Convenience in ordering an item, without traveling for it, is important. These shoppers are often active store shoppers, and they are affluent and well-educated. Many in-home shoppers are self-confident, younger, and venturesome. They like in-store shopping but have low opinions of local shopping. For some catalog shoppers, time is not important. In households with young children, in-home shopping is more likely if the woman works part-time or not at all than if she works full-time. In-home shoppers may be unable to comparison shop; may not be able to touch, feel, handle, or examine products first-hand; are concerned about service (such as returns); and may not have a salesperson to ask questions.

Check out the NUA survey site (www.nua.ie/surveys) to find out more about Web users. Scroll down to "Demographics."

Online shopping: People who shop online are well-educated and have above-average incomes (as noted in Chapter 6). However, unlike many other retail formats, the Web has multiple uses for people that go beyond purchasing online: "Retailers selling online must regard the Internet as a medium through which people not only buy but also sort through their buying decisions. While many online households buy goods or services online, a much higher number have researched goods or services on the Internet, only to buy the items at a store or fax or phone in the order. For retailers, it's really important to avoid judging the success of an online presence simply in terms of sales."[13] This is what U.S. Web users do online: two to three times per week—check or send E-mail; once per week—visit Internet sites for hobbies; play games, read online news or magazines, visit retail sites for merchandise; two to three times per month—conduct business-related activities, look at financial information, view pictures and images, search for or download software, chat online, visit auction sites; once per month—visit sites for tickets/reservations, visit newsgroups, look for job opportunities.[14]

Outshopping: Out-of-hometown shopping, **outshopping**, is important for both local and surrounding retailers. The former want to minimize this behavior, whereas the latter want to maximize it. Outshoppers are often male, young, members of a large family, and new to the community. Income and education vary by situation. Outshoppers differ in their life-styles from those who patronize hometown stores. They enjoy fine foods, like to travel, are active, like to change stores, and read out-of-town newspapers. They also downplay hometown stores and compliment out-of-town stores. This is vital data for suburban shopping centers. Outshoppers have the same basic reasons for out-of-town shopping whether they reside in small or large communities—easy access, liberal credit, store diversity, product assortments, prices, the presence of large chains, entertainment facilities, customer services, and product quality.

SHOPPING ATTITUDES AND BEHAVIOR

In this section, we look at people's attitudes toward shopping, where they shop, and the way in which they make purchase decisions.

ATTITUDES TOWARD SHOPPING

Considerable research has been done on people's attitudes toward shopping. Such attitudes have a big impact on the ways in which people act in a retail setting. Retailers must strive to turn around some negative perceptions that now exist. Let us highlight some recent research findings.

Shopping Enjoyment: In general, people do not enjoy shopping as much as in the past. When the International Mass Retail Association asked shoppers what would make them choose one retailer from a group of similar retailers situated near each other, the shoppers said the retailer whose layout they knew best, the retailer with no stuff in the aisles, the retailer with the best employee attitudes, the cleanest retailer, and the retailer that appeared neatest and nicest inside.[15]

Attitudes Toward Shopping Time: Retail shopping is often viewed as a chore: "Americans no longer regard shopping as a fun pastime. Consumers want to spend fewer hours cruising the mall in search of the perfect item and, instead, get what they need as quickly as possible. This trend has been dubbed 'precision shopping.' The upside of precision shopping is that consumers spend more money each time they visit a store. With less time for idle browsing, they're more purposeful in their shopping ventures."[16]

Shifting Feelings About Retailing: There has been a major change in attitudes toward spending, value, and shopping with established retailers: "Today, the shopper who buys expensive jewelry at Tiffany is just as likely to purchase commodity goods at a BJ's Wholesale Club. This change appears to be a permanent shift in behavior. Another change is that more consumers tend to wait for sales before making their purchases. Indeed, retailers have helped to condition consumers to low prices by offering frequent price promotions. The trend has dampened retailers' potential profits, as consumers who were once loyal to a particular store are now willing to turn on a dime if a well-stocked, lower-priced competitor comes along. This intense focus on price may lead more retailers to adopt an 'everyday low price' strategy in an effort to attract a steady customer base and to eliminate margin-eroding sales."[17]

Why People Buy or Do Not Buy on a Shopping Trip: It is critical for retailers to determine why shoppers leave without making a purchase. Is it prices? A rude salesperson? Not accepting the consumer's credit card? Not having an item in stock? Or some other factor? According to Kurt Salmon Associates, here are the top 10 reasons why shoppers leave an apparel store without buying:

1. Cannot find an appealing style.
2. Cannot find the right size or the item is out of stock.
3. Nothing fits.
4. No sales help is available.
5. Cannot get in and out of the store easily.
6. Prices are too high.
7. In-store experience is stressful.
8. Cannot find a good value.
9. Store is not merchandised conveniently.
10. Seasonality is off.[18]

Attitudes by Market Segment: In their banking activities, upscale consumers are more interested in dealing with "highly professional, competent bankers" than middle-income consumers, who consider "friendliness" and "location" to be more important. Grocery shoppers can be divided into four categories: shopping avoiders, who dislike grocery shopping; time-starved shoppers, who pay more for convenience; responsible shoppers, who feel grocery shopping is a key household task; and traditional shoppers, who plan store trips carefully. Web consumers feel comfortable with technology, like comparison shopping, and are more trusting of online security than nonshoppers. Overall enthusiasm for shopping is much higher in Europe than in the United States; two-thirds of Europeans say they like or love to shop.[19]

Attitudes Toward Private Brands: Many consumers believe private (retailer) brands are as good as or better than manufacturer brands: "For American consumers, private brands are brands like any other brands. In a landmark nationwide study, 75 percent of consumers defined store brands as 'brands' and ascribed to them the same degree of positive product qualities and characteristics—such as guarantee of satisfaction, packaging, value, taste, and performance—that they attribute to manufacturer brands. Moreover, more than 90 percent of all consumers polled were familiar with private brands, and 83 percent said that they purchase these products on a regular basis."[20]

WHERE PEOPLE SHOP

Consumer patronage differs sharply by type of retailer. Thus, it is vital for firms to recognize the venues where consumers are most likely to shop and plan accordingly. Table 7-3 shows where America shops.

Do *you* shop at both Tiffany (www.tiffany.com) and BJ's (www. bjswholesale.com)?

Many consumers do **cross-shopping** whereby they (a) shop for a product category at more than one retail format during the year or (b) visit multiple retailers on one shopping trip. The first occurs because these consumers feel comfortable shopping at different formats throughout the year, their goals vary by occasion (they may want bargains on everyday clothes and fashionable items for weekend wear), they shop wherever sales are offered, and they have a favorite format for themselves and another one for other household members. Visiting multiple retailers on

TABLE 7-3	Where America Shops

Retailers Where Primary Household Shoppers Purchased Within the Past Year
(% of primary household shoppers)

Full-line discount stores	85	Off-price apparel stores	34
Mail-order catalogs	53	Factory outlet stores	34
Self-service shoe stores	51	Full-service shoe stores	21
Traditional department stores	39	Upscale department stores	17
Apparel stores in enclosed malls	38	Fine jewelry stores	13

Shopping Center Monthly Shopper Trends (% of primary household shoppers who shop there at least once per month)

Large strip shopping center with at least one discount department store or one or more category superstores	42
Small to medium strip shopping center with small specialty stores and/or a supermarket	42
Large mall with one or more department stores	29
Strip shopping center with small specialty stores	9
Fashion-oriented shopping center without a department store	6
Downtown shopping district (not a mall)	4

Weekly Shopping (% of primary household shoppers who shop there at least once per month)

Supermarkets	55	Drugstores	21
Convenience stores	45	Small-format value retailers	12
Full-line discount stores	28	Membership clubs	6

Where Travelers Shop (% of travelers who shop there at least once per year while on a trip)

Traditional shopping center or mall	62	Outlet center	38
Downtown shopping district/	53	Megamall	25
Main Street		Airport store	13
Strip center or plaza (not enclosed)	48	Hotel store	13

Source: Compiled by the authors from Retail Forward, "Softgoods," *Shopper Update* (May 2002), p. 5; Retail Forward, "Mass Channel," *Industry Outlook* (March 2002), p. 41; and Travel Industry Association, "Where Travelers Shop," *Chain Store Age* (September 2001), p. 137.

one shopping trip occurs because consumers want to save travel time and shopping time; both can be reduced when visiting more than one retailer per shopping trip. Here are cross-shopping examples:

- Some supermarket customers also regularly buy items carried by the supermarket at convenience stores, full-line department stores, drugstores, and specialty food stores.
- Some department store customers also regularly buy items carried by the department store at factory outlets and full-line discount stores.
- 95 percent of Web shoppers also buy from catalog retailers, 82 percent from mass merchants, 55 percent from apparel chains, and 54 percent from department stores.[21]
- Cross-shopping is especially high for apparel, home furnishings, shoes, sporting goods, and personal care products.

THE CONSUMER DECISION PROCESS[22]

Besides identifying target market characteristics, a retailer should know how people make decisions. This requires familiarity with **consumer behavior**, which is the process by which people determine whether, what, when, how, from whom, and how often to purchase goods and services. Such behavior is influenced by a person's background and traits.

The consumer's decision process must be grasped from two different perspectives: (a) what good or service the consumer is thinking about buying and (b) where the consumer is going to purchase that item (if the person opts to buy). A consumer can make these decisions separately or jointly. If made jointly, he or she relies on the retailer for support (information, assortments, and knowledgeable sales personnel) over the entire decision process. If the decisions are made independently—what to buy versus where to buy—the person gathers information and advice before visiting a retailer and views the retailer merely as a place to buy (and probably more interchangeable with other firms).

The U.S. Consumer Information Center facilitates consumer decision making for such products as cars by providing free online information (www. pueblo.gsa.gov/cars.htm).

In choosing whether or not to buy a given item ("what"), the consumer considers features, durability, distinctiveness, value, ease of use, and so on. In choosing the retailer to patronize for that item ("where"), the consumer considers location, assortment, credit availability, sales help, hours, customer service, and so on. Thus, the manufacturer and retailer have distinct challenges: The manufacturer wants people to buy its brand ("what") at any location carrying it ("where"). The retailer wants people to buy the product, not necessarily the manufacturer's brand ("what"), at its store or nonstore location ("where").

The **consumer decision process** has two parts: the process itself and the factors affecting the process. There are six steps in the process: stimulus, problem awareness, information search, evaluation of alternatives, purchase, and post-purchase behavior. The consumer's demographics and life-style affect the process. The complete process is shown in Figure 7-5.

The best retailers assist consumers at each stage in the process: stimulus (newspaper ads), problem awareness (stocking new models), information search (point-of-sale displays and good salespeople), evaluation of alternatives (clearly noticeable differences among products), purchase (acceptance of credit cards), and post-purchase behavior (extended warranties and money-back returns). The greater the role a retailer assumes in the decision process, the more loyal the consumer will be.

Each time a person buys a good or service, he or she goes through a decision process. In some cases, all six steps in the process are utilized; in others, only a few steps are employed. A consumer who has previously and satisfactorily bought luggage at a local store may not use the same extensive process as one who has never bought luggage.

The decision process outlined in Figure 7-5 assumes that the end result is a purchase. However, at any point, a potential customer may decide not to buy; the process then stops. A good or service may be unneeded, unsatisfactory, or too expensive. Before we consider the ways in which consumers use the decision process, the entire process is explained.

Stimulus: A **stimulus** is a cue (social or commercial) or a drive (physical) meant to motivate or arouse a person to act. When one talks with friends, fellow employees, and others, a social cue is received. The special attribute of a social cue is that it involves an interpersonal, noncommercial source. A commercial cue is a message sponsored by a retailer or some other seller. Ads, sales pitches, and store displays are commercial stimuli. Such cues may not be regarded as highly as

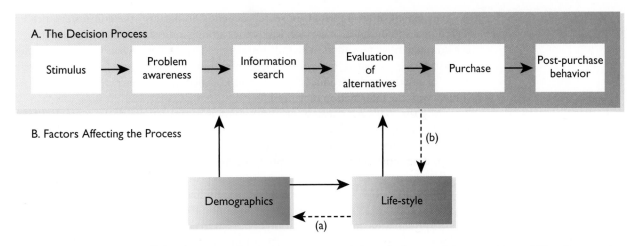

A. The Decision Process

Stimulus → Problem awareness → Information search → Evaluation of alternatives → Purchase → Post-purchase behavior

B. Factors Affecting the Process

Demographics → Life-style
(a)
(b)

Note: Solid arrows connect all the elements in the decision process and show the impact of demographics and life-style upon the process. Dashed arrows show feedback. (a) shows the impact of life-style on certain demographics, such as family size, location, and marital status. (b) shows the impact of a purchase on elements of life-style, such as social class, reference groups, and social performance.

FIGURE 7-5
The Consumer Decision Process

social ones by consumers because they are seller-controlled. A third type of stimulus is a physical drive. It occurs when one or more of a person's physical senses are affected. Hunger, thirst, cold, heat, pain, or fear could cause a physical drive. A potential consumer may be exposed to any or all three types of stimuli. If aroused (motivated), he or she goes to the next step in the process. If a person is not sufficiently aroused, the stimulus is ignored—terminating the process for the given good or service.

Problem Awareness: At **problem awareness**, the consumer not only has been aroused by social, commercial, and/or physical stimuli but also recognizes that the good or service under consideration may solve a problem of shortage or unfulfilled desire. It is sometimes hard to learn why a person is motivated enough to move from a stimulus to problem awareness. Many people shop with the same retailer or buy the same good or service for different reasons, they may not know their own motivation, and they may not tell a retailer their real reasons for shopping there or buying a certain item.

Recognition of shortage occurs when a person discovers a good or service should be repurchased. A good could wear down beyond repair or the person might run out of an item such as milk. Service may be necessary if a good such as a car requires a repair. Recognition of unfulfilled desire takes place when a person becomes aware of a good or service that has not been bought before or a retailer that has not been patronized before. An item (such as contact lenses) may improve a person's life-style, self-image, and so on in an untried manner, or it may offer new performance features (such as a voice-activated computer). People are more hesitant to act on unfulfilled desires. Risks and benefits may be tougher to see. When a person becomes aware of a shortage or an unfulfilled desire, he or she acts only if it is a problem worth solving. Otherwise, the process ends.

Information Search: If problem awareness merits further thought, information is sought. An **information search** has two parts: (1) determining the alternatives that will solve the problem at hand (and where they can be bought) and (2) ascertaining the characteristics of each alternative.

First, the person compiles a list of goods or services that address the shortage or desire being considered. This list does not have to be formal. It may be a group of alternatives the person thinks about. A person with a lot of purchase experience normally uses an internal memory search to determine the goods or services—and retailers—that are satisfactory. A person with little purchase experience often uses an external search to develop a list of alternatives and retailers. This search can involve commercial sources such as retail salespeople, noncommercial sources such as *Consumer Reports*, and social sources such as friends. Second, the person gathers information about each alternative's attributes. An experienced shopper searches his or her memory for the attributes (pros and cons) of each alternative. A consumer with little experience or a lot of uncertainty searches externally for information.

Nonprofit Consumer World has an online, noncommercial guide catalog with over 2,000 sources to aid the consumer's information search (www.consumerworld.org).

The extent of an information search depends, in part, on the consumer's perceived risk regarding a specific good or service. Risk varies among individuals and by situation. For some, it is inconsequential; for others, it is quite important. The retailer's role is to provide enough information for a shopper to feel comfortable in making decisions, thus reducing perceived risk. Point-of-purchase ads, product displays, and knowledgeable sales personnel can provide consumers with the information they need.

Once the consumer's search for information is completed, he or she must decide whether a current shortage or unfulfilled desire can be met by any of the alternatives. If one or more are satisfactory, the consumer moves to the next step in the decision process. The consumer stops the process if no satisfactory goods or services are found.

Evaluation of Alternatives: Next, a person selects one option from among the choices. This is easy if one alternative is superior on all features. An item with excellent quality and a low price is a certain pick over expensive, average-quality ones. However, a choice may not be that simple, and the person then does an **evaluation of alternatives** before making a decision. If two or more options seem attractive, the person determines the criteria to evaluate and their importance. Alternatives are ranked and a choice made.

The criteria for a decision are those good or service attributes that are considered relevant. They may include price, quality, fit, durability, and so on. The person sets standards for these characteristics and rates each alternative according to its ability to meet the standards. The importance of each criterion is also determined, and attributes are usually of differing importance to each person. One shopper may consider price to be most important while another places greater weight to quality and durability.

At this point, the person ranks the alternatives from most favorite to least favorite and selects one. For some goods or services, it is hard to evaluate the characteristics of the available alternatives because the items are technical, intangible, new, or poorly labeled. When this occurs, shoppers often use price, brand name, or store name as an indicator of quality, and choose based on this criterion. Once a person ranks the alternatives, he or she chooses the most satisfactory good or service. In situations where no alternative proves adequate, a decision not to purchase is made.

Purchase Act: A person is now ready for the **purchase act**—an exchange of money or a promise to pay for the ownership or use of a good or service. Important decisions are still made in this step. For a retailer, the purchase act may be the most crucial aspect of the decision process because the consumer is mainly concerned with three factors, as highlighted in Figure 7-6:

● Place of purchase—This may be a store or a nonstore location. Many more items are bought at stores than through nonstore retailing, although the latter are growing more quickly. The place of purchase is evaluated in the same way as the good or the service: Alternatives are listed, their traits are defined, and they are ranked. The most desirable place is then chosen. Criteria for selecting a store retailer include store location, store layout, service, sales help, store image, and prices. Criteria for selecting a nonstore retailer include image, service,

FIGURE 7-6
Key Factors in the
Purchase Act

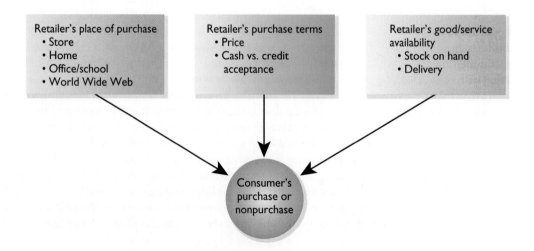

prices, hours, interactivity, and convenience. A consumer will shop with the firm that has the best combination of criteria, as defined by that consumer.

- Purchase terms—These include the price and method of payment. Price is the dollar amount a person must pay to achieve the ownership or use of a good or service. Method of payment is the way the price may be paid (cash, short-term credit, long-term credit).

- Availability—This relates to stock on hand and delivery. Stock on hand is the amount of an item that a place of purchase has in stock. Delivery is the time span between placing an order and receiving an item and the ease with which an item is transported to its place of use.

If a person is pleased with all of the aspects of the purchase act, the good or service is bought. If there is dissatisfaction with the place of purchase, the terms of purchase, or availability, the consumer may not buy, although there is contentment with the item itself:

> Karen wants to buy a stereo. But, after a month of trying, she gave up: "The system I wanted was sold in only three stores and through an online firm. Two stores overpriced the stereo by $75. The third had a good price, but insisted I drive to the warehouse to get the stereo. The Web retailer had a good deal, but it ran out of the model I wanted. When I heard that, I decided to keep my old stereo."

Post-Purchase Behavior: After buying a good or service, a consumer may engage in **post-purchase behavior**, which falls into either of two categories: further purchases or re-evaluation. Sometimes, buying one item leads to further purchases and decision making continues until the last purchase is made. For instance, a car purchase leads to insurance; and a retailer that uses scrambled merchandising may stimulate a shopper to make further purchases, once the primary good or service is bought.

A person may also re-evaluate a purchase. Is the performance as promised? Do actual attributes match the expectations the consumer had of the attributes? Has the retailer acted as expected? Satisfaction typically leads to contentment, a repurchase when a good or service wears out, and favorable ratings to friends. Dissatisfaction may lead to unhappiness, brand or store switching, and unfavorable conversations with friends. The latter situation (dissatisfaction) may result from **cognitive dissonance**—doubt that the correct decision has been made. A consumer may regret that the purchase was made at all or may wish that another alternative had been chosen. To overcome cognitive dissonance and dissatisfaction, the retailer must realize that the consumer decision process does not end with a purchase. After-care (by a phone call, a service visit, or E-mail) may be as important as anything a retailer does to complete the sale. When items are expensive or important, after-care takes on greater significance because the person really wants to be right. In addition, the more alternatives from which to choose, the greater the doubt after a decision is made and the more important the after-care.

Technology in RETAILING — Online Banking: Why Millions Are Attracted

According to many retailing experts, a greater number of consumers now feel comfortable with online financial transactions and have less concern for security-related issues. Whereas about 16 million U.S. consumers used the Web for online banking in 2001, this figure rose to 21 million in 2002—and the number is still growing.

Online banking has advantages for both consumers and banks. To consumers, online banking means faster payments, as well as additional convenience over checks. Consumers can set up their online banking accounts to record the names and addresses of the companies that bill them periodically—such as utilities, rent or mortgage firms, and credit card companies. Online banking also enables consumers to view their account balances at a glance and to transfer money among accounts.

For banks, online transactions often result in high customer loyalty since many people want to avoid the work of establishing new accounts and relisting their frequent bills. Online banking is also allowing banks to expand their retail services. As one online banking software executive says, "Some consumers prefer using the computer for planning instead of making an in-person visit because they want to remain anonymous. You may not want to tell somebody you've got $26,000 in credit card debt."

Source: "More Consumers Switch to Online Banking Due to Convenience," *Dallas Morning News* (January 1, 2002).

Department stores pioneered the money-back guarantee so customers could return items if cognitive dissonance occurred. Realistic sales presentations and ad campaigns minimize dissatisfaction because consumer expectations do not then exceed reality. If overly high expectations are created, a consumer is more apt to be unhappy because performance is not at the level promised. Combining an honest sales presentation with good customer after-care reduces or eliminates cognitive dissonance and dissatisfaction.

TYPES OF CONSUMER DECISION MAKING

Every time a person buys a good or service or visits a retailer, he or she uses a form of the decision process. The process is often used subconsciously, and a person is not even aware of its use. Also, as indicated in Figure 7-5, the process is affected by consumer characteristics. Older people may not spend as much time as younger ones in making decisions due to their experience. Well-educated consumers may consult many information sources before making a decision. Upper-income consumers may spend little time making a decision because they can afford to buy again if they are dissatisfied. In a family with children, each member may have input into a decision, which lengthens the process. Class-conscious shoppers may be more interested in social sources. Consumers with low self-esteem or high perceived risk may use all the steps in detail. People under time pressure may skip steps to save time.

The use of the decision process differs by situation. The purchase of a new home usually means a thorough use of each step in the process; perceived risk is high regardless of the consumer's background. In the purchase of a magazine, the consumer often skips certain steps; perceived risk is low regardless of the person's background. There are three types of decision processes: extended decision making, limited decision making, and routine decision making.

Extended decision making occurs when a consumer makes full use of the decision process. A lot of time is spent gathering information and evaluating alternatives—both what to buy and where to buy it—before a purchase. The potential for cognitive dissonance is great. In this category are expensive, complex items with which the person has had little or no experience. Perceived risk of all kinds is high. Items requiring extended decision making include a house, a first car, and life insurance. At any point in the process, a consumer can stop, and for expensive, complex items, this occurs often. Consumer traits (such as age, education, income, and class consciousness) have the most impact with extended decision making.

Because their customers tend to use extended decision making, such retailers as real-estate brokers and auto dealers emphasize personal selling, printed materials, and other communication to provide as much information as possible. A low-key approach may be best, so shoppers feel comfortable and not threatened. In this way, the consumer's perceived risk is minimized.

With **limited decision making**, a consumer uses each step in the purchase process but does not spend a great deal of time on each of them. It requires less time than extended decision making since the person typically has some experience with both the what and the where of the purchase. This category includes items that have been bought before but not regularly. Risk is moderate, and the consumer spends some time shopping. Priority may be placed on evaluating known alternatives according to the person's desires and standards, although information search is important for some. Items requiring limited decision making include a second car, clothing, a vacation, and gifts. Consumer attributes affect decision making, but the impact lessens as perceived risk falls and experience rises. Income, the importance of the purchase, and motives play strong roles in limited decision making.

This form of decision making is relevant to such retailers as department stores, specialty stores, and nonstore retailers that want to sway behavior and that carry goods and services that people have bought before. The shopping environment and assortment are very important. Sales personnel should be available for questions and to differentiate among brands or models.

Routine decision making takes place when the consumer buys out of habit and skips steps in the purchase process. He or she wants to spend little or no time shopping, and the same brands are usually repurchased (often from the same retailers). This category includes items that are bought regularly. They have little risk because of consumer experience. The key step is problem awareness. When the consumer realizes a good or service is needed, a repurchase is often automatic. Information search, evaluation of alternatives, and post-purchase behavior are unlikely. These steps are not undertaken as long as a person is satisfied. Items involved with routine decision making include groceries, newspapers, and haircuts. Consumer attributes have little impact. Problem awareness almost inevitably leads to a purchase.

This type of decision making is most relevant to such retailers as supermarkets, dry cleaners, and fast-food outlets. For them, these strategic elements are crucial: a good location, long hours, clear product displays, and, most important, product availability. Ads should be reminder-oriented. The major task is completing the transaction quickly and precisely.

IMPULSE PURCHASES AND CUSTOMER LOYALTY

Impulse purchases and customer loyalty merit our special attention.

Impulse purchases arise when consumers buy products and/or brands they had not planned on buying before entering a store, reading a mail-order catalog, seeing a TV shopping show, turning to the Web, and so forth. At least part of consumer decision making is influenced by the retailer. There are three kinds of impulse shopping:

- *Completely unplanned*—A consumer has no intention of making a purchase in a goods or service category before he or she comes into contact with a retailer.
- *Partially unplanned*—A consumer intends to make a purchase in a goods or service category but has not chosen a brand or model before he or she comes into contact with a retailer.
- *Unplanned substitution*—A consumer intends to buy a specific brand of a good or service but changes his or her mind about the brand after coming into contact with a retailer.

With the partially unplanned and substitution kinds of impulse purchases, some decision making takes place before a person interacts with a retailer. In these cases, the consumer may be involved with extended, limited, or routine decision making. Completely unplanned shopping is usually related to routine decision making or limited decision making; there is little or no time spent shopping, and the key step is problem awareness.

Impulse purchases are more influenced by retail displays than are pre-planned purchases: "For most shoppers, the checkout lane is the final hurdle—choose the right lane and get out of the store quickly. Retailers, however, view the checkout lane as a 'last chance' area—the place to sell impulse items such as candy and magazines, and profitable necessities like batteries and razor blades." For retailers, "The key to impulse sales is to have good items on the counter, because it's at the checkout counter that you can really grab your customers' attention. With the impulse item on the counter, they pick one and it's rung up. The customer has no time to think about the purchase at that point. They've grabbed it and bought it."[23]

In studying impulse buying, these are some of the consumer attitudes and behavior patterns that retailers should take into consideration:

- In-store browsing is positively affected by the amount of time a person has to shop.
- Some individuals are more predisposed toward making impulse purchases than others.
- Those who enjoy shopping are more apt to make in-store purchase decisions.
- Impulse purchases are greater if a person has discretionary income to spend.[24]

L.L. Bean (www.llbean. com) has some of the most loyal customers around. See why.

When **customer loyalty** exists, a person regularly patronizes a particular retailer (store or nonstore) that he or she knows, likes, and trusts. This lets a person reduce decision making because he or she does not have to invest time in learning about and choosing the retailer from which to purchase. Loyal customers tend to be time-conscious, like shopping locally, do not often engage in outshopping, and spend more per shopping trip. In a service setting, such as an auto repair shop, customer satisfaction often leads to shopper loyalty; price has little bearing on decisions.

It can be testing to gain customer loyalty—a retailer's greatest asset: " 'What classifies as customer loyalty today only lasts until the next, better deal comes along,' said Britt Beemer, chairman of America's Research Group. 'More people shop somewhere only because that place has the best selection and price of the moment. If someone else comes along with a better offer, loyalty just isn't an issue.' "[25] Applying the retailing concept certainly enhances the chances of gaining and keeping loyal customers: customer orientation, coordinated effort, value-driven, and goal orientation. Relationship retailing helps also!

According to Harte-Hanks Market Research,

- It is tough for any retailer to obtain customer loyalty without shoppers first having a high degree of satisfaction with that retailer.
- Even if retailers get high satisfaction scores, this does not mean they also will earn customer loyalty. Among the factors that create a sense of loyalty beyond satisfaction is the retailer's "value proposition" and an ability to communicate a caring attitude to customers.
- Retailers can receive a higher-than-average degree of loyalty by targeting shoppers who are especially predisposed to being loyal.
- Although two retailers may have the same number of very loyal customers, one of them may deal with more shoppers who are indifferent and do not exhibit any loyalty.[26]

RETAILER ACTIONS

As noted in Chapter 3, in *mass marketing*, a firm such as a supermarket or a drugstore sells to a broad spectrum of consumers; it does not really focus efforts on any one kind of customer. In *concentrated marketing*, a retailer tailors its strategy to the needs of one distinct consumer group, such as young working women; it does not attempt to satisfy people outside that segment. With *differentiated marketing*, a retailer aims at two or more distinct consumer groups, such as men and boys, with a different strategy mix for each; it can do this by operating more than one kind of outlet (such as separate men's and boys' clothing stores) or by having distinct departments grouped by market segment in a single store (as a department store might do). In deciding on a target market approach, a retailer considers its goods/service category and goals, competitors' actions, the size of various segments, the efficiency of each target market alternative for the particular firm, the resources required, and other factors. See Figure 7-7.

After choosing a target market method, the retailer selects the target market(s) to which it wants to appeal; identifies the characteristics, needs, and attitudes of the target market(s); seeks to understand how its targeted customers make purchase decisions; and acts appropriately. The

FIGURE 7-7

ESPNZone: A Clever Target Marketing Approach

ESPNZone restaurants are skillfully targeted toward sports fans. The chain considers itself to be "the ultimate sports dining-and-entertainment complex. Come to the Zone to catch the big game on our 14-foot big screen or check out our interactive games in the sports arena or be part of a live broadcast. The ESPNZone is like ESPN in 3 D." [**http://espn.go.com/ espninc/zone**]

Photo reprinted by permission of Retail Forward, Inc.

FIGURE 7-8
Devising a Target Market Strategy

process for devising a target market strategy is shown in Figure 7-8. Visit our Web site (**www.prenhall.com/bermanevans**) for several useful links on target marketing.

We now present several examples of retailers' target market activities.

RETAILERS WITH MASS MARKETING STRATEGIES

Murray's Discount Auto Parts and Kohl's Department Stores engage in mass marketing.

Find out why Murray's Discount Auto Stores (www.murraysdiscount. com) calls itself "the auto parts supermarket."

Murray's is a Michigan-based regional chain with nearly 100 auto parts stores. Unlike its main competitors, the firm works to attract a broad array of customers—not just seasoned, male do-it-yourselfers. Murray's offers personal shoppers, computer-assisted ordering, and big 10,000-square-foot stores with everyday low prices and merchandise piled high. It is the exception to the stereotype of the intimidating auto parts store: "Let's face it—buying auto parts is not always a pleasant experience. Our job at Murray's is simple—to get you ALL the parts and accessories you need the FIRST time you visit our store. And, as millions of customers in the greater Detroit, Cleveland, Chicago, and Toledo markets will tell you, we do this better than any other auto parts chain in the USA."[27]

Kohl's is one of the fastest-growing general merchandise retailers in the United States. And it is capitalizing on a mass marketing approach. The firm's strategy "doesn't seem revolutionary; but somehow, this chain—a hybrid between discount and department stores—is fast becoming a formidable threat to retailers such as Sears and May Department Stores." And it is "forcing rivals to fight back with new store formats and services that mimic Kohl's mass marketing, even offering shopping carts and express checkouts near the exits at traditional department stores. Kohl's edge over rivals is an emphasis on big brands including Sag Harbor and Reebok that generally aren't available at discounters. Moreover, its prices are lower than at department stores, and it also avoids regional malls where department stores are based, focusing instead on strip centers that are more convenient for customers."[28]

RETAILERS WITH CONCENTRATED MARKETING STRATEGIES

Family Dollar and Zutopia engage in concentrated marketing.

Family Dollar (www. familydollar.com) has carved out a distinctive, narrow niche for itself.

Family Dollar operates 4,200 dollar stores (a type of variety store) in 39 states. It has a very focused target market strategy: "The typical Family Dollar customer is a female who shops for a family with a median annual income of less than $35,000, and in many cases under $20,000. These families depend on Family Dollar to provide them with the good values they must have to stretch their limited disposable income." Stores are rather small and often situated in rural areas and small towns, as well as in urban areas. "The merchandise is sold at everyday low prices in a no-frills, low overhead, self-service environment. Most merchandise is priced under $10.00."[29]

Zutopia is an apparel chain that caters to girls ages 5 to 12. Everything the chain does is aimed at its target market, including an interactive, age-appropriate Web site (**www.zutopia.com**) and the store ambience: "Bright lights, a catwalk, video monitors blasting the latest hits. It is the ultimate shopping experience for trend-conscious tweens. When a girl emerges from the dressing room in the latest look, she walks down a runway to the mirror, sashaying to her favorite songs and putting on a show for people seated nearby."[30]

Ethics in
RETAILING

Trusted Sender E-Mail Differentiates Serious Messages from Spam

Customers of companies that have signed up for "Trusted Sender" will now be able to quickly differentiate a wanted E-mail message from unsolicited junk mail (spam) by clicking on a graphic or a hyperlink that verifies the sender and the recipient. The technology used by Trusted Sender generates a unique encrypted code that allows the recipient to verify the identify of each sender of individual E-mail messages. In addition, each E-mail will provide the consumer with information on a firm's privacy policy, instructions on how to "opt out" of receiving future mailings from a sender, and directions for filing a complaint against firms that continue to send mailings after a customer has opted out.

Trusted Sender is sponsored by direct marketers that want to distinguish themselves from those firms that market questionable products. As the chief privacy officer of ePrivacy (**www.eprivacygroup.com**) says, "Companies want to be able to say 'we are a legitimate sender, we have a legitimate product, and we respect your privacy.' Hopefully, consumers will come to recognize the Trusted Sender program as a symbol of E-mail they can trust, and realize that the sender is going to treat them differently than other people who may be filling their mailbox."

Source: "Marketers Embrace 'Seal' Program for Commercial E-Mail," *Newsbytes* (February 1, 2002).

RETAILERS WITH DIFFERENTIATED MARKETING STRATEGIES

Foot Locker and Big Lots engage in differential marketing.

Besides its mainstream Foot Locker stores, the parent company also operates chains geared specially toward women and children. As the corporate Web site (**www.footlocker. com**) states, the goal of Lady Foot Locker is "to be *the* destination addressing the athletic and fitness needs of women. Born out of the idea that selling footwear to women required a different tact than selling to men, it has thrived to become the only national athletic footwear, apparel, and accessories store devoted to women." And Kids Foot Locker "offers parents a place where they can get the largest selection of quality athletic footwear, apparel, and accessories for their children, as well as expert advice that will meet or exceed their child's needs."

Through its KFC, Pizza Hut, Taco Bell, Long John Silver's, and A&W restaurants, Yum! (www.yum.com) is another retailer practicing differentiated marketing—by food preference.

Even though Big Lots is a deep-discount closeout chain, it still applies differentiated marketing: "We have identified three customer types. The first is our entry price point customers, which represents more than half of our total customer base. They search for the lowest prices and will give up brands to save money. Our next largest group consists of shoppers who look for bargains but prefer brands. Our third customer type has a higher income, shops for fun, and brags about the deals he or she finds. These customers provide some of our best word-of-mouth advertising."[31]

ENVIRONMENTAL FACTORS AFFECTING CONSUMERS

Several environmental factors influence shopping attitudes and behavior, including the:

- State of the economy.
- Rate of inflation (how quickly prices are rising).
- Infrastructure where people shop, such as traffic congestion, the crime rate, and the ease of parking.
- Price wars among retailers.
- Emergence of new retail formats.
- Trend toward more people working at home.
- Government and community regulations regarding shopping hours, new construction, consumer protection, and so forth.
- Evolving societal values and norms.

Although all of these elements may not necessarily have an impact on any particular shopper, they do influence the retailer's overall target market.

When considering the strategy that they offer their customers, retailers should also know the following about the U.S. standard of living:

> The standard of living increased markedly throughout most of the country in the 1990s, bringing gains in education, housing, and mobility along with higher incomes. But if people's homes are bigger, so are their mortgages, and if they own more cars, they also commute more hours to work. In 2000, New York became the first state where residents commuted more than 30 minutes on average each way to their jobs. Today, 40 percent of Californians speak a language other than English at home. And there are still troubling signs of groups being left behind. Nearly 13 percent of the country was living in poverty in 2000. Among the poor are 17 percent of children under 18 and 11 percent of adults 65 or older.[32]

Summary

1. *To discuss why it is important for a retailer to properly identify, understand, and appeal to its customers.* So as to properly develop a strategy mix, a retailer must identify the characteristics, needs, and attitudes of consumers; understand how consumers make decisions; and enact the proper target market plan. It must study environmental influences, too.

2. *To enumerate and describe a number of consumer demographics, life-style factors, and needs and desires—and to explain how these concepts can be applied to retailing.* Demographics are easily identifiable and measurable population statistics. Life-styles are the ways in which consumers live and spend time and money.

   Consumer demographics include gender, age, life expectancy, literacy, languages spoken, income, retail sales, education, and ethnic/racial background. These data usually have to be localized to be useful for retailers. Consumer life-styles comprise social and psychological elements and are affected by demographics. Social factors include culture, social class, reference groups, the family life cycle, and time utilization. Psychological factors include personality, class consciousness, attitudes, perceived risk, and purchase importance. As with demographics, a firm can generate a life-style profile of its target market by analyzing these concepts.

   There are several demographic and life-style trends that apply to retailing. These involve gender roles, consumer sophistication and confidence, the poverty of time, and component life-styles. Research has enumerated consumer profiles in a useful way for retailers.

   When preparing a target market profile, consumer needs and desires should be identified. Needs are basic shopping requirements and desires are discretionary shopping goals. A retail strategy geared toward satisfying consumer needs is appealing to their motives—the reasons for behavior. The better needs and desires are addressed, the more apt people are to buy.

3. *To examine consumer attitudes toward shopping and consumer shopping behavior, including the consumer decision process and its stages.* Many people do not enjoy shopping and no longer feel high prices reflect value. Different segments have different attitudes. More people now believe private brands are of good quality. Consumer patronage differs by retailer type. People often cross-shop, whereby they shop for a product category at more than one retail format during the year or visit multiple retailers on the same shopping trip.

   Retailers should have an awareness of consumer behavior—the process individuals use to decide whether, what, when, where, how, from whom, and how often to buy. The consumer's decision process must be grasped from two perspectives: (a) the good or service the consumer thinks of buying and (b) where the consumer will buy that item. These decisions can be made separately or jointly.

   The consumer decision process consists of stimulus, problem awareness, information search, evaluation of alternatives, purchase, and post-purchase behavior. It is influenced by a person's background and traits. A stimulus is a cue or drive meant to motivate a person to act. At problem awareness, the consumer not only has been aroused by stimulus but also recognizes that a good or service may solve a problem of shortage or unfulfilled desire. An information search determines the available alternatives and their characteristics. Alternatives are then evaluated and ranked. In the purchase act, a consumer considers the place of purchase, terms, and availability. After a purchase, there may be post-purchase behavior in the form of additional purchases or re-evaluation. The consumer may have cognitive dissonance if there is doubt that a correct choice has been made.

   In extended decision making, a person makes full use of the decision process. In limited decision making, each step is used, but not in depth. In routine decision making, a person buys out of habit and skips steps. Impulse purchases occur when shoppers make purchases they had not planned before coming into contact with the retailer. With customer loyalty, a person regularly patronizes a retailer.

4. *To look at retailer actions based on target market planning.* Retailers can deploy mass marketing, concentrated marketing, or differentiated marketing. Several examples are presented.

5. *To note some of the environmental factors that affect consumer shopping.* Consumer attitudes and behavior are swayed by the economy, the inflation rate, the infrastructure where people shop, and other factors. Retailers also need to consider how the standard of living is changing.

Key Terms

demographics (p. 161)	attitudes (opinions) (p. 165)	evaluation of alternatives (p. 174)
life-styles (p. 161)	perceived risk (p. 165)	purchase act (p. 174)
discretionary income (p. 162)	motives (p. 169)	post-purchase behavior (p. 175)
culture (p. 164)	outshopping (p. 169)	cognitive dissonance (p. 175)
social class (p. 164)	cross-shopping (p. 171)	extended decision making (p. 176)
reference groups (p. 164)	consumer behavior (p. 172)	limited decision making (p. 176)
family life cycle (p. 164)	consumer decision process (p. 172)	routine decision making (p. 176)
household life cycle (p. 164)	stimulus (p. 172)	impulse purchases (p. 177)
personality (p. 165)	problem awareness (p. 173)	customer loyalty (p. 177)
class consciousness (p. 165)	information search (p. 173)	

Questions for Discussion

1. Comment on this statement: "Each consumer segment has its own value equation and shops accordingly. Understanding what drives different groups is critical to creating an experience and product offering that satisfies their individual value equations."

2. Analyze the global population data in Table 7-1 from a retailing perspective.

3. How could a national jewelry store chain use the U.S. population data presented in Table 7-2?

4. Explain how a retailer selling expensive, custom-made furniture could reduce the six types of perceived risk.

5. Why is it important for retailers to know the difference between *needs* and *desires*?

6. Why do some consumers engage in outshopping? What could be done to encourage them to shop closer to home?

7. Is cross-shopping good or bad for a retailer? Explain your answer.

8. Describe how the consumer decision process would operate for these products. Include "what" and "where" in your answers: a cell phone, a lawn mower, and a new car. Which elements of the decision process are most important to retailers in each instance? Explain your answers.

9. Differentiate among the three types of impulse purchases. Give an example of each.

10. Contrast the mass market approach used by a fast-food restaurant with the concentrated marketing approach used by an upscale restaurant. What is the key to each firm succeeding?

11. Visit the Web site of Sports Authority (**www.sportsauthority.com**) and then evaluate its target market strategy.

12. Why is it valuable for retailers to know how the standard of living is changing?

Web-Based Exercise

Visit the Web site of J.C. Penney (**www.jcpenney.com**). Click on "about us" at the home page, and then click on "positioning statement" at the toolbar on the next page. Evaluate the target marketing strategy that you find described there.

Note: Stop by our Web site (**www.prenhall.com/bermanevans**) to experience a number of highly interactive, appealing Web exercises based on actual company demonstrations and sample materials related to retailing.

Chapter Endnotes

1. Various company sources.

2. Kurt Salmon Associates, "The Fittest in Today's Environment Are the Most Focused," *Insights* (August 2002), pp. 5–9.

3. *Statistical Abstract of the United States 2002* (Washington, D.C.: U.S. Department of Commerce, 2002), various pages.

4. "Consumer Trends," *Progressive Grocer Annual Report 2002* (April 2002), p. 27.

5. WSL Strategic Retail, *How America Shops 2000.*

6. Pamela N. Danziger, "The Lure of Shopping," *American Demographics* (July–August 2002), p. 46.

7. WSL Strategic Retail, *How America Shops 1998.*

8. Value Retail News, "Who Is the Typical North American Outlet Shopper?" **www.joyofshopping.com/shopper.html** (February 17, 2003).

9. WSL Strategic Retail, *How America Shops 2002.*

10. Marcia Mogelonsky, "Hard-Core Shoppers," *American Demographics* (September 1998), p. 49.

11. "Desire, Not Necessity, Drives $3 Trillion in Consumer Spending," **http://retailindustry.about.com/library/bl/02q3/bl_um071202. htm** (January 23, 2003).

12. Ira P. Schneiderman, "Splitsville: As the Population Becomes Highly Segmented, Retailers Will Have to Choose the Groups They Focus On," *Women's Wear Daily* (March 24, 1999), p. 30.

13. *Second Annual Ernst & Young Internet Shopping Study* (New York: 1999), pp. 9–11.

14. Scott Smith and Bill Swinyard, "The Internet Usability Study," **www.byu.edu/news/releases/archive01/Jul/internet.htm** (July 2001).

15. Calmetta Y. Coleman, "Making Malls (Gasp!) Convenient," *Wall Street Journal* (February 8, 2000), pp. B1, B4.

16. "Retailing: General," *Standard & Poor's Industry Surveys* (May 9, 2002), p. 12.

17. "Retailing: Specialty," *Standard & Poor's Industry Surveys* (January 31, 2002), p. 9.

18. Kurt Salmon Associates, "Which Way to the Emerald City?" *Perspective* (February 2000), p. 3.

19. L. Biff Motley, "Enhance Satisfaction by Targeting Segments," *Bank Marketing* (December 2001), p. 44; Victor J. Orler and David H. Friedman, "The Consumers Behind Consumer-Direct," *Progressive Grocer* (February 1998), p. 40; and "Comparison Shoppers," *Women's Wear Daily* (July 8, 1998), p. 6.

20. Private Label Manufacturers Association, "Store Brands Today," **www.plma.com/storebrands/sbt02.html** (February 28, 2003).

21. Kurt Salmon Associates, "The Fittest in Today's Environment Are the Most Focused," pp. 6–7.

22. For good background reading, see "Special Issue: Retail Consumer Decision Processes," *Journal of Business Research*, Vol. 54 (November 2001).

23. Marcia Mogelonsky, "Keep Candy in the Aisles," *American Demographics* (July 1998), p. 32; and Mary Finn Shapiro, "Impulse Purchases: Location and Demographics Are Key to Hefty Margins for Last-Second Items," *National Petroleum News* (July 2001), p. 41.

24. Sharon E. Beatty and M. Elizabeth Ferrell, "Impulse Buying: Modeling Its Precursors," *Journal of Retailing*, Vol. 74 (Summer 1998), pp. 169–191.

25. Richard Burnett, "Customer Loyalty Is Up for Grabs," *Knight-Ridder/Tribune Business News* (January 27, 2002).

26. Harry Seymour and Laura Rifkin, "Study Shows Satisfaction Not the Same as Loyalty," *Marketing News* (October 26, 1998), p. 40.

27. Isabelle Sender, "Auto Parts for Novices, Supermarket Style," *Chain Store Age* (May 1998), p. 48; "Murray's Discount Auto Stores: The Auto Parts Supermarket," **www.murraysdiscount. com** (February 27, 2003).

28. "Kohl's Focus on Big Brands Gives Rivals Fits; Discount Retailer Expanding with Mass-Market Approach," *Bergen County Record* (June 2, 2002).

29. *Family Dollar 2002 Annual Report.*

30. Kimberly Pfaff, "Wet Seal Repositions Zutopia as Fashion Leader for Young Girls," *Shopping Centers Today* (January 2002), p. 25.

31. *Big Lots (Consolidated Stores) 2000 Annual Report*, p. 14.

32. Eric Schmitt, "Census Data Show a Sharp Increase in Living Standard," *New York Times* (August 6, 2001), p. A1.

Chapter 8

INFORMATION GATHERING AND PROCESSING IN RETAILING

Reprinted by permission.

When Debbi Fields opened her first cookie store in Palo Alto, California, in 1977, she was a 20-year-old housewife with no business experience. At that time, friends told her she was crazy; they felt that a business could not survive on the basis of just selling cookies. They were sure wrong.

Mrs. Field's Cookies (**www.mrsfields.com**) became popular very quickly, and several new stores were set up. To grow even faster, Mrs. Fields started franchising in 1990. Today, the company has several hundred stores, and it is the largest retailer of baked-on-premises cookies in the United States.

Mrs. Fields is among the most widely recognized names in the premium cookie industry with 94 percent brand awareness among consumers. The retailer offers more than 50 different types of cookies, brownies, and muffins. To ensure freshness and quality, products are baked continuously, and all dough is centrally manufactured using only high-quality ingredients.

The chain uses a state-of-the-art retail information system to address the problem of inconsistent performance among stores. When Mrs. Field's Cookies was small, it could ensure consistency by performing on-site inspections. This became more difficult when the chain grew and included foreign units. The problem became apparent when Debbi Fields found that, after only four months in business, the items in a Hawaiian store bore little resemblance to her original products. Unknowingly, the store manager had allowed the cookie formulations to change ever so slightly from their original form and texture. Eventually, the products looked like little cakes instead of cookies.[1]

chapter objectives

1. To discuss how information flows in a retail distribution channel
2. To show why retailers should avoid strategies based on inadequate information
3. To look at the retail information system, its components, and the recent advances in such systems
4. To describe the marketing research process

OVERVIEW

When a retailer forms a new strategy or modifies an existing one, gathering and reviewing information is valuable because it reduces the chances of wrong decisions. The firm can study the attributes and buying behavior of current and potential customers, alternative store and nonstore sites, store management and operations, product offerings, prices, and store image and promotion to prepare the best plan.

Research activity should, to a large degree, be determined by the risk involved. Although it may be risky for a department store to open a new branch store, there is much less risk if a retailer is deciding whether to carry a new line of sweaters. In the branch store situation, thousands of research dollars and many months of study may be necessary. In the case of the new sweaters, limited research may be sufficient.

Information gathering and processing should be conducted in an ongoing manner, yielding enough data for planning and analysis:

iTools (www.itools.com/research-it) offers very useful research tools, including multiple search engines, a dictionary, a thesaurus, a language translator, and more.

Decision makers—merchandisers, financial planners, inventory planners, buyers, and forecasters—throughout retail organizations clamor for the information necessary to gain a competitive advantage. They need the "business intelligence"—the availability of the right information to answer immediate business questions—to improve performance. Today's information systems let retailers interactively investigate performance and trends, and suppliers to assist in managing retail inventory.[2]

Information systems have been a major part of industry-leading Wal-Mart's success. The company invested in most of the waves of retail information technology systems earlier and more aggressively than its competitors: it was among the first retailers to use computers to track inventory (1969), just as it was one of the first to adopt barcodes (1980), electronic data interchange for better coordination with suppliers (1985), and wireless scanning (late 1980s). These investments allowed Wal-Mart to reduce its inventory significantly and to reap savings. Its later investments—such as the Retail Link program, which captures sales data and gives vendors real-time stock and flow information—are aimed more at increasing sales through micromarketing and cutting the incidence of stockouts.[3]

This chapter first looks at the information flows in a retail distribution channel and notes the ramifications of inadequate research. We then describe the retail information system, data-base management and data warehousing, and the marketing research process in detail.

INFORMATION FLOWS IN A RETAIL DISTRIBUTION CHANNEL

In an effective retail distribution channel, information flows freely and efficiently among the three main parties: supplier (manufacturer and/or wholesaler), retailer, and consumer. This enables the parties to better anticipate and address each other's performance expectations. We highlight the flows in Figure 8-1 and describe the information needs of the parties next.

A *supplier* needs these kinds of information: (1) from the retailer—estimates of category sales, inventory turnover rates, feedback on competitors, the level of customer returns, and so on; and (2) from the consumer—attitudes toward given styles and models, the extent of brand loyalty, the willingness to pay a premium for superior quality, and so on. A *retailer* needs these kinds of information: (1) from the supplier—advance notice of new models and model changes, training materials for complex products, sales forecasts, justification for price hikes, and so on; and (2) from the consumer—why people shop with the retailer, what they like and dislike about the retailer, where else people shop, and so on. A *consumer* needs these kinds of information: (1) from the supplier—assembly and operating instructions, the extent of warranty coverage, where to send a complaint, and so on; and (2) from the retailer—where specific merchandise is stocked in the store, the methods of payment accepted, the rain check policy when a sale item is out of stock, and so on.

FIGURE 8-1

How Information Flows
in a Retail Distribution
Channel

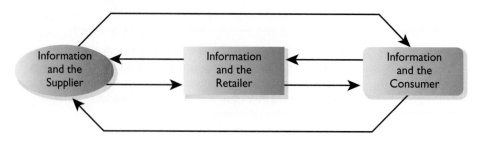

A supplier—the manufacturer or wholesaler—provides information to both the retailer (such as a market forecast) and the consumer (such as an ad describing a new product's features). The supplier determines the information needs of the retailer and the consumer through conversations, surveys, feedback forms, and so forth.

A retailer provides information to both the supplier (such as store unit sales in a product category) and the consumer (such as a salesperson answering questions). The retailer determines the information needs of the supplier and the consumer through conversations, surveys, feedback forms, and so forth.

A consumer provides information to the supplier and retailer through his or her purchases, conversations, credit card data, surveys, feedback forms, complaints, and so forth. In return, the total retail experience is enhanced by the supplier and retailer, since they better understand the consumer—and provide better information to the consumer.

Retailers often play a crucial role in collecting data for other members of the value delivery chain because they have the most direct contact with shoppers. Retailers can assist other channel members by:

- Allowing data to be gathered on their premises. Many research firms like to conduct surveys at shopping centers because of the large and broad base of shoppers.
- Gathering specific data requested by suppliers, such as how shoppers react to displays.
- Passing along information on the attributes of consumers buying particular brands and models. Since credit transactions account for a major portion of sales, many retailers link purchases with consumer age, income, occupation, and other factors.

For the best information flows, collaboration and cooperation are necessary—especially between suppliers and retailers. This is not always easy, as the view of one senior retail executive indicates: "Traditionally, retailers and suppliers just don't like to share supply-chain information with each other. They're more inclined to guard that valuable data than to give it away, even when sharing it would be in their own best interest. As it is, there's friction between retailer and supplier in every step of the supply chain. That's why we still have a messed-up supply chain."[4]

Fortunately, many retailers are working to improve their information-sharing efforts. And as in many aspects of retailing, Wal-Mart is leading the way. Over 10,000 suppliers have online access to Wal-Mart's data base through the firm's Retail Link system, which handles more than 120,000 complex information queries weekly. Retail Link was developed a decade ago to promote more collaboration in inventory planning and product shipping.[5] As the Wal-Mart Web site (**www.walmartstores.com**) notes:

Retail Link provides information and an array of products that allows a supplier to impact all aspects of its business. By using the information available in Retail Link, suppliers can plan, execute, and analyze their businesses—thus providing better service to our common customers. Wal-Mart requires all suppliers to participate in Retail Link because of the benefits it provides.

AVOIDING RETAIL STRATEGIES BASED ON INADEQUATE INFORMATION

Retailers are often tempted to rely on nonsystematic or incomplete ways of obtaining information due to time and costs, as well as a lack of research skills. The results can be devastating. Here are examples.

Using intuition—A movie theater charges $8 for tickets at all times. The manager feels that because all patrons are seeing the same movie, prices should be the same for a Monday matinee as a Saturday evening. Yet, by looking at data stored in the theater's information system, she would learn attendance is much lower on Mondays, indicating that because people prefer Saturday evening performances, they will pay $8 to see a movie then. Weekday customers have to be lured, and a lower price is a way to do so.

Continuing what was done before—A toy store orders conservatively for the holiday season because prior year sales were weak. The store sells out two weeks before the peak of the season, and more items cannot be received in time for the holiday. The owner assumed that last year's poor sales would occur again. Yet, a consumer survey would reveal a sense of optimism and an increased desire to give gifts.

Copying a successful competitor's strategy—A local independent bookstore decides to cut the prices of best-sellers to match the prices of a nearby chain bookstore. The local store then loses a lot of money and has to go out of business. Its costs are too high to match the chain's prices. The firm lost sight of its natural strengths (personal service, a more customer-friendly atmosphere, and long-time community ties).

Devising a strategy after speaking to a few individuals about their perceptions—A family-run gift store decides to have a family meeting to determine the product assortment for the next year. Each family member gives an opinion and an overall "shopping list" is then compiled. Sometimes, the selections are right on target; other times, they result in a lot of excess inventory. The family would do better by also attending trade shows and reading industry publications.

Automatically assuming that a successful business can easily expand—A Web retailer does well with small appliances and portable TVs. It has a good reputation and wants to add other product lines to capitalize on its customer goodwill. However, the addition of furniture yields poor results. The firm did not first conduct research, which would have indicated that people buy standard, branded merchandise via the Web but are more reluctant to buy most furniture that way.

Not having a good read on consumer perceptions—A florist cuts the price of two-day-old flowers from $17 to $5 a dozen because they have a shorter life expectancy, but they don't sell. The florist assumes bargain-hunting consumers will want the flowers as gifts or for floral arrangements. What the florist does not know (due to a lack of research) is that people perceive the older flowers to be of poor quality. The reduced price actually turns off customers!

What conclusion should we draw from these examples? Inadequate information can cause a firm to enact a bad strategy. These situations can be avoided by using a well-conceived retail information system and properly executing marketing research.

RETAILING Around the World   Blockbuster Seeks New Blocks to Expand Outside the United States

Blockbuster (**www.blockbuster.com**) uses both corporate and franchised stores in its international markets. The ratio is about two to one in favor of corporate stores. Now, according to the president of Blockbuster International, the chain plans to further develop its operations in Italy, Spain, Taiwan, Australia, Argentina, Mexico, and other Latin America countries exclusively through franchising.

Blockbuster's new preference for franchising over corporate development stems from its lack of local real-estate knowledge. The president of Blockbuster International acknowledges that "a franchise group can bring local knowledge to the table, which is really beneficial." In selecting international sites, Blockbuster relies on local real-estate professionals; it does not work with any U.S. brokers or developers.

Another advocate of local knowledge is Robert Welanetz, the president of a consulting firm: "Respect is an important criterion going into any international situation. I encourage every retailer to be respectful of local markets and cultures, especially when it's a U.S.-based retailer entering a new country. There's a tendency to think everything should operate as it does in the United States, and that can be offensive and actually retard the retailer's success." Welanetz suggests that retailers need to understand that a brand can travel better than a retailer's U.S. store operations.

Source: "Passport to Global Acceptance," *Chain Store Age* (May 2001), pp. 144, 146.

THE RETAIL INFORMATION SYSTEM

A retail information system requires a lot of background information, which makes the Retailing Resources Web Index (www.crstamu.org/retailing_resources/web-index.asp) valuable.

Data gathering and analysis should not be regarded as a one-shot resolution of a single issue. They should be part of an ongoing, integrated process. A **retail information system (RIS)** anticipates the information needs of retail managers; collects, organizes, and stores relevant data on a continuous basis; and directs the flow of information to the proper decision makers.

These topics are covered next: building and using a retail information system, data-base management, and gathering information through the UPC and EDI.

BUILDING AND USING A RETAIL INFORMATION SYSTEM

Figure 8-2 presents a general RIS. The retailer begins by stating its business philosophy and objectives, which are influenced by environmental factors (such as competitors and the economy). The philosophy and goals provide broad guidelines that direct strategic planning. Some aspects of plans are routine and need little re-evaluation. Others are nonroutine and need evaluation each time they arise.

Once a strategy is outlined, the data needed to enact it are collected, analyzed, and interpreted. If data already exist, they are retrieved from files. When new data are acquired, files are updated. All of this occurs in the information control center. Based on data in the control center, decisions are enacted.

Performance results are fed back to the information control center and compared with preset criteria. Data are retrieved from files or further data are collected. Routine adjustments are made promptly. Regular reports and exception reports (to explain deviations from expected performance) are given to the right managers. Sometimes, managers may react in a way that affects the overall philosophy or goals (such as revising an old-fashioned image or sacrificing short-run profits to introduce a computer system).

All types of data should be stored in the control center for future and ongoing use, and the control center should be integrated with the firm's short- and long-run plans and operations. Information should not be gathered sporadically and haphazardly but systematically.

Retail Info Systems News (www.risnews.com) provides good insights for retailers.

A good RIS has several strengths. Information gathering is organized and company focused. Data are regularly gathered and stored so that opportunities are foreseen and crises averted. Strategic elements can be coordinated. New strategies can be devised more quickly. Quantitative results are accessible, and cost-benefit analysis can be done. Information is routed to the right

FIGURE 8-2
A Retail Information System

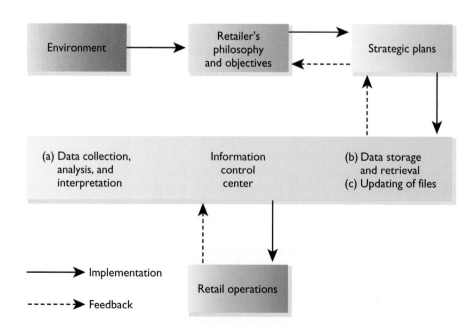

personnel. However, deploying an RIS may require high initial time and labor costs, and complex decisions may be needed to set up such a system.

In building a retail information system, a number of decisions have to be made:

- *How active a role should the RIS have?* Will it proactively search for and distribute any relevant information or will it reactively respond to requests from managers when problems arise? The best systems are more proactive, since they anticipate events.

- *Should an RIS be managed internally or be outsourced?* Although many retailers perform RIS functions, some use outside specialists. Either style can work, as long as the RIS is guided by the retailer's information needs. Several firms have their own RIS and use outside firms for specific tasks (such as conducting surveys or managing networks).

- *How much should an RIS cost?* Retailers typically spend 0.5 to 1.5 percent of sales on an RIS. This lags behind most of the suppliers from which retailers buy goods and services.

- *How technology-driven should an RIS be?* Although retailers can gather data from trade associations, surveys, and so forth, more firms now rely on technology to drive the information process. With the advent of personal computers, inexpensive networks, and low-priced software, technology is easy to use. Even a neighborhood deli can generate sales data by product and offer specials on slow-sellers.

- *How much data are enough?* The purpose of an RIS is to provide enough information, on a regular basis, for a retailer to make the proper strategy choices—not to overwhelm retail managers. This means a balancing act between too little information and information overload. To avoid overload, data should be carefully edited to eliminate redundancies.

- *How should data be disseminated throughout the firm?* This requires decisions as to who receives various reports, the frequency of data distribution, and access to data bases. When a firm has multiple divisions or operates in several regions, information access and distribution must be coordinated.

- *How should data be stored for future use?* Relevant data should be stored in a manner that makes information retrieval easy and allows for adequate longitudinal (period-to-period) analysis.

Larger retailers tend to have a chief information officer (CIO) overseeing their RIS. Information systems departments often have formal, written annual plans. Computers are used by most companies that conduct information systems analysis, and many firms use the Web for some RIS functions. Growth in the use of retail information systems is expected. There are many differences in information systems among retailers, on the basis of revenues and retail format.

Twenty-five years ago, most computerized retail systems were used only to reduce cashier errors and improve inventory control. Today, they often form the foundation for a retail information system and are used in surveys, ordering, merchandise transfers between stores, and other activities. These activities are conducted by both small and large retailers. The vast majority of small and medium retailers—as well as large retailers—have computerized financial management systems, analyze sales electronically, and use computerized inventory management systems. Here are illustrations of the ways in which retailers are using the latest technological advances to computerize their information systems.

Retail Technologies International markets Retail Pro management information software to retailers. See Figure 8-3. This software is used at 24,000 stores around the world. Although popular with several large retailers, Retail Pro software also has an appeal among smaller retailers due to flexible pricing based on the number of users and stores, the type of hardware, and so forth. A small store pays 2 to 3 percent of one year's sales to buy a complete Retail Pro System, including training and support. Retail Pro has the following features, as described at its Web site (**www.retailpro.com**):

OLAP (online analytical processing) processes, analyzes, and views data from different viewpoints on screen instantly without having to generate multiple reports. The *multidimensional data base* can display values by store, vendor, and department for up to 44 dimensions including store, region, day, month, vendor, department, style, size, color, and season. *Drill down* can instantly break out data into more detail. *Pivoting* is the ability to

To see the various ways in which actual retailers are applying Retail Pro, go to the "Sample User List" (www.retailpro.com/public/public_userlist.html). Click on the highlighted retailers for their case histories.

FIGURE 8-3
Retail Pro Management
Information Software

Reprinted by permission of
Retail Technologies
International.

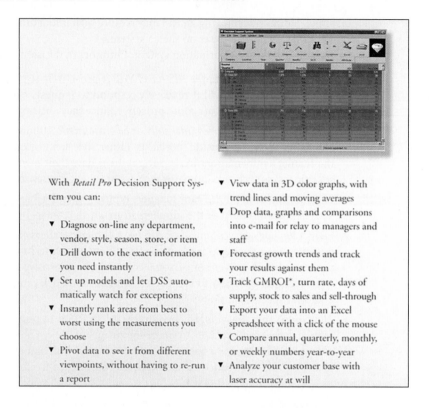

With *Retail Pro* Decision Support System you can:

▼ Diagnose on-line any department, vendor, style, season, store, or item
▼ Drill down to the exact information you need instantly
▼ Set up models and let DSS automatically watch for exceptions
▼ Instantly rank areas from best to worst using the measurements you choose
▼ Pivot data to see it from different viewpoints, without having to re-run a report

▼ View data in 3D color graphs, with trend lines and moving averages
▼ Drop data, graphs and comparisons into e-mail for relay to managers and staff
▼ Forecast growth trends and track your results against them
▼ Track GMROI*, turn rate, days of supply, stock to sales and sell-through
▼ Export your data into an Excel spreadsheet with a click of the mouse
▼ Compare annual, quarterly, monthly, or weekly numbers year-to-year
▼ Analyze your customer base with laser accuracy at will

switch the hierarchy of how you view data. *Ranking* can be done instantly by any value. *Forecast* lets the user project performance along any dimension, using past history or other criteria, and track variances from projections. *Watches* are minimum/maximum levels that can be set for any aspect of performance to activate an alert when exceptions occur.

MicroStrategy typically works with larger retailers—including more than 60 percent of the top 200 retailers in the world—to prepare computerized information systems. Clients include Best Buy, Eddie Bauer, Lowe's, and Victoria's Secret. One of its leading software products is MicroStrategy Desktop, which is described at the firm's Web site (**www.microstrategy.com**):

MicroStrategy Desktop is the business intelligence software component that offers integrated query and reporting, powerful analytics, and decision support workflow on the personal computing desktop. It provides an arsenal of features for online analysis of corporate data. Even complex reports are easy to create; they can be viewed in various presentation formats, polished into production reports, distributed to other users, and extended through a host of features—including data slicing. The interface itself is customizable to different users' skill levels and security profiles.

Wilsons Leather sells men's and women's outerwear, apparel, and accessories at 800 stores in the United States and Canada. Since 1997, it has spent $30 million to revamp its RIS:

Our systems provide all levels of our organization access to information, powerful analytical tools to improve our understanding of sales and operating trends, and the flexibility to anticipate future business needs. Our point-of-sale and back-office systems have been designed to, among other things, free store employees' time so that they can focus on serving our customers. Our point-of-sale system gives each store the ability to view inventory at other store locations, automates store operations, human resource, and inventory management documentation, and enables customer information collection. We obtain sales and inventory data daily from stores, facilitating the allocation of inventory, pricing, and inventory levels. The continuous flow of information to and from our overseas personnel permits us to better control inventory, plan manufacturing capacity, regulate merchandise flow, and ensure product consistency among manufacturers.[6]

DATA-BASE MANAGEMENT

In **data-base management**, a retailer gathers, integrates, applies, and stores information related to specific subject areas. It is a major element in an RIS and may be used with customer data bases, vendor data bases, product category data bases, and so on. A firm may compile and store data on customer attributes and purchase behavior, compute sales figures by vendor, and store records by product category. Each of these would represent a separate data base. Among retailers that have data bases, most use them for frequent shopper programs, customer analysis, promotion evaluation, inventory planning, trading-area analysis, joint promotions with manufacturers, media planning, and customer communications.

Data-base management should be approached as a series of five steps:

1. Plan the particular data base and its components and determine information needs.
2. Acquire the necessary information.
3. Retain the information in a usable and accessible format.
4. Update the data base regularly to reflect changing demographics, recent purchases, and so forth.
5. Analyze the data base to determine company strengths and weaknesses.

Information can come from internal and external sources. A retailer can develop data bases internally by keeping detailed records and arranging them. It could generate data bases *by customer*—purchase frequency, items bought, average purchase, demographics, and payment method; *by vendor*—total retailer purchases per period, total sales to customers per period, the most popular items, retailer profit margins, average delivery time, and service quality; and *by product category*—total category sales per period, item sales per period, retailer profit margins, and the percentage of items discounted.

Donnelley (www. donnelleymarketing.com) offers a number of useful products to help small firms build and manage their data bases.

There are firms that compile data bases and make them available for a fee. Donnelley Marketing, a subsidiary of infoUSA, has a comprehensive data base of the United States, with data on more than 90 percent of all households: "Our DQI[3] data base is the largest, most comprehensive source of insightful demographic and life-style information available. It's a cost-effective way to find new customers and generate more business! We compile our information from more than 3,800 phone directories, auto registration files from available states, public record real-estate information, and self-reported consumer responses. In addition, we integrate dozens of proprietary enrichment sources. The data base allows selection by age, income, types of auto, and credit card holders—to name a few."[7]

To effectively manage a retail data base, these are vital considerations:

- Is senior management knowledgeable in data-base strategies and does it know how company data bases are currently being used?
- Is there a person or department responsible for overseeing the data base?
- Does the firm have data-base acquisition and retention goals?
- Is every data-base initiative analyzed to see if it is successful?
- Is there a mechanism to flag data that indicates potential problems or opportunities?
- Are customer purchases of different products or company divisions cross-linked?
- Is there a clear privacy policy that is communicated to those in a data base? Are there opt-out provisions for those who do not want to be included in a data base?
- Is the data base updated each time there is a customer interaction?
- Are customers, personnel, suppliers, and others invited to update their personal data?
- Is the data base periodically checked to eliminate redundant files?[8]

Let us now discuss two aspects of data-base management: Data warehousing is a mechanism for storing and distributing information. Data mining and micromarketing are ways in which information can be utilized. Figure 8-4 shows the interplay of data warehousing with data mining and micromarketing.

FIGURE 8-4

Retail Data-Base Management in Action

The data warehouse is where information is collected, sorted, and stored centrally. Information is disseminated to retailer personnel, as well as to channel partners (such as alerting them to what merchandise is hot and what is not hot) and customers (such as telling them about order status). In data mining, retail executives and other employees—and sometimes channel partners—analyze information by customer type, product category, and so forth in order to determine opportunities for tailored marketing efforts. With micromarketing, the retailer applies differentiated marketing: Focused retail strategy mixes are planned for specific customer segments—or even for individual customers.

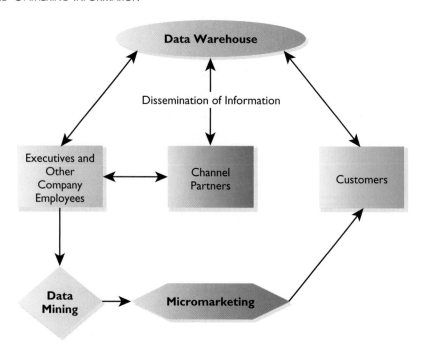

Data Warehousing

NCR publishes a useful online *Data Warehousing Report* (www.teradata.com/dwr) with timely tips and news.

One recent advance in data-base management is **data warehousing**, whereby copies of all the data bases in a firm are maintained in one location and accessible to employees at any locale. The basic premise of data warehousing is "to create a clearinghouse in which to gather and organize critical business data. The data warehouse is a store of integrated data obtained from various internal, and possibly external, sources which represents events or facts as of a given point in time. Properly designed, implemented, and maintained, a data warehouse is a valuable business intelligence tool."[9]

A data warehouse has the following components: (1) the data warehouse, where data are physically stored, (2) software to copy original data bases and transfer them to the warehouse, (3) interactive software to allow inquiries to be processed, and (4) a directory for the categories of information kept in the warehouse.

Data warehousing has several advantages. Executives and other employees are quickly, easily, and simultaneously able to access data wherever they may be. There is more companywide entrée to new data when they are first available. Data inconsistencies are reduced by consolidating records in one location. Better data analysis and manipulation are possible because information is stored in one location.

Computerized data warehouses were once costly to build (an average of $2.2 million a decade ago) and, thus, feasible only for the largest retailers. This has changed. A simple data warehouse can now be put together for less than $25,000, making it affordable to all but very small retailers (which do not have to deal with far-flung executives, making data warehousing less necessary for them).

Federated Department Stores, Hollywood Video, 7-Eleven, and Sears are just a few of the thousands of firms that use data warehousing: "Retailers have collected vast amounts of data for years, but they have not had the means to apply it effectively to their planning and buying because, until a few years ago, no computer or software application could process all of that data. The applications available today offer retailers better results because they incorporate more than just historical sales data."[10] See Figure 8-5.

At Wal-Mart,

Determining the kinds of products carried by its stores used to be the job of merchandisers. Today, computers do the leg work. Every scrap of information about who buys is fed into a huge data warehouse. Wal-Mart has over 100 terabytes of data, which if printed on 8½-by-11 sheets of paper and laid end to end would reach the moon and back 15 times. The system was built in-house and works like this: Scanners located at cash registers read the bar-

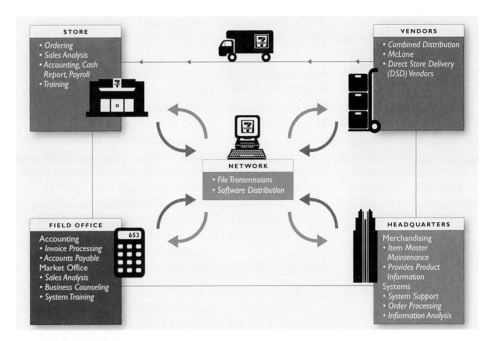

FIGURE 8-5

7-Eleven's Forward-Looking Approach to Data Warehousing

By electronically connecting all parties in the 7-Eleven supply chain, its retail information system creates a higher level of coordination and much better decision making. Store operators have actual sales information presented in logical formats and are able to order more effectively. Receiving exact orders in an organized fashion allows vendors to provide better service to the stores. Field offices are able to reduce administration costs by receiving information in electronic format. Headquarters merchandising staff are able to judge new product acceptance and communicate upcoming advertising and promotions from manufacturers that will affect sales.

Reprinted by permission.

codes on products for price, time of purchase, and the mix of items in each shopper's basket. The info is sent to the data warehouse, where computers slice and dice it to glean who's buying what, and when and where they're buying it. This information is sent to manufacturers through the Internet, telling them what is selling and where it's selling best. They can then quickly resupply—or agree to cut prices if a product isn't moving.[11]

Careers in RETAILING
Women Climb the Information Technology Ladder

Several women have risen to the top information technology (IT) position in their retail companies. Let's take a brief glimpse at three top female IT executives:

- Randy Allen is chief information officer, executive vice-president, and chief strategy officer at Kmart (**www.kmart.com**), where she directs a staff of 1,200 and oversees a $1.4 billion investment in IT. Although Allen admits to being detail-oriented, she says that it has not kept her from being viewed as an astute strategist.
- Norcen Iles is vice-president of retail systems at Sears (**www.sears.com**). She oversees Sears' consumer data warehouse and all of Sears' merchandise planning, assortment planning, and inventory replenishment systems. Iles manages an $85 million budget and a staff of 200, about 40 per-

cent of whom are women. According to Iles, women are even better represented in project management roles at Sears, where they comprise 50 percent of the workforce.
- Debbie Giotti, a data analysis specialist with an excellent knowledge of systems, was one of retailing's most visible chief information officers until she left Starbucks Coffee Co. (**www.starbucks.com**) to join a software company. Because Giotti joined Starbucks when it was a young company, she had a lot of latitude in shaping the organization of its information technology department.

Source: Matt Nannery, "Iron Ladies," *Chain Store Age* (June 2001), pp. 71–80.

Data Mining and Micromarketing

Data mining is the in-depth analysis of information to gain specific insights about customers, product categories, vendors, and so forth. The goal is to learn if there are opportunities for tailored marketing efforts that would lead to better retailer performance. One application of data mining is **micromarketing**, whereby the retailer uses differentiated marketing and develops focused retail strategy mixes for specific customer segments, sometimes fine-tuned for the individual shopper.

Data mining relies on special software to sift through a data warehouse to uncover patterns and relationships among different factors. The software allows vast amounts of data to be quickly searched and sorted. That is why firms such as Bear Creek, the parent of Harry and David (the popular fruit and gift direct marketer), have made the financial commitment to data mining: "We've had to invest in our data bases. They are key to our success in being able to identify and segment customers. They allow us to look at customer purchasing behavior and effectively manage our mailing and E-mail campaigns."[12]

Tesco, the innovative British supermarket chain, is an acknowledged leader in data mining and applying it in the firm's micromarketing efforts:

For an in-depth discussion, go to About Retail Industry (http://retailindustry.about.com) and type "customer data mining" in the search engine.

> The chain's detailed information on customers now forms the basis of Tesco's entire marketing communications strategy—not only on decisions about selling prices, but also about what products are sold in what locations at any given time. As a result, Tesco has reduced its in-store promotions: "It is about focusing on the people who are most price-sensitive. It has changed the way the business is run and saved a lot of money." Every quarter, Tesco sends out a statement to its 10 million regular Clubcard users, yet only one in every 100 will receive the same communication. There are 100,000 variations of the quarterly statement, each offering a different mix of coupons, to provide incentives and reward loyalty. "We don't send customers incentives for goods they don't buy. We see what they buy and send them incentives to get them toward the high watermark of their buying habits. We may also cross-reference people with similar shopping habits to suggest new items they might like. We think about what the customers want rather than what the supermarket wants to sell."[13]

GATHERING INFORMATION THROUGH THE UPC AND EDI

To be more efficient with their information systems, many retailers now rely on the Universal Product Code (UPC) and electronic data interchange (EDI).

With the **Universal Product Code (UPC)**, products (or tags attached to them) are marked with a series of thick and thin vertical lines, representing each item's identification code. UPC-A labeling—the preferred format—includes numbers, as well as lines. The lines are "read" by scanners at checkout counters. Cashiers do not enter transactions manually—although they can, if needed. Because the UPC is not readable by humans, the retailer or vendor must attach a ticket or sticker to a product specifying its size, color, and other information (if not on the package or the product). Given that the UPC does not include price information, this too must be added by a ticket or sticker.

By using UPC-based technology, retailers can record data instantly on an item's model number, size, color, and other factors when it is sold, as well as send the data to a computer that monitors unit sales, inventory levels, and so forth. The goals are to produce better merchandising data, improve inventory management, speed transaction time, raise productivity, reduce errors, and coordinate information. Since its inception, UPC technology has improved substantially. Today, it is the accepted standard in retailing:

> The Uniform Code Council says that several billion UPC scans a day are made. The symbol uniquely identifies each product down to its specific stock-keeping unit. For instance, a 16-ounce bottle of shampoo has a different UPC than a 32-ounce bottle. Over the past three decades, it is estimated that food prices to the consumer would have risen almost twice as fast without the UPC. The value of information in the UPC is estimated to be 20 times more valuable than originally thought."[14]

Virtually every time sales or inventory data are scanned by computer, UPC technology is involved. More than 250,000 manufacturers and retailers worldwide belong to the Uniform Code Council (UCC), an association that has taken the lead in setting and promoting interindustry product identification and communication standards (**www.uc-council.org**). Figure 8-6 shows how far UPC technology has come. The UPC is discussed further in Chapter 16 ("Financial Merchandise Management").

Global eXchange Services is one of the leaders in EDI technology (www.gegxs.com).

With **electronic data interchange (EDI)**, retailers and suppliers regularly exchange information through their computers with regard to inventory levels, delivery times, unit sales, and so on of particular items. As a result, both parties enhance their decision-making capabilities, better con-

FIGURE 8-6

Applying UPC Technology to Gain Better Information

As this photo montage shows, Symbol Technologies has devised a host of scanning products (some of which are wireless) that make UPC data capture and processing quite simple. For example, Symbol products can be used at the point of sale to enter transaction data and transmit them to a central office, at product displays to verify shelf prices, at storage areas to aid in taking physical inventories, at receiving stations to log in the receipt of new merchandise, and at delivery points to track the movement of customer orders.

trol inventory, and are more responsive to demand. UPC scanning is often the basis for product-related EDI data. Thousands of U.S. firms use some form of EDI system. Consider this scenario:

> Virtually every pair of blue jeans sold in a department store today is tracked through a bar-code system. When the retailer's computer system sees that the supply of a particular style and size is low, it automatically generates a purchase order that is transmitted to the apparel manufacturer via EDI. The manufacturer's EDI system imports the information into a computer data base. It is confirmed that the product is in stock, the product is found via bar-code, and a trucking company is notified. When the truck picks up the jeans, the EDI system creates an advance shipment notice and sends it via EDI to the retailer. At the same time, a barcode label for the shipping carton is created. When the truck delivers the jeans, the retailer scans the barcode label. The retailer then automatically generates an electronic funds transfer.[15]

Today, more retailers are expanding their EDI efforts to incorporate Internet communications with suppliers. One such retailer is United Supermarkets, based in Texas. Through its online EDI system, United is saving $400,000 in transaction costs—and reducing the time delays—involving the 60,000 documents a year that it processes. In setting up its system, United first set up its online EDI program with its 20 largest suppliers; it then slowly added its small and medium-size suppliers.[16]

EDI is covered further in Chapter 15 ("Implementing Merchandise Plans"); CPFR (collaborative planning, forecasting, and replenishment) is discussed there.

THE MARKETING RESEARCH PROCESS

Marketing research in retailing entails the collection and analysis of information relating to specific issues or problems facing a retailer. At farsighted firms, marketing research is just one element in a retail information system. At others, marketing research may be the only type of data gathering and processing.

The **marketing research process** embodies a series of activities: defining the issue or problem to be studied, examining secondary data, generating primary data (if needed), analyzing data, making recommendations, and implementing findings. It is not a single act; it is a systematic process. Figure 8-7 outlines the research process. Each activity is done sequentially. Secondary data are not examined until after an issue or problem is defined. The dashed line around the primary data stage means these data are generated only if secondary data do not yield actionable information. The process is described next.

Issue (problem) definition involves a clear statement of the topic to be studied. What information does the retailer want to obtain to make a decision? Without clearly knowing the topic to be researched, irrelevant and confusing data could be collected. Here are examples of issue definitions for a shoe store. The first one seeks to compare three locations and is fairly structured; the second is more open-ended:

1. "Of three potential new store locations, which should we choose?"
2. How can we improve the sales of our men's shoes?"

When **secondary data** are involved, a retailer looks at data that have been gathered for purposes other than addressing the issue or problem currently under study. Secondary data may be internal (such as company records) or external (such as government reports and trade publications). When **primary data** are involved, a retailer looks at data that are collected to address the specific issue or problem under study. This type of data may be generated via survey, observation, experiment, and simulation.

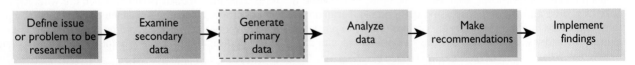

FIGURE 8-7

The Marketing Research Process in Retailing

Technology in RETAILING
Utz Quality Foods: Tracking Snacks from Oven to Store Shelves

The vice-president for key accounts at Utz Quality Foods (**www.utzsnacks.com**), the nation's third-largest manufacturer of salty snacks, had a question when analyzing his sales data on a pre–Super Bowl promotion. Why had two of three Safeway stores in Columbia, Maryland, sold 25 and 40 barrels of Utz's cheese bowls, respectively, while the third store recorded no sales at all? By looking on the Web at his firm's UtzFocus sales-tracking system, the vice-president soon learned that the third store and about 10 others had not ordered any cheese bowls.

Prior to UtzFocus, the firm gave its 500 driver-salespersons handheld computers to upload daily sales data to the firm's corporate headquarters. However, the only department that used this information on a daily basis was accounts receivable. As a result, the sales department only received detailed reports once a month.

The firm's marketing manager and vice-president for sales and marketing insisted that Utz create UtzFocus to provide daily sales breakdowns on a product-by-product and store-by-store basis. As a result, Utz can better track missed deliveries, as well as fast- and slow-selling products by store. The software also provides data that let supermarkets track the impact of promotions.

Source: Timothy J. Mullaney, "Using the Net to Stay Crisp," *Business Week* (April 16, 2001), pp. EB 34–36.

Secondary data are sometimes relied on; other times, primary data are crucial. In some cases, both are gathered. It is important that retailers keep these points in mind: One, there is great diversity in the possible types of data collection (and in the costs). Two, only data relevant to the issue being studied should be collected. Three, primary data are usually acquired only if secondary data are inadequate (thus, the dashed box in Figure 8-7). Both secondary and primary data are described further in the next sections.

These kinds of secondary and primary data can be gathered for the shoe store issues stated previously:

Issue (Problem) Definition	Information Needed to Solve Issue (Problem)
1. Which store location?	1. Data on access to transportation, traffic, consumer profiles, rent, store size, and types of competition are gathered from government reports, trade publications, and observation by the owner for each of the three potential store locations.
2. How to improve sales of shoes?	2. Store sales records for the past five years by product category are gathered. A consumer survey in a nearby mall is conducted.

After data are collected, data analysis is performed to assess that information and relate it to the defined issue. Alternative solutions are also clearly outlined. For example:

Issue (Problem) Definition	Alternative Solutions
1. Which store location?	1. Each site is ranked for all of the criteria (access to transportation, traffic, consumer profiles, rent, store size, and types of competition).
2. How to improve sales of shoes?	2. Alternative strategies to boost sales are analyzed and ranked.

At this point, the pros and cons of each alternative are enumerated. See Table 8-1. Recommendations are then made as to the best strategy for the retailer. Of the available options, which is best? Table 8-1 also shows recommendations for the shoe-store issues discussed in this section.

Last, but not least, the recommended strategy is implemented. If research is to replace intuition in strategic retailing, a decision maker must follow the recommendations from research studies, even if they seem to contradict his or her own ideas.

Let us now look at secondary data and primary data in greater depth.

TABLE 8-1		Research-Based Recommendations	
Issue (Problem)	Alternatives	Pros and Cons of Alternatives	Recommendation
1. Which store location?	Site A.	Best transportation, traffic, and consumer profiles. Highest rent. Smallest store space. Extensive competition.	Site A: the many advantages far outweigh the disadvantages:
	Site B.	Poorest transportation, traffic, and consumer profiles. Lowest rent. Largest store space. No competition.	
	Site C.	Intermediate on all criteria.	
2. How to improve sales of shoes?	Increased assortment.	Will attract and satisfy many more customers. High costs. High level of inventory. Reduces turnover for many items.	Lower prices and increase ads: additional customers offset higher costs and lower margins; combination best expands business.
	Drop some lines and specialize.	Will attract and satisfy a specific consumer market. Excludes many segments. Costs and inventory reduced.	
	Slightly reduce prices.	Unit sales increase. Markup and profit per item decline.	
	Advertise.	Will increase traffic and new customers. High costs.	

SECONDARY DATA

Advantages and Disadvantages

Through Report Gallery (www.reportgallery.com), a retailer can do competitive intelligence on other firms around the globe. Want the most current annual report? Get it here.

Secondary data have several advantages:

- Data assembly is inexpensive. Company records, trade journals, and government publications are all rather low-cost. No data collection forms, interviewers, and tabulations are needed.
- Data can be gathered quickly. Company records, library sources, and Web sites can be accessed immediately. Many firms store reports in their retail information systems.
- There may be several sources of secondary data—with many perspectives.
- A secondary source may possess information that would otherwise be unavailable to the retailer. Government publications often have statistics no private firm could acquire.
- When data are assembled by a source such as *Progressive Grocer*, A.C. Nielsen, *Business Week*, or the government, results are usually quite credible.
- The retailer may have only a rough idea of the topics to investigate. Secondary data can then help to define issues more specifically. In addition, background information about a given issue can be gathered from secondary sources before undertaking a primary study.

Secondary data also have several potential disadvantages:

- Available data may not suit the purposes of the current study because they have been collected for other reasons. Neighborhood statistics may not be found in secondary sources.
- Secondary data may be incomplete. A service station owner would want car data broken down by year, model, and mileage driven, so as to stock parts. A motor vehicle bureau could provide data on the models but not the mileage driven.
- Information may be dated. Statistics gathered every two to five years may not be valid today. The *U.S. Census of Retail Trade* is conducted every five years. Furthermore, there is often a long time delay between the completion of a census and the release of information.

- The accuracy of secondary data must be carefully evaluated. Thus, a retailer needs to decide whether the data have been compiled in an unbiased way. The purpose of the research, the data collection tools, and the method of analysis should each be examined—if they are available for review.

- Some secondary data sources are known for poor data collection techniques; they should be avoided. If there are conflicting data, the source with the best reputation for accuracy should be used.

- In retailing, many secondary data projects are not retested and the user of secondary data has to hope results from one narrow study are applicable to his or her firm.

Whether secondary data resolve an issue or not, their low cost and availability require that primary data not be amassed until after studying secondary data. Only if secondary data are not actionable should primary data be collected. We now present various secondary data sources for retailers.

Sources

There are many sources and types of secondary data. The major distinctions are between internal and external sources.

Internal secondary data are available within the company, sometimes from the data bank of a retail information system. Before searching for external secondary data or primary data, the retailer should look at information available inside the firm.

At the beginning of the year, most retailers develop budgets for the next 12 months. They are based on sales forecasts and outline planned expenditures for that year. A firm's budget and its performance in attaining budgetary goals are good sources of secondary data.

Retailers use sales and profit-and-loss reports to judge performance. Many have data from electronic registers that can be studied by store, department, and item. By comparing data with prior periods, a firm gets a sense of growth or contraction. Overdependence on sales data may be misleading. Sales should be examined along with profit-and-loss data to indicate strengths and weaknesses in operations and management, and lead to improvements.

Through customer billing reports, a retailer learns about inventory movement, sales by different personnel, and sales volume. For credit customers, sales by location, repayment time, and types of purchases can be reviewed. Purchase invoices show the retailer's own buying history and let it evaluate itself against budgetary goals. See Figure 8-8.

Inventory records indicate the merchandise carried throughout the year and the turnover of these items. Knowing the lead time to place and receive orders from suppliers, as well as the extra merchandise kept on hand to prevent running out at different times during the year, aids planning.

If a firm does primary research, the resultant report should be kept for future use (hopefully in the retail information system). When used initially, a report involves primary data. Later reference to it is secondary in nature since the report is no longer used for its primary purpose.

FIGURE 8-8

Internal Secondary Data: A Valuable Source of Information

The sales receipt (invoice) contains a lot of useful data, from the name of the person involved in each sales transaction to the items sold to the selling price. Weekly, monthly, and yearly performance can easily be tracked by carefully storing and retrieving sales receipt data.

Reprinted by permission of Retail Technologies International.

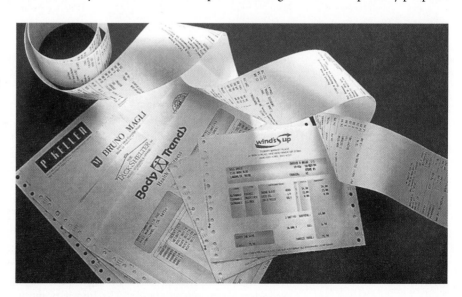

Written reports on performance are another source of internal secondary data. They may be prepared by senior executives, buyers, sales personnel, or others. All phases of retail management can be improved through formal report procedures.

External secondary data are available from sources outside the firm. They should be consulted if internal information is insufficient for a decision to be made on a defined issue. These sources are comprised of government and nongovernment categories.

To use external secondary data well, appropriate reference guides should be consulted. They contain listings of written (computer-based) materials, usually by subject or topic heading, for a specified time. Here are several guides, chosen for their retailing relevance. Most are available through any college library or other large library or via the Web (for online access, you must use your college or local library Web connection—direct entry to the sites is password protected):

- *ABI/INFORM* (data base).   Covers hundreds of journals. Articles are classified by subject.
- *Business Periodicals Index.* Monthly, except for July. Cumulations quarterly, semiannually, and annually. Subject index of hundreds of English-language periodicals.
- *Dialog* (data base).   Contains hundreds of data bases covering various disciplines. Information on public firms, economic data, financial news, and business news.
- *EBSCOhost* (data base).   Covers hundreds of journals, newspapers, and financial reports in business and other disciplines. Full-text articles and abstracts available.
- *InfoTrac* (data base).   Covers hundreds of journals, newspapers, and financial reports in business and other disciplines. Full-text articles and abstracts available.
- *ProQuest* (data base).   Covers hundreds of journals, newspapers, and financial reports in business and other disciplines. Full-text articles and abstracts available.
- *Wall Street Journal Index.* Monthly, with quarterly and annual cumulations.

> The U.S. Census Bureau has a Web site (www. census.gov/econ/www/ retmenu.html) listing its most recent retailing reports, which can be viewed and downloaded from the site.

The government distributes a wide range of materials. Here are several publications, chosen for their retailing value. They are available in any business library or other large library or through the Web:

- *U.S. Census of Retail Trade.* Every five years ending in 2 and 7. Detailed data by retail classification and metropolitan region.
- *U.S. Census of Service Industries.* Every five years ending in 2 and 7. Similar to *U. S. Census of Retail Trade* but covers service industries organized by SIC code.
- *Monthly Retail Trade and Food Services Sales.* Compiled monthly. Data by retail classification.
- *Statistical Abstract of the United States.* Annually. Detailed summary of U.S. statistics.
- *U.S. Survey of Current Business.* Monthly, with weekly supplements. On all aspects of business.
- *Other.* Registration data (births, deaths, automobile registrations, etc.). Available through federal, state, and local agencies.

Government agencies, such as the Federal Trade Commission, also provide pamphlets on topics such as franchising, unit pricing, deceptive ads, and credit policies. The Small Business Administration provides smaller retailers with literature and advice. Pamphlets are distributed free or sold for a nominal fee.

> Looking for secondary data on direct marketing (www. colinear.com/resource.htm) or E-commerce (www. webcommercetoday.com/ research)? Check out these sites.

Nongovernment secondary data come from many sources, often cited in reference guides. Major nongovernment sources are regular periodicals; books, monographs, and other nonregular publications; channel members; and commercial research houses.

Regular periodicals are available at most libraries or by personal subscription. A growing number are also online; some Web sites provide free information, whereas others charge a fee. Periodicals may have a broad scope (such as *Business Week*) and discuss diverse business topics, or they may have narrower coverage (such as *Chain Store Age*) and deal mostly with retail topics.

Many organizations publish books, monographs, and other nonregular retailing literature. Some, such as Prentice Hall (**www.prenhall.com/phbusiness**), produce textbooks and practitioner-oriented books. Others have more distinct goals. The American Marketing Association (**www.marketingpower.com**) offers information to enhance readers' business knowledge. The Better Business Bureau (**www.bbb.org**) wants to improve the public's image of business and expand industry self-regulation. The International Franchise Association (**www.franchise.org**)

and the National Retail Federation (**www.nrf.com**) describe industry practices and trends, and act as spokespersons to advocate the best interests of members. Other associations can be uncovered by consulting Gale's *Encyclopedia of Associations.*

Retailers often get information from channel members such as ad agencies, franchise operators, manufacturers, and wholesalers. When these firms do research for their own purposes and present some or all of the findings to their retailers, external secondary data are involved. Channel members pass on findings to enhance their sales and retailer relations. They usually do not charge for the information.

The last external source is the commercial research house that conducts ongoing studies and makes results available to many clients for a fee. This source is secondary if the retailer is a subscriber and does not request tailored studies. Information Resources Inc., A.C. Nielsen, and Standard Rate & Data Service provide subscriptions at lower costs than a retailer would incur if data were collected only for its use.

Our Web site (**www.prenhall.com/bermanevans**) has links to about 50 online sources of free external secondary data—both government and nongovernment.

PRIMARY DATA

Advantages and Disadvantages

After exhausting the available secondary data, a defined issue may still be unresolved. In this instance, primary data (collected to resolve a specific topic at hand) are needed. When secondary data are sufficient, primary data are not collected. There are several advantages associated with primary data:

- They are collected to fit the retailer's specific purpose.
- Information is current.
- The units of measure and data categories are designed for the issue being studied.
- The firm either collects data itself or hires an outside party. The source is known and controlled, and the methodology is constructed for the specific study.
- There are no conflicting data from different sources.
- When secondary data do not resolve an issue, primary data are the only alternative.

There are also several possible disadvantages often associated with primary data:

- They are normally more expensive to obtain than secondary data.
- Information gathering tends to be more time consuming.
- Some types of information cannot be acquired by an individual firm.
- If only primary data are collected, the perspective may be limited.
- Irrelevant information may be collected if the issue is not stated clearly enough.

In sum, a retailer has many criteria to weigh in evaluating the use of primary data. In particular, specificity, currentness, and reliability must be weighed against high costs, time, and limited access to materials. A variety of primary data sources for retailers are discussed next.

Sources

Want to discover more about the scope of primary data? Go the Business Research Lab Web site (www.busreslab.com) and click the icons on the left-hand tool bar.

The first decision is to determine who collects the data. A retailer can do this itself (internal) or hire a research firm (external). Internal collection is usually quicker and cheaper. External collection is usually more objective and formal. Second, a sampling method is specified. Instead of gathering data from all stores, all products, and all customers, a retailer may obtain accurate data by studying a sample of them. This saves time and money. With a **probability (random) sample**, every store, product, or customer has an equal or known chance of being chosen for study. In a **nonprobability sample**, stores, products, or customers are chosen by the researcher—based on judgment or convenience. A probability sample is more accurate but is also more costly and complex. Third, the retailer chooses among four methods of data collection: survey, observation, experiment, and simulation. All of the methods are capable of generating data for each element of a strategy.

SURVEY With a **survey**, information is systematically gathered from respondents by communicating with them. Surveys are used in many retail settings. Circuit City surveys thousands of customers monthly to determine their satisfaction with the selling process. Spiegel combines a computer-assisted telephone interviewing system with mail questionnaires, personal surveys, and on-site shopper surveys (at its Eddie Bauer stores) to monitor customer tastes and needs. Food Lion uses in-store surveys to find out how satisfied its customers are and what their attitudes are on different subjects.

A survey may be conducted in person, over the phone, by mail, or online. Typically, a questionnaire is used. A *personal survey* is face-to-face, flexible, and able to elicit lengthy responses; unclear questions can be explained. It may be costly, and interviewer bias is possible. A *phone survey* is fast and rather inexpensive. Responses are often short, and nonresponse may be a problem. A *mail survey* can reach a wide range of respondents, has no interviewer bias, and is not costly. Slow returns, high nonresponse rates, and participation by incorrect respondents are potential problems. An *online survey* is interactive, can be adapted to individuals, and yields quick results. Yet, only certain customers shop online or answer online surveys. The technique chosen depends on the goals and requirements of the research project.

A survey may be nondisguised or disguised. In a nondisguised survey, the respondent is told the real purpose of the study. In a disguised survey, the respondent is not told the true purpose so that the person does not answer what he or she thinks a firm wants to hear. Disguised surveys can use word associations, sentence completions, cartoon analysis, or projective questions (such as "Do your friends like shopping at this store?").

The **semantic differential**—a listing of bipolar adjective scales—is a survey technique that may be disguised or nondisguised. The respondent is asked to rate one or more retailers on several criteria, each evaluated by bipolar adjectives (such as unfriendly–friendly). By computing the average rating of all respondents for each criterion, an overall profile can be developed. A semantic differential comparing two furniture retailers appears in Figure 8-9. Store A is a prestige, high-quality store and Store B is a medium-quality, family-run store. The semantic differential graphically portrays the store images.

OBSERVATION The form of research in which present behavior or the results of past behavior are noted and recorded is known as **observation**. Because people are not questioned, observation may not require respondents' cooperation, and survey biases are minimized. Many times, observation is used in actual situations. The key advantages of using observation alone is that attitudes are not elicited.

Retailers use observation to determine the quality of sales presentations (by having researchers pose as shoppers), to monitor related-item buying, to determine store activity by time

FIGURE 8-9
A Semantic Differential
for Two Furniture Stores

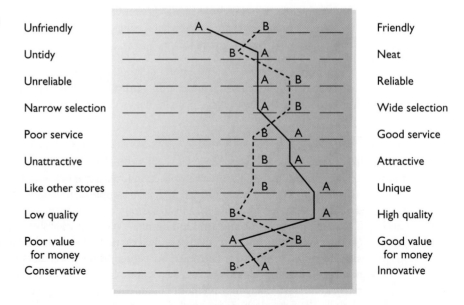

Please check the blanks that best indicate your feelings about Stores A and B.

Ethics in RETAILING

Is Scanning Drivers' Licenses for Information Ethical?

When patrons go to The Rack, a bar in Boston, they are requested to give their driver's license to a doorman or doorwoman who then scans the license. The scanning machine is connected to a data base that determines if the license is a valid one, and if the holder is 21 years old or older.

Although the bar's owner bought the scanner to keep out underage drinkers, he soon realized that he could use it to build a consumer data base. Based on that data base, the bar's owner now knows that a jazz night on Tuesday attracts consumers who are 40 to 45 years old and that his Thursday band attracts consumers from three upscale Boston ZIP codes.

Few of the bar's patrons are aware that the scanning process also reads other information from their driving license, such as the driver's name, address, birth date, and other personal information such as height, weight, eye color, and whether corrective lenses are required. Currently, about 40 states issue driver's licenses with barcodes or magnetic stripes that carry such data. Privacy advocates argue that the increased practice of scanning drivers' licenses could make the license a de facto identity card or internal passport. They are also concerned about a consumer's right to privacy.

Source: Jennifer Lee, "Finding Pay Dirt in Scannable Driver's Licenses," *New York Times on the Web* (March 21, 2002).

and day, to make pedestrian and vehicular traffic counts (to measure the potential of new locations), and to determine the proportion of patrons using mass transit.

With **mystery shoppers**, retailers hire people to pose as customers and observe their operations from sales presentations to how well displays are maintained to service calls.[17] One research firm, Michelson & Associates (**www.michelson.com/mystery**), has a national pool of 80,000 mystery shoppers. As its Web site notes: "We qualify, train, and manage our shoppers to gather factual data and provide objective observations. Our field reps range from 21 to 70 years of age with the majority being women between age 30 and 45. They are pre-selected based on client criteria such as demographics, type of car, shopping habits, etc."

Observation may be disguised or nondisguised, structured or unstructured, direct or indirect, and human or mechanical. In disguised observation, the shopper or company employee is not aware he or she is being watched by a two-way mirror or hidden camera. In nondisguised observation, the participant knows he or she is being observed—such as a department manager watching a cashier's behavior. Structured observation calls for the observer to note specific behavior. Unstructured observation requires the observer to note all of the activities of the person being studied. With direct observation, the observer watches people's present behavior. With indirect observation, the observer examines evidence of past behavior such as food products in consumer pantries. Human observation is carried out by people. It may be disguised, but the observer may enter biased notations and miss behavior. Mechanical observation, such as a camera filming in-store shopping, eliminates viewer bias and does not miss behavior.

EXPERIMENT An **experiment** is a type of research in which one or more elements of a retail strategy mix are manipulated under controlled conditions. An element may be a price, a shelf display, or store hours. If a retailer wants to find out the effects of a price change on a brand's sales, only the price of that brand is varied. Other elements of the strategy stay the same, so the true effect of price is measured.

An experiment may use survey or observation techniques to record data. In a survey, questions are asked about the experiment: Did you buy Brand Z because of its new shelf display? Are you buying more ice cream because it's on sale? In observation, behavior is watched during the experiment: Sales of Brand Z rise by 20 percent when a new display is used. Ice cream sales go up 25 percent during a special sale.

Surveys and observations are experimental if they occur under closely controlled situations. When surveys ask broad attitude questions or unstructured behavior is observed, experiments are not involved. Experimentation can be difficult since many uncontrollable factors (such as the weather, competition, and the economy) come into play. Yet, a well-controlled experiment yields a lot of good data.

The major advantage is an experiment's ability to show cause and effect (a lower price results in higher sales). It is also systematically structured and enacted. The major potential disadvantages are high costs, contrived settings, and uncontrollable factors.

SIMULATION A type of experiment whereby a computer program is used to manipulate the elements of a retail strategy mix rather than test them in a real setting is **simulation**. Two kinds are now being applied in retail settings: those based on mathematical models and those involving "virtual reality."

With the first kind of simulation, a model of the expected controllable and uncontrollable retail environment is constructed. Factors are manipulated by computer so their effects on the overall strategy and specific elements of it are learned. No consumer cooperation is needed, and many combinations of factors can be analyzed in a controlled, rapid, inexpensive, and risk-free manner. This format is gaining popularity because good software is available. However, it is still somewhat difficult to use.

In the second kind of simulation, a retailer devises or buys interactive software that lets participants simulate actual behavior in as realistic a format as possible. This approach creates a "virtual shopping environment." At present, there is limited software for these simulations and personnel must be trained to use it. One exciting application of virtual reality simulations—which has been used with more than 75 clients—is from Simulation Research (**www. simulationresearch.com**). It is depicted in Figure 8-10:

> Visionary Shopper tests in-store variables such as price, promotion, and merchandising. Shoppers are recruited into an interview site, believing they will test a new way of shopping

FIGURE 8-10

Visionary Shopper: A Virtual Reality Simulation

In the Visionary Shopper application, developed by Raymond R. Burke (Indiana University), consumers use a touch-screen monitor to pick up, examine, and purchase products from a simulated shelf display. Virtual reality simulations provide marketers with the realistic competitive context and behavioral measures of a test market along with the low cost, speed, confidentiality, and flexibility of a laboratory experiment.

Reprinted by permission of Raymond R. Burke, Indiana University.

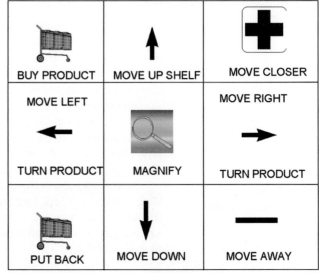

at home (something they might do in the future on their computer or TV). They are seated in front of a computer monitor and taught to maneuver around the shelf. By using a touch-screen and a small control panel, they can go left, right, up, down, zoom in or zoom out, just as in a store. By touching the screen, they can pick up an item from the shelf, turn it around, and look at it more closely. Touching the magnifying glass icon brings up a higher resolution image. Touching the shopping cart icon purchases the product.

Summary

1. *To discuss how information flows in a retail distribution channel.* In an effective retail distribution channel, information flows freely and efficiently among the three main parties (supplier, retailer, and consumer). As a result, the parties can better anticipate and address each other's performance expectations. Retailers often have a vital role in collecting data because they have the most direct contact with shoppers.

2. *To show why retailers should avoid strategies based on inadequate information.* Whether developing a new strategy or modifying an existing one, good data are necessary to reduce a retailer's chances of making incorrect decisions. Retailers that rely on nonsystematic or incomplete research, such as intuition, increase their probabilities of failure.

3. *To look at the retail information system, its components, and the recent advances in such systems.* Useful information should be acquired through an ongoing, well-integrated process. A retail information system anticipates the data needs of retail managers; continuously collects, organizes, and stores relevant data; and directs the flow of information to decision makers. Such a system has several components: environment, retailer's philosophy, strategic plans, information control center, and retail operations. The most important component is the information control center. It directs data collection, stores and retrieves data, and updates files.

   Data-base management is used to collect, integrate, apply, and store information related to specific topics (such as customers, vendors, and product categories). Data-base information can come from internal (company generated) and external (purchased from outside firms) sources. A key advance in data-base management is data warehousing, whereby copies of all the data bases in a firm are kept in one location and can be accessed by employees at any locale. It is a huge repository separate from the operational data bases that support departmental applications. Through data mining and micromarketing, retailers use data warehouses to pinpoint the specific needs of customer segments.

   Retailers have increased their use of computerized retail information systems, and the Universal Product Code (UPC) is now the dominant technology for processing product-related data. With electronic data interchange (EDI), the computers of retailers and their suppliers regularly exchange information, sometimes through the Web.

4. *To describe the marketing research process.* Marketing research in retailing involves these sequential activities: defining the issue or problem to be researched, examining secondary data, gathering primary data (if needed), analyzing the data, making recommendations, and implementing findings. It is systematic in nature and not a single act.

   Secondary data (gathered for other purposes) are inexpensive, can be collected quickly, may have several sources, and may yield otherwise unattainable information. Some sources are very credible. When an issue is ill defined, a secondary data search can clarify it. There are also potential pitfalls: These data may not suit the purposes of the study, units of measurement may not be specific enough, information may be old or inaccurate, a source may be disreputable, and data may not be reliable.

   Primary data (gathered to resolve the specific topic at hand) are collected if secondary data do not adequately address the issue. They are precise and current, data are collected and categorized with the units of measures desired, the methodology is known, there are no conflicting results, and the level of reliability can be determined. When secondary data do not exist, primary data are the only option. The potential disadvantages are the costs, time, limited access, narrow perspective, and amassing of irrelevant information.

Key Terms

retail information system (RIS) (p. 188)

data-base management (p. 191)

data warehousing (p. 192)

data mining (p. 194)

micromarketing (p. 194)

Universal Product Code (UPC) (p. 194)

electronic data interchange (EDI) (p. 195)

marketing research in retailing (p. 196)

marketing research process (p. 196)

issue (problem) definition (p. 196)

secondary data (p. 196)

primary data (p. 196)

internal secondary data (p. 199)

external secondary data (p. 200)

probability (random) sample (p. 201)

nonprobability sample (p. 201)

survey (p. 202)

semantic differential (p. 202)

observation (p. 202)

mystery shoppers (p. 203)

experiment (p. 203)

simulation (p. 204)

Questions for Discussion

1. Relate the information flows in Figure 8-1 to a retailer near to where you live.

2. What would you recommend to guard against this comment? "Traditionally, retailers and suppliers just don't like to share supply-chain information with each other."

3. Can a retailer ever have too much information? Explain your answer.

4. How could a small retailer devise a retail information system?

5. Explain the relationship among the terms *data warehouse*, *data mining*, and *micromarketing*. How can your college bookstore apply these concepts?

6. What are the opportunities and potential problems with electronic data interchange (EDI) for a convenience store chain?

7. Cite the major advantages and disadvantages of secondary data.

8. As a sporting goods store owner, what kinds of secondary data would you use to learn more about your industry and consumer trends in leisure activities?

9. Describe the major advantage of each method of gathering primary data: survey, observation, experiment, and simulation.

10. Develop a 10-item semantic differential for a local theater to judge its image. Who should be surveyed? Why?

11. Why would a retailer use mystery shoppers rather than other forms of observation? Are there any instances when you would not recommend their use? Why or why not?

12. Visit the Simulation Research Web site (**www.simulationresearch. com**) and comment on "virtual shopping" as a research tool for retailers.

Web-Based Exercise

Visit the Web site of A.C. Nielsen (**www.acnielsen.com**), the world's largest marketing research firm. Describe some of the services it offers for retailers. Which service would you most recommend? Why?

Note: Stop by our Web site (**www.prenhall.com/bermanevans**) to experience a number of highly interactive, appealing Web exercises based on actual company demonstrations and sample materials related to retailing.

Chapter Endnotes

1. Various company sources.

2. Kurt Salmon Associates, "Business Intelligence: An Edge for Retailers and Suppliers," *Online Viewpoint* (reprinted from *Retail Asia*, n.d.).

3. Bradford C. Johnson, "Retail: The Wal-Mart Effect," *McKinsey Quarterly* (Number 1, 2002), pp. 41–42.

4. Dan Scheraga, "Disappointment Reigns," *Chain Store Age* (August 2002), p. 83.

5. "Maximizing Relationships," *Chain Store Age* (August 2001), p. 21A.

6. *Wilsons Leather 2001 Annual Report.*

7. "DQI³," **www.donnelleymarketing.com/prodserv/DQI3-1.htm** (February 19, 2003).

8. Adapted by the authors from Jeff St. Onge, "Direct Marketing Credos for Today's Banking," *Direct Marketing* (March 1999), p. 56.

9. "Data Warehousing in the Real World," *America's Network* (May 15, 1999), p. 18; and David Ray Fuller, "The Fundamentals of Data Warehousing: What Is a Data Warehouse?" **www. datawarehouse.com** (January 8, 2002).

10. Meridith Levinson, "They Know What You'll Buy Next Summer (They Hope)," *CIO* (May 2002), p. 116.

11. William J. Holstein, "Data-Crunching Santa," *U.S. News & World Report* (December 21, 1998), pp. 44–45; and Paul Sheldon Foote and Malini Krishnamurthi, "Forecasting Using a Data Warehousing Model: Wal-Mart's Experience," *Journal of Business Forecasting Methods & Systems*, Vol. 20 (Fall 2001), pp. 13–17.

12. "CIOs on CRM," *Chain Store Age* (September 2001), p. 18B.

13. "Dig Deeper into the Data Base Gold Mine," *Marketing* (January 2001), p. 29.

14. "Universal Product Code Turns 25," *Industrial Distribution* (October 1999), p. A7.

15. Stuart Swabini, "EDI and the Internet," *Journal of Business Strategy*, Vol. 22 (January–February 2001), p. 42.

16. Peter Perrotta, "EDI Lowers Transaction Costs for Texas Grocer," *Supermarket News* (February 18, 2002), p. 19.

17. For more information, see Margaret Webb Pressler, "Spies in the Aisles: Companies Use Anonymous Shoppers to Keep Tabs on Service," *Washington Post* (June 16, 2002), p. H5; and Matthew Haeberle, "Corporate Espionage?" *Chain Store Age* (October 2001), pp. 58–60.

part three
Short Cases

1: SHOULD RETAILERS ASK CUSTOMERS WHAT THEY WANT—AND GIVE IT TO THEM?

A popular notion is that a retailer can avoid losing touch with its customers by asking them what they want through focus groups, suggestion boxes, surveys, and so on. Yet, Art Turock (author of a new book entitled *Invent Business Opportunities No One Else Can Imagine*) believes that one of the most crucial errors that a retailer can make is to give customers exactly what they say they really want. Instead, the author contends that a retailer would be better off by giving customers what they might value but could never articulate. According to Turock, these are the six dangers of giving customers just what they want.

Danger 1—Improper expectations of what customers can contribute to a business strategy: Although consumers are able to offer excellent suggestions for improving the goods and services with which they are familiar, they often do not do well when making suggestions with regard to major innovations. After all, consumers are not futurists or technology experts.

Danger 2—Taking customer input as the primary criterion for strategic decisions: Customer feedback should be only one source of information in developing a strategy. Retailers need to study other uncontrollable factors such as industry trends, demographic projections, competitive developments, and value profiles of key market segments.

Danger 3—Listening exclusively to the needs of long-time customers: This approach gives too little consideration to newer customers or newer market segments that may develop into a major part of the business or to small market segments that are highly profitable or have no major competition.

Danger 4—Failing to recognize customers' capacity to accommodate what's familiar: Customers often realize the limitations of existing products only after the next technological breakthrough occurs. Fifteen years ago, few computer users foresaw the need for portable laptop computers that could be run on batteries, cell phones, digital cameras, or DVD players with stereo capability.

Danger 5—Mistaking early customer rejection as a sign of failure: Innovative firms understand that many customers reject truly innovative products during their introduction. To some analysts, immediate acceptance of a new breakthrough may be evidence that the innovation was not a true innovation.

Danger 6—Accommodating customers' lethargic pace of change: Retailers must be wary of serving only customers who resist technological change since they might go out of business with these customers.

Instead of relying exclusively on customer input, Turock feels that the most innovative retailers are those that can recognize customers' latent needs—what customers might value but have never experienced and would never think to ask for—and detect these needs through other means:

- A retailer could determine a customer's implied wishes by carefully evaluating "why can't you give us this" complaints. For example, in response to complaints about why express shippers cannot help firms eliminate their inventory, FedEx designed a procedure whereby the various components would be received at the same time despite coming from multiple manufacturers and multiple shipping points.
- A retailer could observe how some of its practices conflict with common sense. For example, why should a supermarket's best customers have to wait on long lines, while customers with few items are provided with express service?
- Latent needs can be determined by a retailer asking "what's your ideal vision of service from us?" This question gets shoppers away from thinking about small improvements in existing services.

Questions

1. What do you think about Art Turock's six dangers?
2. What mix of research should a retailer conduct to address the issues raised by Art Turock?
3. What are the pros and cons of a retailer quickly reacting to what it feels is an emerging trend?
4. Develop a short customer satisfaction questionnaire for a regional discount auto parts chain, based on Art Turock's suggestions.

The material in this case is drawn from Art Turock, "There's Danger in Listening to Customers," *Supermarket Business* (April 15, 2001), pp. 27–28.

2: LOWE'S: DRAWING WOMEN TO HOME IMPROVEMENT STORES

The duel between Lowe's (**www.lowes.com**) and Home Depot (**www.homedepot.com**) "is one of the best shows in retailing today." In order to maintain its 18 percent annual revenue growth, Lowe's is expanding into large markets such as Boston, New York, and Los Angeles areas where Home Depot has well-established stores. In 2002 alone, Lowe's planned to open 123 new stores and continue its emphasis on cities with populations over 500,000—since Lowe's made only 50 percent of its sales in metropolitan markets. Although Lowe's assumes that its new Northeast stores will each have yearly sales of $50 million (versus a chain average of $32 million), one can never underestimate Home Depot as a competitor.

Until recently, the differences between Lowe's and Home Depot's strategy were straightforward insofar as Lowe's operated smaller stores in smaller towns. But today, its store prototype has a 121,000-square-foot selling area with a lawn and garden center averaging an additional 30,000 square feet.

In contrast to Home Depot, Lowe's current strategy is built on better appealing to women shoppers, especially single women (which is the fastest-growing segment of home buyers). One-half of Lowe's shoppers are women, up from 13 percent in the late 1980s. Lowe's understands that women dislike a "lumber shop atmosphere" and that they prefer wide aisles so two shopping carts can easily pass each other: "Our research says women are not entirely comfortable going into a big old hardware store."

To better appeal to women and first-time home buyers, Lowe's offers solution-based product and installation programs to assure do-it-yourselfers that they can complete the project. Lowe's is also appealing to the "buy-it-yourself consumer" who wants to purchase an item at Lowe's, but wants Lowe's to recommend an installer to complete the task.

Lowe's carries a large selection of small appliances. Its typical store has several different models of toasters and coffee makers, whereas Home Depot may stock one model of each. Lowe's also carries 200 different lamp shades. And, unlike Home Depot, Lowe's focuses on more costly, higher lines of merchandise such as Laura Ashley paints and $899 stainless steel gas barbeque grills. About 30 percent of Lowe's sales involve "fashion" items, including appliances. In the major appliance business, Lowe's market share is second only to Sears'. At Lowe's, appliances account for 12 percent of sales.

Home Depot's strategy has relied on low prices, a large selection of merchandise lines, sales to professional contractors, and the use of "big-box" stores. Yet, in response to Lowe's, Home Depot is changing its strategy to better deal with Lowe's move into larger metropolitan markets. For example, in addition to its big-box stores, Home Depot is building smaller "neighborhood" stores that provide decorating services and more costly items.

Unlike Lowe's, which is aggressively building new stores, Home Depot feels that it has saturated its largest markets and is striving to increase revenues by getting additional sales out of existing stores. At Home Depot, appliances currently account for only 2 percent of sales. So, Home Depot has begun placing its major appliance section in a separate department in hundreds of its current stores, and it is planning to have a major appliance department in all new stores. In response to Lowe's initiative aimed at female shoppers, Home Depot has added more home décor items, made its aisles less cluttered, and added more attractive displays.

Questions

1. Comment on Lowe's strategy to appeal to the needs of female shoppers.
2. How can Home Depot better appeal to females without turning off its contractor customers?
3. From a consumer behavior perspective, what are the advantages and disadvantages of selling major appliances such as ranges and refrigerators in a home improvement center?
4. Contrast the home improvement store needs of "do-it-yourself" versus "buy-it-yourself" consumers.

The material in this case is drawn from Axia M. Pascual, "Lowe's Is Sprucing Up the House," *Business Week* (June 3, 2002), pp. 56–58; "It's All About Women," *Newsday* (July 25, 2002), pp. B18–B19, B21; and *Lowe's Annual Report 2001.*

3: JUSTIFYING AN INVESTMENT IN RETAIL INFORMATION SYSTEMS

This case is based on a roundtable discussion at a recent National Retail Federation Annual Convention in New York. The roundtable discussion dealt with the challenge that chief information officers (CIOs) face when they are asked to increase their efficiency. The participants included the CIOs of Brooks Brothers (**www.**

brooksbrothers.com), Polo Ralph Lauren (**www.polo.com**), Helzberg Diamond Shops (**www.helzberg.com**), and Navy Exchange Service Command (**www.navy-nex.com**).

Each participant agreed that while return on investment was the most crucial measure used by top management to justify a technology proposal, it should not be the only criterion. They also agreed that it was often hard to measure the return on investment of proposed information systems changes. When Polo Ralph Lauren's Judith Formichella was CIO for Charming Shoppes, she proposed a data warehouse project that "would have been hard to cost justify, as it was tough to measure the ROI." Yet, the project succeeded since management realized that the added data that could be obtained were quite valuable.

Among the panelists, Judy Straus, vice-president of information systems for Brooks Brothers, had a particularly difficult job since her firm was being put up for sale and all capital expenditures were frozen. Any plan for increasing efficiency required that existing systems be used. Most of the suggestions that Straus and her team devised involved replacing manual data entry with automated entry and developing a better way to use data across different units of Brooks Brothers. Straus viewed her task in a positive manner, since it required her to look at areas of the business that would otherwise not have received proper attention: "When do you ever get to attend to something that's your third, fourth, or fifth priority?"

Judith Formichella, vice-president of information technology at Polo Ralph Lauren, was asked to reduce her budget by 5 percent, like all departments in the firm. Her plan involved replacing older systems that had high maintenance costs with newer systems. The savings in maintenance costs would pay for other efforts. While she planned to add a few project managers and specialists to staff these capital projects, Polo Ralph Lauren's day-to-day technology operations staff remained at current levels.

Butch Jagoda, divisional vice-president of information services for Herzberg Diamond Shops, said that in a weak economic environment retailers want not only a large return on investment, but they also want it delivered quickly. Until recently, Herzberg stored its information in multiple locations. Jagoda had a tough time convincing management to consolidate the network into a single large data warehouse because of the lengthy time period needed to achieve the savings. However, once management saw how much easier it would be to access and maintain information through a single data warehouse, it decided to go forward with the project. As Jagoda noted, "Some projects are like watching water boil; it sits for a long time before you see a result."

Navy Exchange Service Command's CIO, Bill Finefield, has worked to improve his department's efficiency by increasing labor productivity. According to Finefield, "The hardware to run the organization is relatively cheap, but the cost of people to maintain the hardware is not. To increase productivity, The Navy Exchange is moving toward centralized systems that require little maintenance."

Questions

1. How can a retailer determine how much a retail information system should ideally cost?
2. Why is it so difficult to determine a return on investment for a retail information system? What criteria would you recommend to use in assessing the performance of a retail information system?

3. What can a small independent retailer do to increase the efficiency of its retail information system without spending too much money?

4. What are the pros and cons of managing a company retail information system internally versus having it outsourced?

The material in this case is drawn from Dan Scheraga, "Pinching Pennies," *Chain Store Age* (March 2002), pp. 73–74.

4: 3-D COMPUTER-ASSISTED DESIGN COMES TO RETAILING

While some retailers have yet to try three-dimensional computer-assisted design (CAD), others such as Burger King (**www.burgerking. com**) and Eddie Bauer (**www.eddiebauer.com**) have extensively used 3-D CAD to look at different combinations of colors, fixtures, lighting, and even interior layouts for their stores. While engineers and designers have used CAD for more than 10 years to draw store plans electronically, 3-D adds the perspective of depth. This makes it much easier to visualize a drawing. According to the president of AutoDesSys (**www.autodessys.com**), a provider of 3-D modeling technology, "It's where the future is. Whatever you can do with photographs, you can do with 3-D programs. For a photograph, you need the real thing. With 3-D, you can illustrate virtual situations."

When Burger King wanted to get a focus group's reactions toward a new store design, a 3,300-square-foot, 1950s-style diner, it showed the concept to the group using 3-D computer-assisted design and a video simulation. The focus group could react to the idea without leaving their chairs and without an actual prototype being built. Digital Sculpture, the firm that prepared the video simulation for Burger King, was given hand-drawn sketches, color swatches, graphic boards, and menu boards in digital format. It put these materials into a computer model to devise the 3-D effect. The entire process took Digital Sculpture just over one week. Peter Scott, the president of Digital Sculpture, noted that, "The design was such a radical change that any retailer would hate to build it and be dramatically off. This technology allowed them to do it more cheaply with as much feedback as if consumers were in the store."

Aside from the cost savings, a major research advantage of the 3-D CAD format is its objectivity. The creative director of a brand imaging firm says that hand-drawn sketches are extremely subjective: "By the nature of it, you're going to choose a flattering perspective and make things look good. If there's something you don't understand or haven't thought through, you won't put it in."

Another important application of CAD to retailing is in the area of space management and assortment planning. JDA Software (**www.jdasoftware.com**), for example, recently developed software for supermarkets and suppliers that measures how product placement affects sales: "Whether you're talking about bakery, produce, or health and beauty, you can plug in the sales, units, and other numbers and measure your space-to-sales productivity. So you not only have the 3-D capability, but analytical capability on top of that." A supermarket can use this software to test alternative layouts and assortments. It can then use these designs to reconfigure its space to give additional shelf-facings to high productivity products and departments. A supermarket can also more easily design space to be used differently throughout the year. The space used for lawn furniture in the early summer months can be set up for back-to-school specials in August and early September.

Liquid Presence uses 3-D animation software to create a virtual grocery shopping environment for supermarket Web sites. The company can include such audiovisual effects as showing produce being misted with water to stay fresh and allowing shoppers to select among various musical selections while shopping on the Web. In the future, Liquid Presence foresees incorporating touch and digital-scent devices to the Web experience: "Customers could actually simulate squeezing tomatoes and smell fresh-cooked bread right at their home computer."

Questions

1. Is the new high-tech research environment going to eliminate the use of human researchers? Explain your answer.

2. What are the pros and cons of using 3-D CAD systems for marketing research purposes versus traditional focus groups?

3. Describe the ideal marketing research uses for 3-D animation software in the creation of a virtual grocery shopping environment for supermarkets.

4. Devise a short consumer questionnaire for Burger King to use in assessing its 3-D CAD simulations.

The material in this case is drawn from Jenny Summerour, "Virtual Reality," *Progressive Grocer* (August 2001), pp. 25–28.

part three
Comprehensive Case
A Retailer's Guide to Meeting Consumer Expectations*

INTRODUCTION

What will consumers expect from retail shopping in the future? What can retailers do to deliver? How will consumer trends such as the search for value, the desire to make the most of each shopping trip, the need for customer communication, and an opportunity for customization play out? How can firms use such strategies as marketing partnerships, new store formats, alternative locations, and brand extensions to grow market share? This case examines trends in shopping behavior and firms' responses to these trends.

Consumer Expectations

Expectations for the shopping experience are high—and getting higher. Leisure time is at a premium, and shopping does not rate as a high priority. The bottom line is that consumers are striving to make the shopping experience as productive as possible. People want more selection, service, convenience, information, quality, innovation, and enjoyment for less effort, risk, time, and money.

Consumers are less willing to compromise. If they can't find a specific item at one store, they will go to the next store rather than settle for something else. At the same time, it also seems to be increasingly difficult for consumers to find exactly what they want, even though the stores are packed with products.

According to Harris Interactive, 75 percent of U.S. shoppers "wish there were more goods and services customized to my personal needs and tastes." And 70 percent say, "I am more loyal to companies that make an effort to get to know my needs and tastes." Two-thirds of U.S. consumers are interested in buying clothing and shoes customized to their needs, 65 percent in customized travel planning, 65 percent in customized financial planning, 57 percent in customized electronics, 56 percent in customized food products, 47 percent in customized online information and entertainment, and 42 percent in customized cosmetics. In each category, younger adults are more interested in customization than older adults.

To capture a share of spending, retailers must give consumers a motivation to shop. All segments require this. Older consumers don't really "need" much—they have passed their peak consumption years. Younger shoppers have greater expectations for entertainment, excitement, and novelty when it comes to the shopping experience. To stimulate these shoppers, retailers must be on the lookout for the "next best thing" to keep their interest. But in a world of more choices, the "next best thing" comes along more often, leading to a greater need to cut through the clutter. Nonetheless, WSL Strategic Retail reports that 45 percent of consumers agree that "I'm not finding as many new and interesting things to buy."

Shopping Productivity

Shopping productivity goes up when shoppers get more for less. Ease of shopping and one-stop shopping increase shopping productivity by giving people more choice and more control over the shopping process.

Ease of Shopping

Retailers are exploring ways to make shopping easier by simplifying the steps required to research, find, choose, and purchase products. They are seeking ways to eliminate barriers that can get in the way of the sale. Technology is used to speed the shopping process, chiefly at the order-entry and checkout stages.

In late 2001, Google launched a search service that lets users search the contents of more than 1,500 catalogs (**www.catalogs.google.com**). A search retrieves all catalogs that contain the search term. Each listing shows the catalog cover, an image of the page with the term, and a close-up of the section of the page with the term. Inclusion in Google Catalog Search is now free for publishers, who provide Google with copies of catalogs, which are scanned with a program that converts pages into machine-readable text. Although there is no facility for purchase from Google, the catalog firm's contact information, such as name, phone number, and URL, is provided. Google also is developing fee-based services.

J.C. Penney now uses a classification approach for merchandising its stores to achieve greater clarity of assortment and presentation. Merchandising by classification rather than collection means less duplication and clutter, making it easier to shop. Penney's "big book" mail-order catalog has a more coordinated presentation and offers fewer items per page. Each style is shown in a fully accessorized presentation, giving the consumer guidance and ideas for pulling a look together. Better paper and photography provide greater visual clarity including a realistic representation of colors and textures.

Borders Bookstores has installed self-service kiosks in all U.S. stores. The kiosks let customers check the availability of items. If a desired title is not available at the shopper's location, a "Check Other Stores" feature can look at the inventory of other stores. If another store has the title, a call at the information counter will place it on hold for customer pick-up. If an item is not available in stores, an employee can place an order and have it delivered to the store or the customer's home. Customers can also use a kiosk to read reviews, find out about store events, and order hard-to-find or out-of-print books.

Sam's Club, Kmart, and Home Depot are offering an option whereby customers waiting in line can have shopping baskets pre-scanned and pre-bagged by workers using handheld scanners. Upon reaching the checkout, the customer presents a card for the cashier to scan and process for payment. For Home Depot, portable scanners also enable sales associates to stay in contact with a customer through a multi-item, multi-department, big-ticket purchase, such as a kitchen remodeling project.

Supermarkets are testing drive-through windows to appeal to the consumer on the go. H.E. Butt launched Good to Go!, a full-service, dine-in café that features a take-out, drive-through window in its new 90,000-square-foot supermarket in Austin. The concept caters to those who want the convenience and value of fast food but are looking for more variety and better nutrition.

One-Stop Shopping

Supermarkets and discount department stores have added pharmacies, while drugstores have enhanced their food offers. Supercenters are combination supermarket/discount stores. Among apparel firms, specialty players continue expanding their mix to meet more customer wardrobe and life-style needs. Categories such as footwear and accessories, bath and body products, cosmetics and fragrances, intimate apparel and sleepwear, activewear, and home décor items have been added.

Retailers and real-estate developers have for years created partnerships in which stores are clustered together to facilitate shopping. Now, the store-within-a-store concept is gaining ground by combining complementary offers in one store. For example, Toys "R" Us began selling toys at Giant Food stores in Washington, D.C., to test if supermarket customers like the convenience. Toys "R" Us research showed that an average parent visits a grocery store 96 times a year, compared with 4 to 5 visits to Toys "R" Us.

Some category killer stores are evolving as life-style and solution-oriented retailers that stress solving customer problems rather than just having lots of stuff. PetsMart stores carry a huge selection of products. They also feature pet grooming salons, training classes, and adoption centers. Many stores offer full-service veterinary care at hospitals and wellness clinics operated by Banfield, the Pet Hospital, in which PetsMart has an equity position. The firm's vision is to be the preferred provider for the total lifetime needs of pets.

Providing Greater Personal Relevance

Cultivating More Consumer Segments

Some retailers are going after a more discrete customer segment—a younger or older segment or a group of people who have a different style preference—with "sister-store" concepts. Others are broadening the appeal of their existing concept to more consumer segments via changes in advertising and product mix.

U.S.-based teen retailer Hot Topic developed Torrid, an apparel store targeting women aged 15 to 30 who wear plus sizes and want fashion-forward clothing. About 30 percent of all women in the store's target age range wear size 14 or larger. Billing itself as "the alternative for women sized 14 to 26," Torrid carries the latest trend-setting styles.

CB2 is an offspring of housewares and furniture retailer Crate & Barrel that is designed for a younger, hipper urban customer who wants fresh products. The assortment is priced less than a Crate & Barrel store, but design is key. Merchandise includes housewares; gadgets; home office, storage, and organizing products; and furniture. The target customer is just as apt to be male as female and is a young professional with a strong sense of style but some price constraints.

The Pottery Barn Kids catalog debuted in January 1999. A store rollout followed, with the first unit opening in California in 2000. The chain got its own Web site (**www.potterybarnkids.com**) in 2001. The assortment features the same type of elegant, well-designed merchandise carried by Pottery Barn.

Fashion and Trend Relevance

Part of making the retail offer more relevant is having what's hot when it's hot. That requires a systematic trend and innovation identification process, as well as the ability to react and implement appropriately.

After a year of research into what women want, Nike opened its first NIKEgoddess store in Newport Beach, California, in 2001. The store joined a growing number of Nike's women store-within-a-store concept shops and was joined by a second store in Los Angeles during 2002. At these stores, female consumers can give feedback on the design, performance, and comfort of Nike products. While NikeTown stores stress competitiveness and athletics. NIKEgoddess stores are designed to cater to a women's individuality and personal motivation. Nike has also redesigned its women's lines with greater attention to the mix of performance and style with an extra focus on color and fashion trends.

Instant Gratification

As of mid-March 2002, virtually all Gateway computer stores began offering a selection of PCs to take home immediately. Previously, Gateway PCs had been available on a build-to-order basis only. Consumer research showed that carrying a pre-built inventory of popular systems would improve customer satisfaction and conversion rates.

Personalization

Retailers can cater to consumer desires by personalizing the shopping experience and customer communications. To increase the shopping frequency of new and occasional customers, British-based grocer Tesco has introduced separate home pages for its Tesco.com Web site that address varying levels of experience with the site and different customer segments. The newest users receive a simple Web page. As customers gain more experience with the site, Tesco will expose them to more complex transactions, while minimizing the amount of space and pages devoted to instructions.

Borders sends regular E-mail newsletters to customers who have signed up for them. The E-mail comes in several versions, each catering to different customers with different needs. The program allows Borders to segment people according to their choices. The goal of the E-mail is to drive customers to the store and at the same time give customers special offers.

Lands' End offers a customized Alumni Collection whereby customers can have the logos of 35 American universities embroidered on shirts, sweaters, and turtlenecks. Eighty-eight percent of the firm's customers are college educated and will have an affinity with these universities, whether they are alumni, parents of a student or an alum, or sports fans.

Inspiring Consumers

Today's discriminating consumers want it all—relevant products, good prices, convenient shopping options, more information, and an enjoyable experience. As a result, it is becoming more important for retailers to learn how to "inspire" consumers. To move consumers to action in a crowded marketplace, retailers must give consumers a reason to buy from them that goes beyond product at a price.

Increasingly, consumers will respond to retailing concepts that:

- Promote a sense of discovery.
- Appeal to desires and aspirations rather than needs.
- Stimulate the senses and involve the emotions.
- Create an interactive experience.
- Foster a learning environment.
- Encourage shoppers to have fun.

Inspirational retailers promote a sense of discovery by bringing together an innovative collection of merchandise in a unique shopping environment. Trader Joe's is like a box of chocolates. You never know what you're going to get. The company specializes in its own brand of gourmet and natural foods at discount prices. Items are departures from standard fare, such as artichoke salsa and seven-mushroom marinara—products that cannot be found elsewhere. To keep shopping exciting, the firm introduces 10 to 15 new products each week. The stores' simple layout and displays let products speak for themselves. To keep costs down, there are no service departments, no sales promotions, minimal advertising, and a selection of about 3,000 items (compared to 30,000+ for a supermarket). The company's *Fearless Flyer* circular provides a somewhat irreverent description of products and plays up everyday low prices.

Inspirational retailers appeal to desires rather than needs. Chico's is a specialty apparel retailer that caters to stylish, mature (35- to 60-year-old) women. Its exclusive designs are inspired by cultures from around the world. Belts, jewelry, and footwear are coordinated with the colors and patterns of Chico's clothing, letting customers enhance and individualize wardrobes. It continually introduces new merchandise and designs to complement other Chico's merchandise that customers have in their existing wardrobes. The sales staff is eager to help customers build a casual, sophisticated wardrobe with attitude. To ensure that customers interact with employees, Chico's does not put mirrors in dressing rooms. When a customer goes to the sales floor for a mirror, employees have a chance to help her find coordinating pieces and accessories to pull the look together. Sizing starts at 0 (extra small) and ends with 3 (large). This presents a wide selection of styles without investing in a large number of sizes within a single style.

Inspirational retailers stimulate the senses and connect with the shopper. Sensory stimulation helps to influence the consumer's mood by creating a positive shopping atmosphere. H.E. Butt's Central Market concept is for people with a passion for fresh and unique food. This concept spans 75,000 square feet. Customers can browse among more than 700 varieties of fruits, vegetables, and herbs; 600 cheeses; 90 bread varieties; 2,500 wines; 260 brands of beer; 75 feet of seafood cases; an endless array of meats; and an extensive selection of natural and preventative health care remedies. Café on the Run has homemade meals to go. Gift baskets, flowers, and in-store cooking classes contribute to a European-style experience. "Foodies"—dressed in green and white striped aprons—roam the store to provide culinary advice and meal solutions. Central Market is throughout Texas.

Inspirational retailers create an experiential environment that becomes a selling point. Skinmarket, a retailer of cosmetics, bath and body products, and accessories for teenage girls, provides a place to have fun—just like a best friend's bedroom. Zones in the stores include the Demo Zone where shoppers can sample products and get a free makeover; the Custom Counter where girls can have their favorite scents mixed to order into a selection of bath and body care products; and the Booth, a lounge area where they can look at magazines, listen to music, do their nails, or relax. Experimentation is not only allowed, it's encouraged.

Inspirational retailers foster a learning environment that gives consumers confidence to try something new. Having severed its ties with Circuit City, Apple is opening more Apple-branded stores to provide an opportunity for shoppers to learn about the things they can do with a computer. All of the Macs on display are connected to the Web, and several are connected to digital life-style products that complement the Mac experience, such as digital cameras, camcorders, MP3 players, and handheld organizers. Many of the computers run software applications such as Microsoft Office and Adobe Photoshop. Apple stores have had mixed results. While store traffic and average transaction size are good, sales have been low.

Questions

1. What are the three most important points related to understanding consumers that a retailer could learn from this case? Explain your answer.
2. Discuss the implications of this statement for retailers: "Expectations for the shopping experience are high—and getting higher."
3. Analyze Google's catalog site (**www.catalogs.google.com**). Is it consumer-friendly? Explain your answer.
4. What do you think about this emerging retail strategy? "Some retailers are going after a more discrete customer segment—a younger or older segment or a group of people who have a different style preference—with 'sister-store' concepts."
5. How can retailers do a better job of "having what's hot when it's hot"?
6. What could a competing retailer learn by studying Trader Joe's Web site (**www.traderjoes.com**)?
7. What could a competing retailer learn by studying Chico's Web site (**www.chicos.com**)?

*The material in this case is adapted by the authors from Retail Forward, "What's Next? A Retailer's Guide to Meeting Consumer Expectations," 2002 Strategic Outlook Conference, pp. 1–32. Reprinted by permission of Retail Forward, Inc. (**www.retailforward.com**).

part four

Choosing a Store Location

Once a retailer conducts a situation analysis, sets goals, identifies consumer characteristics and needs, and gathers adequate information about the marketplace, it is ready to develop and enact an overall strategy. In Parts Four through Seven, we examine the elements of such a strategy: choosing a store location, managing a business, merchandise management and pricing, and communicating with the customer. Part Four concentrates on store location.

- **Chapter 9** deals with the crucial nature of store location for retailers and outlines a four-step approach to location planning. We focus on Step 1, trading-area analysis, in this chapter. Among the topics we look at are the use of geographic information systems, the size and shape of trading areas, how to determine trading areas for existing and new stores, and the major factors to consider in assessing trading areas. Several data sources are described.

- **Chapter 10** covers the last three steps in location planning: deciding on the most desirable type of location, selecting a general location, and choosing a particular site within that location. We first contrast isolated store, unplanned business district, and planned shopping center locales. Criteria for rating each location are then outlined and detailed.

Chapter 9

TRADING-AREA ANALYSIS

Reprinted by permission.

Since Blockbuster (**www.blockbuster.com**) opened its first store in 1985, it has grown into the world's largest provider of rentable home videocassettes, DVDs, and video games. Today, on average, more than 3 million customers walk into a U.S. Blockbuster store each day. Blockbuster has thousands of stores throughout the United States, its territories, and dozens of foreign countries. Blockbuster estimates that 64 percent of the U.S. population lives within a 10-minute drive of one of its stores.

In planning new store locations, Blockbuster performs sophisticated trading-area analysis based on its market share, customer transaction, and real-estate data bases. The analysis also includes data on an area's demographics, life-styles, customer concentration levels, and competition. Through this assessment, Blockbuster's store development team is able to minimize cannibalization due to trading-area overlap with existing stores, to determine whether a new store should be built or an existing one acquired, and to decide on the appropriate store format.

Blockbuster seeks out locations that are high in terms of customer convenience and visibility. Its traditional format of 4,000-square-foot or larger units is applied in markets where store-to-population ratios are low and market conditions are optimal. A smaller format is used in rural markets or to reduce cannibalization among its traditional stores. Locations in supermarkets and department stores are used in mature markets where Blockbuster already has a strong presence.[1]

chapter objectives

1. To demonstrate the importance of store location for a retailer and outline the process for choosing a store location
2. To discuss the concept of a trading area and its related components
3. To show how trading areas may be delineated for existing and new stores
4. To examine three major factors in trading-area analysis: population characteristics, economic base characteristics, and competition and the level of saturation

OVERVIEW

Since more than 90 percent of retail sales are made at stores, the selection of a store location is one of the most significant strategic decisions in retailing. Consider the detailed planning of Wilsons Leather:

> We utilize a detailed process to identify favorable store locations in existing or new markets. Within each targeted market, we identify potential sites for new and replacement stores by evaluating market dynamics. Our site selection criteria include customer segment and demographic data derived from our point-of-sale network and outside sources; information relating to population density surrounding the mall; the performance of other stores within the mall; the proposed location within the mall; and projected profitability, cost, return on investment, and cash-flow objectives. Our cross-functional review committee approves proposed store projects, including new sites and lease renewals. We continually evaluate our stores to assess the need for remodeling or the timing of possible closure due to economic factors. We rely upon the familiarity of our name and our national reputation with landlords to enhance our ability to obtain prime store locations and negotiate favorable lease terms.[2]

This chapter and the next explain why the proper store location is so crucial, as well as the steps a retailer should take in choosing a store location and deciding whether to build, lease, or buy facilities. Visit our Web site (**www.prenhall.com/bermanevans**) for many links on store location.

THE IMPORTANCE OF LOCATION TO A RETAILER

The Site Selection Toolkit (www.bizsites.com/Toolkit/ sitetoolkit.html) has a wealth of helpful links for location planning.

Location decisions are complex, costs can be quite high, there is little flexibility once a site is chosen, and locational attributes have a big impact on a strategy. One of the oldest adages in retailing is that "location, location, location" is the major factor leading to a firm's success or failure. See Figure 9-1.

A good location may let a retailer succeed even if its strategy mix is mediocre. A hospital gift shop may do well, although its assortment is limited, prices are high, and it does not advertise. On the other hand, a poor location may be such a liability that even able retailers cannot overcome it. A

FIGURE 9-1

The Importance of Location to Esprit

Why are store locations so important to Esprit? The firm controls several million square feet of retail space in "more than 40 countries spanning five continents. It has approximately 500 directly managed retail outlets and over 2,000 franchised shops. Its Esprit brand has been a leading international life-style fashion brand name applied to an extensive range of women's, men's and children's apparel, footwear, accessories, and other licensed products." [**www.esprit.com**]

Photo reprinted by permission of Retail Forward, Inc.

mom-and-pop store may do poorly if it is across the street from a category killer store; although the small firm features personal service, it cannot match the selection and prices. At a different site, it might prosper.

The choice of a location requires extensive decision making due to the number of criteria considered, including population size and traits, the competition, transportation access, parking availability, the nature of nearby stores, property costs, the length of the agreement, legal restrictions, and other factors.

A store location may necessitate a sizable investment and a long-term commitment. Even a retailer that minimizes its investment by leasing (rather than owning a building and land) can incur large costs. Besides lease payments, the firm must spend money on lighting, fixtures, a storefront, and so on.

Although leases of less than 5 years are common in less desirable retailing locations, leases in good shopping centers or shopping districts are often 5 to 10 years or more. It is not uncommon for a supermarket lease to be 15, 20, or 30 years. Department stores and large specialty stores on major downtown thoroughfares occasionally sign leases longer than 30 years.

Due to its fixed nature, the investment, and the length of the lease, store location is the least flexible element of a strategy. A firm cannot easily move to another site or convert to another format. It may also be prohibited from subleasing to another party during the lease period; and if a retailer breaks a lease, it may be responsible to the property owner for financial losses. In contrast, ads, prices, customer services, and assortment can be altered as the environment (consumers, competition, the economy) changes.

A retailer that owns its store's building and land may also find it hard to change locations. It has to find an acceptable buyer, which might take several months or longer; and it may have to assist the buyer with financing. It may incur a loss, should it sell during an economic downturn.

Any retailer moving from one location to another faces three potential problems. (1) Some loyal customers and employees may be lost; the greater the distance between the old and new sites, the bigger the loss. (2) A new site may not have the same traits as the original one. (3) Store fixtures and renovations at an old site usually cannot be transferred to a new site; their remaining value is lost if they have not been fully depreciated.

Store location affects long- and short-run planning. In the *long run*, the choice of location influences the overall strategy. A retailer must be at a site that is consistent with its mission, goals, and target market for an extended time. It also must regularly study and monitor the status of the location as to population trends, the distances people travel to the store, and competitors' entry and exit—and adapt accordingly.

In the *short run*, the location has an impact on the specific elements of a strategy mix. A retailer in a downtown area with many office buildings may have little pedestrian traffic on weekends. It would probably be improper to sell items such as major appliances there (these items are often bought jointly by husbands and wives). The retailer could either close on weekends and not stock certain products or remain open and try to attract customers to the area by aggressive promotion or pricing. If the retailer closes on weekends, it adapts its strategy mix to the attributes of the location. If it stays open, it invests additional resources in an attempt to alter shopping habits. A retailer that strives to overcome its location, by and large, faces greater risks than one that adapts.

Retailers should follow these four steps in choosing a store location:

1. Evaluate alternate geographic (trading) areas in terms of the characteristics of residents and existing retailers.
2. Determine whether to locate as an isolated store, in an unplanned business district, or in a planned shopping center within the geographic area.
3. Select the general isolated store, unplanned business district, or planned shopping center location.
4. Analyze alternate sites contained in the specified retail location type.

This chapter concentrates on Step 1. Chapter 10 details Steps 2, 3, and 4. The selection of a store location is a process involving each of these steps.

TRADING-AREA ANALYSIS

The first step in the choice of a retail store location is to describe and evaluate alternate trading areas and then decide on the most desirable one. A **trading area** is "a geographic area containing the customers of a particular firm or group of firms for specific goods or services."[3] After a trading area is picked, it should be reviewed regularly.

A thorough analysis of trading areas provides several benefits:

- Consumers' demographic and socioeconomic characteristics are uncovered. For a new store, the study of proposed trading areas reveals opportunities and the retail strategy necessary to succeed. For an existing store, it can be determined if the current strategy still matches consumer needs.

- The focus of promotional activities is ascertained, and the retailer can look at media coverage patterns of proposed or existing locations. If 95 percent of customers live within 3 miles of a store, it would be inefficient to advertise in a paper with a citywide audience.

- A retailer learns whether the location of a proposed branch store will service new customers or take business from its existing stores. Suppose a supermarket chain has a store in Jackson, Mississippi, with a trading area of 2 miles, and it considers adding a new store, 3 miles from the Jackson branch. Figure 9-2 shows the distinct trading areas and expected overlap of the stores. The shaded portion represents the **trading-area overlap**, where the same customers are served by both branches. The chain must find out the overall net increase in sales if it adds the proposed store (total revised sales of existing store + total sales of new store − total previous sales of existing store).

- Chains anticipate whether competitors want to open nearby stores if the firm does not do so itself. That is why TJX has two of its chains, T.J. Maxx and Marshalls, situate within 1.5 miles of each other in more than 100 U.S. markets, even though they are both off-price apparel firms.

- The best number of stores for a chain to operate in a given area is calculated. How many outlets should a retailer have in a region to provide good service for customers (without raising costs too much or having too much overlap)? When CVS entered Atlanta, it opened nine new drugstores in one day. This gave it enough coverage of the city to service residents, without placing stores too close together. A major competitive advantage for Canadian Tire Corporation is that four-fifths of the Canadian population live within a 15-minute drive of a Canadian Tire store.

FIGURE 9-2

The Trading Areas of Current and Proposed Supermarket Outlets

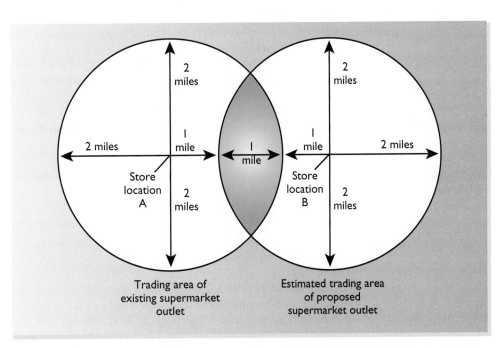

Trading area of existing supermarket outlet

Estimated trading area of proposed supermarket outlet

Technology in
RETAILING   Rack Room Shoes: Pinpointing the Best Locations

Rack Room Shoes (**www.rackroomshoes.com**) had 350 stores in 2002. It plans to open 15 to 20 new stores per year and to remodel 25 to 35 stores annually (some of which will be relocated).

Until 1997, Rack Room tended to downplay the value of marketing research at its site selection meetings. It then spent several years developing a better system for site selection. As of 2001, Rack Room had completed its sales forecasting model that enables it to predict revenues for a new location based on the demographics of its trading area, as well as data on key competitors in each market. The software utilizes desktop geographic information systems and a demographic data engine. Rack Room is also using the software to better focus its advertising campaigns.

There are several major benefits from Rack Room's conducting the analysis on its own versus using a real-estate developer's data base. Although a developer may claim that a mall's trading area is comprised of 250,000 people, the trading area for Rack Room may be significantly smaller. Furthermore, the data analyzed by the developer may not be directly applicable to the shoe market or to a Rack Room store's trading area. Many developers use median income data, but Rack Room prefers income data to be classified by levels.

Source: Connie Robbins Gentry, "Smart Moves," *Chain Store Age* (January 2002), pp. 127–129.

- Geographic weaknesses are highlighted. Suppose a suburban shopping center does an analysis and discovers that most of those residing south of town do not shop there, and a more comprehensive study reveals that people are afraid to drive past a dangerous railroad crossing. Due to its research, the shopping center exerts political pressure to make the crossing safer.

- The impact of the World Wide Web is taken into account. Since the long-run sales relationship between Web and store retailing is far from certain, store-based retailers must examine trading areas even more carefully than before.

- Other factors are reviewed. The competition, financial institutions, transportation, labor availability, supplier location, legal restrictions, and so on can each be learned for the trading area(s) examined.

THE USE OF GEOGRAPHIC INFORMATION SYSTEMS IN TRADING-AREA DELINEATION AND ANALYSIS

Increasingly, retailers are using **geographic information systems (GIS)** software, which combines digitized mapping with key locational data to graphically depict trading-area characteristics such as population demographics, data on customer purchases, and listings of current, proposed, and competitor locations. GIS software lets firms quickly research the attractiveness of different locations and access computer-generated maps. Prior to this software, retailers often placed different color pins on paper maps to show current and proposed locales—and competitors' sites—and had to collect and analyze data.

TIGER (http://tiger.census.gov/cgi-bin/mapbrowse-tbl) can map out any U.S. community. At the bottom of the screen, enter a ZIP code.

Most GIS software programs are extrapolated from the decennial *Census of Population* and the U.S. Census Bureau's national digital map (known as TIGER—topologically integrated geographic encoding and referencing). TIGER incorporates all streets and highways in the United States. GIS software can be accessed through Web site downloads or by CD-ROM disks.

TIGER maps may be downloaded free (**http://tiger.census.gov**) and tailored to reflect census tracts, railroads, highways, waterways, and other physical attributes of any U.S. area. They do not show retailers, other commercial entities, or population traits; the site can be difficult to use; and service may be slow due to heavy site traffic. Figure 9-3 shows a sample TIGER map.

Software from private firms has many more enhancements than TIGER. While these firms often offer free demonstrations, they expect to be paid for their software packages. Although GIS software differs by vendor, it generally can be accessed or bought for as little as under a hundred dollars to as much as several thousand dollars, is designed to work with personal computers, and

FIGURE 9-3
The TIGER Map Service

Reprinted by permission.

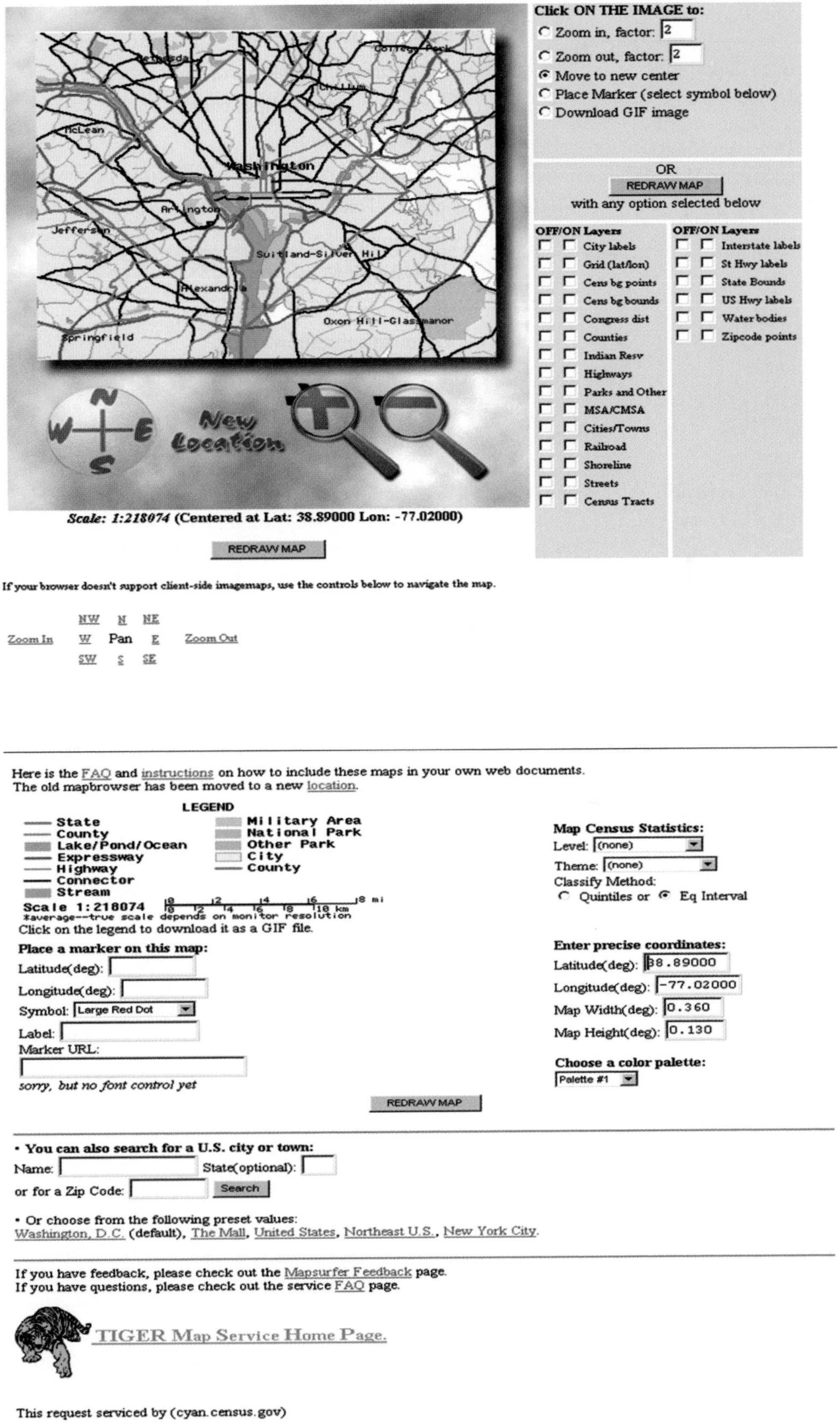

allows for some manipulation of trading-area data. Illustrations appear in Figure 9-4. Private firms that offer mapping software include:

Take a look at sample Claritas reports and maps (http://cluster1.claritas. com/eReports/srhome. wjsp). Click on "Retail."

- Autodesk (**http://usa.autodesk.com**).
- Caliper Corporation (**www.caliper.com**).
- Claritas (**www.claritas.com**).
- ESRI (Environmental Systems Research Institute) (**www.esri.com**).
- GDT (Geographic Data Technology) (**www.geographic.com**).
- geoVue (**www.geovue.com**).
- MapInfo (**www.mapinfo.com**).
- MPSI Systems (**www.mpsisys.com**).
- SRC (**www.demographicsnow.com**).
- Tetrad Computer Applications (**www.tetrad.com**).

At our Web site (**www.prenhall.com/bermanevans**), we provide links to the descriptions of the GIS software for all of these firms. Many of the companies have free demonstrations at their sites.

GIS software can be applied in various ways. A chain retailer could learn which of its stores have trading areas containing households with a median annual income of more than $50,000. That firm could derive the sales potential of proposed new store locations and those stores' potential effect on sales at existing branches. It could use GIS software to determine the demographics of customers at its best locations and set up a computer model to find the potential locations with the most desirable attributes. A retailer could even use the software to pinpoint its geographic areas of strength and weakness.

Do you like *colorful* trading-area maps? Enter SRC's site (www. demographicsnow.com/ default.htm) and "Click here for Map and Report samples."

These examples show how retailers employ GIS software:

- Dunkin' Donuts uses geoVue's iSITE to analyze new store locations: "By screening the trade areas in advance, we can tie up the best locations before others have even started their analysis. This has dramatically cut our time to market."
- CVS has invested in its own proprietary GIS software: "We can identify the prime locations for our stores, right down to a specific corner at an intersection. Through statistical and field research, as well as our own spatial modeling software, we can reach conclusions about the demographic and other factors that drive growth in our stores. When we open a new store or enter a new market, we can be confident in the potential of the investments we are making and their ability to deliver an attractive return on invested capital over the long term."
- Eddie Bauer is now a Claritas client: "Before, we were ordering basic reports from a vendor, pulling out Rand McNally maps, and photocopying them. We would mark stores and trace ZIP code areas by hand. We couldn't map our stores or our competitors. Now, by mapping and using more specialized data, we are making educated decisions on where to locate our stores and how to better serve our customers. This allows us to be more professional and profitable."[4]

THE SIZE AND SHAPE OF TRADING AREAS

Each trading area has three parts: The **primary trading area** encompasses 50 to 80 percent of a store's customers. It is the area closest to the store and possesses the highest density of customers to population and the highest per capita sales. There is little overlap with other trading areas. The **secondary trading area** contains an additional 15 to 25 percent of a store's customers. It is located outside the primary area, and customers are more widely dispersed. The **fringe trading area** includes all the remaining customers, and they are the most widely dispersed. A store could have a primary trading area of 4 miles, a secondary trading area of 5 miles, and a fringe trading area of 10 miles. The fringe trading area typically includes some outshoppers who travel greater distances to patronize certain stores.

FIGURE 9-4

GIS Software in Action

Through GIS mapping software, retailers can pinpoint the trading areas for their stores and the characteristics of the residents in these areas.

Reprinted by permission of ESRI and GDT.

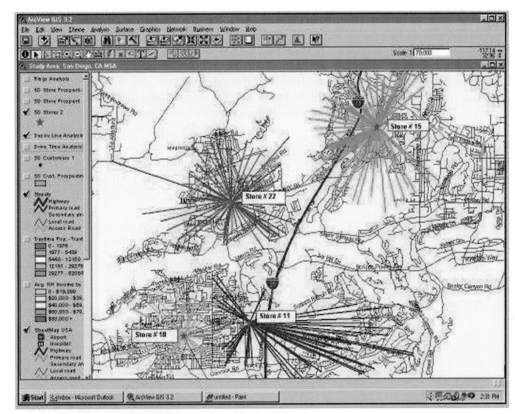

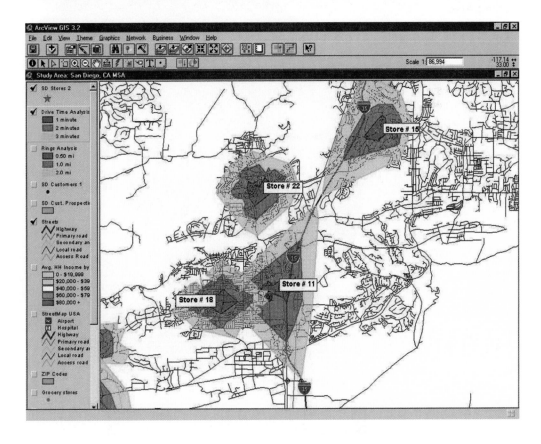

Visit this site to fully see the complexity of factors in site selection (www. conway.com/checklist).

Figures 9-5 and 9-6 show the makeup of trading areas and their segments. In reality, trading areas do not usually follow such circular patterns. They adjust to the physical environment. The size and shape of a trading area are influenced by store type, store size, the location of competitors, housing patterns, travel time and traffic barriers (such as toll bridges), and media availability. These factors are discussed next.

Two stores can have different trading areas even if they are in the same shopping district or shopping center. Situated in one shopping center could be a branch of an apparel chain with a distinctive image and people willing to travel up to 20 miles and a shoe store seen as average and people willing to travel up to 5 miles. When one store has a better assortment, promotes more, and/or creates a stronger image, it may then become a **destination store** and generate a trading area much larger than that of a competitor with a me-too appeal. That is why Dunkin' Donuts used the slogan "It's worth the trip" for many years.

A **parasite store** does not create its own traffic and has no real trading area of its own. This store depends on people who are drawn to the location for other reasons. A magazine stand in a hotel lobby and a snack bar in a shopping center are parasites. Customers patronize these shops while they are there.

The extent of a store's or center's trading area is affected by its own size. As a store or center gets larger, its trading area usually increases, because store or center size generally reflects the assortment of goods and services. Yet, trading areas do not grow proportionately with store or center size. As a rule, supermarket trading areas are bigger than those of convenience stores. Supermarkets have a better product selection and convenience stores appeal to the need for fill-

FIGURE 9-5
The Segments of a Trading Area

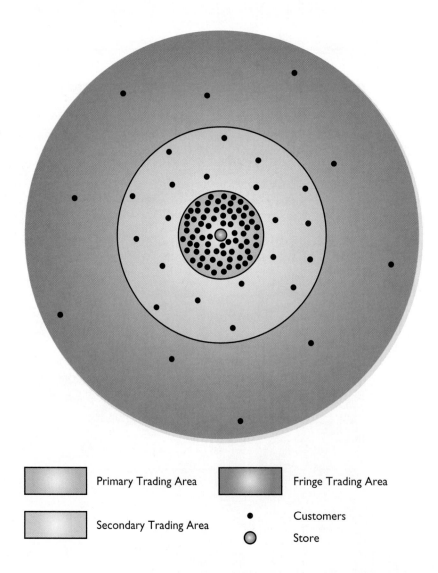

Primary Trading Area

Secondary Trading Area

Fringe Trading Area

• Customers

○ Store

FIGURE 9-6
Delineating Trading-Area Segments

This GIS map clearly depicts primary, secondary, and fringe trading areas for a store. However, the shapes are rarely so concentric.

Reprinted by permission of ESRI and GDT.

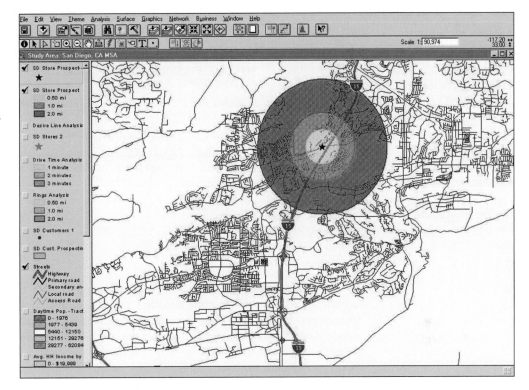

in merchandise. In a regional shopping center, department stores typically have the largest trading areas, followed by apparel stores; gift stores have comparatively small trading areas. See Figure 9-7.

Whenever potential shoppers are situated between two competing stores, the trading area is often reduced for each store. The size of each store's trading area normally increases as the distance between stores grows (target markets do not overlap as much). On the other hand, when stores are situated very near one another, the size of each store's trading area does not necessarily shrink. This store grouping may actually increase the trading area for each store if more consumers are attracted to the location due to the variety of goods and services. Yet, each store's market penetration (its percentage of sales in the trading area) may be low with such competition. Also, the entry of a new store may change the shape or create gaps in the trading areas of existing stores.

FIGURE 9-7
Carrefour Shanghai

Around the world, Carrefour operates huge hypermarkets. The wide selection and low prices attract shoppers who are willing to travel to obtain the Carrefour shopping experience.

Photo reprinted by permission of Retail Forward, Inc.

According to the president of Ikea North America, "My vision is to put Ikea (**www.Ikea.com**) on the map in the United States as a household brand." Since 1985, Ikea has opened a number of stores in the United States, and it plans to open an additional 50 outlets in North America by 2013 (mostly in the United States).

Ikea's strategy also includes replacing some of its smaller and older stores. That is why it moved the store in northern Virginia from its site within a mall to a 10.6-acre site at the edge of the same mall. The new site is twice as large as the old one, and it is visible from a major highway. The larger store enables Ikea to stock 3,000 additional items, to have wider aisles, and to have more display area for its model room layouts. The store should generate sales of about $90 million annually.

Ikea understands that its units are destination stores with huge trading areas. For instance, the northern Virginia store regularly attracts shoppers from Charlotte, North Carolina (about 400 miles away), and Atlanta (over 600 miles away) because these cities have not had Ikea stores.

Source: Gregory J. Gilligan, "Ikea On the Move," *Shopping Centers Today* (April 2002), pp. 51–52.

In many urban communities, people are clustered in multi-unit housing near the center of commerce. With such population density, it is worthwhile for a retailer to be quite close to consumers; and trading areas tend to be small because there are several shopping districts in close proximity to one another, particularly for the most densely populated cities. In many suburbs, people live in single-unit housing—which is more geographically spread out. To produce satisfactory sales volume there, a retailer needs to attract shoppers from a greater distance.

The influence of travel or driving time on a trading area may not be clear from the population's geographic distribution. Physical barriers (toll bridges, poor roads, railroad tracks, one-way streets) usually reduce trading-area size and contribute to their odd shapes. Economic barriers, such as different sales taxes in two towns, also affect the size and shape of trading areas.

In a community where a newspaper or other local media are available, a retailer could afford to advertise and enlarge its trading area. If local media are not available, the retailer would have to weigh the costs of advertising in countywide or regional media against the possibilities of a bigger trading area.

DELINEATING THE TRADING AREA OF AN EXISTING STORE

The size, shape, and characteristics of the trading area for an existing store—or shopping district or shopping center—can usually be delineated quite accurately. Store records (secondary data) or a special study (primary data) can measure the trading area. And many firms offer computer-generated maps that can be tailored to individual retailers' needs.

Store records can reveal customer addresses. For credit customers, the data can be obtained from a retailer's billing department; for cash customers, addresses can be acquired by analyzing deliveries, cash sales slips, store contests (sweepstakes), and checks. In both instances, the task is relatively inexpensive and quick because the data were originally collected for other purposes and are readily available.

Since many big retailers have computerized credit card systems, they can delineate primary, secondary, and fringe trading areas in terms of the

- Frequency with which people from various geographic locales shop at a particular store.
- Average dollar purchases at a store by people from given geographic locales.
- Concentration of a store's credit card holders from given geographic locales.

GDT (www.geographic. com) offers software to provide vehicular traffic counts. Type "Dynamap/ Traffic Counts" in the search engine at the bottom of the page.

Though it is easy to get data on credit card customers, the analysis may be invalid if cash customers are not studied. Credit use may vary among shoppers from different locales, especially if consumer characteristics in the locales are dissimilar. A firm reduces this problem if both cash and credit customers are reviewed.

A retailer can also collect primary data to determine trading-area size. It can record the license plate numbers of cars parked near a store, find the general addresses of those vehicle owners by contacting the state motor vehicle office, and then note them on a map. Only the ZIP code and street of residence are provided to protect people's privacy. When using license plate analysis, nondrivers and passengers—customers who walk to a store, use mass transit, or are driven by others—should not be omitted. To collect data on these customers, questions must often be asked (survey).

Use PRIZM (http://
cluster2.claritas.com/
YAWYL/Default.wjsp)
to study your area's life-
styles and purchasing
preferences.

If a retailer desires more demographic and life-style information about consumers in particular areas, it can buy the data. PRIZM is Claritas' system for identifying communities by life-style clusters. It identifies 62 neighborhood types, including "Gray Power," "Starter Families," and "Suburban Sprawl." PRIZM was based on ZIP codes; it now also incorporates census tracts, block groups and enumeration districts, phone exchanges, and postal routes. Online PRIZM reports can be downloaded for as little as a few hundred dollars; costs are higher if reports are tailored to the individual retailer.

No matter how a trading area is delineated, a time bias may exist. A downtown business district is patronized by different customers during the week (those who work there) than on weekends (those who travel there to shop). Special events may attract people from great distances for only a brief time. Thus, an accurate estimate of a store's trading area requires complete and continuous investigation.

After delineating a trading area, the retailer should map people's locations and densities—either manually or with GIS software. In the manual method, a paper map of the area around a store is used. Different color dots or pins are placed on this map to represent *population* locations and densities, incomes, and other factors. *Customer* locations and densities are then indicated; primary, secondary, and fringe trading areas are denoted by ZIP code. Customers can be lured by promotions aimed at particular ZIP codes. With GIS software, key customer data (such as purchase frequencies and amounts) are combined with other information sources (such as census data) to yield computer-generated digitized maps depicting primary, secondary, and fringe trading areas.

DELINEATING THE TRADING AREA OF A NEW STORE

A new store opening in an established trading area can use the methods just noted. This section refers to a trading area with less-defined shopping and traffic patterns. Such an area must normally be evaluated in terms of opportunities rather than current patronage and traffic (pedestrian and vehicular) patterns. Accordingly, additional tools must be utilized.

Trend analysis—projecting the future based on the past—can be employed by examining government and other data for predictions about population location, auto registrations, new housing starts, mass transportation, highways, zoning, and so on. Consumer surveys can gather information about the time and distance people would be willing to travel to various possible retail locations, the factors attracting people to a new store, the addresses of those most apt to visit a new store, and other topics. Either technique may be a basis for delineating alternate new store trading areas.

Three computerized trading-area analysis models are available for assessing new store locations: An **analog model** is the simplest and most popular trading-area analysis model. Potential sales for a new store are estimated on the basis of revenues for similar stores in existing areas, the competition at a prospective location, the new store's expected market share at that location, and the size and density of the location's primary trading area. A **regression model** uses a series of mathematical equations showing the association between potential store sales and several independent variables at each location, such as population size, average income, the number of households, nearby competitors, transportation barriers, and traffic patterns. A **gravity model** is based on the premise that people are drawn to stores that are closer and more attractive than competitors' stores. The distance between consumers and competitors, the distance between consumers and a given site, and store image are included in this model.[5]

Computerized trading-area models offer several benefits to retailers: They operate in an objective and systematic way. They offer insights as to how each locational attribute should be weighted. They are useful in screening a large number of locations. They can assess management performance by comparing forecasts with results.

More specific methods for delineating new trading areas are described next.

Reilly's Law

The traditional means of trading-area delineation is **Reilly's law of retail gravitation**.[6] It establishes a point of indifference between two cities or communities, so the trading area of each can be determined. The **point of indifference** is the geographic breaking point between two cities (communities) at which consumers are indifferent to shopping at either. According to Reilly's law, more consumers go to the larger city or community because there are more stores; the assortment makes travel time worthwhile. Reilly's law rests on these assumptions: Two competing areas are equally accessible from a major road, and retailers in the two areas are equally effective. Other factors (such as population dispersion) are held constant or ignored.

The law may be expressed algebraically as:[7]

$$D_{ab} = \frac{d}{1 + \sqrt{P_b / P_a}}$$

where

D_{ab} = Limit of city (community) A's trading area, measured in miles along the road to city (community) B
d = Distance in miles along a major roadway between cities (communities) A and B
P_a = Population of city (community) A
P_b = Population of city (community) B

A city with a population of 90,000 (A) would draw people from three times the distance as a city with 10,000 (B). If the cities are 20 miles apart, the point of indifference for the larger city is 15 miles, and for the smaller city, it is 5 miles:

$$D_{ab} = \frac{20}{1 + \sqrt{10,000/90,000}} = 15 \text{ miles}$$

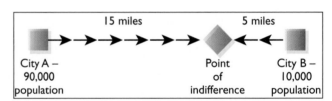

Reilly's law is an important contribution to trading-area analysis because of its ease of calculation. It is most useful when other data are not available or compiling other data is costly. Nonetheless, Reilly's law has three limitations: (1) Distance is only measured by major thoroughfares; some people will travel shorter distances along cross streets. (2) Travel time does not necessarily reflect the distance traveled. Many people are more concerned about time than distance. (3) Actual distance may not correspond with the perceptions of distance. A store with few services and crowded aisles is apt to be a greater perceived distance from the person than a similarly located store with a more pleasant atmosphere.

Huff's Law

Huff's law of shopper attraction delineates trading areas on the basis of the product assortment (of the items desired by the consumer) carried at various shopping locations, travel times from the shopper's home to alternative locations, and the sensitivity of the kind of shopping to travel time. Assortment is rated by the total square feet of selling space a retailer expects all firms in a shopping area to allot to a product category. Sensitivity to the kind of shopping entails the trip's purpose (restocking versus shopping) and the type of good/service sought (such as clothing versus groceries).[8]

Huff's law is expressed as:

$$P_{ij} = \frac{\dfrac{S_j}{(T_{ij})^\lambda}}{\displaystyle\sum_{j=1}^{n} \dfrac{S_j}{(T_{ij})^\lambda}}$$

where

P_{ij} = Probability of a consumer's traveling from home i to shopping location j
S_j = Square footage of selling space in shopping location j expected to be devoted to a particular product category
T_{ij} = Travel time from consumer's home i to shopping location j
λ = Parameter used to estimate the effect of travel time on different kinds of shopping trips
n = Number of different shopping locations

λ must be determined through research or by a computer program.

Assume a leased department operator studies three possible locations with 200, 300, and 500 total square feet of store space allocated to men's cologne (by all retailers in the areas). A group of potential customers lives 7 minutes from the first location, 10 minutes from the second, and 15 minutes from the third. The operator estimates the effect of travel time to be 2. Therefore, the probability of consumers' shopping is 43.9 percent for Location 1, 32.2 percent for Location 2, and 23.9 percent for Location 3:

$$P_{i1} = \frac{(200)/(7)^2}{(200)/(7)^2 + (300)/(10)^2 + (500)/(15)^2} = 43.9\%$$

$$P_{i2} = \frac{(300)/(10)^2}{(200)/(7)^2 + (300)/(10)^2 + (500)/(15)^2} = 32.2\%$$

$$P_{i3} = \frac{(500)/(15)^2}{(200)/(7)^2 + (300)/(10)^2 + (500)/(15)^2} = 23.9\%$$

If 200 men live 7 minutes from Location 1, about 88 of them will shop there.

These points should be considered in using Huff's law:

- To determine Location 1's trading area, similar computations would be made for people living at a driving time of 10, 15, 20 minutes, and so on. The number of people at each distance who would shop there are then summed. Thus, stores in Location 1 could estimate their total market, the trading-area size, and the primary, secondary, and fringe areas for a product category.

- If new retail facilities in a product category are added to a locale, the percentage of people living at every travel time from that location who would shop there goes up.

- The probability of people shopping at a location depends on the effect of travel time. If a product is important, such as men's dress watches, consumers are less sensitive to travel. A λ of 1 leads to these figures: Location 1, 31.1 percent; Location 2, 32.6 percent; and Location 3, 36.3 percent (based on the space in the cologne example). Location 3 is popular for dress watches due to its assortment.

- All the variables are rather hard to calculate; for mapping purposes, travel time must be converted to miles. Travel time also depends on the transportation form used.

- Since people buy different items on different shopping trips, the trading area varies by trip.

Recently, MPSI Systems introduced a new software package called Huff's Market Area Planner.

Access online samples of Huff software at MPSI's Web site (www. datametrix.com).

Other Trading-Area Research

Over the years, a number of other researchers have examined trading-area size in a variety of settings. They have introduced additional factors and sophisticated statistical techniques to explain the consumer's choice of shopping location.

In his model, Gautschi added to Huff's analysis by including shopping-center descriptors and transportation conditions. Weisbrod, Parcells, and Kern studied the attractiveness of shopping centers on the basis of expected population changes, store characteristics, and the transportation network. Ghosh developed a consumer behavior model that takes into consideration multi-purpose shopping trips. LeBlang demonstrated that consumer life-styles could be used to predict sales at new department store locations. Schneider, Johnson, Sleeper, and Rodgers studied trading-area overlap and franchisees. Albaladejo-Pina and Aranda-Gallego looked at the effects of competition among stores in different sections of a trading area. Bell, Ho, and Tang devised a model with both fixed and variable store choice factors. Ruiz studied the influence of shopping center image on its ability to attract shoppers.[9]

CHARACTERISTICS OF TRADING AREAS

PCensus with MapInfo (www.tetrad.com/new/francise.html) is a useful tool for scrutinizing potential franchise locations.

After the size and shape of alternative trading areas are determined, the characteristics of those areas are studied. Of special interest are the attributes of residents and how well they match the firm's definition of its target market. An auto repair franchisee may compare opportunities in several areas by reviewing the number of car registrations; a hearing aid retailer may evaluate the percentage of the population 60 years of age or older; and a bookstore retailer may be concerned with residents' education level.

Among the trading-area factors that should be studied by most retailers are the population size and characteristics, availability of labor, closeness to sources of supply, promotion facilities, economic base, competition, availability of locations, and regulations. The **economic base** is an area's industrial and commercial structure—the companies and industries that residents depend on to earn a living. The dominant industry (company) in an area is important since its drastic decline may have adverse effects on a large segment of residents. An area with a diverse economic base, where residents work for a variety of nonrelated industries, is more secure than an area with one major industry. Table 9-1 summarizes a number of factors to consider in evaluating retail trading areas.

TABLE 9-1	Chief Factors to Consider in Evaluating Retail Trading Areas

Population Size and Characteristics

Total size and density	Total disposable income
Age distribution	Per capita disposable income
Average educational level	Occupation distribution
Percentage of residents owning homes	Trends

Availability of Labor

Management
Management trainee
Clerical

Closeness to Sources of Supply

Delivery costs	Number of manufacturers and wholesalers
Timeliness	Availability and reliability of product lines

Promotion Facilities

Availability and frequency of media
Costs
Waste

Economic Base

Dominant industry	Freedom from economic and seasonal fluctuations
Extent of diversification	Availability of credit and financial facilities
Growth projections	

Competitive Situation

Number and size of existing competitors	Short-run and long-run outlook
Evaluation of competitor strengths/weaknesses	Level of saturation

Availability of Store Locations

Number and type of locations	Zoning restrictions
Access to transportation	Costs
Owning versus leasing opportunities	

Regulations

Taxes	Minimum wages
Licensing	Zoning
Operations	

Much of the data necessary to describe an area can be obtained from the U.S. Bureau of the Census, the *Survey of Buying Power, Editor & Publisher Market Guide, Rand McNally Commercial Atlas & Market Guide, American Demographics, Standard Rate & Data Service*, regional planning boards, public utilities, chambers of commerce, local government offices, shopping-center owners, and renting agents. In addition, GIS software provides data on potential buying power in an area, the location of competitors, and highway access. Both demographic and life-style information may also be included in this software.

Although the yardsticks in Table 9-1 are not equally important in all location decisions, each should be considered. The most important yardsticks should be "knockout" factors: If a location does not meet minimum standards on key measures, it should be immediately dropped from further consideration.

These are examples of desirable trading-area attributes, according to a mix of retailers:

- At Sharper Image: "We have a two-pronged strategy right now in terms of our real-estate. The first is we're looking for grade-A regional malls in urban areas. The other prong is we're looking at drive-up locations in sort of fill-in geographic locations. We believe with our store we can draw people into centers now. That's why we're looking at both prongs."

- Peebles Department Stores has more than 140 stores "strategically located in 'county-seat' towns" throughout 17 states: It's been our experience that small towns are actually better insulated against [economic] problems." Peebles stores "range in size from 15,000 square feet to 30,000 square feet and serve a primary trade area of 15 to 20 miles. The fundamental site-selection criteria are that there are no other department stores in the town and no mall within a 30-minute drive." As Peebles says, "These towns may not be sexy, but they are fairly well-insulated against the wanderings of fortune."

- Dollar General serves more than 3,000 communities that have a population of less than 20,000. This allows it to take advantage of its brand awareness and maximizes operating efficiencies.

- Pathmark "has supermarkets in both urban and suburban marketplaces, and is particularly noted for its historical commitment to opening stores within the inner-cities of its trading area."

- The Syms off-price apparel chain seeks locations near highways or thoroughfares in suburban areas populated by a least 1 million persons and readily accessible by car. In certain areas, with over 2 million people, Syms has more than one store.[10]

Several stages of the process for gathering data to analyze trading areas are shown in Figure 9-8, which includes not only the attributes of residents but also those of the competition. By studying these factors, a retailer sees how desirable an area is for its business.

We next discuss three elements in trading-area selection: population characteristics, economic base characteristics, and the nature of competition and the level of saturation.

Careers in RETAILING
Building Customer Loyalty at Main Street Books

Main Street Books, an independent bookstore in St. Charles, Missouri, has a most unusual location. Mary Fran Rash, the store's owner, says the store is housed in a cottage built around 1830. The building originally served as a kitchen for the main house next door. It also was a school. Part of Main Street Books' popularity is no doubt due to the building's historical heritage.

According to Rash, "To tell you the truth, I've been thinking of moving, but people like the building, so I'm staying." So when she needed additional space, Rash convinced the property owner to rent her the second floor of the building. This additional space used to be an apartment with a kitchen. The kitchen cabinets and oven are now used to store books, and books are displayed on both the sink and stove.

Main Street Books has done well at its location: "Borders [which recently opened nearby] hasn't hurt me. I didn't feel the crunch because people come to Main Street as a destination. Borders does not have the collection of local history books." Rash also specializes in local authors, has frequent book signings, and provides space for book clubs.

Source: Lacey Burnette, "Main Street Books Stays Ahead of the Competition with Customer Service, Ambiance," *St. Louis Post Dispatch* (June 18, 2002).

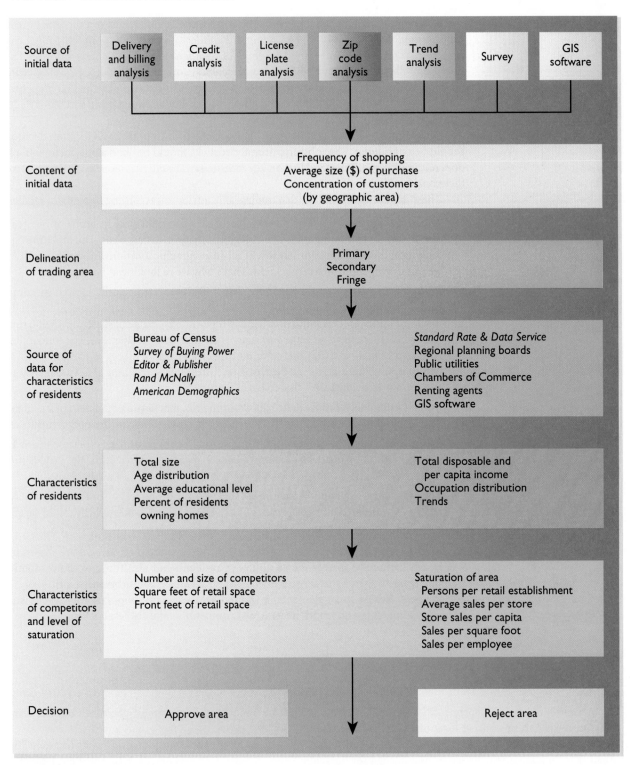

FIGURE 9-8
Analyzing Retail Trading Areas

CHARACTERISTICS OF THE POPULATION

Extensive knowledge about an area's population characteristics can be gained from secondary sources. They offer data about the population size, number of households, income distribution, education level, age distribution, and more. Because the *Census of Population* and the *Survey of Buying Power* are such valuable sources, each is briefly described.

Census of Population

Find out about the 2000 U.S. Census (www.census. gov/dmd/www/2khome. htm).

The **Census of Population** supplies a wide range of demographic data for all U.S. cities and surrounding vicinities. Data are organized on a geographic basis, starting with blocks and continuing to census tracts, cities, countries, states, and regions. There are less data for blocks and census tracts than for larger units due to privacy issues. The major advantage of census data is the information on small geographic units. Once trading-area boundaries are outlined, a firm can look at data for each of the geographic units in that area and study aggregate demographics. There are also data categories that are especially helpful for retailers interested in segmenting the market—including racial and ethnic data, small-area income data, and commuting patterns. Census data are available on CD-ROM disks, on computer tapes, and online.

The U.S. Census Bureau's TIGER computer tapes contain extremely detailed physical breakdowns of areas in the United States. These tapes comprise a computer-readable data base with digital descriptions of geographic areas (area boundaries and codes, latitude and longitude coordinates, and address ranges). Because TIGER tapes must be used in conjunction with population and other data, GIS software is necessary. Many private firms have devised their location analysis programs, based in large part on TIGER. These firms also usually project data to the present year and into the future.

The major drawbacks of the *Census of Population* are that it is undertaken only once every 10 years and that all data are not immediately available when they are collected. For example, the next Census is not until 2010, and information from the 2000 *Census of Population* was released in phases from 2001 through 2003. Census material can, thus, be out-of-date and inaccurate—particularly several years after collection. Supplementary sources, such as municipal building departments or utilities, state government offices, other Census reports (including the *Current Population Survey*), and computerized projections by firms such as Dun & Bradstreet must be used to update *Census of Population* data.

The value of the *Census of Population's* actual 2000 census tract data can be shown by an illustration of Long Beach, New York, which is 30 miles east of New York City on Long Island's south shore. Long Beach encompasses six census tracts: 4164, 4165, 4166, 4167.01, 4167.02, and 4168. See Figure 9-9. Although tract 4163 is contiguous with Long Beach, it represents another community.

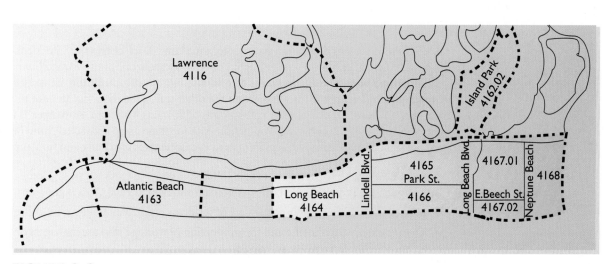

FIGURE 9-9

The Census Tracts of Long Beach, New York

TABLE 9-2	Selected Characteristics of Long Beach, New York, Residents by Census Tract, 1990 and 2000					
	TRACT NUMBER					
	4164	**4165**	**4166**	**4167.01**	**4167.02**	**4168**
<u>Total Population</u>						
1990	7,082	5,694	5,613	4,162	4,479	6,480
1990 population 25 and older	5,315	3,331	4,306	3,003	3,620	5,074
2000	7,406	6,231	6,326	4,471	4,443	6,585
2000 population 25 and older	5,772	4,073	4,904	3,163	3,739	5,173
<u>Number of Households</u>						
1990	2,735	1,812	2,219	1,465	2,295	3,066
2000	3,138	2,002	2,592	1,601	2,440	3,165
<u>Education</u>						
College graduates (% of population 25 and older), 2000	38.4	18.6	44.9	35.8	35.9	43.7
<u>Income</u>						
Median household income, 2000 (estimate)	$59,188	$46,261	$63,716	$68,680	$52,334	$64,348
<u>Selected Occupations</u>						
Managerial, professional, and related occupations (% of employed persons 16 and older), 2000	42.6	25.2	49.1	45.4	40.9	47.6

Sources: Census of Population (Washington, D.C.: U.S. Bureau of the Census, 2000); and authors' computations. Data obtained through "American FactFinder," **http://factfinder.census.gov** (February 21, 2003).

Table 9-2 shows various population statistics for each Long Beach census tract. Resident characteristics in each tract differ; thus, a retailer might choose to locate in one or more tracts but not in others.

Suppose a bookstore chain wants to evaluate two potential trading areas. Because of the demographic differences of tract 4165 from the other tracts, the chain decides not to include this tract in its analysis. Trading area A corresponds with tracts 4164 and 4166. Area B is similar to tracts 4167.01, 4167.02, and 4168. Population data for these areas (extracted from Table 9-2) are presented in Table 9-3. Area A differs from Area B, despite their proximity and similar physical size:

- The population in Area B is 13 percent larger.
- Although the population in both areas rose from 1990 to 2000, Area B grew very little.
- In Area A, a slightly greater percentage of residents aged 25 and older have college degrees.
- The annual median income and the proportion of workers who are managers or professionals are roughly equal in Areas A and B.

The bookstore chain would have a tough time selecting between the areas since they are so similar. Thus, the chain might also consider the location of the sites available in Area A and Area B relative to the locations of its existing stores, before making a final decision.

TABLE 9-3	Selected Population Statistics for Long Beach Trading Areas A and B	
	Area A (Tracts 4164 and 4166)	Area B (Tracts 4167.01, 4167.02, and 4168)
Total population, 2000	13,732	15,499
Population change, 1990–2000 (%)	+8.2	+2.5
College graduates, 25 and older, 2000 (%)	41.4	39.2
Median household income, 2000	$61,236	$61,242
Managerial and professional specialty occupations (% of employed persons 16 and older), 2000	45.3	45.0

Survey of Buying Power

The annual **Survey of Buying Power**, published by *Sales & Marketing Management*, reports current demographic data on metropolitan areas, cities, and states. It also provides some data not available from the *Census of Population*: total annual retail sales by area, annual retail sales for specific product categories, annual effective buying income, and five-year population and retail sales projections. The *Survey's* biggest disadvantage is its use of broad geographic territories, which are often much larger than a store's trading area and cannot be broken down easily.

Two key *Survey* terms must be defined.[11] **Effective buying income (EBI)** is personal income (wages, salaries, interest, dividends, profits, rental income, and pension income) minus federal, state, and local taxes and nontax payments (such as personal contributions for social security insurance). EBI is commonly known as disposable or after-tax personal income.

The **buying power index (BPI)** is a weighted measure that combines effective buying income, retail sales, and population size into one overall indicator of an area's sales potential, expressed in terms of total U.S. sales. Each criterion is assigned a weight, based on its importance:

Buying power index = 0.5 (the area's percentage of U.S. effective buying income)
+ 0.3 (the area's percentage of U.S. retail sales)
+ 0.2 (the area's percentage of U.S. population)

Suppose a prospective new car dealer investigates three countries near Chicago: Du Page, Kane, and Lake. Table 9-4 lists selected population and retail sales data (as well as five-year projections) for these counties. The buying power index for Du Page is over three times greater than Kane's and more than one-third greater than Lake's. Du Page has a larger population and more people 18 and older than either Kane or Lake. In addition, 82.4 percent of Du Page's residents have effective buying incomes of $50,000 or better, compared to 68.1 percent of Kane's residents and 78.6 percent of Lake's. In 2001, motor vehicle and parts dealer sales were $5.3 billion in Du Page, $1 billion in Kane, and $3.3 billion in Lake.

A Cadillac dealer using *Survey of Buying Power* data might select Du Page and a Chevrolet dealer might select Kane. But, because *Survey* statistics are broad in nature, several subsections of Kane may be superior choices to subsections in Du Page for the Cadillac dealer. The competition in each area also must be noted.

The location decision for a fast-food franchise usually requires less data than for a bookstore or an auto dealer. Fast-food franchisors often seek communities with many people living or working within a 3- or 4-mile radius of their stores. However, bookstore owners and auto dealers cannot locate merely on the basis of population density. They must consider a more complex set of population factors.

TABLE 9-4	Selected Data from *Survey of Buying Power* Relating to the Automobile Market in Three Illinois Counties

	COUNTY		
	Du Page	Kane	Lake
December 31, 2001			
Total population	918,200	418,900	663,600
Number of people 18 and over	683,100	293,200	469,200
Number of households	331,300	138,400	222,600
Total effective buying income (EBI)	$27,251,918,000	$8,106,005,000	$19,849,876,000
Median household effective buying income (EBI)	$64,033	$48,636	$62,086
Percentage of households with $35,000–$49,999 EBI	15.2	19.9	15.1
Percentage of households with $50,000+ EBI	67.2	48.4	63.5
Total retail sales	$18,585,209,000	$4,717,959,000	$13,798,830,000
Buying power index (%)	0.4747	0.1477	0.3474
Percentage of U.S. EBI	0.5138	0.1528	0.3743
Percentage of U.S. retail sales	0.5124	0.1301	0.3804
Percentage of U.S. population	0.3201	0.1461	0.2314
Motor vehicle and parts dealer sales, 2001	$5,257,118,000	$1,027,713,000	$3,278,506,000
Projections for December 31, 2006			
Total population	958,300	457,100	715,000
Total EBI	$37,642,539,000	$10,602,263,000	$27,735,924,000
Total retail sales	$24,980,136,000	$6,217,818,000	$19,685,042,000
Buying power index (%)	0.5014	0.1484	0.3782

Source: Adapted from *Sales & Marketing Management: 2002 Survey of Buying Power and Media Markets* (September 2002), pp. 81, 154. Sales & Marketing Management Copyright 2002 by VNU BUS PUBNS USA. Reproduced with permission of VNU BUS PUBNS in the format text via Copy Clearance Center.

Economic Base Characteristics

The economic base reflects a community's commercial and industrial infrastructure and residents' sources of income. A firm seeking stability normally prefers an area with a diversified economic base (a large number of nonrelated industries) to one with an economic base keyed to a single major industry. The latter area is more affected by a strike, declining demand for an industry, and cyclical fluctuations.

In assessing a trading area's economic base, a retailer should investigate the percentage of the labor force in each industry, transportation, banking facilities, the impact of economic fluctuations, and the future of individual industries (firms). Data can be obtained from such sources as Easy Analytic Software, *Editor & Publisher Market Guide*, regional planning commissions, industrial development organizations, and chambers of commerce.

Easy Analytic Software (**www.easidemographics.com**) provides a wide range of inexpensive economic reports. It also produces several "easy-to-use Demographics Reports" by ZIP code that can be downloaded free at "The Right Site" section of its Web site, including: *Employment and Industry Report & Analysis*, *Quality of Life Report & Analysis*, and *Business Profile Report & Analysis*.

Editor & Publisher Market Guide offers annual economic base data for cities, including employment sources, transportation networks, financial institutions, auto registrations, newspaper circulation, and shopping centers. It also has data on population size and total households. Like the *Survey of Buying Power*, *Editor & Publisher Market Guide* data cover broad geographic areas. The bookstore chain noted earlier would find the information on shopping centers to be helpful. The auto dealer would find the information on the transportation network, the availability of financial institutions, and the number of passenger cars to be useful. *Editor & Publisher Market Guide* is best used to supplement other sources.

THE NATURE OF COMPETITION AND THE LEVEL OF SATURATION

Although a trading area may have residents who match the characteristics of the desired market and a strong economic base, it may be a poor location for a new store if competition is too intense. A locale with a small population and a narrow economic base may be a good location if competition is minimal.

When examining competition, these factors should be analyzed: the number of existing stores, the size distribution of existing stores, the rate of new store openings, the strengths and weaknesses of all stores, short-run and long-run trends, and the level of saturation.

Over the past decade, many retailers have expanded into in the Southeast and Southwest due to their growing populations. Tiffany, Target Stores, Marshall Field's, Lord & Taylor, and Macy's are among those that have entered New Orleans, Dallas, Orlando, Phoenix, and other markets. Yet, there is a concern that these locales may become oversaturated due to all the new stores. Furthermore, although the Northeast population has been declining relative to the Southeast and the Southwest, its high population density (the number of persons per square mile) is crucial for retailers. In New Jersey, there are 1,135 people per square mile; in Massachusetts, 810; in Florida, 295; in Louisiana, 105; and in Arizona, 45.

An **understored trading area** has too few stores selling a specific good or service to satisfy the needs of its population. An **overstored trading area** has so many stores selling a specific good or service that some retailers cannot earn an adequate profit. A **saturated trading area** has the proper amount of stores to satisfy the needs of its population for a specific good or service and to enable retailers to prosper.

Despite the large number of areas in the United States that are overstored, there still remain plentiful opportunities in understored communities. For example,

Charlotte, Raleigh-Durham, and the Piedmont Triad (Greensboro/Winston-Salem) are the strongest growth markets in North Carolina. South Carolina is seeing the most growth in the upstate, around Greenville/Spartanburg, as well as in Columbia and Charleston. Myrtle Beach and Florence, South Carolina, are also great for retailing. The population is around 320,000 to 330,000 in this area, but close to 14.5 million tourists visit every year. These tourists are unique because they typically drive to their destination and the average stay is longer than in most resorts, so they shop extensively.[12]

Ethics in RETAILING
Are Communities Out of the Box in Legislating Against Big-Box Stores?

San Francisco recently introduced legislation that would make it more difficult for large box stores from opening within its city limits. The law would require any retailers (except supermarkets) seeking to build new stores larger than 50,000 square feet to have a special review process that would examine such issues as the stores' impact on traffic and on nearby small businesses. The same review process would also be applicable to any small retailer seeking to add 3,000 square feet or more to an existing store.

Two major projects that would have been affected by the proposed legislation were Home Depot's (**www.homedepot.com**) building a 150,000-square-foot store on an old lumber-yard site and Target's (**www.target.com**) constructing its first store in San Francisco. While he acknowledges that legislation against box stores is common, a spokesperson for the International Mass Retail Association (**www.imra.org**) notes, "The unusual thing about San Francisco is the size of the stores being targeted, because 50,000 square feet is not very big. Usually, the laws affect stores in the 80,000- to 120,000-square-foot range."

These zoning laws also pit the interests of local homeowners, who do not want increased traffic or commercial activity in residential areas, against unions seeking jobs.

Source: Doug Desjardins, "Big Box Foes Push for More Legislation," *DSN Retailing Today* (February 25, 2002), p. 1.

Measuring Trading-Area Saturation

Because any trading area can support only a given number of stores or square feet of selling space per goods/service category, these ratios can help to quantify retail store saturation:

- Number of persons per retail establishment.
- Average sales per retail store.
- Average sales per retail store category.
- Average store sales per capita or household.
- Average sales per square foot of selling area.
- Average sales per employee.

The saturation level in a trading area can be measured against a goal or compared with other trading areas. An auto accessory chain might find that its current trading area is saturated by computing the ratio of residents to auto accessory stores. On the basis of this calculation, the owner could then decide to expand into a nearby locale with a lower ratio rather than to add another store in its present trading area.

Data for saturation ratios can be obtained from a retailer's records on its performance, city and state records, phone directories, consumer surveys, economic census data, *Editor & Publisher Market Guide, County Business Patterns,* trade publications, and other sources. Sales by product category, population size, and number of households per market area can be found in the *Survey of Buying Power.*

When investigating an area's saturation for a specific good or service, ratios must be interpreted carefully. Differences among areas may not be reliable indicators of saturation. Car sales per capita are different for a suburban area than an urban area because suburbanites have a much greater need for cars. Each area's level of saturation should be evaluated against distinct standards—based on optimum per capita sales figures in that area.

In calculating saturation based on sales per square foot, a new or growing retailer must take its proposed store into account. If that store is not part of the calculation, the relative value of each trading area is distorted. Sales per square foot decline most if new outlets are added in small communities. The retailer should also consider if a new store will expand the total consumer market for a good or service category in a trading area or just increase its market share in that area without expanding the total market.

These are three examples of how retailers factor trading-area saturation into their decisions:

- Walgreen is quite careful about where its Walgreen's drugstores are located: "Many of our top-performing stores cater to urban neighborhoods underserved by most national chains. We've been doing that for decades—customers count on us to fill in the gap, and we respond by stocking items they need, including expanded food sections in areas where grocery stores are scarce."[13]

- Gottschalk's operates department stores in the Pacific Northwest and Alaska: "Our stores are located primarily in diverse, growing, nonmajor metropolitan or suburban areas in the western United States where management believes there is strong demand and fewer competitors offering similar better to moderate brand-name merchandise and a high level of customer service. We have historically avoided expansion into the center of major metropolitan areas that are well served by the Company's larger competitors, and instead opened new stores in nearby suburban or secondary market areas."[14]

- Supermarket chains buy annual data from Trade Dimensions (**www.tradedimensions.com**) that measure the level of saturation by U.S. city, including the number of supermarkets, overall supermarket sales, supermarket sales per capita, weekly sales per square foot, chain supermarkets versus independents, total supermarket space, the number of supermarket employees, and more.

Download Trade Dimensions' (www. tradedimensions.com) samples of its *Marketing Guide* to see the saturation levels of supermarkets. Click on "Marketing Guide" and choose "Sample Pages."

Summary

1. *To demonstrate the importance of store location for a retailer and outline the process for choosing a store location.* The location choice is critical because of the complex decision making, the high costs, the lack of flexibility once a site is chosen, and the impact of a site on the strategy. A good location may let a retailer succeed even if its strategy mix is relatively mediocre.

The selection of a store location includes (1) evaluating alternative trading areas; (2) determining the best type of location; (3) picking a general site; and (4) settling on a specific site. This chapter looks at Step 1. Chapter 10 details Steps 2, 3, and 4.

2. *To discuss the concept of a trading area and its related components.* A trading area is the geographical area from which customers are drawn. When shopping locales are nearby, they may have trading-area overlap.

Many retailers utilize geographic information systems (GIS) software to delineate and analyze trading areas. The software combines digitized mapping with key data to graphically depict trading areas. This lets retailers research alternative locations and display findings on computerized maps. Several vendors market GIS software, based on TIGER mapping by the U.S. government.

Each trading area has primary, secondary, and fringe components. The farther people live from a shopping area, the less apt they are to travel there. The size and shape of a trading area depend on store type, store size, competitor locations, housing patterns, travel time and traffic barriers, and media availability. Destination stores have larger trading areas than parasites.

3. *To show how trading areas may be delineated for existing and new stores.* The size, shape, and characteristics of the trading area for an existing store or group of stores can be learned accurately—based on store records, contests, license plate numbers, surveys, and so on. Time biases must be considered in amassing data. Results should be mapped and customer densities noted.

Potential trading areas for a new store must often be described in terms of opportunities, rather than current patronage and traffic. Trend analysis and consumer surveys may be used. Three computerized models are available for planning a new store location: analog, regression, and gravity. They offer several benefits.

Two techniques for delineating new trading areas are Reilly's law, which relates the population size of different cities to the size of their trading areas, and Huff's law, which is based on each area's shopping assortment, the distance of people from various retail locales, and sensitivity to travel time.

4. *To examine three major factors in trading-area analysis: population characteristics, economic base characteristics, and competition and the level of saturation.* The best sources for population data are the *Census of Population* and the *Survey of Buying Power*. Census data are detailed and specific but become dated. The *Survey of Buying Power* has current data, but it reports on broader areas.

An area's economic base reflects the community's commercial and industrial infrastructure, as well as residents' income sources. A retailer should look at the percentage of the labor force in each industry, the transportation network, banking facilities, the potential impact of economic fluctuations on the area, and the future of individual industries. Easy Analytic and *Editor & Publisher Market Guide* are good sources of data on the economic base.

A trading area cannot be properly analyzed without studying the nature of competition and the level of saturation. An area may be understored (too few retailers), overstored (too many retailers), or saturated (the proper number of retailers). Saturation may be measured in terms of the number of persons per store, average sales per store, average store sales per capita or household, average sales per square foot of selling space, and average sales per employee.

Key Terms

trading area (p. 217)
trading-area overlap (p. 217)
geographic information systems (GIS) (p. 218)
primary trading area (p. 220)
secondary trading area (p. 220)
fringe trading area (p. 220)
destination store (p. 222)
parasite store (p. 222)
analog model (p. 225)
regression model (p. 225)
gravity model (p. 225)
Reilly's law of retail gravitation (p. 226)
point of indifference (p. 226)
Huff's law of shopper attraction (p. 226)
economic base (p. 228)
Census of Population (p. 231)
Survey of Buying Power (p. 233)
effective buying income (EBI) (p. 233)
buying power index (BPI) (p. 233)
understored trading area (p. 235)
overstored trading area (p. 235)
saturated trading area (p. 235)

Questions for Discussion

1. Comment on this statement: "A good location may let a retailer succeed even if its strategy mix is mediocre." Is it always true? Give examples.

2. If a retailer has a new 10-year store lease, does this mean the next time it studies the characteristics of its trading area should be 5 years from now? Explain your answer.

3. What is trading-area overlap? Are there any advantages to a chain retailer's having some overlap among its various stores? Why or why not?

4. Describe three ways in which a shoe chain could use geographic information systems (GIS) software in its trading-area analysis.

5. How could an off-campus store selling prerecorded music near a college campus determine its primary, secondary, and fringe trading areas? Why should the music store obtain this information?

6. How could a parasite store increase the size of its trading area?

7. Explain Reilly's law. What are its advantages and disadvantages?

8. Use Huff's law to compute the probability of consumers' traveling from their homes to each of three shopping areas: square footage of selling space—Location 1, 5,000; Location 2, 8,000; Location 3, 10,000; travel time—to Location 1, 12 minutes; to Location 2, 18 minutes; to Location 3, 25 minutes; effect of travel time on shopping trip—2. Explain your answer.

9. What are the major advantages and disadvantages of *Census of Population* data in delineating trading areas?

10. Look at the most recent buying power index in the *Survey of Buying Power* for the area in which your college is located. What retailing-related conclusions do you draw?

11. If a retail area is acknowledged to be "saturated," what does this signify for existing retailers? For prospective retailers considering this area?

12. How could a Web-based retailer determine the level of saturation for its product category? What should this retailer do to lessen the impact of the level of saturation it faces?

Note: At our Web site (**www.prenhall.com/bermanevans**), there are several math problems related to the material in this chapter so that you may review these concepts.

Web-Based Exercise

Visit the Web site of *Site Selection* magazine (**www.siteselection. com**). What could a retailer learn from this site? What site feature do you like best? Why?

Note: Stop by our Web site (**www.prenhall.com/bermanevans**) to experience a number of highly interactive, appealing Web exercises

based on actual company demonstrations and sample materials related to retailing.

Chapter Endnotes

1. Various company sources.

2. *Wilsons Leather 2001 Annual Report*, 10-K, p. 8.

3. Peter D. Bennett (Editor), *Dictionary of Marketing Terms*, Second Edition (Chicago: American Marketing Association, 1995), p. 287.

4. "About Dunkin' Donuts," **www.geovue.com/profiles/about_dunkindonuts.htm** (February 28, 2003); *CVS 2000 Annual Report*, pp. 10–11; and "Eddie Bauer: Enter the Next Marketing Generation with Compass & Data," **www.claritas.com/i2_r3/SUB/i2_case_eddie_bauer.htm** (January 28, 2003).

5. For a good overview of gravity models, see "Spatial Modeling," **www.geobusiness.co.uk/products/models/models.htm** (May 21, 2001).

6. William J. Reilly, *Method for the Study of Retail Relationships*, Research Monograph No. 4 (Austin: University of Texas Press, 1929), University of Texas Bulletin No. 2944. See also MacKenzie S. Bottum, "Reilly's Law," *Appraisal Journal*, Vol. 57 (April 1989), pp. 166–172; and Michael D. D'Amico, Jon M. Hawes, and Dale M. Lewison, "Determining a Hospital's Trading Area: An Application of Reilly's Law," *Journal of Hospital Marketing*, Vol. 8 (Number 2, 1994), pp. 121–129.

7. Richard L. Nelson, *The Selection of Retail Locations* (New York: F.W. Dodge, 1959), p. 149.

8. David L. Huff, "Defining and Estimating a Trading Area," *Journal of Marketing*, Vol. 28 (July 1964), pp. 34–38; and David L. Huff and Larry Blue, *A Programmed Solution for Estimating Retail Sales Potential* (Lawrence: University of Kansas, 1966). See also Christophe Benavent, Marc Thomas, and Anne Bergue, "Application of Gravity Models for the Analysis of Retail Potential," *Journal of Targeting, Measurement, and Analysis for Marketing*, Vol. 1 (Winter 1992–1993), pp. 305–315; and Joseph R. Francica, "Are Retail Attractiveness (Huff) Models Misused?" **www.geoplace.com/gw/2002/0206/0206bgeo.asp** (February 2, 2002).

9. David A. Gautschi, "Specification of Patronage Models for Retail Center Choice," *Journal of Marketing Research*, Vol. 18 (May 1981), pp. 162–174; Glen E. Weisbrod, Robert J. Parcells, and Clifford Kern, "A Disaggregate Model for Predicting Shopping Area Market Attraction," *Journal of Retailing*, Vol. 60 (Spring 1984), pp. 65–83; Avijit Ghosh, "The Value of a Mall and Other Insights from a Revised Central Place Model," *Journal of Retailing*, Vol. 62 (Spring 1986), pp. 79–97; Paul LeBlang, "A Theoretical Approach for Predicting Sales at a New Department-Store Location Via Life-Styles," *Direct Marketing*, Vol. 7 (Autumn 1993), pp. 70–74; Kenneth C. Schneider, James C. Johnson, Bradley J. Sleeper, and William C. Rodgers, "A Note on Applying Retail Location Models in Franchise Systems: A View from the Trenches," *Journal of Consumer Marketing*, Vol.

15 (No. 3, 1998), pp. 290–296; Isabel P. Albaladejo-Pina and Joaquin Aranda-Gallego, "A Measure of Trade Centre Position," *European Journal of Marketing*, Vol. 32 (No. 5–6, 1998), pp. 464–479; David R. Bell, Teck-Hua Ho, and Christopher S. Tang, "Determining Where to Shop: Fixed and Variable Costs of Shopping," *Journal of Marketing Research*, Vol. 35 (August 1998), pp. 352–369; and Francisco José Más Ruiz, "Image of Suburban Shopping Malls and Two-Stage Versus Uni-Equational Modelling of the Retail Trade Attraction," *European Journal of Marketing*, Vol. 33 (No. 5–6, 1999), pp. 512–530.

10. "An Off-the-Mall Attitude," *Chain Store Age* (May 2002), p. 60; Connie Robbins Gentry, "Southern Comfort," *Chain Store Age* (August 2001), p. 136; *Dollar General 2001 Annual Report*, 10-K, p. 5; "Company," **www.pathmark.com/company.asp** (January 31, 2003); and *Syms 2002 Annual Report*.

11. "Glossary," *Sales & Marketing Management: 2002 Survey of Buying Power* (September 2002).

12. Gentry, "Southern Comfort," pp. 133–134.

13. *Walgreens 2001 Annual Report*, p. 9.

14. *Gottschalk's 2001 Annual Report*, 10-K, p. 3.

Chapter 10

SITE SELECTION

Reprinted by permission.

After World War II, William Rosenberg started Industrial Luncheon Services to sell donuts, sandwiches, and coffee to factory workers. He purchased 10 unused cab-and-chassis platforms from the New England Telephone Company and had each outfitted with stainless steel bodies and side flaps that could be lifted. Despite the popularity of the sandwiches, coffee and donuts were the real best-sellers. So in 1948, Rosenberg opened his first store, Open Kettle, as an additional outlet for the sale of donuts.

Rosenberg changed the Open Kettle name to Dunkin' Donuts (**www.dunkindonuts.com**) in 1950 and began franchising. Allied Domecq PLC (**ww.allieddomecq.com**) acquired the chain in 1990. Today, Dunkin' Donuts has more than 5,000 locations worldwide, 3,700 of which are in the United States. It is the world's largest donut-and-coffee chain. It sells 6 million donuts and 2 million cups of coffee daily.

To increase the chance of its stores' succeeding, Dunkin' Donuts has developed specific location standards. Its stand-alone store, for example, generally requires a population of 15,000 or more within its drive-time parameters, a median household income of greater than $38,000, and the presence of 10,000 or more workers (since they are frequent customers) within the trading area. Dunkin' Donuts also has specific site requirements. These include a minimum of 20 parking spots, easy access from all traffic directions, high visibility from major arteries (400 feet or more on the approach side), and a 10-year lease with two five-year renewal options.[1]

chapter objectives

1. To thoroughly examine the types of locations available to a retailer: isolated store, unplanned business district, and planned shopping center
2. To note the decisions necessary in choosing a general retail location
3. To describe the concept of the one-hundred percent location
4. To discuss several criteria for evaluating general retail locations and the specific sites within them
5. To contrast alternative terms of occupancy

OVERVIEW

After a retailer investigates alternative trading areas (Step 1), it determines what type of location is desirable (Step 2), selects the general location (Step 3), and evaluates alternative specific store sites (Step 4). At Kohl's Department Stores,

Is there now a Kohl's near you (www.kohls.com)? Click on "store locator."

The objective is to be a national retailer. Our approach is very deliberate, expanding step-by-step into contiguous states and filling in existing markets. We enter new markets with a critical mass of stores that lets us establish a presence and leverage marketing, management, and distribution expenses. Then, we add more stores to further strengthen our market share. Many stores are located in the growing suburban areas of large metropolitan markets, close to the neighborhoods where our customers live and work. In developing new stores, we generally focus on freestanding locations or power strip malls that provide the visibility, parking, and ease of entry that our customers prefer.[2]

Steps 2, 3, and 4 are discussed in this chapter.

TYPES OF LOCATIONS

There are three different location types: isolated store, unplanned business district, and planned shopping center. Each has its own attributes relating to the composition of competitors, parking, nearness to nonretail institutions (such as office buildings), and other factors. Step 2 in the location process is to determine which type of location to use.

THE ISOLATED STORE

An **isolated store** is a freestanding retail outlet located on either a highway or a street. There are no adjacent retailers with which this type of store shares traffic.

The advantages of this type of retail location are many:

- There is no competition.
- Rental costs are relatively low.
- There is flexibility; no group rules must be followed in operations and larger space may be obtained.
- Isolation is good for stores involved in one-stop or convenience shopping.
- Better road and traffic visibility is possible.
- Facilities can be adapted to individual specifications.
- Easy parking can be arranged.
- Cost reductions are possible, leading to lower prices.

There are also various disadvantages to this retail location type:

- Initial customers may be difficult to attract.
- Many people will not travel very far to get to one store on a continuous basis.
- Most people like variety in shopping.
- Advertising expenses may be high.
- Costs such as outside lighting, security, grounds maintenance, and trash collection are not shared.
- Other retailers and community zoning laws may restrict access to desirable locations.
- A store must often be built rather than rented.
- As a rule, unplanned business districts and planned shopping centers are much more popular among consumers; they generate the bulk of retail sales.

Large-store formats (such as Wal-Mart supercenters and Costco membership clubs) and convenience-oriented retailers (such as 7-Eleven) are usually best suited to isolated locations because of the difficulty in attracting a target market. A small specialty store would probably be unable to develop a customer following; people would be unwilling to travel to a store that does not have a large assortment of products or a strong image for merchandise and/or prices.

Years ago, when discount operations were frowned on by traditional retailers, numerous shopping centers forbade the entry of discounters. This forced the discounters to become isolated stores or to build their own centers, and they have been successful. Today, diverse retailers are in isolated locations, as well as at business district and shopping center sites. Retailers using a mixed location strategy include Krispy Kreme, McDonald's, Dairy Queen, Sears, Toys "R" Us, Wal-Mart, and 7-Eleven. Some retailers, including many gas stations and convenience stores, still emphasize isolated locations. See Figure 10-1.

THE UNPLANNED BUSINESS DISTRICT

An **unplanned business district** is a type of retail location where two or more stores situate together (or in close proximity) in such a way that the total arrangement or mix of stores is not due to prior long-range planning. Stores locate based on what is best for them, not the district. Four shoe stores may exist in an area with no pharmacy. There are four kinds of unplanned business district: central business district, secondary business district, neighborhood business district, and string. A description of each follows.

Central Business District

A **central business district (CBD)** is the hub of retailing in a city. It is synonymous with the term *downtown*. The CBD exists where there is the greatest density of office buildings and stores. Both vehicular and pedestrian traffic are very high. The core of a CBD is often no more than a square mile, with cultural and entertainment facilities surrounding it. Shoppers are drawn from the whole urban area and include all ethnic groups and all classes of people. The CBD has at least one major department store and a number of specialty and convenience stores. The arrangement of stores follows no pre-set format; it depends on history (first come, first located), retail trends, and luck.

Here are some strengths that allow CBDs to draw a large number of shoppers:

- Excellent goods/service assortment.
- Access to public transportation.
- Variety of store types and positioning strategies within one area.
- Wide range of prices.
- Variety of customer services.
- High level of pedestrian traffic.
- Nearness to commercial and social facilities.

In addition, chain headquarters stores are often situated in CBDs.

FIGURE 10-1
Site Selection and McDonald's

McDonald's operates its restaurants at all types of locations—and the firm adapts its exterior designs to the standards of the communities in which it situates, such as the lush North Fork of Long Island, New York.

Reprinted by permission.

These are some of the inherent weaknesses of the CBD:

- Inadequate parking, and traffic and delivery congestion.
- Travel time for those living in the suburbs.
- Frail condition of some cities relative to their suburbs, such as aging stores.
- Relatively poor image of central cities to some potential consumers.
- High rents and taxes for the most popular sites.
- Movement of some popular downtown stores to suburban shopping centers.
- Discontinuity of offerings (such as four shoe stores and no pharmacy).

The CBD remains a major retailing force, although, in recent decades, its share of overall sales has fallen, as compared to the planned shopping center. Besides the weaknesses cited, much of the drop-off is due to suburbanization. In the first half of the 20th century, most urban workers lived near their jobs. Gradually, many people moved to the suburbs—where they are served by planned shopping centers.

A number of CBDs are doing quite well and others are striving to return to their former stature. Many use such tactics as modernizing storefronts and equipment, forming cooperative merchants' associations, modernizing sidewalks and adding brighter lighting, building vertical malls (with several floors of stores), improving transportation networks, closing streets to vehicular traffic (sometimes with disappointing results), bringing in "razzmatazz" retailers such as Nike Town, and integrating a commercial and residential environment known as mixed-use facilities.

According to retail location planning experts, "The most successful downtowns are those that are moving back to what they were in the beginning. They are returning to much more of a neighborhood feel, as original city centers. 'Pedestrianization' as we define it today is not to close off cars; it is to make it easy to move through." This means that "most shoppers who arrive downtown in their cars want to park near their shopping area or have easy drop-off access to stores. Pedestrian malls offer neither. Birds and trees are perfectly nice, but no one really goes shopping to see them."[3]

One of the best examples of a strong CBD is New York City, where the business community has strengthened the central city to make it more competitive with suburban shopping centers. Consider the $200 million renovation of Grand Central Terminal:

Grand Central Terminal (www.grandcentralterminal.com) is all dressed up and open for business. Check out the video.

There's a reason why they call it "grand." Just stand on New York City's 42nd Street, across from the Grand Central Terminal. Gaze at one of this country's most magnificent buildings, its rich Beaux Arts design fashioned from granite and limestone, a building that took 10 years to construct before it finally opened in 1913. Today, Grand Central is looking better than ever, thanks to a $200 million restoration project. Before the renovation, most shopping at Grand Central was for a newspaper or a cup of coffee. Now, there's quite a choice of restaurants and specialty shops, including a European-style food market. You can choose from fresh lobster, cakes and pastries, children's toys and clothes, fine chocolates, orchids, stationery, wine, and more. At the same time, Grand Central remains a busy train station; approximately 500,000 people—most commuters—come through the station each day.[4]

Boston's Faneuil Hall is another thriving CBD renovation. When developer James Rouse took over the site containing three 150-year-old, block-long former food warehouses, it had been abandoned for almost 10 years. Rouse used landscaping, fountains, banners, open-air courts, street performers, and colorful graphics to enable Faneuil Hall to capture a festive spirit. Faneuil Hall combines shopping, eating, and watching activities and makes them fun. Today, it has over 70 shops, 14 full-service restaurants, 40 food stalls, and a comedy nightclub. It attracts millions of shoppers and visitors yearly.

As Tower City Center (www.towercitycenter.com) illustrates, CDB renovations are bringing life to downtown.

Other major CBD projects include Riverchase Galleria (Birmingham, Alabama), Tower City Center (Cleveland), Pioneer Place (Portland, Oregon), Harborplace Baltimore, Crown Center (Kansas City), Union Station (Washington, D.C.), Circle Centre (Indianapolis), Peabody Place (Memphis), Horton Plaza (San Diego), New Orleans Centre, and South Street Seaport (New York City). See Figure 10-2.

Visit our Web site (**www.prenhall.com/bermanevans**) for links to all of the CBD projects mentioned in this section.

Secondary Business District

A **secondary business district (SBD)** is an unplanned shopping area in a city or town that is usually bounded by the intersection of two major streets. Cities—particularly larger ones—often have multiple SBDs, each with at least a junior department store (a branch of a traditional department store or a full-line discount store) and/or some larger specialty stores—besides many smaller stores. This format is now more important because cities have "sprawled" over larger geographic areas.

The kinds of goods and services sold in an SBD mirror those in the CBD. However, an SBD has smaller stores, less width and depth of merchandise assortment, and a smaller trading area (consumers will not travel as far) and sells a higher proportion of convenience-oriented items.

Careers in RETAILING — Selling Tenants on Union Station

Robert Mauer is in charge of leasing retail space in historic Union Station, a major railroad station that was converted into a 212,000-square-foot shopping mall in Washington, D.C. Prior to becoming leasing director, Mauer was marketing director at Union Square. When selling his space, he uses such data as average household income, shopping frequency, and number of parking spaces to convince retailers to open an outlet in Union Square.

Like many other major rail stations, Union Station had fallen into disrepair in the 1960s as the auto and the air travel shifted traffic away from the nation's railroads. By the 1980s, Union Station was literally falling apart. In 1998, a public-private partnership restored the building and Union Square reopened with retail stores, a food court, and restaurants. Today, Union Square attracts 25 million visitors each year, and its retail tenants average annual sales of $656 per square foot—more than three times the national average for a shopping center.

Recently, with only two vacant retail slots available in Union Square, Mauer scheduled three full days of meetings with retailers that wanted to open there. Mauer had to weigh the relative merits of a bebe women's clothing store (**www.bebe.com**), a Talbots women's clothing store (**www.talbots.com**), a Museum Company store (**www.museumcompany.com**), and a new women's clothing accessories chain.

Source: Jackie Spinner, "Retailing Success in Track; Union Station Is Among the Region's Top Performers," *Washington Post* (June 4, 200), p. E1.

The SBD's major strengths include a solid product selection, access to thoroughfares and public transportation, less crowding and more personal service than a CBD, and a placement nearer to residential areas than a CBD. The SBD's major weaknesses include the discontinuity of offerings, the sometimes high rent and taxes (but not as high as in a CBD), traffic and delivery congestion, aging facilities, parking difficulties, and fewer chain outlets than in the CBD. These weaknesses have generally not affected the SBD as much as the CBD—and parking problems, travel time, and congestion are less for the SBD.

Neighborhood Business District

A **neighborhood business district (NBD)** is an unplanned shopping area that appeals to the convenience shopping and service needs of a single residential area. An NBD contains several small stores, such as a dry cleaner, a stationery store, a barber shop and/or a beauty salon, a liquor store, and a restaurant. The leading retailer is typically a supermarket or a large drugstore. This type of business district is situated on the major street(s) of its residential area.

An NBD offers a good location, long store hours, good parking, and a less hectic atmosphere than a CBD or SBD. On the other hand, there is a limited selection of goods and services, and prices tend to be higher because competition is less than in a CBD or SBD.

String

A **string** is an unplanned shopping area comprising a group of retail stores, often with similar or compatible product lines, located along a street or highway. There is little extension of shopping onto perpendicular streets. A string may start with an isolated store, success then breeding competitors. Car dealers, antique stores, and apparel retailers often situate in strings.

FIGURE 10-3
Unplanned Business Districts and Isolated Locations

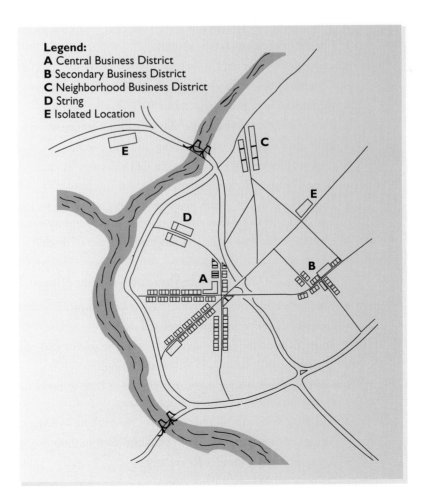

A string location has many of the advantages of an isolated store site (lower rent, more flexibility, better road visibility and parking, and lower operating costs), along with some disadvantages (less product variety, increased travel for many consumers, higher advertising costs, zoning restrictions, and the need to build premises). Unlike an isolated store, a string store has competition at its location. This draws more people to the area and allows for some sharing of common costs. It also means less control over prices and less loyalty toward each outlet. An individual store's increased traffic flow, due to being in a string rather than an isolated site, may be greater than the customers lost to competitors. This explains why four gas stations locate on opposing corners.

Figure 10-3 shows a map with various forms of unplanned business districts and isolated locations.

THE PLANNED SHOPPING CENTER

A **planned shopping center** consists of a group of architecturally unified commercial establishments on a site that is centrally owned or managed, designed and operated as a unit, based on balanced tenancy, and accompanied by parking facilities. Its location, size, and mix of stores are related to the trading area served. Through **balanced tenancy**, the stores in a planned shopping center complement each other as to the quality and variety of their product offerings, and the kind and number of stores are linked to overall population needs. To ensure balanced tenancy, the management of a planned center usually specifies the proportion of total space for each kind of retailer, limits the product lines that can be sold by every store, and stipulates what kinds of firms can acquire unexpired leases. At a well-run center, a coordinated and cooperative long-run retailing strategy is followed by all stores.

Shopping centers in some form have existed for over 1,000 years. Learn more about this phenomenon (www.icsc.org/srch/about/impactofshoppingcenters).

The planned shopping center has several positive attributes:

- Well-rounded assortments of goods and services based on long-range planning.
- Strong suburban population.
- Interest in one-stop, family shopping.
- Cooperative planning and sharing of common costs.
- Creation of distinctive, but unified, shopping center images.
- Maximization of pedestrian traffic for individual stores.
- Access to highways and availability of parking for consumers.
- More appealing than city shopping for some people.
- Generally lower rent and taxes than CBDs (except for enclosed regional malls).
- Generally lower theft rates than CBDs.
- Popularity of malls—both *open* (shopping area off-limits to vehicles) and *closed* (shopping area off-limits to vehicles and all stores in a temperature-controlled facility).
- Growth of discount malls and other newer types of shopping centers.

There are also some limitations associated with the planned shopping center:

- Landlord regulations that reduce each retailer's flexibility, such as required hours.
- Generally higher rent than an isolated store.
- Restrictions on the goods/services that can be sold by each store.
- A competitive environment within the center.
- Required payments for items that may be of little or no value to an individual retailer, such as membership in a merchants' association.
- Too many malls in a number of areas ("the malling of America").
- Rising consumer boredom with and disinterest in shopping as an activity.
- Aging facilities of some older centers.
- Domination by large anchor stores.

Shopping Centers Today, in print and online (www. icsc.org/srch/sct/current), is the bible of the industry.

How important are planned shopping centers? According to the International Council of Shopping Centers (**www.icsc.org**), there are 46,000 U.S. shopping centers, 1,200 of which are fully enclosed shopping malls. Shopping center revenues exceed $1.2 trillion annually and account for almost 40 percent of total U.S. retail-store sales (including autos and gasoline). About 11 million people work in shopping centers. Ninety-four percent of Americans over age 18 visit some type of center in an average month. The Limited, Macy's, and J.C. Penney are among the vast number of chains with a substantial presence at shopping centers. Some big retailers have also been involved in shopping center development. Sears has participated in the construction of dozens of shopping centers, and Publix Supermarkets operates centers with hundreds of small tenants. Each year, numerous new centers of all kinds and sizes are built and millions of square feet of retail space are added to existing centers.

To sustain their long-term growth, shopping centers are engaging in these practices:

● Several older centers have been or are being renovated, expanded, or repositioned. The Florida Mall in Orlando; King of Prussia in Pennsylvania; Park Place in Tucson, Arizona; Roosevelt Field in Long Island, New York; University Towne Center in San Diego; and Westfield Shoppingtown South County in St. Louis are among the centers that have been revitalized. See Figure 10-4. Visit our Web site (**www.prenhall.com/bermanevans**) for links to each of the renovations cited here.

● Certain derivative types of centers are fostering consumer interest and enthusiasm. Three of these, megamalls, life-style centers, and power centers, are discussed a little later in this chapter.

● Shopping centers are responding to shifting consumer life-styles. They have made parking easier, added ramps for baby strollers and wheelchairs, and included more distinctive retailers such as Crate & Barrel, Williams-Sonoma, Grand Cuisine, and The Right Start. They have also introduced more information booths and center directories.

● The retailer mix is broadening at many centers to attract people interested in one-stop shopping. More centers now include banks, stockbrokers, dentists, doctors, beauty salons, TV repair outlets, and/or car rental offices. Many centers also offer "temporary tenants," retailers that lease space (often in mall aisles or walkways) and sell from booths or moving carts. The tenants benefit from the lower rent and short-term commitment; the centers benefit by creating more excitement and diversity in shopping. Consumers often happen on new vendors in unexpected places.

● Some enclosed malls are uncovering: "We look at these centers with a sort of old-town square approach. You can drive up to the store you want to visit and leave or you can park at one store and wander around the center doing some old-fashioned window shopping."[5]

FIGURE 10-4

Roosevelt Field: Renovated, Expanded, *and* Repositioned

Roosevelt Field in Long Island, New York—one of the 10 largest shopping centers in the United States—has been renovated and expanded several times since its opening nearly 45 years ago. In the 1990s alone, $100 million was spent to add a new 170,000-square-foot wing. Today, Roosevelt Field has 2.4 million square feet of store space and it has repositioned itself by adding Bloomingdale's, Nordstrom, Kenneth Cole, Mont Blanc, Tourneau Corner, and Wet Seal (among others) to its mix of 250 stores.

Reprinted by permission of the Simon Property Group.

- More shopping center developers are striving to build their own brand loyalty. Simon, Prime Retail, and Westfield are among those spending millions of dollars to boost their images by advertising their own names—through slogans such as "Simply Simon—Simply the best shopping there is." Simon (**www.simon.com/company**) owns and manages 260 properties in 36 states and Europe.

- Some shopping centers are using frequent-shopper programs to retain customers and track spending. Prizes range from pre-paid calling cards to Caribbean vacations.

There are three types of planned shopping centers: regional, community, and neighborhood. Their characteristics are noted in Table 10-1, and they are described next.

Regional Shopping Center

A **regional shopping center** is a large, planned shopping facility appealing to a geographically dispersed market. It has at least one or two department stores (each with a minimum of 100,000 square feet) and 50 to 150 or more smaller retailers. A regional center offers a very broad and

TABLE 10-1	Characteristics of Typical Neighborhood, Community, and Regional Types of U.S. Planned Shopping Centers		
Features of a Typical Center	**TYPE OF CENTER**		
	Regional	Community	Neighborhood
Total site area (acres)	30–100+	10–30	3–10
Total sq. ft. leased to retailers	400,001–2,000,000+	100,001–400,000	30,000–100,000
Principal tenant	One, two, or more full-sized department stores	Branch department store (traditional or discount), variety store, and/or category killer store	Supermarket or drugstore
Number of stores	50–150 or more	15–25	5–15
Goods and services offered	Largest assortment for customers, focusing on goods that encourage careful shopping and and services that enhance the shopping experience (such as a food court)	Moderate assortment for customers, focusing on a mix of shopping- and convenience-oriented goods and services	Lowest assortment for customers, emphasizing convenience-oriented goods and services
Minimum number of people living/working in trading area needed to support center	100,000+	20,000–100,000	3,000–50,000
Trading area in driving time	Up to 30 minutes	Up to 20 minutes	Fewer than 15 minutes
Location	Outside central city, on arterial highway or expressway	Close to one or more populated residential area(s)	Along a major thoroughfare in a single residential area
Layout	Mall, often enclosed with anchor stores at major entrances/exits	Strip or L-shaped	Strip
Percentage of all centers	5	33	62
Percentage of all centers' selling space	29	46	25
Percentage of all centers' retail sales	30	41	29

Source: Percentage data computed by the authors from *2002 NRB Shopping Center Census.*

deep assortment of shopping-oriented goods and services intended to enhance the consumer's visit. The market is 100,000+ people who live or work up to a 30-minute drive away. On average, people travel less than 20 minutes.

The regional center is the result of a planned effort to re-create the shopping variety of a central city in suburbia. Some regional centers have even become the social, cultural, and vocational focal point of an entire suburban area. Frequently, it is used as a town plaza, a meeting place, a concert hall, and a place for a brisk indoor walk. Despite the declining overall interest in shopping, on a typical visit to a regional shopping center, many people spend an average of an hour or more there.

The first outdoor regional shopping center opened in 1950 in Seattle, anchored by a branch of Bon Marche, a leading downtown department store. Southdale Center (outside Minneapolis), built in 1956 for the Target Corporation (then Dayton Hudson), was the first fully enclosed, climate-controlled mall. Today, there are more than 2,200 U.S. regional centers, and this format is popping up around the world (where small stores still remain the dominant force) from Australia to Malaysia to Brazil.

One type of regional center is the **megamall**, an enormous planned shopping center with 1 million+ square feet of retail space, multiple anchor stores, up to several hundred specialty stores, food courts, and entertainment facilities. It seeks to heighten interest in shopping and greatly expand the trading area. There are 420 U.S. megamalls, including the Mall of America (**www.mallofamerica.com**) in Minnesota. It has four anchors (Bloomingdale's, Macy's, Nordstrom, and Sears), over 500 other stores, a 14-screen movie theater, a health club, 57 restaurants and nightclubs, the world's largest indoor amusement park (Camp Snoopy), and 12,750 parking spaces—on 4.2 million square feet. The mall has stores to fit every budget, attracts 37 percent of visitors from outside a 150-mile radius, and draws 600,000 to 900,000 visitors weekly.[6] Canada's West Edmonton Mall is the largest megamall in the world. See Figure 10-5 for another leading center.

Community Shopping Center

A **community shopping center** is a moderate-sized, planned shopping facility with a branch department store (traditional or discount) and/or a category killer store, as well as several smaller stores (similar to those in a neighborhood center). It offers a moderate assortment of shopping- and convenience-oriented goods and services to consumers from one or more nearby, well-populated, residential areas. About 20,000 to 100,000 people, who live or work within a 10- to 20-minute drive, are served by this location.

There is better long-range planning for a community shopping center than a neighborhood shopping center. Balanced tenancy is usually enforced and cooperative promotion is more apt. Store composition and the center's image are kept pretty consistent with pre-set goals.

Mall of America's Fun Facts (www. mallofamerica.com) are as impressive as the mall itself. Enter the Media Room.

Kramont is a leading retail-estate developer. Visit its properties through online shopping center layouts and photos (www. krt.com/properties.html).

FIGURE 10-5

Festival Walk: Hong Kong Megamall

"Festival Walk is an energized environment of innovation, originality, and pleasure. Boasting a world-class design of natural light and open space, Festival Walk offers an unparalleled environment for business and pleasure: over 200 shops and 25 restaurants, an 11-screen cinema multiplex, Hong Kong's largest ice rink, over 220,000 square feet of office space, an 850-space car park, and direct access to buses, taxis, a train station. Its dramatic setting and accessibility have made it the location of choice for some of the world's best-known retail names and reputable companies." [www.festivalwalk.com]

Photo reprinted by permission of Retail Forward, Inc.

FIGURE 10-6
CocoWalk: A Life-Style Center

CocoWalk is an open-air, life-style shopping center in Coconut Grove, Florida. It is home to legendary restaurants, exclusive retailers, and the AMC 16 "gourmet cinemas." The vibrant Mediterranean ambience, unique shopping and dining experiences, and visitor-friendly surroundings have made it one of the most-frequented destinations in South Florida with over 3.5 million visitors every year.

Reprinted by permission of City Center Retail.

Two noteworthy types of community center are the power center and the life-style center. A **power center** is a shopping site with (a) up to a half-dozen or so category killer stores and a mix of smaller stores or (b) several complementary stores specializing in one product category. A power center usually occupies 200,000 to 400,000 square feet on a major highway or road intersection. It seeks to be quite distinctive to draw shoppers and better compete with regional centers. There are over 2,000 U.S. power centers, such as Pennsylvania's Whitehall Square. That 298,000-square-foot center (operated by Kramont Realty Trust) is a category killer center with a 54,000-square-foot Raymour & Flanigan Furniture Store, a 50,000-square-foot Sports Authority, a 25,000-square-foot Kids "R" Us, and many smaller stores.

A **life-style center** is an open-air shopping site that typically includes 150,000 to 500,000 square feet of space dedicated to upscale, well-known specialty stores. The focus is often on apparel, home products, books, and music—as well as restaurants. Popular stores at life-style centers include Ann Taylor, Banana Republic, Barnes & Noble, Bath & Body Works, Gap, GapKids, Pottery Barn, Talbots, Victoria's Secret, and Williams-Sonoma.[7] Arboretum at Great Hills in Austin, Texas; Aspen Grove in Littleton, Colorado; and CocoWalk in Coconut Grove, Florida, are examples of life-style shopping centers. See Figure 10-6. As of 2002, there were about 40 such centers in the United States—a number that could triple by 2010.

Neighborhood Shopping Center

A **neighborhood shopping center** is a planned shopping facility, with the largest store being a supermarket or a drugstore. Other retailers often include a bakery, a laundry, a dry cleaner, a stationery store, a barbershop or beauty parlor, a hardware store, a restaurant, a liquor store, and a gas station. This center focuses on convenience-oriented goods and services for people living or working nearby. It serves 3,000 to 50,000 people who are within a 15-minute drive (usually less than 10 minutes).

A neighborhood center is usually arranged in a strip. Initially, it is carefully planned and tenants are balanced. Over time, the planned aspects may lessen and newcomers may face fewer restrictions. Thus, a liquor store may replace a barber shop—leaving a void. A center's ability to maintain balance depends on its attractiveness to potential tenants (expressed by the extent of store vacancies). In number, but not in selling space or sales, neighborhood centers account for more than 60 percent of U.S. shopping centers.

THE CHOICE OF A GENERAL LOCATION

The last part of Step 2 in location planning requires a retailer to select a locational format: isolated, unplanned district, or planned center. The decision depends on the firm's strategy and a careful evaluation of the advantages and disadvantages of each alternative.

Charles River Center Turns Green

Concerned with the possible effect on adjacent wetlands, the developer of the Charles River Center, located near Boston, voluntarily redirected relatively clean water from the center's roof and filtered dirty water from the center's parking lot. The rooftop water now flows into pipes allowing it to re-enter the aquifer. The parking lot water, polluted with oil, gasoline, and salt, travels through a different system—where it is filtered prior to returning underground. One of the project's engineers says, "Ten or 15 years ago, we would have just drained the site. Today, not only does the water have to go back down there, it has to be clean."

Some large retailers are also becoming more concerned with the ecological impact of their new construction. Gap (**www.gap.com**), for example, is careful about the use of sustainable materials: "While our store location decisions are made up of many factors, an environmentally-friendly center would certainly be a positive one."

The Green Building Council (**www.usgbc.org**) sets guidelines for designating a building as "green." These guidelines relate to the use of creative landscaping, recycling systems for waste water, solar power, recycled construction materials, and natural ventilation and air-filtering systems. A silver designation means an aggressive commitment to green design.

Source: James McCown, "Going Green: Some Developers Work to Minimize Centers' Ecological Impact," *Shopping Centers Today* (March 2002), pp. 17, 22.

Next, Step 3, the retailer chooses a broadly defined site. Two decisions are needed here. First, the specific kind of isolated store, unplanned business district, or planned shopping center location is picked. If a firm wants an isolated store, it must decide on a highway or side street. Should it desire an unplanned business area, it must decide on a CBD, an SBD, an NBD, or a string. A retailer seeking a planned area must choose a regional, community, or neighborhood shopping center—and whether to use a derivative form such as a megamall or power center. Here are the preferences of three retailers:

- At Wendy's, most "restaurants are freestanding and in urban or heavily populated suburban areas. Success depends on serving a large number of customers. We also operate in travel centers, gas station/convenience stores, military bases, arenas, malls, hospitals, airports, and college campuses."

Guitar Center (www.guitarcenter.com) has a well-conceived location plan.

- The Guitar Center chain views itself as a destination retailer: "Our target real-estate strategy is based on a prominent, recognizable building on a well-known street. It doesn't have to be Main Street, as long as it's a well-known street."

- Sears is one of the mall-based retailers that is opening more stores in CBDs and SBDs: "Expansion opportunities in malls are limited because fewer malls are being built. And Sears' mall-based stores face competition from companies such as Wal-Mart and Home Depot, whose sites are often between shoppers' home and malls."[8]

Second, a firm must select its general store placement. For an isolated store, this means picking a specific highway or side street. For an unplanned district or planned center, this means picking a specific district (e.g., downtown Los Angeles) or center (e.g., Seminary South in Fort Worth, Texas).

In Step 3, the retailer narrows down the decisions made in the first two steps and then chooses a general location. Step 4 requires the firm to evaluate specific alternative sites, including their position on a block (or in a center), the side of the street, and the terms of tenancy. The factors to be considered in assessing and choosing a general location and a specific site within that location are described together in the next section because many strategic decisions are similar to these two steps.

LOCATION AND SITE EVALUATION

The assessment of general locations and the specific sites contained within them requires extensive analysis. In any area, the optimum site for a particular store is called the **one-hundred percent location**. Since different retailers need different kinds of locations, a location labeled as 100

Pedestrian Traffic	Number of people	_____
	Type of people	_____
Vehicular Traffic	Number of vehicles	_____
	Type of vehicles	_____
	Traffic congestion	_____
Parking Facilities	Number and quality of parking spots	_____
	Distance to store	_____
	Availability of employee parking	_____
Transportation	Availability of mass transit	_____
	Access from major highways	_____
	Ease of deliveries	_____
Store Composition	Number and size of stores	_____
	Affinity	_____
	Retail balance	_____
Specific Site	Visibility	_____
	Placement in the location	_____
	Size and shape of the lot	_____
	Size and shape of the building	_____
	Condition and age of the lot and building	_____
Terms of Occupancy	Ownership or leasing terms	_____
	Operations and maintenance costs	_____
	Taxes	_____
	Zoning restrictions	_____
	Voluntary regulations	_____
Overall Rating	General location	_____
	Specific site	_____

percent for one firm may be less than optimal for another. An upscale ladies' apparel shop would seek a location unlike that sought by a convenience store. The apparel shop would benefit from heavy pedestrian traffic, closeness to major department stores, and proximity to other specialty stores. The convenience store would rather be in an area with ample parking and heavy vehicular traffic. It does not need to be close to other stores.

Figure 10-7 contains a location and site evaluation checklist. A retailer should rate every alternative location (and specific site) on all the criteria and develop overall ratings for them. Two firms may rate the same site differently. This figure should be used in conjunction with the trading-area data noted in Chapter 9, not instead of them.

PEDESTRIAN TRAFFIC

The most crucial measures of a location's and site's value are the number and type of people passing by. Other things being equal, a site with the most pedestrian traffic is often best.

Not everyone passing a location or site is a good prospect for all types of stores, so many firms use selective counting procedures, such as counting only those carrying shopping bags. Otherwise, pedestrian traffic totals may include too many nonshoppers. It would be improper for an appliance retailer to count as prospective shoppers all the people who pass a downtown site on the way to work. In fact, much of the downtown pedestrian traffic may be from people who are there for nonretailing activities.

A proper pedestrian traffic count should encompass these four elements:

- Separation of the count by age and gender (with very young children not counted).
- Division of the count by time (this allows the study of peaks, low points, and changes in the gender of the people passing by the hour).
- Pedestrian interviews (to find out the proportion of potential shoppers).
- Spot analysis of shopping trips (to verify the stores actually visited).

RETAILING
Around the World   Home Depot Has Floor Plans for Foreign Site Selection

When Home Depot's (**www.homedepot.com**) current senior vice-president of real-estate joined the firm in 1984, the chain had 19 stores in fewer than 15 markets. As of 2000, Home Depot operated 1,200 stores, and it expects to operate more than 2,000 stores by 2005. The chain has opened stores in every state (including Hawaii and Alaska) and also has stores in Canada, Puerto Rico, Argentina, and Chile.

According to Home Depot's real-estate guru, "Ultimately, we'll be all over the world. Everybody values the place they live and wants to have a nice home; so home improvement is a value that travels well. I can't say how quickly that's going to happen but when you ask 'Will we go to Europe?' or 'Will we go to Asia?' The answer is yes to those places."

Although Home Depot prefers to develop all of its sites and serve as the landlord for the stores, the firm has built on land owned by others through ground leases, and it has remodeled older facilities to meet its needs: "The most important driver for us is to locate the store where we can serve the market."

Source: "Like Clockwork, Orange Covers the World," *Chain Store Age* (May 2001), pp. 97–99.

VEHICULAR TRAFFIC

The quantity and characteristics of vehicular traffic are very important for retailers that appeal to customers who drive there. Convenience stores, outlets in regional shopping centers, and car washes are retailers that rely on heavy vehicular traffic. And automotive traffic studies are essential in suburban areas, where pedestrian traffic is often limited.

As with pedestrian traffic, adjustments to the raw count of vehicular traffic must be made. Some retailers count only homeward-bound traffic, some exclude vehicles on the other side of a divided highway, and some omit out-of-state cars. Data may be available from the state highway department, the county engineer, or the regional planning commission.

Besides traffic counts, the retailer should study the extent and timing of congestion (from traffic, detours, and poor roads). People normally avoid congested areas and shop where driving time and driving difficulties are minimized.

PARKING FACILITIES

Most U.S. retail stores include some provision for nearby off-street parking. In many business districts, parking is provided by individual stores, arrangements among stores, and local government. In planned shopping centers, parking is shared by all stores there. The number and quality of parking spots, their distances from stores, and the availability of employee parking should all be evaluated.

The need for retailer parking facilities depends on the store's trading area, the type of store, the proportion of shoppers using a car, the existence of other parking, the turnover of spaces (which depends on the length of a shopping trip), the flow of shoppers, and parking by non-shoppers. A shopping center normally needs 4 to 5 parking spaces per 1,000 square feet of gross floor area, a supermarket 10 to 15 spaces, and a furniture store 3 or 4 spaces.

Free parking sometimes creates problems. Commuters and employees of nearby businesses may park in spaces intended for shoppers. This problem can be lessened by validating shoppers' parking stubs and requiring payment from nonshoppers. Another problem may occur if the selling space at a location increases due to new stores or the expansion of current ones. Existing parking may then be inadequate. Double-deck parking or parking tiers save land and shorten the distance from a parked car to a store—a key factor since customers at a regional shopping center may be unwilling to walk more than a few hundred feet from their cars to the center.

TRANSPORTATION

Mass transit, access from major highways, and ease of deliveries must be examined.

In a downtown area, closeness to mass transit is important for people who do not own cars, who commute to work, or who would not otherwise shop in an area with traffic congestion. The availability of buses, taxis, subways, trains, and other kinds of public transit is a must for any area not readily accessible by vehicular traffic.

Locations dependent on vehicular traffic should be rated on their nearness to major thoroughfares. Driving time is a consideration for many people. In addition, drivers heading eastbound on a highway often do not like to make a U-turn to get to a store on the westbound side of that highway.

The transportation network should be studied for delivery truck access. Many thoroughfares are excellent for cars but ban large trucks or cannot bear their weight.

STORE COMPOSITION

The number and size of stores should be consistent with the type of location. A retailer in an isolated site wants no stores nearby; a retailer in a neighborhood business district wants an area with 10 or 15 small stores; and a retailer in a regional shopping center wants a location with many stores, including large department stores (to generate customer traffic).

If the stores at a given location (be it an unplanned district or a planned center) complement, blend, and cooperate with one another, and each benefits from the others' presence, **affinity** exists. When affinity is strong, the sales of each store are greater, due to the high customer traffic, than if the stores are apart. The practice of similar or complementary stores locating near each other is based on two factors: (1) Customers like to compare the prices, styles, selections, and services of similar stores. (2) Customers like one-stop shopping and purchase at different stores on the same trip. Affinities can exist among competing stores, as well as among complementary stores. More people travel to shopping areas with large selections than to convenience-oriented areas, so the sales of all stores are enhanced.

One measure of compatibility is the degree to which stores exchange customers. Stores in these categories are very compatible with each other and have high customer interchange:

- Supermarket, drugstore, bakery, fruit-and-vegetable store, meat store.
- Department store, apparel store, hosiery store, lingerie shop, shoe store, jewelry store.

Retail balance, the mix of stores within a district or shopping center, should also be considered. Proper balance occurs when the number of store facilities for each merchandise or service classification is equal to the location's market potential, a range of goods and services is provided to foster one-stop shopping, there is an adequate assortment within any category, and there is a proper mix of store types (balanced tenancy).

SPECIFIC SITE

Visibility, placement in the location, size and shape of the lot, size and shape of the building, and condition and age of the lot and building should be reviewed for the specific site.

Visibility is a site's ability to be seen by pedestrian or vehicular traffic. A site on a side street or at the end of a shopping center is not as visible as one on a major road or at the shopping center entrance. High visibility makes passersby aware of a store. Furthermore, some people hesitate to go down a side street or to the end of a center.

Placement in the location is the site's relative position in the district or center. A corner location may be desirable since it is situated at the intersection of two streets and has "corner influence." It is usually more expensive because of the greater pedestrian and vehicular passersby due to traffic flows from two streets, increased window display area, and less traffic congestion through multiple entrances. Corner influence is greatest in high-volume locations. That is why some Pier 1 stores, Starbucks restaurants, and other retailers occupy corner sites. See Figure 10-8.

A convenience-oriented firm, such as a stationery store, is very concerned about the side of the street, the location relative to other convenience-oriented stores, nearness to parking, access to a bus stop, and the distance from residences. A shopping-oriented retailer, such as a furniture store, is more interested in a corner site to increase window display space, proximity to wallpaper and other related retailers, the accessibility of its pickup platform to consumers, and the ease of deliveries to the store.

When a retailer buys or rents an existing building, its size and shape should be examined. In addition, the condition and age of the lot and the building should be investigated. A department store requires significantly more space than a boutique; and it may desire a square site, whereas the boutique may seek a rectangular one. Any site should be viewed in terms of the total space needed: parking, walkways, selling, nonselling, and so on.

Due to saturation of many desirable locations and the lack of available spots in others, some firms have turned to nontraditional sites—often to complement their existing stores. TGI Friday's, Staples, and Bally have airport stores. McDonald's has outlets in many Wal-Marts and at several gas stations. Some fast-food retailers share facilities to provide more variety and to share costs.

TERMS OF OCCUPANCY

Terms of occupancy—ownership versus leasing, the type of lease, operations and maintenance costs, taxes, zoning restrictions, and voluntary regulations—must be evaluated for each prospective site.

Ownership Versus Leasing

A retailer with adequate funding can either own or lease premises. Ownership is more common in small stores, in small communities, or at inexpensive locations. It has several advantages. There is no chance that a property owner will not renew a lease or double the rent when a lease expires. Monthly mortgage payments are stable. Operations are flexible; a retailer can engage in scrambled merchandising and break down walls. It is also likely that property value will appreciate over time, resulting in a financial gain if the business is sold. Ownership disadvantages are the high initial costs, the long-term commitment, and the inability to readily change sites. Home Depot owns about 75 percent of its store properties.[9]

The Main Street program
(www.mainst.org/
AboutMainStreet) has
revitalized communities
across the United States.

If a retailer chooses ownership, it must decide whether to construct a new facility or buy an existing building. The retailer should consider the purchase price and maintenance costs, zoning restrictions, the age and condition of existing facilities, the adaptability of existing facilities, and the time to erect a new building. To encourage building rehabilitations in small towns (5,000 to 50,000 people), Congress enacted the Main Street program of the National Trust for Historic Preservation. Retailers in over 1,650 U.S. towns have benefited from the program (**www.mainst. org**) through tax credits and low-interest loans.

The great majority of stores in central business districts and regional shopping centers are leased, mostly due to the high investment for ownership. Department stores tend to have renewable 30-year leases, supermarkets usually have renewable 20-year leases, and stores such as T.J. Maxx typically have 10-year leases with options to extend. Some leases give the retailer the right to end an agreement before the expiration date—under given circumstances and for a specific payment by the retailer.

Leasing minimizes the initial investment, reduces risk, allows access to prime sites that could not hold more stores, leads to immediate occupancy and traffic, and reduces the long-term commitment. Many retailers also feel they can open more stores or spend more on other aspects of their strategies by leasing. Firms that lease accept limits on operating flexibility, restrictions on subletting and selling the business, possible nonrenewal problems, rent increases, and not gaining from rising real-estate values.

Through a *sale-leaseback*, some large retailers build stores and then sell them to real-estate investors who lease the property back to the retailers on a long-term basis. Retailers using sale-leasebacks build stores to their specifications and have bargaining power in leasing—while lowering capital expenditures.

Types of Leases

Property owners do not rely solely on constant rent leases, partly due to their concern about interest rates and the related rise in operating costs. Terms can be quite complicated.

Saks Fifth Avenue (www.saks.com), a name synonymous with glamour, is one of the cornerstone retailers on New York's high-rent Fifth Avenue.

The simplest, most direct arrangement is the **straight lease**—a retailer pays a fixed dollar amount per month over the life of the lease. Rent usually ranges from $1 to $75 annually per square foot, depending on the site's desirability and store traffic. At some sites, rent can be much higher. On New York's Fifth Avenue, from 48th to 58th Streets, the average yearly rent is $600 per square foot!

A **percentage lease** stipulates that rent is related to sales or profits. This differs from a straight lease, which provides for constant payments. A percentage lease protects a property owner against inflation and lets it benefit if a store is successful; it also allows a tenant to view the lease as a variable cost—rent is lower when its performance is weak and higher when performance is good. The percentage rate varies by type of shopping district or center and by type of store.

Percentage leases have variations. With a specified minimum, low sales are assumed to be partly the retailer's responsibility; the property owner receives minimum payments (as in a straight lease) no matter what the sales or profits. With a specified maximum, it is assumed that a very successful retailer should not pay more than a maximum rent. Superior merchandising, promotion, and pricing should reward the retailer. Another variation is the sliding scale: the ratio of rent to sales changes as sales rise. A sliding-down scale has a retailer pay a lower percentage as sales go up and is an incentive to the retailer.

A **graduated lease** calls for precise rent increases over a stated period of time. Monthly rent may be $4,800 for the first 5 years and $5,600 for the last 5 years of a lease. Rent is known in advance by the retailer and the property owner, and based on expected increases in sales and costs. There is no problem auditing sales or profits, as there is for percentage leases. This lease is often used with small retailers.

A **maintenance-increase-recoupment lease** has a provision allowing rent to increase if a property owner's taxes, heating bills, insurance, or other expenses rise beyond a certain point. This provision most often supplements a straight rental lease agreement.

A **net lease** calls for all maintenance costs, such as heating, electricity, insurance, and interior repair, to be paid by the retailer. It frees the property owner from managing the facility and gives the retailer control over store maintenance. It is used to supplement a straight lease or a percentage lease.

Technology in RETAILING — Smart Parking: Using High-Tech Garages to Accommodate More Cars

Hoboken, New Jersey, has a new and unusual parking garage. Unlike conventional garages, this one does not have ramps, a public elevator, or a stairwell. And consumers do not go into the garage at all—only their vehicles do. Here's how it works. A consumer picks up a parking ticket and then pulls his or her car into a bay on the ground floor. The bay then hoists the car into an empty space. Upon returning, the driver pays, inserts the ticket into a reader, and his or her car is then automatically returned. Built at a cost of $6.5 million for the Hoboken Parking Authority, this is the first public garage of its kind in the United States.

In contrast to traditional garages, the automated system has many advantages. One, the garage can be built with any façade. Two, since no one enters the garage, crime is greatly reduced. There is less fear among consumers who would otherwise have to go up an empty elevator to retrieve their car late at night. Three, the high-tech garage requires only 200 square feet per car versus an ordinary garage requiring 350 square feet per car. Thus, the automated garage can hold nearly twice as many cars.

Source: Dave Bodamer, "Smart Parking," *Shopping Centers Today* (May 2002), pp. 209, 212.

Other Considerations

After assessing ownership and leasing opportunities, a retailer must look at the costs of operations and maintenance. The age and condition of a facility may cause a retailer to have high monthly costs, even though the mortgage or rent is low. Furthermore, the costs of extensive renovations should be calculated.

What is the sales tax in Utah? California? Go to this site (www.salestaxinstitute.com) to find out the sales tax in all 50 states.

Differences in sales taxes (those that customers pay) and business taxes (those that retailers pay) among alternative sites must be weighed. Business taxes should be broken down into real-estate and income categories. The highest state sales tax is in Mississippi and Rhode Island (7 percent); Alaska, Delaware, Montana, New Hampshire, and Oregon have no state sales tax.

There may be zoning restrictions as to the kind of stores allowed, store size, building height, the type of merchandise carried, and other factors that have to be hurdled (or another site chosen). For example,

> Once welcomed by local communities for their low prices and breadth of assortment, retail companies like Target, Costco, Wal-Mart, and Home Depot now find themselves handcuffed by anti-growth lobbyists and encumbered by land-use rules aimed at containing suburban development. It's not that consumer enthusiasm for competitive pricing and expansive product offerings has fallen. There is an undertow of anti-big-store sentiment that threatens to undermine their future growth. Twenty-two states have passed laws to contain suburban development in the past few years.[10]

Voluntary restrictions—not mandated by the government—are most prevalent in planned shopping centers and may include required membership in merchant groups, uniform hours, and cooperative security forces. Leases for many stores in regional shopping centers have included clauses protecting anchor tenants from too much competition—especially from discounters. These clauses involve limits on product lines, bans against discounting, fees for common services, and so forth. Anchors have been protected by developers since developers need their long-term commitments to finance the centers. The Federal Trade Commission discourages "exclusives"—whereby only a particular retailer in a center can carry specified merchandise and "radius clauses"—whereby a tenant agrees not to operate another store within a certain distance.

Because of overbuilding, some retailers are in a good position to bargain over the terms of occupancy. This differs from city to city and from shopping location to shopping location.

OVERALL RATING

The last task in choosing a store location is to compute overall ratings: (1) Each location under consideration is given an overall rating based on the criteria in Figure 10-7. (2) The overall ratings of alternative locations are compared, and the best location is chosen. (3) The same procedure is used to evaluate the alternative sites within the location.

Lease agreements used to be so simple that they could be written on a napkin—not today (www.icsc.org/srch/sct/current/sct9905/16.htm).

It is often difficult to compile and compare composite evaluations because some attributes may be positive while others are negative. The general location may be a good shopping center, but the site in the center may be poor; or an area may have excellent potential but take two years to build a store. The attributes in Figure 10-7 should be weighted according to their importance. An overall rating should also include *knockout factors*, those that preclude consideration of a site. Possible knockout factors are a short lease, little or no evening or weekend pedestrian traffic, and poor tenant relations with the landlord.

Summary

1. *To thoroughly examine the types of locations available to a retailer: isolated store, unplanned business district, and planned shopping center.* After a retailer rates alternative trading areas, it decides on the type of location, selects the general location, and chooses a particular site. There are three basic locational types.

An isolated store is freestanding, not adjacent to other stores. It has no competition, low rent, flexibility, road visibility, easy parking, and lower property costs. It also has a lack of traffic, no variety for shoppers, no shared costs, and zoning restrictions.

An unplanned business district is a shopping area with two or more stores located together or nearby. Store composition is not based on planning. There are four categories: central business district, secondary business district, neighborhood business district, and string. An unplanned district generally has these favorable points: variety of goods, services, and prices; access to public transit; nearness to commercial and social facilities; and pedestrian traffic. Yet, its shortcomings have led to the growth of the planned shopping center: inadequate parking, older facilities, high rents and taxes in popular CBDs, discontinuity of offerings, traffic and delivery congestion, high theft rates, and some declining central cities.

A planned shopping center is centrally owned or managed and well balanced. It usually has one or more anchor stores and many smaller stores. The planned center is popular, due to extensive goods and service offerings, expanding suburbs, shared strategic planning and costs, attractive locations, parking facilities, lower rent and taxes (except for regional centers), lower theft rates, the popularity of malls (although some people are now bored with them), and the lesser appeal of inner-city shopping. Negative aspects include operations inflexibility, restrictions on merchandise carried, and anchor store domination. There are three forms: regional, community, and neighborhood centers.

2. *To note the decisions necessary in choosing a general retail location.* First, the specific form of isolated store, unplanned business district, or planned shopping center location is determined, such as whether to be on a highway or side street; in a CBD, an SBD, an NBD, or a string; or in a regional, community, or neighborhood shopping center. Then the general store location is specified—singling out a particular highway, business district, or shopping center.

3. *To describe the concept of the one-hundred percent location.* Extensive analysis is required when evaluating each general location and specific sites within it. Most importantly, the optimum site for a given store must be determined. This is the one-hundred percent location, and it differs by retailer.

4. *To discuss several criteria for evaluating general retail locations and the specific sites within them.* Pedestrian traffic, vehicular traffic, parking facilities, transportation, store composition, the attributes of each specific site, and terms of occupancy should be studied. An overall rating is then computed for each location and site, and the best one selected.

Affinity occurs when the stores at the same location complement, blend, and cooperate with one another; each benefits from the others' presence.

5. *To contrast alternative terms of occupancy.* A retailer can opt to own or lease. If it leases, terms are specified in a straight lease, percentage lease, graduated lease, maintenance-increase-recoupment lease, and/or net lease. Operating and maintenance costs, taxes, zoning restrictions, and voluntary restrictions also need to be reviewed.

Key Terms

isolated store (p. 241)

unplanned business district (p. 242)

central business district (CBD) (p. 242)

secondary business district (SBD) (p. 244)

neighborhood business district (NBD) (p. 245)

string (p. 245)

planned shopping center (p. 246)

balanced tenancy (p. 246)

regional shopping center (p. 248)

megamall (p. 249)

community shopping center (p. 249)

power center (p. 250)

life-style center (p. 250)

neighborhood shopping center (p. 250)

one-hundred percent location (p. 251)

affinity (p. 254)

retail balance (p. 254)

terms of occupancy (p. 255)

straight lease (p. 256)

percentage lease (p. 256)

graduated lease (p. 256)

maintenance-increase-recoupment
  lease (p. 256)

net lease (p. 256)

Questions for Discussion

1. A consumer electronics chain has decided to open outlets in a combination of isolated locations, unplanned business districts, and planned shopping centers. Comment on this strategy.

2. From the retailer's perspective, compare the advantages of locating in unplanned business districts versus planned shopping centers.

3. Differentiate among the central business district, the secondary business district, the neighborhood business district, and the string.

4. Develop a brief plan to revitalize a neighborhood business district near your campus.

5. What is a megamall? What is a life-style center? Describe the strengths and weaknesses of each.

6. Evaluate a community shopping center near your campus.

7. Explain why a one-hundred percent location for Pizza Hut may not be a one-hundred percent location for a local pizza restaurant.

8. What criteria should a small retailer use in selecting a general store location and a specific site within it? A large retailer?

9. What difficulties are there in using a rating scale such as that shown in Figure 10-7? What are the benefits?

10. How do the parking needs for a dentist, a TV repair store, and a shoe store differ?

11. Under what circumstances would it be more desirable for a retailer to buy or lease an existing facility rather than to build a new store?

12. What are the pros and cons of a straight lease versus a percentage lease for a prospective retail tenant? For the landlord?

Web-Based Exercise

Visit the Web site of Underground Atlanta (**www.underatl.com**). What is your reaction to this retail urban renewal project? Does the Web site do a good job of conveying why consumers should go to this shopping area? Explain your answer.

Note: Stop by our Web site (**www.prenhall.com/bermanevans**) to experience a number of highly interactive, appealing Web exercises based on actual company demonstrations and sample materials related to retailing.

Chapter Endnotes

1. Various company sources.

2. *Kohl's Corporation 2000 Annual Report*, p. 4.

3. Jennifer Steinhauer, "When Shoppers Walk Away from Pedestrian Malls," *New York Times* (November 5, 1996), pp. D1, D4. See also Jere Merdeith and Clyde Prem, "Central Business District Traffic Circulation Study: Kansas City, Missouri," *ITE Journal*, Vol. 71 (February 2001), pp. 26–31.

4. James H. Roper, "As Grand as It Gets," *Classic American Homes* (October–November 2000), p. 48.

5. Daniel P. Finney, "Open-Air Mall Is Planned for West Omaha," *Knight-Ridder/Tribune Business News* (November 7, 2001), p. ITEM01311003.

6. See Debra Hazel, "10 Years After: How One Megamall Changed the Industry," *Shopping Centers Today* (May 2002), pp. 20–26; and "A Decade of Dominance," *Chain Store Age* (August 2002), p. 174.

7. Michael Baker, "What's in a Life-Style Center?" *Shopping Centers Today* (April 2002), p. 59. See also Susan Reda, "Life-Style Centers Emerge as Solution to Monotony of Traditional Malls," *Stores* (August 2002), pp. 24–28.

8. *Wendy's International 2001 Annual Report*, 10-K, p. 6; "An Off-the-Mall Attitude," *Chain Store Age* (May 2002), p. 60; and "Sears Looking Beyond the Malls," *Chicago Sun-Times* (May 4, 2002).

9. *Home Depot 2002 Annual Report*.

10. Susan Reda, "Boxed In: Growth Curbs Hit Big Retailers," *Stores* (May 2001), pp. 42–46.

part four
Short Cases

1: JONES LANG LASALLE'S PROPERTY WATCH: A NEW TOOL FOR RETAIL SITE SELECTION

Jones Lang LaSalle (JLL) provides real-estate brokerage and management services for all types of retail properties: JLL (**www.joneslanglasalle.com**) operates in 100 cities and in 33 countries. JLL's Property Watch (**www.thepropertywatch.com**) Web site offers customized information for buyers, sellers, and the firm's own brokers.

Through Property Watch, prospective buyers and tenants can obtain detailed information about a property before even speaking to a broker. For sellers and brokers, the Web site provides another way to communicate with buyers and tenants. Brokers are aided by the questionnaire that a buyer/tenant must fill out. The brokers can then assemble a number of potential properties for the tenant/buyer to view based on the responses to these questions.

Prospective buyers and tenants can search the Property Watch Web site by requesting specific property types or locations. They can also develop a "Watchlist" that enables them to immediately track the status of a transaction instead of having to rely on mail or telephone. For example, on one recent day, the site listed 20 big-box store locations on its "Featured Properties" section. Of these, 17 were locations where Wal-Mart was either a current or an immediate past tenant. Each location included a full description of the site and property, including miles from a highway, number of acres, square footage of building, zoning classification, and real-estate taxes. Prospective clients could also look at the location on a map and zoom into a picture. In addition to the Featured Properties section, prospective clients could also search the site by looking at available properties on a state-by-state basis. JLL is planning to add several important features such as online bidding and better legal aspects relating to each locale.

Although buyers/tenants and sellers are restricted in the types of data each can access, JLL's brokers have access to much more information. Daily, brokers receive reports of prospective clients that have created profiles or ordered materials and sellers that have posted properties for sale. Brokers can also search the data base for the types of properties that interest a prospective buyer. This information is useful in reporting sales activity to sellers and for creating lists of prospective buyers for JLL's brokers.

JLL says that Property Watch was designed to enhance—not replace—the traditional interaction among clients, sellers, and brokers: "Property Watch is not its own different thing. It's just one part of a total package and approach. It's not that we want to automate the process or that we do not want to speak with clients. Everyone has the ability to talk with us anytime they want to during a deal."

As of 2002, 1,400 prospective buyers/tenants had registered with Property Watch and 22 companies had sold properties through it. Retail clients include Kimco Realty, Wal-Mart, and Target Stores. Interestingly, the site has been most successful in attracting buyers to rural areas.

Many Web sites are judged largely on the basis of the number of "hits." However, Property Watch is more concerned about getting qualified users. According to an associate at JLL, "We'd rather have 30 qualified individuals than just some exorbitant amount of individuals coming through the site."

Questions

1. What are the pros and cons of using Property Watch from the perspective of a retailer seeking to secure additional locations?
2. What are the pros and cons of using Property Watch from JLL's perspective as a real-estate broker?
3. As a vice-president of real-estate for a regional discount drug store chain, what types of information should be added to each site to make Property Watch more useful to you?
4. Visit Property Watch (**www.thepropertywatch.com**), and describe and evaluate the information you find there.

The material in this case is drawn from Dave Bodamer, "Site Selection," *Shopping Center Times* (November 2001), p. 33; and "The Property Watch," **www.thepropertywatch.com** (September 5, 2002).

2: WAL-MART'S SEARCH FOR GROWTH OUTSIDE THE UNITED STATES

Wal-Mart (**www.walmart.com**) only opened its first foreign store in Mexico in 1991. Yet, by 2002, it had more than 1,200 units located outside the United States. These units accounted for more than $35 billion in annual sales. During 2002 alone, Wal-Mart planned to spend about $2 billion on its foreign expansion for both renovating existing stores and opening 130 new ones.

Although Wal-Mart is the number-one retailer in terms of sales and market share in the United States, Canada, and Mexico—and it is growing at a rapid pace in Asia—it still has relatively low market penetration in Europe and South America. According to the president of Wal-Mart International, China is "the only overseas market where we replicate the scale of our U.S. operations. China offers the potential for 3,000 Wal-Marts by 2028, up from only 19 in 2002." And while French-owned Carrefour (**www.carrefour.com**) has beaten Wal-Mart to the Chinese market, Wal-Mart plans to catch up by aggressively adding new stores.

The presence of Wal-Mart and Carrefour is having a big effect on China's food distribution system, which traditionally had a great deal of spoilage. As the spokesperson for a leading consulting firm notes, "Carrefour and Wal-Mart are so powerful that if you're a supplier, you can't afford to lose them. When they say they want a frozen product on Wednesday, then that's when it arrives. And it is chilled, not swimming in water. If you don't follow their standards, they will look for others who will."

In Japan, Wal-Mart decided to use a local firm, Seiyu, to "run the business for us" after analyzing the difficulties such firms as OfficeMax (**www.officemax.com**), Costco (**www.costco.com**), and Carrefour had in the Japanese market. Wal-Mart plans to streamline Seiyu's operations and supply chain to position Wal-Mart as the price leader.

In Europe, Wal-Mart has had operations in only two countries: Great Britain and Germany. In 1999, it acquired Asda (**www.asda.co.uk**), a British chain. Even though Asda's operations were similar to Wal-Mart's, Wal-Mart Stores' foreign presence was quickly noted by competitors and consumers alike. Wal-Mart Stores' British sales are still below its major competitors, Tesco (**www.tesco.com**) and Sainsbury (**www.j-sainsbury.com**), while Asda has been growing at two times the market average. In 1997, Wal-Mart acquired two German chains, Wertkauf and Interspar (**www.interspar.com**). A major difficulty with the German market-place is its tough zoning laws. As a result, Wal-Mart was only able to build two new stores in Germany in 2001. Enlarging a store in Germany is also quite difficult and the cost of renovations is five times that of the United States. Several estimates by retail analysts suggest that Wal-Mart is losing $100 million annually in Germany. These analysts estimate that Wal-Mart must triple its market share from 2 percent to 6 percent and double its store count in order to get its suppliers to reduce their prices.

Wal-Mart would prefer operating large stores in all of its markets. Nonetheless, it has developed strategies to adapt to foreign market conditions. In Korea, its stores are typically seven stories high—three for shopping and four for parking. And in Mexico, Wal-Mart has developed five different formats, ranging from upscale groceries catering to the upper middle class and wealthy to the Bodega Aurrera chain for low-income consumers.

Questions

1. Describe the pros and cons of foreign expansion for Wal-Mart versus building additional locations in the United States.
2. Discuss the difficulties in conducting a trading-area analysis in a foreign country such as Mexico.
3. Describe the difficulties in site selection in a foreign country such as Mexico.
4. What are the pros and cons of Wal-Mart's use of five different formats in Mexico from a site location perspective?

The material in this case is drawn from Richard Ernsberger, Jr., "Wal-Mart World: Can Arkansas Giant Export Its Price-Cutting Culture Around the World?" *Newsweek* (May 20, 2002), pp. 50 ff.

3: THE WATERFRONT: PITTSBURGH'S NEW MIXED-USE CENTER

The Waterfront is a $300 million mixed-use center located near Pittsburgh that will eventually have over 1.2 million square feet of retail space, offices, homes, and light manufacturing. It is located along the Monongahela River on the site of the Homestead Works, a steel plant that was closed in 1987. With the closing of the mill, the borough of Homestead lost over 60 percent of its tax base. In addition, the borough's population declined from a high of around 20,000 to 4,000. In 1992, Pennsylvania declared Homestead an economically distressed community—which made it eligible for special state funding.

In 1995, Continental Real Estate took over the 260-acre mill site from the Park Corporation, the project's original developer. Continental's chairman stated that he was attracted to the site because it was flat, next to the water, and accessible to a large population base. He added that the site's location in economically depressed communities was not a deterrent.

Three communities in Allegheny County and the state of Pennsylvania have joined together with Continental Real Estate to build The Waterfront. Allegheny County issued $26 million in 20-year bonds to finance infrastructure improvements on the site. These bonds are secured by real-estate taxes on the property. After this 20-year period, each community will get the full taxes from property built in their jurisdiction for 10 years. State and county grant funds paid for ramps off a nearby bridge and nearby roads. The construction is expected to increase the site's fair market value from $8.5 million in 2000 to $179.3 million in 2004, when the construction is to be completed. The Waterfront project is also expected to generate as much s $6.5 million in real-estate taxes and provide employment for about 5,000 people.

The Waterfront has three separate centers. The power center has these anchor tenants: a Giant Eagle (**www.gianteagle.com**) supermarket, a Lowe's home center (**www.lowes.com**), and a Target (**www.target.com**). Its other stores include Bed Bath & Beyond (**www.bedbathandbeyond.com**), Filene's Basement (**www.filenesbasement.com**), and T. J. Maxx (**www.tjmaxx.com**).

Within the life-style center is a 22-screen Cineplex Theater (where patrons in balcony seating are served food and beverages), restaurants, and a mix of local and national tenants such as Ann Taylor (**www.anntaylor.com**) and Victoria's Secret (**www.victoriassecret.com**). The town centers are in smaller-scale buildings, which look like a small-town central business district. According to the design architect, "The idea was to have a lot of major tenants face the town square, which would be a gathering place." The open-air setting will be used for community activities such as band performances.

The Waterfront was designed to keep some of the existing facades. For example, the power center's Target storefront resembles a 1920s' meatpacking plant. The steel plant's 12 brick smokestacks, each of which is 130 feet high, have also been kept intact. These smokestacks provide visibility for the center. Nonretail portions of The Waterfront will include as many as 500 high-end residential units, 200 boat slips, and an office portion. There will also be a park with walking and bicycle paths.

Questions

1. What are the pros and cons of developing a shopping center in an economically depressed area such as Homestead?
2. What are the pros and cons of developing Homestead as a mixed-use center versus a center with only a retail focus?
3. Evaluate the developer's decision to build separate power, life-style, and town centers.
4. How could the principles described in this case be utilized by a neglected business district in your area?

The material in this case is drawn from Donna Mitchell, "From Rust to Retail," *Shopping Centers Today* (May 2002), pp. 39–40, 44; and Suzanne Elliott, "Homestead Set to Benefit from the Promise of Waterfront Development," *Pittsburgh Business Times* (June 15, 2001), p. 36.

4: QUIZNO'S: A STRIP-CENTER STRATEGY FOR RESTAURANTS

Quizno's (**www.quiznos.com**), an Italian deli-style sandwich chain, has grown from 18 units located around Denver in 1991 to 1,500 restaurants in 40 states and 10 foreign countries in 2002. Quizno's is now the third-largest submarine chain in the United States, after Subway (**www.subway.com**) and Blimpie (**www.blimpie. com**). Quizno's plans to have as many as 7,000 to 8,000 restaurants in 40 countries over the next 10 years: "We're opening one restaurant every 18 hours right now." While Quizno's strongest U.S. markets are currently in Texas, California, and Illinois, the chain plans to concentrate its short-run expansion plans in the Northeast.

Although the Quizno's menu consists of hot submarine sandwiches like other Italian-style restaurants, Quizno's can be distinguished from any of its competitors on the basis of its high level of product quality and its presentation. Quizno's serves its submarine sandwiches warm. Each sandwich is prepared open face and then placed in an oven that toasts the bread, melts the cheese, and warms the meat to enhance its flavor. The décor is also distinctly Italian with a green-and-red corporate logo, colorful floor tiling, and bright red chairs. Quizno's management feels that its food and presentation appeal to upscale customers with similar demographics as Starbucks (**www.starbucks.com**). This contributes to Quizno's having one of the highest average checks per customer in its segment.

An important part of Quizno's location strategy is its use of either strip centers or locations on the fringe of shopping centers. According to Quizno's chief executive officer, 98 percent of its restaurants use one of these two types of locations. The chain favors these sites because they capitalize on the traffic of nearby retailers. In newer markets, this is especially vital since some customers have not heard of Quizno's. Strip and fringe locations are also less costly than freestanding units.

Although Quizno's favors strip locations, it does have 50 mall locations. The chain feels that regional mall locations, which are typically in food courts, will always be a small part of Quizno's loca-tional mix. The mall units range in size from 600 to 700 square feet, while its traditional restaurants range in size from 1,200 to 1,800 square feet.

Quizno's also favors locations that are located in what the company refers to as an adult "quick service restaurant" (QSR) cluster. For example, being located close to a Starbucks or a fresh Mexican chain (like Chipotle Mexican Grill or Rubio's) is beneficial since these retailers share a similar customer base with Quizno's. The firm feels that it offers a more upscale alternative to other quick service restaurants: "People are not going to eat a burrito every day."

However, some observers criticize Quizno's site selection approach. One franchising expert says that Quizno's is "missing the boat on the enclosed mall." A vice-president of a restaurant consulting firm concurs: "So much of the traditional shopping center food court fare is hamburgers, tacos, fried food. Quizno's offers variety. It's perceived as a little healthier. I think it should do pretty well in food courts."

Questions

1. What are the advantages and disadvantages of using a location strategy that capitalizes on the traffic of nearby retailers?
2. What do you think about Quizno's choice of locations? Explain your answer.
3. Comment on Quizno's "adult quick service" cluster location strategy.
4. What other types of sites do you think Quizno's should consider (besides those stated in the case)? Why?

The material in this case is drawn from Joseph DiStefano, "Quizno's Raises Stakes in Suburban Warfare," *Shopping Centers Today* (December 2001), pp. 68, 70.

part four
Comprehensive Case
Mall Retailers: The Search for Growth*

INTRODUCTION

In coming years, spending on apparel, accessories, and footwear will show only modest growth. Few new malls will open, while the viability of many existing malls will be more uncertain. Shifts in population growth will leave a number of mall retailers vying for a shrinking customer base. Heightened price sensitivity and a shift in preference toward value retailers will aggravate margins already pressured by persistent price deflation. Off-the-mall and new on-the-mall players will increase competitive intensity.

The Strategies

There are six strategies that make the most sense for the majority of mall retailers to consider:

1. Fill the gaps in existing markets by opening stores in alternative locations.
2. Go national with a multi-channel approach.
3. Go global in new ways that compensate for organizational inexperience and minimize risk.
4. Optimize the existing offer to better serve existing customers.
5. Extend the existing offer by adding new products or services that appeal to existing customers.
6. Create new offers to reach new customers.

The growth strategy that makes the most sense for a specific retailer will depend on three things:

- *The sustainability of the strategy.* Sustainability reflects the extent to which the strategy leverages the retailer's core competencies, the linkages between the strategy and the firm's existing business, and the long-term potential for sales growth, profit growth, new store openings, or building brand equity.
- *The relationship between risk and reward.* Even strategies with significant long-term potential might be poor choices if risk is too high. The risk depends on whether the success of a new strategy relies on unproven skills, is executed in an unfamiliar way, has an uncertain outcome, or is easily copied.
- *The retailer's current position on the retail life cycle.* Retailers that have not yet reached the maturity or decline stage of the life cycle still have lots of opportunities to reach new customers by expanding geographically or filling in existing markets. More mature retailers, however, must focus efforts on getting more sales and profits from existing customers and reaching new customers with new offers.

The Search for Growth

For retailers in the growth stage, geographic expansion is a high reward/low risk strategy. Retailers in this situation include new on-the-mall concepts (most currently targeting teens and tweens), foreign specialty store retailers with U.S. expansion plans, and hot concepts that are regional in scope but have potential to be national. Multi-channel retailing is also extending firms' tenure in the growth stage and providing an opportunity to rejuvenate companies in maturity or decline.

For retailers in maturity (most mall players), new stores will bring incremental growth while raising the likelihood of saturation. While the opportunity exists to go global, few firms have the cultural mind-set, competencies, or money to succeed. Among those that do, few have exportable concepts—those that foreign shoppers would view favorably and that offer something not already offered by firms there. Despite the limits on geographic growth, some opportunities exist for mature mall retailers:

- Open more stores in urban shopping districts within major metropolitan markets.
- Alter the standard format to adapt to smaller markets, entertainment venues, or transportation hubs.
- Reach more customers in more situations by better integrating store and nonstore channels.
- Attain national coverage by regional acquisitions, followed by mergers among leading players.

The lack of substantial new store opening opportunities will prompt most mature mall retailers to focus on getting more out of existing assets. There are many tactics retailers will use to reach this goal:

- Better align the offer with the expectations of the most valuable customers by editing out unwanted products, brands, styles, sizes, and prices, then layering in additions consistent with customer needs.
- Develop a stronger store brand image.
- Create stronger private brands to serve as "umbrella" brands across departments and categories.
- Expand the offer to include new goods and services desired by target customers.

Most mall retailers in the maturity stage will also need to create new offers for new customers. This strategy will appeal to specialty store retailers that excel at developing and rolling out new concepts.

The Situation

Over the long term, many mall retailers will struggle to return to the level of revenue and profit growth that characterized the late 1990s due to a combination of factors.

Subdued Spending

The outlook for spending on apparel, footwear, and accessories is weak. Among three key mall channels—apparel and accessory stores, department stores, and shoe stores—department stores were forecast to post the most significant contraction in sales through 2003, followed by only negligible growth. All three sectors will continue to experience great price pressure, leaving little room for inventory errors.

Store Saturation

For decades, the growth of shopping center space has outpaced population growth. Now, the market has reached saturation, causing numerous mall retailers to slow their new store openings or even retrench.

Mall Malaise

Mall developers will refurbish and expand existing malls, develop smaller malls in smaller markets, and open new types of developments in larger markets, including streetside shopping districts and open-air town centers. Although this provides opportunities for many mall retailers, some mall retailers are not suited to the more upscale life-style positioning. Since these developments are fairly unique in architecture and configuration, retailers also lose benefits associated with the ability to roll out "cookie-cutter" stores.

Compounding the lack of new regional mall growth is greater mall volatility. Malls can see a swift turn in fortunes when key tenants close or changes occur in the mall's trading-area demographics or competitive set. While some declining malls will be transformed into new uses (offices, big-box power centers, etc.), many will simply shut down and add to the blight inside the beltway. At best, the net impact of changes in the property environment indicate that mall retailers will face few opportunities to grow by opening new stores in new malls. At worst, many mature players will see a decrease in their mall stores.

New On-the-Mall Threats

Retailers will face greater competition for space in the best malls. A number of specialty store retailers are rolling out new formats. In addition, some major retailers from Europe plan to open U.S. stores.

More Off-the-Mall Challenges

The recent economic downturn benefited many value retailers, several of whom posted strong growth. It has also exposed a large share of new shoppers to credible fashions at sharp price points, which will increase the overall value orientation among shoppers over the longer term.

Geographic Territory Strategies

Fill the Gaps

An obvious, but productive, growth strategy is to be sure existing markets are fully stored, thus leveraging investments in operations, distribution, and advertising/brand communications. To make sure markets are fully stored, more mall-based retailers will explore alternative sites and develop nonstandard formats to increase shopping frequency or to reach target consumers not currently shopping at the firm's outlets.

Nonmall Stores Opening standard mall formats in nonmall locations like urban street locations, strip centers, and open-air town centers allows mall retailers to offset the inconvenience to many shoppers of reaching mall locations. Some off-mall locations also benefit from lower overhead. Inner-city locations offer a number of benefits, including limited competition from mall-based retailers, pent-up demand from underserved shoppers, and access to shoppers who tend to spend disproportionately on fashion goods.

Reformatted Stores As retailers venture further from the mall, they must often alter the store format to fit alternative sites. Such locales

benefit from a captive audience, as with airports. On the other hand, airports bring added costs and complex management. Merchandise must pass through security before arriving at the store, can be brought in only at certain times, and must be edited to the needs of travelers.

In-Store Shops The store-within-a-store concept can reach different types of shoppers, such as those who frequently shop department stores. It can also be used to intercept customers in nonmall situations.

National Coverage

Operating nationally brings economies of scale for advertising and brand development, merchandising, customer relationship development, store design, real-estate acquisition, store operations, and other corporate support functions. However, many mall specialty retailers are already at or near their growth limits. With few new malls planned, retailers are looking at acquisitions and the integration of store and nonstore channels to provide geographic expansion opportunities.

Ongoing Department Store Acquisitions The leading department store retailers will continue to expand via acquisitions. By 2005, the department store sector will be dominated by a few large, traditional department store players with national coverage. They will be supplemented by a handful of smaller players in the upscale department store sector. Some regionals that aren't acquired will eventually close as major players continue to encroach on their territory.

A Multi-Channel Approach Mall retailers with limited coverage can reach a national customer base by using formats like catalogs and online shopping sites. An effective multi-channel approach leverages the investment in the merchandise, customer service, communications, and brand equity. And it allows the retailer to drive traffic to various formats depending on the needs of the shopper and the retailer, create stronger ties with customers, test new products online before committing to inventory, and improve productivity by offering slow-moving or space-intensive merchandise only online or in the catalog.

Global Expansion

Few mall retailers have aggressively pursued global expansion. But they will be encouraged by a growing middle class, improved infrastructure in developing markets, and the large base of consumers in Europe and Japan with spending power and a willingness to accept foreign retailers. But most international plays will be close to home—crossing the border to Canada. Many U.S. retailers do not have the basic competencies needed to do business in a foreign market, including language skills, experience with legal issues, and experience with different types of real-estate and customer situations.

Northern Exposure In Canada, retailing is less saturated—with 60 percent less shopping center space per person. It has geographic proximity and similar cultural and business norms, language, and fashion tastes. Yet, Canada's relatively small (31 million) and dispersed population makes it hard to attain economies of scale. Canadian labor laws are more erroneous than in the United States. One-fourth of the population speaks French as their first language. Despite the challenges, U.S. retailers are heading north.

South of the Border Over the next few years, U.S. mall retailers will show increased interest in Mexico, reflecting the country's economic growth and consumer demand, a growing middle class, and a large population of young consumers. However, limited opportunities to grow through acquisition of Mexican retailers, strong competition from Mexico's department store sector, and high import taxes and documentation requirements that make it costly to import non-NAFTA apparel will keep U.S. retailers' expansion plans subdued. Most will test the waters to identify opportunities for later expansion.

Overseas Expansion by Nonapparel Players Many markets have few strong specialty chains for bed and bath items, cookware, glassware, lawn and garden furniture, gift/novelty items, accessories/costume jewelry, eyewear, and so on.

Store-Within-a-Store Global Expansion Specialty store retailers can grow globally by operating leased space in department stores. Department stores in Europe and Japan are open to leased space arrangements as a way to provide a more focused offering and improve their image. These department stores also operate in markets where good real estate is hard to come by. This increases the incentive for specialty store retailers to enter into leased arrangements so they can quickly get highly trafficked space.

Private Brand Exports Although there is little need for new department stores around the globe, there is an opportunity for stronger private brands. This will prompt more U.S. department stores to go global by exporting their private brands, thereby leveraging the investment to develop the brands for the U.S. market and further building brand equity through international exposure.

Target Customer Strategies

Optimize the Offer

Over the next several years, more mall retailers will work to get more from existing customers by doing what they already do, but doing it much better. Many will do so because they will have no choice given the dearth of geographic growth opportunities.

Build the Store Brand Store brand-building is a strategic growth initiative because it provides differentiation in a competitive marketplace. Some brand images also let retailers charge a premium in a price-competitive environment.

Insight More mall retailers are scrutinizing merchandise to try to increase their return on investment. They are eliminating slow-moving goods, injecting fashion to invigorate the offer, and increasing the proportion of private brands. They are aided by expanded data storage technologies; marketing automation systems that let retailers build, execute, and measure the impact of various marketing campaigns; and advanced customer analytic systems that allow for multi-channel customer data analysis.

Extend the Offer

Mall retailers will also try to get more from existing customers by extending their offers to include new categories, brands, or services. This should serve to position a retailer higher on the customer's list of preferred stores, increase average transaction size, and boost margins.

More in Store A common strategy of mall retailers is to extend the offer to get a larger "share of wallet" among existing customers. Examples abound of mall retailers adding new categories, such as lingerie, color cosmetics, fragrances, bath and body products, and home fashions. Most times, extensions are within the existing store. A few are being spun off as stand-alone concepts where a separate store allows for presentation of a more complete assortment.

More Online The opportunity to leverage the Internet by introducing more online-only merchandise and using the Web site to test new products is underused by most retailers. This often reflects a mind-set that views online retailing as a copy of the store, rather than an opportunity to complement or extend the store offer. Retailers that test new products online benefit by reducing the inventory risk. They also avoid the need to reconfigure stores to test unproven items. Retailers that sell limited-demand products (e.g., tall-size woman's apparel) only at their online sites can effectively meet most of the special needs of a dispersed customer base while avoiding downward pressure on store productivity.

Create New Offers

Often, the most effective way to grow sales is to tap new customers with a new offer by leveraging the firm's existing core competencies in merchandising, management, sourcing, and brand management. Sometimes, a new offer requires different product development or sourcing skills. Over the next several years, more mall retailers will target new customers with new offers because the potential of such a move is high, while the risks are lower than for many other strategies, such as global expansion.

Questions

1. What are the three most important points related to store location analysis that a retailer could learn from this case? Explain your answer.
2. Discuss how a retailer's current position along the retail life cycle affects its store location decisions. Relate your answer to Wal-Mart.
3. Do you agree or disagree with the following statement? "Over the long term, many mall retailers will struggle to return to the level of revenue and profit growth that characterized the late 1990s." Explain your answer.
4. How can chain retailers better "fill the gaps" in their store location strategies?
5. How can shopping malls increase their trading areas?
6. As a shopping mall developer, what criteria would you use in selecting a new site within 30 miles of your campus? Describe your reasoning.
7. Given the factors noted in the case, should every chain retailer use a multi-channel store format strategy? Why or why not?

*The material in this case is adapted by the authors from Retail Forward, "Mall Retailers: The Search for Growth," *Industry Outlook* (October 2001), pp. 1–35. Reprinted by permission of Retail Forward, Inc. (**www.retailforward.com**).

part five

Managing a Retail Business

In Part Five, the elements of managing a retail enterprise are discussed. We first look at the steps in setting up a retail organization and the special human resource management environment of retailing. Operations management is then examined—from both financial and operational perspectives.

■ **Chapter 11** reports how a retailer can use its organizational structure to assign tasks, policies, resources, authority, responsibilities, and rewards to satisfy the needs of the target market, employees, and management. We also show how human resource management can be applied so that the structure works properly. Human resource management consists of recruiting, selecting, training, compensating, and supervising personnel.

■ **Chapter 12** focuses on the financial dimensions of operations management in enacting a retail strategy. We discuss these topics: profit planning, asset management (including the strategic profit model, other key ratios, and financial trends in retailing), budgeting, and resource allocation.

■ **Chapter 13** presents the operational aspects of operations management. We cover these specific concepts: operations blueprint; store format, size, and space allocation; personnel utilization; store maintenance, energy management, and renovations; inventory management; store security; insurance; credit management; computerization; and crisis management.

Chapter 11

RETAIL ORGANIZATION AND HUMAN RESOURCE MANAGEMENT

Reprinted by permission.

James Nordstrom and Carl Wallin opened their first Wallin & Nordstrom shoe store in downtown Seattle in 1901. Today, Nordstrom (**www.nordstrom.com**) has evolved into a retailing powerhouse with $6 billion in annual sales. The company operates department stores, Nordstrom Rack discount stores, and Façonnable boutiques, as well as two freestanding shoe stores and one clearance store. Although Nordstrom has clearly changed with the times, its core values toward employees and customers remain the same: treat them with respect and empower them.

Nordstrom is committed to a decentralized management style at a time when competitors such as Federated and May are trying to reduce costs and increase bargaining power with their suppliers by centralizing those retailers' staffs. Decisions as to where new stores should be located are largely made by the general managers of Nordstrom's eight regional groups, not executives in the Seattle headquarters. Nordstrom also has 1,000 buyers who make decisions based on specific needs in their markets. As part of the firm's commitment to expansion in Georgia, Texas, and Florida, it recently created a new operating division for the stores there. The division includes a regional buying office, which orders appropriate colors, sizes, and fabric weights for this market.

Nordstrom is considered a model of customer service for the industry and one that competitors often benchmark. As its Web site says: "We remain committed to the simple idea our company was founded on, earning the trust of our customers, one at a time." The firm's strategy is enhanced by its empowering employees to take care of any reasonable customer requests.[1]

chapter objectives

1. To study the procedures involved in setting up a retail organization
2. To examine the various organizational arrangements utilized in retailing
3. To consider the special human resource environment of retailing
4. To describe the principles and practices involved with the human resource management process in retailing

OVERVIEW

Managing a retail business comprises three steps: setting up an organization structure, hiring and managing personnel, and managing operations—financially and nonfinancially. In this chapter, the first two steps are covered. Chapters 12 and 13 deal with operations management.

SETTING UP A RETAIL ORGANIZATION

Through a **retail organization**, a firm structures and assigns tasks (functions), policies, resources, authority, responsibilities, and rewards to efficiently and effectively satisfy the needs of its target market, employees, and management. Figure 11-1 shows various needs that should be taken into account when planning and assessing an organization structure.

As a rule, a firm cannot survive unless its organization structure satisfies the target market, regardless of how well employee and management needs are met. A structure that reduces costs through centralized buying but that results in the firm's being insensitive to geographic differences in customer preferences would be improper. Although many retailers do similar tasks or functions (buying, pricing, displaying, and wrapping merchandise), there are many ways of organizing to perform these functions. The process of setting up a retail organization is outlined in Figure 11-2

FIGURE 11-1
Selected Factors That Must Be Considered in Planning and Assessing a Retail Organization

TARGET MARKET NEEDS
Are there sufficient personnel to provide appropriate customer service?
Are personnel knowledgeable and courteous?
Are store facilities well maintained?
Are the specific needs of branch store customers met?
Are changing needs promptly addressed?

EMPLOYEE NEEDS
Are positions challenging and satisfying enough?
Is there an orderly promotion program from within?
Is the employee able to participate in the decision making?
Are the channels of communication clear and open?
Is the authority-responsibility relationship clear?
Is each employee treated fairly?
Is good performance rewarded?

MANAGEMENT NEEDS
Is it relatively easy to obtain and retain competent personnel?
Are personnel procedures clearly defined?
Does each worker report to only one supervisor?
Can each manager properly supervise all of the workers reporting to him or her?
Do operating departments have adequate staff support (e.g., marketing research)?
Are the levels of organization properly developed?
Are the organization's plans well integrated?
Are employees motivated?
Is absenteeism low?
Is there a system to replace personnel in an orderly manner?
Is there enough flexibility to adapt to changes in customers or the environment?

FIGURE 11-2
The Process of
Organizing a
Retail Firm

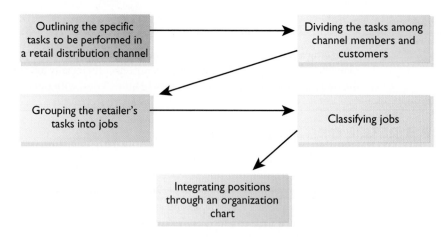

and described next. Visit our Web site (**www.prenhall.com/bermanevans**) for a variety of links on running a retail business.

SPECIFYING TASKS TO BE PERFORMED

The tasks in a distribution channel must be enumerated and then keyed to the chosen strategy mix, for effective retailing to occur:

- Buying merchandise for the retailer.
- Shipping merchandise to the retailer.
- Receiving merchandise and checking incoming shipments.
- Setting prices.
- Marking merchandise.
- Inventory storage and control.
- Preparing merchandise and window displays.
- Facilities maintenance (e.g., keeping the store clean).
- Customer research and exchanging information.
- Customer contact (e.g., advertising, personal selling).
- Facilitating shopping (e.g., convenient site, short checkout lines).
- Customer follow-up and complaint handling.
- Personnel management.
- Repairs and alteration of merchandise.
- Billing customers.
- Handling receipts and financial records.
- Credit operations.
- Gift wrapping.
- Delivery to customers.
- Returning unsold or damaged merchandise to vendors.
- Sales forecasting and budgeting.
- Coordination.

Sysco is a wholesaler serving more than 415,000 restaurants, hotels, schools, and other locales. It offers them a wide range of support services (www.sysco.com/services/services.html).

DIVIDING TASKS AMONG CHANNEL MEMBERS AND CUSTOMERS

Although the preceding tasks are typically performed in a distribution channel, they do not have to be done by a retailer. Some can be completed by the manufacturer, wholesaler, specialist, or consumer. Figure 11-3 shows the types of activities that could be carried out by each party. Following are some criteria to consider in allocating the functions related to consumer credit.

FIGURE 11-3
The Division of Tasks in
a Distribution Channel

Performer	Tasks
Retailer	Can perform all or some of the tasks in the distribution channel, from buying merchandise to coordination.
Manufacturer or Wholesaler	Can take care of few or many functions, such as shipping, marking merchandise, inventory storage, displays, research, etc.
Specialist(s)	Can undertake a particular task: buying office, delivery firm, warehouse, marketing research firm, ad agency, accountant, credit bureau, computer service firm.
Consumer	Can be responsible for delivery, credit (cash purchases), sales effort (self-service), product alterations (do-it-yourselfers), etc.

A task should be carried out only if desired by the target market. For some retailers, liberal credit policies may provide significant advantages over competitors. For others, a cash-only policy may reduce their overhead and lead to lower prices.

A task should be done by the party with the best competence. Credit collection may require a legal staff and computerized records—most affordable by medium or large retailers. Smaller retailers are likely to rely on bank credit cards. There is a loss of control when an activity is delegated to another party. A credit collection agency, pressing for past-due payments, may antagonize customers.

The retailer's institutional framework can have an impact on task allocation. Franchisees are readily able to get together to have their own private-label brands. Independents cannot do this as easily.

Task allocation depends on the savings gained by sharing or shifting tasks. The credit function is better performed by an outside credit bureau if it has expert personnel and ongoing access to financial data, uses tailored computer software, pays lower rent (due to an out-of-the-way site), and so on. Many retailers cannot attain these savings themselves.

GROUPING TASKS INTO JOBS

The National Federation's Web site (www.nrf.com/content/foundation/rcp/all_profiles.htm) highlights the range of jobs available in retailing.

After the retailer decides which tasks to perform, they are grouped into jobs. The jobs must be clearly structured. Here are examples of grouping tasks into jobs:

Tasks	Jobs
Displaying merchandise, customer contact, gift wrapping, customer follow-up	Sales personnel
Entering transaction data, handling cash and credit purchases, gift wrapping	Cashier(s)
Receiving merchandise, checking incoming shipments, marking merchandise, inventory storage and control, returning merchandise to vendors	Inventory personnel
Window dressing, interior display setups, use of mobile displays	Display personnel
Billing customers, credit operations, customer research	Credit personnel
Merchandise repairs and alterations, resolution of complaints, customer research	Customer service personnel
Cleaning store, replacing old fixtures	Janitorial personnel
Personnel management, sales forecasting, budgeting, pricing, coordinating tasks	Management personnel

Ethics in RETAILING

Eddie Bauer: Big Social Responsibility Expectations for Employees

Eddie Bauer (**www.eddiebauer.com**) articulates its social responsibility expectations to employees in two documents. The first, "How We Do Business," describes how the principle of integrity should govern actions affecting all of its employees (called "associates" at Eddie Bauer). Among the principles each associate should follow are avoiding actions that benefit the associate at the expense of the company (such as theft or fraud), treating colleagues with respect and esteem (discrimination, harassment, and violence are not tolerated), maintaining confidentiality, engaging in only ethical business relationships, and communicating with candor and accuracy.

The second document outlines the importance of associate involvement in bettering the community. Eddie Bauer believes that giving back to the community is both a moral and civic responsibility. The company's associates often volunteer for fund-raising walks, serve as mentors for local children, and participate in adopt-a-family and other programs. Eddie Bauer associates annually raise about $2 million during United Way's (**http://national.unitedway.org**) campaign. These monies are obtained through individual contributions by associates, competitive events among the associates to raise money, and fund-raising activities involving the overall community—such as car washes and cake sales.

Sources: "How We Do Business," **www.eddiebauer.com/about/company_info/how_we_do_bus.asp** (March 29, 2003); and "Social Responsibility," **www.eddiebauer.com/about/company_info/corp_resp_all.asp** (March 29, 2003).

While grouping tasks into jobs, specialization should be considered, so each employee is responsible for a limited range of functions (as opposed to performing many diverse functions). Specialization has the advantages of clearly defined tasks, greater expertise, reduced training, and hiring personnel with narrow education and experience. Problems can result due to extreme specialization: poor morale (boredom), people not being aware of their jobs' importance, and the need for more employees. Specialization means assigning explicit duties to individuals so a job position encompasses a homogeneous cluster of tasks.

Once tasks are grouped, job descriptions are constructed. These outline the job titles, objectives, duties, and responsibilities for every position. They are used as a hiring, supervision, and evaluation tool. Figure 11-4 contains a job description for a store manager.

FIGURE 11-4

A Job Description for a Store Manager

JOB TITLE: Store Manager for 34th Street Branch of Pombo's Department Stores

POSITION REPORTS TO: Senior Vice-President

POSITIONS REPORTING TO STORE MANAGER: All personnel in the 34th Street store

OBJECTIVES: To properly staff and operate the 34th Street store

DUTIES AND RESPONSIBILITIES:
- Sales forecasting and budgeting
- Personnel recruitment, selection, training, motivation, and evaluation
- Merchandise display, inventory management, and merchandise reorders
- Transferring merchandise among stores
- Handling store receipts, preparing bank transactions, opening and closing store
- Reviewing customer complaints
- Reviewing computer data forms
- Semiannual review of overall operations and reports for top management

COMMITTEES AND MEETINGS:
- Attendance at monthly meetings with Senior Vice-President
- Supervision of weekly meetings with department managers

CLASSIFYING JOBS

Jobs are then broadly grouped into functional, product, geographic, or combination classifications. *Functional classification* divides jobs by task—such as sales promotion, buying, and store operations. Expert knowledge is utilized. *Product classification* divides jobs on a goods or service basis. A department store hires different personnel for clothing, furniture, appliances, and so forth. This classification recognizes the differences in personnel requirements for different products.

Geographic classification is useful for chains operating in different areas. Employees are adapted to local conditions, and they are supervised by branch managers. Some firms, especially larger ones, use a *combination classification*. If a branch unit of a chain hires its selling staff, but buying personnel for each product line are hired by headquarters, the functional, product, and geographic formats are combined.

DEVELOPING AN ORGANIZATION CHART

The format of a retail organization must be designed in an integrated, coordinated way. Jobs must be defined and distinct; yet, interrelationships among positions must be clear. As a prominent retail official once remarked, "A successful chief executive does not build a business. He or she builds an organization and the organization builds the business. It is done no other way."[2]

The **hierarchy of authority** outlines the job interactions within a company by describing the reporting relationships among employees (from the lowest level to the highest level). Coordination and control are provided by this hierarchy. A firm with many workers reporting to one manager has a *flat organization*. Its benefits are good communication, quicker handling of problems, and better employee identification with a job. The major problem tends to be the number of people reporting to one manager. A *tall organization* has several management levels, resulting in close supervision and fewer workers reporting to each manager. Problems include a long channel of communication, the impersonal impression given to workers regarding access to upper-level personnel, and inflexible rules.

With these factors in mind, a retailer devises an **organization chart**, which graphically displays its hierarchical relationships. Table 11-1 lists the principles to consider in establishing an organization chart. Figure 11-5 shows examples of organization charts.

TABLE 11-1	Principles for Organizing a Retail Firm

An organization should show interest in its employees. Job rotation, promotion from within, participatory management, recognition, job enrichment, and so forth improve worker morale.

Employee turnover, lateness, and absenteeism should be monitored, as they may indicate personnel problems.

The line of authority should be traceable from the highest to the lowest positions. In this way, employees know to whom they report and who reports to them (*chain of command*).

A subordinate should only report to one direct supervisor (*unity of command*). This avoids the problem of workers receiving conflicting orders.

There is a limit to the number of employees a manager can directly supervise (*span of control*).

A person responsible for a given objective needs the power to achieve it.

Although a supervisor can delegate authority, he or she is still responsible for subordinates.

The greater the number of organizational levels, the longer the time for communication to travel and the greater the coordination problems.

An organization has an informal structure aside from the formal organization chart. Informal relationships exercise power in the organization and may bypass formal relationships and procedures.

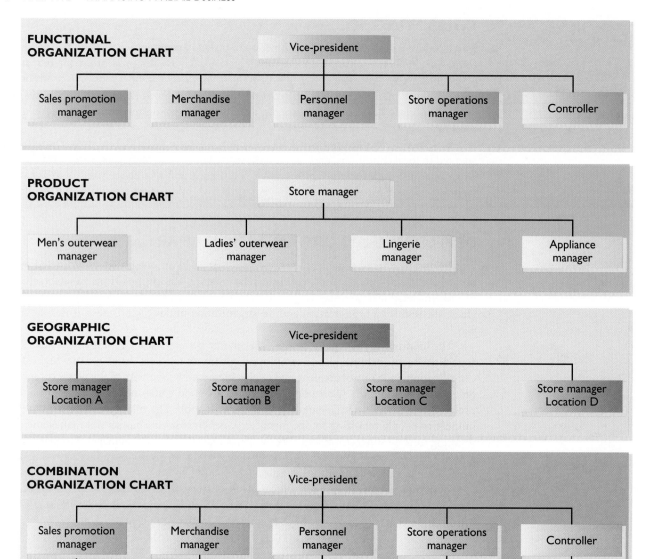

FIGURE 11-5
Different Forms of Retail Organization

ORGANIZATIONAL PATTERNS IN RETAILING

An independent retailer has a simple organization. It operates only one store, the owner-manager usually supervises all employees, and workers have access to the owner-manager if there are problems. In contrast, a chain must specify how tasks are delegated, coordinate multiple stores, and set common policies for employees. The organizational arrangements used by independent retailers, department stores, chain retailers, and diversified retailers are discussed next.

FIGURE 11-6
Organization Structures
Used by Small
Independents

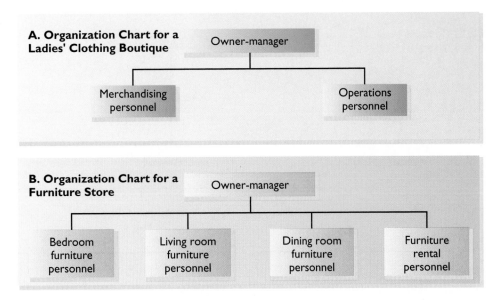

A. Organization Chart for a Ladies' Clothing Boutique

Owner-manager

- Merchandising personnel
- Operations personnel

B. Organization Chart for a Furniture Store

Owner-manager

- Bedroom furniture personnel
- Living room furniture personnel
- Dining room furniture personnel
- Furniture rental personnel

ORGANIZATIONAL ARRANGEMENTS USED BY SMALL INDEPENDENT RETAILERS

Small independents use uncomplicated arrangements with only two or three levels of personnel (owner-manager and employees), and the owner-manager personally runs the firm and oversees workers. There are few employees, little specialization, and no branch units. This does not mean fewer activities must be performed, but that many tasks are performed relative to the number of workers. Each employee must allot part of his or her time to several duties.

Figure 11-6 shows the organizations of two small firms. In A, a boutique is organized by function. Merchandising personnel buy and sell goods and services, plan assortments, set up displays, and prepare ads. Operations personnel are involved with store maintenance and operations. In B, a furniture store is organized on a product-oriented basis, with personnel in each category responsible for selected activities. All products get proper attention, and some expertise is developed. This is important since different skills are necessary to buy and sell each type of furniture.

ORGANIZATIONAL ARRANGEMENTS USED BY DEPARTMENT STORES

Many department stores continue to use organizational arrangements that are a modification of the **Mazur plan**, which divides all retail activities into four functional areas—merchandising, publicity, store management, and accounting and control:

1. Merchandising—buying, selling, stock planning and control, promotion planning.
2. Publicity—window and interior displays, advertising, planning and executing promotional events (along with merchandise managers), advertising research, public relations.
3. Store management—merchandise care, customer services, buying store supplies and equipment, maintenance, operating activities (such as receiving and delivering products), store and merchandise protection (insurance and security), employee training and compensation, workroom operations.
4. Accounting and control—credit and collections, expense budgeting and control, inventory planning and control, recordkeeping.[3]

These areas are organized by *line* (direct authority and responsibility) and *staff* (advisory and support) components. Thus, a controller and a publicity manager provide staff services to merchandisers, but within their disciplines, personnel are organized on a line basis. Figure 11-7 illustrates the Mazur plan.

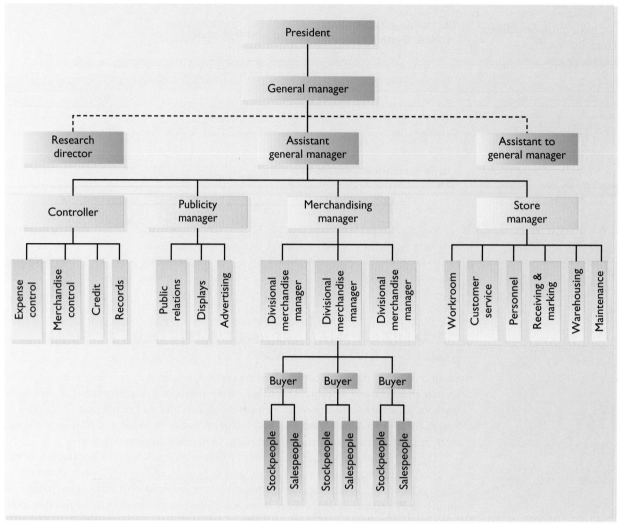

FIGURE 11-7

The Basic Mazur Organization Plan for Department Stores

Source: Adapted from Paul Mazur, *Principles of Organization Applied to Modern Retailing* (New York: Harper & Brothers, 1927), frontispiece. Reprinted by permission.

The merchandising division is responsible for buying and selling. It is headed by a merchandising manager, who is often viewed as the most important area executive. He or she supervises buyers, devises financial controls for each department, coordinates merchandise plans (so there is a consistent image among departments), and interprets the effects of economic data. In some cases, divisional merchandise managers are utilized, so the number of buyers reporting to a single manager does not become unwieldy.

The buyer, in the basic Mazur plan, has complete accountability for expenses and profit goals within a department. Duties include preparing preliminary budgets, studying trends, bargaining with vendors over price, planning the number of salespeople, and informing sales personnel about the merchandise purchased. Grouping buying and selling activities into one job (buyer) may present a problem. Since buyers are not constantly on the selling floor, training, scheduling, and supervising personnel may suffer.

The growth of branch stores has led to three Mazur plan derivatives: *main store control,* by which headquarters executives oversee and operate branches; *separate store organization,* by which each branch has its own buying responsibilities; and **equal store organization,** by which buying is centralized and branches become sales units with equal operational status. The latter is the most popular format.

In the main store control format, most authority remains at headquarters. Merchandise planning and buying, advertising, financial controls, store hours, and other tasks are centrally managed to standardize the performance. Branch store managers hire and supervise employees, but daily operations conform to company policies. This works well if there are few branches and the preferences of their customers are similar to those at the main store. As branch stores increase, buyers, the advertising director, and others may be overworked and give little attention to branches. Since headquarters personnel are not at the branches, differences in customer preferences may be overlooked.

The separate store format places merchandise managers in branch stores, which have autonomy for merchandising and operations. Customer needs are quickly noted, but duplication of tasks is possible. Coordination can also be a problem. Transferring goods between branches is more complex and costly. This format is best if stores are large, branches are dispersed, or local customer tastes vary widely.

In the equal store format, the benefits of both centralization and decentralization are sought. Buying—forecasting, planning, purchasing, pricing, distribution to branches, and promotion—is centralized. Selling—presenting merchandise, selling, customer services, and operations—is managed locally. Outlets, including headquarters, are treated alike. Buyers are freed from managing so many workers. Data gathering is critical since buyers have less customer contact.

ORGANIZATIONAL ARRANGEMENTS USED BY CHAIN RETAILERS

Various chain retailers use a version of the equal store organization, as depicted in Figure 11-8. Although chains' organizations may differ, they generally have these attributes:

- There are many functional divisions, such as sales promotion, merchandise management, distribution, operations, real-estate, personnel, and information systems.
- Overall authority is centralized. Store managers have selling responsibility.
- Many operations are standardized (fixtures, store layout, building design, merchandise lines, credit policy, and store service).
- An elaborate control system keeps management informed.
- Some decentralization lets branches adapt to localities and increases store manager responsibilities. Though large chains standardize most of the items their outlets carry, store managers often fine-tune the rest of the strategy mix for the local market. This is empowerment at the store manager level.

RETAILING
Around the World — Marks & Spencer Looks to Build Positive People Power

Marks & Spencer (**www.marksandspencer.com**) is one of Great Britain's leading retailers of clothing, foods, housewares, and financial services. The firm serves 10 million customers per week in its over 300 British stores. Marks & Spencer also has stores in 30 other countries.

Recently, Marks & Spencer instituted a program to improve its customer service, which had slipped in overall quality. According to Marks & Spencer's chairman, "We have tapped into the values and qualities that customers traditionally associated with our brand but which tended to be obscured in recent years. We may have let our customers down and they may have

punished us by staying away, but the vast majority were waiting for the excuse to come back."

The retailer's program for rebuilding its customer service is based on a customer training program that focuses on "positive people power." Each store now has its own training coach: "Gone are the days when cashiers might chat over the tills to each other. Now, they focus on the customer. Customers are guaranteed a friendly, but unobtrusive, welcome from interested staff."

Sources: "M & S Harnesses Power of Positive Thought," *Grocer* (June 16, 2001), p. 58; and *Marks & Spencer 2002 Annual Report.*

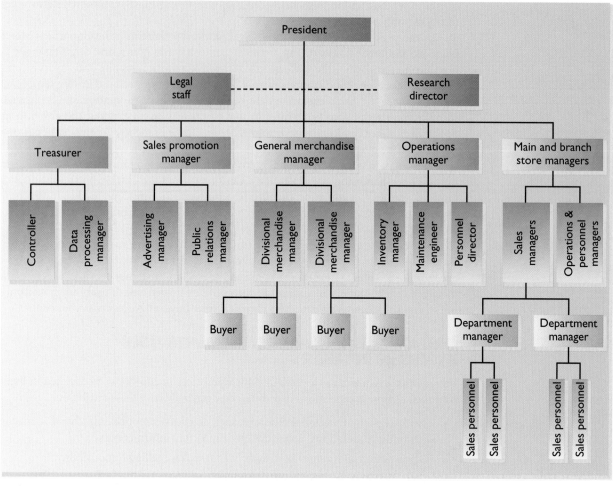

FIGURE 11-8

The Equal-Store Organizational Format Used by Many Chain Stores

ORGANIZATIONAL ARRANGEMENTS USED BY DIVERSIFIED RETAILERS

A **diversified retailer** is a multiline firm operating under central ownership. Like other chains, a diversified retailer operates multiple stores; unlike typical chains, a diversified firm is involved with different types of retail operations. Here are two examples:

To discover how Toys "R" Us operates, go to the "Investor Relations" section of its Web site (http://www2.toysrus. com/investor).

- Toys "R" Us, Inc. (**www.tru.com**) operates Toys "R" Us (toy supermarkets), Kids "R" Us (children's apparel), Babies "R" Us (all types of products for babies, including apparel, furniture, and strollers), and Imaginarium (educational toys) stores—as well as an international division. See Figure 11-9.
- Japan's Aeon Group (**www.aeongroup.net/aeoncorp/english**) comprises superstores, supermarkets, discount stores, home centers, specialty and convenience stores, financial services stores, restaurants, and more. Besides Japan, Aeon has facilities in numerous other countries. It is also a leading shopping center developer.

Due to their multiple strategy mixes, diversified retailers face complex organizational considerations. Interdivision control is needed, with operating procedures and goals clearly communicated. Interdivision competition must be coordinated. Resources must be divided among different divisions. Potential image and advertising conflicts must be avoided. Management skills must adapt to different operations.

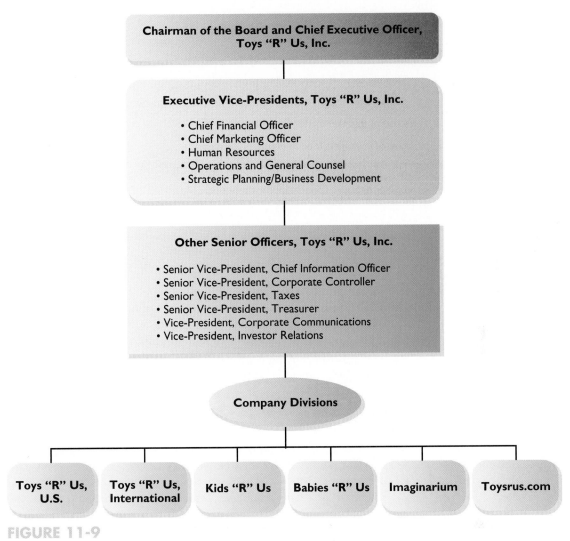

FIGURE 11-9

The Organizational Structure of Toys "R" Us, Inc., Selected Positions

Source: Compiled by the authors from the *Toys "R" Us, Inc. 2002 Annual Report.*

HUMAN RESOURCE MANAGEMENT IN RETAILING

Human resource management involves recruiting, selecting, training, compensating, and supervising personnel in a manner consistent with the retailer's organization structure and strategy mix. Personnel practices are dependent on the line of business, the number of employees, the location of outlets, and other factors. Since good personnel are needed to develop and carry out retail strategies, and labor costs can amount to 50 percent or more of expenses, the value of human resource management is clear:

- U.S. retailing employs 23 million people. Thus, there is a constant need to attract new employees—and retain existing ones. For example, 2 million fast-food workers are aged 16 to 20, and they stay in their jobs for only short periods. In general, retailers need to reduce the turnover rate; when workers quickly exit a firm, the results can be disastrous. See Table 11-2.

Pizzeria Uno (www. pizzeriauno.com/employ. html) has a clear employee development plan.

- The Pizzeria Uno chain is committed to employee development and retention: "If you're ready to move ahead with a dynamic national chain, team up with Uno today. Each restaurant has a team made up of a general manager, assistant general manager, and 1 to 3 managers. In building this team, Uno works hard to offer the right mix to meet career aspirations, training opportunities, work/family considerations, and pay and benefits expectations."[4]

TABLE 11-2	The True Cost of Employee Turnover

Recruiting and hiring new employees.

Training costs—including management time.

Full pay and benefits during training, before full productivity is reached.

Costs of mistakes made by new, inexperienced employees.

Loss of customers loyal to departing employees.

Loss of knowledge and experience of departing employees.

Lost or damaged relationships with suppliers.

Employee morale and customer perceptions of that morale.

Source: Terri Kabachnick, "Turning Against the Tide," *Retailing Issues Letter* (Center for Retailing Studies, Texas A&M University, September 1995), p. 3. Reprinted by permission.

- The highest entry-level position at Home Depot is usually assistant store manager; store managers are typically not hired from outside. Although Home Depot is a huge chain, senior executives are personally involved in training managers.
- At Nordstrom, buying is decentralized and salespeople have considerable input. They can place special orders, get extra merchandise, and resolve customer problems.

THE SPECIAL HUMAN RESOURCE ENVIRONMENT OF RETAILING

The Bureau of Labor Statistics compiles current employment data on such jobs as retail sales worker supervisors and managers (www.bls.gov/oco).

Retailers face a human resource environment characterized by a large number of inexperienced workers, long hours, highly visible employees, a diverse workforce, many part-time workers, and variable customer demand. These factors complicate employee hiring, staffing, and supervision.

The need for a large retail labor force often means hiring persons with little or no prior experience. Sometimes, a position in retailing represents the first "real job." People are attracted to retailing because they find jobs near to home; and retail positions (such as cashiers, stock clerks, and some types of sales personnel) may require limited education, training, and skill. Also, the low wages paid for some positions result in the hiring of inexperienced people. Thus, high employee turnover and cases of poor performance, lateness, and absenteeism may result.

The long working hours in retailing, which may include weekends, turn off certain prospective employees; and many retailers now have longer hours since more shoppers want to shop during evenings and weekends. Accordingly, some retailers require at least two shifts of full-time employees.

Retailing employees are highly visible to the customer. Therefore, when personnel are selected and trained, special care must be taken with regard to their manners and appearance. Some small retailers do not place enough emphasis on employee appearance (neat grooming and appropriate attire).

It is common for retailers to have a diverse labor force, with regard to age, work experience, gender, race, and other factors. This means that firms must train and supervise their workers so that they interact well with one another—and are sensitive to the perspectives and needs of one another. Consider the employee mission of Albertson's: We value the unique qualities that each associate brings to the workplace. It is our goal to attract and retain the best associates in our industry and to provide a courteous and respectful work environment where new ideas and a diverse workforce come together as one team. All Albertson's associates are responsible for creating a working environment where diversity is honored, celebrated, and cherished."[5]

Due to their long hours, retailers regularly hire part-time workers. In many supermarkets, over half the workers are part-time, and problems can arise. Some part-time employees are more lackadaisical, late, absent, or likely to quit than full-time employees. They must be closely monitored.

Variations in customer demand by day, time period, or season may cause difficulties. Most shoppers make major supermarket trips on Thursday, Friday, or Saturday. So, how many employees should there be on Sunday through Wednesday, and how many on Thursday through Saturday? Demand differences by day part (morning, afternoon, evening) and by season (fall, holidays) also affect planning. When stores are especially busy, even administrative and clerical employees may be needed on the sales floor.

As a rule, retailers should consider these points:

- Recruitment and selection procedures must efficiently generate sufficient applicants.
- Some training must be short because workers are inexperienced and temporary.
- Compensation must be perceived as "fair" by employees.
- Advancement opportunities must be available to employees who view retailing as a career.
- Employee appearance and work habits must be explained and reviewed.
- Diverse workers must be taught to work together well and amicably.
- Morale problems may result from high turnover and the many part-time workers.
- Full- and part-time workers may conflict, especially if some full-timers are replaced.

Various retail career opportunities are available to women and minorities—and less of a "glass ceiling" exists than in many other industries. There is still some room for improvement.

Women in Retailing

Women have more career options in retailing than ever before, as the following shows:

Kim Nye started in "Gifts and Linens." Kimberly Baughman sold popcorn at the neighborhood move theater. Karen Daskas and Cheryl Daskas rented a tiny storefront in Birmingham. Nye now tells Saks Fifth Avenue how to market to Detroit's discriminating shoppers. Baughman runs Great Lakes Crossing, one of Michigan's largest malls with a 25-screen movie palace. And the Daskas sisters have bought the building that houses Tender, their boutique and one of Birmingham's most chic shops. In decades past, these women would have remained behind the counter while men with similar qualifications rose to the executive offices. Today, they own, manage, and market some of the most successful retail stores and shopping centers.[6]

May Kay Ash was a true pioneer, beginning her now billion-dollar business in 1963. Learn about her story (www. marykay.com/marykay/ About/marykay/bio.html).

Debbi Fields (Mrs. Fields' Cookies) and Mary Kay Ash (Mary Kay cosmetics) founded retailing empires. At Avon, the chief executive is an Asian-American woman, and 47 percent of its corporate officers are women. The chief executive of J.C. Penney Stores, Catalog, and Internet is a woman. The president of Target Corporation's Marshall Field's division (which includes the recently converted Dayton's and Hudson's) is a woman; and she has boosted performance a lot:

Before Linda Ahlers took over, Dayton's, Hudson's, and Marshall Field's were limping along with operating margins of 5 percent, three points behind the industry leaders. Ahlers dumped the Macy's and Lord & Taylor strategy of stuffing mailboxes with promotion fliers. She cut sale days from 120 to 60, focusing on merchandising and becoming the second-best service provider behind Nordstrom. By deploying global style watchers, she made sure stores had the items in fashion magazines and a knowledgeable, all-smiles, we'll-take-anything-back sales force. The strategy was a hit, enabling Ahlers to boost operating margins while focusing on service and slashing promotions. By 2002, Marshall Field's annual sales had risen to more than $3 billion.[7]

See why Avon calls itself "The Company for Women" (www. avoncompany.com/ women).

Retailing has made a lot of progress in career advancement for women. These retailers are among the top U.S. public companies in the percentage of women who are corporate officers: Avon, Nordstrom, Target Corporation, Foot Locker, and BJ's Wholesale Club. For restaurateurs such as Carlson, Starbucks, Advantica, and IHOP, at least 30 percent of corporate officers are women. The female:male mix for managerial jobs in the lodging and food service sectors is nearly 50 percent. More than two-thirds of supervisors at eating and drinking establishments are women. Target, Gymboree, Marriott, Nordstrom, Patagonia, Sears, and Stride Rite have been rated as excellent opportunities for working mothers.

Despite recent progress, women still account for less than 15 percent of corporate officers at retail firms: "High-ranking women are few. Retail lags behind industry leaders." But this is expected to change. As one woman senior retailing executive remarked, "I think women are comfortable with stores and it makes sense they'd be comfortable running a store."[8]

These are some of the issues for retailers to address with regard to female workers:

- Meaningful training programs.
- Advancement opportunities.
- Flex time—the ability of employees to adapt their hours.
- Job sharing among two or more employees who each work less than full-time.
- Child care.

Minorities in Retailing

DiversityInc.com presents a lot of useful information about minorities in the workplace (www.diversityinc.com).

As with women, retailers have done many good things in the area of minority employment, with more still to be accomplished. Consider these examples.

TJX (parent of off-price T.J. Maxx and Marshalls) is quite involved with diversity in its workforce:

Our culture is built on recognizing people for both their expertise and their individual experiences. Having a diverse workforce gives us all a broader perspective and makes us better able to serve the needs of an ever-changing consumer base. One of the reasons our environment is so vital is because it is made up of many different kinds of ideas, backgrounds, interests, and viewpoints. The primary goal of our Affinity Groups is to make us an even better place to work for everyone. The objectives of these groups are to provide opportunities for associate affinity and self-advocacy; to provide a forum for personal and professional growth and networking; to identify resources for development and support; and to promote the company's values, diversity mission, and vision. Our Minorities & People of Color Affinity Group promotes and encourages an environment of understanding, acceptance, and inclusion among all TJX associates through education and enlightenment.[9]

TJX's corporate philosophy (www.tjx.com/frames/acc_ar.html) encourages diversity and understanding.

Cora Davis, vice-president and divisional merchandise manager for the Wal-Mart Stores division, says that "diversity is a top priority. Wal-Mart is the largest private employer of people of color with more than 140,000 African-Americans and more than 87,000 Hispanic associates." According to Sharon Saunders, vice-president and director of employment at J.C. Penney, "Today, companies are looking to reflect the demographics of the communities they serve. In retailing, having a diverse workforce helps to provide a competitive advantage in selecting appropriate merchandise and services in support of the customer base." Billye Alexander, senior regional vice-president for Sears, says: "Retailing is definitely a viable industry for African-American college graduates. Your success is measured by very objective sales and profit results. There is not much subjectivity in analyzing how you are performing."[10]

More minority workers rate career opportunities as favorable than unfavorable and have a better view of retailing than nonminority workers: Asian-Americans, 45.4 percent favorable, 24.6 percent unfavorable; Hispanic-Americans, 37.8 percent favorable, 27.3 percent unfavorable; African-Americans, 36.3 percent favorable, 34.4 percent unfavorable; Caucasian-Americans, 35.5 percent favorable, 34.7 percent unfavorable. And a 2002 *Fortune* study of the best large U.S. firms for minority employees found that several were retailers—including Denny's (formerly a division of Advantica), Darden restaurants, McDonald's, and Nordstrom. Minority workers make up at least one-third of the employees at these firms.[11]

These are some of the issues for retailers to address with regard to minority workers:

- Clear policy statements from top management as to the value of employee diversity.
- Active recruitment programs to stimulate minority applications.
- Meaningful training programs.
- Advancement opportunities.
- Zero tolerance for insensitive workplace behavior.

THE HUMAN RESOURCE MANAGEMENT PROCESS IN RETAILING

The **human resource management process** consists of these interrelated personnel activities: recruitment, selection, training, compensation, and supervision. The goals are to obtain, develop, and retain employees. When applying the process, diversity, labor laws, and privacy should be considered.

Diversity involves two premises: (1) that employees be hired and promoted in a fair and open way, without regard to gender, ethnic background, and other related factors; and (2) that in a diverse society, the workplace should be representative of such diversity.

There are several aspects of labor laws for retailers to satisfy. They must not

- Hire underage workers.
- Pay workers "off the books."
- Require workers to engage in illegal acts (such as bait-and-switch selling).
- Discriminate in hiring or promoting workers.
- Violate worker safety regulations.
- Disobey the Americans with Disabilities Act.
- Deal with suppliers that disobey labor laws.

Retailers must also be careful not to violate employees' privacy rights. Only necessary data about workers should be gathered and stored, and such information should not be freely disseminated.

We now discuss each activity in human resource management for sales and middle-management jobs. For more insights on the process, go to our Web site (**www.prenhall.com/ bermanevans**).

Recruiting Retail Personnel

Recruitment is the activity whereby a retailer generates a list of job applicants. Table 11-3 indicates the features of several key recruitment sources. In addition to these sources, the Web is playing a bigger role in recruitment. Many retailers have a career or job section at their Web site, and some sections are as elaborate as the overall sites. Visit Target Stores' site (**www.target.com**), for example. Scroll down to "Company" at the bottom of the Target home page and click on "Careers."

For entry-level sales jobs, retailers rely on educational institutions, ads, walk-ins (or write-ins), Web sites, and employee recommendations. For middle-management positions, retailers rely on employment agencies, competitors, ads, and current employee referrals. The retailer's typical goal is to generate a list of potential employees, which is reduced during selection. However, retailers that only accept applications from those who meet minimum background standards can save a lot of time and money.

Selecting Retail Personnel

The firm next selects new employees by matching the traits of potential employees with job requirements. Job analysis and description, the application blank, interviewing, testing (optional), references, and a physical exam (optional) are tools in the process; they should be integrated.

In **job analysis**, information is amassed on each job's functions and requirements: duties, responsibilities, aptitude, interest, education, experience, and physical tasks. It is used to select personnel, set performance standards, and assign salaries. For example, department managers often act as the main sales associates for their areas, oversee other sales associates, have some administrative duties, report to the store manager, are eligible for bonuses, and are paid from $25,000 to $40,000+ annually.

Job analysis should lead to written job descriptions. A **traditional job description** contains a position's title, relationships (superior and subordinate), and specific roles and tasks. Figure 11-4 showed a store manager job description. Yet, using a traditional description alone has been criticized. This may limit a job's scope, as well as its authority and responsibility; not let a person grow; limit activities to those listed; and not describe how positions are coordinated. To complement

TABLE 11-3	Recruitment Sources and Their Characteristics
Sources	Characteristics

Outside the Company

Educational institutions	a. High schools, business schools, community colleges, universities, graduate schools. b. Good for training positions; ensure minimum educational requirements are met; especially useful when long-term contacts with instructors are developed.
Other channel members, competitors	a. Employees of wholesalers, manufacturers, ad agencies, competitors; leads from each of these. b. Reduce extent of training; can evaluate performance with prior firm(s); must instruct in company policy; some negative morale if current employees feel bypassed for promotions.
Advertisements	a. Newspapers, trade publications, professional journals, Web sites. b. Large quantity of applicants; average applicant quality may not be high; cost/applicant is low; additional responsibility placed on screening; can reduce unacceptable applications by noting job qualifications in ads.
Employment agencies	a. Private organizations, professional organizations, government, executive search firms. b. Must be carefully selected; must be determined who pays fee; good for applicant screening; specialists in personnel.
Unsolicited applicants	a. Walk-ins, write-ins. b. Wide variance in quality; must be carefully screened; file should be kept for future positions.

Within the Company

Current and former employees	a. Promotion or transfer of existing full-time employees, part-time employees; rehiring of laid-off employees. b. Knowledge of company policies and personnel; good for morale; honest appraisal from in-house supervisor.
Employee recommendations	a. Friends, acquaintances, relatives. b. Value of recommendations depend on honesty and judgment of current employees.

a traditional description, a **goal-oriented job description** can enumerate basic functions, the relationship of each job to overall goals, the interdependence of positions, and information flows. See Figure 11-10.

An **application blank** is usually the first tool used to screen applicants; providing data on education, experience, health, reasons for leaving prior jobs, outside activities, hobbies, and references. It is usually short, requires little interpretation, and can be used as the basis for probing in an interview. With a **weighted application blank**, factors having a high relationship with job success are given more weight than others. Retailers that use such a form analyze the performance of current and past employees and determine the criteria (education, experience, and so on) best correlated with job success (as measured by longer tenure, better performance, and so on). After weighted scores are awarded to all job applicants (based on data they provide), a minimum total score becomes a cutoff point for hiring. An effective application blank aids retailers in lessening turnover and selecting high achievers.

An application blank should be used along with a job description. Those meeting minimum job requirements are processed further; others are immediately rejected. In this way, the application blank provides a quick and inexpensive method of screening.

FIGURE 11-10

A Goal-Oriented Job Description for a Management Trainee

Attributes Required	Ability	Desire	In the Retailing Environment
ANALYTICAL SKILLS: ability to solve problems; strong numerical ability for analysis of facts and data for planning, managing, and controlling.			Retail executives are problem solvers. Knowledge and understanding of past performance and present circumstances form the basis for action and planning.
CREATIVITY: ability to generate and recognize imaginative ideas and solutions; ability to recognize the need for and be responsive to change.			Retail executives are idea people. Successful buying results from sensitive, aware decisions, while merchandising requires imaginative, innovative techniques.
DECISIVENESS: ability to make quick decisions and render judgments, take action, and commit oneself to completion.			Retail executives are action people. Whether it's new fashion trends or customer desires, decisions must be made quickly and confidently in this ever-changing environment.
FLEXIBILITY: ability to adjust to the ever-changing needs of the situation; ability to adapt to different people, places, and things; willingness to do whatever is necessary to get the task done.			Retail executives are flexible. Surprises in retailing never cease. Plans must be altered quickly to accommodate changes in trends, styles, and attitudes, while numerous ongoing activities cannot be ignored.
INITIATIVE: ability to originate action rather than wait to be told what to do and ability to act based on conviction.			Retail executives are doers. Sales volumes, trends, and buying opportunities mean continual action. Opportunities for action must be seized.
LEADERSHIP: ability to inspire others to trust and respect your judgment; ability to delegate and to guide and persuade others.			Retail executives are managers. Running a business means depending on others to get the work done. One person cannot do it all.
ORGANIZATION: ability to establish priorities and courses of action for self and/or others; skill in planning and following up to achieve results.			Retail executives are jugglers. A variety of issues, functions, and projects are constantly in motion. To reach your goals, priorities must be set and work must be delegated to others.
RISK-TAKING: willingness to take calculated risks based on thorough analysis and sound judgment and to accept responsibility for the results.			Retail executives are courageous. Success in retailing often comes from taking calculated risks and having the confidence to try something new before someone else does.
STRESS TOLERANCE: ability to perform consistently under pressure, to thrive on constant change and challenge.			Retail executives are resilient. As the above description should suggest, retailing is fast-paced and demanding.

The interview seeks information that can be amassed only by personal questioning and observation. It lets an employer determine a candidate's verbal ability, note his or her appearance, ask questions keyed to the application, and probe career goals. Interviewing decisions must be made about the level of formality, the number and length of interviews, the location, the person(s) to do the interviewing, and the interview structure. These decisions often depend on the interviewer's ability and the job's requirements.

Careers in RETAILING — Wal-Mart Prepares for the Next Generation

Three high-level Wal-Mart (**www.walmart.com**) executives, Don Harris, Jim Haworth, and Doug Degn, were recently given new or expanded responsibilities in merchandising and operations. This realignment of responsibilities indicated that all three are in position to further advance within Wal-Mart. According to Tom Coughlin, Wal-Mart's president and chief executive of Wal-Mart's Stores Division, "These new assignments help foster a management team made up of generalists rather than specialists, which is important at Wal-Mart because we ask and expect our people to do a variety of things well."

Here is a little information about Wal-Mart's "Next Generation":

- Don Harris, 45 in 2003, was promoted to executive vice-president of general merchandise in Wal-Mart's Stores Division. He was in his previous position for just 22 months before being promoted. He joined Wal-Mart at 22 as an assistant management trainee.
- Jim Haworth, 41 in 2003, has assumed the position of executive vice-president and chief operating officer of the Stores Division. This is the former position held by Harris. Haworth began as an assistant manager when he was 22.
- While Doug Degn, 46 in 2003, retains his title as executive vice-president of food merchandising, he now has added responsibilities for consumables. Degn was 26 when he began at Wal-Mart as a pharmacy manager.

Source: Mike Troy, "Wal-Mart Taps Next-Generation Leaders," *DSN Retailing Today* (August 6, 2001), pp. 1, 44.

Small firms tend to hire an applicant who has a good interview. Large firms may add testing. In this case, a candidate who does well in an interview then takes a psychological test (to measure personality, intelligence, interest, and leadership) and/or achievement tests (to measure learned knowledge).[12]

Tests must be administered by qualified people. Standardized exams should not be used unless proven effective in predicting job performance. Because achievement tests deal with specific skills or information, like the ability to make a sales presentation, they are easier to interpret than psychological tests, and direct relationships between knowledge and ability can be shown. In administering tests, retailers must not violate any federal, state, or local law. The federal Employee Polygraph Protection Act bars retailers from using lie detector tests in most hiring situations (drugstores are exempt).

CarMax (www.carmax.com) encourages potential employees to submit their resumés online.

To save time and operate more efficiently, some retailers—large and small—use computerized application blanks and testing. Home Depot and Target Stores are among those with in-store kiosks that allow people to apply for jobs, complete application blanks, and answer several questions. This speeds up the hiring process and attracts a lot of applicants.

Many retailers get references from applicants that can be checked either before or after an interview. References are contacted to see how enthusiastically they recommend an applicant, check the applicant's honesty, and ask why an applicant left a prior job. Mail and phone checks are inexpensive, fast, and easy.

Some firms require a physical exam because of the physical activity, long hours, and tensions involved in many retailing positions. A clean bill of health means the candidate is offered a job. Again, federal, state, and local laws must be followed.

Each step in the selection process complements the others; together they give the retailer a good information package for choosing personnel. As a rule, retailers should use job descriptions, application blanks, interviews, and reference checks. Follow-up interviews, psychological and achievement tests, and physical exams depend on the retailer and the position. Inexpensive tools (such as application blanks) are used in the early screening stages; more costly, in-depth tools (such as interviews) are used after reducing the applicant pool. Equal opportunity, nondiscriminatory practices must be followed.

Training Retail Personnel

Every new employee should receive **pre-training**, an indoctrination on the firm's history and policies, as well as a job orientation on hours, compensation, the chain of command, and job duties. New employees should also be introduced to co-workers: "Effective orientation inspires recruits and provides information that they do not know about their jobs and the retailer. What kind of first impression do orientation programs make? Do they confirm the new hire's choice that XYZ is a good place to work?"[13]

Training programs teach new (and existing) personnel how best to perform their jobs or how to improve themselves. Training can range from one-day sessions on operating a computerized cash register, personal selling techniques, or compliance with affirmative action programs to two-year programs for executive trainees on all aspects of the retailer and its operations:

- A Wal-Mart (**www.walmart.com**) assistant store manager trainee gets 20 weeks of instruction in merchandising, people development, and operations. Part of the training is computerized and part is with a management sponsor. After completing the program, the trainee becomes an assistant store manager and oversees a section of a store, known as a "store-within-a-store"—with fiscal, merchandising, and human resource responsibility for it.

- Sears University (**www.sears.com**) offers retail education courses plus self-study options. Annually, several thousand managers enroll in hands-on programs ranging from one day to one week. Some programs involve buying, merchandising, and human resource management. Others involve strategic leadership. Courses are taught by seasoned managers, training and development experts, and university faculty consultants.

Training should be an ongoing activity. New equipment, legal changes, new product lines, job promotions, low employee morale, and employee turnover necessitate not only training but also retraining. Federated Department Stores has a program called "clienteling," which tutors sales associates on how to have better long-term relations with specific repeat customers. Core vendors of Federated teach sales associates about the features and benefits of new merchandise when it is introduced.

There are several training decisions, as shown in Figure 11-11. They can be divided into three categories: identifying needs, devising appropriate training methods, and evaluation.

Short-term training needs can be identified by measuring the gap between the skills that workers already have and skills desired by the firm (for each job). This training should prepare employees for possible job rotation, promotions, and changes in the company. A longer training plan lets a firm identify future needs and train workers appropriately.

There are many training methods for retailers: lectures, demonstrations, films, programmed instruction, conferences, sensitivity training, case studies, role playing, behavior modeling, and competency-based instruction. Some techniques may be computerized (as more firms are doing). The methods' attributes are noted in Table 11-4. Retailers often use more than one technique to reduce employee boredom and cover the material better.

Computer-based training has two formats: personal computer and Web. Advanced Learning Solutions (**www.retail-training.com**) markets cashier training software. Its multimedia CD-ROM for convenience stores takes cashiers "through a series of hands-on exercises and illustrates

To promote its cashier training software, Advanced Learning Systems has an online description of it (www.retail-training.com/pub/docs/c-store.html).

FIGURE 11-11
A Checklist of Selected Training Decisions

✓ When should training occur? (At the time of hiring and/or after being at the workplace?)

✓ How long should training be?

✓ What training programs should there be for new employees? For existing employees?

✓ Who should conduct each training program? (Supervisor, co-worker, training department, or outside specialist?)

✓ Where should training take place? (At the workplace or in a training room?)

✓ What material (content) should be learned? How should it be taught?

✓ Should audiovisuals be used? If yes, how?

✓ Should elements of the training program be computerized? If yes, how?

✓ How should the effectiveness of training be measured?

TABLE 11-4	The Characteristics of Retail Training Methods
Method	Characteristics
Lecture	Factual, uninterrupted presentation of material; can use professional educator or expert in the field; no active participation by trainees
Demonstration	Good for showing how to use equipment or do a sales presentation; applies relevance of training; active participation by trainees
Video	Animated; good for demonstration; can be used many times; no active participation by trainees
Programmed instruction	Presents information in a structured manner; requires response from trainees; provides performance feedback; adjustable to trainees' pace; high initial investment
Conference	Useful for supervisory training; conference leader must encourage participation; reinforces training
Sensitivity training	Extensive interaction; good for supervisors as a tool for understanding employees
Case study	Actual or hypothetical problem presented, including circumstances, pertinent information, and questions; learning by doing; exposure to a wide variety of problems
Role playing	Trainees placed into real-life situations and act out roles
Behavior modeling	Trainees taught to imitate models shown on videotape or in role-playing sessions
Competency-based instruction	Trainees given a list of tasks or exercises that are presented in a self-paced format

how to best service your customer." Pep Boys and Circuit City are among the growing number of retailers that use the Web for at least part of employee training. As Circuit City says, "The Internet gives us a way to more quickly and more efficiently deliver information."[14]

For training to succeed, a conducive environment is needed, based on several principles:

- All people can learn if taught well; there should be a sense of achievement.
- A person learns better when motivated; intelligence alone is not sufficient.
- Learning should be goal-oriented.
- A trainee learns more when he or she participates and is not a passive listener.
- The teacher must provide guidance and adapt to the learner and to the situation.
- Learning should be approached as a series of steps rather than a one-time occurrence.
- Learning should be spread out over a reasonable period of time rather than be compressed.
- The learner should be encouraged to do homework or otherwise practice.
- Different methods of learning should be combined.
- Performance standards should be set and good performance recognized.

A training program must be regularly evaluated. Comparisons can be made between the performance of those who receive training and those who do not, as well as among employees receiving different types of training for the same job. Evaluations should always be made in relation to stated training goals. In addition, training effects should be measured over different time intervals (such as immediately, 30 days later, and 6 months later), and proper records maintained.

Compensating Retail Personnel

Total **compensation**—direct monetary payments (salaries, commissions, and bonuses) and indirect payments (paid vacations, health and life insurance, and retirement plans)—should be fair to both the retailer and its employees. To better motivate employees, some firms also have profit-sharing. Smaller retailers often pay salaries, commissions, and/or bonuses, and have fewer fringe benefits. Bigger ones generally pay salaries, commissions, and/or bonuses and offer more fringe benefits.

This site (www.dol.gov/ esa/minwage/america.htm) shows the minimum wage in every state.

The hourly federal minimum wage is $5.15. In addition, 43 states have their own laws—11 higher than the federal minimum and 3 lower. The minimum wage has the most impact on retailers hiring entry-level, part-time workers. Full-time, career-track retailing jobs are paid an attractive market rate; and to attract part-time workers during good economic times, retailers must often pay salaries above the minimum.

At some large firms, compensation for certain positions is set through collective bargaining. According to the U.S. Bureau of Labor Statistics, about 1 million retail employees are represented by labor unions. However, union membership varies greatly. Unionized grocery stores account for more than one-half of total U.S. supermarket sales, while independent supermarkets are not usually unionized.

With a *straight salary,* a worker is paid a fixed amount per hour, week, month, or year. Advantages are retailer control, employee security, and known expenses. Disadvantages are retailer inflexibility, the limited productivity incentive, and fixed costs. Clerks and cashiers are usually paid salaries. With a *straight commission,* earnings are directly tied to productivity (such as sales volume). Advantages are retailer flexibility, the link to worker productivity, no fixed costs, and employee incentive. Disadvantages are the retailer's potential lack of control over the tasks performed, the risk of low earnings to employees, cost variability, and the lack of limits on worker earnings. Sales personnel for autos, real-estate, furniture, jewelry, and other expensive items are often paid a straight commission—as are direct-selling personnel.

To combine the attributes of salary and commission plans, some retailers pay their employees a *salary plus commission.* Shoe salespeople, major appliance salespeople, and some management personnel are among those paid in this manner. Some bonuses supplement salary and/or commission, normally for outstanding performance. At Finish Line footwear and apparel stores, national, regional, district, and store managers receive fixed salaries and earn bonuses based on the payroll, and theft rate goals. In certain cases, retail executives are paid via a "compensation cafeteria" and choose their own combination of salary, bonus, deferred bonus, fringe benefits, life insurance, stock options, and retirement benefits.

Sears has a generous employee benefits package (www.sears.com/sr/misc/ sears/jobsec/careers_ benefits.jsp).

A thorny issue facing retailers today involves the benefits portion of employee compensation, especially as related to pensions and health care. It is a challenging time due to intense price competition, the use of part-time workers, and escalating medical costs as retailers try to balance their employees' needs with company financial needs.

Technology in RETAILING
Retail Training's Newest Killer Application

Many retailing analysts believe the latest "killer app" corporate training tool is online learning. According to one market research firm's estimate, corporate online learning was expected to reach $11.5 billion in expenditures during 2003. Although an important growth sector for online learning is information technology training, service-oriented training is also a vital niche component.

The analysts cite these as advantages of online training: cost savings, reduced training time (some experts feel that training time can be reduced by 50 percent), reduced employee turnover, and the better transfer of knowledge among stores. Employees can fit the courses around their work schedules and practice material in a self-paced format. All employees are trained in exactly the same way; this is critical in safety-related subjects and in compliance issues (such as alcohol and tobacco sales).

Despite the potential advantages, some experts caution retailers about adopting online training programs without careful consideration. For example, retailers must beware of the quality of video playback when converting from an existing program to the Web. And many analysts do not expect online training to replace traditional training formats. Rather, they advocate a "blended" solution comprised of various training formats.

Source: Jenny Summerour, "Training for Tomorrow," *Progressive Grocer* (April 2001), p. 39.

Supervising Retail Personnel

Supervision is the manner of providing a job environment that encourages employee accomplishment. The goals are to oversee personnel, attain good performance, maintain morale, motivate people, control costs, communicate, and resolve problems. Supervision is provided by personal contact, meetings, and reports.

Every company wants to continually motivate employees so as to harness their energy on behalf of the retailer and achieve its objectives. **Job motivation** is the drive within people to attain work-related goals. It may be positive or negative. Sears believes that 10 attitude questions help predict employee behavior, based on their motivation:

1. Do you like the kind of work you do?
2. Does your work give you a sense of accomplishment?
3. Are you proud to say you work at Sears?
4. How does the amount of work expected from you influence your overall job attitude?
5. How do physical working conditions influence your overall job attitude?
6. How does the way you are treated by supervisors influence your overall job attitude?
7. Do you feel good about the future of the company?
8. Do you think Sears is making the changes necessary to compete effectively?
9. Do you understand Sears' business strategy?
10. Do you see a connection between your work and the company's strategic objectives?[15]

Employee motivation should be approached from two perspectives: What job-related factors cause employees to be satisfied or dissatisfied with their positions? What supervision style is best for both the retailer and its employees? See Figure 11-12.

Each employee looks at job satisfaction in terms of minimum expectations ("dissatisfiers") and desired goals ("satisfiers"). A motivated employee requires fulfillment of both factors. *Minimum expectations* relate mostly to the job environment, including a safe workplace, equitable treatment for those with the same jobs, some flexibility in company policies (such as not

Tom Holmes

SEARS

TYPE OF STORE:
Department Store

HEADQUARTERS:
Hoffman Estates, Ill.

Upcoming grads anxious to climb to the top might take a look at Tom Holmes. At 29, he has already been general store manager at two Sears stores.

This political science major from the University of Illinois worked retail as an undergrad, but planned a career in investment banking. At graduation, he realized retail offered the chance to develop professionally.

"If you're confused about your direction, find an organization that lets you develop a base foundation of skill sets you can use throughout your career," notes Holmes. "Management and leadership skills are important virtually anywhere."

He contacted Sears, and was brought on board in 1993. He started in an executive development program and became a sales manager. Promotions have been quick to come ever since. He presently manages a Sears in West Dundee, Ill.

Holmes values the adventure of dealing with different personalities. "I really like working with people, both having an impact on customers and being able to coach and mentor teams to success," he says.

He is currently earning his MBA from Northwestern University's Kellogg Graduate School of Management, with a focus on strategy and marketing. Sears has tuition reimbursement for graduate and undergraduate students, which helps its employees contribute more to the company and their mutual futures.

With a college degree, employees start higher up on the food chain, get management responsibilities from square one and a sense of accomplishment as a result.

"The first time you're in charge when you realize your boss is two hours away, it makes you feel really responsible," he adds. "I like it that there are lots of plans, direction from Sears as a company, yet there's autonomy as well."

Holmes also enjoys the variety his position offers. "Yes, it's a cliché, but it really is different every day. Sometimes I do human resources things, sometimes presentations, and on other days customer service is the focus. There's a lot of flexibility day-to-day, and in how you shape your career." ■

FIGURE 11-12

Sears: Providing a Motivating Career Path for Employees

Reprinted by permission of *DSN Retailing Today*.

docking pay if a person is 10 minutes late), an even-tempered boss, some freedom in attire, a fair compensation package, basic fringe benefits (such as vacation time and medical coverage), clear communications, and job security. These elements can generally influence motivation in only one way—negatively. If minimum expectations are not met, a person will be unhappy. If these expectations are met, they are taken for granted and do little to motivate the person to go "above and beyond."

Desired goals relate more to the job than to the work environment. They are based on whether an employee likes the job, is recognized for good performance, feels a sense of achievement, is empowered to make decisions, is trusted, has a defined career path, receives extra compensation when performance is exceptional, and is given the chance to learn and grow. These elements can have a huge impact on job satisfaction and motivate a person to go "above and beyond." Nonetheless, if minimum expectations are not met, an employee might still be dissatisfied enough to leave, even if the job is quite rewarding.

There are three basis styles of supervising retail employees:

- Management assumes employees must be closely supervised and controlled, and that only economic inducements really motivate. Management further believes that the average worker lacks ambition, dislikes responsibility, and prefers to be led. This is the traditional view of motivation and has been applied to lower-level retail positions.

- Management assumes employees can be self-managers and assigned authority, motivation is social and psychological, and supervision can be decentralized and participatory. Management also thinks that motivation, the capacity for assuming responsibility, and a readiness to achieve company goals exist in people. The critical supervisory task is to create an environment so people achieve their goals by attaining company objectives. This is a more modern view and applies to all levels of personnel.

- Management applies a self-management approach and also advocates more employee involvement in defining jobs and sharing overall decision making. There is mutual loyalty between the firm and its workers, and both parties enthusiastically cooperate for the long-term benefit of each. This is also a modern view and applies to all levels of personnel.

It is imperative to motivate employees in a manner that yields job satisfaction, low turnover, low absenteeism, and high productivity:

Believe it or not, some of the most effective forms of motivation cost nothing. A sincere word of thanks from the right person at the right time can mean more to an employee than a raise, a formal award, or a wall of certificates or plaques. Part of the power of such rewards comes from the knowledge that someone took the time to notice the achievement, seek out the employee responsible, and personally deliver praise in a timely manner. And the most important things managers can do to develop and maintain motivated employees have no cost, but rather are a function of the daily interactions that managers have with employees pertaining to work. I call these "The Power of I's." There are five of them: (1) Interesting work. (2) Information, communication, and feedback. (3) Involvement and ownership in decisions. (4) Independence, autonomy, and flexibility. (5) Increased visibility, opportunity, and responsibility.[16]

Summary

1. *To study the procedures involved in setting up a retail organization.* A retail organization structures and assigns tasks, policies, resources, authority, responsibilities, and rewards to satisfy the needs of its target market, employees, and management. There are five steps in setting up an organization: outlining specific tasks to be performed in a distribution channel, dividing tasks, grouping tasks into jobs, classifying jobs, and integrating positions with an organization chart.

Specific tasks include buying, shipping, receiving and checking, pricing, and marking merchandise; inventory control; display preparation; facilities maintenance; research; customer contact and follow-up; and a lot more. These tasks may be divided among retailers, manufacturers, wholesalers, specialists, and customers.

Tasks are next grouped into jobs, such as sales personnel, cashiers, inventory personnel, display personnel, customer service personnel, and management. Then jobs are arranged by functional, product, geographic, or combination classification. An organization chart displays the hierarchy of authority and the relationship among jobs, and coordinates personnel.

2. *To examine the various organizational arrangements utilized in retailing.* Retail organization structures differ by institution. Small independents use simple formats, with little specialization. Many department stores use a version of the Mazur plan and place functions into four categories: merchandising, publicity, store management, and accounting and control. The equal store format is used by numerous chain stores. Diversified firms have very complex organizations.

3. *To consider the special human resource environment of retailing.* Retailers are unique due to the large number of inexperienced workers, long hours, highly visible employees, a diverse workforce, many part-time workers, and variations in customer demand. There is a broad range of career opportunities available to women and minorities, although improvement is still needed.

4. *To describe the principles and practices involved with the human resource management process in retailing.* This process comprises several interrelated activities: recruitment, selection, training,

compensation, and supervision. In applying the process, diversity, labor laws, and employee privacy should be kept in mind.

Recruitment generates job applicants. Sources include educational institutions, channel members, competitors, ads, employment agencies, unsolicited applicants, employees, and Web sites.

Personnel selection requires thorough job analysis, creating job descriptions, using application blanks, interviews, testing (optional), reference checking, and physical exams. After personnel are selected, they go through pre-training and job training. Good training identifies needs, uses proper methods, and assesses results. Training is usually vital for continuing, as well as new, personnel.

Employees are compensated by direct monetary payments and/or indirect payments. The direct compensation plans are straight salary, straight commission, and salary plus commission and/or bonus. Indirect payments involve such items as paid vacations, health benefits, and retirement plans.

Proper supervision is needed to sustain superior employee performance. A main task is employee motivation. The causes of job satisfaction/dissatisfaction and the supervisory style must be reviewed.

Key Terms

retail organization (p. 269)

hierarchy of authority (p. 273)

organization chart (p. 273)

Mazur plan (p. 275)

equal store organization (p. 276)

diversified retailer (p. 278)

human resource management (p. 279)

human resource management process (p. 283)

recruitment (p. 283)

job analysis (p. 283)

traditional job description (p. 283)

goal-oriented job description (p. 284)

application blank (p. 284)

weighted application blank (p. 284)

pre-training (p. 286)

training programs (p. 287)

compensation (p. 288)

supervision (p. 290)

job motivation (p. 290)

Questions for Discussion

1. Cite at least five objectives a small independent furniture retailer should set when setting up its organization structure.

2. Why are employee needs important in developing a retail organization?

3. Are the steps involved in setting up a retail organization the same for small and large retailers? Explain your answer.

4. Describe the greatest similarities and differences in the organization structures of small independents, chain retailers, and diversified retailers.

5. How can retailers attract and retain more women and minority workers?

6. How would small and large retailers act differently for each of the following?
   a. Diversity.
   b. Recruitment.
   c. Selection.
   d. Training.

   e. Compensation.
   f. Supervision.

7. Why are the job description and the application blank so important in employee selection?

8. What problems can occur while interviewing and testing prospective employees?

9. Present a plan for the ongoing training of both existing lower-level and middle-management employees without making it seem punitive.

10. Describe the goals of a compensation plan (both direct and indirect components) in a retail setting.

11. Are the minimum job expectations of entry-level workers and middle-level managers similar or dissimilar? What about the desired goals? Explain your answers.

12. How would you supervise and motivate a 19-year-old supermarket cashier? A 65-year-old cashier?

Web-Based Exercise

Visit the Web site that Federated Department Stores has dedicated to college recruiting (**www.retailology.com/college/home.asp**). What do you think of this site as a mechanism for attracting new college graduates to Federated? Why?

Note: Stop by our Web site (**www.prenhall.com/bermanevans**) to experience a number of highly interactive, appealing Web exercises based on actual company demonstrations and sample materials related to retailing.

Chapter Endnotes

1. Various company sources.

2. *Levitz 1995 Annual Report.* See also Mark Gimein, "Sam Walton Made Us a Promise," *Fortune* (March 18, 2002), pp. 121–130.

3. Paul M. Mazur, *Principles of Organization Applied to Modern Retailing* (New York: Harper & Brothers, 1927).

4. Pizzeria Uno, "Employment Opportunities," **www.pizzeriauno. com/employmain.html** (March 30, 2003).

5. *Albertson's, Inc., 2000 Company Profile*, p. 6.

6. Karen Talaski, "Opportunity Knocks for Women in Retail," *Detroit News* (August 20, 2000), p. B1.

7. Michelle Conlin and Wendy Zellner, "The Glass Ceiling: The CEO Still Wears Wingtips," *Business Week Online* (November 22, 1999); and *Target Corporation 2002 Annual Report.*

8. Debby Garbato, "A Woman's Place in Retail," *Retail Merchandiser* (August 2002), p. 6; and "Shattering the Glass Ceiling," *Chain Store Age* (January 2000), pp. 57–59.

9. "The Fabric of Diversity," **www.tjx.com/employment/about_ tjx.html** (October 3, 2002).

10. Thelma Snuggs, "Retailing on the Move: An Era of Change," *Black Collegian* (February 2002), p. 52.

11. David P. Schulz, "Employee Attitude Surveys Focus on the Human Side of the Retail Equation," *Stores* (April 1999), pp. 96–97; and "America's 50 Best Companies for Minorities," *Fortune* (July 8, 2002), p. 110.

12. For a good illustration of the testing resources available for retailers, visit the Web site of Employee Selection & Development Inc. (**www.employeeselect.com**).

13. Marilyn Moats Kennedy, "Setting the Right Tone, Right Away," *Across the Board* (April 1999), pp. 51–52.

14. *Circuit City Stores, Inc. 2001 Annual Report*, p. 8.

15. Anthony J. Rucci, Steven P. Kirn, and Richard T. Quinn, "The Employee-Customer-Profit Chain at Sears," *Harvard Business Review*, Vol. 76 (January–February 1998), pp. 82–97.

16. Bob Nelson, "No-Cost Employee Recognition," *Bank Marketing* (September 2002), p. 14. See also Bryan Fisher, "How to Motivate Employees in Tough Financial Times," *Supervision* (April 2002), pp. 9–11; Janet Wiscombe, "Rewards Get Results," *Workforce* (April 2002), pp. 42–48; and Alison Myers, "Motivate to Accumulate," *Financial Management* (April 2002), p. 19.

Chapter 12

OPERATIONS MANAGEMENT: FINANCIAL DIMENSIONS

Reprinted by permission.

Seventy-five years ago, the top management of Lazarus and the John Shillito Company met with the senior executives of Abraham & Straus, Filene's, and Bloomingdale's. They agreed to merge and form Federated Department Stores so as to reduce their vulnerability to economic downturns. Over the years, Federated (**www.federated-fds.com**) acquired such chains as Bon Marche, Burdines, Goldsmith's, Macy's, and Rich's, and it closed or divested itself of Shillito, Abraham & Straus, and Filene's.

Until relatively recently, the department store sector of retailing was able to attract a large number of customers through one-stop shopping appeals, fashion-forward apparel, and attentive service. Although department store chains were once considered the darlings of retailing, they have been losing market share to discount stores for years. According to the U.S. Department of Commerce, department stores accounted for 50 percent of general merchandise, apparel, and furniture sales (GAF) in 1992. By 2002, their share of GAF sales had fallen to 35 percent.

Of the seven chains that comprise the Standard & Poor's Department Store Index, Federated posted the highest decline in net income (−25 percent) for the fiscal year ended January 2001. The firm's net income (excluding unusual items) as a percentage of sales also dropped from 5.2 percent to 3.9 percent. Furthermore, Federated's net sales declined over the previous year, from $16.6 billion to $15.7 billion. In contrast, Dillard's (**www.dillards.com**), J.C. Penney, (**www.jcpenney.com**), Nordstrom (**www.nordstrom.com**), and Kohl's (**www.kohls.com**) posted improved earnings for the corresponding period. Federated Department Stores has a lot of work to do to regain its past glory.[1]

chapter objectives

1. To define operations management
2. To discuss profit planning
3. To describe asset management, including the strategic profit model, other key business ratios, and financial trends in retailing
4. To look at retail budgeting
5. To examine resource allocation

294

OVERVIEW

After devising an organization structure and a human resource plan, a retailer concentrates on **operations management**—the efficient and effective implementation of the policies and tasks necessary to satisfy the firm's customers, employees, and management (and stockholders, if a public company). This has a major impact on sales and profits. High inventory levels, long hours, expensive fixtures, extensive customer services, and widespread advertising many lead to higher revenues. But at what cost? If a store pays night-shift workers a 25 percent premium, is being open 24 hours per day worthwhile (do higher sales justify the costs and add to overall profit)?

This chapter covers the financial aspects of operations management, with emphasis on profit planning, asset management, budgeting, and resource allocation. The operational dimensions of operations management are explored in detail in Chapter 13. A number of useful financial operations links may be found at our Web site (**www.prenhall.com/ bermanevans**).

PROFIT PLANNING

Learn more about profit-and-loss statement (www.toolkit.cch.com/ text/P06_1578.asp).

A **profit-and-loss (income) statement** is a summary of a retailer's revenues and expenses over a given period of time, usually a month, quarter, or year. It lets the firm review its overall and specific revenues and costs for similar periods (such as January 1, 2003, to December 31, 2003, versus January 1, 2002, to December 31, 2002), and analyze profitability. By having frequent statements, a firm can monitor progress toward goals, update performance estimates, and revise strategies and tactics.

In comparing profit-and-loss performance over time, it is crucial that the same time periods be used (such as the third quarter of 2003 with the third quarter of 2002) due to seasonality. Some fiscal years may have an unequal number of weeks (53 weeks one year versus 51 weeks another). Retailers that open new stores or expand existing stores between accounting periods should also take into account the larger facilities. Yearly results should reflect total revenue growth and the rise in same store sales.

A profit-and-loss statement consists of these major components:

- **Net sales**—The revenues received by a retailer during a given period after deducting customer returns, markdowns, and employee discounts.
- **Cost of goods sold**—The amount a retailer pays to acquire the merchandise sold during a given time period. It is based on purchase prices and freight charges, less all discounts (such as quantity, cash, and promotion).
- **Gross profit (margin)**—The difference between net sales and the cost of goods sold. It consists of operating expenses plus net profit.
- **Operating expenses**—The cost of running a retail business.
- **Taxes**—The portion of revenues turned over to the federal, state, and/or local government.
- **Net profit after taxes**—The profit earned after all costs and taxes have been deducted.

Table 12-1 shows the most recent annual profit-and-loss statement for Donna's Gift Shop, an independent retailer. The firm uses a fiscal year (September 1 to August 31) rather than a calendar year in preparing its accounting reports. These observations can be drawn from the table:

- Annual net sales were $330,000—after deducting returns, markdowns on the items sold, and employee discounts from total sales.
- The cost of goods sold was $180,000, computed by taking the total purchases for merchandise sold, adding freight, and subtracting quantity, cash, and promotion discounts.
- Gross profit was $150,000, calculated by subtracting the cost of goods sold from net sales. This went for operating and other expenses, taxes, and profit.

TABLE 12-1	Donna's Gift Shop, Fiscal 2003 Profit-and-Loss Statement	
Net sales		$330,000
Cost of goods sold		$180,000
Gross Profit		$150,000
Operating expenses		
Salaries	$75,000	
Advertising	4,950	
Supplies	1,650	
Shipping	1,500	
Insurance	4,500	
Maintenance	5,100	
Other	2,550	
Total		$95,250
Other costs		$20,000
Total costs		$115,250
Net profit before taxes		$ 34,750
Taxes		$ 15,500
Net profit after taxes		$ 19,250

- Operating expenses totaled $95,250, including salaries, advertising, supplies, shipping, insurance, maintenance, and other expenses.

- Unassigned costs were $20,000.

- Net profit before taxes was $34,750, computed by deducting total costs from gross profit. The tax bill was $15,500, leaving a net profit after taxes of $19,250.

Over all, fiscal 2003 was pretty good for Donna; her personal salary was $43,000 and the store's after-tax profit was $19,250. A further analysis of Donna's Gift Shop's profit-and-loss statement appears in the budgeting section of this chapter.

Careers in RETAILING — Dorothy Lane Markets Improves Margins by Keeping Employees in the Loop

Dorothy Lane Market (**www.dorothylane.com**) is a three-unit supermarket chain in Ohio. One of its stores (in Washington Township) is surrounded by four Krogers and a Meijer as competitors. Every Monday morning, the store manager there, Ed Flohre, meets with his 220 employees. According to Flohre, "Everybody here knows our sales for the week, our gross margin, what our labor costs were, and how much we spent on supplies." When he first started these meetings, they lasted for an hour. Now, after 15 minutes, employees know what's important, and they leave the meeting knowing what products should be pushed.

Ed Flohre has a good understanding of his customers. He knows that even though 85 percent of his customers go to Kroger for Kroger's weekly specials, they continue to shop at Dorothy Lane Market for high-service, high-margin goods. He is also aware that only 5 to 8 percent of his shoppers cross-shop at Meijer.

Flohre spends just 3 hours of his 50-hour workweek behind his desk. The rest of the time, he's on the floor visiting every single department multiple times per day. This contributes to his awareness of the market and his helpfulness in employee problem solving.

Source: Matt Nannery, "Minding the Stores," *Chain Store Age* (September 2001), pp. 45–54; and "Dorothy Lane Store Locations," **www.dorothylane.com/locations.html** (September 10, 2002).

ASSET MANAGEMENT

Try out the Business Owner's Toolkit's downloadable Excel-based balance sheet template (toolkit.cch.com/tools/ balshe_m.asp).

Each retailer has assets to manage and liabilities to control. This section covers the balance sheet, the strategic profit model, and other ratios. A **balance sheet** itemizes a retailer's assets, liabilities, and net worth at a specific time—based on the principle that assets = liabilities + net worth. Table 12-2 has a balance sheet for Donna's Gift Shop.

Assets are any items a retailer owns with monetary value. Current assets are cash on hand (or in the bank) and items readily converted to cash, such as inventory on hand and accounts receivable (amounts owed to the firm). Fixed assets are property, buildings (a store, warehouse, and so on), fixtures, and equipment such as cash registers and trucks; these are used for a long period. The major fixed asset for many retailers is real-estate. Unlike current assets, which are recorded at cost, fixed assets are recorded at cost less accumulated depreciation. Thus, records may not reflect the true value of these assets. Many retailing analysts use the term **hidden assets** to describe depreciated assets, such as buildings and warehouses, that are noted on a retail balance sheet at low values relative to their actual worth.

Liabilities are financial obligations a retailer incurs in operating a business. Current liabilities are payroll expenses payable, taxes payable, accounts payable (amounts owed to suppliers), and short-term loans; these must be paid in the coming year. Fixed liabilities comprise mortgages and long-term loans; these are generally repaid over several years.

A retailer's **net worth** is computed as assets minus liabilities. It is also called owner's equity and represents the value of a business after deducting all financial obligations.

In operations management, the retailer's goal is to use its assets in the manner providing the best results possible. There are three basic ways to measure those results: net profit margin, asset turnover, and financial leverage. Each component is discussed next.

Net profit margin is a performance measure based on a retailer's net profit and net sales:

$$\text{Net profit margin} = \frac{\text{Net profit after taxes}}{\text{Net sales}}$$

At Donna's Gift Shop, fiscal year 2003 net profit margin was 5.83 percent—a very good percentage for a gift shop. To enhance its net profit margin, a retailer must either raise gross profit as a percentage of sales or reduce expenses as a percentage of sales.[2] It could lift gross profit by purchasing opportunistically, selling exclusive products, avoiding price competition through excellent service, and adding items with higher margins. It could reduce operating costs by stressing self-

TABLE 12-2	A Retail Balance Sheet for Donna's Gift Shop (as of August 31,2003)

Assets		Liabilities	
Current		Current	
Cash on hand	$ 19,950	Payroll expenses payable	$ 6,000
Inventory	36,150	Taxes payable	13,500
Accounts receivable	1,650	Accounts payable	32,100
Total	$ 57,750	Short-term loan	1,050
		Total	$ 52,650
Fixed (present value)			
Property	$187,500	Fixed	
Building	63,000	Mortgage	$ 97,500
Store fixtures	14,500	Long-term loan	6,750
Equipment	2,500	Total	$104,250
Total	$267,600		
		Total liabilities	$156,900
Total assets	$325,350		
		Net Worth	$168,450
		Liabilities + net worth	$325,350

service, lowering labor costs, refinancing the mortgage, cutting energy costs, and so on. The firm must be careful not to lessen customer service to the extent that sales and profit would decline.

Asset turnover is a performance measure based on a retailer's net sales and total assets:

$$\text{Asset turnover} = \frac{\text{Net sales}}{\text{Total assets}}$$

Donna's Gift Shop had a very low asset turnover, 1.0143, and it averaged $1.01 in sales per dollar of total assets. To improve the asset turnover ratio, a firm must generate increased sales from the same level of assets or keep the same sales with fewer assets. A firm might increase sales by having longer hours, accepting Web orders, training employees to sell additional products, or stocking better-known brands. None of these tactics requires expanding the asset base. Or a firm might maintain its sales on a lower asset base by moving to a smaller store, simplifying fixtures (or having suppliers install fixtures), keeping a smaller inventory, and negotiating for the property owner to pay part of the costs of a renovation.

By looking at the relationship between net profit margin and asset turnover, **return on assets (ROA)** can by computed:

$$\text{Return on assets} = \text{Net profit margin} \times \text{Asset turnover}$$

$$\text{Return on assets} = \frac{\text{Net profit after taxes}}{\text{Net sales}} \times \frac{\text{Net sales}}{\text{Total assets}}$$

$$= \frac{\text{Net profit after taxes}}{\text{Total assets}}$$

Donna's Gift Shop had an ROA of 5.9 percent ($.0583 \times 1.0143 = 0.059$). This return is below average for gift stores; the firm's good net profit margin does not adequately offset its low asset turnover.

Financial leverage is a performance measure based on the relationship between a retailer's total assets and net worth:

$$\text{Financial leverage} = \frac{\text{Total assets}}{\text{Net worth}}$$

Donna's Gift Shop's financial leverage ratio was 1.9314. Assets were just under twice the net worth, and total liabilities and net worth were almost equal. This ratio was slightly lower than the average for gift stores (a conservative group). The store is in no danger.

A retailer with a high financial leverage ratio has substantial debt, while a ratio of 1 means it has no debt—assets equal net worth. If the ratio is too high, there may be an excessive focus on cost-cutting and short-run sales so as to make interest payments, net profit margins may suffer, and a firm may be forced into bankruptcy if debts cannot be paid. When financial leverage is low, a retailer may be overly conservative—limiting its ability to renovate and expand existing stores and to enter new markets. Leverage is too low if owner's equity is relatively high; equity could be partly replaced by increasing short- and long-term loans and/or accounts payable. Some equity funds could be taken out of a business by the owner (stockholders, if a public firm).

THE STRATEGIC PROFIT MODEL

The relationship among net profit margin, asset turnover, and financial leverage is expressed by the **strategic profit model**, which reflects a performance measure known as **return on net worth (RONW)**. See Figure 12-1. The strategic profit model can be used in planning or controlling assets.

FIGURE 12-1
The Strategic Profit Model

| Net profit margin | × | Asset turnover | × | Financial leverage | = | Return on net worth |

| $\frac{\text{Net profit}}{\text{Net sales}}$ | × | $\frac{\text{Net sales}}{\text{Total assets}}$ | × | $\frac{\text{Total assets}}{\text{Net worth}}$ | = | $\frac{\text{Net profit}}{\text{Net worth}}$ |

At the *Fortune 500* Web site (www.pathfinder.com/fortune/fortune500/index.html), you can determine the return on net worth (stockholder's equity) for the retailers on this list.

Thus, a retailer could learn that the major cause of its poor return on net worth is weak asset turnover or financial leverage that is too low. A firm can raise its return on net worth by lifting the net profit margin, asset turnover, or financial leverage. Because these measures are multiplied to determine return on net worth, doubling *any* of them would double the return on net worth.

This is how the strategic profit model can be applied to Donna's Gift Shop:

$$\text{Return on net worth} = \frac{\text{Net profit after taxes}}{\text{Net sales}} \times \frac{\text{Net sales}}{\text{Total assets}} \times \frac{\text{Total assets}}{\text{Net worth}}$$

$$= \frac{\$19,250}{\$330,000} \times \frac{\$330,000}{\$325,350} \times \frac{\$325,350}{\$168,450}$$

$$= .0583 \quad \times 1.0143 \quad \times 1.9314$$

$$= .1142 \quad = 11.4\%$$

Over all, Donna's return on net worth was about average for gift stores.

Table 12-3 applies the strategic profit model to various retailers. It is best to make comparisons among firms within given retail categories. For example, the net profit margins of general

TABLE 12-3	Application of Strategic Profit Model to Selected Retailers (2001 Data)			
Retailer	Net Profit Margin	× Asset Turnover	× Financial Leverage	= Return on Net Worth
Apparel Retailers				
Limited Brands	0.38	1.98	1.72	1.29
TJX	0.26	2.98	2.68	2.08
Gap, Inc.	−0.64	1.69	2.52	−2.73
Consumer Electronics Retailers				
Best Buy	2.86	3.16	2.93	26.48
Circuit City	1.39	2.51	1.61	5.62
Drugstore Retailers				
Walgreen	3.54	3.00	1.70	18.05
CVS	0.26	2.58	1.89	1.27
Food Retailers				
Publix	3.67	3.55	1.59	20.72
Albertson's	1.43	2.34	2.70	9.03
Safeway	0.33	1.96	2.97	1.92
General Merchandise Retailers				
Wal-Mart	3.15	2.71	2.38	20.32
Target Corp.	3.56	1.79	3.07	19.56
Sears	2.10	0.99	7.24	15.05
Costco	1.71	3.56	2.07	12.60
Federated Department Stores	3.53	0.93	2.70	8.86
J.C. Penney	0.28	1.77	2.94	1.46
Home Improvement Retailers				
Home Depot	5.87	2.12	1.46	18.17
Lowe's	4.91	1.69	2.06	17.09
Office Supplies Retailers				
Staples	2.95	2.68	1.99	15.74
Office Depot	2.21	2.75	2.34	14.22

Source: Computed by the authors from data in company annual reports.

merchandise retailers have historically been higher than those of food retailers. Because financial performance differs from year to year, caution is advised in studying these data. Furthermore, the individual components of the strategic profit model must be reviewed, not just the return on net worth:

- Sears' return on net worth was not far behind that of Wal-Mart and Target. Yet, an analysis of the individual components of the strategic profit model reveals that Sears' good return on net worth was largely due to high financial leverage. Wal-Mart and Target both had higher net profit margins.
- Costco had a better return on net worth than Federated. Although Federated's net profit margin was double that of Costco, Costco's asset turnover was nearly four times greater.

OTHER KEY BUSINESS RATIOS

Other ratios can also measure retailer success or failure in reaching performance goals. Here are several key business ratios—besides those covered in the preceding discussion:

- *Quick ratio*—cash plus accounts receivable divided by total current liabilities, those due within one year. A ratio above 1 to 1 means the firm is liquid and can cover short-term debt.
- *Current ratio*—total current assets (cash, accounts receivable, inventories, and marketable securities) divided by total current liabilities. A ratio of 2 to 1 or more is good.
- *Collection period*—accounts receivable divided by net sales and then multiplied by 365. If most sales are on credit, a collection period one-third or more over normal terms (such as 40.0 for a store with 30-day credit terms) means slow-turning receivables.
- *Accounts payable to net sales*—accounts payable divided by annual net sales. This compares how a retailer pays suppliers relative to volume transacted. A figure above the industry average indicates that a firm relies on suppliers to finance operations.
- *Overall gross profit*—net sales minus the cost of goods sold and then divided by net sales. This companywide average includes markdowns, discounts, and shortages.[3]

The Census Bureau, online, provides more than a decade of gross profit (gross margin) percentage data by line of business (www.census. gov/svsd/retlann/view/ gmper.txt).

Table 12-4 presents key business ratios—including net profit margin, asset turnover, and return on net worth—for several retail categories. From this table, a hardware store owner would learn that the industry average is a marginal quick ratio of 0.8; liquid assets are slightly less than current liabilities. The current ratio of 3.2 is good, mostly due to the value of inventory on hand. The collection period of 16.4 days is moderate, considering the many small sales paid for in cash. Accounts payable of 4.5 percent of sales is good. The overall gross profit of 34.5 percent covers both operating costs and profit. The net profit margin of 2.1 percent is low for nonfood retailing. Asset turnover is conservative, 2.3, another indicator of the value of inventory. The return on net worth percentage of 6.5 is extremely low. In sum, hardware stores typically require high inventory and other investments and yield low to medium returns.

At our Web site (**www.prenhall.com/bermanevans**), we have links to each of the Yahoo! Finance sites related to retailers' financial performance.

FINANCIAL TRENDS IN RETAILING

Several trends relating to asset management merit discussion: the state of the U.S. economy; funding sources (including initial public offerings); mergers, consolidations, and spinoffs; bankruptcies and liquidations; and questionable accounting and financial reporting practices.

Entrepreneur's "Money" section (www. entrepreneurmag.com) has a lot of valuable advice for small businesses.

Many retailers have been adversely affected by the slow-growth U.S. economy in recent years. When the economy is weak, sales stagnate, cash flow problems may occur, heavy markdowns may be needed (which cut into profit margins), and consumers are more reluctant to purchase big-ticket items. Furthermore, public firms may find that their stock prices plummet, as happened in the United States in the early 2000s: "For much of the 1990s, retailers could mask operational issues and/or inefficiencies behind the blooming market. Today, there is nowhere to hide. Those companies that best manage working capital and cash flow and remain focused on their business

TABLE 12-4	Median Key Business Ratios for Selected Retailer Categories							
Line of Business	QR (times)	CR (times)	CP (days)	AP (%)	OGP (%)[a]	NPM (%)	AT (times)	RONW (%)
Auto & home supply stores	0.8	2.2	23.4	6.3	36.8	2.1	2.8	19.3
Car dealers (new and used)	0.2	1.2	4.4	0.7	12.4	1.1	4.2	16.4
Catalog and mail-order firms	0.7	1.9	13.7	6.2	41.3	1.8	3.0	13.9
Department stores	0.8	3.0	8.0	5.5	35.4	2.3	2.0	6.5
Direct-selling companies	0.6	2.0	10.6	4.6	44.2	2.3	2.9	14.0
Drug & proprietary stores	1.0	2.7	13.9	3.9	24.4	2.7	4.7	14.9
Eating places	0.5	1.0	2.9	3.2	57.5	3.5	2.7	16.2
Family clothing stores	0.9	4.0	5.8	3.9	38.0	5.1	2.3	9.7
Florists	0.8	1.8	17.9	3.3	54.9	2.5	3.1	8.9
Furniture stores	0.8	2.5	18.3	5.5	39.4	3.2	2.5	9.3
Gasoline service stations	0.6	1.3	6.9	3.4	16.6	0.8	4.6	7.2
Gift, novelty, & souvenir shops	0.6	2.8	3.3	3.3	44.5	3.8	2.5	11.1
Grocery stores	0.4	1.5	2.9	3.2	23.4	1.6	4.9	11.1
Hardware stores	0.8	3.2	16.4	4.5	34.5	2.1	2.3	6.5
Hobby, toy, & game shops	0.5	2.7	1.5	5.3	42.2	2.6	2.9	7.8
Jewelry stores	0.6	2.7	11.7	8.7	43.9	4.2	1.7	9.3
Lumber & other materials dealers	1.1	2.7	30.7	4.3	26.7	2.3	2.9	9.1
Men's & boys' clothing stores	0.6	3.1	8.8	5.1	40.9	4.5	2.4	10.1
Radio, TV, & electronics stores	0.6	2.0	13.1	5.1	38.4	4.0	3.1	14.7
Sewing & needlework stores	0.4	3.5	2.4	3.7	41.7	3.9	2.0	9.4
Shoe stores	0.4	2.8	3.1	6.1	39.1	4.2	2.5	10.8
Sporting-goods & bicycle stores	0.4	2.3	4.4	7.7	35.1	2.7	2.7	10.9
Variety stores	0.5	3.1	3.3	4.6	34.6	2.3	2.9	8.9
Women's clothing stores	0.7	3.3	6.2	4.0	39.5	4.6	2.9	12.0

QR = Quick ratio   OGP = Overall gross profit
CR = Current ratio   NPM = Net profit margin after taxes
CP = Collection period   AT = Asset turnover
AP = Accounts payable to net sales   RONW = Return on net worth

[a] Gross profit is reported as means rather than medians and represents net figures, which take into account all deductions (such as markdowns, discounts, and shortages).

Source: Industry Norms and Key Business Ratios (New York: Dun & Bradstreet, 2000–01), pp. 135–152. Reprinted by permission.

are well-positioned to withstand current market conditions. Others, unfortunately, will not survive.[4] Consider these recent occurrences:

- Wal-Mart.com's chief executive resigned and several workers were eliminated because sales were disappointing and high shipping costs caused the online unit to be unprofitable. In general, "the harsh economy caused several retailers to take a harder look at their Internet commerce operations, which were expensive to launch and expensive to maintain."

- To sell more new cars, U.S. firms offered interest-free loans and other financial incentives that averaged nearly $2,500 per vehicle.

- A number of retailers "really kept a very tight reign on inventory. Why throw a bunch of inventory in the stores and have to mark it down?"

- In 2002, the number of retail workers laid off nationwide was the highest amount in two decades.

- "Where people were upgrading before, oblivious to cost, they are now trying to work deals and pinch pennies like you've never seen. And these are people who have the money."[5]

Three sources of funding are proving popular with retailers. First, because interest rates have remained quite low, many companies have refinanced their mortgages—which can dramatically decrease their monthly interest payments. Over all, refinancing is saving retailers billions of dollars yearly.[6]

Second, shopping center developers often use a retail-estate investment trust (REIT) to fund construction. With this strategy, investors buy shares in an REIT as they would a stock. Investors like REITs because real-estate has historically been a good investment: "Simply stated, a REIT is a company dedicated to owning and, in most cases, operating income-producing real-estate, such as shopping centers. Some REITs also are engaged in financing real-estate. Most importantly, to be a REIT, a firm is legally required to pay virtually all of its taxable income (90 percent) to its shareholders every year."[7]

Third, a funding source that has gained more retailing acceptance over the past decade is the initial public offering (IPO), whereby a firm raises money by selling stock. An IPO is typically used to fund expansion. What do investors look for in an IPO? "They want a company to have a history of profitability. They want to see revenue growth and strong backing. And they want a company to match up well against companies already trading." Among the retailers engaging in IPOs over the last few years are Petco, Kirkland's (home decorating products), Overstock.com, and Galyan's Trading. Why? As 99 Cents Only Stores' president remarked: "Being public pushed us to grow faster. Furthermore, having your company traded at a stock exchange provides instant credibility with suppliers and manufacturers. Plus, the stock is a powerful motivational tool for employees in stock-option programs."[8]

Mergers and consolidations represent a way for strong retailers to add to their asset base without building new facilities or waiting for new business units to turn a profit. They also present a way for weak retailers to receive financial transfusions. For example, in recent years, Right Start acquired the FAO Schwarz and Zany Brainy toy chains (and adopted the corporate name of FAO, Inc. because of its familiarity to consumers and investors), Tiffany acquired Little Switzerland, 1-800-flowers.com bought Popcorn Factory, and Camelot Music purchased The Wall. All these deals were driven by the weakness of the acquired firms. Typically mergers and consolidations lead to some stores being shut, particularly those with trading-area overlap, and cutbacks among management personnel.

The leveraged buyout (LBO), in which a retail ownership change is mostly financed by loans from banks, investors, and others, has had a big effect on retail budgeting and cash flow. At times, because debts incurred with LBOs can be high, some well-known retailers have had to focus more on paying interest on their debts than on investing in their businesses, run sales to generate enough cash to cover operating costs and buy new merchandise, and sell store units to pay off debt. Among the major retailers whose operations in the 1990s were affected by LBOs were Macy's, Ralphs, Stop & Shop, and Montgomery Ward. In their weakened state, some LBO

RETAILING
Around the World
Royal Ahold is Taking Hold in the United States

When a leading trade magazine honored the Netherlands' Koninklijke Ahold—known as Royal Ahold (**www.ahold.com**) in English—as the U.S. Mass Retailer of the Year in 2002, many of its U.S. consumers had no idea that the firm was the fifth largest grocery chain in the United States. But if you mention some of Royal Ahold's U.S. chains—Giant Food in Washington, D.C., Stop & Shop in the Northeast, Tops in Ohio, Bruno's in Alabama, and Bi-Lo in the Southeast, you are sure to get instant recognition. Royal Ahold, with U.S. sales of $35.3 billion in 2002, has stores that serve 95 percent of the U.S. population.

According to Ahold's chief executive, "The next step is to buy smaller regional businesses in areas where we are underrepresented and to buy specialist stores." Another important part of Ahold's strategy is to keep the local name of each supermarket acquisition. However, from a financial perspective, Royal Ahold looks for synergies—as well as potential cost savings—due to its combined market power in the United States and around the world. Some retail analysts estimate that the cost savings from the Alliant Bruno acquisition alone totaled $35 million in the first full year of combined operations and increased to $50 million as of the third year.

Sources: Mike Duff, "Royal Ahold Acquires Alliant, Bruno's," *DSN Retailing Today* (September 17, 2001), pp. 7, 68; and Leonard Wiener, "A Helping of Dutch Apple Pie, Made in the United States," *U.S. News & World Report* (February 11, 2002), p. 46.

retailers are acquired by others (such as Macy's acquisition by Federated Department Stores). Safeway, also involved in an LBO, seems to have done well by cutting costs, reducing prices, and improving customer service. The most recent LBO involving a large retailer was the 2002 deal for Burger King.

Some successful retailers use spinoffs to generate more money or to sell a division that no longer meets expectations. Limited Brands spun off the healthy Limited Too and raised funds that were reinvested in its core businesses. Circuit City spun off its CarMax auto retail unit so it could return to its roots and concentrate on consumer electronics: "The split would permit management of the two businesses to better focus on the operational and financial objectives of their respective businesses without the constraints imposed by being affiliates within the same corporate group."[9]

When they want to continue in business, weak retailers file Chapter 11. If they want to liquidate, they file Chapter 7 (www.abiworld.org/media/chapters.html).

To safeguard themselves against mounting debts, as well to continue in business, faltering retailers may seek bankruptcy protection under Chapter 11 of the Federal Bankruptcy Code. With this protection, retailers can renegotiate bills, get out of leases, and work with creditors to plan for the future. Declaring bankruptcy has major ramifications: "While some believe that filing for bankruptcy results in the loss of key executives, disruptions in supply, and demoralization on those who stay, others say it fends off creditors and lets firms pay off debt and survive what may be a temporary upheaval. Executives who are not in favor of filing also cite the cost of legal financial advisory fees of bankruptcy protection."[10]

In 2002, Kmart became the largest retail firm in U.S. history to file for bankruptcy:

Kmart, long criticized for its lack of direction, must finally take a hard look at which categories it should be selling, how it should improve replenishment, what its pricing strategy should be, and how it can reverse an image of sub-par customer service and sloppy stores. The problem is where to start. According to a high-level merchandising executive who left before the bankruptcy, Kmart should start in the stores: "The stores look bad, there aren't enough salespeople, and out-of-stocks are out of control. All these things affect one another. The out-of-stocks often aren't because the product didn't get to the stores. Half the time, it's because the store manager is forced to keep a payroll so low that the staff is insufficient to get products out onto the floor. Kmart has to dedicate the staff to keeping stores clean and putting out merchandise. Kmart has good brands and good products, and when it's done right, the presentation is head and shoulders above Wal-Mart."[11]

See Figure 12-2.

Not all bankruptcies end up with rejuvenated retailers. Many end up in liquidations, where the firms ultimately go out of business. A short time ago, this happened with Montgomery Ward, Ames Department Stores, McCrory, National Record Mart, and Service Merchandise. When a

FIGURE 12-2
Rebuilding Kmart

Kmart is working very hard to turn the corner, as its CEO recently noted at the firm's Web site (**www.kmart.com**): "I want to again emphasize the focused commitment of this management team to work with our employees, vendors, lenders, and other stakeholders to complete our financial and operational restructuring and emerge from Chapter 11 as soon as possible. We are pursuing opportunities to increase store traffic and sales. Recent initiatives include the successful introduction of the Joe Boxer line of fashion and home furnishings for the back-to-school season and the development of new marketing efforts and exclusive brands designed to appeal to Hispanic customers. We have also moved aggressively to ensure that our cost structure is properly aligned with our revenue base."

Reprinted by permission of Kmart.

retailer goes out of business, it is painful for all parties: the owner/stockholders, employees, creditors, landlords (who then have vacant store sites), and customers.

As with several other sectors of business, over the last few years, some retailers have been heavily criticized for questionable accounting and financial practices. Here are two examples:

- Cal Turner Jr., Dollar General's chairman and chief executive, told analysts and investors, "This ship faltered while I was at the helm, but it has been righted. We are on course and, in the end, we have all learned a valuable lesson." According to the *Wall Street Journal*, "In slicing its net income by $199 million over three years due to accounting restatements and settlement of shareholder lawsuits, the discount retailer also took some aggressive and unusual steps. Its goal is to avoid repeating the accounting problems, which concerned leases at 400 stores and other routine expenses. Among other things, stock options for managers will no longer be tied to the company's reaching annual earnings goals. And Mr. Turner will no longer be involved in preparing the company's financial results. Even so, some investors remain wary of the company's management because it refuses to discuss how the accounting errors were made and who was responsible, citing an ongoing investigation by the Securities and Exchange Commission."[12]

- In 2002, three former executives and one current executive of Rite Aid were indicted for fraud, conspiracy, and lying to shareholders: "According to the Securities and Exchange Commission, the executives' creative accounting resulted in a $1.6 billion downward revision of earnings for nine consecutive quarters from 1997 to 1999." Furthermore, the firm's former president and chief operating officer "pleaded guilty to a felony charge of withholding information from the drugstore chain's internal investigators. He agreed to help federal prosecutors build a securities-fraud case against his former colleagues. In separate news, an investigation into Rite Aid's financial reporting and accounting practices has ended. The company will pay no fine under the settlement."[13]

To bolster public confidence and stockholder equity, retailers need to be as "transparent" as possible in their accounting and financial reporting practices:

In the aftermath of the Enron scandal, retailers are being proactive in sharing their views on disclosure and accurate financial reporting with investors. Wal-Mart, in its annual report, noted that, "The financial results reported here will provide you, the stakeholders, with a review of our company, and will provide a detailed discussion about those financial matters that are significant to your company. Although it is not the most exciting reading, our team has worked hard to make these reports comprehensive, yet simple, and I would encourage you to review them." The increased disclosure now practiced by retailers and the relatively straightforward accounting involved in a retail business have made the industry attractive to investors looking for stability in turbulent times. Yet, retailers will almost certainly be forced to live with new and unknown finance-related requirements from elected officials and government regulators who don't want another Enron.[14]

Ethics in RETAILING — A Troubled Kmart Restates Its Earnings

Kmart's (**www.kmart.com**) 2002 announcement that it had to restate its 2001 earnings drew attention to the retailer's use of vendor allowances. After recomputing earnings, Kmart said that its losses for fiscal 2001 would be "significantly higher" than its $244 million loss in 2000.

Vendor allowances constitute supplier payments to Kmart for promotional programs, slotting fees for receiving shelf space, trade allowances for meeting a pre-arranged sales goal, compliance payments that compensate retailers for late delivery of merchandise, and so on. As a spokesperson for the National Association of Credit Management notes, "Many retailers make more money from having a complicated compliance system than they do from the product lines." Although Kmart was paid the allowances up front, it was still liable to return refunds or rebates to its suppliers if sales fell short of expectations. Similarly, Rite Aid had to repay some suppliers and restate earnings for three years after the Securities and Exchange Commission questioned its charges to suppliers for large amounts of damaged goods.

In commenting about retailers' requests for advances and allowances, a financial analyst commented, "It's the Wild West. It is the least scrutinized area of accounting, totally without rhyme or reason or rule."

Source: Constance L. Hays, "Retailer Deals for Cash Back from Suppliers Draw Attention," *New York Times on the Web* (May 11, 2002).

BUDGETING

Why does a new business need a formal budget? Type "Budget Basics" at this site (www. entrepreneurmag.com).

Budgeting outlines a retailer's planned expenditures for a given time based on expected performance. Costs are linked to satisfying target market, employee, and management goals. What should personnel costs be to attain a certain level of customer service? What compensation amount will motivate salespeople? What operating expenses will generate intended revenues and reach profit goals?

There are several benefits from a retailer's meticulously preparing a budget:

- Expenditures are clearly related to expected performance, and costs can be adjusted as goals are revised. This enhances productivity.
- Resources are allocated to the right departments, product categories, and so on.
- Spending for various departments, product categories, and so on is coordinated.
- Because planning is structured and integrated, the goal of efficiency is prominent.
- Cost standards are set, such as advertising equals 5 percent of sales.
- A firm prepares for the future rather than reacts to it.
- Expenditures are monitored during a budget cycle. If a firm allots $50,000 to buy new merchandise, and it has spent $33,000 halfway through a cycle, it has $17,000 remaining.
- A firm can analyze planned budgets versus actual budgets.
- Costs and performance can be compared with industry averages.

A retailer should be aware of the effort in the budgeting process, recognize that forecasts may not be fully accurate (due to unexpected demand, competitors' tactics, and so forth), and modify plans as needed. It should not be too conservative (or inflexible) or simply add a percentage to each expense category to arrive at the next budget, such as increasing spending by 3 percent across the board based on anticipated sales growth of 3 percent. The budgeting process is shown in Figure 12-3 and described next.

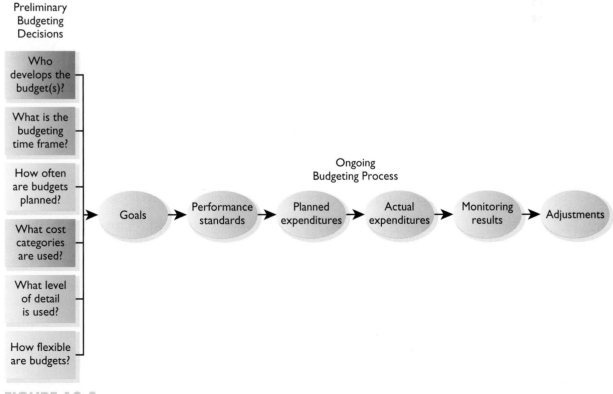

FIGURE 12-3
The Retail Budgeting Process

PRELIMINARY BUDGETING DECISIONS

There are six preliminary decisions.

First, budgeting authority is specified. In top-down budgeting, senior executives make centralized financial decisions and communicate them down the line to succeeding levels of managers. In bottom-up budgeting, lower-level executives develop departmental budget requests; these requests are assembled, and a company budget is designed. Bottom-up budgeting includes varied perspectives, holds managers more accountable, and enhances employee morale. Many firms combine aspects of the two approaches.

Second, the time frame is defined. Most firms have budgets with yearly, quarterly, and monthly components. Annual spending is planned, while costs and performance are regularly reviewed. This responds to seasonal or other fluctuations. Sometimes, the time frame is longer than a year or shorter than a month. When a firm opens new stores over a 5-year period, it sets construction costs for the entire period. When a supermarket orders perishables, it has weekly budgets for each item.

Third, budgeting frequency is determined. Though many retailers review budgets on an ongoing basis, most companies plan them yearly. In some firms, several months may be set aside each year for the budgeting process; this lets all participants have time to gather data and facilitates taking the budgets through several drafts.

Fourth, cost categories are established:

- *Capital expenditures* are long-term investments in land, buildings, fixtures, and equipment. *Operating expenditures* are the short-term expenses of running a business.
- *Fixed costs*, such as store security, remain constant for the budget period regardless of the retailer's performance. *Variable costs*, such as sales commissions, are based on performance. If performance is good, these expenses often rise.
- *Direct costs* are incurred by specific departments, product categories, and so on, such as the earnings of department-based salespeople. *Indirect costs*, such as centralized cashiers, are shared by multiple departments, product categories, and so on.
- *Natural account expenses* are reported by the names of the costs, such as salaries, and not assigned by purpose. *Functional account expenses* are classified on the basis of the purpose or activity for which expenditures are made, such as cashier salaries.

Fifth, the level of detail is set. Should spending be assigned by department (produce), product category (fresh fruit), product subcategory (apples), or product item (McIntosh apples)? With a very detailed budget, every expense subcategory must be adequately covered.

Sixth, budget flexibility is prescribed. A budget should be strict enough to guide planned spending and link costs to goals. Yet, a budget that is too inflexible may not let a retailer adapt to changing market conditions, capitalize on new opportunities, or modify a poor strategy (if further spending is needed to improve matters). Budget flexibility is often expressed in quantitative terms, such as allowing a buyer to increase a quarterly budget by a certain maximum percentage if demand is higher than anticipated.

ONGOING BUDGETING PROCESS

After making preliminary budgeting decisions, the retailer engages in the ongoing budgeting process shown in Figure 12-3:

- Goals are set based on customer, employee, and management needs.
- Performance standards are specified, including customer service levels, the compensation needed to motivate employees, and the sales and profits needed to satisfy management. Typically, the budget is related to a sales forecast, which projects revenues for the next period. Forecasts are usually broken down by department or product category.
- Expenditures are planned in terms of performance goals. In **zero-based budgeting**, a firm starts each new budget from scratch and outlines the expenditures needed to reach that period's goals. All costs are justified each time a budget is done. With **incremental budgeting**, a firm uses current and past budgets as guides and adds to or subtracts from them to

arrive at the coming period's expenditures. Most retailers use incremental budgeting because it is easier, less time-consuming, and not as risky.

- Actual expenditures are made. The retailer pays rent and employee salaries, buys merchandise, places ads, and so on.

- Results are monitored: (1) Actual expenditures are compared with planned spending for each expense category, and reasons for any deviations are reviewed. (2) The firm learns if performance standards have been met and tries to explain deviations.

- The budget is adjusted. Revisions are major or minor, depending on how closely a firm has come to reaching its goals. The funds allotted to some expense categories may be reduced, while greater funds may be provided to other categories.

Table 12-5 compares budgeted and actual revenues, expenses, and profits for Donna's Gift Shop during fiscal 2003. The actual data come from Table 12-1. The variance figures compare expected and actual results for each profit-and-loss item. Variances are positive if performance is better than expected and negative if it is worse.

As Table 12-5 indicates, in *dollar terms*, net profit after taxes was $7,250 higher than budgeted. Sales were $30,000 higher than expected; thus, the cost of goods sold was $15,000 higher. Actual operating expenses were $750 lower than expected, while other costs were $2,000 higher. Table 12-5 also shows results in *percentage terms*. This lets a firm evaluate budgeted versus actual performance on a percent-of-sales basis. In Donna's case, actual net profit after taxes was 5.83 percent of sales—better than planned. The higher net profit was mostly due to the actual operating costs percentage being lower than planned.

A firm must think about **cash flow**, which relates the amount and timing of revenues received to the amount and timing of expenditures for a specific time. In cash flow management, the usual intention is to make sure revenues are received before expenditures are made.[15]

Learn more about cash flow management by typing "Cash Flow" at this site (www. entrepreneurmag.com).

TABLE 12-5	Donna's Gift Shop, Fiscal 2003 Budgeted Versus Actual Profit-and-Loss Statement (in Dollars and Percent)					
	BUDGETED		ACTUAL		VARIANCE[a]	
	Dollars	Percent	Dollars	Percent	Dollars	Percent
Net sales	$300,000	100.000	$330,000	100.00	+$30,000	—
Cost of good sold	$165,000	55.00	$180,000	54.55	−$15,000	+0.45
Gross profit	$135,000	45.00	$150,000	45.45	+$15,000	+0.45
Operating expenses:						
Salaries	$ 75,000	25.00	$ 75,000	22.73	—	+2.27
Advertising	5,250	1.75	4,950	1.50	+$ 300	+0.25
Supplies	1,800	0.60	1,650	0.50	+$ 150	+0.10
Shipping	1,350	0.45	1,500	0.45	−$ 150	—
Insurance	4,500	1.50	4,500	1.36	—	+0.14
Maintenance	5,100	1.70	5,100	1.55	—	+0.15
Other	3,000	1.00	2,550	0.77	+$ 450	+0.23
Total	$ 96,000	32.00	$ 95,250	28.86	+$ 750	+3.14
Other costs	$ 18,000	6.00	$ 20,000	6.06	−$ 2,000	−0.06
Total costs	$114,000	38.00	$115,250	34.92	−$ 1,250	+3.08
Net profit before taxes	$21,000	7.00	$ 34,750	10.53	+$13,750	+3.53
Taxes	$9,000	3.00	$ 15,500	4.70	−$ 6,500	−1.70
Net profit after taxes	$12,000	4.00	$ 19,250	5.83	+$ 7,250	+1.83

There are small rounding errors.

[a] Variance is a positive number if actual sales or profits are higher than expected or actual expenses are lower than expected. Variance is a negative number if actual sales or profits are lower than expected or actual expenses are higher than expected.

TABLE 12-6	The Effects of Cash Flow

A.

A retailer has rather consistent sales throughout the year. Therefore, the cash flow in any given month is positive. This means no short-term loans are needed, and the owner can withdraw funds from the firm if she so desires:

Linda's Luncheonette, Cash Flow for January

Cash inflow:		
Net sales		$11,000
Cash outflow:		
Cost of goods sold	$2,500	
Operating expenses	3,500	
Other costs	2,000	
Total		$ 8,000
Positive cash flow		$ 3,000

B.

A retailer has highly seasonal sales that peak in December. Yet, to have a good assortment of merchandise on hand during December, it must order merchandise in September and October and pay for it in November. As a result, it has a negative cash flow in November that must be financed by a short-term loan. All debts are paid off in January, after the peak selling season is completed:

Dave's Party Favors, Cash Flow for November

Cash inflow:		
Net sales		$14,000
Cash outflow:		
Cost of goods sold	$12,500	
Operating expenses	3,000	
Other costs	2,100	
Total		$17,600
Net cash flow		−$ 3,600
Short-term loan (to be paid off in January)		$ 3,600

Otherwise, short-term loans may be needed or profits may be tied up in inventory and other expenses. For seasonal retailers, this may be unavoidable. Underestimating costs and overestimating revenues, both of which affect cash flow, are leading causes of new business failures. Table 12-6 has cash flow examples.

RESOURCE ALLOCATION

To easily study the financial operating performance of publicly owned retailers, go to EDGAR Online (www.edgar-online.com), do a "Quick Search" with a company name, scroll down to the 10K part of the screen, and click "Glimpse."

In allotting financial resources, both the magnitude of various costs and productivity should be examined. Each has significance for asset management and budgeting.

THE MAGNITUDE OF VARIOUS COSTS

As noted before, spending can be divided into two categories. **Capital expenditures** are long-term investments in fixed assets. **Operating expenditures** are short-term selling and administrative costs in running a business. It is vital to have a sense of the magnitude of various capital and operating costs.

In 2002, these were the average capital expenditures (for the basic building shell; heating, ventilation, and air-conditioning; lighting; flooring; fixtures; ceilings; interior and exterior signage; and roofing) for erecting a single store for a range of retailers: department store—$7.2 million;

Technology in RETAILING — eBay's Winning Approach: High Profits with Very Low Overhead

eBay (**www.ebay.com**) is one of the few major Web-based marketplaces that have survived the dot-com washout. A key factor behind the success of eBay is that its fees are based on a transaction-based business model. According to an eBay spokesperson, "As far as expenses go, we have no real cost of goods, we have no inventory or warehouses, no sales force or commissions." These low costs contribute to eBay's 80 percent profit margin.

Although eBay has a 99 percent recognition rate among consumers and attracts 40 million regular users, it has not spent a single penny on traditional forms of advertising. Instead, it favors partnering with other dot-com sites, such as ESPN

(**www.espn.go.com**) and Sony (**www.sony.com**). For example, if eBay has Spider-man on its Web page, Sony is asked to provide items for sale on eBay.

The Web retailer also uses direct marketing to alert thousands of buyers and sellers about where they can buy or sell their goods and services. eBay carefully targets its direct marketing. A buyer who did not win an auction may also be given a link to a new auction for the same or comparable product.

Source: "eBay Profits with Little Overhead, Executive Tells Colonie, N.Y., Audience," *Knight Ridder/Tribune Business News* (May 15, 2002).

full-line discount store—$4.3 million; supermarket—$3.1 million; home center—$1.5 million; apparel specialty store—$850,000; and drugstore—$750,000.[16] Thus, a typical home center chain must be prepared to invest $1.5 million to build each new outlet (which averaged 37,000 square feet industrywide in 2002), not including land and merchandise costs; the total could be higher if a bigger store is built.

Remodeling can also be expensive. It is prompted by competitive pressures, mergers and acquisitions, consumer trends, the requirement of complying with the Americans with Disabilities Act, environmental concerns, and other factors.

To reduce their investments, some retailers insist that real-estate developers help pay for building, renovating, and fixturing costs. These demands by retail tenants reflect some areas' oversaturation, the amount of retail space available due to the liquidation of some retailers (as well as mergers), and the interest of developers in gaining retailers that generate consumer traffic (such as category killers).

Operating expenses, usually expressed as a percentage of sales, range from 20 percent or so in supermarkets to over 40 percent in some specialty stores. To succeed, these costs must be in line with competitors'. May Department Stores has an edge over many rivals due to lower SGA (selling, general, and administrative expenses as a percentage of sales): May, 21 percent; Saks, 23 percent; Dillard's, 27 percent; Nordstrom, 31 percent; and Federated Department Stores, 31 percent.[17]

Resource allocation must also take into account **opportunity costs**—the possible benefits a retailer forgoes if it invests in one opportunity rather than another. If a supermarket chain renovates 10 existing stores at a total cost of $3.1 million, it cannot open a new outlet requiring a $3.1 million investment (excluding land and merchandise). Financial resources are finite, so firms often face either/or decisions.

PRODUCTIVITY

Look at the various ways in which retailers can improve their financial performance (www. toolkit.cch.com/text/ P06_0100.asp).

Due to erratic sales, mixed economic growth, high labor costs, intense competition, and other factors, many retailers place great priority on improving **productivity**, the efficiency with which a retail strategy is carried out. Productivity can be described in terms of costs as a percentage of sales, the time it takes a cashier to complete a transaction, profit margins, sales per square foot, inventory turnover, and so forth. The key question is: How can sales and profit goals be reached while keeping control over costs?

Because different retail strategy mixes have distinct resource needs as to store location, fixtures, personnel, and other elements, productivity must be based on norms for each type of strategy mix (like department stores versus full-line discount stores). Sales growth should also be measured on the basis of comparable seasons, using the same stores. Otherwise, the data will be affected by seasonality and/or the increased square footage of stores.

There are two ways to enhance productivity: (1) A firm can improve employee performance, sales per foot of space, and other factors by upgrading training programs, increasing advertising, and so forth. (2) It can reduce costs by automating, having suppliers do certain tasks, and so forth. A retailer could use a small core of full-time workers during nonpeak times, supplemented with part-timers in peak periods.

Productivity must not be measured from a cost-cutting perspective alone. This may undermine customer loyalty. One of the more complex dilemmas for store retailers that are also online is how to handle customer returns. To control costs, some of them have decided not to allow online purchases to be returned at their stores. This policy has gotten a lot of customers upset.

These are two strategies that retailers have used to raise productivity:

- Department stores such as Sears are paying more attention to space productivity. Sears has cleared hundreds of thousands of square feet of space by removing some furniture departments, converting space that was previously used by its affiliated home improvement contractors to retail use, and better managing and displaying its merchandise categories.

- Tuesday Morning, a chain selling quality closeouts, shuts its stores for all of January and July—and parts of February, April, and August. Operating costs are low because the stores save on labor expenses (part-time workers are used extensively), utilities, and insurance. The firm reduces its costs by locating in low-rent sites. Tuesday Morning operates destination stores that are sought out by loyal customers.

Tuesday Morning has a *very* unique philosophy about stores dates (www.tuesdaymorning. com/StoreHours.htm).

According to retailing analysts, "It turns out that what worked for manufacturers worked even better for retailers. In the second half of the 1990s, retail productivity skyrocketed. Almost 100 percent of that growth came from closing old stores and opening more efficient ones with the latest equipment at the checkout counter and in the storeroom."[18]

Summary

1. *To define operations management.* Operations management involves efficiently and effectively implementing the tasks and policies to satisfy the retailer's customers, employees, and management. This chapter covered the financial aspects of operations management. Operational dimensions are studied in Chapter 13.

2. *To discuss profit planning.* The profit-and-loss (income) statement summarizes a retailer's revenues and expenses over a specific time, typically on a monthly, quarterly, and/or yearly basis. It consists of these major components: net sales, cost of goods sold, gross profit (margin), operating expenses, and net profit after taxes.

3. *To describe asset management, including the strategic profit model, other key business ratios, and financial trends in retailing.* Each retailer has assets and liabilities to manage. A balance sheet shows assets, liabilities, and net worth at a given time. Assets are items with a monetary value owned by a retailer; some appreciate and may have a hidden value. Liabilities are financial obligations. The retailer's net worth, also called owner's equity, is computed as assets minus liabilities.

Asset management may be measured by reviewing the net profit margin, asset turnover, and financial leverage. Net profit margin equals net profit divided by net sales. Asset turnover equals net sales divided by total assets. By multiplying the net profit margin by asset turnover, a retailer can find its return on assets—which is based on net sales, net profit, and total

assets. Financial leverage equals total assets divided by net worth. The strategic profit model incorporates asset turnover, profit margin, and financial leverage to yield the return on net worth. It allows a retailer to better plan and control its asset management.

Other key ratios for retailers are the quick ratio, current ratio, collection period, accounts payable to net sales, and overall gross profit (in percent).

Current financial trends involve the state of the economy; funding sources; mergers, consolidations, and spinoffs; bankruptcies and liquidation; and questionable accounting and financial reporting practices.

4. *To look at retail budgeting.* Budgeting outlines a retailer's planned expenditures for a given time based on expected performance; costs are linked to goals.

There are six preliminary decisions: (1) Responsibility is defined by top-down and/or bottom-up methods. (2) The time frame is specified. (3) Budgeting frequency is set. (4) Cost categories are established. (5) The level of detail is ascertained. (6) Budgeting flexibility is determined.

The ongoing budgeting process then proceeds: goals, performance standards, planned spending, actual expenditures, monitoring results, and adjustments. With zero-based budgeting, each budget starts from scratch; with incremental budgeting, current and past budgets are guides. The budgeted versus actual profit-

and-loss statement and the percentage profit-and-loss statement are vital tools. In all budgeting decisions, cash flow, which relates the amount and timing of revenues received with the amount and timing of expenditures made, must be considered.

5. *To examine resource allocation.* Both the magnitude of costs and productivity need to be examined. Costs can be divided into capital and operating categories; both must be regularly reviewed. Opportunity costs mean forgoing possible benefits if a retailer invests in one opportunity rather than another. Productivity is the efficiency with which a retail strategy is carried out; the goal is to maximize sales and profits while keeping costs in check.

Key Terms

operations management (p. 295)

profit-and-loss (income) statement (p. 295)

net sales (p. 295)

costs of goods sold (p. 295)

gross profit (margin) (p. 295)

operating expenses (p.295)

taxes (p. 295)

net profit after taxes (p. 295)

balance sheet (p. 297)

assets (p. 297)

hidden assets (p. 297)

liabilities (p. 297)

net worth (p. 297)

net profit margin (p. 297)

asset turnover (p. 298)

return on assets (ROA) (p. 298)

financial leverage (p. 298)

strategic profit model (p. 298)

return on net worth (RONW) (p. 298)

budgeting (p. 305)

zero-based budgeting (p. 306)

incremental budgeting (p. 306)

cash flow (p. 307)

capital expenditures (p. 308)

operating expenditures (p. 308)

opportunity costs (p. 309)

productivity (p. 309)

Questions for Discussion

1. Describe the relationship of assets, liabilities, and net worth for a retailer. How is a balance sheet useful in examining these items?

2. A retailer has net sales of $825,000, net profit of $125,000, total assets of $600,000, and a net worth of $225,000.
   a. Calculate net profit margin, asset turnover, and return on assets.
   b. Compute financial leverage and return on net worth.
   c. Evaluate the financial performance of this retailer.

3. How can a supermarket increase its asset turnover?

4. Is too low a financial leverage ratio good or bad? Why?

5. Differentiate between an IPO and LBO.

6. Present five recommendations for retailers to improve their accounting and financial reporting practices with regard to disclosure ("transparency") of all relevant information to stockholders and others.

7. What is zero-based budgeting? Why do most retailers utilize incremental budgeting, despite its limitations?

8. What is the value of a percentage profit-and-loss statement?

9. How could a seasonal retailer improve its cash flow during periods when it must buy goods for future selling periods?

10. Distinguish between capital spending and operating expenditures. Why is this distinction important to retailers?

11. What factors should retailers consider when assessing opportunity costs?

12. How can these retailers improve their productivity?
    a. Lawn care service.
    b. Laundromat.
    c. Deli.
    d. Discount apparel store.

Note: At our Web site (**www.prenhall.com/bermanevans**), there are several math problems related to the material in this chapter so that you may review these concepts.

Web-Based Exercise

Visit the Web site of QuickBooks (**www.quickbooks.com/products/pro**) and take a "QuickTour." What are benefits of a product such as this for a small retailer?

Note: Stop by our Web site (**www.prenhall.com/bermanevans**) to experience a number of highly interactive, appealing Web exercises

based on actual company demonstrations and sample materials related to retailing.

Chapter Endnotes

1. Various company sources.

2. See Douglas J. Tigert, Lawrence Ring, and Colson Hillier, "The Profit Wedge: How Five Measure Up," *Chain Store Age* (May 1998), pp. 60–68; and Richard Skolnick, "Discount Retail Profitability: A Harbinger for E-Commerce?" *Journal of Business Strategy*, Vol. 18 (Fall 2001), pp. 149–158.

3. *Industry Norms and Key Business Ratios* (New York: Dun & Bradstreet, 2001–01).

4. "Managing Working Capital," *Chain Store Age* (August 2001), p. 26A.

5. Jon Swartz, "Bloomingdale's Joins Big Retailers in Online Retreat," *USA Today* (November 30, 2001), p. B1; Carol Sliwa, "Retailers Mull Pulling Plug on E-Commerce," *Computerworld* (February 18, 2002), p. 14; David Welch, "Can Car Dealers Keep the Profits Rolling?" *Business Week* (January 14, 2002), p. 37; Jenny Strasburg, "Pressure Is On for Retailers," *San Francisco Chronicle* (September 15, 2002), p. G1; "Retail Layoffs Worst in Decades, Firm Says," *Houston Chronicle* (April 5, 2002), p. 4; "Inconspicuous Consumption," *Chain Store Age* (February 2002), pp. 60–62; and Leslie Earnest, Marc Ballon, and Abigail Goldman, "Big Spenders Are Reluctant to Shop Through the Drop," *Wall Street Journal* (July 23, 2002), p. A1.

6. Charlyne H. McWilliams, "Retail Growth Spurt," *Mortgage Banking* (May 2002), pp. 24–29.

7. "The REIT Story," **www.nareit.com/aboutreits/thestorytext. cfm** (February 7, 2003).

8. Ken Clark, "Going Public: Down But Not Out," *Chain Store Age* (January 2002), pp. 55–56.

9. Laura Heller, "Circuit City Restructures, Spins off CarMax Unit," *DSN Retailing Today* (March 11, 2002), p. 3.

10. Michael Hartnett, "Value of Chapter 11 Protections for Retailers Sparks Sharp Debate," *Stores* (April 1999), p. 92.

11. Matt Nannery, "Picking Up the Pieces," *Chain Store Age* (March 2002), pp. 54–62.

12. Chard Terhune and Joann S. Lublin, "Unlike Others, Dollar General Issues a Mea Culpa," *Wall Street Journal* (January 17, 2002), p. B1.

13. "Drug Stores," *Chain Store Age* (August 2002), pp. 16, 18.

14. Mike Troy, "12 Hot Issues Facing Mass Retailing—2: Financial Reform," *DSN Retailing Today* (May 20, 2002), p. 21.

15. See John Mills, Lynn Bible, and Richard Mason, "Defining Free Cash Flow," *CPA Journal*, Vol. 72 (January 2002), pp. 47–51; and Rich Bradshaw, "Keeping the Supply Chain Fluid: Tighter Life-Cycle Management Will Improve Retailers' Cash Flow," *Chain Store Age* (August 2002), p. 178.

16. Computed from "Physical Support Census," *Chain Store Age* (July 2002), pp. 76–82.

17. Company 2002 annual reports.

18. Margaret Popper, "Really Grand Openings: New Stores Boost Retail Productivity," *Business Week* (September 23, 2002), p. 32.

Chapter 13

OPERATIONS MANAGEMENT: OPERATIONAL DIMENSIONS

Reprinted by permission.

The term *black gold* is typically used to describe oil. However, this term is also apropos for the coffee shops created by Howard Schultz, the chief executive of Starbucks (**www.starbucks.com**). While traveling in Italy in 1983, Schultz became excited over the coffee-bar culture there. He was very enthusiastic about the growth prospects in the United States since Milan, a city about the size of Philadelphia, supported 1,500 espresso bars.

Schultz was able to convince his Starbucks bosses to sell espresso at a new store in Seattle in 1984. However, they were reluctant to move into the prepared coffee business. As a result, Schultz began his own coffee-bar operation in 1985.

Today, Starbucks serves 20 million people a week through its thousands of outlets. Each year, it adds as many as 1,000 new stores all over the globe. Since it went public in 1992, Starbucks' sales have increased 20 percent per year and profits an average of 30 percent per year. The Starbucks brand is also one of the fastest-growing global brands according to a recent *Business Week* survey.

Retailing analysts believe that Starbucks' competitive advantages are based on the firm's superior training programs, employee stock option programs, and health and benefits packages (even for part-time employees), as well as the superiority of its coffee blends. This means that Starbucks' stores are generally better operated, have a better atmosphere, and have a warmer feeling than many competitors.[1]

chapter objectives

1. To describe the operational scope of operations management
2. To examine several specific aspects of operating a retail business: operations blueprint; store format, size, and space allocation; personnel utilization; store maintenance, energy management, and renovations; inventory management; store security; insurance; credit management; computerization; outsourcing; and crisis management

OVERVIEW

For a good operations overview, go to About's Retail Industry site (http://retailindustry. about.com/sitesearch.htm? terms=operations).

As defined in Chapter 12, *operations management* is the efficient and effective implementation of the policies and tasks that satisfy a retailer's customers, employees, and management (and stock-holders, if it is publicly owned). While Chapter 12 examined the financial dimensions of operations management, this chapter covers the operational aspects.

For firms to succeed in the long term, operational areas need to be managed well. A decision to change a store format or to introduce new anti-theft equipment must be carefully reviewed since these acts greatly affect performance. In running their businesses, retail executives must make a wide range of operational decisions, such as these:

- What operating guidelines are used?
- What is the optimal format and size of a store? What is the relationship among shelf space, shelf location, and sales for each item in the store?
- How can personnel best be matched to customer traffic flows? Would increased staffing improve or reduce productivity? What impact does self-service have on sales?
- What effect does the use of various building materials have on store maintenance? How can energy costs be better controlled? How often should facilities by renovated?
- How can inventory best be managed?
- How can the personal safety of shoppers and employees be ensured?
- What levels of insurance are required?
- How can credit transactions be managed most effectively?
- How can computer systems improve operating efficiency?
- Should any aspects of operations be outsourced?
- What kind of crisis management plans should be in place?

OPERATING A RETAIL BUSINESS

To address these questions, we now look at the operations blueprint; store format, size, and space allocation; personnel utilization; store maintenance, energy management, and renovations; inventory management; store security; insurance; credit management; computerization; outsourcing; and crisis management.

OPERATIONS BLUEPRINT

To encourage more compatibility among different retail hardware and software systems, the National Retail Federation has established its ARTS program (www.nrf-arts. org).

An **operations blueprint** systematically lists all the operating functions to be performed, their characteristics, and their timing. While developing a blueprint, the retailer specifies, in detail, every operating function from the store's opening to closing—and those responsible for them. For example, who opens the store? When? What are the steps (turning off the alarm, turning on the power, setting up the computer, and so forth)? The performance of these tasks must not be left to chance.

A large or diversified retailer may use multiple blueprints and have separate blueprints for such areas as store maintenance, inventory management, credit management, and store displays. Whenever a retailer modifies its store format or operating procedures (such as relying more on self-service), it must also adjust the operations blueprint(s).

Figure 13-1 has an operations blueprint for a quick-oil-change firm. It identifies employee and customer tasks (in order) and expected performance times for each activity. Among the advantages of this blueprint—and others—are that it standardizes activities (within a location and between locations), isolates points at which operations may be weak or prone to failure (Do employees actually check transmission, brake, and power-steering fluids in one minute?), outlines a plan that can be evaluated for completeness (Should customers be offered different grades of oil?), shows personnel needs (Should one person change the oil and another wash the windshield?), and helps identify productivity improvements (Should the customer or an employee drive a car into and out of the service bay?).

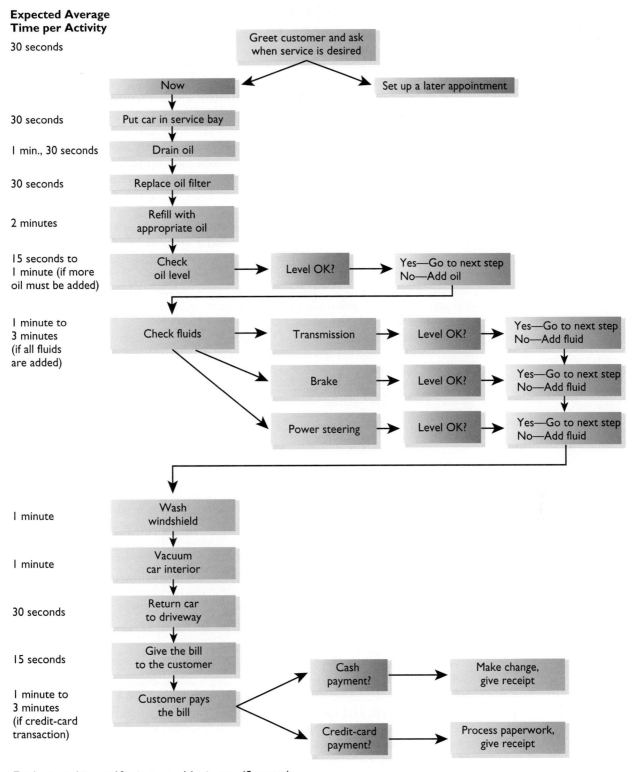

Expected Average Time per Activity

- 30 seconds
- 30 seconds
- 1 min., 30 seconds
- 30 seconds
- 2 minutes
- 15 seconds to 1 minute (if more oil must be added)
- 1 minute to 3 minutes (if all fluids are added)
- 1 minute
- 1 minute
- 30 seconds
- 15 seconds
- 1 minute to 3 minutes (if credit-card transaction)

Total expected time = 10 minutes to 14 minutes, 45 seconds.

FIGURE 13-1

An Operations Blueprint for a Quick-Oil-Change Firm's Employees

STORE FORMAT, SIZE, AND SPACE ALLOCATION

With regard to store format, it should be determined whether productivity can be raised by such tactics as locating in a planned shopping center rather than in an unplanned business district, using prefabricated materials in construction, and applying certain kinds of store design and layouts.

The Retail Group (www.theretailgroup.com) has collaborated with a number of retailers to develop prototype stores.

A key store format decision for chain retailers is whether to use **prototype stores**, whereby multiple outlets conform to relatively uniform construction, layout, and operations standards. Such stores make centralized management control easier, reduce construction costs, standardize operations, facilitate the interchange of employees among outlets, allow fixtures and other materials to be bought in quantity, and display a consistent chain image. Yet, a strict reliance on prototypes may lead to inflexibility, failure to adapt to or capitalize on local customer needs, and too little creativity. Pep Boys, Office Depot, Starbucks, McDonald's, and most supermarket chains are among those with prototype stores.

Together with prototype stores, some chains use **rationalized retailing** programs to combine a high degree of centralized management control with strict operating procedures for every phase of business. Most of these chains' operations are performed in a virtually identical manner in all outlets. Rigid control and standardization make this technique easy to enact and manage, and a firm can add a significant number of stores in a short time. Radio Shack, Toys "R" Us, and Starbucks use rationalized retailing. They operate many stores that are similar in size, layout, and merchandising.

Many retailers use one or both of two contrasting store-size approaches to be distinctive and to deal with high rents in some metropolitan markets. Home Depot, Barnes & Noble, and Sports Authority have category killer stores with huge assortments that try to dominate smaller stores. Food-based warehouse stores and large discount-oriented stores often situate in secondary sites, where rents are low—confident that they can draw customers. Cub Foods (a warehouse chain) and Wal-Mart engage in this approach. At the same time, some retailers believe large stores are not efficient in serving saturated (or small) markets; they have been opening smaller stores or downsizing existing ones because of high rents:

> Best Buy is known for its big-box stores in big cities. But to keep up its growth, the electronics chain is increasingly thinking small. In Wichita Falls, Texas, a city of just over 100,000, the retailer opened a slimmed-down store, choosing a location across from the main regional mall, near restaurants and a movie theater. It has also opened similar-size stores in places such as Cape Girardeau, Missouri; Kokomo, Indiana; and Newington, Connecticut. Those stores are about 30,000 square feet, compared with 45,000 square feet for the urban stores. It is thinking smaller still: Best Buy is experimenting with a 20,000-square-foot store. If the tests are successful, the retailer could open "hundreds" more stores, said the company's chief executive. Although Best Buy still has some urban spaces to fill, including stores in Manhattan and downtown San Francisco, "we're running out of room."[2]

Retailers often focus on allocating store space. They use facilities productively by determining the amount of space, and its placement, for each product category. Sometimes, retailers drop merchandise lines because they occupy too much space. That is why J.C. Penney eliminated home electronics, large sporting goods, and photo equipment from its department stores. With a **top-down space management approach**, a retailer starts with its total available store space (by outlet and for the overall firm, if a chain), divides the space into categories, and then works on product layouts. In contrast, a **bottom-up space management approach** begins planning at the individual product level and then proceeds to the category, total store, and overall company levels.

These are among the tactics that some retailers use to improve store space productivity: Vertical displays, which occupy less room, hang on store walls or from ceilings. Formerly free space now has small point-of-sale displays and vending machines and, sometimes, product displays are in front of stores. Open doorways, mirrored walls, and vaulted ceilings give small stores a larger appearance. Up to 75 percent or more of total floor space may be used for selling; the rest is for storage, rest rooms, and so on. Scrambled merchandising (with high-profit, high-turnover

RETAILING Around the World   Benetton Is Making Its Global Network More Efficient

For many years, the Benetton Group (**www.benetton.com**) was a textbook example of an organization that had gained meaningful efficiencies through outsourcing and subcontracting. Through a network of subcontractors located mainly in northeastern Italy, Benetton outsourced the production of its garments. In addition, Benetton did not own its retail facilities. It used a licensing arrangement similar to franchising.

Today, in a dramatic departure from past practices, Benetton is vertically integrating its operations. The production activities of its subcontractors are to be coordinated by a Benetton subsidiary, which Benetton calls a "production pole." The production pole chooses what is to be produced and allocates production tasks among the subcontractors. To ensure high quality, each production pole concentrates on one type of product.

In its retail operations, Benetton is opening and directly managing its own facilities. As a result, the firm feels that it will be better able to read new fashion trends.

Finally, Benetton is reducing the diversity of its clothing lines. Until recently, more than 20 percent of its clothing and accessories were customized to meet specific demands in each country. Now, in order to communicate a common image across the world, only 5 to 10 percent of styles differ.

Source: Arnaldo Camuffo, Pietro Romano, and Andrea Vinelli, "Back to the Future: Benetton Transforms Its Global Network," *Sloan Management Review*, Vol. 43 (Fall 2001), pp. 46–52.

items) occupies more space in stores, in catalogs, and at Web sites than before. By staying open longer, retailers use space better.

Our Web site (**www.prenhall.com/bermanevans**) has many links on these topics.

PERSONNEL UTILIZATION

From an operations perspective, efficiently utilizing retail personnel is vital: (1) Labor costs are high. For various retailers, wages and benefits may account for up to one-half of operating costs.[3] (2) High employee turnover means increased recruitment, training, and supervision costs. (3) Poor personnel may have weak sales skills, mistreat shoppers, misring transactions, and make other errors. (4) Productivity gains in technology have exceeded those in labor; yet some retailers are labor intensive. (5) Labor scheduling is often subject to unanticipated demand. While retailers know they must increase their staff in peak periods and reduce it in slow ones, they may still be over- or understaffed if weather changes, competitors run specials, or suppliers increase promotions. (6) There is less flexibility for firms with unionized employees. Working conditions, compensation, tasks, overtime pay, performance measures, termination procedures, seniority rights, and promotion criteria are generally specified in union contracts.

These are among the tactics that can maximize personnel productivity:

Kronos' Workforce Smart Scheduler (www.kronos. com/discover/industry/ wf_scheduler.htm) allows retailers to better manage employee scheduling.

- *Hiring process*—By very carefully screening potential employees before they are offered jobs, turnover is reduced and better performance secured.

- *Workload forecasts*—For each time period, the number and type of employees are predetermined. A drugstore may have one pharmacist, one cashier, and one stockperson from 2 P.M. to 5 P.M. on weekdays and add a pharmacist and a cashier from 5 P.M. to 7:30 P.M. (to accommodate people shopping after work). In doing workload forecasts, costs must be balanced against the possibilities of lost sales if customer waiting time is excessive. The key is to be both efficient (cost-oriented) and effective (service-oriented). Many retailers use computer software as an aid in scheduling personnel.

- *Job standardization and cross-training*—Through **job standardization**, the tasks of personnel with similar positions in different departments, such as cashiers in clothing and candy departments, are rather uniform. See Figure 13-2. With **cross-training**, personnel learn tasks associated with more than one job, such as cashier, stockperson, and gift wrapper. A firm increases personnel flexibility and reduces the number of employees needed at any time by job standardization and cross-training. If one department is slow, a cashier could be assigned to a busy one, and a salesperson could process transactions, set up displays, and handle complaints. Cross-training even reduces employee boredom.

FIGURE 13-2
Burger King: Fostering
Job Standardization

Burger King employees are
trained to perform specific
tasks in a standardized
manner, so that customers
receive consistent, high-
quality service each time
they dine with Burger King.

Reprinted by permission of
Douglas Brucker, Burger King
franchisee.

- *Employee performance standards*—Each worker is given clear goals and is accountable for them. Cashiers are judged on transaction speed and misrings, buyers on department revenues and markdowns, and senior executives on the firm's reaching sales and profit targets. Personnel are more productive when working toward specific goals.

- *Compensation*—Financial remuneration, promotions, and recognition that reward good performance help to motivate employees. A cashier is motivated to reduce misrings if there is a bonus for keeping mistakes under a certain percentage of all transactions.

- *Self-service*—Costs are reduced with self-service. However: (1) Self-service requires better displays, popular brands, ample assortments, and products with clear features. (2) By reducing sales personnel, some shoppers may feel service is inadequate, and there is no cross-selling (whereby customers are encouraged to buy complementary goods they may not have been thinking about).

- *Length of employment*—Generally, full-time workers who have been with a firm for an extended time are more productive than those who are part-time or who have worked there for a short time. They are often more knowledgeable, are more anxious to see the firm succeed, need less supervision, are popular with customers, can be promoted, and are adaptable to the work environment. The superior productivity of these workers normally far outweighs their higher compensation.

STORE MAINTENANCE, ENERGY MANAGEMENT, AND RENOVATIONS

Store maintenance encompasses all the activities in managing physical facilities. These are just some of the facilities to be managed: exterior—parking lot, points of entry and exit, outside signs and display windows, and common areas adjacent to a store (e.g., sidewalks); interior—windows, walls, flooring, climate control and energy use, lighting, displays and signs, fixtures, and ceilings. See Figure 13-3.

Domco is a leading maker of retail flooring. Visit its Azrock Commercial Flooring Products division site (www.domco.com/azrock), select "Grocery/Food Store," then choose a flooring application, and see the variety of flooring available.

The quality of store maintenance affects consumer perceptions, the life span of facilities, and operating costs. Consumers do not like stores that are decaying or otherwise poorly maintained. This means promptly replacing burned-out lamps, and periodically repainting room surfaces.

Thorough, ongoing maintenance may extend current facilities for a longer period before having to invest in new ones. At home centers, the heating, ventilation, and air-conditioning equipment lasts an average of 15 years, display fixtures an average of 13 years, and interior signs an average of 8 years. But maintenance is costly. In a typical year, a home center spends $10,000 on floor maintenance alone.[4]

FIGURE 13-3
A Checklist of Selected
Store Maintenance
Decisions

✓ What responsibility should the retailer have for maintaining outside facilities? For instance, does a lease agreement make the retailer or the property owner accountable for snow removal in the parking lot?

✓ Should store maintenance activities be done by the retailer's personnel or by outside specialists? Will that decision differ by type of facility (e.g., air-conditioning versus flooring) and by type of service (e.g., maintenance versus repairs)?

✓ What repairs should be classified as emergencies? How promptly should nonemergency repairs be made?

✓ What should be the required frequency of store maintenance for each type of facility (e.g., daily vacuuming of floors versus weekly washing of exterior windows)? How often should special maintenance activities be done (e.g., restriping spaces in a parking lot)?

✓ How should store maintenance vary by season and by time of day (e.g., when a store is open versus when it is closed)?

✓ How long should existing facilities be utilized before acquiring new ones? What schedule should be followed?

✓ What performance standards should be set for each element of store maintenance? Do these standards adequately balance costs against a desired level of maintenance?

Due to rising costs over the last 30 years, energy management is a major factor in retail operations. For firms with special needs, such as food stores, it is especially critical. To manage their energy resources more effectively, many retailers now:

- Use better insulation in constructing and renovating stores.
- Carefully adjust interior temperature levels during nonselling hours. In summer, air-conditioning is reduced at off-hours; in winter, heating is lowered at off-hours.
- Use computerized systems to monitor temperature levels. Some chains' systems even allow operators to adjust the temperature, lighting, heat, and air-conditioning in multiple stores from one office.
- Substitute high-efficiency bulbs and flourescent ballasts for traditional lighting.
- Install special air-conditioning systems that control humidity levels in specific store areas, such as freezer locations—to minimize moisture condensation.

Ethics in RETAILING

Stop & Shop Stems Energy Consumption

Stop & Shop (**www.stopandshop.com**) has developed an experimental prototype supermarket in Foxboro, Massachusetts, that it hopes will drastically reduce energy consumption. Called the LESS (Low Energy Super Store) project, the supermarket uses fluorescent lighting, skylights, reflectors, energy-efficient compressors for air-conditioning and refrigeration, and energy-saving freezer doors.

In planning the store, Ahold (**www.aholdusa.com**), Stop & Shop's parent company, relied on a team consisting of employees from the various Ahold units that were effectively controlling energy costs, material vendors (such as air-conditioning and heating suppliers), and utility suppliers. According to Stop & Shop's senior vice-president for construction and engineering, "We narrowed our list down based on what was real and what we could expect savings with. Fuel cells are coming, but

they're not here yet. We could not justify them. Windmills will work, but you need the right location."

Even though the project added $500,000 in construction and materials costs above a conventional design, Stop & Shop expects to save 38 percent from its usual energy costs. Most of the savings are forecast to come from reductions in interior lighting costs. Stop & Shop's management planned to study the store for one year before deciding which innovations to incorporate into other stores.

Source: Richard Turcsik, "Low-Energy Activism: Stop & Shop's New Environment-Conscious Store Design Could Cut Electricity Use by 38 Percent," *Progressive Grocer* (April 1, 2002), pp. 26–29.

Here is an example of how seriously some retailers take energy management:

Previously known primarily as the site of the New England Patriots football stadium, Foxboro is sure to enjoy international recognition as the place where supermarkets learned how to shave at least one-third off their energy bills. That's because the Stop & Shop chain, a U.S. subsidiary of the giant Ahold conglomerate, opened a "low-energy superstore." It is the realization of three years of research and development aimed at reducing the energy usage of a single store by a minimum of 30 percent. In addition, the pleasant environment created by the lighting will hopefully encourage shoppers to stay longer, and therefore, increase final checkout totals.[5]

Besides everyday maintenance and energy management, retailers need decision rules regarding renovations: How often are renovations necessary? What areas require renovations more frequently than others? How extensive will renovations be at any one time? Will the retailer be open for business as usual during renovations? How much money must be set aside in anticipation of future renovations? Will renovations result in higher revenues, lower operating costs, or both?

Sometimes, the complexities of store renovations are addressed quite cleverly:

The Bethel Food Market IGA in Connecticut came up with a unique customer retention program designed to keep in-store traffic up through a major expansion: "We have a lot of valued customers that we inconvenienced by having this mess going on," said a company executive. "So we came up with a program to make people feel a part of the whole expansion." The retailer divided the construction into four separate phases, each marked by a milestone that explained what was happening during a particular phase. As each phase was completed, participating customers received a free gift and the chance to compete in a raffle.[6]

INVENTORY MANAGEMENT

A retailer uses inventory management to maintain a proper merchandise assortment while ensuring that operations are efficient and effective. While the role of inventory management in merchandising is covered in Chapter 15, these are some operational considerations:

- How can handling of merchandise from different suppliers be coordinated?
- How much inventory should be on the sales floor versus in a warehouse or storeroom? See Figure 13-4.

FIGURE 13-4

Inventory Management at Costco

Costco has a very efficient approach to inventory management. Virtually all merchandise is displayed on the sales floor in a manner that makes maximum use of floor space. Many of its products are displayed in their original packing cartons, which reduces display and labor costs.

Reprinted by permission of Retail Forward, Inc.

- How often should inventory be moved from nonselling to selling areas of a store?
- What inventory functions can be done during nonstore hours?
- What are the trade-offs between faster supplier delivery and higher shipping costs?
- What supplier support is expected in storing merchandise or setting up displays?
- What level of in-store merchandise breakage is acceptable?
- Which items require customer delivery? When? By whom?

STORE SECURITY

Store security relates to two basic issues: personal security and merchandise security. Personal security is examined here. Merchandise security is covered in Chapter 15.

Many shoppers and employees feel less safe at retail establishments than they did before, with these results: Some people are unwilling to shop at night. Some people age 60 and older no longer go out at all during the night. Almost one-half of shoppers believe malls are not as safe as they once were. Parking is a source of anxiety for people who worry about walking through a dimly lit parking lot. As one industry observer noted, "Retailers must be proactive. They should take precautions to be better prepared and make the shopping experience as safe and enjoyable as possible."[7]

These are among the practices retailers are utilizing to address this issue:

- Uniformed security guards provide a visible presence that reassures customers and employees, and it is a warning to potential thieves and muggers. Some malls even have horse-mounted guards. This is a big change: "Mall management wants us to be less ambassadors of goodwill and is asking us to take a more aggressive approach. They are asking us to not watch and wait too long if we spot suspicious behavior. That lost package that we would have delicately brought to lost and found, we won't do that this year. From a customer's point of view, that lost package is really lost."[8]
- Undercover personnel are used to complement uniformed guards.
- Brighter lighting is used in parking lots, which are also patrolled more frequently by guards. These guards more often work in teams.
- TV cameras and other devices scan the areas frequented by shoppers and employees. 7-Eleven has an in-store cable TV and alarm monitoring system, complete with audio.
- Some shopping areas have curfews for teenagers. This is a controversial tactic.
- Access to store backroom facilities (such as storage rooms) has been tightened.
- Bank deposits are made more frequently—often by armed security guards.

INSURANCE

Among the types of insurance that retailers buy are workers' compensation, product liability, fire, accident, property, and officers' liability. Many firms also offer health insurance to full-time employees; sometimes, they pay the entire premiums, other times, employees pay part or all of the premiums.

Insurance decisions can have a big impact on a retailer: (1) In recent years, premiums have risen dramatically. (2) Several insurers have reduced the scope of their coverage; they now require higher deductibles or do not provide coverage on all aspects of operations (such as the professional liability of pharmacists). (3) There are fewer insurers servicing retailers today than a decade ago; this limits the choice of carrier. (4) Insurance against environmental risks (such as leaking tanks) is more important due to government rules.

To protect themselves financially, a number of retailers have enacted costly programs aimed at lessening their vulnerability to employee and customer insurance claims due to unsafe conditions, as well as to hold down premiums. These programs include no-slip carpeting, flooring, and rubber entrance mats; frequently mopping and inspecting wet floors; doing more elevator and escalator checks; conducting regular fire drills; having fire-resistant facilities; setting up separate storage areas for dangerous items; discussing safety in employee training; and keeping records that proper maintenance has been done.

CREDIT MANAGEMENT

Visa presents a lot of advice (www.visa.com/fb/merch/practice) for retailers to reduce their administrative costs and the fraud associated with the use of credit and debit cards.

These are the operational decisions to be made in the area of credit management:

- *What form of payment is acceptable?* A retailer may accept cash only, cash and personal checks, cash and credit card(s), cash and debit cards, or all of these.
- *Who administers the credit plan?* The firm can have its own credit system and/or accept major credit cards (such as Visa, MasterCard, American Express, and Discover).
- *What are customer eligibility requirements for a check or credit purchase?* With a check purchase, a photo ID might be sufficient. To open a new charge account, a customer must meet age, employment, income, and other conditions; an existing customer would be evaluated in terms of the outstanding balance and credit limit. A minimum purchase amount may be specified for a credit transaction.
- *What credit terms will be used?* A retailer with its own plan must determine when interest charges begin to accrue, the rate of interest, and minimum monthly payments.
- *How are late payments or nonpayments to be handled?* Some retailers with their own credit plans rely on outside collection agencies to follow up on past-due accounts.

The retailer must weigh the ability of credit to increase revenues against the costs of processing payments—screening, transaction, and collection costs, as well as bad debts. If a retailer completes credit functions itself, it incurs these costs; if outside parties (such as Visa) are used, the retailer covers the costs by its fees to the credit organization.

The *Nilson Report* presents information on retail payment methods. At its site (www.nilsonreport.com/issues/recentissues.htm), you can access highlights from recent issues.

In the United States, there are 1.5 billion credit and debit cards in use. During the Christmas holiday season alone (the day after Thanksgiving to the day before Christmas), there are more than 2 billion retail credit and debit card transactions each year. The average sales transaction involving a credit/debit card or a check is much higher than a cash one. Over all, 50 percent of U.S. retail transactions are in cash, 20 percent are by check, and 30 percent are by credit and debit card. Among retailers accepting credit cards, 33 percent have their own card, virtually all accept MasterCard and/or Visa, 80 percent accept Discover, and just over 50 percent accept American Express. Most retailers that accept credit cards handle two or more cards.[9]

Credit card fees paid by retailers range from 1.5 percent to 5.0 percent of sales for Visa, MasterCard, Discover, and American Express—depending on credit volume and the card provider. There may also be transaction and monthly fees. The total costs of retailers' own credit operations as a percent of credit sales are usually lower, at 2.0 percent. Costco has a Merchant Credit Processing program so that small firms may carry Visa or MasterCard. It charges a 1.55 percent of sale fee and a transaction charge of 21 cents for store retailers; the amounts are 2.03 percent and 28 cents per transaction for nonstore retailers.[10]

Many supermarkets, gas stations, and drugstores—among others—have begun placing more emphasis on a **debit card system**, whereby the purchase price of a good or service is immediately deducted from a consumer's bank account and entered into a retailer's account through a computer terminal. The retailer's risk of nonpayment is eliminated and its costs are reduced with debit rather than credit transactions. For traditional credit cards, monthly billing is employed; with debit cards, monetary account transfers are made at the time of the purchase. There is some resistance to debit transactions by consumers who like the delayed-payment benefit of conventional credit cards.

Click on "About Deluxe" (www.deluxe.com) to learn about one of the premier payment systems support companies for retailers.

As the payment landscape evolves, new operational issues must be addressed:

- Retailers have more choices for processing shopper payments: "From ATMs and debit cards to credit cards to emerging technologies such as smart cards and electronic gift cards, the payment field is growing ever more complex. Most retailers want to provide customers with as many payment options as are reasonable and that are likely to be used."[11] Yet, training cashiers is more complicated due to all the formats.
- Hardware and software are available to process paper checks electronically. This means cost savings for the retailer and faster payments from the bank.

- Visa and MasterCard have been sued for requiring retailers to accept both credit and debit cards, if the retailers want to continue carrying Visa and MasterCard credit cards.

- Nonstore retailers have less legal protection against credit card fraud than store retailers that secure written authorization.

- Credit card transactions on the Web must instantly take into account different sales tax rates and currencies (for global sales).

- In Europe, retailers have grappled with the intricacies of converting to the common euro currency.

COMPUTERIZATION

CAM Commerce Solutions (www.camcommerce.com) offers *free* operations software to small retailers in the hope that, as these retailers grow, they will pay for advanced software.

Many retailers have improved their operations productivity through computerization; and with the declining prices of computer systems and related software, more small firms will do so in the near future. At the same time, retailers must consider this observation: "Executives seem to be increasingly comfortable with technology, and most agree that new POS, category management, price management, and employee training systems are having an extreme impact on day-to-day operations. However, executives across different disciplines are mixed on whether technology is improving the bottom line or customer service."[12] Let us look at various examples of the operational benefits of computerization.

Retailers such as Home Depot, Wal-Mart, and J.C. Penney use videoconferencing. This lets them link store employees with central headquarters, as well as interact with vendors. Videoconferencing can be done through satellite technology and by computer (with special hardware and software). In both cases, audio/video communications train workers, spread news, stimulate employee morale, and so on.

SpectraLink (www.spectralink.com) has wireless "Solutions" for "Retail" businesses.

In-store telecommunications aid operations by offering low-cost, secure in-store transmissions. SpectraLink Corporation is one of the firms that markets lightweight pocket phones so personnel can talk to one another anywhere in a store. There are no air time charges or monthly fees. SpectraLink clients include Barnes & Noble, Foot Locker, Ikea, Kmart, Neiman Marcus, and Toys "R" Us. See Figure 13-5.

Software provides computerized inventory control and customer order tracking. For example, "System 2000's Inventory Management features will help your company maintain optimum inventory levels, automate the purchasing process, and dramatically improve product fulfillment to your customers. Advanced formulas analyze seasonal trends, erratic demand, vendor lead times, and cost discounts to create suggested purchase orders for both centralized and distributed

Technology in RETAILING
The Interactive Kiosk: A Tool for Food Chains to Improve Operating Efficiency

There are millions of interactive kiosks in use in the United States. Nearly one-half of them are used in a retail setting. In contrast, banking and finance kiosks account for less than a quarter of the market.

Despite their popularity in various retail settings, the full value of interactive kiosks has not been exploited in supermarkets. Why? Analysts typically cite the small number of appropriate applications, shoppers' concern for speed, and management fear that valuable floor space will be lost.

Nonetheless, the interactive kiosk does have unrealized potential for supermarkets. The store director at Central Market in Poulsbo, Washington, views Healthnotes Online (**www.healthnotes.com**) as "the greatest piece of equipment we could own." The kiosk, which is located in the store's natural foods

department, has an extensive data base that answers consumers' health-related questions. The kiosk attracts as many as 500 to 700 touches per day. Data provided by Healthnotes indicate that this type of kiosk can increase sales by as much as 20 percent. Healthnotes states that the vitamin, mineral, and supplement category also has high kiosk potential: "They're those with the highest margins and that lend themselves to an assisted sell."

Source: Karen Raugust, "Interactive Reluctance; Only a Few Grocery Chains Are Currently Committed to Interactive Kiosks. Several Are Cautiously Testing the Systems, But Some That Use the Devices Extol Them," *Supermarket News* (January 1, 2001), p.15.

FIGURE 13-5
Effective In-Store
Communications

Foot Locker employees are
equipped with battery-
powered headsets that
enable them to communi-
cate easily within individual stores.

Reprinted by permission of
Foot Locker.

environments."[13] And Icode's Everest Enterprise software lets retailers offer online order tracking to customers. See Figure 13-6.

Nowhere is computerization more critical than in the checkout process. Let us examine the computerized checkout, the electronic point-of-sale system, and scanning formats.

The **computerized checkout** is used by both large and small retailers so they can efficiently process transactions and monitor inventory. Firms rely on UPC-based systems; cashiers manually ring up sales or pass items over or past scanners. Computerized registers instantly record and display sales, provide detailed receipts, and store inventory data. See Figure 13-7. This type of check-

FIGURE 13-6
Everest Enterprise:
Integrated E-Commerce
Software

This figure shows the order
tracking function of the software.

Reprinted by permission of
Icode, Inc.

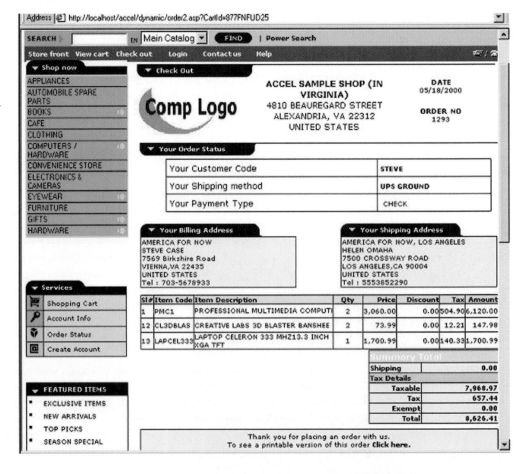

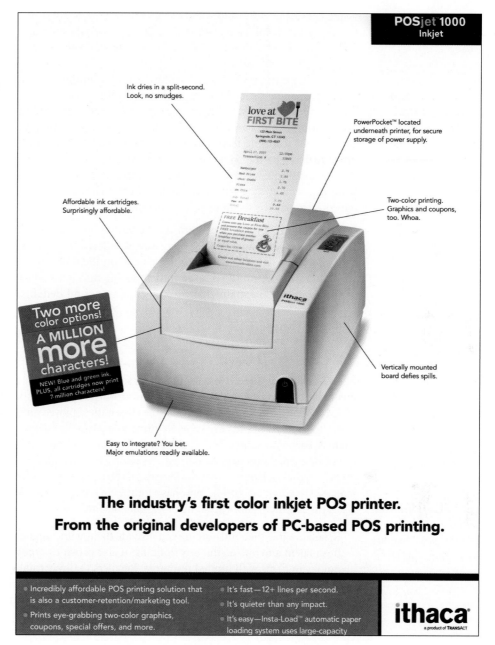

out lowers costs by reducing transaction time, employee training, misrings, and the need for item pricing. Retailers also have better inventory control, reduced spoilage, and improved ordering. They even get item-by-item data—which aid in determining store layout and merchandise plans, shelf space, and inventory replenishment. Recent technological developments related to computerized checkouts include wireless scanners that let workers scan heavy items without lifting them, radio frequency identification tags (RFID) that emit a radio frequency code when placed near a receiver (which is faster than UPC codes and better for harsh climates), and speech recognition (that can tally an order on the basis of a clerk's verbal command).

Retailers do face two potential problems with computerized checkouts. First, UPC-based systems do not reach peak efficiency unless all suppliers attach UPC labels to merchandise; otherwise, retailers incur labeling costs. Second, because UPC symbols are unreadable by humans, some states have laws that require price labeling on individual items. This lessens the labor savings of posting only shelf prices.

Many retailers have upgraded to an **electronic point-of-sale system**, which performs all the tasks of a computerized checkout and verifies check and charge transactions, provides instantaneous sales reports, monitors and changes prices, sends intra- and interstore messages, evaluates personnel profitability, and stores data. A point-of-sale system is often used along with a retail information system. Point-of-sale terminals can stand alone or be integrated with an in-store or a headquarters computer.

Symbol Technologies (www.symbol.com) is one of the leaders in retail scanning equipment, with an extensive product line.

Retailers have specific goals for their scanning equipment: "The dramatic gains in increased efficiency made possible by scanners have served to raise the bar on retailers' expectations. They want systems that are smaller, faster, easier to use, more durable, more affordable, and as useful in distribution centers and backroom storage areas as at the point of sale." Among the recent advances in scanning technology are handheld scanners; wearable, hands-free scanners; and miniaturized data transceivers.[14]

As noted in Chapter 2, one emerging scanning option with greater retailer interest is **self-scanning**, whereby the consumer himself or herself scans the items being purchased at a checkout counter, pays by credit or debit card, and bags the items:

> While unit costs vary depending on the number of lanes and locations, installations range between $85,000 and $100,000 per store. Retailers and vendors cite a return-on-investment payback between 9 and 18 months—based on the lower operational costs associated with self-scanning stations. For every order passing through a lane with a cashier, retailers need $15 to offset lane maintenance, cashier salaries, and benefits, and other front-end labor costs. With a self-service lane, "this cost could drop as low as $6 or $7 per transaction," says the president of IHL Consulting.[15]

OUTSOURCING

More retailers have turned to outsourcing for some of the operating tasks they previously performed themselves. With **outsourcing**, a retailer pays an outside party to undertake one or more of its operating functions. The goals are to reduce the costs and employee time devoted to particular tasks. For example, Limited Brands uses outside firms to oversee its energy use and facilities maintenance. Crate & Barrel outsources the management of its E-mail programs. Kmart uses logistics firms to consolidate small shipments and to process returned merchandise; it also outsources electronic data interchange tasks. Home Depot outsources most trucking operations. J.C. Penney, which for decades managed its credit operations, now has a long-term contract with GE Capital.

GE Capital's Card Services (www.ge.com/capital/retailer/index.html) handles the credit operations for a number of retailers.

This comment sums up some of the benefits of outsourcing:

> Retailers agree that outsourcing can provide them with a higher level of expertise, as well as fresh talent and out-of-the-box thinking. It also provides exposure to state-of-the-art technology to firms with limited resources. Retailers that rely totally on internal resources face the challenge of dealing with the peaks and valleys that are inevitable in business. "All of a sudden, you've got to build a whole team all over again," explained a CompUSA executive. "There is a lot of time involved in staffing back up, bringing people into the fold, and showing them how you do business."[16]

Careers in RETAILING — Today's Store Mangers Rate Their Job Environment

The average retail store manager is 42 years old and a college graduate. He or she has worked in a retail store for 21 years, with 10 of those years being spent as a store manager in his or her current company.

When *Chain Store Age* asked a sample of store mangers to describe the pros and cons of their jobs, they reported that they loved the challenges, responsibility, and leadership aspects. Their most frequently mentioned cons related to the work schedule, salary, and treatment by superiors. As one manager remarked, "Corporate works 9 to 5, Monday to Friday, but will always overwork managers and demand that more be done with the help you have."

In comparing the results of its recent survey with one nearly 20 years before, *Chain Store Age* found that dissatisfaction with salary and lack of recognition from superiors continue to affect manager morale. However, one of the major changes over this period is the increased responsibility for customer service. In the earlier study, 81 percent of the managers stated that their most important responsibility was returning a net profit. Now, 47 percent state that customer service is their most important responsibility, while 51 percent cite sales-volume increases.

Source: Matt Nannery, "Front Lines," *Chain Store Age* (September 2001), pp. 54–58.

CRISIS MANAGEMENT

Despite the best intentions, retailers may sometimes be faced with crisis situations that need to be managed as smoothly as feasible. Crises may be brought on by an in-store fire or broken water pipe, access to a store being partially blocked due to picketing by striking workers, a car accident in the parking lot, a burglary, a sudden illness by the owner or a key employee, a storm that knocks out a retailer's power, unexpectedly high or low consumer demand for a good or service, a sudden increase in a supplier's prices, a natural disaster like a flood or an earthquake, or other factors.

Although some crises may be anticipated, and some adverse effects may occur regardless of retailer efforts, these principles are important:

1. There should be contingency plans for as many different types of crisis situations as possible. That is why retailers buy insurance, install backup generators, and prepare management succession plans. A firm can have a checklist to follow if there is an incident such as a store fire or a parking-lot accident.
2. Essential information should be communicated to all affected parties, such as the fire or police department, employees, customers, and the media, as soon as a crisis occurs.
3. Cooperation—not conflict—among the involved parties is essential.
4. Responses should be as swift as feasible; indecisiveness may worsen the situation.
5. The chain of command should be clear and decision makers given adequate authority.

Crisis management is a key task for both small and large retailers: "While most retailers will never have to invoke responses to many 'what-if' scenarios, few would argue that it does not pay to be prepared."[17]

Visit our Web site (**www.prenhall.com/bermanevans**) for several links related to crisis management.

Summary

1. *To describe the operational scope of operations management.* Operations management efficiently and effectively seeks to enact the policies needed to satisfy customers, employees, and management. In contrast to Chapter 12, which dealt with financial aspects, Chapter 13 covered operational facets.

2. *To examine several specific aspects of operating a retail business.* An operations blueprint systematically lists all operating functions, their characteristics, and their timing, as well as the responsibility for performing the functions.

Store format and size considerations include the use of prototype stores and store dimensions. Firms often use prototype stores in conjunction with rationalized retailing. Some retailers emphasize category killer stores; others open smaller stores. In space allocation, retailers deploy a top-down or a bottom-up approach. They want to optimize the productivity of store space.

Personnel utilization activities that improve productivity range from better screening applicants to workload forecasts to job standardization and cross-training. Job standardization routinizes the tasks of people with similar positions in different departments. With cross-training, people learn tasks associated with more than one job. A firm can advance its personnel flexibility and minimize the total number of workers needed at any given time by these techniques.

Store maintenance includes all activities in managing physical facilities. It influences people's perceptions of the retailer,

the life span of facilities, and operating costs. To better control energy resources, retailers are doing everything from using better-quality insulation materials when building and renovating stores to substituting high-efficiency bulbs. Besides everyday facilities management, retailers need decision rules as to the frequency and manner of store renovations.

Good inventory management requires that retailers acquire and maintain the proper merchandise while ensuring efficient and effective operations. This encompasses everything from coordinating different supplier shipments to planning customer deliveries (if needed).

Store security measures protect both personal and merchandise safety. Because of safety concerns, fewer people now shop at night and some avoid shopping in areas they view as unsafe. In response, retailers are employing security guards, using better lighting in parking lots, tightening access to facilities, and deploying other tactics.

Among the insurance that retailers buy are workers' compensation, product liability, fire, accident, property, and officers' liability. Many firms also have employee health insurance.

Most U.S. adults use credit cards. Check and credit payments generally mean larger transactions than cash payments. One-half of retail transactions are in cash, 20 percent by check, and 30 percent by credit or debit card. Retailers pay various fees to be able to offer noncash payment options to customers, and there is a wide range of payment systems available for retailers.

A growing number of retailers have computerized elements of operations. Videoconferencing and wireless in-store telephone communications are gaining in popularity. Computerized checkouts and electronic point-of-sale systems are quite useful. Electronic point-of-sale systems perform all the tasks of computerized checkouts and verify check and charge transactions, provide instant sales reports, monitor and change prices, send intra- and interstore messages, evaluate personnel and profitability, and store data. Self-scanning is gaining in popularity.

With outsourcing, the retailer pays another party to handle one or more operating functions. The goals are to reduce costs and better utilize employees' time.

Crisis management must handle unexpected situations as smoothly as possible. There should be contingency plans, information should be communicated to those affected, all parties should cooperate, responses should be swift, and the chain of command for decisions should be clear.

Key Terms

operations blueprint (p. 314)

prototype stores (p. 316)

rationalized retailing (p. 316)

top-down space management approach
(p. 316)

bottom-up space management approach
(p. 316)

job standardization (p. 317)

cross-training (p. 317)

store maintenance (p. 318)

debit card system (p. 322)

computerized checkout (p. 324)

electronic point-of-sale system (p. 325)

self-scanning (p. 326)

outsourcing (p. 326)

Questions for Discussion

1. Present a brief operations blueprint for a college bookstore.

2. What are the pros and cons of prototype stores? For which kind of firms is this type of store *least* desirable?

3. Why would a retailer be interested in job standardization and cross-training for its employees?

4. Comment on this statement: "The quality of store maintenance efforts affects consumer perceptions of the retailer, the life span of facilities, and operating expenses."

5. Talk to two local retailers and ask them what they have done to maximize their energy efficiency. Present your findings.

6. As a gift shop owner, you are planning a complete renovation of the greeting card section. What decisions must you make?

7. Present a five-step plan for a retailer to reassure customers that it is safe to shop there.

8. A mom-and-pop store does not accept checks because of the risks involved. However, it does accept Visa and MasterCard. Evaluate this strategy.

9. What potential problems may result if a retailer relies on its computer system to implement too many actions (such as employee scheduling or inventory reordering) automatically?

10. What operations criteria would you use to evaluate the success of self-scanning at Wal-Mart?

11. Are there any operating functions that should *never* be outsourced? Explain your answer.

12. Outline the contingency plan a retailer could have in the event of each of these occurrences:
    a. A shopper's tripping over an on-floor display in the store and sustaining an injury.
    b. Vandalism of the storefront.
    c. A firm's Web site being down for five hours.
    d. The bankruptcy of a key supplier.

Web-Based Exercise

Visit the Web site of Category Management Systems (**www.cmsinc.on.ca**) and surf the "Products" section. What are the benefits of such software for independent pharmacies?

Note: Stop by our Web site (**www.prenhall.com/bermanevans**) to experience a number of highly interactive, appealing Web exercises based on actual company demonstrations and sample materials related to retailing.

Chapter Endnotes

1. Various company sources.

2. Elliot Spagat, "Best Buy Inc. Slims Down to Continue Expansion," *Wall Street Journal* (March 12, 2002), p. B4.

3. See Debbie Howell, "12 Hot Issues Facing Mass Retailing—4: Store Operations," *DSN Retailing Today* (May 20, 2002), p. 26.

4. "Store Size Creeps Up," *Chain Store Age* (July 2002), pp. 76, 81–84.

5. Vilma Barr, "Stop & Shop's Low-Energy Superstore," *Display & Design Ideas* (March 2002), pp. 66–72.

6. Liza Casabona, "Independent Turns Store Remodel into Rewards," *Supermarket News* (October 2001), p. 24.

7. Tony Lisanti, "Security Should Be a Retail Priority," *DSN Retailing Today* (May 6, 2002), p. 11.

8. Leslie Kaufman, "Malls Are Tightening Security as the Holiday Rush Begins," *New York Times* (November 23, 2001), p. C7.

9. Compiled from various sources by the authors.

10. "Credit Card Processing," **www.costco.com/frameset.asp? trg=Info/executivemembership/credit.asp&log=** (March 30, 2003).

11. Sunil Taneja, "The Payment Evolution," *Chain Store Age* (September 1999), p. 178.

12. Michael Friedman and Walter Heller, "Super Tech," *Progressive Grocer* (October 2001), p. 14.

13. "Retail for the 21st Century," **www.vai-software.com/retail.htm** (March 29, 2003).

14. "Special Section: Scanners," *Stores* (August 1999), p. P2. See also "Beyond Barcodes," *Chain Store Age* (January 2002), Supplement.

15. Deena M. Amato-McCoy, "Self-Checkout Shows Promise," *Grocery Headquarters* (June 2002), pp. 43–46.

16. "The Pros and Cons of Outsourcing," *Chain Store Age* (August 2002), p. 8B.

17. Tracy Mullin, "Is Your Business Prepared?" *Chain Store Age* (January 2002), p. 34.

part five
Short Cases

1: THE NEW HIRING SYSTEM OF SHERWIN-WILLIAMS

Sherwin-Williams (**www.sherwinwilliams.com**) is a vertically integrated paint and paint accessories firm with more than 2,200 company-owned retail stores in all 50 states. Each year, the company opens new stores and relocates those that are not performing up to expectations. All of this activity means that Sherwin-Williams constantly has a large number of retail store openings for a variety of positions.

To improve its retail hiring efficiency, Sherwin-Williams has been testing a phone-based program to screen prospective employees for store associate, delivery driver, warehouse employee, and similar positions. Sherwin-Williams first employed this system around New York City; it then expanded the system to include New Jersey and Washington, D.C. As a result, 6,000 applicants looking for a position were directed to a single Sherwin-Williams' toll-free number. This process freed the individual store manager from the tasks of advertising for specific positions, calling local unemployment offices, and conducting preliminary interviews with applicants. According to Sherwin-Williams' area human resources manager, "Its been a life-saver for our hiring managers, saving time and allowing them to focus on other business activities. The cool thing about the system is it's really not a tool to draw people to the store, but to make hiring easier and save time for the hiring manager."

The phone system was devised by Spherion Assessment Group (**www.spherion.com**). Although Spherion has also developed a Web version, Sherwin-Williams uses only the phone-based program. For Sherwin-Williams, "The system eliminates a lot of steps in the recruitment process. The person getting referred has answered 30 to 40 questions. So your store managers are spending the majority of their time interviewing the most qualified candidates."

The first questions ask if the job candidate can perform certain functions. For example, "Do you have a driver's license? Do you have the legal right to work in the United States? Can you lift 50 pounds?" Other questions focus on an applicant's orientation toward the job. For example, "If you're going to be late, do you call in?" and "Do you feel that most customers are too demanding?" Other questions relate to employee ethics, such as: "Should a good employee who steals less than $5 be given a second chance?"

Spherion's proprietary software makes the sequencing of the questions automatic. These questions were developed by interviewing some of Sherwin-Williams' best assistant managers and workers. Some questions were also developed with the assistance of an industrial psychologist or Spherion personnel.

Applicants indicate their answer to each question by pressing the number "1" for "yes" and number "2" for "no". In addition to a candidate's response time being monitored, the questions are branched so that an applicant who responds inappropriately to a customer service question would get additional questions on that topic. Poor applicants are weeded out based on their responses to these questions. Applicants who successfully complete all of the questions in the phone system can then set up a personal interview with the store manager.

Of the 6,000 calls during a one-year testing period, the program identified 11 percent of the respondents as "best matches." Thus, the telephone system saved Sherwin-Williams the expense of conducting more than 5,000 personal interviews.

Questions

1. As a Sherwin-Williams' hiring manager, how would you feel about using this screening system? Explain your answer.
2. As a potential Sherwin-Williams' employee, how would you feel about going through this screening system? Explain your answer.
3. For what kind of positions would this system be most and least effective? Why?
4. Present five questions to assess a job candidate's sensitivity to customer service.

The material in this case is drawn from Ken Clark, "Dial H for Hiring," *Chain Store Age* (May 2002), pp. 157–158; and *Sherwin-Williams 2001 Annual Report*, 10-K.

2: DOLLAR GENERAL SEEKS TO BOUNCE BACK FROM FINANCIAL WOES

In an April 2001 press release, Dollar General (**www.dollargeneral. com**) used the term *accounting irregularities* to describe why its 1998, 1999, and 2000 earnings would have to be revised downward. In January 2002, the firm disclosed that its combined profits for the three years were $100 million less than previously reported. It also said that it would spend $162 million in 2002 to settle stockholder lawsuits.

At a 2002 meeting of security analysts, Dollar General executives discussed the results of the discount variety chain's sale of perishables and new programs aimed at making its inventory management more efficient. According to Dollar General's chairman and chief executive officer, "In this year of silence, we truly have been busier than a bumblebee, and productive." For fiscal 2002, Dollar General had impressive productivity: Overall sales were up 17 percent, and same store sales growth was 7.3 percent.

Dollar General's vice-president of merchandising reported that the chain's sales of food, paper products, and pet food had increased 22 percent. As a result of the strong sales of perishables, Dollar General expanded the number of stores with refrigeration units from 400 to 1,400 in 2002. At the end of 2002, it would also sell bread in 6,000 stores—an increase from 3,800 stores the prior year.

Why are perishables so important? Dollar General's refrigerated perishable products (which include milk, eggs, hot dogs, luncheon meats, and frozen items) are delivered by independent wholesalers: "Our customers love it. The average transaction size in the cooler refrigerated-unit stores is significantly higher." Because of this, Dollar General added 80 new perishable products in 2002.

The chain is applying strategies to make inventory management more efficient. It has a new markdown policy for apparel and seasonal goods that helps foresee oversupply and take markdowns earlier. In the health-and-beauty aids department, vendors are shipping smaller quantities to better reflect local demand. Thus, Dollar General has added new items while keeping shelf space in check.

Dollar General plans to better utilize technology and improve its inventory replenishment process. An automatic replenishment system, tested in three stores, will be expanded. The chain has also recently completed the installation of new IBM cash registers and laser scanning equipment at all of its stores. A new satellite network will also simplify ordering at the store level.

In the past, Dollar General tracked its 2,500-item inventory in each store through a pencil-and-paper method of data collection. It now uses wireless, handheld scanners. These scanners can track each pallet, each carton, and each individual piece of merchandise as it enters the warehouse—and as goods are placed on outbound shipments to stores. The warehouse management system verifies that the inventory ordered is in the warehouse, produces purchase orders to replenish this inventory, and even generates labels for the outbound cartons.

Questions

1. Describe how accounting irregularities can play havoc with a firm's reputation, supplier relations, and manager morale.
2. Discuss other means of measuring and improving financial performance at Dollar General.
3. What are the financial management pros and cons of Dollar General's placing greater emphasis on perishables?
4. Evaluate Dollar General's inventory management initiatives.

The material in this case is drawn from "Dollar General Learns Lesson the Hard Way—Through Devaluation," *DSN Retailing Today* (May 20, 2002), p. 21; Debbie Howell, "Humbled Dollar General Rebounds with Verve," *DSN Retailing Today* (April 8, 2002), pp. 7–8; and Ken Krizner, "Turning Inventory into Profits," *Frontline Solutions* (May 2002), pp. 16–20.

3: TOYS "R" US TIGHTENS ITS BELT

Toys "R" Us (**www.tru.com**) mangement considers the 2000–2001 period to be the "first chapter" in its turnaround. During this part of its revamped strategy, Toys "R" Us transformed 433 of its 702 traditional warehouse-format stores to a new "Mission Possible" format. This format emphasizes targeted "worlds"—sections of the store devoted to boys, girls, games, and so on. Many of the "worlds" include demonstration stations where employees can road test toys for children and their parents. As one retailing analyst observed, "The heavy lifting has been pretty much done on the toy chain conversion, now management is looking at other areas that need attention."

In "chapter two" of its strategic transformation, Toys "R" Us has been highlighting its troublesome apparel division. "It's no secret the Kids "R" Us division has struggled," noted Toys "R" Us' chairman and chief executive. Thus, the firm is seeking to replace many of its stand-alone Kids "R" Us stores in favor of a format wherein toys and apparel are both sold in a single store. Industry observers think the greater focus on the Kids "R" Us division is a positive step in transforming Toys "R" Us as a company.

In the combination format, the middle of each Kids "R" Us store features such new product categories as bedding and bath accessories, electronics, and personal care products. With these stores, Kids "R" Us occupies 5,500-square-foot boutiques within a Toys "R" Us store format. The stores' old design, in which consumers had distinct aisles, has been changed to a teardrop-shaped racetrack format where all consumers have to use the same traffic pattern.

Toys "R" Us planned to have 375 combination stores as of the beginning of 2003. If the new format proved successful, Toys "R" Us planned to convert all remaining Kids "R" Us units to combination stores. Thirty of the new combination stores will come from closing a Kids "R" Us store and then incorporating it into the nearest Toys "R" Us.

These contemporary layouts and store formats are part of the Toys "R" Us strategy to better compete with its rivals. Industry analysts now see Wal-Mart as the market share leader with about 18 to 19 percent of the traditional toy market; in contrast, the Toys "R" Us share is less than 18 percent. Target Stores' share is estimated at 6 to 7 percent, and Kmart has a 5 percent share.

In 2002, Toys "R" Us also announced plans to close 37 Kids "R" Us stores and 27 previous-generation Toys "R" Us stores, and to consolidate five support centers into one unit. The reduction in stores was based on sales reports from 2001. The firm's 2 percent same-store sales increase made it clear that not all unconverted stores were performing as well as necessary: "Some of them [the closed stores] just aren't fixable."

All administrative and financial functions used to be separated by division. In the new "shared services" model, these functions are being performed at the new support headquarters. The cuts in stores, as well as support operation facilities, have reduced the number of Toys "R" Us employees by 1,900 (1,350 from the store level and 55 from support services). This reduction was expected to save Toys "R" Us $25 million in 2002 and $45 million in 2003.

Questions

1. Distinguish between and evaluate the "chapter one" and "chapter two" stages of Toys "R" Us' strategy.
2. Why do you think that Wal-Mart has moved ahead of Toys "R" Us as a toy retailer? Is this trend reversible? Explain your answer.
3. What other operational changes would you suggest for Toys "R" Us? Why?
4. In an area of employee downsizing, what can Toys "R" Us do to attract and retain qualified, enthusiastic workers?

The material in this case is drawn from "TRU Tightens Belt in Stage 2 of Turnaround," *DSN Retailing Today* (February 11, 2002), pp. 5, 58; and David Finnigan, "The New Toy Story," *Brandweek* (February 11, 2002), pp. 26–32.

4: BEALL'S: USING SOFTWARE TO TRACK EMPLOYEE THEFT

This is how employee theft can be tracked today: A manager at a Beall's (**www.bealls.com**) outlet store was stealing money in small amounts—typically ranging from $50 to $90. Before long, the manager had stolen over $1,000. She would take money from the store's register and then fill out a customer refund slip for the amount of the stolen funds. The name of the customer and his or her phone number were looked up in a local phone directory. Within three weeks of the first theft, the manager was highlighted as having an unusually large number of returns and refunds. Beall's security personnel then analyzed prior transactions and installed security cameras. A week later, the manager admitted her theft. If convicted of larceny, the manager would be given three years of probation, fined, and forced to make restitution.

Several years ago, the manager's activity could have gone on for months or, perhaps, even years. Now, Beall's and several other retailers use software that monitors all cash register transactions (every sale, voided transaction, and refund) to look for unusual activities.

Unlike computer scanning systems that track all sales, sales-transaction software focuses on cashiers and looks for unusual sales patterns. Thus, a refund of several hundred dollars at a convenience store would be followed up by a phone call to the store manager within minutes of the refund. Other examples of unusual activity include an increase in credit-card sales that are keyed in by hand rather than swiped (this could mean that an employee is using a customer's credit card from a prior transaction), repeated refunds by the same employee at the same time of day (perhaps when there are fewer people around), or low sales volume at a particular register (which may indicate that the cashier is not ringing up all sales). The latest advance is a software program called Digital Dispatch that matches digital video with cash register transactions; investigators can actually see whether a customer is present when a refund is being made.

Although sales-transaction software has been hailed by some retailing analysts as "the most significant development in retail security since closed circuit cameras were installed 20 years ago," only a limited number of stores have installed the software. The systems can cost $100,000 or more just for the software; yet, they often pay for themselves within months. At Beall's Inc., a 400-unit store chain, the software has identified over 150 instances of fraud since it was installed in 1997. Each of these cases was separately investigated, and all 150 led to employee firings and prosecution. Beall's estimates that this system has saved the firm millions of dollars. It also serves as a major deterrent in employee theft.

Surprisingly, many of the employees who have been caught stealing are more established workers. Why? "The more seasoned employee is more creative in ways of manipulating transactions. To take a $150 refund on a Friday night is what the kids will do. The more seasoned employees will hit you for $25 here, $25 there in different ways. They'll switch."

One criticism of sales-transaction software is that it is too intrusive and that employees may resent having investigators watch over each cash register transaction. Nonetheless, even some civil libertarians agree that the monitoring would be difficult to challenge in court as long as employees have been informed of the firm's policies.

Questions

1. Why do you think many retailers that have installed computer scanning systems have not introduced sales-transaction software into their stores?
2. How would you do a cost-benefit analysis for sales-transaction software? State specific criteria to assess.
3. Identify five types of unusual activities that should trigger a computer scanning system and how a retailer should deal with them.
4. What are the pros and cons of informing employees of the existence of sales-transaction software and in-store video cameras?

The material in this case is drawn from Jennifer Lee, "Tracking Sales and the Cashiers," *New York Times on the Web* (July 11, 2001).

part five
Comprehensive Case

Developing Employees with Good Communication Skills*

INTRODUCTION

"Communication" is a buzzword. Everyone wants to improve communication, to practice more effective communication, or perhaps to settle for just plain good communication. Executives need a more rigorous definition and a useful business model to make communication a key part of corporate strategy. Lacking these, communication is treated like the weather: The assumption is that not much can be done about it.

The Good and the Bad

Recently, I was at home, sick. Our air-conditioning system was being serviced. The serviceperson ended up at my door demanding a credit card. After dragging myself downstairs, calling their office, explaining I had been a customer for 15 years, and always had been billed, the first person on the phone insisted, "It's policy." When I reached the manager, he offered a perfunctory apology but reinforced "it's policy."

The original firm apparently disappeared in two buyouts. I waited a week for an apology. When none arrived, I wrote a letter, terminating the contract for our home, office, and office building and copied the CEO of the parent company. A month later, I received a call from a puzzled manager, who said, "I think you wrote to me. Did you know that we've changed management? I guess it's too late to apologize."

At about that time, I called Wolf Camera. My husband had bought a video camera at one of their stores. I had lost the service contract. Could someone find out if I still qualified and could I bring the camera to the closest store? Maria answered the phone and sounded genuinely interested, "I don't know the answer, but I will find out and call you." Later that day, she called back. She had found the central records, located mine although I had given her the wrong name—my last name and not my husband's. She said that I qualified; if I brought the camera in, she would get it to the right place.

A central question is how to get employees to act like Maria and not the "it's policy" people. The first example shows the mix of operational with communication issues. The Service Experts staff didn't alert a regular customer to a change in procedure. They did not obtain a credit card number over the phone when the appointment was made. When I, the sick customer, objected, the office had no way to confirm a long history with the firm. When the manager came on the phone, he had no discretion. And his interpersonal skills were lacking. He couldn't say "I'm sorry" and really mean it.

After the incident, the firm had more opportunities to communicate. They knew a customer had been inconvenienced. A call, fax, or letter was in order. After I wrote, a prompt response was mandatory. When someone finally phoned, the tone of voice and the conversation were defeatist.

Communication As Corporate Strategy

Our company began our mission to make communication a more useful strategic tool over 15 years ago, when a client said "the cus-

tomer doesn't remember what we thought we told him." We realized that virtually all firms approach communication focused on what they want to say or what they think the customer needs to know. We recommend abandoning the old mind-set and adopting a new one: Good communication is based on what your audience at the moment, frequently your customer, hears, believes, and remembers. And communication as corporate strategy seeks to influence or control these outcomes.

When a firm is really good at this, every employee can be an ambassador. Then, they can enlist their customers to sell for them. Check your firm's definition of communication. Is there an official definition? Is the unofficial one just "more?" Adopt a formal definition as understanding how to influence what your audience hears, believes, and remembers and using these insights to gain a competitive edge and support corporate strategy.

Why Bother?

The goal is to realize the implications of this approach and analyze your own firm. Without understanding the implications, your company potentially misses the opportunity to leverage advertising and marketing and, at worst, undercuts the impact of those communications. The goal is message alignment, whereby what the customer hears via advertising is duplicated by person-to-person comments. This is the single most violated area of business communication today.

PacifiCare, a health-care company, uses well-designed ads offering "straightforward answers." Great promise! How does it do in person? Shortly after PacifiCare bought Harris-Methodist Health Care in Texas, consumer complaints skyrocketed, and elected officials called a town meeting. Here's an exchange: Woman—"Why does it cost me $80 to buy my Celebrex? It used to cost me $10." Company offical—"It's now a closed formulary. It used to be an open formulary. Harris-Methodist made it a closed formulary." The newspaper reported that people left "more confused than when they came." Reading the exchange in writing doesn't show visual images. The executive's facial expression and body language radiated that he wanted to be anywhere else. I showed this video to a group and asked what they thought the official was conveying to the questioner. One person said, "He hopes she'll drop dead."

In contrast, when I complimented Maria at Wolf Camera, she said, "Oh, we want your business!" Almost a direct duplication of Wolf's ad copy. Few firms show employees their ads. The reasons given are: We never did it before, it would cost too much, and our employees would know if the ads aren't true.

Sometimes advertising, marketing, and customer relations seem to exist in separate worlds. Several of our clients in different locales reported the same experience when The Limited distributed $15 certificates by mail. A letter promoting the chain's merchandise accompanied the certificates. One customer tried to buy something for slightly less than $15 and another one for slightly more. Both found store personnel unfamiliar with the coupon. One employee insisted that the purchase had to be exactly $15.

How do you motivate employees to use your own advertising language? In The Limited example, it didn't appear that employees in the store had seen either their ads or the coupons sent to customers. Employees have to believe that executives really believe the message, and it can't be contradicted by internal actions. Assuming those conditions are in place, it's helpful to understand how people "communicate," by which we mean: How do they pick out certain words or concepts and pass them on? What causes your target audience to remember some things and not others?

Influencing Memory: Words Matter

People remember and pass on words. We divide corporate key words into lists of "good" words, those you want repeated, and "bad" words, those you don't. The "good" words list should be closely aligned with advertising, marketing, or recruiting promise. PacifiCare, for example, promised straightforward answers but replied to a patient's question with the jargon term *formulary*.

Our firm conducts a reality check to see if people at all levels of the organization are using "good" words regularly, not just in a pitch situation. A familiar situation is to hear all these "good" words coming out when the speaker is delivering the marketing pitch, but then the moment Q&A takes over, the words disappear. That sends a clear message that these words are just marketing hype.

Texas Commerce Bank, now part of Chase, used the slogan "Star Treatment." Then-chairman and CEO, Marc Shapiro, repeated "star treatment" frequently in one-on-one conversations and corporate communication. Our small firm was trying to buy a building in Dallas, and the loan officer offered to fill out the forms for us. When I thanked her, she said, "It's all part of star treatment." When the officer said "star treatment," she said it with fervor. We not only heard the same words as the ads, we believed that she believed them. Recall that our goal is to influence what the target audience hears, believes, and remembers. Much to the dismay of many clients, "believability" turns first on whether the listener feels the speaker believes what he or she is saying. The perfunctory "I'm sorry" can do more harm than good.

Employees As Ambassadors

How do you turn everyone in a company into an ambassador who promotes the firm? The secret is to understand how people mimic each other combined with training. Mimicry or imitation is key since top management sets the style and communication culture. Training carries it throughout the firm. According to The Container Store's founders, most retailers annually provide seven hours of training, but their chain provides 185. We believe most retailers make meager training investments and always say, "It costs too much." Actually, many firms do use cost-effective training and say it costs too much not to train workers.

Training magazines are filled with articles about effective teaching. Our own experience shows that a company gets the best results by combining peer group dynamics; individualized, real-time scenarios; and video examples. The video examples demonstrate principles. The scenarios illustrate how people react in daily situations, and peer group dynamics produce the shared value that everyone must personally verbalize the firm's message. Peer group experimentation with real situations also allows the opportunity to practice. Grasping the idea intellectually is one thing; getting comfortable doing it requires practice.

In our training, we videotape clients in situations they have experienced. In one case, we asked a group of pharmacists to identify their own problem situations or worst-case scenarios, then to play themselves and the customer to show us exactly what hap-

pened. We videotaped them, had a group session, then taped them again as they practiced the principles we had outlined. Viewing the retaped segment is important because participants must feel they are being honest, professional, and genuine in responding to a complain or situation. They have to decide for themselves and as a group that they are ambassadors and can mirror a firm's advertising and marketing language. Participants learn only by trying it, seeing it, and committing to it. Here's an example of real video from a real client.

A customer complains about getting only half of her pills. The Pharmacist replies, "I'm sorry, but it was kind of busy in here today." We call this *terminal honesty*. I'm sure it was very busy, but when that is highlighted in verbal communication, the customer gets the feeling everything has gone awry. Another comment elicited in the same situation: "That doesn't happen very often, but it does happen." Ouch!

After diagramming the flow of information, role-playing, and watching each other during the group session, the same situation produced this comment. "I'm sorry about this. We aim to be perfect. I'm sorry. I'll get you those pills right now." This employee is using the power of person-to-person, right-on-the-spot communication to reinforce a promise: Since we didn't quite live up to it, we're fixing it.

In complaint situations, the customer is asking the question. However, after saying "I'm sorry" and "we aim to be perfect," the employee can turn the tables on the customer and become the questioner. In the scenario just described, the pharmacist extended the conversation with the customer by asking a question, saying, "I sure appreciate your coming in. Will you give me another chance?"

Educating Versus Communicating

Our training approach resists the temptation to educate the consumer: "It was kind of busy." We're trying to "hear" as the customer does. Statistics can be a problem because they mean one thing to a company and another to the individual. It does no good to say, "We fill hundreds of millions of prescriptions safely. Only one-tenth of 1 percent are misfilled." The customer cares only about the one being picked up now.

Recently, a *Chicago Sun Times* columnist wrote about an experience with Amazon.com. He contacted the help desk and was put on hold. As a reporter, he could contact the head of public relations; after an hour and a half, he did. She looked into it and called him back, saying, "It's a minor glitch, which affects an insignificant number of people." With our approach, such miscommunication is less likely. Although true, *glitch* and *insignificant* are bad words. "Bad" words are the ones you don't want passed from person to person. How do we know about this exchange? The columnist, by writing about it, passed it on.

Why Emphasize Words?

If you ask someone to summarize a meeting or describe an ad, the person recalls words or short phrases and builds a recollection around them. Control the words, and you control communication. Control what people hear, and you can influence what they think. Last summer, our company worked on a product recall. A recall is unpleasant, and products have to be pulled quickly. One customer was taking an item off the shelf when an employee stopped her, saying, "You can't have that." The customer asked, "Why not?" His reply: "It's contaminated." He had heard that word from his manager who got it from a fax. You can guess how many people the customer told about the "contaminated" product. What should have happened? When the worker responded to "why not?" he could have said, "It's not up to our standards."

A client facing an analogous situation asked why the firm should tell the employee anything. Then, maybe he or she would say, "I don't know." I recommend more proactive communication that aims to enlist each hearer in the communication line. If you don't tell people, they'll guess. And, if you accustom people to thinking of themselves as your ambassadors, they'll pass on your intended message. It' a huge mistake to try to deceive any audience. The employee undoubtedly will learn of the situation. Then "I don't know" isn't truthful. It's a huge mistake to leave your employees in the dark. It makes them look foolish and sends the message that they aren't important enough to be included.

Isn't Image Everything?

Understanding and examining the words in a message help capture what people hear. But we "hear" in an environment dramatically changed by television. Several generations have been raised to expect everyone to look and sound like people on television. Visual image is part of television's impact. It's true we have conditioned people to expect a speaker to look them straight in the eye and to smile. People expect the comfortable fluidity of television speech. They are used to speakers who convey they care about them.

People have shorter attention spans and demand "bites" of information; they are less likely to read; they respond to sympathetic anecdotes about individuals. They are used to the question and answer style on television. These expectations have implications for training programs and corporate communication efforts using video. We observe some common mistakes. First, the corporate video often isn't "real." Today's employee instantly can tell when video belongs on the "you control it" network or the "objective media" network. This doesn't mean firms can't produce and use video. It needs to look more like "news" and less like ads. Consider the overall look of the video, the language, and the length of the piece.

Language needs to sound the way people sound on television. Too many internal examples reveal an internal "interviewer" asking, "Mr. Jones, tell us about our company's success in Asia." The executive

replies stiffly, "What a good question, Sarah." A real reporter would have framed the question differently, "Mr. Jones, are you concerned we might not achieve our goals in Asia?" This is exactly the same topic with the question framed differently. This is not a recommendation for an internal interviewer to be hostile. It's a reminder that the audience can spot an easy question, and that the firm loses credibility.

Television has had a definite effect on how long a listener will pay attention. Many videos, speeches, and presentations are much too long. Executives often have the attitude, "What do I want to say" as opposed to "What do I want them to remember?"

Finally, television has conditioned us to expect people to look pleasant. Most presentation skills courses try to address facial expression. A sour expression causes the listener to stop listening. We think, "This person hates me," when the opposite may be true. Understanding that a smile engages people leads to the untrue conclusion that people have to smile all the time. As one expert wrote, "Service with a smile can be emotionally and physically stressful for the employees, especially if it is forced or insincere."

Questions

1. What are the three most important points that a human resources executive in retailing could learn from this case? Explain your answer.
2. Why do you think that some retailers, such as Wolf Camera, "get it" with regard to employee training and employee empowerment, while many others do not?
3. Within the context of reading, what is your definition of "good communication?" Explain your answer.
4. Why is it important for a retailer to know the difference between "educating" and "communicating?"
5. How can a retailer avoid the following operational situation? "Sometimes advertising, marketing, and customer relations seem to exist in separate worlds."
6. Based on the factors noted in the case, offer both employee training and operations tips for a neighborhood luggage store.
7. In recent years, some retailers have gotten themselves into trouble for failing to disclose certain financial data or for obscuring poor performance. What can they learn from this case?

*The material in this case is adapted by the authors from Merrie Spaeth, President, Spaeth Communications, "Just What Is 'Good' Communication?" *Retailing Issues Letter* (May 2000), pp. 1–6. Reprinted by permission.

part six

Merchandise Management and Pricing

In Part Six, we present the merchandise management and pricing aspects of the retail strategy mix. Merchandise management consists of the buying, handling, and financial aspects of merchandising. Pricing decisions deal with the financial aspects of merchandise management and affect their interaction with other retailing elements.

- ■ **Chapter 14** covers the development of merchandise plans. We begin by discussing the concept of a merchandising philosophy. We then look at buying organizations and their processes, as well as the major considerations in formulating merchandise plans. The chapter concludes by describing category management and merchandising software.

- ■ **Chapter 15** focuses on implementing merchandise plans. We study each stage in the buying and handling process: gathering information, selecting and interacting with merchandise sources, evaluation, negotiation, concluding purchases, receiving and stocking merchandise, reordering, and reevaluation. We also examine logistics and inventory management, and their effects on merchandising.

- ■ **Chapter 16** concentrates on financial merchandise management. We introduce the cost and retail methods of accounting. The merchandise forecasting and budgeting process is presented. Unit control systems are discussed. Dollar and unit financial inventory controls are integrated.

- ■ **Chapter 17** deals with pricing. We review the outside factors affecting price decisions: consumers, government, suppliers, and competitors. A framework for developing a price strategy is then shown: objectives, broad policy, basic strategy, implementation, and adjustments.

Chapter 14

DEVELOPING MERCHANDISE PLANS

Reprinted by permission.

In 1993, Millard "Mickey" Drexler, the chief executive of Gap Inc. (**www.gap.com**), realized that his Gap and Banana Republic stores were not effectively reaching consumers who did not want to spend much money on clothes. So, he converted 48 underperforming Gap stores into Gap Warehouse stores. Soon thereafter, Drexler changed the name to Old Navy (**www.oldnavy.com**). Today, Old Navy has achieved a fervent following among its customers, and it generates about $6 billion in annual sales from its more than 800 stores.

Old Navy is able to hold prices at low levels through various merchandising tactics. For example, while a Gap sweater is typically made from merino wool, an Old Navy sweater is more likely made with low-cost acrylic fabric. However, even though the Old Navy sweater may be one-third less expensive than the Gap one, it is designed to look and feel better than acrylic sweaters found at other discounters.

Old Navy also has less consistency in its colors and sizes. Thus, the allowable variance in seam width for a pair of Gap jeans is one-quarter of an inch, while the allowance for Old Navy jeans is one-half inch. As a result, an Old Navy shopper may have to try on several pairs of jeans to find one that fits just right. Despite its low prices, Old Navy apparel is stylish and well displayed, and the sales staff is well trained.[1]

chapter objectives

1. To demonstrate the importance of a sound merchandising philosophy
2. To study various buying organization formats and the processes they use
3. To outline the considerations in devising merchandise plans: forecasts, innovativeness, assortment, brands, timing, and allocation
4. To discuss category management and merchandising software

OVERVIEW

PLANalyst (www.gers. com/products/planalyst/ planalyst1.html) is one of the many software tools to help retailers make better merchandising decisions.

Retailers must have the proper product assortments and sell them in a manner consistent with their overall strategy. **Merchandising** consists of the activities involved in acquiring particular goods and/or services and making them available at the places, times, and prices and in the quantity that enable a retailer to reach its goals. Merchandising decisions can dramatically affect performance. Consider these observations of the late Stanley Marcus, former chief executive of Neiman Marcus:

I believe that retail merchandising is actually very simple: it consists of two factors, customers and goods. If you take good care in the buying of the product, it doesn't come back. If you take good care of your customers, they do come back. It's just that simple and just that difficult. This is obviously an oversimplification of the problems of retailing. It's not quite that easy—but almost.

Yet, no wonder customer loyalty has dropped. There is little reason for a shopper to go across town to a store when it's a forgone conclusion that she'll find the same merchandise in store C that she has already seen in stores A and B. I fully expect to come upon a newspaper headline that proclaims, "Customers Found Bored to Death in the Sportswear Department of the XYZ Department Store."

Merchandise sameness emanates from the training of the buyers who have been taught to play it safe by avoiding risky fashions, to play it cautiously by buying from a limited number of standard vendors who sell the same "packages" to all major accounts, to play it for profit by advertising only the goods supported by manufacturers' advertising allowances. Many retailers erroneously believe the goal is to make a profit and fail to realize that a profit is due to having goods or services that are so satisfactory that the customer is willing to pay a bonus or profit, over and above the distributor's cost.[2]

In this chapter, the *planning* aspects of merchandising are discussed. The *implementation* aspects of merchandising are examined in Chapter 15. The *financial* aspects of merchandising are described in Chapter 16. Retail *pricing* is covered in Chapter 17.

Visit our Web site (**www.prenhall.com/bermanevans**) for a broad selection of links related to merchandising strategies and tactics.

MERCHANDISING PHILOSOPHY

At Cost Plus, "you never know what you'll find" (www.costplus.com).

A **merchandising philosophy** sets the guiding principles for all the merchandise decisions that a retailer makes. It must reflect target market desires, the retailer's institutional type, the marketplace positioning, the defined value chain, supplier capabilities, costs, competitors, product trends, and other factors. The retail merchandising philosophy drives every product decision, from what produce lines to carry to the shelf space allotted to different products to inventory turnover to pricing—and more: "Retailers have to decide on the breadth of assortment across the store (narrow or wide) and the depth of the assortment within each category (deep or shallow). In addition, they must select the quality of the items within the assortment—high or low, national brands or store brands. They need to decide on their pricing policies, across categories and within. Finally, retailers must decide if assortments should generally be stable over time or whether there should be surprises, specials, or customization in assortments."[3] See Figure 14-1.

Costco, the membership club giant, flourishes with its individualistic merchandising philosophy:

We have a selection of about 4,000 items; if you went into a Target or Wal-Mart, you'd find 100,000. We may only select two toasters to sell or two types of peanut butter, but they will be the best values we can find at the time. Those items make up 3,000 of our selection. About 1,000 items constantly change. One week, shoppers see some Levi's relaxed-fit jeans and some Waterford crystal; they come back the next time and we don't have those items, but we have Tommy Hilfiger and Baccarat. It creates an attitude that if you see it, you better buy it. Don't misunderstand me, people really like saving 50 cents on a jar of peanut butter. But what they really love is a Movado watch for $250 that sells for $550 in the jewelry store. That's the conversation of cocktail parties. Peanut butter is not.[4]

FIGURE 14-1

Harry and David's Merchandising Philosophy

What makes this retailer so successful? As its Web site (**www.harryanddavid.com**) states: "Start with the world's finest, freshest ingredients. From fruit to nuts and everything in between, don't cut corners and don't make compromises because just when you think no one will notice the difference, someone will. Pack each gift with pride and personal attention to detail. In short, you need to be a stickler for perfection, every step of the way. Treat the customer the way you'd want to be treated. Guarantee satisfaction 100%. Not just the condition of the package. Not just on-time arrival. If the giver and the receiver aren't delighted, we'll make it right with either a replacement gift or a full refund—whichever you think best. No delays. No questions asked."

Reprinted by permission of Retail Forward, Inc.

In forming a merchandising philosophy, the scope of responsibility for merchandise personnel must be stated. Are these personnel to be involved with the full array of *merchandising functions*, both buying and selling goods and services (including selection, pricing, display, and customer transactions)? Or are they to focus on the *buying function*, with others responsible for displays, personal selling, and so on? Many firms consider merchandising to be the foundation for their success, and buyers (or merchandise managers) engage in both buying and selling tasks. Other retailers consider their buyers to be skilled specialists who should not be active in the selling function, which is done by other skilled specialists. Store managers at full-line discount stores often have great influence on product displays but have little impact on whether to stock or promote particular brands.

With a merchandising-oriented philosophy, the buyer's expertise is used in selling, responsibility and authority are clear, the buyer ensures that items are properly displayed, costs are reduced (fewer specialists), and the buyer is close to consumers through his or her selling involvement. When buying and selling are separated, specialized skills are applied to each task, the morale of store personnel goes up as they get more authority, selling is not viewed as a secondary task, the interaction of salespeople with customers is better exploited, and buying and selling personnel are distinctly supervised. An individual firm must evaluate which format is better for its particular retail strategy.

To capitalize on opportunities, more retailers now use micromerchandising and cross-merchandising. With **micromerchandising**, a retailer adjusts shelf-space allocations to respond to customer and other differences among local markets. Dominick's supermarkets allot shelf space to children's and adult's cereals to reflect demand patterns at different stores. Wal-Mart adapts the space it assigns to product lines at various stores to reflect differences in demographics, weather, and customer activities. Micromerchandising is easier today because of the information generated through data warehouses. As Walgreen says, "This approach puts the correct products in the correct stores for our customers. We want to carry merchandise that appeals to that store's customers, or else we will carry 'dead' inventory."[5]

In **cross-merchandising**, a retailer carries complementary goods and services to encourage shoppers to buy more. That is why apparel stores stock accessories. Cross-merchandising, like scrambled merchandising, can be ineffective if taken too far. Yet, it has tremendous potential. Consider the new approach that Bed Bath & Beyond has been testing for specialty foods:

> Promotional items, such as bottles of Poland Spring water for 50 cents, are featured on the aisle. Much of the array is composed of celebrity brands, including Emeril Legasse and Bobby Flay (of *Food Network* fame). Prices escalate as the shopper moves deeper into the bay, with a bottle of Rao's balsamic vinegar retailing for $19.99. Cross-merchandising opportunities include Rubbermaid food storage products and Pyrex measuring cups displayed next to cookie mixes. Kits for making root beer, lollipops, and other projects are featured. There are other tweaks to the usual format. Adjacent to specialty food is a combined kitchen gadget, kitchen textiles, and kitchen storage department.[6]

BUYING ORGANIZATION FORMATS AND PROCESSES

A merchandising plan cannot be properly devised unless the buying organization and its processes are well defined: Who is responsible for decisions? What are their tasks? Do they have sufficient authority? How does merchandising fit with overall operations? Figure 14-2 highlights the range of organizational attributes from which to choose.

LEVEL OF FORMALITY

With a *formal buying organization*, merchandising (buying) is a distinct retail task and a separate department is set up. The functions involved in acquiring merchandise and making it available for sale are under the control of this department. A formal organization is most often used by larger firms and involves distinct personnel. In an *informal buying organization*, merchandising (buying) is not a distinct task. The same personnel handle both merchandising (buying) and other retail tasks; responsibility and authority are not always clear-cut. Informal organizations generally occur in smaller retailers.

The advantages of a formal organization are the clarity of responsibilities and the use of full-time, specialized merchandisers. The disadvantage is the cost of a separate department. The

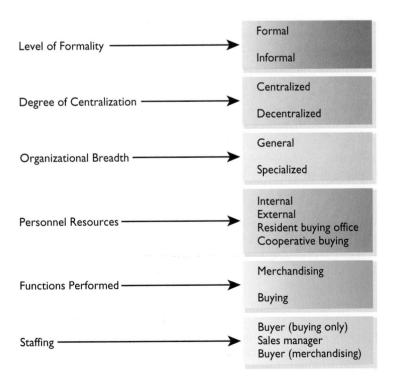

FIGURE 14-2
The Attributes and Functions of Buying Organizations

Level of Formality →
- Formal
- Informal

Degree of Centralization →
- Centralized
- Decentralized

Organizational Breadth →
- General
- Specialized

Personnel Resources →
- Internal
- External
- Resident buying office
- Cooperative buying

Functions Performed →
- Merchandising
- Buying

Staffing →
- Buyer (buying only)
- Sales manager
- Buyer (merchandising)

advantages of an informal format are the low costs and flexibility. The disadvantages are less-defined responsibilities and the lesser emphasis on merchandise planning. Both structures exist in great numbers. It is not critical for a firm to use a formal department. It is crucial that the firm recognizes the role of merchandising (buying) and ensures that responsibility, activities, and operational relationships are aptly defined and enacted.

DEGREE OF CENTRALIZATION

Multiunit retailers must choose whether to have a centralized buying organization or a decentralized one. In a *centralized buying organization,* all purchase decisions emanate from one office. A chain may have eight stores, with all merchandise decisions made at the headquarters store. In a *decentralized buying organization,* purchase decisions are made locally or regionally. A 40-store chain may allow each outlet to select its own merchandise or divide the branches into geographic territories (such as four branches per region) with regional decisions made by the headquarters store in each territory.

The advantages of centralized buying are the integration of effort, strict controls, consistent image, proximity to top management, staff support, and volume discounts. Possible disadvantages are the inflexibility, time delays, poor morale at local stores, and excessive uniformity. Decentralized buying has these advantages: adaptability to local conditions, quick order processing, and improved morale because of branch autonomy. Potential disadvantages are disjointed planning, an inconsistent image, limited controls, little staff support, and a loss of volume discounts.

See what Zara's merchandisers think is "hot" (www.zara.com).

Many chains combine the formats by deploying a centralized buying organization while also giving store managers some input. This is how Zara, the Madrid-based global apparel chain, operates:

> In a bright and vast white room, 200 designers and product managers are deciding what to create. They regularly gather suggestions from more than 500 store managers worldwide—not just specific orders but ideas for cuts, fabrics, or, say, a new line of men's vests. After weighing the managers' ideas, the team in La Coruña decides what to make. Designers draw up the latest ideas on their computers and send them over Zara's Intranet to nearby factories. Within days, cutting, dyeing, stitching, and pressing begin. In just three weeks, the clothes will hang in stores from Barcelona to Berlin to Beirut. Zara isn't just a bit faster than rivals such as Gap. It's 12 times faster.[7]

ORGANIZATIONAL BREADTH

In a general buying organization, one or several people buy all of a firm's merchandise. The owner of a small hardware store may buy the merchandise for his or her store. With a specialized organization, each buyer is responsible for a product category. A department store usually has separate buyers for girls', juniors', and women's clothes.

Careers in RETAILING — 24 Years Old and a Wal-Mart Buyer

Melissa Davies, at 24 years old, became a buyer for Wal-Mart (**www.walmart.com**) with responsibility for purchasing outdoor decorative merchandise in the lawn and garden department. During a typical day, Davies meets with suppliers, corresponds with Wal-Mart's store associates, and answers over 170 E-mails. She says: "It is fast-paced, and I find it exciting to work with suppliers on long-term ideas and strategies." And although she is young, Davies has earned the respect of executives at major corporations that supply her products.

While she was a marketing and management major at Eastern Washington University, Davies was a member of a student group called Students in Free Enterprise. At that time, a Wal-Mart executive heard her give a presentation and invited her to interview with the firm. Since being hired as a buyer trainee, Davies has received several promotions. She is now responsible for a $300 million product category.

Like many other retailing executives, Melissa Davies found that Wal-Mart allows her to follow her gut instincts despite her youth: "At Wal-Mart, it isn't about experience or tenure, it is about performance." And although Davies initially wanted a career in sports marketing, she is now a great supporter of those who wish to pursue a career in retailing.

Source: "Freedom to Follow Her Gut," *Careers in Retailing* (January 2001), p. 15.

A general approach is better if the retailer is small or there are few products involved. A specialized approach is better if the retailer is large or many products are carried. By specializing, there is greater expertise and responsibility is well defined; however, costs are higher and extra personnel are required.

PERSONNEL RESOURCES

A retailer can choose an inside or outside buying organization. An *inside buying organization* is staffed by a retailer's personnel, and merchandise decisions are made by permanent employees. See Figure 14-3. With an *outside buying organization*, a company or personnel external to the retailer are hired, usually on a fee basis. Most retailers use either an inside or an outside organization; some employ a combination.

An inside buying organization is most often used by large retailers and very small retailers. Large retailers do this to have greater control over merchandising decisions and to be more distinctive. They have the financial clout to employ their own specialists. At very small retailers, the owner or manager does all merchandising functions to save money and keep close to the market.

Ross Stores has merchandising career opportunities in New York and Los Angeles. Scroll down to "Buying Office" and click on a job category (www.rossstores.com/jo_jb.jsp).

Ross Stores (**www.rossstores.com**), the off-price-apparel chain with stores in 22 states, is an example of a retailer with an inside buying organization. Its Web site says, "Our commitment to the buying function is key to the company's competitive position. As a team, we provide name brand merchandise at a good price through strong negotiations and vendor relationships. We employ an entrepreneurial buying strategy reflecting regional preferences and trends. Career opportunities often exist in these positions: merchandise managers, buyers, assistant buyers, and merchandise control analysts/planning analysts."

An outside organization is most frequently used by small or medium-sized retailers or those far from supply sources. It is more efficient for them to hire outside buyers than to use company personnel. An outside organization has purchase volume clout in dealing with suppliers, usually services noncompeting retailers, offers research, and may sponsor private brands. Outside buying

---

Melissa Davies

WAL★MART

TYPE OF STORE:
Mass Market

HEADQUARTERS:
Bentonville, Ark.

Networking helped Melissa Davies score a job as a buyer for the nation's largest retailer, Wal-Mart.

While a student and basketball player at Eastern Washington University in Cheney, Wash., Davies was part of a group called Students in Free Enterprise. "The program allows you to network with businesses locally," explains Davies, a business administration marketing and management major. While giving a presentation, a Wal-Mart executive heard her speak and invited her to pursue a career with the chain's training program.

After starting as a buyer trainee, Davies rose through the ranks with four promotions. Now she is a buyer of outdoor decorative merchandise in the lawn and garden department.

"I love the challenge. I find it amazing that I'm 24 years old and have the responsibility for a category that is somewhere in the $300 million range," says Davies. What she finds refreshing at Wal-Mart is that the company is willing to let even young associates follow their gut instincts. "At Wal-Mart, it isn't about experience or tenure, it is about performance," adds Davies, who once vowed she'd never work in retail and wanted to pursue a career in sports marketing because of her college basketball experience. She is now a great supporter of a retail career path. "I've entrusted my career to Wal-Mart," she adds.

During a typical day, Davies finds herself meeting with suppliers, talking to store associates and answering at least 170 e-mails. "It is fast paced, and I find it exciting to work with suppliers on long-term ideas and strategies." Although she's young, she says she's earned the respect of top-level executives from major manufacturers who supply Wal-Mart.

What's her gameplan? "I'd like to stay in merchandising and ultimately have a leadership role in the company." She's still involved in Students in Free Enterprise, and she helps show others the opportunity presented by not only retailing, but Wal-Mart in particular. ■

FIGURE 14-3

At Wal-Mart: Developing an Inside Buying Organization

Reprinted by permission of *DSN Retailing Today.*

organizations may be paid by retailers that subscribe to their services or by vendors that give commissions. An individual retailer may set up its own internal organization if it feels its outside group is dealing with direct competitors or the firm finds it can buy items more efficiently on its own.

The Doneger Group (**www.doneger.com**) is the leading independent resident buying office, with hundreds of retailer clients that operate more than 7,000 stores. As its Web site notes, "Through our daily involvement in all market categories of women's, men's, and children's apparel and accessories, our merchandising and market research specialists are able to offer clients a broad range of services to help them make the right decisions and meet the ever-changing challenges of the fashion and retail business. It is our goal to help retailers generate greater sales, increase profits, and gain market share."

Associated Merchandising Corporation (AMC) is a hybrid buying organization. For more than 70 years, it was a nonprofit organization co-owned by numerous retailers. Target Corporation acquired AMC in 1998, mostly to serve the retailer's Target Stores, Mervyn's, and Marshall Field's chains. AMC still provides merchandising functions for several other retailers, as well. It is involved with international trend identification, product design and development, global product sourcing, quality assurance, and production, delivery, and order tracking. It focuses on apparel, accessories, and home goods.

A **resident buying office**, which can be an inside or outside organization, is used when a retailer wants to keep in close touch with key market trends and cannot do so through just headquarters buying staff. Such offices are situated in important merchandise centers and provide valuable data and contacts. A few large specialized U.S. firms operate resident buying offices that serve several thousand retailers. Each organization just cited (Ross, Doneger, and AMC) has multiple resident buying offices to get a better sense of local markets and merchandise sources. Besides the major players, there are many smaller outside resident buying offices that assist retailers.

Today, independent retailers and small chains are involved with cooperative buying to a greater degree than before to compete with large chains. In **cooperative buying**, a group of retailers gets together to make quantity purchases from suppliers and obtain volume discounts. It is most popular among food, hardware, and drugstore retailers. As an illustration, the Federation of Pharmacy Networks (FPN) comprises 20 buying groups across the United States. It represents 10,000 independent drugstore owners: "FPN negotiates with selected vendors to establish favorable contracts based on the volume purchasing power achieved through our pharmacies. Many of our programs provide the independent pharmacist with significant net savings. Additionally, each member group office benefits from FPN's programs."[8]

Learn more "About Doneger" (www.doneger.com/index_guest.asp), the world's largest outside buying organization.

The Federation of Pharmacy Networks (www.fpn.org) provides many services for its members.

FUNCTIONS PERFORMED

At this juncture, the responsibilities and functions of merchandise and in-store personnel are assigned. With a "merchandising" view, merchandise personnel oversee all buying and selling functions, including assortments, advertising, pricing, point-of-sale displays, employee utilization, and personal selling approaches. With a "buying" view, merchandise personnel oversee the buying of products, advertising, and pricing, while in-store personnel oversee assortments, displays, employee utilization, and sales presentations. The functions undertaken must reflect the retailer's level of formality, the degree of centralization, and personnel resources.

STAFFING

The last organizational decision involves staffing. What positions must be filled and with what qualifications? Firms with a merchandising viewpoint are most concerned with hiring good buyers. Firms with a buying perspective are concerned about hiring sales managers, as well. Many large firms hire college graduates, train them, and promote them to buyers and sales managers.

A **buyer** is responsible for selecting the merchandise to be carried by a retailer and setting a strategy to market that merchandise. He or she devises and controls sales and profit projections for a product category (generally for all stores in a chain); plans proper merchandise assortments, styling, sizes, and quantities; negotiates with and evaluates vendors; and often oversees in-store displays. He or she must be attuned to the marketplace, be able to bargain with suppliers, and be capable of preparing detailed plans; and he or she may travel to the marketplace. A **sales manager** typically supervises the on-floor selling and operational activities for a specific retail department.

He or she must be a good organizer, administrator, and motivator. A *merchandising buyer* must possess the attributes of each. Most retailers feel the critical qualification for good merchandisers is their ability to relate to customers and methodically anticipate future needs. In addition, to some extent, buyers are involved with many of the remaining tasks described in this and the next chapter.

Federated Department Stores, which operates such department store chains as Bloomingdale's and Macy's, has career tracks that recognize the value of both merchandising and in-store personnel. Figure 14-4 shows two distinct career tracks. Here's what it's like at the top of the merchandising world:

Kal Ruttenstein has been, for 25 years, senior vice-president for fashion direction at Bloomingdale's, where he safeguards the store's fashion image. He travels to Europe six to eight times a year to search for new talent and take in the runway antics of established designers. He determines which designers to feature in the coveted New York window displays. He plays soothsayer, presenting his seasonal predictions to a battalion of ready-to-wear and accessories buyers. Ultimately, Ruttenstein determines what will be sold. His task is complicated, risky, and expensive. He has an impressive resumé, with successful runs as a buyer at Lord & Taylor, where he was an early champion of women's trousers, and Saks Fifth Avenue. He was president of Bonwit Teller specialty stores. He has a bachelor's degree in English from Princeton and an MBA from Columbia, which he refrains from advertising because, as he says facetiously, "It's not good for a fashion director to seem too smart." Yet he is both intelligent and savvy, which is how he has managed to survive so long. "I know what it's like to think about the bottom line. I never buy things we don't have a chance of selling."[9]

Federated Department Stores (www.retailology.com/career/career_paths.asp) *has exciting career paths in both merchandising and operations.*

FIGURE 14-4

Merchandising Versus Store Management Career Tracks at Federated Department Stores

Source: Figure developed by the authors based on information at "Career Opportunities," **www.retailology.com/college/career** (March 17, 2003).

Merchandising Track

Divisional Merchandise Manager
Oversees merchandise selection and procurement for a particular business segment. Sets the merchandise direction to ensure continuity on the selling floor. Develops strategy to ensure customer satisfaction and maximize performance and profits.

Buyer
Expected to maximize sales and profitability of a given business area by developing and implementing a strategy, analyzing it, and reacting to trends. Overall support of company sales, gross margin, and turnover objectives.

Associate Buyer
Responsible for merchandise development, marketing, and financial management of a particular business area. This is a developmental step to buyer.

Assistant Buyer
Aids buyer in selecting and procuring merchandise, which supports overall sales, gross margin, and turnover goals. Provides operational support to buyers. Assumes some buying responsibility, once buyer determines proficiency.

Store Management Track

Store Manager
Responsible for all aspects of running a profitable store. Sets the tone to ensure success in customer service, profits, operations, people development, merchandise presentation, and merchandise assortment.

Assistant Store Manager
Directs merchandise flow, store maintenance, expense management, shortage prevention, and store sales support activities for a large portion of store volume. Acts as Store Manager in his or her absence.

Sales Manager
In charge of store activities in a specific merchandise area. Includes merchandise presentation, employee development, customer service, operations, and inventory control.

Assistant Sales Manager
Responsible for supervising daily store activities in a specific merchandise area. Includes selling and service management, selecting and developing associates, merchandising, and business management.

DEVISING MERCHANDISE PLANS

There are several factors to consider in devising merchandise plans, as discussed next. See Figure 14-5.

FORECASTS

Forecasts are projections of expected retail sales for given periods. They are the foundation of merchandise plans and include these components: overall company projections, product category projections, item-by-item projections, and store-by-store projections (if a chain). Consider the process used by Clothestime, an apparel chain with more than 300 stores:

Clothestime (www. clothestime.com) is always looking to stay current with its youthful customers.

Planning starts when top merchandisers meet with financial planners. The group brainstorms—trying to figure out months in advance how the retailer can profit from trends that could quickly fade away. "We start with the finance staff to come up with a corporate goal," says Clothestime's director of planning and allocation. "Then we sit down with the buyer and his or her merchandise planner to talk about where they see their mix going." The buyer and the merchandise planner formulate a detailed plan, which is reviewed and reworked to make sure it meshes with the financial goals the firm has outlined for the next season. "This takes about six weeks from beginning to end."[10]

In this section, forecasting is examined from a general planning perspective. In Chapter 16, the financial dimensions of forecasting are reviewed.

When preparing forecasts, it is essential to distinguish among different types of merchandise. **Staple merchandise** consists of the regular products carried by a retailer. For a supermarket, staples include milk, bread, canned soup, and facial tissues. For a department store, staples include everyday watches, jeans, glassware, and housewares. Because these items have relatively stable sales (sometimes seasonal) and their nature may not change much over time, a retailer can clearly outline the quantities for these items. A **basic stock list** specifies the inventory level, color, brand, style category, size, package, and so on for every staple item carried by the retailer.

Assortment merchandise consists of apparel, furniture, autos, and other products for which the retailer must carry a variety of products in order to give customers a proper selection. This merchandise is harder to forecast than staples due to demand variations, style changes, and the number of sizes and colors to be carried. Decisions are two-pronged: (1) Product lines, styles, designs, and colors are projected. (2) A **model stock plan** is used to project specific items, such as the number of green, red, and blue pullover sweaters of a certain design by size. With a model stock plan, many items are ordered for popular sizes and colors, and small amounts of less popular sizes and colors fill out the assortment.

FIGURE 14-5

Considerations in Devising Merchandise Plans

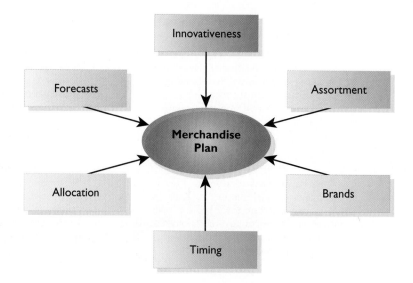

A widespread practice outside the United States is for an established foreign firm with a strong customer reputation and customer following to buy U.S.-branded goods with the understanding that the manufacturer will repackage these goods under the foreign firm's private label.

This strategy is beneficial for both the U.S. manufacturer and the foreign firm. The U.S. firm can have a presence in a foreign country with a minimal investment and a limited commitment. To the foreign firm, the private label strategy gives it exclusive merchandise, a means of developing its own brand, and tested products.

Europe, with $280 billion in private label exports, accounts for over 83 percent of total foreign private label sales. The market is so large that there are premium private labels, specialty private lines that target regional taste preferences, and economy private label lines like "Euroshopper" that are sold in multiple countries. Private label goods will account for 14 percent of total European retail sales. And the private label market in Europe is forecast to continue growing, especially among general merchandise. However, private label food sales are not forecast to grow as rapidly in Northern Europe where the supermarket structure is more fully developed.

Source: "Can Do: Going Private Label Pays in Europe," *AgExporter* (September 2001), p. 4.

Fashion merchandise consists of products that may have cyclical sales due to changing tastes and life-styles. For these items, forecasting can be hard since styles may change from year to year. "Hot" colors often change back and forth. **Seasonal merchandise** consists of products that sell well over nonconsecutive time periods. Items such as ski equipment and air-conditioner servicing have excellent sales during one season per year. Since the strongest sales of seasonal items usually occur at the same time each year, forecasting is straightforward.

With **fad merchandise**, high sales are generated for a short time. Often, toys and games are fads, such as Harry Potter toys that fly off store shelves each time a related movie is released. It is hard to forecast whether such products will reach specific sales targets and how long they will be popular. Sometimes, fads turn into extended fads—and sales continue for a long period at a fraction of earlier sales. Trivial Pursuit board games are in the extended fad category.

In forecasting for best-sellers, many retailers use a **never-out list** to determine the amount of merchandise to purchase for resale. The goal is to purchase enough of these products so they are always in stock. Products are added to and deleted from the list as their popularity changes. Before a new Stephen King novel is released, stores order large quantities to be sure they meet anticipated demand. After it disappears from best-seller lists, smaller quantities are kept. It is a good strategy to use a combination of a basic stock list, a model stock plan, and a never-out list. These lists may overlap.

INNOVATIVENESS

The innovativeness of a merchandise plan depends on a number of factors. See Table 14-1.

An innovative retailer has a great opportunity—distinctiveness (by being first in the market)—and a great risk—possibly misreading customers and being stuck with large inventories. By assessing each factor in Table 14-1 and preparing a detailed plan for merchandising new goods and services, a firm can better capitalize on opportunities and reduce risks. As shown in Figure 14-6, Wendy's takes innovativeness quite seriously. So do companies such as Hammacher Schlemmer and Wal-Mart:

Check out Hammacher Schlemmer's (www. hammacher.com) list of current "Top Picks."

- Hammacher Schlemmer offers an eclectic mix of housewares, personal care products, home and office products, apparel, sports and leisure goods, and gift items. It has stores in major cities, as well as catalogs and a Web site. Its slogan is "Offering the Best, the Only, and the Unexpected since 1848." The firm carries such items as an $1,800 leather massage chair, a $1,460 transparent kayak, and $50 voice-activated clock radio.

- Although the name "Wal-Mart" may not conjure up "innovative retailer," it is extremely innovative: "Gigantic Wal-Mart, with 100,000 products already on its shelves, is surprisingly receptive to new ones, from tooth tattoos to individually wrapped peanut butter slices. Vendors say it has become something of a proving ground for innovative merchandise from suppliers large and small."[11]

TABLE 14-1	Factors to Bear in Mind When Planning Merchandise Innovativeness
Factor	**Relevance for Planning**
Target market(s)	Evaluate whether the target market is conservative or innovative.
Goods/service growth potential	Consider each new offering on the basis of rapidity of initial sales, maximum sales potential per time period, and length of sales life.
Fashion trends	Understand vertical and horizontal fashion trends, if appropriate.
Retailer image	Carry goods/services that reinforce the firm's image. The level of innovativeness should be consistent with this image.
Competition	Lead or follow competition in the selection of new goods/services.
Customer segments	Segment customers by dividing merchandise into established-product displays and new-product displays.
Responsiveness to consumers	Carry new offerings when requested by the target market.
Amount of investment	Consider all of the possible investments for each new good/service: product costs, new fixtures, and additional personnel (or further training for existing personnel).
Profitability	Assess each new offering for potential profits.
Risk	Be aware of the possible tarnishing of the retailer's image, investment costs, and opportunity costs.
Constrained decision making	Restrict franchisees and chain branches from buying certain items.
Declining goods/services	Delete older goods/services if sales and/or profits are too low.

Retailers should assess the growth potential for each new good or service they carry: How fast will a new good or service generate sales? What are the most sales (dollars and units) to be reached in a season or year? Over what period will a good or service continue selling? One tool to assess potential is the **product life cycle**, which shows the expected behavior of a good or service over its life. The basic cycle comprises introduction, growth, maturity, and decline stages—shown in Figure 14-7 and described next.

During introduction, the retailer should anticipate a limited target market. The good or service will probably be supplied in one basic version. The manufacturer (supplier) may limit distribution to "finer" stores. Yet, new convenience items such as food and housewares products are normally mass distributed. Items initially distributed selectively tend to have high prices. Mass distributed products typically involve low prices to foster faster consumer acceptance. Early promotion must be explanatory, geared to informing shoppers. At this stage, there are very few possible suppliers.

As innovators buy a new product and recommend it to friends, sales increase rapidly and the growth stage is entered. The target market includes middle-income consumers who are more innovative than average. The assortment expands, as do the number of retailers carrying the product. Price discounting is not widely used, but competing retailers offer a range of prices and customer service. Promotion is more persuasive and aimed at acquainting shoppers with availability and services. There are more suppliers.

In maturity, sales reach their maximum, the largest portion of the target market is attracted, and shoppers select from very broad product offerings. All types of retailers (discount to upscale) carry the good or service in some form. Prestige retailers stress brand names and customer service, while others use active price competition. Price is more often cited in ads. Competition is intense.

FIGURE 14-6
R&D at Wendy's

Wendy's Research & Development Department is dedicated to continually improving products by refining cooking and serving procedures and ingredients. R&D regularly comes up with new products for testing and possible addition to the menu.

Reprinted by permission

The decline stage is brought on by a shrinking market (due to product obsolescence, newer substitutes, and boredom) and lower profit margins. The target market may become the lowest-income consumers and laggards. Some retailers cut back on the assortment; others drop the good or service. At retailers still carrying the items, promotion is reduced and geared to price. There are fewer suppliers.

Many retailers pay too much attention to new-product additions and not enough to deciding whether to drop existing items. Yet, because of limited resources and shelf space, some items have

FIGURE 14-7
The Traditional Product Life Cycle

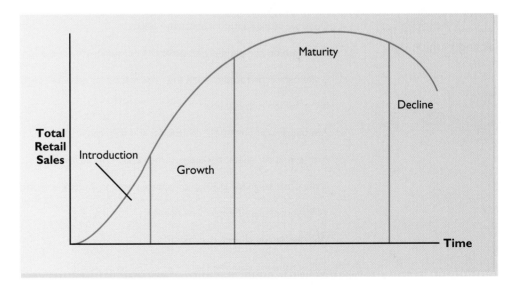

to be dropped when others are added. Instead of intuitively pruning products, a retailer should use structured guidelines:

● Select items for possible elimination on the basis of declining sales, prices, and profits, as well as the appearance of substitutes.

● Gather and analyze detailed financial and other data about these items.

● Consider nondeletion strategies such as cutting costs, revising promotion efforts, adjusting prices, and cooperating with other retailers.

● After making a deletion decision, do not overlook timing, parts and servicing, inventory, and holdover demand.

Sometimes, a seemingly obsolete good or service can be revived. An innovative retailer recognizes the potential in this area and merchandises accordingly. Direct marketers heavily promote "greatest hits" recordings featuring individual music artists and compilations of multiple artists.

Apparel retailers must be familiar with fashion trends. A *vertical trend* occurs when a fashion is first accepted by upscale consumers and undergoes changes in its basic form before it is sold to the general public. A fashion goes through three stages: distinctive—original designs, designer stores, custom-made, worn by upscale shoppers; emulation—modification of original designs, finer stores, alterations, worn by middle class; and economic emulation—simple copies, discount stores, mass produced, mass marketed.

With a *horizontal trend*, a new fashion is accepted by a broad spectrum of people upon its introduction while retaining its basic form. Within any social class, there are innovative customers who act as opinion leaders. New fashions must be accepted by these leaders, who then convince other members of the same social class (who are more conservative) to buy the items. Fashion is sold across the class and not from one class to another. Figure 14-8 has a checklist for predicting fashion adoption.

ASSORTMENT

An **assortment** is the selection of merchandise a retailer carries. It includes both the breadth of product categories and the variety within each category.[12]

A firm first chooses the quality of merchandise. Should it carry top-line, expensive items and sell to upper-income customers? Or should it carry middle-of-the-line, moderately priced items and cater to middle-income customers? Or should it carry lesser-quality, inexpensive items and attract lower-income customers? Or should it try to draw more than one market segment by offering a variety, such as middle- and top-line items for middle- and upper-income shoppers?

FIGURE 14-8
A Selected Checklist for Predicting Fashion Adoption

√ Does the fashion satisfy a consumer need?

√ Is the fashion compatible with emerging consumer life-styles?

√ Is the fashion oriented toward the mass market or a market segment?

√ Is the fashion radically new?

√ Are the reputations of the designer(s) and the retailers carrying the fashion good?

√ Are several designers marketing some version of the fashion?

√ Is the price range for the fashion appropriate for the target market?

√ Will appropriate advertising be used?

√ Will the fashion change over time?

√ Will consumers view the fashion as a long-term trend?

Look at Dollar General's (www.dollargeneral.com) targeted merchandising approach. Click on "Merchandise."

The firm must also decide whether to carry promotional products (low-priced closeout items or special buys used to generate store traffic). Several factors must be reviewed in choosing merchandise quality. See Table 14-2.

Dollar General has an overall merchandising strategy that is very consistent with its approach to merchandise quality:

The Company is committed to offering a focused assortment of quality, consumable basic merchandise in a number of core categories, such as health and beauty aids, packaged food products, home cleaning supplies, housewares, stationery, seasonal goods, basic apparel, and domestics. Because we offer a focused assortment of consumable basic merchandise, customers can shop at Dollar General for everyday household needs. The average customer transaction is about $8.50.[13]

After deciding on product quality, a retailer determines its width and depth of assortment. **Width of assortment** refers to the number of distinct goods/service categories (product lines) a retailer carries. **Depth of assortment** refers to the variety in any one goods/service category (product line) a retailer carries. As noted in Chapter 5, an assortment can range from wide and deep (department store) to narrow and shallow (box store). Figure 14-9 shows advantages and disadvantages for each basic strategy.

Assortment strategies vary widely. Web retailer Discount Art (**www.discountart.com**) says it is geared toward "the artist who demands good-quality art materials but also appreciates good prices." KFC's thousands of worldwide outlets emphasize chicken and related quick-service

TABLE 14-2	Factors to Take into Account When Planning Merchandise Quality
Factor	Relevance for Planning
Target market(s)	Match merchandise quality to the wishes of the desired target market(s).
Competition	Sell similar quality (follow the competition) or different quality (to appeal to a different target market).
Retailer's image	Relate merchandise quality directly to the perception that customers have of retailer.
Store location	Consider the impact of location on the retailer's image and the number of competitors, which, in turn, relate to quality.
Stock turnover	Be aware that high quality and high prices usually yield a lower turnover than low quality and low prices.
Profitability	Recognize that high-quality goods generally bring greater profit per unit than lesser-quality goods; turnover may cause total profits to be greater for the latter.
Manufacturer versus private brands	Understand that, for many consumers, manufacturer brands connote higher quality than private brands.
Customer services offered	Know that high-quality goods require personal selling, alterations, delivery, and so on. Lesser-quality merchandise may not.
Personnel	Employ skilled, knowledgeable personnel for high-quality merchandise. Self-service may be used with lesser-quality merchandise.
Perceived goods/ service benefits	Analyze consumers. Lesser-quality goods attract customers who desire functional product benefits. High-quality goods attract customers who desire extended product benefits (e.g., status, services).
Constrained decision making	Face reality. a. Franchisees or chain store managers have limited or no control over products. b. Independent retailers that buy from a few large wholesalers are limited to the range of quality offered by those wholesalers.

Advantages	Disadvantages

Wide and Deep (many goods/service categories and a large assortment in each category)

Advantages	Disadvantages
Broad market	High inventory investment
Full selection of items	General image
High level of customer traffic	Many items with low turnover
Customer loyalty	Some obsolete merchandise
One-stop shopping	
No disappointed customers	

Wide and Shallow (many goods/service categories and a limited assortment in each category)

Advantages	Disadvantages
Broad market	Low variety within product lines
High level of customer traffic	Some disappointed customers
Emphasis on convenience customers	Weak image
Less costly than wide and deep	Many items with low turnover
One-stop shopping	Reduced customer loyalty

Narrow and Deep (few goods/service categories and a large assortment in each category)

Advantages	Disadvantages
Specialist image	Too much emphasis on one category
Good customer choice in category(ies)	No one-stop shopping
Specialized personnel	More susceptible to trends/cycles
Customer loyalty	Greater effort needed to enlarge the size of the trading area
No disappointed customers	Little (no) scrambled merchandising
Less costly than wide and deep	

Narrow and Shallow (few goods/service categories and a limited assortment in each category)

Advantages	Disadvantages
Aimed at convenience customers	Little width and depth
Least costly	No one-stop shopping
High turnover of items	Some disappointed customers
	Weak image
	Limited customer loyalty
	Small trading area
	Little (no) scrambled merchandising

FIGURE 14-9
Retail Assortment Strategies

products. They do not sell hamburgers, pizza, or many other popular fast-food items. Macy's department stores feature thousands of general merchandise items, and Amazon.com is a Web-based department store with millions of items for sale. Figure 14-10 features Sephora, the cosmetics giant. This is the dilemma that retailers may face in determining how big an assortment to carry:

> A common strategy has been to compete by offering a wide variety of items within a category, designed to appeal to every consumer taste. This can backfire, however, if it causes such information overload that a customer feels overwhelmed or chooses not to make a choice at all. Research shows that dissatisfaction with the shopping process is attributed largely to the retailer, which can impact store traffic and the percentage of customers who purchase. We propose that retailers which offer a large variety in each category ask consumers to explicitly indicate attribute preferences as a way to help them sort through the variety and figure out which option best fits their needs.[14]

FIGURE 14-10

Sephora: A Very Deep Assortment of Cosmetics

Sephora offers 365 shades of lipstick, 150 shades of nail polish, and 150 shades of cosmetic pencils.

Reprinted by permission of Retail Forward, Inc.

Retailers should take several factors into account in planning their assortment: If variety is increased, will overall sales go up? Will overall profits? How much space is required for each product category? How much space is available? Carrying 10 varieties of cat food will not necessarily yield greater sales or profits than stocking 4 varieties. The retailer must look at the investment costs that occur with a large variety. Because selling space is limited, it should be allocated to those goods and services generating the most customer traffic and sales. The inventory turnover rate should also be considered.

A distinction should be made among scrambled merchandising, complementary goods and services, and substitute goods and services. With *scrambled merchandising*, a retailer adds unrelated items to generate more revenues and lift profit margins (such as a florist carrying umbrellas). Handling *complementary goods and services* lets the retailer sell basic items and related offerings (such as stereos and CDs) through cross-merchandising. Although scrambled merchandising and cross-merchandising both increase overall sales, carrying too many *substitute goods and services* (such as competing brands of toothpaste) may shift sales from one brand to another and have little impact on overall retail sales.

These factors are also key as a retailer considers a wider, deeper assortment: (1) Risks, merchandise investments, damages, and obsolescence may rise dramatically. (2) Personnel may be spread too thinly over dissimilar goods and services. (3) Both the positive and negative ramifications of scrambled merchandising may occur. (4) Inventory control may be difficult; overall turnover probably will slow down.

A retailer may not have a choice about stocking a full assortment within a product line if a powerful supplier insists that the retailer carry its entire line or it will not sell at all to that retailer. But large retailers—and smaller ones belonging to cooperative buying groups—are now standing up to suppliers, and many retailers stock their own brands next to manufacturers'.

BRANDS

As part of its assortment planning, a retailer chooses the proper mix of manufacturer, private, and generic brands—a challenge made more complex with the proliferation of brands. **Manufacturer (national) brands** are produced and controlled by manufacturers. They are usually well known, supported by manufacturer ads, somewhat pre-sold to consumers, require limited retailer investment in marketing, and often represent maximum quality to consumers. Such brands dominate sales in many product categories. Popular manufacturer brands include Barbie, Liz Claiborne, Coke, Gillette, Kodak, Levi's, Microsoft, Nike, and Sony. The retailers likely to rely most heavily on manufacturer brands are small firms, Web firms, discounters, and others that want the credibility associated with well-known brands or that have low-price strategies (so consumers can compare the prices of different retailers on name-brand items).

Although they face extensive competition from private bands, manufacturer brands remain the dominant type of brand, accounting for more than 80 percent of all retail sales worldwide: "What would a supermarket without national brands look like? I can describe it in one lonely word—empty. It's hard to imagine a store with no Pepsi, Cheerios, Fritos, or Tide. No Colgate, Oreos, Tylenol, or Hellmann's. No Hershey bars, Campbell's soup, Heinz ketchup, Quaker oatmeal, or Tropicana orange juice. Where are this imaginary store's shoppers? At a supermarket where the aisles are lined with national brands."[15]

Private (dealer) brands, also known as **store brands**, contain names designated by wholesalers or retailers, are more profitable to retailers, are better controlled by retailers, are not sold by competing retailers, are less expensive for consumers, and lead to customer loyalty to retailers. With most private labels, retailers must line up suppliers, arrange for distribution and warehousing, sponsor ads, create displays, and absorb losses from unsold items. This is why retailer interest in private brands is growing:

- Private brands account for nearly 20 percent of U.S. and Canadian retail sales. In Northern Europe, the figure is 24 percent. Private brands account for only 2 percent of sales in Eastern Europe and under 1 percent in Brazil and Argentina.[16]

- Private brands are typically priced 20 to 30 percent below manufacturer brands. This benefits consumers, as well as retailers (costs are lower and revenues are shared by fewer parties). Retailer profits are higher from private brands, despite the lower prices.

- Most U.S. shoppers are aware of private brands—80 percent buy them regularly.

- At Old Navy, The Limited, and McDonald's, private brands represent most or all of company revenues. Costco also does well with its Kirkland brand, featured in Figure 14-11.

- At virtually all large retailers, both private brands and manufacturer brands are strong. Sears' Kenmore appliance line is the market-leading brand—ahead of GE, Maytag, and others. J.C. Penney has set a goal of private brands' accounting for 50 percent of all revenues (up from 27 percent). Penney private brands include Stafford and Hunt Club. Amazon.com sells private brands along with millions of manufacturer-branded items. Take our private brand challenge in Table 14-3.

In the past, private brands were only discount versions of mid-tier products. They are now seen in a different light: "Store brands were viewed as the bargain option, not as well made as name brands but definitely cheaper. Nowadays, the choice is no longer a clear-cut one between price and quality. Research shows that, in many cases, Americans perceive store brands and name

The best-selling appliance brand is not GE or Whirlpool (www.kenmore.com).

FIGURE 14-11

Costco's Approach to Private Brands

Costco has gained great consumer acceptance for its popular Kirkland private brand. The Kirkland brand is used with such diverse products as jeans, auto tires, vitamins, and cookware. It represents a great value to Costco shoppers who respect and trust the company.

Reprinted by permission of Retail Foward, Inc.

TABLE 14-3	The Berman/Evans Private Brand Test

Think you know a lot about private brands? Then take our test. Match the retailers and the brand names. The answers are at the bottom of the table. No peeking. First, take the test.

Please note: Retailers may have more than one brand on the list

Retailer	Brand
1. A&P	a. America's Choice cookies
2. Bloomingdale's	b. Arizona jeans
3. Costco	c. Charter Club apparel
4. Kmart	d. Craftsman tools
5. Macy's	e. Eight O'clock Coffee
6. J.C. Penney	f. Joseph & Lyman men's apparel
7. Saks Fifth Avenue	g. Kenmore appliances
8. Sears	h. Kirkland Signature film
9. Target	i. Martha Stewart home furnishings
10. Wal-Mart	j. Michael Graves home products
	k. Real Clothes apparel
	l. Sam's American Choice detergent

Answers: 1—a, e; 2—f; 3—h; 4—i; 5—c; 6—b; 7—k; 8—d, g; 9—j; 10—l

brands as equal. As these brands approach parity, they provide consumers with a more balanced choice. This trend offers retailers who support both store and national brands multiple opportunities to attract diverse shoppers. The same consumer may even prefer a national brand for one type of product and the store brand for another."[17]

A new form of private branding is also emerging—the *premium private brand*. For example, Premier Selection has been launched by Harris Teeter (the supermarket chain) to give the firm a better chance "to meet and even exceed customer expectations through a higher-quality product than it has made available until now. Harris Teeter has a reputation for quality above and beyond what is generally available in its marketplace. In addition to the moves with Premier Selection, new products will be available under the HT Trader and Harris Teeter labels."[18]

Ethics in RETAILING — Wal-Mart Sells Biodegradable Eco-Crockery

Wal-Mart (www.walmart.com) recently agreed to sell environmentally friendly plates and bowls made by EarthShell (www.earthshell.com) in several of its retail stores. The sale of these products is based on a positive response by consumers to EarthShell products tested at 10 Wal-Mart stores in Portland, Oregon. EarthShell's top marketing executive is thrilled with this development: "Any time you have the largest business in a distribution channel taking on a new product, it sends out a huge message of confidence in that product."

By selling EarthShell products, Wal-Mart wants to help reduce the environmental pollution associated with landfills. Currently, Americans throw away more than 1.8 million tons of quick-serve food packaging, mostly plastic and paper, each year. EarthShell products, which are made from limestone and potato starch, are biodegradable when exposed to moisture. The United States Department of Agriculture (www.usda.gov) has validated EarthShell's claims of biodegradability and compostability.

This is the first time that EarthShell's biodegradable products have been sold in a retail store for personal use. Previously, EarthShell concentrated on business customers such as 500 McDonald's (www.mcdonalds.com) restaurants in the Chicago area and several federal agencies. EarthShell products have also been used by the Department of Interior, which has banned the use of nonbiodegradable food service items in its main cafeteria.

Sources: "EarthShell and the Department of the Interior: A Unique Partnership," www.earthshell.com (September 30, 2002); Environmental Protection Administration, *Greening Your Purchase of Food Serviceware* (n.d.); and "Wal-Mart to Sell Eco-Crockery Made by Santa Barbara, California-Based EarthShell," *Knight Ridder/Tribune Business News* (February 5, 2002).

Care must be taken in deciding how much to emphasize private brands. As previously noted, many consumers are loyal to manufacturer brands and would shop elsewhere if those brands are not stocked or their variety is pruned. See Figure 14-12.

Generic brands feature products' generic names as brands (such as canned peas); they are no-frills goods stocked by some retailers. They are a form of private band. These items usually receive secondary shelf locations, have little or no promotion support, may be of lesser quality, are stocked in limited assortments, and have plain packages. Retailers control generics and price them well below other brands. In supermarkets, generics account for less than 1 percent of sales. In the prescription drug industry, where the quality of manufacturer brands and generics is similar, generics provide one-third of unit sales.

The competition between manufacturers and retailers for shelf space and profits has led to a **battle of the brands**, whereby manufacturer, private, and generic brands fight each other for more space and control. Nowhere is this battle clearer than at large retail chains: "What some believe is that the United States is evolving into the European model where retailers take more and more strength from the marketplace and become more and more brands themselves. Home Depot and Target are examples of this. As these brands are elevated, it lessens the power of those manufacturers who sell to the retailer. What's important for anyone who ends up selling to a Target or a Home Depot is that it's all the more critical that their brand is strong enough to give a balance of power."[19]

TIMING

For new products, the retailer must decide when they are first purchased, displayed, and sold. For established products, the firm must plan the merchandise flow during the year. The retailer should take into account its forecasts and other factors: peak seasons, order and delivery time, routine versus special orders, stock turnover, discounts, and the efficiency of inventory procedures.

Some goods and services have peak seasons. These items (like winter coats) require large inventories in peak times and less stock during off-seasons. Because some people like to shop during off-seasons, the retailer should not eliminate the items.

With regard to order and delivery time, how long does it take the retailer to process an order request? After the order is sent to the supplier, how long does it take to receive merchandise? By adding these two periods together, the retailer can get a good idea of the lead time to restock shelves. If it takes a retailer 7 days to process an order and the supplier another 14 days to deliver goods, the retailer should begin a new order at least 21 days before the old inventory runs out.

Routine orders involve restocking staples and other regularly sold items. Deliveries are received weekly, monthly, and so on. Planning and problems are minimized. Special orders involve merchandise not sold regularly, such as custom furniture. They need more planning and cooperation between retailer and supplier. Specific delivery dates are usually arranged.

Stock turnover (how quickly merchandise sells) greatly influences how often items must be ordered. Convenience items such as milk and bread (which are also highly perishable) have a high turnover rate and are restocked quite often. Shopping items such as refrigerators and color TVs have a lower turnover rate and are restocked less often.

In deciding when and how often to buy merchandise, the availability of quantity discounts should be considered. Large purchases may result in lower per-unit costs. Efficient inventory procedures, such as electronic data interchange and quick response planning procedures, also decrease costs and order times while raising merchandise productivity.

ALLOCATION

The last part of merchandise planning is the allocation of products. A single-unit retailer chooses how much merchandise to place on the sales floor, how much to place in a stockroom, and whether to use a warehouse. A chain also apportions products among stores. Allocation is covered further in Chapter 15.

Some retailers rely on warehouses as distribution centers. Products are shipped from suppliers to these warehouses, and then assigned and shipped to individual stores. Other retailers, including many supermarket chains, do not rely as much on warehouses. They have at least some goods shipped directly from suppliers to individual stores.

It is vital for chains, whether engaged in centralized or decentralized merchandising, to have a clear store-by-store allocation plan. Even if merchandise lines are standardized across the chain, store-by-store assortments must reflect the variations in the size and diversity of the customer base, in store size and location, in the climate, and in other factors.

CATEGORY MANAGEMENT

As noted in Chapter 2, **category management** is a merchandising technique that some firms— including several supermarkets, drugstores, hardware stores, and general merchandise retailers— use to improve productivity. It is a way to manage a retail business that focuses on the performance of product category results rather than individual brands. It arranges product groupings into strategic business units to better meet consumer needs and to achieve sales and profit goals. Retail managers make merchandising decisions that maximize the total return on the assets assigned to them:

> Borders' new category management plan calls for the chain to choose publishers to co-manage each of 250 categories, ranging from thrillers to sports—based on their expertise. These "captains" will be involved with determining which titles will be carried, the number of titles, and how those books will be displayed. In return, they will help pay for market research. Category captains are expected to influence which books are chosen, but Borders has the final say on which books will be purchased. Although book retailers know which titles are selling, Borders believes more research could answer other questions: which books are bought on impulse, which categories may sell better if jacket covers face out, what types of books should be grouped together.[20]

According to one expert, good category management is driven by these considerations:

1. Categories should be arranged as if consumers could stock the shelf themselves.
2. Category configuration should be a function of time, space, and product utilization.
3. Category management should seek to drive multiple-item purchases, not the selection of a single SKU from a like-item category set.
4. Category management is a fluid, dynamic, proprietary set of decisions, not a standard, universal, institutionalized practice.
5. The ultimate aim of category management is to create unique consumer value, not just bolster manufacturer-retailer sales.

6. A category management plan ought to be based on trading-area scenarios.
7. Category management is an exclusionary process—as much a way of deciding what not to sell as what to sell to everyone.
8. The fundamental data base for category management should be drawn from a pre-customer interface analysis of trading-area needs.
9. The supplier's goal is to make the most of purchases and margins within a geographic area. The retailer's goal is to raise store or store cluster profitability and productivity.
10. Category management is a strategy of differentiation.[21]

A fundamental premise is that a retailer must empower specific personnel to be responsible for the financial performance of each product category. As with micromerchandising, category management means adapting merchandise for each store or region to best satisfy customers. In deciding on the space per product category, there are several crucial measures of performance. Comparisons can be made by studying company data from period to period and by looking at categorical statistics in trade magazines:

- Sales per linear foot of shelf space—annual sales divided by the total linear footage devoted to the product category.
- Gross profit per linear foot of shelf space—annual gross profit divided by the total linear footage devoted to the product category.
- Return on inventory investment—annual gross profit divided by average inventory at cost.
- Inventory turnover—the number of times during a given period, usually one year, that the average inventory on hand is sold.
- Days' supply—the number of days of supply of an item on the shelf.
- Direct product profitability (DPP)—an item's gross profit less its direct retailing costs (warehouse and store support, occupancy, inventory, and direct labor costs, but not general overhead).

According to surveys, some collaborative aspects of category management are working well, while others are not:[22]

WHAT MANUFACTURERS FEEL ABOUT RETAILERS

SUCCESSFUL APPLICATIONS OF CATEGORY MANAGEMENT
- Retailers act as equal partners.
- Retailers get input from manufacturers so they put the best possible plan together.
- Retailers are open-minded and willing to change.
- Retailers that give manufacturers proper lead time—and timely goals and suggestions—receive the highest-quality work.

UNSUCCESSFUL APPLICATIONS OF CATEGORY MANAGEMENT
- Different goals among the retailers' senior managers, category managers, and operations managers impede the process.
- Retailers have a "template fixation." Yet, a template alone cannot explain why shoppers choose a given product or category.
- Retailers expect manufacturers to do more than their share or to pay more than their share for gathering and analyzing data.

WHAT RETAILERS FEEL ABOUT MANUFACTURERS

SUCCESSFUL APPLICATIONS OF CATEGORY MANAGEMENT
- Manufacturers gather data on consumer purchasing behavior and make recommendations to retailers.
- Manufacturers with clearly defined and supported plans are viewed favorably.
- Manufacturers help the retailers understand how to get more out of shopper traffic and build shopper loyalty, incremental volume, and return on merchandising assets.

FIGURE 14-13

Applying Category Management to Heavy-Duty Liquid Detergent

Source: Walter H. Heller, "Profitability: Where It's Really At," *Progressive Grocer* (December 1992), p. 27. Copyright *Progressive Grocer.* Reprinted by permission.

	Fewer than 12.3 items per week	**More than 12.3 items per week**
Direct Product Profitability — More than $0.69 per item	**High Potential ("sleepers")** — Action: Promote more, better position, more facings, display more, sample, back with store coupons	**Winners** — Action: Promote more, better position, more facings, display more
Less than $0.69 per item	**Underachievers ("dogs")** — Action: Raise prices, lower position, cut promotions, consider delisting	**Traffic Builders** — Action: Review prices, lower position, expand space, mix with sleepers, display

Unit Sales

Note: The criteria are based on the average profit and movement of the items in the product category of heavy-duty liquid detergent. The averages change for each product category.

UNSUCCESSFUL APPLICATIONS OF CATEGORY MANAGEMENT

- Manufacturers make recommendations that consistently favor their brands.
- Manufacturers just drop a completed template off with their retailers.
- Manufacturers do not maintain confidentiality for shared data or recommendations.

Figure 14-13 indicates how a retailer could use category management to better merchandise liquid detergent. One axis relates to direct product profitability. For the supermarket in this example, $0.69 per item is the average DPP for all liquid detergents. Those with higher amounts would be placed in the top half of the grid and those with lower amounts in the bottom half.

Technology in RETAILING

United Retail Group: Using CommercialWare for Multi-Channel Solutions

United Retail Group (**www.unitedretail.com**) is a specialty retailer of large-size women's fashion apparel, footwear, and accessories. The United Retail Group is a multi-channel retailer that operates 555 Avenue stores, an Avenue catalog, and two Web sites: Avenue.com and Cloudwalkers.com.

The company recently selected CommercialWare's (**www.commercialware.com**) commerce infrastructure software as a means of supporting both Web and catalog orders. This E-commerce software enables customers to research a good's characteristics on the Web, purchase the item through the Web or a call center, verify inventory availability, and determine shipping options and costs. CommercialWare software applications are used by more than 90 retailers, including Jos. A. Banks (**www.josbank.com**), Abercrombie and Fitch (**www.**

abercrombie.com**), Starbucks (**www.starbucks.com**), and Patagonia (**www.Patagonia.com**).

United Retail Group is also using CommercialWare's integration software and its analytics software. Integration.com links CommercialWare's suite to other core applications used by United. The analytics software lets United Retail Group analyze sales data and better interpret fashion trends. As the firm's chief information officer notes, "CommercialWare's suite of products enables us to streamline operational efficiencies in a more productive and cost-effective manner than outsourcing while providing us with the tools to increase customer satisfaction."

Source: "United Retail Group Selects CommercialWare's Multi-Channel Retail Solutions," *Business Wire* (February 25, 2002).

The other axis classifies the detergents in terms of unit sales (an indicator of inventory turnover), with 12.3 items per week being the dividing line between slow- and fast-moving detergents. All detergents could be placed into one of four categories: high potential ("sleepers")—products with high profitability but low sales; winners—products with high profitability and high sales; underachievers ("dogs")—products with low profitability and low sales; and traffic builders—products with low profitability and high sales. Specific strategies are recommended in the figure.

MERCHANDISING SOFTWARE

Forseon's RMSA division has forecasting solutions for retailers in several different sectors (www.forseon.com/Pages/ prod_body.htm).

One of the most significant advances in merchandise planning is the widespread availability of computer software, which gives retailers an excellent support mechanism to systematically prepare forecasts, try out various assortment scenarios, coordinate the data for category management, and so forth. In an era when many retailers carry thousands of items, merchandising software is a part of everyday business life.

Some merchandising software is provided by suppliers and trade associations at no charge—as part of the value delivery chain and relationship retailing. Other software is sold by marketing firms, often for $1,500 or less (although some software sells for $25,000 or more). Let us now discuss the far-reaching nature of merchandising software. The links to several retail merchandising software products, including category management, may be found at our Web site (**www.prenhall.com/bermanevans**).

GENERAL MERCHANDISE PLANNING SOFTWARE

Some retailers prefer functionally driven software, while others use integrated software packages. Limited Brands is an example of the latter. Its software package from Island Pacific Systems (**www.islandpacific.com**) encompasses merchandise planning and forecasting, purchase order management, allocation, inventory management, and price management. Company divisions, including The Limited and Lerner New York, utilize the software. As Island Pacific's Web site says, "The enterprise suite combines the collective wisdom and vision of our extensive customer base to provide a comprehensive and fully integrated merchandise management solution."

FORECASTING SOFTWARE

A number of retailers employ their data warehouses to make merchandise forecasts. JDA Software (**www.jdasoftware.com**) is one of the firms that produces software that lets them do so. With its Arthur Planning software, "A reliable platform enables you to quickly set measurable, enterprisewide strategic goals to ensure your current and future success. At the push of a button, you can spread strategic plans down to any level of detail. Work from the bottom up to accurately reflect sales patterns. Use charts to effortlessly make adjustments to pre-season and in-season trends. Utilize exception management to flag problem areas without sifting through reams of data."[23]

Firms such as ProfitLogic offer sophisticated software for forecasting purposes. Its software addresses four questions: "How can I ensure that my inventory investments support my overall financial goals? How can I make my inventory more productive? How can I be certain store merchandise is reflective of demand? How can I use markdowns and promotions to stimulate demand?"[24]

INNOVATIVENESS SOFTWARE

Since today's software provides detailed data rapidly, it allows retailers to monitor and more quickly react to trends. Processes that once took months now are done in weeks or days. Instead of missing a selling season, retailers are prepared for the latest craze.

Target Corporation, among others, uses Web-based color control software from Datacolor International: "Our Colorite imaging and accurate color enable true-to-life digital sampling. The accuracy eliminates the need for physical samples, making global color communication faster and more precise. E-mail digital samples and make color decisions weeks earlier in the product development cycle. Colorite ensures that the entire supply chain views samples under the same conditions."[25]

ASSORTMENT SOFTWARE

Learn more about Marketmax (www. marketmax.com/aap./ index2.htm).

Many retailers employ merchandising software to better plan assortments. One application is from Marketmax. With its Advanced Assortment Planning software (**www.marketmax. com/aap**), "The information required to plan your product mix resides in one central data base, empowering you to manipulate your data quickly and efficiently and create plans tuned to your customers' needs. Buyers, merchants, and planners are able to spend time building assortments with consistency—using the same process and the same metrics, but with confidence and flexibility by individual category need."

ALLOCATION SOFTWARE

Chains of all sizes and types want to improve how they allocate merchandise to stores. There are several software programs to let them do so. Consider Bombay Company, the furniture and accessories chain using STS Systems Allocation software: "To be successful, we must make purchases that are designed for a group of stores. Buyers need to understand assortment opportunity, and should be shown that every store doesn't necessarily need every thing. Rather, purchases should match certain groups of stores."[26]

CATEGORY MANAGEMENT SOFTWARE

A wide range of software programs is available to help manufacturers and retailers deal with category management's complexities. A few retailers have even developed their own software. Programs typically base space allocation on sales, inventory turnover, and profits at individual stores. Because data are store specific, space allocations reflect actual sales. These are examples of category management software:

At A.C. Nielsen's Category Manager site (http:// acnielsen.com/products/ tools/categorymanager), click on the "Image Gallery" to learn about the software's features.

- A.C. Nielsen (**www.acnielsen.com**) software programs include Category Manager, Spaceman (in multiple versions), and Shelf Builder.
- Information Resources, Inc. (**www.infores.com**) offers several versions of its Apollo software, as well as Account Traffic Builder.
- Logical Planning Systems (**www.shelflogic.com**) markets Shelf Logic category management software for only $750. See Figure 14-14.

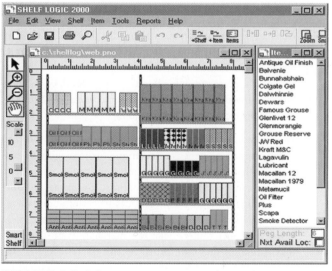
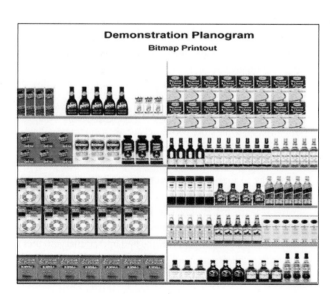

FIGURE 14-14
Shelf Logic: Software for Category Management Planning
Reprinted by permission of Logical Planning Systems.

Summary

1. *To demonstrate the importance of a sound merchandising philosophy.* Developing and implementing a merchandise plan is a key element in a successful retail strategy. Merchandising consists of the activities involved in a retailer's buying goods and services and making them available for sale. A merchandising philosophy sets the guiding principles for all merchandise decisions and must reflect the desires of the target market, the retailer's institutional type, its positioning, its defined value chain, supplier capabilities, costs, competitors, product trends, and other factors.

2. *To study various buying organization formats and the processes they use.* The buying organization and its processes must be defined in terms of its formality, degree of centralization, organizational breadth, personnel resources, functions performed, and staffing.

   With a formal buying organization, merchandising is a distinct task in a separate department. In an informal buying organization, the same personnel handle both merchandising and other retail tasks. Multiunit retailers must choose whether to have a centralized or a decentralized buying organization. In a centralized organization, all purchases emanate from one office. In a decentralized organization, decisions are made locally or regionally. For a general organization, one person or a few people buy all merchandise. For a specialized organization, each buyer is responsible for a product category.

   An inside buying organization is staffed by a retailer's personnel and decisions are made by its permanent employees. An outside buying organization involves a company or personnel external to the retailer. Most retailers use either an inside or an outside buying organization; some employ a combination. A resident buying office, which can be an inside or outside organization, is used when a retailer wants to keep in close touch with key markets and cannot do so through headquarters buying staff. Independents and small chains often use cooperative buying to compete with large chains.

   If a retailer has a "merchandising" view, merchandise personnel oversee all buying and selling functions. If it has a "buying" view, merchandise personnel oversee buying, advertising, and pricing, while store personnel oversee assortments, displays, personnel deployment, and sales presentations.

   A buyer is responsible for selecting merchandise and setting a strategy to market that merchandise. He or she devises and controls sales and profit projections for a product category; plans assortments, styling, sizes, and quantities; negotiates with and evaluates vendors; and oversees store displays. A sales manager supervises the on-floor selling and operational activities for a specific retail department. He or she must be a good organizer, administrator, and motivator.

3. *To outline the considerations in devising merchandise plans: forecasts, innovativeness, assortment, brands, timing, and allocation.*

Forecasts are projections of expected retail sales and form the foundation of merchandise plans. Staple merchandise consists of the regular products a retailer carries. A basic stock list specifies the inventory level, color, brand, and so on for every staple item carried. Assortment merchandise consists of products for which there must be a variety so customers have a proper selection. A model stock plan projects levels of specific assortment merchandise. Fashion merchandise has cyclical sales due to changing tastes and life-styles. Seasonal merchandise sells well over nonconsecutive periods. With fad merchandise, sales are high for a short time. When forecasting for best-sellers, many retailers use a never-out list.

A retailer's innovativeness is related to the target market(s), product growth potential, fashion trends, the retailer's image, competition, customer segments, responsiveness to consumers, investment costs, profitability, risk, constrained decision making, and declining goods and services. Three issues are of particular interest: How fast will a new good or service generate sales? What are the most sales to be achieved in a season or a year? Over what period will a good or service continue to sell? A useful tool is the product life cycle.

An assortment is the merchandise selection carried. The retailer first chooses the quality of merchandise. The assortment is then determined. Width of assortment refers to the number of distinct product categories carried. Depth of assortment refers to the variety in any category. As part of assortment planning, a retailer chooses its mix of brands. Manufacturer brands are produced and controlled by manufacturers. Private brands contain names designated by wholesalers or retailers. Generic brands feature generic names as brands and are a form of private brand. The competition between manufacturers and retailers is called the battle of the brands.

For new goods and services, it must be decided when they are first to be displayed and sold. For established goods and services, the firm must plan the merchandise flow during the year. In deciding when and how often to buy merchandise, quantity discounts should be considered. A single-unit retailer chooses how much merchandise to allocate to the sales floor and how much to the stockroom, and whether to use a warehouse. A chain also allocates items among stores.

4. *To discuss category management and merchandising software.* Category management is a technique for managing a retail business that focuses on product category results rather than the performance of individual brands. It arranges product groups into strategic business units to better address consumer needs and meet financial goals. Category management helps retail personnel make the merchandising decisions that maximize the total return on the assets. There is now plentiful PC- and Web-based merchandising software available for retailers, in just about every aspect of merchandise planning.

Key Terms

merchandising (p. 339)	staple merchandise (p. 346)	assortment (p. 350)
merchandising philosophy (p. 339)	basic stock list (p. 346)	width of assortment (p. 351)
micromerchandising (p. 340)	assortment merchandise (p. 346)	depth of assortment (p. 351)
cross-merchandising (p. 341)	model stock plan (p. 346)	manufacturer (national) brands (p. 353)
resident buying office (p. 344)	fashion merchandise (p. 347)	private (dealer, store) brands (p. 354)
cooperative buying (p. 344)	seasonal merchandise (p. 347)	generic brands (p. 356)
buyer (p. 344)	fad merchandise (p. 347)	battle of the brands (p. 356)
sales manager (p. 344)	never-out list (p. 347)	category management (p. 357)
forecasts (p. 346)	product life cycle (p. 348)	

Questions for Discussion

1. Describe and evaluate the merchandising philosophy of your supermarket.

2. What is the distinction between *merchandising functions* and the *buying function*?

3. Is micromerchandising a good approach? Why or why not?

4. What are the advantages and disadvantages of a centralized buying organization?

5. Interview a local store owner and determine how he or she makes merchandise decisions. Evaluate that approach.

6. How could a toy store use a basic stock list, a model stock plan, and a never-out list?

7. Under what circumstances could a retailer carry a wide range of merchandise quality without hurting its image? When should the quality of merchandise carried be quite narrow?

8. How should a computer retailer use the product life cycle concept?

9. What are the trade-offs in a retailer's deciding how much to emphasize private brands rather than manufacturer brands?

10. Present a checklist of five factors for a chain retailer to review in determining how to allocate merchandise among its stores.

11. What is the basic premise of category management? Why do you think that supermarkets have been at the forefront of the movement to use category management?

12. What do you think are the risks of placing too much reliance on merchandising software? Do the risks outweigh the benefits? Explain your answer.

Web-Based Exercise

Visit the Web site of Sports Authority (**www.sportsauthority.com**). Comment on its merchandising approach. If you ran the company, what kind of buying organization would you use? Why?

Note: Stop by our Web site (**www.prenhall.com/bermanevans**) to experience a number of highly interactive, appealing Web exercises

based on actual company demonstrations and sample materials related to retailing.

Chapter Endnotes

1. Various company sources.

2. Stanley Marcus, "Reflections on Retailing," *Retailing Issues Letter* (July 2000), p. 2.

3. Barbara E. Kahn, "Introduction to the Special Issue: Assortment Planning," *Journal of Retailing*, Vol. 75 (Fall 1999), p. 289.

4. Jim Senegal, "Costco? More Like Costgrow: How America's Biggest Warehouse Club Plans to Get Even Bigger," *Money* (August 2002), p. 44.

5. Rob Eder, "Out-Foxing the Hedgehog's Rivals," *Drug Store News* (March 25, 2002), p. 24.

6. Carole Nicksin, "Bed Bath & Way Beyond: Hybrid Puts Lipstick, Crystal and Pyrex Together," *HFN* (July 22, 2002), p. 1.

7. Miguel Helft, "Fashion Fast Forward," *Business 2.0* (May 2002), pp. 61–62.

8. "FPN History—Who We Are," **www.fpn.org/who.htm** (March 11, 2003).

9. Robin Givhan, "The Eye of Fashion; Bloomingdale's Buyer Kal Ruttenstein Spots Trends—Or Makes Them," *Washington Post* (July 2, 2002), p. C1.

10. "Trend-Spotting," *Chain Store Age* (July 1999), p. 80.

11. Ellen Neuborne, "The World's Largest Focus Group," *Business 2.0* (October 2002), p. 58.

12. For a good, wide-ranging discussion on this topic, see "Special Issue: Assortment Planning," *Journal of Retailing*, Vol. 75 (Fall 1999).

13. *Dollar General Corporation 2001 Annual Report.*

14. Cynthia Huffman and Barbara E. Kahn, "Variety for Sale: Mass Customization or Mass Confusion?" *Journal of Retailing*, Vol. 74 (Fall 1998), pp. 491–492.

15. Gary Rodkin, "A Balancing Act," *Progressive Grocer* (June 1999), p. 29.

16. "Private Label Continues to Gain Share, A.C. Nielsen Study Shows," **www.acnielsen.com** (August 27, 2002).

17. "Store Brands and National Brands Share Space in the Shopping Cart," **www.roper.com/Newsroom/content/news60.htm** (April 6, 2001). See also Judith A. Garretson, Dan Fisher, and Scot Burton, "Antecedents of Private Label Attitude and National Brands Promotion Attitude: Similarities and Differences," *Journal of Retailing*, Vol. 78 (Summer 2002), pp. 91–99.

18. "New Private-Label Alternatives Bring Changes to Supercenters, Clubs," *DSN Retailing Today* (February 5, 2001), p. 66.

19. Arthur Zackiewicz, "The Battle of the Brands," *HFN* (September 10, 2001), p. 12.

20. Jeffrey A. Trachtenberg, "Borders Sets Out to Make the Book Business Businesslike," *Wall Street Journal* (May 20, 2002), p. B1.

21. "Toward a Revised Theory of Category Management," *Progressive Grocer* (August 1995), p. 36. See also Dan Hanor, "Cannondale Associates Finds Category Management Shifting from Analysis to Execution," *Promo* (May 2002), pp. 27–29; Suman Basuroy, Murali K. Mantrala, and Rockney G. Walters, "The Impact of Category Management on Retailer Prices and Performance: Theory and Evidence," *Journal of Marketing*, Vol. 65 (October 2001), pp. 16–32; Sanjay K. Dhar, Stephen J. Hoch, and Nanda Kumar, "Effective Category Management Depends on the Role of the Category," *Journal of Retailing*, Vol. 77 (Summer 2001), pp. 165–184; and "Category Management Starts Here," *Progressive Grocer* (May 2002), pp. 26–32.

22. Information Resources, Inc., "Manufacturer and Retailer Report Cards," *NeoBrief* (Issue 1, 1999), pp. 3–6.

23. "Arthur Planning: Building Optimized Plans with an Eye on Your Bottom Line," **www.jdasoftware.com/file_bin/Collateral/Arthur_planning_Brochure.pdf** (2001).

24. "ProfitLogic—Solutions," **www.profitlogic.com/solutions.html** (March 6, 2003).

25. "Colorite," **www.datacolor.com/uploads/colorite_broch_eng.pdf** (March 14, 2003).

26. "The Bombay Company Increases Sales with Improved Allocation Methods," **www.nsbgroup.com/NSBGROUP/pd/pd_caseStudyArticle.cfm?sect=pd&product=61&id=2&geo=18** (March 10, 2003).

Chapter 15

IMPLEMENTING MERCHANDISE PLANS

Reprinted by permission.

In 1961, Dr. Stanley Pearle had the idea to create a store that combined a complete eye exam, an extensive selection of frames and corrective lenses, and convenient store hours. Pearle could not possibly have foreseen that his first one-stop total eyecare center located in Savannah, Georgia, would grow into Pearle Vision Center. Today, Pearle Vision Center (**www.pearlevision.com**) operates at more than 850 locations—about half of the stores are company owned and the balance are franchised. Cole National Corporation (**www.colenational.com**) acquired the chain in 1996 from Grand Metropolitan.

Pearle Vision stores typically operate in either an "Express" or a "Mainline" format. The Express stores maintain a laboratory that typically produces most glasses in an hour. Although the Mainline stores can fulfill about one-half of their prescriptions on-site in one hour, more difficult prescriptions are sent to Pearle's central lab in Dallas. The Dallas facility also inventories and distributes Pearle's line of frames, lenses, optical supplies, and eyewear to its company-owned and franchise locations.

In addition to Pearle Vision, Cole (the parent company) sells eyewear through its Sears Optical, BJ's Optical, Target Optical, and Cole Managed Vision (which markets eyecare directly to large employers) units. The large number of different types of sites gives Cole the ability to market its products to different segments, as well as clout in negotiating with its key vendors.[1]

chapter objectives

1. To describe the steps in the implementation of merchandise plans: gathering information, selecting and interacting with merchandise sources, evaluation, negotiation, concluding purchases, receiving and stocking merchandise, reordering, and re-evaluation

2. To examine the prominent roles of logistics and inventory management in the implementation of merchandise plans

OVERVIEW

Enter the Seven-Eleven Japan site (www.sej.co.jp) and click on "News Release" to find out what this creative retailer is doing.

This chapter builds on Chapter 14 and covers the implementation of merchandise plans, including logistics and inventory management. Sometimes, it is simple to enact merchandise plans. Other times, it requires hard work, perseverance, and creativity. Home Depot's use of global sourcing for merchandise illustrates the latter situation:

> With more than 1,400 stores throughout the United States, as well as 125 foreign outlets, Home Depot forecasts that its annual sales will exceed $80 billion by 2004 and that its global-sourcing initiative will become an impressive $8 billion business. Currently, 6 percent of its merchandise, more than 4,000 SKUs, originates from international sources. In 2001, the firm shipped 94,000 containers of goods into the United States; during 2002, it shipped 118,000 containers. As the firm's head of global logistics says, "Global sourcing requires an integration of merchandising, logistics, operations, and accounting. The retailer must understand all the manufacturing and supply-chain costs, then ascertain the other costs to make sure it is getting the best value."[2]

IMPLEMENTING MERCHANDISE PLANS

The implementation of merchandise plans comprises the eight sequential steps shown in Figure 15-1 and discussed next.

GATHERING INFORMATION

See how mySimon (www.mysimon.com) can help retailers track competitors.

After overall merchandising plans are set, more information about target market needs and prospective suppliers is required before buying or rebuying merchandise. In gathering data *about the marketplace*, a retailer has several possible sources. The most valuable is the consumer. By regularly researching target market demographics, life-styles, and potential shopping plans, a retailer can learn about consumer demand directly. Loyalty programs are especially useful in tracking consumer purchases and interests.

Other information sources can be used when direct consumer data are insufficient. Suppliers (manufacturers and wholesalers) usually do their own sales forecasts and marketing research (such as test marketing). They also know how much outside promotional support a retailer will get. In closing a deal with the retailer, a supplier may present charts and graphs, showing forecasts and promotional support. Yet, the retailer should remember that it is the party with direct access to the target market and its needs.

Retail sales and display personnel interact with consumers and can pass their observations along to management. A **want book (want slip)** system is a formal way to record consumer requests for unstocked or out-of-stock merchandise. It is very helpful to a retailer's buyers. Outside of customers, salespeople may provide the most useful information for merchandising decisions.

Competitors represent another information source. A conservative retailer may not stock an item until competitors do and employ comparison shoppers to study the offerings and prices of competitors. The most sophisticated comparison shopping involves the use of Web-based shop-

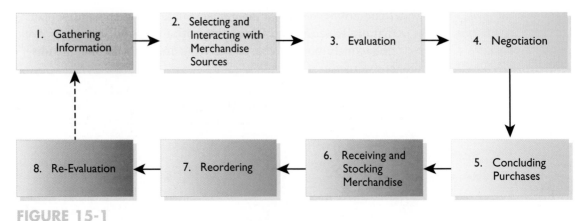

FIGURE 15-1

The Process for Implementing Merchandise Plans

ping bots such as mySimon.com, whereby competitors' offerings and prices are tracked electronically. Buy.com, for one, constantly checks its prices to make sure that it is not undersold. In addition, trade publications report on trends in each aspect of retailing and provide another way of gathering data from competitors. See Figure 15-2 for an example of a competition shopping report.

In addition, government sources indicate unemployment, inflation, and product safety data; independent news sources conduct their own consumer polls and do investigative reporting; and commercial data can be purchased.

To learn about the attributes of *specific suppliers* and their merchandise, retailers can

Learn why High Point (www.ihfc.com) is a world-class market.

- Talk to suppliers, get specification sheets, read trade publications, and seek references.
- Attend trade shows with numerous exhibitors (suppliers). There are hundreds of trade shows yearly in New York. In Paris, the annual International Fashion and Life-Style Exhibition attracts 500 exhibitors and 7,000 attendees. Chicago's National Hardware Show has 2,500 exhibitors and 55,000 attendees each year. The High Point Furniture Market in North Carolina has semi-annual shows that attract more than 3,000 manufacturers and 75,000 attendees—from all 50 states and 110 countries.

CaliforniaMart (www.californiamart.com/retailer/index.htm) offers a lot of online information for retailers.

- Visit year-round merchandise marts such as AmericasMart in Atlanta (**www.americasmart.com**), CaliforniaMart in Los Angeles (**www.californiamart.com**), Dallas Market Center (**www.dallasmarketcenter.com**), and Merchandise Mart in Chicago (**www.merchandisemart.com**). These marts have daily hours for permanent vendor showrooms and large areas for trade shows.
- Search the Web. One newer application is Super Expo (**www.superexpo.com**): "Vendors exhibit to buyers and the press in their online showrooms. This allows buyers to preview the wholesaler's product line directly from their desktops. It also gives Exhibitors a direct exposure of their products to the general public around the world. The shows let the public 'pre-shop' the items directly from the manufacturer and get detailed information such as new products, where sold, press releases, etc."

FIGURE 15-2
A Competition
Shopping Report

COMPETITION SHOPPING REPORT

Store #_____   Date_____

Dept. #_____   Qualified Competition Shopped:

1._____

2._____

Our Style No.	Mfr. Model or Style	Description	Our Price	1st Compet. Price	2nd Compet. Price	Store's Recom. Price	Buyer's Recom. Price

Item Seen at Our Competitor's Store Which We Should Carry:					
Manufacturer	Mfr. Model or Style	Description	Reg. or List Price	Sale Price	Buyer's Comments

_____   _____
Signature of Shopper   *Store Manager*

Whatever the information acquired, a retailer should feel comfortable that it is sufficient for making good decisions. For routine decisions (staple products), limited information may be adequate. On the other hand, new fashions' sales fluctuate widely and require extensive data for forecasts.

At our Web site (**www.prenhall.com/bermanevans**), we have more than a dozen links to leading trade shows and merchandise marts.

SELECTING AND INTERACTING WITH MERCHANDISE SOURCES

The next step is to select sources of merchandise and to interact with them. Three major options exist:

- *Company-owned*—A large retailer owns a manufacturing and/or wholesaling facility. A company-owned supplier handles all or part of the merchandise the retailer requests.
- *Outside, regularly used supplier*—This supplier is not owned by the retailer but used regularly. A retailer knows the quality of merchandise and the reliability of the supplier from its experience.
- *Outside, new supplier*—This supplier is not owned by the retailer, which has not bought from it before. The retailer may be unfamiliar with merchandise quality and supplier reliability.

A retailer can rely on one kind of supplier or utilize a combination (the biggest retailers often use all three formats). The types of outside suppliers (regularly used and new) are described in Figure 15-3. In choosing vendors, the criteria listed in the Figure 15-4 checklist should be considered.

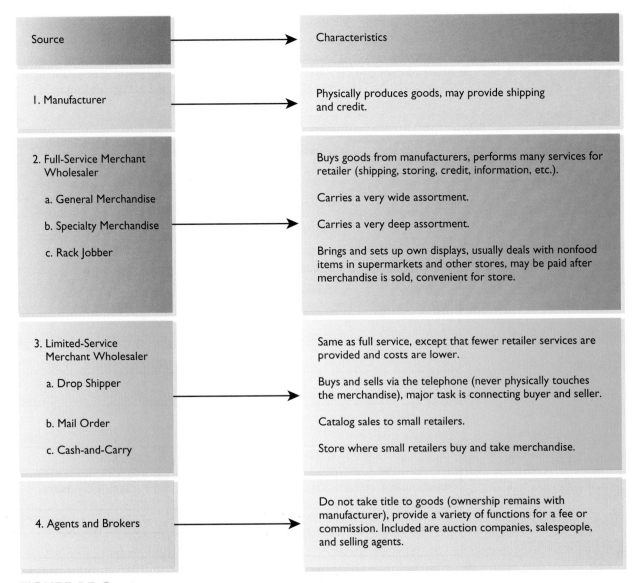

Source	Characteristics
1. Manufacturer	Physically produces goods, may provide shipping and credit.
2. Full-Service Merchant Wholesaler	Buys goods from manufacturers, performs many services for retailer (shipping, storing, credit, information, etc.).
a. General Merchandise	Carries a very wide assortment.
b. Specialty Merchandise	Carries a very deep assortment.
c. Rack Jobber	Brings and sets up own displays, usually deals with nonfood items in supermarkets and other stores, may be paid after merchandise is sold, convenient for store.
3. Limited-Service Merchant Wholesaler	Same as full service, except that fewer retailer services are provided and costs are lower.
a. Drop Shipper	Buys and sells via the telephone (never physically touches the merchandise), major task is connecting buyer and seller.
b. Mail Order	Catalog sales to small retailers.
c. Cash-and-Carry	Store where small retailers buy and take merchandise.
4. Agents and Brokers	Do not take title to goods (ownership remains with manufacturer), provide a variety of functions for a fee or commission. Included are auction companies, salespeople, and selling agents.

FIGURE 15-3
Outside Sources of Supply

✓ Reliability—Will a supplier consistently fulfill all written promises?

✓ Price–quality—Who provides the best merchandise at the lowest price?

✓ Order-processing time—How fast will deliveries be made?

✓ Exclusive rights—Will a supplier give exclusive selling rights or customize products?

✓ Functions provided—Will a supplier undertake shipping, storing, and other functions, if needed?

✓ Information—Will a supplier pass along important data?

✓ Ethics—Will a supplier fulfill all verbal promises and not engage in unfair business or labor practices?

✓ Guarantee—Does a supplier stand behind its offerings?

✓ Credit—Can credit purchases be made from a supplier? On what terms?

✓ Long-term relationships—Will a supplier be available over an extended period?

✓ Reorders—Can a supplier promptly fill reorders?

✓ Markup—Will markup (price margins) be adequate?

✓ Innovativeness—Is a supplier's line innovative or conservative?

✓ Local advertising—Does a supplier advertise in local media?

✓ Investment—How large are total investment costs with a supplier?

✓ Risk—How much risk is involved in dealing with a supplier?

FIGURE 15-4
A Checklist of Points to Review in Choosing Vendors

Big Lots, which buys merchandise to stock its national chain of closeout stores, is a good example of how complicated choosing suppliers can be:

Big Lots places plenty of emphasis on supplier relations (www.biglots. com/invest/x-vendor.htm).

An integral part of our business is buying quality, branded merchandise directly from manufacturers and other vendors at prices substantially below those paid by conventional retailers. We have the ability to buy all of a manufacturer's closeouts in specific product categories and to control distribution according to vendor instructions. We supplement branded closeout purchases with a limited amount of private label goods. Our merchandise is bought from thousands of foreign and domestic suppliers, resulting in multiple sources for each product category. We buy 30 to 35 percent of products directly from overseas suppliers, and a material amount of domestically purchased goods is also made abroad. Thus, a significant portion of our merchandise supply is subject to certain risks including increased import duties and more restrictive quotas.[3]

Retailers and suppliers often interact well together. See Figure 15-5. Other times, there are conflicts. As noted earlier, relationship building can be invaluable. Yet, there remain sore points between retailers and suppliers. On the one hand, many retailers have beefed up their use of private brands because they are upset with firms such as Gucci for opening their own stores in the same shopping centers. Most Gucci sales now come from company-owned and franchised shops. On the other hand, many manufacturers are distressed by what they believe is retailers' excessive use of **chargebacks**, whereby retailers, at their discretion, make deductions in their bills for infractions ranging from late shipments to damaged and expired goods. As one expert noted, "Retailers are applying pressure, asking for larger markdowns and allowances up front. Then, if things don't happen as planned, in terms of margin goals, retailers come back for more later. They are also asking for more support even after goods are shipped."[4]

RETAILING Around the World   Quick-Time Logistics Go from Asian Factories to Limited Stores

Limited Logistics Services supports the retail operations of Limited Brands (**www.limitedbrands.com**). These include Limited Stores, Express, Express for Men, Lerner New York, Bath & Body Works, White Barn Candle Co., and Victoria's Secret. Through its more than 5 million square feet of space, Limited Logistics handles international products that are shipped in bulk and make them store ready. This typically involves breaking down bulk shipments of apparel and accessories by size, color, and style—as well as relabeling them so that they are ready for sale.

About 40 percent of Limited Brands' foreign-made inventory enters the United States by air transportation through Columbus, Ohio (company headquarters), where it is processed within 2 days. From Columbus, the goods can be delivered to any Limited Brands' store within 2-1/2 days. Goods that are shipped over the ocean involve a 3-week trip (versus 3 days by air freight). Yet, Limited Logistics typically arranges for its containers to be the last loaded; in this way, they are the first to be unloaded.

To enable stores to maximize their selling space, Limited Logistics Services seeks to make one to four deliveries each week per store. In peak seasons, some stores receive as many as three to four deliveries daily.

Sources: Connie Robbins Gentry, "Fast Fashion," *Chain Store Age* (July 2001), pp. 86, 88; and "Who We Are," **www.limitedbrands.com/who/index.jsp** (March 9, 2003).

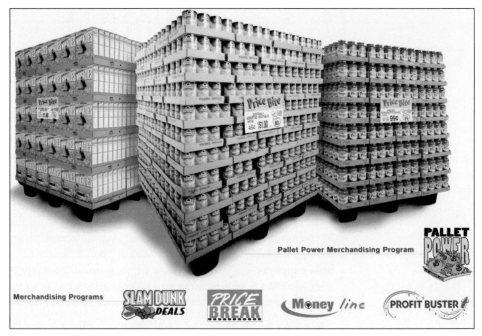

FIGURE 15-5

A Collaborative Supplier-Retailer Program

For Nash Finch (**www.nashfinch.com**), the food wholesaler, "New merchandising programs such as Price Break and Money Line give our independent retailers competitive price breaks to pass on to consumers without reducing their profits. We are able to offer retailers reduced pricing by fully leveraging our $4 billion in purchasing power. Through Slam Dunk Deals, Nash Finch negotiates and spot buys available products for significant savings that are passed along to retailers. Our Pallet Power program provides retailers with an opportunity to sell pallet-ready displays at a lower cost of goods."

Reprinted by permission from Nash-Finch Company, owner of the mark PALLET POWER PROGRAM™ and the registered trademark OUR FAMILY in the U.S.

EVALUATING MERCHANDISE

Whatever source is chosen, there must be a procedure to evaluate the merchandise under consideration. Three procedures are possible: inspection, sampling, and description. The technique depends on the item's cost, its attributes, and purchase regularity.

Inspection occurs when every single unit is examined before purchase and after delivery. Jewelry and art are examples of expensive, rather unique purchases for which the retailer carefully inspects all items.

Sampling is used with regular purchases of large quantities of breakable, perishable, or expensive items. Because inspection is inefficient, items are sampled for quality and condition. A retailer ready to buy several hundred light fixtures, bunches of bananas, or inexpensive watches does not inspect each item. A number of units are sampled, and the entire selection is bought if the sample is okay. An unsatisfactory sample might cause a whole shipment to be rejected (or a discount negotiated). Sampling may also occur upon receipt of merchandise.

Description buying is used with standardized, nonbreakable, and nonperishable merchandise. Items are not inspected or sampled; they are ordered in quantity based on a verbal, written, or pictorial description. A stationery store can order paper clips, pads, and printer paper from a catalog or Web site. After it receives an order, only a count of those items is conducted.

NEGOTIATING THE PURCHASE

Next, a retailer negotiates the purchase and its terms. A new or special order usually results in a negotiated contract, and a retailer and a supplier carefully discuss all aspects of the purchase. A regular order or reorder often involves a uniform contract, since terms are standard or have already been set and the order is handled routinely.

Off-price retailers and other deep discounters may require negotiated contracts for most purchases. These firms employ **opportunistic buying**, by which especially low prices are negotiated for merchandise whose sales have not lived up to expectations, end-of-season goods, items consumers have returned to the manufacturer or another retailer, and closeouts. At TJX, "off-price buying is an art. It requires a savvy team of experienced buyers who are always aware of market dynamics. Buyers are in the marketplace every week and buy very close to need so that we can buy smarter and offer better values."[5]

Several purchase terms must be specified, whether a negotiated or a uniform contract is involved. These include the delivery date, quantity purchased, price and payment arrangements, discounts, form of delivery, and point of transfer of title, as well as special clauses.

The delivery date and the quantity purchased must be clear. A retailer should be able to cancel an order if either provision is not carried out. The purchase price, payment arrangements, and permissible discounts must also be addressed. What is the retailer's cost per item (including handling)? What forms of payment are permitted (cash and credit)? What discounts are given? Retailers' purchase prices are often discounted for early payments ("2/10/net 30" means there is a 2 percent discount if the full bill is paid in 10 days; the full bill is due in 30 days), support activities (setting up displays), and quantity purchases. Stipulations are needed for the form of delivery (truck, rail, and so on) and the party responsible for shipping fees (FOB factory—free on board—means a supplier places merchandise with the shipper, but the retailer pays the freight). Last, the point of transfer of title—when ownership changes from supplier to buyer—must be stated in a contract.

Special clauses may be inserted by either party. Sometimes, they are beneficial to both parties (such as an agreement about the advertising support each party provides). Other times, the clauses are inserted by the more powerful party. As noted in Chapter 1, a major disagreement between vendors and large retailers is the latter's increasing use of **slotting allowances**—payments that retailers require of vendors for providing shelf space.

Food manufacturers, especially small manufacturers, hate slotting allowances because they make it difficult or even impossible to get retail exposure for new products. But retailers complain that most new products are flops, and that if they don't charge up front as a means of self-insurance, they end up holding the bag—losing money on products their customers don't want when they could have stocked the same space with something else their customers do want.[6]

To learn more about the slotting allowance controversy, read this online *Candy Business* article (www.retailmerchandising.net/cbus/archives/0599/599slot.asp).

Unlike many other retailers, industry leader Wal-Mart does not charge any slotting allowances and often gets new products first from suppliers as a result of this policy.

CONCLUDING PURCHASES

There is EDI/QR software (www.gxs.com/gxs/products/product/getw) to fit almost any budget.

At many medium-sized and large firms, computers are used to complete and process orders (based on electronic data interchange [EDI] and quick response [QR] inventory planning), and each purchase is fed into a computer data bank. Smaller retailers often write up and process orders manually, and purchase amounts are added to their inventory in the same way. Yet, with the advances in computerized ordering software, even small retailers may have the capability of placing orders electronically—especially if they are tied to large wholesalers with EDI and QR systems.

Multiunit retailers must determine whether the final purchase decision is made by central or regional management or by local managers. Advantages and disadvantages accrue to each approach.

Several alternatives are possible regarding the transfer of title between parties. The retailer's responsibilities and rights differ in each case:

- The retailer takes title immediately on purchase.
- The retailer assumes ownership after items are loaded onto the mode of transportation.
- The retailer takes title when a shipment is received.
- The retailer does not take title until the end of a billing cycle, when the supplier is paid.
- The retailer accepts merchandise on consignment and does not own the items. The supplier is paid after merchandise is sold.

A consignment or memorandum deal may be possible if a vendor is in a weak position and wants to persuade retailers to carry its items. In a **consignment purchase**, a retailer has no risk because title is not taken; the supplier owns the goods until sold. An electronic version (scan-based trading) is being tried at some supermarkets. It saves time and money for all parties due to the paperless steps in a purchase. In a **memorandum purchase**, risk is still low, but a retailer takes title on delivery and is responsible for damages. In both options, retailers do not pay for items until they are sold and can return items.

RECEIVING AND STOCKING MERCHANDISE

The retailer is now ready to receive and handle items. This involves receiving and storing, checking and paying invoices, price and inventory marking, setting up displays, figuring on-floor assortments, completing transactions, arranging delivery or pickup, processing returns and damaged goods, monitoring pilferage, and controlling merchandise. See Figure 15-6. Distribution management is key.

FIGURE 15-6

Receiving and Stocking Merchandise at Category Killer Stores

Italian-based Salmoiraghi and Vigano operates a chain of category killer eyewear stores. These stores carry prescription and nonprescription glasses, including an extensive line of designer glasses. Because the company carries the products of numerous manufacturers from around the globe, it must coordinate shipments, set up the many displays in each store, and monitor inventory levels by item—challenging tasks.

Reprinted by permission of Retail Forward, Inc.

Items may be shipped from suppliers to warehouses (for storage and disbursement) or directly to retailers' store(s). The Walgreen drugstore chain has fully automated warehouses that stock thousands of products and speed their delivery to stores. Limited Brands orders some apparel by satellite and computer, uses common and contract carriers to pick it up from manufacturers in the United States and Asia (using chartered jets), ships items to its own warehouses in Columbus, Ohio, and then delivers them to stores. J.C. Penney has separate distribution centers for its store and catalog operations.

When orders are received, they must be checked for completeness and product condition. Invoices must be reviewed for accuracy and payments made as specified. This step cannot be taken for granted:

> To improve efficiency, cut costs, and enhance service, manufacturers are seeking to define the "perfect order" and create processes to let them consistently deliver it to retailers and wholesalers. The definition that major firms have agreed upon considers order completeness, timeliness and condition, and invoice accuracy. In the past, manufacturers improved on-time delivery, but did not consider if that affected the condition in which merchandise arrived. And in the effort to ship complete, undamaged orders, they may have missed customer deadlines.[7]

At this point, prices and inventory information are marked on merchandise. Supermarkets estimate that price marking on individual items costs them an amount equal to their annual profits. Marking can be done in various ways. Small firms may hand-post prices and manually keep inventory records. Some retailers use their own computer-generated price tags and rely on preprinted UPC data on packages to keep records. Others buy tags, with computer- and human-readable price and inventory data, from outside suppliers. Still others expect vendors to provide source tagging.

Monarch Marking (www.monarch.com/products/retbarproducts.htm) markets an extensive line of printing devices.

An inventory system works best when there is more data on labels or tags. With Monarch Marking Systems' portable printers, hand-held devices print UPC-based labels and can be connected to store computers. Seagull Scientific's Bar Tender software (**www.seagullscientific.com**) lets firms easily print data-rich tags. See Figures 15-7 and 15-8.

Store displays and on-floor quantities and assortments depend on the retailer and products involved. Supermarkets usually have bin and rack displays and place most inventory on the sales floor. Traditional department stores have all kinds of interior displays and place a lot of inventory in the back room, off the sales floor. Displays and on-floor merchandising are discussed in Chapter 18.

Merchandise handling is not complete until the customer buys and receives it from a retailer. This means order taking, credit or cash transactions, packaging, and delivery or pickup. Automation has improved retailer performance in each of these areas.

FIGURE 15-7

The Monarch 1130
Series Labeler

The 1130 Series labelers
represent a complete family
of identification and pricing solutions. The labelers
are simple and easy to use.
They have ergonomic han-
dle grips, lift-up covers for
quick maintenance, label-
viewing windows, and
other features.

Reprinted by permission of
Monarch Marking Systems.

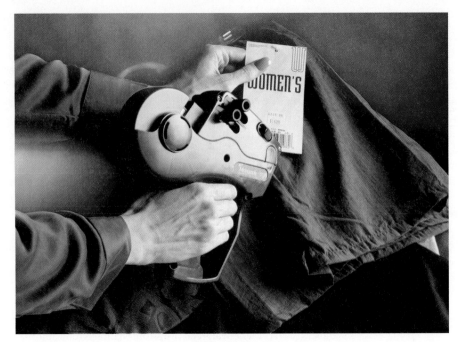

A procedure for processing returns and damaged goods is also needed. The retailer must determine the party responsible for customer returns (supplier or retailer) and the situations in which damaged goods would be accepted for refund or exchange (such as the length of time a warranty is honored).

As discussed later in the chapter, more retailers are taking aggressive actions to monitor and reduce inventory losses. This is a major problem due to the high costs of merchandise theft.

Merchandise control involves assessing sales, profits, turnover, inventory shortages, seasonality, and costs for each product category and item carried. Control is usually achieved by preparing computerized inventory data and doing physical inventories. A physical inventory must be adjusted to reflect damaged goods, pilferage, customer returns, and other factors. A discussion of this topic appears in Chapter 16.

Merchandise receiving and handling is covered further later in this chapter.

FIGURE 15-8

Bar Tender for Windows

Seagull Scientific Systems' Bar Tender for Windows
printing software can be used to generate a wide
variety of label designs.

Reprinted by permission of Seagull Scientific Systems, author
of "Bar Tender" label printing software.

REORDERING MERCHANDISE

Four factors are critical in reordering merchandise that the retailer purchases more than once: order and delivery time, inventory turnover, financial outlays, and inventory versus ordering costs.

How long does it take for a retailer to process an order and a supplier to fulfill and deliver it? It is possible for delivery time to be so lengthy that a retailer must reorder while having a full inventory. On the other hand, overnight delivery may be available for some items.

How long does it take for a retailer to sell out its inventory? A fast-selling product gives a retailer two choices: order a surplus of items and spread out reorder periods, or keep a low inventory and order frequently. A slow-selling item may let a retailer reduce its initial inventory and spread out reorders.

What are the financial outlays under various purchase options? A large order, with a quantity discount, may require a big cash outlay. A small order, while more expensive per item, results in lower total costs at any one time since less inventory is held.

There are trade-offs between inventory holding and ordering costs. A large inventory fosters customer satisfaction, volume discounts, low per item shipping costs, and easier handling. It also means high investments; greater obsolescence and damages; and storage, insurance, and opportunity costs. Placing many orders and keeping a small inventory mean a low investment, low opportunity costs, low storage costs, and little obsolescence. Yet, there may be disappointed customers if items are out of stock, higher unit costs, adverse effects from order delays, a need for partial shipments, service charges, and complex handling. Retailers try to hold enough stock to satisfy customers while not having a high surplus. Quick response inventory planning lowers inventory and ordering costs via close retailer–supplier relationships.

RE-EVALUATING ON A REGULAR BASIS

A merchandising plan should be re-evaluated regularly, with management reviewing the buying organization and that organization assessing the implementation. The overall procedure, as well as the handling of individual goods and services, should be monitored. Conclusions during this stage become part of the information-gathering stage for future efforts.

LOGISTICS

Logistics is the total process of planning, implementing, and coordinating the physical movement of merchandise from manufacturer (wholesaler) to retailer to customer in the most timely, effective, and cost-efficient manner possible. Logistics regards order processing and fulfillment, transportation, warehousing, customer service, and inventory management as interdependent functions in the value delivery chain. If a logistics system works well, firms reduce stockouts, hold down inventories, and improve customer service—all at the same time. See Figure 15-9. Logistics can also be quite challenging:

> When Nestlé Purina launches an item, it typically takes weeks for product information to be printed and sent to retailers. Grocers may need an additional week or more before the data are typed into their procurement systems. Data also need to be entered into warehouse and inventory systems so stock handlers can accept a shipment when it arrives, and into the point-of-sale system so the retailer can price, stock, sell, and reorder an item. If a product arrives before the grocer has all that information, the delivery often sits on a loading dock until Nestlé Purina and the retailer work out the problem. Sometimes, the product just gets sent back from a warehouse. That forces Nestlé Purina to return to the buyer who placed the order and fix the problem manually—an expensive, time-consuming effort. With new technology, the process of entering data into retailers' systems can be automated, so when new information is entered, it's added almost in real time to retailer systems.[8]

In this section, we discuss these logistics concepts: performance goals, the supply chain, order processing and fulfillment, transportation and warehousing, and customer transactions and customer service. Inventory management is covered in the following section.

FIGURE 15-9

The Sophisticated Logistics System of Reitmans

As Canada's largest women's specialty retailer, Reitmans Limited operates stores in five divisions: Reitmans, Smart Set, Dalmys, Penningtons Superstores, and RW & Co. The firm's distribution center consists of 210,000 square feet in Montreal. It ships over 26,000,000 garments and accessories to 660 stores across Canada. This requires sophisticated technology, proven conveyor systems, and dedicated employees. Automated receiving, processing, and shipping systems—with three flat-goods sorters, two hanging-goods sorters, and powered trolleys—have produced excellent results, including increased distribution accuracy, a 30 percent reduction in labor requirements, a 50 percent increase in peak processing throughput, and a two-day reduction in processing time.

Reprinted by permission of Reitmans.

PERFORMANCE GOALS

Among retailers' major logistics goals are to

- Relate the costs incurred to specific logistics activities, thereby fulfilling all activities as economically as possible, given the firms' other performance objectives.
- Place and receive orders as easily, accurately, and satisfactorily as possible.
- Minimize the time between ordering and receiving merchandise.
- Coordinate shipments from various suppliers.
- Have enough merchandise on hand to satisfy customer demand, without having so much inventory that heavy markdowns will be necessary.
- Place merchandise on the sales floor efficiently.
- Process customer orders efficiently and in a manner satisfactory to customers.
- Work collaboratively and communicate regularly with other supply chain members.
- Handle returns effectively and minimize damaged products.
- Monitor logistics performance.
- Have backup plans in case of breakdowns in the system.

At Sears, there is a senior vice-president for supply chain management. This executive is responsible for developing and implementing programs to improve the efficiency and effectiveness of logistics at Sears. Vice-presidents for transportation, distribution, maintenance, information systems, customer relations, and other areas meet periodically to set quantifiable logistics goals, such as reducing the cost of moving cartons through a distribution center by a given time. The vice-presidents suggest goals for one another and vote on each idea proposed.[9]

Ethics in RETAILING

Shoplifting's Big Prize Is the Little Music CD

A study by Loss Prevention Specialists (**www.lossprevention. com**) looked at 166,000 shoplifting incidents in which the thieves were caught, as reported by 101 retailers. The firm then analyzed the data to determine shoplifters' demographic characteristics, when they are most likely to steal, and how much they steal. Of the store types studied, music stores ranked fourth in overall theft amount, after specialty apparel, general merchandise, and consumer electronics stores.

Within music stores, CDs are the most frequently stolen item. Surprisingly, the average theft from a music store is more than $200, about three times the average overall theft. At $15 to $20 or so per CD, the average theft amounts to a dozen CDs.

Shoplifting in music stores is also seasonal—with January and May being the heaviest months, and Tuesdays and Wednesdays being the largest apprehension days of the week.

One theory is that the popularity of Tuesdays and Wednesdays is due to new music releases first appearing on Tuesday. Juveniles comprise 65 percent of those caught stealing recordings.

Sources: Don Jeffrey, "CDs Most Tempting Prize for Shoplifters, Says Study," *Billboard* (December 11, 1999), p. 81; and Retail Prevention Specialists, *Retail Theft Trends Report* (2002).

Bon-Ton (www.bonton. com/scm/main.shtml) is very serious about maximizing its logistics performance.

The Bon-Ton department store chain has a detailed *Domestic Vendor Standards Guide*, as stated at its Web site (**www.bonton.com/scm**):

> Every vendor relationship is important to us, and as you find in any working relationship, it becomes critical to clearly define expectations. Product quality, shipping windows, production, and product availability are just some of the expectations that are defined. In retail, the role of logistics has taken on critical importance in producing higher levels of productivity, improving product flow to the selling floor, reducing inventories, and overall cost reduction for both the retailer and supplier. To this end, we have developed specific supplier and transportation requirements. These are clear and concise expectations and needs, developed by us and consistent with the standard practices prevalent throughout the retail industry. While critical to our mutual success, these provisions allow Bon-Ton to minimize costs and to receive and process merchandise in a timely cost-effective manner, thereby assuring a continuous flow of merchandise to the unit store. All suppliers are required to comply with the instructions, purchase order terms, and the logistical and transportation standards contained here and elsewhere on our Web site.

SUPPLY CHAIN MANAGEMENT

The **supply chain** is the logistics aspect of a value delivery chain. It comprises all of the parties that participate in the retail logistics process: manufacturers, wholesalers, third-party specialists (shippers, order-fulfillment houses, and so forth), and the retailer. Visit our Web site (**www.prenhall.com/bermanevans**) for numerous links related to supply chain management.

The CPFR Committee (www.cpfr.org) is actively working to expand the use of integrated supply chain planning.

Many retailers and suppliers are seeking closer logistical relationships. One technique for larger retailers is **collaborative planning, forecasting, and replenishment (CPFR)**—a holistic approach to supply chain management among a network of trading partners. According to the Collaborative Planning, Forecasting, and Replenishment Committee, a nonprofit organization with about 120 member firms (including Ace Hardware, Best Buy, Circuit City, Federated Department Stores, Kmart, Meijer, J.C. Penney, Safeway, Staples, Target Corporation, Walgreen, and Wal-Mart):

> Retailers and manufacturers have different views of the marketplace. Retailers see and interact with the end consumer in person and infer consumer behavior using POS data. They also see a range of manufacturers, their product offerings, and their plans for marketing those products. Manufacturers see a range of retailers and their merchandising plans. They can also monitor consumer activity, with some delays, through syndicated data. Given these different views, the trading partners can improve their demand planning capabilities through an iterative exchange of data and business intelligence without breaching confidences. The end result is a single shared forecast of consumer demand at the point of sale. A single demand plan can become the foundation for all internal planning activities related to that product for the retailer and the manufacturer. It enables value-chain integration.[10]

Third-party logistics (outsourcing) is becoming more popular. For example, because Sears has very precise vendor standards regarding invoices, purchase orders, advance shipping orders, and barcode labeling—and prefers conducting routine transactions electronically—logistics can be difficult for small suppliers. To remedy this, Sears has used St. Paul Software as an outside logistics specialist to contact the small vendors, determine their abilities, and assist them in meeting Sears' requirements—in some cases, converting vendor faxes into electronic purchase orders (which can then be tracked).[11] Third-party logistics is not limited to just big retailers. Companies such as APL Logistics and UPS Logistics work with retailers of all sizes to ship and warehouse merchandise.

Target Corporation's Partners Online program (www.partnersonline. com) is a proactive relationship retailing activity.

The Web is a growing force in supplier–retailer communications. A number of manufacturers and retailers have set up dedicated sites exclusively to interact with their channel partners. For confidential information exchanges, passwords and secure encryption technology are utilized. Target Corporation has a very advanced Web site called Partners Online, which took four years to develop and test. At the Web site, vendors can access sales data and inventory reports, accounts payable figures, invoices, and report cards on their performance. There are also manuals and newsletters.

ORDER PROCESSING AND FULFILLMENT

To optimize order processing and fulfillment, many firms now engage in **quick response (QR) inventory planning**, by which a retailer reduces the amount of inventory it holds by ordering more frequently and in lower quantity. A QR system requires a retailer to have good relationships with suppliers, coordinate shipments, monitor inventory levels closely to avoid stockouts, and regularly communicate with suppliers by electronic data interchange (via the Web or direct PC connections) and other means.[12]

For the retailer, a QR system reduces inventory costs, minimizes the space required for storage, and lets the firm better match orders with market conditions—by replenishing stock more quickly. For the manufacturer, a QR system can also improve inventory turnover and better match supply and demand by giving the vendor the data to track actual sales. These data were less available in the past. In addition, an effective QR system makes it more unlikely that a retailer would switch suppliers. The most active users of QR are department stores, full-line discount stores, apparel stores, home centers, supermarkets, and drugstores. Among the firms using QR are Dillard's, Federated Department Stores, Giant Food, Home Depot, Limited Brands, J.C. Penney, Sears, Target Corporation, and Wal-Mart.

A QR system works best in conjunction with floor-ready merchandise, lower minimum order sizes, properly formatted store fixtures, and electronic data interchange (EDI). **Floor-ready merchandise** refers to items that are received at the store in condition to be put directly on display without any preparation by retail workers. In this approach, apparel manufacturers are responsible for pre-ticketing garments (with information specified by the retailer) and placing them on hangers, and Wal-Mart requires that vendors ship apples "to stores in collapsible plastic trays that go straight from the truck on the loading dock to the sales floor. When the tray sells out, a full one is put in its place. Wal-Mart employees don't have to handle each apple to restock the display, which saves time and enables them to perform other tasks."[13]

Quick response also means suppliers need to rethink the minimum order sizes they will accept. While a minimum order size of 12 for a given size or color was once required by sheet and towel makers, minimum order size is now as low as 2 units. Minimum order sizes for men's shirts have been reduced from 6 to as few as 2 units.

The lower order sizes have led some retailers to refixture in-store departments. Previously, fixtures were often configured on the basis of a retailer's stocking full inventories. Today, the retailer must make a visual impact with smaller inventories.

Electronic data interchange, EDI (described in Chapter 8), lets retailers do QR inventory planning efficiently—via a paperless, computer-to-computer relationship between retailers and vendors. Research suggests that retail prices could be reduced by an average of 10 percent with the industrywide usage of QR and EDI. This illustration shows the value of QR and EDI:

Implementing a Web-based, electronic data interchange system to communicate with most of its suppliers is saving United Supermarkets of Lubbock, Texas, up to $400,000 a year in transaction costs. "It's very easy to move into this [EDI] world today," said the chief information officer at the 44-store chain. By making the transition to EDI with suppliers, the retailer can now process purchase orders, receipts, and invoices much more efficiently. United is also able to have real-time communication and tracking capabilities. Moreover, the retailer has reduced per-transaction costs by $5 to $6. The implementation was done in two phases. United's 20 major suppliers—who provide about two-thirds of its goods—were put online first. This took about six months. Getting the second-tier suppliers to become EDI-compliant in accordance with United's system took a bit longer.[14]

ECR Europe (www.ecrnet.org) has taken a lead role in trying to popularize this business tool.

A number of firms in the food sector of retailing are striving to use **efficient consumer response (ECR)** planning, which permits supermarkets to incorporate aspects of quick response inventory planning, electronic data interchange, and logistics planning. Here is how: "ECR builds on QR techniques but addresses a much wider scope of issues. Not only is the order cycle addressed, but so are business processes involving new product introductions, item assortments, and promotions. The key enabling methods are similar, however. ECR uses technology to improve every step of the business process, which results in making every step faster and more accurate. ECR also uses collaborative relationships to seek out inefficiencies and reduce costs by looking at the net benefits for all players in the relationship. True efficiency comes only when overall costs are reduced for everyone."[15] Although ECR may allow U.S. supermarkets to cut tens of billions of dollars in distribution costs, implementing it has not been easy. Many supermarkets are still unwilling to trade their ability to negotiate short-term purchase terms with vendors in return for routine order fulfillment without special deals.

Retailers are also addressing two other aspects of order processing and fulfillment: (1) With *advanced ship notices*, retailers that utilize QR and EDI receive an alert when bills of lading are sent electronically as soon as a shipment leaves the vendor. This gives the retailers more time to efficiently receive and allocate merchandise. (2) Since more retailers are buying from multiple suppliers, from multilocation sources, and from overseas, they must better coordinate order placement and fulfillment. Home Depot, among others, has added an import logistics group to coordinate overseas forecasting, ordering, sourcing, and logistics. Supervalu is grappling with its practice of buying products from so many different countries around the globe.

Sometimes, glitches in order processing and fulfillment cause major headaches:

Just a few days before Halloween, the biggest candy binge of the year, the Great North Foods warehouse in Alpena, Michigan, displayed empty shelves where there should have been Hershey's bars. Reese's Peanut Butter Cups were missing, too. The trouble? An order for 20,000 pounds of candy the regional distributor had placed with Hershey in September hadn't arrived. Great North had to stiff 100 of the 700 stores it supplies on orders it couldn't fill. Only on October 28 did a Hershey shipment show up—the first in weeks—and the distributor still didn't know if Hershey had sent enough to meet its needs. For the nation's largest candy maker, new technology that came on line in July had gummed up its ordering and distribution systems, leaving stores nationwide reporting spot shortages of Kisses, Kit Kats, Twizzlers, and other stalwarts.[16]

TRANSPORTATION AND WAREHOUSING

Several transportation decisions are necessary:

- How often will merchandise be shipped to the retailer?
- How will small order quantities be handled?
- What shipper will be used (the manufacturer, the retailer, or a third-party specialist)?
- What transportation form will be used? Are multiple forms required (such as manufacturer trucks to retailer warehouses and retailer trucks to individual stores)?
- What are the special considerations for perishables and expensive merchandise?
- How often will special shipping arrangements be necessary (such as rush orders)?
- How are shipping terms negotiated with suppliers?
- What delivery options will be available for the retailer's customers? This is a critical decision for nonstore retailers, especially those selling through the Web.

Technology in RETAILING

Enhancing Retailer–Vendor Relationships: The Wal-Mart Way

Wal-Mart (**www.walmart.com**) recently announced that it would expand its Retail Link system, an online private exchange. Retail Link facilitates merchandise planning by giving thousands of Wal-Mart's suppliers access to the retailer's sales data on an item level. It is believed that Wal-Mart has invested in excess of $4 billion in the Retail Link supply chain system. This system enables Wal-Mart's vendors to become partners in managing promotions, merchandising, replenishment, and inventory.

Even though Microsoft and Cisco may set technical standards, Wal-Mart often sets business process standards: "When Wal-Mart wants global suppliers like Procter & Gamble or GE or Pfizer to comply with its inventory software and data net-

works, they do or else. It is the 800-pound gorilla in a retail jungle of bonobos and howler monkeys."

Retail Link lets Wal-Mart simultaneously increase sales, shorten shipping lead times, and lower inventory levels. In a recent report by the McKinsey Global Institute, the author (a Nobel award-winning economist) stated that when studying the increase in U.S. productivity from 1995 to 2000, "By far the most important factor in that is Wal-Mart."

Sources: "Assets: Maximizing Relationships," *Chain Store Age* (August 2001), pp. 21A–23A; and Michael Schrage, "Wal-Mart Trumps Moore's Law," *Technology Review* (March 2002), p. 21.

Transportation effectiveness is influenced by the caliber of the logistics infrastructure (including access to refrigerated trucks, airports, waterway docking, and superhighways), traffic congestion, parking, and other factors. Retailers operating outside the United States must come to grips with the logistical problems in many foreign countries: "Food shipments can take 5 days to get across Brazil because there's no superhighway or rail system. In China, 90 percent of roads are dirt."[17]

With regard to warehousing, some retailers focus on warehouses as central or regional distribution centers. Products are shipped from suppliers to these warehouses and then allotted and shipped to individual outlets. Williams-Sonoma, Inc. services its 425 Williams-Sonoma and Pottery Barn stores from a single 1-million-square-foot warehouse in Olive Branch, Mississippi. The building includes nearly 90 receiving and shipping docks, and 6 miles of conveyor belts. Toys "R" Us uses separate regional distribution centers for U.S. Toys "R" Us stores, international Toys "R" Us stores, and Kids "R" Us stores; most centers are owned; some are leased.[18] Figure 15-10 shows Claire's central warehousing system.

FIGURE 15-10

Claire's Aggressive Use of Central Warehousing

Claire's Stores has a central warehouse in Hoffman Estates, Illinois. The mammoth warehouse has been designed to accommodate a second level and can support up to 6,000 stores. At present, the firm operates 3,000 shops, mostly in shopping malls. They sell inexpensive jewelry and accessories for girls. Its stores include Claire's and Icing by Claire's.

Reprinted by permission of Claire's Stores, Inc.

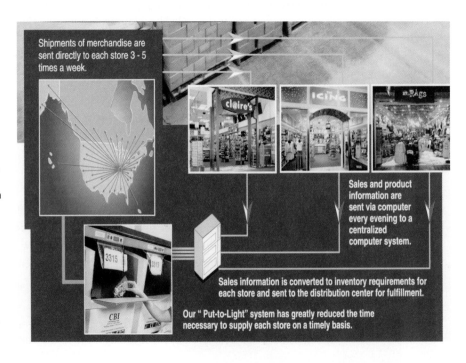

Shipments of merchandise are sent directly to each store 3 - 5 times a week.

Sales and product information are sent via computer every evening to a centralized computer system.

Sales information is converted to inventory requirements for each store and sent to the distribution center for fulfillment.

Our "Put-to-Light" system has greatly reduced the time necessary to supply each store on a timely basis.

Descartes Systems Group (www.descartes.com/customers/directdelivery) is a leader in DSD software.

Other retailers, including many supermarket chains, do not rely as much on central or regional warehouses. Instead, they have at least some goods shipped right from suppliers to individual stores through **direct store distribution** (DSD). This approach works best with retailers that also utilize EDI. It is a way to move high turnover, high bulk, perishable products from the manufacturer directly to the store. The items most apt to involve DSD (such as beverages, bread, and snack foods) have an average shelf life of 70 days, while warehoused items have an average shelf life of more than a year. About 25 percent of the typical supermarket's sales are from items with DSD.[19]

The advantages of central warehousing are the efficiency in transportation and storage, mechanized processing of goods, improved security, efficient merchandise marking, ease of returns, and coordinated merchandise flow. Key disadvantages are the excessive centralized control, extra handling of perishables, high costs for small retailers, and potential ordering delays. Centralized warehousing may also reduce the capability of QR systems by adding another step. These are the pros and cons of DSD:

> DSD is becoming increasingly critical to maintaining high sales levels in food retailing—a trend that is expected to continue as consumer demand for "fresh" requires increased speed of product from manufacturer to retailer shelf. However, any system that has so many deliveries and merchandising services calls to individual stores, creating so many invoices and involving so many logistical and other details, presents a challenge to the industry. While DSD accounts for a growing percentage of profits for the industry, its high turn, high velocity, and high administrative characteristics lead many to seek new and better methods of execution. Most analysts believe DSD could surely benefit from the newer E-commerce technologies that have emerged over the past several years.[20]

CUSTOMER TRANSACTIONS AND CUSTOMER SERVICE

The UPS Logistics Group (www.wwlog.com) is expanding its operations targeted at retailers.

Retailers must plan for outbound logistics (as well as inbound logistics): completing transactions by turning over merchandise to customers. This can be as simple as having a shopper take an item from a display area to the checkout counter or driving his or her car to a loading area. It can also be as complex as concluding a Web transaction that entails shipments from multiple vendors to the customer. A shopper's purchase of a computer, a fax machine, and an answering machine from Buy.com may result in three separate shipments. That is why UPS, Federal Express, DHL, and Airborne are doing more home deliveries. They can readily handle the diversity of shipping requests that retailers often cannot.

Even basic deliveries can have a breakdown. Think of the local pharmacy whose high school deliveryperson fails to come to work one day—or the pizzeria that gets no customer orders between 2:00 P.M. and 5:00 P.M. and 25 delivery orders between 5:00 P.M. and 7:00 P.M.

There are considerable differences between store-based and nonstore retailers. Most retail stores expect the customer to take the purchase or to pick it up when it is ready (such as a new car). All direct marketers, including Web retailers, are responsible for ensuring that products are delivered to the shopper's door or another convenient nearby location.

Customer service expectations are very much affected by logistical effectiveness:

> Looking to reinstall superior customer service, Home Depot is putting greater focus on sales and less on stocking tasks during normal business hours. Under its Service Performance Improvement (SPI) initiative, no wooden pallets will be allowed on the sales floor. Workers will not be allowed to stock merchandise from 8:00 A.M. to 8:00 P.M. Likewise, no forklifts will be allowed on the sales floor during those hours, though in some stores, the hours will change to 10:00 A.M. to 8:00 P.M. Lastly, Home Depot will not showcase more than three smaller sales displays, or "wingstacks," per aisle. Forklifts will be utilized only if a customer needs an item from the top shelf.[21]

INVENTORY MANAGEMENT

As part of its logistics efforts, a retailer utilizes **inventory management** to acquire and maintain a proper merchandise assortment while ordering, shipping, handling, storing, displaying, and selling costs are kept in check. First, a retailer places an order based on a sales forecast or actual customer behavior. Both the number of items and their variety are requested in ordering. Order size and frequency depend on quantity discounts and inventory costs. Second, a supplier fills the order and sends merchandise to a warehouse or directly to the store(s). Third, the retailer receives products, makes items available for sale (by removing them from packing, marking prices, and placing them on the sales floor), and completes customer transactions. Some transactions are not concluded until items are delivered to the customer. The cycle starts anew when a retailer places another order. Let us examine these aspects of inventory management: retailer tasks, inventory levels, merchandise security, reverse logistics, and inventory analysis.

RETAILER TASKS

Due to the comprehensive nature of inventory management, and to be more cost-effective, some retailers now expect suppliers to perform more tasks or they outsource at least part of their inventory management activities: "In 1990, producers shipped products to retailers in a *warehouse-ready* mode. Retailers then reprocessed merchandise to package and price it for sale in the store where consumers make purchases. Today, in the era of *floor-ready*, producers ship products that have already been packaged and prepared for immediate movement to the sales floor. As we move further into the new millennium, there will be a shift to *consumer-ready* manufacturing where the links between producer and consumer are even more direct than traditionally."[22] Here are some examples:

- Wal-Mart and other retailers count on key suppliers to participate in their inventory management programs. Industrywide, this practice is known as **vendor-managed inventory (VMI)**. Procter & Gamble even has its own employees stationed at Wal-Mart headquarters to manage the inventory replenishment of that manufacturer's products.

- Target Corporation is at the forefront of another trend, store retailers outsourcing customer order fulfillment for their online businesses. Its arrangement with Amazon.com "gives customers of the bricks-and-mortar retail giant access to Amazon.com technology that provides personalization, product recommendations, and search capabilities. In addition to Web site technology, Amazon.com handles order-fulfillment and customer-service functions for Target.com. Target.direct, the electronic retailing and direct marketing division of Target, will continue to manage fulfillment for Marshall Field's and Mervyn's."[23]

The National Association for Retailing Merchandising Services offers a national online "JobBank" (www. narms.com/jobbank.html) by category and job location.

- According to the National Association for Retail Merchandising Services (**www.narms.com**), over $1 billion in retail merchandising services are annually provided by third-party specialists, ranging from reordering to display design. One such specialist is Field Marketing (**www.fieldmktg.com**), which provides shelf maintenance, stocking and restocking, category management, visual merchandising, and other services for such clients as Best Buy, Lowe's, and Home Depot.

One contentious inventory management activity involves who is responsible for source tagging, the manufacturer or the retailer. In *source tagging*, anti-theft tags are put on items when they are produced, rather than at the store. Although both sides agree on the benefits of this, in terms of the reduced costs and the floor-readiness of merchandise, there are disagreements about who should pay for the tags.

INVENTORY LEVELS

Having the proper inventory on hand is a difficult balancing act:

1. The retailer wants to be appealing and never lose a sale by being out of stock. Yet, it does not want to be "stuck" with excess merchandise that must be marked down drastically.
2. The situation is more complex for retailers that carry fad merchandise, that handle new items for which there is no track record, and that operate in new business formats where demand estimates are often inaccurate. Thus, inventory levels must be planned in relation to the products involved: staples, assortment merchandise, fashion merchandise, fads, and best-sellers.

3. Customer demand is *never* completely predictable—even for staples. Weather, special sales, and other factors can have an impact on even the most stable items.
4. Shelf space allocations should be linked to current revenues, which means that allocations must be regularly reviewed and adjusted.

One of the advantages of QR and EDI is that retailers hold "leaner" inventories since they receive new merchandise more often. Yet, when merchandise is especially popular or the supply chain breaks down, stockouts may still occur. A Food Marketing Institute study found that even supermarkets, which carry more staples than most other retailers, lose 3 percent of sales due to out-of-stock goods.

This illustration shows just how tough inventory management can be:

Although the pharmacy in a typical chain drugstore may occupy only 10 or 20 percent of the total square footage, it usually accounts for at least 60 percent of the store's revenues. And an average pharmacy carries $175,000 in inventory, half of which is slow-moving items. Thus, inventory management is a critical concern for pharmacies—with carrying costs constantly rising across a carousel of moving targets as new drugs are brought to market, patented drugs become over-the-counter offerings, and the shelf life of every SKU has to be monitored without exception. Logistics processes are compounded because merchandise received in bulk cases and bottles are dispensed as ounces and doses when prescriptions are filled. Pharmacists, unlike other merchants, must determine inventory replenishment based upon SKUs being depleted through incremental percentages.[24]

Inventory level planning is discussed further in the next chapter.

MERCHANDISE SECURITY

Each year, about $35 billion in U.S. retail sales are lost due to **inventory shrinkage** caused by employee theft, customer shoplifting, vendor fraud, and administrative errors. Employees account for $16 billion, customers $11 billion, vendors $2 billion, and administrative errors (faulty paperwork and computer entries) $6 billion. As these figures show, employee theft is much higher than shopper theft.[25] Shrinkage ranges from under 1 percent of sales at supermarkets to more than 2 percent at sporting goods stores. For supermarkets, cigarettes and health-and-beauty-care items represent 60 percent of the items shoplifted. Thus, some form of merchandise security is needed by all retailers.

To reduce merchandise theft, there are three key points to consider: (1) Loss prevention measures should be included as stores are designed and built. The placement of entrances, dressing rooms, and delivery areas is critical. (2) A combination of security measures should be enacted, such as employee background checks, in-store guards, electronic security equipment, and merchandise tags. (3) Retailers must communicate the importance of loss prevention to employees, customers, and vendors—and the actions they will take to reduce losses (such as firing workers and prosecuting shoplifters).

Here are some activities that are reducing losses from merchandise theft:

- Product tags, guards, video cameras, point-of-sale computers, employee surveillance, and burglar alarms are being used by more firms. Storefront protection is also popular.

Sensormatic (www.sensormatic.com) is a leader in electronic security.

- Many general merchandise retailers and some supermarkets use **electronic article surveillance**—whereby special tags are attached to products so that the tags can be sensed by electronic security devices at store exits. If the tags are not removed by store personnel or desensitized by scanning equipment, an alarm goes off. Retailers also have access to nonelectronic tags. These are snugly attached to products and must be removed by special detachers; otherwise products are unusable. Dye tags permanently stain products, if not removed properly. See Figure 15-11.

- Several retailers do detailed background checks for every employee. Some use loss prevention software that detects suspicious employee behavior.

FIGURE 15-11

Sensormatic: The Leader in Store Security Systems

These aesthetically pleasing, acrylic pedestals (part of Sensormatic's Euro Pro Max system) provide an unobstructed vision of exits, as well as the ultimate electronic article surveillance system. An alarm goes off if a person tries to leave a store without a product's security tag being properly removed.

Reprinted by permission of Sensormatic Electronics Corporation.

- Various retailers have employee training programs and offer incentives for reducing merchandise losses. Others use written policies on ethical behavior that are signed by all personnel, including senior management. Target Stores has enrolled managers at problem stores in a Stock Shortage Institute. Neiman Marcus has shown workers a film with interviews of convicted shoplifters in prison to highlight the problem's seriousness.

- More retailers are apt to fire employees and prosecute shoplifters involved with theft. Courts are imposing stiffer penalties; in some areas, store detectives are empowered by police to make arrests. In over 40 states, there are civil restitution laws; shoplifters must pay for stolen goods or face arrests and criminal trials. In most states, fines are higher if goods are not returned or are damaged. Shoplifters must also contribute to court costs.

- Some mystery shoppers are hired to watch for shoplifting, not just to research behavior.

Figure 15-12 presents a list of tactics retailers can use to combat employee and shopper theft, by far the leading causes of losses.

When devising a merchandise security plan, a retailer must assess the plan's impact on its image, employee morale, shopper comfort, and vendor relations. By setting strict rules for fitting rooms (by limiting the number of garments) or placing chains on very expensive coats, a firm may cause some shoppers to avoid this merchandise—or visit another store.

REVERSE LOGISTICS

The term **reverse logistics** encompasses all merchandise flows from the retailer back through the supply channel. It typically involves items returned because of damages, defects, or less-than-anticipated sales. Sometimes, retailers may use closeout firms that buy back unpopular merchandise (at a fraction of the original cost) that suppliers will not take back, and then these firms resell the goods at a deep discount. To avoid channel conflicts, the conditions for reverse logistics should be specified in advance.

Showcase (www.the-showcase.com) buys merchandise from failing retailers and sells it at its stores in Virginia.

According to the Reverse Logistics Executive Council, U.S. firms spend $40 billion per year for the handling, transportation, and processing costs associated with returns. The University of Nevada's Center for Logistics Management says the rate of customer returns is 6 percent for retailing over all, with up to a one-third return rate for some catalog and Web retailers.[26]

These are among the decisions that must be made for reverse logistics:

- Under what conditions (the permissible time, the condition of the product, and so forth) are customer returns accepted by the retailer and by the manufacturer?

FIGURE 15-12
Ways Retailers Can
Deter Employee and
Shopper Theft

A. Employee Theft
- Use honesty tests as employee screening devices.
- Lock up trash to prevent merchandise from being thrown out and then retrieved.
- Verify through cameras and undercover personnel whether all sales are rung up.
- Centrally control all exterior doors to monitor opening and closing.
- Divide responsibilities—have one employee record sales and another make deposits.
- Give rewards for spotting thefts.
- Have training programs.
- Vigorously investigate all known losses and fire offenders immediately.

B. Shopper Theft While Store Is Open
- Use uniformed guards.
- Set up cameras and mirrors to increase visibility—especially in low-traffic areas.
- Use electronic article surveillance for high-value and theft-prone goods.
- Develop comprehensive employee training programs.
- Offer employee bonuses based on an overall reduction in shortages.
- Inspect all packages brought into store.
- Use self-locking showcases for high-value items such as jewelry.
- Attach expensive clothing together.
- Alternate the direction of hangers on clothing near doors.
- Limit the number of entrances and exits to the store, and the dollar value and quantity of merchandise displayed near exits.
- Prosecute all individuals charged with theft.

C. Employee/Shopper Theft While Store Is Closed
- Conduct a thorough building check at night to make sure no one is left in store.
- Lock all exits, even fire exits.
- Utilize ultrasonic/infrared detectors, burglar alarm traps, or guards with dogs.
- Place valuables in a safe.
- Install shatterproof glass and/or iron gates on windows and doors to prevent break-ins.
- Make sure exterior lighting is adequate.
- Periodically test burglar alarms.

- What is the customer refund policy? Is there a fee for returning an opened package?[27]
- What party is responsible for shipping a returned product to the manufacturer?
- What customer documentation is needed to prove the date of purchase and the price paid?
- How are customer repairs handled (an immediate exchange, a third-party repair, or a refurbished product sent by the manufacturer)?
- To what extent are employees empowered to process customer returns?

INVENTORY ANALYSIS

Inventory status and performance must be analyzed regularly to gauge the success of inventory management. Recent advances in computer software have made such analysis much more accurate and timely. According to surveys of retailers, these are the elements of inventory performance that are deemed most important: gross margin dollars, inventory turnover, gross profit percentage, gross margin return on inventory, the weeks of supply available, and the average in-stock position. See Figure 15-13.

Inventory analysis is discussed further in the next chapter.

FIGURE 15-13

Ryder: A Solution for Reducing the Investment in Inventory

Reprinted by permission of Ryder Integrated Logistics.

Summary

1. *To describe the steps in the implementation of merchandise plans.* (1) Information is gathered about target market needs and prospective suppliers. Data about shopper needs can come from customers, suppliers, personnel, competitors, and others. A want book (want slip) is helpful. To acquire information about suppliers, the retailer can talk to prospects, attend trade shows, visit merchandise marts, and search the Web.

    (2) The retailer chooses firm-owned; outside, regularly used; and/or outside, new supply sources. Relationships may become strained with suppliers because their goals differ from those of retailers.

    (3) The merchandise under consideration is evaluated by inspection, sampling, and/or description. The method depends on the product and situation.

    (4) Purchase terms may be negotiated (as with opportunistic buying) or uniform contracts may be used. Terms must be clear, including the delivery date, quantity purchased, price and payment arrangements, discounts, form of delivery, and point of transfer. There may also be special provisions.

    (5) The purchase is concluded automatically or manually. Sometimes, management approval is needed. The transfer of title may take place as soon as the order is shipped or not until after merchandise is sold by the retailer.

    (6) Handling involves receiving and storing, price and inventory marking, displays, floor stocking, customer transactions, delivery or pickup, returns and damaged goods, monitoring pilferage, and control.

    (7) Reorder procedures depend on order and delivery time, inventory turnover, financial outlays, and inventory versus ordering costs.

    (8) Both the overall merchandising procedure and specific goods and services must be reviewed.

2. *To examine the prominent roles of logistics and inventory management in the implementation of merchandise plans.* Logistics includes planning, implementing, and coordinating the movement of merchandise from supplier to retailer to customer. Logistics goals are to relate costs to activities, accurately place and receive orders, minimize ordering/receiving time, coordinate shipments, have proper merchandise levels, place merchandise on the sales floor, process customer orders, work well in the supply chain, handle returns effectively and minimize damaged goods, monitor performance, and have backup plans.

    A supply chain covers all parties in the logistics process. Collaborative planning, forecasting, and replenishment (CPFR) uses a holistic approach. Third-party logistics is more popular than before. Many manufacturers and retailers have Web sites to interact with channel partners.

    Some retailers engage in QR inventory planning. Floor-ready merchandise is received at the store ready to be displayed. EDI lets retailers use QR planning through computerized supply chain relationships. Numerous supermarkets use efficient consumer response. Several transportation decisions are needed, as are warehousing choices. Certain retailers have goods shipped by direct store distribution. Retailers must also plan outbound logistics: completing transactions by turning over merchandise to the customer.

    As part of logistics, a retailer uses inventory management. Due to its complexity, and to reduce costs, retailers may expect suppliers to perform more tasks or they may outsource some inventory activities. Vendor-managed inventory (VMI) is growing in popularity.

Having the proper inventory is a balancing act: The retailer does not want to lose sales due to being out of stock. It also does not want to be stuck with excess merchandise. Each year, $35 billion in U.S. retail sales are lost due to employee theft, customer shoplifting, vendor fraud, and administrative errors.

Many retailers use electronic article surveillance, with special tags attached to products.

Reverse logistics involves all merchandise flows from the retailer back through a supply channel. It includes returns due to damages, defects, or poor retail sales.

Inventory performance must be analyzed regularly.

Key Terms

want book (want slip) (p. 366)
chargebacks (p. 369)
opportunistic buying (p. 371)
slotting allowances (p. 371)
consignment purchase (p. 372)
memorandum purchase (p. 372)
logistics (p. 375)

supply chain (p. 377)
collaborative planning, forecasting, and replenishment (CPFR) (p. 377)
quick response (QR) inventory planning (p. 378)
floor-ready merchandise (p. 378)
efficient consumer response (ECR) (p. 379)

direct store distribution (DSD) (p. 381)
inventory management (p. 381)
vendor-managed inventory (VMI) (p. 382)
inventory shrinkage (p. 383)
electronic article surveillance (p. 383)
reverse logistics (p. 384)

Questions for Discussion

1. What information should a specialty store gather before adding a new stereo brand to its product mix?
2. What are the pros and cons of a retailer's relying too much on a want book?
3. Cite the advantages and disadvantages associated with these merchandise sources for your regular supermarket. How would your answers differ for a local deli?
   a. Company-owned.
   b. Outside, regularly used.
   c. Outside, new.
4. Devise a checklist a retailer could use to negotiate opportunistic buying terms with suppliers.
5. Under what circumstances should a retailer try to charge slotting allowances? How may this strategy backfire?
6. Which is more difficult, implementing a merchandise plan for a small bookstore or a book superstore? Explain your answer.

7. Distinguish between these two terms: logistics and inventory management. Give an example of each.
8. What are the benefits of quick response inventory planning? What do you think are the risks?
9. Why are some retailers convinced that distribution centers must be used as the shipping points for merchandise from manufacturers while other retailers favor direct store distribution?
10. How could a local pharmacy be prepared for the variations in customer demand for home delivery during the day?
11. What is vendor-managed inventory? How do both manufacturers and retailers benefit from its use?
12. Present a seven-item checklist for a retailer to use with its reverse logistics.

Web-Based Exercise

Visit the Web site of UPS e-Logistics (**www.e-logistics.ups.com**). Describe the services that it offers for Web retailers. What are the benefits of using e-Logistics?

Note: Stop by our Web site (**www.prenhall.com/bermanevans**) to experience a number of highly interactive, appealing Web exercises

based on actual company demonstrations and sample materials related to retailing.

Chapter Endnotes

1. Various company sources.
2. Connie Robbins Gentry, "Where Retailers Shop," *Chain Store Age* (March 2002), p. 92.
3. *Big Lots 2002 Annual Report.*
4. Vicki M. Young, "Peak Still Ahead in Chargeback Cycle," *Women's Wear Daily* (December 3, 2001), p. 12.

5. *TJX Companies 2000 Annual Report*, p. 4.

6. "Slotting Allowances in USA Posing Quandary for FTC," *Quick Frozen Foods International* (April 2001), p. 5.

7. Shelly Reese, "Grocery Suppliers Seek the Perfect Order," *Stores* (March 1998), pp. 53–54.

8. Steve Konicki, "Shopping for Savings," *Informationweek* (July 1, 2002), pp. 36–45.

9. "About Sears," **www.sears.com/sr/misc/sears/about/aboutmain/ mainpage.jsp** (March 17, 2003).

10. "CPFR: Guiding Principles," **www.cpfr.org/GuidingPrinciples. html** (March 30, 2003).

11. "Sears, Roebuck and Co. Buyer Case Study," **www.stpaulsoftware. com/cust/cstudy-03.shtml** (November 15, 2002).

12. See Eric Young, "Web Marketplaces That Really Work," *Fortune/ CNET Tech Review* (Winter 2002), pp. 78–86.

13. "Wal-Mart Rewrites Book on Cutting Costs," *DSN Retailing Today* (May 20, 2002), p. 26.

14. Peter Perrotta, "EDI Lowers Transaction Costs for Texas Grocer," *Supermarket News* (February 18, 2002), p. 19.

15. "ECR: Efficient Consumer Response," **www.fmi.org/supply/ ECR** (March 11, 2003).

16. Emily Nelson and Evan Ramstad, "Hershey's Biggest Dud Has Turned Out to Be New Computer System," *Wall Street Journal* (October 29, 1999), pp A1, A6.

17. Len Lewis, "Growing Global," *Progressive Grocer* (September 1999), p. 22.

18. David Maloney, "A New Recipe for Distribution," *Modern Materials Handling* (December 1, 2001), pp. 26–31; and *Toys "R" Us 2002 Annual Report*.

19. Grocery Manufacturers of America, "E-Commerce DSD Opportunities Provide Retailers and Manufacturers with Profit Growth," **www.gmabrands.com/news/docs/NewsRelease.cfm? DocID=915** (March 26, 2002).

20. Grocery Manufacturers of America, *E-Commerce Opportunities in Direct Store Delivery* (2002), p. 1.

21. "Sell by Day, Stock by Night," *Chain Store Age* (April 2001), p. 37.

22. Kurt Salmon Associates, "Vision for the New Millennium," *KSA Brochure* (n.d.).

23. "Target Turns E-Commerce Site, Operations Over to Amazon," **www.internetweek.com/story/INW20020812S0005** (August 12, 2002).

24. "Druggists or Distributors?" *Chain Store Age* (December 2000), p. 148.

25. Updated estimate by the authors based on the *2001 National Retail Security Survey* (Gainesville: University of Florida). See also Harrison Donnelly, "Supermarkets Curb Shrink with Loss Prevention Technology," *Stores* (May 2002), pp. 42–44; and Helen Kolettis, John Mesenbrink, and Bill Zalud, "Guarding the Shelves," *Security* (February 2002), pp. 14–18.

26. Dale S. Rogers, "RLEC Project Plans," Reverse Logistics Executive Council presentation (October 18, 2001).

27. See Jane Spencer, "The Point of No Return," *Wall Street Journal* (May 14, 2002), pp. D1–D2.

Chapter 16
FINANCIAL MERCHANDISE MANAGEMENT

eBay (**www.ebay.com**) was founded in 1995 by Pierre Omidyar as a place for his girlfriend to trade Pez dispensers with fellow collectors. In its first years under Omidyar, eBay quickly grew by popularizing the online auction environment for a host of goods. People love to bargain: "eBay's mission is to help practically anyone trade practically anything on earth."

In 1998, Meg Whitman took over as eBay's chief executive. Under Whitman, more goods are sold at fixed prices, new categories of merchandise have been added, and large retailers now sell goods at their own online eBay stores. Still eBay concentrates on unique or hard-to-find items and used, outdated, and overstocked merchandise. According to its Web site, "The eBay community includes 50 million registered users, and is the most popular shopping site on the Internet when measured by total user minutes." Each year, eBay buyers and sellers exchange billions of dollars worth of goods.

While eBay accounts for only a small fraction of Wal-Mart's sales, Wal-Mart relies on several distribution centers, numerous trucks, thousands of stores, and 1.3 million employees. In comparison, eBay has less than 3,000 employees. And unlike Wal-Mart, eBay does not take title to or possession of a single item. eBay earns its profits by charging sellers a placement fee to list items for sale, an extra fee to highlight "Featured Auction" items, and a success fee, if a transaction is made. Some retailing analysts cite Wal-Mart as the model of the modern, centralized mass marketer, while eBay is the model of the decentralized, virtual marketing company.[1]

chapter objectives

1. To describe the major aspects of financial merchandise planning and management
2. To explain the cost and retail methods of accounting
3. To study the merchandise forecasting and budgeting process
4. To examine alternative methods of inventory unit control
5. To integrate dollar and unit merchandising control concepts

OVERVIEW

Peachtree offers integrated accounting software for small businesses. Try out the free "Trial Version" (www.peachtree.com/trial).

Through **financial merchandise management,** a retailer specifies which products (goods and services) are purchased, when products are purchased, and how many products are purchased. **Dollar control** involves planning and monitoring a retailer's financial investment in merchandise over a stated period. **Unit control** relates to the quantities of merchandise a retailer handles during a stated period. The dollar investment is determined before assortment decisions are made.

Well-structured financial merchandise plans offer these benefits:

- The value and amount of inventory in each department and/or store unit during a given period are delineated. Stock is balanced, and fewer markdowns may be necessary.
- The amount of merchandise (in terms of investment) a buyer can purchase during a given period is stipulated. This gives a buyer direction.
- The inventory investment in relation to planned and actual revenues is studied. This improves the return on investment.
- The retailer's space requirements are partly determined by estimating beginning-of-month and end-of-month inventory levels.
- A buyer's performance is rated. Various measures may be used to set standards.
- Stock shortages are determined, and bookkeeping errors and pilferage are uncovered.
- Slow-moving items are classified—leading to increased sales efforts or markdowns.
- A proper balance between inventory and out-of-stock conditions is maintained.

As one expert noted, "Inventory, cash, and shelf space are among the most precarious resources a retailer has. A firm can hardly afford to manage any of them poorly."[2]

This chapter divides financial merchandise management into four areas: methods of accounting, merchandise forecasting and budgeting, unit control systems, and financial inventory control. The hypothetical Handy Hardware Store illustrates the concepts.

INVENTORY VALUATION: THE COST AND RETAIL METHODS OF ACCOUNTING

The Small Business Administration has an excellent guide on inventory management (www.sba.gov/library/pubs.html#mp-22).

Retail inventory accounting systems can be complex because they entail a great deal of data (due to the number of items sold). A typical retailer's dollar control system must provide such data as the sales and purchases made by that firm during a budget period, the value of beginning and ending inventory, markups and markdowns, and merchandise shortages.

Table 16-1 shows a profit-and-loss statement for Handy Hardware Store for the period from January 1, 2003, through June 30, 2003. The sales amount represents total receipts over this time. Beginning inventory was computed by counting the merchandise in stock on January 1, 2003—recorded at cost. Purchases (at cost) and transportation charges (costs incurred in shipping items from suppliers to the retailer) were derived by adding the invoice slips for all merchandise bought by Handy in the period.

Together, beginning inventory, purchases, and transportation charges equal the cost of **merchandise available for sale.** The **cost of goods sold** equals the cost of merchandise available for sale minus the cost value of ending inventory. Sales less cost of goods sold yields **gross profit,** while **net profit** is gross profit minus retail operating expenses. Because Handy does a physical inventory twice yearly, ending inventory was figured by counting the items in stock on June 30, 2003—recorded at cost (Handy codes each item).

Retailers have different data needs than manufacturers. Assortments are larger. Costs cannot be printed on cartons unless coded (due to customer inspection). Stock shortages are higher. Sales are more frequent. Retailers require monthly, not quarterly, profit data.

Two inventory accounting systems are available: (1) The cost accounting system values merchandise at cost plus inbound transportation charges. (2) The retail accounting system values merchandise at current retail prices. Let us study both methods in terms of the frequency with which data are obtained, the difficulties of a physical inventory and recordkeeping, the ease of settling insurance claims (if there is inventory damage), the extent to which shortages can be computed, and system complexities.

TABLE 16-1	Handy Hardware Store Profit-and-Loss Statement, January 1, 2003–June 30, 2003	
Sales		$417,460
Less cost of goods sold:		
Beginning inventory (at cost)	$ 44,620	
Purchases (at cost)	289,400	
Transportation charges	2,600	
Merchandise available for sale	$336,620	
Ending inventory (at cost)	90,500	
Cost of goods sold		246,120
Gross profit		$171,340
Less operating expenses:		
Salaries	$ 70,000	
Advertising	25,000	
Rental	16,000	
Other	26,000	
Total operating expenses		137,000
Net profit before taxes		$ 34,340

At our Web site (**www.prenhall.com/bermanevans**), there are a number of links related to retail accounting and inventory valuation, including several from the Internal Revenue Service.

THE COST METHOD

With the **cost method of accounting**, the cost to the retailer of each item is recorded on an accounting sheet and/or is coded on a price tag or merchandise container. As a physical inventory is done, item costs must be learned, the quantity of every item in stock counted, and total inventory value at cost calculated. One way to code merchandise cost is to use a 10-letter equivalency system, such as M = 0, N = 1, O = 2, P = 3, Q = 4, R = 5, S = 6, T = 7, U = 8, and V = 9. An item coded with STOP has a cost value of $67.23. This technique is useful as an accounting tool and for retailers that allow price bargaining by customers (profit per item is easy to compute).

A retailer can use the cost method as it does physical or book inventories. A physical inventory means an actual merchandise count; a book inventory relies on recordkeeping.

A Physical Inventory System Using the Cost Method

In a **physical inventory system**, ending inventory—recorded at cost—is measured by counting the merchandise in stock at the close of a selling period. Gross profit is not computed until ending inventory is valued. A retailer using the cost method along with a physical inventory system derives gross profit only as often as it does a full merchandise count. Since most firms do so just once or twice yearly, a physical inventory system alone imposes limits on planning. In addition, a firm might be unable to compute inventory shortages (due to pilferage and unrecorded breakage) because ending inventory value is set by adding the costs of all items in stock. It does not compute what the ending inventory *should be*.

A Book Inventory System Using the Cost Method

View Skandata's online perpetual inventory screens (www.skandata.com/invdemo.html) or download a "Demo."

A **book (perpetual) inventory system** avoids the problem of infrequent financial analysis by keeping a running total of the value of all inventory on hand at cost at a given time. End-of-month inventory values can be computed without a physical inventory, and frequent financial statements can be prepared. In addition, a book inventory lets a retailer uncover stock shortages by comparing projected inventory values with actual inventory values through a physical inventory.[3]

	TABLE 16-2		Handy Hardware Store Perpetual Inventory System, July 1, 2003–December 31, 2003ᵃ				
Date	Beginning-of-Month Inventory (at Cost)	+	Net Monthly Purchases (at Cost)	−	Monthly Sales (at Cost)	=	End-of-Month Inventory (at Cost)
7/1/03	$90,500		$ 40,000		$ 62,400		$ 68,100
8/1/03	68,100		28,000		38,400		57,700
9/1/03	57,700		27,600		28,800		56,500
10/1/03	56,500		44,000		28,800		71,700
11/1/03	71,700		50,400		40,800		81,300
12/1/03	81,300		15,900		61,200		36,000
		Total	$205,900		$260,400		(as of 12/31/03)

ᵃTransportation charges are not included in computing inventory value in this table.

At its Web site, Lifo Systems (www.lifosystems.com/publications/educational.htm) provides good background information.

A book inventory is kept by regularly recording purchases and adding them to existing inventory value; sales are subtracted to arrive at the new current inventory value (all at cost). Table 16-2 shows Handy Hardware's book inventory system for July 1, 2003, through December 31, 2003; the beginning inventory in Table 16-2 is the ending inventory from Table 16-1. Table 16-2 assumes that merchandise costs are rather constant and monthly sales at cost are easy to compute. Yet, suppose merchandise costs rise. How would inventory value then be computed?

FIFO and LIFO are two ways to value inventory. The **FIFO (first-in–first-out) method** logically assumes old merchandise is sold first, while newer items remain in inventory. The **LIFO (last-in–first-out) method** assumes new merchandise is sold first, while older stock remains in inventory. FIFO matches inventory value with the current cost structure—the goods in inventory are the ones bought most recently, while LIFO matches current sales with the current cost structure—the goods sold first are the ones bought most recently. When inventory values rise, LIFO offers retailers a tax advantage because lower profits are shown.

In Figure 16-1, the FIFO and LIFO methods are illustrated for Handy Hardware's snow blowers for 2003; the store carries only one model of snow blower. Handy knows that it sold 220 snow blowers in 2003 at an average price of $320. It began 2003 with an inventory of 30 snow blowers, purchased for $150 each. During January 2003, it bought 100 snow blowers at $175 each; from October to December 2003, Handy bought another 150 snow blowers for $225 apiece. Because Handy sold 220 snow blowers in 2003, as of the close of business on December 31, it had 60 units remaining.

With the FIFO method, Handy assumes its beginning inventory and initial purchases were sold first. The 60 snow blowers remaining in inventory would have a cost value of $225 each, a total cost of goods sold of $42,250, and a gross profit of $28,150. With the LIFO method, Handy assumes the most recently purchased items were sold first and the remaining inventory would consist of beginning goods and early purchases. Of the snow blowers remaining in inventory, 30 would have a cost value of $150 each and 30 a cost value of $175 apiece, resulting in a total cost of goods sold of $46,000 and a gross profit of $24,400. The FIFO method presents a more accurate picture of the cost of goods sold and the true cost value of ending inventory. The LIFO method indicates a lower profit, leading to the payment of lower taxes but an understated ending inventory value at cost.

The retail method of inventory, which combines FIFO and LIFO concepts, is explained shortly.

Disadvantages of Cost-Based Inventory Systems

Cost-based physical and book systems have significant disadvantages. First, both require that a cost be assigned to each item in stock (and to each item sold). When merchandise costs change, cost-based valuation systems work best for firms with low inventory turnover, limited assortments, and high average prices—such as car dealers.

FIGURE 16-1

Applying FIFO and LIFO Inventory Methods to Handy Hardware, January 1, 2003– December 31, 2003.

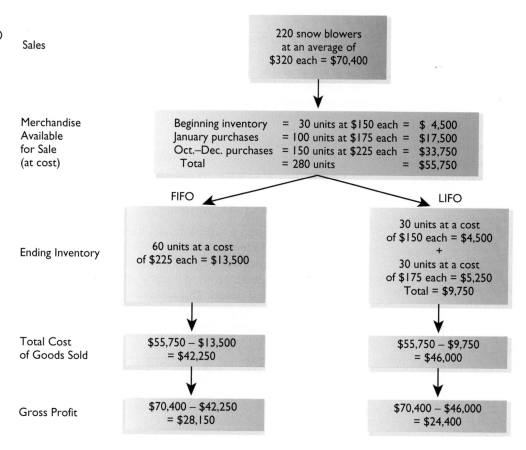

Second, neither cost-based method adjusts inventory values to reflect style changes, end-of-season markdowns, or sudden surges of demand (which may raise prices). Thus, ending inventory value based on merchandise cost may not reflect its actual worth. This discrepancy could be troublesome if inventory value is used in filing insurance claims for losses.

Despite these factors, retailers that make the products they sell—such as bakeries, restaurants, and furniture showrooms—often keep records on a cost basis. A department store with these operations can use the cost method for them and the retail method for other areas.

RETAILING
Around the World   The Barcode Symbol Is Becoming More Globally Uniform

GTIN (pronounced "gee-tin") stands for Global Trade Item Number. This acronym is used as a catchall term to describe the efforts to better standardize the two barcodes used to tag many retail items: the Universal Product Code and its European equivalents (EAN/UCC-13, EAN/UCC-14, and EAN/UCC-8). Whereas the Universal Product Code has a fixed number of digits, the suffix number in the European codes identifies the number of digits used.

The objective of GTIN is to develop a common 14-digit data structure as of January 1, 2005. There are two advantages with a uniform format. First, the 14-digit code will enable more unique numbers to describe each product. Currently, many manufacturers assign the same code number to multiple items; this results in difficulties for retailers using these data for sales

analysis and inventory management. Second, the new standard will also facilitate global trade, such as when U.S. goods are sold to European retailers. Currently, U.S. retailers have to resticker UPC barcodes over their European equivalents. The multiple standards create havoc with the data bases of resellers that sell to both markets.

Although most North American point-of-sale systems and backroom scanners can accommodate the new 14-digit standard, many retailers' and manufacturers' data bases are set up to handle the UPC's 12 digits.

Source: Dan Scheraga, "Banishing Barcode Blues," *Chain Store Age* (July 2001), pp. 59–60.

THE RETAIL METHOD

See a retail-world application of the retail method (www. reacctsoftware.com/ rm_over.html).

With the **retail method of accounting**, closing inventory value is determined by calculating the average relationship between the cost and retail values of merchandise available for sale during a period. Though the retail method overcomes the disadvantages of the cost method, it requires detailed records and is more complex since ending inventory is first valued in retail dollars and then converted to compute gross margin (gross profit).

There are three basic steps to determine ending inventory value by the retail method:

1. Calculating the cost complement.
2. Calculating deductions from retail value.
3. Converting retail inventory value to cost.

Calculating the Cost Complement

The value of beginning inventory, net purchases, additional markups, and transportation charges are all included in the retail method. Beginning inventory and net purchase amounts (purchases less returns) are recorded at both cost and retail levels. Additional markups represent the extra revenues received when a retailer increases selling prices, due to inflation or unexpectedly high demand. Transportation charges are the retailer's costs for shipping the goods it buys from suppliers to the retailer. Table 16-3 shows the total merchandise available for sale at cost and at retail for Handy Hardware from July 1, 2003, through December 31, 2003, using the costs in Table 16-2.

By using Table 16-3 data, the average relationship of cost to retail value for all merchandise available for sale by Handy Hardware—the **cost complement**—can be computed:

$$\text{Cost complement} = \frac{\text{Total cost valuation}}{\text{Total retail valuation}}$$

$$= \frac{\$299,892}{\$496,126} = 0.6045$$

Because the cost complement is 0.6045 (60.45 percent), on average, 60.45 cents of every retail sales dollar went to cover Handy Hardware's merchandise cost.

Calculating Deductions from Retail Value

The ending retail value of inventory must reflect all deductions from the total merchandise available for sale at retail. Besides sales, deductions include markdowns (for special sales and end-of-season goods), employee discounts, and stock shortages (due to pilferage and unrecorded breakage). Although sales, markdowns, and employee discounts can be recorded throughout an accounting period, a physical inventory is needed to learn about stock shortages.

From Table 16-3, it is known that Handy Hardware had a retail value of merchandise available for sale of $496,126 for the period from July 1, 2003 through December 31, 2003. As shown

TABLE 16-3	Handy Hardware Store, Calculating Merchandise Available for Sale at Cost and at Retail, July 1, 2003–December 31, 2003	
	At Cost	At Retail
Beginning inventory	$ 90,500	$139,200
Net purchases	205,900	340,526
Additional markups	—	16,400
Transportation charges	3,492	—
Total merchandise available for sale	$299,892	$496,126

TABLE 16-4	Handy Hardware Store, Computing Ending Retail Book Value, as of December 31, 2003		
Merchandise available for sale (at retail)			$496,126
Less deductions:			
Sales		$422,540	
Markdowns		11,634	
Employee discounts		2,400	
Total deductions			436,574
Ending retail book value of inventory			$ 59,552

in Table 16-4, this was reduced by sales of $422,540 and recorded markdowns and employee discounts of $14,034. The ending book value of inventory at retail as of December 31, 2003, was $59,552.

To compute stock shortages, the retail book value of ending inventory is compared with the actual physical ending inventory at retail. If book inventory exceeds physical inventory, a shortage exists. Table 16-5 shows the results of Handy's physical inventory. Shortages were $3,082 (at retail), and book value was adjusted accordingly. While Handy knows the shortages were from pilferage, bookkeeping errors, and overshipments not billed to customers, it cannot learn the proportion of shortages from each factor.

Occasionally, a physical inventory may reveal a stock overage—an excess of physical inventory value over book value. This may be due to errors in a physical inventory or in keeping a book inventory. If overages occur, ending retail book value is adjusted upward. Inasmuch as a retailer has to conduct a physical inventory to compute shortages (overages), and a physical inventory is usually taken only once or twice a year, shortages (overages) are often estimated for monthly merchandise budgets.

Converting Retail Inventory Value to Cost

The retailer must next convert the adjusted ending retail book value of inventory to cost so as to compute dollar gross profit (gross margin). The ending inventory at cost equals the adjusted ending retail book value multiplied by the cost complement. For Handy Hardware, this was:

$$\text{Ending inventory} = \text{Adjusted ending retail book value} \times \text{Cost complement}$$
$$\text{(at cost)}$$
$$= \$56,470 \times .6045 = \$34,136$$

This computation does not yield the exact inventory cost. It shows the average relationship between cost and the retail selling price for all merchandise available for sale.

The adjusted ending inventory at cost can be used to find gross profit. As Table 16-6 shows, Handy's six-month cost of goods sold was $265,756, resulting in gross profit of $156,784. By deducting operating expenses of $139,000, Handy learns that the net profit before taxes for this period was $17,784.

TABLE 16-5	Handy Hardware Store, Computing Stock Shortages and Adjusting Retail Book Value, as of December 31, 2003
Ending retail book value of inventory	$59,552
Physical inventory (at retail)	56,470
Stock shortages (at retail)	3,082
Adjusted ending retail book value of inventory	$56,470

TABLE 16-6	Handy Hardware Store Profit-and-Loss Statement, July 1, 2003–December 31, 2003	
Sales		$422,540
Less cost of goods sold:		
Total merchandise available for sale (at cost)	$299,892	
Adjusted ending inventory (at cost)[a]	34,136	
Cost of goods sold		265,756
Gross profit		$156,784
Less operating expenses:		
Salaries	$ 70,000	
Advertising	25,000	
Rental	16,000	
Other	28,000	
Total operating expenses		139,000
Net profit before taxes		$ 17,784

[a]Adjusted ending inventory (at cost) = Adjusted retail book value × Cost complement = $56,470 × .6045 = $34,136

Advantages of the Retail Method

Compared to other techniques, there are several advantages of the retail method of accounting:

- Valuation errors are reduced when conducting a physical inventory since merchandise value is recorded at retail and costs do not have to be decoded.

- Because the process is simpler, a physical inventory can be completed more often. This lets a firm be more aware of slow-moving items and stock shortages.

- The physical inventory method at cost requires a physical inventory to prepare a profit-and-loss statement. The retail method lets a firm set up a profit-and-loss statement based on book inventory. The retailer can then estimate the stock shortages between physical inventories and study departmental profit trends.

- A complete record of ending book values helps determine insurance coverage and settle insurance claims. The retail book method gives an estimate of inventory value throughout the year. Since physical inventories are usually taken when merchandise levels are low, the book value at retail lets retailers plan insurance coverage for peak periods and shows the values of goods on hand. The retail method is accepted in insurance claims.

Limitations of the Retail Method

The greatest weakness is the bookkeeping burden of recording data. Ending book inventory figures can be correctly computed only if the following are accurately noted: the value of beginning inventory (at cost and at retail), purchases (at cost and at retail), shipping charges, markups, markdowns, employee discounts, transfers from other departments or stores, returns, and sales. Though personnel are freed from taking many physical inventories, ending book value at retail may be inaccurate unless all required data are precisely recorded. With computerization, this potential problem is lessened.

Another limitation is that the cost complement is an average based on the total cost of merchandise available for sale and total retail value. The ending cost value only approximates the true inventory value. This may cause misinformation if fast-selling items have different markups from slow-selling items or if there are wide variations among the markups of different goods.

Familiarity with the retail and cost methods of inventory is essential for understanding the financial merchandise management material described in the balance of this chapter.

Technology in RETAILING — Windmill Truck Stop: Correcting an Accounting House of Horrors

Many motorists view the Windmill Truck Stop in Rapid City, South Dakota, as a "home away from home." Yet, prior to implementing a new point-of-sale system, the firm's controller had a distinctly different view. He saw the retailer's accounting system as a "house of accounting horrors." The controller was responsible for analyzing both retail fuel sales in the "truckers only" area and sales to motorists in Windmill's convenience store, restaurant, motel, and auto service centers.

The firm's old system was so antiquated that its sales were only broken down by department. As a consequence, "We couldn't tell the difference between a tube of toothpaste and a bottle of shampoo." That's a major problem since Windmill stocks over 20,000 items in its convenience store and restaurant.

The controller searched for a point-of-sale system that was Windows-based, able to support multiple input devices, and easy to use. Windmill now uses PC America's Cash Register Express system (**www.pcamerica.com**), which enables the retailer's cashiers to use touchscreens and barcode scanners to enter orders and update inventory on an item basis. A unique feature is the receipt printer's ability to print special coupons, such as "10 percent off on your next purchase," on the bottom.

Source: "PC America: Inventory Management at Point of Sale," *PC World* (April 2002), p. SSS3.

MERCHANDISE FORECASTING AND BUDGETING: DOLLAR CONTROL

As we noted earlier, dollar control entails planning and monitoring a firm's inventory investment over time. Figure 16-2 shows the six-step dollar control process for merchandise forecasting and budgeting. This process should be followed sequentially since a change in one stage affects all the stages after it. If a sales forecast is too low, a firm may run out of items because it does not plan to have enough merchandise during a selling season and planned purchases will also be too low.

Visit our Web site (**www.prenhall.com/bermanevans**) for a detailed listing of links related to both dollar control and unit control in merchandise management.

DESIGNATING CONTROL UNITS

Merchandise forecasting and budgeting requires the selection of **control units**, the merchandise categories for which data are gathered. Such classifications must be narrow enough to isolate opportunities and problems with specific merchandise lines. A retailer wishing to control goods within departments must record data on dollar allotments separately for each category.

Knowing that total markdowns in a department are 20 percent above last year's level is less valuable than knowing the specific merchandise lines in which large markdowns are being taken. A retailer can broaden its control system by combining categories that comprise a department. However, a broad category cannot be broken down into components.

It is helpful to select control units consistent with other company and trade association data. Internal comparisons are meaningful only when categories are stable. Classifications that shift over time do not permit comparisons. External comparisons are not meaningful if control units are dissimilar for a retailer and its trade associations. Control units may be based on departments, classifications within departments, price line classifications, and standard merchandise classifications. A discussion of each follows.

The broadest practical classification for financial recordkeeping is the department, which lets a retailer assess each general merchandise grouping or buyer. Even the small Handy Hardware needs to acquire data on a departmental basis (tools and equipment, supplies, housewares, and so on) for buying, inventory control, and markdown decisions.

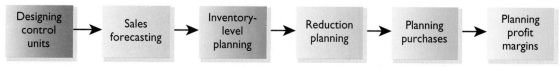

FIGURE 16-2

The Merchandise Forecasting and Budgeting Process: Dollar Control

To obtain more financial data, **classification merchandising** can be used, whereby each department is subdivided into further categories for related types of merchandise. In planning its tools and equipment department, Handy Hardware can keep financial records on both overall departmental performance and the results of such categories as lawn mowers/snow blowers, power tools, hand tools, and ladders.

A special form of classification merchandising uses *price line classifications*—sales, inventories, and purchases are analyzed by price category. This helps if different models of a product are sold at different prices to different target markets (such as Handy's having $20 power tools for do-it-yourselfers and $135 models for contractors). Retailers with deep assortments most often use price line control.

To best contrast its data with industry averages, a firm's merchandise categories should conform to those cited in trade publications. The National Retail Federation devised a *standard merchandise classification* with common reporting categories for a range of retailers and products. It annually produces *Retail Horizons,* using its classifications. Specific classifications are also popular for some retailers. *Progressive Grocer* regularly publishes data based on standard classifications for supermarkets.

Once appropriate dollar control units are set, all transactions—including sales, purchases, transfers, markdowns, and employee discounts—must be recorded under the proper classification number. Thus, if house paint is Department 25 and brushes are 25-1, all transactions must carry these designations.

SALES FORECASTING

Nonstop Solutions (www.nonstop.com/customers/longs_drugs.html) has aided Longs Drugs with forecasting.

A retailer estimates its expected future revenues for a given period by *sales forecasting*. Forecasts may be companywide, departmental, and for individual merchandise classifications. Perhaps the most important step in financial merchandise planning is accurate sales forecasting, because an incorrect projection of sales throws off the entire process. That is why many retailers have state-of-the-art forecasting systems. Longs Drug Stores has dramatically improved its cash flow by using a system from Nonstop Solutions.[4]

Larger retailers often forecast total and department sales by techniques such as trend analysis, time series analysis, and multiple regression analysis. A discussion of these techniques is beyond the scope of this book. Small retailers rely more on "guesstimates," projections based on experience. Even for larger firms, sales forecasting for merchandise classifications within departments (or price lines) relies on more qualitative methods. One way to forecast sales for narrow categories is first to project sales on a company basis and by department, and then to break down figures judgmentally into merchandise classifications.

External factors, internal company factors, and seasonal trends must be anticipated and taken into account. Among the external factors that can affect projected sales are consumer trends, competitors' actions, the state of the economy, the weather, and new supplier offerings. For example, Planalytics offers a patented methodology to analyze and forecast the relationship among consumer demand, store traffic, and the weather.[5] Internal company factors that can impact on future sales include additions and deletions of merchandise lines, revised promotion and credit policies, changes in hours, new outlets, and store remodeling. With many retailers, seasonality must be considered in setting monthly or quarterly sales forecasts. Handy's yearly snow blower sales should not be estimated from December sales alone.

A sales forecast can be developed by examining past trends and projecting future growth (based on external and internal factors). Table 16-7 shows a forecast for Handy Hardware. It is an estimate, subject to revisions. Various factors may be hard to incorporate when devising a forecast, such as merchandise shortages, consumer reactions to new products, the rate of inflation, and new government legislation. That is why a financial merchandise plan needs some flexibility.

After a yearly forecast is derived, it should be broken into quarters or months. In retailing, monthly forecasts are usually required. Jewelry stores know December accounts for nearly one-quarter of annual sales, while drugstores know December sales are slightly better than average. Stationery stores and card stores realize that Christmas cards generate 61 percent of seasonal greeting card sales, while Valentine's Day cards account for 25 percent.[6]

TABLE 16-7	Handy Hardware Store, A Simple Sales Forecast Using Product Control Units		
Product Control Units	Actual Sales 2003	Projected Growth/ Decline (%)	Sales Forecast 2004
Lawn mowers/ snow blowers	$200,000	+10.0	$220,000
Paint and supplies	128,000	+3.0	131,840
Hardware supplies	108,000	+8.0	116,640
Plumbing supplies	88,000	−4.0	84,480
Power tools	88,000	+6.0	93,280
Garden supplies/chemicals	68,000	+4.0	70,720
Housewares	48,000	−6.0	45,120
Electrical supplies	40,000	+4.0	41,600
Ladders	36,000	+6.0	38,160
Hand tools	36,000	+9.0	39,240
Total year	$840,000	+4.9[a]	$881,080

[a]There is a small rounding error.

To acquire more specific estimates, a retailer could use a **monthly sales index**, which divides each month's actual sales by average monthly sales and multiplies the results by 100. Table 16-8 shows Handy Hardware's 2003 actual monthly sales and monthly sales indexes. The store is seasonal, with peaks in late spring and early summer (for lawn mowers, garden supplies, and so on), as well as December (for lighting fixtures, snow blowers, and gifts). Average monthly

TABLE 16-8	Handy Hardware Store, 2003 Sales by Month	
Month	Monthly Actual Sales	Sales Index[a]
January	$ 46,800	67
February	40,864	58
March	48,000	69
April	65,600	94
May	112,196	160
June	103,800	148
July	104,560	149
August	62,800	90
September	46,904	67
October	46,800	67
November	66,884	96
December	94,792	135
Total yearly sales	$840,000	
Average monthly sales	$ 70,000	
Average monthly index		100

[a]Monthly sales index = (Monthly sales/Average monthly sales) × 100

TABLE 16-9	Handy Hardware Store, 2004 Sales Forecast by Month		
Month	Actual Sales 2003	Monthly Sales Index	Monthly Sales Forecast for 2004[a]
January	$ 46,800	67	$73,423 × .67 = $ 49,193
February	40,864	58	73,423 × .58 = 42,585
March	48,000	69	73,423 × .69 = 50,662
April	65,600	94	73,423 × .94 = 69,018
May	112,196	160	73,423 × 1.60 = 117,477
June	103,800	148	73,423 × 1.48 = 108,666
July	104,560	149	73,423 × 1.49 = 109,400
August	62,800	90	73,423 × .90 = 66,081
September	46,904	67	73,423 × .67 = 49,193
October	46,800	67	73,423 × .67 = 49,193
November	66,884	96	73,423 × .96 = 70,486
December	94,792	135	73,423 × 1.35 = 99,121
Total sales	$840,000		Total sales forecast $881,080[b]
Average monthly sales	$ 70,000		Average monthly forecast $ 73,423

[a]Monthly sales forecast = Average monthly forecast × (Monthly index/100). In this equation, the monthly index is computed as a fraction of 1.00 rather than 100.
[b]There is a small rounding error.

2003 sales were $70,000 ($840,000/12). Thus, the monthly sales index for January is 67 [($46,800/$70,000) × 100]; other monthly indexes are computed similarly. Each monthly index shows the percentage deviation of that month's sales from the average month's. A May index of 160 means May sales are 60 percent higher than average. An October index of 67 means sales in October are 33 percent below average.

Once monthly sales indexes are determined, a retailer can forecast monthly sales, based on the yearly sales forecast. Table 16-9 shows how Handy's 2004 monthly sales can be forecast if average monthly sales are expected to be $73,423.

INVENTORY-LEVEL PLANNING

LogicTools (www.logic-tools.com) offers software such as Inventory Analyst to enhance inventory planning.

At this point, a retailer plans its inventory. The level must be sufficient to meet sales expectations, allowing a margin for error. Techniques to plan inventory levels are the basic stock, percentage variation, weeks' supply, and stock-to-sales methods.

With the **basic stock method**, a retailer carries more items than it expects to sell over a specified period. There is a cushion if sales are more than anticipated, shipments are delayed, or customers want to select from a variety of items. It is best when inventory turnover is low or sales are erratic over the year. Beginning-of-month planned inventory equals planned sales plus a basic stock amount:

Basic stock (at retail) = Average monthly stock at retail − Average monthly sales

Beginning-of-month
planned inventory level = Planned monthly sales + Basic stock
  (at retail)

If Handy Hardware, with an average monthly 2004 forecast of $73,423, wants extra stock equal to 10 percent of its average monthly forecast and expects January 2004 sales to be $49,193:

Basic stock (at retail) $= (\$73,423 \times 1.10) - \$73,423 = \$7,342$

Beginning-of-January
planned inventory level $= \$49,193 + \$7,342 = \$56,535$
(at retail)

In the **percentage variation method**, beginning-of-month planned inventory during any month differs from planned average monthly stock by only one-half of that month's variation from estimated average monthly sales. This method is recommended if stock turnover is more than six times a year or relatively stable, since it results in planned inventories closer to the monthly average than other techniques:

Beginning-of-month   Planned average monthly stock at retail
planned inventory level $= \times 1/2\ [1 + ($Estimated monthly sales/
(at retail)   Estimated average monthly sales$)]$

If Handy Hardware plans average monthly stock of 80,765 and November 2004 sales are expected to be 4 percent less than average monthly sales of $73,423, the store's planned inventory level at the beginning of November 2004 would be:

Beginning-of-November
planned inventory level $= \$80,765 \times 1/2\ [1 + (\$70,487/\$73,423)] = \$79,150$
(at retail)

Handy Hardware should not use this method due to its variable sales. If it did, Handy would plan a beginning-of-December 2004 inventory of $94,899, less than expected sales ($99,121).

The **weeks' supply method** forecasts average sales weekly, so beginning inventory equals several weeks' expected sales. It assumes inventory is in proportion to sales. Too much merchandise may be stocked in peak periods and too little during slow periods:

Beginning-of-month   Average estimated   Number of weeks
planned inventory level $=$ weekly sales $\times$ to be stocked
(at retail)

If Handy Hardware forecasts average weekly sales of $10,956.92 from January 1, 2004, through March 31, 2004, and it wants to stock 13 weeks of merchandise (based on expected turnover), beginning inventory would be $142,440:

Beginning-of-January
planned inventory level $= \$10,956.92 \times 13 = \$142,440$
(at retail)

With the **stock-to-sales method**, a retailer wants to maintain a specified ratio of goods on hand to sales. A ratio of 1.3 means that if Handy Hardware plans sales of $69,018 in April 2004, it should have $89,723 worth of merchandise (at retail) available during the month. Like the weeks' supply method, this approach tends to adjust inventory more drastically than changes in sales require.

Yearly stock-to-sales ratios by retail type are provided by sources such as *Industry Norms & Key Business Ratios* (New York: Dun & Bradstreet) and *Annual Statement Studies* (Philadelphia: RMA). A retailer can, thus, compare its ratios with other firms'.

REDUCTION PLANNING

Besides forecasting sales, a firm should estimate its expected **retail reductions**, which represent the difference between beginning inventory plus purchases during the period and sales plus ending inventory. Planned reductions incorporate anticipated markdowns (discounts to stimulate sales), employee and other discounts (price cuts to employees, senior citizens, and others), and stock shortages (pilferage, breakage, and bookkeeping errors):

$$\text{Planned reductions} = \frac{\text{(Beginning inventory + Planned purchases)}}{-\text{ (Planned sales + Ending inventory)}}$$

Reduction planning revolves around two key factors: estimating expected total reductions by budget period and assigning the estimates monthly. The following should be considered in planning reductions: past experience, markdown data for similar retailers, changes in company policies, merchandise carryover from one budget period to another, price trends, and stock-shortage trends.

Past experience is a good starting point. This information can then be compared with the performance of similar firms—by reviewing data on markdowns, discounts, and stock shortages in trade publications. A retailer with higher markdowns than competitors could investigate and correct the situation by adjusting its buying practices and price levels or training sales personnel better.

A retailer must consider its own procedures in reviewing reductions. Policy changes often affect the quantity and timing of markdowns. If a firm expands its assortment of seasonal and fashion merchandise, this would probably lead to a rise in markdowns.

Merchandise carryover, price trends, and stock-shortage trends also affect planning. If such items as gloves and antifreeze are stocked in off-seasons, markdowns are often not used to clear out inventory. Yet, the carryover of fad items merely postpones reductions. Price trends of product categories have a strong impact on reductions. Many full computer systems now sell for less than $1,000, down considerably from earlier amounts. This means higher-priced computers must be marked down. Recent stock-shortage trends (determined by comparing prior book and physical inventory values) can be used to project future reductions due to employee, customer, and vendor theft; breakage; and bookkeeping mistakes. If a firm has total stock shortages of less than 2 percent of annual sales, it is usually deemed to be doing well. Figure 16-3 shows a checklist to reduce shortages from clerical and handling errors. Suggestions for reducing shortages from theft were covered in Chapter 15.

After determining total reductions, they must be planned by month because reductions as a percentage of sales are not the same during each month. Stock shortages may be much higher during busy periods, when stores are more crowded and transactions happen more quickly.

PLANNING PURCHASES

The formula for calculating planned purchases for a period is:

$$\text{Planned purchases (at retail)} = \frac{\text{Planned sales for the month + Planned reductions for the month}}{+ \text{ Planned end-of-month stock} - \text{Beginning-of-month stock}}$$

If Handy Hardware projects June 2004 sales to be $108,666 and total planned reductions to be 5 percent of sales, plans end-of-month inventory at retail to be $72,000, and has a beginning-of-month inventory at retail of $80,000, planned purchases for June are

$$\text{Planned purchases (at retail)} = \$108,666 + \$5,433 + \$72,000 - \$80,000 = \$106,099$$

Because Handy Hardware expects 2004 merchandise costs to be about 60 percent of retail selling price, it is planning to purchase $63,659 of goods at cost in June 2004:

$$\text{Planned purchases (at cost)} = \frac{\text{Planned purchases at retail}}{\times \text{ Merchandise costs as a percentage of selling price}}$$

$$= \$106,099 \times 0.60 = \$63,659$$

Take an online tour of *The OTB Book* (www.otb-retail.com/tour1.htm).

Open-to-buy is the difference between planned purchases and the purchase commitments already made by a buyer for a given period, often a month. It represents the amount the buyer has left to spend for that month and is reduced each time a purchase is made. At the beginning of a month, a firm's planned purchases and open-to-buy are equal if no purchases commitments have been made before that month starts. Open-to-buy is recorded at cost.

FIGURE 16-3

A Checklist to Reduce
Inventory Shortages
Due to Clerical and
Handling Errors

Answer yes or no to each of the following questions. A no means corrective action must be taken.

Buying

1. Is the exact quantity of merchandise purchased always specified in the contract?
2. Are special purchase terms clearly noted?
3. Are returns to the vendor recorded properly?

Marking

4. Are retail prices clearly and correctly marked on merchandise?
5. Are markdowns and additional markups recorded by item number and quantity?
6. Does a cashier check with a manager if a price is not marked on an item?
7. Are old price tags removed when an item's price changes?

Handling

8. After receipt, are purchase quantities checked against the order?
9. Is merchandise handled in a systematic manner?
10. Are items sold in bulk (such as produce, sugar, candy) measured accurately?
11. Are damaged, soiled, returned, or other special goods handled separately?

Selling

12. Do sales personnel know correct prices or have easy access to them?
13. Are misrings by cashiers made on a very small percentage of sales?
14. Are special terms noted on sales receipts (such as employee discounts)?
15. Are sales receipts numbered and later checked for missing invoices?

Inventory Planning

16. Is a physical inventory conducted at least annually and is a book inventory kept throughout the year?
17. Are the differences between physical inventory and book inventory always explained?

Accounting

18. Are permanent records on all transactions kept and monitored for accuracy?
19. Are both retail and cost data maintained?
20. Are inventory shortages compared with industry averages?

At Handy Hardware, the buyer has made purchase commitments for June 2004 in the amount of $55,000 at retail. Accordingly, Handy's open-to-buy at retail for June is $51,099:

$$\text{Open-to-buy} \atop \text{(at retail)} = {\text{Planned purchases for the month} \atop - \text{ Purchase commitments for that month}}$$

$$= \$106{,}099 - \$55{,}000 = \$51{,}099$$

To calculate the June 2004 open-to-buy at cost, $51,099 is multiplied by Handy Hardware's merchandise costs as a percentage of selling price:

$$\text{Open-to-buy} \atop \text{(at cost)} = {\text{Open-to-buy at retail} \atop \times \text{ Merchandise costs as a percentage of selling price}}$$

$$= \$51{,}099 \times 0.60 = \$30{,}659$$

The open-to-buy concept has two major strengths: (1) It maintains a specified relationship between inventory and planned sales; this avoids overbuying and underbuying. (2) It lets a firm adjust purchases to reflect changes in sales, markdowns, and so on. If Handy revises its June 2004 sales forecast to $120,000 (from $108,666), it automatically increases planned purchases and open-to-buy by $11,334 at retail and $6,800 at cost.

It is advisable for a retailer to keep at least a small open-to-buy figure for as long as possible—to take advantage of special deals, purchase new models when introduced, and fill in items that sell out. An open-to-buy limit sometimes must be exceeded due to underestimated demand (low sales forecasts). A retailer should not be so rigid that merchandising personnel are unable to have the discretion (employee empowerment) to purchase below-average-priced items when the open-to-buy is not really open.

PLANNING PROFIT MARGINS

In preparing a profitable merchandise budget, a retailer must consider planned net sales, retail operating expenses, profit, and retail reductions in pricing merchandise:

$$\text{Required initial markup percentage} = \frac{\text{Planned retail expenses} + \text{Planned profit} + \text{Planned reductions}}{\text{Planned net sales} + \text{Planned reductions}}$$

The required markup is a companywide average. Individual items may be priced according to demand and other factors, as long as the average is met. A fuller markup discussion is in Chapter 17. The concept of initial markup is introduced here for continuity in the description of merchandise budgeting.

Handy has an overall 2004 sales forecast of $881,080 and expects annual expenses to be $290,000. Reductions are projected at $44,000. The total net dollar profit margin goal is $60,000 (6.8 percent of sales). Its required initial markup is 42.6 percent:

$$\text{Required initial markup percentage} = \frac{\$290,000 + \$60,000 + \$44,000}{\$881,080 + \$44,000} = 42.6\%$$

$$\text{Required initial markup percentage (all factors expressed as a percentage of net sales)} = \frac{32.9\% + 6.8\% + 5.0\%}{100.0\% + 5.0\%} = 42.6\%$$

In a recent issue of *Management Today*, Alison Reed, the finance director for Marks & Spencer (**www.marksandspencer.com**), was ranked as one of Great Britain's "50 Most Powerful Women." As a senior manager in group accounting, Reed's big break occurred after she was selected by Sir Richard Greenbury, then head of Marks & Spencer, as his executive personal assistant.

Reed says that her work with Greenbury was invaluable: "In terms of a learning experience, it was a highlight. Being at the heart of everything with the city, suppliers, and international operations was a fantastic way of moving from a narrow discipline to a broad discipline."

After two years as executive personal assistant, Reed became the buyer for home furnishings, a product category with annual sales of over 500 million British pounds. According to Greenbury, that move came as "something of a shock" to the then 34-year-old: "Financial people tend to look backwards (at the numbers)—but in buying, you have to look forward and decide on selling prices, products, margins, and markdowns." After four years in this position, Reed then spent two years in logistics and direct selling as group divisional director. She rejoined the finance team in 1996, before being promoted to her current position.

Source: "Accounting for Taste at the Top of M&S: Peter Smith Looks at the Rise of Alison Reed to One of the Senior Jobs at the Retailing Group," *Financial Times* (June 3, 2002), p. 20.

UNIT CONTROL SYSTEMS

RWS Information Systems offers unit control software capabilities in its POS-IM program (www.rwsinfo.com/invcon2.html).

Unit control systems deal with quantities of merchandise in units rather than in dollars. Information typically reveals

- Items selling well and those selling poorly.
- Opportunities and problems in terms of price, color, style, size, and so on.
- The quantity of goods on hand (if book inventory is used). This minimizes overstocking and understocking.
- An indication of inventory age, highlighting candidates for markdowns or promotions.
- The optimal time to reorder merchandise.
- Experiences with alternative sources (vendors) when problems arise.
- The level of inventory and sales for each item in every store branch. This improves the transfer of goods between branches and alerts salespeople as to which branches have desired products. Also, less stock can be held in individual stores, reducing costs.

PHYSICAL INVENTORY SYSTEMS

A *physical inventory unit control system* is similar to a physical inventory dollar control system. However, the latter is concerned with the financial value of inventory, while a unit control system looks at the number of units by item classification. With unit control, inventory levels are monitored either by visual inspection or actual count. See Figure 16-4.

FIGURE 16-4

Physical Inventory Systems Made Simpler

Taking a physical inventory using a Retail Pro portable terminal takes only a fraction of the time required for a traditional manual count. It also yields a more accurate result. After each scan with the laser gun, the physical count is recorded in the portable terminal. Once a section of inventory is complete, an employee connects the portable terminal to a computer and Retail Pro compares the recorded inventory with the physical counts. Any discrepancies are immediately isolated and reported. When the firm is ready, it can automatically adjust the recorded inventory to reflect the physical counts and record this adjustment. The portable terminal can also perform quantity and price verifications by pre-loading inventory quantity and price information. When merchandise is scanned, the unit displays the correct retail price and the expected quantity on hand. This makes it easy to detect pricing errors and missing merchandise.

Reprinted by permission of Retail Technologies International.

In a visual inspection system, merchandise is placed on pegboard (or similar) displays, with each item numbered on the back or on a stock card. Minimum inventory quantities are noted, and sales personnel reorder when inventory reaches the minimum level. This is accurate only if items are placed in numerical order on displays (and sold accordingly). The system is used in the housewares and hardware displays of various discount and hardware stores. Although easy to maintain and inexpensive, it does not provide data on the rate of sales of individual items. And minimum stock quantities may be arbitrarily defined and not drawn from in-depth analysis.

The other physical inventory system, actual counting, means regularly compiling the number of units on hand. This approach records—in units—inventory on hand, purchases, sales volume, and shortages during specified periods. A stock-counting system requires more clerical work but lets a firm obtain sales data for given periods and stock-to-sales relationships as of the time of each count. A physical system is not as sophisticated as a book system. It is more useful with low-value items having predictable sales. Handy Hardware could use the system for its insulation tape:

	Number of Rolls of Tape for the Period 12/1/03–12/31/03
Beginning inventory, December 1, 2003	100
Total purchases for period	70
Total units available for sale	170
Closing inventory, December 31, 2003	60
Sales and shortages for period	110

PERPETUAL INVENTORY SYSTEMS

A *perpetual inventory unit control system* keeps a running total of the number of units handled by a retailer through recordkeeping entries that adjust for sales, returns, transfers to other departments or stores, receipt of shipments, and other transactions. All additions to and subtractions from beginning inventory are recorded. Such a system can be applied manually, use merchandise tags processed by computers, or rely on point-of-sale devices such as optical scanners.

A manual system requires employees to gather data by examining sales checks, merchandise receipts, transfer requests, and other documents. Data are then coded and tabulated. A merchandise tagging system relies on pre-printed tags with data by department, classification, vendor, style, date of receipt, color, and/or material. When an item is sold, a copy of the tag is removed and sent to a tabulating facility for computer analysis. Since pre-printed tags are processed in batches, they can be used by smaller retailers that subscribe to service bureaus and by branches of chains (with data processed at a central location). Point-of-sale (POS) systems feed data from merchandise tags or product labels directly to in-store computers for immediate data processing. Computer-based systems are quicker, more accurate, and of higher quality than manual ones.

Newer POS systems are easy to network, have battery backup capabilities, and run on standard components. Many of these systems use optical scanners to transfer data from products to computers by wands or other devices that pass over sensitized strips on the items. Figure 16-5 shows how barcoding works. As noted earlier, the UPC is the dominant format for coding data onto merchandise. Nonetheless, a big challenge lies ahead:

Want to look up a UPC code? Go here (www.upcdatabase.com/item.pl).

Starting January 1, 2005, the 12-digit codes retailers use to identify everything from cars to candy bars will go to 13 digits. The additional number (and associated bars and spaces) is enough to make checkout scanners seize up and computers crash. The reason for expanding the 12-digit UPC is twofold. First, there is a shortage of UPC numbers. Second, 13-digit bar codes are used almost everywhere else in the world except the United States and Canada. But moving to 13 digits may not be enough. The Universal Code Council and EAN International strongly advise manufacturers and retailers to go a step further and prepare their systems to accommodate a 14-digit code.[7]

FIGURE 16-5

How Does a UPC-Based Scanner System Work?

When a scanner is passed over an item with a UPC symbol, that symbol is read by a low-energy laser. The UPC symbol consists of a series of vertical lines, with numbers below them. Each product has its own unique identification code, and the price is not in the symbol. Scanned information is transmitted to an in-store computer that identifies the item and searches its memory for the current price. This information is then sent back to the checkout terminal.

Reprinted by permission of Beeline Shopper.

Many retailers combine perpetual and physical systems, whereby items accounting for a large proportion of sales are controlled by a perpetual system and other items are controlled by a physical inventory system. Thus, attention is properly placed on the retailer's most important products.

UNIT CONTROL SYSTEMS IN PRACTICE

According to an inventory management practices survey of department stores, discount stores, specialty apparel stores, supermarkets, drugstores, and home centers:

- 94 percent of the firms engage in "wall-to-wall" physical inventories, with 40 percent doing so yearly, 24 percent semiannually, 20 percent quarterly, and 10 percent monthly.
- The majority (57 percent) use a cost inventory system, while 38 percent use the retail method.
- 68 percent of the firms use a perpetual inventory system.[8]

FINANCIAL INVENTORY CONTROL: INTEGRATING DOLLAR AND UNIT CONCEPTS

ProfitLogic (www. grossprofit.com) markets sophisticated inventory analysis software.

Up to now, we have discussed dollar and unit control separately. In practice, they are linked. A decision on how many units to buy is affected by dollar investments, inventory turnover, quantity discounts, warehousing and insurance costs, and so on. Three aspects of financial inventory control are described next: stock turnover and gross margin return on investment, when to reorder, and how much to reorder.

STOCK TURNOVER AND GROSS MARGIN RETURN ON INVESTMENT

Stock turnover represents the number of times during a specific period, usually one year, that the average inventory on hand is sold. It can be measured by store, product line, department, and vendor. With high turnover, inventory investments are productive on a per-dollar basis, items are fresh, there are fewer losses due to changes in styles, and interest, insurance, breakage, and warehousing costs are reduced. A retailer can raise stock turnover by reducing its assortment, eliminating or having little inventory for slow-selling items, buying in a timely way, applying QR inventory planning, and using reliable suppliers.

Stock turnover can be computed in units or dollars (at retail or cost). The choice of a formula depends on the retailer's accounting system:

$$\text{Annual rate of stock turnover (in units)} = \frac{\text{Number of units sold during year}}{\text{Average inventory on hand (in units)}}$$

$$\text{Annual rate of stock turnover (in retail dollars)} = \frac{\text{Net yearly sales}}{\text{Average inventory on hand (at retail)}}$$

$$\text{Annual rate of stock turnover (at cost)} = \frac{\text{Cost of goods sold during the year}}{\text{Average inventory on hand (at cost)}}$$

In computing stock turnover, the average inventory level for the entire period needs to be reflected. Turnover rates are invalid if the true average is not used, as occurs if a firm mistakenly views the inventory level of a peak or slow month as the yearly average. Table 16-10 shows annual turnover rates for various retailers. Eating places, gasoline service stations, and grocery stores have high rates. They rely on sales volume for their success. Jewelry stores, shoe stores, and some clothing stores have low rates. They require larger profit margins on each item sold and maintain a sizable assortment.

Despite the advantages of high turnover, buying items in small amounts may also result in the loss of quantity discounts and in higher transportation charges. Since high turnover might be due to a limited assortment, some sales may be lost, and profits may be lower if prices are reduced to move inventory quickly. The return on investment depends on both turnover and profit per unit.

TABLE 16-10	Annual Median Stock Turnover Rates for Selected Types of Retailers
Type of Retailer	**Annual Median Stock Turnover Rate (Times)**
Auto and home supply stores	7.4
Department stores	4.7
Drugstores and proprietary stores	10.7
Eating places	81.5
Family clothing stores	4.3
Furniture stores	5.1
Gasoline service stations	39.4
Grocery stores	19.7
Hardware stores	4.7
Household appliance stores	6.3
Jewelry stores	2.6
Lumber and other building materials dealers	7.8
Men's and boys' clothing stores	4.1
New and used-car dealers	6.1
Shoe stores	3.9
Women's clothing stores	5.9

Source: Industry Norms & Key Business Ratios (New York: Dun & Bradstreet, 2000–2001), pp. 135–151.

Learn more about GMROI (http://rtfurniture.net/worksheet.html).

Gross margin return on investment (GMROI) shows the relationship between the gross margin in dollars (total dollar operating profits) and the average inventory investment (at cost) by combining profitability and sales-to-stock measures:

$$\text{GMROI} = \frac{\text{Gross margin in dollars}}{\text{Net sales}} \times \frac{\text{Net sales}}{\text{Average inventory at cost}}$$

$$= \frac{\text{Gross margin in dollars}}{\text{Average inventory at cost}}$$

The gross margin in dollars equals net sales minus the cost of goods sold. The gross margin percentage is derived by dividing dollar gross margin by net sales. A sales-to-stock ratio is derived by dividing net sales by average inventory at cost. That ratio may be converted to stock turnover by multiplying it by [(100 − Gross margin percentage)/100].

GMROI is a useful concept for several reasons:

- It shows how diverse retailers can prosper. A supermarket may have a gross margin of 20 percent and a sales-to-stock ratio of 25—a GMROI of 500 percent. A women's clothing store may have a gross margin of 50 percent and a sales-to-stock ratio of 10—a GMROI of 500 percent. Both firms have the same GMROI due to the trade-off between item profitability and turnover.

- It is a good indicator of a manager's performance since it focuses on factors controlled by that person. Interdepartmental comparisons can also be made.

- It is simple to plan and understand, and data collection is easy.

- It can be determined if GMROI performance is consistent with other company goals.[9]

The gross margin percentage and the sales-to-stock ratio must be studied individually. If only overall GMROI is reviewed, performance may be assessed improperly.

WHEN TO REORDER

One way to control inventory investment is to systematically set stock levels at which new orders must be placed. Such a stock level is called a **reorder point**, and it is based on three factors. **Order lead time** is the period from the date an order is placed by a retailer to the date merchandise is ready for sale (received, price-marked, and put on the selling floor). **Usage rate** refers to average sales per day, in units, of merchandise. **Safety stock** is the extra inventory that protects against out-of-stock conditions due to unexpected demand and delays in delivery. It depends on the firm's policy toward running out of items.

Ethics in RETAILING

A Nonprofit Association (SCORE) Helps Small Retailers

SCORE, the Service Corps of Retired Executives (**www. score.org**), is a nonprofit organization that is sponsored by the U.S. Small Business Administration. It helps small and medium-sized businesses through free consulting, mentoring, and educational workshops. SCORE's consultants are volunteers who are retired business owners, business executives, and operations managers who donate their time. Since 1964, more than 4.5 million entrepreneurs have been served by SCORE counselors or have attended a SCORE-sponsored lecture.

The White Plains, New York, chapter of SCORE, a unit with more than 50 counselors, was recently named "Chapter of the Year." According to Bill Owen, a counselor at this chapter, a firm using SCORE "is not any different than a company hiring a consultant to come in and find problems. The consultant is a

worker. The consultant is a teacher." In addition to its consulting activities, the chapter offers weekly business workshop programs to local businesses.

Scott Greenbaum is a client of the White Plains branch of SCORE who has seen the program work for him: "I was seeing Bill an average of once every two to three weeks. We would discuss business planning strategies to increase my business and what I needed to move forward. I would always have to report back to him and that helps give you some discipline."

Source: "Looking to SCORE," *Westchester County Business Journal* (December 10, 2001).

This is the formula for a retailer that does not plan to carry safety stock. It believes customer demand is stable and that its orders are promptly filled by suppliers:

$$\text{Reorder point} = \text{Usage rate} \times \text{Lead time}$$

If Handy Hardware sells 10 paintbrushes a day and needs 8 days to order, receive, and display them, it has a reorder point of 80 brushes. It would reorder brushes once inventory on hand reaches 80. By the time brushes from that order are placed on shelves (8 days later), stock on hand will be zero, and the new stock will replenish the inventory.

This strategy is proper only when Handy has a steady customer demand of 10 paintbrushes daily and it takes exactly 8 days to complete all stages in the ordering process. This does not normally occur. If customers buy 15 brushes per day during the month, Handy would run out of stock in 5-1/3 days and be without brushes for 2-2/3 days. If an order takes 10 days to process, Handy would have no brushes for 2 days, despite correctly estimating demand. Figure 16-6 shows how stockouts may occur.

For a retailer interested in keeping a safety stock, the reorder formula becomes:

$$\text{Reorder point} = (\text{Usage rate} \times \text{Lead time}) + \text{Safety stock}$$

Suppose Handy Hardware decides on safety stock of 30 percent for paintbrushes; its reorder point is $(10 \times 8) + (.30 \times 80) = 80 + 24 = 104$. Handy still expects to sell an average of 10 brushes per day and receive orders in an average of 8 days. The safety stock of 24 extra brushes is kept on hand to protect against unexpected demand or a late shipment.

By combining a perpetual inventory system and reorder point calculations, ordering can be computerized and an **automatic reordering system** can be mechanically activated when stock-on-hand reaches the reorder point. However, intervention by a buyer or manager must be possible, especially if monthly sales fluctuate greatly.

FIGURE 16-6
How Stockouts
May Occur

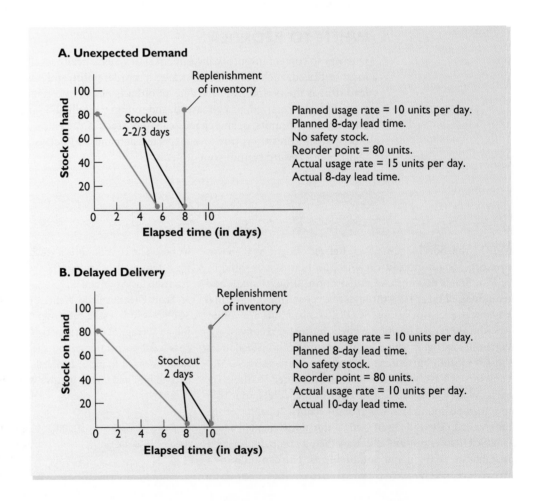

HOW MUCH TO REORDER

A firm placing large orders generally reduces ordering costs but increases inventory-holding costs. A firm placing small orders often minimizes inventory-holding costs while ordering costs may rise (unless EDI and a QR inventory system are used).

Economic order quantity (EOQ) is the quantity per order (in units) that minimizes the total costs of processing orders and holding inventory. Order-processing costs include computer time, order forms, labor, and handling new goods. Holding costs include warehousing, inventory investment, insurance, taxes, depreciation, deterioration, and pilferage. EOQ calculations can be done by large and small firms.

As Figure 16-7 shows, order-processing costs drop as the order quantity (in units) goes up because fewer orders are needed for the same total annual quantity, and inventory-holding costs rise as the order quantity goes up because more units must be held in inventory and they are kept for longer periods. The two costs are summed into a total cost curve. Mathematically, the economic order quantity is

$$EOQ = \sqrt{\frac{2DS}{IC}}$$

where

$$
\begin{aligned}
EOQ &= \text{quantity per order (in units)} \\
D &= \text{annual demand (in units)} \\
S &= \text{costs to place an order (in dollars)} \\
I &= \text{percentage of annual carrying cost to unit cost} \\
C &= \text{unit cost of an item (in dollars)}
\end{aligned}
$$

Handy estimates it can sell 150 power tool sets per year. They cost $90 each. Breakage, insurance, tied-up capital, and pilferage equal 10 percent of the costs of the sets (or $9 each). Order costs are $25 per order. The economic order quantity is 29.

$$EOQ = \sqrt{\frac{2(150)(\$25)}{(0.10)(\$90)}} = \sqrt{\frac{\$7,500}{\$9}} = 29$$

The EOQ formula must often be modified to take into account changes in demand, quantity discounts, and variable ordering and holding costs.

FIGURE 16-7
Economic Order Quantity

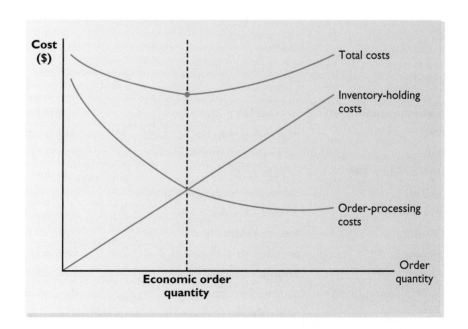

Summary

1. *To describe the major aspects of financial merchandise planning and management.* The purpose of financial merchandise management is to stipulate which products are bought by the retailer, when, and in what quantity. Dollar control monitors inventory investment, while unit control relates to the amount of merchandise handled. Financial merchandise management encompasses accounting methods, merchandise forecasts and budgets, unit control, and integrated dollar and unit controls.

2. *To explain the cost and retail methods of accounting.* The two accounting techniques for retailers are the cost and retail methods of inventory valuation. Physical and book (perpetual) procedures are possible with each. Physical inventory valuation requires counting merchandise at prescribed times. Book inventory valuation relies on accurate bookkeeping and a smooth data flow.

   The cost method obligates a retailer to have careful records or to code costs on packages. This must be done to find the exact value of ending inventory at cost. Many firms use LIFO accounting to project that value, which lets them reduce taxes by having a low ending inventory value. In the retail method, closing inventory value is tied to the average relationship between the cost and retail value of merchandise. This more accurately reflects market conditions but is more complex.

3. *To study the merchandise forecasting and budgeting process.* This is a form of dollar control with six stages: designating control units, sales forecasting, inventory-level planning, reduction planning, planning purchases, and planning profit margins. Adjustments require all later stages to be modified.

   Control units—merchandise categories for which data are gathered—must be narrow to isolate problems and opportunities with specific product lines. Sales forecasting may be the key stage in the merchandising and budgeting process. Through inventory-level planning, a firm sets merchandise quantities for specified periods through the basic stock, percentage variation, weeks' supply, and/or stock-to-sales methods. Reduction planning estimates expected markdowns, discounts, and stock shortages. Planned purchases are linked to planned sales, reductions, and ending and beginning inventory. Profit margins depend on planned net sales, operating expenses, profit, and reductions.

4. *To examine alternative methods of inventory unit control.* A unit control system involves physical units of merchandise. It monitors best-sellers and poor-sellers, the quantity of goods on hand, inventory age, reorder time, and so on. A physical inventory unit control system may use visual inspection or stock counting. A perpetual inventory unit control system keeps a running total of the units handled through recordkeeping entries that adjust for sales, returns, transfers, and so on. A perpetual system can be applied manually, by merchandise tags processed by computers, or by point-of-sale devices. Virtually all larger retailers conduct regular complete physical inventories; two-thirds use a perpetual inventory system.

5. *To integrate dollar and unit merchandising control concepts.* Three aspects of financial inventory management integrate dollar and unit control concepts: stock turnover and gross margin return on investment, when to reorder, and how much to reorder. Stock turnover is the number of times during a period that average inventory on hand is sold. Gross margin return on investment shows the relationship between gross margin in dollars (total dollar operating profits) and average inventory investment (at cost). A reorder point calculation—when to reorder—includes the retailer's usage rate, order lead time, and safety stock. The economic order quantity—how much to reorder—shows how big an order to place, based on both ordering and inventory costs.

Key Terms

financial merchandise management (p. 390)
dollar control (p. 390)
unit control (p. 390)
merchandise available for sale (p. 390)
cost of goods sold (p. 390)
gross profit (p. 390)
net profit (p. 390)
cost method of accounting (p. 391)
physical inventory system (p. 391)
book (perpetual) inventory system (p. 391)
FIFO method (p. 392)

LIFO method (p. 392)
retail method of accounting (p. 394)
cost complement (p. 394)
control units (p. 397)
classification merchandising (p. 398)
monthly sales index (p. 399)
basic stock method (p. 400)
percentage variation method (p. 401)
weeks' supply method (p. 401)
stock-to-sales method (p. 401)
retail reductions (p. 401)

open-to-buy (p. 402)
stock turnover (p. 407)
gross margin return on investment (GMROI) (p. 409)
reorder point (p. 409)
order lead time (p. 409)
usage rate (p. 409)
safety stock (p. 409)
automatic reordering system (p. 410)
economic order quantity (EOQ) (p. 411)

Questions for Discussion

1. Which retailers can best use a perpetual inventory system based on the cost method? Explain your answer.

2. The FIFO method seems more logical than the LIFO method, because it assumes the first merchandise purchased is the first merchandise sold. So, why do more retailers use LIFO?

3. Explain the basic premise of the retail method of accounting. Present an example.

4. Why should a small florist designate control units, even though this may be time-consuming?

5. Why use sophisticated weather forecasting services if daily weather predictions tend to be inaccurate?

6. Contrast the weeks' supply method and the percentage variation method of merchandise planning.

7. Present two situations in which it would be advisable for a retailer to take a markdown instead of carry over merchandise from one budget period to another.

8. A retailer has yearly sales of $650,000. Inventory on January 1 is $260,000 (at cost). During the year, $500,000 of merchandise (at cost) is purchased. The ending inventory is $275,000 (at cost). Operating costs are $90,000. Calculate the cost of goods sold and net profit, and set up a profit-and-loss statement. There are no retail reductions in this problem.

9. A retailer has a beginning monthly inventory valued at $60,000 at retail and $35,000 at cost. Net purchases during the month are $140,000 at retail and $70,000 at cost. Transportation charges are $7,000. Sales are $150,000. Markdowns and discounts equal $20,000. A physical inventory at the end of the month shows merchandise valued at $10,000 (at retail) on hand. Compute the following:
   a. Total merchandise available for sale—at cost and at retail.
   b. Cost complement.
   c. Ending retail book value of inventory.
   d. Stock shortages.
   e. Adjusted ending retail book value.
   f. Gross profit.

10. The sales of a full-line discount store are listed. Calculate the monthly sales indexes. What do they mean?

Jan. $200,000 May $240,000 Sept. $240,000
Feb. 210,000 June 220,000 Oct. 200,000
Mar. 210,000 July 180,000 Nov. 260,000
Apr. 240,000 Aug. 220,000 Dec. 340,000

11. If the planned average monthly stock for the discount store in Question 10 is $280,000 (at retail), how much inventory should be planned for August if the retailer uses the percentage variation method? Comment on this retailer's choice of the percentage variation method.

12. The store in Questions 10 and 11 knows its cost complement for all merchandise purchased last year was 0.61; it projects this to remain constant. It expects to begin and end December with inventory valued at $160,000 at retail and estimates December reductions to be $12,000. The firm already has purchase commitments for December worth $120,000 (at retail). What is the open-to-buy at cost for December?

Note: At our Web site (**www.prenhall.com/bermanevans**), there are several math problems related to the material in this chapter so that you may review these concepts.

Web-Based Exercise

Visit the Web site of e-Data Technologies (**www.geodata.com**). Click on "Smart ACCT Retail Management." Read the online brochure and watch the demonstration. What are the benefits of accounting software such as this for retailers?

Note: Stop by our Web site (**www.prenhall.com/bermanevans**) to experience a number of highly interactive, appealing Web exercises based on actual company demonstrations and sample materials related to retailing.

Chapter Endnotes

1. Various company sources.

2. "Inventory Planning: The Key to Profitability," *Chain Store Age* (January 2002), p. 2C.

3. For a good example, see Connie Robbins Gentry, "The Road to Perpetual Progress," *Chain Store Age* (August 2002), pp. 100, 102.

4. "Longs Drugs," **www.nonstop.com/customers/longs_drugs.html** (March 21, 2003).

5. "Retail & Manufacturing Products/Applications," **www.planalytics.com/app/corp/start.jsp?p=retail_products** (March 8, 2003).

6. National Retail Federation, "December Defense," *Promo* (December 2001), p. 28; and "Greeting Card Industry General Facts and Trends," **www.greetingcard.org/gcindustry_generalfacts.html** (March 3, 2003).

7. Kate Murphy, "Bigger Bar Code Inches Up on Retailers," *New York Times* (August 12, 2002), p. C3.

8. "Overview: Inventory Management," *Chain Store Age* (December 2001), pp. 3A–6A.

9. See Connie Robbins Gentry, "The Bombay Co. Scores Savings," *Chain Store Age* (September 2002), p. 90.

Chapter 17

PRICING IN RETAILING

Reprinted by permission.

Fifty years ago, Sol Price founded FedMart, the nation's first membership club. Initially, FedMart was open only to government employees due to strict laws regarding discounting. In 1975, Price sold his interest in FedMart and a year later opened Price Club in an aircraft hanger in an industrial section of San Diego. In 1983, some former Price Club executives opened their own membership club and named it Costco. Price Club and Costco merged as Price Costco in 1993, and the name of the company was changed to Costco (**www.costco.com**) in 1995.

There are now 1,200 membership clubs in the United States, operated mostly by Costco, Sam's Club (**www.samsclub.com**), and BJ's (**www.bjswholesale.com**). Costco concentrates on the high end for all of its merchandise categories. To encourage impulse purchasing and browsing, Costco does not use aisle markers. This creates more of a treasure hunt for the shopper. Costco was also the first membership club chain to offer gasoline. To encourage consumers to visit its stores, Costly aggressively prices gasoline. Its prices are so low that motorists are willing to wait as long as 20 minutes to purchase gasoline at Costco.

To attract upscale customers, Costco carries wine and charges a retail markup of no more than 14 percent. In contrast, local merchants may mark up wine as much as 50 percent. As a result, Costco is probably the largest retailer of premium wines in the United States.[1]

chapter objectives

1. To describe the role of pricing in a retail strategy and to show that pricing decisions must be made in an integrated and adaptive manner

2. To examine the impact of consumers; government; manufacturers, wholesalers, and other suppliers; and current and potential competitors on pricing decisions

3. To present a framework for developing a retail price strategy: objectives, broad policy, basic strategy, implementation, and adjustments

OVERVIEW

Learn about the complexities of setting prices (http://retailindustry.about.com/cs/retail_pricing).

Nordstrom is now the world's largest online shoe retailer (http://shoes2.nordstrom.com/shoes), with its usual upscale prices and service.

Goods and services must be priced in a way that both achieves profitability for the retailer and satisfies customers. A pricing strategy must be consistent with the retailer's overall image (positioning), sales, profit, and return on investment goals.

There are three basic pricing options for a retailer: (1) A *discount orientation* uses low prices as the major competitive advantage. A low-price image, fewer shopping frills, and low per-unit profit margins mean a target market of price-oriented customers, low operating costs, and high inventory turnover. Off-price retailers and full-line discount stores are in this category. (2) With an *at-the-market orientation*, the retailer has average prices. It offers solid service and a nice atmosphere to middle-class shoppers. Margins are moderate to good, and average to above-average quality products are stocked. This firm may find it hard to expand its price range, and it may be squeezed by retailers positioned as discounters or prestige stores. Traditional department stores and many drugstores are in this category. (3) Through an *upscale orientation*, a prestigious image is the retailer's major competitive advantage. A smaller target market, higher expenses, and lower turnover mean customer loyalty, distinctive services and products, and high per-unit profit margins. Upscale department stores and specialty stores are in this category.

As we have mentioned several times, a big key to successful retailing is providing a good *value* in the consumer's mind—for the price orientation chosen: "Costco is successful because of the things it doesn't do. No advertising. No loss leaders. No escalators. No shopping bags. No big buck salaries for executives. 'We stack merchandise on the floor with a price and a sign on it telling what it is.'"[2]

Every customer, whether buying an inexpensive $4 ream of paper or a $40 ream of embossed, personalized stationery, wants to feel the purchase represents a good value. The consumer is not necessarily looking only for the best price. He or she is often interested in the best value—which may be reflected in a superior shopping experience:

> Twenty-first century shoppers are quite price-conscious. With nine out of 10 consumers frequenting discount stores, it's obvious that low prices are the determining factor for many people—and they place retailers in a real predicament. Overhead dictates that traditional retailers can only cut prices so far; so what are they to do? If you can't win in the price war, you're got to show shoppers what they are getting for their money. Despite the overall cost-conscious mentality, a significant segment of the new shopper population will pay more when they receive personalized customer service. This may mean a radical readjustment for many stores.[3]

See Figure 17-1.

Another factor shaping today's pricing environment for retailers of all types is the ease by which a shopper can compare prices on the Web. When a consumer could only do price comparisons by visiting individual stores, the process was time consuming—which limited many people's willingness to shop around. Now, with a few clicks of a computer mouse, a shopper can gain online price information from several retailers in just minutes—without leaving home. Web sites such as mySimon.com and CNET make comparison shopping even simpler: "Comparison sites are free and easy for shoppers to use, and they operate much like search services. The sites don't sell anything; instead, they simply link shoppers to the places that do. The best part is, consumers are visiting these sites in droves."[4]

The interaction of price with other retailing mix elements can be shown by BE's Toy City, a hypothetical discounter. It has a broad strategy consisting of:

- A target market of price-conscious families that shop for inexpensive toys ($9 to $12).
- A limited range of merchandise quality ("better" merchandise consists of end-of-season closeouts and manufacturer overruns).
- Self-service in an outlet mall location.
- A good assortment supported by quantity purchases at deep discounts from suppliers.
- An image of efficiency and variety.

In this chapter, we divide retail pricing into two major sections: the external factors affecting a price strategy and the steps in a price strategy. At our site (**www.prenhall.com/bermanevans**), there are several links to information on setting a price strategy.

EXTERNAL FACTORS AFFECTING A RETAIL PRICE STRATEGY

Several factors (discussed next) have an impact on a retail pricing strategy, as shown in Figure 17-2. Sometimes, the factors have a minor effect. In other cases, they severely restrict a firm's pricing options.

THE CONSUMER AND RETAIL PRICING[5]

Retailers should understand the **price elasticity of demand**—the sensitivity of customers to price changes in terms of the quantities they will buy—because there is often a relationship between price and consumer purchases and perceptions. If small percentage changes in price lead to sub-

FIGURE 17-2
Factors Affecting Retail
Price Strategy

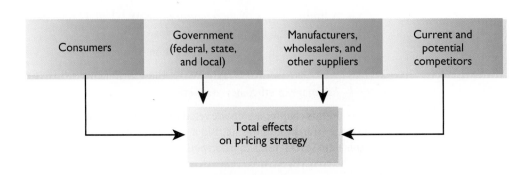

stantial percentage changes in the number of units bought, demand is *price elastic*. This occurs when the urgency to purchase is low or there are acceptable substitutes. If large percentage changes in price lead to small percentage changes in the number of units bought, demand is *price inelastic*. Then purchase urgency is high or there are no acceptable substitutes (as takes place with brand or retailer loyalty). *Unitary elasticity* occurs when percentage changes in price are directly offset by percentage changes in quantity.

Price elasticity is computed by dividing the percentage change in the quantity demanded by the percentage change in the price charged. Because purchases generally decline as prices go up, elasticity tends to be a negative number:

One look at Godiva's Web site (www.godiva.com) and you'll know why demand for its products is inelastic.

$$\text{Elasticity} = \frac{\dfrac{\text{Quantity 1} - \text{Quantity 2}}{\text{Quantity 1} + \text{Quantity 2}}}{\dfrac{\text{Price 1} - \text{Price 2}}{\text{Price 1} + \text{Price 2}}}$$

Table 17-1 shows the price elasticity for a 1,000-seat movie theater (with elasticities converted to positive numbers). The quantity demanded (tickets sold) declines at every price from $6.00 to $10.00. Demand is inelastic from $6.00 to $7.00 and $7.00 to $8.00; total ticket receipts increase since the percentage change in price is greater than the percentage change in tickets sold. Demand is unitary from $8.00 to $9.00; total ticket receipts are constant since the percentage change in tickets sold exactly offsets the percentage change in price. Demand is elastic from $9.00 to $10.00; total ticket receipts decline since the percentage change in tickets sold is greater than the percentage change in price.

For our example, total ticket receipts are highest at $8.00 or at $9.00. But what about total revenues? If patrons spend an average of $4.00 each at the concession stand, the best price is $6.00 (total overall revenues of $10,000). This theater is most interested in total revenues since its operating costs are the same whether there are 1,000 or 550 patrons. But typically, retailers should evaluate the costs, as well as the revenues, from serving additional customers.

In retailing, computing price elasticity is difficult. First, as with the movie theater, demand for individual events or items may be hard to predict. One week, the theater may attract 1,000 patrons to a movie, and the next week it may attract 400 patrons to a different movie. Second, many retailers carry thousands of items and cannot possibly compute elasticities for every one. As a result, they usually rely on average markup pricing, competition, tradition, and industrywide data to indicate price elasticity.

Price sensitivity varies by market segment, based on shopping orientation. After identifying potential segments, retailers determine which of them form their target market:

TABLE 17-1	A Movie Theater's Elasticity of Demand		
Price	Tickets Sold (Saturday Night)	Total Ticket Receipts	Elasticity of Demand (E)[a]
$6.00	1,000	$6,000	
			E = 0.68
7.00	900	6,300	
			E = 0.79
8.00	810	6,480	
			E = 1.00
9.00	720	6,480	
			E = 2.54
10.00	550	5,500	

Computation example = [(1,000 − 900)/(1,000 + 900)]/[($6.00 − $7.00)/($6.00 + $7.00)] = 0.68

[a]Expressed as a positive number.

American Express (**www.americanexpress.com**) and other credit card companies see the conversion to the Euro currency as a way of increasing the adoption and use of credit cards throughout Europe. In one advertising campaign, American Express states that by using a credit card, the issuer—not the consumer—handles the currency conversion. A secondary benefit is that by using a credit card instead of a debit card, the consumer does not have to concern himself or herself with overdrawing his or her account due to misjudging a price or a currency conversion.

Interestingly, American Express has run this ad campaign in Great Britain—where the Euro has not been adopted. Why? Many British people travel to Continental Europe and are subject to currency conversion errors. According to a Europroject spokesperson for American Express London, "Now, using the card outside of country borders is the same as using it locally."

Currency conversion issues have led to other advantages for credit cards. Passengers with credit cards are eligible to use special toll booth lanes at country borders. Some supermarkets have even opened separate lines for credit card customers. These lanes/lines move much faster than cash- or check-based lines due to the absence of currency conversion complexities.

Source: "Card Companies Sell Euro's Convenience," *American Banker* (September 1, 2001).

Dell (www.dell.com) appeals to multiple market segments—from novice to advanced computer user, with prices set accordingly.

- *Economic consumers*—They perceive competing retailers as similar and shop around for the lowest possible prices. This segment has grown dramatically in recent years.
- *Status-oriented consumers*—They perceive competing retailers as quite different. They are more interested in prestige brands and customer services than in price.
- *Assortment-oriented consumers*—They seek retailers with a strong selection in the product categories being considered. They want fair prices.
- *Personalizing consumers*—They shop where they are known and feel a bond with employees and the firm itself. These shoppers will pay slightly above-average prices.
- *Convenience-oriented consumers*—They shop because they must, want nearby stores with long hours, and may use catalogs or the Web. These people will pay higher prices for convenience.

THE GOVERNMENT AND RETAIL PRICING

Three levels of government may affect retail pricing decisions: federal, state, and local. When laws are federal, they apply to interstate commerce. A retailer operating only within the boundaries of one state may not be restricted by some federal legislation. Major government rules relate to horizontal price fixing, vertical price fixing, price discrimination, minimum price levels, unit pricing, item price removal, and price advertising.

Horizontal Price Fixing

An agreement among manufacturers, among wholesalers, or among retailers to set prices is known as **horizontal price fixing**. Such agreements are illegal under the Sherman Antitrust Act and the Federal Trade Commission Act, regardless of how "reasonable" prices may be. It is also illegal for retailers to get together regarding the use of coupons, rebates, or other price-oriented tactics.

Although few large-scale legal actions have been taken in recent years, the penalties for horizontal price fixing can be severe:

A. Alfred Taubman said Monday that he will work with Sotheby's to find a new owner for the storied auction house that brought him social cachet, then disgrace and a conviction for price-fixing. Taubman, 78, is to report to federal prison on August 1 to begin serving his sentence of a year and a day. He was convicted for conspiring with the chairman of rival Christie's International, Sir Anthony Tennant, to fix the prices the companies charged sellers of fine art, jewels, rugs, and furniture. The houses control about 90 percent of the world's auctions of fine art. Taubman was also fined $7.5 million in connection with his conviction.[6]

Vertical Price Fixing

When manufacturers or wholesalers seek to control the retail prices of their goods and services, **vertical price fixing** occurs. According to the Consumer Goods Pricing Act, retailers in the United States cannot be forced to adhere to *minimum retail prices* set by manufacturers and wholesalers. The Act encourages competition among retailers. However, as a result of a Supreme Court ruling, manufacturers and wholesalers are allowed to set *maximum retail prices*. This ruling "opened the door for manufacturers and wholesalers to cap the prices retailers charge for their products. It reversed a decision that barred such limits and left retailers and franchisees free to raise prices above suppliers' suggested prices. Now, manufacturers can set a maximum price as long as they show they aren't stifling competition."[7]

There have been various legal actions in this area. For example, in late 2002,

The nation's five major music labels, as well as three music retailers, agreed to cough up $143.1 million to settle a case brought by New York and Florida. The cases against the music majors and retailers Tower Records, Musicland Stores, and Transworld Entertainment (parent of Coconuts) were filed after the labels reached a settlement in 2000 with the Federal Trade Commission. At that time, the music companies agreed to stop an industry practice known as "minimum advertised pricing." The suits alleged that from 1995 through 2000, the five major labels, BMG Entertainment, Warner Music Group, Sony Music Entertainment, Universal Music Group, and EMI, artificially inflated the prices of CDs by having retailers agree not to sell albums below a pre-determined minimum price. In exchange, the music retailers received advertising dollars from the record companies.[8]

Other than by setting maximum prices, manufacturers and wholesalers can legally control retail prices only by one of these methods: They can screen retailers. They can set realistic list prices. They can pre-print prices on products (which retailers do not have to use). They can set regular prices that are accepted by consumers (such as 50 cents for a newspaper). They can use consignment selling, whereby the supplier owns items until they are sold and assumes costs normally associated with the retailer. They can own retail facilities. They can refuse to sell to retailers that advertise discount prices in violation of written policies. A supplier has a right to announce a policy for dealer pricing and can refuse to sell to those that do not comply. It cannot use coercion to prohibit a retailer from advertising low prices.

Price Discrimination

The **Robinson-Patman Act** bars manufacturers and wholesalers from discriminating in price or purchase terms in selling to individual retailers if these retailers are purchasing products of "like quality" and the effect of such discrimination is to injure competition. The intent of this Act is to stop large retailers from using their power to gain discounts not justified by the cost savings achieved by suppliers due to big orders. There are exceptions that allow justifiable price discrimination when:

- Products are physically different.
- The retailers paying different prices are not competitors.
- Competition is not injured.
- Price differences are due to differences in supplier costs.
- Market conditions change—costs rise or fall, or competing suppliers shift their prices.

Discounts are not illegal, as long as suppliers follow the preceding rules, make discounts available to competing retailers on an equitable basis, and offer discounts sufficiently graduated so small retailers can also qualify. Discounts for cumulative purchases (total yearly orders) and for multistore purchases by chains may be hard to justify.

Although the Robinson-Patman Act restricts sellers more than buyers, retailers are covered under Section 2(F): "It shall be unlawful for any person engaged in commerce, in the course of such commerce, knowingly to induce or receive a discrimination in price which is prohibited in this section." Thus, a retail buyer must try to get the lowest prices charged to any competitor, yet not bargain so hard that discounts cannot be justified by acceptable exceptions.

Minimum-Price Laws

About half the states have **minimum-price laws** that prevent retailers from selling certain items for less than their cost plus a fixed percentage to cover overhead. Besides general laws, some state rules set minimum prices for specific products. For instance, in New Jersey and Connecticut, the retail price of liquor cannot be less than the wholesale cost (including taxes and delivery charges).

Minimum-price laws protect small retailers from **predatory pricing**, in which large retailers seek to reduce competition by selling goods and services at very low prices, thus causing small retailers to go out of business. In one widely watched case, three pharmacies in Arkansas filed a suit claiming Wal-Mart had sold selected items below cost in an attempt to reduce competition. Wal-Mart agreed it had priced some items below cost to meet or beat rivals' prices but not to harm competitors. The Arkansas Supreme Court ruled that Wal-Mart did not use predatory pricing since the three pharmacies were still profitable.

With **loss leaders**, retailers price selected items below cost to lure more customer traffic for those retailers. Supermarkets use loss leaders to increase overall sales and profits because people buy more than one item once in a store. And consider this: "When Burger King and Wendy's began to cut into the profits of McDonald's, McDonald's wasted no time in countering with the 99-cent Big Mac. But how, you may ask, does one make a profit out of loss leaders? The secret is that the price cut wasn't the whole tactic. McDonald's was able to cut its prices on Big Macs by training its staff to more aggressively cross-sell the real profit-generators: French fries, shakes, large beverages, and desserts."[9] Although loss leaders are restricted by some minimum-price laws, because the tactic is usually consumer-oriented, the laws are rarely applied (as long as there is no predatory pricing).

Unit Pricing

In some states, the proliferation of package sizes has led to **unit pricing** laws—whereby some retailers must express both the total price of an item and its price per unit of measure. Food stores are most affected by unit price rules because grocery items are more regulated than nongrocery items. There are exemptions for firms with low sales. The aim of unit pricing is to enable consumers to better compare the prices of products available in many sizes. Thus, a 6.5-ounce can of tuna fish priced at 99 cents would also have a shelf label showing this as $2.44 per pound. With unit pricing, a person learns that a 12-ounce can of soda selling for 35 cents (2.9 cents per ounce) costs more than a 67.6-ounce—2-liter—bottle for $1.49 (2.2 cents per ounce).

Retailer costs include computing per-unit prices, printing product and shelf labels, and keeping computer records. These costs are influenced by the way prices are attached to goods (by the supplier or the retailer), the number of items subject to unit pricing, the frequency of price changes, sales volume, and the number of stores in a chain.

Unit pricing can be a good strategy for retailers to follow, even when not required. Giant Food's unit pricing system more than pays for itself because of decreased price-marking errors, better inventory control, and improved space management.

Item Price Removal

The boom in computerized checkout systems has led many firms, especially supermarkets, to advocate **item price removal**—whereby prices are marked only on shelves or signs and not on individual items. Scanning equipment reads pre-market product codes and enters price data at the checkout counter. This practice is banned in several states and local communities.

Many retailers oppose item pricing laws: "In the eyes of the typical retailer, item-pricing laws are relics of a bygone era, inappropriate for the world of scanners and shelf labeling, electronic or manual. And instead of serving customers and cutting costs, employees are forced to work the aisles with a sticker gun." Yet, consumer advocates support them: "Price tags help people shop and help reduce checkout errors. Consumers have the right to compare a price tag to the amount charged at the checkout."[10]

Price Advertising

The FTC has guidelines pertaining to advertising price reductions, advertising prices in relation to competitors' prices, and bait-and-switch advertising. To access several FTC publications on acceptable pricing practices, visit our Web site (**www.prenhall.com/bermanevans**).

According to the Federal Trade Commission (**www.ftc.gov**), complaints about unordered merchandise and services billed to consumers jumped 169 percent from 1998 to 2000. Why? Many firms used strategies in which consumers continued to receive unsolicited merchandise until they notified the retailers by letter or phone. According to an assistant district attorney in Florida, "Companies are pushing the envelope to see what they can get away with."

Unlike in previous years, when most complaints involved small fly-by-night firms, businesses now under investigation or that have become involved in litigation include much larger firms with well-established reputations. For example, the Florida attorney general investigated Burdines (**www. burdinesflorida.com**), a major department store chain, for allegedly failing to notify customers that they had been enrolled in a company buying club. Fleet Mortgage (**www. fleetmortgagesolutions.com**) was sued by the attorney general of Minnesota for enrolling its home borrowers in an insurance program and then adding these charges onto the borrower's monthly bill. To stop the additional insurance, borrowers had to notify the mortgage company.

Some retailing analysts state that companies are engaging in this questionable behavior as a means of pumping up weak sales and as a means of taking "advantage of people's inherent laziness."

Source: Charles Haddad and Brian Grow, "Wait a Second—I Didn't Order That!" *Business Week* (July 16, 2001). p. 45.

A retailer cannot claim or imply that a price has been reduced from some former level (a suggested list price) unless the former price was one that the retailer had actually offered for a good or service on a regular basis during a reasonably substantial, recent period of time.

When a retailer says its prices are lower than competitors', it must make certain that its comparisons pertain to firms selling large quantities in the same trading area. A somewhat controversial, but legal, practice is price matching. For the most part, a retailer makes three assumptions when it "guarantees to match the lowest price of any competing retailer:" (1) This guarantee gives shoppers the impression that the firm always offers low prices or else it would not make such a commitment. (2) Most shoppers will not return to a store after a purchase if they see a lower price advertised elsewhere. (3) The guarantee can exclude most deep discounters by stating they are not really competitors.

Bait-and-switch advertising is an illegal practice in which a retailer lures a customer by advertising goods and services at exceptionally low prices; once the customer contacts the retailer (by entering a store, calling a toll-free number, or going to a Web site), he or she is told the good/service of interest is out of stock or of inferior quality. A salesperson (or Web script) tries to convince the person to buy a more costly substitute. The retailer does not intend to sell the advertised item. In deciding if a promotion uses bait-and-switch advertising, the FTC considers how many sales are made at the advertised price, whether a sales commission is paid on sale items, and total sales relative to advertising costs.

MANUFACTURERS, WHOLESALERS, AND OTHER SUPPLIERS— AND RETAIL PRICING

There may be conflicts between manufacturers (and other suppliers) and retailers in setting final prices since each would like some control. Manufacturers usually want a certain image and to let all retailers, even inefficient ones, earn profits. In contrast, most retailers want to set prices based on their own image, goals, and so forth. A supplier can control prices by using an exclusive distribution system, not selling to price-cutting retailers, or being its own retailer. A retailer can gain control by being vital as a customer, threatening to stop carrying suppliers' lines, stocking private brands, or selling gray market goods.

Many manufacturers set their prices to retailers by estimating final retail prices and then subtracting required retailer and wholesaler profit margins. In the men's apparel industry, the common retail markup is 50 percent of the final price. Thus, a man's shirt retailing at $50 can be sold to the retailer for no more than $25. If a wholesaler is involved, the manufacturer's wholesale price must be far less than $25.

Retailers sometimes carry manufacturers' brands and place high prices on them so rival brands (such as private labels) can be sold more easily. This is called "selling against the brand" and is disliked by manufacturers since sales of their brands are apt to decline. Some retailers also sell **gray market goods**, brand-name products bought in foreign markets or goods transshipped from other retailers. Manufacturers object to gray market goods because they are often sold at low prices by unauthorized dealers. Some of them limit gray market goods on the basis of copyright and trademark infringement.

When suppliers are unknown or products are new, retailers may seek price guarantees. For example, to get its radios stocked, a new supplier might have to guarantee the $30 suggested retail price. If the retailers cannot sell the radios for $30, the manufacturer pays a rebate. Should the retailers have to sell the radios at $25, the manufacturer gives back $5. Another guarantee is one in which a supplier tells the retailer that no competitor will buy an item for a lower price. If anyone does, the retailer gets a rebate. The relative power of the retailer and its suppliers determines whether such guarantees are provided.

A retailer also has other suppliers: employees, fixtures manufacturers, landlords, and outside parties (such as ad agencies). Each has an effect on price because of their costs to the retailer.

COMPETITION AND RETAIL PRICING

See how differently Auto-by-Tel (www.autobytel.com) and CarsDirect.com (www.carsdirect.com) approach the selling of cars.

Market pricing occurs when shoppers have a large choice of retailers. In this instance, retailers often price similarly to each other and have less control over price because consumers can easily shop around. Supermarkets, fast-food firms, and gas stations may use market pricing due to their competitive industries. Demand for specific retailers may be weak enough so that some customers would switch to a competitor if prices are raised much.

With *administered pricing*, firms seek to attract consumers on the basis of distinctive retailing mixes. This occurs when people consider image, assortment, service, and so forth to be important and they are willing to pay above-average prices to unique retailers. Upscale department stores, fashion apparel stores, and expensive restaurants are among those with unique offerings and solid control over their prices.

Most price-oriented strategies can be quickly copied. Thus, the reaction of competitors is predictable when the leading firm is successful. This means a price strategy should be viewed from both short-run and long-run perspectives. If competition becomes too intense, a price war may erupt—whereby various firms continually lower prices below regular amounts and sometimes below their cost to lure consumers from competitors. Price wars are sometimes difficult to end and can lead to low profits, losses, or even bankruptcy for some competitors. This is especially so for Web retailers.

DEVELOPING A RETAIL PRICE STRATEGY

Nielsen's Priceman (http://acnielsen.com/products/tools/priceman) is a powerful software tool for strategic pricing.

As Figure 17-3 shows, a retail price strategy has five steps: objectives, policy, strategy, implementation, and adjustments. Pricing policies must be integrated with the total retail mix, which occurs in the second step. The process can be complex due to the often erratic nature of demand, the number of items carried, and the impact of the external factors already noted.

RETAIL OBJECTIVES AND PRICING

A retailer's pricing strategy has to reflect its overall goals and be related to sales and profits. There must also be specific pricing goals to avoid such potential problems as confusing people by having too many prices, spending too much time bargaining with customers, offering frequent dis-

FIGURE 17-3
A Framework for Developing a Retail Price Strategy

counts to stimulate customer traffic, having inadequate profit margins, and placing too much emphasis on price.

Overall Objectives and Pricing

CDnow (www.cdnow.com) sells its "Top 100" at a discount. The Cheesecake Factory (www.cheesecake-factory.net/cake.html) has great cakes—although they can be a little pricey.

Sales goals may be stated in terms of revenues and/or unit volume. An aggressive strategy, known as **market penetration pricing**, is used when a retailer seeks large revenues by setting low prices and selling many units. Profit per unit is low, but total profit is high if sales projections are reached. This approach is proper if customers are price sensitive, low prices discourage actual and potential competition, and retail costs do not rise much with volume.

With a **market skimming pricing** strategy, a firm sets premium prices and attracts customers less concerned with price than service, assortment, and prestige. It usually does not maximize sales but does achieve high profit per unit. It is proper if the targeted segment is price insensitive, new competitors are unlikely to enter the market, and added sales will greatly increase retail costs. See Figure 17-4.

Return on investment and early recovery of cash are other possible profit-based goals for retailers using a market skimming strategy. *Return on investment* is sought if a retailer wants profit to be a certain percentage of its investment, such as 20 percent of inventory investment. *Early recovery of cash* is used by retailers that may be short on funds, wish to expand, or be uncertain about the future.

BE's Toy City, the discounter we introduced earlier in this chapter, may be used to illustrate how a retailer sets sales, profit, and return-on-investment goals. The firm sells inexpensive toys and overruns to avoid competing with mainstream toy stores, has one price for all toys (to be set within the $9 to $12 range), minimizes operating costs, encourages self-service, and carries a good selection. Table 17-2 has data on BE's Toy City pertaining to demand, costs, profit, and return on inventory investment at prices from $9 to $12. The firm must select the best price within that range. Table 17-3 shows how the figures in Table 17-2 were derived. Several conclusions can be drawn from Table 17-2:

- A sales goal would lead to a price of $10. Total sales are highest ($1,040,000).
- A dollar profit goal would lead to a price of $11. Total profit is highest ($132,000).
- A return on inventory investment goal would also lead to a price of $10. Return on inventory investment is 127 percent.
- Although a lot can be sold at $9, that price would lead to the least profit ($55,600).
- A price of $12 would yield the highest profit per unit and as a percentage of sales, but total dollar profit is not maximized at this price.
- High inventory turnover would not necessarily lead to high profits.

FIGURE 17-4
A Marketing Skimming Approach in an Upscale Shopping Environment

As the company says at its Web site (**www.saksfifthavenue.com**), "Saks Fifth Avenue today is renowned for its superlative selling services and merchandise offerings. The best of European and American designers for men and women are sold throughout its 62 stores servicing customers in 24 states. Key women's designer collections include Gucci, Ferragamo, Chanel, Prada, Michael Kors, Giorgio Armani, Donna Karan, Jil Sander, St. John, Ralph Lauren, Dolce & Gabbana, Zoran, Versace, Thierry Mugler, Christian Lacroix, Oscar de la Renta, Bill Blass, and Calvin Klein."

Reprinted by permission of Retail Forward, Inc.

TABLE 17-2		BE's Toy City: Demand, Costs, Profit, and Return on Inventory Investment[a]						
Selling Price ($)	Demand (units)	Total Sales Revenue ($)	Average Cost of Goods ($)	Total Cost of Goods ($)	Total Operating Costs ($)	Total Costs ($)	Average Total Costs ($)	Total Profit ($)
9.00	114,000	1,026,000	7.60	866,400	104,000	970,400	8.51	55,600
10.00	104,000	1,040,000	7.85	816,400	94,000	910,400	8.75	129,600
11.00	80,000	880,000	8.25	660,000	88,000	748,000	9.35	132,000
12.00	60,000	720,000	8.75	525,000	80,000	605,000	10.08	115,000

Selling Price ($)	Profit/ Unit ($)	Markup at Retail (%)	Profit/ Sales (%)	Average Inventory on Hand (units)	Inventory Turnover (units)	Average Inventory Investment at Cost ($)	Inventory Turnover ($)	Return on Inventory Investment (%)
9.00	0.49	16	5.4	12,000	9.5	91,200	9.5	61
10.00	1.25	22	12.5	13,000	8.0	102,050	8.0	127
11.00	1.65	25	15.0	14,000	5.7	115,500	5.7	114
12.00	1.92	27	16.0	16,000	3.8	140,000	3.8	82

Note: Average cost of goods reflects quantity discounts. Total operating costs include all retail operating expenses.
[a]Numbers have been rounded.

TABLE 17-3	Derivation of BE's Toy City Data
Column in Table 17-2	**Source of Information or Method of Computation**
Selling price	Trade data, comparison shopping, experience
Demand (in units) at each price	Consumer surveys, trade data, experience
Total sales revenue	Selling price × Quantity demanded
Average cost of goods	Supplier contacts, quantity discount structure, estimates of order sizes
Total cost of goods	Average cost of goods × Quantity demanded
Total operating costs	Experience, trade data, estimation of individual retail expenses
Total costs	Total cost of goods + Total operating costs
Average total costs	Total costs/Quantity demanded
Total profit	Total sales revenue − Total costs
Profit per unit	Total profit/Quantity demanded
Markup (at retail)	(Selling price − Average cost of goods)/Selling price
Profit as a percentage of sales	Total profit/Total sales revenue
Average inventory on hand	Trade data, inventory turnover data (in units), experience
Inventory turnover (in units)	Quantity demanded/Average inventory on hand (in units)
Average inventory investment (at cost)	Average cost of goods × Average inventory on hand (in units)
Inventory turnover (in $)	Total cost of goods/Average inventory investment (at cost)
Return on inventory investment	Total profit/Average inventory investment (at cost)

As a result, BE's Toy City decides a price of $11 would earn the highest dollar profits, while generating good profit per unit and profit as a percentage of sales.

Specific Pricing Objectives

Figure 17-5 lists specific pricing goals other than sales and profits. Each retailer must determine their relative importance given its situation—and plan accordingly. Some goals may be incompatible, such as "to not encourage shoppers to be overly price-conscious" and a " 'we-will-not-be-undersold' philosophy."

BROAD PRICE POLICY

KSS presents several case studies (www.kssg.com/markets/petrol/casestudies.asp) as to how gasoline retailers are integrating their price strategies.

Through a broad price policy, a retailer generates an integrated price plan with short- and long-run perspectives (balancing immediate and future goals) and a consistent image (vital for chains and franchises). The retailer interrelates its price policy with the target market, the retail image, and the other elements of the retail mix. These are some of the price policies from which a firm could choose:

- No competitors will have lower prices; no competitors will have higher prices (for prestige purposes); or prices will be consistent with competitors'.
- All items will be priced independently, depending on the demand for each; or the prices for all items will be interrelated to maintain an image and ensure proper markups.
- Price leadership will be exerted; competitors will be price leaders and set prices first; or prices will be set independently of competitors.
- Prices will be constant over a year or season; or prices will change if costs change.

FIGURE 17-5
Specific Pricing Objectives from Which Retailers May Choose

✓ To maintain a proper image.

✓ To encourage shoppers not to be overly price-conscious.

✓ To be perceived as fair by all parties (including suppliers, employees, and customers).

✓ To be consistent in setting prices.

✓ To increase customer traffic during slow periods.

✓ To clear out seasonal merchandise.

✓ To match competitors' prices without starting a price war.

✓ To promote a "we-will-not-be-undersold" philosophy.

✓ To be regarded as the price leader in the market area by consumers.

✓ To provide ample customer service.

✓ To minimize the chance of government actions relating to price advertising and antitrust matters.

✓ To discourage potential competitors from entering the marketplace.

✓ To create and maintain customer interest.

✓ To encourage repeat business.

PRICE STRATEGY

See how firms can "price for profits" (www.incsight.com/resources/articles/pricing.htm).

In **demand-oriented pricing**, a retailer sets prices based on consumer desires. It determines the range of prices acceptable to the target market. The top of this range is called the demand ceiling, the most people will pay for a good or service. With **cost-oriented pricing**, a retailer sets a price floor, the minimum price acceptable to the firm so it can reach a specified profit goal. A retailer usually computes merchandise and operating costs and adds a profit margin to these figures. For **competition-oriented pricing**, a retailer sets its prices in accordance with competitors'. The price levels of key competitors are studied and applied.

As a rule, retailers should combine these approaches in enacting a price strategy. The approaches should not be viewed as operating independently.

Demand-Oriented Pricing

Retailers use demand-oriented pricing to estimate the quantities that customers would buy at various prices. This approach studies customer interests and the psychological implications of pricing. Two aspects of psychological pricing are the price–quality association and prestige pricing.

According to the **price–quality association** concept, many consumers feel high prices connote high quality and low prices connote low quality. This association is especially important if competing firms or products are hard to judge on bases other than price, consumers have little experience or confidence in judging quality (as with a new retailer), shoppers perceive large differences in quality among retailers or products, and brand names are insignificant in product choice. Though various studies have documented a price–quality relationship, research also indicates that if other quality cues, such as retailer atmospherics, customer service, and popular brands, are introduced, these cues may be more important than price in a person's judgment of overall retailer or product quality.

Prestige pricing—which assumes that consumers will not buy goods and services at prices deemed too low—is based on the price–quality association. Its premise is that consumers may feel too low a price means poor quality and status. Some people look for prestige pricing when selecting retailers and do not patronize those with prices viewed as too low. Saks Fifth Avenue and Neiman Marcus do not generally carry inexpensive items because their customers may feel they are inferior. Prestige pricing does not apply to all shoppers. Some people may be economizers and always shop for bargains, and neither the price–quality association nor prestige pricing may be applicable for them.

Cost-Oriented Pricing

One form of cost-oriented pricing, markup pricing, is the most widely used pricing technique. In **markup pricing**, a retailer sets prices by adding per-unit merchandise costs, retail operating expenses, and desired profit. The difference between merchandise costs and selling price is the **markup**. If a retailer buys a desk for $200 and sells it for $300, the extra $100 covers operating costs and profit. The markup is 33-1/3 percent at retail or 50 percent at cost. The level of the markup depends on a product's traditional markup, the supplier's suggested list price, inventory turnover, competition, rent and other overhead costs, the extent to which a product must be serviced, and the selling effort.

Markups can be computed on the basis of retail selling price or cost but are typically calculated using the retail price: (1) Retail expenses, markdowns, and profit are always stated as a percentage of sales. Thus, markups expressed as a percentage of sales are more meaningful. (2) Manufacturers quote selling prices and discounts to retailers as percentage reductions from retail list prices. (3) Retail price data are more readily available than cost data. (4) Profitability seems smaller if expressed on the basis of price. This can be useful in dealing with the government, employees, and consumers.

This is how a **markup percentage** is calculated. The difference is in the denominator:

$$\text{Markup percentage (at retail)} = \frac{\text{Retail selling price} - \text{Merchandise cost}}{\text{Retail selling price}}$$

$$\text{Markup percentage (at cost)} = \frac{\text{Retail selling price} - \text{Merchandise cost}}{\text{Merchandise cost}}$$

TABLE 17-4	Markup Equivalents
Percentage at Retail	Percentage at Cost
10.0	11.1
20.0	25.0
30.0	42.9
40.0	66.7
50.0	100.0
60.0	150.0
70.0	233.3
80.0	400.0
90.0	900.0

Table 17-4 shows several markup percentages at retail and at cost. As markups go up, the disparity between the percentages grows. Suppose a retailer buys a watch for $20 and considers whether to sell it for $25, $40, or $100. The $25 price yields a markup of 20 percent at retail and 25 percent at cost, the $40 price a markup of 50 percent at retail and 100 percent at cost, and the $80 price a markup of 80 percent at retail and 400 percent at cost.

These three examples indicate the usefulness of the markup concept in planning:

1. A discount clothing store can buy a shipment of men's jeans at $12 each and wants a 30 percent markup at retail.[11] What retail price should the store charge to achieve this markup?

$$\text{Markup percentage (at retail)} = \frac{\text{Retail selling price} - \text{Merchandise cost}}{\text{Retail selling price}}$$

$$0.30 = \frac{\text{Retail selling price} - \$12.00}{\text{Retail selling price}}$$

Retail selling price = $17.14

2. A stationery store desires a minimum 40 percent markup at retail.[12] If the envelopes retail at 79 cents per box, what is the maximum price the store can pay for them?

$$\text{Markup percentage (at retail)} = \frac{\text{Retail selling price} - \text{Merchandise cost}}{\text{Retail selling price}}$$

$$0.40 = \frac{\$0.79 - \text{Merchandise cost}}{\$0.79}$$

Merchandise cost = $0.474

3. A sporting goods store has been offered a closeout purchase for bicycles. The cost of each bike is $105, and it should retail for $160. What markup at retail would the store obtain?

$$\text{Markup percentage (at retail)} = \frac{\text{Retail selling price} - \text{Merchandise cost}}{\text{Retail selling price}}$$

$$= \frac{\$160.00 - \$105.00}{\$160.00} = 34.4$$

A retailer's markup percentage may also be determined by examining planned retail operating expenses, profit, and net sales. Suppose a florist estimates yearly operating expenses to be

$55,000. The desired profit is $50,000 per year, including the owner's salary. Net sales are forecast to be $250,000. The planned markup would be:

$$\text{Markup percentage (at retail)} = \frac{\text{Planned retail operating expenses} + \text{Planned profit}}{\text{Planned net sales}}$$

$$= \frac{\$55,000 + \$50,000}{\$250,000} = 42$$

If potted plants cost the florist $8.00 each, the retailer's selling price would be:

$$\text{Retail selling price} = \frac{\text{Merchandise cost}}{1 - \text{Markup}}$$

$$= \frac{\$8.00}{1 - 0.42} = \$13.79$$

The florist must sell about 18,129 plants at $13.79 apiece to achieve its sales and profit goals. To reach these goals, all plants must be sold at the $13.79 price.

Because it is rare for a retailer to sell all items in stock at their original prices, the initial markup, maintained markup, and gross margin should be computed. **Initial markup** is based on the original retail value assigned to merchandise less the costs of the merchandise. **Maintained markups** are based on the actual prices received for merchandise sold during a time period less merchandise cost. Maintained markups relate to actual prices received, so they can be hard to predict. The difference between the initial and maintained markups is that the latter reflect adjustments from markdowns, added markups, shortages, and discounts.

The initial markup percentage depends on planned retail operating expenses, profit, reductions, and net sales:

$$\text{Initial markup percentage (at retail)} = \frac{\text{Planned retail operating expenses} + \text{Planned profit} + \text{Planned retail reductions}}{\text{Planned net sales} + \text{Planned retail reductions}}$$

If planned retail reductions are 0, the initial markup percentage equals planned retail operating expenses plus profit, both divided by planned net sales. To resume the florist example, suppose the firm projects that retail reductions will be 20 percent of estimated sales, or $50,000. To reach its goals, the initial markup and the original selling price would be:

$$\text{Initial markup percentage (at retail)} = \frac{\$55,000 + \$50,000 + \$50,000}{\$250,000 + \$50,000} = 51.7$$

$$\text{Retail selling price} = \frac{\text{Merchandise cost}}{1 - \text{Markup}} = \frac{\$8.00}{1 - 0.517} = \$16.56$$

The original retail value of 18,129 plants is about $300,000. Retail reductions of $50,000 lead to net sales of $250,000. Thus, the retailer must begin by selling plants at $16.56 apiece if it wants an average selling price of $13.79 and a maintained markup of 42 percent.

The maintained markup percentage can be viewed as:

$$\text{Maintained markup percentage (at retail)} = \frac{\text{Actual retail operating expenses} + \text{Actual profit}}{\text{Actual net sales}}$$

or

$$\text{Maintained markup percentage (at retail)} = \frac{\text{Average selling price} - \text{Merchandise cost}}{\text{Average selling price}}$$

Gross margin is the difference between net sales and the total cost of goods sold (which adjusts for cash discounts and additional expenses):

$$\text{Gross margin (in \$)} = \text{Net sales} - \text{Total cost of goods}$$

The florist's gross margin (the dollar equivalent of maintained markup) is roughly $105,000.

Although a retailer must set a companywide markup goal, markups for categories of merchandise or individual products may differ—sometimes dramatically. At many full-line discount stores, maintained markup as a percentage of sales ranges from under 20 percent for consumer electronics to more than 40 percent for jewelry and watches.

With a **variable markup policy**, a retailer purposely adjusts markups by merchandise category. Such a policy:

- Recognizes that the costs of different goods/service categories may fluctuate widely. Some items require alterations or installation. Even within a product line, expensive items may require greater end-of-year markdowns than inexpensive ones. The high-priced line needs a larger initial markup.

- Allows for differences in product investments. For major appliances, where the retailer orders regularly from a wholesaler, lower markups are needed than with fine jewelry, where the retailer must have a complete stock of unique merchandise.

- Accounts for differences in sales efforts and merchandising skills. A food processor may require a substantial effort, whereas a toaster may involve much less effort.

- May help a retailer to generate more customer traffic by advertising certain products at deep discounts. This entails leader pricing (discussed later in the chapter).

One way to plan variable markups is **direct product profitability (DPP)**, a technique that enables a retailer to find the profitability of each category of merchandise by computing adjusted per-unit gross margin and assigning direct product costs for such expense categories as warehousing, transportation, handling, and selling. The proper markup for each category or item is then set. DPP is used by some supermarkets, discounters, and other retailers. The major problem is the complexity of assigning costs.

Figure 17-6 illustrates DPP for two items with a selling price of $20. The retailer pays $12 for Item A, whose per-unit gross margin is $8. Since the retailer gets a $1 per unit allowance to set up a special display, the adjusted gross margin is $9. Total direct retail costs are estimated at $5. Direct product profit is $4—20 percent of sales. The retailer pays $10 for Item B, whose per-unit gross margin is $10. There are no special discounts or allowances. Since Item B needs more selling effort, total direct retail costs are $6. The direct profit is $4—20 percent of sales. To attain the same direct profit per unit, Item A needs a 40 percent markup (per-unit gross margin/selling price), and Item B needs 50 percent.

Cost-oriented (markup) pricing is popular among retailers. It is simple, because a retailer can apply a standard markup for a product category more easily than it can estimate demand at various prices. The firm can also vary prices according to demand or segment a market. Markup

Careers in RETAILING
Forman Mills: Growing a Discount Business from Scratch

Richard Forman never completed his business undergraduate degree from Rutgers University–Camden because he was too busy selling T-shirts. While other students may have been copying notes, "I was in the back of the class figuring out how many shirts I was going to buy, and hiring people from school." Today, Forman is president and chief executive of Forman Mills (**www.formanmills.com**), a privately held company with more than a dozen stores in Pennsylvania, New Jersey, and Delaware.

In describing the merchandising strategy for his off-price clothing chain, Forman says, "Brands are important for everybody, and I always like to say, 'We sell BMWs at Chevy prices.'" The firm's niche is that it opens stores in urban markets where there is less competition.

One of his first retail locations, opened in 1986, was a burned-out store in northeast Philadelphia. Forman blacktopped the store's parking lot, brought in trailers on wheels, and created an outdoor 30,000-square-foot flea market for a three-day period. About 3,000 people showed up, validating Forman's notion that the market was underserved then. Another early location had no heat or air-conditioning. These facilities set the stage for Forman to sell name-brand merchandise more cheaply due to very low rents.

Source: Suzette Parmley, "Philadelphia-Area Discount Retailer's Founder Builds Success on Niche Market," *Knight-Ridder/Tribune Business News* (June 20, 2002).

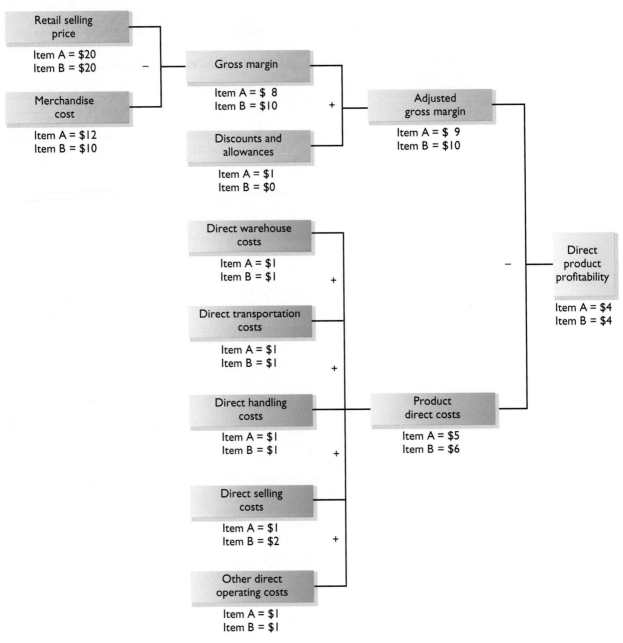

FIGURE 17-6
How to Determine Direct Product Profitability

pricing has a sense of equity given that the retailer earns a fair profit. When retailers have similar markups, price competition is reduced. Markup pricing is efficient if it takes into account competition, seasonal factors, and the intricacies in selling some products.

Competition-Oriented Pricing

A retailer can use competitors' prices as a guide. That firm might not alter prices in reaction to changes in demand or costs unless competitors alter theirs. Similarly, it might change prices when competitors do, even if demand or costs remain the same.

As shown in Table 17-5, a competition-oriented retailer can price below, at, or above the market. A firm with a strong location, superior service, good assortments, a favorable image, and exclusive brands can set prices above competitors. However, above-market pricing is not suitable for a retailer that has an inconvenient location, relies on self-service, is not innovative, and offers no real product distinctiveness.

TABLE 17-5	Competition-Oriented Pricing Alternatives		
	ALTERNATIVE PRICING STRATEGIES		
Retail Mix Variable	Pricing Below the Market	Pricing at the Market	Pricing Above the Market
Location	Poor, inconvenient site; low rent	Close to competitors, no location advantage	Few strong competitors, convenient to consumers
Customer service	Self-service, little salesperson support, limited displays	Moderate assistance by sales personnel	High levels of personal selling, delivery, etc.
Product assortment	More emphasis on best-sellers	Medium or large assortment	Small or large assortment
Atmosphere	Inexpensive fixtures, racks for merchandise	Moderate atmosphere	Attractive and pleasant decor
Innovativeness in assortment	Follower, conservative	Concentration on best-sellers	Leader
Special services	Not available	Not available or extra fee	Included in price
Product lines carried	Some name brands, private labels, closeouts	Selection of name brands, private labels	Exclusive name brands and private labels

Competition-oriented pricing does not require calculations of demand curves or price elasticity. The average market price is assumed to be fair for both the consumer and the retailer. Pricing at the market level does not disrupt competition and, therefore, does not usually lead to retaliation.

Integration of Approaches to Price Strategy

To properly integrate the three approaches, questions such as these should be addressed:

- If prices are reduced, will revenues increase greatly? (Demand orientation)
- Should different prices be charged for a product based on negotiations with customers, seasonality, and so on? (Demand orientation)
- Will a given price level allow a traditional markup to be attained? (Cost orientation)
- What price level is necessary for a product requiring special costs in purchasing, selling, or delivery? (Cost orientation)
- What price levels are competitors setting? (Competitive orientation)
- Can above-market prices be set due to a superior image? (Competitive orientation)

IMPLEMENTATION OF PRICE STRATEGY

Implementing a price strategy involves a variety of separate but interrelated specific decisions, in addition to those broad concepts already discussed. A checklist of selected decisions is shown in Figure 17-7. In this section, the specifics of a pricing strategy are detailed.

Customary and Variable Pricing

In **customary pricing**, a retailer sets prices for goods and services and seeks to maintain them for an extended period. Examples of items with customary prices are newspapers, candy, arcade games, vending machine items, and foods on restaurant menus. In each case, the retailer wants to establish set prices and have consumers take them for granted.

Bi-Lo, the southeastern supermarket chain, offers everyday low prices and "Weekly Specials" (www.bi-lo.com). Click on "Save" to see this week's.

A version of customary pricing is **everyday low pricing (EDLP)**, in which a retailer strives to sell its goods and services at consistently low prices throughout the selling season. Low prices are set initially, and there are few or no advertised specials, except on discontinued items or end-of-season closeouts. The retailer reduces its advertising and product repricing costs, and increases

FIGURE 17-7

A Checklist of Selected
Specific Pricing
Decisions

✓ How important is price stability? How long should prices be maintained?

✓ Is everyday low pricing desirable?

✓ Should prices change if costs and/or customer demand vary?

✓ Should the same prices be charged to all customers buying under the same conditions?

✓ Should customer bargaining be permitted?

✓ Should odd pricing be used?

✓ Should leader pricing be utilized to draw customer traffic? If yes, should leader prices be above, at, or below costs?

✓ Should consumers be offered discounts for purchasing in quantity?

✓ Should price lining be used to provide a price range and price points within that range?

✓ Should pricing practices vary by department or product line?

the credibility of its prices in the consumer's mind. On the other hand, with EDLP, manufacturers tend to eliminate the special trade allowances designed to encourage retailers to offer price promotions during the year. Wal-Mart and Ikea are among the retailers successfully utilizing EDLP. See Figure 17-8.

In many instances, a retailer cannot or should not use customary pricing. A firm *cannot* maintain constant prices if its costs are rising. A firm *should not* hold prices constant if customer demand varies. Under **variable pricing**, a retailer alters its prices to coincide with fluctuations in costs or consumer demand. Variable pricing may also provide excitement due to special sales opportunities for customers.

Cost fluctuations can be seasonal or trend-related. Supermarket and florist prices vary over the year due to the seasonal nature of many food and floral products. When seasonal items are scarce, the cost to the retailer goes up. If costs continually rise (as with luxury cars) or fall (as with computers), the retailer must change prices permanently (unlike temporary seasonal changes).

FIGURE 17-8

Ikea and Everyday Low Pricing

This is the Ikea approach to EDLP (www.ikea.co.uk): "Our designers work with manufacturers to find smart ways to make furniture using existing production processes. Then our buyers look all over the world for good suppliers with the most suitable materials. Next, we buy in bulk—on a global scale—so we can get the best deals and you can get the lowest price. Then you do your part. Using our catalog and visiting the store, you choose the furniture yourself and pick it up at the self-serve warehouse. Because most items are packed flat, you can get them home easily, and assemble them yourself. This means we don't charge you for things you can easily do on your own."

Reprinted by permission of Retail Forward, Inc.

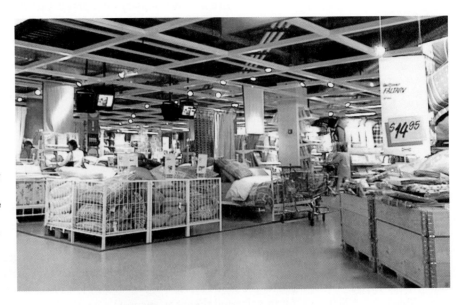

Demand fluctuations can be place- or time-based. Place-based fluctuations exist for retailers selling seat locations (such as concert halls) or room locations (such as hotels). Different prices can be charged for different locations, such as tickets close to the stage commanding higher prices. Time-based fluctuations occur if consumer demand differs by hour, day, or season. Demand for a movie theater is greater on Saturday than on Wednesday. Prices should be lower during periods of less demand.

Yield management pricing is a computerized, demand-based, variable pricing technique, whereby a retailer (typically a service firm) determines the combination of prices that yield the greatest total revenues for a given period. It is widely used by airlines and hotels. A crucial airline decision is how many first-class, full-coach, intermediate-discount, and deep-discount tickets to sell on each flight. With this approach, an airline offers fewer discount tickets for flights during peak periods than for ones in off-peak times. The airline has two goals: to fill as many seats as possible on every flight and to sell as many full-fare tickets as it can ("You don't want to sell a seat for $99 when someone will pay $599"). Yield management pricing may be too complex for small retailers, and it requires complex software. Our Web site (**www.prenhall.com/bermanevans**) has many links that illustrate the uses of yield management and other pricing software.

It is possible to combine customary and variable pricing. A movie theater can charge $5 every Wednesday night and $9 every Saturday. A bookstore can lower prices by 20 percent for best-sellers that have been out for three months.

One-Price Policy and Flexible Pricing

Under a **one-price policy**, a retailer charges the same price to all customers buying an item under similar conditions. This policy may be used together with customary pricing or variable pricing. With variable pricing, all customers interested in a particular section of concert seats would pay the same price. This approach is easy to manage, does not require skilled salespeople, makes shopping quicker, permits self-service, puts consumers under less pressure, and is tied to price goals. One-price policies are the rule for most U.S. retailers, and bargaining is often not permitted.

Looking to bargain? Go to eBay (www.ebay.com) or BargainandHaggle.com, (www.bargainandhaggle. com).

Flexible pricing lets consumers bargain over prices; those who are good at it obtain lower prices. Many jewelry stores, auto dealers, and others use flexible pricing. They do not clearly post bottom-line prices; shoppers need prior knowledge to bargain successfully. Flexible pricing encourages consumers to spend more time, gives an impression the firm is discount-oriented, and generates high margins from shoppers who do not like haggling. It requires high initial prices and good salespeople.

A special form of flexible pricing is **contingency pricing**, whereby a service retailer does not get paid until after the service is performed and payment is contingent on the service's being satisfactory. In some cases, such as real-estate, consumers prefer contingency payments so they know the service is done properly. This represents some risk to the retailer since a lot of time and effort may be spent without payment. A real-estate broker may show a house 25 times and not sell it and, therefore, not be paid.

Odd Pricing

Retail prices are set at levels below even dollar values, such as $0.49, $4.98, and $199, in **odd pricing**. The assumption is that people feel these prices represent discounts or that the amounts are beneath consumer price ceilings.[13] Odd pricing is a form of psychological pricing. Realtors hope consumers with a price ceiling of less than $250,000 are attracted to houses selling for $249,500. See Figure 17-9.

Odd prices that are 1 cent or 2 cents below the next highest even price ($0.29, $0.99, $2.98) are common up to $10.00. Beyond that point and up to $50.00, 5-cent reductions from the highest even price ($19.95, $49.95) are more usual. For more expensive items, prices are in dollars ($399, $4,995).

Leader Pricing

In **leader pricing**, a retailer advertises and sells selected items in its goods/services assortment at less than the usual profit margins. The goal is to increase customer traffic for the retailer so as to sell regularly priced goods and services in addition to the specially priced items. This is different from bait-and-switch, in which sale items are not sold.

FIGURE 17-9
Odd Pricing: A Popular
Retailing Tactic

At Toys "R" Us, odd pricing
is widely employed so that
the chain projects a value-
driven image to shoppers.

Reprinted by permission of
Retail Forward, Inc.

Leader pricing typically involves frequently purchased, nationally branded, high turnover goods and services because it is easy for customers to detect low prices. Supermarkets, home centers, discount stores, drugstores, and fast-food restaurants are just some of the retailers that utilize leader pricing to draw shoppers. There are two kinds of leader pricing: loss leaders and sales at lower than regular prices (but higher than cost). Loss leaders are regulated on a statewide basis under minimum-price laws.

Multiple-Unit Pricing

With **multiple-unit pricing**, a retailer offers discounts to customers who buy in quantity or who buy a product bundle. By selling items at two for $0.75, a retailer attempts to sell more products than at $0.39 each. There are three reasons to use multiple-unit pricing: (1) A firm could seek to have shoppers increase their total purchases of an item. (If people buy multiple units to stockpile them, instead of consuming more, the firm's overall sales do not increase.) (2) This approach can help sell slow-moving and end-of-season merchandise. (3) Price bundling may increase sales of related items.

In **bundled pricing**, a retailer combines several elements in one basic price. A 35-mm camera bundle could include a camera, batteries, a telephoto lens, a case, and a tripod for $289. This approach increases overall sales and offers people a discount over unbundled prices. However, it is unresponsive to different customers. As an alternative, many retailers use **unbundled pricing**—they charge separate prices for each item sold. A TV rental firm could charge separately for TV set rental, home delivery, and a monthly service contract. This closely link prices with costs and gives people more choice. Unbundled pricing may be harder to manage and may result in people buying fewer related items.

Price Lining

Marriott International
(www.marriott.com) really
knows how to use price
lining.

Rather than stock merchandise at all different price levels, retailers often employ **price lining** and sell merchandise at a limited range of price points, with each point representing a distinct level of quality. Retailers first determine their price floors and ceilings in each product category. They then set a limited number of price points within the range.[14] Department stores generally carry good, better, and best versions of merchandise consistent with their overall price policy—and set individual prices accordingly.

Price lining benefits both consumers and retailers. If the price range for a box of handkerchiefs is $6 to $15 and the price points are $6, $9, and $15, consumers know that distinct product qualities exist. However, should a retailer have prices of $6, $7, $8, $9, $10, $11, $12, $13, $14, and $15, the consumer may be confused about product differences. For retailers, price lining aids merchandise planning. Retail buyers can seek those suppliers carrying products at appropriate prices, and they can better negotiate with suppliers. They can automatically disregard products not fitting within price lines and thereby reduce inventory investment. Also, stock turnover goes up when the number of models carried is limited.

Difficulties do exist: (1) Depending on the price points selected, price lining may leave excessive gaps. A parent shopping for a graduation gift might find a $30 briefcase to be too cheap and a $200 one to be too expensive. (2) Inflation can make it tough to keep price points and price ranges. (3) Markdowns may disrupt the balance in a price line, unless all items in a line are reduced proportionally. (4) Price lines must be coordinated for complementary product categories, such as blazers, skirts, and shoes.

PRICE ADJUSTMENTS

Retailers need to be focused in making price adjustments (www.bizmove.com/general/m6h4.htm).

Price adjustments let retailers use price as an adaptive mechanism. Markdowns and additional markups may be needed due to competition, seasonality, demand patterns, merchandise costs, and pilferage. Figure 17-10 shows a price change authorization form.

A **markdown** from an item's original price is used to meet the lower price of another retailer, adapt to inventory overstocking, clear out shopworn merchandise, reduce assortments of odds and ends, and increase customer traffic. An **additional markup** increases an item's original price because demand is unexpectedly high or costs are rising. In today's competitive marketplace, markdowns are applied much more frequently than additional markups.

A third price adjustment, the employee discount, is noted here since it may affect the computation of markdowns and additional markups. Although an employee discount is not an adaptive mechanism, it influences morale. Some firms give employee discounts on all items and also let workers buy sale items before they are made available to the general public.

FIGURE 17-10
A Price Change Authorization Form

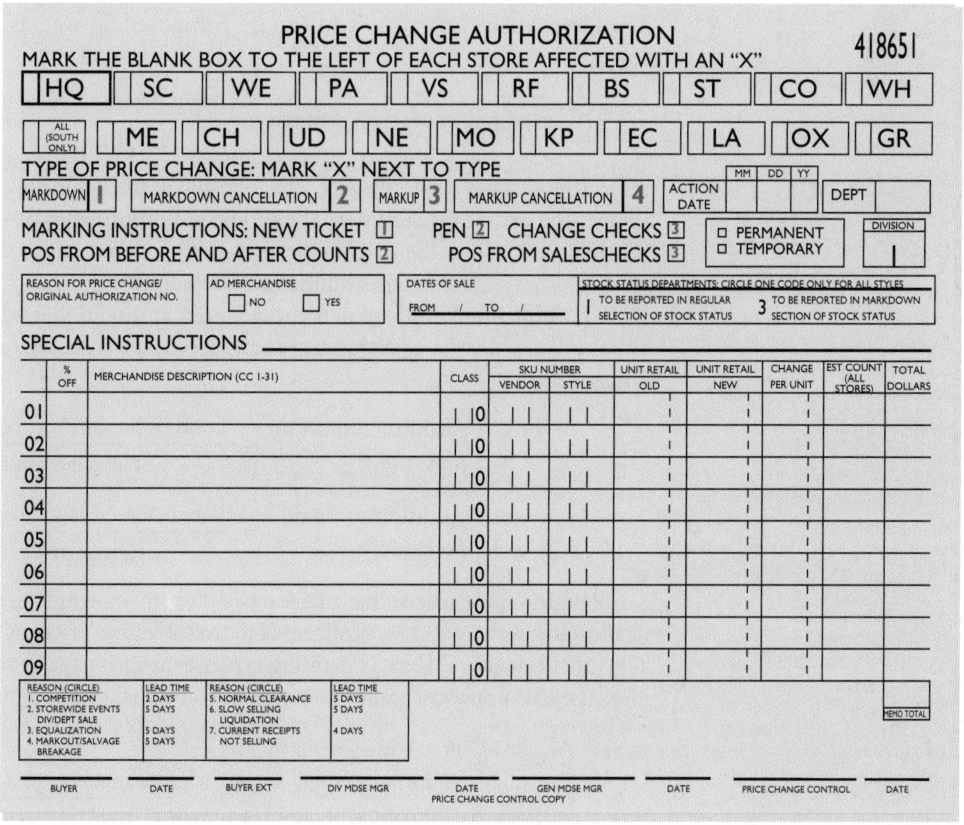
PRICE CHANGE AUTHORIZATION 418651
MARK THE BLANK BOX TO THE LEFT OF EACH STORE AFFECTED WITH AN "X"
HQ | SC | WE | PA | VS | RF | BS | ST | CO | WH
ALL (SOUTH ONLY) | ME | CH | UD | NE | MO | KP | EC | LA | OX | GR
TYPE OF PRICE CHANGE: MARK "X" NEXT TO TYPE
MARKDOWN 1 | MARKDOWN CANCELLATION 2 | MARKUP 3 | MARKUP CANCELLATION 4 | ACTION DATE MM DD YY | DEPT
MARKING INSTRUCTIONS: NEW TICKET 1 PEN 2 CHANGE CHECKS 3
POS FROM BEFORE AND AFTER COUNTS 2 POS FROM SALESCHECKS 3
□ PERMANENT □ TEMPORARY | DIVISION 1
REASON FOR PRICE CHANGE/ ORIGINAL AUTHORIZATION NO. | AD MERCHANDISE □ NO □ YES | DATES OF SALE FROM / TO /
STOCK STATUS DEPARTMENTS: CIRCLE ONE CODE ONLY FOR ALL STYLES
1 TO BE REPORTED IN REGULAR SELECTION OF STOCK STATUS 3 TO BE REPORTED IN MARKDOWN SECTION OF STOCK STATUS
SPECIAL INSTRUCTIONS

	% OFF	MERCHANDISE DESCRIPTION (CC 1-31)	CLASS	SKU NUMBER VENDOR	SKU NUMBER STYLE	UNIT RETAIL OLD	UNIT RETAIL NEW	CHANGE PER UNIT	EST COUNT (ALL STORES)	TOTAL DOLLARS
01			10							
02			10							
03			10							
04			10							
05			10							
06			10							
07			10							
08			10							
09			10							

REASON (CIRCLE)	LEAD TIME	REASON (CIRCLE)	LEAD TIME
1. COMPETITION	2 DAYS	5. NORMAL CLEARANCE	5 DAYS
2. STOREWIDE EVENTS DIV/DEPT SALE	5 DAYS	6. SLOW SELLING LIQUIDATION	5 DAYS
3. EQUALIZATION	5 DAYS	7. CURRENT RECEIPTS NOT SELLING	4 DAYS
4. MARKOUT/SALVAGE BREAKAGE	5 DAYS		

MEMO TOTAL

BUYER | DATE | BUYER EXT | DIV MDSE MGR | DATE | GEN MDSE MGR | DATE | PRICE CHANGE CONTROL | DATE
PRICE CHANGE CONTROL COPY

Welcome to the new world where you may be fingerprinted at a supermarket—if that is okay with you. Some large supermarket chains, such as Kroger (**www.kroger.com**), have begun testing a system that allows customers to pay for purchases by simply placing their index finger on a scanning pad, which then checks the fingerprint against its data base. After the customer's fingerprint is verified, the purchase is automatically linked to either the customer's debit or credit card.

These scanners offer significant benefits for both the consumer and the retailer. The consumer no longer has to carry cash, credit cards, or a checkbook—and the new system also cuts down on identity theft. The retailer benefits through increased checkout productivity due to a fast processing time of 5 seconds and a reduction in both credit card and check fraud.

Duther Family Foods, a three-store supermarket chain in Grand Rapids, Michigan, recently installed a fingerprint scanning system after being burned by too many bad checks. The small chain cashes as much as $500,000 weekly in checks. After installing a $9,000 fingerprint scanning system in each store, check fraud was reduced by 75 percent. Although the firm's founder realizes that some customers dislike having their fingerprints taken, he says, "If they don't do it, they can take their checks elsewhere."

Source: Constance Gustke, "Pressing the Flesh: Biometric Scanners Let Shoppers Pay at the Touch of a Finger and Speed Things Up at the Front End," *Progressive Grocer* (February 1, 2002), p. 20.

Computing Markdowns and Additional Markups

Markdowns and additional markups can be expressed in dollars or percentages.

The **markdown percentage** is the total dollar markdown as a percentage of net sales (in dollars):

$$\text{Markdown percentage} = \frac{\text{Total dollar markdown}}{\text{Net sales (in \$)}}$$

While it is simple to compute, this formula does not enable a retailer to learn the percentage of items that are marked down relative to those sold at the original price.

A complementary measure is the **off-retail markdown percentage**, which looks at the markdown for each item or category of items as a percentage of original retail price. The markdown percentage for every item can be computed, as well as the percentage of items marked down:

$$\text{Off-retail markdown percentage} = \frac{\text{Original price} - \text{New price}}{\text{Original price}}$$

Suppose a gas barbecue grill sells for $400 at the beginning of the summer and is reduced to $280 at the end of the summer. The off-retail markdown is 30 percent [($400 − $280)/$400]. If 100 grills are sold at the original price and 20 are sold at the sale price, the percentage of items marked down is 17 percent, and the total dollar markdown is $2,400.

The **additional markup percentage** looks at total dollar additional markups as a percentage of net sales, while the **addition to retail percentage** measures a price rise as a percentage of the original price:

$$\frac{\text{Additional markup}}{\text{percentage}} = \frac{\text{Total dollar additional markups}}{\text{Net sales (in \$)}}$$

$$\frac{\text{Addition to retail}}{\text{percentage}} = \frac{\text{New price} - \text{Original price}}{\text{Original price}}$$

Retailers must realize that many more customers would have to buy at reduced prices for the retailers to have a total gross profit equal to that at higher prices. A retailer's judgment regarding price adjustments is affected by its operating expenses at various sales volumes and customer price elasticities. The true impact of a markdown or an additional markup can be learned from this formula:

$$\frac{\text{Unit sales required to earn the same total gross profit with a price adjustment}}{} = \frac{\text{Original markup (\%)}}{\text{Original markup (\%)} + / - \text{Price change (\%)}} \times \frac{\text{Expected unit sales at original price}}{}$$

Suppose a Sony Walkman with a cost of $50 has an original retail price of $100 (a markup of 50 percent). A retailer expects to sell 500 units over the next year, generating a total gross profit of $25,000 ($50 × 500). How many units does the retailer have to sell if it reduces the price to $85 or raises it to $110—and still earn a $25,000 gross profit? Here's the answer:

$$\text{Unit sales required (at \$85)} = \frac{50\%}{50\% - 15\%} \times 500 = 1.43 \times 500 = 714$$

$$\text{Unit sales required (at \$110)} = \frac{50\%}{50\% + 10\%} \times 500 = 0.83 \times 500 = 417$$

Markdown Control

Through markdown control, a retailer evaluates the number of markdowns, the proportion of sales involving markdowns, and the causes. The control must be such that buying plans can be altered in later periods to reflect markdowns. A good way to evaluate the cause of markdowns is to have retail buyers record the reasons for each markdown and then examine them periodically. Possible buyer notations are "end of season," "to match the price of a competitor," "worn merchandise," and "obsolete style."

Markdown control lets a retailer monitor its policies, such as the way items are displayed. Careful planning may also enable a retailer to avoid some markdowns by running more ads, training workers better, shipping goods more efficiently among branch units, and returning items to vendors.

The need for markdown control should not be interpreted as meaning that all markdowns can or should be minimized or eliminated. In fact, too low a markdown percentage may indicate that a retailer's buyers have not assumed enough risk in purchasing goods.

Timing Markdowns

Although there are different perspectives among retailers about the best markdown timing sequence, much can be said about the benefits of an *early markdown policy*: It requires much lower markdowns to sell products than markdowns late in the season. Merchandise is offered at reduced prices while demand is still fairly active. Early markdowns free selling space for new merchandise. The retailer's cash flow position can be improved. The main advantage of a *late markdown policy* is that a retailer gives itself every opportunity to sell merchandise at original prices. Yet, the advantages associated with an early markdown policy cannot be achieved under a late markdown policy.

Retailers can also use a *staggered markdown policy* and discount prices throughout a selling period. One pre-planned staggered markdown policy is an *automatic markdown plan*, in which the amount and timing of markdowns are controlled by the length of time merchandise remains in stock. Syms, the off-price chain, uses this approach to ensure fresh stock and early markdowns:

> All garments are sold with the brand name affixed by the manufacturer. Syms has long utilized a 10-day automatic markdown pricing policy to promote movement of merchandise. The date of placement on the selling floor of each item is stamped on the back of the price ticket. The front of each ticket contains what we believe to be the nationally advertised price, the initial Syms price, and three reduced prices. Each reduced price becomes effective after the passage of 10 selling days. We also offer "dividend" prices consisting of additional price reductions on various merchandise.[15]

A *storewide clearance*, conducted once or twice a year, is another way to time markdowns. It often takes place after peak selling periods like Christmas and Mother's Day. The goal is to clean out merchandise before taking a physical inventory and beginning the next season. The advantages of a storewide clearance are that a longer period is provided for selling merchandise at original prices and that frequent markdowns can destroy a consumer's confidence in regular prices: "Why buy now, when it will be on sale next week?" Clearance sales limit bargain hunting to once or twice a year. See Figure 17-11.

In the past, many retailers would introduce merchandise at high prices and then mark down many items by as much as 60 percent to increase store traffic and improve inventory turnover. This caused customers to wait for price reductions and treat initial prices skeptically. Today, more retailers start out with lower prices, run fewer sales, and apply fewer markdowns than before. Nonetheless, a big problem facing some retailers is that they have gotten consumers too used to buying when items are discounted.

FIGURE 17-11

Promoting Markdowns

Sometimes, retailers are subtle when they offer special sales on their merchandise. Other times, they want to make sure that shoppers are quite aware that a clearance sale is going on. It's pretty hard to miss this sign!

Reprinted by permission of Goran Petkovic.

Summary

1. *To describe the role of pricing in a retail strategy and to show that pricing decisions must be made in an integrated and adaptive manner.* Pricing is crucial to a retailer because of its interrelationship with overall objectives and the other components of the retail strategy. A price plan must be integrated and responsive—and provide a good value to customers.

2. *To examine the impact of consumers; government; manufacturers, wholesalers, and other suppliers; and current and potential competitors on pricing decisions.* Before designing a price plan, a retailer must study the factors affecting its decisions. Sometimes, the factors have a minor effect on pricing discretion; other times, they severely limit pricing options.

   Retailers should be familiar with the price elasticity of demand and the different market segments that are possible. Government restrictions deal with horizontal and vertical price fixing, price discrimination, minimum prices, unit pricing, item price removal, and price advertising. There may be conflicts about which party controls retail prices; and manufacturers, wholesalers, and other suppliers may be asked to provide price guarantees (if they are in a weak position). The competitive environment may foster market pricing, lead to price wars, or allow administered pricing.

3. *To present a framework for developing a retail price strategy.* This framework consists of five stages: objectives, broad price policy,

price strategy, implementation of price strategy, and price adjustments.

Retail pricing goals can be chosen from among sales, dollar profits, return on investment, and early recovery of cash. Next, a broad policy outlines a coordinated series of actions, consistent with the retailer's image and oriented to the short and long run.

A good price strategy incorporates demand, cost, and competitive concepts. Each of these orientations must be understood separately and jointly. Psychological pricing, markup pricing, alternative ways of computing markups, gross margin, direct product profitability, and pricing below, at, or above the market are among the key aspects of strategy planning.

When enacting a price strategy, specific tools can be used to supplement the broad base of the strategy. Retailers should know when to use customary and variable pricing, one-price policies and flexible pricing, odd pricing, leader pricing, multiple-unit pricing, and price lining.

Price adjustments may be required to adapt to internal and external conditions. Adjustments include markdowns, additional markups, and employee discounts. It is important that adjustments are controlled by a budget, the causes of markdowns are noted, future company buying reflects prior performance, adjustments are properly timed, and excessive discounting is avoided.

Key Terms

price elasticity of demand (p. 416)

horizontal price fixing (p. 418)

vertical price fixing (p. 419)

Robinson-Patman Act (p. 419)

minimum-price laws (p. 420)

predatory pricing (p. 420)

loss leaders (p. 420)

unit pricing (p. 420)

item price removal (p. 420)

bait-and-switch advertising (p. 421)

gray market goods (p. 422)

market penetration pricing (p. 423)

market skimming pricing (p. 423)

demand-oriented pricing (p. 426)

cost-oriented pricing (p. 426)

competition-oriented pricing (p. 426)

price–quality association (p. 426)

prestige pricing (p. 426)

markup pricing (p. 426)

markup (p. 426)

markup percentage (p. 426)

initial markup (p. 428)

maintained markups (p. 428)

gross margin (p. 428)

variable markup policy (p. 429)

direct product profitability (DPP) (p. 429)

customary pricing (p. 431)

everyday low pricing (EDLP) (p. 431)

variable pricing (p. 432)

yield management pricing (p. 433)

one-price policy (p. 433)

flexible pricing (p. 433)

contingency pricing (p. 433)

odd pricing (p. 433)

leader pricing (p. 433)

multiple-unit pricing (p. 434)

bundled pricing (p. 434)

unbundled pricing (p. 434)

price lining (p. 434)

markdown (p. 435)

additional markup (p. 435)

markdown percentage (p. 436)

off-retail markdown percentage (p. 436)

additional markup percentage (p. 436)

addition to retail percentage (p. 436)

Questions for Discussion

1. Why is it important for retailers to understand the concept of price elasticity even if they cannot compute it?

2. Comment on each of the following from the perspective of a small retailer:
   a. Horizontal price fixing.
   b. Vertical price fixing.
   c. Price discrimination.
   d. Minimum-price laws.
   e. Unit pricing.

3. Give an example of a price strategy that integrates demand, cost, and competitive criteria.

4. Explain why markups are usually computed as a percentage of selling price rather than of cost.

5. A floor tile retailer wants to receive a 40 percent markup (at retail) for all merchandise. If one style of tile retails for $11 per tile, what is the maximum that the retailer would be willing to pay for a tile?

6. A car dealer purchases multiple-disc CD players for $175 each and desires a 40 percent markup (at retail). What retail price should be charged?

7. A photo store charges $11.00 to process a roll of slides; its cost is $7.75. What is the markup percentage (at cost and at retail)?

8. A firm has planned operating expenses of $220,000, a profit goal of $160,000, and planned reductions of $50,000 and expects sales of $875,000. Compute the initial markup percentage.

9. At the end of the year, the retailer in Question 8 determines that actual operating expenses are $200,000, actual profit is $145,000, and actual sales are $870,000. What is the maintained markup percentage? Explain the difference in your answers to Questions 8 and 9.

10. What are the pros and cons of everyday low pricing to a retailer? To a manufacturer?

11. Under what circumstances do you think unbundled pricing is a good idea? A poor idea? Why?

12. A retailer buys items for $50. At an original retail price of $85, it expects to sell 1,000 units.
    a. If the price is marked down to $75, how many units must the retailer sell to earn the same total gross profit it would attain with an $85 price?
    b. If the price is marked up to $100, how many units must the retailer sell to earn the same total gross profit it would attain with an $85 price?

Note: At our Web site (**www.prenhall.com/bermanevans**), there are several math problems related to the material in this chapter so that you may review these concepts.

Web-Based Exercise

Visit the Web site of Costco (**www.costco.com**). What are the least expensive products sold through this site? The most expensive? Do you feel that this price range is consistent with Costco's image as a discount-oriented membership club chain? Explain your answer.

Note: Stop by our Web site (**www.prenhall.com/bermanevans**) to experience a number of highly interactive, appealing Web exercises based on actual company demonstrations and sample materials related to retailing.

Chapter Endnotes

1. Various company sources.

2. "No Frills Costco Chain Leads Way in Annual Sales," *Knight Ridder/Tribune Business News* (April 28, 2002), p. ITEM02118021.

3. C. Britt Beemer, "Don't Discount Customer Service," *Chain Store Age* (March 2002), p. 34.

4. Melissa Campanelli, "Price Check, Please," *Entrepreneur* (August 2002), p. 40.

5. See Sangman Han, Sunil Gupta, and Donald R. Lehmann, "Consumer Price Sensitivity and Price Thresholds," *Journal of Retailing*, Vol. 77 (Winter 2001), pp. 435–456; and Kristy E. Reynolds, Jaishankar Ganesh, and Michael Luckett, "Traditional Malls Vs. Factory Outlets: Comparing Shopper Typologies and Implications for Retail Strategy," *Journal of Business Research*, Vol. 55 (September 2002), pp. 687–696.

6. Jennifer Dixon, "Sotheby's Likely to Be Sold; Taubman's 'Ultimate Toy' Marred by Price-Fixing," *Knight Ridder/Tribune Business News* (June 4, 2002), p. ITEM02155006.

7. Edward Felsenthal, "Manufacturers Allowed to Cap Retail Prices," *Wall Street Journal* (November 5, 1997), pp. A3, A8.

8. Phyllis Furman, "Music Industry Must Pay $141.3 Million in CD Price-Fixing Settlement," *Knight Ridder/Tribune Business News* (October 1, 2002), p. ITEM02274109.

9. Richard Turen, "Loss Leader Is No Loss," *Travel Weekly* (December 13, 2001), p. 59.

10. Ken Clark, "Sticker Shock," *Chain Store Age* (September 2000), p. 88.

11. Selling price may also be computed by transposing the markup formula into

$$\text{Retail selling price} = \frac{\text{Merchandise cost}}{1 - \text{Markup}} = \$17.14$$

12. Merchandise cost may also be computed by transposing the markup formula into

$$\text{Merchandise cost} = (\text{Retail selling price}) (1 - \text{Markup}) = \$0.474$$

13. See Robert M. Schindler and Thomas M. Kibarian, "Image Communicated by the Use of 99 Endings in Advertised Prices," *Journal of Advertising*, Vol. 30 (Winter 2001), pp. 95–99.

14. See Steven M. Shugan and Ramarao Desiraju, "Retail Product-Line Pricing Strategy When Costs and Products Change," *Journal of Retailing*, Vol. 77 (Spring 2001), pp. 17–38.

15. *Syms 2002 Annual Report.*

part six
Short Cases

1: PRODUCT INNOVATIONS AND BURGER KING

Burger King (**www.burgerking.com**) is in the midst of a $300-million-plus brand relaunch that includes 14 new products and a host of promotions with such marketing partners as eBay, AOL Time Warner, Nickelodeon, and Universal Studios. According to Burger King's chairman and chief executive, the firm's goal is to increase its average store sales by $250,000 (that's a 23 percent increase) by 2005. This would give Burger King a 22.8 percent market share of the fast-food hamburger business. As of 2002, Burger King had an 18.1 percent share versus McDonald's 43.1 percent share.

These goals will not be easy to achieve. In 2001, Burger King's average transactions per store dropped to 20,000 per month, from a peak of 25,000 in 1995. Burger King executives acknowledge that "Our underlying customer base has been eroding precipitously. Our task is to turn around top-line sales by bringing more customers into our restaurants. If that was so simple, it would have been done before."

Burger King is counting on two parties to make its turnaround successful: its franchisees and its marketing partners. Since franchisees own 92 percent of the chain's total restaurants, Burger King needs an 80 percent participation rate for any plan to be successful. Burger King franchisees each contribute 4 percent of their sales for national advertising, as well as less than 0.5 percent for local advertising. If franchisees approve, local advertising may be increased to 1 percent of sales as of 2004.

Burger King's most ambitious marketing partnership is its BK Rewards, a frequent-eater program launched in 2002 with eBay (**www.ebay.com**) as the partner. For six months, Burger King customers received codes on each purchase that were banked at a special Web site. They could then bid on rewards at the site. The rewards came in three levels: first tier—including CDs and magazine subscriptions; second tier—including personal digital assistants and TV sets; and third tier—including cruises and walk-on movie roles. The chain could afford these rewards since it bartered for the prizes and there were no up-front costs.

Other tie-ins focus on movie-related partnerships and children's promotions. Burger King likes to work with several movie studios because it "gives us a better inventory to choose from. If you sign with one studio, they tell you how many of their movies and which ones to promote each year." In contrast, McDonald's has an exclusive 10-year partnership with Walt Disney. Promotional foods are often used by Burger King with its film tie-ins. Nonetheless, "we want kids to come in because they love our food, not because they want the toy we have."

To streamline promotional planning, Burger King has reduced the number of advertising agencies it works with by one-half. Separate agencies now handle television, print and radio, the Web, kids' advertising, local creative, and promotions and point-of-sale. Another agency handles premiums.

Burger King has been launching many new products, such as several new salads, a Chicken Whopper, an Egg'wich muffin (to compete against McDonald's Egg McMuffin), and a Veggie Burger.

The introduction of some new products has been tied to specific events. For example, vanilla ice cream and blue-cherry frozen drinks were tied to the movie *Ice Age*, and shake flavors such as King Praline were tied to the Super Bowl.

Questions

1. Describe and evaluate Burger King's merchandising philosophy.
2. What must Burger King do to persuade franchisees to carry the new products that it develops?
3. Is Burger King placing too much emphasis on promotions as a part of its merchandising strategy? Explain your answer.
4. Are Burger King's goals realistic based on the plans described in the case? Explain your answer.

The material in this case is drawn from Betsy Spethmann, "Cooking with Gas," *Promo* (April 2002), pp. 41–44.

2: WET SEAL STAYS AHEAD OF THE FASHION CURVE

In addition to its Wet Seal (**www.wetseal.com**) stores, Wet Seal Inc. (**www.wetsealinc.com**) operates Arden B. (**www.ardenb.com**) and Zutopia (**www.zutopia.com**) stores. Wet Seal Inc. had sales of $600 million in 2002 from its 570 nationwide stores and catalog operations. Wet Seal Inc.'s chief executive Kathy Bronstein is one of the few women heading a publicly held company. This case concentrates on the Wet Seal brand of stores.

In her role as chief executive, Kathy Bronstein has a difficult job. As one retailing analyst notes, "The firm is in a race that never ends, trying to stay ahead of a fashion curve that's constantly shifting. It also is continuing to expand in a niche where some analysts think there are already too many stores." The director of the California Fashion Association (**www.californiafashionassociation.org**) adds that Bronstein "is probably the most proactive retailer I've heard of in terms of acting upon a suggestion, a piece of advice, news. That's the key to her success."

The Wet Seal chain's target market consists of girls and young women who desire trendy clothing at moderate prices. To be an effective retailer in this segment, a firm must be able to quickly respond to trends, as well as to implement markdowns to clear inventory when a trend is misjudged. The segment is an especially complex one to satisfy: "Junior apparel retailing is not for the faint-of-heart. Teens are a notoriously fickle bunch and what's in one day is often old hat the next."

Bronstein views her knowledge of the market as coming from a combination of instinct and experience. For example, on a recent trip to Rome, a young woman who was wearing a shirt that was crocheted at the wrist and neckline caught her eye. So Bronstein ordered crocheted sweaters for Wet Seal, and they sold well.

Wet Seal subscribes to several trend-forecasting services. In addition, Bronstein regularly visits Europe's fashion centers to better understand global trends. And she carefully monitors sales reports to see what is selling. Unlike Gap and Old Navy, which are 100-percent private label, Wet Seal stores mix private-label items with national brands. Bronstein says, "Wet Seal shoppers like branded goods, primarily in bottoms and particularly in denim." In 2002,

Wet Seal increased the amount of private-label goods in its product assortment to 25 percent, up from less than 20 percent in 2001.

Besides the chain's knowledge of the market, Wet Seal is viewed as a hardy bargainer. For example, Wet Seal has been known to reduce an order commitment with a supplier when it sees that a given fashion does not take hold or when customer sales start to decline. Bronstein acknowledges that she's tough, but she also feels that she is fair: "We don't cancel orders unless terms of the orders have not been adhered to—that is delivery date, quality, and fit."

Wet Seal has been negotiating with music companies to create videos that will debut at its stores. The chain wants the videos so that "Our customers can dress like the performers they watch each week." It has also relaunched a catalog to be mailed to 1.3 million households, and it has just introduced a line of cosmetics.

Questions

1. Evaluate Wet Seal's overall merchandising approach.
2. What additional sources of market information can Wet Seal utilize?
3. Discuss the pros and cons of Wet Seal's planned increase in private-label goods.
4. As a supplier, how would you respond to Wet Seal's canceling an order for a style that does not sell well? Why?

The material in this case is drawn from Leslie Earnest, "Wet Seal CEO Fit for Tough Business: Kathy Bronstein's Eye for Trends Has Led to Solid Sales," *Los Angeles Times* (April 15, 2002), p. C1; and Marianne Wilson, "Wet Seal's Primo Performance," *Chain Store Age* (November 2001), pp. 50–55.

3: THE BOTTOM LINE ON REVERSE LOGISTICS

Because customer returns are inevitable, especially with Web transactions, retailers need to manage the return process so that expenses are held in check. A failure to do so can jeopardize a firm's overall financial well-being. Research indicates that approximately 7 percent of all Web purchases are returned. And the figure can be as high as 40 percent for fashion items. Recently, returns at ZoZa, an online retailer of high-fashion activewear, were so extensive that it ended up going out of business.

The first line of defense in reducing return costs is to enact a number of procedures to minimize their occurrence. At Recreational Equipment Inc., REI (**www.rei.com**) company specialists use Returns Analysis Tool software to better track the reasons for returns. When these specialists found that women were returning a particular pair of hiking boots at an unusually high rate, the software determined that shoppers found the boot to be one-half size too small. After the boot was resized, its returns dropped "almost to zero." REI also attempts to minimize returns by being especially careful in keeping its Web site up-to-date. This ensures that its delivered goods will match customer expectations.

Another way to reduce the costs associated with returns is to switch from a manual return process to automated technology. One marketing research firm estimates that manually processing a returned item costs an average of $32.40. This amount is twice the cost of initially sending the item to the customer, not counting ship-

ping fees. The automated technology that uses the Web and barcodes can reduce the total costs of processing a return to $8.69. A large part of the savings through automation is due to the customer's looking up the order history on the Web, as well as a scannable barcode on the return label. While it costs an average of $12.00 for a phone call center to search for an initial order, the customer's looking up the order history reduces these costs to $3.00. Furthermore, it costs $11.70 to manually key in a return at a warehouse versus $2.00 with the scannable barcode return label.

Janice Parker, the chief executive of Sincerely Yours (**www.sincerelyyours.com**), a home décor catalog business, says, "The biggest issue with returns is to turn them around quickly." The longer a returned item stays in a firm's warehouse, the less its resale value and the higher its inventory holding costs. To maximize the opportunity to sell a good and to reduce storage costs, Parker set a 24-hour goal for returns to be processed. Her firm consistently meets that goal, except at the end of the holiday season.

Recently, Sincerely Yours decided to outsource returns to a reverse logistics specialist, which now handles the whole returns process for a fee. After contracting with Newgistics (**www.newgistics.com**), Sincerely Yours was able to close the entire section of its warehouse that once stored returned goods. For fees typically ranging from $1 to $5 per return, specialists such as Newgistics, Genco (**www.genco.com**), and UPS E-Logistics (**www.e-logistics.com**) will handle a selected part of the return process, such as selling returned goods to a closeout merchant, or the entire process.

Questions

1. What is the risk of reducing customer returns too much? Explain your answer.
2. Present a plan for a Web-only retailer to reduce returns. The plan should not significantly reduce sales or increase consumer dissatisfaction.
3. Present a plan for a multi-channel retailer to handle customer returns. Balance the customer's desire for convenience with the retailer's desire to control its return costs.
4. Under what conditions should a retailer handle the entire return process? Under what conditions should it outsource the entire return process? Explain your answers.

The material in this case is drawn from Owen Thomas, "Gone Today, Here Tomorrow," *Business 2.0* (December 2001), pp. 116–117.

4: CAN RETAILERS SUCCESSFULLY EXPLOIT THE POWER OF OPTIMAL PRICING?

Price optimization software helps a retailer determine prices by estimating a consumer's demand curve for each product based on a computer analysis of data from a store's point-of-sale terminals and its seasonal sales. This analysis helps identify the most price-sensitive items. On the basis of these data, store managers can then adjust prices based on each store's objectives: profit, revenue, or market share. The key insight this software provides is "the crossover point between driving sales and giving away margin unnecessarily."

New software designed by DemandTec (**www.demandtec.com**), a San Carlos, California, firm, is now used in all of Longs' more than 400 drugstores (**www.longs.com**) to determine the ideal price for every item, at each store, at a given time. An item priced at $2.07 in a Longs' Walnut Creek, California, store might sell for $1.86 in a Seattle location.

Longs' chief executive says the new software has helped Longs to maintain its overall profit margins during a time when the firm has used more store promotions. Longs' chief operating officer adds that the software has also led to "category-by-category increases in sales and margins," mostly in the nonpharmacy sales areas—which account for most of Longs' profits.

Longs is not the only retailer having excellent success with DemandTec. D'Agostino, a New York supermarket chain (**www.dagnyc.com**), has experimented with the price optimization system. During its test, sales increased almost 10 percent, unit volume rose by 6 percent, and net profit jumped by 2 percent. Similarly, ShopKo stores (**www.shopko.com**) experienced a 24 percent increase in gross profits during its test. According to a recent study by a marketing research firm in conjunction with *Retail Information News*, close to one-half of the retailers that use price-optimization software expect it to cover their costs within 12 months based on increased sales and profitability.

Retailing experts say that it is about time that retailers apply scientific methods to their price setting. They believe that even though many retailers have fine-tuned their inventory management and supply chain management activities, most simply continue to set prices based on traditional markups, on comparisons with competition, and on manufacturer list prices. As a result, these retailers often overprice or underprice their merchandise.

DemandTec's founder stated that—prior to adopting his firm's software—one of its retailer clients bargain-priced diapers under the mistaken belief that this product was very price sensitive. After analyzing the retailer's sales, DemandTec found that most of the retailer's price-conscious diaper shoppers purchased diapers at discounters like Wal-Mart. As a result, the client was able to increase its diaper prices and its gross profit without hurting either sales or customer traffic.

Despite the success of DemandTec, there are obstacles to more widespread use. Depending on the number of stores and the product assortment, the costs of adopting this software can be between $1 million and $10 million. This limits the use of DemandTec to relatively large retail chains. Another problem is that the software's recommendations may be contrary to a manager's experience or judgment. Managers may be upset that the computer program suggests a price of $2.07 instead of $1.99. Or they may be concerned that the software misprices a popular item viewed as a way to generate more customer traffic than a nearby competitor. In sum, "You have to trust it. That's probably the toughest thing initially."

Questions

1. Discuss the pros and cons of using price optimization software.
2. Visit DemandTec's Web site (**www.demandtec.com**) and comment on it.
3. What is the impact of DemandTec's strategy on a chain retailer that uses centralized advertising for its prices? How can any problems be overcome?
4. Cite additional obstacles to the use of price optimization software by retailers and how you would try to overcome them.

The material in this case is drawn from Amy Cortese, "The Power of Optimal Pricing," *Business 2.0* (September 2002), pp. 68–70.

part six
Comprehensive Case
Kohl's: Keeping the Momentum Going*

Introduction

Kohl's, the Wisconsin-based promotional department store retailer, is neither the fastest-growing retailer nor the most profitable. It isn't the biggest or the most exciting to watch. But Kohl's has tremendous momentum, and it continues to steal market share from competitors. There are lessons to be learned by understanding what makes Kohl's tick and by paying attention to where the company is heading.

Strategic Perspective

What's in Store at Kohl's

National coverage Kohl's expansion is continuing. Its freestanding and strip center location strategy provides the flexibility to grow in major metro markets wherever feasible. In addition, there are lots of midsized communities that are not served by a department store where Kohl's can offer shoppers an option to discount department stores. It will continue seizing opportunities as they arise, capitalizing on the bankruptcies of lesser rivals by buying and converting selected stores to bolster the pace of expansion.

More flagship brands Kohl's will add store brands that are meaningful to its customers. More branded manufacturers looking for new growth will see Kohl's as a major reseller. While its fashion position is not trend forward, these brands will help to ensure that it is trend right. We don't expect it to seek unknown vendors to offer more distinctive products, but we wouldn't be surprised to see Kohl's enter partnerships with makers of top brands for exclusive lines that leverage the flagship brand's caché.

Improved shopping environment Convenience and ease of shopping are cornerstones. Kohl's is in the enviable position of being able to devote significant resources to remodeling stores to create a more spacious, functional, and visually appealing shopping environment. We expect Kohl's to continue to upgrade stores, resulting in greater merchandising flexibility and further improving ease of shopping.

Building the Kohl's brand The firm is just beginning to build the store itself as a brand. Television and radio are becoming more important marketing tools. Brand-building spots are designed to convey the message that "Kohl's is part of everyday life" and support its strong brand names, value, and convenience offer. Increased spending on image advertising will also help Kohl's.

Key Lessons

Shopping efficiency counts Retailers can't waste shoppers' time with inefficient assortments, layouts, and processes. Department stores have underrated the importance of this simple edict. While each firm's customers will have different expectations for merchandise depth and breadth, prices, service, ambiance, and amenities, all shoppers expect to find what they want, when they want it, quickly, and easily.

The importance of being focused Kohl's has taught us that a key to shopping efficiency is focusing only on what's most relevant to customers and eliminating the rest. Although most stores are packed with products, it is now harder for consumers to find exactly what they want. They will be loyal to those firms that make an effort to get to know their needs and preferences, and focus their offers accordingly.

Need for differentiation Many retailers are striving to emulate parts of Kohl's strategy and will likely benefit from the effort. However, rather than just follow in Kohl's footsteps, each retailer must focus on what makes it different and special to a significant group of customers if it is to succeed long term. To break out of their doldrums, retailers need to leverage their own unique strengths. In addition, they should identify weaknesses at Kohl's, at least as perceived by some consumers, and provide what Kohl's cannot.

Need for experimentation Department store retailers must work within the confines of their mall locations and learn to use space more flexibly to attract mall customers, who tend to be younger and more fashion-driven than Kohl's customers. They must experiment with new brands and create an exciting shopping environment, and they should try nonmall formats that allow different approaches to the product and service mix. Are Kohl's advantages sustainable? We think so. But if competition heats up, it won't be as easy for Kohl's to continue taking market share simply by rolling out more stores.

A Consistently Strong Performer

Kohl's is enjoying remarkable success at a time when most other retailers have been struggling. For the Kohl's customer, it's all about getting more for less. More brands, convenience, and value for less time, effort, and risk. Since going public in 1992, when it was a 79-store chain located solely in the Midwest, Kohl's has established a record of consistently strong performance and continued expansion. With 382 stores in 29 states at year-end 2001, it is on the road to becoming a nationwide chain.

Why It Works: The Retail Positioning Model for Kohl's

As depicted in Figure 1, Kohl's has a well-conceived retail positioning model that incorporates positioning variables and retail mix variables.

Positioning Variables

The retail positioning model provides a good framework for understanding why the Kohl's concept works. The positioning variables on the left side identify Kohl's strategic goals: target customers, target competition, core merchandise, and key appeals. Kohl's stated objective is to sell moderately priced, branded apparel, footwear, accessories, and home products to middle-income consumers shopping for their families and homes. Retail Forward's consumer shopping behavior survey data confirm that target customers like the company's offer. Compared to shoppers of key competitors, as well as to all primary household shoppers, Kohl's frequent shoppers are much more apt to be ages 35 to 54, have incomes of $50,000+ (traditional department stores excepted), be married, and have children under age 18 at home.

Kohl's considers its main competitors to be Sears, J.C. Penney, and midrange department stores that also target the middle-class

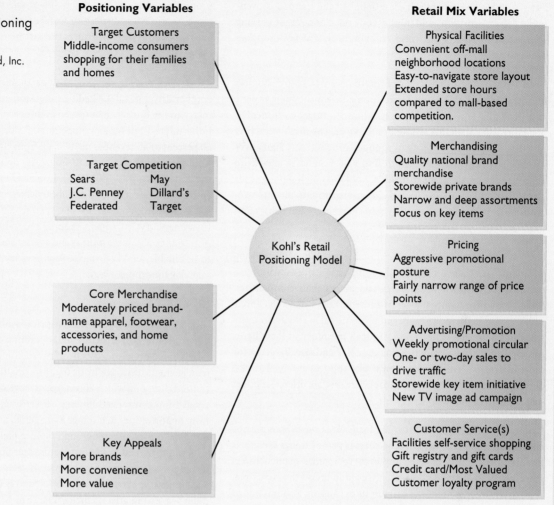

FIGURE 1
Kohl's Retail Positioning Model

Source: Retail Forward, Inc.

Positioning Variables

Target Customers
Middle-income consumers shopping for their families and homes

Target Competition
Sears   May
J.C. Penney   Dillard's
Federated   Target

Core Merchandise
Moderately priced brand-name apparel, footwear, accessories, and home products

Key Appeals
More brands
More convenience
More value

Kohl's Retail Positioning Model

Retail Mix Variables

Physical Facilities
Convenient off-mall neighborhood locations
Easy-to-navigate store layout
Extended store hours compared to mall-based competition.

Merchandising
Quality national brand merchandise
Storewide private brands
Narrow and deep assortments
Focus on key items

Pricing
Aggressive promotional posture
Fairly narrow range of price points

Advertising/Promotion
Weekly promotional circular
One- or two-day sales to drive traffic
Storewide key item initiative
New TV image ad campaign

Customer Service(s)
Facilities self-service shopping
Gift registry and gift cards
Credit card/Most Valued Customer loyalty program

American family. The profiles of frequent shoppers of these retailers show much overlap. We would include Target in Kohl's competitive set, despite Target's more fashion-forward position. The profile of the frequent Target shopper is much more akin to Kohl's than to its discount department store counterparts Wal-Mart and Kmart.

Apparel and accessories account for 70 percent of Kohl's business, footwear 10 percent, and home products 20 percent. On the apparel side, the focus on moderate brands competes most directly with Sears and Penney and the low end of traditional department stores. In the late 1990s, Kohl's took advantage of a void in the marketplace as many department stores moved up market in response to the economic expansion—downplaying the moderate business. In women's, Sag Harbor, Villager, and Norton McNaughton—brands given second-class treatment by department stores—are highlighted at Kohl's. By focusing on traditional styles and practical looks that are the everyday preference of nearly half of female shoppers, Kohl's has grown its women's business to comprise 30 percent of company sales.

Among Kohl's female frequent shoppers, 3.3 percent want the latest styles; 19.4 percent want contemporary fashions but not necessarily the "latest" trends; 30.5 percent want traditional styles that never go out of fashion; 31.9 percent want practical styles; and 14.9 percent want basic, durable clothes. (The comparable percentages at Sears are 4.6, 16.2, 26.1, 28.6, and 24.5; at J.C. Penney, they are 5.6,

21.0, 27.5, 27.7, and 18.2; and at traditional department stores, they are 4.0, 35.8, 33.2, 21.6, and 5.4.)

On the home goods side, Kohl's also faces competition from superstore operators such as Bed Bath & Beyond and Linens 'N Things, as well as from discount department stores. In recent years, Wal-Mart, Kmart, and Target have strengthened their home furnishings by trading up to better-quality products, offering exclusive lines, and becoming more fashion-driven. Kohl's home goods business will get a boost from a revamped home goods presentation being rolled out in new and remodeled stores.

Perhaps the most significant factor in Kohl's success is that its concept is clear, consistent, and easily understood. It appeals to target customers through three factors: (1) quality national brand merchandise (2) priced to provide exceptional value to its customers (3) through convenient neighborhood locations.

Retail Mix Variables

Off-mall location strategy Kohl's location approach benefits from the shift in shopping preferences away from malls. Touting itself as "your neighborhood Kohl's store," the firm offers convenient shopping at sites close to where customers live and work. Most stores are in strip shopping centers or are freestanding. The balance are in community or regional malls. Stores average 86,800 gross square feet (76,200 selling square feet), less than half the size of a conventional department store, and most occupy one floor. Ample parking and extended store hours also contribute to greater shopping convenience.

Easy-to-shop stores Unlike many firms that want to keep customers in stores longer, Kohl's wants to create an efficient shopping experience. The question that Kohl's asks is how it can get customers to buy more while spending less time in the store. The firm's attractive, easy-to-navigate layout leads to shopper productivity. Signs over each department make it easy to find a merchandise area from almost any point along the main aisle. Kohl's has high standards for cleanliness and neatness. Central checkouts simplify buying from multiple departments. Shopping cards accommodate babies and products.

Narrow and deep assortments Kohl's achieves a big merchandising advantage—and offers a simpler shopping experience—by having a more edited assortment of styles and prices than competitors. Rather than offer a dozen styles of an item, Kohl's may offer three, using a good/better/best strategy to promote value and avoid overwhelming shoppers with choices. Its deep inventory in these items lets the firm keep a strong position on color and size. Targeted for those in a hurry, "everyday essentials," like knit tees and turtlenecks, denim jeans and khaki pants, and cookware sets, are offered at prices that are hard to pass up.

Embracing well-known brands The focus on popular brands associated with traditional department stores is part of Kohl's success. It understands the value of being important to branded manufacturers and is committed to their growth and profitability. At the same time, Kohl's seeks vendors that can support its expansion. Kohl's is one of the few U.S. growth platforms for many branded apparel makers.

While keeping a narrow vendor list, Kohl's is adding key brands. It introduced Nine & Company, developed with Jones Apparel, in 2001 in about half its stores and chainwide by the end of 2002. The line is modeled after the Nine West line in conventional departments stores and includes misses' sportswear, shoes, accessories, and handbags. In 2002, Kohl's reintroduced OshKosh B'Gosh, a children's brand. OshKosh had pulled out of Kohl's in 1997, thinking it would do better if sold only in more upscale stores. Kohl's has made a strong commitment to OshKosh and will carry a full assortment of its merchandise.

Private brands complement national brand strategy Although Kohl's is committed to national brands, there is still room for strong private brands. Consisting primarily of Sonoma and Croft & Barrow—which extend across all major product categories—private brands are 20 percent of sales. Kohl's believes these brands complement the name brands as an opening price point and help differentiate the firm. While not currently an area of emphasis for growth, Kohl's private brands have done well, providing a tremendous opportunity to develop items to sell in larger quantities, such as knit tops, sweaters, denim, and fleece.

Aggressive promotional posture focuses on key items Kohl's is a beneficiary of an increasingly value-conscious consumer. It stresses value by reportedly selling more than two-thirds of merchandise on promotion. One- or two-day point-of-sale markdowns drive customer traffic. Mass displays of featured items are supported by circulars, as well as by new fixtures and attention-getting signage in the stores.

Credit card and loyalty programs drive sales Kohl's credit card is another driver of sales. Credit-card customers get discounts on sale merchandise during eight special events each year. And Kohl's offers lower interest rates than competitors. Proprietary credit sales were 30 percent of all revenues in 2000, up from 20 percent in 1995, when Kohl's moved the business in-house. By doing so, Kohl's increased the active accounts and transaction size. Proprietary credit sales (projected to soon reach the mid-30 percent range) mean lower fees to credit-card companies and better data. The Most Valued Customer (MVC) frequent shopper program represents 20 percent of accounts. Shoppers must spend at least $600 annually on the card to be eligible for MVC status. Privileges include picking your own sales day four times a year.

Low Cost Structure

Kohl's offers customers low prices without sacrificing profits due to its low cost structure and operating discipline. This advantage is based on lower costs from freestanding stores, a smaller store management team, sophisticated information systems, and a centralized checkout, which allows leaner store staffing. Efficiencies also result from centralized buying, advertising, and distribution, and from opportunities to leverage managerial, merchandising, and promotional infrastructure through rapid expansion.

Improvement in the firm's gross margin reflects a gradual shift in the product mix to higher-margin categories, such as women's and juniors' apparel and accessories, and better inventory management—a strong area of focus. The firm is also proactive with its clearance strategy, taking markdowns early when they tend to be most effective and least expensive—further boosting margins.

Kohl's enjoys high turnover as measured by the sales-to-stock ratio. Its narrow vendor structure and concentration on relatively few styles bought in large quantity also contribute to better inventory turnover, simpler inventory management, and a lower cost of goods. The higher gross margin and turnover are both reflected in the improvement in Kohl's gross margin return on inventory investment (GMROI).

National Expansion Plans

Kohl's is in the enviable position of generating large amounts of capital with which to invest in new stores, refurbishing existing stores, and upgrading systems and distribution centers. Its objective to be a national retailer brings with it important economies of scale. Continued expansion also will help Kohl's diversify its geographic risk by reducing regional setbacks from bad weather or economic slowdowns.

The growth strategy is deliberate, expanding into contiguous states and filling in existing markets. Markets range from small cities like Rochester, Minnesota (population 82,000), with a single store, to the New York City metropolitan area, where there are 35 units. Kohl's enters major markets with a critical mass of stores that enables it to quickly establish a presence and leverage expenses.

During 2002, Kohl's planned to open 70 stores, including continued expansion in the Northeast (Boston), further expansion in Texas with a significant entry into Houston, and four stores in Nashville, another new market. The Northeast expansion included the acquisition of 15 former Bradlees stores of which 12 stores were an initial entry into the Boston market. In 2003, Kohl's planned to begin a major expansion into the Southwest region of the country with an entry into Los Angeles. Further expansion into Southern California, Arizona, and Nevada was planned for 2003 and 2004.

Questions

1. Describe and evaluate Kohl's overall merchandising strategy.
2. What merchandising considerations should Kohl's keep in mind as it seeks to expand?
3. How should Kohl's merchandising strategy differ by region of the country?
4. Comment on Kohl's retail positioning model, which is shown in Figure 1.
5. What could other retailers learn by studying Figure 1?
6. As Kohl's looks to the future, do you think its product mix of 70 percent apparel and accessories, 20 percent home products, and 10 percent footwear should be modified? Why or why not?
7. What must Kohl's do to continue to attract price-conscious shoppers?

*The material in this case is adapted by the authors from Retail Forward, "Kohl's—Why It Works and What You Can Learn," *Industry Brief* (January 2002), pp. 1–21. Reprinted by permission of Retail Forward, Inc. (**www.retailforward.com**).

part seven

Communicating with the Customer

In Part Seven, the elements involved in a retailer's communicating with its customers are discussed. First, we cover the role of a retail image and how it is developed and sustained. Various aspects of a promotional strategy are then detailed.

■ **Chapter 18** discusses the importance of communications for a retailer. We review the significance of image in the communications effort and the components of a retailer's image. Creating an image depends heavily on a retailer's atmosphere—which is comprised of all of its physical characteristics, such as the store exterior, the general interior, layouts, and displays. This applies to both store and nonstore retailers. Ways of encouraging customers to spend more time shopping and the value of community relations are also described.

■ **Chapter 19** focuses on promotional strategy, specifically how a retailer can inform, persuade, and remind its target market about its strategic mix. In the first part of the chapter, we deal with the four basic types of retail promotion: advertising, public relations, personal selling, and sales promotion. The second part describes the steps in a promotional strategy: objectives, budget, mix of forms, implementation of mix, and review and revision of the plan.

Chapter 18

ESTABLISHING AND MAINTAINING A RETAIL IMAGE

Reprinted by permission.

For the past several years, Target Stores (**www.target.com**) has been busy building its image as a fashion-forward full-line discount store chain. And it has succeeded. The firm has come a very long way since its 1962 founding. While many upper-middle-class customers feel uncomfortable shopping for clothing or housewares at Wal-Mart (**www.walmart.com**) or Kmart (**www.kmart.com**), their general view of Target can be summarized by the statement "It's hip to be cheap."

At one time, Target was not perceived as an upscale discounter. It has now achieved that status through strategic partnerships with trendy firms and designers such as housewares by prominent architect Michael Graves (**www.michaelgraves.com**), pots by Calphalon (**www.calphalon.com**), seating by French architect Phillipe Starck, and an exclusive line of apparel by Mossimo (**http://biz.yahoo.com/p/m/moss.html**).

Target's success in redefining its image can be seen by examining the demographics of its target customer: typically a suburban, professional, well-educated female with a family and an average household annual income of $45,000 per year. This is significantly higher than the demographics of the average shopper at either Wal-Mart or Kmart.

Target's fashionable strategy was borne from the realization that it could not compete against Wal-Mart on price. It instead decided to use its department store roots to develop fashion merchandise that was attractive to upscale shoppers. Yet, despite its upscale merchandising, Target is still clearly a discounter as seen by its optical, pharmacy, and photo-finishing departments—as well as its self-service merchandising philosophy.[1]

chapter objectives

1. To show the importance of communicating with customers and examine the concept of retail image

2. To describe how a retail store image is related to the atmosphere it creates via its exterior, general interior, layout, and displays, and to look at the special case of non-store atmospherics

3. To discuss ways of encouraging customers to spend more time shopping

4. To consider the impact of community relations on a retailer's image

OVERVIEW

There are many trade associations (www. visualstore.com/events/ associations.html) in the retail image arena. Visit a few online.

A retailer needs a superior communications strategy to properly position itself in customers' minds, as well as to nurture their shopping behavior. Once customers are attracted, it is then imperative for the retailer to create a proper shopping mood for them. Various physical and symbolic cues can be used to do this. See Figure 18-1. As mentioned in Chapter 1, it is imperative to maximize the total retail experience:

> The consumer/retailer relationship is simply all about perception. Consider some of the strong brands in retailing. Starbucks brings to mind, in one word, the concept "relax." Almost immediately, one thinks about a casual, albeit expensive, cup of coffee in a comfortable atmosphere. The single most important strategy for Wal-Mart is its everyday low price strategy which others have tried to establish, but very few have been able to execute. Wal-Mart's image is reinforced with one word—"rollback." When it comes to fashion and cool products, Target has nurtured its perception among consumers for being the destination for "cheap chic." Sears, one of the nation's oldest chains, is an example of how a retailer has tried time and again to alter its stodgy company image and become more contemporary, yet it is still known best for the quality and dependability of its private brands (Kenmore and Craftsman). Over the years, Eckerd has exploited its strengths in photos while CVS has focused on health care to help differentiate the chains among consumers.[2]

This chapter describes how to establish and maintain an image. Retail atmosphere, storefronts, store layouts, and displays are examined. We also explore the challenge of how to encourage people to spend more time shopping and the role of community relations. Chapter 19 focuses on the common promotional tools available to retailers: advertising, public relations, personal selling, and sales promotion.

FIGURE 18-1

Positioning and Retail Image

At FAO Schwarz, every aspect of its retail image is carefully planned and executed so that the retailer projects a very distinctive retail position in the marketplace. It is true to this Web site description (**www.fao.com/aboutfao/history.cfm**): "FAO prides itself in offering unique products in an unforgettable environment. Management designed stores to interact with customers in a manner which distinguishes itself from other retailers. Considered the leading specialty seller of toys and collectibles in the United States, FAO is a mecca for toy lovers from all over the world."

Reprinted by permission of Goran Petkovic.

While our discussion looks more at store retailers, the basic principles do apply to nonstore retailers. For a mail-order firm, the catalog cover is its storefront, and the interior layouts and displays are the pages devoted to product categories and the individual items within them. For a Web retailer, the home page is its storefront, and the interior layouts and displays are represented by the links within the site.

THE SIGNIFICANCE OF RETAIL IMAGE

Display & Design Ideas (www.ddimagazine.com) is a leading trade magazine that often deals with retail image topics.

As defined in Chapter 3, *image* refers to how a retailer is perceived by customers and others, and *positioning* refers to a firm's devising its strategy so as to project an image relative to its retail category and its competitors—and to elicit a positive consumer response. To succeed, a firm must communicate a distinctive, clear, and consistent image. Once its image is established in consumers' minds, a retailer is placed in a niche relative to competitors. For global retailers, it can be challenging to convey a consistent image worldwide, given the different backgrounds of consumers.[3]

COMPONENTS OF A RETAIL IMAGE

Numerous factors contribute to a retailer's image, and it is the totality of them that forms an overall image. See Figure 18-2. We examined these factors in earlier chapters: target market, firm's positioning, customer service, store location, merchandise attributes, and pricing. Our focal points for Chapters 18 and 19 are the attributes of physical facilities, shopping experiences, community service, advertising, public relations, personal selling, and sales promotion.

THE DYNAMICS OF CREATING AND MAINTAINING A RETAIL IMAGE

Creating and maintaining a retail image is a complex, multistep, ongoing process. It encompasses far more than store "atmosphere," which is discussed shortly. Furthermore, with so many people having little time for shopping and others having less interest in it, retailers must work hard to *entertain* shoppers:

> The definition of entertainment differs widely across the board. Some shoppers get a kick out of cooking lessons at the local supermarket. Others love giving themselves a makeover at the cosmetics counter. Still others enjoy relaxing at a bookstore café. Some retailers have taken their

FIGURE 18-2
The Elements of a Retail Image

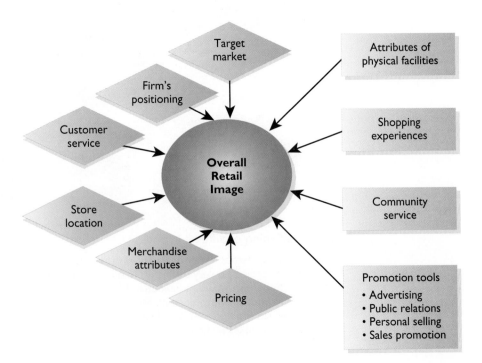

whole image or core offering and turned it into an experience. Entertainment retailing has evolved to the point where it's more about making the emotional connection with your customer than entertainment per se. It's about driving the experience and customer connection.[4]

As one industry expert says: "A shopper should be able to determine the following about a store *in three seconds*: its name, its line of trade, its claim to fame, its price position, and its personality. All that must be conveyed quickly because people are generally unwilling to buy things from retailers. Those who need what you are selling will find you. Thus, everyone else must be enticed—in very short order—to enter your store. The glut of pitches out there only ups the ante. Without a distinct image, you don't have a chance of being seen or heard through all the clutter that is retailing."[5]

See how Best Buy's Web site (www.bestbuy.com) reinforces its retail image.

Let's look at two examples. Best Buy is the leading consumer electronics chain (in revenues)—and wants to stay that way. It has invested millions of dollars in a new store design to update the firm's image, based on three principles: (1) "We will stand for price, but we are not going to build our brand off price because Wal-Mart can eat anybody's lunch when it comes to that." (2) "We put it together for the consumer, much like fashion retailers have done. We've created value-packaged elements such as home theater in a box." (3) The end-of-aisle displays will "turn customers' attention to new products with informative graphics and interactive technology." Best Buy's goal is to show that "we're not just in the business of selling commodities or pushing products, we are selling experiences, and we want to be first to market with the best offerings for high-end technology for the mass market."[6]

Would you name a store Chapter 11? An Atlanta bookstore chain has: "Barbara Babbit Kaufman, founder of Chapter 11 Books, has never been superstitious: 'I wanted a name that would draw people's attention. I also wanted something that would get across the idea that we sell at bargain prices'" There are several reasons for the firm's success. "We fulfill a niche that large bookstores find impossible to fill by virtue of their superstore format. When the customer comes into the store, she can turn her head from side to side and see the entire store. There's signage over everything, so every section is easy to find." There is also a help desk in front. Chapter 11 communicates its image by the slogan, "Prices so low, you'd think we were going bankrupt." Its strategy is also based on in-store events. "We spend less on ads in one year than our neighbor Wolf Camera spends every week. But our brand recognition in the area we serve is nearly 100 percent."[7] The firm also does well through its Web site (**www.chapter11books.com**).

A key goal for chain retailers, franchisors, and global retailers is to maintain a consistent image among all branches. Yet, despite the best planning, a number of factors may vary widely among branch stores and affect the image. They include management and employee performance, consumer profiles, competitors, the convenience in reaching stores, parking, safety, the ease of finding merchandise, and the qualities of the surrounding area. Sometimes, retailers with

Careers in RETAILING

Hot Topics Uses Store Managers to Reinforce Its Image

Charlene Rogers is a twenty-something year-old, self-described punk rocker who manages Hot Topics Brea, California, store (**www.hottopic.com**). Her store is one of the chain's top 10 highest-grossing units, with average sales per square foot of $669.

Rogers is successful because she knows what groups of 17-year-olds want to purchase: "My enthusiasm came out at Hot Topic, since this was the first company that ever stopped to tell me why I was doing what I was doing. At other retailers, the company tells you what to sell."

She gathers much of her information about consumer trends by going to clubs and shows and seeing what's new.

Rogers' store is often one of the first outlets to have trendy items in stock. She encourages her staff of 13 employees, four of whom are assistant managers, to do the same: "I'll put one associate in charge of the CD deaprtment. Once a week, he'll call the CD buyer and they'll talk about what's selling and what the customers are asking for. When a new associate starts, I'll tell him or her, 'Hey, dude, you know you can call the company and tell them what we should be carrying.'"

Source: Matt Nannery, "Minding the Stores," *Chain Store Age* (September 2001), pp. 45–54.

good images receive negative publicity. This must be countered in order for them to maintain their desired standing with the public.

ATMOSPHERE

The National Association of Visual Merchandisers (www.visualmerch.com) profiles the real-world experiences of its members through the "Newsletter" section of its site.

A retailer's image depends heavily on its "atmosphere," the psychological feeling a customer gets when visiting that retailer. It is the personality of the store, catalog, vending machine, or Web site. "Retail image" is a much broader and all-encompassing term relative to the communication tools a retailer uses to position itself. For a store-based retailer, **atmosphere (atmospherics)** refers to the store's physical characteristics that project an image and draw customers. For a nonstore-based firm, atmosphere refers to the physical characteristics of catalogs, vending machines, Web sites, and so forth. A retailer's sights, sounds, smells, and other physical attributes all contribute to customer perceptions.

A retailer's atmosphere may influence people's shopping enjoyment, as well as their time spent browsing, willingness to converse with personnel, tendency to spend more than originally planned, and likelihood of future patronage. Many people even form impressions of a retailer before entering its facilities (due to the store location, storefront, and other factors) or just after entering (due to displays, width of aisles, and other things). They often judge the firm prior to examining merchandise and prices.

Check out the advantages of "Visual Stimulation" (www.facit.co.uk/retail_planning.htm) in planning atmospherics.

When a retailer takes a proactive, integrated atmospherics approach to create a certain "look," properly display products, stimulate shopping behavior, and enhance the physical environment, it engages in **visual merchandising**. According to Cahill, an interior design firm, "Visual merchandising is more than the enhancement of retail space for the purpose of increasing sales. By creatively using lighting, props, and customized displays, selling space can inform, stimulate the senses, entertain, and ultimately reinforce the shopper's relationships with the product."[8] It includes everything from store display windows to the width of aisles to the materials used for fixtures to merchandise presentation, as highlighted in Figure 18-3. Visit our Web site (**www.prenhall.com/bermanevans**) for numerous links related to visual merchandising.

A STORE-BASED RETAILING PERSPECTIVE

Store atmosphere (atmospherics) can be divided into these key elements: exterior, general interior, store layout, and displays. Figure 18-4 contains a detailed breakdown of them.

FIGURE 18-3
Visual Merchandising and Gap

This chain places great reliance on its visual merchandising efforts. Gap stores are well known for their unique "look."

Reprinted by permission of Retail Forward, Inc.

FIGURE 18-4
The Elements of
Atmosphere

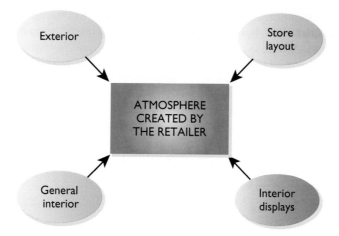

Exterior

A store's exterior has a powerful impact on its image and should be planned accordingly.

A **storefront** is the total physical exterior of the store itself. It includes the marquee, entrances, windows, lighting, and construction materials. With its storefront, a retailer can present a conservative, trendy, upscale, discount, or other image. Consumers who pass through an unfamiliar business district or shopping center often judge a store by its exterior. Besides the storefront itself, atmosphere can be enhanced by trees, fountains, and benches in front of the store. These intensify consumer feelings about shopping and about the store by establishing a relaxed environment. There are various alternatives in planning a basic storefront. Here are a few of them:

- Modular structure—a one-piece rectangular or square that may attach several stores.
- Prefabricated (pre-fab) structure—a frame built in a factory and assembled at the site.
- Prototype store—used by franchisors and chains to foster a consistent atmosphere.
- Recessed storefront—lures people by being recessed from the level of other stores. Customers must walk in a number of feet to examine the storefront.
- Unique building design—a round structure, for example.

A **marquee** is a sign that displays the store's name. It can be painted or a neon light, printed or script, and set alone or mixed with a slogan (trademark) and other information. The marquee should attract attention, as Macy's Herald Square does. See Figure 18-5. Image is influenced because a marquee can be gaudy and flashy or subdued and subtle. The world's best-known marquee is McDonald's golden arch.

FIGURE 18-5

Using a Marquee to Generate a Powerful Retail Image

Reprinted by permission of Goran Petkovic.

Store entrances require three major decisions. First, the number of entrances is determined. Many small stores have only one entrance. Department stores may have four to eight or more entrances. A store hoping to draw both vehicular and pedestrian traffic may need at least two entrances (one for pedestrians, another near the parking lot). Because front and back entrances serve different purposes, they should be designed separately. A factor that may limit the number of entrances is potential pilferage.

Second, the type of entrance(s) is chosen. The doorway can be revolving; electric, self-opening; regular, push-pull; or climate-controlled. The latter is an open entrance with a curtain of warm or cold air, set at the same temperature as inside the store. Entrance flooring can be cement, tile, or carpeting. Lighting can be traditional or fluorescent, white or colors, and/or flashing or constant. Look at how impressive MAC's entrances are, as depicted in Figure 18-6.

Third, walkways are considered. A wide, lavish walkway creates a different atmosphere and mood than a narrow one. Large window displays may be attractive, but customers would not be pleased if there is insufficient space for a comfortable entry into the store.

Display windows have two main purposes: to identify the store and its offerings, and to induce people to enter. By showing a representative merchandise offering, a store can create an overall mood. By showing fashion or seasonal goods, it can show it is contemporary. By showing sale items, a store can lure price-conscious consumers. By showing eye-catching displays that have little to do with its merchandise offering, a store can attract pedestrians' attention. By showing public service messages (such as a sign for the Special Olympics), the store can indicate its community involvement.

A lot of planning is needed to develop good display windows, which leads many retailers to hire outside specialists. Decisions include the number, size, shape, color, and themes of display windows and the frequency of changes per year. Retailers in shopping malls may not use display windows for the side of the building facing the parking lot; there are solid building exteriors. They feel vehicular patrons are not lured by expensive outside windows; they invest in displays for storefronts inside the malls.

Exterior building height can be disguised or nondisguised. With disguised building height, part of a store or shopping center is beneath ground level. Such a building is not as intimidating to people who dislike a large structure. With nondisguised building height, the entire store or center can be seen by pedestrians. An intimate image cannot be fostered with a block-long building. Nor can a department store image be linked to a small site.

Few firms succeed with poor visibility. This means pedestrian and/or vehicular traffic must clearly see storefronts or marquees. A store located behind a bus stop has poor visibility for vehicular traffic and pedestrians across the street. Many firms near highways use billboards since drivers go by quickly.

FIGURE 18-6

How a Store Entrance Can Generate Shopper Interest

MAC store entrances are visually appealing and inviting.

Reprinted by permission of Retail Forward, Inc.

In every case, the goal is to have the store or center appear unique and catch the shopper's eye. A distinctive storefront, an elaborate marquee, recessed open-air entrances, decorative windows, and unusual building height and size are one set of features that could attract consumers by their uniqueness. Nonetheless, uniqueness may not be without its shortcomings. An example is the multilevel "shopping-center-in-the-round." Because this center (which often occupies a square city block) is round, parking on each floor level makes the walking distances very short. Yet, a rectangular center may have greater floor space on a lot of the same size, on-floor parking may reduce shopping on other floors, added entrances increase chances for pilferage, many people dislike circular driving, and architectural costs are higher.

As a retailer plans its exterior, the surrounding stores and the surrounding area should be studied. Surrounding stores present image cues due to their price range, level of service, and so on. The surrounding area reflects the demographics and life-styles of those who live nearby. An overall area image rubs off on individual retailers because people tend to have a general perception of a shopping center or a business district. An unfavorable atmosphere would exist if vandalism and crime are high, people living near the store are not in the target market, and the area is rundown.

Parking facilities can add to or detract from store atmosphere. Plentiful, free, nearby parking creates a more positive image than scarce, costly, distant parking. Some potential shoppers may never enter a store if they must drive around for parking. Other customers may run in and out of a store to finish shopping before parking meters expire. A related potential problem is that of congestion. Atmospherics are diminished if the parking lot, sidewalks, and/or entrances are jammed. Consumers who feel crushed in the crowd spend less time shopping and are in poorer moods than those who feel comfortable.

General Interior

Gladson Interactive (www.gladson.com/sd.html) has designed interiors for a variety of retailers. Several are profiled here.

Once customers are inside a store, numerous elements affect their perceptions. At Toys "R" Us, an expensive, multiyear plan to upgrade its stores is nearing completion: "We are enhancing the look and creating a new attitude that guests will notice. Our updated stores emphasize a unique merchandise assortment, a format that is more convenient, open, and easy to shop—with improved guest service." And the firm's rather new flagship store in New York (costing an estimating $35 million to construct) offers much more than a vast selection of toys: "The multilevel store has indoor retail attractions such as a 60-foot Ferris wheel, a 4,000-square-foot Barbie Dollhouse, and a 20-foot-tall animatronic Jurassic Park T-Rex that roars."[9] See Figure 18-7. The general interior elements of store atmosphere were cited in Figure 18-4. They are described next.

FIGURE 18-7
Eye-Catching Displays from Toys "R" Us

At Toys "R" Us outlets around the world, the store interior plays a prominent role in creating a total retail experience. From the linoleum floors to the plain metal fixtures to the bold colors and sounds, the chain sets the proper tone for its shoppers.

Reprinted by permission of Retail Forward, Inc.

Flooring can be cement, wood, linoleum, carpet, and so on. A plush, thick carpet creates one kind of atmosphere and a concrete floor another. Thus, 100 percent of department stores have carpeted floors, 95 percent of discount stores have vinyl floors, and 90 percent of home centers have concrete floors.[10]

Bright, vibrant colors contribute to a different atmosphere than light pastels or plain white walls. Lighting can be direct or indirect, white or colors, constant or flashing. A teen-oriented apparel boutique might use bright colors and vibrant, flashing lights to foster one atmosphere, and a maternity dress shop could use pastel colors and indirect lighting to form a different atmosphere. In its Plano, Texas, store, Neiman Marcus has created a "comfortably modern feel and bold contemporary style. Unexpected materials, including mother-of-pearl counters, Murano glass light fixtures, and tinted polished plasters, add to the luxurious ambiance."[11]

Scents and sounds influence the customer's mood. A restaurant can use food aromas to increase people's appetites. A cosmetics store can use an array of perfume scents to attract shoppers. A pet store can let its animals' natural scents and sounds woo customers. A beauty salon can play soft music or rock, depending on its customers. Slow-tempo music in supermarkets encourages people to move more slowly.

Store fixtures can be planned on the basis of both their utility and aesthetics. Pipes, plumbing, beams, doors, storage rooms, and display racks and tables should be considered part of interior decorating. An upscale store usually dresses up and disguises its fixtures. A discount store might leave fixtures exposed because this portrays the desired image.

Wall textures enhance or diminish atmospherics. Prestigious stores often use raised wallpaper. Department stores are more apt to use flat wallpaper, while discount stores may have barren walls. Chic stores might have chandeliers, while discounters have fluorescent lighting.

The customer's mood is affected by the store's temperature and how it is achieved. Insufficient heat in winter and no air-conditioning in summer can shorten a shopping trip. And image is influenced by the use of central air-conditioning, unit air-conditioning, fans, or open windows.

Wide, uncrowded aisles create a better atmosphere than narrow, crowded ones. People shop longer and spend more if they are not pushed while walking or looking at merchandise. In Boston, although the basement in Filene's department store offers bargains, overcrowding keeps some customers away.

Dressing facilities can be elaborate, plain, or nonexistent. An upscale store has carpeted, private dressing rooms. An average-quality store has linoleum-floored, semiprivate rooms. A discount store has small stalls or no facilities. For some apparel shoppers, dressing facilities are a factor in store selection.

Multilevel stores must have vertical transportation: elevator, escalator, and/or stairs. Larger stores may have a combination of all three. Traditionally, finer stores relied on operator-run elevators and discount stores on stairs. Today, escalators are quite popular. They provide shoppers with a quiet ride and a panoramic view of the store. Finer stores decorate their escalators with fountains, shrubs, and trees. Stairs remain important for some discount and smaller stores.

Light fixtures, wood or metal beams, doors, rest rooms, dressing rooms, and vertical transportation can cause **dead areas** for the retailer. These are awkward spaces where normal displays cannot be set up. Sometimes, it is not possible for such areas to be deployed profitably or attractively. However, retailers have learned to use dead areas better. Mirrors are attached to exit doors. Vending machines are located near rest rooms. Ads appear in dressing rooms. One creative use of a dead area involves the escalator. It lets shoppers view each floor, and sales of impulse items go up when placed at the escalator entrance or exit. Many firms plan escalators so customers must get off at each floor and pass by appealing displays.

Polite, well-groomed, knowledgeable personnel generate a positive atmosphere. Ill-mannered, poorly groomed, uninformed personnel engender a negative one. A store using self-service minimizes its personnel and creates a discount, impersonal image. A store cannot develop an upscale image if it is set up for self-service.

The merchandise a retailer sells influences its image. Top-line items yield one kind of image, and lower-quality items yield another. The mood of the customer is affected accordingly.

Price levels foster a perception of retail image in consumers' minds; and the way prices are displayed is a vital part of atmosphere. Upscale stores have few or no price displays, rely on discrete price tags, and place cash registers in inconspicuous areas behind posts or in employee rooms. Discounters accentuate price displays, show prices in large print, and locate cash registers centrally, with signs pointing to them.

A store with state-of-the-art technology impresses people with its operations efficiency and speed. One with slower, older technology may have impatient shoppers. A store with a modern building (new storefront and marquee) and new fixtures (lights, floors, and walls) fosters a more favorable atmosphere than one with older facilities. Remodeling can improve store appearance, update facilities, and reallocate space. It typically results in strong sales and profit increases after completion.

Last, but certainly not least, there must be a plan for keeping the store clean. No matter how impressive the exterior and interior, an unkempt store will be perceived poorly. As the chief executive of Casey's General Stores once said, "We sell clean. People open the door and form an image right away."[12]

Store Layout

At this point, the specifics of store layout are *sequentially* planned and enacted.

ALLOCATION OF FLOOR SPACE Each store has a total amount of floor space to allot to selling, merchandise, personnel, and customers. Without this allocation, the retailer would have no idea of the space available for displays, signs, rest rooms, and so on:

- *Selling space* is used for displays of merchandise, interactions between salespeople and customers, demonstrations, and so on. Self-service retailers apportion most space to selling.

- *Merchandise space* is used to stock nondisplayed items. At a traditional shoe store, this area takes up a large percentage of total space.

- *Personnel space* is set aside for employees to change clothes and to take lunch and coffee breaks, and for rest rooms. Because retail space is valuable, personnel space is strictly controlled. Yet, a retailer should consider the effect on employee morale.

- *Customer space* contributes to the shopping mood. It can include a lounge, benches and/or chairs, dressing rooms, rest rooms, a restaurant, a nursery, parking, and wide aisles. Discounters are more apt to skimp on these areas.

Nielsen markets planogram services (www.marketdec.com/ planogram) as part of its retail solutions package.

More firms now use planograms to assign space. A **planogram** is a visual (graphical) representation of the space for selling, merchandise, personnel, and customers—as well as for product categories. It also lays out their in-store placement. A planogram may be hand-drawn or computer-generated. Visit our Web site (**www.prenhall.com/bermanevans**) for several planogram links.

CLASSIFICATION OF STORE OFFERINGS A store's offerings are next classified into product groupings. Many retailers use a combination of groupings and plan store layouts accordingly. Special provisions must be made to minimize shoplifting and pilferage. This means placing vulnerable products away from corners and doors. Four types of groupings (and combinations of them) are most commonly used:

- **Functional product groupings** display merchandise by common end use. A men's clothing store might group shirts, ties, cuff links, and tie pins; shoes, shoe trees, and shoe polish; T-shirts, undershorts, and socks; suits; and sport jackets and slacks.

- **Purchase motivation product groupings** appeal to the consumer's urge to buy products and the amount of time he or she is willing to spend on shopping. A committed customer with time to shop will visit a store's upper floors; a disinterested person with less time will look at displays on the first floor. Look at the first level of a department store. It includes impulse products and other rather quick purchases. The third floor has items encouraging and requiring more thoughtful shopping.

- **Market segment product groupings** place together various items that appeal to a given target market. A women's apparel store divides products into juniors', misses', and ladies' apparel. A music store separates CDs into rock, jazz, classical, R&B, country, and other sections. An art gallery places paintings into different price groups.

- **Storability product groupings** may be used for products needing special handling. A supermarket has freezer, refrigerator, and room-temperature sections. A florist keeps some items refrigerated and others at room temperature, as do a bakery and a fruit store.

DETERMINATION OF A TRAFFIC-FLOW PATTERN The traffic-flow pattern of the store is then set. A **straight (gridiron) traffic flow** places displays and aisles in a rectangular or gridiron pattern, as shown in Figure 18-8. A **curving (free-flowing) traffic flow** places displays and aisles in a free-flowing pattern, as shown in Figure 18-9. Piggly Wiggly's innovative layout, which combines both approaches, is highlighted in Figure 18-10.

A straight traffic pattern is often used by food retailers, discount stores, drugstores, hardware stores, and stationery stores. It has several advantages:

- An efficient atmosphere is created.
- More floor space is devoted to product displays.
- People can shop quickly.
- Inventory control and security are simplified.
- Self-service is easy, thereby reducing labor costs.

The disadvantages are the impersonal atmosphere, the more limited browsing by customers, and the rushed shopping behavior.

FIGURE 18-8

How a Supermarket Uses a Straight (Gridiron) Traffic Pattern

Illustration by Steve Cowden for *Progressive Grocer.* Reprinted by permission.

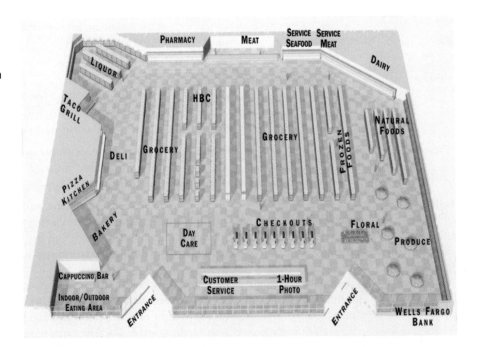

FIGURE 18-9
How a Department Store
Uses a Curving (Free-
Flowing) Traffic Pattern

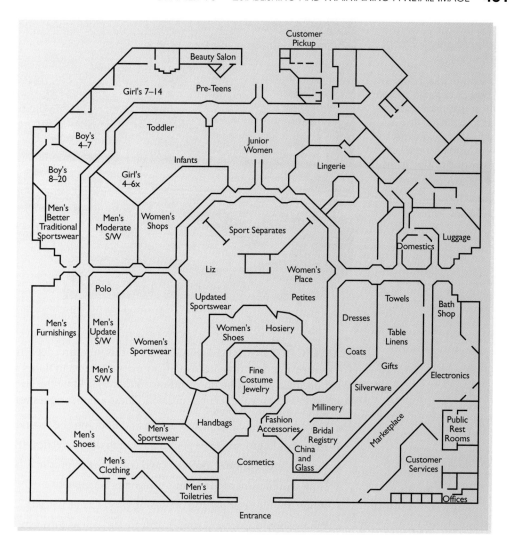

FIGURE 18-9
How a Department Store Uses a Curving (Free-Flowing) Traffic Pattern

A curving traffic pattern is used by department stores, apparel stores, and other shopping-oriented stores. Apparel retailer Wet Seal's interiors are "intentionally chaotic to echo the atmosphere of a teenage girl's bedroom."[13] This approach has several benefits:

- A friendly atmosphere is presented.
- Shoppers do not feel rushed and will browse around.
- People are encouraged to walk through the store in any direction or pattern.
- Impulse or unplanned purchases are enhanced.

The disadvantages are the possible customer confusion, wasted floor space, difficulties in inventory control, higher labor intensity, and potential loitering. Also, these displays often cost more.

DETERMINATION OF SPACE NEEDS The space for each product category is now calculated, with both selling and nonselling space considered. There are two different approaches: the model stock method and the space-productivity ratio.

The **model stock approach** determines the floor space necessary to carry and display a proper merchandise assortment. Apparel stores and shoe stores are among those using this method. The **sales-productivity ratio** assigns floor space on the basis of sales or profit per foot. Highly profitable product categories get large chunks of space; marginally profitable categories get less. Food stores and bookstores are among those that use this technique.

FIGURE 18-10
Piggly Wiggly's Open Traffic Design

This supermarket captures the best of both the straight and curving traffic patterns, so as to optimize its customers' shopping experience. Customers are encouraged to stay in the store longer.

Reprinted by permission of Fresh Brands, Inc.

MAPPING OUT IN-STORE LOCATIONS At this juncture, department locations are mapped out. For multilevel stores, that means assigning departments to floors and laying out individual floors. What products should be on each floor? What should be the layout of each floor? A single-level store addresses only the second question. These are some questions to consider:

- What items should be placed on the first floor, on the second floor, and so on?
- How should groupings be placed relative to doors, vertical transportation, and so on?
- Where should impulse products and convenience products be situated?
- How should associated product categories be aligned?
- Where should seasonal and off-season products be placed?
- Where should space-consuming categories such as furniture be located?
- How close should product displays and stored inventory be to each other?
- What shopping patterns do consumers follow once they enter the store?
- How can the overall appearance of store crowding be averted?

Saks Fifth Avenue knows men "don't like having to walk past perfume spritzers or go up 10 flights." At Kohl's, "a key part of the success formula is its unique store design. The store layout is smaller and simpler than those of most department stores. Its design is geared to smoothly lead shoppers past all the merchandise, in what the retailer hopes is a continuous circuit of temptation."[14]

ARRANGEMENT OF INDIVIDUAL PRODUCTS The last step in store layout planning is arranging individual products. The most profitable items and brands could be placed in the best locations; and products could be arranged by package size, price, color, brand, level of personal service required, and/or customer interest. End-aisle display positions, eye-level positions, and checkout-counter positions are the most likely to increase sales for individual items. Continuity of locations is also important; shifts in store layout may decrease sales by confusing shoppers. The least desirable display position is often knee or ankle level, because consumers do not like to bend down.

Retailer goals often differ from their manufacturers. While the latter want to maximize their brands' sales and push for eye-level, full-shelf, end-aisle locations, retailers seek to maximize total store sales and profit, regardless of brand. Self-service retailers have special considerations. Besides using a gridiron layout to minimize shopper confusion, they must clearly mark aisles, displays, and merchandise.

Consider some of the tactics that supermarkets have employed:

- Many have produce near the entrance; most of the rest have flowers. "The idea is to tantalize the customer, to draw you in with eye-catching displays."
- "Cereal theory" means placing boxes on lower shelves, which are at eye level for children.
- People buy more soup if the varieties are not shelved in alphabetical order.
- Store brands do better when located to the left of manufacturer brands. "After seeing the name brand, the eye automatically moves left (as if on a new page) to compare prices."
- Since "the best viewing angle is 15 degrees below the horizontal, the choicest display level has been measured at 51 to 53 inches off the floor."[15]

Interior (Point-of-Purchase) Displays

Cahill specializes in creative retail displays (www.cahilldisplay.com).

Once store layout is fully detailed, a retailer devises its interior displays. Each **point-of-purchase (POP) display** provides shoppers with information, adds to store atmosphere, and serves a substantial promotional role. Here's what Point-of-Purchase Advertising International (POPAI) has to say:

P-O-P advertising is persuasive. Serving as the last three feet of the marketing plan, it is the only mass medium executed at the critical point of confluence for the three elements needed for any commercial transaction: the product, the consumer, and the dollars to purchase the product. With 74 percent of all purchase decisions in mass merchandisers made in store, an increasing number of brand marketers and retailers invest in this medium. *P-O-P advertising serves as the silent salesperson.* Displays, signs, and in-store media educate and inform consumers about product availability and attributes. Coming at a time when retailers have reduced staffing levels, P-O-P performs a vital service and augments cost-reduction efforts. *P-O-P advertising is flexible.* It is the only mass advertising medium that can convey the same overall strategic message in differing languages to varying audiences. *P-O-P advertising is increasingly sophisticated in its construction and utilization.* P-O-P is more easily assembled and maintained and, at the same time, more powerful in entertaining and informing in the retail environment. *P-O-P advertising is used increasingly by retailers to enhance the shopping experience.* It is used to help overhaul a store's image, re-direct store traffic, and bolster merchandising plans.[16]

Several types of displays are described here. Most retailers use a combination of them.

An **assortment display** exhibits a wide range of merchandise. With an *open assortment*, the customer is encouraged to feel, look at, and/or try on products. Greeting cards, books, magazines, and apparel are the kinds of products for which retailers use open assortments. In addition, food stores have expanded their open displays for fruit, vegetables, and candy; and some department stores have opened up their cosmetics and perfume displays. With a *closed assortment*, the customer is encouraged to look at merchandise but not touch it or try it on. Computer software and CDs are pre-packaged items that cannot be opened before buying. Jewelry is usually kept in closed glass cases that employees must unlock.

At this site (http://dir. yahoo.com/Business_and_ Economy), retailers can choose from many display firms. Click on "Business to Business," "Retail Management," and then "Point of Purchase Displays."

A **theme-setting display** depicts a product offering in a thematic manner and sets a specific mood. Retailers often vary their displays to reflect seasons or special events; some even have employees dress for the occasion. All or part of a store may be adapted to a theme, such as Columbus Day, Valentine's Day, or another concept. Each special theme seeks to attract attention and make shopping more fun.

With an **ensemble display**, a complete product bundle (ensemble) is presented—rather than showing merchandise in separate categories (such as a shoe department, sock department, pants department, shirt department, and sports jacket department). Thus, a mannequin may be dressed in a matching combination of shoes, socks, pants, shirt, and sports jacket, and these items would be available in one department or adjacent departments. Customers like the ease of a purchase and envisioning an entire product bundle.

A **rack display** has a primarily functional use: to neatly hang or present products. It is often used by apparel retailers, housewares retailers, and others. This display must be carefully maintained because it may lead to product clutter and shoppers' returning items to the wrong place. Current technology enables retailers to use sliding, disconnecting, contracting/expanding, lightweight, attractive rack displays. A **case display** exhibits heavier, bulkier items than racks hold. Records, books, pre-packaged goods, and sweaters typically appear in case displays.

A **cut case** is an inexpensive display that leaves merchandise in the original carton. Supermarkets and discount stores frequently use cut cases, which do not create a warm atmosphere. Neither does a **dump bin**—a case that holds piles of sale clothing, marked-down books, or other products. Dump bins have open assortments of roughly handled items. Both cut cases and dump bins reduce display costs and project a low-price image.

Posters, signs, and cards can dress up all types of displays, including cut cases and dump bins. They provide information about product locations and stimulate customers to shop. A mobile, a hanging display with parts that move in response to air currents, serves the same purpose—but stands out more. Electronic displays are also widely used today. They can be interactive, be tailored to individual stores, provide product demonstrations, answer customer questions, and incorporate the latest in multimedia capabilities. These displays are much easier to reprogram than traditional displays are to remodel.

A NONSTORE-BASED RETAILING PERSPECTIVE

Interact with this demo E-store (http://sm.kemford.com/webstore/store) to experience the many components of online retailing.

Many atmospherics' principles apply to both store and nonstore retailers. However, there are also some distinctions. Let us look at the storefront, general interior, store layout, displays, and checkout counter from the vantage point of one type of direct marketer, the Web retailer.

Storefront

The storefront for a Web retailer is the home page. Thus, it is important that the home page:

- Prominently show the company name and indicate the positioning of the firm.
- Be inviting. A "virtual storefront" must encourage customers to enter.
- Make it easy to enter the store.
- Show the product lines carried.
- Use graphics as display windows and icons as access points.
- Have a distinctive look and feel.
- Include the retailer's E-mail address, mailing address, and phone number.
- Be highlighted at various search engines.

See Figure 18-11.

General Interior

As with store retailers, a Web retailer's general interior sets a shopping mood. Colors run the gamut from plain white backgrounds to stylish black backgrounds. Some firms use audio to generate shopper interest. "Fixtures" relate to how simple or elaborate the Web site looks. "Width of aisles" means how cluttered the site appears and the size of the text and images. The general interior also involves these elements:

- Instructions about how to use the site.
- Information about the company.
- Product icons.
- News items.
- The shopping cart (how orders are placed).
- A product search engine.
- Locations of physical stores (for multi-channel retailers).
- A shopper login for firms that use loyalty programs and track their customers.

Store Layout

A Web retailer's store layout has two components: the layout of each individual Web page and the links to move from page to page. Web retailers spend a lot of time planning the traffic flow for their stores. Online consumers want to shop efficiently, and they get impatient if the "store" is not laid out properly.

Some online firms use a gridiron approach, while others have more free-flowing Web pages and links. Web companies often have a directory on the home page that indicates product categories. The shopper clicks on an icon to enter the area of the site housing the category (department) of interest. Many retailers encourage customers to shop for any product from any section of the Web site by providing an interactive search engine. In that case, a person types in the product name or category and is automatically sent to the relevant Web page. Like physical stores, online retailers allocate more display space to popular product categories and brands, and give them a better position. On pages that require scrolling down, best-sellers usually appear at the top of the page and slower-sellers at the bottom.

Displays

Web retailers can display full product assortments or let shoppers choose from tailored assortments. This decision affects the open or cluttered appearance of a site, the level of choice, and possible shopper confusion. Online firms often use special themes, such as Valentine's Day. It is easy for them to show ensembles—and for shoppers to interactively mix and match to create their own ensembles. Through graphics and photos, a site can give the appearance of cut cases and dump bins for items on sale.

Checkout Counter

The checkout counter can be complicated for Web retailers: (1) Online shoppers tend to worry more about the security and privacy of purchase transactions than those who buy in a store. (2) Online shoppers often have to work harder to complete transactions. They must carefully enter the model number and quantity, and their shipping address, E-mail address, shipping preference, and credit card number. They may also be asked for their phone number, job title, and so on, because some retailers want to build their data bases. (3) Online shoppers may feel surprised by shipping and handling fees, if these are not revealed until they go to checkout.

Learn how Amazon.com (www.amazon.com) enables shoppers to use "1-Click Settings" for easy ordering.

To simplify matters, Amazon.com has a patented checkout process—a major competitive advantage. Amazon.com's "1-Click" program lets shoppers securely store their shipping address, preferred shipping method, and credit card information. Each purchase requires just one click to set up an order form.

Special Considerations

Let us examine two other issues: how to set up a proper Web site, and the advantages and disadvantages of Web atmospherics versus those of traditional stores.

New online retailers often have little experience with Web design or the fundamentals of store design and layout. These firms typically hire specialists to design their sites. When business grows, they may take Web design in-house. Here is a sampling of specialists that design online stores for small retailers: Bigstep.com (**www.bigstep.com**), Entrabase (**www.econgo.com**), Global Mall (**www.globalmall.com**), Storefront Development (**www.store-front.com**), Unisoft (**http://e-storefront.com**), and Yahoo! Store (**http://store.yahoo.com**). In this grouping, design and hosting costs are as low as $14.95 monthly.

Compared with physical stores, online stores have several advantages. A Web site:

- Has almost unlimited space to present product assortments, displays, and information.
- Can be tailored to the individual customer.
- Can be modified daily (or even hourly) to reflect changes in demand, new offerings from suppliers, and competitors' actions.
- Can promote cross-merchandising and impulse purchases with little shopper effort.
- Enables a shopper to enter and exit an online store in a matter of minutes.

Online stores also have potential disadvantages. A Web site:

- Can be slow for dialup shoppers. The situation worsens as more graphics and video clips are added.
- Can be too complex. How many clicks must a shopper make from the time he or she enters a site until a purchase is made?
- Cannot display the three-dimensional aspects of products as well as physical stores.
- Requires constant updating to reflect stockouts, new merchandise, and price changes.
- Is more likely to be exited without a purchase. It is easy to visit another Web site.

ENCOURAGING CUSTOMERS TO SPEND MORE TIME SHOPPING

Underhill's Envirosell Inc. (www.envirosell.com) is a leader in shopping behavior research.

Paco Underhill, the guru of retail anthropology, has a simple explanation for why consumers should be encouraged to spend more time in a store or at a Web site: "The amount of time a shopper spends in a store (shopping, not waiting in line) is perhaps the single most important factor in determining how much he or she will buy. In an electronics store that we studied, nonbuyers spent an average of 5 minutes and 6 seconds in the store, compared with the 9 minutes and 29 seconds buyers spent there. In a toy store, buyers averaged more than 17 minutes, compared with 10 minutes for nonbuyers. In some stores, buyers are there three or four times longer."[17] Our Web site (**www.prenhall.com/bermanevans**) has links to a number of research projects and video clips from Underhill's company Envirosell.

Among the tactics to persuade people to spend more time shopping are experiential merchandising, solutions selling, an enhanced shopping experience, retailer co-branding, and wish list programs.

The aim of **experiential merchandising** is to convert shopping from a passive activity into a more interactive one, by better engaging customers. See Figure 18-12. Retailers must meet this challenge: "When did shopping become a task instead of a pastime? Stores need to reverse the growing reluctance of shoppers to spend more time browsing there, and to counter the allure of E-shopping by providing an incentive to show up to shop."[18] Many firms are doing so:

> Retailers who are entertaining, such as Nike Town, where customers shop 45 minutes to one hour; REI, where they stay one to two hours; or Oshman's Sporting Goods, where customers shop at least 30 minutes, find longer stays mean bigger sales. "We call this 'experiential merchandising,' the art of providing merchandise in a creative environment that encourages customers to interact with store items and personnel," says Oshman's chief executive.[19]

> Bass Pro Shops is famous for its in-store outdoor-sport facilities, including trout ponds, waterfalls, archery and rifle ranges, and putting greens. The freestanding Bass Pro Shops flagship store in Missouri even has a barber shop where customer hair trimmings are made into "hair trigger" fishing lures. Barnes & Noble and Borders bookstore chains are both famous for book and poetry readings, signings, and presentations, along with comfy chairs and in-store cafés to keep customers reading.[20]

FIGURE 18-12

Making the Shopping Experience More Pleasant

Ikea understands the value of creating a pleasant shopping environment for customers. By taking a restaurant break, customers extend the length of their shopping visits.

Reprinted by permission of Goran Petkovic.

Hungry? Thirsty? Tired? Take a break in the Restaurant.

A full meal, a quick snack, a cup of coffee or a giant chocolate bar. Shopping can make you hungry, so stop by the Café to rest and recharge. On your way home, get some treats and Swedish specialties at the Swede Shop.

Solutions selling takes a customer-centered approach and presents "solutions" rather than "products." It goes a step beyond cross-merchandising. At holiday times, some retailers group gift items by price ("under $25, under $50, under $100, $100 and above") rather than by product category. This provides a solution for the shopper who has a budget to spend but a fuzzy idea of what to buy. Many supermarkets sell fully prepared, complete meals that just have to be heated and served. This solves the problem of "What's for dinner?" without requiring the consumer to shop for meal components.

An *enhanced shopping experience* means the retailer does everything possible to make the shopping trip pleasant—and to minimize annoyances. Given all of the retail choices facing consumers, a pleasing experience is a must: "A well-designed merchandising system might attract you, but what happens next? Don't you need to be engaged? Don't you need to know all of your options? Don't you need information, presented in the right way? And don't you want all of this in a matter of seconds?"[21]

See how retailers can create an enhanced shopping experience (http://merchandiseconcepts.com/frames/newsF.htm).

Retailers can provide an enhanced shopping experience by setting up wider aisles so people do not feel cramped, adding benches and chairs so those accompanying the main shopper can relax, using kiosks to stimulate impulse purchases and answer questions, having activities for children (such as Ikea's playroom), and opening more checkout counters. What 75-year-old shopping accessory is turning out to be one of the greatest enhancements of all? It is the humble shopping cart, as highlighted in Figure 18-13:

> As old-fashioned as they seem, carts are perfectly suited for the way people shop today. They're pressed for time and buy more in fewer trips. Mothers struggling to corral children love them. The growing ranks of senior citizens lean on carts for support and appreciate not having to carry their purchases. Carts empower an impulse. From cateogry killers such as Home Depot to mass merchandisers such as Target Stores and Kmart, stores are getting bigger, carrying a wider array of goods, and pushing prices lower. They need customers to stay longer, cruise through the whole store, and load up. Why would any sane retailer deny its customers a cart? Some, it seems, are just too classy to have stainless steel contraptions junking up their stores. "I'm not sure I could see someone buying a $2,000 suit and hanging it over a cart," says the director of stores for Saks Fifth Avenue.[22]

More firms participate in *co-branding*, whereby two or more well-known retailers situate under the same roof (or at one Web site) to share costs, stimulate consumers to visit more often, and attract people shopping together who have different preferences. Here are several examples: McDonald's in Wal-Mart stores, Starbucks in Barnes & Noble stores, joint Dunkin' Donuts and Baskin-Robbins outlets, and Amazon.com featuring Target and Toys "R" Us as partners at its Web site. As one expert noted, "You see co-branding partners everywhere. The most visible are highway travel centers that combine fast-food franchises, convenience stores, and gas stations. In

FIGURE 18-13

The Shopping Cart's Role in an Enhanced Shopping Experience

One look at this Kmart photo shows why the "humble" shopping cart can be such a powerful in-store marketing tool.

Reprinted by permission of Kmart.

one stop, you can fill up your belly, your car, and your pantry. In any city's commerce corridors, you're sure to find two-in-one shops: a dessert and coffee store, sandwich shop and car wash, tuxedo rental and dry cleaner, etc. If it's not there now, it will be."[23]

Another tactic in use by a growing number of retailers is the *wish list program.* It is a technique borrowed from Web retailers that enables customers to prepare shopping lists for gift items they'd like to receive from a particular store or shopping center:

> No more itchy wool sweaters, books you've already read, or ties from the boutique that doesn't take returns. But no more touching surprises that show how well the gift-giver knows you, either. This season, several store-based retailers have introduced holiday gift registries, usually called wish lists, on their Web sites. The tradition, long reserved for brides and grooms, apparently is now appropriate for baby showers, birthdays, and the biggest bonanza of all: Christmas. While the holiday gift registry is primarily an online phenomenon now—with an estimated 50 percent of online merchants offering a wish list service—Marshall Field's also is testing the concept for its stores, so that eventually you could print out a Christmas registry at an in-store kiosk, the way customers are in the habit of doing for weddings. J.C. Penney already includes holiday registries on its in-store kiosks and encourages shoppers to sign up at the store or online.[24]

COMMUNITY RELATIONS

The way that retailers interact with the communities around them can have a significant impact on their image—and performance. Their stature can be enhanced by engaging in such community-oriented actions as these:

- Making sure that stores are barrier-free for disabled shoppers.
- Showing a concern for the environment by recycling trash and cleaning streets.
- Supporting charities and noting that support at the company Web site.
- Participating in anti-drug programs.
- Employing area residents.
- Running special sales for senior citizens and other groups.
- Sponsoring Little League and other youth activities.
- Cooperating with neighborhood planning groups.
- Donating money and/or equipment to schools.
- Carefully checking IDs for purchases with age minimums.

Ethics in RETAILING   Is Slip-and-Fall Good Atmospherics or a Legal Nightmare?

According to a recent ruling by the Florida Supreme Court, if a shopper falls in a retail store, the burden of proof is now on the store to show that "reasonable care" was taken to keep its floors free of hazards. Before this ruling, the plaintiff had the responsibility to prove negligence on the part of the store. Two separate slip-and-fall cases in which shoppers allegedly slipped on a banana and were thereby injured formed the basis of the judgment.

Legal experts predict that this ruling will increase the slip-and-fall litigation in Florida, as well as other states. A spokesperson for the National Floor Safety Institute (**www.nfsi.org**) believes that "this is a huge wake-up call to retailers nationwide." Among business groups, the Florida Retail Federation (**www.frf.org**), which represents 6,000 independent

and chain retailers, has been particularly vocal. It says the court has created "a new profit center for the trial lawyer industry."

Among the measures that retailers will now have to implement to defend themselves against slip-and-fall claims are better training employees to carefully examine floor areas, inspecting the floor on a more regular basis, quickly responding to spills, and keeping a detailed log of inspections and cleanups.

Sources: "A Slippery Slope," *Chain Store Age* (March 2002), pp. 104, 106; and Meg Major, "Slipping Beneath a Heavy Burden: Until They Can Get Some Legislative Help, Florida Retailers Have a Lot More to Worry About When Customers File Slip-and-Fall Suits," *Progressive Grocer* (February 1, 2001), p. 10.

Each year, 7-Eleven makes more than $2 million in charitable contributions of cash and goods to support programs addressing issues such as literacy, reading, crime, and multicultural understanding. It also donates hundreds of thousands of pounds of food to local food banks throughout the United States. Wal-Mart, Kmart and Big Lots are among the numerous retailers participating in some type of anti-drug program. Borders, Barnes & Noble, Target Stores, and others participate in the national "Read-In" literacy program. Safeway and Giant Food are just two of the supermarket chains that give money or equipment to schools in their neighborhoods.

As with any aspect of retail strategy planning, community relations efforts can be undertaken by companies and organizations of any size and format:

The only mall in Morgan County (Decatur, Alabama), Colonial Mall is the area's biggest youth hangout. On Friday and Saturday nights, teenagers jam the aisles, blocking store access, and cruise the parking lot in smoke-filled cars with music blaring. Though most of the teens don't misbehave, they simply have nothing better to do. Most troubling is the unsupervised socializing, especially in the parking lot, because this is fertile ground for alcohol, drug, and tobacco use. The mall didn't want to keep losing adult shoppers on those nights, but more important, mall officials wondered how they could reduce the teens' risky behavior. So Colonial Mall created MochaTeen, a supervised coffeehouse just for teens. It's an inviting, ongoing opportunity for drug-free socializing with friends, something that reduces the risk of substance abuse. The mall teamed up with a division of the Mental Health Association in Morgan County and other local agencies and businesses to build, staff, and run MochaTeen. To give area teens a sense of ownership in the project, the mall also enlisted a number of them to help create, build, paint, and decorate the space, creating murals and painting a coffee motif on the floors and walls. MochaTeen operates from 6:00 P.M. to 9:00 P.M. on Friday and Saturday nights, with a menu of beverages at teen-friendly prices.[25]

Summary

1. *To show the importance of communicating with customers and examine the concept of retail image.* Customer communications are crucial for a store or nonstore retailer to position itself in customers' minds. Various physical and symbolic cues can be used.

Presenting the proper image—the way a firm is perceived by its customers and others—is an essential aspect of the retail strategy mix. The components of a firm's image are its target market characteristics, retail positioning and reputation, store location, merchandise assortment, price levels, physical facilities, shopping experiences, community service, advertising, public relations, personal selling, and sales promotion. A retail image requires a multistep, ongoing approach. For chains, there must be a consistent image among branches.

2. *To describe how a retail store image is related to the atmosphere it creates via its exterior, general interior, layout, and displays, and to look at the special case of nonstore atmospherics.* For a store retailer, atmosphere (atmospherics) is based on the physical attributes of the store utilized to develop an image; it is composed of the exterior, general interior, store layout, and displays. For a nonstore firm, the physical attributes of such elements as catalogs, vending machines, and Web sites affect the image.

The store exterior is comprised of the storefront, marquee, entrances, display windows, building height and size, visibility, uniqueness, surrounding stores and area, parking, and congestion. It sets a mood before a prospective customer even enters a store.

The general interior of a store encompasses its flooring, colors, lighting, scents and sounds, fixtures, wall textures, temperature, width of aisles, dressing facilities, vertical transportation, dead areas, personnel, self-service, merchandise, price displays, cash register placement, technology/modernization, and cleanliness. An upscale retailer's interior is far different from a discounter's—reflecting the image desired and the costs of doing business.

In laying out a store interior, six steps are necessary: (1) Floor space is allocated among selling, merchandise, personnel, and customers based on a firm's overall strategy. More firms now use planograms. (2) Product groupings are set, based on function, purchase motivation, market segment, and/or storability. (3) Traffic flows are planned, using a straight or curving pattern. (4) Space per product category is computed by a model stock approach or sales-productivity ratio. (5) Departments are located. (6) Individual products are arranged within departments.

Interior (point-of-purchase) displays provide information for consumers, add to the atmosphere, and have a promotional role. Interior display possibilities include assortment displays, theme displays, ensemble displays, rack and case displays, cut case and dump bin displays, posters, mobiles, and electronic displays.

For Web retailers, many principles of atmospherics are similar to those for store retailers. There are also key differences. The home page is the storefront. The general interior consists of site instructions, company information, product icons, the shopping cart, the product search engine, and other factors. The store layout includes individual Web pages, as well as the links that connect them. Displays can feature full or more selective assortments. Sales are lost if the checkout counter does not function well. There are specialists that help in Web site design. Compared to traditional stores, Web stores have various pros and cons.

3. *To discuss ways of encouraging customers to spend more time shopping.* To persuade consumers to devote more time with the retailer, these tactics are often employed: experiential merchandising, solutions selling, enhancing the shopping experience, retailer co-branding, and wish list programs.

4. *To consider the impact of community relations on a retailer's image.* Consumers react favorably to retailers involved in such activities as establishing stores that are barrier-free for persons with disabilities, supporting charities, and running special sales for senior citizens.

Key Terms

atmosphere (atmospherics) (p. 454)

visual merchandising (p. 454)

storefront (p. 455)

marquee (p. 455)

dead areas (p. 458)

planogram (p. 459)

functional product groupings (p. 460)

purchase motivation product groupings (p. 460)

market segment product groupings (p. 460)

storability product groupings (p. 460)

straight (gridiron) traffic flow (p. 460)

curving (free-flowing) traffic flow (p. 460)

model stock approach (p. 461)

sales-productivity ratio (p. 461)

point-of-purchase (POP) display (p. 463)

assortment display (p. 463)

theme-setting display (p. 463)

ensemble display (p. 463)

rack display (p. 463)

case display (p. 464)

cut case (p. 464)

dump bin (p. 464)

experiential merchandising (p. 467)

solutions selling (p. 468)

Questions for Discussion

1. Why is it sometimes difficult for a retailer to convey its image to consumers? Give an example of an on-campus retailer with a fuzzy image.

2. How could a realtor selling new homes project an upscale retail image? How could a realtor selling 20-year-old homes project such an image?

3. Define the concept of *atmosphere*. How does this differ from that of *visual merchandising*?

4. Which aspects of a store's exterior are controllable by a retailer? Which are uncontrollable?

5. What are meant by *selling*, *merchandise*, *personnel*, and *customer space*?

6. Present a planogram for a nearby clothing store.

7. Develop a purchase motivation product grouping for an online bookstore.

8. Which stores should *not* use a curving (free-flowing) layout? Explain your answer.

9. Visit the Web site of eToys (**www.etoys.com**) and then comment on its storefront, general interior, store layout, displays, and checkout counter.

10. How could a neighborhood hardware store engage in solutions selling?

11. Do you agree with upscale retailers' decision not to provide in-store shopping carts? What realistic alternatives would you suggest? Explain your answers.

12. Present a community relations program for a local bakery.

Web-Based Exercise

Visit the Web site of Godiva Chocolatier (**www.godiva.com**). How would you rate the atmospherics and ambience of this site? Why? Also comment on Godiva's use of multi-channel retailing.

Note: Stop by our Web site (**www.prenhall.com/bermanevans**) to experience a number of highly interactive, appealing Web exercises based on actual company demonstrations and sample materials related to retailing.

Chapter Endnotes

1. Various company sources.

2. Tony Lisanti, "Retailers, Too, Need to Build a Brand Image," *Drug Store News* (June 2002), p. 27.

3. See A. Coskun Samli, J. Patrick Kelly, and H. Keith Hunt, "Improving the Retail Performance by Contrasting Management- and Customer-Perceived Store Images: A

Diagnostic Tool for Corrective Action," *Journal of Business Research*, Vol. 43 (September 1998), pp. 27–38; Steve Burt and Jose Carralero-Encinas, "The Role of Store Image in Retail Internationalisation," *International Marketing Review*, Vol. 17 (Number 4-5, 2000), pp. 433–453; and Robert V. Kozinets, John F. Sherry, Jr., Benet DeBerry-Spence, Adam Duhachek, Krittinee Nuttavuhtisit, and Diana Storm, "Themed Flagship Brand Stores in the New Millennium: Theory, Practice, Prospects," *Journal of Retailing*, Vol. 78 (Spring 2002), pp. 17–29.

4. Marianne Wilson, "Redefining Retailtainment," *Chain Store Age* (March 2001), p. 71.

5. Edward O. Welles, "The Diva of Retail," *Inc.* (October 1999), p. 48.

6. Julie Clark, "Best Buy Shakes Up the Box," *Display & Design Ideas* (June 2002), p. 25.

7. "Turn the Page," *Chain Store Age* (November 1999), pp. 80, 84; and "Chapter 11," **www.chapter11books.com** (March 25, 2003).

8. Tom Lyons, "Visual Merchandising Today," **www.cahilldisplay. com/resources.htm** (March 20, 2001).

9. Marianne Wilson, "Toys "R" Us Takes Manhattan," *Chain Store Age* (December 2001), p. 80; and "About Toys "R" Us, Inc.," **http://www7.toysrus.com/about** (March 5, 2003).

10. "Types of Flooring Used," *Chain Store Age* (July 2002), p. 90.

11. "Retail Stores of the Year," *Chain Store Age* (February 2002), p. 4RSOY.

12. "Retail Entrepreneur of the Year: Donald F. Lamberti," *Chain Store Age* (December 1997), p. 54.

13. Miles Socha, "Display: Engaging All the Senses," *Women's Wear Daily* (May 24, 1999), p. 13.

14. Jean E. Palmieri, "Saks Out to Be Men's Best Friend in Chicago," *Daily News Record* (December 3, 1999), p. 24; and Calmetta Coleman, "Kohl's Retail Racetrack—Big Discount Chain Tempts Shoppers, Posts Big Gains with Unique Store Layout," *Wall Street Journal* (March 2001), p. B1.

15. Jack Hitt, "The Theory of Supermarkets," *New York Times Magazine* (March 10, 1996), pp. 56–61, 94, 98.

16. "The Point-of-Purchase Advertising Industry," **www.popai. com/about/pop_industry.html** (March 9, 2003).

17. Paco Underhill, *Why We Buy* (New York: Simon & Schuster, 1999). See also Paul Keegan, "The Architect of Happy Customers," *Business 2.0* (August 2002), pp. 85–87.

18. Laurie Joan Aron, "Looking For Shoppers? Make It Fun," **www.bizsites.com/locationstrategies/archives/prototype/ feature.html** (April 1, 2003).

19. Dick Silverman, "Making Shopping Fun Again," *Footwear News* (November 9, 1998), p. 31.

20. Aron, "Looking for Shoppers? Make It Fun."

21. "Category Merchandising: The Finishing Touch to Category Management," *Aftermarket Business* (October 1999), p. 63.

22. Joseph B. Cahill, "The Secret Weapon of Big Discounters: Lowly Shopping Cart," *Wall Street Journal* (November 24, 1999), pp. A1, A10. See also Renee DeGross, "Department Stores Try on New Ideas," *Atlanta Journal-Constitution* (August 18, 2002), p. F1.

23. Rhonda Bauer, "Co-Branding: Growing Family or Family Feud?" *Franchising World* (May–June 2002), pp. 22–23.

24. Allison Kaplan, "Retail Gift Registries Now Target Christmas," *Houston Chronicle* (December 12, 2001), p. 7.

25. "Meet Me at MochaTeen," *Shopping Centers Today* (November 2002), MAXI 2002 Awards Supplement, p. 6.

Chapter 19

PROMOTIONAL STRATEGY

Reprinted by permission of Mary Kay.

In her second year selling Stanley Home Products, Mary Ash was named "queen of sales." Unfortunately, a younger male associate was then promoted instead of her. So, in 1963, she quit in frustration. One month later, with a $5,000 investment, Ash started her own skin care business with just five items for sale. Today, Mary Kay Inc. (**www.marykay.com**) has annual sales in excess of $1.4 billion and is the largest direct seller of skin products in the United States, with an independent sales force of more than 900,000 consultants. All of its salespeople can order products on the Web and are eligible to get a personal Web site designed and maintained by the company for $50 per year.

Associates characterized Mary Kay Ash as a tough businesswoman who stressed the empowerment of women, as well as positive thinking. Many feel that she offered women career opportunities that were not otherwise available to them. *Fortune* magazine named Mary Kay as among the "Best Companies to Work for in America" and as one of the 10 best companies for women. Ash believed that "given the opportunity, encouragement, and awards, they will soar."

Ash is also remembered for her reward dinners where top sales consultants were (and still are) given jewelry and cars. The reward for the top independent sales consultants? The use of a new pink Cadillac. Currently, Mary Kay independent sales force members drive an estimated 1,500 Cadillacs and 7,000 assorted other General Motors cars—making the firm one of General Motors' largest commercial passenger-fleet customers.[1]

chapter objectives

1. To explore the scope of retail promotion
2. To study the elements of retail promotion: advertising, public relations, personal selling, and sales promotion
3. To discuss the strategic aspects of retail promotion: objectives, budgeting, the mix of forms, implementing the mix, and reviewing and revising the plan

OVERVIEW

Sephora, the European and U.S. beauty chain, has an integrated promotion plan—from its colorful Web site (www.sephora.com) to its stores.

Retail promotion includes any communication by a retailer that informs, persuades, and/or reminds the target market about any aspect of that firm. In the first part of this chapter, the elements of retail promotion are detailed. The second part centers on the strategic aspects of promotion.

Consider the effort that Wal-Mart puts into its promotion strategy. The firm does not rely on low prices alone. Here are excerpts from an interview with Wal-Mart's vice-president of marketing:

What role do marketing managers play in promotion? Ideas often originate with marketing managers, who also coordinate the marketing plan to be executed in stores. Our success is the result of this collaborative effort that typically begins with our marketing managers but sometimes with suppliers or buyers. Promotions are coordinated by marketing managers but managed at store level. We give stores a core program and challenge them to enhance it.

What has Wal-Mart learned about consumers and about marketing? We believe customers want to feel a connection with associates in their store, their community. Take our Good Works Program. We need to let our customers know our stores have charitable programs that benefit their hometowns. We also achieve that connection with retailtainment—our Oreo Stacking Contest, Grandparents Day, and live broadcasts of exclusive performances from Garth Brooks, Britney Spears, Faith Hill, and others.

What promotion has been Wal-Mart's best? Not every promotion has sold a lot, but that's all right. Most times it's about retailtainment—letting people know Wal-Mart is a place for socializing.[2]

In 2002, *DSN Retailing Today* called Wal-Mart "the retailer of the century" for the twentieth century.[3]

ELEMENTS OF THE RETAIL PROMOTIONAL MIX

This site (www.office.com/promoteyourbusiness.htm) is a good place to start learning about retail promotion.

Advertising, public relations, personal selling, and sales promotion are the elements of promotion. In this section, we discuss each in terms of goals, advantages and disadvantages, and basic forms. A good plan integrates these elements—based on the overall strategy. A movie theater concentrates on ads and sales promotion (food displays), while an upscale specialty store stresses personal selling. See Figure 19-1.

FIGURE 19-1

Communicating Through the Retail Promotion Mix

Toys "R" Us uses a full spectrum of promotion tools. It advertises a lot in newspapers and through freestanding circulars. It seeks out publicity when it opens new stores or engages in community activities. Employees are available to answer customer questions and to direct them to the proper section of the store (personal selling). Sales promotions are quite popular, such as the Disney back-to-school display shown here.

Reprinted by permission of Goran Petkovic.

Retailers devote significant sums to promotion. For example, a typical department store spends nearly 4 percent of sales on ads and 8 to 10 percent on personal selling and support services. And most department store chains invest heavily in sales promotions and use public relations to generate favorable publicity and reply to media information requests. We have more than a dozen links related to the retail promotion mix at our Web site (**www.prenhall.com/ bermanevans**).

ADVERTISING

Advertising is paid, nonpersonal communication transmitted through out-of-store mass media by an identified sponsor. Four aspects of this definition merit clarification: (1) Paid form—This distinguishes advertising from publicity (an element of public relations), for which no payment is made by the retailer for the time or space used to convey a message. (2) Nonpersonal presentation—A standard message is delivered to the entire audience, and it cannot be adapted to individual customers (except with the Web). (3) Out-of-store mass media—These include newspapers, radio, TV, the Web, and other mass channels, rather than personal contacts. In-store communications (such as displays) are considered sales promotion. (4) Identified sponsor—The sponsor's name is clearly divulged, unlike publicity. See Figure 19-2.

Sears has the highest annual dollar advertising expenditures among U.S. retailers—$1.5 billion, about 4 percent of its U.S. sales. Many firms, such as Federated Department Stores (5 percent), have higher advertising-to-sales ratios, despite lower dollar spending. On the other hand, Wal-Mart spends just 0.3 percent of sales on ads, relying more on word of mouth, in-store events, and everyday low prices.[4] Table 19-1 shows advertising ratios for several retailing categories.

Differences Between Retailer and Manufacturer Advertising Strategies

Retailers usually have more geographically concentrated target markets than manufacturers. This means they can adapt better to local needs, habits, and preferences. However, many retailers are unable to utilize national media as readily as manufacturers. Only the largest retail chains and franchises can advertise on national TV programs. An exception is direct marketing (including the World Wide Web) because trading areas for even small firms can be geographically dispersed.

Retail ads stress immediacy. Individual items are placed for sale and advertised over short time periods. Manufacturers are more often concerned with developing favorable attitudes.

FIGURE 19-2

Lands' End's Dominant Business: Mail-Order Retailing

Lands' End is one of the leading mail-order retailers in the world, with a large and growing global presence. It regularly advertises its catalogs in a number of media. And its catalogs are the firm's best form of advertising.

Photo by Barry Berman.

TABLE 19-1	Selected U.S. Advertising-to-Sales Ratios by Type of Retailer	
Type of Retailer	Advertising Dollars as Percentage of Sales Dollars[a]	Advertising Dollars as Percentage of Margin[b]
Apparel and accessories stores	6.6	16.7
Auto and home supply stores	1.0	2.3
Department stores	3.6	10.3
Drug and proprietary stores	0.8	3.2
Eating places	3.6	16.1
Family clothing stores	2.5	8.3
Furniture stores	4.6	13.8
Grocery stores	1.2	4.9
Hobby, toy, and game shops	1.2	3.8
Hotels and motels	1.8	8.1
Lumber and building materials	0.5	1.7
Mail-order firms	6.7	23.4
Movie theaters	2.5	10.0
Radio, TV, and consumer electronics stores	3.6	15.0
Shoe stores	2.6	7.9

[a]Advertising dollars as percentage of sales = Advertising expenditures/Net company sales
[b]Advertising dollars as percentage of margin = Advertising expenditures/(Net company sales − Cost of goods sold)

Source: Schonfeld & Associates, "2002 Advertising-to-Sales Ratios for the 200 Largest Ad Spending Industries," *Advertising Age* (September 16, 2002), p. 41. Reprinted by permission. Copyright Crain Communications Inc.

Many retailers stress prices in ads, whereas manufacturers usually emphasize key product attributes. In addition, retailers often display several different products in one ad, whereas manufacturers tend to minimize the number of products mentioned in a single ad.

Media rates tend to be lower for retailers. Because of this, and the desire of many manufacturers and wholesalers for wide distribution, the costs of retail advertising are sometimes shared by manufacturers or wholesalers and their retailers. Two or more retailers may also share costs. Both of these approaches entail **cooperative advertising**.

Objectives

Find our how to devise ads that work (www.inc.com/articles/marketing/pr/advertising).

A retailer would select one or more of these goals and base advertising efforts on it (them).

- Lifting short-term sales.
- Increasing customer traffic.
- Developing and/or reinforcing a retail image.
- Informing customers about goods and services and/or company attributes.
- Easing the job for sales personnel.
- Developing demand for private brands.

Advantages and Disadvantages

The major advantages of advertising are that:

- A large audience is attracted. And for print media, circulation is supplemented by the passing of a copy from one reader to another.

Store receipts were once considered to be "plain vanilla" because they included just basic information, such as the price for individual items, the total amount, and the store's name and address. Now, some receipts have taken on a new dimension as a combination of scorecard and mini-marketing program on a single sheet of paper.

Here are some interesting applications of receipts as promotional tools:

● Carter's Foods (**www.cartersfoods.com**), a 25-store Michigan grocery chain, uses the receipt as part of its customer loyalty program. The receipt shows current purchases, as well as the total points earned in the store's loyalty program. These points are redeemable for merchandise available through the S&H greenpoints.com Web site (**www.greenpoints.com**).

● To improve customer service, a Wal-Mart (**www.walmart. com**) store in Pennsylvania places the name of the store manager and his/her phone number on each receipt.
● Some retailers are using receipts as a means of building loyalty by printing targeted coupons, based on a customer's past buying behavior.
● Various retailers include barcodes so that the original purchase amount can be easily retrieved when a customer returns an item. This is particularly useful with gifts.

Source: Ken Clark, "Watch This Space," *Chain Store Age* (May 2001), pp. 74, 76.

● The costs per viewer, reader, or listener are low.
● A number of alternative media are available, so a retailer can match a medium to the target market.
● The retailer has control over message content, graphics, timing, and size (or length), so a standardized message in a chosen format can be delivered to the entire audience.
● In print media, a message can be studied and restudied by the target market.
● Editorial content (a TV show, a news story, and so on) often surrounds an ad. This may increase its credibility or the probability it will be read.
● Self-service or reduced-service operations are possible since a customer becomes aware of a retailer and its offerings before shopping.

The major disadvantages of advertising are that:

● Standardized messages lack flexibility (except for the Web and its interactive nature). They do not focus on the needs of individual customers.
● Some media require large investments. This may reduce the access of small firms.
● Media may reach large geographic areas, and for retailers, this may be wasteful. A small supermarket chain might find that only 40 percent of an audience resides in its trading area.
● Some media require a long lead time for placing ads. This reduces the ability to advertise fad items or to react to some current events themes.
● Some media have a high throwaway rate. Circulars may be discarded without being read.
● A 30-second TV commercial or small newspaper ad does not have many details.

The preceding are broad generalities. The pros and cons of specific media are covered next.

Media

Retailers can choose from the media highlighted in Table 19-2 and described here.

Papers (dailies, weeklies, and shoppers) represent the most preferred medium for retailers, having the advantages of market coverage, short lead time, reasonable costs, flexibility, longevity, graphics, and editorial association (ads near columns or articles). Disadvantages include the possible waste (circulation to a wider area than necessary), the competition among retailers, the black-and-white format, and the appeal to fewer senses than TV. To maintain a dominant position, many papers have

TABLE 19-2	Advertising Media Comparison Chart	
Medium	**Market Coverage**	**Particular Suitability**
Daily papers	Single community or entire metro area; local editions may be available.	All larger retailers.
Weekly papers	Single community usually; may be a metro area.	Retailers with a strictly local market.
Shopper papers	Most households in one community; chain shoppers can cover a metro area.	Neighborhood retailers and service businesses.
Phone directories	Geographic area or occupational field served by the directory.	All types of goods and service-oriented retailers.
Direct mail	Controlled by the retailer.	New and expanding firms, those using coupons or special offers, mail order.
Radio	Definable market area surrounding the station.	Retailers focusing on identifiable segments.
TV	Definable market area surrounding the station.	Retailers of goods and services with wide appeal.
World Wide Web	Global.	All types of goods and service-oriented retailers.
Transit	Urban or metro community served by transit system.	Retailers near transit routes, especially those appealing to commuters.
Outdoor	Entire metro area or single neighborhood.	Amusement and tourist-oriented retailers, well-known firms.
Local magazines	Entire metro area or region, zoned editions sometimes available.	Restaurants, entertainment-oriented firms, specialty shops, mail-order firms.
Flyers/circulars	Single neighborhood.	Restaurants, dry cleaners, service stations, and other neighborhood firms.

The Yellow Pages (www. yellowpages.com) remains a key medium for retailers.

revamped their graphics, and some run color ads. Free-distribution shopper papers ("penny savers"), with little news content and delivery to all households in a geographic area, are popular today.

In a White Pages telephone directory, retailers get free alphabetical listings along with all other phone subscribers, commercial and noncommercial. The major advantage of the White over the Yellow Pages is that people who know a retailer's name are not exposed to competitors' names. The major disadvantage, in contrast with the Yellow Pages, is the alphabetical rather than type-of-business listing. A customer unfamiliar with repair services will usually look in the Yellow Pages under "Repair" and choose a firm. In the Yellow Pages, firms pay for listings (and larger display ads, if desired) in their business category. Most retailers advertise in the Yellow Pages. The advantages include their widespread usage by people who are ready to shop and their long life (one year or more). The disadvantages are that retailer awareness may not be stimulated and there is a lengthy lead time for new ads.

With direct mail, retailers send catalogs or ads to customers by the mail or private delivery firms. Advantages are the targeted audience, tailored format, controlled costs, quick feedback, and tie-ins (including ads with bills). Among the disadvantages are the high throwaway rate ("junk mail"), poor image to some people, low response rate, and outdated mailing lists (addressees may have moved).

Radio is used by a variety of retailers. Advantages are the relatively low costs, its value as a medium for car drivers and riders, its ability to use segmentation, its rather short lead time, and its wide reach. Disadvantages include no visual impact, the need for repetition, the need for brevity, and waste. The use of radio by retailers has gone up in recent years.

TV ads, although increasing due to the rise of national and regional retailers, are far behind papers in retail promotion expenditures. Among the advantages are the dramatic effects of messages, the large market coverage, creativity, and program affiliation (for sponsors). Disadvantages include high minimum costs, audience waste, the need for brevity and repetition, and the limited availability of popular times for nonsponsors. Because cable TV is more focused than conventional stations, it appeals to local retailers.

From an advertising perspective, retailers use the Web to provide information to customers about store locations, to describe the products carried, to let people order catalogs, and so forth. Retailers have two opportunities to reach customers: advertising on search engines and other firms' Web sites; and communicating with customers at their own sites.

Transit advertising is used in areas with mass transit systems. Ads are displayed on buses and in trains and taxis. Advantages are the captive audience, mass market, high level of repetitiveness, and geographically defined market. Disadvantages are the ad clutter, distracted audience, lack of availability in small areas, restricted travel paths, and graffiti. Many retailers also advertise on their delivery trucks.

At the Outdoor Advertising Association Web site (www.oaaa.org), click on "creative library" and then type in "retail."

Outdoor (billboard) advertising is sometimes used by retailers. Posters and signs may be displayed in public places, on buildings, and alongside highways. Advantages are the large size of the ads, the frequency of exposure, the relatively low costs, and the assistance in directing new customers. Disadvantages include the clutter of ads, a distracted audience, the limited information, and some legislation banning outdoor ads. See Figure 19-3.

Magazine usage is growing for three reasons: the rise in retail chains, the creation of regional and local editions, and the use by nonstore firms. Advantages are the tailoring to specific markets, creative options, editorial associations, longevity of messages, and color. Disadvantages include the long lead time, less sense of consumer urgency, and waste.

Single-page (flyers) or multiple-page (circulars) ads are distributed in parking lots or to consumer homes. Advantages include the targeted audience, low costs, flexibility, and speed. Among the disadvantages are the level of throwaways, the poor image to some, and clutter. Flyers are good for smaller firms, while circulars are used by larger ones.

Types

Advertisements can be classified by content and payment method. See Figure 19-4.

Pioneer ads have awareness as a goal and offer information (usually on new firms or locations). *Competitive ads* have persuasion as a goal. *Reminder ads* are geared to loyal customers and stress the attributes that have made the retailers successful. *Institutional ads* strive to keep retailers names before the public without emphasizing the sale of goods or services. Public service messages are institutional.

Retailers may pay their own way or seek cooperative ventures in placing ads. Firms paying their own way have total control and incur all costs. With cooperative ventures, two or more parties share the costs and the decision making. About $15 billion is spent annually on U.S. cooperative advertising, most in vertical agreements. Newspapers are preferred over other media for cooperative ads related to retailing.

FIGURE 19-3
Billboard Advertising for Pedestrians and Motorists

Around the globe, billboard advertising is a rather inexpensive and attention-getting medium. Shown here is a Burger King billboard in Lugano, Switzerland.

Photo by Barry Berman.

FIGURE 19-4
Types of Advertising

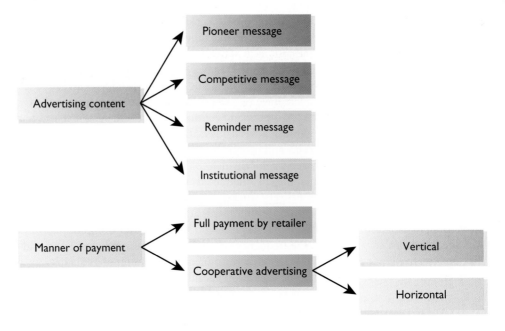

In a **vertical cooperative advertising agreement**, a manufacturer and a retailer or a whole-saler and a retailer share an ad.[5] Responsibilities are specified contractually, and retailers are typically not reimbursed until after ads run. Vertical cooperative advertising is subject to the Robinson-Patman Act; similar arrangements must be offered to all retailers on a proportional basis. Advantages to a retailer are the reduced ad costs, assistance in preparing ads, greater market coverage, and less planning time. Disadvantages to a retailer include less control, flexibility, and distinctiveness. Some retailers are concerned about the eligibility requirements to participate and the emphasis on the supplier's name in ads. In response, manufacturers and other suppliers are being more flexible and understanding.

Carol Wright (www.carolwright.com) is a leader in horizontal cooperative promotions.

With a **horizontal cooperative advertising agreement**, two or more retailers share an ad. A horizontal agreement is most often used by small noncompeting retailers (such as independent hardware stores), retailers in the same shopping center, and franchisees of a given firm. Advantages and disadvantages are similar to those in a vertical agreement. Two further benefits are the bargaining power of retailers in dealing with the media and the synergies of multiple retailers working together.

When planning a cooperative strategy, these questions should be considered:

- What ads qualify, in terms of merchandise and special requirements?
- What percentage of advertising is paid by each party?
- When can ads be run? In what media?
- Are there special provisions regarding message content?
- What documentation is required for reimbursement?
- How does each party benefit?
- Do cooperative ads obscure the image of individual retailers?

PUBLIC RELATIONS

At Wendy's (www.wendys.com), public relations means community relations. After entering the site, select "In the Community."

Public relations entails any communication that fosters a favorable image for the retailer among its publics (consumers, investors, government, channel members, employees, and the general public). It may be nonpersonal or personal, paid or nonpaid, and sponsor controlled or not controlled. **Publicity** is any nonpersonal form of public relations whereby messages are transmitted through mass media, the time or space provided by the media is not paid for, and there is no identified commercial sponsor.

The basic distinction between advertising and publicity is that publicity is nonpaid. As a result, publicity is not as readily controllable. A story on a store opening may not appear at all, appear after the fact, or not appear in the form desired. Yet, to consumers, publicity is often more credible and valuable than ads. Advertising and publicity (public relations) should complement each other. Many times, publicity should precede advertising.

Public relations can benefit both large and small retailers. While the former often spend a lot of money to publicize events such as the Macy's Thanksgiving Day Parade, small firms can creatively generate attention for themselves on a limited budget. They can feature book signings by authors, sponsor school sports teams, donate goods and services to charities, and so forth.

Objectives

Public relations seeks to accomplish one or more of these goals:

- Increase awareness of the retailer and its strategy mix.
- Maintain or improve the company image.
- Show the retailer as a contributor to the public's quality of life.
- Demonstrate innovativeness.
- Present a favorable message in a highly believable manner.
- Minimize total promotion costs.

Advantages and Disadvantages

The major advantages of public relations are that:

- An image can be presented or enhanced.
- A more credible source presents the message (such as a good restaurant review).
- There are no costs for the message's time or space.
- A mass audience is addressed.
- Carryover effects are possible (if a store is perceived as community-oriented, its value positioning is more apt to be perceived favorably).
- People pay more attention to news stories than to clearly identified ads.

The major disadvantages of public relations are that:

- Some retailers do not believe in spending any funds on image-related communication.
- There is little retailer control over a publicity message and its timing, placement, and coverage by a given medium.
- It may be more suitable for short-run, rather than long-run, planning.
- Although there are no media costs for publicity, there are costs for a public relations staff, planning activities, and the activities themselves (such as store openings).

Types

Public relations can be planned or unexpected and image enhancing or image detracting.

With planned public relations, a retailer outlines its activities in advance, strives to have media report on them, and anticipates certain coverage. Community services, such as donations and special sales; parades on holidays (such as the Macy's Thanksgiving Day Parade); the introduction of "hot" new goods and services; and a new store opening are activities a retailer hopes will gain media coverage. The release of quarterly sales figures and publication of the annual report are events a retailer knows will be covered.

When unexpected publicity occurs, the media report on a company without its having advance notice. TV and newspaper reporters may anonymously visit restaurants and other retailers to rate their performance and quality. A fire, an employee strike, or other newsworthy event may be mentioned in a story. Investigative reports on company practices may appear.

There is positive publicity when media reports are complimentary, with regard to the excellence of a retailer's practices, its community efforts, and so on. However, the media may also provide negative publicity. A story could describe a store opening in less than glowing terms, rap a firm's environmental record, or otherwise be critical. That is why public relations must be viewed as a component of the promotion mix, not as the whole mix.

FIGURE 19-5

J.C. Penney's Tips for Sales Associates

Source: J.C. Penney.

✓ Greet the customer. This sets the tone for the customer's visit to your department.
✓ Listen to customers to determine their needs.
✓ Know your merchandise. For example, describe the quality features of Penney's private brands.
✓ Know merchandise in related departments. This can increase sales and lessen a customer's shopping time.
✓ Learn to juggle several shoppers at once.
✓ Pack merchandise carefully. Ask if customer wants an item on a hanger to prevent creasing.
✓ Constantly work at keeping the department looking its best.
✓ Refer to the customer by his or her name; this can be gotten from the person's credit card.
✓ Stress Penney's "hassle-free" return policy.

PERSONAL SELLING

Selling tips are helpful (www.inc.com/guides/sales/directory.html).

Personal selling involves oral communication with one or more prospective customers for the purpose of making a sale. The level of personal selling used by a retailer depends on the image it wants to convey, the products sold, the amount of self-service, and the interest in long-term customer relationships—as well as customer expectations. Retail salespeople may work in a store, visit consumer homes or places of work, or engage in telemarketing.

J.C. Penney believes in training superior sales associates. Why? First, higher levels of selling are needed to reinforce its image as a fashion-oriented department store. Unlike self-service discounters, Penney wants its sales staff to give advice to customers. Second, Penney wants to stimulate cross-selling, whereby associates recommend related items to customers. Third, Penney wants sales associates to "save the sale," by suggesting that customers who return merchandise try different colors, styles, or quality. Four, Penney believes it can foster customer loyalty. Figure 19-5 highlights Penney's sales associate tips.

Objectives

The goals of personal selling are to:

- Persuade customers to buy (since they often enter a store after seeing an ad).
- Stimulate sales of impulse items or products related to customers' basic purchases.
- Complete customer transactions.
- Feed back information to company decision makers.
- Provide proper levels of customer service.
- Improve and maintain customer satisfaction.
- Create awareness of items also marketed through the Web, mail, and telemarketing.

Careers in RETAILING — A $4 Million Retail Sales Associate

Ann Wang is the top-selling salesperson for Escada (**www. escada.com**), a high-end women's clothing and accessories designer. She has a sales quota of about $4 million a year.

There are several secrets to Ann Wang's success:

- She feels that if she cannot gain potential customers' interest within the first 10 minutes, she will lose them. She always compliments customers on how well they look.
- She facilitates shopping for repeat customers by offering delivery and by traveling to customers' homes or offices with a tailor. Wang knows shopping is not a top priority.
- She sends her customers handwritten notes telling them about important fashion trends so that they can shop accordingly.

- Key customers receive evening bags, key chains, and perfume on occasions such as birthdays, anniversaries, and holidays.

In discussing her approach with newer sales associates, Wang cautions them not to sell clients aggressively—as many already have "black belts in shopping." Instead, they should make customers feel comfortable and entertain them: "I never consider selling as a job; I always consider it one great party. You talk to the customer, you gossip, you laugh."

Source: Stephanie Clifford, "Party Girl," *Business 2.0* (December 2001), p. 75.

Advantages and Disadvantages

The advantages of selling relate to its personal nature:

- A salesperson can adapt a message to the needs of the individual customer.
- A salesperson can be flexible in offering ways to address customer needs.
- The attention span of the customer is higher than with advertising.
- There is less waste; most people who walk into a store are potential customers.
- Customers respond more often to personal selling than to ads.
- Immediate feedback is provided.

The major disadvantages of personal selling are that:

- Only a limited number of customers can be handled at a given time.
- The costs of interacting with each customer can be high.
- Customers are not initially lured into a store through personal selling.
- Self-service may be discouraged.
- Some customers may view salespeople as unhelpful and as too aggressive.

Types

Most sales positions involve either order taking or order getting. An **order-taking salesperson** performs routine clerical and sales functions—setting up displays, stocking shelves, answering simple questions, and ringing up sales. This type of selling is most likely in stores that are strong in self-service but also have some personnel on the floor. An **order-getting salesperson** is actively involved with informing and persuading customers, and in closing sales. This is a true "sales" employee. Order getters usually sell higher-priced or complex items, such as real-estate, autos, and consumer electronics. They are more skilled and better paid than order takers. See Figure 19-6.

A manufacturer may sometimes help fund personal selling by providing **PMs** (promotional or push monies) for retail salespeople selling its brand. PMs are in addition to regular salesperson compensation. Many retailers dislike this practice because their salespeople may be less responsive to actual customer desires (if customers desire brands not yielding PMs).

Functions

Store sales personnel may be responsible for all or many of the tasks shown in Figure 19-7 and described next. Nonstore sales personnel may also have to generate customer leads (by knocking on doors in residential areas or calling people who are listed in a local phone directory).

FIGURE 19-6

Personal Selling: When Self-Service Isn't Appropriate

Despite the greater emphasis on self-service retailing, many products (such as Goodyear tires) lend themselves to a more personal approach, where salespeople can present information and answer questions.

Reprinted by permission of Goodyear.

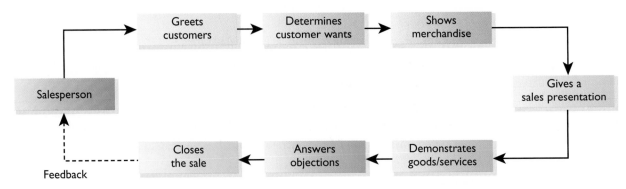

FIGURE 19-7
Typical Personal Selling Functions

On entering a store or a department in it (or being contacted at home), a salesperson greets the customer. Typical in-store greetings are: "Hello, may I help you?" "Hi, is there anything in particular you are looking for?" With any greeting, the salesperson seeks to put the customer at ease and build rapport.

The salesperson next finds out what the person wants: Is the person just looking, or is there a specific good or service in mind? For what purpose is the item to be used? Is there a price range in mind? What other information can the shopper provide to help the salesperson?

At this point, the salesperson may show merchandise. He or she selects the product most apt to satisfy the customer. The salesperson may try to trade up (discuss a more expensive version) or offer a substitute (if the retailer does not carry or is out of the requested item).

The salesperson now makes a sales presentation to motivate the customer to purchase. The **canned sales presentation** is a memorized, repetitive speech given to all customers interested in a particular item. It works best if shoppers require little assistance and sales force turnover is high. The **need-satisfaction approach** is based on the principle that each customer has different wants; thus, a sales presentation should be geared to the demands of the individual customer. It is being utilized more in retailing.

A demonstration can show the utility of an item and allow customer participation. Demonstrations are often used with stereos, autos, health clubs, and watches.

A customer may have questions, and the salesperson must address them properly. After all questions are answered, the salesperson tries to close the sale. This means getting the shopper to purchase. Typical closing lines are: "Will you take it with you or have it delivered?" "Cash or charge?" "Would you like this gift wrapped?"

For personal selling to work well, salespeople must be enthusiastic, knowledgeable, interested in customers, and good communicators. Figure 19-8 cites several ways that retail sales can be lost through poor personal selling and how to avoid these problems.[6]

SALES PROMOTION

SCA (www.scapromotions. com) offers numerous online sales promotions.

Sales promotion encompasses the paid communication activities other than advertising, public relations, and personal selling that stimulate consumer purchases and dealer effectiveness. It includes displays, contests, sweepstakes, coupons, frequent shopper programs, prizes, samples, demonstrations, referral gifts, and other limited-time selling efforts outside of the ordinary promotion routine. The value and complexity of sales promotion are clear from this commentary:

> Three of every four shoppers are open to new experiences as they browse the aisles of super-markets and search for bargains at drugstores and mass merchandisers. This means an opportunity to make a measurable impact when they're free of distractions and most receptive to new ideas. Some retailers must work harder to get shoppers' attention and use more displays and special signs. While shopping varies by store, there are exceptions based on the product. For shampoos and pain relievers bought at drugstores and mass merchandisers, more browsing takes place than at supermarkets. Shampoos and pain relievers need more intrusive promotion at supermarkets. In drug and discount stores, it's the food items that need to use them.[7]

FIGURE 19-8
Selected Reasons Why
Retail Sales Are Lost—
and How to Avoid Them

✗ *Poor qualification of the customer.* ✓ Obtain information from the customer so the sales presentation is properly tailored.
✗ *Salespersons not demonstrating the good or service.* ✓ Show the good or service in use so that benefits are visualized.
✗ *Failure to put feeling into the presentation.* ✓ Encourage salespeople to be sincere and consumer-oriented.
✗ *Poor knowledge.* ✓ Train salespeople to know the major advantages and disadvantages of the goods and services, as well as competitors', and be able to answer questions.
✗ *Arguing with a customer.* ✓ Avoid arguments in handling customer objections, even if the customer is wrong.
✗ *No suggestion selling.* ✓ Attempt to sell related items (such as service contracts, product supplies, and installation).
✗ *Giving up too early.* ✓ Try again if an attempt to close a sale is unsuccessful.
✗ *Inflexibility.* ✓ Be creative in offering alternative solutions to a customer's needs.
✗ *Poor follow-up.* ✓ Be sure that orders are correctly written, that deliveries arrive on time, and that customers are satisfied.

Objectives

Sales promotion goals include:

- Increasing short-term sales volume.
- Maintaining customer loyalty.
- Emphasizing novelty.
- Complementing other promotion tools.

Advantages and Disadvantages

The major advantages of sales promotion are that:

- It often has eye-catching appeal.
- Themes and tools can be distinctive.
- The consumer may receive something of value, such as coupons or free merchandise.
- It helps draw customer traffic and maintain loyalty to the retailer.
- Impulse purchases are increased.
- Customers can have fun, particularly with contests and demonstrations.

RETAILING Around the World — For Conoco's Customers, Smile Is a Real Gas

Conoco (**www.conoco.com**) operates over 500 Jet service stations throughout Great Britain. Its London advertising agency, Clark Hooper Momentum, recently won a first-place award in the "Best Activity Generating Brand Loyalty Category" for a major Conoco advertising campaign.

The campaign, dubbed "Smile," was tied to an electronic loyalty program that provides customers with points that can be accumulated for cash, air travel, or retail goods. Consumers can earn points by purchasing gasoline, auto service, or car washes. There is no limit to the number of points a shopper can accrue; consumers can also withdraw their points in multiples of 5 British pounds.

The program was designed for both family and group accounts. Family members can request multiple Smile cards and pool the earned points. Nonprofit organizations, such as schools, hospitals, and charities, can also sign up for group accounts. This enables them to benefit from the combined purchases of their members.

The campaign generated more than 250,000 Big Smile members. About 7,000 parents, teachers, and government officials are using Smile for school accounts, and about 3,500 office workers are saving for their companies. The Smile promotion generated a 29 percent increase in volume and the average consumer purchase increased by 20 percent.

Source: Amie Smith, "Gas Attack: Conoco's U.K. Loyalty Scheme Gives Consumers a Reason to Smile," *Promo* (April 2001), p. 112.

The major disadvantages of sales promotion are that:

- It may be hard to terminate certain promotions without adverse customer reactions.
- The retailer's image may be hurt if trite promotions are used.
- Frivolous selling points may be stressed rather than the retailer's product assortment, prices, customer services, and other factors.
- Many sales promotions have only short-term effects.
- It should be used mostly as a supplement to other promotional forms.

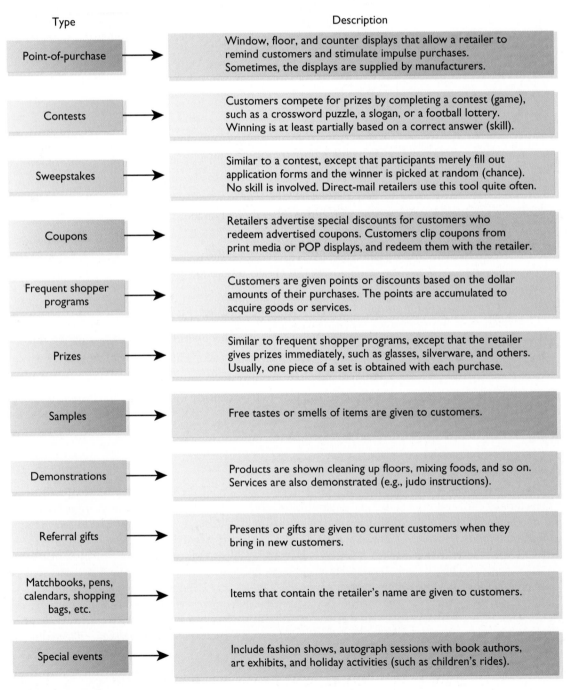

Type	Description
Point-of-purchase	Window, floor, and counter displays that allow a retailer to remind customers and stimulate impulse purchases. Sometimes, the displays are supplied by manufacturers.
Contests	Customers compete for prizes by completing a contest (game), such as a crossword puzzle, a slogan, or a football lottery. Winning is at least partially based on a correct answer (skill).
Sweepstakes	Similar to a contest, except that participants merely fill out application forms and the winner is picked at random (chance). No skill is involved. Direct-mail retailers use this tool quite often.
Coupons	Retailers advertise special discounts for customers who redeem advertised coupons. Customers clip coupons from print media or POP displays, and redeem them with the retailer.
Frequent shopper programs	Customers are given points or discounts based on the dollar amounts of their purchases. The points are accumulated to acquire goods or services.
Prizes	Similar to frequent shopper programs, except that the retailer gives prizes immediately, such as glasses, silverware, and others. Usually, one piece of a set is obtained with each purchase.
Samples	Free tastes or smells of items are given to customers.
Demonstrations	Products are shown cleaning up floors, mixing foods, and so on. Services are also demonstrated (e.g., judo instructions).
Referral gifts	Presents or gifts are given to current customers when they bring in new customers.
Matchbooks, pens, calendars, shopping bags, etc.	Items that contain the retailer's name are given to customers.
Special events	Include fashion shows, autograph sessions with book authors, art exhibits, and holiday activities (such as children's rides).

FIGURE 19-9
Types of Sales Promotion

Types

Visit the site of the leading point-of-purchase trade association (www.popai. org).

Figure 19-9 describes the major types of sales promotions. Each is explained here.

Point-of-purchase promotion consists of in-store displays designed to lift sales. From a promotional perspective, displays may remind customers, stimulate impulse behavior, facilitate self-service, and reduce retailer costs if manufacturers provide the displays. See Figure 19-10. These data show the extent of displays:

- U.S. manufacturers and retailers together annually spend $16 billion on in-store displays, with retailers using about two-thirds of all displays provided by manufacturers.
- Virtually all retailers have some type of POP display.
- Restaurants, apparel stores, music/video stores, toy stores, and sporting goods stores are among the retail categories with above-average use of in-store displays.
- Retailers spend one-sixth of their sales promotion budgets on displays.
- Display ads appear on shopping carts in most U.S. supermarkets. And thousands of supermarkets have electronic signs above their aisles promoting well-known brands.[8]

Contests and sweepstakes are similar; they seek to attract customers who participate in events with large prizes. A contest requires a customer to show some skill. A sweepstakes only requires participation, with the winner chosen at random. Disadvantages of contests and sweepstakes are their costs, customer reliance on these tools for continued patronage, the customer effort, and entries by nonshoppers. Together, U.S. manufacturers and retailers spend over $1 billion yearly on contests and sweepstakes.[9]

Each year, 250 billion coupons—discounts from regular selling prices—are distributed in the United States, with grocery products accounting for 75 percent of them. Consumers actually redeem 4 billion coupons annually, resulting in their saving $3 billion; retailers receive several hundred million dollars for processing coupon redemptions. Coupons are offered through freestanding inserts in Sunday papers and placements in daily papers, direct mail, Web sites, regular magazines, and Sunday newspaper magazines. They are also placed in or on packages and dispensed from in-store machines.[10]

Coupons have four key advantages: (1) In many cases, manufacturers pay to advertise and redeem them. (2) According to surveys, 99 percent of consumers redeem coupons at least once during the year. (3) They contribute to the consumer's perception that a retailer offers good value. (4) Ad effectiveness can be measured by counting redeemed coupons. Disadvantages

FIGURE 19-10

Using Point-of-Purchase Displays to Generate Consumer Enthusiasm

Albertson's sure knows how to create mouth-watering point-of-purchase displays to encourage impulse shopping and make its products look tasty.

Reprinted by permission of Retail Forward, Inc.

include the possible negative effect on the retailer's image, consumers shopping only if coupons are available, the low redemption rates, the clutter of coupons, retailer and consumer fraud, and handling costs. Less than 2 percent of coupons are redeemed by consumers due to the large number of them that are received.

Frequent shopper programs foster customer relationships by awarding discounts or prizes to people for continued patronage. In most programs, customers accumulate points (or their equivalent)—which are then redeemed for cash, discounts, or prizes. Some programs, such as Blockbuster Rewards (**www.blockbuster.com/bb/rewards**), are very successful:

(1) With every five paid movie or game rentals during each calendar month, you'll get one rental FREE. You can earn up to two of these FREE rentals per month! (2) Get one FREE Blockbuster Favorites movie rental every month. (3) Rent one paid movie or game every Monday through Wednesday, get one Blockbuster Favorites movie rental FREE. Includes holidays! *Automatic Tracking:* We'll keep track of your rentals and tell you when you've earned a free one. Simply pay the $9.95 annual fee at the checkout counter. There are no forms to fill out. You'll get two Blockbuster Rewards Membership Cards plus two key ring cards. Give the extra cards to household members authorized on your account—their paid rentals help you earn free rentals even faster!

All sorts of retailers participate in online loyalty programs, such as e-Rewards (www.e-rewards.com/redeem/body.asp).

The advantages of frequent shopper programs for retailers are the loyalty (customers amass points only by shopping at a specific firm or firms), the increased shopping, and the competitive edge for a retailer similar to others. However, some consumers feel these programs are not really free and would rather shop at lower-priced stores without loyalty programs, it may take a while for shoppers to gather enough points to earn meaningful gifts, and their profit margins may be smaller if retailers with these programs try to price competitively with firms without the programs.

Prizes are similar to frequent shopper programs, but they are given with each purchase. They are most effective when sets of glasses, silverware, dishes, place mats, and so on are distributed one at a time to shoppers. These encourage loyalty. Problems are the cost of prizes, the difficulty of termination, and the possible impact on image.

Free samples (food tastings) and demonstrations (cooking lessons) can complement personal selling. About $800 million is spent annually on sampling and demonstrations in U.S. stores—mostly at supermarkets, membership clubs, specialty stores, and department stores.[11] They are effective because customers become involved and impulse purchases increase. Loitering and costs may be problems.

Referral gifts may encourage existing customers to bring in new ones. Direct marketers, such as book and music clubs, often use this tool. It is a technique that has no important shortcomings and recognizes the value of friends in influencing purchases.

Matchbooks, pens, calendars, and shopping bags may be given to customers. They differ from prizes since they promote retailers' names. These items should be used as supplements. The advantage is longevity. There is no real disadvantage.

Retailers may use special events to generate consumer enthusiasm. Events can range from store grand openings to fashion shows. When Toys "R" Us opens stores, it has giveaways and children's activities, and there is a guest appearance by the firm's Geoffrey the giraffe (a human in a costume). Generally, in planning a special event, the potential increase in consumer awareness and store traffic needs to be weighed against that event's costs.

PLANNING A RETAIL PROMOTIONAL STRATEGY

A systematic approach to promotional planning is shown in Figure 19-11 and explained next. Our Web site (**www.prenhall.com/bermanevans**) has several links related to promotional strategy, including word of mouth.

DETERMINING PROMOTIONAL OBJECTIVES

A retailer's broad promotional goals may be drawn from this list:

- Increase sales.
- Stimulate impulse and reminder buying.

FIGURE 19-11
Planning a Retail
Promotional Strategy

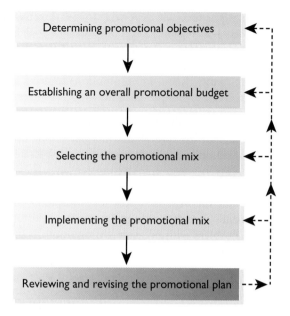

- Raise customer traffic.
- Get leads for sales personnel.
- Present and reinforce the retailer's image.
- Inform customers about goods and services.
- Popularize new stores and Web sites.
- Capitalize on manufacturer support.
- Enhance customer relations.
- Maintain customer loyalty.
- Have consumers pass along positive information to friends and others.

In developing a promotional strategy, the firm must determine which of these are most important. See Figure 19-12.

FIGURE 19-12
The Ikea Playroom

Since one of its goals is to attract parents with young children, Ikea actively promotes its glass-enclosed playrooms. Parents can shop in an undistracted manner while their children have a great time playing.

Reprinted by permission of Retail Forward, Inc.

It is vital to state goals as precisely as possible to give direction to the choice of promotional types, media, and messages. Increasing sales is not a specific goal. However, increasing sales by 10 percent is directional, quantitative, and measurable. With that goal, a firm could prepare a thorough promotional plan and evaluate its success. McDonald's, which has won numerous awards for creative advertising, wants its ads and promotions to drive sales, introduce new products, push special offers, and create an emotional bond with customers:

> McDonald's new national ad campaign will revolve around a national "dollar value menu" that will eventually include the Big 'N' Tasty burger, the McChicken sandwich, and special sizes of fries, soda, salad, and various desserts. It may not strike anyone as anything particularly new, but it will transmit a unified, consistent message about a bargain. By moving away from sporadic deep discounting in favor of a permanent two-tier menu that keeps signature products like the Big Mac at the top, Mickey D's is following the model that Wendy's has successfully used to lure in penny-pinching customers and then sell them on costlier items. The problem with occasional promotions is that "you train customers to come only when there's a blue-light special."[12]

See what leads to good WOM (www.geocities. com/wallstreet/6246/ tactics1.html).

Perhaps the most vital long-term promotion goal for any retailer is to gain positive **word of mouth (WOM)**, which occurs when one consumer talks to others.[13] If a satisfied customer refers friends to a retailer, this can build into a chain of customers. No retailer can succeed if it receives extensive negative WOM (such as "The hotel advertised that everything was included in the price. Yet it cost me $50 to play golf"). Negative WOM will cause a firm to lose substantial business.

Service retailers, even more than goods-oriented retailers, must have positive word of mouth to attract and retain customers. They credit WOM referrals with generating most new customers/clients/patients. As consultant Michael Cafferky says (**www.geocities.com/WallStreet/6246/main.html**): "We are bombarded with thousands of advertising messages every day. So many advertising messages rush at us daily, we cut through all that hype to get to the essence of the messages we need. Word of mouth (which usually we trust) allowed us to sort it out."

ESTABLISHING AN OVERALL PROMOTIONAL BUDGET

There are five main procedures for setting the size of a retail promotional budget. Retailers should weigh the strengths and weaknesses of each technique in relation to their own requirements and constraints. To assist firms in their efforts, there is now computer software available.

With the **all-you-can-afford method**, a retailer first allots funds for each element of the retail strategy mix except promotion. The remaining funds go to promotion. This is the weakest technique. Its shortcomings are that little emphasis is placed on promotion as a strategic variable; expenditures are not linked to goals; and if little or no funds are left over, the promotion budget is too small or nonexistent. The method is used predominantly by small, conservative retailers.

The **incremental method** relies on prior promotion budgets to allocate funds. A percentage is either added to or subtracted from one year's budget to determine the next year's. If this year's promotion budget is $100,000, next year's would be calculated by adjusting that amount. A 10 percent rise means that next year's budget would be $110,000. This technique is useful for a small retailer. It provides a reference point. The budget is adjusted based on the firm's feelings about past successes and future trends. It is easy to apply. Yet, the budget is rarely tied to specific goals. "Gut feelings" are used.

With the **competitive parity method**, a retailer's promotion budget is raised or lowered based on competitors' actions. If the leading competitor raises its budget by 8 percent, other retailers in the area may follow. This method is useful for small and large firms, uses a comparison point, and is market-oriented and conservative. It is also an imitative approach, takes for granted that tough-to-get competitive data are available, and assumes that competitors are similar (as to years in business, size, target market, location, merchandise, prices, and so on). That last point is critical because competitors often need very different promotional budgets.

In the **percentage-of-sales method**, a retailer ties its promotion budget to revenue. A promotion-to-sales ratio is developed. Then, during succeeding years, this ratio remains constant. A firm could set promotion costs at 10 percent of sales. Since this year's sales are $600,000, there is a $60,000 promotion budget. If next year's sales are estimated at $720,000, a $72,000 budget is planned. This process uses sales as a base, is adaptable, and correlates promotion and sales. Nonetheless, there is no relation to goals (for an established firm, sales growth may not require increased promotion); promotion is not used to lead sales; and promotion drops during poor periods, when increases might be helpful. This technique provides excess financing in times of high sales and too few funds in periods of low sales.

Under the **objective-and-task method**, a retailer clearly defines its promotion goals and prepares a budget to satisfy them. A goal might be to have 70 percent of the people in its trading area know a retailer's name by the end of a one-month promotion campaign, up from 50 percent. To do so, it determines the tasks and costs required to achieve that goal:

Objective	Task	Cost
1. Gain awareness of working women.	Use eight 1/4-page ads in four successive Sunday editions of two area papers.	$20,000
2. Gain awareness of motorists.	Use 20 30-second radio ads during prime time on local radio stations.	12,000
3. Gain awareness of pedestrians.	Give away 5,000 shopping bags.	10,000
	Total budget	$42,000

The objective-and-task method is the best budgeting technique. Goals are clear, spending relates to goal-oriented tasks, and performance can be assessed. It can be time-consuming and complex to set goals and specific tasks, especially for small retailers.

SELECTING THE PROMOTIONAL MIX

After a budget is set, the promotional mix is determined: the retailer's combination of advertising, public relations, personal selling, and sales promotion. A firm with a limited budget may rely on store displays, flyers, targeted direct mail, and publicity to generate customer traffic, while one with a big budget may rely more on newspaper and TV ads. Retailers often use an assortment of promotional forms to reinforce each other. A melding of media ads and POP displays may be more effective than either form alone. See Figure 19-13.

The promotional mix is affected by the type of retailer involved. In supermarkets, sampling, frequent shopper promotions, theme sales, and bonus coupons are among the techniques used most. At upscale stores, there is more attention to personal selling and less to advertising and sales promotion as compared with discounters. Table 19-3 shows a number of small-retailer promotional mixes.

Freestanding inserts (www.fsicouncil.org) offer retailers many advertising and sales promotion possibilities.

IEE's color LCD dual input display, **ShopVue®**, is revolutionizing the way retail establishments present sales and advertising information to customers. The display will run advertising spots when not displaying a sales transaction. Retailers have the opportunity to sell advertising to their suppliers and thus the displays can become a source of revenue.

In reacting to a retailer's communication efforts, consumers often go through a sequence of steps known as the **hierarchy of effects**, which takes them from awareness to knowledge to liking to preference to conviction to purchase. Different promotional mixes are needed in each step. Ads and public relations are best to develop awareness; personal selling and sales promotion are best in changing attitudes and stimulating desires. This is especially true for expensive, complex goods and services. See Figure 19-14.

TABLE 19-3	The Promotional Mixes of Selected Small Retailers			
Type of Retailer	Favorite Media	Personal Selling Emphasis	Special Considerations	Promotional Opportunities
Apparel store	Weekly papers; direct mail; radio; Yellow Pages; exterior signs.	High.	Cooperative ads available from manufacturers.	Fashion shows for community groups and charities.
Auto supply store	Local papers; Yellow Pages; POP displays; exterior signs.	Moderate.	Cooperative ads available from manufacturers.	Direct mail.
Bookstore	Local papers; shoppers; Yellow Pages; radio; exterior signs.	Moderate.	Cooperative ads available from publishers.	Author-signing events.
Coin-operated laundry	Yellow Pages; flyers in area; local direct mail; exterior signs.	None.	None.	Coupons in newspaper ads.
Gift store	Weekly papers; Yellow Pages; radio; direct mail; exterior signs.	Moderate.	None.	Special events; Web ads.
Hair grooming/ beauty salon	Yellow Pages; mentions in feature articles; exterior signs.	Moderate.	Word-of-mouth communication key.	Participation in fashion shows; free beauty clinics.
Health food store	Local papers; shoppers; POP displays; exterior signs.	Moderate.	None.	Display windows.
Restaurant	Newspapers; radio; Yellow Pages; outdoor; entertainment guides; exterior signs.	Moderate.	Word-of-mouth communication key.	Write-ups in critics' columns; special events.

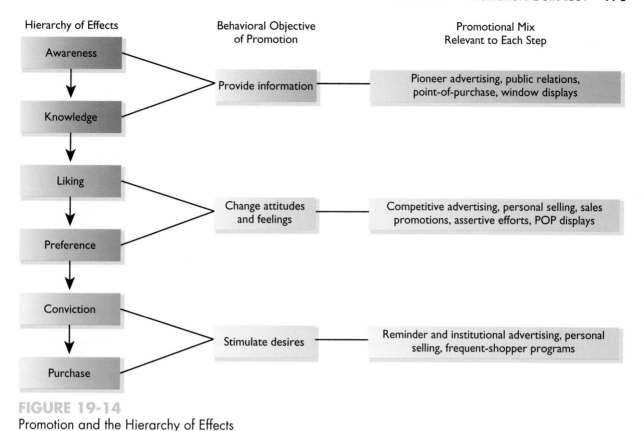

FIGURE 19-14
Promotion and the Hierarchy of Effects

IMPLEMENTING THE PROMOTIONAL MIX

The implementation of a promotional mix involves choosing which specific media to use (such as Newspaper A and Newspaper B), timing, message content, the makeup of the sales force, specific sales promotion tools, and the responsibility for coordination. Consider this example:

> When one bank chain decided to open branches in supermarkets, its employees were turned into active promotion partners. Shoppers never knew when a bank employee would pop up in the meat department or dairy section to dispense brochures on loans, checking accounts, or certificates of deposit. With 30,000 monthly shoppers, grocery aisles provided a captive audience for the bank. Its staffers used juice and soup cans as props. They donned supermarket aprons and gave out flowers or vegetable seeds to show the "home-grown" quality of home loans. In-store efforts were supported with a jungle safari instant-win game tied to the Walt Disney Animal Kingdom park.[14]

Media Decisions

Is 3D shopping on the Web ahead of its time or on target (www. 3dshopper.net)?

The choice of specific media is based on their overall costs, efficiency (the cost to reach the target market), lead time, and editorial content. Overall costs are important since heavy use of one expensive medium may preclude a balanced promotional mix, and a firm may not be able to repeat a message in a costly medium.

A medium's efficiency relates to the cost of reaching a given number of target customers. Media rates are often expressed in terms of cost per 1,000 readers, watchers, or listeners:

$$\text{Cost per thousand} = \frac{\text{Cost per message} \times 1,000}{\text{Circulation}}$$

A newspaper with a circulation of 400,000 and a one-page advertising rate of $10,000 has a per-page cost per thousand of $25.

In this computation, total circulation was used to measure efficiency. Yet, because a retailer usually appeals to a limited target market, only the relevant portion of circulation should be considered. If 70 percent of readers are target customers for a particular firm (and the other 30 percent live outside the trading area), the real cost per thousand is

$$\text{Cost per thousand} \atop \text{(target market)} = \frac{\text{Cost per page} \times 1,000}{\text{Circulation} \times \dfrac{\text{Target market}}{\text{Circulation}}}$$

$$= \frac{\$10,000 \times 1,000}{400,000 \times 0.70} = \$35.71$$

Different media require different lead time. A newspaper ad can be placed shortly before publication, whereas a magazine ad sometimes must be placed months in advance. In addition, the retailer must decide what kind of editorial content it wants near ads (such as a sports story or a personal care column).

Media decisions are not simple. Despite spending billions of dollars on TV and radio commercials, banner ads at search engines, and other media, many Web retailers have found that the most valuable medium for them is E-mail. It is fast, inexpensive, and targeted. Consider the following.

To generate greater *awareness* of Web retailers, costly advertising may be necessary in today's competitive and cluttered landscape: "E-Trade has a new name. Well, almost. Starting with two glitzy, multimillion-dollar ads during the Super Bowl, the firm unveiled its new moniker: E-Trade Financial. The advertising blitz continued with full-page newspaper ads in papers across the country."[15] Once customers have visited a Web site, E-mail can help *sustain relationships*: "Many firms are on a first-name basis with their opt-in E-mail customers (those who choose to receive E-mail). When they send out E-mail, they address their customers by name. But personalization can go much further. One customer of a gifts marketer may prefer to receive information only about jewelry, while another may wish to receive E-mails about novelty products such as singing fish. A survey by the E-tailing Group indicated that 22 percent of online marketers allow customers to choose E-mail by product category or interest."[16]

Timing of the Promotional Mix

Reach refers to the number of distinct people exposed to a retailer's promotion efforts in a specific period. **Frequency** is the average number of times each person reached is exposed to a retailer's promotion efforts in a specific period. A retailer can advertise extensively or intensively. Extensive media coverage often means ads reach many people but with relatively low frequency. Intensive media coverage generally means ads are placed in selected media and repeated frequently. Repetition is important, particularly for a retailer seeking to develop an image or sell new goods or services.

Decisions are needed about how to address peak selling seasons and whether to mass or distribute efforts. When peak seasons occur, all elements of the promotional mix are usually utilized; in slow periods, promotional efforts are typically reduced. A **massed promotion effort** is used by retailers, such as toy retailers, that promote seasonally. A **distributed promotion effort** is used by retailers, such as fast-food restaurants, that promote throughout the year. Although they are not affected by seasonality in the same way as other retailers, massed advertising is practiced by supermarkets, many of which use Wednesday for weekly newspaper ads. This takes advantage of the fact that a high proportion of their consumers do their major shopping trip on Thursday, Friday, or Saturday.

Sales force size can vary by time (morning versus evening), day (weekdays versus weekends), and month (December versus January). Sales promotions also vary in their timing. Store openings and holidays are especially good times for sales promotions (and public relations).

Content of Messages

The CarMax message: "Car Buying the Way It *Should* Be" is clear and information packed (www.carmax. com/CompanyInfo/ compinfo.htm).

Whether written or spoken, personally or impersonally delivered, message content is important. Advertising themes, wording, headlines, the use of color, size, layout, and placement must be selected. Publicity releases must be written. In personal selling, the greeting, sales presentation, demonstration, and closing need to be applied. With sales promotion, the firm's message must be composed and placed on the promotional device.

To a large extent, the characteristics of the promotional form influence the message. A shopping bag often contains no more than a retailer's name, a billboard (seen at 55 miles per hour) is good for visual effect but can hold only limited information, and a salesperson may be able to hold a customer's attention for a while. Some shopping centers use a glossy magazine to communicate a community-oriented image, introduce new stores to consumers, and promote the goods and services carried at stores in the center. Cluttered ads displaying many products suggest a discounter's orientation, while fine pencil drawings and selective product displays suggest a specialty store focus.

Some retailers use comparative advertising to contrast their offerings with competitors'. These ads help position a retailer relative to competitors, increase awareness of the firm, maximize the efficiency of a limited budget, and offer credibility. Yet, they provide visibility for competitors, may confuse people, and may lead to legal action. Fast-food and off-price retailers are among those using comparative ads.

Makeup of Sales Force

Sales personnel qualifications must be detailed, and these personnel must be recruited, selected, trained, compensated, supervised, and monitored. Personnel should also be classified as order takers or order getters and assigned to the appropriate departments.

Sales Promotion Tools

Specific sales promotion tools must be chosen from among those cited in Figure 19-9. The combination of tools depends on short-term goals and the other aspects of the promotion mix. If possible, cooperative ventures should be sought. Tools inconsistent with the firm's image should never be used; and retailers should recognize the types of promotions that customers really want: "Store promotions are a way of life. Indeed, an intensive promotional activity allows the store to maintain/increase its sales by achieving a higher penetration rate in the market area, an increase in the frequency of visits, and/or an increase in the average amount spent in a store. Moreover, store-level promotions help reinforce a low-price positioning, a key to performance."[17]

Responsibility for Coordination

Regardless of the retailer's size or format, someone must be responsible for the promotion function. Larger retailers often assign this job to a vice-president, who oversees display personnel, works with the firm's ad agency, supervises the firm's advertising department (if there is one), and supplies branch outlets with POP materials. In a large retail setting, personal selling is usually under the jurisdiction of the store manager. For a promotional strategy to succeed, its components have to be coordinated with other retail mix elements. Sales personnel must be informed of special sales and know product attributes; featured items must be received, marked, and displayed; and accounting entries must be made. Often, a shopping center or a shopping district runs theme promotions, such as "Back to School." In those instances, someone must coordinate the activities of all participating retailers.

REVIEWING AND REVISING THE PROMOTIONAL PLAN

An analysis of the success of a promotional plan depends on its objectives. Revisions should be made if pre-set goals are not achieved. Here are some ways to test the effectiveness of a promotional effort:

Examples of Retail Promotion Goals	Approaches for Evaluating Promotion Effectiveness
Inform current customers about new credit plans; acquaint potential customers with new offerings.	Study company and product awareness before and after promotion; evaluate size of audience.
Develop and reinforce a particular image; maintain customer loyalty.	Study image through surveys before and after public relations and other promotion efforts.
Increase customer traffic; get leads for salespeople; increase revenues above last year's; reduce customer returns from prior year's.	Evaluate sales performance and the number of inquiries; study customer intentions to buy before and after promotion; study customer trading areas and average purchases; review coupon redemption.

NET-ADS (www.net-ads. com/articles/advertising) presents a lot of information on the performance of Web advertising.

Although it may at times be tough to assess promotion efforts (for instance, increased revenues might be due to several factors, not just promotion), it is crucial for retailers to systematically study and adapt their promotional mixes. Wal-Mart provides suppliers with store-by-store data and sets up-front goals for cooperative promotion programs. Actual sales are then compared against the goals. Lowe's, the home center chain, applies computerized testing to review thousands of different ideas affecting the design of circulars and media mix options. And consider this:

A few food retailers are beginning to venture into new territory with the availability of predictive software that can produce dramatic results for targeted promotions. At the Paw Paw Shopping Center in Michigan, a new generation of predictive software from New York-based AdPilot is helping the retailer better target its customers. The program uses complex algorithms to generate queries without user intervention, uncovering buying patterns and relationships not easily discernible. "When we were generating our own queries, we would look at how often and last purchased." By looking outside of these historical parameters, AdPilot is able to find potential customers in those shoppers (or nonusers), who have never even purchased in a specific category before.[18]

Summary

1. *To explore the scope of retail promotion.* Any communication by a retailer that informs, persuades, and/or reminds the target market about any aspect of the retailer through ads, public relations, personal selling, and sales promotion is retail promotion.

2. *To study the elements of retail promotion.* Advertising involves paid, nonpersonal communication. It has a large audience, low costs per person, many alternative media, and other factors. It also involves message inflexibility, high absolute costs, and a wasted portion of the audience. Key advertising media are papers, phone directories, direct mail, radio, TV, the Web, transit, outdoor, magazines, and flyers/circulars. Especially useful are cooperative ads, in which a retailer shares costs and messages with manufacturers, wholesalers, or other retailers.

Public relations includes all communications fostering a favorable image. It may be nonpersonal or personal, paid or nonpaid, and sponsor controlled or not controlled. Publicity is the nonpersonal, nonpaid form of public relations. Public relations creates awareness, enhances the image, involves credible sources, and has no message costs. It also has little control over messages, is short term, and can entail nonmedia costs. Publicity can be expected or unexpected and positive or negative.

Personal selling uses oral communication with one or more potential customers and is critical for persuasion and in closing sales. It is adaptable, flexible, and provides immediate feedback. The audience is small, per-customer costs are high, and shoppers are not lured into the store. Order-taking and/or order-getting salespeople can be employed. Functions include greeting the customer, determining wants, showing merchandise, making a sales presentation, demonstrating products, answering objections, and closing the sale.

Sales promotion comprises the paid communication activities other than advertising, public relations, and personal selling. It may be eye-catching, unique, and valuable to the customer. It also may be hard to end, have a negative effect on image, and rely on frivolous selling points. Tools include POP displays, contests and sweepstakes, coupons, frequent shopper programs, prizes, samples, demonstrations, referral gifts, matchbooks, pens, calendars, shopping bags, and special events.

3. *To discuss the strategic aspects of retail promotion.* There are five steps in a promotion strategy: (1) Goals are stated in specific and measurable terms. Positive word of mouth (WOM) is an important long-term goal. (2) An overall promotion budget is set on the basis of one of these techniques: all you can afford, incremental, competitive parity, percentage of sales, and objective and task. (3) The promotional mix is outlined, based on the budget, the type of retailing, the coverage of the media, and the hierarchy of effects. (4) The promotional mix is enacted. Included are decisions involving specific media, promotional timing, message content, sales force composition, sales promotion tools, and the responsibility for coordination. (5) The retailer systematically reviews and adjusts the promotional plan, consistent with pre-set goals.

Key Terms

retail promotion (p. 474)

advertising (p. 475)

cooperative advertising (p. 476)

vertical cooperative advertising agreement (p. 480)

horizontal cooperative advertising agreement (p. 480)

public relations (p. 480)

publicity (p. 480)

personal selling (p. 482)

order-taking salesperson (p. 483)

order-getting salesperson (p. 483)

PMs (p. 483)

canned sales presentation (p. 484)

need-satisfaction approach (p. 484)

sales promotion (p. 484)   *competitive parity method (p. 490)*   *reach (p. 494)*

word of mouth (WOM) (p. 490)   *percentage-of-sales method (p. 491)*   *frequency (p. 494)*

all-you-can-afford method (p. 490)   *objective-and-task method (p. 491)*   *massed promotion effort (p. 494)*

incremental method (p. 490)   *hierarchy of effects (p. 492)*   *distributed promotion effort (p. 494)*

Questions for Discussion

1. How would an advertising plan for a Web retailer differ from that for a bricks-and-mortar chain?

2. How do manufacturer and retailer cooperative advertising goals overlap? How do they differ?

3. How may a local restaurant try to generate positive publicity?

4. Are there any retailers that should *not* use personal selling? Explain your answer.

5. Are there any retailers that should *not* use sales promotion? Explain your answer.

6. How can advertising, public relations, personal selling, and sales promotion complement each other for a retailer?

7. What are the pros and cons of coupons?

8. Develop sales promotions for each of the following:

a. A nearby regional shopping center.

b. A new dry cleaner.

c. A pharmacy offering free delivery for the first time.

9. Which method of promotional budgeting should a small retailer use? A large retailer? Why?

10. Explain the hierarchy of effects from a retail perspective. Apply your answer to a new shoe store.

11. Develop a checklist for a discount furniture store chain to coordinate its promotional plan.

12. For each of these promotional goals, explain how to evaluate promotional effectiveness:

a. Increase customer traffic.

b. Project an innovative image.

c. Maintain customer loyalty rates.

Web-Based Exercise

Visit the Web site of Point-of-Purchase Advertising International (**www.popai.com**), the biggest trade association in the field of display promotions. What could a retailer learn by surfing this site?

Note: Stop by our Web site (**www.prenhall.com/bermanevans**) to experience a number of highly interactive, appealing Web exercises based on actual company demonstrations and sample materials related to retailing.

Chapter Endnotes

1. Various company sources.

2. "10 Years in Five Questions," *Promo* (December 1999), p. 65.

3. Tony Lisanti, "The Legacy of Sam Walton Lives On," *DSN Retailing Today* (June 10, 2002), p. 17.

4. Computed by the authors from data in "100 Leading National Advertisers," *Advertising Age* (June 24, 2002), p. S-30.

5. See Zhimin Huang and Susan X. Li, "Co-op Advertising Models in Manufacturer-Retailer Supply Chains: A Game Theory Approach," *European Journal of Operational Research*, Vol. 135 (December 16, 2001), pp. 527–544.

6. See also John R. Graham, "The Ten Most Deadly, Detrimental, and Destructive Sales Mistakes," *American Salesman* (October 2002), pp. 16–21.

7. "Special Report: Impact in the Aisles," *Promo* (January 1996), pp. 25, 28.

8. *Promo's Sourcebook 2003*; and authors' estimates.

9. Ibid.

10. Ibid.

11. Ibid.

12. Daniel Eisenberg, "Can McDonald's Shape Up?" *Time* (September 30, 2002), pp. 52–57.

13. See Alex M. Susskind, "I Told You So!: Restaurant Customers' Word-of-Mouth Communication Patterns," *Cornell Hotel and Restaurant Administration Quarterly*, Vol. 43 (April 2002), pp. 75–85; and L. Jean Harrison Walker, "The Measurement of Word-of-Mouth Communication and an Investigation of Service Quality and Customer Commitment as Potential Antecedents," *Journal of Service Research*, Vol. 4 (August 2001), pp. 60–75.

14. Richard Sale, "Bankers Go to Market," *Promo* (August 1999), pp. 85–86.

15. Susanne Craig and Suzanne Vranica, "Ditching Its Dot-Com: E-Trade Group Plans Super-Bowl Regroup—Multimillion-Dollar Ad Effort Will Launch Rebranding to Reflect Product Range," *Wall Street Journal* (February 1, 2002), p. B3.

16. Moria Cotlier, "Improving Upon Generic E-Mails," *Catalog Age* (December 2001), p. 43.

17. Pierre Volle, "The Short-Term Effect of Store-Level Promotions on Store Choice, and the Moderating Role of Individual Variables," *Journal of Business Research*, Vol. 53 (August 2001), p. 63.

18. Sarah Mulholland, "Stimuli and Response; Retailers Are Applying Sophisticated Analytic Tools to Get into the Heads of Their Customers," *Supermarket News* (March 25, 2002), p. 14.

part seven
Short Cases

1: PACO UNDERHILL, CONSULTING GURU, ON RETAIL ATMOSPHERICS

Paco Underhill is founder and marketing director of Envirosell (**www.envirosell.com**), a research firm that specializes in studying consumers and their shopping environment. Envirosell discreetly follows shoppers around stores with in-store video cameras. Unlike other research firms that use focus groups and questionnaires, Envirosell's respondents do not know that their behavior is being measured. There is also no bias from respondents telling the interviewer what they think he or she wants to hear. Envirosell's 150 clients include Gap (**www.gap.com**), CVS (**www.cvs.com**), Estée Lauder (**www.esteelauder.com**)—which has leased departments in more than 2,000 stores—and McDonald's (**www.mcdonalds.com**).

Understanding shopping habits is more important than ever. Recent studies have found that the average time a shopper spends in a shopping mall is now just over one hour per visit; this is the lowest time ever recorded. And while Underhill has found that purchasers spend an average of 11.27 minutes in a store, nonbuyers average only 2.36 minutes. Underhill says that converting nonbuyers to buyers is largely dependent on store design and displays since so many consumer purchases are unplanned. Among the retailing techniques that may increase a consumer's time in the store are displaying complementary items together (books and bookcases), suggesting adjacency sales (selling handbags with dresses), and working merchandising into the original design for cash register areas (rather than as an afterthought).

Underhill has five "Golden Rules" for retailers to enhance their customers' shopping experiences:

- *Break It Down:* Different age groups may interpret a retailer's marketing campaign differently, so the retailer should target each group with a distinct campaign. Firms selling to older shoppers might place goods at waist and eye levels since some seniors may have trouble bending down. Retailers also need to evaluate their lighting and the size of lettering on packages. Some Eckerd drugstores place magnifiers at points of purchase so seniors can better read ingredients, directions, and so on.
- *Women Rule:* Women are an important part of the retail economy. Retailers should recognize that many women are uncomfortable browsing in narrow aisles. Hardware and technology retailers also need to make women feel they are an important target market. Stores that better appeal to one gender should consider placing comfortable chairs for the less-involved companion to relax or read. This increases the browsing time for the involved shopper.
- *The Times They Are A-Changing:* Factors such as convenience are much more important now than a decade ago. What constitutes "acceptable" waiting time at the register needs to be reconsidered.
- *Market to Minorities:* Retailers need to better understand and react to markets whose primary language is not English since many of these markets are not well served. Firms should develop distinctive merchandise and displays for these markets. Tourists are also an important buying group.
- *Have Fun:* Unless consumers are having fun, they will not return to a store. Firms should consider special demonstrations, product samples, MTV videos, and constantly changing window displays. Choosing employees who enjoy working also helps create and maintain the proper atmosphere.

Questions

1. Discuss the implications of Underhill's statement that "converting nonbuyers to buyers is largely dependent on store design and display."
2. Design a program for a music retailer to increase a consumer's time in its store.
3. Should an upscale retailer interpret Underhill's research differently than a low-end retailer? Explain your answer.
4. Relate Underhill's "Golden Rules" to a Web retailer.

The material in this case is drawn from Scott Smith, "Attention Shoppers!" *Entrepreneur* (December 2001), pp. 73–75.

2: SPORTS AUTHORITY: UPGRADING THE IN-STORE EXPERIENCE

According to Sports Authority's (**www.thesportsauthority.com**) chief operating officer, the goals of the chain with regard to the customer's in-store experience are to promote Sports Authority as the "authority" and to provide product information that communicates value, price, and savings. The company's chief executive says, "We are the number one sporting goods brand in the United States. We reference it in our name, and we try to create in-store the message that we're the authority with the information."

In comparison to its old atmosphere that was disjointed, Sports Authority's new efforts use consistent tools and a dramatic value message. The two key parts of the new Sports Authority in-store experience are the revamped store design and the in-store television network: WTSA.

The company is in the midst of creating a new look for its stores that reinforces its position as "the authority" on athletics. Instead of its previous warehouse look, where merchandise was "stockpiled high to the rafters," Sports Authority is now using separate boutiques. Whereas the old store design had an apparel department in the center and departments such as footwear and fitness at the store's edge, the new design features such specialty shops as a water shop (with beach toys and fishing supplies), a wheel shop (with roller blades and bicycles), and a team shop for seasonal sports. Many departments have unique floor treatments. At the Ft. Lauderdale store's water shop, for example, the floor tiles look like water.

To brighten up each store and facilitate shopping, each department has a different color band to identify it. A blue band is used for water sports and a red band for the team sports shop. Departments are also color coded to highlight products for specific gender or age groups. And to reinforce "the authority" image, each aisle has detailed information about the vendor, the correct size for sports equipment, vital safety information, and how to maintain or repair a product. The Sports Authority's end-of-aisle displays are color coded to match the departments. When displays contain a brand's logo, that logo is de-emphasized in comparison to the item's price and savings relative to its list price.

A big part of Sports Authority's new in-store experience is WTSA, its in-store television network. WTSA provides sports-related news, product information, and tips by sports celebrities. The network broadcasts half-hour segments—with 20 minutes of entertainment (such as tips and information from professional athletes and experts, and professional team and player profiles) and 10 minutes of advertising. The content is produced by RMS Networks, a media firm having a five-year agreement with Sports Authority. RMS designs WTSA content based on what is being sold at Sports Authority.

Jeff Handler, Sports Authority's senior vice-president of marketing and advertising, says, "We saw the programming RMS was doing for other retailers, and it seemed perfect for the sporting goods environment." The WTSA network is being broadcast in new Sports Authority stores and in those that are being renovated. During its testing phase, the stores with the WTSA network saw sales increase by 10 percent.

Questions

1. Evaluate Sports Authority's new store design in light of the retailer's objectives.
2. Discuss the pros and cons of Sports Authority's use of specialty boutiques instead of its previous warehouse format.
3. Develop a promotional campaign for Sports Authority to capitalize on "the authority" image.
4. Do you think the WTSA network will prove to be a major contributor to Sports Authority's atmospherics or will it turn out to be a fad? Explain your answer.

The material in this case is drawn from "The Sports Authority: Where POP Is the MVP," *Point of Purchase* (September 2001), pp. 14, 16.

3: CAN GAP REGAIN ITS ADVERTISING LUSTER?

Industry analysts, once strong supporters of Gap's advertising efforts, are now much more critical: "Gap, the brand that was named after the generation gap and built its business targeting baby boomers, is suffering its own mid-life crisis." Gap (**www.gap.com**) admits that 2001 was its "most difficult year ever" as an $877 million profit in 2000 turned into an $8 million loss in 2001. By mid-2002, Gap was witnessing the 26th consecutive month of declines in same-store sales.

When asked what went wrong, Anita Borzyszkowska, head of Gap's European public relations, stated: "We lost focus on our core brand, our core operation, and key items. We ignored the fundamentals and we got too swept up on trends. The Gap brand is about simple, classic, confident clothing for everyday wear and we didn't deliver on that." Other observers agree that Gap erred when it moved away from its basic product lines to more high-fashion products: "Gap has lost its edge. It has not delivered the desirable basics we associate with its brand—or the right fashions when it

tried to make its lines more fashion-driven. You're either right or wrong when you go with fashion lines—and Gap has been wrong."

Despite the concern over its product choices, many experts point out that Gap's problems can also be attributed to its ineffective advertising. For example, in late 2001, a Prudential Securities retailing analyst said Gap's advertising was "ineffective" and noted that its advertising was one reason he had downgraded Gap stock from a "hold" to a "sell" rating. In February 2002, Gap fired the Modernista ad agency—after only 16 months. Analysts were relieved in March 2002, when Gap hired a new agency to run its account. This agency was led by Trey Laird, a former creative director at Donna Karan. It also brought back Lisa Prisco, a freelance creative director who directed some of Gap's best ads, including "Khakis Groove."

In the past, Gap's ads—mostly produced in-house—were viewed as a big part of its overall strategy. Many of the ads had a music/dance video style and a distinctive tone and look. Under Modernista, the ads shifted to include celebrity performances by such singers as Alanis Morissette, Sheryl Crow, and Seal.

Will Gap's ads get back on target? One advertising expert says, "I suspect it [Gap] will try to keep the underlying tone of the messages that have worked well for it in the past. They suggest the warmth that Gap is all about. I think the key issue is what they showcase—the clothes they pick, the artists they work with, and the music." He suggests that Gap's U.S. heritage and global presence may work against it with young European and other foreign consumers who may not respond well to standardized advertising.

Although Gap spent a great deal of effort on its 2002 advertising campaign, the campaign was not viewed positively by advertising critics. The creative director of a New York agency, for example, described the campaign as lacking: "The goal is obviously to give the brand a kind of inside buzz. But when you are the Starbucks of clothing, it is impossible to have cachet."

Questions

1. What should the role of advertising be in Gap's overall promotion mix? Explain your answer.
2. What would you recommend for Gap advertising to get back on track?
3. Describe the pros and cons of Gap's using a standardized global promotional program.
4. Comment on the statement, "But when you are the Starbucks of clothing, it is impossible to have cachet." How would you address the underlying criticism in the statement?

The material in this case is drawn from Conor Dignam, "Can Gap Regain Its Cool?" *Marketing* (April 2002), pp. 22–23; and Vanessa O'Connell and Amy Merrick, "Gap's New TV Ad Campaign Leaves Some Viewers Puzzled," *Wall Street Journal* (May 30, 2002), p. B7.

4: BEST BUY USES PROMOTIONS TO PUMP UP THE SALES

Best Buy (**www.bestbuy.com**) is a 500-store technology and entertainment retailer. Its promotion planning and implementation are conducted on two levels: through a 92-person corporate Strategic

Marketing Group and regionally. Each Best Buy operating region has a marketing manager with a specific budget for local programs.

The chain develops and aims its promotional programs at various target markets. The "young fun" target market represents Best Buy's core customer; this group consists of young, tech-savvy shoppers. According to Best Buy's senior vice-president for strategic marketing, "This is the target consumer that often doesn't watch TV spots or read circulars. Until recently, promotion was underutilized. But we now know we need to reach this crowd." Best Buy also targets these segments: "digital home" (married couples with children), "technojock" (active single males who are music and sports enthusiasts), and "traditional entertainment" (casual users).

One of the difficulties Best Buy faces in planning its promotional strategy is the diversity of its product line. Best Buy sells a wide variety of technology and entertainment products that include audio/visual products, cordless phones, cameras, computers and peripherals, movies, music, and major appliances. Although some of the products are very technical, Best Buy does not want to alienate the nontechnical customer who wants to purchase an inexpensive cordless phone. Thus, Best Buy's promotional message "needs to be consistent, relevant, and not too heavy handed—while expressing the diverse inventory that exists under the Best Buy banner. We have a signal brand that represents a lot of things to different people. We need to create programs that represent all that."

A recent Best Buy campaign used a "Fun Zone" 53-foot-long truck that toured various destinations. The "Fun Zone" showed how technology is invading everyday life. Among the products demonstrated were refrigerators with built-in Web browsers, high-definition home theater systems, and a gaming area with space-age chairs. The truck visited baseball stadiums, tourist areas (such as the Santa Monica pier), and the New York City Marathon. At some locations, as many as 5,000 people visited daily.

Another campaign had a back-to-school theme. In mid-August, shoppers with school identification cards received gift bags filled with coffee mugs, compilation CDs, popcorn, batteries, and other goodies. Students who charged their purchases with Discover cards were also entered to win one of four $25,000 scholarships. About 500,000 students entered.

Best Buy is a big believer of cross-promotions; its music and home video departments most heavily use this strategy. One observer remarked that Best Buy "develops promotions that work for everybody involved." One recent holiday cross-promotion consisted of two parts. The first part was at a time when Best Buy was the only retailer selling a particular U2 DVD. The first 500 people in each store on a given Saturday were given samplers containing unreleased songs. On the same day the samplers were given out, Best Buy started another promotional offer entitling customers to buy an N'Sync bobble-head toy for $9.99 with a $25 minimum purchase. Supplementing this offer was a sweepstakes of five trips for two to an N'Sync concert and a backstage visit.

Questions

1. Evaluate Best Buy's overall promotion strategy.
2. What different promotion appeals would you use to reach "young fun," "digital home," "technojock," and "traditional entertainment" customers? Assume you are promoting a 20-inch flat screen television with built-in stereo speakers.
3. How would you assess the effectiveness of Best Buy's "Fun Zone" truck?
4. Describe potential cross-promotions for Best Buy that could be aimed at the college student market.

The material in this case is drawn from Dan Hanover, "Pump Up the Volume," *Promo* (December 2001), pp. 42–45.

part seven
Comprehensive Case
Build-A-Bear Workshop: Putting the Heart Back in Retailing*

INTRODUCTION

When I started my company, I wanted to re-create the excitement and magic I felt as a child in certain stores, when going shopping was an event. My mother, sister, and I would look forward to our shopping excursions in downtown Miami in those days; this was our version of Disneyland. From the minute you walked into Burdines, you became part of the store; it was special. The truth is that what it takes to engage and retain retail customers today is really not much different from the past.

The Build-A-Bear Niche

Build-A-Bear Workshop epitomizes "good-old-fashioned-it's-just-about-the-customer retailing." We are unique because Build-A-Bear Workshop—Where Best Friends Are Made is a retailer that invites participation and makes you smile. It is a place where families and kids from 3 to 103 come together to have fun while creating a special memory. You can't hang on to a birthday cake too long, nor can you expect balloons to keep you company when you are sick. A Build-A-Bear Workshop bear, frog, bunny, cow, or dog endures, makes you feel better, and more. This is why our guests come back. We are, to my knowledge, the first truly interactive family entertainment concept developed for mall-based retailing.

I have been in retailing a long time and have heard many opinions about what it takes to succeed in business. It no longer takes $5,000 and a good idea, as it did for Sam Walton (Wal-Mart) or Les Wexner (The Limited). Today, a month's mall rent exceeds that number. It takes a lot of capital, knowledge, experience, and partnership to bring an idea into the market and succeed, especially in America's malls.

Success in retailing is also about details and their implementation. Due to my experience with one of the finest retailers in the industry, May Department Stores, and as president of Payless ShoeSource, I could develop Build-A-Bear Workshop with the proper background, know-how, and contacts.

During my third week as an executive trainee at the Hecht Company in Washington, D.C., the then-CEO of May Company talked about retailing as entertainment and the store as a theater. I remember his statement, as if he were saying it to me alone: "When customers have fun, they spend more money."

Bringing Back the Theater

I left corporate America to bring the theater back to retailing and to give back to the industry that was so good to me. At that time, my financial rewards were very high, but my psychic bank account was nearly empty. I wanted to create something unique. I knew my strengths were in merchandising and marketing and that the children's toy and entertainment business would require me to use my

talents on a daily basis. I wanted to take children's interactive and entertainment retailing a step further and turn it into experience retailing, which would let me use my skills and encourage creativity in children. Little opportunity exists in retailing for kids to get involved and participate, even in the best entertainment stores.

I examined what was available in children's retail and discovered that few places are targeted to children, and even fewer to both boys and girls. In my research, I visited a factory that offered tours to grade schools and scout troops. When I went on the tour, I saw a special look in the children's eyes. They were enthralled by the process of seeing products made. Unable to convince the owners to sell, I decided to reinvent the concept for mall-based retail. After all, Ray Kroc (McDonald's) didn't invent hamburgers, and Howard Schultz (Starbucks) didn't invent coffee—they invented how to sell more and better.

I've always been a student of retailing. Shopping is my hobby and my profession. I've learned from the best, be it a department store, specialty store, or restaurant. I took all of my favorite ideas and rolled them into one. Then I gathered my ideas and went straight to customers and the best source—children. Their input is the basis of Build-A-Bear Workshop.

I spoke with lots of children, who eventually became my advisory board with children ages 6 through 14. Remember the old department store teen boards? I was on one, and it was so much fun—I have never forgotten that experience. It was a major reason to even consider retail as my career. I couldn't wait to get up each morning, don my Bobbie Brooks wool skirt and knee socks, and go out in 100-degree Miami heat to make minimum wage. It was so much fun that I thought I should be paying the store rather than them paying me. Why couldn't I recreate that feeling for my advisory board and young employees?

When I first opened Build-A-Bear Workshop, I expected children would be enthusiastic customers. Not as obvious is the other huge segment of our business. Grandparents, parents, aunts, uncles, and teenagers all love making their own bears. Teddy bears are ageless and so is the bear-making process.

Every Day Is a Holiday to Cele-Bear-Ate

Build-A-Bear Workshop involves much more than visiting and buying a bear. Although we have many pre-made bears that are dressed and ready to go, people want to make their own bears. They take the time to pick out their skin, their heart—the whole thing. The store is designed to bring out the creative side of guests, regardless of age or gender. The universal reaction is amazing. People love to personalize bears, and we are happy to provide an environment that encourages creativity.

Just another toy store? Strictly seasonal? Think again. During the holiday season, a toy store does 40 to 50 percent of its sales and an even bigger share of profits, but not Build-A-Bear Workshop. With birthdays, every day is a holiday, and business is more evenly distributed throughout the year. Since we launched our Build-A-Party program, we have hosted parties for scouts, school classes, and all types of cele-bear-ations. The guest of honor at a birthday party receives a free gift, and scouts get free patches.

Corporations have also scheduled parties for their customers, as well as employees and their families. People come from miles around to cele-bear-ate with us. Most Workshops are booked solid for parties throughout the year. This is my first experience with guests making reservations to shop, and it creates a cash flow and schedule-planning advantage.

Most toy introductions occur in the second half of the year, but not at Build-A-Bear Workshop. Our tradition is to introduce a new Limited Edition item on the day after every holiday. We've created an event for our guests to anticipate that isn't driven by discounts but by what I believe the customer really wants—newness.

At Build-A-Bear Workshop, we celebrate Teddy Roosevelt's birthday as a national holiday. Why? When President Roosevelt was on a hunting trip, and after three unsuccessful days, his fellow hunters found a bear cub and tied it to a tree. Roosevelt refused to shoot. This touching scene was depicted in a *Washington Post* cartoon. The story captured the heart of the nation and led to the teddy bear.

Many people ask if I miss the fashion business. Fashion is what teddy bears are all about. Valentine's Day is a bear's favorite Hugday, so in February we are the Love Stuff Headquarters. In spring, our bears, bunnies, and other animals cele-bear-ate a Spring Fling. Summer brings out the beach bears. In October, Halloween costumes for our furry friends are beary popular. Because we design and develop our products, we can control our own destiny. Metal scooters for bears? We call our bear-sized version Scootfur, and it is a huge success.

Bear Business Facts

We set ourselves apart from other retailers in numerous ways. We do our entire business on 300 SKUs, which creates a highly productive business model. We also peak inventory at a different time from the traditional toy store. Every item is in stock after Christmas. We sell a huge amount of Bear Bucks gift certificates, and we don't want to disappoint any of our guests when they come in to redeem them.

Build-A-Bear Workshop is both a store and a brand. Thanks to Adrienne Weiss Corporation, a Chicago-based brand think tank, I was able to bring the store of my dreams to reality. Adrienne's mission was to create a brand and a store that would make people smile. I gave her just two rules: use our already researched and protected name and tag line, Build-A-Bear Workshop—Where Best Friends Are Made, and use bright primary colors. Both being kids at heart, we began the brainstorming and the Build-A-Bear Workshop brand was born.

It is designed to be a theme park in a mall. At the entry to our Workshop, two animated bear sentries greet guests. The Workshop is divided into eight stations: Choose Me, Stuff Me, Hear Me, Stitch Me, Fluff Me, Name Me, Dress Me, and Take Me Home. Each defines a key step in the bear-making process.

At Choose Me, each guest selects from 30 stuffed animal choices, including bears, dogs, frogs, kitties, and bunnies. Guests proceed to Stuff Me, where Master Bear Builders help them fill their bear with the right amount of stuffing and let guests give their bear a hug test. At Hear Me, guests choose from various sounds and songs. In 2000, we introduced Build-A-Sound, our record-your-own message chip. We have had many marriage proposals and loving messages recorded, making personalizing their furry friend even more special.

One of the most important steps is the "Heart Stuff," a Build-A-Bear Workshop trademark. Guests select their bear's heart, warm it in the palms of their hands, make a special wish, and place the heart into the bear. Children say they can actually hear their bear's heart beating, making this a magical experience for adults also. At this sta-

tion, the bond between the new owner and the bear is secured, and this is one of the most popular parts of the process.

Stitch Me finalizes the technical part of the process. At Fluff Me, guests give their furry friend an air bath and brush the fur. It adds more fun to the process because the guest takes part in creating the final look of the bear. At Name Me, the computer asks a series of questions, such as the bear's name and birth date, and prints a storybook or a birth certificate. All bears are entered into our Find-A-Bear tracking system. If the bear is lost and returned to us, we trace the owner and send the bear safely home. Through our proprietary computerized naming system, we have built a huge data base that lets us serve guests even better. It provides us with extensive demographic information that helps us plan our marketing and future Workshop locations.

The next-to-last station is Dress Me, where the owner picks out bear apparel from complete outfits, such as golf, prom, soccer, and cheerleader, to accessories like hats, backpacks, and briefcases. Guests like to bring their own items to add to their bears, making them unique. We receive considerable feedback on this feature from guests, and it assures us that we have accomplished one of our goals: we have engaged them. Costumes such as pilot and camouflage outfits are examples of ideas contributed by our guests. The Take Me Home station completes the process. The bear and the personalized storybook or birth certificate are placed in our Cub Condo, a box designed to be a keepsake, as well as a handy travel carrier.

Our Cub Condo is also a promotional tool as children carry them proudly through the mall. They have also become collectible. We have a winter ski lodge, a Valentine's Day red love nest, a summer beach shack, and a Halloween haunted house. In addition, we offer a clothing gift box known as a Beararmoire, another walking mall billboard.

A few more attractions make us unique. I have always loved music in a store, and it was clear that if I wanted music for kids from 3 to 103, we would have to create it. Our 10-song compact disc is available for purchase and is a part of the Workshop's atmosphere. We also have our beary own holiday bear tunes and are expanding our collection.

Each station is unique and fun for everyone. And besides being a totally creative experience, we are priced right. When I began devising the store, I knew that success meant being affordable for children across all economic lines. Thus, our stuffed animals are priced from $10 to $25, clothes range from $3 to $15 (for a five-piece outfit), and accessories start at $2.

We developed Build-A-Bear Workshop so the entire store staff would talk to the guest. It's hard to know which element tugs at the heartstrings and says "buy me" more than another. Take away any one ingredient, and I am sure our sales would be less. We've created a brand that is part of a total package, including our award-winning Web site.

At **www.buildabear.com**, you'll see a whimsical version of our Workshop. It is a successful site, and we keep working to make the site fun and interactive. We have games, electronic and printable greeting cards, invitations to parties, and more—all designed to enable us to stay connected to our guests. Our Web site also enables us to communicate by E-mail. It's another easy and economical way to interact and engage guests.

Life According to Bearisms

Build-A-Bear Workshop challenges the creative mind and brings out the child in us. Something happened to retailing over the last decade. We started taking ourselves too seriously, and fun seemed to go away.

I am charged with sustaining this business as a special place. Our Bearisms are the values we live by. Simply put, we treat our guests and associates the way that we would want to be treated. We're known for creating holidays and reasons for bear-giving.

Our interest in associates is evident from the day they are hired. Everyone goes to World Bearquarters in St. Louis for three weeks of training. I strive to meet every associate personally. I attend every Workshop set-up and/or grand opening. It's hectic, but each opening is meaningful and a part of our family culture.

I have long believed that you can be the same person at work and at home, and we are creating a workplace that makes this a reality. Our environment is casual. While we have suggested work hours, our office is accessible around the clock every day of the year to meet the demands of family, and associates can log onto our intranet from home.

Children visit World Bearquarters, and they have their own Cub Stuff room complete with games, a computer, TV/VCR, and other comforts. World Bearquarters is a themed environment, just like our Workshops. Bearisms line the wall and stuffing floats on the ceiling. Our office is filled with cuddly teddy bears, and we label everything the way we think a teddy would. Every employee's opinions, including college interns', are welcome. Everyone at Build-A-Bear Workshop is a teacher and a mentor—that, too, is part of who we are. It is also about the future of our company.

We integrate customer satisfaction with store performance, and we have implanted an innovative Guest Satisfaction program that is tied to financial rewards for Workshop managers. Scores are reported weekly to managers and posted for all associates to see. A store does not qualify for a sales bonus unless it reaches a minimum pre-determined Guest Satisfaction score. The ultimate test—"Did we make you smile?"—is at the top of the list. These results are as important as weekly sales, and stores wait anxiously to see them. We are continually looking for ways to raise guest satisfaction, which is the best indicator of how truly successful we are.

We don't wait for opportunities to come to us—we are in charge of our own destiny. We developed a Teddy Bear Tea program that debuted in Boston. What better place to throw a giant tea party? We believe in our philosophy of being good partners. Malls know they can rely on us to participate in events and in the community, and we create our own promotions. Building this relationship is key to continued success.

In 2000, we launched the first in a series of World Wildlife Fund co-branded animals with the introduction of a plush giant panda. By purchasing this stuffed animal, our guests help save the giant panda, as well as other endangered animals, and fulfill the partnership's motto, "Making Friends That Make a Difference."

At Build-A-Bear Workshop, our products are recognized for their uniqueness and standard-setting quality. Call them what you will—cute, huggable, lovable, soft, cuddly, and always affordable—everyone has to have at least one. Our goal is to be the best that we can be. We don't ever want this business not to be fun for our guests or for us. We are in a fast growth mode. It will be a balancing act to succeed while maintaining our integrity, heeding a vision, and meeting the needs of suppliers, associates, landlords, shareholders, and guests.

Questions

1. What are the three most important points that a retailing executive could learn from this case? Explain your answer.
2. Comment on the strategic implications of this statement from Build-A-Bear's founder: "Shopping is my hobby and my profession."
3. Why do Build-A-Bear stores appeal to both young children and those age 65 and older?
4. How could a drugstore be more interactive and entertaining for shoppers? A consumer electronics store?
5. Visit **www.buildabear.com** and discuss whether the firm has successfully re-created the store atmosphere online.
6. How should Build-A-Bear utilize advertising?
7. What kinds of store promotions would be *in*appropriate for Build-A-Bear? Why?

*The material in this case is adapted by the authors from Maxine Clark, Chief Executive, Build-A-Bear Workshop, "Putting the Heart Back in Retailing," *Retailing Issues Letter* (January 2001), pp. 1–5. Reprinted by permission.

part eight

In Part Eight, we "put it all together."

■ **Chapter 20** ties together the elements of a retail strategy that have been described all through this book. We examine planning and opportunity analysis, productivity, performance measures, and scenario analysis. The value of data comparisons (benchmarking and gap analysis) is indicated. Strategic control via the retail audit is covered.

INTEGRATING AND CONTROLLING THE RETAIL STRATEGY

Reprinted by permission

Bernard Marcus and Arthur Blank, the co-founders of Home Depot (**www.homedepot.com**), met while they worked for Handy Dan, a regional hardware store chain based in Los Angeles. After a personality clash with their boss, Marcus and Blank were both fired. The two executives were convinced that a store offering home improvement products (some of which were previously available only to contractors) could provide excellent customer service and change the way these products were sold. In 1979, the partners opened their first Home Depot store in Atlanta. Today, Home Depot dominates the do-it-yourself home improvement market with annual sales approaching $60 billion, 1,500 stores (including EXPO Design Centers), and more than 250,000 associates.

Home Depot is certainly not complacent with its success as the firm plans for the future. It is rolling out a larger appliance showroom format in as many as 350 locations in an attempt to move up from its number four position in the appliance business (after Sears, Lowe's, and Best Buy). It is testing a new distribution system that can deliver in-stock appliances to its customers within 24 hours.

The retailer is also working on a neighborhood store prototype intended for high-density market areas where its full-size units are impractical. Lastly, Home Depot is aggressively opening new stores in the United States and internationally. The company has opened as many as 17 stores on a single day![1]

chapter objectives

1. To demonstrate the importance of integrating a retail strategy
2. To examine four key factors in the development and enactment of an integrated retail strategy: planning procedures and opportunity analysis, defining productivity, performance measures, and scenario analysis
3. To show how industry and company data can be used in strategy planning and analysis (benchmarking and gap analysis)
4. To show the value of a retail audit

OVERVIEW

This site (www.bizmove. com/marketing/m2c.htm) raises a lot of good questions for retailers to think about in integrating their strategies.

This chapter focuses on integrating and controlling a retail strategy. We tie together the material detailed previously, show why retailers need coordinated strategies, and describe how to assess performance.

By integrating and regularly monitoring their strategies, firms of any size or format can take a proper view of the retailing concept and create a superior total retail experience. Consider the independent hardware store, which is threatened by Home Depot and other power retailers:

> Village Hardware in Southport Village (Connecticut) has become a community landmark, which helps it retain customers in the face of competition from Home Depot and Lowe's. Founded in 1912, Village Hardware is a central component of the traditional Southport community. Brooms, cast-iron firewood holders, and benches are set up just outside the store. Glenn Oesterle took out a home-equity loan in 1986 to buy the store. After years of working for hardware store owners, he decided to put his experience to work for himself. Oesterle is a fixture of the community; he greets his customers by first name and they him. On a recent visit, many customers are shopping and his shelves are stocked with everything from paints to plumbing tools to lawn-care supplies. Additionally, Village Hardware has become the community fix-it shop. Oesterle repairs everything from chandeliers to bicycles: "At the end of the day, people shop where they feel at home."[2]

As today's retailers look to the future, they must deal with new strategic choices due to the globalization of world markets, evolving consumer life-styles, competition among formats, and rapid technology changes. They would also be wise to study the strategies of successful firms, as well as those encountering significant challenges. Here are the observations of a retailing executive who worked for both Target and Kmart:

> While at Target, I saw a model of retailing efficiency. New programs are carefully planned and tested. Caution is the operating principle for all moves. Underperforming elements of the business, whether stores or strategies, are eradicated. Leadership is valued for its consistency and tenure. Idea sharing is encouraged on all levels. Speed in replenishment, service, and execution is ingrained in the company mind-set. At Kmart, the top leadership was always impressive and I was surrounded by a sense of pride and tradition. But operations left much to be desired. The company has many long-term, experienced, and dedicated employees. Turnover, however, is a huge issue, especially in the mid-level to vice-president ranks. Training programs suffer because of the rapid turnover. The transition to Fleming food distribution was extremely rocky, even if the decision to use Fleming over Supervalu was a huge coup. Technology is archaic.[3]

INTEGRATING THE RETAIL STRATEGY

A major goal of *Retail Management* has been to describe the relationships among the elements of a retail strategy and show the need to act in an integrated way. Figure 20-1 highlights the integrated strategy of bebe, the apparel chain. Annually, bebe has been cited by *Chain Store Age* as one of the leading U.S. "high performance retailers."[4] At our Web site (**www.prenhall.com/bermanevans**), there are links to several integrated retail strategies using Bplans.com software templates.

Four fundamental factors especially need to be taken into account in devising and enacting an integrated retail strategy: planning procedures and opportunity analysis, defining productivity, performance measures, and scenario analysis. These factors are discussed next.

PLANNING PROCEDURES AND OPPORTUNITY ANALYSIS

Planning procedures are enhanced by undertaking three coordinated activities. The process is then more systematic and reflects input from multiple parties:

1. Senior executives outline the firm's overall direction and goals. This provides written guidelines for middle- and lower-level managers, who get input from various internal and external sources. These managers are encouraged to generate ideas at an early stage.
2. Top-down plans and bottom-up or horizontal plans are combined.
3. Specific plans are enacted, including checkpoints and dates.

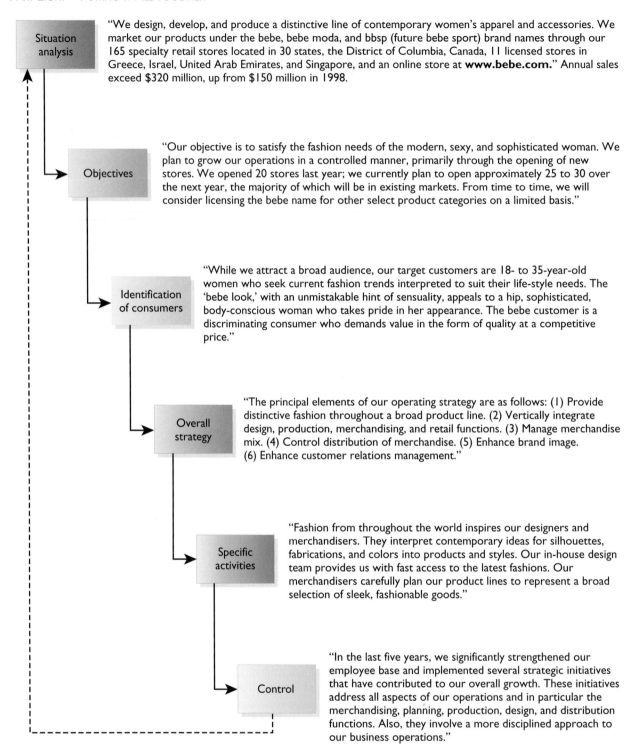

Situation analysis

"We design, develop, and produce a distinctive line of contemporary women's apparel and accessories. We market our products under the bebe, bebe moda, and bbsp (future bebe sport) brand names through our 165 specialty retail stores located in 30 states, the District of Columbia, Canada, 11 licensed stores in Greece, Israel, United Arab Emirates, and Singapore, and an online store at **www.bebe.com.**" Annual sales exceed $320 million, up from $150 million in 1998.

Objectives

"Our objective is to satisfy the fashion needs of the modern, sexy, and sophisticated woman. We plan to grow our operations in a controlled manner, primarily through the opening of new stores. We opened 20 stores last year; we currently plan to open approximately 25 to 30 over the next year, the majority of which will be in existing markets. From time to time, we will consider licensing the bebe name for other select product categories on a limited basis."

Identification of consumers

"While we attract a broad audience, our target customers are 18- to 35-year-old women who seek current fashion trends interpreted to suit their life-style needs. The 'bebe look,' with an unmistakable hint of sensuality, appeals to a hip, sophisticated, body-conscious woman who takes pride in her appearance. The bebe customer is a discriminating consumer who demands value in the form of quality at a competitive price."

Overall strategy

"The principal elements of our operating strategy are as follows: (1) Provide distinctive fashion throughout a broad product line. (2) Vertically integrate design, production, merchandising, and retail functions. (3) Manage merchandise mix. (4) Control distribution of merchandise. (5) Enhance brand image. (6) Enhance customer relations management."

Specific activities

"Fashion from throughout the world inspires our designers and merchandisers. They interpret contemporary ideas for silhouettes, fabrications, and colors into products and styles. Our in-house design team provides us with fast access to the latest fashions. Our merchandisers carefully plan our product lines to represent a broad selection of sleek, fashionable goods."

Control

"In the last five years, we significantly strengthened our employee base and implemented several strategic initiatives that have contributed to our overall growth. These initiatives address all aspects of our operations and in particular the merchandising, planning, production, design, and distribution functions. Also, they involve a more disciplined approach to our business operations."

FIGURE 20-1

The Integrated Strategy of bebe

Source: Figure developed by the authors based on data from *bebe stores, inc., 2002 Annual Report,* various pages.

FIGURE 20-2
Opportunity Analysis
with the SBA

Opportunities need to be studied with regard to their impact on overall strategy, and not in an isolated manner. See Figure 20-2. Just for Feet stumbled badly by overexpanding and adding smaller stores that did not fit with its category killer format. As a result, Just for Feet filed for bankruptcy. In 2000, it was acquired by Footstar (owner of Meldisco and Footaction). Today, Just for Feet focuses on superstores.

A useful retailer tool for evaluating opportunities is the **sales opportunity grid**, which rates the promise of new and established goods, services, procedures, and/or store outlets across a variety of criteria. It enables opportunities to be evaluated on the basis of the integrated strategies the firms would follow if the opportunities are pursued. Computerization makes it possible to apply such a grid.

Table 20-1 shows a sales opportunity grid for a supermarket that wants to decide which of two salad dressing brands to carry. The store manager has outlined the integrated strategy for each brand; A is established; B is new. Due to its newness, the manager believes initial Brand B sales would be lower, but first-year sales would be similar. The brands would be priced the same and occupy identical space. Brand B requires higher display costs but offers a larger markup. Brand B would return a greater gross profit and net profit than Brand A by the end of the first year. Based on the overall grid, the manager picks Brand B. Yet, if the store is more concerned about immediate profit, Brand A might be chosen.

DEFINING PRODUCTIVITY IN A MANNER CONSISTENT WITH THE STRATEGY

Intellilink's UltraLite Plus system (www.ilsa.com) can improve a retailer's productivity. See how.

As we noted in Chapters 12 and 13, productivity refers to the efficiency with which a retail strategy is carried out; it is in any retailer's interest to reach sales and profit goals while keeping control over costs. On the one hand, a retailer looks to avoid unnecessary expenses. It does not want eight salespeople working at one time if four can satisfactorily handle all customers. Likewise, it does not want to pay high rent for a site in a regional shopping center if customers would willingly travel a few miles farther to a less costly site. On the other hand, a firm is not looking to

TABLE 20-1	Supermarket's Sales Opportunity Grid for Two Brands of Salad Dressing	
Criteria	Brand A (established)	Brand B (new)
Retail price	$1.29/8-ounce bottle	$1.29/8-ounce bottle
Floor space needed	8 square feet	8 square feet
Display costs	$10.00/month	$20.00/month for 6 mos. $10.00/month thereafter
Operating costs	$0.12/unit	$0.12/unit
Markup	19%	22%
Sales estimate		
During first month		
Units	250	50
Dollars	$323	$65
During first six months		
Units	1,400	500
Dollars	$1,806	$645
During first year		
Units	2,500	2,750
Dollars	$3,225	$3,548
Gross profit estimate		
During first month	$61	$14
During first six months	$343	$142
During first year	$613	$781
Net profit estimate		
During first month	$21	−$12
During first six months	$115	−$38
During first year	$193	$271

Example 1:
Gross profit estimate = Sales estimate − [(1.00 − Markup percentage) × (Sales estimate)]

Brand A gross profit estimate during first six months = $1,806 − [(1.00 − 0.19) × ($1,806)] = $343

Example 2:
Net profit estimate = Gross profit estimate − (Display costs + Operating costs)

Brand A net profit estimate during first six months = $343 − ($60 + $168) = $115

lose customers because there are insufficient sales personnel to handle the rush of shoppers during peak hours. It also does not want a low-rent site if this means a significant drop in customer traffic.[5]

Potential trade-offs often mean neither the least expensive strategy nor the most expensive one is the most productive strategy; the former approach might not adequately service customers and the latter might be wasteful. An upscale retailer could not succeed with self-service, and it would be unnecessary for a discounter to have a large sales staff. The most productive approach applies a specific integrated retail strategy (such as a full-service jewelry store) as efficiently as possible.

Food Lion (**www.foodlion.com/companyinfo.htm**) is a leading retailer due to its well-integrated, productive strategy:

Food Lion's success is based on the principle of offering customers quality products at extra low prices in clean, conveniently located stores. Stores sell more than 24,000 different products and offer nationally and regionally advertised brand name merchandise, as well as a growing number of quality private-label products manufactured and packaged for Food Lion. The company maintains its low price leadership and quality assurance through technological advances and operating efficiencies such as standard store formats, innovative warehouse design and management, energy efficient facilities, and data synchronization and integration with suppliers. Food Lion's commitment to quality is evident in its more than 86,000 associates. The Company actively supports its associates through ongoing training programs and continuing advancement opportunities.

PERFORMANCE MEASURES

By outlining relevant **performance measures**—the criteria used to assess effectiveness—and setting standards (goals) for each of them, a retailer can better develop and integrate its strategy. Among the measures frequently used by retailers are total sales, average sales per store, sales by goods/service category, sales per square foot, gross margins, gross margin return on investment, operating income, inventory turnover, markdown percentages, employee turnover, financial ratios, and profitability.

A retailer can gain insights from a visit to the Benchmarking Report Center (www. reportcenter.com).

To properly gauge a strategy's effectiveness, a firm should use **benchmarking**, whereby the retailer sets standards and measures its performance based on the achievements of its sector of retailing, specific competitors, high-performance firms, and/or the prior actions of the firm itself: "Benchmarking can identify good business practices, innovative ideas, effective operating procedures, and winning strategies to be adopted by a firm to accelerate its own progress by ensuring quality, productivity, and cost gains. It involves investigating how things are done elsewhere and where they are done differently or better, to see whether a firm could adapt the processes of another organization to improve its own processes."[6]

A good source is the *Annual Benchmark Report for Retail Trade*, available free from the U.S. Census Bureau (**www.census.gov/svsd/www/artstbl.html**). It shows a 10-year monthly comparison of sales, purchases, gross margins, inventories, and inventory-to-sales ratios by retail category.

Learn about best practices, both retail and nonretail, from APQC (www.apqc. org/best).

Retailers of varying sizes—and in different goods or service lines—can also obtain comparative data from such sources as the Internal Revenue Service, Small Business Administration, *Progressive Grocer, Stores, Chain Store Age, DSN Retailing Today,* Dun & Bradstreet, the National Retail Federation, RMA, and annual reports. Those retailers can then compare their performance with others.

Table 20-2 contains revenue, expense, and income benchmarking data for small retailers in 20 different business categories. The cost of goods sold as a percentage of revenues is highest for gas stations and grocery stores, gross profit is greatest for barber shops and dentists, operating expenses are the most for coin laundries and motels, and net income is highest for barber shops and dentists.

One popular, independent, ongoing benchmarking survey is the American Customer Satisfaction Index (ACSI). It addresses two questions: (1) Are customer satisfaction and evaluations of quality improving or declining in the United States? (2) Are they improving or declining for particular sectors of industry and for specific companies? It is based on a scale of 0 to 100, with 100 the highest possible score. A national sample of 65,000 people takes part in phone

Careers in RETAILING
The Best Retailers to Work For

Fortune (**www.fortune.com/lists/bestcompanies**) annually publishes its "Best 100 Companies to Work For" list. The 2002 list of best firms was chosen from 279 that applied for this designation. Each firm was rated on the basis of a questionnaire given to employees, as well as *Fortune*'s evaluation of each company's response to its Culture Audit.

In 2002, the top three retailers and their overall rank were Container Store (2), CDW Computer Centers (13), and JM Family Enterprises (20). Let's look at some of their strategies:

● Container Store (**www.containerstore.com**) pays above-average salaries, has excellent fringe benefits (the retailer matches an employee's contribution to his or her pension plan up to 4 percent of pay), and has an excellent reputation for respecting employees.

● CDW Computer Centers (**www.cdw.com**) is an online computer and accessories reseller headed by a fun-loving CEO who once vowed to shave his head if the firm met revenue targets. Despite poor overall performance in its industry, the head of CDW's president is now clean-shaven.

● JM Family Enterprises (**www.jmfamily.com**)—which operates Lexus and Toyota dealerships, among its many businesses—has outstanding programs for employees, including on-site medical centers and child-care facilities, free prescriptions and flu shots, free haircuts and manicures, 30 paid days off per year, tuition reimbursement, profit sharing, and more.

Source: Robert Levering and Milton Moskowitz, "100 Best Companies to Work For," *Fortune* (January 20, 2003), pp. 127–152.

TABLE 20-2	Benchmarking Through Annual Operating Statements of Typical Small Retailers (Expressed in Terms of Revenues = 100%)				
Type of Retailer	Total Revenues	Cost of Goods Sold	Gross Profit	Total Operating Expenses	Net Income
Apparel stores	100	66.7	33.3	29.2	4.1
Auto parking	100	32.9	67.1	59.1	8.0
Auto repair shops	100	53.9	46.1	33.7	12.4
Barber shops	100	4.1	95.9	41.3	54.6
Bars/drinking places	100	54.3	45.7	41.2	4.5
Beauty salons	100	20.0	80.0	54.0	26.0
Bicycle stores	100	69.8	30.2	24.5	5.7
Coin laundries	100	11.3	88.7	85.1	3.6
Dentists	100	8.5	91.5	49.6	41.9
Drugstores	100	69.0	31.0	22.5	8.5
Eating places	100	53.0	47.0	41.4	5.6
Gas stations	100	84.0	16.0	12.2	3.8
Gift stores	100	63.2	36.8	34.0	2.8
Grocery stores	100	83.1	16.9	14.4	2.5
Hardware stores	100	74.8	25.2	20.9	4.3
Motels	100	12.8	87.2	84.4	2.8
Photography studios	100	29.0	71.0	54.8	16.2
Real-estate brokers	100	9.1	90.9	52.2	38.7
Repair services	100	40.1	59.9	41.5	18.4
Used car dealers	100	83.5	16.5	14.3	2.2

Source: U.S. Internal Revenue Service, as reported at **www.score114.org/Docs/OpStmts/mTypOps.htm** (March 9, 2003).

interviews, with at least 250 interviews of current customers for each of the 200 firms studied (**www.theacsi.org**). Table 20-3 shows that the highest score by any of the listed retailers was 81 for Publix, while the lowest was 62 for McDonald's.

There is now more interest in the benchmarking of service retailing. One well-known measurement tool is SERVQUAL, which lets service retailers assess their quality by asking customers to react to a series of statements in five areas of performance:

- *Reliability*—Providing services as promised. Dependability in handling service problems. Performing services right the first time. Providing services at the promised time. Maintaining error-free records.

- *Responsiveness*—Keeping customers informed about when services will be done. Prompt service. Willingness to help customers. Readiness to act on customer requests.

- *Assurance*—Employees who instill customer confidence and make customers feel safe in transactions. Employees who are consistently courteous and who have the knowledge to answer questions.

- *Empathy*—Giving customers individual attention in a caring way. Having the customer's best interest at heart. Employees who understand the needs of their customers. Convenient business hours.

- *Tangibles*—Modern equipment. Visually appealing facilities. Employees who have a neat, professional appearance. Visually appealing materials associated with the service.[7]

TABLE 20-3	Benchmarking Through the American Customer Satisfaction Index		
Retailer	Fourth Quarter 1995 Index Score	Fourth Quarter 1998 Index Score	Fourth Quarter 2001 Index Score
Department/Discount Stores	75	73	75
Target Corporation (discount stores)	76	74	77
Nordstrom	83	79	76
Sears	75	74	76
Wal-Mart	81	75	75
J.C. Penney	77	75	75
May	75	72	75
Dillard's	74	71	75
Target Corporation (department stores)	76	74	74
Kmart	72	71	74
Federated	71	67	69
Supermarkets	75	73	75
Publix	82	79	81
Supervalu	77	77	76
Kroger	76	73	75
Safeway	73	71	75
Albertson's	77	70	72
Winn-Dixie	75	74	72
Hotels	72	72	71
Marriott	77	77	76
Hilton (including Doubletree, Embassy Suites, etc.)	75	74	76
Hyatt	77	73	75
Holiday Inn	69	68	69
Ramada Inns	70	67	67
Restaurants/Fast-Food Firms	70	69	71
Domino's Pizza	70	70	73
Wendy's	73	73	72
Pizza Hut	66	71	71
Little Caesar's	69	71	70
Taco Bell	66	64	66
Burger King	65	64	65
KFC	68	64	63
McDonald's	63	61	62

Sources: University of Michigan Business School, American Society for Quality Control, and CFI Group, "Fourth Quarter Scores 2001," **www.theacsi.org/industry_scores.htm** (November 1, 2002). Reprinted by permission.

In reviewing the performance of others, a firm should look at the *best practices* in retailing—whether involving companies in its own business sector or other sectors: "Find someone who does a great job, observe and monitor them, benchmark their results, and apply the most appropriate techniques they use. From the firm that scrutinizes a best practice in one territory or store and tries to clone it to the rest of its organization, to the merchant that scrupulously studies the best of its competitors, the value of analyzing, adopting, or adapting best practices is a technique that cannot be overestimated."[8]

The Retail Forward consulting company regularly publishes a best practices list of "global high performance retailers." This list is derived from the top 100 global retailers ranking produced by Retail Forward. It includes firms performing well above average on a **retail performance index**, encompassing 5-year trends in revenue growth and profit growth, and a 6-year average return on assets. Due to its importance, return on assets is weighted twice as much as revenue growth or profit growth. An overall performance index of 100 is average. Table 20-4 shows leading high-performance retailers and reveals that there are various ways to be one. The overall leader, TJX (parent of T.J. Maxx and Marshalls), was strong in

TABLE 20-4	Benchmarking Global High-Performance Retailers					
Company	Compound Annual Revenue Growth, 1995–2000	Compound 5-Year Revenue Growth Index	Annual Profit Growth, 1995–2000	5-Year Profit Growth Index	Average Annual Return on Assets, 1995–2000	5-Year Return on Assets Index	Retail Performance Index[a]
TJX (U.S.)	6.6	180	82.9	791	13.2	284	385
Dixons (Great Britain)	19.6	212	53.5	511	11.4	246	304
Gap Inc. (U.S.)	25.5	277	19.9	190	17.2	371	302
Kohl's (U.S.)	26.1	284	38.6	369	9.2	199	262
Home Depot (U.S.)	24.2	263	28.7	274	11.3	244	256
Royal Ahold (Netherlands)	31.3	340	40.0	382	5.6	121	241
Best Buy (U.S.)	16.3	176	52.5	501	6.0	129	234
Lowe's (U.S.)	21.6	234	29.1	277	7.0	151	203
Walgreen (U.S.)	15.3	166	19.4	185	10.4	224	200
Costco (U.S.)	12.0	130	36.4	347	5.6	121	180
Publix (U.S.)	9.2	100	17.0	162	10.6	229	180
Safeway (U.S.)	14.3	155	27.3	261	6.9	149	179
Wal-Mart (U.S.)	15.3	166	18.1	173	7.9	170	170
Kroger (U.S.)	15.4	167	23.7	226	5.8	125	161
Target Corporation (U.S.)	9.4	102	32.4	309	5.1	109	157
Kingfisher (Great Britain)	18.1	196	12.5	120	7.2	156	157
Loblaw (Canada)	15.3	167	26.4	252	4.7	102	156
Tesco (Great Britain)	11.7	126	10.5	100	7.1	152	133
Global Top 100 Retailers' Medians	*9.2*	*100*	*10.5*	*100*	*4.6*	*100*	*100*

[a]Retail performance index = [Revenue growth index + Profit growth index + 2 (Return on assets index)]/4

Source: "2000 Global High Performance Retailers," *Global Retail Intelligencer* (October 2001), p. 2. Reprinted by permission of Retail Forward, Inc.

profitability and return on assets. On the other hand, Royal Ahold (the sixth-best retailer) was first in revenue growth but only tied for 15th in return on assets—among the 18 high performers in Table 20-4. By learning about high-performance firms in different retail categories, a prospective or existing company can study the strategies of those retailers and try to emulate their best practices.

A retailer can also benchmark its own internal performance, conduct gap analysis, and plan for the future. Through **gap analysis**, a company compares its actual performance against its potential performance and then determines the areas in which it must improve. As Figure 20-3 indicates, gap analysis has four main steps.

Let us apply gap analysis to Home Depot. Table 20-5 indicates the firm's financial results for the period from 1999 through 2001. The data in the table may be used to benchmark Home Depot in terms of its own performance. Between 1999 and 2001, Home Depot increased its gross margin percentage and decreased its general and administrative expenses and pre-opening expenses from 2.1 to 1.9 percent of sales. Net earnings in dollars rose accordingly; however, net earnings as a percent of sales declined because profit growth did not keep up with sales growth.

What makes a good retail Web site? Companies can close the gap by checking here (www.waller.co.uk/eval.htm).

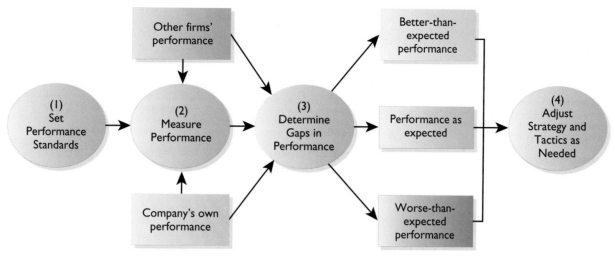

FIGURE 20-3
Utilizing Gap Analysis

Likewise, the current ratio, return on invested capital, and sales per square foot all declined. These results were due to "gaps" that Home Depot must correct to sustain its financial momentum. Over all, Home Depot's 1999 to 2001 performance was strong.

To ensure that gaps are minimized in relationship retailing, firms should undertake the following:

Retail Forward (www. retailforward.com/ FreeContent) makes various forward-looking retail research reports available online. Click on "Free Info" and then "Free Newsletters."

1. *Customer Insight:* Analyze known consumer information, such as sales, cost, and profits by segment.
2. *Customer Profiling:* Regularly gather and merge transaction and life-style data to get a fuller picture of individual shoppers. Identify noncustomers who fit the profile of the firm's best segment.
3. *Customer Life-Cycle Model:* Study the firm's interactions with shoppers at various stages in the shoppers' life span. Analyze demographic data by market segment. Determine the cost of serving each life cycle within each segment and the resultant profitability.
4. *Extended Business Model:* Based on steps 2 and 3, draw conclusions about which customers to focus on, the best ways to interact with them, and the best strategy to foster relationships. Survey individual customers to find out how to tailor the retail strategy to best satisfy their needs.
5. *Relationship Program Planning and Design:* Identify all points of contact (in person, pick-up, delivery, kiosk, phone, fax, computer) between the firm and its customers, and the communications that should flow back and forth during each contact. Select processes that please existing customers and attract new ones, promote retention, increase spending, and lift profitability per customer.
6. *Implementation:* Integrate marketing, customer service, and selling efforts.[9]

At our Web site (**www.prenhall.com/bermanevans**), we have a number of links related to benchmarking and gap analysis.

SCENARIO ANALYSIS

Predicting the future is not easy (www.futurist.com/ ssp.htm).

In **scenario analysis**, a retailer projects the future by studying factors that affect long-run performance and then forms contingency ("what if") plans based on alternate scenarios (such as low, moderate, and high levels of competition). Planning for the future is not easy:

Most sectors of U.S. retailing are saturated compared to other developed markets. This largely reflects the big-box retailers in the United States, as well as ongoing upsizing of store formats across most retail sectors. Market saturation will drive (1) an innovation imperative, forcing growth-minded firms to look for new ways to grow sales and profits, including an emphasis on getting more out of existing stores and customers and devising

TABLE 20-5	Home Depot: Internal Benchmarking and Gap Analysis		
	1999	2000	2001
Statement of Earnings Data			
Net sales (in 000,000s)	$38,434	$45,738	$53,553
Earnings before taxes (in 000,000s)	$3,804	$4,217	$4,957
Net earnings (in 000,000s)	$2,320	$2,581	$3,044
Gross margin (% of sales)	29.7	29.9	30.2
General and administrative expenses (% of sales)	1.8	1.7	1.7
Pre-opening expenses (% of sales)	0.3	0.3	0.2
Net earnings (% of sales)	6.0	5.6	5.7
Balance Sheet Data and Financial Ratios			
Total assets (in 000,000s)	$17,081	$21,385	$26,394
Working capital (in 000,000s)	$2,734	$3,392	$3,860
Merchandise inventories (in 000,000s)	$5,489	$6,556	$6,725
Current ratio (times)	1.75	1.77	1.59
Inventory turnover (times)	5.4	5.1	5.4
Return on invested capital (%)	22.5	19.6	18.3
Customer and Store Data			
Number of stores	930	1,134	1,333
Square footage at year-end (in 000,000s)	100	123	109
Number of customer transactions (in 000,000s)	757	937	1,091
Average sale per transaction	$47.87	$48.65	$48.64
Comparable-store sales increase (%)	10	4	1
Weighted-average sales per square foot	$423	$415	$388

Source: Home Depot 2001 Annual Report.

RETAILING Around the World
Is the H&M Apparel Chain a Hit or Miss in the United States?

Swedish-based H&M (Hennes & Mauritz AB) operates stores (www.hm.com) that feature basic clothing in trendy styles and at moderate prices for men, women, and children. As of mid-2002, the company operated 32 East Coast stores in the United States. It plans to double that number by 2005.

There is some disagreement among retailing analysts as to whether H&M's U.S. popularity will be no more than a "flash in the pan." Its supporters state that shoppers still wait for the doors of its Fifth Avenue, New York, store to open each morning and that during lunch hours and weekends the store is literally packed with customers.

However, its detractors question whether H&M can compete in the long run with other competitors that are more established, such as Old Navy (www.oldnavy.com), Target (www.target.com), Abercrombie & Fitch (www.abercrombie.com), and Zara (www.zara.com). They also question how well H&M's strategy will play out in regional markets and in smaller malls.

H&M understands that it needs to fine-tune its U.S. strategy. For example, it recently had to take $4.9 million in markdowns as the result of the chain's disproportionate focus on high fashion rather than basic fashion. It is expanding beyond its original target market to include fashion-focused 18- to 45-year-olds.

Sources: "Expanding at the Speed of Fashion: Eriksen Wants Young Buyers to Get Hooked on Hip Styles at Affordable Prices," *Business Week* (June 17, 2002), p. 78; and Emily Scardino, "H&M: Can It Adapt to America's Landscape?" *DSN Retailing Today* (September 17, 2001), pp. A10, A11.

new concepts; (2) increased stress on struggling retailers, with more store closings by those in bankruptcy, as well as by financially solvent retailers looking to reduce the impact of saturation on profits by closing stores and exiting unprofitable areas; (3) more retail consolidation, resulting in bigger, bolder retailers that will grow their private brands and enter into more exclusive brand arrangements with suppliers; and (4) a sticky situation for suppliers, forcing them to address tough questions about where and how to grow.[10]

These are among the likely aspects of the global economy of the early 21st century: Retailing will be more global, more consolidated, more efficient, and more focused. Consumers worldwide will be more sophisticated, more price-conscious, more discerning, and more demanding of efficient shopping experiences. Some competitive surprises will come from home-grown retailers in emerging markets. There will be fewer currencies. Asia will recover. Russia will not—at least not anytime soon. Japan will muddle along. Inflation will remain dead. Growth will be robust in areas with strong human capital, open financial markets, strong banking laws and weak regulation of other industries, and independent central banks. Good potential retail markets are Poland, Argentina, Chile, Philippines, China, Korea, and Thailand.[11]

As they rein in costs in response to the economic slowdown, supermarkets and drugstores are refocusing on key markets in an intensified competitive environment. These retailers can never take their customers for granted. In a slow economy, this is especially true. Although consumers must still buy food and medication, they are likely to be even more diligent about seeking the best prices and greatest convenience. In this difficult environment, customer loyalty is as important as ever. Supermarket and drugstore chains are broadening their product lines to meet more of consumers' needs, remodeling their units to improve the shopping experience, and adding more stores to fill in their markets and become more recognizable, if not ubiquitous.[12]

How are individual firms reacting to their environment? Consider the vision of Lowe's, as expressed in Figure 20-4. Let's also look at Kohl's (**www.kohls.com**), whose well-conceived plan will continue in the future:

- *Organizational Mission and Positioning:* "The thing that sets it apart is an intense customer focus. It is very narrow in terms of price lines and it hits the ball right up the fairway. The firm concentrates on people 30 to 50 years old, basically the people who spend money."

Ethics in RETAILING — Home Depot's Road to Number One in Social Responsibility

According to a recent online poll by Harris Interactive (**www.harrisinteractive.com**) and the Reputation Institute (**www.reputationinstitute.com**), Home Depot (**www.homedepot.com**) ranks number one in social responsibility in the eyes of U.S. consumers. Home Depot also ranks in the top five in the categories of emotional appeal, goods and services, workplace environment, and corporate reputation.

Three important parts of Home Depot's commitment to social responsibility involve preserving the forests, employee and customer health and safety, and forging strong relationships in its communities.

- Home Depot is striving to better conserve energy, to increase its recycling activities, to stock more environmentally correct products, and to implement a unique lumber purchasing policy. Its vendors are now required to document the source of its lumber products.

- Employee and customer safety initiatives include better measures to keep its aisles free during restocking activities, requiring forklift operators to earn annual re-certification, setting up in-house exercise programs for employees, and placing new signs aimed at reminding customers that they are in a "working warehouse."

- Home Depot believes in giving back to its communities through donations of time and money. Each year, more than 6 million hours are spent by employees who volunteer for local projects and work with national nonprofit groups.

Source: "Company Information: Community Involvement," **www.homedepot.com** (March 17, 2003).

FIGURE 20-4
Lowe's Home Improvement: A Well-Conceived Vision

Reprinted by permission of Lowe's.

We're expanding our vision.

At Lowe's, we're keeping our promise of *Improving Home Improvement*. Our innovative new concepts in home improvement retailing are not only attracting new customers from previously untapped markets, they're keeping our present customers coming back, time after time.

Our product knowledge is unmatched. Our superior customer service skills continue to elevate our position among our retail and commercial customers. And most importantly, the tools and processes we continue to perfect will help us serve customers better — and continue to drive our growth. In 2001, our strategy goes far beyond our preferred product selection and everyday low prices. Our 21st century strategy involves identifying and leveraging new opportunities and focusing on geographic expansion. By seizing these crucial opportunities as they present themselves, Lowe's continues to build on our previous successes for the good of our shareholders, employees, customers and the communities in which we operate.

- *Overall Strategy:* "Kohl's cost structure allows the retailer to promote labels such as Arrow, Levi's, Villager, Sag Harbor, Columbia, Jockey, and Warner's—just to give you a sampling—at 25 percent to 40 percent off so-called 'regular price.' Sears and J.C. Penney typically promote at 20 percent to 30 percent off."

- *Growth:* According to one industry expert, "Our saturation study suggests the United States could support 1,978 Kohl's stores. This means Kohl's could continue to grow square footage at its targeted rate of 20 percent for another nine years before facing saturation issues."

- *Promotion:* "Like most retailers, Kohl's utilizes weekly newspaper circulars to promote its private and national brands. However, the stores have a significantly higher number of 'events' than the competition."

- *Management Team:* As the chain's chief executive says, "Our concept has proven to be very successful, and we are confident in our ability to execute our strategy over the long term."[13]

At our Web site (**www.prenhall.com/bermanevans**), there are several links related to scenario analysis and future planning.

CONTROL: USING THE RETAIL AUDIT

After a retail strategy is devised and enacted, it must be continuously assessed and necessary adjustments made. A vital evaluation tool is the **retail audit**, which systematically examines and evaluates a firm's total retailing effort or a specific aspect of it. The purpose of an audit is to study what a retailer is presently doing, appraise performance, and make recommendations for the future. An audit investigates a retailer's objectives, strategy, implementation, and organization. Goals are reviewed and evaluated for their clarity, consistency, and appropriateness. The strategy and the methods for deriving it are analyzed. The application of the strategy and how it is received by customers are reviewed. The organizational structure is analyzed with regard to lines of command and other factors.

Good auditing includes these elements: Audits are conducted regularly. In-depth analysis is involved. Data are amassed and analyzed systematically. An open-minded, unbiased perspective is maintained. There is a willingness to uncover weaknesses to be corrected, as well as strengths to be exploited. After an audit is completed, decision makers are responsive to the recommendations made in the audit report.

UNDERTAKING AN AUDIT

There are six steps in retail auditing. See Figure 20-5 for an overview of the process, which is described next: (1) Determine who does an audit. (2) Decide when and how often an audit is done. (3) Establish the areas to be audited. (4) Develop audit form(s). (5) Conduct the audit. (6) Report to management.

FIGURE 20-5
The Retail Audit Process

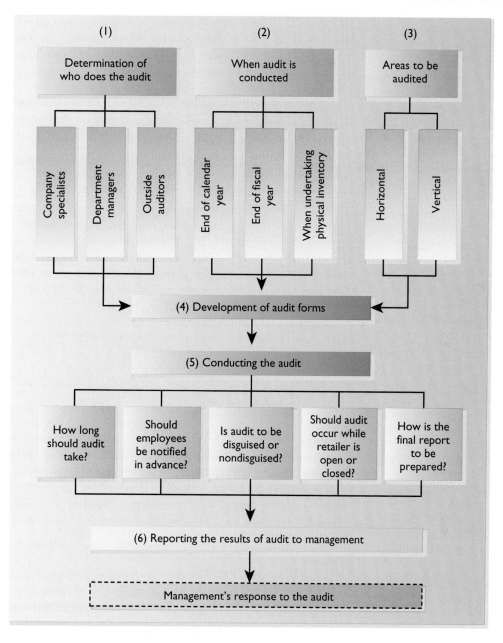

Determining Who Does the Audit

One or a combination of three parties can be involved: a company audit specialist, a company department manager, and an outside auditor.

A company audit specialist is an internal employee whose prime responsibility is the retail audit. The advantages of this person include the auditing expertise, thoroughness, level of knowledge about the firm, and ongoing nature (no time lags). Disadvantages include the costs (especially for retailers that do not need full-time auditors) and the auditor's limited independence.

A company department manager is an internal employee whose prime job is operations management; that manager may also be asked to participate in the retail audit. The advantages are that there are no added personnel expenses and that the manager is knowledgeable about the firm and its operations. Disadvantages include the manager's time away from the primary job, the potential lack of objectivity, time pressure, and the complexity of companywide audits.

An outside auditor is not a retailer's employee but a paid consultant. Advantages are the auditor's broad experience, objectivity, and thoroughness. Disadvantages are the high costs per day or hour (for some retailers, it may be cheaper to hire per-diem consultants than full-time auditors; the opposite is true for larger firms), the time lag while a consultant gains familiarity with the firm, the failure of some firms to use outside specialists continuously, and the reluctance of some employees to cooperate.

Determining When and How Often the Audit Is Conducted

Logical times for auditing are the end of the calendar year, the end of the retailer's annual reporting year (fiscal year), or when a complete physical inventory is conducted. Each of these is appropriate for evaluating a retailer's operations during the previous period. An audit must be enacted at least annually, although some retailers desire more frequent analysis. It is important that the same period(s), such as January–December, be studied to make meaningful comparisons, projections, and adjustments.

Determining Areas to Be Audited

A retail audit typically includes more than financial analysis; it reviews various aspects of a firm's strategy and operations to identify strengths and weaknesses. There are two basic types of audits. They should be used in conjunction with one another because a horizontal audit often reveals areas that merit further investigation by a vertical audit.

This site has a detailed online vertical pricing audit (www.bizmove.com/ marketing/m2y3.htm) for retailers.

A **horizontal retail audit** analyzes a firm's overall performance, from the organizational mission to goals to customer satisfaction to the basic retail strategy mix and its implementation in an integrated, consistent way. It is also known as a "retail strategy audit." A **vertical retail audit** analyzes—in depth—a firm's performance in one area of the strategy mix or operations, such as the credit function, customer service, merchandise assortment, or interior displays. A vertical audit is focused and specialized.

Developing Audit Forms

To be systematic, a retailer should use detailed audit forms. An audit form lists the area(s) to be studied and guides data collection. It usually resembles a questionnaire and is completed by the auditor. Without audit forms, analysis is more haphazard and subjective. Key questions may be omitted or poorly worded. Auditor biases may appear. Most significantly, questions may differ from one audit period to another, which limits comparisons. Examples of retail audit forms are presented shortly.

Conducting the Audit

Next, the audit itself is undertaken. Management specifies how long the audit will take. Prior notification of employees depends on management's perception of two factors: the need to compile some data in advance to save time versus the desire to get an objective picture and not a distorted one (which may occur if employees have too much notice). With a disguised audit, employees are unaware that it is taking place. It is useful if the auditor investigates an area like personal selling and wishes to act as a customer to elicit employee responses. With a nondisguised audit, employees know an audit is being conducted. This is desirable if employees are asked specific operational questions and help in gathering data.

Some audits should be done while the retailer is open, such as assessing parking adequacy, in-store customer traffic patterns, the use of vertical transportation, and customer relations. Others should be done when the firm is closed, such as analyses of the condition of fixtures, inventory levels and turnover, financial statements, and employee records.

An audit report can be formal or informal, brief or long, oral or written, and a statement of findings or a statement of findings plus recommendations. It has a better chance of acceptance if presented in the format desired by management.

Reporting Audit Findings and Recommendations to Management

The last auditing step is to present findings and recommendations to management. It is the role of management—not the auditor—to see what adjustments (if any) to make. Decision makers must read the report thoroughly, consider each point, and enact the needed strategic changes.

Technology in RETAILING · The Retail Store of the Future: What Will It Be Like?

According to one retailing analyst, every retailer has two conflicting goals: (1) to keep shoppers in a store longer to increase impulse sales and (2) to get them out faster at the checkout counter. A number of new technologies are now emerging to accomplish each objective. Let's examine how these technologies may be used in the store of the future.

Retailers can increase impulse sales by strategically placing electronic signs that can be programmed to change on a scheduled or random basis. These signs can present special offers for current in-store shoppers and direct customers to complementary departments. In conjunction with electronic signs, retailers may use electronic shelf labels. Not only do these reduce labor costs, but they also virtually guarantee pricing accuracy.

Some experts feel that "cyber communications," whereby customers are electronically recognized as they enter the store and receive promotions based on past purchase behavior, are inevitable.

The store of the future will lessen customer waiting time through more extensive use of smart cards that display remaining balances. And self-checkouts are expected to expand to "parts of the store like the deli or garden department."

Source: George L. Colicchio, "The Store of the Future: A Look at the Technologies That Will Be Driving Your Stores—and Your Customers—Within the Next Five Years," *Progressive Grocer* (February 2002), pp. 13–14.

They should treat each audit seriously and react accordingly. No matter how well an audit is done, it is not a worthwhile activity if management fails to enact recommendations.

RESPONDING TO AN AUDIT

TJX (www.tjx.com) is very open about its performance. Enter the "Corporate Web Site" and see how much information is available about the firm's plans and results.

After management studies audit findings, appropriate actions are taken. Areas of strength are continued and areas of weakness are revised. These actions must be consistent with the retail strategy and noted in the firm's retail information system (for further reference).

J.C. Penney, the veteran department store chain, places great reliance on its retail audits. Consider this commentary by *Chain Store Age* on the occasion of the firm's 100th anniversary:

As significant as that milestone might seem, Penney executives are more concerned with another anniversary. They're focused on what is now year two of a five-year turnaround plan to recapture past glories of the all-American chain. While many chains talk about turning around their sales, their profits, and their businesses, Penney's comeback story is noteworthy during its centennial because it includes some encouraging results in black and white. The strategy to change a 100-year-old company is not only complicated, it's difficult—especially in an arena dominated by the increasing punching power of Wal-Mart, Kohl's, and Target: "Penney's most significant issue today is the fact that its sales per square foot lag the industry by a tremendous gap." The department store niche is fighting a war on two fronts—one front with the discounters that have better prices, and one with upscale retailers with better products or service or both. Yet, the middle road of retail is precisely the one traveled by Penney, which according to its chief executive is "a moderate-priced department store" serving "mainstream American families."[14]

POSSIBLE DIFFICULTIES IN CONDUCTING A RETAIL AUDIT

AuditNet (www.auditnet.org) has a number of good examples of auditing applications. Click on "Audit Programs."

Several obstacles may occur in doing a retail audit. A retailer should be aware of them:

- An audit may be costly.
- It may be quite time-consuming.
- Performance measures may be inaccurate.
- Employees may feel threatened and not cooperate as much as desired.
- Incorrect data may be collected.
- Management may not be responsive to the findings.

At present, many retailers—particularly small ones—do not understand or perform systematic retail audits. But this must change if they are to assess themselves properly and plan correctly for the future.

Planning

1. Have you thought about the long-term direction of your business? ___
2. Have you developed a realistic set of plans for the year's operations? ___
3. Do your plans provide methods to deal with competition? ___
4. Is there a system for auditing your objectives? ___

Customer Analysis (Who are your target customers and what are they seeking from you?)

1. Have you profiled your customers by age, income, education, occupation, etc.? ___
2. Are you aware of the reasons why customers shop with you? ___
3. Do you ask your customers for suggestions on ways to improve your operation? ___
4. Do you know what goods and services your customers most prefer? ___

Organization and Human Resources

1. Are job descriptions and authority for responsibilities clearly stated? ___
2. Have you an effective system for communication with employees? ___
3. Do you have a formal program for motivating employees? ___
4. Have you taken steps to minimize shoplifting and internal theft? ___

Operations and Special Services

1. Do you monitor every facet of your operations in terms of specific goals? ___
2. Do you provide time-saving services for greater customer convenience? ___
3. Do you have a policy for handling merchandise returned by customers? ___
4. Do you get feedback through customer surveys? ___

Financial Analysis and Control

1. Do your financial records give you the information to make sound decisions? ___
2. Can sales be broken down by department? ___
3. Do you understand the pros and cons of the retail method of accounting? ___
4. Have you taken steps to minimize shoplifting and internal theft? ___

Buying

1. Do you have a merchandise budget (planned purchases) for each season that is broken down by department and merchandise classification? ___
2. Does it take into consideration planned sales, planned gross margin, planned inventory turnover, and planned markdowns? ___
3. Do you plan exclusive or private brand programs? ___
4. Do you take advantage of cash discounts and allowances offered by your vendor/supplier? ___

Pricing

1. Have you determined whether to price below, at, or above the market? ___
2. Do you set specific markups for each product category? ___
3. Do you know which products are slow-movers and which are fast? ___
4. Have you developed a markdown policy? ___

Atmospherics

1. Are the unique appeals of your business reflected in your image? ___
2. Have you figured out the best locations for displays? ___
3. Do you know which items are bought on "impulse?" ___
4. Do you use signs to aid your customers in shopping? ___

Promotion

1. Are you familiar with the strengths and weaknesses of various promotional methods? ___
2. Do you participate in cooperative advertising? ___
3. Do you ask customers to refer your business to friends and relatives? ___
4. Do you make use of community projects or publicity? ___

FIGURE 20-6

A Management Audit Form for Small Retailers—Selected Questions

These questions cover areas that are the basis for retailing. You can use this form to evaluate your current status and, perhaps, to rethink certain decisions. Answer YES or NO to each question.

Source: Adapted by the authors from Michael W. Little, *Marketing Checklist for Small Retailers* (Washington, D.C.: U.S. Small Business Administration, Management Aids Number 4.012).

ILLUSTRATIONS OF RETAIL AUDIT FORMS

Here, we present a management audit form and a retailing effectiveness checklist to show how small and large retailers can inexpensively, yet efficiently, conduct retail audits. An internal or external auditor (or department manager) could periodically complete one of these forms and then discuss the findings with management. The examples noted are both horizontal audits. A vertical audit would involve an in-depth analysis of any one area in the forms.

A Management Audit Form for Small Retailers

Under the auspices of the U.S. Small Business Administration, a *Marketing Checklist for Small Retailers* was developed. Although written for small firms, it is a comprehensive horizontal audit applicable to all retailers. Figure 20-6 shows selected questions from this audit form. "Yes" is the desired answer to each question. For questions answered negatively, the firm must learn the causes and adjust its strategy.

A Retailing Effectiveness Checklist

Figure 20-7 has another type of audit form to assess performance and prepare for the future: a retailing effectiveness checklist. It can be used by small and large firms alike. The checklist is more strategic than the *Management Audit for Small Retailers*—which is more tactical. Unlike the yes-no answers in Figure 20-6, the checklist lets a retailer rate its performance from 1 to 5 in each

✓ A long-term organizational mission is clearly articulated.	_____
✓ The current status of the firm is taken into consideration when setting future plans.	_____
✓ Sustainable competitive advantages are actively pursued.	_____
✓ Company weaknesses have been identified and minimized.	_____
✓ The management style is compatible with the firm's way of doing business.	_____
✓ There is a logical short-run and long-run approach to the firm's chosen line of business.	_____
✓ There are specific, realistic, and measurable short- and long-term goals.	_____
✓ These goals guide strategy development and resource allocation.	_____
✓ The characteristics and needs of the target market are known.	_____
✓ The strategy is tailored to the chosen target market.	_____
✓ Customers are extremely loyal.	_____
✓ There are systematic plans prepared for each element of the strategy mix.	_____
✓ All important uncontrollable factors are monitored.	_____
✓ The overall strategy is integrated.	_____
✓ Short-, moderate-, and long-term plans are compatible.	_____
✓ The firm knows how each merchandise line, for-sale service, and business format stands in the marketplace.	_____
✓ Tactics are carried out in a manner consistent with the strategic plan.	_____
✓ The strategic plan and its elements are adequately communicated.	_____
✓ Unbiased feedback is regularly sought for each aspect of the strategic plan.	_____
✓ Information about new opportunities and threats is sought out.	_____
✓ After enacting a strategic plan, company strengths and weaknesses, as well as successes and failures, are studied on an ongoing basis.	_____
✓ Results are studied in a manner that reduces the firm's chances of overreacting to a situation.	_____
✓ Strategic modifications are made when needed and before crises occur.	_____
✓ The firm avoids strategy flip-flops (that confuse customers, employees, suppliers, and others).	_____
✓ The company has a well-executed Web site or plans to have one shortly.	_____

FIGURE 20-7

A Retailing Effectiveness Checklist

Rate your company's effectiveness in each of the following areas on a scale of 1 to 5, with 1 being strongly agree (excellent effort) and 5 being strongly disagree (poor effort). An answer of 3 or higher signifies that improvements are necessary.

area; this provides more in-depth information. However, a total score should not be computed (unless items are weighted), because all items are not equally important. A simple summation would not be a meaningful score.

Summary

1. *To demonstrate the importance of integrating a retail strategy.* This chapter shows why retailers need to plan and apply coordinated strategies, and describes how to assess success or failure. The stages of a retail strategy must be viewed as an ongoing, integrated system of interrelated steps.

2. *To examine four key factors in the development and enactment of an integrated retail strategy: planning procedures and opportunity analysis, defining productivity, performance measures, and scenario analysis.* Planning procedures can be optimized by adhering to a series of specified actions, from situation analysis to control. Opportunities need to be studied in terms of their impact on overall strategy. The sales opportunity grid is good for comparing various strategic options.

   To maximize productivity, retailers need to define exactly what productivity represents to them when they enact their strategies. Though firms should be efficient, this does not necessarily mean having the lowest possible operating costs (which may lead to customer dissatisfaction), but rather keying spending to the performance standards required by a retailer's chosen niche (such as upscale versus discount).

   By applying the right performance measures and setting standards for them, a retailer can better integrate its strategy. Measures include total sales, average sales per store, sales by goods/service category, sales per square foot, gross margins, gross margin return on investment, operating income, inventory turnover, markdown percentages, employee turnover, financial ratios, and profitability. Retail Forward's performance index combines sales growth, profit growth, and return on assets.

   With scenario analysis, a retailer projects the future by examining the major factors that will have an impact on its long-term performance. Contingency plans are then keyed to alternative scenarios. This is not easy.

3. *To show how industry and company data can be used in strategy planning and analysis (benchmarking and gap analysis).* With benchmarking, a retailer sets its own standards and measures performance based on the achievements of its sector of retailing, specific competitors, the best companies, and/or its own prior actions. Through gap analysis, a retailer can compare its actual performance against its potential performance and see the areas in which it must improve.

4. *To show the value of a retail audit.* A retail strategy must be regularly monitored, evaluated, and fine-tuned or revised. The retail audit is one way to do this. It is a systematic, thorough, and unbiased review and appraisal.

   The audit process has six sequential steps: (1) determining who does the audit, (2) deciding when and how often it is conducted, (3) setting the areas to be audited, (4) preparing forms, (5) conducting the audit, and (6) reporting results and recommendations to management. After the right executives read the audit report, necessary revisions in strategy should be made.

   In a horizontal audit, a retailer's overall strategy and performance are assessed. In a vertical audit, one element of a strategy is reviewed in detail. Among the potential difficulties of auditing are the costs, the time commitment, the inaccuracy of performance standards, the poor cooperation from some employees, the collection of incorrect data, and unresponsive management. Some firms do not conduct audits; thus, they may find it difficult to evaluate their positions and plan for the future.

   Two audit forms are presented in the chapter: a management audit for retailers and a retailing effectiveness checklist.

Key Terms

sales opportunity grid (p. 509)

performance measures (p. 511)

benchmarking (p. 511)

retail performance index (p. 513)

gap analysis (p. 514)

scenario analysis (p. 516)

retail audit (p. 518)

horizontal retail audit (p. 520)

vertical retail audit (p. 520)

Questions for Discussion

1. Why is it imperative for a firm to view its strategy as an integrated and ongoing process?

2. Develop a sales opportunity grid for a movie theater planning to add an ATM to its services mix.

3. Cite five performance measures commonly used by retailers, and explain what can be learned by studying each.

4. What is benchmarking? Present a five-step procedure to do retail benchmarking.

5. What do you think are the pros and cons of the retail performance index highlighted in Table 20-4?

6. How are the terms *gap analysis* and *scenario analysis* interrelated?

7. Distinguish between horizontal and vertical retail audits. Develop a vertical audit form for a jewelry store.

8. What are the attributes of good retail auditing?

9. Distinguish among these auditors. Under what circumstances would each be preferred?
   a. Outside auditor.
   b. Company audit specialist.
   c. Company department manager.

10. Under what circumstances should a nondisguised audit be used?

11. How should management respond to the findings of an audit? What can happen if the findings are ignored?

12. Why do many retailers not conduct any form of retail audit? Are these reasons valid? Explain your answer.

Web-Based Exercise

Visit the industry section of the Web site of the American Customer Satisfaction Index (**www.theacsi.org/industry_scores. htm**) and click on each of the retailing industry links. What do you conclude from reviewing these scores?

Note: Stop by our Web site (**www.prenhall.com/bermanevans**) to experience a number of highly interactive, appealing Web exercises based on actual company demonstrations and sample materials related to retailing.

Chapter Endnotes

1. Various company sources.

2. Mark S. Bassett, "Hardware Store Competes Successfully with Big Chains," *Knight Ridder/Tribune Business News* (March 7, 2002), p. ITEM02066008.

3. Rick Wingate, "Target Vs. Kmart—A Store-Level View (Opinions from the Field)," *DSN Retailing Today* (May 6, 2002), p. 12.

4. See "2002 High-Performance Retailers," *Chain Store Age* (November 2002), p. 39.

5. See Chris Dubelaar, Nukesh Bhargava, and David Ferrarin, "Measuring Retail Productivity: What Really Matters?" *Journal of Business Research*, Vol. 55 (May 2002), pp. 417–426.

6. Sue Henczel, "Benchmarking—Measuring and Comparing for Continuous Improvement," *Information Outlook* (July 2002), p. 12. See also Jeffrey T. Resnick, "Reputation Matters," *Chain Store Age* (May 2002), pp. 40–41.

7. A. Parasuraman, Valarie A. Zeithaml, and Leonard L. Berry, "Alternative Scales for Measuring Service Quality: A Comparative Assessment Based on Psychometric and Diagnostic Criteria," *Journal of Retailing*, Vol. 70 (Fall 1994), pp. 201–230. See also Terry Grapentine, "The History and Future of Service Quality Assessment," *Marketing Research* (Winter 1998/Spring 1999), pp. 5–20; Richard S. Lytle, Peter W. Hom, and Michael P. Mokwa, "SERV*OR: A Managerial Measure of Organizational

Service-Orientation," *Journal of Retailing*, Vol. 74 (Fall 1998), pp. 455–489; and Michael K. Brady, J. Joseph Cronin, and Richard R. Brands, "Performance-Only Measurement of Service Quality: A Replication and Extension," *Journal of Business Research*, Vol. 55 (January 2002), pp. 17–31.

8. "Best Practices in Retailing," *Chain Store Age* (November 1995), pp. 49–108. See also "Global Supply Chain Benchmarking and Best Practices Study: Phase II," *Stores* (September 1999), pp. K1–K22.

9. Austen Mulinder, "Hear Today . . . Or Gone Tomorrow? Winners Listen to Customers," *Retailing Issues Letter* (September 1999), p. 5.

10. Lois Huff, "Retail Industry Change Agents in the Next Economy," *2002 Strategic Outlook Conference* (Columbus, Ohio: Retail Forward, 2002), p. 4.

11. Ira Kalish, "Global Outlook: The Economy and the Retail Industry," *Winning Strategies for the New World of Global Retailing* (Columbus, Ohio: PricewaterhouseCoopers, 1999), pp. 15–16.

12. *Standard & Poor's Industry Surveys: Supermarkets & Drugstores* (June 27, 2002), p. 1.

13. Jeffrey Arlen, "Can Kohl's Keep It Up?" *DSN Retailing Today* (August 20, 2001), pp. A8–A9.

14. "At 100, J.C. Penney Looks Ahead," *Chain Store Age* (June 2002), pp. 45–47.

part eight
Short Cases

1: LOOKING AHEAD WITH 7-ELEVEN

7-Eleven (**www.7-eleven.com**) is a huge retail entity that operates 22,000 convenience stores worldwide—nearly 6,000 stores in the United States. As part of the chain's 75th Birthday Initiative, the marketing team made a decision to not only revamp the convenience chain's marketing blueprint but also to change its corporate structure as well. 7-Eleven's director of marketing said, "We're bolstering our entire marketing mix, bridging it with merchandising, and inviting partners along for the ride." He promised that the new plan will be focused, have a consistent communication message, and be carefully coordinated with channel partners. The main focus in long-run planning is to attract and retain 7-Eleven's manufacturing partners and to use the strength of co-marketing to generate brand and store loyalty.

In one co-branding campaign, 7-Eleven received a 30-day exclusive on single-serving bottles of Code Red, a Mountain Dew spin-off. 7-Eleven promoted the product with 15-second-spot TV commercials. After the brand was launched, 7-Eleven introduced a Code Red Slurpee that was served with customized cups. According to an executive at Pepsi-Cola (Mountain Dew's parent company), "With that campaign, 7-Eleven sent a message to all manufacturers: 'Look what we can do.'" Shortly thereafter, 7-Eleven attracted nine additional vendors for a holiday campaign. That effort revolved around a 12-page coupon booklet containing $9 in discounts from a number of manufacturers. The booklets also contained "peel and reveal" instant-win games with such prizes as cell phones, small TV sets, and gasoline cards.

In addition to its theme-based promotions, 7-Eleven is looking to develop 60-day promotional campaigns for its private-label merchandise: "There's no reason why account-specific programs and dedicated private-label efforts cannot run their respective courses, without bleeding into each other, even if the goals of each are very different." In order to control space allocation and to make for a more uniform store environment, 7-Eleven manufactures all point-of-purchase materials. The number of point-of-purchase materials sent monthly to the stores has also been reduced from 85 to 50 promotions.

Special product combinations are also gaining in importance to 7-Eleven and its customers. "Meal deals" that combine beverages and snacks with 7-Eleven's fresh-item menu are popular. So is the chain's communications center that consists of such items as phone cards, pre-paid cell phone kits, and pre-paid Internet access.

Although 7-Eleven's core market continues to be 18- to 44-year-old males, the chain wants to better appeal to women, as well as to build the teen market (for both genders). For example, women find fresh food, delicatessen sandwiches, fruit, and new wine items to be appealing. As for the teen market, 7-Eleven is increasing its spending on targeted promotions, such as a recent campaign offering customers a free Britney Spears poster and customized fountain cups with the purchase of a 12-pack of Pepsi. The offer was coordinated with a Britney Spears concert.

The prototype store is also to be revised as part of the new marketing plan. Among the revisions being considered are a larger store with easier-to-navigate aisles, more sophisticated end-of-aisle displays, and drive-in windows. One factor that has not been finalized is whether 7-Eleven should revise its decades-old tagline: "Thank Heaven for 7-Eleven." While the tagline is closely associated with the company, its continued use may be in conflict with the retailer's new desired image.

Questions

1. What techniques should 7-Eleven use to monitor the future of the convenience store industry and its place in it?
2. What performance measures should 7-Eleven use in assessing its new initiatives?
3. Can 7-Eleven effectively practice both co-branding and a private-label strategy? Explain your answer.
4. Present a brief vertical audit for 7-Eleven to rate its channel partner programs.

The material in this case is drawn from Dan Hanover, "Marriage of Convenience," *Promo* (February 2002), pp. 32–38.

2: CAN JIFFY LUBE CONTINUE GETTING THE JOB DONE?

Jiffy Lube (**www.jiffylube.com**) invented the quick-change oil-and-lubrication business in 1979. Its 2,200 service centers (78 percent franchised) now serve over 31 million consumers per year. Jiffy Lube, with 13 percent of the installed-oil segment of the auto after-care market, has the most recognized name in its retail segment. *Entrepreneur* magazine recently ranked Jiffy Lube as the fifth-best overall franchise organization on the basis of such criteria as financial strength and growth.

Despite these positive characteristics, Jiffy Lube's sales have been stagnant in recent years. While this is largely due to the sale or closing of more than 600 store locations after Jiffy Lube merged with Quaker State (**www.quakerstate.com**), new car dealers and specialty repair shops have been successful in their efforts to target the quick-change oil segment.

In 2001, Anne Tawney was appointed senior vice-president of marketing at Jiffy Lube. She has responsibility for advertising, promotions, and brand development. One of Tawney's primary tasks is to better understand consumers' relationships with their cars and then to tailor Jiffy Lube's promotional messages. For example, many new car purchasers mistakenly feel that Jiffy Lube's technicians do not have the competency to perform oil changes and lubrication services. Some new car buyers also wrongly assume that using Jiffy Lube will void their new car warranty. Furthermore, new car service manuals typically recommend an oil change only every 10,000 miles—unless driving conditions are severe. Few motorists realize that short "stop-and-go" trips should be categorized as severe driving conditions.

As part of Jiffy Lube's brand repositioning strategy, the retailer undertook a major study of consumer attitudes and competitor strategies. It found that most consumers perceived Jiffy Lube as a "me too" brand with no distinctive positioning. In addition, Jiffy Lube's competitors sought to differentiate themselves on the basis of pricing, different services, and misrepresentations about warranties. Because of this research, Jiffy Lube decided to define itself as the category leader, with a secondary theme that Jiffy Lube is "the well-oiled machine" with personnel who are dependable professionals.

When implementing its repositioning strategy, Jiffy Lube knows it must have a single image for all of its franchised and company-owned dealerships. Although there are some regional differences, all dealerships use the same central message. About two-thirds of Jiffy Lube's advertising budget is devoted to 30- and 60-second commercials. Its message is made more memorable through Sheryl Crow's hit song "A Change (Would Do You Good)" as the musical backdrop. TV ads account for 30 percent of the budget. The balance consists of radio, direct-mail, point-of-purchase, outdoor, and print advertising.

Jiffy Lube has a data base with 34 million names. The retailer is now working on a way to tailor its messages to specific classes of customers. One message, for example, would remind customers that their car needs an oil change based on the customer's driving habits and time since their last oil change. Different groups of customers may also receive different promotional offers.

A significant challenge to Jiffy Lube is that its current corporate owner is Pennzoil, a lubricant manufacturer that sells its oils and lubricants to a wide variety of retailers—including a large number of Jiffy Lube's competitors. Jiffy Lube accounts for 10 percent of Pennzoil's total sales. Yet, Pennzoil has a 36 percent share of the total motor oil market.

Questions

1. In planning for the future, what kinds of information should Jiffy Lube seek out? Explain your answer.
2. How can Jiffy Lube avoid the "me too" perception among its target customers?
3. What are Jiffy Lube's competitive advantages and disadvantages in comparison to new car dealers? How can it reduce the disadvantages?
4. Devise a brief horizontal audit for Jiffy Lube to assess its retail strategy.

The material in this case is drawn from Keven T. Higgins, "Quick Change Branding Strategy," *Marketing Management* (June 2002), pp. 12–15.

part eight
Comprehensive Case

Who's Minding the Future?*

INTRODUCTION

Although answers to questions about the future are filled with uncertainty, that uncertainty can be framed by analyzing major trends transforming business practices. A major force behind retail change is the ever-shifting customer. They continue to demand more from retailers than quality merchandise at fair prices; are harder to identify, segment, and target than before; exercise new forms of power; and are filled with contradictions—such as wanting a stimulating yet serene shopping environment—making it much more difficult for retailers to meet customers' product, service, and store expectations. Consumer changes can dramatically impact traditional store design, merchandising, information systems, personal selling, communications, supply chain systems, and other elements of the retail mix—all of which begs the question: Who will emerge as the retailing leaders of tomorrow and what will they look like?

The Six Faces of the Changing Consumer

Tomorrow's retailing leaders will be truly customer-centered. They will begin the journey toward success armed with superior knowledge of customer needs and wants. They will demonstrate superior skill at designing and executing strategies to better serve the changing customer.

What are the key consumer trends transforming retailing practices? While we know they exist, we haven't seen them clearly articulated in a form that readily translates into retail strategy. Through our research, we've attempted to close this knowledge gap. We've studied the marketplace and consulted with retail thought leaders to uncover six consumer mega-trends that should be at the forefront of all strategic thinking as retailers prepare to compete in the brave new world some three to five years from now.

In our research, we uncovered more than 300 consumer trends, identified commonalities among them, and delineated the major shifts that will characterize shoppers for some time. This was done by subjecting the trends to an analysis by a team of more than 20 industry experts. Initially, team members collapsed the 300 trends into 46 major patterns and further refined those to 14 broader trends. Next, the team identified six mega-trends to describe consumer behavior. These trends were then subjected to roundtable discussions with senior executives from ten leading retailers. The six mega-trends are summarized next.

Composite Nation

America has moved from a society that recognizes and accepts Caucasian nuclear families to a society that recognizes and accepts multi-ethnic, diverse households. While diversity has always been a part of our landscape, its scope continues to intensify. The "American family" as we know it is being redefined. It may be made up of the traditional two parents and kids, a single mom and kid, a same-sex couple, an extended family with grandparents, aunts, uncles, and even friends. What's more, Americans come from more diverse racial, ethnic, and cultural backgrounds than ever before.

Mysterious Customers

Gauging the customer is more difficult than ever. As society embraces individuality, diversity, and self-expression, the once-clear clues to life-style and potential spending power—such as age, gender, style of dress, and even vernacular—seem to have disappeared. The emergence of "young" old people and "old" young people (children taking on more and more adult roles and adults maintaining younger life-styles), stay-at-home dads and working moms, more urban and ethnic influence, multi-community memberships, and wider availability of "knock-off" items have all contributed to a harder-to-read customer. People come from households we didn't have 15 years ago and were brought up on relatively new values. Their tastes range widely. They have short attention spans and less patience compared to traditional customers.

Consumer Power Shift

Consumers now have more power, and they are using it to create better and more informed decisions, purchases, and service experiences. Through access to unlimited information from external sources, chiefly the Internet, consumers have almost perfect information on the terms of sale and the service and product options available, before they enter the store. They are empowered and independent information gatherers and decision makers. "Transactions in glass houses" means that consumers can immediately and confidently assess levels of fairness in any transaction, which they are doing with increased frequency. They also are more conscious of the opportunity cost of their time. What is different today is that with countless choices at their disposal, consumers are increasingly intolerant of anyone or any entity that fails to respect their time. They want concepts such as convenience to be defined and executed on their terms.

Stimulation and Sanctuary

Consumers are involved in a balancing act between a desire for stimulation and a need for sanctuary. *Multi-tasking* used to be a computer term. Today, it describes people trying to squeeze as much activity as possible into shrinking slivers of time. Inundated with stimuli, consumers have developed an appetite for speed, excitement, and extremism. This is fueled in part by new technology that allows 24/7 access to everything and simulates a "real experience." Such fast-paced lives have also led to an intensified desire for spaces of retreat, reflection, comfort, and security. More consumers are attending church and spas are booming, as are yoga classes, candle sales, and other mood creators. Just as consumers seek greater stimulation, they also seek greater solace—often from the same retailer and often at the same time.

Amorphous Codes and Spaces

Well-established norms have given way to codes that are loose and flexible. With the rise of diversity and individuality, ubiquitous communities, and redefined households (as well as interchangeable roles, such as father as mother and mother as father), common customs and standards are up for grabs as we struggle to make sense of it all. Much of what consumers do is shape themselves on the fly. Many people create momentary realities, switch between roles, and take on different personalities as the situation warrants. Current codes of conduct no longer draw heavily from the past. The future will likely see more consumers applying multiple codes. People have gone from multi-tasking at a single site to multi-tasking in a multi-functional environment. Space is whatever the consumer perceives it to be.

Communities Everywhere

Online communities, neighborhood associations, self-help groups, antique clubs, gardening clubs, and volunteer groups are proliferating. Not long ago, memberships were clearly delineated, defined by space, or passed down from one generation to the next. But with the breakup of the nuclear family, more single-person households, increased connectivity afforded by the Internet, the rise of individuality, and a greater sense of isolation, people are actively exploring and seeking out community membership, often in previously uncharted forms. These new communities are designed quickly and virtually; they come and go based on individual needs and preferences, with individuals free to join and leave as they please.

Experiential-Based Versus Commodity-Based Competition

One outcome of the changes in needs, wants, and behaviors is that store choice is not only driven by value assessments (consumer benefits for the costs they incur), but that the consumer value equation is also changing. What people are looking for in retailing, and what they will demand in the future, is growing in scope, sophistication, and complexity. A historical perspective of value assessment shows that consumers have gone from defining value in terms of price (with lower price being equated to higher value) to looking at value as quality of the merchandise received relative to its price. Value estimations now also include assessments of the shopping experience. The consumer value equation has assumed this form:

$$V_t = w_1 V_o + w_2 V_e$$

V_t is the total value of the retailing exchange; V_o is the value of the offering, which equals quality/price; V_e is the value of the retailing experience; and w_1 and w_2 are the relative weights placed on the two major components of value by consumers. Thus, you might view consumers as dividing 100 importance points between V_o and V_e when assessing the overall value received from shopping at a particular store.

We see consumers focusing on total value and giving more emphasis (w_2) to the retailing experience (V_e) in making assessments. While changing economic and personal conditions can cause fluctuations in the emphasis placed (w_1 versus w_2) in assessing total value, the overriding trend has been to give more weight to the retailing experience. FAO Schwarz has long recognized this by offering fair prices and an engaging shopping experience. Competing on quality and further competing on the experiential aspects that define the retailing engagement are alternatives to pursue for increasing customer value.

Yet, for decades, many retailers have focused on the product side of the value equation, pursuing a commodity-based strategy of competition that stresses winning with price and merchandise assortments. The result has been similar product offerings and intense retail price competition. As a consequence, several retailers have turned to in-house brands and exclusive product agreements with manufacturers to move away from this sea of sameness. Even these private brands are often composed of similar offerings.

The expanded value equation reveals that differentiation strategies can be enhanced by switching to an experiential-based strategy of competition, thereby creating value not only through superior offerings but also with a concerted effort to maximize consumer value through the in-store shopping experience. A positive benefit of this is the creation of store and shopping elements that are not easily duplicated by competitors in the short run (such as superior customer service, stimulating environments, superior communities). The elements may be nonduplicable by competitors even in the long run. Just as failure to provide value in offerings creates openings for competitors, failing to provide valuable experiences can give competitors a chance to steal customers via superior levels of total shopping value.

Some experiential facets become clear from a convergence of the six faces of the changing consumer. One could even say the "new retail values" will be competitive imperatives. To some, these values will be completely new to their way of doing business. To others, they represent new forms of executing classical strategies (e.g., community leadership instead of community involvement). To still others, the new values will reinforce concepts currently at the early developmental stage of the strategic planning process.

Five New Retail Values

(1) Customer respect as central to success, not tangential: The changing face of the customer points to respect as a key to future retail success. The diversity in ethnicity, sexual orientations, and relationships, as well as other factors, argues for the need to respect individual differences. The further blurring of gender roles, the exercising of power by more women, the amorphous nature of conduct codes, and how people use retail space also point to respect for individualism as a cornerstone of success.

As consumers become more time-pressed and time-pressured, respect for their time also becomes critical. Providing fast, efficient, and effortless shopping experiences is integral to demonstrating a respect for time. Similarly, as consumers tailor the retail experience to their tastes and preferences, respect for consumer choices is more critical to providing customers with total retail value. Trust, commitment, patronage, positive word of mouth, repeat buying, satisfaction, and customer enthusiasm are among the positive outcomes to retailers from respecting shoppers. Making customer respect an explicit and integral component of corporate culture, therefore, is a new value that can pay important dividends.

(2) Soul of the customer, not superficial understanding: The changing face of the consumer in regard to a composite nation and the lack of clear shopping cues implies that getting to know customers will be harder in the future. Customers are no longer who they may appear to be. Older people acting younger, younger people

acting older; stay-at-home dads; the rich dressing down and the poor dressing up; doctors and lawyers driving Harleys—what's going on? Retailers will have to learn each person's interests, attitudes, opinions, and corresponding wants and needs as traditional, observational cues lose their value as indicators of shopping behavior. More intimate information must be gathered. The role of sales associates in identifying customers and effectively interacting with them may become more critical.

(3) Customer enthusiasm, not satisfaction: Future consumers will want retailers to do more than just satisfy them. They will expect to be delighted, with outcomes exceeding expectations, so they are enthusiastic or fanatical patrons. Retailers will then have customer advocates who spread the word about the firm, its offerings, and their experiences. The passion of such customers is heartfelt, long-lasting, and infectious. The emotional trends in consumer behavior suggest that more consumers actually want to be enthusiastic if given a chance. Enthusiasm can be due to community, customization, knowing customer expectations intimately, and respecting customers. It can also result from being innovative; understanding the value of freshness in merchandise and store design; creating holidays or celebrations within the store; and celebrating the store experience with managers, employees, senior executives, and customers.

(4) Customers customize, not retailers: A major benefit touted in the days of the dot-com euphoria was the ability of online retailers to customize shopping for each customer when he or she logged on. Yet, online customization never materialized in the form promised to shoppers, and did anyone really care? Customers do not want any firm to define their shopping experience. Offering customers the opportunity to tailor their own experiences by simple, multi-optioned navigation is valued. Customers want to exercise power and to define their own experiences. Enabling them to easily and efficiently customize the experience to their needs and wants is a competitive mandate. Retailers should not be the customizer; rather, they should be enablers. The store of the future will be filled with contradictions—personal service (sales associates) and no service (self-checkout), wide arrays of merchandise (to customers who shop the whole store) and narrow assortments (to destination-oriented customers), simple (straightforward) yet memorable (different enough to be compelling) experiences, and so on.

(5) Community leadership, not participation: There is a subtle but important difference in what retailers need to do in the future relative to what generally is the situation today. Community leadership rather than community participation is what consumers value. Leading causes, not supporting causes, is what people want. A firm's efforts must be organized and meaningful so it is seen as making a difference in the local community and in society at large. Specialty

clubs, chat rooms or information exchanges, and interest groups offer ways for people to connect, share views, and seek validation in their commonalities and stimulation from overlapping interests. Strong bonds, customer commitment, improved customer relationships, and greater feedback are among the positive outcomes of creating such communities.

Concluding Thoughts

Where do we go from here? Effective implementation and execution of concepts is critical for competing in the future. Successful execution will likely be aided by technology. Somewhat paradoxically, a discussion of the future of retailing might have been expected to be dominated by technological discussions and how they might fundamentally change business practice and consumer shopping experiences. However, when placed in proper perspective, technology can be viewed as one of the enablers that will facilitate the execution of strategies designed to improve the experiential value of retailing. In many instances, the application of technology has occurred in the absence of a keen understanding of consumer trends and values. The results have been mixed at best and disappointing in many other instances.

While this research is timely, the significance of our report is its potential impetus for retailers to constantly monitor the retail landscape for changes in consumer behavior and to interpret these changes for their effects on retailing practice.

Questions

1. Why is it so difficult to predict the future? What are the implications of this for retailers?
2. What do you think about the methodology used to come up with the six consumer mega-trends noted in the case?
3. Which of the six mega-trends do you believe is the most important for retailers? Why?
4. How will the impact of the six mega-trends vary by type of retailer? Explain your reasoning.
5. Distinguish experiential-based and commodity-based competition. Why is it important to know the difference between the two?
6. Which of the five new retail values do you believe is the most important for retailers? Why?
7. How will the impact of the five new retail values vary by type of retailer? Explain your reasoning.

*The material in this case is adapted by the authors from Jay A. Scansaroli, Global Managing Partner, Andersen's Retail Industry Services, and David M. Szymanski, Director, Center for Retailing Studies, Texas A&M University, "Who's Minding the Future?" *Retailing Issues Letter* (January 2002), pp. 1–8. Reprinted by permission.

Appendix A

CAREERS IN RETAILING

OVERVIEW

A person looking for a career in retailing has two broad possibilities: owning a business or working for a retailer. One alternative does not preclude the other. Many people open their own retail businesses after getting experience as employees. A person can also choose franchising, which has elements of both entrepreneurship and managerial assistance (as discussed in Chapter 4).

Regardless of the specific retail career path chosen, recent college graduates often gain personnel and profit-and-loss responsibilities faster in retailing than in any other major sector of business. After an initial training program, an entry-level manager supervises personnel, works on in-store displays, interacts with customers, and reviews sales and other data on a regular basis. An assistant buyer helps in planning merchandise assortments, interacting with suppliers, and outlining the promotion effort. Our Web site (**www.prenhall.com/bermanevans**) has loads of career-related materials: We

- Have a table describing 35 selected positions in retailing.
- Present career paths for Bon-Ton (a department store chain), Sherwin-Williams (a specialty chain), and Walgreens (a drugstore chain).
- Offer advice on resumé writing (complete with a sample resumé), interviewing, and internships.
- Highlight retailing-related information from the *Occupational Outlook Handbook*.
- Present links to a number of popular career sites, including over 100 retailers' sites.

THE BRIGHT FUTURE OF A CAREER IN RETAILING

Consider these observations from *DSN Retailing Today's Careers in Retailing* and the National Retail Federation. According to *Careers in Retailing*:

Not long ago, doomsayers were predicting the death of traditional bricks-and-mortar stores. Faced with so many look-alike choices, shoppers were becoming bored and disinterested. It was the end of shopping as we knew it—or so said the pessimists. But retailers fought back, using state-of-the-art technology to transform the shopping experience, improving the way goods are ordered and delivered, as well as overall store operations. This technology has put retailers more in tune with consumers' wants and needs, quickening the flow of goods from suppliers to shoppers and allowing a more targeted and immediate response. The emphasis on technology is just part of retailers' new-found focus on providing value to consumers. Other ways include quality customer service, brand equity, unique and compelling merchandise selection, and exciting stores. Many firms are luring shoppers by providing entertaining one-of-a-kind experiences.[1]

The hard-hit economic environment has taken a bite out of many career opportunities. The job market in fields like technology, telecommunications, consumer products, and manufacturing, for example, is tight. However, that's not the case in retailing. If anything, options in retailing are expanding. Retail career paths have expanded from buying and operations, and now encompass everything from information technology to logistics. Retailing also offers the chance to combine personal interests and a career. Like sports? The

531

Athlete's Foot has many career options. Those who love to design apparel might want to look into positions at Jo-Ann Stores. From toys at Toys "R" Us to the latest in electronic gadgets at Electronics Boutique, there's something for everyone in retailing.[2]

The National Retail Federation, through its Retail Employer Link to Education program, makes these points regarding some of the negative perceptions of retailing careers:[3]

Myth: Retailing offers good summer and part-time jobs, especially for younger and older workers, but it's not a career. **Fact:** The salaries available in the retail industry are often much higher than those offered in other industries at comparable experience levels. Retailing is a career that offers many opportunities for promotions and advancement, and provides greater responsibility earlier in a career than many other industries. That's right. No matter what kind of work setting you prefer—whether you'd like to be your own boss, or work within a large, well-known company, there is a place for you in the ever-changing world of retail. Not only will you meet all different types of people, but if you are creative and like taking on new challenges, you will go far.

Myth: Retail jobs only consist of cashier and sales clerk positions. **Fact:** Retailing offers perhaps the greatest variety of opportunities for ambitious and hardworking employees. With dedication and commitment, a sales associate can be promoted into many retail career path options, such as merchandising and buying; store, regional, and corporate management; inventory control; distribution; finance and internal auditing; marketing, sales promotion, and public relations; information systems; E-commerce; and human resources.

Myth: Retail positions do not prepare young people for challenging, upwardly mobile careers. **Fact:** Career paths in the dynamic, expanding retail industry are exciting, varied, and lucrative. At the store level alone, a general manager of a mass merchandiser department store oversees an average sales volume of $25 million to $30 million and employs an average of 150 people. Average department store manager salaries start at $80,000 and exceed $100,000. In addition, most of the skills needed to succeed in the retail industry are necessary to succeed in any industry.

OWNING A BUSINESS

Owning a retail business is popular, and many opportunities exist. Three-quarters of retail outlets are sole proprietorships, and many of today's giants began as independents, including Wal-Mart, J.C. Penney, Kmart, Filene's, Toys "R" Us, McDonald's, Sears, and Mrs. Fields'. Consider the saga of Wendy's (www.wendys.com/wendys_story.pdf):

When Dave Thomas opened the first "Wendy's Old Fashioned Hamburgers" restaurant, he had created something new and different in the restaurant industry. He offered high quality food made with the freshest ingredients and served the way the customer wanted it. To Dave, quality was so important that he put the phrase "Quality is our Recipe" on the logo. Dave had an uncompromising passion for quality—food, people, and the way we run our business. His passion for quality remains our number one priority at every Wendy's restaurant around the world. And it all began in 1969 with one restaurant in Columbus, Ohio. In 1970, Wendy's broke new ground by opening a second restaurant in Columbus, featuring a Pick-Up Window with a separate grill, a unique feature in quick-service restaurants. Wendy's is credited with creating the first modern-day, Drive-Thru Window. During 1972, Wendy's first franchisee, L.S. Hartzog, signed an agreement for Indianapolis, Indiana. As of 2002, Wendy's was the third largest quick-service hamburger restaurant chain in the world, with more than 6,000 restaurants in the United States, Canada, and 25 other countries and territories.

Too often, people overlook the possibility of owning a retail business. Initial investments can be quite modest (several thousand dollars). Direct marketing (both mail order and Web retailing), direct selling, and service retailing often require relatively low initial investments—as do various franchises. Financing may also be available from banks, suppliers, store-fixture firms, and equipment companies.

OPPORTUNITIES AS A RETAIL EMPLOYEE

As we've noted before, in the United States, 23 million people work for traditional retailers. This does not include millions of others employed by firms such as banks, insurance companies, and airlines. More people work in retailing than in any other industry.

Career opportunities are plentiful because of the number of new retail businesses that open and the labor intensity of retailing. Thousands of new outlets open each year in the United States, and certain segments of retailing are growing at particularly rapid rates. Retailers such as Wal-Mart and Costco also plan to open many new stores in foreign markets. The increased employment from new store openings and the sales growth of retail formats (such as membership clubs) also mean there are significant opportunities for personal advancement for talented retail personnel. Every time a chain opens a new outlet, there is a need for a store manager and other management-level people.

Selected retailing positions, career paths, and compensation ranges are described next.

TYPES OF POSITIONS IN RETAILING

Employment is not confined to buying and merchandising. Retail career opportunities also encompass advertising, public relations, credit analysis, marketing research, warehouse management, data processing, personnel management, accounting, and real-estate. Look at the table ("Selected Positions in Retailing") in the career section of our Web site for a list and description of a wide range of retailing positions. Some highly specialized jobs may be available only in large retail firms.

The type of position a person seeks should be matched with the type of retailer likely to have such a position. Chain stores and franchises may have real-estate divisions. Department stores and chain stores may have large human resource departments. Mail-order firms may have advertising production departments. If one is interested in travel, a buying position or a job with a retailer having geographically dispersed operations should be sought.

Figures 1 to 3 show the retailing experiences of three diverse college graduates.

Glorie Delamin

TYPE OF STORE:
Office Superstore

HEADQUARTERS:
Framingham, Mass.

Glorie Delamin knew what she wanted before graduating last May, and she got it. She went from a career fair to a career at Staples. Originally an accounting major, she realized she wanted to pursue the retail route after a good experience as an assistant manager at a Conroy's store. She switched to a major in business administration with an emphasis in retail and earned a certificate in marketing at California State University in Los Angeles.

She started last June, and is presently operations manager at a Staples store in Glendale, Calif. "Staples is currently a great opportunity. I'm fortunate that I got in at such a good time. We're expanding and growing at a rapid rate. There's new Web site opportunities now as well."

Like many in retail, she loves that she's not anchored down to a desk from 9 to 5. Her workday is flexible. One day she works on plan-o-grams and store layouts; another, she is hiring people and always making sure everyone's duties are completed. About 60 percent of the time, she's roaming the sales floor, and she enjoys this one-on-one contact with customers.

"The most challenging part of my job is being able to satisfy customers' needs, but it's one of the best parts as well," she adds. "Our store is in an area where we get a lot of regular customers, and we're constantly talking to them. We feel really close to them because of the personal contact we get on a daily basis."

Recruits learn about satisfying customer's needs in the in-store manager trainee program that also covers merchandising and taking inventory—basically the ropes of the operation. Staples' program features workshops where trainees role-play in-store scenarios. Stores usually have three managers—general, sales and operations—and trainees see firsthand what the different positions entail.

Delamin's advice to upcoming graduates? "Take advantage of your school's career fairs, career center and contacts. They're really useful and could lead you right into a job after school."

It worked for her. ■

FIGURE 1
Staples

Reprinted by permission of *DSN Retailing Today.*

Michael Hines

TYPE OF STORE:
Consumer Electronics Chain

HEADQUARTERS:
Eden Prairie, Minn.

After teaching abroad, working in real estate and getting his MBA, retail was the last place Michael Hines thought he would end up. But, he's found it to be the perfect career for him.

He earned his bachelor's degree in psychology from the University of Notre Dame and his MBA from Vanderbilt University before working for Best Buy, where he is presently project manager for small business development. He's proof that there's a lot of room to move up in retail, even with an advanced degree. In fact, Best Buy offers scholarships to help workers pay for MBAs. And getting your MBA pays: according to Hines, starting salaries, not including the stock options, are around $70,000 to $80,000 annually with this additional degree.

As school ended, he took advantage of an alumni contact at Best Buy, adding that many college Web sites and career centers make similar information available.

"The best part of my job is that I get to work with bright, dynamic people from very diverse backgrounds," says Hines. "It's very intellectually stimulating and very rewarding."

Hines works on cross-functional teams, addressing issues like logistics, advertising, development and brand management. There's a lot to retail that's behind-the-scenes. He's only been with the company a few months, but he's already well into the swing of things.

"It's very challenging. The company puts a lot of trust in me and really respects my opinion. What we're doing is very entrepreneurial, and I get a lot of hands-on assignments on different sides of the company."

What kind of people fit in at Best Buy? "You have to be a fun-loving person, not take yourself too seriously, enjoy life outside of the workplace," adds Hines. "Best Buy wants its employees to have time to play. They feel it makes employees well rounded and more productive overall."

Respect, fun, challenges, growth opportunity all at one job? Hines should know, that's why he's sticking with retail. ■

FIGURE 2
Best Buy

Reprinted by permission of *DSN Retailing Today.*

M.J. Marlinski

JO-ANN
stores inc

TYPE OF STORE:
Specialty Craft

HEADQUARTERS:
Hudson, Ohio

When M.J. Marlinski joined Jo-Ann Stores in 1981, she expected the position to be temporary. Marlinski, a Cornell University graduate with a design and marketing degree, dreamed of designing apparel. Today, after 19 years with Jo-Ann she's senior vice president of joann.com and has never looked back.

She took a job at Jo-Ann because "the idea of running a store, hiring a staff and having control over the merchandising and displays of a store intrigued me."

After training at a Buffalo, N.Y., store for three months, she became a store manager in State College, Pa., for a year, then at a high volume store in Detroit. After three years in the field, she moved to the chain's headquarters as a merchandise coordinator.

During her next 12 years with Jo-Ann, Marlinski served as a buyer, merchandise manager, vice president and senior vice president, growing existing categories and exploring new business methods. "I really like starting things and envisioning what the results will be," she explains. "I had the opportunity to explore what it would take for us to become, for example, a destination quilting shop, then to create that business. We are no longer just small fabric stores but 45,000-sq.-ft. creative destination stores, and I have been part of that change."

Marlinski heads the company's on-line venture, Joann.com. "We partnered with a dot.com company to create the site, and my team decides what and how much material will be on line, gets it there and helps merchandise products."

Marlinski is still excited about Jo-Ann, which operates over 1,000 stores in 49 states. "I've always loved what we're about," she says.

"Our mission statement is 'To serve and inspire creativity,' and I love the merchandise that I touch everyday. I have traveled all over the world and have had the chance to be part of a start-up business, adapt to a changing business and sustain existing business. It's been a great career path. Who would have thought?" ■

FIGURE 3
Jo-Ann

Reprinted by permission of *DSN Retailing Today.*

CAREER PATHS AND COMPENSATION IN RETAILING

For college graduates, executive training programs at larger retailers offer good learning experiences and advancement potential. These firms often offer careers in merchandising and nonmerchandising areas.

Here is how a new college graduate could progress in a career path at a typical department store or specialty store chain: He or she usually begins with a training program (lasting from three months to a year or more) on how to run a merchandise department. That program often involves on-the-job and classroom experiences. On-the-job training includes working with records, reordering stock, planning displays, and supervising salespeople. Classroom activities include learning how to evaluate vendors, analyze computer reports, forecast fashion trends, and administer store policy.

After initial training, the person becomes an entry-level operations manager (often called a sales manager, assistant department manager, or department manager—depending on the firm) or an assistant buyer. An entry-level manager or assistant buyer works under the direction of a seasoned department (group) manager or buyer and analyzes sales, assists in purchasing goods, handles reorders, and helps with displays. The new manager supervises personnel and learns store operations; the assistant buyer is more involved in purchases than operations. Depending on the retailer, either person may follow the same type of career path, or the entry-level operations manager may progress up the store management ladder and the assistant buyer up the buying ladder.

During this time, the responsibilities and duties depend on the department (group) manager's or buyer's willingness to delegate and teach. In a situation where a manager or buyer has authority to make decisions, the entry-level manager or assistant buyer will usually be given more responsibility. If a firm has centralized management, a manager (buyer) is more limited in his or her responsibilities, as is the entry-level manager or assistant buyer. Further, an assistant buyer will gain more experience if he or she is in a firm near a wholesale market center and can make trips to the market to buy merchandise.

The next step in a department store or specialty store chain's career path is promotion to department (group) manager or buyer. This position is entrepreneurial—running a business. The manager or buyer selects merchandise, develops a promotional campaign, decides which items to reorder, and oversees personnel and recordkeeping. For some retailers, *manager* and *buyer* are synonymous. For others, the distinction is as just explained for entry-level positions. Generally, a person is considered for promotion to manager or buyer after two years.

Large department store and specialty store chains have additional levels of personnel to plan, supervise, and assess merchandise departments. On the store management side, there can be group managers, store managers, branch vice-presidents, and others. On the buying side, there can be divisional managers, merchandising vice-presidents, and others.

At many firms, advancement is indicated by specific career paths. This lets employees monitor their performance, know the next career step, and progress in a clear manner. Selected career paths at Bon-Ton department stores, Sherwin-Williams' specialty stores, and Walgreens' drugstores are shown in the careers section of our Web site.

Table 1 lists compensation ranges for personnel in a number of retailing positions.

GETTING YOUR FIRST POSITION AS A RETAIL PROFESSIONAL

The key steps in getting your first professional position in retailing are the search for opportunities, interview preparation, and the evaluation of options. You must devote sufficient time to these steps so your job hunt progresses as well as possible.

SEARCHING FOR CAREER OPPORTUNITIES IN RETAILING

Various sources should be consulted. These include your school placement office, company directories and Web sites, classified ads in your local newspapers, Web job sites, and networking (with professors, friends, neighbors, and family members). Here are some hints to consider:

- *Do not "place all your eggs in one basket."* Do not rely too much on friends and relatives. They may be able to get you an interview but not a guaranteed job offer.

TABLE 1	Typical Compensation Ranges for Personnel in Selected Retailing Positions

Position	Compensation Range
Operations	
Department manager—soft-line retailer	$18,000–$32,000+
Store management trainee	$22,000–$35,000+
Department manager—department store	$22,000–$35,000+
Department manager—mass merchandiser	$22,000–$35,000+
Department manager—hard-line retailer	$24,000–$35,000+
Customer service representative	$25,000–$50,000+
Warehouse director	$30,000–$90,000+
Store manager—specialty store, home center, drugstore	$32,000–$70,000+
Store manager—soft-line retailer	$35,000–$75,000+
Customer service supervisor	$40,000–$60,000+
Security director	$42,000–$70,000+
Store manager—department store	$45,000–$85,000+
Operations director	$60,000–$100,000+
Merchandising	
Assistant buyer	$23,000–$35,000+
Buyer—specialty store, home center, drugstore, department store	$28,000–$80,000+
Buyer—discount store	$35,000–$85,000+
Buyer—national chain	$45,000–$85,000+
Divisional merchandise manager	$60,000–$90,000+
General merchandise manager—drugstore, home center	$65,000–$90,000+
General merchandise manager—specialty store, department store	$70,000–$125,000+
General merchandise manager—discount store, national chain	$70,000–$125,000+
Senior merchandising executive	$80,000–$250,000+
Marketing Research	
Market research junior analyst	$28,000–$32,000+
Market research analyst	$33,000–$45,000+
Market research senior analyst	$37,000–$55,000+
Market research assistant director	$40,000–$65,000+
Market research director	$50,000–$75,000+
Top Management	
Senior human resources executive	$55,000–$140,000+
Senior advertising executive	$60,000–$110,000+
Senior real-estate executive	$65,000–$120,000+
Senior financial executive	$80,000–$200,000+
President	$250,000–$3,000,000+
Chairman of the board	$350,000–$10,000,000+
Other	
Public relations specialist	$35,000–$85,000+
Retail sales analyst	$38,000–$90,000+

Source: Estimated by the authors from various sources.

- *Be serious and systematic in your career search.* Plan in advance and do not wait until the recruiting season starts at your school to generate a list of retail employers.
- *Use directories with lists of retailers and current job openings.* Online directories include *Careers in Retailing* (**www.careersinretailing.com**), *Retail Job Mart* (**www.retailjobmart.com**), *Retail Jobnet* (**www.retailjobnet.com**), *RetailManager.net* (**www.retailmanager.net**), and *RetailRecruiter.com* (**www.retail-recruiter.com**). Also visit our Web site (**www.prenhall.com/bermanevans**).
- *Rely on the "law of large numbers."* In sending out resumés, you may have to contact at least 10 to 20 retailers to get just two to four interviews.

- *Make sure your resumé and accompanying cover letter highlight your best qualities.* These may include school honors, officer status in an organization, work experience, special computer expertise, and the proportion of college tuition you paid. Our Web site shows a sample resumé geared to an entry-level position in retailing.
- *Show your resumé to at least one professor.* Be receptive to constructive comments. Remember, your professor's goal is to help you get the best possible first job.

PREPARING FOR THE INTERVIEW

The initial and subsequent interviews for a position, which may last for 20 to 30 minutes or longer, play a big part in determining if you get a job offer. For that reason, you should be prepared for all interviews:

- *Adequately research each firm.* Be aware of its goods/service category, current size, overall retail strategy, competitive developments, and so on.
- *Anticipate questions and plan general responses:* "Tell me about yourself." "Why are you interested in a retailing career?" "Why do you want a job with us?" "What are your major strengths?" "Your major weaknesses?" "What do you want to be doing five years from now?" "What would your prior boss say about you?" In preparation, role-play your answers to these questions with someone.
- *Treat every interview as if it is the most important one.* Otherwise, you may not be properly prepared if the position turns out to be more desirable than you originally thought. And remember that you represent both your college and yourself at all interviews.
- *Be prepared to raise your own questions when asked to do so in the interview.* They should relate to career paths, training, and opportunities for advancement.
- *Dress appropriately and be well groomed.*
- *Verify the date and place of the interview.* Be prompt.
- *Have a pen and pad available to record information after the interview is over.*
- *Write a note to the interviewer within a week to thank him or her for spending time with you and to express a continuing interest in the company.*

EVALUATING RETAIL CAREER OPPORTUNITIES

Job seekers often place too much emphasis on initial salary or the firm's image in assessing career opportunities. Many other factors should be considered, as well:

- What activities do you like?
- What are your personal strengths and weaknesses?
- What are your current and long-term goals?
- Do you want to work for an independent, a chain, or a franchise operation?
- Does the opportunity offer an acceptable and clear career path?
- Does the opportunity include a formal training program?
- Will the opportunity enable you to be rewarded for good performance?
- Will you have to relocate?
- Will each promotion in the company result in greater authority and responsibility?
- Is the compensation level fair relative to other offers?
- Can a good employee move up the career path much faster than an average one?
- If owning a retail firm is a long-term goal, which opportunity is the best preparation?

ENDNOTES

1. "Retail Growth Brings New Opportunities," *Careers in Retailing* (January 1999), p. 9.
2. "Retail: Diverse Opportunity, Dynamic Growth," *Careers in Retailing* (Fall 2001), p. 2.
3. "Retail Employer Link to Education," **www.nrf.com/content/default.asp?folder=foundation &file=rele.htm&bhcp=1** (April 5, 2003).

Appendix B

ABOUT THE WEB SITE THAT ACCOMPANIES *RETAIL MANAGEMENT*

(WWW.PRENHALL.COM/BERMANEVANS)

OVERVIEW

Retail Management: A Strategic Approach is accompanied by a comprehensive, dynamic, interactive Web site that includes everything from chapter links to career data to a comprehensive listing of retail company sites on the World Wide Web. Once you have connected to the Internet, it is designed to easily run on your Web browser. Our site is user-friendly, real-world in nature, and keyed to the concepts covered in *Retail Management*. In this appendix, we present an overview of the site's components.

From within your browser, enter our home page by going to **www.prenhall.com/bermanevans**. All of the components of the site can be accessed from this home page. The first time you visit the site, read the description. It explains each of the various components. You can print this (or any) material for later reference by clicking on the "Print" icon at the top of the screen. All necessary instructions appear at the home page or in the various sections. From the menu screen, you can click your mouse on the icon of any of the components of the Web site. You then enter that specific section.

WEB SITE COMPONENTS

Our site has these components:

- There is a chapter-by-chapter listing (including the appendixes).
- For each of the 20 chapters in *Retail Management*, there are chapter objectives, a chapter overview (summary), a listing of key terms (with their definitions), interactive study guide questions, hot links to relevant Web sites (several hundred in all), and more.
- For each of the eight parts in *Retail Management*, there are four real-world exercises drawn from company Web sites. These exercises ask you to apply a variety of retailing concepts in an interactive manner. In addition, each part has other links to free downloads and demonstrations.
- In the sections of our Web site devoted to Chapters 9, 12, 16, and 17, there are a number of extra online math problems so that you may enhance your understanding of the mathematical concepts in these chapters.
- We provide the full glossary in an easily scrollable manner.
- There is a plethora of career material, including a directory of hundreds of retailers—complete with links to their home pages.
- Author biographies and photos are shown.
- There are numerous resources for professors, including a large packet of PowerPoint slides, teaching notes, and a lot more.

538

INTERACTIVE STUDY GUIDE

The interactive study guide contains multiple-choice, true-false, and fill-in questions for each chapter (with answers and text references). And you can look at the glossary section of the Web site to further brush up on key terms. You may even E-mail your results to yourself or your professor.

CHAPTER OBJECTIVES/CHAPTER OVERVIEWS

These two sections enable you to view the objectives and overviews of each of the book's 20 chapters.

KEY TERMS AND GLOSSARY

There is a listing of key terms (with their definitions) by chapter. These terms are presented in the order in which we covered them in the chapter. You may also access glossary terms alphabetically.

TEXT-RELATED WEB SITE LINKS

This section has links to well over 1,000 retailing-related Web sites, divided by category. Click on the link to any of the Web sites and you are immediately transported there.

CAREERS IN RETAILING

This section contains advice on resumé writing, how to take an interview, and internships. There is a lot of information from the *Occupational Outlook Handbook*, as well as actual career paths and links to popular career sites. There are also a listing of positions in retailing, a listing of retail career search engines, and links to the career sections of retailers' Web sites.

RETAIL RESOURCES ON THE WEB

Still more information on the world of retailing is contained here: a retailer directory, Federal Trade Commission business tips, and Small Business Administration business tips.

WEB EXERCISES

At the end of each chapter in Retail Management, there is a short Web exercise. In addition, our site offers 32 more in-depth Web-based exercises (four per part). Look at our site for more information on applying these exercises, which are divided by text part. The exercises contain links to actual company Web sites, as well as questions for you to answer.

COMPUTER EXERCISES

Sixteen user-friendly computer exercises, noted by a computer symbol throughout this book, can be downloaded from our Web site. The exercises are divided by text part.

TRADE ASSOCIATIONS

This section lists nearly 60 retail-related associations, complete with mailing addresses and URLs.

GLOSSARY

Additional Markup Increase in a retail price above the original markup when demand is unexpectedly high or costs are rising.

Additional Markup Percentage Looks at total dollar additional markups as a percentage of net sales:

$$\frac{\text{Additional markup}}{\text{percentage}} = \frac{\text{Total dollar additional markups}}{\text{Net sales (in \$)}}$$

Addition to Retail Percentage Measures a price rise as a percentage of the original price:

$$\frac{\text{Addition to}}{\text{retail percentage}} = \frac{\text{New price} - \text{Original price}}{\text{Original price}}$$

Advertising Paid, nonpersonal communication transmitted through out-of-store mass media by an identified sponsor.

Affinity Exists when the stores at a given location complement, blend, and cooperate with one another, and each benefits from the others' presence.

All-You-Can-Afford Method Promotional budgeting procedure in which a retailer first allots funds for each element of the strategy mix except promotion. The funds that are left go to the promotional budget.

Americans with Disabilities Act (ADA) Mandates that persons with disabilities be given appropriate access to retailing facilities.

Analog Model Computerized site selection tool in which potential sales for a new store are estimated based on sales of similar stores in existing areas, competition at a prospective location, the new store's expected market share at that location, and the size and density of a location's primary trading area.

Application Blank Usually the first tool used to screen applicants. It provides data on education, experience, health, reasons for leaving prior jobs, outside activities, hobbies, and references.

Assets Any items a retailer owns with a monetary value.

Asset Turnover Performance measure based on a retailer's net sales and total assets. It is equal to net sales divided by total assets.

Assortment Selection of merchandise carried by a retailer. It includes both the breadth of product categories and the variety within each category.

Assortment Display An open or closed display in which a retailer exhibits a wide range of merchandise.

Assortment Merchandise Apparel, furniture, autos, or other products for which the retailer must carry a variety of products in order to give customers a proper selection.

Atmosphere (Atmospherics) Reflection of a store's physical characteristics that are used to develop an image and draw customers. The concept is also applicable to non-store retailers.

Attitudes (Opinions) Positive, neutral, or negative feelings a person has about different topics.

Augmented Customer Service Encompasses the actions that enhance the shopping experience and give retailers a competitive advantage.

Automatic Reordering System Computerized approach that combines a perpetual inventory and reorder point calculations.

Bait-and-Switch Advertising Illegal practice in which a retailer lures a customer by advertising goods and services at exceptionally low prices, and then tries to convince the person to buy a better, more expensive substitute that is available. The retailer has no intention of selling the advertised item.

Balanced Tenancy Occurs when stores in a planned shopping center complement each other as to the quality and variety of their product offerings.

Balance Sheet Itemizes a retailer's assets, liabilities, and net worth at a specific time—based on the principle that assets equal liabilities plus net worth.

Basic Stock List Specifies the inventory level, color, brand, style category, size, package, and so on for every staple item carried by a retailer.

Basic Stock Method Inventory level planning tool wherein a retailer carries more items than it expects to sell over a specified period:

$$\text{Basic stock} = \frac{\text{Average monthly stock at retail}}{- \text{Average monthly sales}}$$

Battle of the Brands The competition between manufacturers and retailers for shelf space and profits, whereby manufacturer, private, and generic brands fight each other for more space and control.

Benchmarking Occurs when the retailer sets its own standards and measures performance based on the achievements in its sector, specific competitors, high-performance firms, and/or its own prior actions.

Bifurcated Retailing Denotes the decline of middle-of-the-market retailing due to the popularity of both mass merchandising and niche retailing.

Book Inventory System Keeps a running total of the value of all inventory at cost as of a given time. This is done by recording purchases and adding them to existing inventory value; sales are subtracted to arrive at the new current inventory value (all at cost). It is also known as a perpetual inventory system.

Bottom-Up Space Management Approach Exists when planning starts at the individual product level and then proceeds to the category, total store, and overall company levels.

Box (Limited-Line) Store Food-based discounter that focuses on a small selection of items, moderate hours of operation (compared to supermarkets), few services, and limited manufacturer brands.

Budgeting Outlines a retailer's planned expenditures for a given time based on expected performance.

Bundled Pricing Involves a retailer combining several elements in one basic price.

Business Format Franchising Arrangement in which the franchisee receives assistance in site location, quality control, accounting, startup practices, management training, and responding to problems—besides the right to sell goods and services.

Buyer Person responsible for selecting the merchandise to be carried by a retailer and setting a strategy to market that merchandise.

Buying Power Index (BPI) Single weighted measure combining effective buying income, retail sales, and population size into one overall indicator of an area's sales potential. It is expressed as:

$$BPI = 0.5 \text{ (the area's percentage of U.S. effective buying income)}$$
$$+ 0.3 \text{ (the area's percentage of U.S. retail sales)}$$
$$+ 0.2 \text{ (the area's percentage of U.S. population)}$$

Canned Sales Presentation Memorized, repetitive speech given to all customers interested in a particular item.

Capital Expenditures Retail expenditures that are long-term investments in fixed assets.

Case Display Interior display that exhibits heavier, bulkier items than racks hold.

Cash Flow Relates the amount and timing of revenues received to the amount and timing of expenditures made during a specific time.

Category Killer (Power Retailer) Very large specialty store featuring an enormous selection in its product category and relatively low prices. It draws consumers from wide geographic areas.

Category Management Merchandising technique that improves productivity. It focuses on product category results rather than the performance of individual brands or models.

Census of Population Supplies a wide range of demographic data for all U.S. cities and surrounding vicinities. These data are organized on a geographic basis.

Central Business District (CBD) Hub of retailing in a city. It is synonymous with "downtown." The CBD has the greatest density of office buildings and stores.

Chain Retailer that operates multiple outlets (store units) under common ownership. It usually engages in some level of centralized (or coordinated) purchasing and decision making.

Channel Control Occurs when one member of a distribution channel can dominate the decisions made in that channel by the power it possesses.

Channel of Distribution All of the businesses and people involved in the physical movement and transfer of ownership of goods and services from producer to consumer.

Chargebacks Practice of retailers, at their discretion, making deductions in the manufacturers' bills for infractions ranging from late shipments to damaged and expired merchandise.

Class Consciousness Extent to which a person desires and pursues social status.

Classification Merchandising Allows firms to obtain more financial data by subdividing each specified department into further categories for related types of merchandise.

Cognitive Dissonance Doubt that occurs after a purchase is made, which can be alleviated by customer after-care, money-back guarantees, and realistic sales presentations and advertising campaigns.

Collaborative Planning, Forecasting, and Replenishment (CPFR) Emerging technique for larger firms whereby there is a holistic approach to supply chain management among a network of trading partners.

Combination Store Unites supermarket and general merchandise sales in one facility, with general merchandise typically accounting for 25 to 40 percent of total sales.

Community Shopping Center Moderate-sized, planned shopping facility with a branch department store and/or a category killer store, in addition to several smaller stores. About 20,000 to 100,000 people, who live or work within 10 or 20 minutes of the center, are served by this location.

Compensation Includes direct monetary payments to employees (such as salaries, commissions, and bonuses) and indirect payments (such as paid vacations, health and life insurance benefits, and retirement plans).

Competition-Oriented Pricing Approach in which a firm sets prices in accordance with competitors'.

Competitive Advantages Distinct competencies of a retailer relative to competitors.

Competitive Parity Method Promotional budgeting procedure by which a retailer's budget is raised or lowered based on competitors' actions.

Computerized Checkout Used by large and small retailers to efficiently process transactions and monitor inventory. Cashiers ring up sales or pass items by scanners. Computerized registers instantly record and display sales, customers get detailed receipts, and inventory data are stored in a memory bank.

Concentrated Marketing Selling goods and services to one specific group.

Consignment Purchase Items not paid for by a retailer until they are sold. The retailer can return unsold merchandise. Title is not taken by the retailer; the supplier owns the goods until sold.

Constrained Decision Making Limits franchisee involvement in the strategic planning process.

Consumer Behavior The process by which people determine whether, what, when, where, how, from whom, and how often to purchase goods and services.

Consumer Cooperative Retail firm owned by its customer members. A group of consumers invests in the company, elects officers, manages operations, and shares the profits or savings that accrue.

Consumer Decision Process Stages a consumer goes through in buying a good or service: stimulus, problem awareness, information search, evaluation of alternatives, purchase, and post-purchase behavior. Demographics and life-style factors affect this decision process.

Consumerism Involves the activities of government, business, and other organizations that protect people from practices infringing on their rights as consumers.

Consumer Loyalty (Frequent Shopper) Programs Reward a retailer's best customers, those with whom it wants long-lasting relationships.

Contingency Pricing Arrangement by which a service retailer does not get paid until after the service is satisfactorily performed. This is a special form of flexible pricing.

Control Phase in the evaluation of a firm's strategy and tactics in which a semiannual or annual review of the retailer takes place.

Controllable Variables Aspects of business that the retailer can directly affect (such as hours of operation and sales personnel).

Control Units Merchandise categories for which data are gathered.

Convenience Store Well-located food-oriented retailer that is open long hours and carries a moderate number of items. It is small, with average to above-average prices and average atmosphere and services.

Conventional Supermarket Departmentalized food store with a wide range of food and related products; sales of general merchandise are rather limited.

Cooperative Advertising Occurs when manufacturers or wholesalers and their retailers, or two or more retailers, share the costs of retail advertising.

Cooperative Buying Procedure used when a group of retailers make quantity purchases from suppliers.

Core Customers Consumers with whom retailers seek to nurture long relationships. They should be singled out in a firm's data base.

Corporation Retail firm that is formally incorporated under state law. It is a legal entity apart from individual officers (or stockholders).

Cost Complement Average relationship of cost to retail value for all merchandise available for sale during a given time period.

Cost Method of Accounting Requires the retailer's cost of each item to be recorded on an accounting sheet and/or coded on a price tag or merchandise container. When a physical inventory is done, item costs must be learned, the quantity of every item in stock counted, and total inventory value at cost calculated.

Cost of Goods Sold Amount a retailer has paid to acquire the merchandise sold during a given time period. It equals the cost of merchandise available for sale minus the cost value of ending inventory.

Cost-Oriented Pricing Approach in which a retailer sets a price floor, the minimum price acceptable to the firm so it can reach a specified profit goal. A retailer usually computes merchandise and retail operating costs and adds a profit margin to these figures.

Cross-Merchandising Exists when a retailer carries complementary goods and services so that shoppers are encouraged to buy more.

Cross-Shopping Occurs when consumers shop for a product category through more than one retail format during the year or visit multiple retailers on one shopping trip.

Cross-Training Enables personnel to learn tasks associated with more than one job.

Culture Distinctive heritage shared by a group of people. It passes on beliefs, norms, and customs.

Curving (Free-Flowing) Traffic Flow Presents displays and aisles in a free-flowing pattern.

Customary Pricing Used when a retailer sets prices for goods and services and seeks to maintain them for an extended period.

Customer Loyalty Exists when a person regularly patronizes a particular retailer (store or nonstore) that he or she knows, likes, and trusts.

Customer Satisfaction Occurs when the value and customer service provided through a retailing experience meet or exceed consumer expectations.

Customer Service Identifiable, but sometimes intangible, activities undertaken by a retailer in conjunction with the basic goods and services it sells.

Cut Case Inexpensive display, in which merchandise is left in the original carton.

Data-Base Management Procedure a retailer uses to gather, integrate, apply, and store information related to specific subject areas. It is a key element in a retail information system.

Data-Base Retailing Way to collect, store, and use relevant information on customers.

Data Mining Involves the in-depth analysis of information so as to gain specific insights about customers, product categories, vendors, and so forth.

Data Warehousing Advance in data-base management whereby copies of all the data bases in a company are maintained in one location and accessible to employees at any locale.

Dead Areas Awkward spaces where normal displays cannot be set up.

Debit Card System Computerized process whereby the purchase price of a good or service is immediately deducted from a consumer's bank account and entered into a retailer's account.

Demand-Oriented Pricing Approach by which a retailer sets prices based on consumer desires. It determines the range of prices acceptable to the target market.

Demographics Objective, quantifiable, easily identifiable, and measurable population data.

Department Store Large store with an extensive assortment (width and depth) of goods and services that has separate departments for purposes of buying, promotion, customer service, and control.

Depth of Assortment The variety in any one goods/service category (product line) with which a retailer is involved.

Destination Retailer Firm that consumers view as distinctive enough to become loyal to it. Consumers go out of their way to shop there.

Destination Store Retail outlet with a trading area much larger than that of a competitor with a less unique appeal. It offers a better merchandise assortment in its product category(ies), promotes more extensively, and/or creates a stronger image.

Differentiated Marketing Aims at two or more distinct consumer groups, with different retailing approaches for each group.

Direct Marketing Form of retailing in which a customer is first exposed to a good or service through a nonpersonal medium and then orders by mail, phone, or fax—and increasingly by computer.

Direct Product Profitability (DPP) Method for planning variable markups whereby a retailer finds the profitability of each category or unit of merchandise by computing adjusted per unit gross margin and assigning direct product costs for such expenses as warehousing, transportation, handling, and selling.

Direct Selling Includes both personal contact with consumers in their homes (and other nonstore locations such as offices) and phone solicitations initiated by a retailer.

Direct Store Distribution (DSD) Exists when retailers have at least some goods shipped directly from suppliers to individual stores. It works best with retailers that also utilize EDI.

Discretionary Income Money left after paying taxes and buying necessities.

Distributed Promotion Effort Used by retailers that promote throughout the year.

Diversification Way in which retailers become active in business outside their normal operations—and add stores in different goods/service categories.

Diversified Retailer Multiline firm with central ownership. It is also known as a retail conglomerate.

Dollar Control Planning and monitoring the financial merchandise investment over a stated period.

Downsizing Unprofitable stores closed or divisions sold off by retailers unhappy with performance.

Dual Marketing Involves firms engaged in more than one type of distribution arrangement. This enables those firms to appeal to different consumers, increase sales, share some costs, and maintain a good degree of strategic control.

Dump Bin Case display that houses piles of sale clothing, marked-down books, or other products.

Ease of Entry Occurs due to low capital requirements and no, or relatively simple, licensing provisions.

Economic Base Area's industrial and commercial structure—the companies and industries that residents depend on to earn a living.

Economic Order Quantity (EOQ) Quantity per order (in units) that minimizes the total costs of processing orders and holding inventory:

$$EOQ = \sqrt{\frac{2DS}{IC}}$$

Effective Buying Income (EBI) Personal income (wages, salaries, interest, dividends, profits, rental income, and pension income) minus federal, state, and local taxes and nontax payments (such as personal contributions for social security). It is commonly known as disposable or after-tax personal income.

Efficient Consumer Response (ECR) Form of order processing and fulfillment by which supermarkets are incorporating aspects of QR inventory planning, EDI, and logistics planning.

Electronic Article Surveillance Involves special tags that are attached to products so that the tags can be sensed by electronic security devices at store exits.

Electronic Banking Includes both automatic teller machines (ATMs) and the instant processing of retail purchases.

Electronic Data Interchange (EDI) Lets retailers and suppliers regularly exchange information through their computers with regard to inventory levels, delivery times, unit sales, and so on, of particular items.

Electronic Point-of-Sale System Performs all the tasks of a computerized checkout and also verifies check and charge transactions, provides instantaneous sales reports, monitors and changes prices, sends intra- and interstore messages, evaluates personnel and profitability, and stores data.

Employee Empowerment Way of improving customer service in which workers have discretion to do what they feel is needed—within reason—to satisfy the customer, even if this means bending some rules.

Ensemble Display Interior display whereby a complete product bundle (ensemble) is presented rather than showing merchandise in separate categories.

Equal Store Organization Centralizes the buying function. Branch stores become sales units with equal operational status.

Ethics Involves activities that are trustworthy, fair, honest, and respectful for each retailer constituency.

Evaluation of Alternatives Stage in the decision process where a consumer selects one good or service to buy from a list of alternatives.

Everyday Low Pricing (EDLP) Version of customary pricing whereby a retailer strives to sell its goods and services at consistently low prices throughout the selling season.

Exclusive Distribution Takes place when suppliers enter agreements with one or a few retailers to designate the latter as the only firms in specified geographic areas to carry certain brands or product lines.

Expected Customer Service Level of service that customers want to receive from any retailer, such as basic employee courtesy.

Experiential Merchandising Tactic whose intent is to convert shopping from a passive activity into a more interactive one, by better engaging the customer.

Experiment Type of research in which one or more elements of a retail strategy mix are manipulated under controlled conditions.

Extended Decision Making Occurs when a consumer makes full use of the decision process, usually for expensive, complex items with which the person has had little or no experience.

External Secondary Data Available from sources outside a firm.

Factory Outlet Manufacturer-owned store selling its closeouts, discontinued merchandise, irregulars, canceled orders, and, sometimes, in-season, first-quality merchandise.

Fad Merchandise Items that generate a high level of sales for a short time.

Family Life Cycle How a traditional family moves from bachelorhood to children to solitary retirement.

Fashion Merchandise Products that may have cyclical sales due to changing tastes and life-styles.

Feedback Signals or cues as to the success or failure of part of a retail strategy.

FIFO Method Logically assumes old merchandise is sold first, while newer items remain in inventory. It matches inventory value with the current cost structure.

Financial Leverage Performance measure based on the relationship between a retailer's total assets and net worth. It is equal to total assets divided by net worth.

Financial Merchandise Management Occurs when a retailer specifies exactly which products (goods and services) are purchased, when products are purchased, and how many products are purchased.

Flea Market Location where many vendors offer a range of products at discount prices in plain surroundings. Many flea markets are located in nontraditional sites not normally associated with retailing.

Flexible Pricing Strategy that lets consumers bargain over selling prices; those consumers who are good at bargaining obtain lower prices than those who are not.

Floor-Ready Merchandise Items that are received at the store in condition to be put directly on display without any preparation by retail workers.

Food-Based Superstore Retailer that is larger and more diversified than a conventional supermarket but usually smaller and less diversified than a combination store. It caters to consumers' complete grocery needs and offers them the ability to buy fill-in general merchandise.

Forecasts Projections of expected retail sales for given time periods.

Franchising Contractual arrangement between a franchisor (a manufacturer, a wholesaler, or a service sponsor) and a retail franchisee, which allows the franchisee to conduct a given form of business under an established name and according to a given pattern of business.

Frequency Average number of times each person who is reached by a message is exposed to a retailer's promotion efforts in a specific period.

Fringe Trading Area Includes customers not found in primary and secondary trading areas. These are the most widely dispersed customers.

Full-Line Discount Store Type of department store with a broad, low-priced product assortment; all of the range of products expected at department stores; centralized checkout service; self-service; private-brand nondurables and well-known manufacturer-brand durables; less fashion-sensitive merchandise; relatively inexpensive building, equipment, and fixtures; and less emphasis on credit.

Functional Product Groupings Categorize and display a store's merchandise by common end use.

Gap Analysis Enables a company to compare its actual performance against its potential performance, and then determine the areas in which it must improve.

Generic Brands No-frills goods stocked by some retailers. These items usually receive secondary shelf locations, have little or no promotion support, are sometimes of less quality than other brands, are stocked in limited assortments, and have plain packages. They are a form of private brand.

Geographic Information Systems (GIS) Combine digitized mapping with key locational data to graphically depict such trading-area characteristics as the demographic attributes of the population, data on customer purchases, and listings of current, proposed, and competitor locations.

Goal-Oriented Job Description Enumerates a position's basic functions, the relationship of each job to overall goals, the interdependence of positions, and information flows.

Goods Retailing Focuses on the sale of tangible (physical) products.

Goods/Service Category Retail firm's line of business.

Graduated Lease Calls for precise rent increases over a stated period of time.

Gravity Model Computerized site selection tool based on the premise that people are drawn to stores that are closer and more attractive than competitors'.

Gray Market Goods Brand-name products bought in foreign markets or goods transshipped from other retailers. They are often sold at low prices by unauthorized dealers.

Gross Margin Difference between net sales and the total cost of goods sold. It is also called gross profit.

Gross Margin Return on Investment (GMROI) Shows relationship between total dollar operating profits and the average inventory investment (at cost) by combining profitability and sales-to-stock measures:

$$GMROI = \frac{Gross\ margin\ in\ dollars}{Net\ sales}$$
$$\times \frac{Net\ sales}{Average\ inventory\ at\ cost}$$
$$= \frac{Gross\ margin\ in\ dollars}{Average\ inventory\ at\ cost}$$

Gross Profit Difference between net sales and the total cost of goods sold. It is also known as gross margin.

Hidden Assets Depreciated assets, such as store buildings and warehouses, that are reflected on a retailer's balance sheet at low values relative to their actual worth.

Hierarchy of Authority Outlines the job interactions within a company by describing the reporting relationships among employees. Coordination and control are provided.

Hierarchy of Effects Sequence of steps a consumer goes through in reacting to retail communications, which leads him or her from awareness to knowledge to liking to preference to conviction to purchase.

Horizontal Cooperative Advertising Agreement Enables two or more retailers (most often small, situated together, or franchisees of the same company) to share an ad.

Horizontal Price Fixing Agreement among manufacturers, among wholesalers, or among retailers to set certain prices. This is illegal, regardless of how "reasonable" prices may be.

Horizontal Retail Audit Analyzes a retail firm's overall performance, from mission to goals to customer satisfaction to basic retail strategy mix and its implementation in an integrated, consistent way.

Household Life Cycle Incorporates the life stages of both family and nonfamily households.

Huff's Law of Shopper Attraction Delineates trading areas on the basis of the product assortment carried at various shopping locations, travel times from the shopper's home to alternative locations, and the sensitivity of the kind of shopping to travel time.

Human Resource Management Recruiting, selecting, training, compensating, and supervising personnel in a manner consistent with the retailer's organization structure and strategy mix.

Human Resource Management Process Consists of these interrelated activities: recruitment, selection, training, compensation, and supervision. The goals are to obtain, develop, and retain employees.

Hypermarket Combination store pioneered in Europe that blends an economy supermarket with a discount department store. It is even larger than a supercenter.

Image Represents how a given retailer is perceived by consumers and others.

Impulse Purchases Occur when consumers buy products and/or brands they had not planned to before entering a store, reading a catalog, seeing a TV shopping show, turning to the Web, and so forth.

Incremental Budgeting Process whereby a firm uses current and past budgets as guides and adds to or subtracts from them to arrive at the coming period's expenditures.

Incremental Method Promotional budgeting procedure by which a percentage is either added to or subtracted from one year's budget to determine the next year's.

Independent Retailer that owns one retail unit.

Infomercial Program-length TV commercial (most often, 30 minutes in length) for a specific good or service that airs on cable television or on broadcast television, often at a fringe time. It is particularly worthwhile for products that benefit from visual demonstrations.

Information Search Consists of two parts: determining alternatives to solve the problem at hand (and where they can be bought) and learning the characteristics of alternatives. It may be internal or external.

Initial Markup (at Retail) Based on the original retail value assigned to merchandise less the merchandise costs, expressed as a percentage of the original retail price:

Initial markup percentage (at retail) =

$$\frac{\substack{Planned\ retail\ operating\ expenses \\ +\ Planned\ profit\ +\ Planned\ retail\ reductions}}{\substack{Planned\ net\ sales \\ +\ Planned\ retail\ reductions}}$$

Intensive Distribution Takes place when suppliers sell through as many retailers as possible. This often maximizes suppliers' sales and lets retailers offer many brands and product versions.

Internal Secondary Data Available within a company, sometimes from the data bank of a retail information system.

Internet Global electronic superhighway of computer networks that use a common protocol and that are linked by telecommunications lines and satellite.

Inventory Management Process whereby a firm seeks to acquire and maintain a proper merchandise assortment while ordering, shipping, handling, storing, displaying, and selling costs are kept in check.

Inventory Shrinkage Encompasses employee theft, customer shoplifting, vendor fraud, and administrative errors.

Isolated Store Freestanding retail outlet located on either a highway or a street. There are no adjacent retailers with which this type of store shares traffic.

Issue (Problem) Definition Step in the marketing research process that involves a clear statement of the topic to be studied.

Item Price Removal Practice whereby prices are marked only on shelves or signs and not on individual items. It is banned in several states and local communities.

Job Analysis Consists of gathering information about each job's functions and requirements: duties, responsibilities, aptitude, interest, education, experience, and physical tasks.

Job Motivation Drive within people to attain work-related goals.

Job Standardization Keeps tasks of employees with similar positions in different departments rather uniform.

Leader Pricing Occurs when a retailer advertises and sells selected items in its goods/service assortment at less than the usual profit margins. The goal is to increase customer traffic so as to sell regularly priced goods and services in addition to the specially priced items.

Leased Department Site in a retail store—usually a department, discount, or specialty store—that is rented to an outside party.

Liabilities Financial obligations a retailer incurs in operating a business.

Life-Style Center An open-air shopping site that typically includes 150,000 to 500,000 square feet of space dedicated to upscale, well-known specialty stores.

Life-Styles Ways that individual consumers and families (households) live and spend time and money.

LIFO Method Assumes new merchandise is sold first, while older stock remains in inventory. It matches current sales with the current cost structure.

Limited Decision Making Occurs when a consumer uses every step in the purchase process but does not spend a great deal of time on each of them.

Logistics Total process of planning, enacting, and coordinating the physical movement of merchandise from supplier to retailer to customer in the most timely, effective, and cost-efficient manner possible.

Loss Leaders Items priced below cost to lure more customer traffic. Loss leaders are restricted by some state minimum price laws.

Maintained Markup (at Retail) Based on the actual prices received for merchandise sold during a time period less merchandise cost, expressed as a percentage:

$$\text{Maintained markup percentage (at retail)} = \frac{\text{Actual retail operating expenses} + \text{Actual profit}}{\text{Actual net sales}}$$

or

$$\frac{\text{Average selling price} - \text{Merchandise cost}}{\text{Average selling price}}$$

Maintenance-Increase-Recoupment Lease Has a provision allowing rent to increase if a property owner's taxes, heating bills, insurance, or other expenses rise beyond a certain point.

Manufacturer (National) Brands Produced and controlled by manufacturers. They are usually well known, supported by manufacturer ads, somewhat pre-sold to consumers, require limited retailer investment in marketing, and often represent maximum product quality to consumers.

Markdown Reduction from the original retail price of an item to meet the lower price of another retailer, adapt to inventory overstocking, clear out shopworn merchandise, reduce assortments of odds and ends, and increase customer traffic.

Markdown Percentage Total dollar markdown as a percentage of net sales (in dollars):

$$\text{Markdown percentage} = \frac{\text{Total dollar markdown}}{\text{Net sales (in \$)}}$$

Marketing Research in Retailing Collection and analysis of information relating to specific issues or problems facing a retailer.

Marketing Research Process Embodies a series of activities: defining the issue or problem, examining secondary data, generating primary data (if needed), analyzing data, making recommendations, and implementing findings.

Market Penetration Pricing Strategy in which a retailer seeks to achieve large revenues by setting low prices and selling a high unit volume.

Market Segment Product Groupings Place together various items that appeal to a given target market.

Market Skimming Pricing Strategy wherein a firm charges premium prices and attracts customers less concerned with price than service, assortment, and status.

Markup Difference between merchandise costs and retail selling price.

Markup Percentage (at Cost) Difference between retail price and merchandise cost expressed as a percentage of merchandise cost:

$$\text{Markup percentage (at cost)} = \frac{\text{Retail selling price} - \text{Merchandise cost}}{\text{Merchandise cost}}$$

Markup Percentage (at Retail) Difference between retail price and merchandise cost expressed as a percentage of retail price:

$$
\text{Markup percentage (at retail)} = \frac{\text{Retail selling price} - \text{Merchandise cost}}{\text{Retail selling price}}
$$

Markup Pricing Form of cost-oriented pricing in which a retailer sets prices by adding per unit merchandise costs, retail operating expenses, and desired profit.

Marquee Sign used to display a store's name and/or logo.

Massed Promotion Effort Used by retailers that promote mostly in one or two seasons.

Mass Marketing Selling goods and services to a broad spectrum of customers.

Mass Merchandising Positioning approach whereby retailers offer a discount or value-oriented image, a wide and/or deep merchandise selection, and large store facilities.

Mazur Plan Divides all retail activities into four functional areas: merchandising, publicity, store management, and accounting and control.

Megamall Enormous planned shopping center with at least 1 million square feet of retail space, multiple anchor stores, up to several hundred specialty stores, food courts, and entertainment facilities.

Membership (Warehouse) Club Appeals to price-conscious consumers, who must be members to shop.

Memorandum Purchase Occurs when items are not paid for by the retailer until they are sold. The retailer can return unsold merchandise. However, it takes title on delivery and is responsible for damages.

Merchandise Available for Sale Equals beginning inventory, purchases, and transportation charges.

Merchandising Activities involved in acquiring particular goods and/or services and making them available at the places, times, and prices and in the quantity to enable a retailer to reach its goals.

Merchandising Philosophy Sets the guiding principles for all the merchandise decisions a retailer makes.

Mergers The combinations of separately owned retail firms.

Micromarketing Application of data mining whereby the retailer uses differentiated marketing and focused strategy mixes for specific segments, sometimes fine-tuned for the individual shopper.

Micromerchandising Strategy whereby a retailer adjusts its shelf-space allocations to respond to customer and other differences among local markets.

Minimum Price Laws State regulations preventing retailers from selling certain items for less than their cost plus a fixed percentage to cover overhead. These laws restrict loss leaders and predatory pricing.

Model Stock Approach Method of determining the amount of floor space necessary to carry and display a proper merchandise assortment.

Model Stock Plan Planned composition of fashion goods, which reflects the mix of merchandise available based on expected sales. It indicates product lines, colors, and size distributions.

Monthly Sales Index Measure of sales seasonality that is calculated by dividing each month's actual sales by average monthly sales and then multiplying the results by 100.

Motives Reasons for consumer behavior.

Multi-Channel Retailing A distribution approach whereby a retailer sells to consumers through multiple retail formats (points of contact).

Multiple-Unit Pricing Discounts offered to customers who buy in quantity or who buy a product bundle.

Mystery Shoppers People hired by retailers to pose as customers and observe their operations, from sales presentations to how well displays are maintained to service calls.

Need-Satisfaction Approach Sales technique based on the principle that each customer has a different set of wants; thus, a sales presentation should be geared to the demands of the individual customer.

Neighborhood Business District (NBD) Unplanned shopping area that appeals to the convenience shopping and service needs of a single residential area. The leading retailer is typically a supermarket or a large drugstore, and it is situated on the major street(s) of its residential area.

Neighborhood Shopping Center Planned shopping facility with the largest store being a supermarket or a drugstore. It serves 3,000 to 50,000 people within a 15-minute drive (usually less than 10 minutes).

Net Lease Calls for all maintenance costs, such as heating, electricity, insurance, and interior repair, to be paid by the retailer.

Net Profit Equals gross profit minus retail operating expenses.

Net Profit After Taxes The profit earned after all costs and taxes have been deducted.

Net Profit Margin Performance measure based on a retailer's net profit and net sales. It is equal to net profit divided by net sales.

Net Sales Revenues received by a retailer during a given time period after deducting customer returns, markdowns, and employee discounts.

Net Worth Retailer's assets minus its liabilities.

Never-Out List Used when a retailer plans stock levels for best-sellers. The goal is to purchase enough of these products so they are always in stock.

Niche Retailing Enables retailers to identify customer segments and deploy unique strategies to address the desires of those segments.

Nongoods Services Area of service retailing in which intangible personal services are offered to consumers—who experience the services rather than possess them.

Nonprobability Sample Approach in which stores, products, or customers are chosen by the researcher—based on judgment or convenience.

Nonstore Retailing Utilizes strategy mixes that are not store-based to reach consumers and complete transactions. It occurs via direct marketing, direct selling, and vending machines.

Objective-and-Task Method Promotional budgeting procedure by which a retailer clearly defines its promotional goals and prepares a budget to satisfy them.

Objectives Long-term and short-term performance targets that a retailer hopes to attain. Goals can involve sales, profit, satisfaction of publics, and image.

Observation Form of research in which present behavior or the results of past behavior are observed and recorded. It can be human or mechanical.

Odd Pricing Retail prices set at levels below even dollar values, such as $0.49, $4.98, and $199.

Off-Price Chain Features brand-name apparel and accessories, footwear, linens, fabrics, cosmetics, and/or housewares and sells them at everyday low prices in an efficient, limited-service environment.

Off-Retail Markdown Percentage Markdown for each item or category of items computed as a percentage of original retail price:

$$\text{Off-retail markdown percentage} = \frac{\text{Original price} - \text{New price}}{\text{Original price}}$$

One-Hundred Percent Location Optimum site for a particular store. A location labeled as 100 percent for one firm may be less than optimal for another.

One-Price Policy Strategy wherein a retailer charges the same price to all customers buying an item under similar conditions.

Open Credit Account Requires a consumer to pay his or her bill in full when it is due.

Open-to-Buy Difference between planned purchases and the purchase commitments already made by a buyer for a given time period, often a month. It represents the amount the buyer has left to spend for that month and is reduced each time a purchase is made.

Operating Expenditures (Expenses) Short-term selling and administrative costs of running a business.

Operations Blueprint Systematically lists all the operating functions to be performed, their characteristics, and their timing.

Operations Management Process used to efficiently and effectively enact the policies and tasks to satisfy a firm's customers, employees, and management (and stockholders, if a publicly owned company).

Opportunistic Buying Negotiates low prices for merchandise whose sales have not met expectations, end-of-season goods, items returned to the manufacturer or another retailer, and closeouts.

Opportunities Marketplace openings that exist because other retailers have not yet capitalized on them.

Opportunity Costs Possible benefits a retailer forgoes if it invests in one opportunity rather than another.

Option Credit Account Form of revolving account that allows partial payments. No interest is assessed if a person pays a bill in full when it is due.

Order-Getting Salesperson Actively involved with informing and persuading customers, and in closing sales. This is a true "sales" employee.

Order Lead Time Period from when an order is placed by a retailer to the date merchandise is ready for sale (received, price marked, and put on the selling floor).

Order-Taking Salesperson Engages in routine clerical and sales functions, such as setting up displays, placing inventory on shelves, answering simple questions, filling orders, and ringing up sales.

Organizational Mission Retailer's commitment to a type of business and a distinctive marketplace role. It is reflected in the attitude to consumers, employees, suppliers, competitors, government, and others.

Organization Chart Graphically displays the hierarchical relationships within a firm.

Outshopping When a person goes out of his or her hometown to shop.

Outsourcing Situation whereby a retailer pays an outside party to undertake one or more operating tasks.

Overstored Trading Area Geographic area with so many stores selling a specific good or service that some retailers will be unable to earn an adequate profit.

Owned-Goods Services Area of service retailing in which goods owned by consumers are repaired, improved, or maintained.

Parasite Store Outlet that does not create its own traffic and has no real trading area of its own.

Partnership Unincorporated retail firm owned by two or more persons, each with a financial interest.

Perceived Risk Level of risk a consumer believes exists regarding the purchase of a specific good or service from a given retailer, whether or not the belief is actually correct.

Percentage Lease Stipulates that rent is related to a retailer's sales or profits.

Percentage-of-Sales Method Promotional budgeting method in which a retailer ties its budget to revenue.

Percentage Variation Method Inventory level planning method where beginning-of-month planned inventory during any month differs from planned average monthly stock by only one-half of that month's variation from estimated average monthly sales. Under this method:

$$\begin{array}{l} \text{Beginning-of-month} \\ \text{planned inventory} \\ \text{level (at retail)} \end{array} = \begin{array}{l} \text{Planned average monthly} \\ \text{stock at retail} \times 1/2 \\ [1 + (\text{Estimated monthly sales/} \\ \text{Estimated average monthly sales})] \end{array}$$

Performance Measures Criteria used to assess effectiveness, including total sales, sales per store, sales by product category, sales per square foot, gross margins, gross margin return on investment, operating income, inventory turnover, markdown percentages, employee turnover, financial ratios, and profitability.

Personality Sum total of an individual's traits, which make that individual unique.

Personal Selling Oral communication with one or more prospective customers to make sales.

Physical Inventory System Actual counting of merchandise. A firm using the cost method of inventory valuation and relying on a physical inventory can derive gross profit only when it does a full inventory.

Planned Shopping Center Group of architecturally unified commercial facilities on a site that is centrally owned or managed, designed and operated as a unit, based on balanced tenancy, and accompanied by parking.

Planogram Visual (graphical) representation of the space for selling, merchandise, personnel, and customers—as well as for product categories.

PMs Promotional money, push money, or prize money that a manufacturer provides for retail salespeople selling that manufacturer's brand.

Point of Indifference Geographic breaking point between two cities (communities), so that the trading area of each can be determined. At this point, consumers would be indifferent to shopping at either area.

Point-of-Purchase (POP) Display Interior display that provides shoppers with information, adds to store atmosphere, and services a substantial promotional role.

Positioning Enables a retailer to devise its strategy in a way that projects an image relative to its retail category and its competitors, and elicits consumer responses to that image.

Post-Purchase Behavior Further purchases or re-evaluation based on a purchase.

Power Center Shopping site with (a) up to a half dozen or so category killer stores and a mix of smaller stores or (b) several complementary stores specializing in one product category.

Predatory Pricing Involves large retailers that seek to reduce competition by selling goods and services at very low prices, thus causing small retailers to go out of business.

Prestige Pricing Assumes consumers will not buy goods and services at prices deemed too low. It is based on the price–quality association.

Pre-Training Indoctrination on the history and policies of the retailer and a job orientation on hours, compensation, the chain of command, and job duties.

Price Elasticity of Demand Sensitivity of customers to price changes in terms of the quantities bought:

$$\text{Elasticity} = \frac{\dfrac{\text{Quantity 1} - \text{Quantity 2}}{\text{Quantity 1} + \text{Quantity 2}}}{\dfrac{\text{Price 1} - \text{Price 2}}{\text{Price 1} + \text{Price 2}}}$$

Price Lining Practice whereby retailers sell merchandise at a limited range of price points, with each point representing a distinct level of quality.

Price–Quality Association Concept stating that many consumers feel high prices connote high quality and low prices connote low quality.

Primary Data Those collected to address the specific issue or problem under study. This type of data may be gathered via surveys, observations, experiments, and simulation.

Primary Trading Area Encompasses 50 to 80 percent of a store's customers. It is the area closest to the store and possesses the highest density of customers to population and the highest per capita sales.

Private (Dealer, Store) Brands Contain names designated by wholesalers or retailers, are more profitable to retailers, are better controlled by retailers, are not sold by competing retailers, are less expensive for consumers, and lead to customer loyalty to retailers (rather than to manufacturers).

Probability (Random) Sample Approach whereby every store, product, or customer has an equal or known chance of being chosen for study.

Problem Awareness Stage in the decision process at which the consumer not only has been aroused by social, commercial, and/or physical stimuli, but also recognizes that the good or service under consideration may solve a problem of shortage or unfulfilled desire.

Productivity Efficiency with which a retail strategy is carried out.

Product Life Cycle Shows the expected behavior of a good or service over its life. The traditional cycle has four stages: introduction, growth, maturity, and decline.

Product/Trademark Franchising Arrangement in which the franchisee acquires the identify of the franchisor by agreeing to sell the latter's products and/or operate under the latter's name.

Profit-and-Loss (Income) Statement Summary of a retailer's revenues and expenses over a particular period of time, usually a month, quarter, or year.

Prototype Stores Used with an operations strategy that requires multiple outlets in a chain to conform to relatively uniform construction, layout, and operations standards.

Publicity Any nonpersonal form of public relations whereby messages are transmitted by mass media, the time or space provided by the media is not paid for, and there is no identified commercial sponsor.

Public Relations Any communication that fosters a favorable image for the retailer among its publics (consumers, investors, government, channel members, employees, and the general public).

Purchase Act Exchange of money or a promise to pay for the ownership or use of a good or service. Purchase variables include the place of purchase, terms, and availability of merchandise.

Purchase Motivation Product Groupings Appeal to the consumer's urge to buy products and the amount of time he or she is willing to spend in shopping.

Quick Response (QR) Inventory Planning Enables a retailer to reduce the amount of inventory it keeps on hand by ordering more frequently and in lower quantity.

Rack Display Interior display that neatly hangs or presents products.

Rationalized Retailing Combines a high degree of centralized management control with strict operating procedures for every phase of business.

Reach Number of distinct people exposed to a retailer's promotional efforts during a specified period.

Recruitment Activity whereby a retailer generates a list of job applicants.

Reference Groups Influence people's thoughts and behavior. They may be classified as aspirational, membership, and dissociative.

Regional Shopping Center Large, planned shopping facility appealing to a geographically dispersed market. It has at least one or two full-sized department stores and 50 to 150 or more smaller retailers. The market for this center is 100,000+ people, who live or work up to a 30-minute drive time from the center.

Regression Model Computerized site selection tool that uses equations showing the association between potential store sales and several independent variables at each location under consideration.

Reilly's Law of Retail Gravitation Traditional means of trading-area delineation that establishes a point of indifference between two cities or communities, so the trading area of each can be determined.

Relationship Retailing Exists when retailers seek to establish and maintain long-term bonds with customers, rather than act as if each sales transaction is a completely new encounter with them.

Rented-Goods Services Area of service retailing in which consumers lease and use goods for specified periods of time.

Reorder Point Stock level at which new orders must be placed:

Reorder point = (Usage rate × Lead time) + Safety stock

Resident Buying Office Inside or outside buying organization used when a retailer wants to keep in close touch with market trends and cannot do so with just its headquarters buying staff. Such offices are usually situated in important merchandise centers (sources of supply) and provide valuable data and contacts.

Retail Audit Systematically examines the total retailing effort or a specific aspect of it to study what a retailer is presently doing, appraise how well it is performing, and make recommendations.

Retail Balance The mix of stores within a district or shopping center.

Retail Information System (RIS) Anticipates the information needs of managers; collects, organizes, and stores relevant data on a continuous basis; and directs the flow of information to proper decision makers.

Retailing Business activities involved in selling goods and services to consumers for their personal, family, or household use.

Retailing Concept An approach to business that is customer-oriented, coordinated, value-driven, and goal-oriented.

Retail Institution Basic format or structure of a business. Institutions can be classified by ownership, store-based retail strategy mix, and nonstore-based, electronic, and nontraditional retailing.

Retail Life Cycle Theory asserting that institutions—like the goods and services they sell—pass through identifiable life stages: introduction (early growth), growth (accelerated development), maturity, and decline.

Retail Method of Accounting Determines closing inventory value by calculating the average relationship between the cost and retail values of merchandise available for sale during a period.

Retail Organization How a firm structures and assigns tasks, policies, resources, authority, responsibilities, and rewards so as to efficiently and effectively satisfy the needs of its target market, employees, and management.

Retail Performance Index Encompasses five-year trends in revenue growth and profit growth, and a 6-year average return on assets.

Retail Promotion Any communication by a retailer that informs, persuades, and/or reminds the target market about any aspect of that firm.

Retail Reductions Difference between beginning inventory plus purchases during the period and sales plus ending inventory. They encompass anticipated markdowns, employee and other discounts, and stock shortages.

Retail Strategy Overall plan guiding a retail firm. It influences the firm's business activities and its response to market forces, such as competition and the economy.

Return on Assets (ROA) Performance ratio based on net sales, net profit, and total assets:

$$\frac{\text{Return}}{\text{on assets}} = \frac{\text{Net profit}}{\text{Net sales}} \times \frac{\text{Net sales}}{\text{Total assets}} = \frac{\text{Net profit}}{\text{Total assets}}$$

Return on Net Worth (RONW) Performance measure based on net profit, net sales, total assets, and net worth:

$$\frac{\text{Return on}}{\text{net worth}} = \frac{\text{Net profit}}{\text{Net sales}} \times \frac{\text{Net sales}}{\text{Total assets}} \times \frac{\text{Total assets}}{\text{Net worth}}$$

Reverse Logistics Encompasses all merchandise flows from the retailer back through the supply channel.

Revolving Credit Account Allows a customer to charge items and be billed monthly on the basis of the outstanding cumulative balance.

Robinson-Patman Act Bars manufacturers and wholesalers from discriminating in price or purchase terms in selling to individual retailers if these retailers are purchasing products of "like quality" and the effect of such discrimination is to injure competition.

Routine Decision Making Takes place when a consumer buys out of habit and skips steps in the purchase process.

Safety Stock Extra inventory to protect against out-of-stock conditions due to unexpected demand and delays in delivery.

Sales Manager Person who typically supervises the on-floor selling and operational activities for a specific retail department.

Sales Opportunity Grid Rates the promise of new and established goods, services, procedures, and/or store outlets across a variety of criteria.

Sales-Productivity Ratio Method for assigning floor space on the basis of sales or profit per foot.

Sales Promotion Encompasses the paid communication activities other than advertising, public relations, and personal selling that stimulate consumer purchases and dealer effectiveness.

Saturated Trading Area Geographic area with the proper amount of retail facilities to satisfy the needs of its population for a specific good or service, as well as to enable retailers to prosper.

Scenario Analysis Lets a retailer project the future by studying factors that affect long-term performance and then forming contingency plans based on alternate scenarios.

Scrambled Merchandising Occurs when a retailer adds goods and services that may be unrelated to each other and to the firm's original business.

Seasonable Merchandise Products that sell well over non-consecutive time periods.

Secondary Business District (SBD) Unplanned shopping area in a city or town that is usually bounded by the intersection of two major streets. It has at least a junior department store and/or some larger specialty stores—in addition to many smaller stores.

Secondary Data Those gathered for purposes other than addressing the issue or problem currently under study.

Secondary Trading Area Geographic area that contains an additional 15 to 25 percent of a store's customers. It is located outside the primary area, and customers are more widely dispersed.

Selective Distribution Takes place when suppliers sell through a moderate number of retailers. This lets suppliers have higher sales than in exclusive distribution and lets retailers carry some competing brands.

Self-Scanning Enables the consumer himself or herself to scan the items being purchased at a checkout counter, pay electronically by credit or debit card, and bag the items.

Semantic Differential Disguised or nondisguised survey technique, whereby a respondent is asked to rate one or more retailers on several criteria; each criterion is evaluated along a bipolar adjective scale.

Service Retailing Involves transactions in which consumers do not purchase or acquire ownership of tangible products. It encompasses rented goods, owned goods, and nongoods.

Simulation Type of experiment whereby a computer program is used to manipulate the elements of a retail strategy mix rather than test them in a real setting.

Single-Channel Retailing A distribution approach whereby a retailer sells to consumers through one retail format.

Situation Analysis Candid evaluation of the opportunities and threats facing a prospective or existing retailer.

Slotting Allowances Payments that retailers require of vendors for providing shelf space in stores.

Social Class Informal ranking of people based on income, occupation, education, and other factors.

Social Responsibility Occurs when a retailer acts in society's best interests—as well as its own. The challenge is to balance corporate citizenship with fair profits.

Sole Proprietorship Unincorporated retail firm owned by one person.

Solutions Selling Takes a customer-centered approach and presents "solutions" rather than "products." It goes a step beyond cross-merchandising.

Sorting Process Involves the retailer's collecting an assortment of goods and services from various sources, buying them in large quantity, and offering to sell them in small quantities to consumers.

Specialog Enables a retailer to cater to the specific needs of customer segments, emphasize a limited number of items, and reduce catalog production and postage costs.

Specialty Store Retailer that concentrates on selling one goods or service line.

Staple Merchandise Consists of the regular products carried by a retailer.

Stimulus Cue (social or commercial) or a drive (physical) meant to motivate or arouse a person to act.

Stock-to-Sales Method Inventory level planning technique wherein a retailer wants to maintain a specified ratio of goods on hand to sales.

Stock Turnover Number of times during a specific period, usually one year, that the average inventory on hand is sold. It can be computed in units or dollars (at retail or cost):

$$\text{Annual rate of stock turnover (in units)} = \frac{\text{Number of units sold during year}}{\text{Average inventory on hand (in units)}}$$

$$\text{Annual rate of stock turnover (in retail dollars)} = \frac{\text{Net yearly sales}}{\text{Average inventory on hand (at retail)}}$$

$$\text{Annual rate of stock turnover (at cost)} = \frac{\text{Cost of goods sold during the year}}{\text{Average inventory on hand (at cost)}}$$

Storability Product Groupings Used for products that need special handling.

Storefront Total physical exterior of a store, including the marquee, entrances, windows, lighting, and construction materials.

Store Maintenance Encompasses all the activities in managing a retailer's physical facilities.

Straight (Gridiron) Traffic Flow Presents displays and aisles in a rectangular or gridiron pattern.

Straight Lease Requires the retailer to pay a fixed dollar amount per month over the life of a lease. It is the simplest, most direct leasing arrangement.

Strategic Profit Model Expresses the numerical relationship among net profit margin, asset turnover, and financial leverage. It can be used in planning or controlling a retailer's assets.

Strategy Mix Firm's particular combination of store location, operating procedures, goods/services offered, pricing tactics, store atmosphere and customer services, and promotional methods.

String Unplanned shopping area comprising a group of retail stores, often with similar or compatible product lines, located along a street or highway.

Supercenter Combination store blending an economy supermarket with a discount department store.

Supermarket Self-service food store with grocery, meat, and produce departments and minimum annual sales of $2 million. The category includes conventional supermarkets, food-based superstores, combination stores, box (limited-line) stores, and warehouse stores.

Supervision Manner of providing a job environment that encourages employee accomplishment.

Supply Chain Logistics aspect of a value delivery chain. It comprises all of the parties that participate in the retail logistics process: manufacturers, wholesalers, third-party specialists, and the retailer.

Survey Research technique which systematically gathers information from respondents by communicating with them.

Survey of Buying Power Reports current demographic data on metropolitan areas, cities, and states. It also provides such information as total annual retail sales by area, annual retail sales for specific product categories, annual effective buying income, and five-year population and retail sales projections.

Tactics Actions that encompass a retailer's daily and short-term operations.

Target Market Customer group that a retailer seeks to attract and satisfy.

Taxes The portion of revenues turned over to the federal, state, and/or local government.

Terms of Occupancy Consist of ownership versus leasing, the type of lease, operations and maintenance costs, taxes, zoning restrictions, and voluntary regulations.

Theme-Setting Display Interior display that depicts a product offering in a thematic manner and portrays a specific atmosphere or mood.

Threats Environmental and marketplace factors that can adversely affect retailers if they do not react to them (and sometimes, even if they do).

Top-Down Space Management Approach Exists when a retailer starts with its total available store space, divides the space into categories, and then works on in-store product layouts.

Total Retail Experience All the elements in a retail offering that encourage or inhibit consumers during their contact with a retailer.

Trading Area Geographic area containing the customers of a particular firm or group of firms for specific goods or services.

Trading-Area Overlap Occurs when the trading areas of stores in different locations encroach on one another. In the overlap area, the same customers are served by both stores.

Traditional Department Store Type of department store in which merchandise quality ranges from average to quite good, pricing is moderate to above average, and customer service ranges from medium levels of sales help, credit, delivery, and so forth to high levels of each.

Traditional Job Description Contains each position's title, supervisory relationships (superior and subordinate), committee assignments, and the specific ongoing roles and tasks.

Training Programs Used to teach new (and existing) personnel how best to perform their jobs or how to improve themselves.

Unbundled Pricing Involves a retailer's charging separate prices for each item sold.

Uncontrollable Variables Aspects of business to which the retailer must adapt (such as competition, the economy, and laws).

Understored Trading Area Geographic area that has too few stores selling a specific good or service to satisfy the needs of its population.

Unit Control Looks at the quantities of merchandise a retailer handles during a stated period.

Unit Pricing Practice required by many states, whereby retailers (mostly food stores) must express both the total price of an item and its price per unit of measure.

Universal Product Code (UPC) Classification for coding data onto products via a series of thick and thin vertical lines. It lets retailers record information instantaneously on a product's model number, size, color, and other factors when it is sold, as well as send the information to a computer that monitors unit sales, inventory levels, and other factors. The UPC is not readable by humans.

Unplanned Business District Type of retail location where two or more stores situate together (or nearby) in such a way that the total arrangement or mix of stores is not due to prior long-range planning.

Usage Rate Average sales per day, in units, of merchandise.

Value Embodied by the activities and processes (a value chain) that provide a given level of value for the consumer—from manufacturer, wholesaler, and retailer perspectives. From the customer's perspective, it is the perception the shopper has of a value chain.

Value Chain Total bundle of benefits offered to consumers through a channel of distribution.

Value Delivery System All the parties that develop, produce, deliver, and sell and service particular goods and services.

Variable Markup Policy Strategy whereby a firm purposely adjusts markups by merchandise category.

Variable Pricing Strategy wherein a retailer alters prices to coincide with fluctuations in costs or consumer demand.

Variety Store Outlet that handles a wide assortment of inexpensive and popularly priced goods and services, such as apparel and accessories, costume jewelry, notions and small wares, candy, toys, and other items in the price range.

Vending Machine Format involving the cash- or card-operated dispensing of goods and services. It eliminates the use of sales personnel and allows around-the-clock sales.

Vendor-Managed Inventory (VMI) Practice of retailers counting on key suppliers to actively participate in their inventory management programs. Suppliers have their own employees stationed at retailers' headquarters to manage the inventory replenishment of the suppliers' products.

Vertical Cooperative Advertising Agreement Enables a manufacturer and a retailer or a wholesaler and a retailer to share an ad.

Vertical Marketing System All the levels of independently owned businesses along a channel of distribution. Goods and services are normally distributed through one of three types of systems: independent, partially integrated, and fully integrated.

Vertical Price Fixing Occurs when manufacturers or wholesalers seek to control the retail prices of their goods and services.

Vertical Retail Audit Analyzes—in depth—performance in one area of the strategy mix or operations.

Video Kiosk Freestanding, interactive, electronic computer terminal that displays products and related information on a video screen; it often uses a touchscreen for consumers to make selections.

Visual Merchandising Proactive, integrated approach to atmospherics taken by a retailer to create a certain "look," properly display products, stimulate shopping, and enhance the physical environment.

Want Book Notebook in which retail store employees record requests for unstocked or out-of-stock merchandise.

Want Slip Slip on which retail store employees enter requests for unstocked or out-of-stock merchandise.

Warehouse Store Food-based discounter offering a moderate number of food items in a no-frills setting.

Weeks' Supply Method An inventory level planning method wherein beginning inventory equals several weeks' expected sales. It assumes inventory is in direct proportion to sales. Under this method:

$$\begin{matrix} \text{Beginning-of-month} \\ \text{planned inventory} \\ \text{level (at retail)} \end{matrix} = \begin{matrix} \text{Average estimated weekly sales} \\ \times \text{ Number of weeks to} \\ \text{be stocked} \end{matrix}$$

Weighted Application Blank Form whereby criteria best correlating with job success get more weight than others. A minimum total score becomes a cutoff point for hiring.

Wheel of Retailing Theory stating that retail innovators often first appear as low-price operators with low costs and low profit margins. Over time, they upgrade the products carried and improve facilities and customer services. They then become vulnerable to new discounters with lower cost structures.

Width of Assortment Number of distinct goods/service categories (product lines) a retailer carries.

Word of Mouth (WOM) Occurs when one consumer talks to others.

World Wide Web (Web) Way of accessing the Internet, whereby people work with easy-to-use Web addresses and pages. Users see words, colorful charts, pictures, and video, and hear audio.

Yield Management Pricing Computerized, demand-based, variable pricing technique whereby a retailer (typically a service firm) determines the combination of prices that yield the greatest total revenues for a given period.

Zero-Based Budgeting Practice followed when a firm starts each new budget from scratch and outlines the expenditures needed to reach that period's goals. All costs are justified each time a budget is done.

Photo Credits

Chapter 1

CO-1 (**page 2**) Reprinted by permission. **Fig. 1-1** (**page 3**) Reprinted by permission of Retail Forward, Inc. **Fig. 1-2** (**page 5**) Reprinted by permission of *DSN Retailing Today*. **Fig. 1-6** (**page 8**) Reprinted by permission of Retail Forward, Inc. **Fig. 1-9** (**page 11**) Reprinted by permission of Retail Forward, Inc. **Fig. 1-11** (**page 14**) Reprinted by permission of Retail Forward, Inc.

Chapter 2

CO-2 (**page 19**) Reprinted by permission. **Fig. 2-1** (**page 20**) Reprinted by permission of Retail Forward, Inc. **Fig. 2-3** (**page 23**) Reprinted by permission of CVS Corporation. **Fig. 2-5** (**page 26**) Reprinted by permission of Giant Food, Inc. **Fig. 2-10** (**page 35**) Reprinted by permission of Stores Automated Systems, Inc. **Fig. 2-11** (**page 37**) Reprinted by permission of Eddie Bauer, Inc. **Fig. 2-13** (**page 41**) Reprinted by permission of Target Stores.

Chapter 3

CO-3 (**page 48**) Reprinted by permission. **Fig. 3-2** (**page 51**) Reprinted by permission of Frisch's Restaurants, Inc. **Fig. 3-6** (**page 59**) Reprinted by permission of Retail Forward, Inc. **Fig. 3-8** (**page 63**) Reprinted by permission of Retail Forward, Inc. **Fig. 3-10** (**page 64**) Reprinted by permission of Meristar Hotels & Resorts, Inc.

Chapter 4

CO-4 (**page 84**) Reprinted by permission. **Fig. 4-3** (**page 89**) Reprinted by permission of Retail Forward, Inc. **Fig. 4-4** (**page 90**) Reprinted by permission of Regis Corporation.

Chapter 5

CO-5 (**page 104**) Reprinted by permission. **Fig. 5-5** (**page 111**) Reprinted by permission of Eckerd Corporation. **Fig. 5-6** (**page 114**) Reprinted by permission of Wendy's International. **Fig. 5-7** (**page 115**) Reprinted by permission of Retail Forward, Inc. **Fig. 5-8** (**page 118**) Reprinted by permission. **Fig. 5-9** (**page 122**) Reprinted by permission of Retail Forward, Inc.

Chapter 6

CO-6 (**page 127**) Reprinted by permission. **Fig. 6-2** (**page 129**) Reprinted by permission. **Fig. 6-3** (**page 130**) Reprinted by permission. **Fig. 6-5** (**page 139**) Reprinted by permission of Mary Kay Cosmetics. **Fig. 6-10** (**page 146**) Reprinted by permission. **Fig. 6-11** (**page 147**) Reprinted by permission. **Fig. 6-12** (**page 148**) Reprinted by permission of Borders Group Inc. **Fig. 6-13** (**page 149**) Reprinted by permission of Borders Group Inc.

Chapter 7

CO-7 (**page 160**) Reprinted by permission. **Fig. 7-3** (**page 167**) Reprinted by permission of the Great Atlantic and Pacific Tea Company. **Fig. 7-4** (**page 167**) Reprinted by permission of Retail Forward, Inc. **Fig. 7-7** (**page 178**) Reprinted by permission of Retail Forward, Inc.

Chapter 8

CO-8 (**page 184**) Reprinted by permission. **Fig. 8-3** (**page 190**) Reprinted by permission of Retail Technologies International. **Fig. 8-5** (**page 193**) Reprinted by permission of 7-Eleven, Inc. **Fig. 8-6** (**page 195**) Reprinted by permission of Symbol Technologies. **Fig. 8-8** (**page 199**) Reprinted by permission of Retail Technologies International. **Fig. 8-10** (**page 204**) Reprinted by permission of Raymond R. Burke, Indiana University.

Chapter 9

CO-9 (**page 214**) Reprinted by permission. **Fig. 9-1** (**page 215**) Reprinted by permission of Retail Forward, Inc. **Fig. 9-3** (**page 219**) Reprinted by permission. **Fig. 9-4** (**page 221**) Reprinted by permission of ESRI and GDT. **Fig. 9-6** (**page 223**) Reprinted by permission of ESRI and GDT. **Fig. 9-7** (**page 223**) Reprinted by permission of Retail Forward, Inc.

Chapter 10

CO-10 (**page 240**) Reprinted by permission. **Fig. 10-1** (**page 242**) Reprinted by permission. **Fig. 10-2** (**page 244**) Reprinted by permission of The Rouse Company. **Fig. 10-4** (**page 247**) Reprinted by permission of the Simon Property Group. **Fig. 10-5** (**page 249**) Reprinted by permission of Retail Forward, Inc. **Fig. 10-6** (**page 250**) Reprinted by permission of City Center Retail Trust. **Fig. 10-8** (**page 255**) Reprinted by permission of Retail Forward, Inc.

Chapter 11

CO-11 (**page 268**) Reprinted by permission. **Fig. 11-12** (**page 290**) Reprinted by permission of *DSN Retailing Today*.

Chapter 12

CO-12 (**page 294**) Reprinted by permission. **Fig. 12-2** (**page 303**) Reprinted by permission of Kmart.

Chapter 13

CO-13 (**page 313**) Reprinted by permission. **Fig. 13-2** (**page 318**) Reprinted by permission of Brucker Enterprises, Inc., a franchise of Burger King Corporation. **Fig. 13-4** (**page 320**) Reprinted by permission of Retail Forward, Inc. **Fig. 13-5** (**page 324**) Reprinted by permission of Foot Locker. **Fig. 13-6** (**page 324**) Reprinted by permission of Icode, Inc. **Fig. 13-7** (**page 325**) Reprinted by permission of TransAct Technologies, Inc.

Chapter 14

CO-14 (**page 338**) Reprinted by permission. **Fig. 14-1** (**page 340**) Reprinted by permission of Retail Forward, Inc. **Fig. 14-3** (**page 343**) Reprinted by permission of *DSN Retailing Today*. **Fig. 14-6** (**page 349**) Reprinted by permission of Wendy's International, Inc. **Fig. 14-10** (**page 353**) Reprinted by permission of Retail Forward, Inc. **Fig. 14-11** (**page 354**) Reprinted by permission of Retail Forward, Inc. **Fig. 14-12** (**page 356**) Reprinted by permission of Retail Forward, Inc. **Fig. 14-14** (**page 361**) Reprinted by permission of Logical Planning Systems.

Chapter 15

CO-15 (**page 365**) Reprinted by permission. **Fig. 15-5** (**page 370**) Reprinted by permission from Nash-Finch Company, owner of the mark PALLET POWER PROGRAM™ and the registered trademark OUR FAMILY in the U.S. **Fig. 15-6** (**page 372**) Reprinted by permission of Retail Forward, Inc. **Fig. 15-7** (**page 374**) Reprinted by permission of Monarch Marking Systems. **Fig. 15-8** (**page 374**) Reprinted by permission of Seagull Scientific Systems, author of "Bar Tender" label printing software. **Fig. 15-9** (**page 376**) Reprinted by permission of Reitmans (Canada) Limited. **Fig. 15-10** (**page 380**) Reprinted by permission of Claire's Stores, Inc. **Fig. 15-11** (**page 384**) Reprinted by permission of Sensormatic Electronics Corporation. **Fig. 15-13** (**page 386**) Reprinted by permission of Ryder Systems, Inc.

Chapter 16

CO-16 (**page 389**) Reprinted by permission of eBay, Inc. Copyright EBAY INC. All rights reserved. **Fig. 16-4 (page 405)** Reprinted by permission of Retail Technologies International. **Fig. 16-5 (page 407)** Reprinted by permission of Beeline Shopper.

Chapter 17

CO-17 (**page 414**) Reprinted by permission. **Fig. 17-1 (page 416)** Reprinted by permission of Weingarten Realty Investors. **Fig. 17-4 (page 423)** Reprinted by permission of Retail Forward, Inc. **Fig. 17-8 (page 432)** Reprinted by permission of Retail Forward, Inc. **Fig. 17-9 (page 434)** Reprinted by permission of Retail Forward, Inc. **Fig. 17-11 (page 438)** Reprinted by permission of Goran Petkovic.

Chapter 18

CO-18 (**page 450**) Reprinted by permission. **Fig. 18-1 (page 451)** Reprinted by permission of Goran Petkovic. **Fig. 18-3 (page 454)** Reprinted by permission of Retail Forward, Inc. **Fig. 18-5 (page 455)** Reprinted by permission of Goran Petkovic. **Fig. 18-6 (page 456)** Reprinted by permission of Retail Forward, Inc. **Fig. 18-7 (page 457)** Reprinted by permission of Retail Forward, Inc. **Fig. 18-8 (page 460)** Reprinted by permission of *Progressive Grocer*. **Fig. 18-10 (page 461)** Reprinted by permission of Fresh Ideas, LLC.

Fig. 18-11 (page 465) Reprinted by permission of Costco Wholesale. **Fig. 18-12 (page 467)** Reprinted by permission of Goran Petkovic. **Fig. 18-13 (page 468)** Reprinted by permission of Kmart Corporation.

Chapter 19

CO-19 (**page 473**) Reprinted by permission of Mary Kay Inc. **Fig. 19-1 (page 474)** Reprinted by permission of Goran Petkovic. **Fig. 19-2 (page 475)** Reprinted by permission. **Fig. 19-3 (page 479)** Reprinted by permission. **Fig. 19-6 (page 483)** Reprinted by permission of Goodyear. **Fig. 19-10 (page 487)** Reprinted by permission of Retail Forward, Inc. **Fig. 19-12 (page 489)** Reprinted by permission of Retail Forward, Inc. **Fig. 19-13 (page 492)** Reprinted by permission of Industrial Electronic Engineers (IEE).

Chapter 20

CO-20 (**page 506**) Reprinted by permission. **Fig. 20-4 (page 518)** Reprinted by permission of Lowe's Companies Inc.

Appendix

Fig. 1 (page 533) Reprinted by permission of *DSN Retailing Today*. **Fig. 2 (page 534)** Reprinted by permission of *DSN Retailing Today*. **Fig. 3 (page 534)** Reprinted by permission of *DSN Retailing Today*.

Name Index

A

Aamco Transmissions, 101
Abercrombie & Fitch, 14, 359, 516
ABI/INFORM, 200
Abraham & Straus, 153, 294
Accor, 75
Ace Hardware, 31, 88, 92, 377
AdPilot, 496
Adrienne Weiss Corporation, 503
Advance Auto Parts, 110
Advanced Learning Systems, 287
Advantica, 281, 282
Aeon Group, 75, 278
Aerus, 4
Agins, Teri, 18n4
Ahlers, Linda, 281
Airborne, 381
Albaladejo-Pina, Isabel P., 227, 238n9
Albertson's, 6, 36, 63, 115, 116, 280, 299,
    487, 513
Aldi, 116
Alexander, Billye, 282
Allen, Randy, 193
Alliant Bruno, 302
Allied Domecq PLC, 240
Alloy.com, 158
Amato-McCoy, Deena M., 329n15
Amazon.com, 11, 127, 145–146, 158, 334, 352,
    354, 382, 466, 468
American Association of Franchisees and
    Dealers, 103
American Booksellers Association, 86
American Eagle, 157
American Express, 57, 74, 322, 418
American Franchisee Association, 103
American Marketing Association, 200
American Outpost, 59
America's Research Group, 178
AmericasMart, 367
Ames Department Stores, 203
Amway, 139
Ann Taylor, 250, 261
AOL Time Warner, 441
A&P. See Great Atlantic & Pacific
APL Logistics, 378
Apple, 212
APQC, 511
Aramark Refreshment Services, 140
Aranda-Gallego, Joaquin, 227, 238n9
Arboretum at Great Hills, 250
Arden B, 441
Arlen, Jeffrey, 525n13
Aron, Laurie Joan, 472nn18, 20
ASDA, 16, 260–261
Ash, Mary Kay, 281, 473
Ask Jeeves, 158
Aspen Grove, 250
Associated Food, 92

Associated Merchandising Corporation (AMC),
    344
AuditNet, 521
Auto-by-Tel, 422
Autodesk, 220
AutoDesSys, 209
AutoZone, 25
Avenue.com, 359
Avon, 74, 96, 139, 167, 281
A&W, 180
Azrock Commercial Flooring Products, 318

B

Babies "R" Us, 59
Baccarat, 339
Bahls, Jane Easter, 70n5
Bahls, Steven C., 70n5
Baird, Bill, 152n21
Baker, Michael, 259n7
Ballon, Marc, 312n5
Bally, 255
Banana Republic, 250, 338
Banks, Jos. A., 359
BargainandHaggle, 433
Barnes & Noble, 22, 86, 111, 118, 250, 316, 323,
    467, 468, 470
Barr, Vilma, 329n5
Baskin-Robbins, 468
Bass (footwear), 122
Bass Pro Shops, 467
Bassett, Mark S., 525n2
Basuroy, Suman, 364n21
Bates, Albert D., 26
Bath & Body Works, 111, 250, 370
Bauer, Rhonda, 472n23
Baughman, Kimberly, 281
Bazinet, Dan, 43n10
Beall's Inc., 332
Bean, L.L., 130, 133, 158, 177
Bear Creek, 194
Beatty, Sharon E., 183n24
bebe, 244, 507, 508
Bebko, Charlene Pleger, 44n19
Bed Bath & Beyond, 261, 341, 445
Beemer, C. Britt, 178, 440n3
Bell, David R., 227, 238n9
Benavent, Chrisophe, 238n8
Benchmarking Report Center, 511
Benetton Group, 317
Bennett, Peter D., 238n3
Bergue, Anne, 238n8
Berman, Barry, 152n8
Berry, Leonard L., 15, 18n6, 33, 34, 44n19, 47n3,
    525n7
Best Buy Inc., 70n3, 118, 190, 299, 316, 377, 382,
    453, 500–501, 506, 514
Best Products, 109
Bethel Food Market IGA, 320

Better Business Bureau, 38, 67, 200
Bezos, Jeff, 127
Bhargava, Nukesh, 525n5
Bible, Lynn, 312n15
Big Lots, 60, 121, 180, 369, 470
Bigstep.com, 466
Bi-Lo, 75, 302, 431
BJ's Wholesale Club, 170, 171, 281, 365
Blank, Arthur, 506
Blattberg, Robert, 43n4
Blinds Depot, 146
Blockbuster, 31, 99, 107, 118, 187, 214, 488
Bloomingdale's, 119, 133, 154, 247, 249, 294,
    345, 355
Blue, Larry, 238n8
BMG Entertainment, 419
Bodamer, Dave, 256, 260
Body Shop International, 75
Bombay Company, 361
Bon Marche, 249, 294
Bon-Ton, 377
Bonwit Teller, 345
Borders Bookstores, 22, 86, 111, 118, 148, 210,
    211, 229, 357, 467, 470
Borzyskowska, Anita, 500
Boston Consulting Group, 152nn15, 17, 18,
    21
Bottum, MacKenzie S., 238n6
Bplans.com, 507
Bradlees stores, 447
Bradshaw, Rich, 312n15
Brady, Michael K., 47n2, 525n7
Brands, Richard R., 525n7
Bresler's Ice Cream and Premium Frozen Yogurt,
    99
Bristol-Meyers Squibb, 36
Bronstein, Kathy, 441, 442
Brooks Brothers, 122, 208
Brown, Stephen W., 46, 126n2
Bruno's, 75, 302
Buechner, Maryanne Murray, 79
Build-A-Bear Workshop, 14, 502–504
Builders Square, 111
BuildHost.com, 152n24
Burdines, 294, 421, 502
Burger King, 203, 209, 318, 420, 441, 479,
    513
Burke, Raymond R., 204
Burlington Coat Factory, 51, 121
Burnett, Richard, 183n25
Burnette, Lacey, 229
Burt, Steve, 471n3
Burton, Scot, 364n17
Bush, George H.W., 2, 117
Business Research Lab Web, 201
Butt, H.E., 210, 212
Buy.com, 367, 381
Buzzell, Robert D., 43n16

C

Cachon, Gérard P., 43n17
Cafferky, Michael, 490
Cahill, Joseph B., 454, 463, 472n22
California Fashion Association, 441
CaliforniaMart, 367
Caliper Corporation, 220
Calphalon, 450
CAM Commerce Solutions, 323
Camelot Music, 302
Camp Snoopy, 249
Campanelli, Melissa, 440n4
Camuffo, Arnaldo, 317
Canadian Tire Corporation, 217
Canteen Corporation, 140
Cap Gemini Ernst & Young, 164
Carlson, 281
CarMax, 203, 286, 494
Carol Wright, 480
Carralero-Encinas, Jose, 471n3
Carrefour, 89, 116, 223, 260
CarsDirect, 422
Carson Pirie, 119
Carter's Foods, 477
Casabona, Liza, 329n6
Casey's General Stores, 112, 459
Casio, 21
Catherine's Stores, 59, 168
CB2, 211
CCH Business Owner's Toolkit, 86
CDnow, 423
CDW Computer Centers, 511
Centerlinq, 467
Central Market, 212, 323
Chabrow, Eric, 97
ChainDrugStore.net, 36
Champion Auto, 92
Chapter 11 Books, 453
Charles River Center, 251
Charming Shoppes, 208
Cheap Tickets, 32
Cheesecake Factory, 423
Chico's, 212
Chiger, Sherry, 152nn6, 9
Chipotle Mexican Grill, 262
Chiu, Hung-Chang, 34
Christie's International, 418
Circle Centre, 243
Circle K, 112
Circuit City, 3, 118, 202, 203, 212, 288, 299,
    377
Cirrus networks, 34
Cisco, 380
Claire's Stores, 380
Claritas, 220, 225
Clark, Ken, 44nn18, 22, 99n6, 312n8, 330,
    440n10, 477
Clark, Maxine, 504
Clark Hooper Momentum, 485
Clifford, Stephanie, 482
Clothestime, 346
Cloudwalkers.com, 359
CNET, 415
Coach, 156, 157
Coca-Cola, 353
Coconuts, 419
CocoWalk, 250

Cohen, Norma, 123
Cole National Corporation, 365
Coleman, Calmetta Y., 183n15, 472n14
Colicchio, George L., 521
Collaborative Planning, Forecasting, and
    Replenishment Committee, 377
Colonial Mall, 470
CommercialWare, 359
CompUSA, 326
Concentric Network, 146
Conlin, Michelle, 293n7
Conoco, 485
Consumer WebWatch, 143
Consumers Distributing, 109
Consumers Union, 143
Container Store, The, 90, 334, 511
Continental Real Estate, 261
Cooke, Gordon R., 154
CoolBrands International, 99, 101
Cornell, Lisa, 44n25
Cortese, Amy, 443
Costco, 3, 6, 14–15, 21, 61, 123, 167, 241, 257,
    260, 299, 300, 320, 322, 339, 354, 355,
    414, 415, 465, 514
Cotlier, Moria, 498n16
Coughlin, Tom, 286
Council of Better Business Bureaus, 38
Coyles, Stephanie, 43n6
CPI Corporation, 95
Craig, Susanne, 498n15
Crate & Barrel, 75, 211, 326
Cronin, J. Joseph, Jr., 47n2, 525n7
Crow, Sheryl, 527
Crown Center, 243
Cub Foods, 316
CustomerSat.com, 29
CVS, 23, 77–78, 217, 220, 299, 451

D

Daffy's, 356
D'Agostino, 443
Dairy Queen, 242
Dallas Market Center, 367
Dalmys, 376
D'Amico, Michael D., 238n6
Danziger, Pamela N., 182n6
Darden restaurants, 282
Daskas, Cheryl, 281
Daskas, Karen, 281
Datacolor International, 360
Davies, Melissa, 342
Davis, Cora, 282
Days Inn, 92
Dayton's, 11, 281
DeBerry-Spence, Benet, 471n3
Degn, Doug, 286
DeGross, Renee, 472n22
Delhaize America, 110
Delhaize Le Lion, 75
DeLise, Jacqueline T., 152n33
Dell, 155, 418
Deloitte & Touche, 74
Deloitte Touche Tohmatsu, 76n1
Deluxe, 322
DemandTec, 443
Denny's, 282, 373
Department of Commerce, 5

Derryberry, Jennifer, 152n12
Descartes Systems Group, 381
Desiardins, Doug, 21
Desiraju, Ramarao, 440n14
Desjardins, Doug, 235
Dhar, Sanjay K., 364n21
DHL, 381
Dickey, Jay, 117
Digital Sculpture, 209
Dignam, Conor, 500
Dillard's, 20, 294, 309, 378, 513
Direct Marketing Association, 38, 67, 133, 138
Direct Selling Association, 138
Discount Art, 351
Discount Auto Parts, 110
Discover, 322
Disney, Walt, Company, 46, 155, 158
DiStefano, Joseph, 262
DiversityInc.com, 282
Dixon, Jennifer, 440n6
Dixons, 514
Dollar General, 121, 229, 304, 330–331, 351
Dominick's supermarkets, 340
Domino's Pizza, 513
Domco, 318
Doneger Group, 344
Donnelley Marketing, 191
Donnelly, Harrison, 388n25
Dorothy Lane Market, 296
Drexler, Millard "Mickey," 338
Duane Reade, 77, 78
Dubelaar, Chris, 525n5
Duff, Mike, 302
Duhachek, Adam, 471n3
Dun & Bradstreet, 231, 401, 511
Dunkin' Donuts, 101, 220, 240, 468
Dutch Boy paints, 96
Duther Family Foods, 436

E

EAN International, 406
Earnest, Leslie, 312n5, 442
EarthShell, 355
EasyAsk, 157
eBay, 124, 129, 155, 289, 309, 433, 441
Eckerd Corporation, 8, 111, 451
ECR Europe, 379
Eddie Bauer, Inc., 37, 75, 134, 156, 190, 202, 209,
    220, 272
Eder, Rob, 363n5
EDGAR Online, 308
Eisenberg, Daniel, 497n12
Elbogdady, Dina, 126n4
Electrolux, 4
Electronic Retailing Association, 134
Elliott, Suzanne, 261
eMarketer, 152n18
EMI, 419
Entrabase, 466
Envirosell Inc., 466, 499
ePrivacy, 180
e-Rewards, 488
Ernsberger, Richard, Jr., 261
Ernst & Young, 142, 152n18
Escada, 482
ESPNZone, 178
Esprit de Corp, 65, 215

ESRI (Environmental Systems Research Institute), 220
Estée Lauder, 499
E-Trade Financial, 494
Evans, Joel R., 152n8
Everest Enterpirse, 324
EXPO Design Centers, 506
Express, 48, 111, 370
Express for Men, 111, 370
ExxonMobil, 3, 92
EZsize, 157

F

Façonnable, 268
Family Dollar, 121, 179
Faneuil Hall, 243
Fantastic Sams, 101
FAO Schwarz, 302, 451
Fay, 111
Federal Express, 133, 381
Federated Department Stores, 94, 154, 192, 203, 268, 287, 294, 299, 300, 309, 345, 377, 378, 475, 513
Federation of Pharmacy Networks (FPN), 344
FedMart, 414
Felsenthal, Edward, 440n7
Ferrarin, David, 525n5
Ferrell, M. Elizabeth, 183n24
Festival Walk, 249
Field Marketing, 382
Fields, Debbi, 184, 281
Filene's, 294, 458
Filene's Basement, 261
Finefield, Bill, 208
Finish Line footwear, 289
Finney, Daniel P., 259n5
Finnigan, David, 331
Fisher, Bryan, 293n16
Fisher, Dan, 364n17
Flay, Bobby, 341
Fleet Mortgage, 421
Fleming Companies, 153
Flohre, Ed, 296
Florida Mall, 247
Florida Retail Federation, 469
Food Lion, 75, 202, 510–511
Food Marketing Institute, 114, 383
Foot Locker, 180, 281, 323, 324
Footaction, 509
Foote, Paul Sheldon, 206n11
Footstar, 509
Ford, 92
Ford, Robert C., 46
Foreman, George, Grill, 134
Forest City Enterprises, 467
Forman, Richard, 429
Forman Mills, 429
Formichella, Judith, 208
Forrester Research, 141, 157
Forseon, 360
Fox, Richard J., 152n15
Francica, Joseph R., 238n8
Franklin Mint, 74, 130
Fred Meyer, 110, 116
Fresh Brands, 153
Friedman, David H., 183n19
Friedman, Michael, 329n12

Frisch's Restaurants, 51
FUBU, 157
Fuller, David Ray, 206n9
Fuller Brush, 139
Furman, Phyllis, 440n8

G

Galyan's Trading, 302
Ganesh, Jaishankar, 440n5
Gap Inc., 15, 61, 118, 149, 250, 251, 299, 338, 441, 454, 499, 500, 514
GapKids, 250
Garbato, Debby, 293n8
Garretson, Judith A., 364n17
Gartner, 135
Gateway, 211
Gautschi, David A., 227, 238n9
GDT (Geographic Data Technology), 220, 224
GE Capital, 326
Genco, 442
General Electric (GE), 354, 380
General Motors, 3, 92, 473
Genovese, 111
Gentry, Connie Robbins, 99n6, 218, 239nn10, 12, 370, 387n2, 413nn3, 9
George's Forest Park Auto Service, 491
geoVue, 220
Getz, Gary, 43n4
Ghosh, Avijit, 227, 238n9
Giant Eagle, 261
Giant Food, Inc., 26, 40, 75, 211, 302, 378, 420, 470
Gifts and Linens, 281
Gillette, 353
Gilligan, Gregory J., 224
Gimein, Mark, 293n2
Giotti, Debbie, 193
Givhan, Robin, 364n9
Gladson Interactive, 457
Global Mall, 466
Godiva, 417
Gokey, Timothy C., 43n6
Goldman, Abigail, 312n5
Goldsmith's, 294
Good to Go!, 210
Goodwill, 147
Goody, Sam, 52, 118
Goodyear, 483
Google, 210
Gottschalk's, 236
Graham, John R., 497n6
Grand Central Terminal, 243
Grant, Lorrie, 79
Grapentine, Terry, 525n7
Graves, Michael, 450
Great Atlantic & Pacific (A&P), 40, 75, 167, 355
Great Lakes Crossing, 281
Great North Foods warehouse, 379
Green Building Council, 251
Greenbaum, Scott, 409
Greenbury, Sir Richard, 404
Grewal, Dhruv, 34
Grimm, Mathew, 18n4
Grocery Manufacturers of America, 388nn19, 20
Grow, Brian, 421
Gucci, 369
Guitar Center, 158, 251
Gustke, Constance, 436

Gutner, Toddi, 130
Gymboree, 281

H

Haddad, Charles, 421
Haeberle, Matthew, 206n17
Hale, Todd, 43n14
Haller, Susan, 44n32
Hammacher Schlemmer, 347
Han, Sangman, 440n5
Handler, Jeff, 500
Handy Dan, 506
Hanna, Robin, 77
Hannaford Bros., 39, 110
Hanor, Dan, 364n21
Hanover, Dan, 501, 526
Hansotia, Behram J., 152n2
Harborplace Baltimore, 243, 244
Harris, Don, 286
Harris, Nicole, 152n32
Harris Interactive, 210, 517
Harris-Methodist Health Care, 333
Harris Teeter, 355
Harry and David, 122, 194, 340
Harte-Hanks Market Research, 178
Hartnett, Michael, 312n10
Hawes, Jon M., 238n6
Haworth, Jim, 286
Hays, Constance L., 18n4, 79, 304
Hazel, Debra, 259n6
Heaton, Cherrill P., 46
Hecht Company, 502
Helft, Miguel, 363n7
Heller, Laura, 312n9
Heller, Walter H., 329n12, 359
Helzberg Diamond Shops, 208
Henczel, Sue, 525n6
Henri Bendel, 111
Hertz, 32, 45, 67, 92
Higgins, Keven T., 527
High Point Furniture Market, 367
Hilton, 513
Hitt, Jack, 472n15
H&M (Hennes & Mauritz AB), 516
Ho, Teck-Hua, 227, 238n9
Hoboken Parking Authority, 256
Hoch, Stephen J., 364n21
Hodara, Susan, 126n5
Holiday Inn, 513
Hollander, Stanley, 126n2
Hollywood Video, 192
Holstein, William J., 206n11
Hom, Peter W., 525n7
Home Depot, 6, 15, 25, 61, 88, 118, 129, 155, 207, 208, 210, 235, 251, 253, 255, 257, 280, 286, 299, 316, 323, 326, 356, 366, 378, 379, 381, 382, 506, 507, 514–515, 517
Home Shopping Network (HSN), 134
Homestead Works, 261
Horton Plaza, 243
Hoskins, Michele, 373
Hot Topic, 211, 453
Howell, Debbie, 70n9, 328n3, 331
Hu, Ting, 373
Huang, Zhimin, 497n5
Hudson's, 281
Huff, David L., 238n8

Huff, Lois, 525n10
Huffman, Cynthia, 364n14
Hult, G. Tomas M., 47n2
Hunt, H. Keith, 471n3
Hunt Club, 354
Hyatt, 513

I

I Can't Believe It's Yogurt, 99
IBM, 155, 331
IGA, 115
IHOP, 281
Ikea, 50, 75, 104, 224, 323, 432, 467, 468, 489
Iles, Norcen, 193
iMall, 146
Imus, Marv, 13
Information Resources, Inc., 201, 361
infoUSA, 136
Integration.com, 359
Intellilink, 509
International Council of Shopping Centers, 153, 247
International Fashion and Life-Style Exhibition, 367
International Franchise Association, 91, 103, 200–201
International Mass Retail Association, 170, 235
International Trade Administration, 71
Internet Antique Shop, 155
Interspar, 261
IntuiFind, 157
iQVC, 158
Island Pacific Systems, 360
iTools, 185
Ito-Yokado, 75

J

Jagoda, Butch, 208
Jaguar, 54
Java Coast Fine Coffees, 99
Jazzercise, 92, 101
JDA Software, 209, 360
Jeffrey, Don, 377
Jiffy Lube, 526–527
Jill, J., 154
JM Family Enterprises, 511
Jo-Ann's fabrics and crafts stores, 106
Johnson, Bradford C., 206n3
Johnson, James C., 227, 238n9
Jollibee, 168
Jones Apparel, 446
Jones Lang LaSalle (JLL), 260
Joy of Socks, 119
Jupiter Media Metrix, 109, 157
Just for Feet, 509

K

Kabachnick, Terri, 280
Kadlec, Daniel, 43n17
Kahn, Barbara E., 363n3, 364n14
Kalish, Ira, 525n11
Kamprad, Ingvar, 104
Kaon Interactive, 156
Kaplan, Allison, 472n24
Kaufman, Barbara Babbit, 453
Kaufman, Leslie, 329n8
K-B Toys, 60, 118

Keegan, Paul, 472n17
Kelly, J. Patrick, 471n3
Kelly, Kevin, 142
Kennedy, John F., 39, 40
Kennedy, Marilyn Moats, 293n13
Kennedy Airport, 149
Kenneth Cole, 247
Kentucky Fried Chicken Franchise Association, 103
Kern, Clifford, 227, 238n9
Kerr, 111
KFC, 180, 351–352, 513
Kibarian, Thomas M., 440n13
Kids "R" Us, 250, 331, 380
Kimco Realty, 260
King, Stephen, 347
Kingfisher, 514
King of Prussia Mall, 247
Kiosks.org, 148
Kirby, 139
Kirkland's, 302
Kirkpatrick, David D., 86
Kirn, Steven P., 293n15
Kmart, 6, 11, 94, 111, 116, 117n, 120, 121, 193, 203, 210, 304, 323, 326, 355, 377, 445, 450, 468, 470, 507, 513
Koch, Bill, 44n21
Kodak, 353
Kohl's Department Stores, 3, 62, 179, 241, 294, 444–447, 462, 514, 517–518, 521
Kolettis, Helen, 388n25
Konicki, Steve, 388n8
Koopman, John C., 76nn2, 4
Kozinets, Robert V., 471n3
Kozmo, 109
Kramont Realty Trust, 249, 250
Krishnamurthi, Malini, 206n11
Krispy Kreme Doughnuts, 3, 242
Krizner, Ken, 331
Kroc, Ray, 84, 502
Kroger Company, 6, 20, 57, 95, 96, 110, 115, 296, 436, 513, 514
Kronos, 317
KSS, 425
Kumar, Nanda, 364n21
Kurt Salmon Associates, 170, 182n2, 183nn18, 21, 206n2, 388n12
Kwak, Hyokjin, 152n15

L

Laird, Trey, 500
Lamson, George, 149
Lands' End, 10, 14, 79, 96, 110, 134, 154, 157, 158, 211, 475
Lane Bryant, 157
Lariviere, Martin A., 43n17
Lawn Doctor, 4, 92
Lawson, Richard, 152n3
Lazarus, 294
LeBlang, Paul, 227, 238n9
Lee, Jennifer, 203, 332
Legasse, Emeril, 341
Lemon, Katherine N., 47n2
LensCrafters, 75
Lerner New York, 48, 360, 370
Leung, Shirley, 77
Levering, Robert, 511

Levinson, Meridith, 206n10
Levi's, 122, 339, 353
Lewis, Len, 44n20, 388n17
Lewison, Dale M., 238n6
Lexus, 511
Li, Susan X., 497n5
Lifo Systems, 392
Limited Brands, 48, 111, 203, 299, 326, 360, 370, 373, 378
Limited Stores, 370
Limited, The, 48, 118, 247, 333, 354, 360, 502
    See also Limited Brands
Limited Too, 157, 203
Linens 'N Things, 445
Liquid Presence, 209
Lisanti, Tony, 28, 329n7, 471n2, 497n3
Little, Michael W., 522
Little Caesar's, 513
Little Switzerland, 302
LivePerson, 158
Liz Claiborne, 122, 353
Loblaw, 514
Logical Planning Systems, 361
LogicTools, 400
Lohr, Steve, 152n16
Long John Silver's, 180
Longs Drug Stores, 398, 443
Lord & Taylor, 235, 281, 345
Loss Prevention Specialists, 377
Lowe's, 190, 207–208, 261, 299, 382, 496, 506, 507, 514, 517, 518
Lublin, Joann S., 312n12
Luckett, Michael, 440n5
Luxottica, 75
Lyons, Tom, 472n8
Lytle, Richard S., 525n7

M

McCown, James, 251
McCrory, 121, 203
McDonald, Maurice and Richard, 84
McDonald, William J., 76n3
McDonald's, 38, 74–75, 84, 91, 92, 100, 149, 168, 242, 255, 282, 316, 354, 355, 420, 441, 455, 468, 490, 499, 502, 512, 513
McIntosh, Robert, 103n1
McKinsey Global Institute, 380
McNair, Malcolm P., 126n2
MAC's, 456
McWilliams, Charlyne H., 312n6
Macy's, 10, 40, 119, 154, 157, 203, 235, 247, 249, 281, 294, 302, 345, 352, 355, 455, 481
Mail Boxes Etc., 101
Main Street Books, 229
Main Street program, 255
Major, Meg, 469
Mall of America, 249
Maloney, David, 388n18
Mantrala, Murali K., 364n21
MapInfo, 220, 228
Marcus, Bernard, 506
Marcus, Stanley, 28, 339, 363n2
Mardesich, Jodi, 152n22
Marketmax, 361
Marks & Spencer, 277, 404
Marriott International, 46, 281, 434, 513
Marshall Field's, 11, 62, 235, 281, 344, 382, 469

Marshalls, 121, 217, 282, 513–514
Mary Kay Cosmetics, 73, 139, 281
Más Ruiz, José, 238n9
Mason, Richard, 312n15
MasterCard, 322, 323
MasterCuts Family Haircutters, 90
Mauer, Robert, 244
Maxim, 157
Maxx, T.J., 62, 121, 217, 255, 261, 282, 513–514
May Department Stores, 179, 268, 309, 502, 513
Maytag, 354
Mazur, Paul M., 293n3
Medicine Shoppe, 101
Meijer, 116, 296, 377
Meldisco Corporation, 94, 509
Mendelsohn, Francis, 148
Mercado Software, 131
Merchandise Mart, 367
Meredith, Jere, 259n3
Merrick, Amy, 99n8, 500
Mervyn's, 11, 344, 382
Mesenbrink, John, 388n25
Michelson & Associates, 203
Micro Warehouse, 130
Microsoft, 140, 353, 380
MicroStrategy, 190
Midas Muffler, 92
Mills, John, 312n15
Mitchell, Donna, 261
Modernista ad agency, 500
Mogelonsky, Marcia, 183nn10, 23
Mokwa, Michael P., 525n7
Monarch Marking System, 373, 374
Mont Blanc, 247
Montgomery Ward, 153, 203, 302
Moskowitz, Milton, 511
Mossimo, 450
Motel 6, 54, 75
Motley, L. Biff, 183n19
Moto Photo, 101
Movado, 339
Mowatt, Jeff, 29
MPSI Systems, 220, 227
Mrs. Fields' Cookies, 184, 281
MSN eShop, 158
Mulholland, Sarah, 498n18
Mulinder, Austen, 525n9
Mullaney, Timothy J., 197
Mullin, Tracy, 144, 152n20, 329n17
Murphy, Kate, 413n7
Murray's Discount Auto Parts, 179
Museum Company, 244
MusiciansFriend.com, 158
Musicland Stores, 419
My Virtual Model, 157
Myers, Alison, 293n16
mySimon.com, 366, 367, 415

N

Nannery, Matt, 61, 90, 193, 296, 312n11, 326, 453
Nash Finch, 370
National Association for Retailing
    Merchandising Services, 382
National Association of Chain Drug Stores, 36
National Association of Credit Management, 304
National Association of Visual Merchandisers, 454
National Floor Safety Institute, 469

National Franchise Mediation Program, 103
National Hardware Show, 367
National Record Mart, 203
National Retail Federation, 67, 144, 201, 208,
    271, 314, 398, 413, 511
National Trust for Historic Preservation, 255
Navy Exchange Service Command, 208
Naylor, Mary, 130
NCR, 36, 192
Neighborhood Market, 128
Neiman Marcus Group, 28, 36, 60, 158, 323, 339,
    384, 426, 458
Nelson, Bob, 293n16
Nelson, Emily, 388n16
Nelson, Richard L., 238n7
Nelson, Taylor, 152n15
Nestlé Purina, 375
NET-ADS, 496
Netflix, 146
Netscape, 140
Neuborne, Ellen, 364n11
New Orleans Centre, 243
Newgistics, 442
Nicastro, Ernest W., 43n9
Nickelodeon, 441
Nicksin, Carole, 363n6
Nielsen, A.C., 29, 198, 201, 361, 422, 459
Nike, 211, 353
Nike Town, 243, 467
99 Cents Only Stores, 302
Noble Wheeler Foundation, 117
Nonprofit Consumer World, 173
Nonstop Solutions, 398
Nordstrom, 15, 22, 133, 247, 249, 268, 280, 281,
    282, 294, 309, 415, 513
Nordstrom, James, 268
North Communications, 152n28
Nuttavuhtisit, Krittinee, 471n3
Nye, Kim, 281

O

O'Connell, Vanessa, 500
Oesterle, Glenn, 507
Office Depot, 158, 160, 299, 316
OfficeMax, 111, 160, 260
Old Navy, 15, 61, 338, 354, 441, 516
Omidyar, Pierre, 289
1-800-flowers, 302
Opinion Research Corp. International, 36
Orler, Victor J., 183n19
Osborne, Suzanne Barry, 43n13
OshKosh B'Gosh, 446
Oshman's Sporting Goods, 467
Otto Versand Gmbh, 75
Outdoor Advertising Association, 479
Overstock.com, 302
Owen, Bill, 409

P

PacifiCare, 333, 334
Palmieri, Jean E., 472n14
Pal's Sudden Service, 47
Papa John's, 61
Parasuraman, A., 33, 525n7
Parcells, Robert J., 227, 238n9
Parisian department stores, 119
Park Corporation, 261

Park Place, 247
Parker, Janice, 442
Parmley, Suzette, 429
Pascual, Axia M., 208
Patagonia, 281, 359
Pathmark, 229
Paw Paw Shopping Center, 13, 496
Pay Less drugstores, 111
Payless ShoeSource, 502
PC America, 397
PCensus, 228
Peabody Place, 243–244
Peachtree, 390
Peapod, 21, 26, 109
Pearle, Stanley, 365
Pearle Vision Center, 365
Peebles Department Stores, 229
Penney, J.C., 6, 7, 8, 39, 40, 60, 106, 108, 111, 120,
    130, 133, 139, 157, 210, 247, 281, 282,
    294, 299, 316, 323, 326, 354, 355, 373,
    377, 378, 444, 445, 469, 482, 513, 521
Penningtons Superstores, 376
Pennzoil, 527
Pep Boys, 288, 316
Pepperidge Farm, 122
Pepsi-Cola, 526
Perrotta, Peter, 206n16, 388n14
Petco, 131, 302
Peters, Tom, 19
Petland, 101
PetsMart, 51–52, 70n3, 211
Pfaff, Kimberly, 183n30
Pfizer, 36, 380
Pier 1 stores, 254
Piggly Wiggly, 153, 460, 462
Pike, Laus, 152n12
Pilot, 114
Pioneer Place, 243
Pizza Hut, 180, 513
Pizzeria Uno, 279
Planalytics, 398
Plus networks, 34
PlusSize.com, 157
Point-of-Purchase Advertising International
    (POPAI), 463
Poland Spring water, 341
Pollack, Elaine, 126n8
Polo Ralph Lauren, 8, 208
Popcorn Factory, 302
Popeil, Ron, 134
Popper, Margaret, 312n18
Porsche, 168
Potter, Harry, 347
Pottery Barn, 211, 250, 380
Prem, Clyde, 259n3
Prentice Hall, 200
Pressler, Margaret Webb, 206n17
Price, Sol, 414
Price Club, 414
Price Costco, 414
PriceChopper, 36
Priceline.com, 147
Prime Retail, 248
Prisco, Lisa, 500
Procter & Gamble, 36, 380, 382
ProfitLogic, 360, 407
Profitt's department stores, 119

Publishers Clearinghouse, 130, 137
Publix Super Market, 117, 299, 512, 513, 514
Pyrex, 341

Q

Quaker State, 526
Quinn, Richard T., 293n15
Quizno's, 261–262
QVC, 134

R

Rack, The, 203
Rack Room Shoes, 218
Radio Shack, 89, 92, 316
Ralphs, 302
Ramada Inn, 513
Ramstad, Evan, 388n16
Ranco Rotisserie, 134
Rao, 341
Rash, Mary Fran, 229
Raska, Danielle, 90
Raugust, Karen, 323
Raymour & Flanigan Furniture Store, 250
Reader's Digest, 74
Recreational Equipment Inc. (REI), 96, 97, 442, 467
Reda, Susan, 18n8, 43n8, 77, 78, 110, 152n19, 259n7, 259n10
RedEnvelope, 158
Reebok, 179
Reed, Alison, 404
Reese, Shelly, 388n7
Reichheld, Frederick R., 43n6
Reidy, Chris, 126n22
Reilly, William J., 238n6
Reitmans, 376
Report Gallery, 198
Reputation Institute, 517
Resnick, Jeffrey T., 525n6
Retail Forward, Inc., 144, 156, 158, 513, 515
Retail Group, 316
Retail Pro, 405
Retail Technologies International, 189–190, 405
Reverse Logistics Executive Council, 384
Reynolds, Kristy E., 440n5
Richard, P.C., & Sons, 14–15
RichFX, 156
Rich's, 294
Rifkin, Laura, 183n26
Riggio, Leonard, 86
Right Start, 302
Ring, Lawrence, 312n2
Rite Aid, 77, 78, 94, 111, 304
Ritz-Carlton, 46
Riverchase Galleria, 243
RMA, 401, 511
Rodgers, William C., 227, 238n9
Rodkin, Gary, 364n15
Rogers, Charlene, 453
Rogers, Dale S., 388n26
Rolex, 21
Romano, Pietro, 317
Ronald McDonald House, 38
Roosevelt Field, 247
Roper, James H., 259n4
Rose Bowl Flea Market, 124
Rosenberg, William, 240

Ross Stores, 121, 343, 344
Rouse, James, 243
Royal Ahold, 75, 302, 319, 320, 514
RTKL Associates, 459
Rubbermaid, 341
Rubio's, 262
Rucci, Anthony J., 293n15
Rukstales, Bradley, 152n2
Rust, Roland T., 47n2
Ruttenstein, Kal, 345
RW & Co., 376
RWS Information Systems, 405
Ryder Integrated Logistics, 386

S

Safeway, 6, 25, 30, 36, 115, 203, 299, 377, 470, 513, 514
Sag Harbor, 179
Sainsbury, 261
St. Onge, Jeff, 206n8
St. Paul Software, 378
Saks Fifth Avenue, 15, 119, 156, 256, 281, 309, 345, 355, 423, 426, 462
Sale, Richard, 497n14
Salmoiraghi and Vigano, 372
Samli, A. Coskun, 471n3
Sam's Club, 123, 128, 210, 414
Samsonite, 122
Sandler, Barbara, 373
Saturn, 168
Saunders, Sharon, 282
Save-A-Lot, 116
SCA, 484
Scansaroli, Jay A., 530
Scheraga, Dan, 206n4, 209, 393
Schindler, Robert M., 440n13
Schlotzsky's, 77
Schmitt, Eric, 183n32
Schneider, Kenneth C., 227, 238n9
Schneiderman, Ira P., 183n12
Schonfeld, Erick, 155
Schonfeld & Associates, 476
Schrage, Michael, 380
Schultz, Howard, 313, 502
Schulz, David P., 126n16, 293n11
SCORE (Service Corps of Retired Executives), 409
Scott department stores, 119
Seagull Scientific, 373, 374
Sears, Roebuck & Company, 6, 22, 40, 61, 79, 89, 95, 106, 108, 110, 120, 154, 179, 192, 193, 242, 249, 251, 281, 282, 287, 290, 299, 300, 310, 354, 355, 365, 376, 378, 444, 445, 451, 475, 506, 513
Segal, Eric, 51
Seiders, Kathleen, 34
Seiyu, 260
Sender, Isabelle, 183n27
Senegal, Jim, 363n4
Sensormatic Electronics Corporation, 384
Sephora, 118, 353, 474
Serruya brothers, 99
Service Merchandise, 109, 203
Setlow, Carolyn, 43n15
7-Eleven, 32, 75, 112, 192, 193, 241, 242, 470, 526
Seven-Eleven Japan, 366
Seymour, Harry, 183n26

Shaklee, 139
Shapiro, Marc, 334
Shapiro, Mary Finn, 183n23
Sharper Image, 107, 134, 229
Shaw's Supermarkets, 36
Sheraton Safari Hotel, 64
Sherry, John F., Jr., 471n3
Sherwin-Williams, 8, 96, 99n7, 330
Shillito, John, Company, 294
ShopKo stores, 443
Showcase, 384
Shugan, Steven M., 440n14
Silverman, Dick, 472n19
Simon, Rosa, 146
Simon Property Group, 247, 248
Simpson, Jill, 109
Simulation Research, 204–205
Sincerely Yours, 442
Site Selection Toolkit, 215
Skandata, 391
Skinmarket, 212
Skolnick, Richard, 312n2
Sleeper, Bradley J., 227, 238n9
Sliwa, Carol, 312n5
Smart Set, 376
Smith, Amie, 485
Smith, Scott, 183n14, 499
Snuggs, Thelma, 293n10
Socha, Miles, 472n13
Sofres Interactive, 152n15
Sony, 353, 419
Sotheby's, 418
South Street Seaport, 244
Southdale Center, 249
Southwest Airlines, 46
Spaeth, Merrie, 335
Spagat, Elliot, 328n2
Spears, Britney, 526
SpectraLink Corporation, 323, 324
Speedway SuperAmerica, 112
Spencer, Jane, 18n9, 388n27
Spethmann, Betsy, 441
Spherion Assessment Group, 330
Spiegel, 75, 133, 156, 202
Spinner, Jackie, 244
Sports Authority, 59, 111, 118–119, 250, 316, 499–500
SRC, 220
Stafford, 354
Standard Rate & Data Service, 201
Stanley Home Products, 473
Staples, 27, 118, 148–149, 158, 160, 255, 299, 377
Starbucks Coffee Co., 147, 193, 254, 262, 281, 313, 316, 359, 468, 502
Starck, Phillipe, 450
Steinauer, Joan M., 43n4
Steinhauer, Jennifer, 259n3
Stemberg, Thomas, 160
Stern's, 153
Steve's Ice Cream, 99
Stew Leonard's, 19
Stillerman Jones & Company, 43n5
Stop & Shop, 75, 109, 302, 319, 320
Storefront Development, 466
Stores Automated Systems, Inc., 35
Storm, Diane, 471n3
Strasburg, Jenny, 312n5

Straus, Judy, 208
Streamline.com, 109
Stride Rite, 281
Structure, 48, 111
STS Systems Allocation, 361
Subway fast food, 100, 262
Suman, Alicia Orr, 152n9
Summerour, Jenny, 209, 289
Sunglass Hut, 119
Super 8 Motels, 101
Super Expo, 367
Supercuts Franchisee Association, 103
Supervalu, 115, 379, 513
Susskind, Alex M., 497n13
Swabini, Stuart, 206n15
Swartz, Jon, 79, 312n5
Swensen's Ice Cream, 99
Swinyard, Bill, 183n14
Symbol Technologies, 195, 326
Syms, 229, 437
Sysco, 270
System 2000, 323
Szymanski, David M., 530

T

Taco Bell, 50, 180, 513
Taco John's International, 101–102
Talaski, Karen, 293n6
Talbots, 75, 154, 244, 250
Tan, Tony, 168
Taneja, Sunil, 329n11
Tang, Christopher S., 227, 238n9
Target Corporation, 6, 11, 12, 62, 116, 121, 235,
        249, 257, 281, 299, 300, 344, 360, 377,
        378, 382, 513, 514
Target Stores, 10–12, 40, 41, 62, 117n, 120, 121,
        127, 139, 235, 260, 261, 283, 286, 339,
        344, 355, 356, 365, 384, 445, 450, 451,
        468, 470, 507, 516, 521
Taubman, A. Alfred, 418
Tawney, Anne, 526
Taylor Nelson Sofres Interactive, 142
Tedeschi, Bob, 152n24
Templin, Neal, 44n26
Tender, 281
Tengelmann, 75
Tennant, Sir Anthony, 418
Terhune, Chard, 312n12
Tesco, 158, 194, 211, 261, 514
Tetrad Computer Applications, 220
Texas Commerce Bank, 334
TGI Friday's, 255
Thomas, Dave, 28
Thomas, Jacquelyn, 43n4
Thomas, Marc, 238n8
Thomas, Owen, 442
Thrift Drug, 111
Tie Rack, 119
Tiffany, 61, 62, 78, 171, 235, 302
Tigert, Douglas J., 312n2
Time-Life books, 134
TJX, 121, 217, 282, 299, 371, 513–514, 521
T-Mobile HotSpot, 147
Tomkins, Doug and Susie, 65
Tommy Hilfiger, 157, 339
Tops Markets, 75, 302
Torres, Nicole L., 99n9

Torrid, 211
Tortola, Jane Olszeski, 13, 99n4
Totes, 122
TouchVision, 109
Tourneau Corner, 247
Tower Records, 419
Toyota, 511
Toys "R" Us, Inc., 74, 118, 127, 211, 242, 278, 279,
        316, 323, 331, 380, 434, 457, 468, 474, 488
Trachtenberg, Jeffrey A., 364n20
Trade Dimensions, 236
Trader Joe's, 212
TransAct Technologies, Inc., 325
Transworld Entertainment, 419
Travelsmith, 133
Trivial Pursuit, 347
Troy, Mike, 121, 286, 312n14
Tuesday Morning, 310
Tupperware, 139
Turcsik, Richard, 319
Turen, Richard, 440n9
Turner, Cal, Jr., 304
Turock, Art, 207

U

uBid.com, 147
Underhill, Paco, 466, 472n17, 499
Uniform Code Council (UCC), 195
Unilever, 158
Union Station, 243, 244
Unisoft, 466
United Nations, 71
United Retail Group, 359
U.S. Consumer Information Center, 172
U.S. Trade Information Center, 71
United Supermarkets, 196, 378–379
Universal Code Council, 406
Universal Music Group, 419
Universal Studios, 441
University Towne Center, 247
UPS (United Parcel Service), 28, 381
UPS E-Logistics, 442
UPS Logistics Group, 378, 381
Urbanski, Al, 153
Utz Quality Foods, 197

V

Vavra, Bob, 44n27
Victoria's Secret, 48, 111, 190, 250, 261, 370
Village Hardware, 507
Vinelli, Andrea, 317
VIPdesk, 130
Visa, 322, 323
Vision Care Franchisee Association, 103
Volle, Pierre, 498n17
Vranica, Suzanne, 498n15

W

Waldenbooks, 149
Walgreen, 236, 299, 340, 373, 377, 514
Walker, L. Jean Harrison, 497n13
Wall, The, 302
Wallin, Carl, 268
Wallin & Nordstrom, 268
Wal-Mart, 2, 3, 6, 11, 14, 16, 38–39, 40, 59, 61,
        73–74, 78, 106, 116, 117n, 120, 121, 128,
        155, 185, 186, 192–193, 241, 242, 251,

        255, 257, 260–261, 286, 287, 289, 299,
        300, 301, 316, 323, 331, 339, 340, 342,
        343, 347, 355, 372, 377, 378, 380, 382,
        420, 432, 443, 445, 450, 451, 453, 468,
        470, 474, 475, 477, 496, 502, 513, 514, 521
Walters, Rockney G., 364n21
Walton, Sam, 2, 502
Wanamaker, John, 153
Wang, Ann, 482
Warner Music Group, 419
Waterford, 339
Waterfront, 261
Webvan, 109
Wegmans, 36
Weisbrod, Glen E., 227, 238n9
Weitzman, Jennifer, 154
Welanetz, Robert, 187
Welch, David, 312n5
Welcome Wagon, 139
Welles, Edward O., 472n5
Wells Fargo, 57
Wendy's, 28, 54, 114, 251, 347, 349, 420, 480, 513
Wertkauf, 261
West Edmonton Mall, 249
Westfield Shoppingtown South County, 247, 248
Wet Seal Inc., 247, 441–442, 461
Wexner, Leslie, 48, 502
White Barn Candle, 370
Whitehall Square, 250
Whitman, Meg, 155, 289
Wiener, Leonard, 302
Williams-Sonoma, 134, 250, 380
Wilson, Marianne, 18n5, 44n31, 65, 154, 442,
        472nn4, 6
Wilsons Leather, 190, 215
Windmill Truck Stop, 397
Wingate, Rick, 525n3
Winn-Dixie, 115, 513
Winston, House of Harry, 78
Wiscombe, Janet, 293n16
Wolf Camera, 333, 453
Woolworth, 121
World Wildlife Fund, 504
WSL Strategic Retail, 13, 43n5

Y

Yadav, Manjit S., 47n3
Yahoo! Store, 146, 466
Yogen Früz, 99, 101
Young, Eric, 388n12
Young, Vicki M., 387n4
Yum!, 180

Z

Zackiewicz, Arthur, 364n19
Zalud, Bill, 388n25
Zane, Christopher J., 80–82
Zane's Cycles, 80–82
Zany Brainy, 302
Zara, 342, 516
Zeithaml, Valarie A., 33, 47n2, 525n7
Zellner, Wendy, 293n7
Zinkhan, George M., 152n15
Zoza, 442
Zutopia, 179

Subject Index

Note: An asterisk before term indicates Glossary entry

A

Accident insurance, 321
Accounting, in department store, 275, 276
    See also Financial merchandise management;
        Operations management, financial
        dimensions of
Accounts payable to net sales, 300, 301
Achievement tests, in selection of retail
    personnel, 286
ACSI. *See* American Customer Satisfaction Index
Actual counting, as physical inventory system,
    406
ADA. *See* Americans with Disabilities Act
*Additional markup, 435–437
*Additional markup percentage, 436
*Addition to retail percentage, 436
Administered pricing, 422
Advanced ship notices, 379
*Advertising, 474, 475–480
    advantages/disadvantages of, 476–477
    advertising-to-sales ratios and, 475, 476
    agencies, 201
    awareness and, 492, 493
    bait-and-switch, 67, 420, 421
    cognitive dissonance and dissatisfaction and,
        176
    comparative, 495
    competitive, 479
    cooperative, 476, 479–480, 495
    definition of, 475
    direct marketing and, 136
    distributed, 494
    effectiveness of, 495–496
    extensive, 494
    franchising and, 475
    frequency and, 494
    global, 479
    by independents, 88
    institutional, 479
    intensive, 494
    legal environment and, 67, 480
    by manufacturers, 475–476
    massed, 494
    media for, 475, 477–479
    message and, 475, 494–495
    objectives of, 476
    outdoor, 478, 479, 495
    pioneer, 479
    of prices, 420–421
    public relations/publicity *versus*, 475, 480–481
    public service, 479
    reach and, 494
    as recruitment source, 284
    reminder, 479
    by retailer *versus* manufacturer, 475–476
    retail institution and, 113–114, 475, 476
    tactical decisions on, 68

    timing and, 494
    truth-in, 67
    types of, 479–480
    World Wide Web and, 475, 478, 479, 494
    See also Point-of-purchase (POP) display
*Affinity, 254
After-tax personal income. *See* Effective buying
    income
Agents, 368
Airport retailing, 105, 129, 149–150
Aisles
    enhanced shopping experience and, 468
    of stores, 458
    of Web retailer, 464
Allocation, in merchandise planning, 346, 357,
    361
*All-you-can-afford method, 490
Alterations, as customer service, 28
Alternatives. *See* Evaluation of alternatives
American Customer Satisfaction Index (ACSI),
    29, 511–512, 513
American Demographics, 229
*Americans with Disabilities Act (ADA), 39, 40,
    283, 309
*Analog model, 225
Annual Benchmark Report for Retail Trade, 511
Annual Statement Studies, 401
Antitrust laws, 66, 67, 418
*Application bank, for selection of retail
    personnel, 284, 286
Asset management. *See* Operations manage-
    ment, financial dimensions of
*Assets, 297
*Asset turnover, 298, 300, 301
Assistant buyer, 4, 345
Assistant sales manager, 345
Assistant store manager, 345
Associate buyer, 345
*Assortment, 346, 350–353, 361
*Assortment display, 463
*Assortment merchandise, 346
Assortment-oriented consumers, 418
*Atmosphere (atmospherics), 105, 454–466
    chain and, 90
    as controllable variable, 65
    exterior, 455–457, 459
    general interior, 457–459
    global retailing and, 459
    independent and, 87
    retail institution and, 113–114
    technology and, 467
    Web site and, *see* World Wide Web
    See also Image; Point-of-purchase (POP) dis-
        play; Store layout
At-the-market price orientation, 415, 431
*Attitudes (opinions), 165, 166
    See also Shopping attitudes and behavior

*Augmented customer service, 25–26, 27
Augmented retail strategy, 22
Automatic markdown plan, 437
*Automatic reordering system, 410
Automatic teller machines (ATMs), 34
Availability, purchase act and, 175

B

Baby boomers, 169
*Bait-and-switch advertising, 67, 420, 421
*Balanced tenancy, 246, 249, 254
*Balance sheet, 297
Baldrige Award, 47
Bankruptcy, 111, 303
Banks/banking
    consumers' attitudes toward, 170
    electronic, 34, 322, 323
    online, 175
    smart cards and, 61
*Basic stock list, 346
*Basic stock method, 400–401
*Battle of the brands, 356
Behavior modeling, 287, 288
*Benchmarking, 511–515, 516
Benelux, smart cards and, 61
*Bifurcated retailing, 60
Billboards. *See* Outdoor advertising
Billing reports, secondary data from, 199
Birth rate, 163
Blue laws, 66–67
Bonuses, 288, 289
*Book (perpetual) inventory system, 391
    cost method of accounting and, 391–395
    physical inventory system combined with, 407
    retail method of accounting and, 390, 394–396
    unit control systems and, 406–407
Boston, as central business district, 243
Bottom-up budgeting, 306
*Bottom-up space management approach, 316
*Box (limited-line) store, 113, 114, 115, 116, 117,
    235, 316
BPI. *See* Buying power index
Brands, 353–356
    battle of the, 356
    generic, 356
    global retailing and, 347
    manufacturer, 351, 353–354
    private, 347, 351, 354–356
    selling against the, 421–422
Broad price policy, 425
Brokers, 368
*Budgeting
    promotional, 475, 490–491
    secondary data from, 199
    See also Financial merchandise management;
        Operations management, financial
        dimensions of

*Bundled pricing, 434
Bureau of Census. *See* Census Bureau
Bureau of Labor Statistics, 280, 289
Business definition, in direct marketing strategy, 135
Business district. *See* Unplanned business district
*Business format franchising, 91
Business Owner's Toolkit, 297
Business Periodicals Index, 200
Business ratios, 297–300, 301
Business Week, 198, 200
*Buyer, 4, 51, 276, 277, 340, 342, 344, 345
    See also under Merchandising
Buying clubs, 88, 96
Buying function, merchandising philosophy and, 340, 344
Buying organization. *See* Merchandise buying and handling process
*Buying power index (BPI), 233

C

Cable television, advertising in, 479
Calendars, 486, 488
Cancellation policy, as purchase term, 371
*Canned sales presentation, 484
*Capital expenditures, 306, 308–309
Careers in retailing, 4, 5
    advancement and, 286
    best companies to work for and, 511
    leadership and, 28
    number of jobs in retailing and, 5–6
    quantities of candidates for, 4
    salaries and, 121
    success in, 51
    See also Human resource management; Retail institution; Service retailing; *specific careers*; World Wide Web
*Case display, 464
Case study, 287, 288
Cash-and-carry, 368
*Cash flow, 307–308
Cashiers, 271, 289
Catalog Age, 129
Catalogs, 7, 10, 131, 133–134, 136, 137
    See also Direct marketing
*Category killer (power retailer), 60, 61, 118–119, 211, 316, 372
*Category management, 31, 357–360, 361
Category manager, 51
Caveat emptor ("Let the buyer beware"), 58
CBD. *See* Central business district
Census Bureau, 200, 229
    benchmarking and, 511
    gross profit (gross margin) and, 300
    TIGER maps and, 218, 219, 231
Census of Population, 218, 231–233
Census of Retail Trade, 85, 198, 200
Census of Service Industries, 200
*Central business district (CBD), 242–244, 245, 251, 255
Centralized buying organization, 342
Centralized structure, 52, 53
*Chain, 62, 89–91
    advantages/disadvantages of, 87, 88, 89–91
    advertising and, 475
    buying organization of, 342

closeout, 121
convenience store and, 112
conventional supermarket and, 115
cooperative, 92
cooperative buying and, 344
diversified retailer and, 278–279
dollar discount store and, 121
independent *versus*, 86
location of, 242
manufacturer-retailer, 92
niche of, 86
off-price, 106, 114, 121–122
organizational arrangements used by, 274, 277, 278
service sponsor-retailer, 92
specialty store and, 118
store format and, 316
store location and, 217, 220
voluntary, 92
wholesaler-retailer, 92
    See also Supermarket
Chain of command, 273
Chain Store Age, 68, 200, 511
*Channel control, 96
*Channel of distribution
    allocation of tasks in, 270–271
    information flows in, 185–186
    as recruitment source, 284
    relationships among, 30–31, *see also* Retailer/supplier relationship
    retailing as last stage in, 7
    secondary data from, 201
    tasks in, 270
    value chain and, 20–21
    See also Manufacturer; Wholesaler/wholesaling
Chapter 11, 303
Charge account. *See* Credit cards
*Chargebacks, 369
Checkout process
    computerized, 324–325
    impulse purchases and, 177
    point-of-sale scanning equipment and, 35–36, 110, 326
    Universal Product Code and, 194–195, 196, 324, 325, 373, 393, 406, 407
    Web retailers and, 465–466
Check purchase, 322
Chief executive officer (CEO), 121
Chief information officer (CIO), 189
CIBER (Michigan State University), 70
*Class consciousness, 165, 166
*Classification merchandising, 398
Clayton Act, 66
Cleanliness, store atmosphere and, 459
Clerks, 289
Closed assortment, 463
Closed corporation, 52
Closeout chain, 121
Co-branding, 468–469
*Cognitive dissonance, 175–176
Collaborative planning, forecasting, and replenishment (CPFR), 377
Collection period, 300, 301
Collective bargaining, 289
Collusion laws, 67
Combination job classification, 273
Combination organization chart, 274

*Combination store, 113, 114, 115, 116, 117
Commercial research house, 201
Commercial stimulus, 172
    See also Advertising
Commissions, 288, 289
Communication skills, 333–335
Communications strategy, 451
    See also Atmosphere (atmospherics); Image
Community relations, 65
    image and, 456, 469–470
    See also Relationship retailing; Retail information system; World Wide Web
*Community shopping center, 249–250, 251
Company audit specialist, 519
Company department manager, 519
Comparative advertising, 495
*Compensation, 288–289, 318
Compensation cafeteria, 289
Competency-based instruction, 287, 288
Competition
    direct marketing and, 133
    franchising and, 94
    merchandise planning and, 351, 366–367
    price strategy and, 105, 422, 426, 430–431
    proximity of, 10
    as recruitment source, 284
    trading-area analysis and, 228, 235
    as uncontrollable variable, 65
*Competition-oriented pricing, 105, 422, 426, 430–431
Competitive ads, 479
*Competitive advantages, 62–63
*Competitive parity method, 490
Complaints, as customer service, 28
Complementary goods and services, 353
Completely unplanned shopping, 177
Component Life-Styles, 166–167
*Computerized checkout, 324–325
Computers. *See* Technology; World Wide Web
*Concentrated marketing, 61, 62, 178, 179
Conferences, training and, 287, 288
*Consignment purchase, 372
Consolidations, 302
*Constrained decision making, 93, 351
*Consumer behavior, 172
    See also Consumer decision making; Shopping attitudes and behavior
Consumer bill of rights, 39, 40
*Consumer cooperative, 86, 96–97
Consumer decision making
    constrained decision making and, 93, 351
    customer loyalty and, 177–178
    decision process, 172–176
        evaluation of alternatives, 172, 173, 174
        information search, 172, 173–174
        post-purchase behavior, 172, 173, 175–176
        problem awareness, 172, 173
        purchase act, 172, 173, 174–175
        stimulus, 172–173
    impulse purchases and, 177
    types of, 176–177
        consumer traits and, 176
        extended, 176
        limited, 176
        routine, 176–177
*Consumer decision process. *See* Consumer decision making

Consumer Goods Pricing Act, 419
*Consumerism, 36, 39–41
Consumer life-styles. *See* Consumers
*Consumer loyalty (frequent shopper) pro-
    grams, 29–30, 77–78, 366, 488
Consumer-ready manufacturing, 382
Consumer Reports, 173
Consumers, 160–183
    demographics and, 161, 162–164, 366, *see also*
        life-styles and, *below*
        consumer decision making and, 172, 173
        global, 162
        retail implications of, 162–164, 166–168
    environmental factors and, 180–181
    expectations of, 210–212
    information flows and, 185–186
    life-styles and, 161, 164–168, 366
        component life-styles and, 166–167
        consumer decision making and, 172, 173
        consumer sophistication and confidence
            and, 166
        direct marketing and, 132–133
        gender roles and, 24, 162, 163, 166, 167
        global, 164
        poverty of time and, 132–133, 166, 167
        psychological factors and, 165–166,
            173–174, 176
        retailing implications of, 166–168
        social factors and, 164, 165
        trends and, 24
    merchandise plans and, 366
    needs and desires of, 168–169
    price strategy and, 416–418
    profiles of, 165, 168
    retailer actions and, *see* Target market
    retail tasks performed by, 271
    store location and, 217, 228, 231–235
    as uncontrollable variable, 65
    Web use and, 142–143
    See also Consumer decision making;
        Shopping attitudes and behavior
Contests, 486, 487
*Contingency pricing, 46, 433
Contracts, in negotiating purchase, 371–372
*Control, in retail strategy, 68
    See also Retail audit
*Controllable variables, 63–65
    See also Atmosphere; Human resource man-
        agement; Merchandise buying and han-
        dling process; Operations management;
        Price strategy; Promotional strategy;
        Retail organization; Store location
Controller, 275, 276
*Control units, 397
Convenience-oriented consumers, 418
*Convenience store, 112, 113, 114, 115, 117, 241,
    252
*Conventional supermarket, 110, 113, 114–115,
    117
Cooling-off laws, 67
Cooperative. *See* Consumer cooperative
*Cooperative advertising, 476, 479–480, 495
*Cooperative buying, 344
Cooperative franchising, 92
Cooperative marketing, franchising and, 92
*Core customers, 24
*Corporation, 52, 55

Cost categories, in budgets, 306
*Cost complement, 394
Cost containment, 111–112
Cost leadership, 46
*Cost method of accounting, 390, 391–393
*Cost of goods sold, 295, 296, 390, 391
*Cost-oriented pricing, 426–430, 431
Counting system, as physical inventory system,
    406
County Business Patterns, 236
Coupons, 486, 487–488
CPFR. *See* Collaborative planning, forecasting,
    and replenishment
Credit bureau, 271
Credit cards, 27
    banks and commercial, 28
    collection and, 271
    extent of, 322
    fees paid by retailers and, 322
    fraud and, 323
    major, 322
    operational issues and, 323
    retailer-sponsored, 27
    secondary data from, 199
    trading area analysis and, 224
Credit management, 322–323, 373
    careers in, 271
    collection and, 271
    department store and, 275, 276
    functions related to, 270–271
    legal environment and, 67
    operational decisions on, 322–323
    See also Credit cards
Crisis management, 327
*Cross-merchandising, 341
*Cross-shopping, 171–172
*Cross-training, 317
*Culture, 164, 165
Current Population Survey, 231
Current ratio, 300, 301
*Curving (free-flowing) traffic flow, 460, 461,
    462
*Customary pricing, 431–432, 433
Customer base, 24
Customer insight, 515
Customer life-cycle model, 515
*Customer loyalty, 170, 177–178
    global retailing and, 485
    prizes and, 488
    store location and, 229
    See also Consumer loyalty (frequent shopper)
        programs
Customer profiling, 515
Customer relationships. *See* Relationship
    retailing
Customer respect checklist, 15
*Customer satisfaction, 29, 58
*Customer service, 3, 12, 14–15, 24–29, 65, 105
    augmented, 25–26, 27
    careers in, 271
    choice of, 26
    classification of, 26
    cost of, 27
    destination retailer and, 105
    employee empowerment and, 25, 90
    evaluation of, 27
    expected, 25, 26, 27

    global retailing and, 277
    image and, 26
    individual services and, 27–29
    level of, 26
    logistics and, 375
    merchandise plans and, 351
    retail institution and, 113–114
    service retailing *versus*, 32
    strategy for, 25–27
    termination of, 27
    World Wide Web and, 145, 157–158
Customer space, allocation of, 459
Customer/supplier interactions, technology and,
    35–36
*Cut case, 464

D

Damaged goods
    processing, 374
    reverse logistics and, 384–385
Data analysis, in marketing research process,
    188, 196, 197, 198
*Data-base management. *See* Retail information
    system
*Data-base retailing, 132
*Data mining, 191, 194
*Data warehousing, 191, 192–193
Days' supply, category management and, 358
*Dead areas, 458
Dealer brands. *See* Private (dealer, store) brands
*Debit card system, 34, 322, 323
Decentralized buying organization, 342
Decentralized structure, 52, 53
Decline stage
    in product life cycle, 349
    in retail life cycle, 108, 109–110
Delivery, 175, 373
    as customer service, 28
    nonstore retailing and, 381
    as purchase term, 371
    reordering merchandise and, 375
    time of in merchandise plans, 356
Demand, cost fluctuations and, 432–433
    See also Price elasticity of demand
*Demand-oriented pricing, 426, 431
*Demographics. *See* Consumers
Demonstration
    in personal selling, 484, 494
    in training, 287, 288
Department manager, 4, 283
Departments
    financial recordkeeping and, 397–398
    mapping out locations for, 462
*Department store, 119–120
    advertising and, 476
    affinity and, 254
    benchmarking and, 513
    branch stores and, 276–277
    buyers and, 342
    capital expenditures and, 308–309
    decline of, 294
    discount, 60, 61, 62
    exterior of, 456
    full-line discount store, 106, 113, 119,
        120–121, 415, 429
    interior of, 458
    inventory management and, 407

*Department store (*cont.*)
  leases and, 216, 255
  money-back guarantee and, 176
  one-stop shopping and, 210
  operating expenses and, 309
  organization arrangements used by, 275–277
  price strategy and, 415, 422, 434
  productivity and, 310
  promotional strategy and, 475
  sales transaction per shopping trip and, 9
  staffing in, 344–345
  target market and, 62
  trading areas of, 223
  traditional, 60–61, 62, 106, 113, 119–120, 153–154
  traffic flow in, 460, 461, 462
  upscale, 60
*Depth of assortment, 112, 351–353
Description, for evaluating merchandise, 371
Desired goals, job satisfaction and, 291
Desires, of consumers, 168–169
*Destination retailer, 105, 251
*Destination store, 222
Dialog, 200
*Differentiated marketing, 62, 178, 180
Direct costs, 306
Direct mail, 129, 136, 137, 478
  See also Direct marketing
*Direct marketing, 4, 5, 129–138, 368
  advantages of, 130
  advertising and, 475
  catalogs and, 131, 133–134, 136, 137
  competition and, 133
  consumer dissatisfaction and, 137
  data-based retailing and, 132
  delivery and, 381
  domain of, 131–132
  general, 129
  global, 74, 129, 134–135
  legal environment and, 138
  life-styles and, 132–133
  limitations of, 131
  mail-order clubs and, 137
  multi-channel retailing and, 132, 133, 135, 138, 154
  privacy and, 132, 137–138
  selection of retailer and, 133
  specialty, 129
  strategy for, 135–137
    business definition, 135
    customer contact, 135, 136–137
    customer generation, 135, 136
    customer response, 135, 137
    measuring results and maintaining data base, 135, 137
    media selection, 135, 136
    message presentation, 135, 136
    order fulfillment, 135, 137
  technology and, 131, 132, 134
  television and, 134
  30-day rule and, 131
  See also World Wide Web
Direct monetary payments, 288, 289
Direct observation, 203
*Direct product profitability (DPP), 358, 359, 429–430
*Direct selling, 4, 5, 66, 67, 131–132, 138–139, 289

*Direct store distribution (DSD), 381
Discount department store, 24, 60, 61, 62
Discount price orientation, 415
Discounts
  price discrimination and, 67, 419
  as purchase term, 371
  quantity, 357
  as retail reduction, 402
Discount store
  benchmarking and, 513
  box (limited-line) store, 113, 114, 115, 116, 117, 235, 316
  capital expenditures and, 309
  closeout chain, 121
  dollar, 121
  factory outlets, 106, 114, 122–123
  flea markets, 106, 114, 123–124
  full-line, 106, 113, 119, 120–121, 415, 429
  growing from scratch, 429
  interior of, 458, 459
  inventory management and, 407
  locations of, 242
  negotiating purchases from retailers and, 371
  off-price chain, 106, 114, 121–123
  one-stop shopping and, 210
  price strategy and, 415, 429, 434
  promotional strategy and, 495
  store size and, 316
  traffic flow in, 460, 462
  warehouse stores, 113, 114, 115, 116–117
  Web retailers, 106
*Discretionary income, 162
Disguised audit, 520
Disguised building height, 456
Disguised observation, 203
Disguised survey, 202
Display & Design Ideas, 452
Display personnel, merchandise plans and, 366
Displays. *See* Point-of-purchase (POP) display
Display windows, 456, 457
Disposable income. *See* Effective buying income
*Distributed promotional effort, 494
Distribution
  exclusive, 8, 9
  intensive, 8, 9
  receiving and stocking merchandise and, 372–374
  retail functions in, 7–8
  scrambled merchandising and, 108
  selective, 8, 9
  vertical marketing system and, 86, 95–96
  See also Channel of distribution; Retailer/supplier relationship
*Diversification, 110–111
*Diversified retailers, 278–279
Diversity. *See* Minorities
Divisional merchandise manager, 345
DNS Retailing Today, 511
Do-it-yourselfers, 46
*Dollar control (merchandise forecasting and budgeting). *See* Financial merchandise management
Dollar discount store, 121
Door-to-door selling, 139
  See also Direct selling
Doorways, of stores, 456
*Downsizing, 111

Downtown. *See* Central business district
DPP. *See* Direct product profitability
DQI data base, 191
Dressing facilities, of stores, 458
Drop shipper, 368
DSD. *See* Direct store distribution
*Dual marketing, 96
*Dump bin, 464
Durable goods, sales in, 5
Durable goods stores, 55

E
Early markdown policy, 437
Early recovery of cash, 423
*Ease of entry, 86–87
Easy Analytic Software, 234
EBI. *See* Effective buying income
EBSCOhost, 200
*Economic base, 228, 234–235
Economic consumers, 418
*Economic order quantity (EOQ), 411
Economies of scale, independent and, 88
Economy
  impact of retailing on, 4–6
  slow-growth, 300–301
  as uncontrollable variable, 66
ECR. *See* Efficient consumer response
EDI. *See* Electronic data interchange
Editor & Publisher Market Guide, 234–235, 236
EDLP. *See* Everyday low pricing
Education
  target market and, 162, 164
  Web use and, 142
Educational institutions, as recruitment source, 284
*Effective buying income (EBI), 233
Efficiency pricing, 46
*Efficient consumer response (ECR), 379
*Electronic article/surveillance, 383, 384
*Electronic banking, 34, 35–36, 322, 323
*Electronic data interchange (EDI), 194, 195–196, 372, 378–379, 383
Electronic displays, 464
Electronic gift card, 36
*Electronic point-of-sale system, 325
Electronic retailing. *See* World Wide Web
E-mail
  as promotional medium for World Wide Web, 494
  spam and, 180
Employee discount, 435
*Employee empowerment, 25, 90
Employee Polygraph Protection Act, 286
Employees
  appearance of, 280
  merchandise theft and, 383–384, 385
  motivation of, 290–291
  part-time, 280, 289
  as recruitment source, 284
  retail organization and, 269
  satisfaction of, 59
  store atmosphere and, 458
  turnover and, 279, 280
  See also Human resource management
Employment agencies, as recruitment source, 284
Employment status, target market and, 162, 163

Encyclopedia of Associations, 201
Energy management, 319–320
Enhanced shopping experience, 468
*Ensemble display, 463
Entertainment, shopping as, 452–453
Entrances to stores, 456, 457
Entrepreneur Magazine, 54, 300
Environmental factors
    retail information system and, 188
    shopping attitudes and behavior and, 180–181
Environmental laws, 67
Environmental protection, 355
EOQ. *See* Economic order quantity
*Equal store organization, 276–277, 278
Escalators, 458
*Ethics, 36–38
    box stores and, 235
    chain *versus* independent and, 86
    codes of, 38
    energy management and, 319
    environmental protection and, 355
    franchising and, 103
    honesty and, 491
    questionable accounting and financial prac-
        tices and, 304
    scanning drivers' licenses and, 203
    shoplifting and, 377, 382, 383–384, 385,
        459–460
    slip-and-fall claims and, 469
    small businesses and, 409
    social responsibility and, 36, 38–39, 272, 517
    spam and, 180
    standard of business conduct and, 10
    store location and, 251
    supermarkets and, 117
    telemarketing and, 66
    unethical behavior and, 37–38
    unordered merchandise and, 421
    World Wide Web and, 38
    See also Consumerism; Privacy
Ethnic groups. *See* Minorities
Euro, 323, 418
*Evaluation of alternatives, 172, 173, 174
*Everyday low pricing (EDLP), 170, 431–432
*Exclusive distribution, 8, 9
Exclusives, 257
Executives, 51, 289
Existing business
    buying, 52–53, 54, 255
    trading-area analysis of, 224–225
*Expected customer service, 25, 26, 27
Expected retail strategy, 22
*Experiential merchandising, 467
*Experiment, 196, 203–204
Extended business model, 515
*Extended decision making, 176
Exterior building height, 456, 457
Exterior of store, 455–457, 459
*External secondary data, 196, 200–201

F
*Factory outlet, 106, 114, 122–123
*Fad merchandise, 347
*Family life cycle, 164, 166
Family status, 163
*Fashion merchandise, 347
Fashion trends, 350

Fast food, global retailing and, 168
Federal Bankruptcy Code, 303
Federal Trade Commission (FTC), 66, 67
    bait-and-switch advertising and, 420, 421
    exclusives and, 257
    franchising and, 93
    point-of-sale scanning and, 35
    price advertising and, 420–421
    radius clauses and, 257
    secondary data from, 200
    Telemarketing Sales Rule and, 139
    30-day rule and, 131
    vertical price fixing and, 419
Federal Trade Commission Act, 418
*Feedback
    direct marketing and, 137
    retail strategy and, 68
    World Wide Web and, 140–141
*FIFO (first-in-first-out) method, 392, 393
Financial inventory control. *See* Financial mer-
    chandise management
*Financial leverage, 298
Financial management. *See* Financial merchan-
    dise management; Operations manage-
    ment, financial dimensions of
*Financial merchandise management, 389–413
    benefits of, 390
    financial inventory control, 407–411
        economic order quantity and, 411
        gross margin return on investment and,
            408
        reorder point and, 409–410
        stock turnover and, 407–408
    inventory valuation, 390–396
        book inventory and, 391–393
        cost method of accounting and, 390,
            391–393
        FIFO method and, 392, 393
        LIFO method and, 392, 393
        physical inventory and, 391, 392–393
        profit-and-loss statement and, 390, 391,
            395, 396
        retail method of accounting and, 390,
            394–396
    merchandise forecasting and budgeting (dol-
        lar control), 390, 397–404
        control units selected and, 397–398
        inventory-level planning and, 400–401
        planning purchases and, 402–404
        profit-margin planning and, 404
        retail-reduction planning and, 401–402, 403
        sales forecasting and, 398–400
        unit control system integrated with, *see*
            financial inventory control, *above*
    unit control systems and, 390, 405–407
        merchandise forecasting and budgeting
            (dollar control) integrated with, *see*
            financial inventory control, *above*
        perpetual inventory systems and, 406–407
        physical inventory systems and, 405–406
        in practice, 407
Financial perceived risk, 165
Financial resources, for running a business,
    55–57
Fire insurance, 321
First-in-first-out method. *See* FIFO (first-in-
    first-out) method

Fixed costs, 306
Fixtures
    of stores, 458, 459
    for Web retailer, 464
Flat organization, 273
*Flea market, 106, 114, 123–124
*Flexible pricing, 433
Flooring
    for exterior of store, 456
    for interior of store, 458
    maintenance of, 318
*Floor-ready merchandise, 378, 382
Floor space, allocation of, 316–317, 459, 461
Flyers/circulars, 478, 479
FOB factory, 371
*Food-based superstore, 113, 114, 115–116, 117
Food-oriented retailer. *See* Retail institution
*Forecasts, in merchandise plans, 344, 346–347,
    360
    See also Financial merchandise management
Formal buying organization, 341, 342
Fortune, 511
Franchisee, 91
*Franchising, 53, 91–94, 99–103
    advantages/disadvantages of, 92–94, 100–102
    advertising and, 475
    assessing opportunities in, 102
    business format, 91
    buying and selling, 100–101
    ethics and, 103
    failure rate of, 101
    financial resources and, 55
    franchisor-franchisee relationships and,
        101–103
    global retailing and, 99
    investment and start-up costs for, 100, 101
    legal environment and, 67, 93, 103
    management and, 100–101
    niche of, 86
    people suited for, 100
    product/trademark, 91
    retail tasks performed by, 271
    royalties and, 93, 100
    secondary data from, 201
    size and structural arrangements and, 92
    Web sites and, 99
Franchisor, 91
Free-flowing traffic flow. *See* Curving (free-
    flowing) traffic flow
Freestanding inserts, 491
*Frequency, 494
Frequent shopper programs. *See* Consumer loy-
    alty (frequent shopper) programs
Fringe benefits, 288–289
*Fringe trading area, 220, 222, 223, 225
FTC. *See* Federal Trade Commission
*Full-line discount store, 106, 113, 119, 120–121,
    415, 429
Full-service merchandise wholesaler, 368
Fully integrated vertical marketing system,
    95–96
Functional account expenses, in budgets, 306
Functional job classification, 273
Functional organization chart, 274
Functional perceived risk, 165
*Functional product groupings, 460
Funding, sources of, 302

Future
  retail store of, 521
  scenario analysis and, 515, 517–518
  trends transforming business practices and,
    528–530

G

*Gap analysis, 514–515, 516
Gender
  roles, 24, 162, 163, 166, 167
  target market and, 163
  Web use and, 142
  See also Women
General buying organization, 342–343
General direct marketer, 130
General interior
  of store, 457–459
  of Web retailer, 454
General merchandise retailer. *See* Retail
  institution
General merchandise wholesaler, 368
*Generic brands, 356
*Geographic information systems (GIS),
    218–220, 221, 223, 225, 231
Geographic job classification, 273
Geographic organization chart, 274
Gift card, 36
Gift certificate, 28
GIS. *See* Geographic information systems
Global retailing, 3, 21, 141
  advertising and, 479
  atmosphere and, 459
  barcode symbol and, 393
  benchmarking and, 513–514, 516
  brands and, 347
  chain and, 89
  consumer cooperatives and, 97
  consumer life styles and, 164
  consumers' attitudes toward shopping and,
    171
  customer service and, 277
  demographics and, 162
  direct marketing and, 74, 129, 134–135
  efficiency and, 317
  euro and, 323, 418
  factory outlets and, 123
  fast food and, 168
  franchising and, 92, 99
  image and, 71, 452
  information needed for, 187
  joint ventures and, 73
  logistics and, 370, 380
  mature markets and, 73, 74
  merchandise buying and handling process
    and, 342, 366
  optical scanning and, 406
  order processing and fulfillment and, 379
  pillars in, 70
  planned shopping centers and, 249
  promotional strategy and, 485
  retail strategy for, 70–76
    foreign retailers in U.S. market, 75
    immature markets and, 73, 74
    opportunities in, 72
    standardization and, 72–73
    steps in, 71–72
    success of, 73

  threats in, 72
  U.S. retailers and, 73–75
  sales in, 70
  shopping attitudes and behavior and, 171
  store location and, 73, 223, 224, 253
  supermarket and, 302
  video kiosk and, 147
  World Wide Web and, 140, 141
GMROI. *See* Gross margin return on investment
*Goal-oriented job description, 284, 285
Good Neighbor Awards, 117
*Goods retailing, 32, 55
*Goods/service category, 54, 55, 62, 88, 92, 94, 105
  See also Goods retailing; Retail institution;
    Service retailing
Government
  merchandise plans and, 367
  price strategy and, 418–421
  satisfaction of, 59
  secondary data from, 200
  See also Legal environment; *specific legislation*
*Graduated lease, 256
*Gravity model, 225
*Gray market goods, 422
Gridiron traffic flow. *See* Straight (gridiron) traf-
  fic flow
Grocery store. *See* Supermarket
*Gross margin, 428–429
*Gross margin return on investment (GMROI),
    409
*Gross profit (margin), 295, 296, 390, 391, 395,
    396
Gross profit per linear foot of shelf space, 358
Growth stage
  in product life cycle, 348
  in retail life cycle, 108, 109
GTIN (Global Trade Item Number), 393
Guarantees, money-back, 176

H

Health care, employee compensation and, 289
Height of buildings, 456
*Hidden assets, 297
*Hierarchy of authority, 273
*Hierarchy of effects, 492, 493
High-end strategy, 106, 107
Home page, 464, 465
Honesty, ethics and, 491
*Horizontal cooperative advertising agreement,
    480
*Horizontal price fixing, 418
*Horizontal retail audit, 520
Horizontal trend, 350
*Household life cycle, 164, 166
Household size, 163
*Huff's law of shopper attraction, 226–227
Huff's Market Area Planner, 227
Human observation, 203
*Human resource management, 279–291
  chain and, 90, 91
  communications skills and, 333–335
  as controllable variable, 64
  efficient employee utilization and, 317–318
  employee relations and, 12
  independent and, 87, 88
  leased departments and, 94
  legal environment and, 67, 283, 286

  length of employment and, 318
  merchandise buying and handling and,
    344–345
  merchandise plans and, 351
  minorities and, 280, 282, 283, 286
  personnel productivity and, 317–318
  process, 283–291
    compensation, 288–289, 318
    recruitment, 283, 284
    selection, 283–286, 317
    supervision, 290–291
    training, 286–288, 289
  tactical decisions on, 68
  women and, 281–282, 404
  See also Careers in retailing; Employees; Retail
    organization
*Human resource management process. *See*
    Human resource management
Hybrid buying organization, 344
*Hypermarket, 116, 223

I

*Image, 11–12, 59, 65, 450, 451, 452
  chain and, 88
  community relations and, 456, 469–470
  components of, 452
  creating and maintaining, 452–454
  customer service and, 26
  global retailing and, 71, 452
  independent and, 88
  leased departments and, 94
  merchandise planning and, 351
  publicity and, 481
  scrambled merchandising and, 108
  semantic differential and, 202
  wheel of retailing and, 106
  World Wide Web and, 140
  See also Atmosphere (atmospherics);
    Positioning
Immature markets, in global market, 73, 74
Implementation, in marketing research process,
    196, 197, 198
Importers, 4
*Impulse purchases, 9–10, 177
Income
  effective buying, 233
  target market and, 162, 163
  Web use and, 142
Income statement. *See* Profit-and-loss (income)
    statement
*Incremental budgeting, 306–307
*Incremental method, 490
*Independent, 86–89, 274, 275, 344
Independent vertical marketing system, 95
Indirect costs, 306
Indirect observation, 203
Indirect payments, 288, 289
Industry Norms & Key Business Ratios, 401
*Infomercial, 134
Informal buying organization, 341, 342
Information gathering and processing, 184–209
  electronic data interchange and, 194, 195–196,
    372, 378–379, 383
  global retailing and, 187
  inadequate information and, 186–187
  information flows in channels of distribution
    and, 185–186

merchandise plan implementation and, 366–368
nonsystematic research for, 186–187
See also Marketing research in retailing; Retail information system
*Information search, 172, 173–174
InfoTrac, 200
In-home shopping, 169
*Initial markup (at retail), 428
Initial public offering (IPO), 302
Innovation, 12
in merchandise plans, 346, 347–350, 360
Innovators, 105
Inside buying organization, 343
Inspection, for evaluating merchandise, 371
Installations, as customer service, 28
Institutional ads, 479
Insurance, 321
Integrated retail strategy. *See* Retail strategy
*Intensive distribution, 8, 9
Interior displays. *See* Point-of-purchase (POP) display
Interior of stores. *See* General interior
Internal Revenue Service, 511, 512
*Internal secondary data, 196, 199–200
International retailing. *See* Global retailing
*Internet, 140
See also World Wide Web
Interview, for selection of retail personnel, 285–286
Introduction stage
in product life cycle, 348
in retail life cycle, 108, 109
Inventory, holding *versus* ordering costs and, 375
Inventory analysis, 385, 386
Inventory-level planning, 400–401
*Inventory management, 381–386, 391
careers in, 271
chain and, 89
computerized, 9
computers for, 323
control and, 374
conventional supermarkets and, 115
electronic data interchange and, 194, 195–196, 372, 378–379, 381, 383
independent and, 88
inventory analysis and, 385–386
inventory levels and, 382–383
inventory marking and, 373, 374
legal environment and, 67
operational considerations and, 320–321
outsourcing online order fulfillment and, 382
quick response inventory planning and, 372, 375, 378–379, 381, 383
retailer tasks in, 382
retail reductions and, 401–402, 403, *see also* security and, *below*
reverse logistics and, 384–385
scrambled merchandising and, 108
security and, 374, 377, 382, 383–384, 385, 459, 461
source tagging and, 382
stock overage and, 395
stock turnover and, 351, 357, 358, 375, 407–408
technology and, 397

vendor-managed inventory and, 382
See also Financial merchandise management
Inventory records, secondary data from, 199
*Inventory shrinkage, 382, 383–384, 385
Inventory valuation. *See* Financial merchandise management
Invoices
review of, 373
secondary data from, 199
IPO. *See* Initial public offering
iSITE, 220
*Isolated store, 216, 241–242, 245, 250, 251, 254
*Issue (problem) definition, 196–197, 198
*Item price removal, 420

J

Janitorial personnel, 271
Japan, membership clubs in, 21
*Job analysis, 283
Job classification, 273
Job description, 272, 283–284, 285
application blank with, 284
goal oriented, 284, 285
traditional, 283–284
*Job motivation, 290
Jobs
retail tasks grouped into, 270, 271–272, *See also* Careers in retailing
target market and, 162, 164
Job satisfaction, 290–291
*Job standardization, 317, 318
Joint ventures, 73
Junk mail, 478

K

Keirsey Temperament Sorter, 165
Kiosk, 109, 148
Knockout factors, in store location, 257

L

Labeling laws, 67
Labor availability, trading-area analysis and, 228
Last-in-last-out method. *See* LIFO (last-in-last-out) method
Late markdown policy, 437
LBO. *See* Leveraged buyout
*Leader pricing, 433–434
*Leased department, 86, 94–95
Leasing, 67, 216, 255–256
Lecture, training and, 287, 288
Legal environment
advertising and, 67, 480
antitrust and, 66, 67, 418
consumerism and, 39, 40
direct marketing and, 138
direct selling and, 66, 67, 139
franchising and, 93, 103
human resource management process and, 67, 283, 286
inventory management and, 67
renovations and, 309
shoplifting and, 384
slip-and-fall claims and, 469
store location and, 216, 257
trading-area analysis and, 228
as uncontrollable variable, 66, 67
See also Government; Privac

Lemon laws, 67
Leveraged buyout (LBO), 302–303
*Liabilities, 297
Liability insurance, 321
Liability laws, 67
Licensing provisions, 67
Lie detector tests, 286
*Life-style center, 250
*Life-styles. *See* Consumers
*LIFO (last-in-first-out) method, 392, 393
Lighting
for exterior of store, 456
for interior of store, 458
*Limited decision making, 176
Limited-line store. *See* Box (limited-line) store
Limited-service merchant wholesaler, 368
Line positions, 275, 276
Liquidations, 303–304
Liquor stores, 109
Local ordinances, 67
Location. *See* Store location
*Logistics, 375–381
customer service and, 381
customer transactions and, 381
global retailing and, 370, 380
order processing and fulfillment and, 378–379
performance goals and, 376–377
reverse, 384–385
supply chain management and, 376, 377–378
third-party, *see* Outsourcing
transportation and, 379–380
warehousing and, 380–381
See also Inventory management
*Loss leaders, 420
Low-end strategy, 106, 107
Loyalty. *See* Consumer loyalty (frequent shopper) programs; Customer loyalty

M

Magazines
advertising and, 478, 479
sales promotion and, 495
secondary data from, 200
Mailing lists, 136, 137
Mail-order business. *See* Direct marketing
Mail survey, 202
Main store control, for branch stores, 276, 277
*Maintained markups (at retail), 428
*Maintenance-increase-recoupment lease, 256
Malls
megamalls, 249, 251
outlet, 122
pedestrian, 243
See also Planned shopping center
Management
careers in, 271
chain and, 89, 90–91
franchising and, 92, 93, 100–102
independent and, 89
retail organization and, 269
See also Human resource management; *under* Operations management; Retail organization
Management alternatives, 52, 53
See also Retail institution
Manual system, for perpetual inventory unit control system, 406

Manufacturer, 4, 8, 368
    advertising and, 475–476
    personal selling and, 483
    price strategy and, 421–422
    retailer and, 7–8, 358–359
    retail tasks performed by, 271
    secondary data from, 201
    value and, 21
    vertical marketing system and, 86, 95–96
    See also Supplier
*Manufacturer (national) brands, 351, 353–354
Manufacturer-retailer franchising, 92
Marital status, 163
*Markdown, 397, 401–402, 435–437
Markdown control, 437–438
*Markdown percentage, 436
*Marketing research in retailing, 196–205
    marketing research process, 196, *see also*
        Primary data; Secondary data
    data analysis, 188, 196, 197, 198
    implementation, 196, 197, 198
    issue definition, 196–197, 198
    recommendations, 196, 197, 198
*Marketing research process. See Marketing
        research in retailing
*Market penetration pricing, 105, 423
Market pricing, 422
*Market segment product groupings, 460, 461
Market share, as goal, 58
Market size, 162, 163
*Market skimming pricing, 423
*Markup, 426–430, 440nn11, 12
    initial, 428
    maintained, 428
    required initial, 404
    variable, 429
*Markup percentage, 426–428
    at cost, 426–427
    merchandise cost and, 440n12
    planned retail operating expenses, profit, and
        net sales and, 427–428
    at retail, 426–427
    selling price and, 440n11
*Markup pricing, 426–430, 440nn11, 12
*Marquee, 455, 456, 457, 459
*Massed promotion effort, 494
*Mass marketing, 61, 62, 178, 179
*Mass merchandising, 59, 60
Matchbooks, 486, 488
Mathematical models, 204
Mature markets, in global market, 73, 74
Maturity stage
    in product life cycle, 348
    in retail life cycle, 108, 109
Maximum retail prices, 419
*Mazur plan, 275–277
Mechanical observation, 203
Media
    advertising and, 475, 477–479
    direct marketing and, 136
    lead time and, 494
    promotion and, 493
    rates and, 493–494
Medium strategy, 106, 107
*Megamall, 249, 251
*Membership (warehouse) club, 21, 60, 61, 114,
        115, 123, 241, 339, 414

Memorandum deal, 372
*Memorandum purchase, 372
*Merchandise available for sale, 390, 391
Merchandise buying and handling process
    buying organization and, 341–345, *see also*
        Merchandise plans
    centralized, 341, 342
    cooperative buying and, 344
    decentralized, 341, 342
    formal, 341, 342
    functions performed and, 341, 344
    general, 341–342
    hybrid, 344
    informal, 341, 342
    inside, 343
    merchandising philosophy and, 339–341
    outside, 343–344
    resident buying office and, 344
    specialized, 341, 342
    staffing and, 341, 344–345
    careers in, 51, 276, 277, 340, 342, 344–345
    category management and, 357–360, 361
    chain and, 89, 90
    competition and, 351, 366–367
    complementary goods/services and, 353
    as controllable variable, 64
    cross-merchandising and, 341
    department store and, 275, 276
    franchising and, 92, 93
    global retailing and, 342, 366
    independent and, 87, 88
    kinds of merchandise and, 346–347
    legal environment and, 67
    in Mazur plan, 275–277
    merchandising philosophy and, 339–341
    micromerchandising and, 340
    order tracking and, 323–324
    retail institution and, 113–114
    scrambled merchandising and, 106–108, 175,
        316–317, 341, 353
    substitute goods and services and, 353
    tactical decisions on, 68
    See also Financial merchandise management;
        Inventory management; Merchandise
        plans; Price strategy
Merchandise cost, 440n12
    See also Markup
Merchandise forecasting and budgeting. *See*
        Financial merchandise management
Merchandise marts, 367
Merchandise plans, 346–353
    allocation and, 346, 347, 357, 360, 361
    assortment and, 346, 350–353, 360
    buying organizations and, *see under*
        Merchandise buying and handling
    forecasts and, 344, 346–347, 360
    innovativeness and, 346, 347–350, 360
    quality and, 350–351
    software for, 359, 360–361
    space allocation and, 316–317, 459, 461
    timing and, 346, 356–357
    See also Brands
Merchandise plans, implementation of, 366–375
    concluding purchase, 372
    evaluating merchandise, 371
    gathering information, 366–368
    global sourcing and, 366

    merchandise control, 374, 382, 383–384, 385
    negotiating purchase, 371–372
    receiving and stocking merchandise, 372–374
    re-evaluation, 375
    reordering merchandise, 375
    selecting and interacting with merchandise
        sources, 368–370
    See also Inventory management; Logistics;
        Point-of-purchase (POP) display
Merchandise restrictions, 67
Merchandise space, allocation of, 316–317, 459,
        461
Merchandise tagging system, 406
*Merchandising, 339
    philosophy of, 339–341
Merchandising buyer, 345
Merchandising function, 340, 344
Merchandising manager, 276, 277
*Merchandising philosophy, 339–341
*Mergers, 79, 110, 111, 302
Message
    advertising and, 475
    direct marketing and, 135, 137
    promotion and, 494
Michigan State University, CIBER and, 70
*Micromarketing, 191, 194
*Micromerchandising, 340
MicroStrategy Desktop, 190
Middle-management, 283
Minimum expectations, job satisfaction and,
        290–291
*Minimum price laws, 419, 420
Minimum wage, 289
Minorities
    in retailing, 280, 282, 283, 286
    target market and, 162, 164
Mixed location strategy, 242
Mobile, 464
Mobility, target market and, 162, 163
*Model stock approach, 461
*Model stock plan, 346
Modular structure, for storefront, 455
Monthly Retail Trade and Food Services Sales, 200
*Monthly sales index, 399–400
Mortgages, 67, 302
Motivation, of employees, 291
*Motives, 169
*Multi-channel retailing, 7, 8, 96, 128, 132, 133,
        135, 138, 154
Multiple regression, 398
*Multiple-unit pricing, 434
*Mystery shoppers, 203

N

National brands. *See* Manufacturer brands
National Small Business Poll, 88
Natural account expenses, 306
NBD. *See* Neighborhood business district
Needs, of consumers, 168–169
*Need-satisfaction approach, 484
Negative feedback, 68
Negative publicity, 481
Negotiated pricing, 46
*Neighborhood business district (NBD), 245,
        254
*Neighborhood shopping center, 248, 250, 251
Netherlands, smart cards and, 61

*Net lease, 256
*Net profit, 390, 391
*Net profit after taxes, 295, 296
*Net profit margin, 297–298, 300, 301
*Net sales, 295, 296
*Net worth, 297
*Never-out list, 347
New business, 52, 53, 55, 56, 255
    See also Trading area analysis
New contacts, direct marketing and, 136
Newspapers, advertising and, 477–478, 479
New York City
    as central business district, 243
    leases in, 256
*Niche retailing, 59, 60
Nilson Report, 322
Nondisguised audit, 520
Nondisguised building height, 456
Nondisguised observation, 203
Nondisguised survey, 202
Nondurable goods, sales in, 5
Nondurable goods stores, 55
*Nongoods services, 32
Nongovernment secondary data, 200–201
*Nonprobability sample, 201
Nonprofit firms, 4
Nonregulars, direct marketing and, 136
Nonrespondents, direct marketing and, 136, 137
*Nonstore retailing. *See* Retail institution
Nontraditional retailing. *See* Retail institution;
    World Wide Web
North American Free Trade Agreement, 99
NUA survey, 169

O

*Objective-and-task method, 491
*Objectives. *See* Retail strategy
*Observation, 196, 201–203
Occupancy, terms of. *See* Store location
Occupation. *See* Jobs
Occupational Outlook Handbook, 5
*Odd pricing, 433, 434
*Off-price chain, 106, 114, 121–123
*Off-retail markdown percentage, 436
*One-hundred percent location, 251–252
*One-price policy, 433
On-floor merchandising, 373
Online shopping, 169
    See also World Wide Web
Open assortment, 463
Open corporation, 52
*Open credit account, 28
*Open-to-buy, 402–404
Operating efficiency, 58
*Operating expenditures (expenses), 295, 296,
    306, 308, 309
*Operations blueprint, 316–317
*Operations management, 105, 295, 314
    as controllable variable, 64
    tactical decisions on, 68
*Operations management, financial dimensions
    of, 294–311
    asset management, 297–304
        balance sheet, 297
        key business ratios, 297–300, 301
        strategic profit model, 298–300
        trends in retailing and, 300–304

budgeting, 305–308
    bottom-up, 306
    cash flow and, 307–308
    cost categories and, 306
    incremental, 306–307
    ongoing process, 305, 306–308
    preliminary decisions, 305, 306
    reasons for, 305
    top-down, 306
    zero-based, 306
costs of operations and maintenance and, 257
location and site evaluation and, 257
profit planning and, 295–296
questionable practices and, 304
resource allocation and, 308–310
    capital expenditures and, 308–309
    operating expenditures and, 308, 309
    opportunity costs and, 309
    productivity and, 309–310
*Operations management, operational dimen-
    sions of, 313–329
computerization, 323–325
credit management, 322–323
crisis management, 327
energy management, 319–320
insurance, 321
inventory management, 320–321
operations blueprint, 314–315
outsourcing, 326
personnel utilization, 317–318
renovations, 309, 320, 459
space allocation, 316–317, 459, 461
store format, 316
store maintenance, 318–320
store security, 321
store size, 316
*Opportunistic buying, 371
*Opportunities, 50
    in global retail strategy, 72
Opportunity analysis, 509, 510
*Opportunity costs, 309
Optical scanners, 406, 407
*Option credit account, 28
*Order-getting salesperson, 483
*Order lead time, 409–410
Order processing and fulfillment
    direct marketing and, 135, 137
    logistics and, 378–379
    software tracking, 323–324
    See also under Merchandise
*Order-taking salesperson, 483
Order time, in merchandise plans, 356–357
Organization. *See* Retail organization
*Organizational mission, 50–52
*Organization chart, 270, 273–274
Organizations, secondary data from, 200–201
Orientation. *See* Pre-training
Outdoor advertising, 478, 479, 495
*Outshopping, 169
Outside auditor, 519–520
Outside buying organization, 343–344
*Outsourcing, 326, 378, 382
Overall gross profit, 300, 301
Overall net increase in sales, 217
Overall ratings, in store location, 257
Overall retail strategy. *See* Retail strategy
*Overstored trading area, 235

*Owned-goods services, 32
Owner-manager, 52, 53
Ownership alternatives. *See* Retail institution

P

Packaging, 373
    gift wrapping and, 28
*Parasite store, 222
Parking facilities
    atmosphere and, 457
    location/site evaluation and, 216, 252, 253,
        256
Partially integrated vertical marketing system, 95
Partially unplanned shopping, 177
*Partnership, 52, 55
Part-time employees, 280, 289
Payment arrangements, as purchase term, 371
Pedestrian malls, 243
Pedestrian traffic, location/site evaluation and,
    252
Penetration pricing. *See* Market penetration
    pricing
Penny savers. *See* Shopper papers
Pens, for sales promotion, 486, 488
Pensions, 289
*Perceived risk, 165, 166, 173–174, 176
*Percentage lease, 256
*Percentage-of-sales method, 491
*Percentage variation method, 401
Performance goals, logistics and, 376–377
*Performance measures, 11, 12, 511–516
Performance standards, 306, 318
Periodicals. *See* Magazines; Newspapers
Perpetual inventory system. *See* Book (perpet-
    ual) inventory system
Personal abilities, for running a business, 54–55
Personal drawing account, 55, 56
*Personality, 165, 166
Personalizing consumers, 418
*Personal selling. *See* Promotional strategy
Personal survey, 202
Personnel space, allocation of, 459
Phone directories, advertising in, 478
Phone survey, 202
Physical drive, 172–173
Physical exam, in selection of retail personnel,
    286
*Physical inventory system
    book (perpetual) inventory system combined
        with, 407
    cost method of accounting and, 391, 392–393
    retail method of accounting and, 390,
        394–396
    unit control system and, 405–406
Physical perceived risk, 165
Pioneer ads, 479
Place-based demand fluctuations, 433
Placement, in specific site, 254, 255
PLANalyst, 339
Planned public relations, 481
*Planned shopping center, 216, 246–250, 251
    balanced tenancy and, 246, 249, 254
    community, 248, 249–250, 251
    global, 249
    growth of, 263–265
    importance of, 246–247
    leased department and, 86, 94–95

*Planned shopping center (*cont.*)
  life-style center, 250
  limitations of, 246
  long-term growth of, 247–248
  megamall, 249, 251
  multilevel "shopping-center-in-the-round"
    and, 457
  neighborhood, 248, 250, 251
  positive attributes of, 246
  power centers, 250, 251
  promotional strategy of, 495, 496
  real-estate investment trusts and, 302
  rectangular, 457
  regional, 248–249, 251, 253, 254, 255, 257
  retail life cycle and, 108
  safety in, 321
  voluntary restrictions in, 257
Planning procedures, in integrated retail strat-
    egy, 507
*Planogram, 459
*PMs (promotional or push monies), 483
*Point-of-purchase (POP) display, 10, 373,
    463–464
  assortment, 463
  careers in, 271
  case, 464
  cut case, 464
  direct marketing and, 136
  dump bin, 464
  electronic, 464
  ensemble, 463
  free space as, 316
  in front of store, 316
  hanging, 464
  impulse purchases and, 177
  rack, 463–464
  for sales promotion, 475, 486, 487
  self-service and, 318
  store space and, 316
  tactical decisions on, 68
  theme-setting, 463
  vertical, 316
  for Web retailer, 465
Point-of-sale system
  book (perpetual) inventory systems and, 406
  electronic, 325
  scanning and, 35–36, 110, 326
POP. *See* Point-of-purchase (POP) display
Population
  customer base analysis and, 24
  of trading area, 228, 231–235, *See also*
    Consumers
*Positioning, 59–61, 78–79, 452
  See also Image
Positive feedback, 68
Positive publicity, 481
*Post-purchase behavior, 172, 173, 175–176
Potential retail strategy, 22
Poverty-of-time, 132–133, 166, 167
*Power center, 250, 251
Power retailer. *See* Category killer
*Predatory pricing, 420
Prefabricated (pre-fab) structure, for storefront,
    455
Premium private brand, 355
*Prestige pricing, 105, 426
*Pre-training, 286–287

Price discrimination, 67, 419
*Price elasticity of demand, 416–418
Price fixing
  horizontal, 418
  vertical, 419
Price guarantees, 422
Price inelasticity, 417
Price line classifications, 398
*Price lining, 434–435
Priceman, 422
Price marking, 373
Price optimization software, 442–443
Price-oriented shoppers, 21
*Price-quality association, 426
Price-sensitive shoppers, 105–106
Price strategy, 414–440
  above market, 431
  additional markups, 435–437
  administered pricing, 422
  at-the-market orientation, 415, 431
  bait-and-switch, 67
  below market, 431
  broad, 425
  bundled, 434
  chain and, 90
  collusion, 67
  competitive, 105, 422, 430–431, 436
  contingency pricing, 68, 433
  as controllable variable, 64
  cost-oriented, 426–430, 431
  customary pricing, 431–432, 433
  demand-oriented, 426, 431
  destination retailer and, 105
  discount, 415
  discounts to employees, 435
  early recovery of cash, 423
  efficiency pricing, 46
  everyday low pricing, 170, 431–432
  factors affecting, 416–422
    competitors, 422
    consumers, 416–418
    government, 418–421
    suppliers, 421–422
  flexible pricing, 438
  global retailing and, 418
  horizontal price fixing, 418–419
  implementation of, 431–435
  integration of approaches to, 431
  item price removal and, 420
  leader pricing, 433–434
  legal environment and, 67, 418–421
  loss leaders, 420
  markdowns, 435–437
  market penetration, 105, 423
  market pricing, 422
  market skimming, 423
  marking, 373
  markup pricing, 426–430, 440nn11, 12
  maximum retail prices, 419
  minimum-price laws and, 419, 420
  multiple-unit pricing, 434
  negotiated, 46
  objectives in, 422–425
    overall, 423–425
    specific, 425
  odd pricing, 433, 434
  one-price policy, 433

predatory pricing, 420
  prestige pricing, 105, 426
  price adjustments, 435–437
  price advertising, 420–421
  price discrimination, 67, 419
  price elasticity of demand and, 416–418
  price guarantees, 422
  price lining, 434–435
  price optimization software and, 442–443
  price-quality association and, 426
  relationship pricing, 46
  retail institution and, 113–114
  return on investment and, 423, 424
  sale prices, 67
  satisfaction-based, 46
  service retailing and, 46, 60
  store atmosphere and, 458–459
  store image and, 458–459
  tactical decisions on, 68
  target market and, 62
  unbundled, 434
  unit pricing, 67, 420
  upscale, 415
  value, 415, 416
  variable pricing, 432–433
  vertical price fixing, 419
  yield management pricing, 433
Price wars, 422
Pricing objectives. *See* Price strategy
*Primary data, 196, 197, 201–205
  advantages/disadvantages of, 201
  report on, 199–200
  sources of, 201–205
    experiment, 196, 203–204
    observation, 196, 201–203
    sampling, 201
    simulation, 196, 204–205
    survey, 196, 201, 202, 203
  trading area of existing store and, 224–225
*Primary trading area, 220, 222, 223, 225
Privacy
  consumers and, 39–40
  direct marketing and, 132, 137–138
  door-to-door selling laws and, 67
  spam and, 180
  World Wide Web and, 38, 145, 465
*Private (dealer, store) brands, 171, 347, 351,
    354–356
Prizes, for sales promotion, 486, 488
PRIZM, 225
*Probability (random) sample, 201
*Problem awareness, 172, 173
Problem definition. *See* Issue (problem) definition
Product diversification, job classification and,
    273
*Productivity, 309–310, 317–318, 509–511
*Product life cycle, 348–349
Product lines
  depth of assortment and, 112
  destination retailer and, 105
  scrambled merchandising and, 106–108
  store atmosphere and, 458
  width of assortment and, 112
  See also Merchandise buying and handling
    process
Product organization chart, 274
Products, arrangement of in store, 462–463

*Product/trademark franchising, 91
Professional manager, 52, 53
Profiles, of consumers, 165, 168
Profit
    merchandise planning and, 351
    objectives related to, 58
*Profit-and-loss (income) statement, 199,
    295–296, 390, 391, 395, 396
Profit margins, 404
Profit planning, 295–296
Profit-sharing, 289
Programmed instruction, training and, 287, 288
Progressive Grocer, 198, 398, 511
Promotional mix. *See* Promotional strategy
Promotional monies. *See* PMs
Promotional strategy, 473–498
    budget for, 475, 490–491
    chain and, 89, 90
    as controllable variable, 65
    displays and, *see* Point-of-purchase (POP)
        display
    distributed, 494
    frequency and, 494
    global retailing and, 485
    independent and, 88
    legal environment and, 67
    massed, 494
    objectives of, 488–490, 495
    personal selling and, 474, 482–484
        advantages/disadvantages of, 482
        attitudes and desires and, 492, 493
        coordination of, 495
        functions of, 482–483, 494
        legal environment and, 67
        losing sales and, 484, 485
        merchandise plans and, 366
        objectives of, 482
        sales force and, 494, 495
        sales presentation and, 176, 484, 494
        small retailers and, 492
        types of, 482
    promotional mix for, 474–475, 491–495
        coordination and, 495
        hierarchy of effects and, 492, 493
        implementation of, 493–495
        media decisions and, 493–494
        message content and, 494–495
        small retailers and, 492
        timing and, 494
    publicity, 174, 275, 276, 474, 475, 480–481, 494
    public relations, 474, 475, 480–481, 492, 493,
        see also publicity, *above*
    reach and, 494
    retail institution and, 113–114
    reviewing and revising, 495–496
    sales promotion, 474, 475, 484–488, *see also*
        Point-of-purchase (POP) display
        advantages/disadvantages of, 485–486
        attitudes and desires and, 492, 493
        message of, 494
        objectives of, 485
        timing of, 494
        types of, 487–488, 495
    store location and, 217
    store receipts and, 477
    target market selection and, 62
    See also Advertising

Property insurance, 321
ProQuest, 200
*Prototype stores, 316, 455
Psychological factors, consumer life-styles and,
    165–166, 173–174, 176
Psychological perceived risk, 165
Psychological tests, in selection of retail person-
    nel, 286
*Publicity, 174, 275, 276, 474, 475, 480–481, 494
*Public relations, 474, 475, 480–481, 492, 493
Publics, satisfaction of, 58–59
Public service messages, 479
Purchase
    importance of, 165, 166
    impulse, 177
    planning, 402–404
    post-purchase behavior and, 172, 173,
        175–176
    retailer concluding, 372
    retailer negotiating, 371–372
    Web use and, 143
    See also Consumer decision process; Purchase
        act; Shopping attitudes and behavior
*Purchase act, 172, 173, 174–175
    availability and, 175
    place of purchase and, 174, 175
    purchase terms and, 175
    See also Merchandise plans, implementation
        of
*Purchase motivation product groupings, 460
Purchase price, 371
Purchase terms, 371–372
Push monies. *See* PMs

Q

QR. *See* Quick response inventory planning
Quality, of merchandise, 350–351
Quantity discounts, 357
Quantity purchased, as purchase term, 371
Quick ratio, 300, 301
*Quick response (QR) inventory planning, 372,
    375, 378–379, 381, 383

R

*Rack display, 463–464
Rack jobber, 368
Radio, advertising on, 478
Radio frequency identification tags (RFID), 325
Radius clauses, 257
*Rand McNally Commercial Atlas & Market
    Guide*, 229
Random sample. *See* Probability (random) sample
*Rationalized retailing, 316
"Razzmatazz" retailers, 243
*Reach, 494
Recessed storefront, 455
Recommendations, in marketing research
    process, 196, 197, 198
*Recruitment, 283, 284
Recycling laws, 67
Reductions. *See* Retail reductions
*Reference groups, 164, 166
References, in selection of retail personnel, 286
Referral gifts, 486, 488
*Regional shopping center, 248–249, 253, 254,
    255, 257
Registers, secondary data from, 199

Registration data, secondary data from, 200
*Regression model, 225
Regular order, negotiating, 371
Regulars, direct marketing and, 136
*Reilly's law of retail gravitation, 226
REIT. *See* Real-estate investment trust
Relationship pricing, 46
Relationship program planning and design, in
    gap analysis, 515
*Relationship retailing, 15–16, 22, 23
    channel relationships and, 30–31, *See also*
        Channel of distribution
    customer relationships and, 23–30, *see also*
        Customer satisfaction; Customer service
    consumer loyalty (frequent shopper) pro-
        grams and, 29–30, 77–78, 366, 488
    customer base and, 24
    customer respect checklist and, 15
    goods retailing *versus* service retailing and, 9,
        32–34
    technology and, 15–16, 34–36
    customer and supplier interactions and,
        35–36
    electronic banking and, 34–35, 322, 323
Reminder ads, 479
Renovations, 309, 320, 459
*Rented-goods services, 32
Reordering, 371, 375
*Reorder point, 409–410
Reports, secondary data from, 199–200
*Resident buying office, 344
Resource allocation. *See* Operations manage-
    ment, financial dimensions of
*Retail audit, 518–524
    areas audited in, 520
    conducting, 520
    determining who conducts, 519–520
    difficulties with, 521
    disguised, 520
    forms for, 520, 523–524
        retailing effectiveness checklist, 523–524
        for small retailer, 522, 523
    horizontal, 520
    nondisguised, 520
    reporting findings of, 520–521
    responding to, 521
    steps in, 518
    time when conducted, 520
    vertical, 520
*Retail balance, 254
Retail catalog showroom, 106, 109–110
Retailer/supplier relationship, 8–9
    collaboration and, 370
    communications and, 378
    conflicts and, 369
    information flow and, 185–186
    merchandise planning and, 380
    off-price chain and, 122
    slotting allowances and, 371–372
    value delivery system and, 30–31
    Web portals and, 36
Retail-estate investment trust (REIT), 302
Retail Horizons, 398
Retail image. *See* Image
*Retail information system (RIS), 188–196
    building and using, 188–190
    career in, 113, 189

*Retail information system (*cont.*)
    data-base management and, 191–194
    data mining and, 191, 194
    data warehousing and, 191, 192–193
    micromarketing and, 191, 194
  decisions in, 189
  electronic data interchange and, 194, 195–196,
    372, 378–379, 383
  investment in, 208–209
  report on primary research in, 199
  strengths of, 188–189
  technology and, 189
  Universal Product Code and, 194–195, 196,
    324, 325, 373, 393, 406, 407
Retail Info Systems News, 188
*Retailing, 2–18
  challenges of, 2, 14
  characteristics of, 9–10
  costs and profits of, 6
  definition of, 3
  framework of, 3–4
  largest retailers and, 5, 6
  reasons for studying, 4–8
  See also Careers in retailing
*Retailing concept, 12–15, 178
  See also Customer service; Relationship retail-
    ing; Total retail experience
Retailing effectiveness checklist, 523–524
*Retail institution, 84–158
  advertising and, 475, 476
  capital expenditures and, 308–309
  evolution of, 110–112
    cost containment and, 111–112
    diversification and, 110–111
    downsizing and, 111
    mergers and, 110, 111
    value-driven retailing and, 112
  financial resources and, 55–57
  food-oriented retailers, 85, 112–117, *see also*
    Supermarket
    box (limited-line) store, 113, 114, 115, 116,
      117, 235, 316
    combination store, 113, 114, 115, 116, 117
    convenience store, 112, 113, 114, 115, 117,
      241, 252
    food-based superstore, 113, 114, 115–116,
      117
    warehouse store, 113, 114, 115, 116–117, 316
  general merchandise retailers, 85, 113–114, *see*
    also Department store
    category killer (power retailer), 60, 61,
      118–119, 211, 316, 372
    combination store, 113, 114, 115, 116, 117
    factory outlet, 106, 114, 122–123
    flea market, 106, 114, 123–124
    full-line discount store, 106, 113, 119,
      120–121, 415, 429
    membership (warehouse) club, 21, 60, 61,
      114, 115, 123, 241, 339, 414
    off-price chain, 106, 114, 121–122
    retail catalog showroom, 106, 109–110
    specialty store, 9, 60, 61, 109, 113, 118–119,
      216, 241–242, 252, 309, 407, 415, 422, 495
    variety store, 113, 121
  management alternatives and, 52, 53
  multi-channel retailing and, 7, 8, 96, 128, 132,
    133, 135, 138, 154

nonstore retailing, 85, 128–140, *see also* Direct
  marketing; nontraditional retailing,
  below
  deliveries and, 381
  direct selling, 4, 5, 66, 67, 131–132,
    138–139, 289
  vending machine, 4, 5, 132, 139–140, 316
nontraditional retailing, 85, 129, *see also*
  World Wide Web
  airport retailing, 105, 129, 149–150
  video kiosk, 36, 105, 109, 129, 132, 136,
    147–149, 323, 467, 468
organization of, *see* Retail organization
ownership type, 52–54, 84–99, *see also* Chain;
  Franchising
  consumer cooperative, 86, 96–97
  corporation, 52, 55
  existing business, 52–53, 54, 224–225, 255
  independent, 86–89, 274, 275, 344
  leased department, 86, 94–95
  leasing *versus* ownership and, 67, 216,
    255–256
  new business, 52, 53, 55, 56, 255
  partnership, 52, 55
  sole proprietorship, 52
  vertical marketing system, 86, 95–96
  personal abilities and, 54–55
  single-channel retailing and, 128
  by store-based retail strategy mix, 85,
    112–126, *see also* food-oriented retailers,
    above; general merchandise retailers,
    above; Strategy mix
  time demands and, 57
  See also Service retailing
*Retail life cycle, 108–110
Retail management trainee, 4
*Retail method of accounting, 390, 394–396
*Retail organization, 269–279
  centralized *versus* decentralized, 52, 53
  as controllable variable, 64
  independent and, 87
  by institutional type, 274–279
    chain, 274, 277, 278
    department store, 275–277
    diversified retailer, 278–279
    independent, 274, 275
  planning and assessing, 269
  setting up, 269–274, *see also* Job description
    job classification for, 270, 273
    organization chart for, 270, 273–274, *see*
      also by institutional type, *above*
    task allocation for, 270–271
    tasks grouped into jobs for, 270, 271–272
    tasks to be performed determined for,
      270
  tactical decisions on, 68
*Retail performance index, 513–514
Retail Pro management information software,
  189–190
*Retail promotion, 474
  See also Promotional strategy
*Retail reductions, 401–402, 403
*Retail strategy, 10–12, 48–70
  chain and, 90
  control in, 68, *see also* Retail audit
  example of, 10–12
  features of, 49

  feedback in, 68
  franchising and, 93
  goods/service category and, 10, 11, 54, 55, 62,
    88, 92, 94, 105, *see also* Goods retailing;
    Service retailing
  independent and, 87
  integrated, 506–518
    benchmarking for, 511–515, 516
    controlling, *see* Retail audit
    gap analysis for, 514–515, 516
    global retailing and, 513–514, 516
    opportunity analysis for, 509, 510
    performance measures for, 10, 11, 511–516
    planning procedures for, 507
    productivity and, 509–511
    scenario analysis for, 515, 517–518
  objectives in, 10, 11, 57–61
    image (positioning), 59–61
    pricing, *see* Price strategy
    profit, 58
    sales, 57–58
    satisfaction of publics, 58–59
    selection of, 61
  overall strategy, 63–67, *see also* Controllable
    variables; Information gathering and
    processing; Uncontrollable variables
    integrating, 67
  retailing concept and, 12–15, *see also*
    Customer service; Relationship retailing;
    Total retail experience
  situation analysis, 50–57, *see also* Goods
    retailing; Goods/service category; Retail
    institution; Service retailing
    organizational mission and, 50–52
    ownership and management alternatives
      and, 52–57, *see also* Retail institution
  steps in, 10, 49
  tactical decisions on, 68
  target market and, 10, 11, 61–63, 163, *see also*
    Consumer behavior
  value-oriented, 22, 23
  See also Consumers; Direct marketing;
    Global retailing; Information gathering
    and processing; Service retailing;
    Strategy mix
Retail strategy audit. *See* Horizontal retail audit
Returned goods
  as customer service, 28
  processing, 374
  reverse logistics and, 384–385
*Return on assets (ROA), 298
Return on inventory investment, 358
Return on investment (ROI), 58, 423, 424
*Return on net worth (RONW), 298–300, 301
*Reverse logistics, 384–385
*Revolving credit account, 28
RFID. *See* Radio frequency identification tags
RIS. *See* Retail information system
Rite Site, The, 162
ROA. *See* Return on assets
*Robinson-Patman Act, 66, 419, 480
ROI. *See* Return on investment
Role playing, training and, 287, 288
RONW. *See* Return on net worth
*Routine decision making, 176–177
Routine orders, 357
Royalties, franchising and, 93, 100

S

*Safety stock, 409–410
Salaries, 288, 289
Salary plus commission, 289
Sale-leaseback, 256
Sale prices, 67
Sales, consumers waiting for, 170
Sales data, secondary data from, 199
Sales events, 29
Sales forecast, 163, 398–400
Sales jobs, 283
    sales manager, 4, 344–345
    See also Salespeople
*Sales manager, 4, 344–345
Sales & Marketing Management, 233
Sales objectives, 57–58
*Sales opportunity grid, 509, 510
Salespeople, 271, 280, 289, 482–484
    merchandise plans and, 366
    order-getting, 484
    order-taking, 483
    personal selling and, See Promotional strategy
Sales per linear foot of shelf space, 358
Sales presentation, 176, 484, 494
*Sales-productivity ratio, 461
*Sales promotion. See Promotional strategy
Sales tax, 67, 130, 138, 257
Samples
    primary data from, 201
    for sales promotion, 486, 488
Sampling, for evaluating merchandise, 371
Satisfaction-based pricing, 46
*Saturated trading area, 93, 235, 236
SBD. See Secondary business district
Scan-based trading, 372
Scanning
    optical, 406, 407
    point-of-sale system and, 35–36, 110, 326
*Scenario analysis, 515, 517–518
Scents, for interior of store, 458
*Scrambled merchandising, 106–108, 175,
        316–317, 341, 353
Seasonality
    cost fluctuations and, 432
    merchandise plans and, 356
    profit-and-loss statements and, 295
    as uncontrollable variable, 66
*Seasonal merchandise, 347
*Secondary business district (SBD), 244–245,
        251
*Secondary data, 196, 197, 198–201
    advantages/disadvantages of, 198–199
    external, 196, 200–201
    internal, 196, 199–200
    trading-area analysis and, 231–235
    trading area of existing store and, 224, 225
*Secondary trading area, 220, 222, 223, 225
Securities and Exchange Commission, 304
Security
    merchandise, 377, 382, 383–384, 385, 386,
        459, 461
    personal, 321
Selection, in human resource management
        process, 283–286
*Selective distribution, 8, 9
Self-management approach, 291
*Self-scanning, 35–36, 326

Self-service, 318
Selling. See Promotional strategy; Sales
        promotion
Selling against the brand, 421–422
Selling price, 440n11
    See also Markup
Selling space, allocation of, 316–317, 459, 461
*Semantic differential, 202
Sensitivity training, 287, 288
Separate store organization, 276, 277
Service-oriented shoppers, 21
*Service retailing, 4, 44–47, 162
    award for, 47
    benchmarking for, 512
    extent of, 44
    in global retailing, 73
    goods retailing versus, 32–34
    improving performance in, 45–46
    location of, 45–46
    nongoods services and, 32
    owned-goods services and, 32
    price strategy and, 46, 60
    rented-goods services and, 32
    requirements for success in, 44–45
    sales in, 5
    scope of, 55
    standardization and, 45
    tangibility and, 32, 33, 45
    technology and, 44, 45
    word of mouth and, 490
Service sponsor-retailer franchising, 92
SERVQUAL, 512
Sherman Antitrust Act, 66, 418
Shipping fees, as purchase term, 371
Shoplifting, 377, 382, 383–384, 385, 459–460
Shopper papers, 478
Shopping attitudes and behavior, 170–172
    consumer sophistication and confidence and,
        166
    cross-shopping and, 171–172
    environmental factors and, 180–181
    failure to make purchase and, 170
    global marketing and, 171
    location of shopping and, 171–172
    loyalty to retailers and, 170
    market segment and, 170–171
    private brands and, 171
    reasons for purchase and, 170
    sales and, 170
    shopping enjoyment and, 170
    shopping time and, 132–133, 170
    Web use and, 142–143
    See also Consumer decision making
Shopping bags, for sales promotion, 486, 488,
        495
Shopping cart, enhanced shopping experience
        and, 468
Shopping center. See Planned shopping center
Shopping-center-in-the-round, 457
Shopping Centers Today, 246
Shopping network, 134
Shopping time, lengthening, 466–469
    enhanced shopping experience and, 468
    experiential merchandising and, 467
    retailer co-branding and, 468–469
    solutions selling and, 468
    wish list programs and, 469

*Simulation, 196, 204–205
*Single-channel retailing, 128
Site evaluation. See Store location
*Situation analysis. See Retail strategy
Sliding-down scale lease, 256
Sliding scale percentage lease, 256
Slip-and-fall claims, 469
*Slotting allowances, 371–372
Small business. See Independent
Small Business Administration (SBA), 390
    benchmarking and, 511
    franchising and, 100
    management audit form for small retailers
        and, 522, 523
    Marketing Checklist for Small Retailers and,
        522, 523
    opportunity analysis with, 509
    planning tools and, 49
    SCORE and, 409
    secondary data from, 200
    Small Business Development Center and, 87
Smart card, 35, 61
*Social class, 164, 165
Social factors, consumer life-styles and, 164, 165
Social perceived risk, 165
*Social responsibility, 36, 38–39, 272, 517
    See also Ethics
Social stimulus, 172
*Sole proprietorship, 52
*Solutions selling, 468
*Sorting process, 7
Sounds, for interior of store, 458
Source tagging, 382
Space allocation, operations management and,
        316
    floor space and, 316–317, 459, 461–462
Spam, 180
Span of control, 273
Special events, 486, 488
Specialists, retail tasks performed by, 271
Specialization, grouping tasks into jobs and, 272
Specialized buying organization, 343
*Specialog, 133–134, 137
Special order, 357, 371
Specialty direct marketer, 130
Specialty merchandise wholesaler, 368
*Specialty store, 9, 61, 109, 113, 118–119, 216,
        241–242, 252, 309, 407, 415, 422, 495
    category killer (power retailer) and, 60, 61,
        118–119, 211, 316, 372
Specified maximum percentage lease, 256
Specified minimum percentage lease, 256
Spinoffs, 303
Stability, as goal of retailers, 58
Staff positions, 275, 276
Staggered markdown policy, 437
Standardization
    in global retail strategy, 72–73
    in service retailing, 45
Standard merchandise classification, 398
Standard of living, shopping attitudes and
        behavior and, 181
Standard Rate & Data Service, 229
*Staple merchandise, 346
Statement stuffers, direct marketing and, 136
Statistical Abstract of the United States, 200
Status-oriented consumers, 21, 418

*Stimulus, 172–173
Stockholders, satisfaction of, 58
Stock on hand, 175
Stockouts, 410
Stock overage, 395
Stock shortages, 402, 403
    calculating, 394–395
*Stock-to-sales method, 401
*Stock turnover, 351, 357, 358, 375, 407–408
*Storability product groupings, 460
Store atmosphere. *See* Atmosphere
        (atmospherics)
Store-based retail strategy mix. *See* Retail
        institution
Store-based shopping orientation, 10
Store brands. *See* Private (dealer, store) brands
Store composition, location/site evaluation and,
        216, 252, 253
Store format, 316
*Storefront, 65, 68, 455, 456, 457, 459
    for Web retailer, 464, 465
Store hours, 10
    destination retailer and, 105
    human resources and, 280
Store layout, 10, 459–464
    department locations and, 462
    floor space allocation and, 316–317, 459, 461
    individual product location and, 462–463
    store offerings classification and, 459–460
    tactical decisions on, 68
    traffic flow patterns and, 460–461, 462
    World Wide Web and, 465
    See also Point-of-purchase (POP) display
Store location, 10, 105, 213–266
    alternative sites and, 251
    chain and, 87, 90
    choosing, 216
    consumers and, 231–235
    as controllable variable, 64
    destination retailer and, 105
    general location for, 250–251
    global retailing and, 73, 223, 224, 253
    importance of, 215–216
    independent and, 87
    legal environment and, 67, 216, 257
    location and site evaluation and, 251–255, *see
        also* terms of occupancy, *below*
        checklist for, 252
        parking facilities, 216, 252, 253, 256
        pedestrian traffic, 252
        specific site, 252, 254–255
        store composition, 216, 252, 254
        transportation, 216, 252, 253–254
        vehicular traffic, 252, 253
    long-run planning and, 216
    merchandise planning and, 351
    moving from location to location and, 216
    one-hundred percent, 251–252
    overall rating and, 252, 257
    retail institution and, 113–114, 217, 220,
        241–242, 252
    service retailing and, 45–46
    short-run planning and, 216
    strategy mix and, 216
    tactical decisions on, 68
    target market selection and, 62

    taxes and, 257
    technology and, 218–220, 221, 225, 229
    terms of occupancy and, 252, 255–257
        leasing, 67, 216, 255–256
        legal environment and, 216
        operations and maintenance costs and, 216,
            257
        ownership, 216, 255
        taxes and, 257
        voluntary regulations and, 257
        zoning restrictions and, 257
    types of, 241–250, *see also* Planned shopping
        center; Unplanned business district
        isolated store, 216, 241–242, 245, 250, 251,
            254
        mixed-location strategy, 242
    See also under Trading area
*Store maintenance, 318–320
Store management, in department store, 275, 276
Store manager, 272, 280, 289, 326, 340, 345, 453,
        495
Store offerings, classification of, 459–460
Store receipts, promotional strategy and, 477
Stores, 511
Store security. *See* Security
Store size, 316
Storewide clearance, 437, 438
Store-within-a-store concept, 211
Straight commission, 289
*Straight lease, 256
Straight salary, 289
*Straight (gridiron) traffic flow, 460, 462
    for Web retailer, 465
Strategic planning. *See* Retail strategy
*Strategic profit model, 298–300
*Strategy mix, 105–110
    destination retailer and, 105
    retail life cycle and, 108–110
    scrambled merchandising and, 106–108
    store-based, *see* Retail institution
    wheel of retailing and, 105–106, 107
    See also Customer service; Goods/service cate-
        gory; Operations management; Price
        strategy; Promotional strategy; Store
        atmosphere; Store location
*String, 245–246, 251
Structured observation, 203
Substitute goods and services, 353
*Supercenter, 116, 210–211
*Supermarket, 24, 114, 115
    affinity and, 211
    attitudes of shoppers and, 170
    benchmarking for, 513
    box (limited-line) store, 113, 114, 115, 116,
        117, 235, 316
    capital expenditures and, 309
    category management and, 31
    combination store, 113, 114, 115, 116, 117
    consumers' attitudes toward, 170
    conventional, 113, 114–115, 117
    debit cards and, 322
    displays and, 373
    energy management and, 320
    ethics and, 117
    fingerprinting at, 436
    food-based superstore, 113, 114, 115–116, 117

    global retailing and, 302
    human resource planning and, 281
    inventory management and, 383, 407
    item price removal and, 420
    leases and, 216, 255
    one-stop shopping and, 210
    online grocery store and, 109
    operating expenses and, 309
    order processing and fulfillment and, 378,
        379
    price marking and, 373
    price strategy and, 429, 432, 434
    pricing strategy and, 422
    product locations in, 463
    promotional strategy and, 491, 494
    prototype stores and, 316
    regional, 111
    sales transaction per shopping trip and, 9
    scan-based trading and, 372
    scrambled merchandising and, 107–108
    target market and, 62
    technology and, 110
    trading areas and, 222–223
    trading-area saturation and, 236
    traffic flow in, 460, 462
    warehouse store, 113, 114, 115, 116–117, 316
    warehousing and, 381
    See also Checkout process
Superstore. *See* Food-based superstore
*Supervision, 290–291
Supplier
    chain and, 89
    company-owned, 368
    independent and, 88
    information flows and, 185–186
    merchandise plans and, 366, 367
    outside, new, 368
    outside, regularly used, 368
    price strategy and, 421–422
    retailer relationship with, *see* Retailer/supplier
        relationship
    satisfaction of, 59
    selecting and interacting with, 368–370
    trading-area analysis and, 228
    See also Manufacturer; Merchandise plans,
        implementation of; Wholesaler/whole-
        saling
*Supply chain, 376, 377–378
Support activities, as purchase term, 371
Surrounding area, atmosphere and, 457
*Survey, 196, 201, 202, 203
Survey of Buying Power, 233–234, 236
Survey of Current Business, 200
Sweepstakes, 486, 487

T

*Tactics, 68
Tall organization, 273
*Target market
    concentrated marketing and, 178, 179
    demographics and, 161, 162–164
    differentiated marketing and, 178, 180
    independent and, 87
    mass marketing and, 178, 179
    merchandise planning and, 351
    retail organization and, 269

selection of, 61–63, *see also* Consumer
  behavior
wheel of retailing and, 106
See also Consumers
Tasks. *See* Retail organization
*Taxes
  in profit-and-loss statement, 295, 296
  sales, 67, 130, 138, 257
Technology, 12
  atmosphere and, 467
  chain and, 90
  connecting with customers and, 13
  data analysis and, 197
  direct marketing and, 132, 134
  fingerprinting in supermarket and, 436
  independent and, 88
  in-store telecommunications and, 323, 324
  inventory management and, 323, 397
  merchandise buying and handling process
    and, 359, 360–361
  operations management and, 323–324
  parking lots and, 256
  price optimization software and, 442–443
  retailer/supplier relationship and, 380
  retail information system and, 189
  retail store of future and, 521
  service retailing and, 44, 45
  smart card and, 35, 61
  store atmosphere and, 459
  store location and, 218–220, 221, 225, 229
  3-D computer-assisted design, 209
  total retail experience and, 77
  as uncontrollable variable, 66
  videoconferencing and, 323
  See also Checkout process; Relationship retail-
    ing; Retail information system; Video
    kiosk; World Wide Web
Telemarketing. *See* Direct selling
Telemarketing Sales Rule, 66, 67, 139
Telephone sales. *See* Direct marketing; Direct
  selling
Television
  advertising and, 478–479
  direct marketing and, 134
Temperature, of stores, 458
Tenancy, terms of, 64
10-letter equivalency system, 391
Terms of occupancy. *See* Store location
Tests, in selection of retail personnel, 286
Theft. *See* Shoplifting
*Theme-setting display, 463
Third-party logistics. *See* Outsourcing
*Threats, 50, 72
3-D computer-assisted design, 209
TIGER, 218, 219, 231
Time
  attitudes towards shopping time and, 170
  demands on for running retail business, 57
  global retailing strategy and, 73
  poverty of, 132–133, 166, 167
Time-based demand fluctuations, 433
Time bias, trading-area analysis and, 225
Time perceived risk, 165
Time series analysis, 398
Time utilization, 164, 166
Timing, in merchandise plans, 346, 356–357

Top-down budgeting, 306
*Top-down space management approach, 316
*Total retail experience, 13–14, 15–16, 24, 58, 77,
  451
Trade-ins, 28–29
Trademarks, 67
Trade publications, merchandise plans and, 367
Trade shows, merchandise plans and, 367
*Trading area, 217
  characteristics of, 228–230
    availability of store locations, 228
    closeness to sources of supply, 228
    competition, 228, 235
    data for, 229, 230, 231–235
    economic base, 228, 234–235
    examples of, 229
    labor availability, 228
    population, 228, 231–235
    promotion facilities, 228
    regulations, 228
  fringe, 220, 222, 223, 225
  overstored, 235
  primary, 220, 222, 223, 225
  saturated, 235, 236
  secondary, 220, 222, 223, 225
  size and shape of, 163, 220, 222–224
  understored, 235
Trading-area analysis, 217–239
  benefits of, 217–218
  for existing store, 224–225
  geographic information systems in, 218–220,
    221, 223, 225, 229, 231
  global retailing and, 223, 224
  for new store, 225–227
    computerized trading-area models for,
      225
    Huff's law for, 226–227
    Reilly's law for, 226
    trend analysis for, 225
    trading-area size and shape and, 220,
      222–224
  See also Store location; Trading area
*Trading-area overlap, 217
*Traditional department store, 60, 62, 106, 113,
  119–120, 153–154
*Traditional job description, 283–284
Traffic. *See* Vehicular traffic
Traffic-flow patterns
  for store, 460–461, 462
  for Web retailer, 465
*Training programs, 286–288, 289
Transfer of title, as purchase term, 371
Transit advertising, 478, 479
Transportation, 10
  independent and, 88
  location/site evaluation and, 216, 252, 253
  logistics and, 379–380
Trend analysis
  sales forecasting and, 398
  trading area of new stores delineated with,
    225
Trial purchases, 29
Trusted Sender, 180
Truth-in-advertising and -selling laws, 67
Truth-in-credit laws, 67
"2/10/net 30," 371

U
*Unbundled pricing, 434
*Uncontrollable variables, 65–67
  See also Competition; Consumers; Economy;
    Legal environment; Seasonality;
    Technology
*Understored trading area, 235
Unexpected publicity, 481
Unions, 289
  collective bargaining and, 289
  personnel productivity and, 317
Unitary elasticity, 417
*Unit control. *See* Financial merchandise
  management
*Unit pricing, 67, 420
Unity of command, 273
*Universal Product Code (UPC); 194–195, 196,
  324, 325, 373, 393, 406, 407
*Unplanned business district, 216, 242–246, 250,
  251
  central business district, 242–244, 245, 251, 255
  neighborhood business district, 245, 251, 254
  secondary business district, 244–245, 251
  string, 245–246, 251
Unplanned substitution shopping, 177
Unstructured observation, 203
Upscale price orientation, 415
*Usage rate, 409–410

V
VALS Survey, 168
*Value, 20–21, 112
  retail strategy and, 22, 23
  See also Value chain
*Value chain, 21
  information flow in, 186
  supply chain and, 377–378
  value delivery system and, 30–31
*Value delivery system, 30–31
Value pricing, 415, 416
Variable costs, 306
*Variable markup policy, 429
*Variable pricing, 432–433
Variables. *See* Controllable variables;
  Uncontrollable variables
*Variety store, 113, 121
Vehicular traffic, location/site evaluation and,
  252, 253
*Vending machine, 4, 5, 132, 139–140, 316
Vendor. *See* Supplier
*Vendor-managed inventory (VMI), 382
*Vertical cooperative advertising agreement, 480
*Vertical marketing system, 86, 95–96
*Vertical price fixing, 419
*Vertical retail audit, 520
Vertical transportation, 458
Vertical trend, 350
Videoconferencing, 323
*Video kiosk, 36, 105, 109, 129, 132, 136,
  147–149, 323, 467, 468
Virtual reality, 204–205
Visibility
  of specific site, 254
  of stores, 456
Visual inspection system, as physical inventory
  system, 406

*Visual merchandising, 454
VMI. *See* Vendor-managed inventory
Voluntary franchising, 92

W

Walkways, of stores, 456
Wall Street Journal Index, 200
Wall textures, of stores, 458
*Want book (want slip), 366
Warehouse club. *See* Membership (warehouse) club
Warehouse-ready manufacturing, 382
*Warehouse store, 113, 114, 115, 116–117, 316
Warehousing, 373, 380–381
Web. *See* World Wide Web
Web site. *See* World Wide Web
*Weeks' supply method, 401
*Weighted application blank, 284
*Wheel of retailing, 105–106, 107
White Pages, advertising in, 478
Wholesaler-retailer franchising, 92
Wholesaler/wholesaling, 4
    full-service merchant, 368
    limited-service merchant, 368
    price strategy and, 421–422
    retailers and, 7–8
    retail tasks performed by, 271
    secondary data from, 201
    value and, 21
    vertical marketing system and, 86, 95–96
    See also Retailer/supplier relationship; Supplier
*Width of assortment, 112, 351–353
Window displays, 456, 457
Wish list program, 469
WOM. *See* Word of mouth

Women
    in labor force, 132, 139, 162, 163, 193
    in retailing, 281–282, 404
*Word of mouth (WOM), 490
Workers' compensation, 321
Workload forecasts, 317
*World Wide Web, 3, 4, 5, 140–147
    advantages of, 143
    advertising and, 475, 478, 479, 494
    atmosphere and, *see* Web site and, *below*
    attitudes of shoppers and, 170–171
    banner ads and, 136
    concierge service based on, 130
    consumers' attitudes toward, 170–171
    customer service and, 157–158
    customers of, 142–143
    disadvantages of, 144
    discount Web retailers and, 106
    ease of searching and, 131
    E-mail as promotional medium for, 494
    ethics and, 38
    examples of, 145–147, 154–155
    flea markets and, 124
    global retailing and, 140, 141
    hot links and, 136
    merchandise plans and, 366–367
    multi-channel retailing and, 128
    online banking and, 175
    online grocery store and, 109
    operational issues and, 156–157
    personalization and, 158
    price comparisons on, 415
    price wars and, 422
    privacy and, 145
    product imaging and, 156–157
    profile of shoppers and, 169

    recruitment and, 283
    retailer/supplier relationship and, 36
    role of, 140–141
    scope of, 141–142
    searching and, 157
    secondary data from, 200, 201
    security and, 145
    spam and, 180
    store location and, 218
    successful retailers on, 309
    supplier-retailer communication and, 378
    surfing, 140
    3D shopping on, 493
    for training, 287–288, 289
    trust in, 143
    video kiosk and, 109
    Web site and, 7, 10, 143–145, 464–466
        checkout counter and, 465–466
        design and, 466
        displays and, 465
        general interior and, 464
        home page (storefront), 464, 465
        links and, 465
        shopping time and, 466
        store layout and, 465
        traditional stores *versus*, 466
        traffic flow and, 465
    wish list program and, 469

Y

Yellow Pages, advertising in, 478
*Yield management pricing, 433

Z

*Zero-based budgeting, 306
Zoning restrictions, 66, 67, 257

| Yamada Denki | www.yamadadenki.jp/stores/webshop/usr/info/index-e.html |
| Yodobashi Camera | www.yodobashi.com (J) |

GREAT BRITAIN

Arcadia	www.arcadiagroup.co.uk
Boots	www.wellbeing.com
Compass Group	www.compass-group.com
Cooperative Group (CWS)	www.co-op.co.uk
Dixons	www.dixons.co.uk
Great Universal Stores	www.gusplc.co.uk
Iceland	www.iceland.co.uk
J Sainsbury	www.j-sainsbury.co.uk
John Lewis	www.johnlewis.com
Kingfisher	www.kingfisher.co.uk
Littlewoods	www.littlewoodsextra.com
Marks and Spencer	www.marksandspencer.com
Safeway	www.safeway.co.uk
Somerfield	www.somerfield.co.uk
Tesco	www.tesco.com
WH Smith	www.whsmith.co.uk
Wm Morrison	www.morereasons.co.uk

GERMANY (G MEANS SITE IS IN GERMAN)

Aldi Einkauf	www.aldi.de
Anton Schlecker	http://uk.schlecker.com
Bertelsmann	www.bertelsmann.com
Edeka/AVA	www.edeka.de (G)
Globus Handelshof	www.globus-handelshof.de (G)
KarstadtQuelle	www.karstadtquelle.com/englisch/1003.asp
Lidl & Schwarz	www.lidl-schwarz.de (G)
Metro	www.metrogroup.de (select English language version)
Otto Versand	www.otto.de (G)
Rewe	www.rewe.de (select flag at bottom to change to English)
Tchibo Holding	www.tchibo-holding.de/holding/en/index.html
Tengelmann	www.tengelmann.de (G)

FRANCE (F MEANS SITE IS IN FRENCH)

Auchan	www.auchan.com (select English language version)
Carrefour	www.carrefour.com/english/homepage/index.jsp
Casino	www.groupe-casino.fr/index.php?lang=en
Cora	www.cora.fr (F)
E. Leclerc	www.e-leclerc.com (F)
Galeries Lafayette	www.galerieslafayette.com/inter/index.asp
Intermarche	www.intermarche.com (F)
LeRoy Merlin	www.leroymerlin.com/html/en/home.htm
LVMH	www.lvmh.fr/default.asp (select English at bottom of screen)
Pinault-Printemps-Redoute	www.pprgroup.com (select English at bottom of screen)
Systeme U	www.systeme-u.fr (F)

CANADA

Canadian Tire	www.canadiantire.ca
Empire	www.empireco.ca
Hudson's Bay	www.hbc.com
Loblaw	www.loblaw.com
Metro	www.metro.ca
Sears Canada	www.sears.ca

ITALY (I MEANS SITE IS IN ITALIAN)

Conad	www.conad.it (I)
Coop Italia	www.coop.it (I)
Esselunga	www.esselunga.it (select English at bottom of screen)
Gruppo Mega	www.megamark.it (I)
Interdis	www.interdis.it (I)
Rinascente	www.rinascente.it (select English at top of screen)

MEXICO (S MEANS SITE IS IN SPANISH)

Controladora Comercial Mexicana	www.comerci.com.mx
Grupo Carso	www.gcarso.com.mx (select English at top of screen)
Grupo Gigante	www.gigante.com.mx (S)

Notes

Notes

Notes

Notes

Notes

Notes